The Cambridge Handbook of Motivation and Learning

Written by leading researchers in neuroscience, learning science, and developmental, educational, and social psychology, the contributions to this edited volume are suitable for a wide academic readership. The chapters provide definitions of key terms related to motivation and learning, alongside developed explanations of significant findings in the field. They present cohesive descriptions of how motivation relates to learning, in addition to multiple perspectives on motivational constructs and their measurement. This handbook is meant to be a resource for a range of scientific communities, both basic and applied.

K. ANN RENNINGER is the Dorwin P. Cartwright Professor of Social Theory and Social Action, as well as Chair of the Department of Educational Studies, at Swarthmore College, USA.

SUZANNE E. HIDI is Adjunct Professor in the Department of Curriculum, Teaching, and Learning, Ontario Institute for Studies in Education at the University of Toronto, Canada.

The Cambridge Handbook of Motivation and Learning

K. Ann Renninger
Swarthmore College

Suzanne E. Hidi
University of Toronto

CAMBRIDGE
UNIVERSITY PRESS

CAMBRIDGE
UNIVERSITY PRESS

University Printing House, Cambridge CB2 8BS, United Kingdom

One Liberty Plaza, 20th Floor, New York, NY 10006, USA

477 Williamstown Road, Port Melbourne, VIC 3207, Australia

314-321, 3rd Floor, Plot 3, Splendor Forum, Jasola District Centre, New Delhi - 110025, India

79 Anson Road, #06-04/06, Singapore 079906

Cambridge University Press is part of the University of Cambridge.

It furthers the University's mission by disseminating knowledge in the pursuit of education, learning and research at the highest international levels of excellence.

www.cambridge.org
Information on this title: www.cambridge.org/9781107177932
DOI: 10.1017/9781316823279

First published 2019

A catalogue record for this publication is available from the British Library

ISBN 978-1-107-17793-2 Hardback
ISBN 978-1-316-63079-2 Paperback

Although psychology can continue to deal with the loftiest human aspirations, it also must become rooted in the evolutionary realities of the brain if it is to become a true science.

Jaak Panksepp

p. viii, Affective neuroscience: The foundations of human and animal emotions (Oxford University Press, 1998)

Contents

Figures

Tables

Contributors

R. ALISON ADCOCK Department of Psychiatry and Behavioural Sciences, Duke University

HYUN SEON AHN Lee Kong Chian School of Medicine, Nanyang Technological University

JOHN AINLEY Australian Council for Educational Research

MARY AINLEY Melbourne School of Psychological Sciences, University of Melbourne

JOYCE M. ALEXANDER Dean, College of Education, and Department of Educational Psychology, Texas A&M University

PATRICK ANSELME Department of Biopsychology, University of Bochum

KENNETH E. BARRON Department of Psychology, James Madison University

MIMI BONG Department of Education and the Brain and Motivation Research Institute, Korea University

ELIZABETH A. CANNING Department of Psychological and Brain Science, University of Indiana

KIMBERLY S. CHIEW Center for Cognitive Neuroscience, Duke University

JAMES DANCKERT Department of Psychology, University of Waterloo

AVANTI DEY Department of Neuroscience, Columbia University

THERESA DICKE Institute for Positive Psychology and Education, Australian Catholic University

JOHN EASTWOOD Faculty of Health, Department of Psychology, York University

JACQUELYNNE S. ECCLES School of Education, University of California, Irvine

TERRI FLOWERDAY Department of Individual, Family, & Community Education, University of New Mexico

JENNIFER A. FREDRICKS Dean of Academic Departments and Programs and Department of Psychology, Union College

DANIELLE M. GEERLING Department of Psychology, University of Utah

THOMAS GOETZ Department of Empirical Educational Research, University of Konstanz and Thurgau University of Teacher Education

JACQUELINE GOTTLIEB Department of Neuroscience, Columbia University

MATTHIAS J. GRUBER Cardiff University Brain Research Imaging Centre (CUBRIC), School of Psychology, Cardiff University

NATHAN C. HALL Department of Educational and Counselling Psychology, McGill University

JUDITH M. HARACKIEWICZ Department of Psychology, University of Wisconsin-Madison

DANIEL T. HICKEY Learning Science Program, School of Education, Indiana University at Bloomington

SUZANNE E. HIDI Department of Curriculum, Teaching, and Learning, Ontario Institute for Studies in Education, University of Toronto

TARA L. HOFKENS Center for Advanced Study of Teaching and Learning, Curry School of Education, University of Virginia

SOPHIA YANG HOOPER Department of Educational Psychology, The University of Texas at Austin

MARCUS S. HORWOOD Institute of Positive Psychology and Education, Australian Catholic University

CHRIS S. HULLEMAN Center for Advanced Study of Teaching and Learning, Curry School of Education, University of Virginia

MIZUKO ITO Connected Learning Lab, University of California, Irvine

KATHY E. JOHNSON Department of Psychology, Indiana University-Purdue University Indianapolis

SUNG-IL KIM Department of Education and the Brain and Motivation Research Institute, Korea University

JEFF J. KOSOVICH Center for Creative Leadership

MAIKE KRANNICH Department of Empirical Educational Research, University of Konstanz

REED W. LARSON Department of Human Development and Family Studies, University of Illinois Urbana-Champaign

GLONA LEE Department of Education and the Brain and Motivation Research Institute, Korea University

HYUN JI LEE Department of Education and the Brain and Motivation Research Institute, Korea University

LISA LINNENBRINK-GARCIA Department of Counseling, Educational Psychology, and Special Education, Michigan State University

JORDAN LITMAN University of Maine at Machias

OLIVER LÜDTKE Department of Educational Measurement, Leibniz Institute for Science and Mathematics Education

HERBERT W. MARSH Institute of Positive Psychology and Education, Australian Catholic University

CRYSTLE MARTIN Department of Library and Learning Resources, El Camino College

GINA MCGOVERN Department of Human Development and Family Studies, University of Illinois Urbana-Champaign

JHOTISHA MUGON Department of Psychology, University of Waterloo

KOU MURAYAMA Department of Psychology, University of Reading

BENJAMIN NAGENGAST Hector Research Institute of Education Sciences and Psychology, University of Tübingen

CARIN NEITZEL Department of Educational Psychology, Black Hills State University

MARKKU NIEMIVIRTA Department of Education, University of Oslo; Department of Education, University of Helsinki

SUSAN BOBBITT NOLEN College of Education, University of Washington

GEORG NORTHOFF Mind, Brain Imaging, and Neuroethics Research Unit, University of Ottawa Institute of Mental Health Research

CAROLYN ORSON Department of Human Development and Family Studies, University of Illinois Urbana-Champaign

PHILIP D. PARKER Institute of Positive Psychology and Education, Australian Catholic University

ERIKA A. PATALL Rossier School of Education, University of Southern California

RACHEL CODY PFISTER Department of Communication, University of California, San Diego

ANTTI-TUOMAS PULKKA Department of Leadership and Military Pedagogy, National Defence University

MATTHEW RAFALOW YouTube

CHARAN RANGANATH Psychology Department and Center for Neuroscience, University of California, Davis

K. ANN RENNINGER Department of Educational Studies, Swarthmore College

BRENT ROBERTS Social and Behavioral Sciences Research Initiative, University of Illinois Urbana-Champaign

MIKE J. F. ROBINSON Department of Psychology, Wesleyan University

EMILY Q. ROSENZWEIG Department of Human Development and Quantitative Methodology, University of Maryland

KATIE SALEN TEKINBAŞ Department of Infomatics, University of California, Irvine

CAROL SANSONE Department of Psychology, University of Utah

KATERINA SCHENKE School of Education and Information Studies, University of California, Los Angeles

BARRY SCHWARTZ Haas School of Business, University of California

MARJORIE SEATON Institute of Positive Psychology and Education, Australian Catholic University

DUANE F. SHELL Department of Educational Psychology, University of Nebraska-Lincoln

DA-JUNG DIANE SHIN Department of Education and the Brain and Motivation Research Institute, Korea University

JESSI L. SMITH Associate Vice Chancellor for Research, Department of Psychology, University of Colorado, Colorado Springs

ANNA TAPOLA Department of Education, University of Helsinki

DUSTIN B. THOMAN Motivation and Social Identity Lab, Department of Psychology, San Diego State University

ULRICH TRAUTWEIN Hector Research Institute of Education Sciences and Psychology, University of Tübingen

HETA TUOMINEN Department of Education, University of Helsinki

ASHVANTI VALJI Cardiff University Brain Research Imaging Centre (CUBRIC), School of Psychology, Cardiff University

MING-TE WANG School of Education and Department of Psychology, and Learning Research and Development Center, University of Pittsburgh

ALLAN WIGFIELD Department of Human Development and Quantitative Methodology, University of Maryland

STEPHANIE V. WORMINGTON Curry School of Education, Center for Advanced Study of Teaching and Learning, University of Virginia

AMANDA WORTMAN Connected Learning Lab, University of California, Irvine

AMY WRZESNIEWSKI Yale School of Management, Yale University

Foreword

How do you motivate your children to study in school and university, interact with friends, find a nice profession that interests and satisfies them, and stay honest and healthy, all at the same time? There are wide-ranging (and sometimes wild) opinions on this, ranging from generously pampering and bribing them via coaching and tutoring to the carrot-and-stick approach and the somewhat radical tiger moms. We all have our ideas about how to induce motivation for learning, how the two are related, and how to improve each. In addition, there are plenty of cultural prejudices and folk psychology that may have the best of intentions, but ultimately may not go far enough for the demands of modern societies built on evidence rather than irrational beliefs. What is needed is a coherent scientific approach that assures humane, rational, thoughtful, flexible, and open procedures. In these modern times, this approach should involve evidence derived from studying the properties of the underlying hardware, which in these cases is the brain. The current collection of chapters is exactly that. A number of psychologists, educators, and neuroscientists have written about their thoughts and draw on their empirical research to analyze the evidence, make predictions, and give advice.

Motivation is a funny thing. If you have too much, you may go around in circles, and if do not have enough, you cannot fulfill your dreams and intentions (and those of your parents and friends). You can derive motivation from rewards that you get from having done something well, and you may try again and again to get more of the reward. Reward is a powerful goal of motivated behavior and reinforces it. In particular, surprising rewards will make you go for more; they are often more efficient than rewards that are predicted. Goethe once famously said, "Nothing is harder than a succession of fair days." Surprise generates attention and interest; it motivates you to get more of it. Thus, surprising rewards are good motivators. They are also very effective for learning. Once you get a surprising reward, you want more of it, and to do so, you may need to change your behavior, which is exactly what learning is all about.

But rewards are not the only motivators. Punishing an underperforming child reflects a general intuition that children will do things to avoid punishment and that punishment is a motivator. When it comes to carrot and stick, a good reward will go a long way, but sometimes a little pushing can help (although, luckily enough, the proverbial stick no longer exists in its physical implementation). Another big motivator is novelty, which also attracts attention. Has there ever been a child that did not seek novel things? The child's drive is the curiosity that acts to seek out unknown things. But where children are full of curiosity and just love the novel stuff, we adults often avoid it as much as possible. As Douglas Adams, the author of the *The hitchhiker's guide to the galaxy*, famously quipped, "Anything invented after you're thirty-five is against the natural order of things." Adults just cannot understand how children always seek novel things. Let us give them a chance!

Of course, as with everything important and good, motivation has enemies. How can our children stay motivated in the presence of the great distractors, such as prejudice (class paranoia: only the rich can make it), social interaction (it is too tempting to play with others, rather than sitting down alone and studying things), celebrity (no higher effort required other than posturing and talking useless rubbish), and asset inequality (why do they have what I can't get?). Some children just do not understand why they need to spend time and effort to achieve something that may turn out to be beneficial only at some future point, when others seemingly can be big, famous, and rich without the effort. The social media on the Internet tells them so! The children are too young to anticipate the consequences of their compromised motivation.

All of the above could be interpreted to say that the brain is responsible for all of these behaviors. Yes, there are hardware systems for reward, punishment, attention, and curiosity, but these systems are not all that hard-wired. They are amenable to modification through experience, one of the great feats of neuroscience. Hopefully you will find it interesting to read about what is now available in the quest for understanding and improving motivation and learning. Happy reading!

Wolfram Schultz
University of Cambridge

Acknowledgments

The editors gratefully acknowledge the ongoing support of David Repetto as they worked on this volume, the insight of Patrick Anselme, and editorial support from Eliana Yankelev. In addition, the editors would like to acknowledge support for their work on this volume from Swarthmore College and the University of Toronto.

Introduction

Motivation and Its Relation to Learning

Suzanne E. Hidi and K. Ann Renninger

This volume brings together chapters that address present understanding of motivation and learning, as well as the relation between them.[1] Neuroscientists, learning scientists, and developmental, educational, and social psychologists have contributed chapters, in which they describe research on motivation and learning, its potential to contribute to practice – both in and out of school – and future directions for inquiry.

Historically, research on motivation explores conscious as well as unconscious (implicit) responses to social and cultural circumstances, the will to engage (connect, participate), the influence of feelings about the self (self-concept, self-efficacy) and the work needed to address those feelings (self-regulation, self-motivation). It includes whether and when information search, rewards, incentives, or choice are operative, as well as the contributions of interest and internal motivation, curiosity and boredom, and goals and values.

Research addressing learning is similarly broad, in that it encompasses a wide range of foci. It addresses how and when individuals engage their attention, recognition and recall memory, and information processing (self-specificity, perception, affordances), as well as the acquisition and use of learning strategies. Research on learning also considers outcomes that can range from sustained participation and interest to achievement and deeper learning.

Even though motivation and learning are always mutually supportive, research that considers their relation has tended to focus on how motivation contributes to learning. For example, researchers have shown that (a) proximal goals motivate individuals, leading them to increased effort and improved performance (e.g., Bandura & Schunk, 1981; Zimmerman & Kitsantas, 2002); (b) developing and well-developed interests facilitate learning (e.g., Harackiewicz et al., 2008; Jansen et al., 2016); and (c) rewards contribute to increased attention and have cognitive benefits, such as improving memory for events due to enhanced dopaminergic activity in the midbrain and hippocampus (Adcock et al., 2006; Anderson et al., 2011). Researchers

---

1 All references to the contributing authors' work refer to their chapters in this handbook, unless otherwise noted.

in the learning sciences have examined the role of context and culture to provide detail about commonalities and their potential to inform design (e.g., the quality of interactions, activities in the learning environment; see Järvelä & Renninger, 2014). Together, findings from these approaches provide a basis for understanding how deeper learning may be promoted, and how unmotivated learners, in particular, can be enabled to meaningfully engage with content.

Consideration of how and when motivation can support learning is especially timely, as declines in students' motivation, interest, and value for academic subjects have been widely reported in recent years (Frenzel et al., 2010; Hidi & Harackiewicz, 2000; Hyde et al., 2016; Rosenzweig & Wigfield, 2016). In fact, in their review of the literature, Lazowski and Hulleman (2016) concluded that declines in student motivation span grade levels, beginning in elementary school, and are a systemic problem that threatens educational equality.

Furthermore, attention is needed that focuses on how the development of learning may change motivation. Some scholars have recognized that knowledge acquisition – even when it is not voluntary – can have positive motivational outcomes. For example, having students take physics courses that they would not choose on their own may expose them to ideas that promote learning and voluntary re-engagement.

Emerging neuroscientific work helps us explain why motivation functions as it does and, specifically, how it contributes to learning. One of the best examples of such findings – one that is reported in several chapters of this volume – reveals information-seeking to be an intrinsic reward that activates the reward circuitry in the brain just as extrinsic rewards do. This finding is critical for explaining the way motivation can lead to learning without extrinsic rewards. As Hidi (2006, 2016) pointed out, the relevance of neuroscientific findings has tended to be underestimated by social and educational psychologists, particularly in the area of motivational research. Indeed, many educational and social psychologists have argued for skepticism about how neuroscience can be relevant to educational practice and policy (e.g., Bruer, 1997).

Thus, although neuroscientific research has examined a plethora of issues about the human brain that are relevant to motivation and learning, the findings from this literature, by and large, have not been integrated with psychological research. For example, Rushworth et al. (2011) defined the areas of the brain that are critical in learning about reward associations, selecting reward goals, choosing actions to obtain rewards, and decision-making. This article is not cited in many papers on these topics in the motivation literature. Another example is the neuroscientific research on the reward circuitry: the literature on this topic contains hundreds of investigations that only recently have begun to be seriously considered by learning scientists and psychologists.

The importance of neuroscientific research has become obvious in the last two decades, and specifications of neural substrates of information processing have led to findings that behavioral investigations have not been in a position to provide. The benefits of linking neuroscientific research to domain-specific educational investigations are many. For example, De Smedt et al. (2010) demonstrated the relevance of cognitive neuroscientific research for mathematics education. Neuroscientific examinations are now able to provide information about the way that various circuits in the brain are activated. As such, they provide more direct observation of motivation than was available when Kanfer (1990) wrote that motivation is not directly observable and suggested that we can only observe behavior and infer motivational processes. In turn, the learning sciences – and developmental, educational, and social psychologists – are positioned to provide neuroscience with information about variables on which to focus their studies: which variables, in which contexts, have already been identified as critical, and open questions that neuroscience may be in a position to address (De Smedt et al., 2010).

Describing the scientific and pragmatic challenges of bridging education and neuroscience, Varma et al. (2008) suggested that neuroscientists and educational researchers should view themselves as collaborators, rather than competitors, in the pursuit of knowledge. This handbook has been compiled in the spirit of this suggestion.

In undertaking the editing of this volume, we had in mind commonalities that are present in the published findings of domains that have traditionally been distinct. We specifically invited contributions from those whose work, in juxtaposition with others', would enable readers to consider their synergies. Chapters in this handbook have been organized into six sections: I. The Self and Its Impact; II. Rewards, Incentives, and Choice; III. Interest and Internal Motivation; IV. Curiosity and Boredom; V. Goals and Values; and VI. Methods, Measures, and Perspective.

The reader may note that many of the chapters address more than a single topic and could have been assigned to more than one section. This situation reflects a movement toward consideration (or the integration) of topics across and within fields that formerly had been isolated or siloed. For example, in Chapter 21, Chiew and Adcock use neuroscientific methods to show the critical role of motivation in encoding information in long-term memory. They describe the pursuit of learning goals based on their interrogative/imperative model of information-seeking. Although they are addressing goals and values, their chapter also involves serious consideration of reward, incentive, and choice, as well as curiosity and boredom. As such, their chapter could easily have been included in a number of sections. Similarly, in Chapter 15, Schwartz and Wrzesniewski distinguish between activities that are internally motivated (pursued for consequences related to the activity itself that can yield lasting effects on well-being) and intrinsically motivated activity (undertaken due to pleasure). Their chapter appears in the section concerning interest and internal motivation. However, it could have been assigned to the section on rewards, incentives, and choice, or that on goals and values. In fact, most of the chapters in this volume bridge a number of topics.

In making section assignments, we chose to facilitate readers' consideration of differences and synergies in conceptualizations, questions, and approaches. Readers will also notice that some chapters address the same construct (e.g., boredom, curiosity, goals), yet represent distinct points of view and differing research questions or methods. For example, in Chapter 19, Goetz and his colleagues report on the negative consequences of boredom (defined as an emotion) and ways by which those consequences could be avoided; whereas, in Chapter 20, Mugon et al. investigate the state of boredom as a signal of disengagement rather than as a cause of disengagement. This is not a case of one group of researchers being more correct than another; rather, each view presents a different focus and related questions.

Readers will also note that the concept of curiosity is addressed in several different chapters. In Chapter 16, Gruber et al. first discuss trait curiosity (i.e., curiosity that is considered to be a specific personality characteristic). Subsequently, they describe neuroscientific research that demonstrates the memory benefits of information-seeking during temporary states of curiosity. These benefits were established not only for associated information, but also for incidentally encoded information. In Chapter 17, Litman, who describes two types of curiosity (interest and deprivation), examines the relation between trait and state measures, and weighs the implications of neuroscientific findings for his model. Finally, in Chapter 18, Shin et al. lay out reasons to distinguish between interest and curiosity (see also Grossnickle, 2016), although they acknowledge that both can have a positive impact on individuals' motivation, learning, creativity, and well-being.

In the sections that follow, we point to some of the themes that emerge and to future directions that the respective research suggests. We pose no grand theory in this handbook. Rather, readers are invited to partner with an incredible group of authors to think on both the breadth and depth of available research on motivation and learning.

Emergent Themes

Across the chapters, several emergent themes can be identified. These include: integrative approaches to inquiry (across and within domains); the centrality of reward in human functioning; the importance of personal connections, social practices, and cultural identities; and the need to reconsider methods and measures. We review each of these themes next, drawing examples from this volume. We note that not all instances are mentioned, and that the examples we do provide may not come from the same sections.

Integrative Approaches

Fields (or domains) and topics that, in the past, have been studied as distinct because of differences in researchers' training and methods, are now beginning to be considered in relation to each other. We found that some form of integration characterizes all of the chapters in this volume in one way or another, suggesting that authors' efforts to contextualize their foci in relation to others' may be a harbinger of new directions in the field. Here, we point to examples of this integration across domains as well as between psychological constructs.

Across domains. In Chapter 6, Murayama points out that cross-disciplinary work between neuroscience and psychology is vitally important for understanding motivation and learning, and provides a rationale for studies of incentives. He explains that whereas neuroscientists have determined that extrinsic and intrinsic incentives form a single psychological process, psychologists have tended to focus on the differences between the two types of incentives. Murayama concludes that these two perspectives should productively inform each other.

Another example of integration across domains involves affective neuroscientific research on self-related information processing; in Chapter 1, Hidi et al. consider how it is related to rewards and interest. They also point to its potential to explain why an educational intervention (such as utility-value) is beneficial for some individuals but not for others. Similarly, in Chapter 10, Patall and Hooper's discussion of choice provision highlights motivational, cognitive, social, and neuroscientific perspectives, which provide a complex picture of the role of choice in educational settings. For example, they explain that the broader social and interpersonal context can change the meaning and effects of choice.

Between psychological constructs. In their discussions of psychological constructs, the authors of some chapters in this volume also reflect the movement toward integration. However, rather than integrating across domains, the focus in these chapters is between topics within the domain of psychology. For instance, in Chapter 2, Marsh et al. describe their studies of academic self-concept in the context of positive psychology. Their multifaceted model of academic self-concept includes multiple aspects of the self: academic, social, physical, and emotional. Similarly, in considering the relationship between interest and conscientiousness, in Chapter 14, Trautwein et al. draw on two psychological literatures that have been almost completely distinct: personality and educational psychology. They introduce and provide evidence for the Conscientiousness × Interest Compensation (CONIC) model, in which they describe how conscientiousness and interest at least partly compensate for each other in predicting academic achievement. Finally, in Chapter 24, Rosenzweig et al. discuss the relation among psychological constructs in their review of expectancy-value theory (Eccles et al., 1983). They describe findings demonstrating the development of expectancies, task values, and perceptions of cost, as well as their implications.

In Chapter 29, person-oriented approaches, in which variables are studied in combination within a person, represent yet another form of integration that offers additional insight about educational outcomes. Linnenbrink-Garcia and Wormington point out that motivation in classrooms is far more complicated than variable-centered analyses (e.g., analyses that focus on a single motivational variable such as self-efficacy) can describe and address. They present an integrative, person-oriented approach for studying student motivation. In Chapter 23, Niemivirta et al. further elaborate on the benefits of a person-oriented approach, focusing on its use in the study of multiple goals to address a long-standing debate in the literature on the advantages of endorsing different goals. Niemivirta and his colleagues state that person-centered approaches allow study of the individual as an active agent, as well as developments in individual learning and engagement over time – information that they note as critical for both researchers and practitioners.

Chapter 11, our chapter on interest development and learning, provides an illustration of how person-oriented, or within-person, analyses extend findings from previous variable-centered studies. We point to findings detailing a distinct set of relations among learner understanding, effort, feedback preferences, goals, self-efficacy, and self-regulation for each of the four phases of interest development. As our discussion demonstrates, integrative findings of this type have implications for theory building and research, as well as practice.

The Centrality of Reward in Human Functioning

Neuroscientists have established that the reward circuitry in the brain involves dopaminergic systems related to motivation and value, as well as cortical systems related to attention and memory. Reward anticipation and receipt of rewards activate this circuitry, suggesting that understanding the relation between motivation and learning results in having to acknowledge centrality of reward in human functioning. Several contributors consider the motivating power of such activation, and its effect on learning and performance.

An example of a dopamine-dependent motivational process, incentive salience, is the focus of Chapter 7, by Anselme and Robinson. They provide evidence that incentive salience not only plays a direct role in determining individuals' responses, but also contributes to the variability of performance that learning alone cannot explain. Furthermore, Anselme and Robinson relate the invigorating effect of reward uncertainty to incentive salience, and they introduce the novel construct of incentive hope to explain its power.

For years, research on incentives has been focused on extrinsic rewards. However, findings from neuroscience indicate that extrinsic and intrinsic rewards activate the same areas in the reward circuitry (see Gottlieb et al.,

2013; Murayama, Chapter 6). Subsequently, findings on intrinsic rewards established that searching for information is such a reward. Curiosity and interest that are both associated with information search are intrinsically rewarding.

Contributors addressing these topics acknowledge the power of intrinsic rewards. For example, in Chapter 8, Dey and Gottlieb consider intrinsic rewards and information-seeking. They focus on the neuroscience of attention and describe the mechanisms coordinating individuals' decision-making, beliefs, goals, and actions. They suggest that attention is used to reduce uncertainty and obtain reward, and they explore the role of cognitive control in directing attention. They also point to the strong reward-dependent attentional effects related to novelty and introduce the concept of savoring, which explains that people obtain utility not only from actual rewards they receive, but also from future-oriented "anticipatory" feelings. Both the concepts of incentive hope and savoring touch on strong motivation related to anticipation of rewards.

In Chapter 9, Hickey and Schenke do not deal with the neuroscientific findings of rewards but focus on the educational relevance of a particular type of incentive: the use of digital badges for tracking and sharing accomplishment online. They distinguish the use of badging from many people's working assumptions about the negative effects of extrinsic rewards and point, instead, to findings indicating the utility and transparency provided by badging systems, especially in inquiry-based environments.

Social Practices and Cultural Identities

A recurring theme in the chapters written by learning scientists and developmental, educational, and social psychologists is the essential role of social practices and cultural identities in motivating engagement and learning. For example in Chapter 12, Ito et al. describe the connected learning that occurs in online affinity networks (online communities that share a specific focus) as motivating learning and promoting interest development. They point to the roles of shared interests, identity, culture, and values as binding people together, and to shared practice as providing a focus of activity and engagement. Similarly, in Chapter 5, Larson et al. characterize effective after-school programming as sustaining motivation by providing opportunities for adolescent youth to develop relationships and have experiences that promote feelings of competence and camaraderie.

In Chapter 13, Alexander et al. using longitudinal data, provide evidence that with support from other people such as peers, parents, and teachers, the potential to trigger and maintain interest in science exists in every developmental time period. In order for social context and practices to support learners at different points in their development, understanding the way those learners ascribe meaning is essential. In Chapter 30, Shell and Flowerday describe how people learn from the affordances that are available and that they perceive. They point to the impact of culture on the opportunities and affordances and its subsequent impact on the processes involved in knowing and motivation, as well as what is learned.

In Chapter 22, Nolen focusing on the goals that people have and develop, explains that goals are not context-free. She points to the range of ways in which goals have been studied (e.g., in relation to action, beliefs across settings, or a more situated analysis of how goals are specific to context) and calls for studying goals in relation to the systems of meanings under study. In Chapter 25, Canning and Harackiewicz consider mechanisms that explain the success of utility value interventions. They point, in particular, to the possibility that background knowledge may be critical. This is not the same point that Nolen makes, but the role of learner understanding is critical to each consideration. Similarly, in Chapter 4, Sansone et al. draw on the Self-Regulation of Motivation (SRM) model to demonstrate how experiencing interest is both a process and an outcome, and provide an explanation of the role of individual differences (e.g., having an interpersonal orientation) in goal adoption and strategy use. They also explain that the anticipated, perceived, or experienced congruence between a student's goals, and the way that science, technology, engineering, and math (STEM) learning tasks are presented and structured, can be an important source of student motivation to begin and persist in learning, and may influence whether and how students attempt to make learning tasks more interesting.

In Chapter 3, Ahn and Bong in reviewing the literature on the development of self-efficacy beliefs and the relation between self-efficacy and other constructs (such as motivation, strategy use, self-regulation, and achievement)also point to the possibility that before their self-efficacy beliefs start shaping motivation and learning, students need to understand the characteristics of the school subject. These authors also suggest that differences in educational systems and policies need to be considered in studies of the use of self-efficacy information that have been attributed to cultural diversity.

Methodological Considerations

All of the chapters in this handbook address the methods and measures used in motivation research and point to needed adaptations and consideration. In Chapter 26, Ainley and Ainley review the methods and measures being used to study motivation, pointing to the expansion of tools and techniques that are available to researchers. They provide detail about their use, data reduction, analyses, and point to the increasing interest of motivation researchers in acknowledging the interactive influences of the person and context. They also underscore the need for researchers to align the methods and measures they employ with their research questions, rather than relying exclusively on various forms of self-reports to provide information about motivation and learning. In Chapter 27, Fredricks et al. review examples of the measures employed in the study of engagement specifically and the challenges of each. Subsequently, decisions to combine methods to address measurement challenges in their studies are explained. They describe the use of interviews and focus groups to validate a survey tool, and the use of observational approaches to measure behavioral engagement, along with tests of their predictive validity.

In Chapter 28, Kosovich et al. also draw on examples from their own work to illustrate the application of pragmatic measurement, which involves adapting commonly accepted measurement practices to situational constraints (e.g., limited time for survey completion) that are common to data collection in educational settings. They argue for the utility of pragmatic measurement in educational settings, where it can address research questions as effectively as high-quality measures that require substantial resources.

Concluding Thoughts

The chapters of this handbook provide a foundation for considering both present knowledge and the next steps for understanding motivation, learning, and the relation between them. As we noted earlier, we propose no grand theory, but our sense is that this handbook makes a case for encouraging consideration of the synergies that can be identified when topics are considered across and within domains. Considering similarities and differences in findings about topics in motivation and learning, as well as the relations that exist among them, is critical if research is to inform policy and practice.

Some open questions include:

- How can researchers working on related constructs, but with different perspectives, find common ground?
- How are beliefs, goals, and expectancies – all conscious – related to possibly unconscious motivation, such as incentive salience?
- How is motivation, such as striving for excellence, related to neuroscientific research?
- How are cultural influences related to reward anticipation?

It is our "incentive hope" that the chapters of this handbook will lead researchers to undertake investigations that can answer these questions and the many more that can be generated in the course of reading.

References

Adcock, R. A., Thangavel, A., Whitfield-Gabrieli, S., Knutson, B., & Gabrieli, J. D. E. (2006). Reward-motivated learning: Mesolimbic activation precedes memory formation. *Neuron, 50*, 507–17.

Anderson, B. A., Laurent, P. A., & Yantis, S. (2011). Value-driven attentional capture. *Proceedings of the National Academy of Sciences of the United States of America, 108*(3), 10367–71.

Bandura, A. & Schunk, D. H. (1981). Cultivating competence, self-efficacy, and intrinsic interest through proximal self-motivation. *Journal of Personality and Social Psychology, 41*, 586–98.

Bruer, J. T. (1997). Education and the brain: A bridge too far. *Educational Researcher, 26*(8), 4–16.

De Smedt, B., Ansari, D., Grabner, R. H., Hannula, M. M., Schneider, M., & Verschaffel, L. (2010). Cognitive neuroscience meets mathematics education. *Educational Research Review, 5*, 97–105.

Eccles, J., Adler, T. F., Futterman, R., Goff, S. B., Kaczala, C. M., Meece, J., & Midgley, C. (1983). Expectancies, values, and academic behaviors. In J. T. Spence (Ed.), *Achievement and Achievement Motives* (pp. 75–146). San Francisco, CA: W. H. Freeman.

Frenzel, A. C., Goetz, T., Pekrun, R., & Watt, H. M. (2010). Development of mathematics interest in adolescence: Influences of gender, family and school context. *Journal of Research on Adolescence, 20*(2), 507–37.

Gottlieb, J., Oudeyer, P.-Y., Lopes, M., & Baranes, A. (2013). Information seeking, curiosity and attention: Computational and neural mechanisms. *Trends in Cognitive Sciences, 17*(11), 585–93. doi: 10.1016/j.tics.2013.09.001.

Grossnickle, E. M. (2016). Disentangling curiosity: Dimensionality, definitions, and distinctions from interest in educational contexts. *Educational Psychology Review, 28*, 23–60.

Harackiewicz, J. M., Durik, A. M., Barron, K. E., Linnenbrink, L., & Tauer, J. M. (2008). The role of achievement goals in the development of interest: Reciprocal relations between achievement goals, interest, and performance. *Journal of Educational Psychology, 100*(1), 105–22. doi: 10.1037/0022-0663.100.1.105.

Hidi, S. (2006). Interest: A unique motivational variable. *Educational Research Review, 1*, 69–82.

Hidi, S. (2016). Revisiting the role of rewards in motivation and learning: Implications of neuroscientific research. *Educational Psychology Review, 28*(1), 61–93. doi: 10.1007/s10648-015-9307-5.

Hidi, S. & Harackiewicz, J. M. (2000). Motivating the academically unmotivated: A critical issue for the 21st century. *Review of Educational Research, 70*(2), 151–79. doi: 10.2307/1170660.

Hyde, J. S., Canning, E. A., Rozek, C. S., Clarke, E., Hulleman, C. S., & Harackiewicz, J. M. (2016). The role of mothers' communication in promoting motivation for math and science course-taking in high school. *Journal of Research on Adolescence, 27*, 49–64. doi: 10.1111/jora.12253.

Jansen, M., Lüdtke, O., & Schroeders, U. (2016). Evidence for a positive relationship between interest and achievement: Examining between-person and within-person variation in five domains. *Contemporary Educational Psychology*, *46*, 116–27. doi: 10.1016/j.cedpsych.2016.05.004.

Järvelä, S. & Renninger, K. A. (2014). Designing for learning: Interest, motivation, and engagement. In D. Keith Sawyer (Ed.), *The Cambridge handbook of the learning sciences* (2nd ed, pp. 668–85). New York, NY: Cambridge University Press.

Kanfer, R. (1990). Motivation theory and industrial organizational psychology. In M. D. Dunnette and L. Hough (Eds.), *Handbook of industrial and organizational psychology, Vol. 1: Theory in industrial and organizational psychology* (pp. 75–170). Palo Alto, CA: Consulting Psychologists Press.

Lazowski, R. A. & Hulleman, C. S. (2016). Motivation interventions in education: A meta-analytic review. *Review of Educational Research*, *86*(2), 602–40. doi: 10.3102/0034654315617832.

Rosenzweig, E. Q. & Wigfield, A. (2016). STEM motivation interventions for adolescents: A promising start, but further to go. *Educational Psychologist*, *51*(2), 146–63. doi: 10.1080/00461520.2016.1154792.

Rushworth, M. F. S., Noonan, M. P., Boorman, E. D., Walton, M. E., & Behrens, T. E. (2011). Frontal cortex and reward-guided learning and decision-making. *Neuron*, *70*(6), 1054–69.

Varma, S., McCandliss, B. D., & Schwartz, D. L. (2008). Scientific and pragmatic challenges for bridging education and neuroscience. *Educational Researcher*, *37*, 140–52.

Zimmerman, B. J. & Kitsantas, A. (2002). Acquiring writing revision and self-regulatory skill through observation and emulation. *Journal of Educational Psychology*, *94*, 660–8.

PART I

The Self and Its Impact

1 The Educational Benefits of Self-Related Information Processing

Suzanne E. Hidi, K. Ann Renninger,
and Georg Northoff

Abstract: In this chapter, we describe psychological and neuroscientific research that demonstrates the unique characteristics of self-related information processing. These characteristics have been shown to produce beneficial effects on basic functions (such as perception, attention, and actions), as well as on higher-order cognitive activities (including memory). The findings are explained by their correspondence to the neurocorrelates of self-related information processing. Northoff's (2016) basic model of the self, which describes self-specificity to be a fundamental aspect of the brain's spontaneous (resting) activity, provides further clarification of these results. After considering the unique characteristics of self-related information processing, we describe the potential benefits of considering findings from neuroscience for educational practice by pointing to the positive outcomes of utility value interventions. More specifically, these types of interventions, which are grounded in the expectancy-value theory of student motivation, are examples of how self-related information processing can have educational benefits by increasing motivation and learning.

Philosophers and psychologists have long debated the nature of the way information relevant to the self is processed (Denny et al., 2012). In philosophical discussions, the self traditionally has been considered a higher-order function. Based on this view, neuroscientists have tended to focus on the relation of the self to cognitive activities such as remembering things or making judgments. However, more recent neuroscientific investigations have demonstrated that self-specificity (also referred to as self-relatedness) – the degree to which internal or external stimuli are related to the self – influences not only higher-order functions like memory, but also the activation of more basic functions such as perception, emotion, and reward (Northoff, 2016).

In this chapter, we first examine relevant behavioral and neuroscientific findings that demonstrate the unique characteristics of self-related information processing. Next, we briefly review Northoff's basis model of the self, which

The authors would like to thank Chris Hulleman for his helpful comments and suggestions on an earlier version of this manuscript. The editorial assistance provided by William Kenny and Melissa Running is appreciated. Research support from the Swarthmore College Faculty Research fund is gratefully acknowledged.

describes self-specificity to be a fundamental feature of the brain's spontaneous (resting) activity. We close the chapter by considering how self-related information processing could be utilized in educational settings. Considering the way that findings from neuroscience can inform educational practice is essential, given the confirmed and puzzling declines in the academic interest and performance of students as they progress through schooling. More specifically, we suggest that utility value interventions are an example of how self-related information processing can benefit motivation and learning,[1] and argue that their positive outcomes are a demonstration of the benefits of such processing.

Self-Related Information Processing

For several decades now, psychologists have reported that activities involving the self have beneficial influences on what is remembered. For example, many investigations have shown that items a person chooses are better remembered than items assigned by an experimenter (see also Patall & Hooper, Chapter 10). In their meta-analysis of over 100 studies, Symons and Johnson (1997) pointed to the self-reference effect in memory, specifically to the superior memory that results from relating material to the self. They confirmed that self-referent encoding strategies yield superior memory, relative to both semantic and other-referent encoding strategies, and concluded that because the concept of the self is a well-developed and frequently used construct, it promotes elaboration and organization of encoded information. More recently, researchers have also found that stimuli such as trait adjectives related to the self result in enhanced memory and shorter reaction times when compared to non-self-related stimuli (see Cunningham et al., 2011, 2008).

Many years after psychologists were examining the role of the self in cognition, neuroscientists began to focus on the unique characteristics of processing self-relevant information and reported that people are biased toward information related to the self, rather than to other people (e.g., Humphreys & Sui, 2015). Northoff (2016), in particular, posited that self-related processing refers to processing stimuli at a neural (rather than a psychological) level and is automatic as well as implicit. Furthermore, he suggested that self-related processing involves the assignment of self-specificity to internal or external stimuli: an automatic and involuntary process, rather than a voluntary and controlled one. This type of automatic assignment is assumed to be rooted in the resting state of the brain (Northoff, 2016).

More specifically, self-specificity can be assigned automatically, both to external stimuli from the environment and to internal stimuli from one's own

---

1 Utility interventions are used in schooling to highlight the value of a given experience (e.g., doing mathematics) for students. They typically involve participants writing or working with scenarios designed to link content to themselves.

body or brain. For instance, the brain's resting state continuously encounters external stimuli from the environment, like auditory stimuli, as well as changes from internal stimuli from one's own body. Together, these various stimuli continuously modulate the ongoing spontaneous activity in the brain that operationally is also described as the resting state. As Northoff explained: "Even content like one's own name, which appears to be intrinsically self-related, must undergo self-related processing in order for it to assign self-specificity" (Northoff, 2016, p. 4). The process of assigning self-specificity has also been referred to by Sui and colleagues (e.g., Sui et al., 2012) as self-association or self-expansion.

Benefits of Self-Related Information Processing

Studies comparing the processing of self-related with non-self-related stimuli have demonstrated beneficial effects of the former, not only on memory but also on basic psychological functions like perception. For example, Sui and colleagues (Sui et al., 2012, 2014) had participants form associations between three types of geometrical shapes (circles, triangles, and squares) and three types of labels (self, friend, or stranger). Individuals were presented with pairs of shapes and labels that either did or did not match the previously learned associations. Faster reaction times and better accuracy were found for pairings in which the self was involved, whereas performance decreased when pairings included a friend and even more so for pairings with a stranger. In a related study, Frings and Wentura (2014) paired movements (left, right, up, and down) with four different labels (self, mother, stranger, and neutral). After learning the associations between movements and labels, participants were asked to respond to matching and non-matching pairs with cue-based movements and judgments. Pairings that involved the self had faster reaction times and were more accurate than other pairings. Results such as these demonstrate the beneficial effects of self-labels, not only on perception but also on actions.

Neural Activity and Self-Related Information Processing

Neuroscientists have also been exploring the likelihood that people encode information in the brain differently depending on how related it is to their experience and sense of self. Using functional magnetic resonance imaging (fMRI),[2] they have investigated the neural correlates of self-related information processing. This type of research describes how individuals experience

---

2 fMRI is a neuroimaging technique in which changes in blood flow are used to assess the presence and location of brain activity.

their self in daily life: perceiving certain objects, persons, or events. Here, we highlight some of the main findings of recent imaging studies on self-relatedness, which include research of spatial and temporal patterns of brain activity and of social patterns of neural activity during self-related processing.

Spatial Patterns of Neural Activity

The results of various imaging studies have shown that activation of certain brain regions is domain-specific, and clear differences between self- and non-self-related stimuli in these regions could not be observed (see Northoff et al., 2006). However, regions that are domain-independent (not domain-specific) show specific patterns of activation when involved in the neural processing of the self. These patterns have been observed in the cortical midline structure of the brain and have involved trait adjectives, movements, memories, and social communications (see Hu et al., 2016; Northoff et al., 2006; van der Meer et al., 2010). More specifically, in this region, self-specific stimuli induced higher neural activity than non-self-specific stimuli that were irrelevant and unrelated to the person. In addition, researchers also demonstrated that, depending on the nature of the tasks, different areas in the brain may be activated. Participants who were asked to make judgments (involving cognitive operations) showed a greater degree of activation in the dorsal and posterior regions. In contrast, when individuals had only to perceive stimuli without making judgments (not involving cognitive operations), the ventral and anterior regions were more involved (Grimm et al., 2009).

In other words, these findings indicate that different regions are mediating various aspects of self-relatedness and that the cortical midline structures are involved in the neural processing of self-relatedness when attributing self-relevance to stimuli. Furthermore, in a study that also used fMRI measures and focused on the relation between emotions and the self, Phan et al. (2004) reported neural overlap in the two recruited areas. They asked participants to view emotional pictures while they were being scanned and, subsequently, to rate the degree of self-relatedness (personal relevance) of the same set of pictures. Comparisons of the ratings correlated with the fMRI signals and indicated that the degree of activation in the ventromedial prefrontal cortex (VMPFC) predicted the degree of self-relatedness that the subjects attributed to the emotional pictures post-scanning. Other studies (e.g., Moran et al., 2006; Northoff et al., 2009) have also indicated a close relationship of neural activity between self-specificity and emotions.

Social Patterns of Neural Activity

Researchers have suggested that there may be an intrinsically social dimension in neural activity that is essential for consciousness of both one's self and others' sense of self (Humphreys & Sui, 2015; Pfeiffer et al., 2013). For example, Schilbach et al. (2012) investigated the neural overlap between emotional processing, resting state activity (activation that is always present without a particular stimulus), and social-cognitive processing. More specifically, they conducted a meta-analysis including imaging studies from all three kinds of investigations. Their analyses of the brain regions that were implicated in each of the three tasks showed significant recruitment of neural activity in the midline regions, including the ventromedial and dorsomedial prefrontal cortex and the posterior cingulate cortex. In addition, the authors overlaid the activation of emotional, social-cognitive, and resting state tasks in order to detect commonly activated areas. Their data revealed that the midline regions of the dorsomedial prefrontal cortex and the posterior cingulate cortex are commonly shared among emotional and social-cognitive tasks, as well as the resting state. Based on their findings, Schilbach et al. (2012) concluded that neural activity may have an intrinsically social dimension and, as such, may hold implications for consciousness of one's own self and others' selves.

Temporal Patterns of Neural Activity

In addition to establishing spatial patterns of self-related processing based on fMRI studies, temporal patterns associated with self-related stimuli have also been demonstrated using electroencephalogram (EEG) measures.[3] For example, Knyazev's (2013) investigations revealed that when self-related stimuli were compared to non-self-related stimuli, they induced different electrical activity changes in the brain at both 100–200 ms and 300–500 ms after stimulus onset. The temporal patterns between self- and non-self-related stimuli showed both early and late differences in individuals' responses.

Reward, Interest, Self-Related Information Processing, and the Brain

To help explain the benefits of self-related information processing, researchers examined the association of self-relatedness with activation of the reward circuitry. Before discussing this relation, we briefly review aspects of the reward circuitry and its activation.

The reward circuitry is activated by responses to either the anticipation or the receipt of reward. Such activation is considered to be a basic motivational function of the brain and has been shown to generate approach and consummatory behavior and to increase the probability of learning (see Hidi, 2016, for a partial review of the literature). This significant role of reward derives from

---

3 An EEG is a procedure in which electrodes are attached to the scalp with wires in order to test and track patterns in brain waves.

the brain's dopamine-fueled reward circuitry, and from the affective and cognitive benefits of its activation. The reward circuitry includes cortical regions such as the VMPFC, and subcortical regions such as the substantia nigra, ventral tegmental area (VTA), and ventral striatum (VS). The activation of the reward circuitry is associated not only with motivation but also with the constitution of value. By being processed in the brain's dopamine-based reward system, an otherwise value-neutral stimulus attains a certain value – that is, a reward value – and hence increases motivation for the respective content.

Although early research studies focused on how extrinsic rewards activate the reward circuitry (e.g., Schultz, 2007), subsequent neuroscientific investigations have indicated that intrinsic rewards, such as seeking/searching for information, activate the same areas of the reward circuitry as extrinsic rewards (e.g., Gottlieb et al., 2013; Gruber et al., 2014; Kang et al., 2009). Given that information search is fundamental to interest experience, the activation of the reward circuitry associated with information search is also critical for explaining the powerful beneficial effects of interest on performance and learning (Ainely & Hidi, 2014; Renninger & Hidi, 2016). Establishing that interest has a physiological basis also indicates that interest is universal, and that it is not simply a product of socio-cultural circumstance. In other words, all persons regardless of age and context, may be supported to develop interest.

Neuroscientific investigations have pointed to a close neural relationship between reward and the self, and have concluded that reward-self neural overlap occurs in the brain. This finding has been supported by several studies from Northoff and colleagues. For example, using fMRI, de Greck et al. (2008) studied the neural overlap of reward and self-relatedness. They presented participants with different pictures of alcohol, gambling, and food and asked them to evaluate both their rewarding and self-related features. Stimuli evaluated as highly self-related by the participants elicited high signal changes in the reward-related regions (VS, VTA, and VMPFC), whereas those assessed as low self-related did not show these signal changes.

Similarly using fMRI, Ersner-Hershfield et al., (2009) also found evidence that reward and self-relatedness are linked. Their participants were asked to judge personality traits, in relation to themselves and other people, in two time frames: the present and ten years in the future. After one week, participants were asked to choose between immediate monetary rewards and delayed, but larger, rewards. The VMPFC showed greater activity for self-versus-other trials, as well as for self-present versus self-future trials. Interestingly, the researchers found that the greater the VMPFC activity for the present self, the greater the tendency to choose immediate, rather than delayed, monetary rewards (see analogous results by Mitchell et al., 2011).

In another study, Zhan et al. (2016) pointed to the neural overlap of reward-related and self-related tasks in the reward system. These researchers demonstrated that activation by reward expectation enhanced self-face processing.

They recorded event-related potentials during judgments of faces, including those of self, friends, and strangers, as well as judgments of monetary rewards, and concluded that the activation of the reward circuitry yields "a robust and sustained modulation over their overlapped brain areas where reward and self-related processing mechanisms may operate together" (p. 735). On the basis of these findings, Zhan et al. suggested that the reward circuits activated by monetary rewards drive the neural networks associated with self-relevant processing and may enhance neural responses for self-relevant stimuli.

There is also evidence of links between reward and the self in activities that involve personal relevance. For example, using fMRI, Carter et al. (2009) examined the interaction of motivational salience and affective valence with the reward system. They manipulated motivational salience by postulating potential monetary rewards for the self or for charity. For self-directed trials, rather than charity-directed trials, increased activation was found in reward-related regions of the brain. Other studies have shown that the reward circuitry is activated if participants actively engage to earn rewards rather than receiving them passively (Elliot et al., 2004; Tricomi et al., 2004; Zink et al., 2004). It should be noted that the results of these investigations tend to be explained as demonstrating the importance of the saliency of the activity and do not address the role of the self. However, one may conclude that self-related processing is likely to be implicated, if one acknowledges that actively earning rewards involves attention, decision-making, and performance.

Although a significant number of studies provide evidence of reward-self overlap, Northoff and colleagues (Northoff, 2016; Northoff & Hayes, 2011) caution that these findings do not mean that reward and self are identical. Both may dissociate from each other; in other words, even though the two can result in the same brain activation, changes in the task conditions could result in different outcomes. For example, Sui and Humphreys (2015) demonstrated this dissociation behaviorally. They found that an increase in the size of stimuli did not affect reward-related behavior bias, but did increase the self-bias effect.[4] This disassociation also was demonstrated neurally. They observed that reward-related activity signals in three reward regions were normal in recovered alcoholic and gambling patients, whereas the patients' self-related activity was virtually absent, indicating no distinction between high and low self-related stimuli in VS, VTA, and VMPFC.

In sum, the noted studies point to close relations between reward value and interest, as well as between reward value and self-related processing. This latter association is evident in the subcortical-cortical reward circuitry and can be described as reward-self overlap. Neural reward value is likely to be associated with self-relatedness, but both functions, i.e., reward and self-relatedness may also dissociate from each other. That is, even if stimuli attain reward value,

---

4 Self-bias refers to the effect of the self on processing information; individuals process information differently than they would without the bias.

self-related processing is not guaranteed. Furthermore, such disassociation may affect interest. For instance, abstinent alcoholics and pathological gamblers, in their recovery phase, show "normalization" of reward-related activity in the reward system, whereas their self-related activity is depleted and they also show reduced interest (de Greck et al., 2009, 2010). Thus, even the abstinent addicted subjects show decreased interest in others and their own environment as they focus instead on the substance to which they are addicted. One would consequently suppose that the diminished self-related activity in the reward regions may index diminished interest on the behavioral side.

More generally, interest is not only associated with reward circuitry but also with self-related processing. Hence, to generate and yield interest, the respective stimulus or task may need to be associated with self-relatedness. In other words, stimuli may remain "indifferent" for the subject and not trigger interest without a relation to the self. Simple reward or motivation may remain insufficient to yield interest, as in the case of addiction.

However, we also note that triggers for interest have been identified that do not appear to be self-related. For example, intensity or activity level has been found to contribute to the interestingness of text that triggers situational interest (Anderson et al., 1987; Hidi & Baird, 1986). Nevertheless, the self may be a critical aspect of emerging or well-developed individual interest. Hidi et al. (2017) provide further detail about this relation of the self and interest. They point to change in the relationship as interest develops (see Renninger, 2009). In early phases of its development, triggered interest may initiate a connection between the object of interest and the self. In later phases of interest development, the interest-self relation becomes more elaborated; triggers for interest support the deepening of information search about content and support self-identification (identity) with that content. These suggestions need further empirical investigations in order to establish the precise relation between the self and the development of interest.

The Basis Model of Self-Specificity

Northoff's (2016) basis model suggests that self-specificity is a fundamental feature of the brain's spontaneous activity, independent of specific stimuli or tasks that are external to the brain itself. Operationally, the spontaneous activity is investigated in what is described as the "resting state" (when participants are at rest), where no specific stimuli or tasks need to be processed by the brain. The resting state can be tested with eyes closed or eyes open. Several studies have reported a strong neural overlap between the resting state and brain regions recruited during self-specificity (D'Argembeau et al., 2005; Lou et al., 2016; Whitfield-Gabrieli et al., 2011). In order to investigate the special relationship between self-specific activity and resting state activity in subcortical and anterior cortical midline regions of the brain,

Qin and Northoff (2011) conducted a meta-analysis of imaging studies of self and resting state. They concluded that a "rest-self overlap" describes the regional convergence between resting state activity and self-related activity in the cortical midline structures.

Northoff (2016) has also pointed to rest-self containment with the following premises: (a) the resting state contains self-specific information, (b) activity dependence exists between resting state and self-related activity, and (c) self-specificity is encoded in spatiotemporal schemata. Although Northoff noted that these premises need further verification, he suggested that self-specificity in the brain's spontaneous activity may be central in linking the self to either internal or external stimuli.

The Educational Potential of Self-Related Information Processing: The Case of Utility Value Interventions

Although there are aspects of reward, interest, and self-specificity association that still require investigation, neuroscientific research has demonstrated that there is significant modulation of perception, emotion, memory, and reward by self-specificity, especially in the midline brain regions, and that – as Northoff (2016) suggested – the basis model of self-specificity may account for most of these findings. The importance of considering the implications of findings from studies of self-related processing for educational practice is suggested by both present understanding of the influence of self-related information processing, and questions from researchers involved in studying utility value interventions (UVI) who are trying to understand how and why utility value interventions work at certain times and not at others (e.g., Harackiewicz, Smith, et al., 2016; Rosenzweig & Wigfield, 2016).

Educational and social psychologists have acknowledged the importance of the self for how we think, act, and perform (e.g., see Marsh et al., Chapter 2), but in many cases have not yet linked their research to those of neuroscientists.[5] Here, we suggest that utility value interventions linking educational content to personal relevance provide a good example of the way neuroscientific research on self-related processing can help to explain findings from psychological research. Utility value interventions are relatively simple and effective educational interventions that encourage participants to make connections between their lives and content, such as course materials. They have been found to increase value and interest, as well as to result in improved performance. However, these interventions often benefit some groups of students more than others, leading researchers to wonder why this is the case.

---

5 To be fair, neuroscientists also have tended not to link their work to that of psychologists.

When these interventions do work, it is because students find their content personally relevant. Studies of utility value interventions have repeatedly demonstrated that students can be supported to make connections to disciplinary content (e.g., through class activities such as writing), and that these result in improved performance, increased interest, and course re-enrollment (e.g., Hulleman et al., 2016). These interventions have also been found to be most effective for students who are considered to be at-risk (e.g., first-generation and/or underrepresented minority students), suggesting, on the one hand, that they have the potential to close the achievement gaps between students (Harackiewicz, Canning, et al., 2016) and, on the other hand, that they do not function the same way for all individuals. This has led researchers to call for studies that could clarify the intervention's critical features (Harackiewicz et al., 2014).

Hulleman et al. (2016) suggested that targeted psychological mechanisms (e.g., thinking frequently about connections) provide an explanation for the success of the utility value intervention. In a slight revision of this explanation, we suggest that the pervasiveness of the self throughout the whole array of psychological functions may be especially relevant for understanding the impact of utility value interventions. Learning includes perception, action, memory, reward, and emotion (e.g., Shell et al., 2010), and only if these functions are properly recruited will students be able to learn and develop interest in the learning material. Given findings from research on self-relatedness, it appears that when these functions are permeated and driven by self-specificity of information as a basis of interest, they can be properly recruited. Additionally, students are better positioned to learn material that otherwise could feel meaningless because it is neither self-related nor interesting.

Conceptually, the design of utility value interventions is grounded in the expectancy-value theory of student motivation (e.g., Eccles & Wigfield, 2002; Eccles et al., 1983; Hulleman & Barron, 2016; Hulleman et al., 2016; see also reviews by Canning & Harackiewicz, Chapter 25). In this framework, two components determine students' motivation to learn: how well students expect to do on a task (expectancy beliefs) and how much students value the outcome of the task engagement (subjective task value). Researchers have described three types of perceived task values: intrinsic value (enjoyment and interest), attainment value (importance of the task for identity and self-worth), and utility value (usefulness of the task for future goals) (see discussions in Wigfield & Cambria, 2010; Wigfield & Eccles, 2002a, b).[6]

Utility value has been shown to be predictive of students' interest and performance in coursework. For example, in one of the first reported studies of utility value interventions (relevance interventions), Hulleman and Harackiewicz (2009) helped students to focus on the personal relevance and

---

6 Originally, cost was considered as a fourth component of task value, or more specifically, as a negative consequence of task engagement. However, in more recent conceptualizations (e.g., Hulleman et al., 2016), cost is viewed as a unique construct that is independent of expectancy and value.

utility value of school materials by linking them to students' lives using writing exercises.[7] They randomly assigned high school science students to either write about how the materials they were studying related to their lives or to write summaries of the materials. The results confirmed that the intervention was effective for students who had low expectancies of success at the beginning of the course. Hulleman and Barron (2016) have since described a series of studies that similarly involved dividing high school and undergraduate students randomly into experimental and control groups before a learning session. In the experimental groups, students wrote about how the topics of the assigned tasks applied to their lives. In the control condition, students wrote summaries of the topics assigned. The studies involved undergraduates in statistics and psychology classes, as well as high school students in science classrooms. The overall results of these studies showed that the interventions in the experimental group, but not the control group, enhanced students' interest (Hulleman et al., 2010), maintained their interest over time (Harackiewicz et al., 2009), and increased their academic performance (Hulleman & Harackiewicz, 2009). Across all studies, the findings were particularly strong for students who had low expectations of academic success and/or who performed poorly on initial exams (i.e., low perceived or actual competence).

Similarly, Gaspard et al. (2015) examined how, in classrooms, students' value beliefs in mathematics could be promoted by relevance interventions that had several design features aimed at increasing their effectiveness. First, they had 82 classes (1,916 students in ninth grade) participate, allowing between-classroom designs of two intervention groups and a control group. Second, in addition to the usual writing condition, they devised a second category of interventions called the quotation condition. Students in the quotation condition were asked to read six quotations from interviews with young adults who were describing situations in which mathematics was useful for them, and then to evaluate the personal relevance of the quotations. Specifically, the students were asked to (a) rate the novelty of the statements, (b) describe whether they found them convincing and why, and (c) rank them for personal relevance. The results indicated that the quotation condition was beneficial for all of the three perceived values in the expectancy model (intrinsic value, attainment value, and utility value), whereas the writing condition increased only utility value. This finding suggests that the intervention is more effective when students are given personally relevant information to evaluate than when they have to generate personal associations on their own.

---

7 As reported by Lazowski and Hulleman (2016), their research was foreshadowed by Oyserman et al.'s (2002) nine-week, after-school "possible selves intervention" that was undertaken with African American middle school students who were asked to imagine themselves as successful adults and connect these images to their current school involvement. By the end of the year, students who received the intervention showed many positive outcomes, such as having more concerns about doing well in school, better attendance records, and more balanced perceptions of their possible selves.

Hulleman et al. (2016) replicated prior work in a college-level, general education course by demonstrating that utility value interventions encouraging students to make connections between their lives and their course materials increase both interest and performance. As in earlier studies, the researchers found that low-performing students benefited the most from the intervention. They also extended prior research by both measuring and manipulating the frequency of the students' abilities to provide connections between the materials and their lives. In the first study, they found that making more connections was positively related to expecting to do well in the course, valuing the course material, and continuing interest. In the second study, the results showed that with increased numbers of connections, students became more confident that they could learn the material and had better course performance. Again, the utility value intervention was particularly effective for the lowest performing students. Compared to those in the control condition who showed a steady decline in performance across the semester, low-performing male students increased their performance across the semester. The difference between the utility value and control conditions for low-performing male students was strongest on the final exam (d = 0.76).

In addition to developing utility value in the classroom, researchers have also examined interventions that encourage parents to talk to their children about the utility value of math and science in order to influence their own and their children's interest in these subjects (Harackiewicz et al., 2012). Relevant materials (two brochures and access to a website) were delivered to parents whose children were in the intervention groups. The findings indicated that those 10th and 11th grade students whose parents received the interventions took nearly one more math or science course in their last two years of high school than the classmates whose parents did not receive the materials.

In a follow-up study, Hyde et al. (2016) focused on the role of mothers and their communications with their adolescent children about mathematics and science courses. While the results of this study were complex, one of the more relevant findings was that mothers' scores on supporting personal connections (e.g., child-specific reasons that the mathematics or science class would be relevant) directly predicted the adolescents' interest in and utility value measures for STEM. These scores also had an indirect effect on STEM course-taking through the variable of adolescents' interest. Hyde et al. noted that these research findings are consistent with investigations on the effectiveness of personalization in mathematics instruction in schools reported by Walkington and colleagues (Walkington, 2013; Walkington et al., 2013). They further observe:

> Making personal connections can become a powerful tool for parents in their communications with their children about school. Moreover, any parent can use personalization, even if they have not taken the relevant class and cannot elaborate about its usefulness. The effect of personal connections demonstrates how important parents can be. Parents may even

be more effective than teachers at making personal connections as they have more detailed knowledge of their own children's interests, experiences and aspirations (Hyde, et al., 2016, p. 602).

The authors also concluded that many mothers were quite adept at making personal connections. The most common themes of these connections were the everyday usefulness of materials from a class and the importance of materials for the adolescents' intended careers. Connections to the adolescents' personal interests were also common. Less frequently, mothers made connections to adolescents' ability or talent and to adolescents' past experiences. It may be concluded that parents' socialization practices can be particularly effective if parents use personal connections when explaining the usefulness of mathematics or science classes.

Utility value interventions have been especially effective in promoting the interest and/or performance of students with low performance expectations, as well as those with histories of low performance. Based on these findings, Harackiewicz, Canning, et al. (2016) examined the effectiveness of these types of interventions for underrepresented minority (URM) and first-generation (FG) students. Their intervention involved 1,040 students enrolled in an introductory biology course. Individuals in the utility value condition received three assignments in which they wrote about how the course content was relevant to their own lives. The control participants wrote summaries of course content. Analysis of participants' writing indicated not only that students in the utility value condition were more engaged in their tasks, but also that even though the intervention was successful in helping all students to find utility value in the course content, it was particularly helpful for the URM and FG participants.

Harackiewicz, Canning, et al. (2016) noted that utility value interventions help students discover connections between their lives and course topics in their own terms, and suggested that discovering such connections helps students appreciate the value of their coursework and leads to deeper levels of engagement and improved performance. Lazowski and Hulleman (2016) have concluded that careful conceptual work is required to understand which interventions and constructs strengthen each other, and how they should be ordered developmentally (which should come before the other). Hulleman and Baron (2016), moreover, suggested that relevance interventions encouraging students to discover the connections between their lives and their topics of study are effective because they encourage students to see greater purpose and utility in what they are studying. In their view, there is a clear and causal relation between the interventions and students' improved interest and performance.

What do these data imply for addressing why and when utility value interventions work? They suggest that there is a set of related associations explaining the success of the utility value intervention: because the utility value intervention encourages the linkage of academic content to the self through personal relevance, it can activate the reward circuitry and trigger interest. In other words, reward and self-activation overlap in the brain and can propel interest to develop and benefit learning. However, once individuals experience self-involvement and/or interest prior to the utility value intervention, there is likely to be an existing activation of the reward system and of the self that makes the utility value intervention ineffective. That is, the brain activation may not be additive to the existing condition for these students. Instead, the students who are most likely to benefit from utility value interventions are those who are not interested or involved with the content, and thus are at risk in terms of academic success. These students need support to make personally relevant (self-related), meaningful connections to the content they are to learn. When they make such connections, they activate the part of the brain where the self and reward overlap, setting up the potential for interest to develop.

Concluding Thoughts

In this chapter, we point to the importance of the self, reward processes, and interest in addition to their interactions in providing students with the opportunity to make connections between themselves and academic content. In order to motivate the unmotivated learner, it appears that linking content to the self is a critical starting point, one that may have educational benefits throughout development. In other words, self-relatedness is interest enhancing.

Further empirical support is needed in order to address the degree to which stimuli related to the self have an impact on cognitive functioning. The benefits of self-relatedness may be a key to better understanding how to support motivation for learning. We took utility value interventions as a particular case illustration in this chapter. A wide range of interventions have addressed support for student learning (e.g., belongingness, cooperative learning, cognitive reappraisal, growth mindset, mindfulness meditation, possible selves, self-affirmations); in addition to utility value, none of these seem to have addressed neuroscientific research on the self or reward. A number have highlighted the role of the self (e.g., belongingness [Hurtado & Carter, 1997], careers [Woolley et al., 2013], cognitive reappraisal [Schweder, 1993], self-affirmations [Cohen et al., 2006]), but the association of reward activation, the self, and interest development in the support of increases in learning, value, and interest has not been articulated as such.

Neuroscience provides substantive evidence of self-related information processing that can be distinguished from other forms of information processing. Specifically, self-related information processing has been shown to benefit perception, activity, and memory. The neuro-mechanisms of this type of processing have also been identified and reveal overlaps in the brain with activation of the reward circuitry and links to interest. In other words, the self may be a trigger for interest and may also provide an explanation of why interest, once triggered, is then maintained and continues to develop. Unaddressed, however, are details of this relation and consideration of developmental changes. That is, we do not know if the self has, indeed, an increasingly coordinated and important relation to interest development as we suggest, and research on the case of utility value interventions reviewed here does not answer this question. Longitudinal data may provide more answers. Moreover, future studies may be conducted in which utility value interventions are accompanied by brain imaging, testing for the neural responses to self-related stimuli in each individual participant before and after the intervention. One would predict that, if the participant learned successfully, there should be increased neural responsivity in the cortical midline structure to learning material-relevant self-related stimuli after UVI when compared to before UVI. In contrast, participants with low or absent learning effects should not show any change in the cortical midline structure responsivity UVI and, even more importantly, should show decreased connection from the cortical midline structures to the reward circuitry including the ventral striatum. Ideally, extending even further into the future, fMRI may be used to test for those stimuli that are highly self-related to participants by measuring such responsivity; these stimuli may then be applied in subsequent UVI. This would amount to a neurally guided individualized UVI.

The literature on self-related processing also suggests that other possible studies could be undertaken. For example, a study might compare the effects of utility value interventions on students who are considered to be at risk on the basis of their race, ethnicity, or social class with students who are attending institutions identified as successfully targeting minority STEM retention, through what Estrada et al. (2016) describe as

> deliberate development of co-curricular activities that include strong opportunities for research participation; participation in special workshops, seminars, and courses; careful academic and career advisement; and incorporation into the campus scientific community through the interaction with science faculty, academic and industrial scientists, and other successful science students (p. 6).

(e.g., Hernandez et al., 2013; Matsui et al., 2003; Slovacek et al., 2011). In this case, we would predict that the utility value intervention would be less effective for students with similar backgrounds who were not in the same type of supportive programming, or for those who already have interest and/or have made academic connections because of self-related processing. Another suggestion for further study comes from findings concerning the dissociation of the self and reward, which would predict that students with addictive issues may be less likely to benefit from utility value intervention support to make connections to academic content that is self-related.

References

Ainely, M. & Hidi, S. (2014). Interest and engagement. In R. Pekrun & L. Linnenbrink-Gracia (Eds.), *International handbook of emotions and education* (pp. 205–27). New York, NY: Routledge.

Anderson, R. C., Shirey, L. L., Wilson, P. T., & Fielding, L. G. (1987). Interestingness of children's reading material. In R. E. Snow & M. J. Farr (Eds.), *Aptitude, learning, and instruction, Vol. III: Cognitive and affective process analyses* (pp. 287–99). Hillsdale, NJ: Erlbaum.

Carter, R. M., MacInnes, J. J., Huettel, S. A., & Adcock, R. A. (2009). Activation in the VTA and nucleus accumbens increases in anticipation of both gains and losses. *Frontiers in Behavioral Neuroscience, 3*(21). doi:10.3389/neuro.08.021.2009

Cohen, G. L., Garcia, J., Apfel, N., & Master, A. (2006). Reducing the racial achievement gap: A social-psychological intervention. *Science, 313*(5791), 1307–10. doi:10.1126/science.1128317

Cunningham, S. J., Brady-Van den Bos, M., & Turk, D. J. (2011). Exploring the effects of ownership and choice on self-memory biases. *Memory, 19*(5), 449–61. doi:10.1080/09658211.2011.584388

Cunningham, S. J., Turk, D. J., Macdonald, L. M., & Macrae, C. N. (2008). Yours or mine? Ownership and memory. *Consciousness and Cognition, 17*(1), 312–18. doi:10.1016/j.concog.2007.04.003

D'Argembeau, A., Collette, F., Van der Linden, Laureys, S., Del Fiore, G., Degueldre, C., … Salmon, E. (2005). Self-referential reflective and its relationship with rest: A PET study. *NeuroImage, 25*(2), 616–24. doi:10.1016/j.neuroimage.2004.11.048

de Greck, M., Enzi, B., Prösch, U., Gantman, A., Tempelmann, C., & Northoff, G. (2010). Decreased neuronal activity in reward circuitry of pathological gamblers during processing of personal relevant stimuli. *Human Brain Mapping, 31*(11), 1802–12. doi:10.1002/hbm.20981

de Greck, M., Rotte, M., Paus, R., Moritz, D., Thiemann, R., Proesch, U., … Northoff, G. (2008). Is our self based on reward? Self-relatedness recruits neural activity in the reward system. *NeuroImage, 39*(4), 2066–75.

de Greck, M., Supady, A., Thiemann, R., Tempelmann, C., Bogerts, B., Forschner, L., … Northoff, G. (2009). Decreased neural activity in reward circuitry during personal reference in abstinent alcoholics – A fMRI study. *Human Brain Mapping, 30*(5), 1691–704. doi:10.1002/hbm.20634

Denny, B. T., Kober, H., Wager, T. D., & Oschner, K. N. (2012). A meta-analysis of functional neuroimaging studies of self and other judgements reveals a spatial gradient for mentalizing in medical prefrontal cortex. *Journal of Cognitive Neuroscience, 24*(8) 1742–52. doi:10.1162/jocn_a_00233

Eccles, J. S. & Wigfield, A. (2002). Motivational beliefs, values, and goals. *Annual Review of Psychology, 53*(1), 109–32. doi:10.1146/annurev.psych.53.100901.135153

Eccles, J. S., Adler, T. F., Futterman, R., Goff, S. B., Kaczala, C. M., Meece, J., & Midgley, C. (1983). Expectancies, values and academic behaviors. In J. T. Spence (Ed.), *Achievement and achievement motives* (pp. 75–146). San Francisco, CA: W. H. Freeman.

Elliott, R., Newman, J. L., Longe, O. A., & William Deakin, J. F. (2004). Instrumental responding for rewards is associated with enhanced neuronal response in subcortical reward systems. *NeuroImage, 21*, 984–90.

Ersner-Hershfield, H., Wimmer, G. E., & Knutson, B. (2009). Saving for the future self: Neural measures of future self-continuity predict temporal discounting. *Social Cognitive and Affective Neuroscience, 4*(1), 85–92. doi:10.1093/scan/nsn042

Estrada, M., Burnett, M., Campbell, A. G., Campbell, P. B., Denetclaw, W. F., Gutiérriz, C. G., ... Zavala, M. (2016). Improving underrepresented minority student persistence in STEM. *CBE – Life Science Education, 15*(3), Es5. doi:10.1187/cbe.16-01-0038

Frings, C. & Wentura, D. (2014). Self-priorization processes in action and perception. *Journal of Experimental Psychology: Human Perception and Performance, 40*(5), 1737. doi:10.1037/a0037376

Gaspard, H., Dicke, A. L., Flunger, B., Brisson, B. M., Hafner, I., Nagengast, B., & Trautwein, U. (2015). Fostering adolescents' value beliefs for mathematics with a relevance intervention in the classroom. *Developmental Psychology, 51*(9), 1226–40. doi:10.1037/dev0000028

Gottlieb, J., Oudeyer, P.-Y., Lopes, M., & Baranes, A. (2013). Information seeking, curiosity and attention: Computational and neural mechanisms. *Trends in Cognitive Sciences, 17*(11) 585–93. doi:10.1016/j.tics.2013.09.001

Grimm, S., Ernst, J., Boesiger, P., Schuepbach, D., Hell, D., Boeker, H., & Northoff, (2009). Increased self-focus in major depressive disorder is related to neural abnormalities in subcortical-cortical midline structures. *Human Brain Mapping, 30*(8), 2617–27. doi:10.1002/hbm.20693

Gruber, M. J., Gelman, B. D., & Ranganath, C. (2014). States of curiosity modulate hippocampus-dependent learning via the dopaminergic circuit. *Neuron, 84*(2), 486–96. doi:10.1016/j.neuron.2014.08.060

Harackiewicz, J. M., Canning, E., Priniski, S. J., & Tibbetts, Y. (2016, April). *Why is writing about value so powerful?* Paper presented as part of the symposium, The roles of value and interest in promoting learning. (K. A. Renninger, Chair). American Educational Research Association, Washington, DC.

Harackiewicz, J. M., Canning, E. A., Tibbetts, Y., Giffen, C., Blair, S. S., Rouse, D. I., & Hyde, J. S. (2014). Closing the social class achievement gap for first-generation students in undergraduate biology. *Journal of Educational Psychology, 106*(2), 375–89. doi:10.1037/a0034679

Harackiewicz, J. M., Canning, E. A., Tibbetts, Y., Prinski, S. J., & Hyde, J. S. (2015). Closing the achievement gaps with a utility-value intervention: Disentangling race and social class. *Journal of Personality and Social Psychology, 111*(5), 745–65. doi:10.1037/pspp0000075

Harackiewicz, J. M., Hulleman, C. S., & Pastor, D. A. (2009, August). *Developmental trajectories of interest within semester-long courses in high school science and introductory psychology.* Paper presented at the European Association for Research on Learning and Instruction (EARLI) Biennial Conference. Munich, Germany.

Harackiewicz, J. M., Rozek, C. R., Hulleman, C. S., & Hyde, J. S. (2012). Helping parents motivate their teens in mathematics and science: An experimental test of a utility-value intervention. *Psychological Science, 23*(8), 899–906. doi:10.1177/0956797611435530

Harackiewicz, J. M., Smith, J. L., & Priniski, S. J. (2016). Interest matters: The importance of promoting interest in education. *Policy Insights from the Behavioral and Brain Sciences, 3*(2), 220–7. doi:10.1177/2372732216655542

Harackiewicz, J. M., Tibbetts, Y., Canning, E., & Hyde, J. S. (2014). Harnessing values to promote motivation in education. In S. A. Karabenick & T. C. Urdan (Eds.), *Motivational interventions* (Vol. 18, pp. 71–105). UK: Emerald. doi:10.1108/S0749-742320140000018002

Hernandez, P. R., Schultz, P. W., Estrada, M., Woodcock, A., & Chance, R. C. (2013). Sustaining optimal motivation: A longitudinal analysis of interventions to broaden participation of underrepresented students in STEM. *Journal of Educational Psychology, 105*(1), 1–36. doi:10.1037/a0029691

Hidi, S. (2016). Revisiting the role of rewards in motivation and learning: Implications of neuroscientific research. *Educational Psychology Review, 28*(1), 61–93.

Hidi, S. & Baird, W. (1986). Interestingness: A neglected variable in discourse processing. *Cognitive Science, 10*(2), 179–94.

Hidi, S. E., Renninger, K. A., & Northoff, G. (2017). The development of interest and self-related processing. In F. Guay, H. W. Marsh, D. M. McInerney, & R. G. Craven (Eds.), *International advances in self research, Volume 6: SELF – Driving positive psychology and well-being.* Charlotte, NC: Information Age Press.

Hu, C., Di, X., Eickhoff, S. B., Zhang, M., Peng, K., Guo, H., & Sui, J. (2016). Distinct and common aspects of physical and psychological self-representation in the brain: A meta-analysis of self-bias in facial and self-referential judgements. *Neuroscience & Biobehavioral Reviews, 61,* 197–207. doi:10.1016/j.neubiorev.2015.12.003

Hulleman, C. S. & Barron, K. E. (2016). Motivation interventions in education: Bridging theory, research, and practice. In L. Corno & E. M. Anderman (Eds.), *Handbook of educational psychology* (3rd ed., pp. 160–71). New York, NY: Routledge, Taylor and Francis.

Hulleman, C. & Harackiewicz, J. (2009). Promoting interest and performance in high school science classes. *Science, 326*(5698), 1410–12. doi:10.1126/science.1177067

Hulleman, C. S., Godes, O., Hendricks, B. L., & Harackiewicz, J. M. (2010). Enhancing interest and performance with a utility value intervention. *Journal of Educational Psychology, 102,* 880–95. doi:10.1037/a0019506

Hulleman, C. S., Kosovich, J. J., Barron, K. E., & Daniel, D. B. (2016). Making connections: Replicating and extending the utility value intervention in the classroom. *Journal of Educational Psychology, 109*(3), 387–404. doi:10.1037/edu0000146

Humphreys, G. W. & Sui, J. (2015). The salient self: Social saliency effects based on self-bias. *Journal of Cognitive Psychology, 27*(2), 129–40.

Hurtado, S. & Carter, D. F. (1997). Effects of college transition and perceptions of campus climate on Latino college students' sense of belonging. *Sociology of Education, 70*(4), 324–45. doi:10.2307/2673270

Hyde, J. S., Canning, E. A., Rozek, C. S., Clarke, E., Hulleman, C. S., & Harackiewicz, J. (2016). The role of mothers' communication in promoting motivation for math and science course-taking in high school. *Journal of Research on Adolescence, 27,* 49–64. doi:10.1111/jora.12253

Kang, M. J., Hsu, M., Krajbich, I. M., Loewenstein, G., McClure, S. M., Wang, J. T., & Camerer, C. F., (2009). The wick in the candle of learning: Epistemic curiosity activates reward circuitry and enhances memory. *Psychological Science, 20,* 963–73. doi:10.1111/j.1467-9280.2009.02402.x

Knyazev, G. G. (2013). EEG correlates of self-referential processing. *Frontiers in Human Neuroscience, 7,* 1–14. doi:10.3389/fnhum.2013.00264

Lazowski, R. A. & Hulleman, C. S. (2016). Motivation interventions in education: A meta-analytic review. *Review of Educational Research, 86*(2), 602–40. doi:10.3102/0034654315617832

Lou, H. C., Changeux, J. P., & Rosenstand, A. (2016). Towards a cognitive neuroscience of self-awareness. *Neuroscience and Biobehavioral Reviews. 83*, 765–73. doi:10.1016/j.neubiorev.2016.04.004

Matsui, J., Liu, R., & Kane, C. M. (2003). Evaluating a science diversity program at UC Berkeley: More questions than answers. *Cell Biology Education, 2*, 117–21. doi:10.1187/cbe.02-10-0050

van der Meer, L., Costafreda, S., Aleman, A., & David, A. S. (2010). Self-reflection and the brain: A theoretical review and meta-analysis of neuroimaging studies with implications for schizophrenia. *Neuroscience & Behavioral Reviews, 34*(6), 935–46. doi:10.1016/j.neubiorev.2009.12.004

Mitchell, J. P., Schirmer, J., Ames, D. L., & Gilbert, D. T. (2011). Medial prefrontal cortex predicts intertemporal choice. *Journal of Cognitive Neuroscience, 23*(4), 857–66. doi:10.1162/jocn.2010.21479

Moran, J. M., Macrae, C. N., Heatherton, T. F., Wyland, C. L., & Kelley, W. M. (2006). Neuroanatomical evidence for distinct cognitive and affective components of self. *Journal of Cognitive Neuroscience, 18*(9), 1586–94.

Northoff, G. (2016). Is the self a higher-order or fundamental function of the brain? The "basis model of self-specificity" and its encoding by the brain's spontaneous activity. *Cognitive Neuroscience, 7*(1–4), 203–22. doi:10.1080/17588928.2015.1111868

Northoff, G. & Hayes, D. J. (2011). Is our self nothing but reward? *Biological Psychiatry, 69*(11), 1019–25. doi:10.1016/j.biopsych.2010.12.014

Northoff, G., Heinzel, A., de Greck, M. D., Bermpohl, F., Dobrowolny, H., & Panksepp, J. (2006). Self-referential processing in our brain–A meta-analysis of imaging studies on the self. *NeuroImage, 31*(1), 440–57. doi:10.1016/j.neuroimage.2005.12.002

Northoff, G., Schneider, F., Rotte, M., Matthiae, C., Tempelmann, C., Wiebking, C., ... Panksepp, J., (2009). Differential parametric modulation of self-relatedness and emotions in different brain regions. *Human Brain Mapping, 30*(2), 369–82. doi:10.1002/hbm.20510

Oyserman, D., Terry, K., & Bybee, D., (2002). A possible selves intervention to enhance school involvement. *Journal of Adolescence, 25*, 313–26. doi:10.1006/jado.2002.0474

Pfeiffer, U. J., Vogeley, K., & Schilbach, L. (2013). From gaze cueing to dual eye-tracking: Novel approaches to investigate the neural correlates of gaze in social interaction. *Neuroscience & Biobehavioral Reviews, 37*(10), 2516–28. doi:10.1016/j.neubiorev.2013.07.017

Phan, K. L., Taylor, S. F., Welsh, R. C., Ho, S. H., Britton, J. C., & Liberzon, I. (2004). Neural correlates of individual ratings of emotional salience: A trial-related fMRI study. *NeuroImage, 21*(2), 768–80. doi:10.1016/j.neuroimage.2003.09.072

Qin, P. & Northoff, G. (2011). How is our self related to midline regions and the default-mode network? *NeuroImage, 57*(3), 1221–33.

Renninger, K. A. (2009). Interest and identity development in instruction: An inductive model. *Educational Psychologist, 44*(2), 1–14. doi:10.1080/00461520902832392

Renninger, K. A. & Hidi, S. (2016). *The power of interest for motivation and engagement*. New York, NY: Routledge.

Rosenzweig, E. Q. & Wigfield, A. (2016). STEM motivation interventions for adolescents: A promising start, but further to go. *Educational Psychologist, 51*(2), 146–63. doi:10.1080/00461520.2016.1154792

Schilbach, L., Bzdok, D., Timmermans, B., Fox, P. T., Laird, A. R., Vogeley, K., & Eickhoff, S. B. (2012). Introspective minds: Using ALE meta-analyses to study commonalities in the neural correlates of emotional processing, social & unconstrained cognition. *PLoS One, 7*(2), e30920.

Schilbach, L., Timmermans, B., Reddy, V., Costall, A., Bente, G., Schlicht, T., & Vogeley, K. (2013, August). Toward a second person. *Behavioural Brain Science, 36*(4), 393–414. doi:10.1017/S0140525X1200066

Schultz, W. (2007). Behavioural theories and the neurophysiology of reward. *Annual Review of Psychology, 57*, 87–115.

Schweder, R. (1993). The cultural psychology of the emotions. In M. Lewis & J. M. Haviland (Eds.), *Handbook of emotions* (pp. 417–31). New York, NY: Guilford Publications.

Shell, D. F., Brooks, D. W., Trainin, G., Wilson, K. M., Kauffman, D. F., & Herr, L. M. (2010). *The unified learning model: How motivational, cognitive, and neurobiological sciences inform best teaching practices.* Dordrecht: Springer. doi:10.1007/978-90-481-3215-7

Slovacek, S. P., Whittinghill, J. C., Tucker, S., Rath, K. A., Peterfreund, A. R., Kuehn, G. D., & Reinke, Y. G. (2011). Minority students severely underrepresented in science, technology engineering and math. *Journal of STEM Education, 12*(1), 5–16.

Sui, J. & Humphreys, G. W. (2015). Super-size me: Self biases increase to larger stimuli. *Psychonomic Bulletin & Review, 22*(2), 550–8. doi:10.3758/s13423-014-0690-6

Sui, J., He, X., & Humphreys, G. W. (2012). Perceptual effects of social salience: Evidence from self-prioritization effects on perceptual matching. *Journal of Experimental Psychology: Human Perception and Performance, 38*(5), 1105–17. doi:10.1037/a0029792

Sui, J., Liu, M., Mevorach, C., & Humphreys, G. W. (2013). The salient self: The left intraparietal sulcus responds to social as well as perceptual-salience after self-association. *Cerebral Cortex, 25*(4), 1060–8. doi:10.1093/cercor/bht302

Sui, J., Rotshtein, P., & Humphreys, G. W. (2014). Coupling social attention to the self forms a network for personal significance. *Proceedings of the National Academy of Sciences, 110*(19), 7607–12. doi:10.1073/pnas.1221862110

Symons, C. S. & Johnson, B. T. (1997). The self-reference effect in memory: A meta-analysis. *Psychological Bulletin, 121*(3), 371–94.

Tricomi, E. M., Delgado, M. R., & Fiez, J. A. (2004). Modulation of caudate activity by action contingency. *Neuron, 41*, 281–92. doi:10.1016/S0896-6273(03)00848-1

Walkington, C. (2013). Using adaptive learning technologies to personalize instruction to student interests: The impact of relevant contexts on performance and learning outcomes. *Journal of Educational Psychology, 105*(94), 932–45. doi:10.1037/a0031882

Walkington, C., Petrosino, A., & Sherman, M. (2013). Supporting algebraic reasoning through personalized story scenarios: How situational understanding mediates performance and strategies. *Mathematical Thinking and Learning, 15*(2), 89–120. doi:10.1080/10986065.2013.770717

Whitfield-Gabrieli, S., Moran, J. M., Nieto-Castanon, A., Triantafyllou, C., Saxe, R., & Gabrieli, J. D. (2011). Associations and dissociations between default and self-reference networks in the human brain. *NeuroImage*, *55*(1), 225–32. doi:10.1016/j.neuroimage.2010.11.048

Wigfield, A. & Cambria, J. (2010). Students' achievement values, goal orientations, and interest: Definitions, development, and relations to achievement outcomes. *Developmental Review*, *30*(1), 1–35. doi:10.1016/j.dr.2009.12.001

Wigfield, A. & Eccles, J. S. (2002a). Children's motivation during the middle school years. In J. Aronson (Ed.), *Improving academic achievement: Contributions of social psychology* (pp. 159–84). San Diego, CA: Academic Press. doi:10.1016/b978-012064455-1/50011-7

Wigfield, A. & Eccles, J. S. (2002b). The development of competence beliefs, expectancies for success, and achievement values from childhood through adolescence. In A. Wigfield & J. S. Eccles (Eds.), *Development of achievement motivation. A volume in the Educational Psychology Series* (pp. 249–84). San Diego, CA: Acade5mic Press. doi:10.1016/B978-012750053-9/50012-7

Woolley, M. E., Rose, R. A., Orthner, D. K., Akos, P. T., & Jones-Sanpei, H. (2013). Advancing academic achievement through career relevance in the middle grades: A longitudinal evaluation of CareerStart. *American Educational Research Journal*, *50*(6), 1309–35. doi:10.3102/0002831213488818

Zhan, Y., Xiao, X., Li, F., Fan, W., & Zhong, Y. (2016). Reward promotes self-face processing: An event-related potential study. *Frontiers in Psychology*, *7*, 735. doi:10.3389/fpsyg.2016.00735

Zink, C. F., Pagnoni, G., Martin-Skurski, M. E., Chappelow, J. C., & Berns, G. S. (2004). Human striatal responses to monetary reward depend on saliency. *Neuron*, *42*, 509–17. doi:10.1016/S0896-6273(04)00183-7

2 The Centrality of Academic Self-Concept to Motivation and Learning

Herbert W. Marsh, Marjorie Seaton, Theresa Dicke,
Philip D. Parker, and Marcus S. Horwood

Abstract: The construct of self-concept lies at the core of the positive psychology revolution. Historically, as one of the cornerstone constructs in the social sciences, the approach to self-concept has been adapted to focus on how healthy individuals can thrive in life. In this chapter we differentiate between the historical unidimensional perspective of self-concept (centered on self-esteem) and the evolving multifaceted models discriminating between different aspects of self (such as specific academic, social, physical, and emotional components).

We review:

- *the definition of self-concept and the reason it is so important;*
- *historical and evolving perspectives of self-concept;*
- *general and domain-specific theoretical models with associated empirical research regarding self-concept, motivation, and performance;*
- *the way different self-concept domains vary as a function of gender and age;*
- *the impact of specific psychological and social traits on self-concept development;*
- *the differentiation between multidimensional perspectives of personality and self-concept;*
- *theoretical models of academic self-concept formation and its relation to achievement;*
- *frame of reference effects in self-concept formation;*
- *a construct-validity approach to self-concept enhancement interventions; and directions for further research.*

Self-concept is one of the oldest constructs in psychology. The idea of the self-concept existed long before the science of psychology was born. Hattie (1992) noted that the foundations of self-concept theory went back as far as Socrates and Plato in the fourth century BC, and subsequently to Descartes, James, Freud,

The authors gratefully acknowledge the generous funding from the Australian Research Council over the last 30 years, which enabled much of the research presented in this monograph.

Bandura, and Rogers. Typing "self-concept" into a search engine produces more than 29,000,000 hits. While it is entirely probable that not all of these will relate to self-concept per se, this staggering number of hits demonstrates just how important self-concept is, even in today's technologically advanced world. This chapter begins by discussing the definition, significance, and structure of self-concept, focusing on its multidimensionality, and continues by reviewing developmental, gender, and educational perspectives, the relation between self-concept and achievement, frame of reference models, and personality perspectives.

What Is Self-Concept and Why Is It Important?

Self-concept and related self-beliefs are key psychological constructs. The formation of self-concept represents: "a basic psychological need that has a pervasive impact on daily life, cognition and behavior, across age and culture ... an ideal cornerstone on which to rest the achievement motivation literature but also a foundational building block for any theory of personality, development and well-being" (Elliot & Dweck, 2005, p. 8); a "cornerstone of both social and emotional development" in early childhood (Kagan et al., 1995, p. 18;); "a major (perhaps the major) structure of personality" (Greenwald, 1988, p. 30); and a widely accepted critical psychological construct that leads to success in educational settings (Chen, et al., 2013), social and emotional situations (Harter, 2012), and daily life more generally (Elliot & Dweck, 2005). Thus, Guo et al. (2015) found that academic self-concept (ASC) in high school had stronger effects on long-term occupational aspirations and educational attainment five years after high school graduation than did IQ or intrinsic and utility-value motivation.

For over a century, theorists have disputed the nature and structure of self-concept. As far back as 1890, James interpreted self-concept from a multidimensional, hierarchical perspective. He distinguished between the material, social, and spiritual self. He proposed that these three components of the self are grouped together in a hierarchical structure, with the material self at the base, the social self in the middle, and the spiritual self at the pinnacle of the hierarchy. Subsequent theorists (e.g., Marx & Winne, 1978), however, argued that self-concept was unidimensional in structure, with self-concept being denoted by a single construct such as self-esteem, self-appraisal, or self-worth. Hence, notwithstanding James' insights into the structure of self-concept, by the 1970s the area was lacking in sound methodology, measurement instruments, definition, and theoretical perspectives (e.g., Shavelson, et al., 1976; Wells & Marwell, 1976; Wylie, 1979). For these reasons, Hattie (1992) labeled this period as one of "dustbowl empiricism" as most self-concept researchers tended to "throw it in and see what happens". Thus, in reviewing self-concept research, Byrne (2002) asserted:

> Without question, the most profound happening in self-concept research during the past century was the wake-up call sounded regarding the sorry state of its reported findings, which was followed by a conscious effort on the part of methodologically oriented researchers to rectify the situation (p. 898).

The wake-up call was trumpeted by Shavelson et al. (1976). While criticizing deficiencies in self-concept research, they proposed a mature construct definition of self-concept and suggested that self-concept is multidimensional and hierarchical in structure. Integrating key features from 17 different conceptual definitions of self-concept, they defined self-concept as a "person's perception of himself ... formed through his experience with his environment ... and influenced especially by environmental reinforcements and significant others" (Shavelson et al., 1976, p. 411). Thus, not only does self-concept influence behavior, but behavior in turn influences one's self-perceptions, and how one views oneself is a function of one's interactions with others. In a sense, others are a mirror through which one catches glimpses of who and what one is. This conceptualization of self-concept, being influenced by both oneself and others, has led to self-concept being regarded as a critical variable in a variety of research areas.

The multidimensional hierarchical model proposed by Shavelson et al. (1976) had general self-concept (also known as self-esteem) at the pinnacle of the hierarchy, divided into two second-order components: ASC and non-ASC (see Figure 2.1a). These two factors were further partitioned, with ASC being divided into subject-specific self-concepts and non-ASC comprising physical, social, and emotional components. At the time, Shavelson et al. were unable to empirically test their model, as appropriate measurement instruments were unavailable. This was rectified by Marsh and Shavelson (1985) with the Self-Description Questionnaire (SDQ), which was based on the Shavelson et al. model. Their results produced a revised model (Figure 2.1b) showing that a singular ASC factor was inappropriate. Instead two factors, verbal self-concept and mathematics self-concept, were required to ascertain relationships between the lower-order factors (see Figure 2.1b). Subsequent SDQ instruments (see Marsh, 2007; also see review by Byrne, 1996) were developed for children (SDQI), adolescents (SDQII), and late-adolescents/young adults (SDQIII), as well as specialized instruments for very young children aged four to seven (SDQ-P), elite athletes (Elite Athlete SDQ), and physical self-concept (PSDQ) more generally.

The multidimensional, hierarchal structure, as well as the specific domains in the Marsh and Shavelson (1985) and Shavelson et al. (1976) models (Figure 2.1), has provided a blueprint for most self-concept instruments developed in the last 40 years. Indeed, widely used multidimensional self-concept instruments, stimulated at least in part by Shavelson et al. (1976), differ in

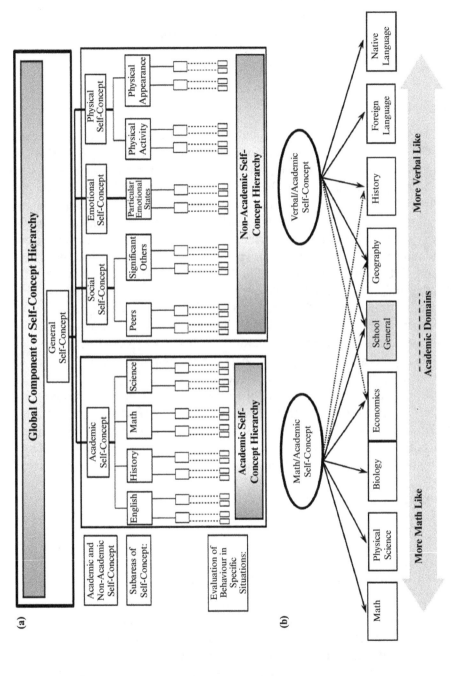

Figure 2.1 *The structure of academic self-concept. (a) The original Shavelson Model. (b) The Marsh/Shavelson revision of the academic component of the self-concept structure. Adapted from Self-Concept Theory, Measurement, and Research into Practice: the Role of Self-Concept in Educational Psychology, by H. W. Marsh, 2007.*

the self-concept dimensions included (see review by Byrne, 1996), but typically include at least one or more factors representing the specific academic (e.g., mathematics self-concept [MSC] in mathematics, and verbal self-concept [VSC] in verbal domains), social (e.g., relationships with friends and family), physical (e.g., physical competence, attractiveness), and emotional spheres of self-concept, as well as a global self-esteem (general self-concept) scale as posited in the Shavelson et al. model.

Domain Specificity

A critical feature of the Marsh and Shavelson (1985) and Shavelson et al. (1976) models (Figure 2.1) is the domain specificity, particularly of ASC. The relation between self-concept and academic achievement was investigated in an early meta-analysis by Hansford and Hattie (1982). The correlation between non-domain-specific measures of self-concept and academic achievement was positive but moderately low ($r = .21$). However, when a more specific measure of ASC was used, this correlation increased to $r = .42$, supporting the multidimensional and domain-specific nature of self-concept. Shavelson and Bolus (1982) similarly reported that the correlation between subject-specific grades and subject-specific self-concepts was stronger when compared with a specific domain of ASC. Hence, ASC and academic achievement appear to be positively related and this relationship is domain specific. So, for example, mathematics self-concept is more strongly related to mathematics achievement than to verbal achievement, and verbal self-concept is more strongly related to verbal achievement than to mathematics achievement.

A study of German high school students emphasizes this domain specificity. Marsh et al. (2006d) demonstrated that mathematics, German, and English self-concepts were substantially positively related to their corresponding outcome measures, whereas a global self-esteem measure was uncorrelated with them. For example, mathematics self-concept was significantly correlated with achievement in a standardized mathematics test ($r = .59$), with taking advanced mathematics courses ($r = .51$), and with mathematics grades ($r = .71$). Although we touch on this issue only briefly, this issue of domain specificity is central to each of the sections that follow.

Does Self-Concept Vary as a Function of Age and Gender?

Reviews (e.g., Wylie, 1979) have historically acknowledged that general self-concept is mostly unrelated with gender and/or age, although subsequent meta-analyses (Kling et al., 1999) found small differences favoring boys. Wylie (1979), however, proposed that small gender differences in general self-concept may reflect greater gender differences within specific self-concept components. When specific self-concept components were considered, Marsh (1989, 2007) reported the following gender differences that were consistent with traditional gender stereotypes: (1) boys had higher physical ability, appearance, mathematics, emotional stability, problem solving, and general self-concepts, and (2) girls had higher verbal, honesty, and spiritual self-concepts. Marsh (1989) also found a reasonably consistent pattern of self-concepts decreasing from a young age, leveling out in middle adolescence, and finally increasing at least through early adulthood. The interactions between age and gender, however, were typically small, suggesting that the reported gender differences were relatively stable from preadolescence to at least early adulthood. Such consistent gender differences further support a domain-specific approach to self-concept.

Self-concept formation in very young children were given an age range of four to seven: developmental perspectives. As noted earlier, a positive self-concept is seen as a key construct for many developmental and early childhood researchers (Eder & Mangelsdorf, 1997). Major advances in theoretical models and the development of self-concept instruments during the 1980s and 1990s, described earlier, emphasized specific self-concept domains rather than one global component. A lack of measurement research with young children, however, led Marsh et al. (2005) to argue that better multidimensional instruments, based on a rigorous approach to the construct validation, would stimulate progress in theory, research, and practice for young children, much as it had already done for older students.

When considering responses from young children, a difficulty in identifying the a priori factors may result from problems with the specific instrument or the incapacity of the children to reliably express their self-concepts with standardized paper-and-pencil assessments. An adaptive procedure has, however, been developed by Marsh et al. (1998) for measuring multiple facets of self-concept for children aged five to eight. Similarly to older children, the researchers found that these preschool children could distinguish between different self-concept components, but that there were differences. Thus, for example, their mathematics and verbal self-concepts were more highly correlated than was the case with older children. In their study consisting of even younger children (aged four and five years old), Marsh et al. (2002) reported good psychometric properties. Achievements correlated modestly with ASC factors but were either non-significantly or significantly negatively related to non-ASC scales.

Shavelson et al. (1976) hypothesized that self-concept factors would become more distinct and less correlated as an individual grows older. In testing this hypothesis, Marsh and Ayotte (2003) proposed, and found support for, a differential distinctiveness hypothesis: with increasing age and cognitive development, there are counterbalancing processes of self-concept integration and differentiation. Integration occurs when closely related areas of self-concept become more strongly related; differentiation refers to the increasing differentiation of disparate areas of self-concept (e.g., mathematics and verbal self-concepts).

There are many theoretical perspectives that endeavor to explain how self-concept changes with age (e.g., Harter, 1998). For example, Marsh and Craven (1997) proposed that the high self-concepts children held in childhood become more realistic and differentiated with age such that relations with external indicators increase. Thus, self-concepts in areas of relative strength might remain high, but self-concepts in areas of relative weakness drop so that self-concepts averaged across all children tend to decrease with age.

In summary, research with young children supports the feasibility and validity of adapted self-report instruments for young children as a basis for validating claims based on theoretical models of self-concept development. Further, children as young as four and five years of age are likely to be capable of distinguishing between multiple dimensions of self-concept. The combination of more appropriate assessment tools, improved methodology, and sound statistical procedures should facilitate high-quality self-concept research when assessing younger children, as has been the case for self-concept research with older children, adolescents, and adults.

Are Personality and Self-Concept Related?

Historically, personality researchers have differentiated personality from self-concept: they view self-concept as more malleable than fundamental personality traits such as the Big Five (neuroticism, extraversion, conscientiousness, agreeableness, and openness; see Marsh, 2008). Both self-concept and personality researchers consider their constructs to be multidimensional. However, Marsh et al. (2006d) noted that in personality research, when self-concept was considered, it was typically treated as a unidimensional construct based on global self-esteem measures. Global self-esteem is typically positively correlated with conscientiousness, openness, and agreeableness, and negatively correlated with neuroticism (see Watson et al., 2002).

Integrating multidimensional perspectives for both personality and self-concept, Marsh et al. (2006d) examined the relations between 17 self-concept factors (an extended version of the SDQIII), Big Five personality factors, and well-being and academic outcomes (i.e., school grades, test scores, and coursework selection). Both self-concept and personality were shown to be multidimensional constructs with limited support for a strong, well-defined hierarchical structure. Convergent validity was supported by substantial correlations between self-concept and personality factors that were logically related to each other (e.g., conscientiousness with honesty and trustworthiness, $r = .40$; neuroticism with emotional stability, $r = -.82$). Divergent validity was evidenced by little or no relation between self-concept and personality factors that were not logically related to each other (e.g., agreeableness with physical ability self-concept, $r = .04$; openness with physical appearance self-concept, $r = .02$). Self-concept factors were highly and systematically related to achievement measures (e.g., mathematics self-concept with mathematics grades, $r = .71$; verbal [German] self-concept with German grades, $r = .51$). Interestingly, the relations between the Big Five personality and well-being factors with academic outcomes were mostly low and did not add to the prediction of academic outcomes beyond the contribution of ASC factors. Marsh et al.'s (2006d) findings also indicated that particular self-concept factors predicted considerable amounts of variance in each of the Big Five personality and well-being factors. For the personality factors, the predicted variance fluctuated between 23 percent and 60 percent ($M = 39$ percent) and for the well-being factors the variance was between 14 percent and 19 percent ($M = 17$ percent). Conversely, self-esteem by itself explained almost none of the variance in the personality or well-being factors. Taken together, these results indicate that multidimensional self-concept measures would be better suited for use in personality research than the unidimensional global self-esteem measures in common use.

Theoretical Models of ASC Formation and Its Relationship to Achievement

Although self-concept and a person's actual ability in the same domain are reciprocally related and mutually reinforcing, it is important to keep in mind that self-concept and ability are two distinct constructs. Thus, naturally a psychometrically sound measure of self-concept will be an accurate representation of that person's self-concept. Taken together, this means that self-concept and ability in the same domain are closely related, and self-concept will to some extent reflect a person's ability while, simultaneously, due to the reciprocal nature of the constructs, ability will to some extent reflect a person's self-concept. Nevertheless, the extent to which self-concept reflects (or predicts) the actual ability of a person is affected by a set of processes commonly referred to as frames of reference (Marsh, 2007). These frames of reference are crucial for the development of self-beliefs and, in particular, self-concept.

Thus, in this section we make the case for the domain specificity of relations between ASC and achievement consistent with the Marsh and Shavelson (1985) and Shavelson et al. (1976) models, and then review the following three major frames of reference that characterize the development of ASC and its relationship to achievement (see Figure 2.2): (a) reciprocal effects model (REM) of relations between academic achievement and ASC over time (temporal frame of reference); (b) big-fish-little-pond effect (BFLPE): the negative effect of school-average achievement on ASC (external frame of reference); and (c) internal/external (I/E) frame of reference model (internal frame of reference), which relates mathematics and verbal achievement to corresponding measures of ASC.

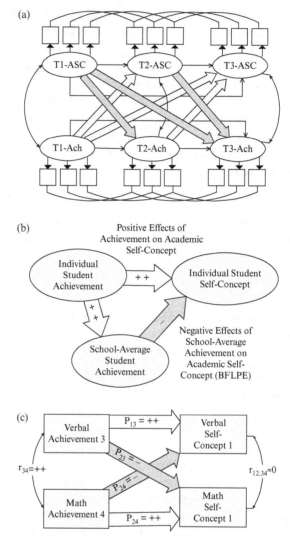

Figure 2.2 *Three theoretical models of relations between academic self-concept (ASC) and academic achievement. (a) Reciprocal effects model. (b) Big-fish-little-pond effect. (c) Internal/External frame of reference model. From* Self-Concept Theory, Measurement, and Research into Practice: the Role of Self-Concept in Educational Psychology, *by H. W. Marsh, 2007.*

Reciprocal Effects Model: The Causal Relationship Between Self-Concept and Academic Achievement

Having demonstrated that self-concept and achievement are substantially correlated, the key question became whether a causal link existed between the two: Was one the cause or effect of the other? This is an especially important question, as it has wide-reaching implications for self-concept theory and for teaching practices that can successfully improve academic success. Traditional approaches to this issue (Calsyn & Kenny, 1997) took an "either-or" approach – either prior achievement leads to subsequent ASC (a skill development model) or prior ASC leads to subsequent achievement (a self-enhancement model). However, integrating theoretical and statistical perspectives, Marsh (1990a) argued for a dynamic REM that incorporates both the skill development and the self-enhancement models, such that both ASC and achievement are posited to be causes and also effects of each other.

The research evidence supporting the REM has grown steadily, showing that prior self-concept and subsequent achievement are positively related, as are prior achievement and subsequent self-concept (e.g., Chen et al., 2013; Pinxten et al., 2010). In meta-analyses of these studies, Valentine and DuBois (2005; Valentine et al., 2004; also see Huang, 2011) found consistent support for the REM. Consistent with ASC theory and research, it is not surprising that prior achievement has an effect on ASC. However, the meta-analysis revealed that the effect of prior ASC on subsequent achievement, after controlling for the effects of prior achievement, was also highly significant overall and positive in 90 percent of the studies they considered. In these meta-analyses, support for the REM generalized over country, age, gender, and different ASC instrument.

The REM has also been shown to be valid for young children. Using a multicohort-multioccasion design, Guay et al., (2003) measured ASC and achievement for three cohorts of students, ranging in age from eight to ten years, at three time points. Results demonstrated strong support for the REM in this sample of young students, leading the authors to conclude that the REM generalizes well across preadolescent students.

The REM research has also been extended to elite swimmers (see Marsh & Perry, 2005), the physical domain (Marsh et al., 2006a), and academically gifted students. For example, Seaton et al. (2015) compared the size of the REM in a sample of gifted students who attended academically selective schools and students who attended mixed-ability comprehensive schools. They found that the REM was similar in size and direction in both samples, supporting the importance of ASCs in both academically selective and mainstream schools.

The REM researchers have also questioned whether individual student characteristics can mediate the relation between ASC and academic achievement. In a longitudinal study based on two large samples of German high school students, Marsh et al. (2006d) assessed the relation between ASC, academic achievement (measured by grades and standardized tests), and academic interest. In addition to support for the REM, they found that prior self-concept was significantly associated with subsequent academic interest when previous grades, test scores, and interest were controlled. Other research has found reciprocal effects relating interest and academic performance (e.g.,

Harackiewicz et al., 2008) when ASC was not included in the model. However, Marsh et al. found that after controlling for prior ASC, prior academic interest was only minimally associated with subsequent ASC and had little effect on subsequent achievement. In sum, this study showed that the effect of prior ASC on subsequent achievement was not mediated by academic interest.

Baumeister et al. (2003) challenged the view that high self-esteem leads to better academic achievement. Instead, they ascertained that high self-esteem was partly the outcome of good academic achievement, and that boosting students' self-esteem had "not been shown to improve academic performance and may sometimes be counterproductive" (p. 1). However, as argued by Marsh and Craven (2006), Baumeister et al. based their review on self-esteem as a unidimensional construct and, although they recognized its existence, ignored the multidimensionality of self-concept. In doing so, they did not consider any of the domain-specific studies that would have demonstrated reciprocity between ASC and achievement. In integrating these apparently inconsistent claims, Marsh and O'Mara (2008) demonstrated that, whereas general self-esteem was only weakly associated with grade point average (GPA) or educational attainment, ASC was positively and reciprocally related with both these measures of achievement.

Thus, the REM has played a significant role in the advancement of self-concept theory. Not only has it demonstrated the mutually positive reinforcing relationship between self-concept and achievement, but it has also established self-concept as fundamental to success and achievement.

Are Different Frames of Reference Important for Self-Concept?

To evaluate abilities and opinions, individuals often use others to obtain a sense of their relative standing. This was recognized even as early as the time of James (1890, 1963), who noted that "we have the paradox of a man shamed to death because he is only the second pugilist or the second oarsman in the world" (p. 310). These comparative processes, or frames of reference, serve an important purpose in forming self-perceptions. Multiple frames of reference can be used to assess one's accomplishments that form the basis of self-concept self-perceptions (Shavelson et al., 1976; Skaalvik & Skaalvik, 2002). Such frames of reference can include, for example, an external criterion (the five-minute mile), a personal goal (running 100 meters in less than 12 seconds), social comparisons (class- or school-average levels of achievement), temporal comparisons (improvement over time), dimensional comparisons (accomplishments in one domain relative to those in others), or a personal internal standard (a personal best).

In this section we focus on two frame of reference models. The first is the BFLPE, in which the frames of reference are comparisons with the achievement of classmates and the negative effect that school- or class-average achievement has on ASC (see Figure 2.2b). The second is the I/E model and its extension Dimensional Comparison Theory (DCT), in which individuals use dimensional comparisons (comparing achievement in one domain with that in another) and social comparisons with their classmates.

The BFLPE: theoretical BFLPE model. The BFLPE model has its theoretical basis in psychophysical and social judgment, sociology, relative deprivation theory, and social comparison theory (see review by Marsh, 2007). In essence, the BFLPE proposes that students form their ASCs by comparing their academic achievements with those of their classmates. Thus, whereas there is a positive relation between individual ability and ASC, class- or school-average is negatively related to ASC (see Figure 2.2b). Consider this example: Alex and Bill are above-average mathematics students of similar ability, but Alex attends an academically selective school and Bill attends a mixed-ability school. In the academically selective school, the school-average mathematics ability is higher than that of the surrounding mixed-ability schools. In the mixed-ability school, the school-average mathematics ability is similar to that of other mixed-ability schools. Bill's mathematics ability is extremely good compared to his classmates, so his mathematics self-concept is high, as he is a big fish in a little pond. However, in Alex's school there are many highly capable mathematics students and, compared to them, his mathematics ability is average. As a result, Alex's mathematics self-concept is low, as he is a little fish in a big pond. Here we see the frame of reference of the BFLPE at work: by attending the academically selective school Alex feels less competent in mathematics than Bill, even though they are both of similar mathematics ability. Hence, ASC is influenced not only by a student's own academic achievement, but also by the accomplishments of the student's classmates.

Early BFLPE research. In the foundational BFLPE study, Marsh and Parker (1984) found that although there was a positive relation between individual academic ability and ASC, when individual academic ability was controlled for, school-average ability and ASC were negatively related. Consistent with the BFLPE, equally able students had lower ASCs in high-ability schools than those in low-ability schools. In subsequent research based on a large database, Marsh (1987) replicated the results and showed that the BFLPE was driven by school-average achievement rather than school-average socioeconomic status (SES).

Since the Marsh and Parker (1984) study, results from BFLPE research have provided further support for the multidimensionality of self-concept (Marsh & Seaton, 2015).When examined in academic settings, results indicate that the BFLPE is specific to ASC, as school- and class-average achievement has little effect, either positively or negatively, on global self-esteem or on non-ASC (for a review, see Marsh et al., 2008). Additionally, the BFLPE has been shown to exist at different levels of education, both in primary schools (e.g., Marsh et al., 1995) and in high schools (e.g., Marsh et al., 2001a).

Over the ensuing years there has also been widespread support for the predictions of the BFLPE, spanning such areas as: its effect on educational outcomes (Marsh, 1987); its durability (Marsh et al., 2007); and its generalizability across educational levels, countries, and cultures (e.g., Marsh & Seaton, 2015;

Seaton, et al., 2009, 2010; Zeidner & Schleyer, 1998). For example, it has been shown that, apart from ASC, school-average achievement can have a negative effect on many other desirable educational outcomes including: educational aspirations, general self-concept, school grades, standardized test scores, advanced coursework selection, subsequent college attendance, and occupational aspirations (Marsh, 1991). The BFLPE can also affect psychosocial constructs, such as importance, effort persistence, and rehearsal, elaboration, and control strategies (Xu, 2010). These findings imply that attending a high-ability school has negative effects on more educational outcomes than just ASC alone, meaning that such students may not be reaching their full academic potential.

Researchers have suggested strategies to reduce these negative effects of the BFLPE (e.g., Marsh et al., 2008). These include avoidance of highly competitive environments and of feedback based on comparisons of the performance of other students. However, there is very little evidence to support such strategies (see Marsh & Seaton, 2015).

How long-lasting is the BFLPE? Although some researchers (Dai, 2004; Dai & Rinn, 2008) have suggested that the BFLPE is nothing more than a short-term ephemeral effect, research has shown that it is long-lasting. Two large longitudinal studies with German high school students provided evidence of the long-term durability and persistence of the BFLPE. In the first study, Marsh et al. (2007) found that, two years after graduation from high school, the effect of school-average achievement on mathematics self-concept was still negative. In the second study, these authors demonstrated evidence of the BFLPE four years after students had left high school. Furthermore, Marsh and O'Mara (2010) demonstrated that school-average achievement had a negative effect on school grades and that this effect remained for up to five years after graduation from high school. Evidence from other longitudinal studies (e.g., Marsh et al., 2001a) has also shown that the BFLPE is no short-term effect, but is stable and persistent over time.

The BFLPEs for academically disadvantaged students. Research has also shown that the BFLPE affects academically disadvantaged students who attend mainstream classes. Labeling theory predicts that placing academically disadvantaged students in special classes instead of mainstream classes should result in lower ASCs and stigmatization for these students. However, Marsh et al. (2006c) found the opposite: It was the academically disadvantaged students in mainstream classes who had lower ASCs than their equally able peers who were placed in special classes with similarly academically disadvantaged students. From a BFLPE perspective this finding makes perfect sense. In mainstream classes, the academically disadvantaged students have students of higher ability with whom to compare their achievements, with the resulting drop in ASC.

The BFLPE: cross-national generalizability. There is now considerable support for the generalizability of the negative effects of school-average achievement on ASC (see review by Marsh et al., 2008). Demonstrating that the

BFLPE is one of psychology's most cross-culturally universal phenomena, four successive Programme for International Student Assessment (PISA) data collections with 15-year-old students (Marsh & Hau, 2003: 103,558 students from 26 countries; Seaton et al., 2010: 265,180 students from 41 countries; Nagengast & Marsh, 2012: 397,500 students from 57 countries; Marsh et al., 2018a: 485,490 students, 18,292 schools, 68 countries) showed that the effect of school-average achievement on ASC was negative in all but one of the 191 samples, and significantly so in 182 samples. These multiple country studies have provided very strong support for Seaton et al.'s (2009) conclusion that the BFLPE is a pan-human theory as it "is not only a symptom of developed countries and individualist societies, but it is also evident in developing nations and collectivist countries of the world" (p. 414).

Moderators of the BFLPE. A critically important method for extending knowledge of a theory is to test whether there are any variables that can moderate the effect. If strong BFLPE moderators were found, this information would aid in understanding the underlying processes of the BFLPE and allow the development of interventions that could lessen its negative consequences. However, if the BFLPE were to generalize across diverse student characteristics, then such evidence would strengthen support for its generalizability. In one of the most encompassing studies searching for BFLPE moderators, using the PISA 2003 database, Seaton et al. (2010) examined 17 potential moderators (e.g., student background, learning styles, and the perceived learning environment) of the BFLPE. Statistically significant moderating effects were found for some of these potential BFLPE moderators. However, in relation to the large sample size ($N = 265,180$), most were considered too small to be practically important and none were sufficiently large to change the direction of the BFLPE. Overall, they concluded that results supported the generalizability of the BFLPE "as it was reasonably consistent across the specific constructs examined" (p. 390).

Personality factors have also been evaluated as moderators of the BFLPE. Using the Big Five traits and narcissism, Jonkmann et al. (2012) found that if students had high narcissism levels, then they had higher ASCs and the BFLPE was smaller. However, if students reported high levels of neuroticism, then the BFLPE was stronger. As was the case with the Seaton et al. (2010) study, the moderating effects were modest as the direction of the BFLPE was not changed, thus providing further support for the generalizability of the BFLPE.

Extensions of BFLPE theory: negative effects of year in school. The BFLPE effect is based on the assumption that the academic accomplishments of classmates form a frame of reference or standard of comparison that students use to form their own ASCs. However, being in a school environment with more or less able students, as operationalized by school-average achievement, is not the only way in which a student's frame of reference can be altered. For a variety of reasons, such as acceleration or starting school at an early age, students can find themselves in classes with older, more academically advanced students who form a potentially more demanding frame of reference than would same-age classmates. Similarly, due to starting school at a later age or being held back to repeat a grade, students may find themselves in classes with younger, less academically advanced students.

Based on the logic of frame of reference effects and BFLPE theory, Marsh (2016) posited and found that the relative year in school (being one or more years ahead of or behind the year in school of same-age students) had a negative effect on ASC: the effects on ASC were negative for de facto acceleration (e.g., starting early and skipping grades – both resulting in a higher year in school) and positive for de facto retention (e.g., starting late and repeating grades – both resulting in a lower year in school). In apparently the first large-scale study of this effect, Marsh demonstrated, using PISA 2003 (276,165 fifteen-year-olds), that the negative effects of relative year in school on ASC were consistent across the 41 countries. Although negative effects of year in school were independent of the negative BFLPEs, it is important to emphasize that these negative effects of year in school were consistent with a priori predictions based on the logic of frame of reference effects and BFLPE theory. Marsh et al. (2018a) subsequently replicated these negative effects of year in school with 68 countries using the PISA 2012 database. Extending this research, they showed that there were negative effects on ASC associated with starting school at a younger age and acceleration or skipping grades, and positive effects for starting school at an older age (an increasingly popular strategy used by parents to advantage their children, also referred to as "red shirting" by Gladwell, 2008) and repeating a grade.

Each of these effects is controversial (see Hattie, 2012 for reviews in relation to academic achievement) in that evidence in relation to the effects of skipping grades and red shirting is mixed, while the prediction of the positive effects of repeating a grade contradicts the "accepted wisdom" that this practice has negative effects (but see Marsh et al., 2017). The remarkable feature of the negative year-in-school effect is that it encapsulates all four of these effects based on a single variable. Regardless of how students end up as older than their same-grade classmates, the negative year-in-school effect leads to higher ASCs. Thus, year in school captured all or at least most of the variance explicable by retention, acceleration, and starting age. These results have potentially important implications, providing a link between research on starting age, retention, and acceleration, where there has been surprisingly little cross-fertilization.

The Internal/External Model (I/E Model)

Theoretical basis for the I/E model. This model relates mathematics and verbal achievement to corresponding measures of ASC. Most people think of themselves as a mathematics person or a verbal person. However, students who excel at one tend to excel at the other too (Marsh, 1986). Why does this disparity between academic self-perceptions and corresponding objective measures of academic performance exist? This relative lack of correlation between mathematics and verbal self-concepts also led to the Marsh and Shavelson (1985) revision of the original Shavelson et al. (1976) model (see Figure 2.1). The I/E model (Figure 2.2c) endeavors to explain this contradiction. According to this model, students use external and internal comparisons to form their self-concepts. The external or social comparisons are those with peers in which students use the accomplishments of other students to evaluate their ability. The internal or dimensional comparisons are those between performances in different school subjects by the same student.

Empirical support for the I/E model. The I/E model predicts that, although the paths leading from mathematics achievement to mathematics self-concept and verbal achievement to verbal self-concept will be substantial and positive, the paths from mathematics achievement to verbal self-concept and from verbal achievement to mathematics self-concept will be small and negative. For example, Marsh (1986) noted consistently high correlations between mathematics and verbal achievement ($rs = .42$ to $.94$), but weak or even negative correlations between mathematics and verbal self-concept ($rs = -.10$ to $+.19$). He further noted that the paths from the relevant achievement to the corresponding self-concept domain (i.e., mathematics achievement to mathematics self-concept and verbal achievement to verbal self-concept) were substantial and positive. The paths from mathematics achievement to verbal self-concept and from verbal achievement to mathematics self-concept, however, were significant and negative. Hence, according to the I/E model, individuals whose verbal achievement is high tend to have lower mathematics self-concept due to dimensional comparison processes, and those with high mathematics achievement tend to have lower verbal self-concept.

There has been wide support for the I/E model in numerous studies differing in nationality, in age, and in their use of self-concept instruments, achievement measures, and methodology (see Marsh, 1990b, 1993). Additionally, cross-cultural comparisons have been important in validating the model (Marsh & Hau, 2004). Results have indicated that the I/E model generalizes not only across the domains of mathematics and science, but also across age and nationality (Marsh et al., 2015).

The model has also been supported longitudinally (Marsh et al., 2001b), using experimental manipulation (Möller & Köller, 2001; Pohlmann & Möller, 2009), and in diary studies (Möller & Husemann, 2006). Importantly, the model has been validated by meta-analyses. For example, using 69 data sets ($N = 125,308$) Möller et al. (2009) confirmed predictions from the I/E model that generalized across age, gender, and nationality. They found that although mathematics and verbal achievements were highly correlated, MSCs and VSCs were nearly uncorrelated across all studies. Moreover, as the I/E model predicts, the paths leading from achievement in one domain to its matching ASC were positive (.61 for mathematics, .49 for verbal) but those to non-matching domains were negative (mathematics achievement to VSC = −.21; verbal achievement to MSC = −.27).

The I/E effects in perceptions by significant others. Although there is strong support for I/E predictions based on self-perceptions, there is little support for predictions based on the inferred self-concept by significant others (e.g., parents, teachers, or peers asked to rate the self-concept of child, student, or classmate; see Marsh, 2007). For example, primarily on the basis of a single study of responses by students and their parents (Dai, 2002), previous reviews (e.g., Möller et al., 2009) concluded inferred self-concepts by parents apparently do not reflect internal comparison processes. However, Dai tested the I/E model with parent perceptions of their child's abilities, rather than parent inferences of their child's self-concepts (i.e., inferred self-concept ratings). In order to address this issue, van Zanden et al. (2016) conducted a study assessing parents' perceptions of their children's abilities (as in the Dai study), but also their perceptions of their children's self-concepts in the verbal and the mathematical areas. As reported by Dai, there were no dimensional comparison effects for parent perceptions of their child's abilities, but there was support for the I/E model for student self-concept ratings inferred by their parents as well as students' own self-concept ratings. Thus, for example, mathematics achievement had positive effects on children's mathematics self-concepts and those inferred by their parents, but negative effects on verbal self-concept ratings by the children and those inferred by parents. Particularly in high school settings, teachers in one subject area might not know the abilities of their students in other subject areas. Dickhäuser (2005) used an experimental design to address this issue, providing teachers with experimentally manipulated mathematics and verbal achievement scores for hypothetical students. Consistent with I/E predictions, teachers inferred that students had relatively higher verbal self-concepts when their mathematics achievement scores were relatively lower. However, it will be important to replicate these results based on non-hypothetical students in actual classroom settings, and more research is needed to determine the circumstances under which there is support for the I/E model based on responses by significant others.

Extensions of the I/E model. The DCT expands the focus of the I/E model on mathematics and verbal subjects to include all academic subjects that vary along the continuum between mathematics and verbal domains (see Figure 2.1b). Moreover, DCT positioned the I/E model squarely within frame of reference research by acknowledging the importance of dimensional comparisons (see Möller & Marsh, 2013). In essence, DCT predicts that if subjects are "near" to each other (e.g., Dutch and English for Dutch-speaking students who also study English), then the path coefficient relating academic achievement in one subject to the ASC of the other should be positive. If subjects are "far" from each other (e.g., mathematics and English, as in the original I/E model), then the path coefficient relating academic achievement in one subject to the ASC of the other should be negative (Guo et al., 2017).

Research supporting DCT has been growing steadily (Jansen et al., 2015). For example, Marsh et al. (2014) showed that the cross paths relating Dutch and English achievement to Dutch and English self-concepts were positive, but that the cross paths relating mathematics achievement to both language self-concepts were negative. Likewise, Guo et al. (2017) found positive associations between achievement and self-concept for physics and chemistry and negative associations for both physics and chemistry with biology. Consistent with the generalized I/E model, a similar pattern was noted for intrinsic value. The generalized I/E model has also been evaluated beyond the realms of achievement and self-concept, although this research is still rare (see Möller & Husemann, 2006; Möller & Savyon, 2003). In summary, these extensions of the original I/E model have been richly heuristic in terms of generating new research. In particular, DCT provided a clearly defined structure in terms of a priori predictions and the distinction between near and far dimensions.

An Integrated ASC Model

Marsh et al. (2018b) recently proposed the integration of the three theoretical models of ASC formation (i.e., REM, BFLPE, and I/E) into a single, unified model. The overarching aim of this unified model is to systematically explain the relations between ASC and academic achievement in relation to: temporal comparisons (e.g., one's current accomplishments relative to past accomplishments; REM), social comparisons (one's accomplishments relative to those of one's peer group; BFLPE), and dimensional comparisons (one's accomplishments in one domain relative to accomplishments in other domains; DCT). Using a large longitudinal database, Marsh et al. demonstrated support for predictions from all three ASC theories based on parameter estimates from a single multi-level statistical model. They also added a developmental perspective, demonstrating that support for theoretical predictions was consistent across five years of compulsory secondary education, suggesting that the self-system had achieved developmental equilibrium during this potentially volatile early-to-middle adolescent period.

Self-Concept Interventions

Interventions to enhance self-concept typically aim to target self-concept, either directly through praise and performance feedback or directly by targeting a related construct that is posited to affect self-concept (see Craven, et al., 1991 for an overview). And indeed, O'Mara et al. (2006), in their meta-analysis on self-concept enhancement interventions, found feedback or praise to show the strongest effect size for such interventions ($d = 1.13$). In particular, attributional or internally focused feedback seems to be effective in this regard. However, when approaching self-concept with a multidimensional perspective, the different ways in which an intervention impacts an individual can be mapped to the specific, relevant dimensions of self-concept. As such, the extent an intervention impacts the different self-concept dimensions that it is designed to change, and has less impact on other self-concept factors that are less relevant, is a strong test of the construct validity of a multifaceted perspective of self-concept.

This construct validation approach is evident in academic interventions in which successful interventions impact ASCs more than non-academic and global components (e.g., Marsh et al., 2006b) and physical interventions in which the effects are greater for physical components of self-concept (Marsh & Peart, 1988). This construct validity approach was evident in the juxtaposition of two Outward Bound studies based on residential wilderness interventions. The "standard" Outward Bound course focused largely on non-academic outcomes (Marsh et al., 1986a, 1986b): effects were significantly larger for domains posited a priori to be most relevant to the intervention, were consistent across 27 different programs, and were maintained over 18 months. The Outward Bound "bridging" course (Marsh & Richards, 1988) was designed to produce significant gains in the academic domain for under-achieving adolescents: ASC effects were significantly more positive than non-academic effects and there were corresponding effects on mathematics and reading achievement. If these studies had taken a unidimensional perspective and only measured global self-esteem, both interventions would have been judged much weaker, and a rich understanding of the match between specific intended goals and actual outcomes would have been lost.

Haney and Durlak's (1998) meta-analysis of self-concept interventions found significantly positive effect sizes, leading to their conclusion that:

> it is possible to significantly improve children's and adolescents' levels
> of SE/SC [self-esteem/self-concept] and to obtain concomitant positive
> changes in other areas of adjustment. There is even the suggestion that SE/
> SC programs do at least as well as other types of interventions in changing
> other domains of functioning such as behaviors, self-reported personality
> functioning, and academic performance (p. 429).

Consistent with typical approaches to meta-analysis of the time, Haney and Durlak considered only one effect size per intervention (i.e., the mean effect size averaged across different self-concept dimensions) where more than one had been considered. In contrast to this implicit unidimensional approach, O'Mara et al. (2006) updated and extended this meta-analysis to embrace a multidimensional perspective, coding the relevance of each self-concept domain in relation to the aims of the intervention. Similar to Haney and Durlak, they found interventions were significantly effective overall ($d = .51$, 460 effect sizes). However, supporting a multidimensional perspective, interventions targeting a specific self-concept domain and subsequently measuring that domain were much more effective ($d = 1.16$). They also found that studies that targeted global self-esteem were much less successful compared to those that targeted specific components of self-concept. These results demonstrate that the Haney and Durlak meta-analysis substantially underestimated the effectiveness of self-concept interventions and provide further support for the usefulness of a multidimensional, domain-specific perspective in relation to self-concept interventions.

Concluding Thoughts

As emphasized in this chapter, positive self-beliefs serve as an influential platform for facilitating life potential and getting the most out of life. Indeed, positive self-beliefs are at the heart of the positive psychology evolution in psychological research more generally (Bandura, 2008a, 2008b; Hunter & Csikszentmihalyi, 2003). Since the seminal work by Shavelson et al. (1976), research in the field of self-concept has boomed. However, there is still much work to be done. For example:

- Notwithstanding theoretical contributions, understanding of the relationship between self-concept and age would benefit from more targeted research examining the issue;
- Personality research would benefit from using multidimensional self-concept measures rather than the global self-esteem measures in common use;
- The REM research could be advantaged by investigating the mediating role of individual characteristics in the REM;
- Strategies to reduce the negative effects of the BFLPE should be examined, as there is a paucity of research in this area;
- More studies are needed to examine I/E predictions based on the inferred self-concept by significant others;
- Further research is needed to establish when dimensional comparisons result in assimilation (for near subjects) and contrast (for far subjects), but also the conditions under which I/E-like effects generalize to other constructs; and
- An integrated approach to interventions is necessary, targeting a specific self-concept domain and subsequently measuring that domain.

Future research to address these questions should build on the substantial growth in the theoretical, methodological, and statistical sophistication in self-concept research summarized in this chapter.

References

Bandura, A. (2008a). An agentic perspective on positive psychology. In S. J. Lopez (Ed.), *Positive psychology: Exploring the best in people, Vol. 1: Discovering human strengths* (pp. 167–96). Westport, CT: Praeger/Greenwood.

Bandura, A. (2008b). Toward an agentic theory of the self. In H. Marsh, R. G. Craven, & D. M. McInerney (Eds.), *Advances in self research, Vol. 3: Self-processes, learning, and enabling human potential* (pp. 15–49). Charlotte, NC: Information Age.

Baumeister, R. F., Campbell, J. D., Krueger, J. I., & Vohs, K. D. (2003). Does high self-esteem cause better performance, interpersonal success, happiness, or healthier lifestyles? *Psychological Science in the Public Interest, 4*, 1–44.

Byrne, B. M. (1996). *Measuring self-concept across the life span: Issues and instrumentation*. Washington, DC: American Psychological Association.

Byrne, B. M. (2002). Validating the measurement and structure of self-concept: Snapshots of past, present, and future research. *American Psychologist, 57*, 897–909.

Calsyn, R. & Kenny, D. (1997). Self-concept of ability and perceived evaluations by others: Cause or effect of academic achievement? *Journal of Educational Psychology, 69*, 136–45.

Chen, S., Yeh. Y., Hwang, F., & Lin, S. S. J. (2013). The relationship between academic self-concept and achievement: A multicohort–multioccasion study. *Learning and Individual Differences, 23*, 172–8.

Craven, R. G., Marsh, H. W., & Debus, R. L. (1991). Effects of internally focused feedback and attributional feedback on enhancement of academic self-concept. *Journal of Educational Psychology, 83*(1), 17–27.

Dai, D. Y. (2002). Incorporating parent perceptions: A replication and extension study of the internal-external frame of reference model of self-concept development. *Journal of Adolescent Research, 17*(6), 617–45.

Dai, D. Y. (2004). How universal is the big-fish-little-pond effect? *American Psychologist, 59*, 267–68. doi:10.1037/0003-066X.59.4.267.

Dai, D. Y. & Rinn, A. N. (2008). The big-fish–little-pond effect: What do we know and where do we go from here? *Educational Psychology Review, 20*, 283–317. doi:10.1007/s10648-008-9071-x.

Dickhäuser, O. (2005). Teachers' inferences about students' self-concepts – the role of dimensional comparison. *Learning and Instruction, 15*(3), 225–35. doi:10.1016/j.learninstruc.2005.04.004.

Eder, R. A. & Mangelsdorf, S. C. (1997). The emotional basis of early personality development: Implications for the emergent self-concept. In R. Hogan, J. Johnson, & S. Briggs (Eds.), *Handbook of personality psychology* (pp. 209–40). San Diego, CA: Academic Press.

Elliot, A. J. & Dweck, C. S. (2005). Competence and motivation: Competence as the core of achievement motivation. In A. J. Elliot & C. S. Dweck (Eds.), *Handbook of competence and motivation* (pp. 3–12). New York, NY: Guilford Press.

Gladwell, M. (2008). *Outliers*. New York, NY: Little, Brown and Company.

Greenwald, A. G. (1988). A social-cognitive account of the self's development. In D. K. Lapsley & F. C. Power (Eds.), *Self, ego, and identity: Interpretative approaches* (pp. 30–42). New York, NY: Springer-Verlag.

Guay, F., Marsh, H. W., & Boivin, M. (2003). Academic self-concept and academic achievement: Developmental perspectives on their causal ordering. *Journal of Educational Psychology, 95*, 124–36.

Guo, J., Marsh, H. W., Morin, A. J. S., Parker, P. D., & Kaur, G. (2015). Directionality of the associations of high school expectancy-value, aspirations, and attainment: A longitudinal study. *American Educational Research Journal, 52*(2), 371–402. doi:10.3102/0002831214565786.

Guo, J., Marsh, H. W., Parker, P. D., Morin, A. J. S., & Dicke, T. (2017). Extending expectancy-value theory predictions of achievement and aspirations in science: Dimensional comparison processes and expectancy-by-value interactions. *Learning and Instruction, 49*, 81–91.

Haney, P. & Durlak, J. A. (1998). Changing self-esteem in children and adolescents: A meta-analytic review. *Journal of Clinical Child Psychology*, *27*, 423–33.

Hansford, B. C. & Hattie, J. A. (1982). The relationship between self and achievement/performance measures. *Review of Educational Research*, *52*, 123–42.

Harackiewicz, J. M., Durik, A. M., Barron, K. E., Linnenbrink-Garcia, L., & Tauer, J. M. (2008). The role of achievement goals in the development of interest: Reciprocal relations between achievement goals, interest, and performance. *Journal of Educational Psychology*, *100*(1), 105–22. doi:10.1037/0022-0663.100.1.105.

Harter, S. (1998). The development of self-representations. In W. Damon & N. Eisenberg (Eds.), *Handbook of child psychology* (5th ed., pp. 553–617) Hoboken, NJ: John Wiley & Sons.

Harter, S. (2012). *The construction of the self: Developmental and sociocultural foundations*. New York, NY: Guilford Press.

Hattie, J. (1992). *Self-concept*. Hillsdale, NJ: Erlbaum.

Hattie, J. A. (2012). *Visible learning: A synthesis of over 800 meta-analyses relating to achievement*. Abingdon: Routledge.

Huang, C. (2011). Self-concept and academic achievement: A meta-analysis of longitudinal relations. *Journal of School Psychology*, *49*, 505–28.

Hunter, J. P. & Csikszentmihalyi, M. (2003). The positive psychology of interested adolescents. *Journal of Youth and Adolescence*, *32*, 27–35.

James, W. (1890/1963). *The principles of psychology*. New York, NY: Holt, Rinehart & Winston.

Jansen, M., Schroeders, U., Lüdtke, O., & Marsh, H. W. (2015). Contrast and assimilation effects of dimensional comparisons in five subjects: An extension of the I/E model. *Journal of Educational Psychology*, *107*(4), 1086–101.

Jonkmann, K., Becker, M., Marsh, H. W., Lüdtke, O., & Trautwein, U. (2012). Personality traits moderate the big-fish-little-pond effect of academic self-concept. *Learning and Individual Differences*, *22*, 736–46.

Kagan, S. L., Moore, E., & Bredekamp, S. (1995). *Considering children's early development and learning: Toward common views and vocabulary* (Report N. 95-03). Washington, DC: National Education Goals Pane.

Kling, K. C., Hyde, J. S., Showers, C. J., & Buswell, B. N. (1999). Gender differences in self-esteem: A meta-analysis. *Psychological Bulletin*, *125*, 470–500.

Marsh, H. W. (1986). Verbal and math self-concepts: An internal/external frame of reference model. *American Educational Research Journal*, *23*, 129–49.

Marsh, H. W. (1987). The big-fish-little-pond effect on academic self-concept. *Journal of Educational Psychology*, *79*(3), 280–95.

Marsh, H. W. (1989). Age and sex effects in multiple dimensions of self-concept: Preadolescence to early adulthood. *Journal of Educational Psychology*, *81*, 417–30.

Marsh, H. W. (1990a). The causal ordering of academic self-concept and academic achievement: A multiwave, longitudinal panel analysis. *Journal of Educational Psychology*, *82*, 646–56.

Marsh, H. W. (1990b). A multidimensional, hierarchical self-concept: Theoretical and empirical justification. *Educational Psychology Review*, *2*, 77–172.

Marsh, H. W. (1991). Failure of high ability schools to deliver academic benefits commensurate with their students' ability levels. *American Educational Research Journal*, *28*(2), 445–80.

Marsh, H. W. (1993). Academic self-concept: Theory, measurement, and research. In J. Suls (Ed.), *Psychological perspectives on the self* (pp. 59–98). Hillsdale, NJ: Erlbaum.

Marsh, H. W. (2007). *Self-concept theory, measurement, and research into practice: The role of self-concept in educational psychology.* (pp. 59–98). Leicester: British Psychological Society.

Marsh, H. W. (2008). A multidimensional, hierarchical model of self-concept: An important facet of personality. In G. J. Boyle, G. Matthews, & D. H. Saklofske (Eds.), *The SAGE handbook of personality theory and assessment, Vol. 1: Personality theories and models* (pp. 447–69). Thousand Oaks, CA: Sage Publications, Inc.

Marsh, H. W. (2016). Cross-cultural generalizability of year in school effects: Negative effects of acceleration and positive effects of retention on academic self-concept. *Journal of Educational Psychology, 108*(2), 256–73. doi:10.1037/edu0000059.

Marsh, H. W., Abduljabbar, A. S., Parker, P. D., Morin, A. J. S., Abdelfattah, F., Nagengast, B., ... Abu-Hilal, M. M. (2015). The internal/external frame of reference model of self-concept and achievement relations: Age-cohort and cross-cultural differences. *American Educational Research Journal, 52*(1), 168–202.

Marsh, H. W. & Ayotte, V. (2003). Do multiple dimensions of self-concept become more differentiated with age? The differential distinctiveness hypothesis. *Journal of Educational Psychology, 95*, 687–706.

Marsh, H. W., Chanal, J. P., & Sarrazin, P. G. (2006a). Self-belief does make a difference: A reciprocal effects model of the causal ordering of physical self-concept and gymnastics performance. *Journal of Sports Sciences, 24*, 101–11.

Marsh, H. W., Chessor, D., Craven, R. G., & Roche, L. (1995). The effects of gifted-and-talented programmes on academic self-concept: The big fish strikes again. *American Educational Research Journal, 32*, 285–319.

Marsh, H. W. & Craven, R. G. (1997). Academic self-concept: Beyond the dustbowl. In G. Phye (Ed.), *Handbook of classroom assessment: learning, achievement, and adjustment* (pp. 131–93). San Diego, CA: Academic Press.

Marsh, H. W. & Craven, R. G. (2006). Reciprocal effects of self-concept and performance from a multidimensional perspective: Beyond seductive pleasure and unidimensional perspectives. *Perspectives on Psychological Science, 1*, 133–63.

Marsh, H. W., Craven, R. G., & Debus, R. L. (1998). Structure, stability, and development of young children's self-concepts: A multicohort–multioccasion study. *Child Development, 69*, 1030–53.

Marsh, H. W., Debus, R., & Bornholt, L. (2005). Validating young children's self-concept responses: Methodological ways and means to understand their responses. In D. M. Teti (Ed.), *Handbook of research methods in developmental science* (pp. 138–60). Oxford: Blackwell Publishing.

Marsh, H. W., Ellis, L. A., & Craven, R. G. (2002). How do preschool children feel about themselves? Unravelling measurement and multidimensional self-concept structure. *Developmental Psychology, 38*, 376–93.

Marsh, H. W. & Hau, K. T. (2003). Big-fish-little-pond effect on academic self-concept: A cross-cultural (26 country) test of the negative effects of academically selective schools. *American Psychologist, 58*, 364.

Marsh, H. W. & Hau, K. T. (2004). Explaining paradoxical relations between academic self-concepts and achievements: Cross-cultural generalizability of the internal/external frame of reference predictions across 26 countries. *Journal of Educational Psychology, 96*, 56–67.

Marsh, H. W., Köller, O., & Baumert, J. (2001a). Reunification of East and West German school systems: Longitudinal multilevel modeling study of the big-fish-little-pond effect on academic self-concept. *American Educational Research Journal*, *38*(2), 321–50.

Marsh, H. W., Kong, C. K., & Hau, K. (2001b). Extension of the internal/external frame of reference model of self-concept formation: Importance of native and non-native languages for Chinese students. *Journal of Educational Psychology*, *93*, 543–3. doi:10.1037/0022-0663.93.3.543.

Marsh, H. W., Kuyper, H., Morin, A. J. S., Parker, P. D., & Seaton, M. (2014). Big-fish-little-pond social comparison and local dominance effects: Integrating new statistical models, methodology, design, theory, and substantive implications. *Learning and Instruction*, *33*, 50–66. doi: https://doi.org/10.1016/j.learninstruc.2014.04.002

Marsh, H. W., Martin, A. J., & Hau, K. (2006b). A multimethod perspective on self-concept research in educational psychology: A construct validity approach. In M. Eid & E. Diener (Eds.), *Handbook of multimethod measurement in psychology* (pp. 441–56). Washington, DC: American Psychological Association.

Marsh, H. W. & O'Mara, A. (2008). Reciprocal effects between academic self-concept, self-esteem, achievement, and attainment over seven adolescent years: Unidimensional and multidimensional perspectives of self-concept. *Personality and Social Psychology Bulletin*, *34*, 542–52.

Marsh, H. W. & O'Mara, A. J. (2010). Long-term total negative effects of school-average ability on diverse educational outcomes: Direct and indirect effects of the big-fish-little-pond effect. *German Journal of Educational Psychology*, *24*, 51–72.

Marsh, H. W. & Parker, J. (1984). Determinants of student self-concept: Is it better to be a relatively large fish in a small pond even if you don't learn to swim as well? *Journal of Personality and Social Psychology*, *47*, 213–31.

Marsh, H. W., Parker, P. D., & Pekrun, R. (2018a). Three paradoxical effects on academic self-concept across countries, schools, and students: Frame-of-reference as a unifying theoretical explanation. *European Psychologist*. doi:10.1027/1016-9040/a000332.

Marsh, H. W. & Peart, N. (1988). Competitive and cooperative physical fitness training programs for girls: Effects on physical fitness and on multidimensional self-concepts. *Journal of Sport and Exercise Psychology*, *10*, 390–407.

Marsh, H. W., Pekrun, R., Murayama, K., Arens, A. K., Parker, P. D., Guo, J., & Dicke, T. (2018b). An integrated model of academic self-concept development: Academic self-concept, grades, test scores, and tracking over 6 years. *Developmental Psychology*. *54*(2), 263–80.

Marsh, H. W., Pekrun, R., Murayama, K., Guo, J., Dicke, T., Lichtenfeld, S. (2017). Long-term positive effects of repeating a year in school: Six-year longitudinal study of self-beliefs, anxiety, social relations, school grades, and test scores. *Journal of Educational Psychology*, *109*(3), 425–38. doi:10.1037/edu0000144.

Marsh, H. W. & Perry, C. (2005). Self-concept contributes to winning gold medals: Causal ordering of self-concept and elite swimming performance. *Journal of Sport & Exercise Psychology*, *27*, 71–91.

Marsh, H. W. & Richards, G. (1988). The Outward Bound bridging course for low achieving high-school males: Effect on academic achievement and multidimensional self-concepts. *Australian Journal of Psychology*, *40*, 281–98.

Marsh, H. W., Richards, G., & Barnes, J. (1986a). Multidimensional self-concepts: A long-term follow-up of the effect of participation in an Outward Bound program. *Personality and Social Psychology Bulletin*, *12*, 475–92.

Marsh, H. W., Richards, G., & Barnes, J. (1986b). Multidimensional self-concepts: The effect of participation in an Outward Bound program. *Journal of Personality and Social Psychology*, *45*, 173–87.

Marsh, H. W. & Seaton, M. (2015). The big-fish–little-pond effect, competence self-perceptions, and relativity: Substantive advances and methodological innovation. In A. J. Elliott (Ed.), *Advances in Motivation Science*, *2*, 127–84. New York, NY: Elsevier.

Marsh, H. W., Seaton, M., Trautwein, U., Lüdtke, O., Hau, K. T., O'Mara, A. J., & Craven, R. G. (2008). The big-fish-little-pond-effect stands up to critical scrutiny: Implications for theory, methodology, and future research. *Educational Psychology Review*, *20*, 319–50.

Marsh, H. W. & Shavelson, R. (1985). Self-concept: Its multifaceted, hierarchical structure. *Educational Psychologist*, *20*, 107–25.

Marsh, H. W., Tracey, D. K., & Craven, R. G. (2006c). Multidimensional self-concept structure for preadolescents with mild intellectual disabilities: A hybrid multigroup-mimic approach to factorial invariance and latent mean differences. *Educational and Psychological Measurement*, *66*, 795–818.

Marsh, H. W., Trautwein, U., Lüdtke, O., & Baumert, J. (2007). The big-fish–little-pond effect: Persistent negative effects of selective high schools on self-concept after graduation. *American Educational Research Journal*, *44*(3), 631–69.

Marsh, H. W., Trautwein, U., Lüdtke, O., Köller, O., & Baumert, J. (2006d). Integration of multidimensional self-concept and core personality constructs: Construct validation and relations to well-being and achievement. *Journal of Personality*, *74*, 403–56.

Marx, R. W. & Winne, P. H. (1978). Construct interpretations of three self-concept inventories. *American Educational Research Journal*, *15*(1), 99–109.

Möller, J. & Husemann, N. (2006). Internal comparisons in everyday life. *Journal of Educational Psychology*, *98*, 342–53. doi:10.1037/0022-0663.98.2.342.

Möller, J. & Köller, O. (2001). Dimensional comparisons: An experimental approach to the internal/external frames of reference model. *Journal of Educational Psychology*, *93*, 826–35.

Möller, J. & Marsh, H. W. (2013). Dimensional comparison theory. *Psychological Review*, *120*(3), 544–60. doi:10.1037/a0032459.

Möller, J., Pohlmann, B., Köller, O., & Marsh, H. W. (2009). A meta-analytic path analysis of the internal/external frame of reference model of academic achievement and academic self-concept. *Review of Educational Research*, *79*, 1129–67.

Möller, J. & Savyon, K. (2003). Not very smart thus moral: Dimensional comparisons between academic self-concept and honesty. *Social Psychology of Education*, *6*, 95–106. doi:10.1023/A:1023247910033.

Nagengast, B. & Marsh, H. W. (2012). Big fish in little ponds aspire more: Mediation and cross-cultural generalizability of school-average ability effects on self-concept and career aspirations in science. *Journal of Educational Psychology*, *104*, 1033–53.

O'Mara, A. J., Marsh, H. W., Craven, R. G., & Debus, R. (2006). Do self-concept interventions make a difference? A synergistic blend of construct validation and meta-analysis. *Educational Psychologist*, *41*, 181–206.

Pinxten, M., De Fraine, B., Damme, J., & D'Haenens, E. (2010). Causal ordering of academic self-concept and achievement: Effects of type of achievement measure. *British Journal of Educational Psychology*, *80*, 689–709.

Pohlmann, B. & Möller, J. (2009). On the benefit of dimensional comparisons. *Journal of Educational Psychology*, *101*(1), 248–58. doi:10.1037/a0013151.

Seaton, M., Marsh, H. W., & Craven, R. G. (2009). Earning its place as a pan-human theory: Universality of the big-fish-little-pond effect across 41 culturally and economically diverse countries. *Journal of Educational Psychology*, *101*, 403–19.

Seaton, M., Marsh, H. W., & Craven, R. G. (2010). Big-fish-little-pond effect generalizability and moderation – two sides of the same coin. *American Educational Research Journal*, *47*, 390–433.

Seaton, M., Marsh, H. W., Parker, P. D., Craven, R. G., & Yeung, A. S. (2015). The reciprocal effects model revisited: Extending its reach to gifted students attending academically selective schools. *Gifted Child Quarterly*, *59*(3), 143–56. doi:10.1177/0016986215583870.

Shavelson, R. J. & Bolus, R. (1982). Self-concept: The interplay of theory and methods. *Journal of Educational Psychology*, *74*(1), 3–17.

Shavelson, R. J., Hubner, J. J., & Stanton, G. C. (1976). Self-concept: Validation of construct interpretations. *Review of Educational Research*, *46*, 407–41.

Skaalvik, E. M. & Skaalvik, S. (2002). Internal and external frames of reference for academic self-concept. *Educational Psychologist*, *37*, 233–44.

Valentine, J. C. & DuBois, D. L. (2005). Effects of self-beliefs on academic achievement and vice-versa: Separating the chicken from the egg. In H. W. Marsh, R. G. Craven, & D. M. McInerney (Eds.), *International advances in self research* (pp. 203–30). Greenwich, CT: Information Age.

Valentine, J. C., DuBois, D. L., & Cooper, H. (2004). The relations between self-beliefs and academic achievement: A systematic review. *Educational Psychologist*, *39*, 111–33.

Van Zanden, B. E., Marsh, H. W., Seaton, M., Parker, P. D., Guo, J., & Duineveld, J. J. (2016). How well do parents know their adolescent children? Extending the internal/external frame of reference model of self-concept to parents. *Learning and Instruction*, *47*, 25–32.

Watson, D., Suls, J., & Haig, J. (2002). Global self-esteem in relation to structural models of personality and affectivity. *Journal of Personality and Social Psychology*, *83*, 185.

Wells, L. E. & Marwell, G. (1976). *Self-esteem: Its conceptualisation and measurement*. Beverly Hills, CA: Sage Publications.

Wylie, R. C. (1979). *The Self-concept, Vol. 2: Theory and research on selected topics*. Lincoln: University of Nebraska Press.

Xu, M. K. (2010). *Frame of reference effects in academic self-concept: An examination of the big-fish-little-pond effect and the internal/external frame of reference model for Hong Kong adolescents*. PhD thesis, University of Oxford.

Zeidner, M. H. & Schleyer, E. J. (1999). The big-fish-little-pond effect for academic self-concept, test anxiety, and school grades in gifted children. *Contemporary Educational Psychology, 24*(4), 305–29.

3 Self-Efficacy in Learning

Past, Present, and Future

Hyun Seon Ahn and Mimi Bong

Abstract: Self-efficacy is a popular construct among researchers interested in student learning and performance. It has been used successfully to explain and predict a variety of cognitive, affective, and behavioral outcomes in diverse academic settings. Evidence has accumulated that unanimously points to the functional advantage of having strong self-efficacy beliefs. While so much has been documented on this important construct during the past several decades, it is our judgment that the time has come to reflect on past research findings and revisit some of the unresolved issues that have held up further development in academic self-efficacy research. In this chapter, we summarize existing research on self-efficacy beliefs in academic settings and suggest directions for future research in this area. Specifically, we present a brief overview of self-efficacy theory, along with relevant empirical findings, paying particular attention to the development of self-efficacy beliefs and their relationships with academic outcomes and other motivation constructs. We then turn to unresolved issues in self-efficacy theory and research, such as the growth trajectories of self-efficacy beliefs across time and academic domains, the benefits of modeling, and cross-cultural issues.

Self-efficacy refers to an individual's subjective conviction in her or his capabilities to perform a specific task successfully to achieve a desired outcome (Bandura, 1977). The construct has been studied by many researchers in various domains, since its initial conception, due to its proposed significance in adaptive human functioning. Considerable evidence has indeed accumulated, which points to self-efficacy as a powerful socio-cognitive determinant of human motivation, behavior, and affect (Bandura, 1997). In particular, self-efficacy plays a critical role in academic contexts, predicting choice of activities and courses, interest, persistence, effort expenditure, use of learning strategies, self-regulation, and eventual achievement of students (Bandura & Schunk, 1981; Pajares, 1996, 1997; Schunk, 1995).

Research on self-efficacy in the education literature can be classified into several representative strands. The first research strand focuses on the

The writing of this chapter was supported by a National Research Foundation of Korea grant funded by the Korean government (NRF-2014S1A5B8060944).

development of self-efficacy beliefs (Usher, 2009), while the second examines the relationship between self-efficacy and other constructs such as motivation, strategy use, self-regulation, and achievement (Pajares, 1996, 1997). The third research strand comprises studies on the role of self-efficacy beliefs in students' choice behaviors, especially college majors and career-related choices in the fields of mathematics and science (Hackett, 1995), which has been a more popular topic in counseling than in education. The fourth major strand represents research on teacher efficacy (Tschannen-Moran et al., 1998).

In this chapter, we focus on the first and second research strands, because those two are most relevant in understanding the function of self-efficacy in student learning and performance. We first present a brief overview of self-efficacy theory, followed by past research findings on the development of self-efficacy beliefs and their relationship with other constructs. We then turn to some of the unresolved issues, which, in our opinion, have held up further advancement in self-efficacy theory and research.

Research on Self-Efficacy: What We Already Know

A vast majority of published studies on self-efficacy have investigated the relationship of self-efficacy to motivation and performance. In this section, we discuss findings of previous studies in education. After a short introduction of self-efficacy theory, we discuss the development of self-efficacy beliefs, along with relevant findings from educational research. We then introduce further empirical findings on the relationship of self-efficacy beliefs with student learning, motivation, and self-regulation.

Brief Overview of Self-Efficacy Theory

Bandura's (1986) social cognitive theory posits that human behavior is explained by reciprocal determinism or a model of triadic reciprocity, in which personal, behavioral, and environmental factors interact with each other as determinants of human behavior. As an agentic perspective forms the foundation of social cognitive theory (Bandura, 2001),[1] self-efficacy is a pivotal component in these reciprocal relationships. Individuals appraise their self-efficacy to determine what actions to take, how much effort to invest, how long to persevere, and what strategies to use before performing a task, especially under taxing circumstances (Pajares & Schunk, 2001).

---

1 An agentic perspective refers to the view that people are self-organizing, proactive, self-reflective, and self-regulating toward their own development, adaptation, and change in given situations. In social cognitive theory, agentic perspective includes four core properties of human agency, namely intentionality, forethought, self-reactiveness, and self-reflectiveness.

Perceptions of self-efficacy differ from other perceptions of the self in many important respects. For example, self-concept and self-esteem, like self-efficacy, also represent subjective recognition of the self and its attributes, including competence. However, these two perceptions entail highly evaluative assessments of the recognized attributes and incorporate affective reactions toward the self, such as liking or disliking oneself. Judgments of self-efficacy can likewise result in emotional responses but, unlike self-concept or self-esteem, these emotions stay as separate constructs and do not comprise self-efficacy beliefs (Bong & Clark, 1999; Bong & Skaalvik, 2003). Table 3.1 summarizes these and other differences between academic self-concept and academic self-efficacy.

Although self-concept is less global than self-esteem and may be tied closely to each academic domain, neither perception is as specific as self-efficacy (Bong & Clark, 1999; Bong & Skaalvik, 2003). As can be seen in the sample assessment items presented in Table 3.2, self-concept also relies more heavily on one's past performance history compared to self-efficacy, which necessarily makes the construct more stable and resistant to change, especially in the short run. Self-efficacy is relatively more malleable compared to self-concept or self-esteem, which renders itself a desirable target of instructional interventions. Self-efficacy is a competence-based construct and represents personal estimation of the confidence toward the task at hand (Pajares & Schunk, 2001; Schunk & Pajares, 2002). Because one needs to foretell the imminent performance situation to arrive at such judgment, it is best viewed as a predictive construct that goes beyond the appraisal of one's past accomplishments (Bandura, 1997). Interested readers are referred to Bong and Skaalvik (2003) for a more detailed discussion of the similarities and differences between self-concept and self-efficacy.

Students with strong self-efficacy beliefs are likely to enjoy higher academic achievement, because they are more willing to approach challenging tasks (Pajares, 1996); exert more effort toward and persist longer at difficult tasks (Zimmerman, 2000); use self-regulated learning strategies more effectively (Zimmerman & Martinez-Pons, 1990); and experience lower levels of anxiety (Bandura, 1997) compared to those with weak self-efficacy beliefs. Self-efficacy is acquired and modified through four major sources of self-efficacy information (Bandura, 1977, 1997): mastery experience (e.g., enactive performance accomplishments; Joët et al., 2011); vicarious experience (e.g., modeling; Schunk & Hanson, 1985, 1989); social persuasion (e.g., encouragement; Usher & Pajares, 2009); and physiological states (e.g., feelings of anxiety; Usher & Pajares, 2008). Below we summarize the findings of previous studies on the development of self-efficacy beliefs.

Development of Self-Efficacy Beliefs

Sources of self-efficacy information. Bandura (1997) claimed that the major sources of information individuals use in forming their efficacy beliefs could

Table 3.1 *Comparison between the self-constructs in achievement situations*

Comparison dimension	Self-esteem	Self-concept	Self-efficacy
Conceptual definition	Evaluative judgments of oneself, which include one's feelings of and satisfaction toward oneself	Knowledge and perceptions about one's competencies and attributes, along with resultant emotional reactions	Subjective convictions for successfully executing a course of action to achieve a desired outcome
Judgment specificity	Global	Domain-specific	Domain- and context-specific
Dominant reference point	Past experiences	Past experiences	Future possibilities
Temporal stability	Stable	Stable	Malleable
	Academic self-esteem	Academic self-concept	Academic self-efficacy
Conceptual definition	Evaluative judgments of oneself in achievement situations, which include one's feelings of and satisfaction toward oneself	Knowledge and perceptions about one's competencies and attributes in achievement situations, along with resultant emotional reactions	Subjective convictions for successfully performing given academic tasks to a desired level
Levels of formation	Overall judgments formed at the global levels of functioning	Formed at the global as well as domain- and subject-specific levels	Formed in reference to specific domains, subjects, or tasks
Relevant constructs	Academic self-esteem	Academic self-concept, subject-specific self-concept	Academic self-efficacy, subject-specific self-efficacy, task-specific self-efficacy
Example constructs	Academic self-esteem	Academic self-concept, English self-concept, mathematics self-concept, etc.	Academic self-efficacy, mathematics self-efficacy, self-efficacy for solving subtraction problems, etc.
Example statements	I like myself in school I am satisfied with the way I am at school	I have always done well in English I am a good student in mathematics	I am confident that I can receive a grade of B or better in English I am confident that I can perform well in mathematics I am confident that I can successfully solve the subtraction problems

Table 3.2 *Examples of self-concept and self-efficacy items for predicting mathematics performance*

Self-concept items	Self-efficacy items
	How confident are you that you can...
Mathematics is one of my best subjects	Solve equations containing square roots?
I often need help in mathematics*	Solve for x in quadratic equations?
I look forward to mathematics classes	Solve functions from given vertex and/or Cartesian coordinates?
I have trouble understanding anything with mathematics in it*	Compute the mean, standard deviation, and variance using a frequency table?
I enjoy studying for mathematics	Determine whether a given triangle is acute or obtuse using its three sides?
I do badly in tests of mathematics*	Compute the area of a figure with known perimeters?
I get good marks in mathematics	Solve for a particular angle of figures inscribed in a circle?
I never want to take another mathematics course*	Compute the area of a circle inscribed in a triangle with known sides?
I have always done well in mathematics	Compute the length of a line connecting a particular point on a circle and a tangent line?
I hate mathematics*	Solve equations containing cos, sin, tan, $\cos^2$, $\sin^2$, or $\tan^2$?

Note. Self-concept items are from the Self-Description Questionnaire II (Marsh, 1999b). Self-efficacy items are from Bong (2002) for tenth grade mathematics in Korea.
*Negatively worded items.

be categorized into the following four types: mastery experience, vicarious experience, social persuasion, and physiological states.

Mastery experience, or one's past achievement, is the most prominent source of self-efficacy information (Usher & Pajares, 2008). Whereas past experiences that are successful and positive nourish and enrich one's self-efficacy beliefs (Britner & Pajares, 2006), those that are unsuccessful and negative weaken and lower these beliefs (Pajares, 2003). It is easier for failure experiences to dampen one's self-efficacy toward the task than for successful experiences to boost one's self-efficacy toward it (Bandura, 1997). What is most important in self-efficacy estimation, however, is not the success and failure in an objective sense but one's subjective recognition and interpretation of one's own prior experiences.

Vicarious experience is the next powerful source of self-efficacy information (Bandura, 1977), acquired through observing others. To obtain information concerning their potential performance on a given task, especially when lacking direct mastery experience, students compare themselves to others in similar learning situations. Observing a model successfully performing a task raises the self-efficacy of observers toward the same task (Bandura, 1986, 1997) and influences their subsequent performance positively (Schunk & Hanson, 1985, 1989; Schunk et al., 1987). Competent models that demonstrate effective learning strategies for dealing with difficult tasks enhance the efficacy beliefs of the observing students, whereas incapable and unsuccessful models that display learning and performance difficulties weaken the self-efficacy beliefs of the observers toward the same or related tasks (Bandura, 1986, 1997; Schunk, 1987; Zeldin & Pajares, 2000).

Social persuasion, verbal and non-verbal reactions by others to one's actual and potential performance, is another source of self-efficacy information. Positive feedback from significant others augments the efficacy beliefs of students (Zeldin & Pajares, 2000), while little or negative feedback undermines their efficacy beliefs (Bandura, 1997; Usher, 2009). Social persuasion is effective when delivered by powerful, competent, and credible social agents (Bandura, 1997).

Physiological states, such as sweating, nervousness, and heartbeat, are the last and presumably the weakest source of self-efficacy information (Bandura, 1977). The awareness that one feels anxious about performing any upcoming task lowers one's self-efficacy toward the very task (Usher & Pajares, 2008).

Over the past several decades, a number of researchers have developed scales for measuring the four sources of self-efficacy information (e.g., Hampton, 1998; Lent et al., 1991; Matsui, et al., 1990), and they have tested the relationship between the sources so assessed and the resultant self-efficacy beliefs across a wide range of academic domains (Britner & Pajares, 2006; Joët et al., 2011; Lopez & Lent, 1992). A detailed review of the existing source scales can be found in Usher and Pajares (2008). Among the available efficacy source scales, the following three have been most widely used in educational research: the Mathematics Efficacy Information developed by Matsui et al. (1990); the Sources of Mathematics Self-Efficacy Scale developed by Lent et al. (1991); and the Sources of Middle School Mathematics Self-Efficacy Scale developed by Usher and Pajares (2009). Among these three, the Sources of Middle School Mathematics Self-Efficacy Scale is arguably the most psychometrically sound and feasible instrument, closely aligned with Bandura's (1997) self-efficacy theory (Chen & Usher, 2013).

By adopting the aforementioned scales, investigators have found repeatedly that mastery experience is the most powerful predictor of student self-efficacy, which supports Bandura's claim (Britner & Pajares, 2006; Joët et al., 2011; Lopez & Lent, 1992). Vicarious experience and social persuasion also predict self-efficacy positively, although the predictive utility of vicarious experience has not always been consistent (Lent et al., 1991; Matsui et al., 1990; Phan, 2012; Usher & Pajares, 2009). Social persuasion tends to demonstrate more stable predictive power over student self-efficacy beliefs than vicarious experience does, a finding that deviates from theoretical prediction. The complexity associated with the assessment of vicarious experience is suspected to have prevented researchers from accurately capturing its influence on self-efficacy formation (Usher & Pajares, 2009). Physiological states are the negative predictor of student self-efficacy (Joët et al., 2011), whose relative predictive capacity often surpasses that expected by theory.

Role of social agents. A large body of research on the development of self-efficacy has verified the importance of social agents, especially in vicarious experience and social persuasion. As indicated earlier, effects of vicarious experience fluctuate considerably by the characteristics and types of models that demonstrate the target skill (Bandura, 1997; Schunk, 1987; Schunk & Hanson, 1985; Schunk et al., 1987). Effects of social persuasion are expected to vary likewise, depending on the perceived expertise, knowledgeableness, and credibility of the persuader (Bandura, 1997). However, empirical research to date has mainly centered on discovering the characteristics of models that make vicarious experience, rather than social persuasion, more influential on the formation of self-efficacy beliefs.

Characteristics of models. Modeling has proved effective in raising the efficacy beliefs of children in various school subjects, such as mathematics (Schunk & Hanson, 1985, 1989; Schunk et al., 1987), reading and writing (Braaksma et al., 2002; Couzijn, 1999; Schunk, 2003; Zimmerman & Kitsantas, 2002), as well as creative domains (Groenendijk et al., 2011). The effectiveness of this vicarious experience depends partly on the individual model involved.

For instance, Schunk and Hanson (1985, 1989) employed mastery and coping models in their series of classroom research, which demonstrated the targeted arithmetic skills to children lacking arithmetic competence. Mastery models demonstrated rapid and flawless performance of the skills. They also verbalized statements that reflected their positive attitudes (e.g., "I like doing these"), strong confidence (e.g., "I can do that one"), high perceived ability (e.g., "I'm good at this"), and low levels of task difficulty (e.g., "That looks easy"). In contrast, coping models initially performed the task with hesitation and occasional mistakes, verbalizing statements reflecting their negative attitudes (e.g., "That isn't much fun"), weak confidence (e.g., "I'm not sure I can do that one"), low perceived ability (e.g., "I'm not very good at this"), and high levels of task difficulty (e.g., "That looks tough"). As time passed, however, they showed gradual improvement in performance and began to verbalize coping statements (e.g., "I'll have to work hard on this one"), which resulted in successful performance. Coping models were significantly more beneficial than mastery models for the participating children, who had previously experienced learning difficulties in mathematics.

A recent study by Groenendijk et al. (2011) has further shown that the superiority of coping models to mastery models is not confined to academic domains or students at particular performance levels. When videotaped modeling of mastery and coping performance in visual (collage) and verbal arts (poetry writing) were presented, students who observed coping models in visual arts reported stronger self-efficacy and more creative performance than those who observed mastery models. Similar effects were not obtained in poetry writing.

The perceived similarity of the model to the observer is an important source of information to formulate efficacy perceptions (Schunk et al., 1987). In general, children judge themselves to be more similar to a coping model than to a mastery model, which explains the stronger influence of coping models on their self-efficacy formation and performance. Children also exhibit stronger efficacy beliefs and performance after watching a peer model than a teacher model (Schunk & Hanson, 1985), presumably because of the greater degree of perceived similarity in competence to the same-aged peer than to the adult teacher. Presenting multiple models is more effective than presenting a single model for improving observers' self-efficacy for the same reason; it increases the probability that observers find a model they perceive to be similar to themselves (Schunk, 2012).

Types of social agents. Although the relationship between self-efficacy and its four principal sources of information is rather firmly established, there have been inconsistent findings nonetheless. Specifically, vicarious experience and social persuasion theorized by Bandura (1977, 1997) have proved less effective or reliable as predictors of self-efficacy, particularly when they are assessed along with mastery experience or physiological states. Some researchers found that both were significant predictors of self-efficacy (Matsui et al., 1990; Usher & Pajares, 2006), whereas others reported no such effect (Britner & Pajares, 2006; Joët et al., 2011; Lopez & Lent, 1992). Often, social persuasion predicted self-efficacy better than vicarious experience did (Lent et al., 1991; Matsui et al., 1990; Phan, 2012; Usher & Pajares, 2009).

It is interesting to note that this inconsistency may be attributed to the lack of distinction between social agents, such as parents, teachers, and peers, in the existing vicarious experience and social persuasion scales. Self-efficacy development is sensitive to life-stage transitions, which induce changes in personal and social relationships (Schunk & Meece, 2006; Schunk & Pajares, 2002). Previous research suggests that the impact of social models on the sources of efficacy information varies depending on the students' developmental stage and the perceived competence of the person modeling the performance (Schunk, 1987; Schunk & Pajares, 2002). Compared to younger children, adolescents are more prone to evaluate the similarities of their peers to themselves and adopt feedback from those peers when estimating their efficacy beliefs (Schunk & Miller, 2002; Usher, 2009; Wigfield & Wagner, 2005).

Not only does vicarious experience function differently depending on the social model, social persuasion may also differ in its effectiveness by the social model that delivers efficacy-relevant messages. Ahn, Bong and Kim (2017) tested this possibility by developing new vicarious experience and social persuasion scales. These scales assess the vicarious experience and social persuasion from family members, teachers, and peers separately. The new vicarious experience scale thus contains three subscales: vicarious experience from family members, vicarious experience from teachers, and vicarious experience from peers. The new social persuasion scale contains three subscales as well: social persuasion by family members, social persuasion by teachers, and social persuasion by peers. Korean high school and college students responded to these items in reference to mathematics (e.g., "I have a family member who is really good at math") and English as a foreign language (e.g., "When I am struggling with English, my teacher tells me that I can do well").

Exploratory and confirmatory factor analysis revealed that Korean high school and college students alike clearly distinguished between the efficacy sources conveyed by different social agents in both mathematics and English. Multitrait-multimethod analysis also confirmed the necessity of distinguishing between efficacy sources as well as between social models. In addition to mastery experience and physiological states, social persuasion by teachers, but not vicarious experience from teachers or social persuasion by family members and peers, predicted student self-efficacy in mathematics; vicarious experience from teachers, but not social persuasion by teachers or vicarious experience from family members and peers, predicted student self-efficacy in English. These results further justify the need for independent assessment of the self-efficacy sources by the social model.

Relationships of Self-Efficacy Beliefs to Other Constructs

Relationships to academic achievement. A wealth of literature has substantiated that self-efficacy is a powerful predictor of academic behaviors (Bandura, 1997; Schunk, 1995). Numerous studies have documented the strong positive relationship between self-efficacy and academic achievement across grade levels (Alivernini & Lucidi, 2011; Joët et al., 2011; Zimmerman et al., 1992). A meta-analysis conducted by Multon, Brown, and Lent (1991) has shown that self-efficacy is positively related to both academic persistence and achievement. The effect was stronger for high school and college students than for elementary school students. The positive tie between academic self-efficacy and achievement was replicated in another meta-analysis (Honicke & Broadbent, 2016). Researchers generally agree that, among diverse self-beliefs and motivation constructs, self-efficacy is by far the strongest predictor of academic performance (Bong & Clark, 1999; Bong & Skaalvik, 2003).

Relationships to learning and self-regulation. Self-efficacy also influences self-regulatory processes such as goal setting, self-monitoring, self-evaluation, and strategy use (Zimmerman, 2000; Zimmerman & Cleary, 2006). Students with strong self-efficacy are more likely to engage in challenging tasks, set more difficult goals, demonstrate more efficient use of self-regulatory strategies, and persist longer than are those with weak self-efficacy. Zimmerman et al.

(1992) demonstrated that self-efficacy for self-regulated learning reported by students predicted their self-efficacy for academic achievement, which in turn predicted their final grades. Students' self-efficacy for academic achievement predicted students' final grades directly as well as indirectly via students' grade goals. Pintrich and De Groot (1990) also reported that students with high self-efficacy were more likely to use cognitive and self-regulatory strategies compared to students with low self-efficacy.

A sense of self-efficacy is enhanced when students set proximal goals. Bandura and Schunk (1981) randomly assigned students into the proximal-goal (to complete six pages of the problem set during each of the seven sessions in the remedial instructional program), distal-goal (to complete all 42 pages of the problem set by the end of the entire program), no-goal (to complete simply as many pages as possible during the program), and no-treatment conditions. All students, except for those in the no-treatment condition, learned how to solve subtraction problems using self-instructional materials. Self-efficacy and skill development in subtraction, assessed at the end of the program, were significantly higher among the students who had worked with proximal goals than among those in any other condition, including the students who had worked with distal goals.

Zimmerman and Kitsantas (1997) provided additional evidence detailing the effects of goal setting and self-monitoring on self-efficacy and skill development. In their experiment, high school girls were asked to participate in a study of dart-throwing and were subsequently provided with demonstration, instructions, and practice time for dart-throwing skills in one of nine conditions. Eight experimental conditions were created by different combinations of outcome and process goals, with or without self-recording; a practice-only control group involved neither goal setting nor self-recording. The results showed that students in the shifting-goal condition with self-recording ended up with the highest dart-throwing skill, strongest self-efficacy beliefs, most positive self-reactions, and greatest interest in the dart-throwing game. In contrast, students in the outcome-goal condition without self-recording displayed the lowest levels of skills, self-efficacy, self-reactions, and interest in dart throwing. The students in the shifting-goal condition started their dart-throwing practice with a process goal of following the correct steps for the throw but, once their throwing skills had become automatized, shifted to an outcome goal of hitting the bull's-eye on the target.

These experiments demonstrate the advantage of short-term process goals for augmenting student self-efficacy and skill development, especially during the initial stage of learning. The specific and proximal nature of these goals is conducive to effective self-monitoring, because they offer students clear standards and opportunities to evaluate their progress toward the goals. After students become proficient and reasonably confident with the execution of target skills, their self-efficacy and performance can be further enhanced by pursuing specific outcome goals.

More recently, Lee, et al. (2014) compared the relative function of self-efficacy and interest in the self-regulatory pathway, leading to achievement in the subject domain. Self-efficacy predicted the grade goal that students set for the subject, which predicted their achievement in the domain directly and indirectly via their self-regulatory strategy use. Self-efficacy of the students also predicted their achievement directly. In contrast, interest linked to achievement only through students' use of self-regulatory strategies was not able to predict achievement directly. The same pattern was obtained repeatedly in four different subject areas that included Korean, English, mathematics, and science, lending credibility to the finding. The authors suggested that there might be two pathways to successful self-regulation and that self-efficacy beliefs constituted the most crucial component in the cognitive pathway to academic self-regulation and achievement.

Relationships to academic motivation. Finally, research on self-efficacy demonstrates significant relationships of self-efficacy to a variety of motivation constructs. Self-efficacy typically covaries positively with adaptive variables, such as task value, interest, and mastery achievement goals, and negatively with maladaptive variables, such as anxiety. Below we introduce relevant empirical findings on the relationship of self-efficacy with each of these motivation constructs.

Self-efficacy and task value. Expectancy for success and task value are important predictors of students' academic choice and performance behaviors in expectancy-value theory (Wigfield & Eccles, 2000). Expectancy for success refers to the subjectively estimated probability of success on a given task, which is considered conceptually similar to self-efficacy. Task value refers to an incentive for engaging in the task and consists of attainment value (i.e., perceived importance of doing well on the task for one's self-concept), intrinsic value (i.e., perceived interest in and enjoyment while performing the task), and utility value (i.e., perceived usefulness of doing well on the task; Eccles & Wigfield, 2002). Many studies have attested to the positive relationship between self-efficacy and task value in various academic domains.

Wolters et al. (1996), for instance, present evidence for a positive correlation between self-efficacy and task value across mathematics, English, and social studies. Seventh and eighth graders at a junior high school participated in the survey at the beginning and end of the school year. The self-efficacy beliefs of the students correlated positively with their task value perceptions in all three academic subjects at both time points. Corroborating evidence for the efficacy-value link was provided in a study by Bong (2001). Self-efficacy beliefs of both Korean middle and high school students correlated positively with their task value in Korean, English, mathematics, and science. Findings from these two studies affirm the robust association between self-efficacy and task value across multiple subject areas and grade levels that is unaffected by the characteristics of specific subjects or the time of assessments. Students who expressed strong confidence for performing well in a given school subject also tend to believe that the subject is important, interesting, and useful.

Whereas beliefs of self-efficacy and task value typically maintain positive relationships, an inside look at their connections reveals relationships that are not always as simple or straightforward. Lee et al. (2013) reasoned that when students are faced with abundant social comparative cues, fierce competition, and high-stakes testing in their learning environment, perceptions of high task value unsupported by strong self-efficacy can be a source of self-worth threat for them. Empirical results showed that this was indeed the case. The researchers analyzed the survey responses of almost 7,000 Korean middle school students, collected when they were eighth (T1) and ninth graders (T2), on their perceptions of self-efficacy and task value toward English and mathematics, as well as their use of self-handicapping strategies and test stress in these two subjects. Significant interactions emerged between T1 task value and self-efficacy on T2 self-handicapping and test stress. Students with strong self-efficacy engaged in less self-handicapping as they perceived greater intrinsic value and utility value in the subject; those with weak self-efficacy, however, reported greater self-handicapping as they perceived greater task value. Similarly, all students experienced greater test stress as they perceived greater task value in the subjects; however, this tendency was significantly stronger among students with weak self-efficacy than among those with strong self-efficacy.

Lee et al. (2014) replicated this pattern with another group of Korean high school students. Beliefs of self-efficacy in English again interacted significantly with the task value perceptions students held toward English. Highly self-efficacious students reported less cheating and less academic procrastination as they perceived greater task value in English; students lacking self-efficacy, on the contrary, displayed stronger tendency to cheat and procrastinate in English as their perceptions of task value in English became stronger.

Self-efficacy and interest. Alternatively, some researchers focus more specifically on the relationship of self-efficacy to interest. Bandura and Schunk's (1981) study is one of the earliest works that investigated the connection between self-efficacy, proximal goals, and interest. They hypothesized that proximal goals would serve as an important tool in the development of competencies, self-efficacy, and interest. Students who displayed weak competence and low interest in arithmetic computations were randomly assigned to the proximal-goal, distal-goal, no-goal, and no-treatment conditions and attended remedial classes with self-instructional materials. At the end of the program, children in the proximal-goal condition made the most substantial improvements in arithmetic skills and self-efficacy, as well as interest toward the arithmetic activities. This result is consistent with the co-development in skills, self-efficacy, and interest in dart throwing reported by Zimmerman and Kitsantas (1997), described earlier.

The observations of Bandura and Schunk (1981) as well as Zimmerman and Kitsantas (1997) suggest that learners may need to feel reasonably competent before finding the activity to be interesting. Bong et al. (2015) tested this possibility. In Study 1, the cross-sectional association between self-efficacy and interest in three subject areas was examined among Korean middle and high school students. They observed that the self-efficacy and interest correlated significantly more strongly in mathematics and science than in language arts. In Study 2, the longitudinal association between self-efficacy and interest was explored in mathematics among a nationally representative sample of Korean middle school students. The two constructs displayed significant reciprocal relationships across the four assessment points, spanning the three middle school years and one high school year. Contrary to the authors' hypothesis, student interest in mathematics during the previous year was a stronger predictor of student self-efficacy in mathematics in the subsequent year than student self-efficacy was of student interest. These results suggest that interest may be an important prerequisite for developing self-efficacy beliefs, especially in science and mathematics.

Niemivirta and Tapola's (2007) study with students in Finland provides additional insight into the relationship between self-efficacy and interest. The researchers examined how changes in self-efficacy and changes in interest related to each other, and whether these changes independently predicted overall performance on dynamic problem-solving tasks. There was a significant positive correlation between the initial self-efficacy scores and the initial interest scores, as well as between the changes in self-efficacy scores and those in interest scores (i.e., slopes). Not only self-efficacy beliefs during the beginning phase of the task correlated with interest, but also subsequent increases in self-efficacy beliefs correlated with similar increases in interest. Taken together, these studies illustrate the strong tie and co-development of self-efficacy and interest, corroborating the finding of meta-analysis (Rottinghaus et al., 2003).

Self-efficacy and achievement goals. Another motivational variable that has received fairly extensive attention in self-efficacy research is achievement goals. Achievement goals represent the reasons for engaging in achievement-oriented pursuits that most typically include a mastery goal and a performance goal, with the latter separated into a performance-approach goal and a performance-avoidance goal. Students with mastery goals strive for self-improvement and task mastery, whereas those with performance goals are most concerned with validating their competence, either by demonstrating their superior competence (i.e., performance-approach goal) or by concealing their relative incompetence (i.e., performance-avoidance goal) compared to others (Elliot, 1999; Elliot & Church, 1997). Self-efficacy correlates positively with mastery and performance-approach goals and negatively with performance-avoidance goals across academic domains (Bong, 2001).

Pajares et al. (2000) sought to explain the relationship between achievement goals and self-efficacy in writing and science. Self-efficacy beliefs of the middle school students in both writing and science correlated positively with their mastery goals and negatively with their performance-avoidance goals. Moreover, self-efficacy was predicted independently by achievement goals. Specifically, self-efficacy was predicted positively by mastery goals in both writing and science. Writing self-efficacy was also predicted positively by performance-approach goals but negatively by performance-avoidance goals.

Not surprisingly, the firm linkage between self-efficacy and achievement goals was replicated in a study of Korean adolescents by Noh et al. (2011). Analyzing a longitudinal database across three waves, the investigators found a significant reciprocal association between self-efficacy and achievement goals across time. Prior self-efficacy predicted later mastery goals positively and later performance-avoidance goals negatively; mastery goals in turn predicted subsequent self-efficacy positively, while performance-avoidance goals did so negatively. Whereas self-efficacy during the first wave positively predicted performance-approach goals during the second wave, the path disappeared during the third wave. Performance-approach goals predicted subsequent self-efficacy in none of the waves, hinting at the stronger role efficacy beliefs play in performance-approach goal adoption than vice versa.

Self-efficacy and anxiety. Self-efficacy often determines the emotional state of individuals in achievement situations (Bandura, 1997). In particular, a vicious cycle operates between self-efficacy and anxiety. Nervousness before performing a task lowers one's self-efficacy toward the impending task, and the weakened sense of self-efficacy intensifies the worries and negative affect while one performs the task, further lowering the efficacy toward it. The strong negative association between judgments of self-efficacy and anxiety has been observed repeatedly in educational research (e.g., Bong et al., 2012; Wolters et al., 1996).

Cross-Cultural Differences in the Relative Utility of Self-Efficacy Information

Self-efficacy has proven its significance as an important determinant of motivation and performance across a multitude of countries and cultures (Bandura, 2002). Despite this cross-cultural generality in the functional value of self-efficacy, some have nevertheless suspected culture-related differences in the formation of self-efficacy beliefs. Oettingen (1995) asserts, "culture may affect not only the type of information provided by the various sources, but also which information is selected and how it is weighted and integrated in people's self-efficacy judgments" (p. 151). She has presented three possibilities as a basis of her claim: (1) individuals in different cultures may experience different degrees of exposure to certain sources of self-efficacy information; (2) communication of efficacy-relevant information can take different forms across cultures; and (3) the extent to which each self-efficacy information source is deemed valuable varies across cultures.

Self-efficacy researchers have acknowledged the potential role of culture in the development and operation of self-efficacy beliefs. Bandura (2002) stated, "Although efficacy beliefs have generalized functional value, how they are developed and structured, the ways in which they are exercised, and the purposes to which they are put vary cross-culturally" (p. 273). Likewise, Pajares (2007) called for "culturally attentive" research to understand different cultural practices for cultivating academic self-efficacy beliefs of students.

Answering this call, a number of researchers have investigated differences in the strength of self-efficacy beliefs, as well as in the relationship between efficacy sources and resultant self-efficacy judgments, across countries and ethnic groups. After reviewing studies of self-efficacy that contain cultural components, Klassen (2004b) concluded that individuals from collectivistic cultures tend to rate their self-efficacy lower than do those from individualistic cultures. He observed that these modest self-efficacy beliefs of collectivists nonetheless demonstrate predictive utility that is comparable or superior to that associated with the self-efficacy beliefs of individualists. The findings of Stigler et al. (1985) are consistent with this observation. Taiwanese fifth graders rated their general self-worth, as well as their perceived competence in the cognitive and physical domains, significantly lower in comparison to the ratings US children had provided on the same scale in previous studies. However, perceived competence of the Taiwanese children in the cognitive domain was still a significant predictor of their reading, mathematics, social studies, and average grades, to the degree commensurate to that witnessed in the US samples.

Klassen (2004a) provided further evidence that individualism and collectivism could make a difference in the relative weight students assign to each source of self-efficacy information. For collectivistic Indo-Canadian seventh graders, both self-oriented (i.e., mastery experience and physiological states) and other-oriented (i.e., vicarious experience and social persuasion) sources of efficacy information were significant antecedents of their academic self-efficacy in mathematics. For individualistic Anglo-Canadian students, in contrast, only the two self-oriented sources were significant predictors of their mathematics self-efficacy. This study shows that students of individualistic and collectivistic heritage place different weights on the sources of self-efficacy information when gauging their self-efficacy in the domain.

In a more recent study, Ahn et al. (2016) compared the predictive utility of other-oriented sources of self-efficacy information from multiple social agents in the formation of mathematics self-efficacy beliefs of adolescents in Korea, the Philippines, and the United States. Both vicarious experience and social persuasion exhibited prediction power that differed not only by the social agents but also by the cultural backgrounds of the adolescents. Mathematics self-efficacy beliefs of the American and Korean students were predicted equally by the vicarious experience from their teachers and the social persuasion by their family members and peers, whereas those of the Filipino students were best predicted by the social persuasion by their peers.

Future Research Directions: What We Need to Know Further

In this final section of the chapter, we suggest directions for future research on academic self-efficacy based on the gaps we identified in contemporary literature. It is our assessment that research on the following topics is currently lacking and appears particularly promising for making contributions to the field, once conducted. Specifically, future research is recommended on the growth trajectories of self-efficacy beliefs, the benefits of modeling, and cross-cultural issues.

Growth Trajectories of Self-Efficacy Beliefs across Contexts and Time

Many researchers have invested a lot of effort into uncovering the relationship of self-efficacy to its antecedents and consequences. Interestingly, a considerable majority of the extant literature involves the domain of mathematics. The heavy focus on the role of self-efficacy in mathematics learning and performance may be attributable to the inherent nature of the domain. Pajares and Miller (1994) stated, "the solving of math problems afforded a clearer and more reliable assessment than was possible in other academic contexts" (p. 200).

However, Butz and Usher (2015) pointed out that the strength of the source-to-efficacy connection can fluctuate, depending on the individual or contextual factors. Obviously, contextual differences in self-efficacy beliefs are not limited to their associations with their antecedents. Nevertheless, relationships of efficacy perceptions with their information sources are suspected to swing more than their relationships with other constructs such as academic motivation and performance. For instance, the same mastery experience may strengthen student self-efficacy better in learning environments where task mastery and individual progress are appreciated than in learning environments where test performance and relative superiority receive the greatest rewards and recognition. In fact, that was exactly what Ahn et al. (2013) observed. In their study, the mastery experience of the participating students interacted significantly with their perceptions of the classroom goal structure such that the same mastery experience augmented students' self-efficacy beliefs significantly more strongly in mastery-oriented classrooms than in performance-oriented ones. The effect of self-efficacy on motivation and achievement may likewise differ depending on the context or the academic domain.

A clear need also exists for more investigations on the relationship between self-efficacy and academic motivation over time. Bong (2005) observed an interesting pattern when she repeatedly assessed Korean students' self-efficacy and achievement goals in Korean, English, mathematics, and general school learning over an academic year: once before a midterm examination and once after a final examination during both the first and second semesters. Beliefs of self-efficacy increased from the beginning to the end of the first semester in all four contexts but, when assessed again before the midterm during the second semester, dropped to a level equivalent to that in the beginning of the first semester. By the end of the second semester, the weakened self-efficacy recovered to a level similar to that at the end of the first semester. In addition, self-efficacy predicted mastery goals positively and performance-avoidance goals negatively, but these predictive paths emerged largely during the second semester and seldom during the first semester.

The findings of Bong (2005) hint at two possibilities: (1) increases in self-efficacy beliefs generally take a linear form, especially in the long run, but vary considerably around major achievement events such as midterm and final examinations; and (2) it may be necessary for students to grasp the characteristics of the school subjects or the learning environments before their self-efficacy beliefs start shaping their motivation and performance. More longitudinal studies can address how the growth trajectories and predictive relationships of self-efficacy differ across contexts, domains, and time.

Benefits of Modeling

Schunk et al. have generated many findings on modeling that have strong implications for classroom instruction (e.g., Schunk & Hanson, 1985, 1989; Schunk et al., 1987). Still, there are areas in which further research can prove useful. One such area is the model similarity hypothesis that explains the unequal impact of modeling on self-efficacy development. Up to date, perceived model-observer similarity in competence is assumed to underlie the stronger relationship between coping models and student self-efficacy compared to that between mastery models and self-efficacy beliefs. We need to learn whether this effect of similarity is largely restricted to competence or entails other model characteristics as well.

The type of modeling may also interact with observer characteristics. In a study by Braaksma et al. (2002), eighth graders were randomly assigned to the weak-model, good-model, and control conditions. Students assigned to the two modeling conditions watched videos of coping and mastery peer-model pairs performing argumentative writing tasks. Students in the weak-model condition were asked to focus on the coping model's performance, while those in the good-model condition focused on the mastery model's performance. Low-ability participants learned more after observing coping models, whereas high-ability participants learned more after observing mastery models. Though the researchers did not assess students' perceptions of model similarity, it seems probable that low-ability students found coping models more similar to themselves, as high-ability students did mastery models.

Adoption of new technologies could help researchers pursue this line of research on effective modeling. Levels of proficiency displayed by models and degrees of similarity of models to observers in age, gender, appearance, and other traits can be manipulated easily in videos and computer programs. Performance features that can inform instructional decisions, such as the degree of coping or the time taken to eventual task mastery, are also much easier to exemplify in varying degrees in technological environments than in live modeling. This type of inquiry would produce results that can help optimize the effects of instructional modeling on students' self-efficacy beliefs.

Cross-Cultural Issues

Despite the promising early findings, a great deal more work is required to clarify how the diverse sources of self-efficacy information are selected, interpreted, and integrated differently because of different cultural practices. As described earlier, recent studies found some evidence of cultural diversity in the relative use of self-efficacy information sources (Ahn et al., 2016; Klassen, 2004a). These studies, although enlightening, illustrate cultural differences at a very broad level and fall short of detailing the mechanism responsible for the observed differences. We are left to wonder whether the difference between individualistic and collectivistic cultures (Klassen, 2004a, 2004b) or that between adolescent learners in Korea, the Philippines, and the United States (Ahn et al., 2016) in the degree each self-efficacy source is consulted is truly due to cultural norms and, if so, whether these norms apply equally to various subject domains, phases of learning, and groups of students at different developmental stages.

Often, cultural differences are closely intertwined with differences in educational systems and policies. It will be informative to disentangle differences due mainly to cultural practices from those due to systems, so as not to make an erroneous conclusion regarding the cultural features in self-efficacy development. If we understand why students from certain cultural backgrounds are drawn more to one efficacy source or the other, we will be in a better position to devise practical strategies to help improve the self-efficacy beliefs of more learners in need.

Concluding Thoughts

Self-efficacy is a popular construct among educational researchers, because it explains and predicts a variety of cognitive, affective, and behavioral outcomes in diverse learning situations. In achievement contexts, it represents the subjective confidence of students to learn and perform given academic tasks successfully to a desired level (Schunk, 1991). Abundant evidence has accumulated during the past several decades that unanimously points to the functional advantage of having strong self-efficacy beliefs in academic settings. We have traced the evolution of self-efficacy research within the domain of education, focusing on the development of self-efficacy beliefs and their relationships with other constructs.

Self-efficacy beliefs are cultivated through acquiring relevant information from four major sources, namely mastery experience, vicarious experience, social persuasion, and physiological states (Bandura, 1997). Academic self-efficacy so constructed is a powerful predictor of students' academic achievement (Schunk, 1995) as well as students' self-regulatory processes and outcomes (Zimmerman, 2000; Zimmerman & Cleary, 2006). The sense of self-efficacy of learners in any academic domain correlates positively with their task value (Bong, 2001), interest (Bong et al., 2015), and mastery achievement goals in the same domain (Bong, 2005; Noh et al., 2011).

We have recounted these and other important findings from previous research and offered directions for future investigations on academic self-efficacy. Although many investigators have already studied, and continue to study, the sources and consequences of self-efficacy beliefs, several vexing problems remain. The growth trajectories of self-efficacy beliefs across contexts, domains, and time; the benefits of modeling; and the relative utility of self-efficacy sources, as well as the relative power of self-efficacy beliefs as determinants of student learning, motivation, and performance across cultures, are the topics that require urgent attention, in our view. We hope this chapter provides some useful information and guidelines for researchers and educators interested in self-efficacy theory and research.

References

Ahn, H. S., Bong, M., & Kim, S. (2013). *Interaction between implicit theories, classroom goal structures, and sources of efficacy information on math self-efficacy.* Poster Session presented at the annual meeting of the American Educational Research Association, San Francisco, CA.

Ahn, H. S., Bong, M., & Kim, S. (2017). Social models in the cognitive appraisal of self-efficacy information. *Contemporary Educational Psychology, 48,* 149–66. doi:10.1016/j.cedpsych.2016.08.002.

Ahn, H. S., Usher, E. L., Butz, A. R., & Bong, M. (2016). Cultural differences in the understanding of modelling and feedback as sources of self-efficacy information. *British Journal of Educational Psychology, 86,* 112–36. doi:10.1111/bjep.12093.

Alivernini, F. & Lucidi, F. (2011). Relationship between social context, self-efficacy, motivation, academic achievement, and intention to drop out of high school: A longitudinal study. *The Journal of Educational Research, 104,* 241–52. doi:10.1080/00220671003728062.

Bandura, A. (1977). Self-efficacy: Toward a unifying theory of behavioral change. *Psychological Review, 84,* 191–215. doi:10.1037/0033-295X.84.2.191.

Bandura, A. (1986). *Social foundations of thought and action: A social cognitive theory.* Englewood Cliffs, NJ: Prentice Hall.

Bandura, A. (1997). *Self-efficacy: The exercise of control.* New York, NY: Freeman.

Bandura, A. (2001). Social cognitive theory: An agentic perspective. *Annual Review of Psychology, 52,* 1–26. doi:10.1146/annurev.psych.52.1.1.

Bandura, A. (2002). Social cognitive theory in cultural context. *Applied Psychology: An International Review, 51*(2), 269–90. doi:10.1111/1464-0597.00092.

Bandura, A. & Schunk, D. H. (1981). Cultivating competence, self-efficacy, and intrinsic interest through proximal self-motivation. *Journal of Personality and Social Psychology, 41*, 586–98. doi:10.1037/0022-3514.41.3.586.

Bong, M. (2001). Between- and within-domain relations of academic motivation among middle and high school students: Self-efficacy, task-value, and achievement goals. *Journal of Educational Psychology, 93*, 23–34. doi:10.1037/0022-0663.93.1.23.

Bong, M. (2005). Within-grade changes in Korean girls' motivation and perceptions of the learning environment across domains and achievement levels. *Journal of Educational Psychology, 97*, 656–72. doi:10.1037/0022-0663.97.4.656.

Bong, M., Cho, C., Ahn, H. S., & Kim, H. J. (2012). Comparison of self-beliefs for predicting student motivation and achievement. *The Journal of Educational Research, 105*, 336–52. doi:10.1080/00220671.2011.627401.

Bong, M. & Clark, R. E. (1999). Comparison between self-concept and self-efficacy in academic motivation research. *Educational Psychologist, 34*, 139–54. doi:10.1207/s15326985ep3403_1.

Bong, M., Lee, S. K., & Woo, Y.-K. (2015). The role of interest and self-efficacy in pursuing mathematics and science. In K. A. Renninger, M. Nieswandt, & S. Hidi (Eds.), *Interest in mathematics and science learning* (pp. 33–48). Washington, DC: American Educational Research Association.

Bong, M. & Skaalvik, E. M. (2003). Academic self-concept and self-efficacy: How different are they really? *Educational Psychology Review, 15*, 1–40. doi:10.1023/A:1021302408382.

Braaksma, M. A. H., Rijlaarsdam, G., & van den Bergh, H. (2002). Observational learning and the effects of model-observer similarity. *Journal of Educational Psychology, 94*, 405–15. doi:10.1037/0022-0663.94.2.405.

Britner, S. L. & Pajares, F. (2006). Sources of science self-efficacy beliefs of middle school students. *Journal of Research in Science Teaching, 43*, 485–99. doi:10.1002/tea.20131.

Butz, A. R. & Usher, E. L. (2015). Salient sources of early adolescents' self-efficacy in two domains. *Contemporary Educational Psychology, 42*, 49–61. doi:10.1016/j.cedpsych.2015.04.001.

Chen, J. A. & Usher, E. L. (2013). Profiles of the sources of science self-efficacy. *Learning and Individual Differences, 24*, 11–21. doi:10.1016/j.lindif.2012.11.002.

Couzijn, M. (1999). Learning to write by observation of writing and reading processes: Effects on learning and transfer. *Learning and Instruction, 9*, 109–42. doi:10.1016/S0959-4752(98)00040-1.

Eccles, J. S. & Wigfield, A. (2002). Motivational beliefs, values, and goals. *Annual Review of Psychology, 53*, 109–32. doi:10.1146/annurev.psych.53.100901.135153.

Elliot, A. J. (1999). Approach and avoidance motivation and achievement goals. *Educational Psychologist, 34*, 169–89. doi:10.1207/s15326985ep3403_3.

Elliot, A. J. & Church, M. A. (1997). A hierarchical model of approach and avoidance achievement motivation. *Journal of Personality and Social Psychology, 72*, 218–32. doi:10.1037/0022-3514.72.1.218.

Groenendijk, T., Janssen, T., Rijlaarsdam, G., & van den Bergh, H. (2011). The effect of observational learning on students' performance, processes, and motivation in two creative domains. *British Journal of Educational Psychology, 83*, 1–26. doi:10.1111/j.2044-8279.2011.02052.x.

Hackett, G. (1995). Self-efficacy in career choice and development. In A. Bandura (Ed.), *Self-efficacy in changing societies* (pp. 232–58). New York, NY: Cambridge University Press.

Hampton, N. Z. (1998). Sources of academic self-efficacy scale: An assessment tool for rehabilitation counselors. *Rehabilitation Counseling Bulletin, 41*, 260–77.

Honicke, T. & Broadbent, J. (2016). The influence of academic self-efficacy on academic performance: A systematic review. *Educational Research Review, 17*, 63–84. doi:10.1016/j.edurev.2015.11.002.

Joët, G., Usher, E. L., & Bressoux, P. (2011). Sources of self-efficacy: An investigation of elementary school students. *Journal of Educational Psychology, 103*, 649–63. doi:10.1037/a0024048.

Klassen, R. M. (2004a). A cross-cultural investigation of the efficacy beliefs of South Asian immigrant and Anglo Canadian nonimmigrant early adolescents. *Journal of Educational Psychology, 96*, 731–42. doi:10.1037/0022-0663.96.4.731.

Klassen, R. M. (2004b). Optimism and realism: A review of self-efficacy from a cross-cultural perspective. *International Journal of Psychology, 39*, 205–30. doi:10.1080/0020759 0344000330.

Lee, J., Bong, M., & Kim, S. (2014). Interaction between task values and self-efficacy on maladaptive achievement strategy use. *Educational Psychology, 34*, 538–60. doi:10.1080/01443410.2014.895296.

Lee, J., Lee, M., & Bong, M. (2013). High value with low perceived competence as an amplifier of self-worth threat. In D. McInerney, H. Marsh, R. Craven, & F. Guay (Eds.), *Theory driving research: New wave perspectives on self-processes and human development* (pp. 205–31). Charlotte, NC: Information Age.

Lee, W., Lee, M. J., & Bong, M. (2014). Testing interest and self-efficacy as predictors of academic self-regulation. *Contemporary Educational Psychology, 39*, 86–99. doi:10.1016/j.cedpsych.2014.02.002.

Lent, R. W., Lopez, F. G., & Bieschke, K. J. (1991). Mathematics self-efficacy: Sources and relation to science-based career choice. *Journal of Counseling Psychology, 38*, 424–30. doi:10.1037/0022-0167.38.4.424.

Lopez, F. G. & Lent, R. W. (1992). Sources of mathematics self-efficacy in high school students. *Career Development Quarterly, 41*, 3–12. doi:10.1002/j.2161-0045.1992.tb00350.x.

Matsui, T., Matsui, K., & Ohnishi, R. (1990). Mechanisms underlying math self-efficacy learning of college students. *Journal of Vocational Behavior, 37*, 225–38. doi:10.1016/0001-8791(90)90042-Z.

Multon, K. D., Brown, S. D., & Lent, R. W. (1991). Relation of self-efficacy beliefs to academic outcomes: A meta-analytic investigation. *Journal of Counseling Psychology, 1*, 30–8. doi:10.1037/0022-0167.38.1.30.

Niemivirta, M. & Tapola, A. (2007). Self-efficacy, interest, and task performance: Within-task changes, mutual relationships, and predictive effects. *Zeitschrift für Pädagogische Psychologie, 21*(3), 241–50. doi:10.1024/1010-0652.21.3.241.

Noh, A., Song, J., Hwang, A., & Bong, M. (2011). Longitudinal investigation on causal predominance between self-efficacy and achievement goal. *Korean Journal of Educational Methodology Studies, 23*(1), 213–33.

Oettingen, G. (1995). Cross-cultural perspectives on self-efficacy. In A. Bandura (Ed.), *Self-efficacy in changing societies* (pp. 149–76). New York, NY: Cambridge University Press.

Pajares, F. (1996). Self-efficacy beliefs in academic settings. *Review of Educational Research, 66*, 543–78. doi:10.3102/00346543066004543.

Pajares, F. (1997). Current directions in self-efficacy research. In M. Maehr & P. R. Pintrich (Eds.), *Advances in motivation and achievement* (Vol. 10, pp. 1–49). Greenwich, CT: JAI.

Pajares, F. (2003). Self-efficacy beliefs, motivation, and achievement in writing: A review of the literature. *Reading & Writing Quarterly, 19*, 139–58. doi:10.1080/10573 560308222.

Pajares, F. (2007). Culturalizing educational psychology. In F. Salili & R. Hoosain (Eds.), *Culture, motivation, and learning: A multicultural perspective* (pp. 19–42). Charlotte, NC: Information Age.

Pajares, F., Britner, S. L., & Valiante, G. (2000). Relation between achievement goals and self-beliefs of middle school students in writing and science. *Contemporary Educational Psychology, 25*, 406–22. doi:10.1006/ceps.1999.1027.

Pajares, F. & Miller, M. D. (1994). Role of self-efficacy and self-concept beliefs in mathematical problem solving: A path analysis. *Journal of Educational Psychology, 86*, 193–203. doi:10.1037/0022-0663.86.2.193.

Pajares, F. & Schunk, D. H. (2001). Self-beliefs and school success: Self-efficacy, self-concept, and school achievement. In R. Riding & S. Ryner (Eds.), *Perception* (pp. 239–66). London: Ablex Publishing.

Phan, H. P. (2012). Relations between informational sources, self-efficacy and academic achievement: A developmental approach. *Educational Psychology, 32*, 81–105. doi:10.1080/01443410.2011.625612.

Pintrich, P. R. & De Groot, E. V. (1990). Motivational and self-regulated learning components of classroom academic performance. *Journal of Educational Psychology, 82*, 33–40. doi:10.1037/0022-0663.82.1.33.

Rottinghaus, P. J., Larson, L. M., & Borgen, F. H. (2003). The relation of self-efficacy and interests: A meta-analysis of 60 samples. *Journal of Vocational Behavior, 62*, 221–36. doi:10.1016/S0001-8791(02)00039-8.

Schunk, D. H. (1987). Peer models and children's behavior change. *Review of Educational Research, 57*, 149–74. doi:10.3102/00346543057002149.

Schunk, D. H. (1991). Self-efficacy and academic motivation. *Educational Psychologist, 26*, 207–31. doi:10.1080/00461520.1991.9653133.

Schunk, D. H. (1995). Self-efficacy and education and instruction. In J. E. Maddux (Ed.), *Self-efficacy, adaptation, and adjustment: Theory, research, and application* (pp. 281–303). New York, NY: Plenum.

Schunk, D. H. (2003). Self-efficacy for reading and writing: Influence of modeling, goal setting, and self-evaluation. *Reading & Writing Quarterly, 19*, 159–72. doi:10.1080/ 10573560308219.

Schunk, D. H. (2012). *Learning theories: An educational perspective* (6th ed.). Boston, MA: Pearson.

Schunk, D. H. & Hanson, A. R. (1985). Peer models: Influence on children's self-efficacy and achievement. *Journal of Educational Psychology, 77*, 313–22. doi:10.1037/0022-0663.77.3.313.

Schunk, D. H. & Hanson, A. R. (1989). Influence of peer-model attributes on children's beliefs and learning. *Journal of Educational Psychology, 81*, 431–4. doi:10.1037/0022-0663.81.3.431.

Schunk, D. H., Hanson, A. R., & Cox, P. D. (1987). Peer-model attributes and children's achievement behaviors. *Journal of Educational Psychology, 79*, 54–61. doi:10.1037/0022-0663.79.1.54.

Schunk, D. H. & Meece, J. L. (2006). Self-efficacy development in adolescence. In F. Pajares & T. Urdan (Eds.), *Self-efficacy beliefs of adolescents* (pp. 71–96). Greenwich, CT: Information Age.

Schunk, D. H. & Miller, S. D. (2002). Self-efficacy and adolescents' motivation. In F. Pajares & T. Urdan (Eds.), *Academic motivation of adolescents* (pp. 29–52). Greenwich, CT: Information Age.

Schunk, D. H. & Pajares, F. (2002). The development of academic self-efficacy. In A. Wigfield & J. Eccles (Eds.), *Development of achievement motivation* (pp. 15–31). San Diego, CA: Academic Press.

Stigler, J. W., Smith, S., & Mao, L.-W. (1985). The self-perception of competence by Chinese children. *Child Development, 56*, 1259–70. doi:10.2307/1130241.

Tschannen-Moran, M., Woolfolk-Hoy, A., & Hoy, W. K. (1998). Teacher efficacy: Its meaning and measure. *Review of Educational Research, 68*, 202–48. doi:10.3102/00346543068002202.

Usher, E. L. (2009). Sources of middle school students' self-efficacy in mathematics: A qualitative investigation. *American Educational Research Journal, 46*, 275–314. doi:10.3102/0002831208324517.

Usher, E. L. & Pajares, F. (2006). Sources of academic and self-regulatory efficacy beliefs of entering middle school students. *Contemporary Educational Psychology, 31*, 125–41. doi:10.1016/j.cedpsych.2005.03.002.

Usher, E. L. & Pajares, F. (2008). Sources of self-efficacy in school: Critical review of the literature and future directions. *Review of Educational Research, 78*, 751–96. doi:10.3102/0034654308321456.

Usher, E. L. & Pajares, F. (2009). Sources of self-efficacy in mathematics: A validation study. *Contemporary Educational Psychology, 34*, 89–101. doi:10.1016/j.cedpsych.2008.09.002.

Wigfield, A. & Eccles, J. S. (2000). Expectancy-value theory of achievement motivation. *Contemporary Educational Psychology, 25*, 68–81. doi:10.1006/ceps.1999.1015.

Wigfield, A. & Wagner, A. L. (2005). Competence, motivation, and identity development during adolescence. In A. J. Elliot & C. S. Dweck (Eds.), *Handbook of competence and motivation* (pp. 222–39). New York, NY: Guilford.

Wolters, C. A., Yu, S. L., & Pintrich, P. R. (1996). The relation between goal orientation and students' motivational beliefs and self-regulated learning. *Learning and Individual Differences, 8*, 211–38. doi:10.1016/S1041-6080(96)90015-1.

Zeldin, A. L. & Pajares, F. (2000). Against the odds: Self-efficacy beliefs of women in mathematical, scientific, and technological careers. *American Educational Research Journal, 37*, 215–46. doi:10.3102/00028312037001215.

Zimmerman, B. J. (2000). Self-efficacy: An essential motive to learn. *Contemporary Educational Psychology, 25*, 82–91. doi:10.1006/ceps.1999.1016.

Zimmerman, B. J., Bandura, A., & Martinez-Pons, M. (1992). Self-motivation for academic attainment: The role of self-efficacy beliefs and personal goal setting. *American Educational Research Journal, 29*, 663–76. doi:10.3102/00028312029003663.

Zimmerman, B. J. & Cleary, T. J. (2006). Adolescents' development of personal agency: The role of self-efficacy beliefs and self-regulatory skill. In F. Pajares & T. Urdan (Eds.), *Adolescence and education: Self-efficacy beliefs of adolescents* (pp. 45–69). Greenwich, CT: Information Age.

Zimmerman, B. J. & Kitsantas, A. (1997). Developmental phases in self-regulation: Shifting from process goals to outcome goals. *Journal of Educational Psychology, 89*, 29–36. doi:10.1037/0022-0663.89.1.29.

Zimmerman, B. J. & Kitsantas, A. (2002). Acquiring writing revision and self-regulatory skill through observation and emulation. *Journal of Educational Psychology, 94*, 660–8. doi:10.1037/0022-0663.94.4.660.

Zimmerman, B. J. & Martinez-Pons, M. (1990). Student differences in self-regulated learning: Relating grade, sex, and giftedness to self-efficacy and strategy use. *Journal of Educational Psychology, 82*, 51–9. doi:10.1037/0022-0663.82.1.51.

4 Self-Regulation of Motivation

A Renewable Resource for Learning

Carol Sansone, Danielle M. Geerling,
Dustin B. Thoman, and Jessi L. Smith

Abstract: In this chapter, we review our Self-Regulation of Motivation (SRM) model, which identifies the important role that interest plays in students' motivational experiences. When learning requires persistence and re-engagement over time, activities, and contexts, the ability to maintain motivation becomes a critical self-regulatory task. The SRM model proposes that while motivation to attain goals can be sufficient to start a learning activity, experiencing interest becomes important once engaged. Aspects of the goal striving process (such as goal congruence and the expectancy-value of goals) affect the interest experience, over and above objective activity characteristics. Moreover, when interest is low but reaching a goal is important, students purposely engage in actions that make the experience more interesting (e.g., by making it more congruent with their goals or by exploratory engagement with the activity and context). Further, the ways in which students try to make the experience interesting can influence performance in both positive and negative ways (e.g., potential trade-offs between short-term output and longer-term persistence, re-engagement, and learning). We discuss evidence for this model across a variety of contexts (including online learning and science classrooms) and discuss the implications for understanding group-level differences (e.g., in gender or ethnicity) in students' interest and motivation.

Motivation is essential for learning. Although this premise is not new, the motivation–learning connection remains an important area of study because it relates to the problem of how to *maintain* motivation over time and contexts. Take, for example, individuals faced with learning a topic such as how to use HyperText Markup Language (HTML) and JavaScript programming to create a web page. What are their perceptions of the learning tasks involved? How do they feel as they work on the tasks? Some individuals might be motivated to learn how to create a website for themselves or for others. Others might be fascinated by learning how different "hidden" commands change the appearance or function of web pages. Still others might have little motivation, finding

Preparation of and research reported in this chapter was supported in part by grants from the National Science Foundation and the National Institutes of Health. Any opinions, findings, and conclusions or recommendations expressed in this material are our own and do not necessarily reflect the views of the NSF or NIH.

the material to be "over their heads", or having their attention pulled away to more interesting things or more pressing concerns. In light of this variability, an educator should select a different strategy to help motivate each learner (e.g., providing mastery feedback for the student who feels that the lesson is too hard versus limiting access to "off task" materials for the student who appears distracted).

Instead of thinking about these as different learners, however, what if we consider that these different perceptions and reactions represent a different snapshot in time *within the same person*? When learning things that are easily mastered or soon abandoned (e.g., learning something to pass a test, never to be used again), the problem of maintaining motivation is less central. However, different levels and sources of motivation are most likely to occur when learning requires persistence and re-engagement over time, activities, and contexts – such as when people are mastering a new skill, exploring new fields, or developing in-depth knowledge. In these circumstances, people not only need to have sufficient motivation to begin learning, but they also need to be able to maintain motivation over the long term. Because of the flexible and dynamic nature of motivation over time, we have suggested that the problem of sustaining motivation is in fact a critical *self*-regulatory task (Sansone et al., 1992). To be effective, a person must learn to recognize what motivates them at a particular point in time, implement relevant strategies, and continue to monitor and adjust as the person, the learning requirements, and the contexts change. To help learners maintain motivation, then, it is important for them, and for educators, to recognize the self-regulatory nature of the motivation process. Motivation energizes learning; thankfully, it is a renewable source of energy.

Self-Regulation of Motivation

Over several decades, we have developed and worked with the Self-Regulation of Motivation (SRM) model (Sansone & Harackiewicz, 1996; Sansone & Smith, 2000; Sansone & Thoman, 2005). In this model, we integrate two distinct sources of motivation: motivation that is defined in terms of striving to reach a particular goal or outcome (e.g., getting a good grade; becoming a programmer), and motivation that is defined in terms of the experience itself (i.e., whether the experience is interesting and engaging).

Goals-defined motivation typically involves a combination of a person's feelings about the value of achieving the goal and their expectancy of reaching it (e.g., Atkinson, 1964; Eccles & Wigfield, 2002). This perspective is in line with decades of scholarship within educational and developmental psychology (e.g., Expectancy-Value Theory [Eccles et al., 1983] and Social Cognitive Career Theory [Lent et al., 1996]). If a person sees a goal as valuable (e.g., they think that being able to program is important) but their expectancy of reaching that goal is low (e.g., they think the assignments will be too difficult), then they are likely to have low motivation (e.g., they don't bother to learn much about programming). Likewise, a person who expects they could figure out how to reach a goal but does not think it would be very useful would have lower motivation, compared to someone who both values the goal and expects that they can achieve it. In these examples, engagement with the learning tasks is a means to reaching the learning goal but is not the source of motivation itself.

Experience-defined motivation, in contrast, derives from the way a person feels as they engage with the activity. Does the person lose track of time? Feel distracted? Feel energized? We focus in particular on how much working on the activity triggers and sustains an experience of interest. Defining "interest" can be challenging; it is often defined in different ways and at different levels (see Renninger and Hidi [2011, 2016] for recent overviews), ranging from momentary reactions elicited by the situation to well-developed individual interests that can help define the person (Hidi & Renninger, 2006). We have focused on the *phenomenological experience* of interest (Sansone & Morgan, 1992) (similar to what Renninger and Hidi [2016] describe as the *psychological state of interest*), whereby a person's attention is directed and focused; they are actively engaged and more likely to persist (they "feel like it" [Sansone & Smith, 2000]); and they are more likely to re-engage in the same or similar activities in the future (e.g., Sansone et al., 1999). Interest is experienced as a rewarding internal state (Berlyne, 1966), which neuroscience research suggests can trigger the same reward brain mechanisms as traditional rewards (e.g., incentives) (Panksepp, 1998; Panksepp & Moskal, 2008; see also Hidi, 2016). Students who experience interest while learning have many positive outcomes (e.g., Renninger et al., 2015), including feeling inoculated from competence-related stereotypes (Master et al., 2016), experiencing greater psychological involvement and positivity (Brown et al., 2015), feeling rejuvenated after depletion (Thoman et al., 2011), and feeling more identified with the domain in which they are working (Smith et al., 2015). Overall, interest is experienced positively, although momentary negative feelings of frustration or confusion can also be part of the interest experience (Hidi & Harackiewicz, 2000; Turner & Silvia, 2006).

Historically, researchers have distinguished between motivation defined in terms of the goals and outcomes a person is working toward and motivation defined in terms of the (anticipated, actual, or sought) experience of interest, viewing them as opposite sides of the motivational coin. For example, researchers have referred to the former as "extrinsic motivation" (i.e., the activity is a means to an end) and to the latter as "intrinsic motivation" (i.e., when motivated by the activity for its own sake, because of the interest it generates) (Deci & Ryan, 2000; Lepper et al., 1973). One reason for this is that each source, on its own, is sufficient to motivate behavior, at least for a time. For example, a person could complete a programming assignment because they feel it is important to get a good grade *or* because they find the assignment interesting. Second, there is evidence that motivational "solutions" appearing to enhance one of these sources of motivation can end up hurting the other source of motivation (Sansone & Harackiewicz, 2000). For example, adding incentives (e.g., rewards) or constraints (e.g., deadlines) can increase motivation to complete an assignment, but these same factors can result in lower interest and reduce subsequent motivation to re-engage or work on related material once the incentives have been received or the constraints lifted (e.g., Deci & Ryan, 2000; Lepper & Henderlong, 2000). Conversely, adding features that make a one-time experience more "fun" (e.g., adding graphics, videos, or games to an assignment) can make the experience more interesting but can result in poorer learning of the materials (Garner et al., 1989; Mayer, 2008), and interest may not generalize to other assignments or related materials that do not have these same embellishments. In fact, individuals might see "fun" things as less important (Bianco et al., 2003).

What gets lost when viewing sources of motivation as this two-sided coin is most evident when considering motivation over the long term. Understanding fluctuations in motivation over time requires understanding how factors that enhance motivation to reach goals influence the experience of interest and how factors that impact the experience of interest fit with reaching a longer-term learning goal.

In our SRM model, we embed the motivational properties of the interest experience within the process of goal striving. We suggest that once a person begins an activity, their subsequent actions are in service of reaching goals *and* in service of maintaining motivation to reach those goals. Both goals-defined and experience-defined motivation are essential for maintaining persistence and engagement over the long term, and they can influence each other in both positive and negative ways. For example, valuing the goal of becoming a programmer can lead to greater interest in programming tasks (Smith et al., 2005); however, it could also lead to concerns about performing well, which can interfere with interest (Smith et al., 2007). In turn, interest (or lack thereof) while engaged with programming tasks can direct future goal striving, shaping decisions to pursue or abandon future learning. From this perspective, then, it is important to consider a learner's experience while engaged with learning tasks, in the context of why they started. Moreover, this vantage point makes it possible to consider how people's experience while engaged influences subsequent selection and pursuit of goals (e.g., whether to persist or re-engage, whether to expand into related areas, or whether to decide to pursue something completely different) (Harackiewicz et al., 2008; Sansone & Harackiewicz, 1996).

Given the strong motivational force of interest, one important question is: What will make learning interesting? Much research has identified features of the learner (e.g., self-efficacy; prior knowledge), the context (e.g., autonomy-supportive), or the activity (e.g., optimal challenge) that can make a particular activity more or less interesting (Renninger & Hidi, 2016). To these, we add a factor that becomes important when considering interest as embedded within a self-regulatory process – that is, whether the activity is congruent with goals (e.g., whether learning how to use JavaScript is congruent with being able to create one's own website or become a programmer). *Goal congruence*, over and above features of the activity itself, can make the experience more interesting. This effect becomes stronger the greater the person's motivation to attain the goal (e.g., the more that a person values learning how to code, the more interesting they are likely to find the programming assignment [Durik & Harackiewicz, 2007; Harackiewicz & Manderlink, 1984]). Further, once a person engages with the activity, they can do so in ways that are congruent with their goals (e.g., they might experiment with coding to make a web page load faster, even though this was not part of the assignment). As a result, they can make the experience more interesting. In this case, the person's actions were in service of reaching goals, but their actions also had beneficial effects for experience-defined motivation.

When an activity is not (or is no longer) interesting, however, then regulation in service of one or both sources of motivation becomes necessary for persistence. The SRM model suggests that the person then considers whether there are good reasons to continue with the activity despite the lack of interest. If the person sees no sufficient reason to persist with the (now) uninteresting activity, they are likely to quit. One way that a person can regulate motivation at this point is to find, create, or remind themselves about good reasons to persist (e.g., Wolters, 1998). For example, students can remind themselves about the importance of getting a good grade, or how mastering programming will help them create their own web page.

If the person perceives good reasons to persist, the model suggests several further choices. For one, a person may persist at the uninteresting activity as it is. This may be a good choice if the uninteresting activity is short-term, serving just as a necessary step to progressing to areas that are more interesting or to goal attainment itself. However, if this experience is prolonged, the person is more likely to suffer stress-related effects, quit as soon as possible, and choose to not re-engage in the future (e.g., Sansone et al., 1999).

On the other hand, when there are good reasons to persist, people can also choose a different option – they can purposely change how they engage with the activity to make the experience more interesting. For example, the student can experiment with programming code or vary how they do the activity. If successful in making the experience more interesting, then motivation is more likely to be maintained and persistence or re-engagement is more likely. However, this option requires more effort, and because the student has changed how they do the activity, these changes could also impact performance (e.g., running out of time to complete an assignment). Thus, there might be trade-offs between the actions used to make the experience more interesting and the actions that would maximize immediate performance outcomes, especially if the things that a person does to regulate interest come at a cost to limited resources (e.g., time and attention).

In sum, the SRM model posits:

- Motivation to attain goals can be sufficient to start a learning activity, but it may not be sufficient to maintain motivation over the longer term. Whether people experience interest while working toward the goals also becomes important.
- The *process* of goal striving (e.g., goal congruence; value and expectancy of reaching goals; actions in service of goals) can impact the interest experience, over and above characteristics of the activity itself.
- When interest is low *and* persistence is important, people can purposely engage in actions to make the experience more interesting.
- How people try to make the experience interesting has implications for performance, both in the short term and the long term.

Laying the Empirical Building Blocks of the SRM Framework

Much of the research guided by the SRM framework has been conducted with college students, for whom completion of learning tasks requires a greater reliance on *self*-regulation, compared to past reliance on parents and teachers, to help regulate their learning process. One of the first directions we pursued when developing the SRM model was to examine the relationships between goals and interest (Harackiewicz & Sansone, 1991). Rather than seeking to identify whether certain goals were more reflective of and conducive to experiencing interest, we considered whether seeing an activity as congruent with goals helped to make the activity more interesting. Sansone et al. (1989) published the results of what was the first test of how the same activity can generate different experiences of interest as a function of goal congruence. In this study, introductory college students came into a lab and played a fantasy-based computer game. The structure and content of the game prompted all participants to adopt experience-defined goals to become involved in the fantasy adventure. From there, some students were randomly assigned to conditions that, instead, prompted adoption of competence-related goals (e.g., they received performance feedback relative to other students [Study 1]; the game was described as a test of skill [Study 2]). Students then received feedback that provided suggestions for ways to increase their scores. When contextual cues had first prompted the adoption of skill-related goals, this instructional feedback was associated with *greater* subsequent interest and with participants being more likely to take a company brochure when they left (which would facilitate access to similar games by the same company in the future). However, the same feedback was associated with *decreases* in interest and participants were *less* likely to take the brochure when individuals' goals were focused on the fantasy adventure. Although performing ostensibly the same activity, individuals experienced different levels of interest depending on whether or not the instruction was congruent with their initial goals.

Later research, also conducted with college student samples, found similar goal-congruence effects for achievement goals (e.g., Harackiewicz & Elliot, 1993), promotion and prevention goals (Smith et al., 2009), and interpersonal goals (e.g., Isaac et al., 1999; Morf et al., 2000; Smith & Ruiz, 2007). The extension to interpersonal goals is important, because it demonstrates that the elements making up the experience of the "activity" include features of the context and how individuals interact with them. Although the presence of others might make an activity more interesting for most people (e.g., Plass et al., 2013; Sansone et al., 1992; Smith & Ruiz, 2007; Tauer & Harackiewicz, 2004), the presence of others can be most impactful for those for whom interpersonal goals are especially important. For example, in Isaac et al. (1999), college students worked on a math-related activity (designing and calculating an infrastructure budget for a satellite college campus). Students higher in characteristic interpersonal orientation (i.e., those who characteristically approach activities with interpersonal goals) experienced greater interest in the activity when they worked with, or even just alongside, another person (a confederate), as opposed to when they worked alone. They were also more likely to subsequently request further information about the topic of campus planning by signing up for a real campus planning newsletter.

Isaac et al. also videotaped the work sessions to explore *how* the presence of others might have resulted in a more interesting experience. Isaac et al. found that individuals higher in interpersonal orientation reached out and engaged with the other person present, displaying a more interpersonally involving interaction style (e.g., expressing thoughts to a greater degree). These actions elicited more off-task conversations from the other person, and these conversations in turn predicted greater interest in the activity (and being more likely to seek additional information about the topic in the future). These results demonstrate that the goals individuals bring to the activity not only influence how they engage with the task, but also how they engage with the surrounding context. If they can, individuals will actively create experiences that are congruent with their goals, resulting in greater interest. In turn, greater interest can lead to students becoming more likely to adopt goals for future engagement and learning.

Regulating the interest experience directly. In addition to goal congruence creating interest, the SRM model suggests that individuals can purposely engage in actions with the intent of making the experience more interesting, whether or not these actions are congruent with goals. Initial tests of this hypothesis were reported by Sansone et al. (1992), who outlined the conditions under which individuals should be most likely to actively engage in strategic actions to enhance interest: (1) when the activity is currently not interesting (i.e., there is a need to regulate), (2) there is a good reason to persist anyway, and (3) the actions that would make the experience more interesting (e.g., varying how the activity is performed) are possible in that situation. They created an experimental paradigm to test these hypotheses using identical materials across conditions, comparing an initially boring task (copying letters matrices) and an initially interesting task (finding words hidden in those same matrices). A subset of participants doing the copying task were also provided a reason to value the task (i.e., health benefits when performed regularly). Those who performed the copying task with knowledge of the health benefits were most likely to engage in interest-enhancing actions (e.g., varying the procedure) while doing the copying. For example, they attempted to copy the particular typeface displayed in each matrix (although that was not necessary for the task) or varied the pattern with which they copied the letters (e.g., did all the diagonals first). Those who performed the hidden-words task were least likely to vary how they performed the task, and individuals who performed the copying task without the health benefit information fell between the two. Moreover, varying the procedure predicted a greater likelihood of doing the activity in the future (i.e., participants were more likely to request matrices to take with them after the session). Importantly, the health benefit information in itself did not predict greater likelihood of doing the activity again. Rather, the health benefit information made it more likely that individuals would do the interest-enhancing actions, and it was these actions that predicted greater likelihood of future engagement. In sum, this research shows that when an activity is perceived as boring but important, people can and do purposely choose to take action to change the task into one that is more interesting. As a result, they are more likely to engage with the activity in the future.

Sansone et al. (1992) also suggested that individuals' beliefs about the effectiveness of regulating interest would be important for whether and when people attempt to regulate interest, but they did not assess these beliefs in a learning context. Research has previously demonstrated that learning is influenced by students' meta-motivational beliefs or mind-sets (e.g., Miele & Scholer, 2016; Wolters et al., 1996). However, the focus of this research has been primarily on people's interpretations of why they perform an activity (e.g., Lepper et al., 1982) and why they struggle or succeed (e.g., Blackwell et al., 2007). In contrast, Thoman et al. (2018) examined undergraduates' lay theories about the possibility of regulating interest; Thoman et al. proposed that students would only regulate interest if they believed that interest *could* be regulated. College students' theories about the malleability of interest (versus the fixed nature of interest) were assessed via an adaption of Dweck et al.'s (1995) measure of implicit theory of intelligence. Students were also asked if they could recall any recent boring assignments from their actual classes and, if so, whether they used any interest-enhancing strategies (selected from a list) when completing the assignments. Across a range of academic domains, results revealed that students who believed the level of interest in an activity could be changed were more likely to report having used interest-enhancing strategies than students who believed that experiences of interest were stable. These findings were also conceptually replicated across two experimental studies (Thoman et al., 2018). These findings suggest that meta-motivational beliefs about the malleability of the interest experience can be an important influence on whether students are able to sustain motivation, by influencing whether and when they regulate the interest experience.

Relationship between regulating interest and performance. If people change how they perform an activity in order to create interest, there is the potential for an unintended effect on performance. We would expect this to depend on how individuals chose to create interest and whether those actions were compatible with performance. For example, if students chose to attempt more challenging assignments or seek out additional information related to the topic as strategies for creating interest, they could also end up with greater learning. However, time and effort spent on these more challenging assignments or searching for more information could also negatively impact what was accomplished in a set period of time. In Sansone et al. (1992), for example, although individuals who varied the procedure were more likely to do the activity again, they also copied fewer letters in the time allowed, and Smith et al. (2009) subsequently found a similar negative relationship between strategy use and number of letters copied. However, when people were free to choose how long they worked on the copying task, those who varied the procedure persisted longer and, thus, copied more letters than individuals who did not engage in these strategies (Sansone et al., 1999). Taken together, these results suggest that there can be trade-offs, at least in the short term, between regulating the interest experience and performance outcomes. However, these results were also limited to an experimental paradigm developed as an analog for everyday experiences; unlike many everyday experiences, there were no consequences for poor performance. Thus, it was important that we look for similar patterns in more naturalistic settings, and in the next section we describe research conducted in learning contexts.

In sum, this brief review provides empirical support for the idea that the interest experience is embedded within the process of goal striving over time. The same activity can be associated with different levels of interest depending on individuals' goals, whether those goals are characteristic goals that differentiate people or reflect goals that shift within the same person over time and across contexts. These goals could include learning more about topics for which people are developing individual interests, goals that reflect a desire to demonstrate competence to others, or goals for enjoying the experience (Harackiewicz et al., 2008; Renninger & Hidi, 2016). Moreover, these include goals having to do with other people, not just goals for personal accomplishments. This research also shows that individuals do not simply react to contexts but, rather, actively create experiences and appear to do so differentially as a function of whether they see persistence as important. The strategies they use to create interest can be interpersonal as well as intrapersonal, and people may use these strategies even if they hurt short-term performance outcomes. Finally, the SRM research illustrates the reciprocal relationship between experiencing interest in a specific moment and the greater likelihood that people will re-engage with and learn more about the same or related activities in the future, even though the path by which they came to experience interest might differ because of different initial goals, strategies, and contexts. Harackiewicz et al.'s (2008) findings illustrate that this reciprocal relationship can have important implications for selection and persistence in college coursework. In their study, students who began an introductory course with greater interest in the topic were more likely to subsequently adopt mastery goals for learning (i.e., wanting to learn more about the topic); in turn, mastery goals predicted greater situational interest later in the course (i.e., greater enjoyment of course lectures), and this greater interest experienced during the class predicted students' being more likely to have enrolled in related classes when tracked seven semesters later.

The SRM in Action: Lessons from Learning Contexts

Learning Online: A Greater Challenge for Self-Regulation

Online learning provides many benefits and opportunities for educational innovation, but this format can also pose a greater challenge to students' self-regulation, in the absence of set times, places, and supervision of learning activities (e.g., Azevedo et al., 2008). Online learning also provides researchers with the ability to capture individual student behaviors as they occur, providing opportunities for glimpses of self-regulation processes as they unfold over time. For example, research conducted in a Massive Online Open Course found that behavioral engagement in the course (i.e., watching lecture videos) was associated with increases in levels of situational interest throughout the course, which then resulted in better performance outcomes (de Barba et al., 2016). Notably, in this research, individual interest (defined as a relatively stable predisposition toward a topic, assessed at the beginning of the class – e.g., "I've always been fascinated by micro-economics") *negatively* predicted final grades, which underscores the importance of assessing how students engage with a class *over time*, rather than relying solely on self-reports of interest at one time point.

An ideal scenario for studying the self-regulation of interest within the online learning classroom would have a comparable face-to-face classroom available for study simultaneously. Methodologically speaking, comparing students' self-regulation of motivation processes while learning the same content in different formats (e.g., online versus on-campus) allows the researcher some control over extraneous variables when random assignment is not possible. Sansone et al. (2012) examined the self-regulation of interest in this manner by following undergraduates in both an online section and an on-campus section of the same upper division psychology course. Results showed students in the online course were more likely than students in the on-campus course to report attempting to make studying for an exam more enjoyable by exploring material on the class web page, which was available to students in both class sections. Although students in the online section reported overall lower interest than students in the on-campus section, those online students who reported exploring material on the class web page had interest levels equivalent to students in the on-campus section. The more that students in the online section reported using the web-browsing strategy, however, the greater their interest but the poorer their exam performance. The results are consistent with interest/performance trade-offs found in experimental lab settings (e.g., Smith et al., 2009). However, because students self-selected into taking the course online versus on-campus, it was not possible to know whether these differences emerged because of the self-regulatory process or because the two groups of students constituted two different populations (e.g., students who took the class online might have cared less about grades, might be drawn to situations that afford more autonomy, or might have been more likely to be nontraditional students who were not as "schooled" in strategies that aided exam performance).

We were able to address these potential alternative explanations in a hybrid paradigm that provided many of the controls that are part of an experimental paradigm, but that also allowed students the time and freedom to work through online lessons as they would in a class (e.g., Sansone et al., 2011). College student participants came to the computer lab, where they participated in a 90-minute learning session on the use of HTML for creating web pages. This session combined several lessons from an actual computer science class offered online, including a final assignment (reproducing a sample web page) to submit before the end of the session. Piloting had suggested that the materials could be completed in about 75 minutes if students worked straight through on the main lesson pages, and so we allowed students 90 minutes to submit their assignments. How they worked through the online lesson (e.g., whether they accessed and experimented with examples and exercises), and whether they submitted the assignment in time, was left up to the individual students.

Using this paradigm, we could test multiple hypotheses generated from the SRM model. Case in point, the SRM model posits that external interventions increasing the value of a learning goal (i.e., increased goal-defined motivation) can directly enhance interest, or indirectly enhance interest by motivating active engagement with the material in ways that make the experience more interesting. The literature shows that one effective way to increase the value of learning is through interventions that support students in finding the usefulness or utility of the content (e.g., Hulleman & Harackiewicz, 2009).

Results from Sansone et al. (2011) showed that, when provided with information about the usefulness of learning HTML (e.g., ability to enhance personal or organizational web pages or to collect information from customers), students displayed a greater degree of exploration and experimentation with sample tags and commands during a lesson. Greater exploratory engagement during the lesson predicted higher interest at the end of the session, which in turn predicted requests for the ability to access code to the entire online course. Greater engagement during the lesson also tended to predict higher quiz scores.

However, the results also reflected the trade-offs found in the more artificial copying task situations (Sansone et al., 1999; Smith et al., 2009). That is, about 20 percent of the participants received a zero score on the assignment because they failed to submit it before the session ended, and this failure was predicted by greater exploration and experimentation during the lesson. This pattern suggests that students are more likely to create interesting experiences when they value the goal of learning, and that their actions can potentially hurt short-term performance measures while increasing the odds of longer-term learning and re-engagement.

We followed up these findings by collecting data in two semester-long online computer science courses. In addition to the measures used in the paradigm above, we added assessments of what students were feeling "in the moment" by programming pop-up questionnaires into the class server. These questionnaires appeared either at random intervals while the student was logged into the class (i.e., experience-sampling), or when the student chose to engage with class examples and exercises (i.e., event-sampling, where the "events" mapped onto similar engagement measures used in the laboratory paradigm). Using this methodology, we could track how students' interest levels changed over time, both in general and while students were known to be actively engaged with the course materials. Initial results suggest that students' in-the-moment reactions predicted interest and performance outcomes differently when assessed at the point that students had chosen to actively engage with the examples and exercises, in comparison to reactions assessed at random intervals when they were logged into the course (Geerling, 2017).

Together, findings from research in the context of online learning support the SRM model and suggest that students' actions during the learning process over time are critical for whether interest is developed and maintained. Students appear to engage in these actions differentially as a function of the need to enhance interest, their reasons for learning, and how much they value those reasons. Our research also supports the contention that actions enhancing the interest experience can result in performance trade-offs, particularly when learning activities are constructed in ways that create conflicts in time management. Utilizing an online learning paradigm has thus given us a better sense of the ways in which students can use course materials to regulate their own interest experiences and maintain motivation over time.

Science Classroom Context: Learning *and* Doing Science

Unlike online learning environments where student behaviors can be relatively easily tracked at granular levels, our research in science classrooms has relied on self-report survey methodologies and interventions that vary classroom assignments across students. These studies have primarily focused on the goal-congruence prediction of the SRM model, examining effects on student interest, including both expectations of interest (in classes and related careers) and actual class experiences of interest.

Given the systematic underrepresentation of students from certain groups (e.g., women) in science, the science classroom offers a unique opportunity to explore how different groups of students might hold and value different types of goals, and the implications for their motivation. Some theoretical explanations suggest that certain groups are underrepresented in STEM (science, technology, engineering, and mathematics) because they are "choosing" to opt-out (Ceci & Williams, 2011) and are perhaps less interested in the topics of STEM (Woodcock et al., 2012). Indeed, people are pushed and pulled to different learning paths depending on interest and feelings of belonging (Thoman et al., 2013, 2014). However, the SRM model highlights how the goal-matching mechanism can explain (at least in part) why individuals from groups traditionally underrepresented in STEM (e.g., underrepresented minority students) tend to report lower interest in STEM fields than those from well-represented groups.

The first SRM study to focus on group differences and implications of goal congruence was conducted by Morgan et al. (2001), who asked college students to rate the importance of various work goals (Study 1) and asked their perceptions of whether different types of career fields would allow them to fulfill various work goals (Study 2). Although men and women reported many similarities in work goals, women undergraduates were more likely than men to cite a desire to work with and help others as an important reason for choosing the type of work they want to do. In Study 2, STEM fields were perceived to be less likely to afford these communal goals compared to other careers, across all participants, and these perceptions predicted lower anticipated interestingness of these careers. This pattern of mismatch between the high value of communal work goals and a perceived lack of opportunity to fulfill these goals in STEM careers is one leading explanation for low STEM interest among women (e.g., Diekman et al., 2010).

These initial results suggested that the perception of goal incongruence can lead students to anticipate that a STEM field will be less interesting to pursue. In more recent research, we have examined whether similar perceptions of goal *in*congruence can help to explain differential reactions in STEM learning contexts. The classroom context of STEM is built on epistemologies that privilege majority group members (e.g., white, male, continuing generation students)

(Cech et al., 2017). As such, STEM learning activities are often created in ways that (unintentionally) do not appeal to first-generation college students, women, and underrepresented minorities, making these groups at risk for opting out (Allen et al., 2015; Jackson et al., 2016; Smith et al., 2014). Indeed, underrepresented students are more likely to cite wanting to work with others and to give back to their communities as important career goals. When these students pursue STEM majors, the extent to which they see the "big picture" – how potential STEM careers can fulfill communal goals – positively predicts their experience of interest in STEM classes and their anticipated experience of interest in future STEM careers (Smith et al., 2014, 2015). This same pattern emerges when examining the research and career interests of advanced undergraduates who are working in faculty-led laboratories, where science majors learn to do science. Thoman et al. (2015) found that the degree to which underrepresented student research assistants believed that the research they were working on in the lab could be used to help society or give back to their community predicted greater subsequent interest in that research and in science careers.

The good news is that the learning context can be restructured in ways that allow students to see the communal value of STEM without harming majority group students who often do not endorse these values to the same degree (e.g., Smith et al., 2014). One example is an intervention conducted in a large undergraduate biology course that served as a gateway course for biology majors (Harackiewicz et al., 2016a). Students were asked to write short essays in which they identified the ways that specific concepts covered at three different points during the semester were relevant to their lives or were useful to them. The researchers found that the utility value intervention narrowed the achievement gap (as measured by final grades) between the most at-risk students (the "first generation" in their families to attend college from "underrepresented minority" [FG-URM] groups) and continuing generation students. When examining students' essays, Harackiewicz et al. found that students from FG-URM backgrounds were more likely to write about connections that were congruent with their communal values. In fact, the amount of text that they generated while engaged in identifying the potential value of learning mediated the positive effect of the utility value intervention on grades. Although Harackiewicz et al. did not report differential findings for class interest, they did suggest that students became more engaged with the class material when they were able to see it as being more consistent with their communal goals and values (see also Harackiewicz et al., 2016b). Thus, these results suggest that, when provided with a structured opportunity, students from FG-URM backgrounds expended more effort to make what they were learning more congruent with their goals and values.

In sum, this research suggests that the anticipated, perceived, or experienced congruence between a student's goals and the way that STEM learning tasks are presented and structured can be an important source of whether students experience sufficient motivation to begin and persist in learning, and may influence whether and how students attempt to make the learning tasks more interesting. This research also suggests that the issue of goal congruence can help to explain apparent group-level differences (e.g., gender; culture; socio-economic status (SES)) in interest.

Everyone Has a Stake in the Self-Regulation of Motivation: The Take-Away Messages

The SRM model offers a useful framework to develop hypotheses, to test predictions, and to understand the parameters, processes, and consequences of students' goal striving. At its core, the SRM model illustrates how the experience of interest is both a process and an outcome. The empirical evidence for the SRM model is rich and robust in places, and emerging and unexplored in others.

One take-away message is that the SRM model may help to understand and deconstruct what appears to be group-level differences in learning interests. That is, what may appear in analyses as group differences in interests may really reflect group differences in *goals* that are less congruent with how the learning activity and the context are constructed. For example, even if students start at similar levels of interest, those from underrepresented groups might find fewer opportunities, given curricular constraints, to make the activity more interesting for them and might be more focused on avoiding the confirmation of negative performance stereotypes (e.g., Smith et al., 2007). Thus, they could lose interest at faster rates, or have much more variability in their experiences. They could thus be less likely to subsequently adopt goals to persist or re-engage in the future (Geerling, 2017).

These points also suggest that we should see significant variability among people from the same group, as a function of the intersectionality of multiple identities with which individuals define themselves (e.g., ethnicity and gender; ethnicity and social class [Else-Quest & Hyde, 2016]). We should also expect variability within groups as a function of the unique experiences and contexts that contribute to the goals an individual brings to the learning context (e.g., Allen et al., 2015; Sansone & Thoman, 2006; Shechter et al., 2011).

For educators and parents, the self-regulation lens suggests that the way learning activities are presented and constructed might work best for different subsets of students. Rather than trying to identify the "perfect" activity, therefore, one implication is that it may be more important to allow enough flexibility in learning activities for individuals to construct the experiences that are most beneficial for their own motivation, without being penalized for these efforts. Furthermore, parents and educators might consider ways to model the process of finding or creating interest when it is important to maintain motivation. Do they convey to students that it is possible to regulate interest, along with strategies about when, why, and how to regulate interest effectively (without creating unwanted performance trade-offs)?

Such questions have important implications for the development of interventions targeting the self-regulatory process. Although our work illustrates the way individual differences can influence different inputs into the process (e.g., differences in interpersonal orientation can influence the goals adopted and the strategies used; see Sansone and Thoman [2006] and Sansone et al. [2010] for reviews), we have not found any consistent individual differences in the process itself. That is, we have been unable to reliably identify individuals who are characteristically more likely to regulate interest, across settings or time. This means that interventions cannot be developed in the style of "X habits of successful people," but must be more nuanced and include recognition of when and where it might be good to regulate interest and motivation, and when it might not.

Supporting student motivational processes requires educational administrators to make space for confronting, challenging, and championing new teaching practices. The key is for administrators to see motivation and learning as compatible and to reward teachers for efforts that enable student self-regulatory processes (Harackiewicz et al., 2016a, 2016b). Of course, we are not suggesting that anyone ignore learning and performance outcomes. Indeed, another take-away from the SRM research is the potential trade-offs that might emerge between maintaining motivation and performance evaluations, particularly when the ways in which students might make learning more interesting conflict with spending time and attention on features of the activity that are more directly relevant to what is assessed. The same process can lead to better, deeper learning over time *and* short-term decrements in evaluated performance. Recognizing the latter as trade-offs, rather than reflecting motivational or ability deficits, is key to promoting greater learning over the longer term.

This recognition of possible trade-offs is needed by students themselves, as well as by parents, educators, and others concerned with student success. The self-regulation of motivation is not necessarily an intentional or explicit process (Sansone & Thoman, 2005). Once students can tune in to their motivational needs, they can decide for themselves when it is okay to experience some short-term performance decrements in favor of motivational boosts, knowing that the experience of interest is important to long-term achievement and career outcomes over time (for reviews, see Cerasoli et al. [2014], and Nye et al. [2012]).

With that said, an important component of effective self-regulation is recognizing when a person can afford the trade-off – or whether a certain activity, domain, or career is worth the trade-off. Some evaluations are more important than others (e.g., when a poor grade rules out the possibility of access to advanced programs or is interpreted as indicating that the student is "not a science person"); some passions can negatively impact one's physical and psychological well-being (e.g., Vallerand et al., 2003). An important area of future study is to place the process of self-regulation for a particular activity within the larger context of a person's life over time. For example, there may be key transition points or certain points in development when the process of self-regulating motivation becomes particularly important or the failure to recognize trade-offs becomes particularly problematic (e.g., Thoman et al., 2014).

The developmental trajectory of this self-regulation process is indeed an area that is underexplored, and there are many important empirical questions that remain unanswered. For example, at what point do students recognize that they *can* make the experience more interesting? When do they learn that by doing so, they are more likely to be able to persist at important activities? Once learned, do people continue to regulate motivation similarly across the life span? Or might they become less likely to learn new things that they do not initially find interesting? Do the ways in which someone tries to make an activity more interesting change over time? And *should* they change over time? For example, as the ways in which a person approaches and performs learning tasks become routinized, might they become less conscious of the strategies they employed and continue to use them mindlessly without attending to whether they still work?

Additional important questions to explore come from the possibilities associated with online learning. The ability to unobtrusively collect vast quantities of information about people's online learning behaviors can be an important source of information on how students construct their learning process. Our research also suggests a caution, however, in that the same behaviors can predict both positive and negative outcomes for students. Thus, future research is needed to identify the best ways to assess "small data" (i.e., students' perceptions and experiences) that map onto the "big data" of students' online behaviors. It is still unclear *when* the best times are to sample things like motivation, affect, and engagement, and answering that question will be an important step for further research in this area.

More generally, as SRM researchers, we have many lessons yet to learn, which are highly dependent upon the methods we choose. For example, it is possible that different *patterns* in the experience of interest while engaged with a learning task (e.g., stable; ascending; descending) have different implications for motivational and performance outcomes (Knogler et al., 2015), and certain patterns might distinguish people who are underrepresented in certain fields (Geerling, 2017). Patterns in the interest experience can only be examined through methodological approaches and analyses that allow the dynamic process inherent in a regulatory process to emerge (e.g., Butner et al., 2014). As these newer approaches become more common, we expect there will be new insights and greater in-depth knowledge about the self-regulation of motivation process.

Concluding Thoughts

Our approach suggests that motivation is not stable, even when an activity is connected with an area, field, or domain in which a person has well-established interests or passions. That is, although there may be average differences in interest between individuals faced with the same learning task, there will still be variability within individuals as the process of learning extends over time. This flexibility in interest means that just because someone has "low" motivation at one point does not mean they could not have new or renewed levels of interest. An important factor in whether interest is created or renewed is the person's own actions, and whether these actions and the person's larger goals are supported by the activity and the surrounding context.

By embedding the interest experience within the process of goal striving over time, the SRM model provides a framework for understanding whether, when, and how interest can motivate learning. The SRM model suggests that students will experience greater interest when their goals are congruent with the learning context because they match initially, the context is altered by external forces to match, or the context is made to match through individuals' own actions while engaged with an activity. The learning activity is thus an ever-changing situation, unfolding over time as contexts change and actions are taken (or not) to create and maintain interest. Interest is not always necessary for motivation, but the need to experience some interest, at least part of the time, becomes clearer when we examine the learning process over time. Students spontaneously engage in strategies to make something more interesting when they think it is important to persist, and they may do so even when those strategies inadvertently lead to more negative performance outcomes.

Thus, our research has focused on identifying the important role that the experience of interest plays in students' motivation (whether or not that role is recognized). It is our hope that researchers, educators, administrators, parents, and students themselves retire the traditional metaphor of the two-sided motivational coin in favor of recognizing the roles of both goals-defined *and* experience-defined motivation, as well as the important relationship between them. Although motivation can ebb, it can also be replenished and renewed. It is important to recognize the significant role that self-regulation plays in the renewal of this valued resource and the way that the experience of interest is embedded within this process. The good news is that we can renew this valuable resource for ourselves, and we can also help support its renewal by others.

References

Allen, J. M., Muragishi, G. A., Smith, J. L., Thoman, D. B., & Brown, E. R. (2015). To grab and to hold: Cultivating communal goals to overcome cultural and structural barriers in first-generation college students' science interest.

Translational Issues in Psychological Science, 1(4), 331–41. doi:10.1037/tps0000046.

Atkinson, J. W. (1964). *An introduction to motivation.* Princeton, NJ: Van Nostrand.

Azevedo, R., Moos, D., Greene, J., Winters, F., & Cromley, J. (2008). Why is externally facilitated regulated learning more effective than self-regulated learning with hypermedia? *Educational Technology Research and Development, 56*(1), 45–72.

Berlyne, D. E. (1966). Curiosity and exploration. *Science, 153*(3731), 25–33. doi:10.1126/science.153.3731.25.

Bianco, A. T., Higgins, E. T., & Klem, A. (2003). How "fun/importance" fit affects performance: Relating implicit theories to instruction. *Personality and Social Psychology Bulletin, 29*, 1091–103.

Blackwell, L. S., Trzesniewski, K. H., & Dweck, C. S. (2007). Implicit theories of intelligence predict achievement across an adolescent transition: A longitudinal study and an intervention. *Child Development, 78*(1), 246–63. doi:10.1111/j.1467-8624.2007.00995.x.

Brown, E. R., Smith, J. L., Thoman, D. B., Allen, J. M., & Muragishi, G. (2015). From bench to bedside: A communal utility value intervention to enhance students' biomedical science motivation. *Journal of Educational Psychology, 107*(4), 1116–35. doi:10.1037/edu0000033.

Butner, J. E., Gagnon, K. T., Geuss, M. N., Lessard, D. A., & Story, T. N. (2015). Utilizing topology to generate and test theories of change. *Psychological Methods, 20*(1), 1–25. doi:10.1037/a0037802.

Cech, E. A., Metz, A., Smith, J. L., & deVries, K. (2017). Epistemological dominance and social inequality: Experiences of Native American science, engineering, and health students. *Science, Technology & Human Values, 42*(5), 3157–62. doi:10.1073/pnas.1014871108.

Ceci, S. J. & Williams, W. M. (2011). Understanding current causes of women's underrepresentation in science. *Proceedings of the National Academy of Sciences of the United States of America, 108*(8), 3157–62. doi:10.1073/pnas.1014871108.

Cerasoli, C. P., Nicklin, J. M., & Ford, M. T. (2014). Intrinsic motivation and extrinsic incentives jointly predict performance: A 40-year meta-analysis. *Psychological Bulletin, 140*(4), 980–1008. doi:10.1037/a0035661.

de Barba, P. G., Kennedy, G. E., & Ainley, M. D. (2016). The role of students' motivation and participation in predicting performance in a MOOC. *Journal of Computer Assisted Learning, 32*(3), 218–31. doi:10.1111/jcal.12130.

Deci, E. L. & Ryan, R. M. (2000). The "what" and "why" of goal pursuits: Human needs and the self-determination of behavior. *Psychological Inquiry, 11*, 227–68.

Diekman, A. B., Brown, E. R., Johnston, A. M., & Clark, E. K. (2010). Seeking congruity between goals and roles: A new look at why women opt out of science, technology, engineering, and mathematics careers. *Psychological Science, 21*(8), 1051–7. doi:10.1177/0956797610377342.

Durik, A. M. & Harackiewicz, J. M. (2007). Different strokes for different folks: How individual interest moderates the effects of situational factors on task interest. *Journal of Educational Psychology, 99*(3), 597–610. doi:10.1037/0022-0663.99.3.597.

Dweck, C. S., Chiu, C., & Hong, Y. (1995). Implicit theories and their role in judgements and reactions: A world from two perspectives. *Psychological Inquiry*, *6*, 267–85.

Eccles, J., Adler, T. F., Futterman, R., Goff, S. B., Kaczala, C. M., Meece, J. L., & Midgley, C. (1983). Expectancies, values, and academic behaviors. In J. T. Spence (Ed.), *Achievement and achievement motives: Psychological and sociological approaches* (pp. 75–146). San Francisco, CA: W. H. Freeman.

Eccles, J. S. & Wigfield, A. (2002). Motivational beliefs, values, and goals. *Annual Review of Psychology*, *53*, 109–32.

Else-Quest, N. M. & Hyde, J. S. (2016). Intersectionality in quantitative psychological research II: Methods and techniques. *Psychology of Women Quarterly*, *40*(3), 319–36. doi:10.1177/0361684316647953.

Garner, R., Gillingham, M. G., & White, C. S. (1989). Effects of "seductive details" on macroprocessing and microprocessing in adults and children. *Cognition and Instruction*, *6*(1), 41–57. doi:10.1207/s1532690xci0601_2.

Geerling, D. M. (2017). *Dynamical systems analysis of gender-related interest development in online coursework*. Unpublished master's thesis, University of Utah, Salt Lake City, UT.

Harackiewicz, J. M., Canning, E. A., Tibbetts, Y., Priniski, S. J., & Hyde, J. S. (2016a). Closing achievement gaps with a utility-value intervention: Disentangling race and social class. *Journal of Personality and Social Psychology*, *111*(5), 745–65. doi:10.1037/pspp0000075.

Harackiewicz, J. M., Durik, A. M., Barron, K. E., Linnenbrink-Garcia, L., & Tauer, J. M. (2008). The role of achievement goals in the development of interest: Reciprocal relations between achievement goals, interest, and performance. *Journal of Educational Psychology*, *100*(1), 105–22. doi:10.1037/0022-0663.100.1.105.

Harackiewicz, J. M. & Elliot, A. J. (1993). Achievement goals and intrinsic motivation. *Journal of Personality and Social Psychology*, *65*(5), 904–15. doi:10.1037/0022-3514.65.5.904.

Harackiewicz, J. M. & Manderlink, G. (1984). A process analysis of the effects of performance-contingent rewards on intrinsic motivation. *Journal of Experimental Social Psychology*, *20*(6), 531–51. doi:10.1016/0022-1031 (84)90042-8.

Harackiewicz, J. M. & Sansone, C. (1991). Goals and intrinsic motivation: You can get there from here. *Advances in Motivation and Achievement*, *7*, 21–49.

Harackiewicz, J. M., Smith, J. L., & Priniski, S. J. (2016b). Interest matters: The importance of promoting interest in education. *Policy Insights from the Behavioral and Brain Sciences*, *3*(2), 220–7. doi:10.1177/2372732216655542.

Hidi, S. (2016). Revisiting the role of rewards in motivation and learning: Implications of neuroscientific research. *Educational Psychology Review*, *28*, 61–93. doi:10.1007/s10648-015-9307-5.

Hidi, S. & Harackiewicz, J. (2000). Motivating the academically unmotivated: A critical issue for the 21st century. *Review of Educational Research*, *70*, 151–79.

Hidi, S. & Renninger, K. A. (2006). The four-phase model of interest development. *Educational Psychologist*, *41*(2), 111–27. doi:10.1207/s15326985ep4102_4.

Hulleman, C. S. & Harackiewicz, J. M. (2009). Promoting interest and performance in high school science classes. *Science*, *326*(5958), 1410–12. doi:10.1126/science.1177067.

Isaac, J. D., Sansone, C., & Smith, J. L. (1999). Other people as a source of interest in an activity. *Journal of Experimental Social Psychology, 35*(3), 239–65. doi:10.1006/jesp.1999.1385.

Jackson, M. C., Galvez, G., Landa, I., Buonora, P., & Thoman, D. B. (2016). Science that matters: the importance of a cultural connection in underrepresented students' science pursuit. *CBE-Life Sciences Education, 15*(3), 1–12. doi:10.1187/cbe.16-01-0067.

Knogler, M., Harackiewicz, J. M., Gegenfurtner, A., & Lewalter, D. (2015). How situational is situational interest? Investigating the longitudinal structure of situational interest. *Contemporary Educational Psychology, 43*, 39–50. doi:10.1016/j.cedpsych.2015.08.004.

Lent, R. W., Hackett, G., & Brown, S. D. (1996). A social cognitive framework for studying career choice and transition to work. *Journal of Vocational Education Research, 21*, 3–31.

Lepper, M.R., Greene, D., & Nisbett, R.E. (1973). Undermining children's intrinsic interest with extrinsic reward: A test of the "overjustification" hypothesis. *Journal of Personality and Social Psychology, 28*, 129–37.

Lepper, M. R. & Henderlong, J. (2000). Turning "play" into "work" and "work" into "play": 25 years of research on intrinsic versus extrinsic motivation. In C. Sansone & J. M. Harackiewicz (Eds.). *Intrinsic and extrinsic motivation: The search for optimal motivation and performance* (pp. 257–307). New York, NY: Academic Press.

Lepper, M. R., Sagotsky, G., Dafoe, J. L., & Greene, D. (1982). Consequences of superfluous social constraints: Effects on young children's social inferences and subsequent intrinsic interest. *Journal of Personality and Social Psychology, 42*(1), 51–65. doi:10.1037/0022-3514.42.1.51.

Master, A., Cheryan, S., & Meltzoff, A. N. (2016). Computing whether she belongs: Stereotypes undermine girls' interest and sense of belonging in computer science. *Journal of Educational Psychology, 108*(3), 424–37. doi:10.1037/edu0000061.

Mayer, R. E. (2008). Applying the science of learning: Evidence-based principles for the design of multimedia instruction. *American Psychologist, 63*(8), 760–9. doi:10.1037/0003-066X.63.8.760.

Miele, D. B. & Scholer, A. A. (2016). Self-regulation of motivation. In K. R. Wentzel & D. B. Miele (Eds.). *Handbook of motivation at school* (pp. 363–384). New York, NY: Routledge.

Morf, C. C., Weir, C., & Davidov, M. (2000). Narcissism and intrinsic motivation: The role of goal congruence. *Journal of Experimental Social Psychology, 36*(4), 424–38. doi:10.1006/jesp.1999.1421.

Morgan, C., Isaac, J. D., & Sansone, C. (2001). The role of interest in understanding the career choices of female and male college students. *Sex Roles, 44*(5–6), 295–320. doi:10.1023/A:1010929600004.

Nye, C. D., Su, R., Rounds, J., & Drasgow, F. (2012). Vocational interests and performance: A quantitative summary of over 60 years of research. *Perspectives on Psychological Science, 7*(4), 384–403. doi:10.1177/1745691612449021.

Panksepp, J., 1998. *Affective neuroscience: The foundations of human and animal emotions.* New York, NY: Oxford University Press.

Panksepp, J. & Moskal, J. (2008). Dopamine and seeking: Subcortical "reward" systems and appetitive urges. In A. J. Elliot (Ed.), *Handbook of Approach and Avoidance Motivation* (pp. 67–87). New York: Psychology Press.

Plass, J. L., O'Keefe, P. A., Homer, B. D., Case, J., Hayward, E. O., Stein, M., & Perlin, K. (2013). The impact of individual, competitive, and collaborative mathematics game play on learning, performance, and motivation. *Journal of Educational Psychology*, *105*(4), 1050–66. doi:10.1037/a0032688.

Renninger, K. A. & Hidi, S. (2011). Revisiting the conceptualization, measurement, and generation of interest. *Educational Psychologist*, *46*(3), 168–84. doi:10.1080/00461520.2011.587723.

Renninger, K. A. & Hidi, S. (2016). *The power of interest for motivation and learning.* New York, NY: Routledge.

Renninger, K. A., Nieswandt, M., & Hidi, S. (2015). *Interest in K-16 mathematics and science learning.* Washington, DC: American Educational Research Association.

Sansone, C., Fraughton, T., Zachary, J. L., Butner, J., & Heiner, C. (2011). Self-regulation of motivation when learning online: The importance of who, why and how. *Educational Technology Research and Development*, *59*(2), 199–212. doi:10.1007/s11423-011-9193-6.

Sansone, C. & Harackiewicz, J. M. (1996). "I don't feel like it": The function of interest in self-regulation. In L. M. Martin & A. Tesser (Eds.) *Striving and feeling: Interactions among goals, affect, and self-regulation* (pp. 203–28). New Jersey, NJ: Lawrence Erlbaum Associates.

Sansone, C. & Harackiewicz, J. M. (2000). *Intrinsic and extrinsic motivation: The search for optimal motivation and performance.* New York, NY: Academic Press.

Sansone, C. & Morgan, C. (1992). Intrinsic motivation and education: Competence in context. *Motivation and Emotion*, *16*, 249–70.

Sansone, C., Sachau, D. A., & Weir, C. (1989). Effects of instruction on intrinsic interest: The importance of context. *Journal of Personality and Social Psychology*, *57*(5), 819–29. doi:10.1037/0022-3514.57.5.819.

Sansone, C. & Smith, J. L. (2000). Interest and self-regulation: The relation between having to and wanting to. In C. Sansone & J. M. Harackiewicz (Eds.), *Intrinsic and extrinsic motivation: The search for optimal motivation and performance* (pp. 341–72). San Diego, CA: Academic Press.

Sansone, C., Smith, J. L., Thoman, D. B., & MacNamara, A. (2012). Regulating interest when learning online: Potential motivation and performance trade-offs. *The Internet and Higher Education*, *15*(3), 141–9. doi:10.1016/j.iheduc.2011.10.004.

Sansone, C. & Thoman, D. B. (2005). Interest as the missing motivator in self-regulation. *European Psychologist*, *10*(3), 175–86. doi:10.1027/1016-9040.10.3.175.

Sansone, C. & Thoman, D. B. (2006). Maintaining activity engagement: Individual differences in the process of self-regulating motivation. *Journal of Personality*, *74*, 1697–720.

Sansone, C., Thoman, D. B., & Smith, J. L. (2010). Interest and self-regulation: Understanding individual variability in choices, efforts and persistence over time. In R. Hoyle (Ed.) *Handbook of personality and self-regulation* (pp. 191–217). Hoboken, NJ: Wiley-Blackwell.

Sansone, C., Weir, C., Harpster, L., & Morgan, C. (1992). Once a boring task always a boring task? Interest as a self-regulatory mechanism. *Journal of Personality and Social Psychology*, *63*(3), 379–90. doi:10.1037/0022-3514.63.3.379.

Sansone, C., Wiebe, D. J., & Morgan, C. (1999). Self-regulating interest: The moderating role of hardiness and conscientiousness. *Journal of Personality*, *67*(4), 701–33. doi:10.1111/1467-6494.00070.

Shechter, O. G., Durik, A. M., Miyamoto, Y., & Harackiewicz, J. M. (2011). The role of utility value in achievement behavior: The importance of culture. *Personality and Social Psychology Bulletin*, *37*(3), 303–17. doi:10.1177/0146167210396380.

Smith, J. L., Brown, E. R., Thoman, D. B., & Deemer, E. D. (2015). Losing its expected communal value: How stereotype threat undermines women's identity as research scientists. *Social Psychology of Education*, *18*(3), 443–66. doi:10.1007/s11218-015-9296-8.

Smith, J. L., Deemer, E. D., Thoman, D. B., & Zazworsky, L. (2014). Motivation under the microscope: Understanding undergraduate science students' multiple motivations for research. *Motivation and Emotion*, *38*(4), 496–512. doi:10.1007/s11031-013-9388-8.

Smith, J. L., Morgan, C. L., & White, P. H. (2005). Investigating a measure of computer technology domain identification: A tool for understanding gender differences and stereotypes. *Educational and Psychological Measurement*, *65*(2), 336–55. doi:10.1177/0013164404272486.

Smith, J. L. & Ruiz, J. M. (2007). Interpersonal orientation in context: Correlates and effects of interpersonal complementarity on subjective and cardiovascular experiences. *Journal of Personality*, *75*(4), 679–708. doi:10.1111/j.1467-6494.2007.00453.x.

Smith, J. L., Sansone, C., & White, P. H. (2007). The stereotyped task engagement process: The role of interest and achievement motivation. *Journal of Educational Psychology*, *99*(1), 99–114. doi:10.1037/0022-0663.99.1.99.

Smith, J. L., Wagaman, J., & Handley, I. M. (2009). Keeping it dull or making it fun: Task variation as a function of promotion versus prevention focus. *Motivation and Emotion*, *33*(2), 150–60. doi:10.1007/s11031-008-9118-9.

Tauer, J. M. & Harackiewicz, J. M. (2004). The effects of cooperation and competition on intrinsic motivation and performance. *Journal of Personality and Social Psychology*, *86*(6), 849–61. doi:10.1037/0022-3514.86.6.849.

Thoman, D. B., Arizaga, J. A., Smith, J. L., Story, T. S., & Soncuya, G. A., (2014). The grass is greener in non-STEM: Examining the role of competing belonging in undergraduate women's vulnerability to being pulled away from science. *Psychology of Women Quarterly*, *38*, 246–58. doi:10.1177/0361684313499899.

Thoman, D. B., Brown, E. R., Mason, A. Z., Harmsen, A. G., & Smith, J. L. (2015). The role of altruistic values in motivating underrepresented minority students for biomedicine. *BioScience*, *65*, 183–8. doi:10.1093/biosci/biu199.

Thoman, D. B., Sansone, C., Robinson, J., & Helm, J. (2018). *Implicit theories of interest regulation*. Manuscript under review.

Thoman, D. B., Smith, J. L., Brown, E. R., Chase, J. P., & Lee, J. K. (2013). Beyond performance: The motivational experience model of stereotype threat. *Educational Psychology Review*, *25*, 211–43. doi:10.1007/s10648-013-9219-1.

Thoman, D. B., Smith, J. L., & Silvia, P. J. (2011). The resource replenishment function of interest. *Social Psychological and Personality Science*, *2*(6), 592–9. doi:10.1177/1948550611402521.

Turner, S. A., Jr. & Silvia, P. J. (2006). Must interesting things be pleasant? A test of competing appraisal structures. *Emotion*, *6*, 670–4.

Vallerand, R. J., Blanchard, C., Mageau, G. A., Koestner, R., Ratelle, C., Léonard, M., & Marsolais, J. (2003). Les passions de l'âme: On obsessive and harmonious passion. *Journal of Personality and Social Psychology*, *85*(4), 756–67. doi:10.1037/0022-3514.85.4.756.

Wolters, C. A. (1998). Self-regulated learning and college students' regulation of motivation. *Journal of Educational Psychology*, *90*, 224.

Wolters, C. A., Yu, S. L., & Pintrich, P. R. (1996). The relation between goal orientation and students' motivational beliefs and self-regulated learning. *Learning and Individual Differences*, *8*, 211–38.

Woodcock, A., Graziano, W. G., Branch, S. E., Habashi, M. M., Ngambeki, I., & Evangelou, D. (2012). Person and thing orientations: Psychological correlates and predictive utility. *Social Psychological and Personality Sciences. 4*, 116.

5 Youth Development Programs

Supporting Self-Motivation in Project-Based Learning

Reed W. Larson, Gina McGovern, and Carolyn Orson

Abstract: Afterschool youth development programs (including, arts, leadership, and STEM programs) are significant learning contexts for adolescents. Participation in high-quality programs is related to the acquisition of cognitive, social-emotional, and occupational skills. It is notable that youth in programs report high motivation, markedly higher than in school. Furthermore, motivation increases over time and becomes more self-sustained. This chapter draws on our extensive qualitative interview research with youth and staff to examine questions about how programs – using a project-based learning model – facilitate high and sustained motivation. We find, first, that effective programs create an interpersonal environment of belonging and safety that allows youth to engage in high-functioning relationships, and that projects facilitate motivation because youth experience agency, increasing competency and comradery in their work. Second, although projects periodically confront youth with difficult challenges, which are sometimes overwhelming and can disrupt motivation, youth are typically resilient, and experienced leaders have well-developed strategies for helping youth navigate and learn from these experiences. Third, youth develop sustained motivation because they develop personal connections to program goals and learn techniques to regulate and preempt situations that disrupt motivation. Some youth report learning strategies to help them sustain motivation in the complex, open-ended work of projects.

Before she joined, Devin Mitchell's[1] impression of the Emerson theater program was: "I would never do that. Why would they put on makeup and act all weird?" But two years after joining, Devin, now sixteen, described how the program had become highly motivating for her:

> The atmosphere, the people. It was just a good feeling. I can't even explain it. It's just being surrounded by so many different people. I think that's why I keep wanting to do it. It's an experience I've never experienced before. Getting to know people. Just feeling the love. It just makes me want to do more. I'm like in a whole 'nother world.

We would like to thank the William T. Grant Foundation and the Susan Crown Exchange for their generous support of this research, and the youth and adult leaders who shared their experiences with us.

1 All names of people and programs are pseudonyms.

Devin went on to explain that her motivation in this "whole 'nother world" was elevated by: the other youth ("feeling the love"), the director ("she's a teacher who cares"), and the comradery of working together to develop a successful production ("the best team I've ever been part of"). It was a world created by all these elements. The types of motivation Devin reported included a frequent *state* of intrinsic motivation: rehearsals were often "really, really fun". She also reported that, after completing several shows, she had developed longer-term *sustained motivation* in the work and learning: She was invested in creating a show that would "put smiles and tears on people's faces". This goal kept her going when rehearsals were exhausting or difficult.

The high motivation Devin described is frequent among teenagers in after-school and out-of-school youth development programs. "Youth development programs" includes community-based programs and extracurricular school activities, such as arts, leadership, STEM, civic, and other organized activities (Roth & Brooks-Gunn, 2003a). Research finds that these programs are the most consistently motivating learning context in adolescents' lives. When signaled to report on their psychological states at random times across a week, teens in three large studies reported high average state motivation in youth programs – much higher than during schoolwork (Csikszentmihalyi et al., 1993; Larson, 2011; Vandell et al., 2006). Additional evidence suggests that motivation increases over the course of program participation and, importantly, that youth develop longer-term, sustained motivation (Dawes & Larson, 2011; Smith et al., 2016b). Both the state and sustained motivation that youth report in programs is "self-motivation": it is intrinsic (rather than extrinsic); it originates from the self (Ryan & Deci, 2000).

What makes the experience of after-school programs so motivating, especially for adolescents who are often bored and unmotivated in other settings (Eccles & Roeser, 2009; Larson & Richards, 1991)? There is much to be gained from delving into this puzzle, as we do in this chapter. Programs are important learning contexts: Youth in high-quality programs learn cognitive, social-emotional, and occupational skills (Catalano et al., 2014; Smith et al., 2016b; Vandell et al., 2015). Educators and motivational theorists can benefit from understanding how programs successfully engage teens in learning these skills. Programs for adolescents typically have them do projects – produce plays, create videos, lobby officials, or plan events – which are vehicles for much of this learning (Heath, 1999; Larson, 2011). So, part of the puzzle is how projects support youth's experience of self-motivation in learning activities – and how projects might put it in jeopardy.

This chapter examines three central questions about youth's motivation in programs. The first is: How does the *environment* of programs support motivation? What creates the kind of highly motivating "world" that Devin experienced? Theorists argue that the environment is critical to understanding motivation (Bevan & Michalchik, 2013; Kaplan & Maehr, 2007).

Our second question focuses on fluctuations and possible disruptions in youth's day-to-day motivation. Average motivation in programs is high, but participants like Devin also report experiences of frustration and setbacks in their projects, which can create substantial motivational downturns, including wanting to quit (Larson et al., (in press)). Blumenfeld et al. (1991) suggested that the work of projects is open-ended, making them "complex and inherently ambiguous and risky" (p. 380). We ask: Does the open-ended nature of projects create significant risks to youth's continued motivation?

Our third question is: How might youth in programs develop sustained motivation? This question is important to teens' preparation for adulthood: To function in a career, contribute to society, and navigate adult life, they need the ability to sustain attention and effort in goal pursuits (Bandura, 2006; Larson, 2000). Devin reported developing more stable investment in the long-term goals of producing shows. Motivational theorists suggest a range of other possible contributors to sustained motivation: developing individual interest, developing dispositions like grit, and learning skills for the regulation of motivation (Duckworth, 2016; Renninger & Hidi, 2016; Zimmerman & Campillo, 2003).

Each of these three questions – on the motivational environment, risks to youth's day-to-day motivation, and development of sustained motivation – is the topic of a separate section in the chapter. We address these questions from a social-cultural-ecological perspective, which views motivation as grounded in complex, unfolding human–environment transactions. Our focus is on *experiences-in-context*. To understand motivation in a complex learning context (like youth's projects), we believe it essential to understand these human–environment transactions as they are experienced and enacted by youth and staff. Such "context-sensitive" understanding, it is argued, is especially important to the development of knowledge that is useful to practice (Donovan, 2013; Kaplan et al., 2012, p. 177). We think the findings here will be helpful to practitioners, not only in programs, but in schools – where projects are often advocated as a valuable method of learning, but concerns about their complexity are a frequent obstacle to their use (Barron et al., 1998).

This chapter is based on a family of grounded-theory studies we conducted that obtained hundreds of interviews with youth on motivation-related experiences: interacting with peers, struggling with challenging projects, and learning to control their motivation. We augment the findings from youth with findings from program staff on how they facilitate youth's experiences.

Background: Programs and Methods

Before addressing the questions, we provide further background on youth development programs and on the methods of the studies used here.

Project-Based Programs: A Distinct Learning Model

Youth programs have some basic advantages in supporting youth's experiences of self-motivation. Compared to schools, programs are subject to fewer top-down mandates, which gives them greater flexibility to adapt programming to youth (Walker et al., 2005). Further, youth's participation is voluntary: youth choose programs fit to their interests (Akiva & Horner, 2016) and can quit if they wish.

The project-based learning model in most programs contains additional components that may contribute to youth's self-motivation. The primary mode of learning is *experiential*. Learning occurs through cycles of reflective trial-and-error (Halpern, 2009; Roth & Brooks-Gunn, 2003b). Most programs are *rooted in a specific disciplinary tradition* (e.g., theater, agriculture, social activism), and youth learn through taking on authentic tasks and employing tools and techniques of that discipline. Effective programs are *youth-centered*: staff support youth in taking ownership and responsibility for their work (Roth & Brooks-Gunn, 2003a). Projects are often *collaborative*: youth work together, and returning peers from prior years often help newer youth (Walker et al., 2005).

Youth's projects are structured in ways that might also be helpful to understanding youth's motivation. In some programs, youth receive initial training in basic skills or do smaller projects that lead to larger ones. Projects typically follow a schedule with deadlines; youth may receive staff or peer feedback on their work at significant milestones. Some programs model their schedule on the "production cycle" in the discipline, for example, the sequence of steps to building a boat or rehearsing a play. Finally, projects typically conclude with an outcome, performance, or showcase event that provides authentic feedback and reinforcement (Smith et al., 2016a).

Understand Experience-in-Context: Research Methods

For 20 years, our team has been studying how youth learn social-emotional competencies (e.g., responsibility, strategic thinking, self-motivation, emotion-management skills) through experiences in project-based programs. In this chapter, we present both published and new findings from this research. Many of our articles on these competencies contribute to knowledge of motivation-in-context, and are often cited herein. This is because the experiences related to each of the competencies are intertwined: Events in projects, interactions with peers and staff, and the internal thought processes associated with responsibility, emotions, etc., are part of an interconnected stream. For example, youth's ongoing work, emotions, and motivations affect each other (as described below). Likewise, developing both responsibility and strategic thinking depends on youth having some form of motivation that propels them through critical learning experiences in their projects. The new findings we report here build on these published findings.

Description of studies. Interviews were our method of choice for obtaining accounts of experiences-in-context. Our findings come primarily from the three major studies summarized in Table 5.1. The first two were conducted by our team at the University of Illinois, the third by the Weikart Center (with our

Table 5.1 *Description of the grounded-theory studies used in the chapter*

Name of study, PI, & institution	Description of youth programs	Criteria used to select programs	N of youth (N of interviews)	N of leaders (N of interviews)	Publications cited in this chapter
TYDE Larson, PI University of Illinois	12 programs for high-school-aged youth from Chicago and Central Illinois	Recommended by local youth professionals, had experienced leaders, youth-centered philosophy, low youth turnover, high youth engagement	113 (661)	26 (125)	**On motivation:** Dawes and Larson (2011), Larson (2011), Pearce and Dawes (2015), Pearce and Larson (2007); **On strategic thinking:** Larson and Angus (2011), Larson and Hansen (2005); **On responsibility development:** Wood, Larson, and Brown (2009); **On emotions:** Larson and Brown (2007)
Pathways Project Larson, PI University of Illinois	Pilot Study: 4 programs in Central Illinois, Chicago, and Minneapolis	Same as main study	38	8	**On responsibility development** Salusky et al. (2014); **On emotional learning:** Rusk et al. (2013)
	Main Study: 13 programs for high-school-aged youth in Central Illinois, Chicago, and Minneapolis	Recommended by local youth professionals, had experienced leaders, youth-centered philosophy, low youth turnover	108 (280)	25 (96)	**On motivation:** Larson et al. (2017); Orson (2017); **On youth-leader relationships:** Griffith and Larson (2016), Griffith et al. (n.d.); **On youth's program roles:** Larson et al. (in press); **On leader practices:** Larson et al. (2016)
	Additional Program Leaders: 14 programs for middle school youth	Selected to approximately match the high school programs	0	25 (97)	
SEL Challenge Smith, PI Weikart Center	8 programs for high-school- and middle-school-aged youth from cities across the United States	Selection criteria: demonstrable high quality; a focus on social and emotional learning; the ability to articulate and describe how youth learn in relation to the design of the program; target vulnerable youth	52 (8 individual interviews; 8 focus groups)	19 (34)	**On social-emotional learning, including motivation:** Smith et al. (2016a, 2016b)

Note. TYDE is the acronym for The Youth Development Experience; SEL is the acronym for Social and Emotional Learning (SEL) Challenge.

participation).[2] All three studies focused on programs that served ethnically-diverse youth (African-American, White, Latinx) from low- to middle-income families. For all, we selected programs identified as "high quality" – because we wanted to maximize procurement of accounts of developmental processes.[3] The Illinois studies included multiple interviews with youth and staff (at four points in time for Pathways), which allowed us to examine how projects unfolded and youth–staff relationships developed over time, among other things. All three studies obtained additional data from observations, questionnaires, and parents, which provided a deep base of knowledge for understanding the context of youth's experiences.

Youth's experiences and staff practices. The youth interviews in the two Illinois studies were our main source of findings on youth's motivational experiences. The first Illinois study, The Youth Development Experience (TYDE), provided valuable initial discoveries; the Pathways study, which is the source of our new findings, then sought "second-generation" knowledge based on more targeted questioning. Interviewers asked semi-structured questions aimed at obtaining youth's accounts of day-to-day experiences in projects and how these led to development. The Pathways interviews included questions about what influenced youth's motivation and what caused it to "grow or change". Most Pathways youth reported that their motivation had increased since they joined the program, and their explanations for this increase were a major source of the findings we present on the motivational environment (Q1), and on how formation of goals contributed to sustained motivation (Q3). Findings about motivational flux and disruptions (Q2) came mostly from questions about how program activities influenced youth's motivation but also from other questions in the interview (e.g., on emotions, responsibility).

The eight programs in the Weikart study were selected for exemplary quality, including the expertise of their staff. Therefore, we used the published Weikart findings as our primary source on staff practices that support youth's experiences of self-motivation. We also use published findings on these practices from the Illinois studies.

Grounded-theory analyses. The published and new findings for youth and staff were obtained from grounded-theory data analysis, a methodology designed to systematically examine the variety of human experiences and processes in complex contexts (Strauss & Corbin, 2008). Our use of these procedures involved iterative cycles of: identifying patterns in the interviews that addressed specific research questions; conceptualizing those patterns; confirming the sturdiness of those conceptualizations to the data among multiple coders; and repeating

---

2 David P. Weikart Center for Youth Program Quality at the Forum for Youth Investment.
3 Programs in the Illinois studies were selected following procedures for identifying high-quality programs formulated by McLaughlin et al. (1994). The eight programs in the Weikart study were selected through a competitive application process with 242 applicants (see Smith et al., 2016b).

these analytic processes as higher-order concepts and findings were identified (Charmaz, 2014). Following grounded-theory methods, we gave priority to the language and concepts employed by interviewees. At the same time we used findings and concepts from motivational theories as "sensitizing concepts" to help interpret and frame the patterns emerging in later iterations of the analyses (Charmaz, 2014). Thus, for example, we found youth consistently reported that feelings of belonging and safety were important to their experience of a motivating program environment. So, we drew on relevant motivational literature to help conceptualize that pattern, but we also present representative quotes in the text to maintain the connection to the patterns of experience-in-context. As a whole, this chapter should be seen as providing preliminary grounded theory about motivation-in-context in youth programs.

Youth Programs as Motivating Environments: "A Whole 'Nother World"

As in other studies, youth in our research described being highly motivated. They repeatedly described the program and its activities as "fun" and "exciting." Youth in the Pathways study reported being "passionate" about program activities, "intensely involved," "supermotivated," and "really into it." They described repeated experiences where they were "hyped up" or "everyone's motivation skies up." Some described a cascade of motivation, for example, "You get more interested and you want to do more things." High motivation was evident in youth's accounts of their actions: exercising new initiative; generating ideas and plans, developing their own style, taking ownership, and enduring hardships. Alonzo, in an urban agriculture program, described how he likes to stay clean: "I don't like to get dirty. [But] now I can get in the sun and work for hours. I don't mind getting dirty." Nearly all Pathways youth reported their motivation had increased over time (one said it increased "exponentially") as they discovered opportunities in the program. One said, "It was just kind of like, 'Whoa! We can do stuff like that?'"

What makes programs so motivating? Like Devin, many youth in our studies and others attribute their high motivation to experiencing programs as a world where things are done differently (McLaughlin et al., 1994). They relate to people in different ways, have new kinds of conversations, and become absorbed in serious work in ways that didn't happen elsewhere. The environment of the program provided affordances for them to actively engage with people and activities in new ways that were highly motivating. Blyth et al. (2015) suggest that programs afford youth new, active *ways of being*, including "ways of feeling, relating, and doing." In this section, we describe how these affordances are related to the culture and other features of the environment. By culture we refer to values, norms, language, meanings, ways of relating to people, and ways of engaging in activities that are shared among members of a group (Shweder et al., 2006). Other features include the structure of program activities and the intentional professional practices of staff.

We began our analyses for this section by identifying all passages in which the 108 Pathways youth identified experiences related to the environment as reasons for their increased motivation. We found that youth's explanations could readily be separated into descriptions of the social environment and the activity environment. Within each of these, our grounded-theory analyses identified elements of youth's experiences-in-context that supported motivation, most of which accorded with motivational theory.

Motivating Social Environment

Cultivating a positive social environment is a high priority in most programs (Roth & Brooks-Gunn, 2003b). We identified two elements of youth's experiences in the social environment that contributed to their motivation: belonging and principled relationships.

Belonging. Feeling that one belongs, research shows, is a precondition to motivation (Baumeister & Leary, 1995). Many Pathways youth pointed to the experience of belonging and interpersonal safety as reasons for high motivation in the programs. When asked to describe why her motivation increased, Katie, a first-year member of Rising Leaders, explained: "Other people are happy to see me and are glad when I come up with opinions and ideas. Just knowing I am needed." Youth reported feeling safe with each other – free from fears that inhibited them in other contexts. Jessica at The Station made a comparison to school: "I feel like people at school judge me more, I can trust people here." She went on to say: "I feel more motivated here because people know me and won't make fun of me." Youth experienced a culture of inclusion, which is created through deliberate staff practices in high-quality programs (Smith et al., 2016a).

Youth's relationships with staff contributed to this collective experience of belonging and safety. In explaining their high motivation, many Pathways youth said program leaders were different and more caring than other adults. Aurelia at The Station said, "He would actually talk to us. You felt like he was another friend, rather than just an older person." Many American adolescents experience disrespect and hostility from adults in their lives (teachers, principals, police), which undermines how secure they feel in many adult-occupied settings (Cohen & Steele, 2002). Carisa at Visionaries attributed her motivation to the leader being different: "She is one of the best people you can meet because ... she knows we are teenagers so she understands us; She doesn't yell." We found that nearly all youth in Pathways reported a trusting relationship with at least one staff member; and they said this trust transformed their program experience, including increasing their motivation (Griffith & Larson, 2016).

Participation in principled high-functioning relationships. Research finds that belonging, safety, and trust provide a foundation for other powerful relationship processes (Eccles & Gootman, 2002; Rhodes, 2002), and this appeared to happen for Pathways youth. They described being motivated by their experience of high-functioning relationships, both among individuals and in the group. In recounting what was distinct about these relationships, youth described core values and principles that appeared to guide them.

One set of core principles included acting respectfully and maturely towards each other (see also Deutsch & Jones, 2008). One youth explained his motivation: "No one is ever mad at each other." Another said: "Mostly, kids here, they're not having tantrums or trying to own the situation by themselves." A youth in another program explained her high motivation by saying: "Staying positive – that's what Rising Leaders is about." Program members' embrace of these principles was motivating because it allowed them to have honest, mutual, and caring conversations and to work more effectively together.

Another shared core principle was taking their work seriously. Youth described being motivated by the ways youth and staff valued the importance of the work. Nadir in the theater program said: "We held ourselves to a higher standard, which made it more fun." A youth who was interviewing community members for a video said it "was motivating because you could tell [everyone] was serious about it." In some programs, discussions about society, inequality, and their own place in the world were important activities, and the covenant of seriousness (and mutual respect) made them highly engaging (e.g., Larson et al., 2012).

Smith et al. (2016a) found that leaders in high-quality programs are intentional in cultivating these and related core principles for high-functioning relationships (including listening, turn-taking, and "all are different, equal, and important"). In some programs, youth are enlisted to help formulate rules for them to follow. Leaders also model principles in their relationships with youth. Pathways youth described experiencing their relationships with leaders as blueprints for mature relationships, which they applied to their relationships with people in the program and beyond (Griffith & Larson, 2016).

In sum, this research suggests that the social environment of effective programs appears to be highly motivating, because a shared culture of inclusion and principled relationships allows youth to relate to each other in powerful, new ways.

Motivating Activity Environment

Educational research has identified features of activity environments that support (and disrupt) motivation in classrooms (Kaplan & Maehr, 2007), but little is known about how such features might apply to programs. Our analyses of youth's accounts of what increased their motivation identified three elements of youth's experiences in program activities. These elements, we find, represent environmental affordances provided by projects, program culture, and staff practices. Further, when we brought in the motivational literature, we found that these elements were closely aligned with motivational theory,

especially the three basic human motivators (autonomy, competence, relatedness) that Ryan and Deci (2000) identified from reviewing decades of motivational research.

Experience of agency. First, many youth attributed their motivation to participation in work that granted them a high degree of agency. Their projects
were open-ended. Youth had freedom to make choices, experiment, and be in
charge of their work, as individuals or as part of a team. A youth in an arts
program was motivated because: "We had to be independent; we had to learn
how to do our own thing, we had to learn our own style." A youth making a
film was motivated because: "I can work it into something great, with the help
of my partners." Youth described enjoying the process of trial-and-error and
"seeing" what happens. Alonzo in Urban Farmers became highly motivated
by "messing with the dirt. It was interesting seeing, 'Wow, dirt can actually do
all of that to just a seed!'" Projects afforded youth experiences of individual or
group agency over a long time span. In a leadership program, Alexis was motivated by: "Seeing things develop: our plans, the step-by-step that we're taking,
leading to bigger things." Motivational research shows that the experience of
agency (or "autonomy") is a basic motivator (Ryan & Deci, 2000), and that
motivation is enhanced in environments where learners can make decisions, be
creative, and learn from trial-and-error (Kaplan & Maehr, 2007). Leaders in
high-quality programs intentionally maximize youth's experience of agency as
much as is pragmatically feasible within the constraints of the situation and
program (Larson et al., 2016; Smith et al., 2016a).

Learning skills for action. Closely related, youth attributed their motivation to their experience of developing competencies. Imani, in a graffiti arts
program, said: "Every day I improve my skills, which improves my motivation." These competencies included action skills for managing open-ended
work: using "if-then" thinking, weighing trade-offs, navigating open-ended
challenges, and employing strategic concepts from the discipline of their work
(e.g., film-making, leadership, teaching children [Larson & Angus, 2011]). For
example, youth at Nutrition Rocks, who ran a summer camp for children,
described being motivated by learning and practicing action skills that helped
their work of teaching. These included skills for how to get the children's
"brains working" and "take them out of their shell," and being able to "raise
my voice but not all the way" (Diaz et al., 2015). Research shows that developing and using competencies is a basic motivator (Ryan & Deci, 2000). What is
especially important here is that youth were being motivated by learning skills
they could then apply to the unstructured challenges of projects.

Leaders in high-quality programs deliberately create affordances for youth's
development of these action skills (Smith et al., 2016a). Heath (1999) discovered that strategies for dealing with unstructured challenges were embedded
in the language and culture of high-quality programs. Leaders deliberately
cultivated this language and culture; youth internalized it and helped pass it
on to new youth (see also Larson & Hansen, 2005).

Collaboration. Third, youth attributed their high motivation to positive experiences of collaborative work, and relatedness to others is Ryan and Deci's third basic motivator. When youth worked on projects together, they motivated each other. Rosanna at High Definition said, "We each helped each other motivate ourselves." Some youth described their motivation as contagious: Excitement flowed from one person to another. Youth were also motivated from discovering that they accomplished more when working in a team – particularly a team that followed the core principles described earlier. Lorelei provided an example in which brainstorming with others led to a better product than she could have created on her own: "It won't just be my ideas. It would be, with the help of someone else's, too, that we mold it into something that's really cool." In separate articles we report findings on how youth's experiences of cooperation and mutual accountability created "good pressure" that is a powerful force in motivating their work (Larson et al., (in press); Salusky et al., 2014). Program leaders support a positive culture of collaboration by cultivating group norms and helping ensure they are followed, and by modeling teamwork and coaching youth on group processes (Smith et al., 2016a).

This third element represents the convergence of the social and activity environment. Feeling safe and trusting others allows youth to take risks in ways that lead to groups developing ideas successfully. Following core principles of high-functioning relationships allows youth to experience group agency, learn together, and, by their accounts, help them do higher-quality work than they would have done working alone.

Conclusion

The explanation for youth's experience of high motivation in programs, then, appears to be that programs successfully create the favorable affordances identified by motivational research: belonging, safety, agency, competence, and connection. The environment and culture of high-quality programs support youth's active experiences of ways of relating and working with others that are known to be motivating. This general picture of a highly motivating environment, however, is incomplete unless we also examine how motivation can be disrupted.

Motivational Flux and Disruptions in the Day-to-Day Work of Projects

Dahlia Sanchez was writing an article for a program magazine, and her frustration mounted as she realized that her topic wasn't going to work. She became so distraught, she wanted to quit the project: "I didn't want to do it anymore. I just wanted to be done." In the prior section, we focused on stable elements of programs that create high motivation. In this section, we zoom in on emergent situations in projects that impact youth's motivation, including – as Dahlia experienced – disrupting it. Blumenfeld et al. (1991) observed that the open-ended nature of projects can lead to situations that put youth's continued motivation at risk. We focus here on accounts of specific unfolding episodes in youth's work. Can these episodes create fluctuations in motivation? What kind of situations cause downturns or major disruptions like Dahlia's? When downturns and disruptions occur, are youth – or staff – able to respond in ways that successfully restore youth's motivation?

We first describe general patterns in youth's day-to-day motivational fluctuations and downturns. Then we examine a subset of situations in which youth's motivation is significantly disrupted or blocked and, lastly, present findings on staff responses to these disruptive episodes.

Motivation in Flux

We found that fluctuations in motivation were normative among youth we studied. In describing their motivation, youth in the Pathways and TYDE research reported ups and downs related to shifting situations and circumstances in their projects (Griffith et al., 2017; Larson, 2011). Their motivation changed as they became excited about an idea, encountered obstacles, lost direction, and experienced breakthroughs. Joseph at High Definition described multiple motivational changes while making a video:

> At first, I was really, really into it – but not the theme. I wanted to do "how high school affects your identity" and, within that, how people, drugs, and your surroundings influence you. I just didn't have enough time and that aggravated me. So we changed to skateboarding and then I was not that into it. Then we changed to "how music influences your identity," and I was a little more interested. So that motivated me to try to have creative ideas and put out something I would be proud of.

As is apparent in Joseph's accounts, it was not just the situation but his experience of the situation that affected his motivation (e.g., his interest in topics, perceptions of the time they will take).

Researchers agree on a number of *experiential conditions* in person-situation interactions that influence intrinsic motivation, and several of these are helpful in describing youth's fluctuations. Motivation is highest when someone experiences the challenges in an activity as matched to their skill level (not too easy, not overwhelmingly hard), and when they experience control and self-efficacy (Kaplan et al., 2012; Larson & Rusk, 2011). Youth and leader accounts often identified the absence of these experiential conditions as contributors to motivational downturns, thus we incorporated them into our analysis of general patterns.

Setbacks. Downturns in motivation, we found, were often attributed to youth encountering setbacks or challenges they experienced as above their skill level (Griffith & Larson, 2016; Larson & Dawes, 2015). For example, John, who (like Joseph) was making a film, described how unsuccessful attempts shook his perception of his ability to make a good film: "I kind of lost faith in it. I made two films that were not that good, and I was like, 'Ugh.' I kind of gave up." These setbacks undercut his self-efficacy.

Setbacks and situations in which youth perceived challenges as too difficult appeared to be almost inherent in youth's projects. Most youth reporting these experiences were novices trying new things and taking risks; they often overestimated what they could achieve, leading to situations where they felt overwhelmed (Blumenfeld et al., 1991; Griffith & Larson, 2016). We also found this pattern when youth accepted program roles (e.g., news reporter, team leader). As they took on roles, the majority of youth discovered that it was harder than they expected: unanticipated challenges, complexities, and obligations emerged. For example, they discovered that holding a leadership role did not mean people would do what you asked (Larson et al., (in press); Salusky et al., 2014).

Experiencing lack of control. A contributing factor was youth's frequent experience of motivational fluctuations as outside their control. This occurred often for downturns. Youth often felt helpless – that they could not influence whatever caused their motivation to fall. For example, Caleb, who was practicing for a 4-H archery contest, reported, "When I'm shooting good, I just want to keep shooting." But, "When I don't shoot right I get mad, because I'm doing everything I'm supposed to do and it's just not going right." Rather than being inspired to work on his shot, Caleb got angry. This perceived helplessness was also evident in diminished motivation when a role a youth accepted required dealing with difficult emergent demands (Larson et al., (in press)).

Youth's experience of helplessness was sometimes due to *not knowing* what caused their low motivation. "I knew I could do it," one youth said, "but something was holding me back." Youth also reported lack of knowledge and control over upswings in motivation. Lorelei said her artistic motivation "comes and goes – I don't know how that happens." She explained: "Sometimes I don't feel creative, but then inspiration hits me and I feel like drawing something ... But it can't be forced or it won't come out as good."

Motivational resilience. Despite this vulnerability to motivational downturns, youth were typically resilient. When they got caught up on sleep or had time away from the work, they were able to approach difficult challenges with fresh energy. The collaborative culture of the program also helped restore youth's motivation: Peers provided encouragement, members of a team solved problems together, and experienced peers provided tips that helped youth surmount difficulties (Larson et al., (in press)).

Some youth were proactive in addressing conditions that undermined their motivation. John, whose motivation fell after two unsuccessful films, learned new camera techniques that helped him regain his self-confidence and work on a new film. Some youth reported having a pre-existing disposition for perseverance – to "never give up" or "not back outta things" – which helped them rally to overcome setbacks and difficult challenges (Salusky et al., 2014; Wood et al., 2009).

Leaders' role in modulating downturns. Our studies indicate that program leaders can be effective in helping youth respond to downturns and restore the experiential conditions for intrinsic motivation. Youth report that, when they need assistance, leaders are available to help (Larson & Angus, 2011); when they experience self-doubts, leaders often provide helpful encouragements (e.g., "they're always there to fire you up when you're down"; Griffith & Larson, 2016); and when they feel helplessness, skilled staff can help them see that progress comes through effort and perseverance (Smith et al., 2016a).

Youth's Experiences of Disrupted Motivation

Despite youth's resilience and the availability of staff, sometimes youth's downturns in motivation went from bad to worse and became paralyzing. Youth reported situations in which a challenge grew to become overwhelmingly hard, leading to major disruptions in motivation. Episodes like these were frequent and disruptive enough that we felt it important to understand how they happened. To do this, we searched the Pathways data for all accounts of episodes where youth experienced a major disruption in motivation, then we analyzed how they unfolded.

These episodes, we found, began when a setback or difficult challenge led to a swell of frustration, worry, or self-doubt. Youth encountered a vexing problem, felt overwhelmed by a complex task, or felt they had "messed up." For example, Delphia was helping paint a mural and had progressed from the easy step of outlining a picture of "the ice cream man" to the harder step of using spray paint to try to bring the outline to life. The spray-painted picture, however, clashed with her mental image of how the man should look. This led to mounting anxiety from successive failed attempts.

These swells of emotion then disrupted motivation. They led to loss of interest, constricted attention, wanting to quit, and active avoidance. During rehearsals for a musical in a theater program, Amanda reported a "meltdown," after which she was not able to land the steps of a dance. She was rehearsing with other cast members when the emotional swell started: "It was kind of a buildup of a bunch of things. I had a fight with my father. I was having trouble with my knee. I couldn't get the dance. It was just kind of a modge-podge of crap." Amanda was so angry and frustrated that she "went and hid backstage while everybody else was on stage practicing." Her earlier investment in the musical had been transformed into active avoidance. Other youth in similar episodes reported, "I just keep thinking about how mad I was ... you go into zombie mode" and "I'm not gonna be able to do this. Why am I even in here?"

Psychological research and theory suggest the psychological mechanisms driving this sequence of experiences. People who are novices in a domain (e.g., using spray paint) are prone to becoming overwhelmed with information (Zimmerman & Campillo, 2003). Repeated frustration and failure in a task readily leads to helplessness and self-doubt (Bandura, 1991a). The emotions created by challenging experiences do not inevitably disrupt motivation (Pekrun et al., 2007) but, when they are extreme and feel inescapable, they can distract attention (e.g., "I just keep thinking about how mad I am"), compromise performance, and reduce motivation through other means (Carver & Scheier, 2007). Fisher (2013) suggested the term "spiral" for this set of convergent processes, a term that fits youth's experience of an uncontrollable downward swirl of feelings leading to "I can't do this" or "I don't want to do this."

Leaders' Responses to Youth's Disrupted Motivation

When youth experienced spirals of emotion and demotivation they sometimes recovered on their own. But other times, leaders intervened to help them become re-engaged. Understanding how leaders do this successfully is a vital topic for motivational theory and practice. To gain insight, we asked leaders to describe a situation they encountered when "youth's anxieties or worries about a project interfered with making progress" and how they responded (Orson, 2018). The sample for this analysis was 40 experienced leaders from the Pathways study.[4] The situations they described were similar to those mentioned by youth – they often began with a setback or situation that was overwhelmingly challenging.

Leader's reframing. Leaders recounted using a variety of strategies for responding to youth in these situations. These included asking an experienced program member to help a struggling youth and helping youth understand that mistakes help them learn (Orson, 2018). We focus here on the most common strategy, *reframing* (used by 20 of 40 leaders), which appears to have been well-fitted to youth's needs in these episodes. Reframing involves helping youth look at situations from new and different perspectives. Often leaders suggested a specific framework – or several – to help youth reinterpret the circumstance that created the emotional spiral. In a few cases, leaders provided a frame to help youth understand their emotions. The new frameworks that leaders suggested contextualized the difficulties youth were facing, challenged youth's assumptions, or drew attention to situational dimensions that youth hadn't seen, often including strengths in youth's ideas (Orson, 2018).

When the difficulty of a challenge created anxiety, leaders suggested new frames that made the situation more manageable. They showed youth alternative, easier pathways or worked to shift youth's expectations by, for example, introducing different criteria for evaluating progress, success, or failure. Desiree Bustamante, a leader at the graffiti arts programs, described helping a youth who (like Delphia) was frustrated by the imprecision of spray paint.

---

4 Leaders had an average of 12 years' professional experience.

Desiree explained that detail and perfection aren't goals with graffiti art. She suggested a different perspective: stepping back to see how the spray-painted figure looked from a distance.

In situations when self-doubt was the main driver of blocked motivation, leaders helped youth reframe their perceptions of themselves and their abilities. Cathy Murphy, a middle-school theater director, described how the actress in the lead role of "Annie" suddenly lost all confidence midway through rehearsals. She was in great distress, telling Cathy, "I'm not good enough. I can't do it." Cathy spent 20 or 30 minutes "rebuilding" the actress's confidence, using evidence of her competence in previous productions. Leaders' reframing addressed the cause of anxiety and helped restore experiential conditions for youth's motivation (Orson, 2018).

A case example of reframing. A more in-depth example is useful to illustrate how leaders adapt reframing strategies to the complex situations youth face. Allie, a young woman who had been working on a film at Reel Makers, explained to leader Tyler Bates through a flow of tears: "I just want to give up. I want to scrap the whole thing." Allie was a first-time filmmaker, and she had put much effort into the film – a story she'd written about a girl who is abused by her boyfriend. But her lead actor quit before she could finish filming her 20-page script. Now she had hours of footage for an unfinished story.

Tyler's first objective with Allie was to provide a framework to help her understand and deal with her intense feelings of distress. He sat down with her, acknowledged the seriousness of the situation, and told her, "This is not the end of the world. This is serious, but you are physically okay, so let's work on the emotional place you are in." This framing helped Allie move through her strong emotions.

When ready, Tyler began helping Allie reframe the cause of her emotions. He explained that her experience was frequent in creative work and "it can feel like absolutely everything that could go wrong has gone wrong." But, Tyler emphasized, "This is something in your control." Like Cathy Murphy, he helped build up Allie's confidence with evidence from previous successes: "I know you're capable of doing this. I don't just have blind faith. This is grounded in the work you've shown me."

Tyler then helped Allie reframe the situation with her film. He drew on his experience to suggest ways she might organize the footage into a strong film. "You can mold something out of this that is close to your original idea … there's absolutely a way to work with what you have and create something in the spirit of that story." He helped her construct a viable plan to reorganize her footage in a powerful way. Tyler had used several different frames aimed at helping Allie understand her emotions, see setbacks as normal, recognize her abilities, and re-plan her film.

The effectiveness of leaders' responses. When faced with difficult challenges, novice problem solvers (like these youth) tend to persist with their initial framework and approach (Zimmerman & Campillo, 2003). As a result, when they experience mounting frustration and anxiety, they often remain stuck and demotivated. The experienced leaders in our research, however, appeared to have well-developed strategies for helping youth reconceptualize difficult situations and restore the experiential conditions for motivation (Orson, 2018).

Did these interventions work? A number of youth in Pathways and TYDE provided accounts that suggested leaders' reframing helped them restore their motivation. After being frustrated by how an art project turned out, Eloise at Voces Unidas was "mad, upset, and did not want to do it anymore." But the leader reassured her that the project she was attempting was really difficult – "It rarely works the first time" – and helped her devise a new approach, which produced a result she liked. Some youth said leaders were especially helpful because they were not prescriptive. Leaders had given them multiple choices and, as expressed by Xavier at High Definition, "then we could make our own decision on whether we still wanted to do our thing or take the advice that he [was] giving us" (Griffith et al., 2017). This example illustrates how leaders provided "autonomy support," which facilitates youth motivation (Ryan & Deci, 2000) by providing helpful suggestions while supporting youth's ideas and agency.

We were fortunate to have Allie's account of her episode, which illustrates the nuances of autonomy support. Allie did *not* follow the plan Tyler had made with her, but the discussion with him helped her think through another framework for her footage: organizing it into a movie trailer. Using this concept, she became highly motivated editing her material around the goal of making viewers interested in a (hypothetical) full-length film. Allie also reported being motivated by wanting to prove to Tyler that she could achieve success *on her own*.

Importantly, Allie said this experience with her film was "a good thing because the next time [it happens] I'll be able to control it, and I won't be too nervous." She felt she had gained insights that would help her control anxiety and motivational disruptions in the future. We cannot verify whether Allie had actually become less vulnerable, but she expressed a phenomenon identified by resilience research: when people successfully overcome setbacks, it can lead to valuable social-emotional learning (Masten, 2013). Indeed, many youth in our research report learning resilience from these challenging episodes (Larson et al., (in press); Larson & Walker, 2006). Helping youth develop motivational resilience from overcoming difficult challenges is a deliberate pedagogical strategy in some programs (Priest & Gass, 2005).

Conclusion

In sum, youth conducting projects experience downturns in motivation that, in some cases, are severe enough to threaten continued motivation. However, most youth bounce back on their own or do so with skilled support from leaders. Moreover, we found evidence that the process of bouncing back and overcoming challenges can lead to valuable learning that helps youth control motivation.

Development of Sustained Motivation in Challenging Work

We turn now to the question of whether youth who do projects gain abilities to sustain motivation for the longer haul. What skills might teens develop or learn to help them remain engaged through distractions and downturns? Answers to these questions are important, not only for teens' projects in programs, but for the open-ended, real-world projects of adulthood that lie ahead in their lives (Csikszentmihalyi, 1990; Duckworth, 2016). We had reason to be optimistic. Research shows that adolescents develop an expanded future perspective and can learn to think systematically about how their present actions influence what happens in the minutes, days, and months ahead (Nurmi, 2004; Steinberg, 2014). Indeed, teens doing projects in programs learn skills to plan their work and anticipate future contingencies, including twists and turns (Heath, 1999; Larson & Angus, 2011). How might this expanded future perspective contribute to the development of sustained motivation? Youth in our research identified two ways: by developing personal investments in long-term goals and by learning techniques for regulating their motivation.

Development of Personal Investment in Goals

Investment in goals is known to be a significant contributor to stable motivation, especially when people have confidence that a goal is achievable (Eccles, 2005). Self-set goals are particularly powerful motivators (Bandura, 1991b). We found that many youth in programs became invested in self-set goals related to their work. In a major analysis of the TYDE data, Dawes and Larson (2011) identified this investment process as one of *forming a personal connection* to goals. Over time, these TYDE youth had formulated goals for their work that were personally meaningful – significant to their personal values, ambitions, and identity. Dawes and Larson (2011) describe this process as "convergence between self and the activity" (p. 263). It involved youth not just picking a goal but developing the self in ways that made the goal come alive with meaning.

Youth in TYDE reported that their increased motivation came from forming connections to three types of self-set goals (Dawes & Larson, 2011), and these three types were replicated in new analyses of the Pathways data.

First, we found that as youth developed skills and had success in their work, they became more invested in *experiencing competency* through their projects. For youth who were creating works of art, planning events, and growing a garden, it became a personally meaningful and motivating goal to achieve a high-quality outcome. Yesenia recounted how gaining skills in a graffiti arts program transformed her motivation: "When I was first starting, I was really hesitant in my abilities, and I couldn't do a fill or anything." But as she gained experience and skills with spray painting, that hesitancy receded, and she was able to plan a picture and know she would feel good about it. "Now I can put up a piece on a wall ... do my *own* pieces, and I'm proud of it." As a result, the episodes of low or disrupted motivation became less of a threat for Yesenia and other youth. As Devin Mitchell, the actress we started with, said: "Knowing the outcome will be good – that's what motivates me. Just picturing it all at the end and being satisfied with what I've done. That's what keeps me going." This ability for confidently "picturing" or visualizing a pathway to a personally satisfying goal outcome can be an important contributor to stable motivation in complex work (Bandura, 2006).

Second, as youth gained competence, some also reported becoming motivated by long-term *future goals* (e.g., for post-secondary education or adult employment) that were served by their program work and learning. Forming personal connections to these goals often involved youth doing identity work concurrently with the work of the program. They developed values, ambitions, and visions of future selves that converged with – and gave meaning to – their learning in the program (Dawes & Larson, 2011; Rickman, 2009).When asked what increased her motivation, Adalyn at Emerson theater, described this process:

> When I first started, it was something that I really enjoyed. I loved being on stage in middle school. Then I slowly realized that, "I'm decent at this. Maybe this is what I love doing, and I have a lot of passion for it. I feel like I've grown as a person, I've grown as a performer." That's when I realized I wanted to do it for the rest of my life and I wanted to go in a college and learn and just do more with it.

The third category of goals youth developed was altruistic: It involved *pursuing purpose*. Damon (2008) defines "purpose" as a goal "that is at the same time meaningful to the self and consequential to the world beyond the self" (p. 121). Youth in programs reported increased motivation when they experienced their actions as consequential to their communities or the people they served. At Nutrition Rocks, youth planned and ran a summer camp for children. Evelyn initially viewed the work as just tending children, but that changed:

> When I first started, I had this mindset: "It's just kids. You're just gonna do activities with them, and they're gonna go about their day." *It's not about that.* It's teaching kids how to live a healthier life, learn things they never learned before. And it just motivates you to do better for yourself and for them.

Evelyn came to see how her work influenced the children's future lives, and she became motivated by the conjoined goals of doing "better for yourself and for them."

Youth's development of goals contributes to sustained motivation, because it reduces dependence on immediate rewards and susceptibility to motivational downturns. Youth often cited these long-term goals as the thing that kept them going in the face of instrumental and motivational challenges in their work (Larson et al., (in press)). A significant takeaway in these findings is that formation of personal connections may need to come from youth's own *active processes* of building meaning. Staff in high-quality programs, however, support this meaning-making by encouraging youth to choose topics they feel passionate about and by helping youth use their expanding future perspective to explore connections between program work and life goals (Larson & Rusk, 2011; Smith et al., 2016a).

Learning Techniques for Regulating Motivation

Goals help youth persevere through downturns; we wondered if they also learned skills to *control* these downturns. Adolescents gain capabilities to develop meta-cognitive skills for understanding and regulating their own mental processes (Johnson et al., 2014; Steinberg, 2014), possibly including skills for influencing their motivation (Renninger & Hidi, 2016). We were interested in what youth in programs might learn for regulating motivation in projects – where challenges and setbacks can emerge unexpectedly.

We found that youth reported learning techniques that specifically addressed the causes of downturns discussed in the section on motivation flux. These included use of self-encouragements – aimed at directly raising their motivational state – and more nuanced strategies for regulating the person-situation interactions that influenced their state.[5]

Self-encouragements. Self-doubt was a frequent cause of motivational downturns, and the most frequent regulation technique youth learned was self-talk to rally their self-confidence and determination. They repeated words of encouragement to themselves: "try your best," "it depends on effort," and "there is nothing you can't do regardless of the situation." A number of youth reported picking up these encouragements from a leader. Findings in sports psychology suggests that this encouraging self-talk can aid motivation, partly by counteracting negative self-talk (Hardy, 2006). Javier recounted how early in the program: "I would say 'I can't do this,' and then I knew I couldn't. But I learned that I actually could, and now I know not to ever let myself down." He had learned that self-doubt easily became a self-fulfilling prophesy – but that he could countermand it. These youth appeared to be learning the positive or "optimistic" self-talk associated with grit (Duckworth, 2016).

Strategies for regulating the person-situation interaction. Fewer youth, mostly program veterans, reported learning strategies to regulate conditions in the *person-situation interaction* that disrupt their motivation. For example,

---

5 Findings come from a subset of Pathways youth who were asked what they had learned about "how to motivate yourself or keep your motivation going," including "when your motivation is low."

John said that, when his motivation was low, he had learned to: "Just analyze everything around me, just slow down everything, and do hundreds of little tests on whatever *I'm doing and the situation* (emphasis added)." He was analyzing conditions in his person-situation interactions. We didn't find out what John's "little tests" were or how he acted on them. Other youth, however, described two specific strategies for regulating person-situation conditions.

Regulating challenges to match skills. We previously found that overwhelming challenges were a frequent cause of downturns. Several youth described learning to control the challenges they were taking on, so as to be within their abilities. For example, in previous years, Xavier at High Definition had been overwhelmed when he finished filming and faced trying to organize hundreds of video segments. But he had developed strategies for this situation: "Try looking at it from a different way. Or break it down into parts so it doesn't seem like as much of a load on you." These strategies resemble the reframing techniques that Tyler at Reel Makers had used to help Allie deal with being overwhelmed. Xavier, an experienced filmmaker, had learned to reframe on his own.

Evelyn, who ran activities for children at Nutrition Rocks, had learned to *both* control challenges and elevate her use of skills. She said, "You learn what to expect out of yourself. What you can do, what you can't do. When do you need to stop? When has it gone overboard?" She had learned to restrain her tendency to get too ambitious and set challenges that were too high. At the same time, she had learned that working with children required using all her skills: "You always have to be on top of your game ... You can't slack off or they slack off ... You learn how to keep yourself up high." It appears that she had developed a meta-cognitive balancing act: keeping challenges manageable, but also devoting all the skills and effort she could.

Regulating emotions. Finally, many youth reported learning skills for regulating emotions (Rusk et al., 2013). They described gaining strategies to manage disruptive emotions; several learned strategies for avoiding the downward emotional spiral that can disrupt motivation. Dani at 4-H Shooting Sports had discovered (as Caleb mentioned earlier) that: "You miss a few targets in a row, and your motivation drops down really, really far." But (unlike Caleb) she had learned "to step away, take a deep breath, count to ten, and try again." This strategy, she found, helped her preempt the spiral of anxiety and self-doubt. We also found that many learned to *use* excitement, pride, and, sometimes, righteous anger as sources of motivation in their projects (Kirshner, et al., 2011; Larson & Brown, 2007; Rusk et al., 2013).

These youth appeared to be developing meta-cognitive strategies for managing the abstract conditions that influence motivation. These strategies included slowing down thoughts to analyze the issues affecting their motivation, adjusting the challenges they were trying to address, and understanding how emotions affect motivation. They also included recognizing that missing several targets in a row can make your motivation drop quickly and that taking a break can recharge your mind. Youth were developing tools to control their motivation. They were learning to use flexible meta-cognitive *structures* (i.e., models of person-situation processes) to help them sustain motivation in the *unstructured* situations of complex work.

Conclusion

Youth's development of goals and strategies is important, we think, because it represents youth's active process of constructing control over their motivation. But humility is warranted. We suspect goals and strategies are components of a larger set of overlapping processes that contribute to development of sustained self-motivation. These are likely to include coming to feel at home in the activity, gradual accumulation of experiences, gaining knowledge and skills, and developing individual interest and dispositions like grit (Duckworth, 2016).

Concluding Thoughts

This chapter has examined motivation from the inside-out: starting from teens' accounts of experiences that shaped their motivation. These accounts indicate that project-based youth programs are highly motivating, because they provide an environment with new and "different" values, norms, and ways of being. These include ways of participating in human relationships that are based on a shared ethos of mutual respect, trust, and principles of high-functioning communication. They also include new ways of acting – conducting long-term projects, plunging into the unknown, taking responsibility, and experiencing ups and downs and learning from them. This chapter suggests that, when environments support these ways of being and acting, adolescents become self-motivated and "intensely involved," have "fun," and invest themselves in the challenges and goals of the work.

Elsewhere we have argued that the high self-motivation youth experience in programs and projects may be a particularly valuable catalyst for social-emotional learning (Larson et al., 2017). Research shows that experiencing intrinsic motivation is associated with deeper cognitive processing, more strategy use, and more expansive and integrative reasoning (Larson & Rusk, 2011). Combined with high self-motivation, these active mental processes might help youth engage in the important social-emotional learning work of questioning assumptions, unpacking emotions, navigating knotty real-world challenges, and developing skills for action (Larson, 2011; Smith et al., 2016a).

The skills of frontline staff, we believe, are key to youth's self-motivation and the accompanying social-emotional learning. The day-to-day running of a project-based program is not a simple matter. The open-ended and challenging nature of youth's projects creates open-ended (emergent) challenges for staff as well. When do they step in to help youth? When do they "pump up" youth's motivation with encouragements – and when do they let youth take responsibility for their own motivation? Throughout the chapter, we have cited findings on effective practices, but all of these need to be adapted to specific situations (Larson & Rusk, 2011; Smith et al., 2016a). Kaplan et al. (2012) detail how educators need to be attuned and responsive to a myriad of contextual dynamics that may affect students' motivation (e.g., youth who are influenced by different motivational processes or interpret information from different frames of reference). A major challenge with adolescents is how to balance providing the right amount of structure and guidance *with* granting youth latitude for their agency and learning from experience. We have found that experienced program leaders have the situational knowledge to achieve this (Larson et al., 2016).

The state of scientific knowledge on motivation in youth programs is limited. Much work needs to be done to follow up on the findings here and to better understand variations across youth and types of programs and projects. A valuable line of study would be intensive time-sampling research on the fluctuations in youth's motivation and how they are related to episodes in youth's work and to the actions of leaders. Comparison of "expert" and novice leaders can be a helpful starting point for understanding the application of effective strategies. Further interview and observational research could lead to better understanding of the trade-offs associated with different strategies.

References

Akiva, T. & Horner, C. G. (2016). Adolescent motivation to attend youth programs: A mixed-methods investigation. *Applied Developmental Science, 20*(4), 278–93. doi: 10.1080/10888691.2015.1127162.

Bandura, A. (1991a). Anticipatory and self-reactive mechanisms. In R. A. Dienstbier (Ed.), *Nebraska Symposium on Motivation, Perspectives on Motivation* (Vol. *38*). Lincoln, NE: University of Nebraska Press.

Bandura, A. (1991b). Social cognitive theory of self-regulation. *Organizational Behavior and Human Decision Processes, 50*(2), 248–87. doi: 10.1016/0749-5978(91)90022-L.

Bandura, A. (2006). Toward a psychology of human agency. *Perspectives on Psychological Science, 1*(2), 164–80. doi: 10.1111/j.1745-6916.2006.00011.x.

Barron, B., Schwartz, D., Vye, N., Moore, A., Petrosino, A., Zech, L., & Brandsford, J. (1998). Doing with understanding: Lessons from research on problem and project-based learning. *Journal of the Learning Sciences, 7*(3), 271–311. doi: 10.1207/s15327809jls0703&4_2.

Baumeister, R. F. & Leary, M. R. (1995). The need to belong: Desire for interpersonal attachments as a fundamental human motivation. *Psychological Bulletin, 117*(3), 497–529. doi: 10.1037/0033-2909.117.3.497.

Bevan, B. & Michalchik, V. (2013). Where it gets interesting: Competing models of STEM learning after school. *Afterschool Matters, 17*, 1–8.

Blumenfeld, P. C., Soloway, E., Marx, R. W., Krajcik, J. S., Guzdial, M., & Palincsar, A., (1991). Motivating project-based learning: Sustaining the doing, supporting the learning. *Educational Psychologist, 26*(3–4), 369–98. doi: 10.1080/00461520.1991.9653139.

Blyth, D., Olson, B., & Walker, K. (2015). Ways of being: A model for social & emotional learning. *University of Minnesota Extension: Youth Development Issue Brief*. Retrieved from www.ostrc.org/newsletter/documents/WaysofBeing_000.pdf.

Carver, C. S. & Scheier, M. F. (2007). Feedback processes in the simultaneous regulation of action and affect. In J. Y. Shah & W. L. Gardner (Eds.), *Handbook of motivation science* (1st ed., pp. 308–24). New York, NY: Guilford.

Catalano, R. F., Toumbourou, J. W., & Hawkins, J. D. (2014). Positive youth development in the United States: History, efficacy, and links to moral and character education. In L. Nucci, D. Narvaez, & T. Krettenauer (Eds.), *Handbook of moral and character education* (2nd ed., pp. 423–40). New York, NY: Routledge.

Charmaz, K. (2014). *Constructing grounded theory* (2nd ed.). Los Angeles, CA: Sage.

Cohen, G. L. & Steele, C. M. (2002). A barrier of mistrust: How negative stereotypes affect cross-race mentoring. In J. Aronson (Ed.), *Improving academic achievement* (pp. 303–27). New York, NY: Emerald. doi: 10.1016/B978-012064455-1/50018-X.

Csikszentmihalyi, M. (1990). *Flow: The psychology of optimal experience*. New York, NY: Harper Perennial.

Csikszentmihalyi, M. Rathunde, K., & Whalen, S. (1993). *Talented teenagers: A longitudinal study of their development*. New York, NY: Cambridge University Press.

Damon, W. (2008). *The path to purpose: Helping our children find their calling in life*. New York, NY: Free Press.

Dawes, N. P. & Larson, R. W. (2011). How youth get engaged: Grounded-theory research on motivational development in organized youth programs. *Developmental Psychology*, *47*(1), 259–69. doi: 10.1037/a0020729.

Deutsch, N. L. & Jones, J. N. (2008). "Show me an ounce of respect": Respect and authority in adult-youth relationships in after-school programs. *Journal of Adolescent Research*, *23*(6), 667–88. doi: 10.1177/0743558408322250.

Diaz, L., Larson, R. W., Armstrong, J., & Perry, S. C. (2015). *A case study of youth learning to lead: The power of iterative cycles of situated learning*. Paper presented at Annual Meetings of AERA, Chicago.

Donovan, M. S. (2013). Generating improvement through research and development in education systems. *Science*, *340*(6130), 317–19. doi: 10.1126/science.1236180.

Duckworth, A. (2016). *Grit: The power of passion and perseverance*. New York, NY: Scribner.

Eccles, J. S. (2005). Studying gender and ethnic differences in participation in math, physical science, and information technology. *New Directions for Child and Adolescent Development*, *2005*(110), 7–14. doi: 10.1002/cd.146.

Eccles, J. S. & Roeser, R. W. (2009). Schools, academic motivation, and stage-environment fit. In R. M. Lerner & L. Steinberg (Eds.), *Handbook of adolescent psychology* (3rd ed., Vol. *1*, pp. 404–34). Hoboken, NJ: Wiley. doi: 10.1002/9780470479193.adlpsy001013.

Fisher, L. J. (2013). Motivational spiral models (MSM): Common and distinct motivations in context. *SpringerPlus*, *2*(1), 565. doi: 10.1186/2193-1801-2-565.

Griffith, A. N. & Larson, R. W. (2016). Why trust matters: How confidence in leaders transforms what adolescents gain from youth programs. *Journal of Research on Adolescence*, *26*(4), 790–804. doi: 10.1111/jora.12230.

Griffith, A. N., Larson, R. W., & Johnson, H. E. (2017). How trust grows: Teenagers' accounts of forming trust in youth program staff. *Qualitative Psychology*. Advance online publication. http://dx.doi.org/10.1037/qup0000090.

Halpern, R. (2009). *The means to grow up: Reinventing apprenticeship as a developmental support in adolescence*. New York, NY: Routledge. doi: 10.4324/9780203885970.

Hardy, J. (2006). Speaking clearly: A critical review of the self-talk literature. *Psychology of Sport and Exercise*, *7*(1), 81–97. doi: 10.1016/j.psychsport.2005.04.002.

Heath, S. B. (1999). Dimensions of language development: Lessons from older children. In A. S. Masten (Ed.), *Cultural processes in child development: The Minnesota Symposia on Child Psychology* (Vol. *29*, pp. 59–75). Mahwah, NY: Erlbaum.

Johnson, E. L., Munro, S. E., & Bunge, S. A. (2014). Development of neural networks supporting goal-directed behavior. In P. D. Zelazo & M. D. Sera (Eds.), *Developing cognitive control processes: Mechanisms, implications, and interventions: Minnesota Symposia on Child Psychology* (Vol. *37*, pp. 21–54). Hoboken, NJ: Wiley. doi: 10.1002/9781118732373.

Kaplan, A., Katz, I., & Flum, H. (2012). Motivation theory in educational practice: Knowledge claims, challenges, and future directions. In K. R. Harris, S. Graham, & T. Urdan (Eds.), *APA educational psychology handbook* (pp. 165–94). Washington, DC: American Psychological Association.

Kaplan, A. & Maehr, M. L. (2007). The contributions and prospects of goal orientation theory. *Educational Psychology Review*, *19*(2), 141–84. doi: 10.1007/s10648-006-9012-5.

Kirshner, B., Pozzoboni, K., & Jones, H. (2011). Learning how to manage bias: A case study of youth participatory action research. *Applied Developmental Science*, *15*(3), 140–55. doi: 10.1080/10888691.2011.587720.

Larson, R. W. (2000). Toward a psychology of positive youth development. *American Psychologist*, *55*(1), 170–83. doi: 10.1037//0003-066X.55.1.170.

Larson, R. W. (2011). Positive development in a disorderly world. *Journal of Research on Adolescence*, *21*(2), 317–34. doi: 10.1111/j.1532-7795.2010.00707.x.

Larson, R. W. & Angus, R. M. (2011). Adolescents' development of skills for agency in youth programs: Learning to think strategically. *Child Development*, *82*(1), 277–94. doi: 10.1111/j.1467-8624.2010.01555.x.

Larson, R. W. & Brown, J. R. (2007). Emotional development in adolescence: What can be learned from a high school theater program? *Child Development*, *78*(4), 1083–99. doi: 10.1111/j.1467-8624.2007.01054.x.

Larson, R. W. & Dawes, N. P. (2015). How to cultivate adolescents' motivation: Effective strategies employed by the professional staff of American youth programs. In S. Joseph (Ed.), *Positive psychology in practice* (pp. 313–26). New York, NY: Wiley.

Larson, R., Raffaelli, M., Guzman, S., Salusky, I., Orson, C., & Kenzer, A., (in press). The important (but neglected) developmental value of roles: Findings from youth programs. *Developmental Psychology*.

Larson, R. W. & Hansen, D. (2005). The development of strategic thinking: Learning to impact human systems in a youth activism program. *Human Development*, *48*, 327–49. doi: 10.1159/000088251.

Larson, R. W., Izenstark, D., Rodriguez, G., & Perry, S. C. (2016). The art of restraint: How experienced program leaders use their authority to support youth agency. *Journal of Research on Adolescence*, *26*(4), 845–63. doi: 10.1111/jora.12234.

Larson, R. W., Jensen, L., Kang, H., Griffith, A. N., & Rompala, V. (2012). Peer groups as a crucible of positive value development in a global world. In G. Trommsdorff & X. Chen (Eds.), *Values, religion, and culture in adolescent development* (pp. 164–87). New York, NY: Cambridge University Press.

Larson, R. W. & Richards, M. H. (1991). Boredom in the middle school years: Blaming schools versus blaming students. *American Journal of Education*, *99*(4), 418–43. doi: 10.1086/443992.

Larson, R. W. & Rusk, N. (2011). Intrinsic motivation and positive development. In R. M. Lerner, J. V. Lerner, & J. B. Benson (Eds.), *Advances in child development and behavior* (Vol. *41*, pp. 89–130). Oxford: Elsevier. doi: 10.1016/B978-0-12-386492-5.00005-1.

Larson, R. W. & Walker, K. C. (2006). Learning about the "real world" in an urban arts youth program. *Journal of Adolescent Research*, *21*(3), 244–68. doi: 10.1177/0743558405285824.

Masten, A. S. (2013). Risk and resilience in development. In P. D. Zelazo (Ed.), *Oxford handbook of developmental psychology* (Vol. 2, pp. 579–607). New York, NY: Oxford Press. doi: 10.1093/oxfordhb/9780199958474.013.0023.

McLaughlin, M. W., Irby, M. A., & Langman, J. (1994). *Urban sanctuaries: Neighborhood organizations in the lives and futures of inner-city youth*. San Francisco, CA: Jossey-Bass.

Nurmi, J. E. (2004). Socialization and self-development: Channeling, selection, adjustment, and reflection. In R. M. Lerner & L. Steinberg (Eds.), *Handbook of adolescent psychology* (2nd ed., pp. 85–124). Hoboken, NJ: Wiley. doi: 10.1002/9780471726746.ch4.

Orson, C. (2018). *Reframing: How staff help youth overcome episodes of anxiety in youth programs*. Masters Thesis. Urbana-Champaign, IL: University of Illinois.

Pekrun, R., Frenzel, A. C., Goetz, T., & Perry, R. P. (2007). The control-value theory of achievement emotions: An integrative approach to emotions in education. In P. A. Schutz & R. Pekrun (Eds.), *Emotion in education* (pp. 13–36). Amsterdam: Academic Press.

Priest, S. & Gass, M. A. (2005). *Effective leadership in adventure programming* (2nd ed.). Champaign, IL: Human Kinetics.

Renninger, K. A. & Hidi, S. E. (2016). *The power of interest for motivation and engagement*. New York, NY: Routledge. doi: 10.4324/9781315771045.

Rickman, A. N. (2009). *A challenge to the notion of youth passivity: Adolescents' development of career direction through youth programs*. Urbana-Champaign, IL: University of Illinois.

Roth, J. L. & Brooks-Gunn, J. (2003a). What exactly is a youth development program? Answers from research and practice. *Applied Developmental Science, 7*(2), 94–111. doi: 10.1207/S1532480XADS0702.

Roth, J. L. & Brooks-Gunn, J. (2003b). Youth development programs and healthy development: A review and next steps. In D. Romer (Ed.), *Reducing adolescent risk: Toward an integrated approach* (pp. 355–65). Thousand Oaks, CA: Sage.

Rusk, N., Larson, R. W., Raffaelli, M., Walker, K., Washington, L., Gutierrez, V., ... Cole Perry, S. (2013). Positive youth development in organized programs: How teens learn to manage emotions. In C. Proctor & P. A. Linley (Eds.), *Research, applications, and interventions for children and adolescents: A positive psychology perspective* (pp. 247–61). Dordrecht: Springer Netherlands. doi: 10.1007/978-94-007-6398-2_15.

Ryan, R. M. & Deci, E. L. (2000). Self-determination theory and the facilitation of intrinsic motivation, social development, and well-being. *American Psychologist, 55*(1), 68–78. doi:10.1037/0003-066X.55.1.68.

Salusky, I., Larson, R. W., Griffith, A. N., Wu, J., Raffaelli, M., Sugimura, N., & Guzman, M. (2014). How adolescents develop responsibility: What can be learned from youth programs. *Journal of Research on Adolescence, 24*(3), 417–30. doi: 10.1111/jora.12118.

Shweder, R. A., Goodnow, J. J., Hatano, G., LeVine, R. A., Markus, H. R., & Miller, P. J. (2006). The cultural psychology of development: One mind, many mentalities. In W. Damon & R. Lerner (Gen. Eds.) & R. Lerner (Vol. Ed.), *Handbook of child psychology: Vol. 1. Theoretical models of human development* (6th ed., pp. 716–792). Hoboken, NJ: Wiley. doi: 10.1002/9780470147658.chpsy0113.

Smith, C., McGovern, G., Larson, R. W., Hillaker, B., & Peck, S. C. (2016a). *Preparing youth to thrive: Promising practices for social and emotional learning.* Washington, DC: David P. Weikart Center for Youth Program Quality at the Forum for Youth Investment. Retrieved from http://selpractices.org.

Smith, C., McGovern, G., Peck, S. C., Larson, R. W., & Roy, L. (2016b). *Preparing youth to thrive: Methodology and findings from the Social and Emotional Learning Challenge.* Washington, DC: David P. Weikart Center for Youth Program Quality at the Forum for Youth Investment. Retrieved from http://selpractices.org.

Steinberg, L. (2014). *Age of opportunity: Lessons from the new science of adolescence.* Boston, MA: Houghton Mifflin Harcourt.

Strauss, A. L. & Corbin, J. (2008). *Basics of qualitative research.* (3rd ed.) Thousand Oaks, CA: Sage.

Vandell, D. L., Larson, R. W., Mahoney, J. L., & Watts, T. W. (2015). Children's organized activities. In M. H. Bornstein, T. Leventhal, & R. Lerner (Eds.), *Handbook of child psychology and developmental science* (pp. 1–40). New York, NY: Wiley. doi: 10.1002/9781118963418.childpsy408.

Vandell, D. L., Reisner, E. R., Pierce, K. M., Brown, B. B., Lee, D., Bolt, D., & Pechman, E. M., (2006). *The study of promising after-school programs: Examination of longer term outcomes after two years of program experiences.* Retrieved from http://gseweb.oit.uci.edu/childcare/pdf/afterschool/PP Examination in Year 3.pdf.

Walker, J., Marczak, M., Blyth, D., & Borden, L. (2005). Designing youth development programs: Toward a theory of developmental intentionality. In J. L. Mahoney, R. W. Larson, & J. S. Eccles (Eds.), *Organized activities as contexts of development: Extracurricular activities, after-school and community programs* (pp. 399–418). Mahwah, NJ: Erlbaum.

Wood, D., Larson, R. W., & Brown, J. R. (2009). How adolescents come to see themselves as more responsible through participation in youth programs. *Child Development, 80*(1), 295–309. doi: 10.1111/j.1467-8624.2008.01260.x.

Zimmerman, B. J. & Campillo, M. (2003). Motivating self-regulated problem solvers. In J. E. Davidson & R. J. Sternberg (Eds.), *The psychology of problem solving.* (pp. 233–62) Cambridge: Cambridge University Press.

PART II

Rewards, Incentives, and Choice

6 Neuroscientific and Psychological Approaches to Incentives

Commonality and Multifaceted Views

Kou Murayama

Abstract: While research on neuroscience posits that intrinsic and extrinsic incentives involve a single, common psychological process based on a reinforcement learning model (forming a "commonality view" on motivation), research in psychology has made a strong distinction between these two types of incentives (forming a "multifaceted view" on motivation), often even viewing them as competitive. Although they are not necessarily contradictory, I argue that these two meta-theoretical views have biased and prevented our comprehensive understanding of motivation and its relation to learning. I suggest ways that these different perspectives can inform each other, contributing to our broader understanding of human motivation and learning. These examples include the effects of reward on learning, the way people can transform one type of motivation to another, and a rewarding view for effort, challenge, and negative feedback. The arguments presented in this chapter underscore the vital importance of cross-disciplinary work on motivation and learning in future studies.

Motivation constitutes a fundamental element in human functioning. In fact, both in neuroscience and psychology, the topic of motivation has attracted considerable attention, and researchers have provided a variety of views and theories on motivation that attempt to reveal the nature of human motivated behavior. However, when one digs into the literature of motivation, both in psychology and neuroscience, one notices a sobering fact: The way that motivation is conceptualized and analyzed is fundamentally different between neuroscience and psychology (Braver et al., 2014; Reeve & Lee, 2012). Indeed, as you will see, motivation research in psychology and in neuroscience has been developed relatively independently within the respective disciplines, with little communication between them. They now seem to have very different, or even, apparently, opposite views and languages on motivation. This is puzzling, because

This research was supported by a Marie Curie Career Integration Grant (CIG630680), JSPS KAKENHI (15H05401 and 16H06406), a grant from the American Psychological Foundation (the F. J. McGuigan Early Career Investigator Prize), a Leverhulme Trust Project Grant (RPG-2016-146), and a Leverhulme Research Leadership Award (RL-2016-030).

both psychology and neuroscience have attempted to understand the same concepts of motivation (Hidi, 2016).

The aim of this chapter is to highlight and discuss such different meta-theoretical views on motivation between psychology and neuroscience, especially focusing on the distinction between intrinsic and extrinsic incentives. In addition, I attempt to accommodate these meta-theoretical views, and discuss the implications and importance of being aware of these views to comprehensively understand human motivation and learning.

Motivation in Neuroscience: A Commonality View

Until recently, most research in neuroscience had focused on extrinsic rewards or incentives (i.e., tangible incentives such as food, juice, and money) to empirically investigate motivation (Berridge, 2004; Niv et al., 2006). That is, to examine the role of motivation, researchers manipulated the amount of food, juice, or money for a task and investigated the neural correlates associated with such extrinsic incentives. These studies repeatedly showed that extrinsic rewards are primarily represented and valued in the so-called reward network, especially in the ventral striatum (Haber & Knutson, 2010; O'Doherty, 2004; Rangel & Hare, 2010; Shohamy, 2011; other brain areas of this network include the ventral tegmental area and the orbitofrontal cortex). In fact, using functional magnetic resonance imaging (fMRI) and positron emission tomography (PET), researchers revealed that the striatum showed increased activation in response to a variety of extrinsic rewards (Berns et al., 2001; Delgado et al., 2005; Knutson & Greer, 2008; McCabe et al., 2013; O'Doherty et al., 2001; Valentin & O'Doherty, 2009).

Importantly, recent neuroimaging work has also presented evidence that the same brain area shows activation in response to *intrinsic* rewards or incentives[1] – that is, incentives that are abstract and do not have tangible entity. For example, research observed activation in the ventral striatum in response to positive task feedback, even when no tangible reward was provided (Campbell-Meiklejohn et al., 2010; Daniel & Pollmann, 2010, 2012; Han et al., 2010; Murayama et al., 2015; Tricomi et al., 2006). Several studies also indicated that the striatum is involved with representing and updating the value of other various forms of intrinsic rewards. For example, Salimpoor et al., (2011) showed that the pleasurable feeling ("chill" experience) participants experienced while

---

1 Incentives often refer to motivational properties of a stimulus and are distinguished from rewards (e.g., Berridge, 2001). In this chapter, however, I use the terms rather interchangeably.

listening to their favorite choice of music was associated with activation in the ventral striatum (the nucleus accumbens). Koepp et al. (1998) found that playing enjoyable video games is associated with dopaminergic activation in the ventral striatum (see also Klasen et al., 2012). In fact, the ventral striatum is one of the brain areas implicated in the hedonic hotspot, which is responsible for so-called "liking" responses or subjective feelings of pleasantness (Kringelbach & Berridge, 2016). The reward network has also been shown to be related to other various types of intrinsic incentives, such as curiosity (Gruber et al., 2014; Jepma et al., 2012; Kang et al., 2009), aesthetic experience (Aharon et al., 2001; Pearce et al., 2016), and social value (Davey et al., 2010; Izuma, 2012; Izuma et al., 2008; Jones et al., 2011; Lin et al., 2011). Some other researchers also took the activation in the reward network as evidence that a certain type of behavior acts as an intrinsic reward. For example, Leotti and Delgado (2011) showed that the opportunity of making a choice activates the reward network in the brain, indicating that personal choice serves as an intrinsic reward or incentive (for reviews, see Leotti et al., 2010; Murayama, Izuma, et al., 2016).

These studies together led researchers to an important observation about the neural process of human motivation that I shall call a *commonality view*: All types of rewards, including both extrinsic and intrinsic rewards, are processed in the common brain network, indicating a common single mechanism to produce motivated behavior (Figure 6.1). In fact, based on the empirical studies discussed above, researchers have considered the ventral striatum as the hub of the human valuation process, converting and integrating different types of incentives onto a common scale (Dayan & Niv, 2008; Montague & Berns, 2002; Seymour & McClure, 2008). A theoretical background underpinning the commonality view is reinforcement learning (RL), which has dominated the neuroscience literature on motivational decision-making behavior over the past decade (Daw & Doya, 2006; Dayan & Niv, 2008; Rushworth, et al., 2009; Schultz et al., 1997). The RL was a computational framework that was originally developed to enable reward-guided decision-making in artificial systems (Sutton & Barto, 1998), but gained considerable attention from neuroscience because accumulating evidence suggested that RL algorithms appeared to be instantiated in neural mechanisms (Daw & Doya, 2006; Dayan & Niv, 2008; Kakade & Dayan, 2002). In (so-called "model free") RL, agents are supposed to learn the values of different actions in different states through trial and error. Thus, rewards are treated as the events that update the values of actions and states. Importantly, because RL represents the values as abstract entities on an arbitrary metric (i.e., "common currency"; Montague & Berns, 2002), specific identities of rewards (e.g., "can I get a juice or a chocolate if I make an action?") do not need to be encoded. In other words, RL concerns the outcome-general value

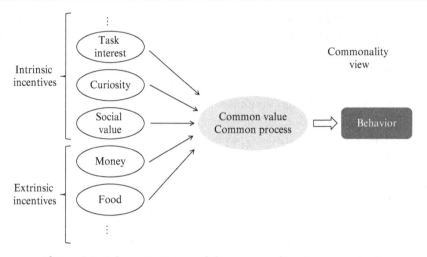

Figure 6.1. *Schematic picture of the commonality view on motivation*

that integrated different types of rewards (e.g., food, juice, intrinsic pleasantness; Daw et al., 2005; Niv et al., 2006; Niv & Schoenbaum, 2008). Reinforcement learning fits nicely with the empirical findings that the ventral striatum is similarly responsive to different types of incentives, presumably the common currency; the neuroscientific findings and RL have jointly shaped the commonality view of motivation in neuroscience.

Motivation in Psychology: A Multifaceted View

In some theories of behaviorism in psychology, the concept of motivation was incorporated with the aim to better explain behavior (Berridge, 2004; Dickinson & Balleine, 2002). Different early theories have somewhat different ideas of motivation, such as drive (Hull, 1943) and incentive motivation (Bindra, 1974; Bolles, 1972), but one commonality is that they tend to assume a single motivational system in learning models, bearing resemblance to the commonality view in neuroscience. A big paradigmatic change, however, came in the 1970s and 1980s, when cognitive revolution and humanistic psychology dethroned behaviorism and operant learning theory, and a number of "contemporary" theories of motivation were proposed. These theories initially focused on documenting motivational phenomena that cannot be reduced to a single learning mechanism, emphasizing the qualitative difference among different types of motivation. This historical background shaped a meta-theoretical perspective on motivation that I shall call a *multifaceted view*, which is in marked contrast to the commonality view in neuroscience. The multifaceted view presumes that different motivation elicits behavior through different processes. In other words, the multifaceted view supposes

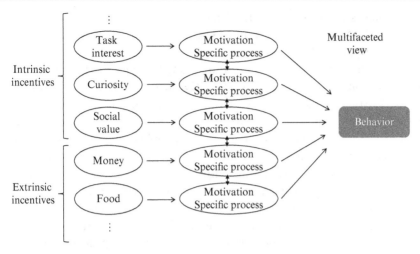

Figure 6.2. *Schematic picture of the multifaceted view on motivation*

that human motivated behavior is not governed by a unitary process (such as RL), but is a function of several unique motivational processes that interact with each other (Figure 6.2).

One hallmark of the multifaceted view is the distinction between *extrinsic motivation* and *intrinsic motivation*. Extrinsic motivation refers to the motivation driven by extrinsic incentives such as money, whereas intrinsic motivation is motivation activated by intrinsic incentives such as task pleasure and curiosity (Deci & Ryan, 1985). Unlike the neuroscientific literature, researchers in psychology have argued that they are qualitatively different types of motivation and should involve different psychological processes. Of course, this is not the only distinction that is made in psychology – indeed, contemporary theories of motivation in psychology propose myriad types of motivation in human behavior (which commonly correspond to different types of intrinsic incentives). For example, in the literature of social psychology, Baumeister and Leary (1995) argued that the need to belong (i.e., the motivation to form and maintain interpersonal relationships) is one of the fundamental motivations in human functioning, playing a unique role to regulate human behavior. In educational psychology, researchers have posited that learners have qualitatively different types of goals and motives, such as the distinction between mastery goals (i.e., motivation to develop one's own competence) and performance goals (i.e., motivation to compete with other people; Ames, 1992; Murayama et al., 2012). The list of motivational constructs in psychology is too long to name here, but other popular motivation-relevant constructs commonly discussed in textbooks include self-enhancement motive (Sedikides & Strube, 1997); achievement motive (McClelland et al., 1989); self-efficacy (Bandura, 1997); approach-avoidance motivation (Elliot, 2008); locus of control or control belief (Rotter, 1966; Skinner,

1996); mind-sets (or theory of intelligence; Dweck, 1999); and needs for competence, relatedness, and autonomy (which are often called basic psychological needs; Ryan & Deci, 2000).

One of the most provocative examples supporting the multifaceted view of motivation is the *undermining effect* (Deci, 1971; Deci et al., 1999; Ryan et al., 1983) – also called the "motivation crowding-out effect" (Camerer & Hogarth, 1999; Frey & Jegen, 2001) or the "over justification effect" (Lepper et al., 1973) – a phenomenon in which people's intrinsic motivation is *decreased* after receiving performance-contingent extrinsic rewards. In a typical experiment of the undermining effect, participants are randomly divided into an extrinsic reward group and a control group, and both groups work on an interesting (i.e., intrinsically motivating) task. Participants in the extrinsic reward group obtain (or expect) extrinsic rewards contingent on their performance, whereas participants in the control group do not. After the session, participants are left to engage in any activity, including more of the target task if they wish, for a brief period in which they believe they are no longer being observed (the "free-choice period"). A number of studies found that the extrinsic reward group spent significantly *less* time than the control group engaging in the target activity during the free-choice period, providing evidence that extrinsic rewards undermine intrinsic motivation for the task (Deci et al., 1999; Tang & Hall, 1995; Wiersma, 1992). This is a counterintuitive phenomenon (Murayama et al., 2016) and seems to support the idea that intrinsic motivation and extrinsic motivation are qualitatively different, or even competitive. In fact, RL presumes that performance-based extrinsic rewards monotonically increase the value of behavior, making people motivated to perform that behavior again. However, the undermining effect shows that this does not seem to apply to intrinsically motivated behavior, indicating a unique motivational mechanism associated with intrinsic motivation. Such special mechanisms pose an inconsistency with the commonality view.

Another line of evidence that supports the multifaceted view is *outcome discrimination*, where researchers claim that two motivational constructs are qualitatively different if these types of motivation lead to different outcomes. For example, using a longitudinal survey study that tracks students' mathematics achievement over years, Murayama et al. (2013) showed that extrinsic motivation (as assessed by self-reported questions) predicts the concurrent math achievement but not the growth of achievement, whereas intrinsic motivation predicts long-term growth but not the concurrent achievement (see also Murayama & Elliot, 2011; Vansteenkiste et al., 2005). A recent meta-analysis also showed that intrinsic motivation predicts the quality (e.g., creativity) of performance more than the quantity (e.g., the number of tasks solved) of performance, whereas extrinsic motivation mostly predicts the quantity of performance (Cerasoli et al., 2014). These double-dissociations of the outcome variables predicted by respective motivation suggest that these types of motivation work differently in learning. Even beyond the distinction of intrinsic motivation and extrinsic motivation, outcome differentiation (using either behavioral experiments or survey methods) is the gold standard in the literature of psychology to claim that one type of motivation is qualitatively different from the other. For example, to claim that implicit and self-attributed motives represent different motivational constructs, McClelland et al. (1989) presented evidence that implicit motives predict spontaneous and automatic behavior patterns, whereas self-attributed motives predict deliberate choice and behavior (for other examples, see Burton et al., 2006; Elliot & Harackiewicz, 1996).

Opposing Views?

I have pointed out that there have been seemingly opposing views on how to conceptualize motivation – the commonality view in neuroscience and the multifaceted view in psychology. I would like, however, to point out that this is a meta-theoretical difference, and at the level of implementation, these views are not contradictory. The commonality view concerns people's decision-making processes, and in our daily life, we frequently face different decision options that are incommensurable. Sometimes we may need to compare the values of different types of incentives, such as extrinsic incentives and intrinsic incentives (e.g., "should I work for money or take a break for leisure?"). One potential solution to such a situation is to transform the qualitatively different values of these options onto a common value metric (common currency) so that we can easily compare them and make a decision (e.g., "I currently feel that the value of taking a break is more precious than the value of working to obtain extra money"). Given the number of decisions (at different levels) we have to make every moment, it is reasonable that humans are equipped with the capacity to align incommensurable values, however idiosyncratically and imperfectly, onto a common metric (Levy & Glimcher, 2012; Seymour & McClure, 2008). From this perspective, the idea that extrinsic and intrinsic incentives share common reward processing is essential to understanding the human decision-making process in complex environments.

However, this is only the downstream of the entire decision-making process. Intrinsic and extrinsic incentives are obviously different in many facets. At a surface level, extrinsic incentives have tangible sensory properties, whereas intrinsic incentives are not visible and do not have specific sensory properties. Many extrinsic incentives can physically be consumed, but intrinsic incentives are basically subjective, making it difficult to define the consumption. Intrinsic and extrinsic incentives also evoke different emotional and memory processes. For example, intrinsic incentives often involve the process of self-concept and, thus, may be related more to the self-evaluative emotions (e.g., self-esteem). Given these various differences between intrinsic and extrinsic incentives in the

	Session 1	Free-choice Period	Session 2	Free-choice Period (follow-up)
Control group	**No performance-based Reward**	Intrinsic motivation assessment	**No performance-based reward**	Follow-up assessment
Reward group	*Performance-based Reward*	Intrinsic motivation assessment	**No performance-based reward**	Follow-up assessment

Scanning   Scanning

Figure 6.3. *Basic procedure of Murayama et al. (2010)*

pre-decision processes, it is not surprising that these incentives have different behavioral and psychological consequences. Motivation is not a single entity but a process by which activities are instigated and sustained (Pintrich & Schunk, 2002), and when we consider motivation as a process in our behavioral regulation, the commonality and multifaceted views are no longer incompatible.

In fact, more recent models in neuroscience and computational modeling incorporate different types of incentives more explicitly while maintaining the idea of common currency. For example, model-based RL, an extension of the previously explained RL (often called "model-free" RL), assumes that agents encode the information regarding the identity of incentives (e.g., "do I get a juice or a chocolate if I make an action?"), as well as the general value, on a common metric, making it possible to distinguish motivated behavior guided by different incentives (Balleine et al., 2008; Daw et al., 2005; McDannald et al., 2012; Niv et al., 2006; Sutton & Barto, 1998). Some researchers proposed computational models of learning that incorporate different types of intrinsic incentives, such as information search (Oudeyer & Kaplan, 2009; Oudeyer et al., 2016). Although there has been a limited number of empirical studies utilizing these models, they do indicate that the commonality view and the multifaceted view of motivation should be considered as complementary, rather than competitive.

An fMRI study that examined neural correlates of the undermining effect also gives some insights into this idea. In Murayama et al.'s (2010) study (see Figure 6.3), brain activation was compared between two groups that both played a simple computer game called the stopwatch task. In the first session, one group received performance-based extrinsic rewards (money), while the other group played the same game but did not receive performance-based extrinsic rewards. The fMRI analysis showed that both groups of participants exhibited increased activation in the striatum (i.e., one of the reward areas), but the activation was especially salient for the participants in the reward group, indicating that these participants were more motivated for the task. After the session, participants were asked to wait alone for the next session in a small room, where they could play the stopwatch task

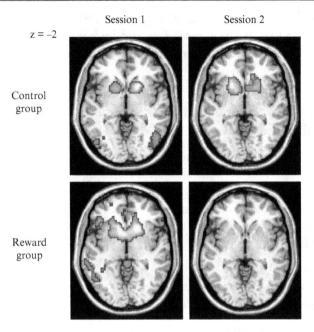

Figure 6.4. *Brain activation in response to success feedback in comparison to failure feedback*

with a computer if they wanted. Unbeknownst to the participants, their voluntary play with the stopwatch task during this free-choice period was recorded.

Consistent with the previous findings, the behavioral results showed the undermining effect – participants in the reward group showed *less* voluntary engagement in the task (i.e., less intrinsic motivation for the task) than those in the control group. In the second session, to track the brain activation associated with the observed undermining effect, both groups of participants played with the task inside the scanner without performance-based extrinsic rewards (like the free-choice period). The results showed stark contrast with the first session. Whereas the activation in the striatum was sustained in the control group, the reward group no longer exhibited activation in the reward areas, which mirrors the behavioral undermining effect (Figure 6.4).

These findings apparently support the multifaceted view, as extrinsic rewards worked in competition with intrinsic motivation. The findings are, however, also consistent with the commonality view, as both extrinsic incentives (the first session in the reward group) and intrinsic motivation (both sessions in the control group) seem to be represented by the common striatal area. These results indicate that the dichotomy of the commonality view versus the multifaceted view is inaccurate, or even misleading, for understanding the nature of the human motivational process. The study clearly showed that extrinsic incentives can undermine people's intrinsic motivation (for the discussion of potential underlying mechanism, see Deci et al., 1999), but this does not contradict the fact that extrinsic incentives and intrinsic incentives activate the shared reward network to represent the common value.

What Are the Implications for Studying Motivation and Learning?

Although the commonality and multifaceted views are not necessarily contradictory, it is important to notice that these different meta-theoretical perspectives have influenced and shaped our way of approaching, conceptualizing, and empirically testing motivation. In fact, recognizing these meta-theoretical views makes one aware of some implicit assumptions and biases underlying the current research on motivation and its implications for learning.

Implications of the Commonality View for Psychological Research on Motivation

In the research of psychology (i.e., multifaceted view), there have been arguments that intrinsic motivation and extrinsic motivation are qualitatively different or even antagonistic. In light of the commonality view, however, this idea may be in danger of overlooking some important commonalities between these types of motivation (Hidi, 2016; Murayama, FitzGibbon, & Sakaki, 2018). For instance, recent research on cognitive neuroscience has shown that extrinsic rewards facilitate long-term consolidation of learning through the link between the dopaminergic reward system (e.g., the striatum) and the hippocampal memory system in the brain (Adcock et al., 2006; Murty & Adcock, 2014; Shohamy & Adcock, 2010; Wittmann et al., 2005). Several behavioral studies also provided supportive evidence for this hypothesis (Mather & Schoeke, 2011; Spaniol et al., 2014). In one of such studies, Murayama and Kitagami (2014) presented a series of trials where a neutral picture was followed by either a task in which participants could acquire money (reward task) or a similar task in which participants had no chance to receive money (control task). The results showed that participants' recognition memory for the neutral pictures after a week's delay was enhanced when these pictures were followed by the reward task in comparison to when these pictures were followed by the neutral task. As reward was manipulated in the post-encoding phase, these findings indicate that extrinsic rewards can directly consolidate learning even without modulating participants' encoding strategies.

According to the multifaceted view of motivation, these findings should bring little or no information about the relationship between intrinsic motivation and learning. Given that the reward network in the brain is activated by intrinsic as well as extrinsic incentives, however, it is in fact possible to infer from these studies that any type of intrinsic incentive can also directly consolidate learning. This hypothesis seems to have received supportive evidence. Gruber et al. (2014) showed that the state of curiosity induced by trivia questions enhanced long-lasting memory for irrelevant materials (i.e., face pictures), and this effect was mediated by activation in the reward network (Kang et al., 2009). Indeed, there is an accumulating body of evidence showing that curiosity or interest supports long-lasting memory performance (Marvin & Shohamy, 2016; McGillivray et al., 2015; Fastrich et al., 2018) in press). Similarly, as the opportunity to make personal choices also activates the reward network in the brain (Leotti & Delgado, 2011), we can hypothesize that making a personal choice also consolidates learning. Indeed, this hypothesis has received supportive evidence. An fMRI study by Murty et al. (2015) found that participants' declarative memory for the objects they voluntarily chose to see was better than that for the objects they were forced to select, and the striatal activation in response to the choice opportunity cue predicted memory performance after a 24-hour delay.

The commonality view also indicates that extrinsic motivation and intrinsic motivation are not completely opposite to each other, and even suggests the possibility that people can transform one type of motivation into the other and that this transformation might be mediated by the common reward processing in the brain (see also Hidi, 2016). In fact, if you reflect upon your own experiences, it is not difficult to find examples of such transformation of motivation. For example, the activities that people currently enjoy (e.g., swimming) were often originally uninteresting to them or even extrinsically motivated (e.g., parents forced you to learn it). People sometimes develop an interest that was initially triggered by a teacher's casual rewarding behavior (e.g., "Your drawing is very good – let's display it in our classroom"). On the other hand, like the undermining effect, it is also the case that people enjoyed an activity in the first place, but it became contingent on extrinsic rewards or punishment ("I enjoyed playing piano, but now I am playing it just to win open competitions"). Indeed, there are several recent empirical studies showing that immediate extrinsic rewards can be a source of continuing intrinsic motivation. For example, Woolley and Fishbach (2016) showed that immediate (but not performance-contingent) rewarding experiences, such as eating snacks, increased high school students' enjoyment and persistence for school assignments (see also Harackiewicz et al., 1984).

It is worth noting that the idea of different types of motivation being transformable has already been suggested, even in some contemporary theories of motivation. For example, Ryan and Deci (2000) argued that extrinsically motivated behavior can be internalized and transformed into autonomous behavior, as people find and attach personal value to the behavior. In the four-phase model of interest development, Hidi and Renninger (2006) distinguished situational interest (momentary rewarding experiences triggered by external stimuli) and individual interest (internally driven, enduring predispositions to engage or re-engage in an activity). Interest develops from situational interest through interactions with the environment, knowledge development, and internal valuation processes (see also Murayama et al., 2018 for a reward learning model of interest). Although there is now a good amount of evidence for this model (see Renninger & Hidi, 2016), such transformation of motivation has still been paid relatively little attention in the empirical literature. Rather, consistent with the multifaceted view of motivation, research testing these models has been more interested in the differential contributions of different types of motivation on outcomes (outcome discrimination). On the contrary, the commonality view has the potential to shed light on the importance of examining the transformative process of people's motivation.

Implications of the Multifaceted View for the Neuroscientific Research on Motivation

The multifaceted view can also provide some insights into the neuroscientific literature on motivation. As the commonality view focuses on the similarities of intrinsic incentives with extrinsic incentives, neuroscientific research tends to overlook some unique but important aspects associated with intrinsic incentives. It is also often the case that researchers in neuroscience underestimate the power of intrinsic incentives in our daily experiences.

For example, the fundamental principle in the commonality view (and model-free RL) is that positive feedback strengthens and negative feedback inhibits motivated behavior. However, research in psychology suggests that negative feedback on some occasions triggers people's achievement motivation (Atkinson, 1957; McClelland et al., 1976; Murray, 1938); similar constructs have been labeled *mastery motivation* or *mastery goals* (Ames, 1992; Elliot, 2005; MacTurk & Morgan, 1995). Achievement motivation is defined as a desire to achieve a standard of excellence in order to attain an inner feeling of personal accomplishment. In other words, these studies suggest the possibility that negative feedback serves as a source of intrinsic incentive to cause persistent behavior. In fact, Tanaka and Murayama (2014) found that students who have mastery goals do not lose task interest even when they perceive the class as difficult. Some researchers argue that achievement motivation is maximized when the task at hand is moderately difficult relative to their ability level – called optimal challenge (Atkinson, 1957; Csikszentmihalyi, 1990; Locke & Latham, 1990; MacTurk & Morgan, 1995; Metcalfe & Kornell, 2005). Although simple and obvious, these phenomena pose some challenges to the commonality view on motivation. A somewhat different, yet similar challenge is presented when participants have different levels of interest in the subject on which they are receiving feedback. Lipstein and Renninger (2007) reported that middle school students with less developed interest did not appreciate feedback unless it told them what to do, whereas those with more developed interest appreciated even negative feedback if it supported them to develop their capacity as a writer.

Similar arguments can also be made for the concept of effort. In the literature of neuroscience, researchers have assumed that effort is aversive – something that should be avoided. The aversive nature of effort has been demonstrated in a popular "effort discounting" paradigm in which participants work on an effortful task to obtain monetary rewards (Westbrook et al., 2013). Researchers have shown that effortful tasks decrease both task value and activation of the brain's reward network (Botvinick et al., 2009; Kool et al., 2010). Humans, however, often *love* effort, especially when interested. Many people have attempted to climb up to the summit of Mt. Chomolungma, even though it is extremely tough and difficult and can pose a risk to their lives (Loewenstein, 1999). In our daily life, countless daily newspapers set effortful puzzles – like Sudoku, anagrams, and crossword puzzles – which thousands of people tackle, habitually, with no offer of external reward. Consistent with these observations, classic psychological literature revealed that people often add value to effortful tasks (a classic "effort justification" phenomenon; Aronson & Mills, 1959). For example, Klein et al. (2005) showed that when participants were presented with a neutral cue and spent substantial effort to obtain extrinsic rewards following the cue, people preferred that cue (in comparison to a control cue). These results suggest that the investment of effort actually increased the value of the cue.

These observations indicate the possibility that negative feedback or effort investment can have both negative and positive rewarding properties, and its positive rewarding properties can even overcome the negative aspects. Examination of the potential intrinsic incentives associated with negative feedback or effort are essential to understanding our motivation in daily life. At schools, for example, it is almost impossible for students to receive only positive feedback and avoid effortful challenge, and successful students seem to have a good capability to sustain (or even boost) their motivation in the face of negative feedback and challenge (Dweck, 1999). Predominated by the commonality view, however, these important aspects of our motivation have not been sufficiently investigated in the literature (for an exception, see Bhanji & Delgado, 2014).

Another example is the role of choice in the context of learning. As discussed earlier, research in neuroscience has found that personal choice has inherent rewarding properties (for reviews, see Leotti et al., 2010 and Murayama et al., 2017; but see also Flowerday & Shell, 2015 and Reeve et al., 2003, for a more nuanced view on the effects of choice). These findings indicate that making personal choices is motivating, but the commonality view tells little about *how* personal choice sustains our motivated behavior. On the other hand, looking at the motivational theories in psychology, there have been a number of studies that examined the psychological process underlying the facilitative effects of personal choice on motivation. One such critical factor is how choice influences people's perceptions about feedback. Researchers have argued that making one's own choice makes one resilient to negative feedback, because personal choice increases self-responsibility and directs people's attention to the informative aspects of negative feedback (e.g., "this feedback is important to improve my behavior"; Deci & Ryan, 1985).

A recent neuroscientific study examined the relationship between personal choice and the feedback process using fMRI (Murayama et al., 2015). In this experiment, participants played with the stopwatch task, which was used in the experiment explained earlier. There were two types of trials: choice trials and control trials. In the choice trials, participants were presented with two different designs for the stopwatch and could freely choose the design that they wanted to play with. In the control trials, participants were also presented with the two different designs of stopwatch, but they were forced to choose a specific design as suggested by a computer. Consistent with previous findings, the results showed that the opportunity to make a choice activated the reward network in the brain, indicating that choice is inherently rewarding (see also Aoki et al., 2014). Indeed, task performance was better in choice trials than in control trials.

Importantly, the research further showed that this enhanced task performance in the choice trials was also related to feedback processing in the ventromedial prefrontal cortex (vmPFC), which has been implicated in representing task values (Daw & Doya, 2006; Kable & Glimcher, 2009). Specifically, whereas negative feedback decreased activation in the vmPFC in control trials, this decrease was not observed in the choice trials, suggesting that negative feedback was no longer aversive in the choice trials. The authors suggested that making personal choices allows people to offset the negative emotional value of failure by treating the feedback informationally. In other words, consistent with the previous literature in psychology, personal choice enhances people's motivation by making them embrace the positive experience of receiving feedback.

Concluding Thoughts

The current chapter aimed to uncover two different meta-theoretical views (implicitly) underlying the concept of motivation in neuroscience and psychology – the commonality view and the multifaceted view on motivation. The difference in these views is especially apparent when it comes to the distinction between intrinsic and extrinsic incentives. Although these two meta-theoretical views are not necessarily opposing each other, I suggest that they have biased our thoughts and ideas about motivation, producing an unnecessary gap between neuroscience and psychology. To understand the nature of motivation broadly and comprehensively, future research on motivation should take a more balanced, interdisciplinary perspective, incorporating a variety of views from psychology, neuroscience, and other relevant areas. I offered some promising examples for future studies, and I hope that the current chapter serves as leverage for moving toward more active cross-disciplinary interaction and integration in studying the science of motivation.

References

Adcock, R. A., Thangavel, A., Whitfield-Gabrieli, S., Knutson, B., & Gabrieli, J. D. E. (2006). Reward-motivated learning: Mesolimbic activation precedes memory formation. *Neuron, 50*(3), 507–17. doi:10.1016/j.neuron.2006.03.036.

Aharon, I., Etcoff, N., Ariely, D., Chabris, C. F., O'Connor, E., & Breiter, H. C. (2001). Beautiful faces have variable reward value: fMRI and behavioral evidence. *Neuron, 32*(3), 537–51. doi:10.1016/s0896-6273(01)00491-3.

Ames, C. (1992). Achievement goals and the classroom motivational climate. In D. H. Schunk & J. L. Meece (Eds.), *Student perceptions in the classroom* (pp. 327–48). Hillsdale, NJ: Lawrence Erlbaum Associates.

Aoki, R., Matsumoto, M., Yomogida, Y., Izuma, K., Murayama, K., Sugiura, A., ... Adolphs, R. (2014). Social equality in the number of choice options is represented in the ventromedial prefrontal cortex. *Journal of Neuroscience, 34*, 6413–21.

Aronson, E. & Mills, J. (1959). The effect of severity of initiation on liking for a group. *The Journal of Abnormal and Social Psychology, 59*(2), 177–81. doi:10.1037/h0047195.

Atkinson, J. W. (1957). Motivational determinants of risk-taking behavior. *Psychological Review, 64*, 359–72.

Balleine, B. W., Daw, N. D., & O'Doherty, J. P. (2008). Multiple forms of value learning and the function of dopamine. In P. W. Glimcher, C. F. Camerer, R. A. Poldrack, & E. Fehr (Eds.), *Neuroeconomics: Decision-making and the brain* (pp. 367–88). New York, NY: Academic Press.

Bandura, A. (1997). *Self-efficacy: The exercise of control*. New York, NY: Freeman.

Baumeister, R. F. & Leary, M. R. (1995). The need to belong: Desire for interpersonal attachments as a fundamental human motivation. *Psychological Bulletin, 117*, 497–529.

Berns, G. S., McClure, S. M., Pagnoni, G., & Montague, P. R. (2001). Predictability modulates human brain response to reward. *Journal of Neuroscience, 21*(8), 2793–8.

Berridge, K. C. (2001). Reward learning: Reinforcement, incentives, and expectations. *The Psychology of Learning and Motivation: Advances in Research and Theory, 40*, 223–78.

Berridge, K. C. (2004). Motivation concepts in behavioral neuroscience. *Physiology & Behavior, 81*, 179–209.

Bhanji, J. P. & Delgado, M. R. (2014). Perceived control influences neural responses to setbacks and promotes persistence. *Neuron, 83*(6), 1369–75. doi:10.1016/j.neuron.2014.08.012.

Bindra, D. (1974). A motivational view of learning, performance, and behavior modification. *Psychological Review, 81*(3), 199–213. doi:10.1037/h0036330.

Bolles, R. C. (1972). Reinforcement, expectancy, and learning. *Psychological Review, 79*, 394–409.

Botvinick, M. M., Huffstetler, S., & McGuire, J. T. (2009). Effort discounting in human nucleus accumbens. *Cognitive, Affective & Behavioral Neuroscience, 9*(1), 16–27. doi:10.3758/CABN.9.1.16.

Braver, T. S., Krug, M. K., Chiew, K. S., Kool, W., Westbrook, J. A., Clement, N. J., ... Somerville, L. H. (2014). Mechanisms of motivation-cognition interaction:

Challenges and opportunities. *Cognitive Affective & Behavioral Neuroscience*, *14*(2), 443–72.

Burton, K. D., Lydon, J. E., D'Alessandro, D. U., & Koestner, R. (2006). The differential effects of intrinsic and identified motivation on well-being and performance: Prospective, experimental, and implicit approaches to self-determination theory. *Journal of Personality and Social Psychology*, *91*(4), 750–62. doi:10.1037/0022-3514.91.4.750.

Camerer, C. F. & Hogarth, R. M. (1999). The effects of financial incentives in experiments: A review and capital-labor-production framework. *Journal of Risk and Uncertainty*, *19*, 7–42.

Campbell-Meiklejohn, D. K., Bach, D. R., Roepstorff, A., Dolan, R. J., Frith, C. D. (2010). How the opinion of others affects our valuation of objects. *Current Biology*, *20*(13), 1165–70. doi:10.1016/j.cub.2010.04.055.

Cerasoli, C. P., Nicklin, J. M., & Ford, M. T. (2014). Intrinsic motivation and extrinsic incentives jointly predict performance: A 40-year meta-analysis. *Psychological Bulletin*, *140*(4), 980–1008. doi:10.1037/a0035661.

Csikszentmihalyi, M. (1990). *Flow: The psychology of optimal experience*. New York, NY: Harper and Row.

Daniel, R. & Pollmann, S. (2010). Comparing the neural basis of monetary reward and cognitive feedback during information-integration category learning. *Journal of Neuroscience*, *30*(1), 47–55. doi:10.1523/jneurosci.2205-09.2010.

Daniel, R. & Pollmann, S. (2012). Striatal activations signal prediction errors on confidence in the absence of external feedback. *Neuroimage*, *59*(4), 3457–67. doi:10.1016/j.neuroimage.2011.11.058.

Davey, C. G., Allen, N. B., Harrison, B. J., Dwyer, D. B., & Yucel, M. (2010). Being liked activates primary reward and midline self-related brain regions. *Human Brain Mapping*, *31*(4), 660–8. doi:10.1002/hbm.20895.

Daw, N. D. & Doya, K. (2006). The computational neurobiology of learning and reward. *Current Opinion in Neurobiology*, *16*, 199–204.

Daw, N. D., Niv, Y., & Dayan, P. (2005). Uncertainty-based competition between prefrontal and dorsolateral striatal systems for behavioral control. *Nature Neuroscience*, *8*(12), 1704–11. www.nature.com/neuro/journal/v8/n12/suppinfo/nn1560_S1.html.

Dayan, P. & Niv, Y. (2008). Reinforcement learning and the brain: The good, the bad, and the ugly. *Current Opinion in Neurobiology*, *18*(2), 185–96.

Deci, E. L. (1971). Effects of externally mediated rewards on intrinsic motivation. *Journal of Personality and Social Psychology*, *18*, 105–15.

Deci, E. L., Koestner, R., & Ryan, R. M. (1999). A meta-analytic review of experiments examining the effects of extrinsic rewards on intrinsic motivation. *Psychological Bulletin*, *125*, 627–68.

Deci, E. L. & Ryan, R. M. (1985). *Intrinsic motivation and self-determination in human behavior*. New York, NY: Plenum.

Delgado, M. R., Miller, M. M., Inati, S., & Phelps, E. A. (2005). An fMRI study of reward-related probability learning. *Neuroimage*, *24*(3), 862–73. doi:10.1016/j.neuroimage.2004.10.002.

Dickinson, A. & Balleine, B. (2002). The role of learning in the operation of motivational systems. In H. Pashler & R. Gallistel (Eds.), *Stevens' handbook of experimental psychology: learning, motivation and emotion* (Vol. 3, pp. 497–534). New York, NY: John Wiley & Sons, Inc.

Dweck, C. S. (1999). *Self-theories: Their role in motivation, personality, and development*. New York, NY: Psychology Press.

Elliot, A. J. (2005). A conceptual history of the achievement goal construct. In A. J. Elliot & C. S. Dweck (Eds.), *Handbook of competence and motivation* (pp. 52–72): New York, NY: Guilford Publications.

Elliot, A. J. (2008). *Handbook of approach and avoidance motivation*. New York, NY: Psychology Press.

Elliot, A. J. & Harackiewicz, J. M. (1996). Approach and avoidance achievement goals and intrinsic motivation: A mediational analysis. *Journal of Personality and Social Psychology, 70*, 461–75.

Fastrich, G. M., Kerr, T., Castel, A. D., & Murayama, K. (2018). The role of interest in memory for trivia questions: An investigation with a large-scale database. *Motivation Science, 4*(3), 227–250. doi: http://dx.doi.org/10.1037/mot0000087.

Flowerday, T. & Shell, D. F. (2015). Disentangling the effects of interest and choice on learning, engagement, and attitude. *Learning and Individual Differences, 40*, 134–40. doi:http://dx.doi.org/10.1016/j.lindif.2015.05.003.

Frey, B. S. & Jegen, R. (2001). Motivation crowding theory. *Journal of Economic Surveys, 15*, 589–611.

Gruber, M. J., Gelman, B. D., & Ranganath, C. (2014). States of curiosity modulate hippocampus-dependent learning via the dopaminergic circuit. *Neuron, 84*(2), 486–96. doi:http://dx.doi.org/10.1016/j.neuron.2014.08.060.

Haber, S. N. & Knutson, B. (2010). The reward circuit: Linking primate anatomy and human imaging. *Neuropsychopharmacology, 35*(1), 4–26. doi:10.1038/npp.2009.129.

Han, S., Huettel, S. A., Raposo, A., Adcock, R. A., & Dobbins, I. G. (2010). Functional significance of striatal responses during episodic decisions: Recovery or goal attainment? *Journal of Neuroscience, 30*(13), 4767–75. doi:10.1523/jneurosci.3077-09.2010.

Harackiewicz, J. M., Manderlink, G., & Sansone, C. (1984). Rewarding pinball wizardry: Effects of evaluation and cue value on intrinsic interest. *Journal of Personality and Social Psychology, 47*(2), 287–300.

Hidi, S. (2016). Revisiting the role of rewards in motivation and learning: Implications of neuroscientific research. *Educational Psychology Review, 28*, 61–93. doi:10.1007/s10648-015-9307-5.

Hidi, S. & Renninger, K. A. (2006). The four-phase model of interest development. *Educational Psychologist, 41*(2), 111–27. doi:http://dx.doi.org/10.1207/s15326985ep4102_4.

Hull, C. L. (1943). *Principles of behavior: An introduction to behavior theory*. Oxford: Appleton-Century.

Izuma, K. (2012). The social neuroscience of reputation. *Neuroscience Research, 72*(4), 283–8. doi:10.1016/j.neures.2012.01.003.

Izuma, K., Saito, D. N., & Sadato, N. (2008). Processing of social and monetary rewards in the human striatum. *Neuron, 58*(2), 284–94. doi:10.1016/j.neuron.2008.03.020.

Jepma, M., Verdonschot, R. G., van Steenbergen, H., Rombouts, S., & Nieuwenhuis, S. (2012). Neural mechanisms underlying the induction and relief of perceptual curiosity. *Frontiers in Behavioral Neuroscience, 6*. doi:10.3389/fnbeh.2012.00005.

Jones, R. M., Somerville, L. H., Li, J., Ruberry, E. J., Libby, V., Glover, G., ... Casey, B. J. (2011). Behavioral and neural properties of social reinforcement learning. *The Journal of Neuroscience, 31*(37), 13039–45. doi:10.1523/jneurosci.2972-11.2011.

Kable, J. W. & Glimcher, P. W. (2009). The neurobiology of decision: Consensus and controversy. *Neuron, 63*(6), 733–45. doi:10.1016/j.neuron.2009.09.003.

Kakade, S. & Dayan, P. (2002). Dopamine: Generalization and bonuses. *Neural Networks, 15*(4–6), 549–59. doi:10.1016/s0893-6080(02)00048-5.

Kang, M. J., Hsu, M., Krajbich, I. M., Loewenstein, G., McClure, S. M., Wang, J. T-y., & Camerer, C. F. (2009). The wick in the candle of learning: Epistemic curiosity activates reward circuitry and enhances memory. *Psychological Science, 20*(8), 963–73. doi:10.1111/j.1467-9280.2009.02402.x.

Klasen, M., Weber, R., Kircher, T. T. J., Mathiak, K. A., & Mathiak, K. (2012). Neural contributions to flow experience during video game playing. *Social Cognitive and Affective Neuroscience, 7*(4), 485–95. doi:10.1093/scan/nsr021.

Klein, E. D., Bhatt, R. S., & Zentall, T. R. (2005). Contrast and the justification of effort. *Psychonomic Bulletin & Review, 12*(2), 335–9. doi:10.3758/bf03196381.

Knutson, B. & Greer, S. M. (2008). Anticipatory affect: Neural correlates and consequences for choice. *Philosophical Transactions of the Royal Society B-Biological Sciences, 363*(1511), 3771–86. doi:10.1098/rstb.2008.0155.

Koepp, M. J., Gunn, R. N., Lawrence, A. D., Cunningham, V. J., Dagher, A., Jones, T., ... Grasby, P. M. (1998). Evidence for striatal dopamine release during a video game. *Nature, 393*(6682), 266–8.

Kool, W., McGuire, J. T., Rosen, Z. B., & Botvinick, M. M. (2010). Decision-making and the avoidance of cognitive demand. *Journal of Experimental Psychology: General, 139*(4), 665–82. doi:10.1037/a0020198.

Kringelbach, M. L. & Berridge, K. C. (2016). Neuroscience of reward, motivation, and drive. In S. Kim, J. Reeve, & M. Bong (Eds.), *Recent developments in neuroscience research on human motivation (Advances in Motivation and Achievement, Vol. 19)*, pp. 23–35. Bingley, UK: Emerald Group Publishing Limited.

Leotti, L. A. & Delgado, M. R. (2011). The inherent reward of choice. *Psychological Science, 10*, 1310–8. doi: 10.1177/0956797611417005.

Leotti, L. A., Iyengar, S. S., & Ochsner, K. N. (2010). Born to choose: The origins and value of the need for control. *Trends in Cognitive Sciences, 14*(10), 457–63. doi:10.1016/j.tics.2010.08.001.

Lepper, M. R., Greene, D., & Nisbett, R. E. (1973). Undermining childrens' intrinsic interest with extrinsic reward: Test of the "overjustification" hypothesis. *Journal of Personality and Social Psychology, 28*(1), 129–37.

Levy, D. J. & Glimcher, P. W. (2012). The root of all value: A neural common currency for choice. *Current Opinion in Neurobiology, 22*(6), 1027–38. doi:10.1016/j.conb.2012.06.001.

Lin, A., Adolphs, R., & Rangel, A. (2011). Social and monetary reward learning engage overlapping neural substrates. *Social Cognitive and Affective Neuroscience, 7*(3), 274–81.

Lipstein, R. L. & Renninger, K. A. (2007). Interest for writing: How teachers can make a difference. *The English Journal*, *96*, 79–85.

Locke, E. A. & Latham, G. P. (1990). *A theory of goal setting & task performance.* Englewood Cliffs, NJ: Prentice-Hall.

Loewenstein, G. (1999). Because it is there: The challenge of mountaineering … for utility theory. *Kyklos*, *52*, 315–43. doi:10.1111/j.1467-6435.1999 .tb00221.x.

MacTurk, R. H. & Morgan, G. A. (Eds.) (1995). *Mastery motivation: Origins, conceptualizations, and applications.* Norwood, NJ: Ablex.

Marvin, C. B. & Shohamy, D. (2016). Curiosity and reward: Valence predicts choice and information prediction errors enhance learning. *Journal of Experimental Psychology: General*, *145*(3), 266–72. doi:10.1037/xge0000140.

Mather, M. & Schoeke, A. (2011). Positive outcomes enhance incidental learning for both younger and older adults. *Frontiers in Neuroscience*, *5*. doi:10.3389/ fnins.2011.00129.

McCabe, C., Harwood, J., Brouwer, S., Harmer, C. J., & Cowen, P. J. (2013). Effects of pramipexole on the processing of rewarding and aversive taste stimuli. *Psychopharmacology*, *228*(2), 283–90. doi:10.1007/s00213-013-3033-9.

McClelland, D. C., Atkinson, J. W., Clark, R. A., & Lowell, E. L. (1976). *The achievement motive*: Oxford: Irvington.

McClelland, D. C., Koestner, R., & Weinberger, J. (1989). How do self-attributed and implicit motives differ? *Psychological Review*, *96*, 690–702.

McDannald, M. A., Takahashi, Y. K., Lopatina, N., Pietras, B. W., Jones, J. L. & Schoenbaum, G. (2012). Model-based learning and the contribution of the orbitofrontal cortex to the model-free world. *European Journal of Neuroscience*, *35*(7), 991–6. doi:10.1111/j.1460-9568.2011.07982.x.

McGillivray, S., Murayama, K., & Castel, A. D. (2015). Thirst for knowledge: The effects of curiosity and interest on memory in younger and older adults. *Psychology and Aging*, *30*(4), 835–41.

Metcalfe, J. & Kornell, N. (2005). A region of proximal learning model of study time allocation. *Journal of Memory and Language*, *52*(4), 463–77. doi:10.1016/ j.jml.2004.12.001.

Montague, P. R. & Berns, G. S. (2002). Neural economics and the biological substrates of valuation. *Neuron*, *36*, 265–84.

Murayama, K. & Elliot, A. J. (2011). Achievement motivation and memory: Achievement goals differentially influence immediate and delayed remember–know recognition memory. *Personality and Social Psychology Bulletin*, *37*(10), 1339–48. doi:10.1177/0146167211410575.

Murayama, K., Elliot, A. J., & Friedman, R. (2012). Achievement goals and approach-avoidance motivation. In R. M. Ryan (Ed.), *Oxford handbook of motivation* (pp. 191–207). Oxford: Oxford University Press.

Murayama, K., FitzGibbon, L., & Sakaki, M. (2018). Process account of curiosity and interest: A reward learning model of knowledge acquisition. https://doi.org/ 10.31219/osf.io/hbcz5.

Murayama, K., Izuma, K., Aoki, R., & Matsumoto, K. (2016). "Your choice" motivates you in the brain: The emergence of autonomy neuroscience. In S. Kim, J. Reeve, & M. Bong (Eds.), *Recent developments in neuroscience research on human motivation (Advances in Motivation and Achievement, Vol. 19)*, pp. 95–125. Bingley, UK: Emerald Publishing Group Limited.

Murayama, K. & Kitagami, S. (2014). Consolidation power of extrinsic rewards: Reward cues enhance long-term memory for irrelevant past events. *Journal of Experimental Psychology: General, 143*, 15–20.

Murayama, K., Kitagami, S., Tanaka, A., & Raw, J. A. (2016). People's naiveté about how extrinsic rewards influence intrinsic motivation. *Motivation Science, 2*(3), 138–42. doi: https://doi.org/10.1037/mot0000040.

Murayama, K., Matsumoto, M., Izuma, K., & Matsumoto, K. (2010). Neural basis of the undermining effect of monetary reward on intrinsic motivation. *PNAS Proceedings of the National Academy of Sciences of the United States of America, 107*(49), 20911–16.

Murayama, K., Matsumoto, M., Izuma, K., Sugiura, A., Ryan, R. M., Deci, E. L., & Matsumoto, K. (2015). How self-determined choice facilitates performance: A key role of the ventromedial prefrontal cortex. *Cerebral Cortex, 25*(5), 1241–51. doi:10.1093/cercor/bht317.

Murayama, K., Pekrun, R., Lichtenfeld, S., & vom Hofe, R. (2013). Predicting long-term growth in students' mathematics achievement: The unique contributions of motivation and cognitive strategies. *Child Development, 84*(4), 1475–90. doi:10.1111/cdev.12036.

Murray, H. A. (1938). *Explorations in personality*. New York, NY: Oxford University Press.

Murty, V. P. & Adcock, R. A. (2014). Enriched encoding: Reward motivation organizes cortical networks for hippocampal detection of unexpected events. *Cerebral Cortex, 24*(8), 2160–8. doi:10.1093/cercor/bht063.

Murty, V. P., DuBrow, S., & Davachi, L. (2015). The simple act of choosing influences declarative memory. *The Journal of Neuroscience, 35*(16), 6255–64.

Niv, Y., Joel, D., & Dayan, P. (2006). A normative perspective on motivation. *Trends in Cognitive Sciences, 10*, 375–81.

Niv, Y. & Schoenbaum, G. (2008). Dialogues on prediction errors. *Trends in Cognitive Sciences, 12*(7), 265–72. doi:10.1016/j.tics.2008.03.006.

O'Doherty, J., Kringelbach, M. L., Rolls, E. T., Hornak, J., & Andrews, C. (2001). Abstract reward and punishment representations in the human orbitofrontal cortex. *Nature Neuroscience, 4*, 95–102.

O'Doherty, J. P. (2004). Reward representations and reward-related learning in the human brain: Insights from neuroimaging. *Current Opinion in Neurobiology, 14*, 769–76.

Oudeyer, P. Y., Gottlieb, J., & Lopes, M. (2016). Intrinsic motivation, curiosity, and learning: Theory and applications in educational technologies. In S. Bettina & K. Stefan (Eds.), *Progress in brain research* (Vol. 229, pp. 257–84). Amsterdam, Netherlands: Elsevier.

Oudeyer, P.-Y. & Kaplan, F. (2009). What is intrinsic motivation? A typology of computational approaches. *Frontiers in Neurorobotics, 1*. doi:10.3389/neuro.12.006.2007.

Pearce, M. T., Zaidel, D. W., Vartanian, O., Skov, M., Leder, H., Chatterjee, A., & Nadal, M. (2016). Neuroaesthetics. *Perspectives on Psychological Science, 11*(2), 265–79. doi:10.1177/1745691615621274.

Pintrich, P. R. & Schunk, D. H. (2002). *Motivation in education: Theory, research, and applications* (2nd ed.). Columbus, OH: Merrill-Prentice Hall.

Rangel, A. & Hare, T. (2010). Neural computations associated with goal-directed choice. *Current Opinion in Neurobiology, 20*(2), 262–70. doi:10.1016/j.conb.2010.03.001.

Reeve, J. & Lee, W. (2012). Neuroscience and human motivation. In R. M. Ryan (Ed.), *The Oxford handbook of human motivation* (pp. 365–80). Oxford: Oxford University Press.

Reeve, J., Nix, G., & Hamm, D. (2003). Testing models of the experience of selfdetermination in intrinsic motivation and the conundrum of choice. *Journal of Educational Psychology, 95*, 375–92.

Renninger, K. A. & Hidi, S. (2016). *The power of interest for motivation and engagement.* New York, NY: Routledge.

Rotter, J. B. (1966). Generalized expectancies for internal versus external control of reinforcement. *Psychological Monographs: General & Applied, 80*(1), 1–28.

Rushworth, M. F. S., Mars, R. B., & Summerfield, C. (2009). General mechanisms for making decisions? *Current Opinion in Neurobiology, 19*(1), 75–83.

Ryan, R. M. & Deci, E. L. (2000). Intrinsic and extrinsic motivations: Classic definitions and new directions. *Contemporary Educational Psychology, 25*, 54–67.

Ryan, R. M., Mims, V., & Koestner, R. (1983). Relation of reward contingency and interpersonal context to intrinsic motivation: A review and test using cognitive evaluation theory. *Journal of Personality and Social Psychology, 45*(4), 736–50. doi:10.1037/0022-3514.45.4.736.

Salimpoor, V. N., Benovoy, M., Larcher, K., Dagher, A., & Zatorre, R. J. (2011). Anatomically distinct dopamine release during anticipation and experience of peak emotion to music. *Nature Neuroscience, 14*(2), 257–355. doi:10.1038/nn.2726.

Schultz, W., Dayan, P., & Montague, P. R. (1997). A neural substrate of prediction and reward. *Science, 275*(5306), 1593–9. doi:10.1126/science.275.5306.1593.

Sedikides, C. & Strube, M. J. (1997). Self-evaluation: To thine own self be good, to thine own self be sure, to thine own self be better. *Advances in Experimental Social Psychology, 29*, 209–69.

Seymour, B. & McClure, S. M. (2008). Anchors, scales and the relative coding of value in the brain. *Current Opinion in Neurobiology, 18*(2), 173–8. doi:10.1016/j.conb.2008.07.010.

Shohamy, D. (2011). Learning and motivation in the human striatum. *Current Opinion in Neurobiology, 21*(3), 408–14. doi:10.1016/j.conb.2011.05.009.

Shohamy, D. & Adcock, R. A. (2010). Dopamine and adaptive memory. *Trends in Cognitive Sciences, 14*(10), 464–72. doi:10.1016/j.tics.2010.08.002.

Skinner, E. A. (1996). A guide to constructs of control. *Journal of Personality and Social Psychology, 71*, 549–70.

Spaniol, J., Schain, C., & Bowen, H. J. (2014). Reward-enhanced memory in younger and older adults. *Journals of Gerontology Series B-Psychological Sciences and Social Sciences, 69*(5), 730–40. doi:10.1093/geronb/gbt044.

Sutton, R. S. & Barto, A. G. (1998). *Reinforcement learning.* Cambridge, MA: MIT Press.

Tanaka, A. & Murayama, K. (2014). Within-person analyses of situational interest and boredom: Interactions between task-specific perceptions and achievement goals. *Journal of Educational Psychology, 106*, 1122–34.

Tang, S. H. & Hall, V. C. (1995). The overjustification effect – a metaanalysis. *Applied Cognitive Psychology, 9*(5), 365–404. doi:10.1002/acp.2350090502.

Tricomi, E., Delgado, M. R., McCandliss, B. D., McClelland, J. L., & Fiez, J. A. (2006). Performance feedback drives caudate activation in a phonological learning task. *Journal of Cognitive Neuroscience, 18*(6), 1029–43. doi:10.1162/jocn.2006.18.6.1029.

Valentin, V. V. & O'Doherty, J. P. (2009). Overlapping prediction errors in dorsal striatum during instrumental learning with juice and money reward in the human brain. *Journal of Neurophysiology, 102*(6), 3384–91. doi:10.1152/jn.91195.2008.

Vansteenkiste, M., Simons, J., Lens, W., Soenens, B., & Matos, L. (2005). Examining the motivational impact of intrinsic versus extrinsic goal framing and autonomy-supportive versus internally controlling communication style on early adolescents' academic achievement. *Child Development, 76*(2), 483–501.

Westbrook, A., Kester, D., & Braver, T. S. (2013). What is the subjective cost of cognitive effort? Load, trait, and aging effects revealed by economic preference. *PLoS One, 8*(7), e68210. doi:10.1371/journal.pone.0068210.

Wiersma, U. J. (1992). The effects of extrinsic rewards in intrinsic motivation – a metaanalysis. *Journal of Occupational and Organizational Psychology, 65,* 101–14.

Wittmann, B. C., Schott, B. H., Guderian, S., Frey, J. U., Heinze, H. J., & Duzel, E. (2005). Reward-related fMRI activation of dopaminergic midbrain is associated with enhanced hippocampus-dependent long-term memory formation. *Neuron, 45*(3), 459–67. doi:10.1016/j.neuron.2005.01.010.

Woolley, K. & Fishbach, A. (2016). For the fun of it: Harnessing immediate rewards to increase persistence in long-term goals. *Journal of Consumer Research, 42*(6), 952–66. doi:10.1093/jcr/ucv098.

7 Incentive Motivation

The Missing Piece between Learning and Behavior

Patrick Anselme and Mike J. F. Robinson

Abstract: In the behavioral sciences, it is common to explain behavior in terms of what was learned in a task, as if any subsequent change in performance had to denote a change in learning. However, learning alone cannot account for variability in performance. Instead, incentive motivation plays a direct role (and is more effective) in controlling moment-to-moment changes in an individual's responses than the learning process. After briefly introducing the history of the study of incentive motivation, we explain that incentive motivation consists of a dopamine-dependent process that does not require consciousness to influence responding to a task. We analyze two Pavlovian situations in which incentive motivation can modulate performance, irrespective of additional learning: the instant transformation of disgust into attraction for salt and the invigoration of responses under reward uncertainty. Finally, we consider drug addiction as an example of motivational dysregulation rather than as a consequence of the habit to consume substances of abuse.

Traditionally, motivation is viewed as a conscious goal that leads us to learn to perform specific actions in order to reach need-related, pleasurable rewards. Although this definition may seem intuitive, it fails to capture the subtle relationships that exist between motivation, learning, and behavior. Here, we present the concept of incentive motivation (called the incentive salience hypothesis), showing how motivational processes are produced in the brain, their potential dissociation from pleasure and learning, and the evidence that their computation occurs in the absence of conscious awareness. Basically, incentive motivation is the psychological process that makes specific stimuli (e.g., food, sex, money, games) attractive, approached, and physically contacted. We show how the incentive salience hypothesis can explain specific phenomena that are more problematic for typical reinforcement learning theories. In particular, we discuss how a sudden change in physiological state can transform disgust into attraction without additional learning and the invigorating effect of reward uncertainty on Pavlovian responses – which occur when

Patrick Anselme's research was supported in part by the Deutsche Forschungsgemeinschaft. Mike Robinson's research was supported in part by a National Center for Responsible Gaming grant. The authors thank Kent Berridge for graceful comments on an earlier version of this manuscript.

an individual comes to respond to the presentation of a stimulus (e.g., lever, light, sound) that predicts the delivery of reward (e.g., food).

What Is Incentive Motivation?

Incentive motivation is the psychological process that transforms the "cold" memory of stimuli into appetizing incentives (or rewards), such as a glass of fresh water for a thirsty person. This process is responsible for reward attraction, which consists of approaching conditioned cues and unconditioned rewards, and is often referred to as "wanting" (Berridge & Robinson, 1998). The modern incentive interpretation originated from the works of Bolles, Bindra, and Toates (Bindra, 1976; Bolles, 1972; Toates, 1986), and differs from the concept of incentive that was initially formulated within the drive theory (Hull, 1943; Spence, 1956). Here we present a short historical background showing why and how incentive theories have replaced drive theories.

Historical Background

Drive theory, many versions of which were proposed throughout the twentieth century, posits that a need for specific rewards (e.g., food, water, sex) induces a motivational drive that urges organisms to get those rewards. As their consumption satisfies the need in question, need satisfaction is accompanied with drive reduction. Drive concepts all describe motivation as an energizing, homeostatic process. This simple view fits well the intuitive description people have about motivational changes, especially with respect to hunger and thirst. However, despite undeniable successes, only the convenience of its use can explain why this interpretation has been maintained for so long in the scientific literature. A number of empirical data provide evidence against the existence of drive (Archer, 1988; Bodor et al., 2010; Hinde, 1960; Holst & Saint Paul, 1963; Laumann et al., 1994; McFarland, 1969; Robinson et al., 2015b; Valenstein et al., 1970). For example, drive reduction does not prevent motivation. The intravenous administration of nutrients or the introduction of food and water directly into the stomach by means of a gastric fistula should reduce the drive associated with hunger and thirst. Yet, such treatments are ineffective at reducing appetite in animals and humans (Miller & Kessen, 1952; Myers & Hall, 1998; Turner et al., 1975; Wolf & Wolff, 1943).

The accumulation of findings that could not be explained by drive theory suggested the need for a theoretical shift. Bolles (1972) initiated this change, suggesting that motivation originated in incentive expectancies (pleasure anticipation) rather than in drive induction. He emphasized the relevance of stimulus–stimulus (S–S) associations; drive theories were only focused on stimulus–response (S–R) associations. He argued that a conditioned stimulus (CS) (e.g., a light) acquires its incentive properties due to repeated pairing with a hedonic reward (e.g., food), because it caused the expectancy of that reward. However, it remained unclear how expectancy alone could produce motivation rather than simply a passive anticipation of reward. Therefore Bindra adopted Bolles' incentive prediction approach, while rejecting the idea that expectation was the critical factor for motivation (Bindra, 1976). Instead, he suggested that a CS not only acquires a predictive value, but also the incentive motivational state normally caused by the unconditioned stimulus (UCS) with which it was repeatedly paired. The acquisition of incentive motivation properties can explain why CSs are approached when associated with appetitive UCSs (such as food) and avoided when associated with aversive UCSs (such as shock). However, in Bindra's conceptual framework, the motivational salience of CSs became permanent once acquired; a CS predictive of food should always be attractive whether hungry or sated. Yet it was clear that the internal physiological state of an individual is important to motivation, even if physiological drive alone cannot account for motivation. Accordingly, Toates (1986) proposed and showed that an individual's physiological state modulates the incentive value of a stimulus, whether it is a CS or a UCS. While drive theorists also discussed the incentive property of a stimulus (Hull, 1943; Spence, 1956), to them, incentives were independent of the motivation (drive) for the stimulus. Instead, in the modern incentive perspective (Bindra, 1976; Berridge & Robinson, 1998), the incentive salience of a stimulus directly depends on motivational strength, which possesses a "magnetic" (reward attraction) rather than "energetic" effect (need-triggered behavior). As such, hunger will make the smell of baked goods attractive, rather than simply trigger an increase in sniffing for odorants.

The Bolles–Bindra–Toates model of incentive motivation presupposes that the incentive value of a CS is a consequence of the hedonic impact of the UCS. However, this presumption has revealed itself to be untrue: the incentive salience of a CS ("wanting"), although often influenced and informed by the hedonic reactions ("liking") felt during consumption of the reward UCS or the learning of the CS–UCS association, is a separate psychological and neuroanatomical process (Berridge & Robinson, 1998; Robinson & Berridge, 1993). This raises the following questions: How is incentive motivation controlled in the brain? Does it depend on consciousness? And why is it not equivalent to the anticipated pleasure of the reward or the strength of the learned association between the predictor and the reward? We discuss these questions and then describe their implications for the understanding of behavioral performance and addiction, especially in the context of human gambling (for additional details on the history of motivational theory, see Berridge, 2004; Robinson & Berridge, 2001).

The Role of Dopamine in Motivation

For centuries, it had been believed that motivation and pleasure were two sides of the same coin and, early in the 1980s, some findings suggested that the neurotransmitter dopamine was strongly involved in pleasurable experiences (Wise, 1982). For example, when rats were injected with a dopamine antagonist (which reduces the action of dopamine in the brain), they stopped seeking rewards such as food. The belief was that dopamine antagonists abolished pleasure, thereby causing a loss of motivation for previously pleasurable rewards. In contrast, more thorough studies gave us a new insight of dopamine's role: Reward is not a unitary process, and dopamine only influences the motivational component of reward ("wanting"), not the hedonic reactions ("liking") or the predictive learning component (Berridge & Robinson, 1998; Robinson & Berridge, 1993). Dopamine-deficient (DD) mice – whose brains produce no dopamine – would die of starvation, even if hungry and surrounded by appetizing food, because they simply do not "want" to approach it. But when food is placed directly into their mouths, DD mice enjoy and ingest the same amount of food and learn Pavlovian associations as well as normal mice (Cannon & Bseikri, 2004; Peciña et al., 2003). In contrast, hyperdopaminergic (DATkd) mice, which overproduce extra-cellular dopamine, exhibit a greater incentive performance for sucrose and proceed more directly to the goal in a runway, but show no enhanced "liking" reactions to sweet tastes (Peciña et al., 2003). These mice do tend to learn the CS–UCS association more rapidly, although this is likely due to high motivation facilitating learning speed – as it does in both animal training and human learning.

Although other neurotransmitters and brain regions are known to play a role in reward (Ikemoto, 2010), mesolimbic dopamine has been shown to be both necessary and sufficient to alter incentive motivation (Berridge, 2007, 2012). However, we recognize that the incentive salience hypothesis is not the only interpretation of dopamine's role in reward (Salamone & Correa, 2002; Schultz, 1998; Wise, 1982). Alternative views of dopamine's role have been extensively discussed in the literature and cannot be presented in detail in the present chapter. One example, known as the prediction error view, sees dopamine as a learning signal (Rescorla & Wagner, 1972; Schultz, 1998). It is based on evidence that phasic dopamine release is high after the delivery of unexpected rewards, but gradually reduces to baseline levels as conditioning and acquisition of a predictive cue progress. This view suggests that dopamine is a prediction error signal used to correct (and learn from) inaccurate predictions (Schultz, 1998, 2010). However, if we assumed that any change in performance necessarily resulted from a change in learning, any immediate shift in performance, as might be adaptive following a sudden physiological change, would be impossible in the absence of new learning. However, recent evidence (explored in further detail later in the chapter) suggests that a dramatic change in incentive motivation can occur in rats suddenly placed in a state of salt deprivation (Robinson & Berridge, 2013). Indeed, the reward prediction error hypothesis implies that a modulation of performance should only occur if the CS-reward association is gradually relearned in the new motivational state (McClure et al., 2003). In addition, the prediction error hypothesis has trouble accounting for the enhanced conditioned responding seen under uncertainty, because the predicted higher dopamine release is not assumed to reflect a motivational process. In fact, if dopamine was a teaching or learning signal, animals should perform less under uncertainty, as predicted by the Rescorla–Wagner model of learning (Rescorla & Wagner, 1972).

Yet another theory proposes to interpret dopamine as a neurotransmitter involved in motor control or the exertion of effort (Salamone & Correa, 2002). This hypothesis relies on data showing that low doses of dopamine antagonists (such as haloperidol) reduce lever pressing, running speed, and the propensity of rats to expend additional effort (e.g., climb a barrier) for more palatable food (Cousins et al., 1993; Ikemoto & Panksepp, 1996; Salamone et al., 1994). Evidence from patients with Parkinson's disease (characterized by a difficulty in initiating motor movements) who present a degeneration of the substantia nigra (a midbrain nucleus that produces dopamine) lends support to this view. But, overall, it is hard to find evidence for effort-control theory that cannot also be accounted for by incentive motivation theory: Why would animals modulate their effort in a task if this modulation was not a consequence of the strength with which rewards are "wanted"? In addition, an increase in dopamine function tends to promote gambling behavior in Parkinson's patients (Dodd et al., 2005; Voon et al., 2006), which the effort-control theory is unlikely to capture, along with the specific effects described in more detail later (uncertainty and salt depletion).

Incentive Motivation as an Unconscious Process

Contrary to a widespread idea that desire comes only with conscious experience, we can "want" stimuli in the absence of any subjective consciousness. For example, recovering addicts were asked to freely choose between two intravenous injections: one of them contained cocaine (lowest dose: 4 mg; highest dose: 50 mg) and the other was a saline solution (Fischman & Foltin, 1992). Addicts systematically selected the cocaine option, for which subjective feelings and cardiovascular responses were recorded. At the lowest dose of cocaine tested, they also pressed the button that delivered cocaine more often than the button for saline. However, they reported no more subjective feelings for cocaine than with saline, and no cardiovascular responses were observed. Self-reports from addicts indicated that they thought of sampling both options equally (cocaine and saline). This result suggests that their choice was influenced by unconscious "wanting." Similarly, irrational cue attraction occurs in crack cocaine addicts who, when found inspecting the floor for a white speck that is more likely to be an ordinary pebble than crack cocaine, can then be attracted to pick it up, inspect it, and even try to smoke the non-cocaine pebble (Rosse et al., 1993). This type of behavior appears to defy more cognitive forms of motivation; it will occur repeatedly despite the individual's conscious knowledge that, although it possesses some of the reward's properties, the cue is not, in fact, the reward itself. In animals, this can be seen in Pavlovian autoshaping – a procedure in which the presentation of a CS is automatically followed by limited delivery of food – where pigeons might make eating pecks at a keylight (CS) predictive of a food (UCS) and perform drinking pecks when the same CS predicts water (Jenkins & Moore, 1973). Another example is provided by male Japanese quail that, under some circumstances, will approach and copulate with an inanimate object CS that had been previously paired with the opportunity to copulate with a female UCS (Burns & Domjan, 1996; Domjan et al., 1988).

Of course, this is not to say that cognitive processes have no impact on motivation. For example, a learned expectation may magnify the attractiveness of a reward. But an expectation is not a motivation per se; it can be expressed independently of any kind of motivation. Some experiments have shown that young children have some expectations about the world and exhibit surprise when these expectations are violated (Baillargeon, 1987; Woodward et al., 1993). Their reactions depend on their internal model of the world's laws, rather than on their motivation for the manipulated objects. In contrast, "wanting" computations might be necessary to desire something one expects. If I wish to go to a movie, I may have some conscious expectations about a specific movie or about the good time spent doing this activity. As a result, I can infer that my wish to go to a movie is also conscious. But this desire would be unlikely to exist if the deep subcortical structures involved in "wanting" were not activated. Desires such as successful performance in a video game (Koepp et al., 1998) or the anticipation of possible wins in a gambling task release dopamine in the nucleus accumbens of human participants (Chase & Clark, 2010; Clark et al., 2009; Kassinove & Schare, 2001; Linnet et al., 2010). The attractiveness of a task, whether simple (seeking food) or complex (playing chess), depends on the ability of specific task-related stimuli to activate dopamine neurons in the ventral tegmental area. To date, no "desire area" has ever been found in the cortical structures, although unconscious "wanting" can naturally alter cortical processing of information (Belayachi et al., 2015).

In this respect, incentive motivation may be related to human interest for specific topics, where this interest could be classified as a psychological state that predisposes individuals to re-engage contents that apply to various contexts of life (Hidi & Renninger, 2006; Renninger & Hidi, 2016). Contrary to traditional reward-directed motivational processes, interest typically occurs in the absence of potential external reward (e.g., money, food); it is a self-reinforcing activity. Interest combines motivational, emotional, attentional, learning, and cognitive components, in addition to being a conscious state of mind. But current evidence suggests that incentive motivation is the core process controlling its occurrence and development. Panksepp (1998) had initially proposed that interest was related to a "seeking" system: a hypothetical dopamine-dependent brain architecture allowing animals and humans to explore their environment in order to find rewards. Further research has confirmed this general view, as dopamine seems to be involved in each developmental phase of interest (Hidi & Renninger, 2006; Renninger & Hidi, 2016). In addition, although interest is correlated with some knowledge of a topic, knowledge itself is neither necessary nor sufficient to trigger it (Renninger, 2000; Renninger et al., 2002). Some people may come to be interested in something while having little knowledge of it (e.g., the origin of the universe for a non-physicist) or have detailed knowledge of a topic for which they develop no interest at all (e.g., the Highway Code). Even well-developed interests, supported by strong background knowledge, require more than cortical activity – as the brain signature of cognitive processing of information (Panksepp, 1998). In short, despite its complex psychological organization, interest might directly depend on the activation of the reward circuitry in the brain.

Why do we have the strong impression that our motivations are a product of consciousness? One possibility is that human cognition incessantly attempts to rationalize thoughts, beliefs, and actions. Rationalizations are at the origin of the perception of our motivations as conscious goals. Sometimes, they may correctly identify the causes of unconscious "wanting," but often they fail to do so accurately (Nisbett & Wilson, 1977). For example, in a consumerist society, many items (such as recent advances in technology) are "wanted" far more than they are needed, yet individuals will sometimes justify impulse purchases by arguing that they are needed (Litt et al., 2010; Robinson & Berridge, 2015). Correctly identifying the cause of a particular behavior is often epiphenomenal to its occurrence and does not mean consciousness was required to initially generate the behavior.

Learning and Performance

Psychologists have long noted that learning and performance are two distinct components of behavior. Hull (1943), for example, suggested that two major causes of behavior are learned habits and a non-specific motivational drive, which was assumed to provide "energy" for action. Other early theorists criticized the concept of drive (Hinde, 1960; Young, 1961) while recognizing that the explanation of performance requires a strong motivation concept. In human studies, the distinction established between effort and competence (Nicholls, 1984) or between learning goal and performance goal (Dweck & Leggett, 1988) also reflects the emphasis on learning and performance as two different, complementary aspects of behavior.

Surprisingly, however, a number of modern interpretations of behavior tend to forget the role of motivation in controlling performance, presupposing that learning rules are sufficient to capture it. The influential Rescorla–Wagner model of associative learning is at the origin of those interpretations (Rescorla & Wagner, 1972). This model predicts that the association between a CS and an UCS is strengthened from trial to trial (based on an error correction principle) and that the gradual enhancement of conditioned responding to a CS (performance) simply reflects the strength of the CS–UCS association (learning and acquisition). This presumption can be problematic, given that a change in learning can only be inferred from a change in performance (because learning is not measurable directly). In fact, many other processes (e.g., emotions, motivations) can influence performance besides learning, and perhaps more directly. Many current learning models are based on the temporal difference (TD) algorithm, where the difference between what is predicted and the actual outcome is translated into neuronal activity. This neuronal activity is believed to act as an error signal that would help modify future predictions in order to reduce that error. However, current learning models derived or inspired by the TD algorithm reduce performance to learning in quite a similar way to early models (Glimcher, 2011; McClure et al., 2003; Redish et al., 2008; Schultz et al., 1997). Error-correction mechanisms are supported by empirical findings that activity of dopamine neurons in the ventral tegmental area correlates with that prediction error signal (for reviews, see Schultz, 1998, 2010). Indeed, dopaminergic activity reaches higher levels than background activity when a reward occurs unexpectedly (positive prediction error), lower levels when a reward does not occur at the expected time (negative prediction error), and remains stable when reward occurrence fits the predicted time (Dreher et al., 2006; Fiorillo et al., 2003). Some authors therefore assume that mesolimbic dopamine codes how much learning is required to complete a prediction task rather than being involved in motivation.

However, failing to differentiate between learning and performance has negative implications for our understanding of the mechanisms of behavior. A classic example of how learning alone cannot fully account for the degree of motivation registered through performance is the so-called Crespi effect (Crespi, 1942). In this seminal study, rats from three groups were initially trained to run for 1, 16, or 64 food morsels. At test, all the rats ran for 16 food morsels. Crespi observed that their running speed depended on the contrast between the current amount of reward (16 morsels) and the number of morsels received during training, rather than being based solely on the current learned outcome of the task. Running speed therefore increased for those animals that were initially trained on 1 morsel of food and then tested with 16 food morsels (1-16 group) and decreased in the 64-16 group, while speed remained constant in the 16-16 group. The fact that running speed was related to the reward magnitude obtained on previous trials cannot be the simple consequence of a learning process, because the rats of all groups received the same amount of training and were given the same amount of learning of the new contingency. These results were later attributed to the incentive properties of rewards by Tolman, Hull, and Spence (Hull, 1943; Spence, 1956; Tolman, 1949).

Two recent illustrations of the necessity to distinguish performance from learning come from our own work. The first one examines the instant shift in Pavlovian responses that follows a physiological change, such as a sudden state of deprivation. It is known that when an animal progressively learns that a particular cue predicts a positive outcome UCS (reward), it will learn to approach and be attracted to that cue. The same is true of avoiding a cue paired with a negative outcome UCS (punishment). However, if the animal learns to associate a cue with an unpleasant outcome, but this outcome then becomes suddenly necessary for its survival, performance can instantly change without having to slowly re-evaluate the association (i.e., without the requirement of any further learning). Robinson and Berridge trained salt non-deprived rats to receive a 9 percent salty solution (three times the concentration of seawater) in their mouths by means of oral cannulas predicted by the presentation of a lever CS (Robinson & Berridge, 2013). These rats developed strong aversion for the CS, actively avoiding it when it was presented. Two days later and in the absence of additional training, the rats were injected with two substances (deoxycorticosterone and furosemide) to produce an intense state of sodium deficiency, and they were placed again in the test chambers. Despite their highly aversive past experience with the lever CS, and having never tasted the salt solution as anything other than disgusting, the rats became avidly and immediately attracted by the lever, showing an instant shift in behavior as soon as the first lever presentation occurred, despite never tasting the salt solution in this new state. This result suggests that incentive motivation can instantly transform a learned association from disgust into attraction, independently of the learned value of the CS and without requiring any additional learning of the new contingencies (for a related experiment based on electrophysiological recordings, see Tindell et al., 2009).

A second example of how performance and motivation can be independent of learning comes from the invigorating effect of reward uncertainty on Pavlovian responses. Learning models suggest that the stronger the predictive value of a CS regarding its outcome UCS (reward or punishment), the more the animal is inclined to respond to the predictive CS (approach or avoidance). In this view, a CS that predicts UCS delivery with 100 percent probability (certainty) should lead animals to produce stronger conditioned responses than a CS that unreliably predicts UCS delivery (uncertainty: 50 percent probability). However, a number of studies have revealed that an unreliable CS enhances responding compared to a reliable CS (Anselme et al., 2013; Collins et al., 1983; Gottlieb, 2004; Robinson et al., 2014a). Thus, this effect shows something uncaptured by learning theories. For example, we accustomed rats to obtaining a sucrose pellet on each trial during three autoshaping sessions, where a trial consisted of one pellet delivered after short presentation of a lever and tone CS. In this procedure, rats spontaneously come to approach, sniff, nibble, and press the available lever – a behavior called sign-tracking (by opposition to the goal-tracking propensity of other individuals, who prefer to approach and interact with the food dish). Sign-tracking behavior is used as a measure of attraction and incentive motivation attributed to a reward-related cue. After three days of training under certain conditions, half of the rats were switched to uncertain conditions, while the other half were maintained on the previous certainty schedule for five additional days. Under uncertainty, animals received nothing on 50 percent of trials and one, two, or three pellets, on a random basis, on the remaining 50 percent of trials, in contrast to certain conditions where animals received one pellet on 100 percent of trials. The number of reward pellets and cue presentations were perfectly matched between the certain and uncertain conditions, so that any differences could not be accounted for by differences in the amount of reinforcement or the number of learning pairings (cue presentations). Although sign-tracking performance was similar in the two groups on training days one through three, rats exposed to uncertain pellets quickly came to approach the lever faster and pressed and nibbled the lever at higher rates than rats exposed to certain conditions (Anselme et al., 2013). The opportunity to receive larger rewards (three pellets) was not the reason for enhanced performance under uncertainty. In fact, receiving one, two, or three pellets per trial at random, without omission of reward delivery, made no difference in the rats' attraction to the lever, compared to a situation of 100 percent chance of only one pellet per trial (Anselme et al., 2013).

Homeostatic mechanisms can readily explain why a state of deprivation would momentarily increase motivation, such as why desire for sweet and salty foods may result from a prolonged period without anything to eat. However, the link between food uncertainty and motivation may seem a bit counterintuitive: Logically, a degraded CS–UCS association should reduce the attractiveness of the CS. Yet, some behavioral findings suggest that invigorated responding under uncertainty results from increased incentive motivation (or "wanting") for the CSs. For example, rats trained under reward uncertainty sign-track toward a lever CS located farther from the food dish than rats trained under reward certainty, suggesting that the CS has acquired a greater capacity to attract attention and motivated behavior (Robinson et al., 2014a). In the same vein, responding decreases toward the end of a fully predictable CS, but does not when the CS is unreliable (Gibbon et al., 1980). After training the same pigeons in uncertainty versus certainty conditions, it appeared that they chose to peck at the CS previously associated with uncertainty more than that previously associated with certainty (Collins & Pearce, 1985). Finally, reward uncertainty generates a higher number of sign-trackers and stronger sign-tracking responses than reward certainty (Robinson et al., 2015a).

Of course, we are not trying to say that animals prefer uncertainty to certainty, but rather that *unavoidable* uncertainty enhances food-seeking motivation. A hypothesis allowing us to understand the motivational effects of reward uncertainty is that of incentive hope (Anselme, 2015, 2016). To hope something is to "want" it, while having no guarantee that it will be obtained. In this view, organisms "want" uncertain rewards (just as certain rewards), but they also "hope" for their delivery. Incentive hope adds its motivational effect to that of hunger-induced motivation and makes the food reward more attractive when it is eventually obtained. Increased attractiveness of uncertain rewards is unlikely to be learned in the traditional sense but might sensitize brain mechanisms in a similar way to drugs of abuse. For example, we showed that rats initially exposed to high uncertainty maintained more vigorous CS-directed behaviors after uncertainty was dramatically reduced (Robinson et al., 2014a). This somewhat irrational behavior might play a determining role in the problematic attraction to gambling-related cues, particularly in slot-machine gambling (Anselme et al., 2013). However, the motivational effects of reward uncertainty could basically be an adaptive process, allowing animals experiencing unpredictable food access to seek and consume more food items than if those items were easy to find (Anselme, 2013, 2016). A large body of literature in behavioral ecology indicates that, when exposed to unpredictable food in many different conditions (e.g., winter, social subordination, poor foraging capacity), animals (especially small birds) consume more food and become fatter (Cresswell, 2003; Ekman & Hake, 1990; Gosler, 1996; Pravosudov & Grubb, 1997). Higher fat reserves are thought to act as insurance against the risk of starvation, given that more time and energy must be spent when food density is low. The incentive hope hypothesis is a plausible mechanism for explaining *how* increased seeking is possible. Taken together, these findings suggest not only that uncertainty increases reward-seeking motivation, but also that this process was put in place by evolution due to its usefulness for survival.

In support of our claim that uncertainty has motivational properties that enhance "wanting," it is interesting to note that uncertainty processing requires dopamine. Indeed, a number of studies have revealed that midbrain dopamine release is higher when uncertainty of a CS is maximal (de Lafuente & Romo, 2011; Dreher et al., 2006; Fiorillo et al., 2003; Hart et al., 2015; Preuschoff et al., 2006; Singer et al., 2012; Tan & Bullock, 2008; Zack et al., 2014). We found that uncertainty elevates sign-tracking in a similar fashion to amphetamine, a dopamine agonist-like drug known to increase motivation (Robinson et al., 2015a). D'Souza and Duvauchelle (2008) showed that rats exposed to visual and olfactory cues previously associated with uncertain cocaine access (self-administration) exhibited enhanced extracellular dopamine release compared to rats for which those cues fully predicted cocaine access. The incentive hope hypothesis fits well with those results, because hope can easily be understood as a motivational factor:

Hope is what motivates people to seek longer or more intensely. It is therefore unsurprising that it contributes to increasing incentive salience as a dopaminergic process.

Upon the assumption that human interest is basically an incentive motivational process (see next section), it can be hypothesized that individuals are more likely to develop incentive hope relative to a topic of interest. For example, Costikyan (2013), a game developer, points out that the reason many people like to play games is that the uncertainty associated with the outcome or with the game's path holds their interest. More thorough investigation is needed, but there is some evidence that playing a video game activates the brain reward circuit (Koepp et al., 1998).

In conclusion, considering Pavlovian conditioning from a pure learning perspective is unsatisfactory. Learning is a necessary step, allowing the CS to acquire some predictive value, but this predictive value is not, in itself, what controls the observed performance. Performance is a consequence of the individual's motivation in the task. In particular, incentive motivation is a crucial factor capable of explaining the instant shift and the reward uncertainty effects.

Addictions: The Dysregulation of Motivational Processes

Addiction is characterized by the compulsive pursuit of a specific reward to the detriment of others. It often occurs despite repeated adverse (e.g., health, social, legal) consequences, and is characterized by excessive "wanting" for certain rewards and their cues, often referred to as incentive sensitization. Evidence suggests that addiction, whether for drugs, food, sex or gambling, involves the sensitization of dopamine neurons in subcortical structures that permanently alter an individual's capacity for making appropriate decisions about many aspects of everyday life (Robinson & Berridge, 1993, 2008). The excessive desire and craving that result from sensitized motivational systems is believed to make addiction a pathological problem, followed by frequent relapse, despite repeated intentions to quit. Addiction is often portrayed as a powerful habit (Everitt & Robbins, 2015) that develops as a transition from recreational use to compulsive reward-seeking. Through repeated learning and "stamping-in" of reward associations, neural activity is believed to shift from the ventral to the dorsal striatum. However, although it may be true that reward consumption can become an overly ritualized habitual act, this may be less true of the preceding motivation to obtain the reward. Learned habits alone cannot account for the excessive motivational attraction of rewards and their cues that develops through addiction. The idea that addiction is merely a rigid S–R habit does not account for how motivation imbues the act of drug-taking with characteristic flexibility and innovation of new means of obtaining the reward when required. Nor does it explain the compulsive overtones that cannot be easily overridden by the resolution to abstain. Other extremely well-learned

habits (such as brushing one's teeth or tying one's shoelaces) are not compulsive in the motivational sense. Those habits can easily be left undone or halted
midway without the emergence of a compulsive urge to continue. Furthermore,
recent evidence suggests that the learning of strong associations does not mean
that well-learned predictors carry the most incentive motivation. Instead, as
can be seen with gambling, highly uncertain and therefore weak predictors can
invigorate motivation and at times sensitize reward pathways (Linnet et al.,
2010; Robinson et al., 2015a).

Addiction has also been associated with a loss of cognitive control
(Robinson et al., 2014b, 2015c). The excessive motivation for drugs and
other rewards may go beyond the ability to use rational thought to influence decisions. In particular, it appears that decisions are no longer linked
to learned and experienced outcomes. Whereas addiction is often accompanied by sensitization of "wanting" systems, evidence seems to suggest
that the pleasure or "liking" associated with the reward is either reduced
(through a process known as tolerance) or stays relatively the same. As a
result, addicts often require ever-increasing consumption and abuse of the
reward to attain near-equivalent levels of euphoria. In addition, addiction
is often accompanied by growing negative outcomes, including loss of family and social connections, loss of employment, increased legal problems,
health issues, and (in some cases) powerful withdrawal symptoms. If learning were at the root of motivation, these growing adverse effects would
progressively come to outweigh the benefits of the addiction and would
attenuate use, mitigating any prior overconsumption. Instead, increased
adverse effects fail to deter compulsive use. One report even suggested that
within a group of inpatients treated for cocaine rehabilitation, those that
reported growing negative side effects (sensitization) over the course of their
history of drug use (in this case paranoid psychosis) were most likely to
relapse, as indicated by re-hospitalization for addiction treatment (Bartlett
et al., 1997). These results suggest that negative outcomes no longer seem
able to shape the direction of motivation and, in extreme cases in which
negative outcomes outweigh the pleasure of the reward, the addict may
perpetually struggle to relearn old or learn new healthy behaviors to overcome their addiction.

One reason addicts struggle with using the rise of adverse consequences to
overcome addiction is that the desire to pursue the reward has become pathological. Excessive "wanting" for the reward and its cues is believed to result
from incentive sensitization, where cues and the reward develop the ability to
trigger increasingly intense peaks in craving that make pursuit of the reward
almost irresistible. However, evidence initially gathered from animal models
of addiction has shown that sensitization of "wanting" is not restricted to
the reward of choice. In fact, repeated exposure to a particular reward can
result in a sensitized response to other rewards – a phenomenon known as
cross-sensitization, which implies a greater response to a treatment, even on

the first exposure, due to prior experience with another treatment. For example, cross-sensitization occurs between drugs of different classes. So pretreatment with either amphetamine or nicotine can accelerate the acquisition of cocaine self-administration. Cross-sensitization also occurs between drugs and stress, where repeated stress can produce greater motivation to consume amphetamine. Finally, cross-sensitization can occur between drugs and natural rewards or between drugs and gambling. For example, amphetamine sensitization can lead to sugar hyperphagia (and the reverse is true of intermittent sugar consumption; Avena & Hoebel, 2003a, 2003b) and, in humans, pathological gamblers show a greater dopamine response to amphetamine, which is correlated with gambling severity (Boileau et al., 2013). Cross-sensitization is further evidence that motivation can occur relatively independently of prior learning. Thus, although addiction may involve disorders of learning and the creation of powerful habits, learning alone is unable to explain the excessive desire and motivation that addicts experience for their rewards and its cues.

Concluding Thoughts

Motivation is directed. For motivation to be more than a sudden peak in activity, a target is required, upon which motivation can be focused. In most cases this target requires learning. Individuals must learn to associate certain cues or actions with a specific reward for it to be imbued with motivation. However, learning alone does not generate motivation. As we have shown here, the weak association between a cue and a reward that results from uncertainty can actually enhance motivation. This is contrary to the predictions that would be made by learning theories. In addition, as we showed with the case of salt depletion, motivation can be generated spontaneously, even out of disgust, without any new learning, simply through a sudden change in physiological state. Finally, although addiction is accompanied by powerful learned habits, these habits cannot account for the excessive "wanting" that develops with addiction and is responsible for the compulsive, and often flexible, pursuit of reward and the craving that can lead to relapse even after years of abstinence.

Outstanding questions include the following:

- What are the subjective feelings of problem gamblers playing their favorite game?
- Which neurotransmitters (other than dopamine) influence gambling behavior?
- Is the preference often shown for variable schedules controlled by the same brain processes as the higher response rates shown in Pavlovian autoshaping?
- Is there a link between the interest in a topic and the hope of obtaining responses to questions related to that topic?
- Small birds exposed to an unpredictable food access come to consume more food, but is this activity correlated with enhanced dopamine release?

References

Anselme, P. (2013). Dopamine, motivation, and the evolutionary significance of gambling-like behaviour. *Behavioural Brain Research, 256C*, 1–4. doi:10.1016/j.bbr.2013.07.039.

Anselme, P. (2015). Incentive salience attribution under reward uncertainty: A Pavlovian model. *Behavioural Processes, 111*, 6–18. doi:10.1016/j.beproc.2014.10.016.

Anselme, P. (2016). Motivational control of sign-tracking behaviour: A theoretical framework. *Neuroscience and Biobehavioral Reviews, 65*, 1–20. doi:10.1016/j.neubiorev.2016.03.014.

Anselme, P., Robinson, M. J. F., & Berridge, K. C. (2013). Reward uncertainty enhances incentive salience attribution as sign-tracking. *Behavioural Brain Research, 238*, 53–61. doi:10.1016/j.bbr.2012.10.006.

Archer, J. (1988). *The behavioural biology of aggression.* Cambridge University Press Archive.

Avena, N. M. & Hoebel, B. G. (2003a). A diet promoting sugar dependency causes behavioral cross-sensitization to a low dose of amphetamine. *Neuroscience, 122*(1), 17–20.

Avena, N. M. & Hoebel, B. G. (2003b). Amphetamine-sensitized rats show sugar-induced hyperactivity (cross-sensitization) and sugar hyperphagia. *Pharmacology, Biochemistry, and Behavior, 74*(3), 635–9.

Baillargeon, R. (1987). Object permanence in 3½- and 4½-month-old infants. *Developmental Psychology, 23*(5), 655–64.

Bartlett, E., Hallin, A., Chapman, B., & Angrist, B. (1997). Selective sensitization to the psychosis-inducing effects of cocaine: a possible marker for addiction relapse vulnerability? *Neuropsychopharmacology, 16*(1), 77–82. doi:10.1016/S0893-133X(96)00164-9.

Belayachi, S., Majerus, S., Gendolla, G., Salmon, E., Peters, F., & Van der Linden, M. (2015). Are the carrot and the stick the two sides of same coin? A neural examination of approach/avoidance motivation during cognitive performance. *Behavioural Brain Research, 293*, 217–26. doi:10.1016/j.bbr.2015.07.042.

Berridge, K. C. (2004). Motivation concepts in behavioral neuroscience. *Physiology & Behavior, 81*(2), 179–209. doi:10.1016/j.physbeh.2004.02.004.

Berridge, K. C. (2007). The debate over dopamine's role in reward: the case for incentive salience. *Psychopharmacology, 191*(3), 391–431. doi:10.1007/s00213-006-0578-x.

Berridge, K. C. (2012). From prediction error to incentive salience: mesolimbic computation of reward motivation. *European Journal of Neuroscience, 35*(7), 1124–43. doi:10.1111/j.1460-9568.2012.07990.x.

Berridge, K. C. & Robinson, T. E. (1998). What is the role of dopamine in reward: hedonic impact, reward learning, or incentive salience? *Brain Research Reviews, 28*(3), 309–69.

Bindra, D. (1976). *A theory of intelligent behavior.* Oxford: Wiley-Interscience.

Bodor, J. N., Rice, J. C., Farley, T. A., Swalm, C. M., & Rose, D. (2010). The association between obesity and urban food environments. *Journal of Urban Health, 87*(5), 771–81. doi:10.1007/s11524-010-9460-6.

Boileau, I., Payer, D., Chugani, B., Lobo, D. S., Houle, S., Wilson, A. A., ... Zack, M. (2013). In vivo evidence for greater amphetamine-induced dopamine release in pathological gambling: A positron emission tomography study with [11C]-(+)-PHNO. *Molecular Psychiatry*, *19*(12), 1305–13. doi:10.1038/mp.2013.163.

Bolles, R. C. (1972). Reinforcement, expectancy, and learning. *Psychological Review*, *79*(5), 394–409.

Burns, M. & Domjan, M. (1996). Sign tracking versus goal tracking in the sexual conditioning of male Japanese quail (Coturnix japonica). *Journal of Experimental Psychology Animal Behavior Processes*, *22*(3), 297–306. doi:10.1037/0097-7403.22.3.297.

Cannon, C. M. & Bseikri, M. R. (2004). Is dopamine required for natural reward? *Physiology & Behavior*, *81*(5), 741–8. doi:10.1016/j.physbeh.2004.04.020.

Chase, H. W. & Clark, L. (2010). Gambling severity predicts midbrain response to near miss outcomes. *Journal of Neuroscience*, *30*(18), 6180–7. doi:10.1523/JNEUROSCI.5758-09.2010.

Clark, L., Lawrence, A. J., Astley-Jones, F., & Gray, N. (2009). Gambling near-misses enhance motivation to gamble and recruit win-related brain circuitry. *Neuron*, *61*(3), 481–90. doi:10.1016/j.neuron.2008.12.031.

Collins, L. & Pearce, J. M. (1985). Predictive accuracy and the effects of partial reinforcement on serial autoshaping. *Journal of Experimental Psychology: Animal Behavior Processes*, *11*, 548–64.

Collins, L., Young, D. B., Davies, K., & Pearce, J. M. (1983). The influence of partial reinforcement on serial autoshaping with pigeons. *The Quarterly Journal of Experimental Psychology B, Comparative and Physiological Psychology*, *35*(4), 275–90. doi:10.1080/14640748308400893.

Costikyan, G. (2013). *Uncertainty in games*. Cambridge: MIT Press.

Cousins, M. S., Sokolowski, J. D., & Salamone, J. D. (1993). Different effects of nucleus accumbens and ventrolateral striatal dopamine depletions on instrumental response selection in the rat. *Pharmacology, Biochemistry, and Behavior*, *46*(4), 943–51.

Crespi, L. P. (1942). Quantitative variation of incentive and performance in the white rat. *The American Journal of Psychology*, *55*(4), 467–517. doi:10.2307/1417120?ref=-search-gateway:18b91fd28dc7c135471d0d97bddee0b1.

Cresswell, W. (2003). Testing the mass-dependent predation hypothesis: In European blackbirds poor foragers have higher overwinter body reserves. *Animal Behaviour*, *65*, 1035–44.

D'Souza, M. S. & Duvauchelle, C. L. (2008). Certain or uncertain cocaine expectations influence accumbens dopamine responses to self-administered cocaine and non-rewarded operant behavior. *European Neuropsychopharmacology*, *18*(9), 628–38. doi:10.1016/j.euroneuro.2008.04.005.

de Lafuente, V. & Romo, R. (2011). Dopamine neurons code subjective sensory experience and uncertainty of perceptual decisions. *Proceedings of the National Academy of Sciences of the United States of America*, *108*(49), 19 767–71. doi:10.1073/pnas.1117636108.

Dodd, M. L., Klos, K. J., Bower, J. H., Geda, Y. E., Josephs, K. A., & Ahlskog, J. E., (2005). Pathological gambling caused by drugs used to treat Parkinson disease. *Archives of Neurology*, *62*(9), 1377–81. doi:10.1001/archneur.62.9.noc50009.

Domjan, M., O'Vary, D., & Greene, P. (1988). Conditioning of appetitive and consummatory sexual behavior in male Japanese quail. *Journal of the Experimental Analysis of Behavior*, *50*(3), 505–19. doi:10.1901/jeab.1988.50-505.

Dreher, J.-C., Kohn, P., & Berman, K. F. (2006). Neural coding of distinct statistical properties of reward information in humans. *Cerebral Cortex, 16*(4), 561–73. doi:10.1093/cercor/bhj004.

Dweck, C. S. & Leggett, E. L. (1988). A social-cognitive approach to motivation and personality. *Psychological Review, 95*(2), 256–73.

Ekman, J. B. & Hake, M. K. (1990). Monitoring starvation risk: adjustments of body reserves in greenfinches (*Carduelis chloris* L.) during periods of unpredictable foraging success. *Behavioral Ecology, 1*, 62–7.

Everitt, B. J. & Robbins, T. W. (2015). Drug addiction: updating actions to habits to compulsions ten years on. *Annual Review of Psychology, 67*, 23–50. doi:10.1146/annurev-psych-122414-033457.

Fiorillo, C. D., Tobler, P. N., & Schultz, W. (2003). Discrete coding of reward probability and uncertainty by dopamine neurons. *Science, 299*(5614), 1898–902. doi:10.1126/science.1077349.

Fischman, M. W. & Foltin, R. W. (1992). Self-administration of cocaine by humans: a laboratory perspective. *Ciba Foundation Symposium, 166*, 165–80.

Gibbon, J., Farrell, L., Locurto, C. M., Duncan, H. J., & Terrace, H. S. (1980). Partial reinforcement in autoshaping with pigeons. *Animal Learning & Behavior, 8*(1), 45–59.

Glimcher, P. W. (2011). Understanding dopamine and reinforcement learning: the dopamine reward prediction error hypothesis. *Proceedings of the National Academy of Sciences of the United States of America, 108* Suppl 3, 15 647–54. doi:10.1073/pnas.1014269108.

Gosler, A. G. (1996). Environmental and social determinants of winter fat storage in the great tit (Parus major). *Journal of Animal Ecology, 65*(1), 1–17. doi:10.2307/5695?ref=search-gateway:1604b76cc4918de863817a1952f0beff.

Gottlieb, D. A. (2004). Acquisition with partial and continuous reinforcement in pigeon autoshaping. *Learning & Behavior, 32*(3), 321–34.

Hart, A. S., Clark, J. J., & Phillips, P. E. M. (2015). Dynamic shaping of dopamine signals during probabilistic Pavlovian conditioning. *Neurobiology of Learning and Memory, 117*, 84–92. doi:10.1016/j.nlm.2014.07.010.

Hidi, S. & Renninger, K. A. (2006). The four-phase model of interest development. *Educational Psychologist, 41*(2), 111–27.

Hinde, R. A. (1960). Energy models of motivation. *Symposia of the Society for Experimental Biology, 14*, 199–213.

Holst, von, E. & Saint Paul, von, U. (1963). On the functional organisation of drives. *Animal Behaviour, 11*(1), 1–20.

Hull, C. L. (1943). *Principles of behavior: An introduction to behavior theory.* (R. M. Elliott, Ed.). Appleton-Century.

Ikemoto, S. (2010). Brain reward circuitry beyond the mesolimbic dopamine system: A neurobiological theory. *Neuroscience and Biobehavioral Reviews, 35*(2), 129–50. doi:10.1016/j.neubiorev.2010.02.001.

Ikemoto, S. & Panksepp, J. (1996). Dissociations between appetitive and consummatory responses by pharmacological manipulations of reward-relevant brain regions. *Behavioral Neuroscience, 110*(2), 331–45.

Jenkins, H. M. & Moore, B. R. (1973). The form of the auto-shaped response with food or water reinforcers. *Journal of the Experimental Analysis of Behavior, 20*(2), 163–81. doi:10.1901/jeab.1973.20-163.

Kassinove, J. I. & Schare, M. L. (2001). Effects of the "near miss" and the "big win" on persistence at slot machine gambling. *Psychology of Addictive Behaviors*, *15*(2), 155–8. doi:10.1037//0893-164X.15.2.155.

Koepp, M. J., Gunn, R. N., Lawrence, A. D., Cunningham, V. J., Dagher, A., Jones, T., ... Grasby, P. M. (1998). Evidence for striatal dopamine release during a video game. *Nature*, *393*(6682), 266–8. doi:10.1038/30498.

Laumann, E. O., Gagnon, J. H., Michael, R. T., & Michaels, S. (1994). *The social organization of sexuality: Sexual practices in the United States*. University of Chicago Press.

Linnet, J., Peterson, E., Doudet, D. J., Gjedde, A., & Møller, A. (2010). Dopamine release in ventral striatum of pathological gamblers losing money. *Acta Psychiatrica Scandinavica*, *122*(4), 326–33. doi:10.1111/j.1600-0447.2010.01591.x.

Litt, A., Khan, U., & Shiv, B. (2010). Lusting while loathing: parallel counter-driving of wanting and liking. *Psychological Science*, *21*(1), 118–25. doi:10.1177/0956797609355633.

McClure, S. M., Daw, N. D., & Montague, P. R. (2003). A computational substrate for incentive salience. *Trends in Neurosciences*, *26*(8), 423–8.

McFarland, D. (1969). Separation of satiating and rewarding consequences of drinking. *Physiology & Behavior*, *4*(6), 987–9. doi:10.1016/0031-9384(69)90054-7.

Miller, N. E. & Kessen, M. L. (1952). Reward effects of food via stomach fistula compared with those of food via mouth. *Journal of Comparative and Physiological Psychology*, *45*(6), 555–64.

Myers, K. P. & Hall, W. G. (1998). Evidence that oral and nutrient reinforcers differentially condition appetitive and consummatory responses to flavors. *Physiology & Behavior*, *64*(4), 493–500.

Nicholls, J. G. (1984). Achievement motivation: Conceptions of ability, subjective experience, task choice, and performance. *Psychological Review*, *91*(3), 328–46.

Nisbett, R. E. & Wilson, T. D. (1977). Telling more than we can know: Verbal reports on mental processes. *Psychological Review*, *84*, 231–59.

Panksepp, J. (1998). *Affective neuroscience: The foundations of human and animal emotions*. Oxford: Oxford University Press.

Peciña, S., Cagniard, B., Berridge, K. C., Aldridge, J. W., & Zhuang, X. (2003). Hyperdopaminergic mutant mice have higher "wanting" but not "liking" for sweet rewards. *The Journal of Neuroscience*, *23*(28), 9395–402.

Pravosudov, V. V. & Grubb, T. C. (1997). Management of fat reserves and food caches in tufted titmice (Parus bicolor) in relation to unpredictable food supply. *Behavioral Ecology*, *8*, 332–9.

Preuschoff, K., Bossaerts, P., & Quartz, S. R. (2006). Neural differentiation of expected reward and risk in human subcortical structures. *Neuron*, *51*(3), 381–90. doi:10.1016/j.neuron.2006.06.024.

Redish, A. D., Jensen, S., & Johnson, A. (2008). A unified framework for addiction: Vulnerabilities in the decision process. *Behavioral and Brain Sciences*, *31*(4), 415–37. doi:10.1017/S0140525X0800472X.

Renninger, K. A. (2000). Individual interest and its implications for understanding intrinsic motivation. In C. Sansone & J. M. Harackiewicz (Eds.), *Intrinsic and extrinsic motivation: The search for optimal motivation and performance* (pp. 375–407). New York, NY: Elsevier. doi:10.1016/B978-012619070-0/50035-0.

Renninger, K. A., Ewen, L., & Lasher, A. K. (2002). Individual interest as context in expository text and mathematical word problems. *Learning and Instruction*, *12*, 467–91.

Renninger, K. A. & Hidi, S. (2016). Interest, attention, and curiosity. In K. A. Renninger & S. Hidi (Eds.), *The power of interest for motivation and engagement* (pp. 32–51). New York, NY and London: Routledge.

Rescorla, R. A. & Wagner, A. R. (1972). A theory of Pavlovian conditioning: Variations in the effectiveness of reinforcement and nonreinforcement. In A. H. Black & W. F. Prokasy (Eds.), *Classical conditioning II: Current theory and research* (pp. 64–99). New York, NY: Appleton-Century-Crofts.

Robinson, M. J. F. & Berridge, K. C. (2013). Instant transformation of learned repulsion into motivational "Wanting". *Current Biology*, *23*(4), 282–9. doi:10.1016/j.cub.2013.01.016.

Robinson, M. J. F. & Berridge, K. C. (2015). Wanting vs needing. In J. D. Wright (Ed.), *International encyclopedia of the social & behavioral sciences* (2nd ed., Vol. 25, pp. 351–6). Oxford: Elsevier. doi:10.1016/B978-0-08-097086-8.26091-1.

Robinson, M. J. F., Anselme, P., Fischer, A. M., & Berridge, K. C. (2014a). Initial uncertainty in Pavlovian reward prediction persistently elevates incentive salience and extends sign-tracking to normally unattractive cues. *Behavioural Brain Research*, *266*, 119–30. doi:10.1016/j.bbr.2014.03.004.

Robinson, M. J. F., Anselme, P., Suchomel, K., & Berridge, K. C. (2015a). Amphetamine-induced sensitization and reward uncertainty similarly enhance incentive salience for conditioned cues. *Behavioral Neuroscience*, *129*(4), 502–11. doi:10.1037/bne0000064.

Robinson, M. J. F., Burghardt, P. R., Patterson, C. M., Nobile, C. W., Akil, H., Watson, S. J., ... Ferrario, C. R. (2015b). Individual differences in cue-induced motivation and striatal systems in rats susceptible to diet-induced obesity. *Neuropsychopharmacology*, *40*(9), 2113–23. doi:10.1038/npp.2015.71.

Robinson, M. J. F., Fischer, A. M., Ahuja, A., Lesser, E. N., & Maniates, H. (2015c). Roles of "wanting" and "liking" in motivating behavior: Gambling, food, and drug addictions. In P. D. Balsam & E. H. Simpson (Eds.), (Vol. 27, pp. 105–36). *Current topics in behavioral neurosciences*. doi:10.1007/7854_2015_387.

Robinson, M. J. F., Robinson, T. E., & Berridge, K. C. (2014b). Incentive salience in addiction and over-consumption. In S. Preston, M. L. Kringelbach, B. Knutson, & P. C. Whybrow (Eds.), *The interdisciplinary science of consumption* (pp. 185–97). Cambridge, MA: MIT Press.

Robinson, T. E. & Berridge, K. C. (1993). The neural basis of drug craving: an incentive-sensitization theory of addiction. *Brain Research Brain Research Reviews*, *18*(3), 247–91.

Robinson, T. E. & Berridge, K. C. (2001). Incentive-sensitization and addiction. *Addiction*, *96*(1), 103–14. doi:10.1046/j.1360-0443.2001.9611038.x.

Robinson, T. E. & Berridge, K. C. (2008). The incentive sensitization theory of addiction: some current issues. *Philosophical Transactions of the Royal Society of London Series B, Biological Sciences*, *363*(1507), 3137–46. doi:10.1098/rstb.2008.0093.

Rosse, R. B., Fay-McCarthy, M., Collins, J. P., Risher-Flowers, D., Alim, T. N., & Deutsch, S. I. (1993). Transient compulsive foraging behavior associated with crack cocaine use. *The American Journal of Psychiatry*, *150*(1), 155–6.

Salamone, J. D. & Correa, M. (2002). Motivational views of reinforcement: Implications for understanding the behavioral functions of nucleus accumbens dopamine. *Behavioural Brain Research*, *137*, 3–25.

Salamone, J. D., Cousins, M. S., & Bucher, S. (1994). Anhedonia or anergia? Effects of haloperidol and nucleus accumbens dopamine depletion on instrumental response selection in a T-maze cost/benefit procedure. *Behavioural Brain Research, 65*(2), 221–9. doi:10.1016/0166-4328(94)90108-2.

Schultz, W. (1998). Predictive reward signal of dopamine neurons. *Journal of Neurophysiology, 80*(1), 1–27.

Schultz, W. (2010). Subjective neuronal coding of reward: temporal value discounting and risk. *The European Journal of Neuroscience, 31*(12), 2124–35. doi:10.1111/j.1460-9568.2010.07282.x.

Schultz, W., Dayan, P., & Montague, P. R. (1997). A neural substrate of prediction and reward. *Science, 275*(5306), 1593–9.

Singer, B. F., Scott-Railton, J., & Vezina, P. (2012). Unpredictable saccharin reinforcement enhances locomotor responding to amphetamine. *Behavioural Brain Research, 226*(1), 340–4. doi:10.1016/j.bbr.2011.09.003.

Spence, K. W. (1956). *Behavior theory and conditioning.* New Haven, CT: Yale University Press. doi:10.1037/10029-000.

Tan, C. O. & Bullock, D. (2008). A local circuit model of learned striatal and dopamine cell responses under probabilistic schedules of reward. *Journal of Neuroscience, 28*(40), 10 062–74. doi:10.1523/JNEUROSCI.0259-08.2008.

Tindell, A. J., Smith, K. S., Berridge, K. C., & Aldridge, J. W. (2009). Dynamic computation of incentive salience: "wanting" what was never "liked." *The Journal of Neuroscience, 29*(39), 12220–8. doi:10.1523/JNEUROSCI.2499-09.2009.

Toates, F. (1986). *Motivational systems.* New York, NY: Cambridge University Press.

Tolman, E. C. (1949). The nature and functioning of wants. *Psychological Review, 56*(6), 357–69.

Turner, L. H., Solomon, R. L., Stellar, E., & Wampler, S. N. (1975). Humoral factors controlling food intake in dogs. *Acta Neurobiologiae Experimentalis, 35*(5-6), 491–8.

Valenstein, E. S., Cox, V. C., & Kakolewski, J. W. (1970). Reexamination of the role of the hypothalamus in motivation. *Psychological Review, 77*(1), 16–31.

Voon, V., Hassan, K., Zurowski, M., Duff-Canning, S., de Souza, M., Fox, S., … Miyasaki, J. (2006). Prospective prevalence of pathologic gambling and medication association in Parkinson disease. *Neurology, 66*(11), 1750–2. doi:10.1212/01.wnl.0000218206.20920.4d.

Wise, R. A. (1982). Neuroleptics and operant behavior: The anhedonia hypothesis. *Behavioral and Brain Sciences, 5*(1), 39–53.

Wolf, S. G. & Wolff, H. G. (1943). *Human gastric function: An experimental study of a man and his stomach.* London: Oxford University Press.

Woodward, A., Phillips, A., & Spelke, E. S. (1993). Infants' expectations about the motions of inanimate vs. animate objects. In *Proceedings of the Cognitive Science Society*, Hillsdale, NJ: Erlbaum.

Young, P. T. (1961). *Motivation and emotion: A survey of the determinants of human and animal activity.* Oxford: Wiley.

Zack, M., Featherstone, R. E., Mathewson, S., & Fletcher, P. J. (2014). Chronic exposure to a gambling-like schedule of reward predictive stimuli can promote sensitization to amphetamine in rats. In B. F. Singer, P. Anselme, M. J. Robinson, & P. Vezina (Eds.), *Neuronal and Psychological Underpinnings of Pathological Gambling. Lausanne: Frontiers in Behavioral Neuroscience, 8,* 36. doi:10.3389/fnbeh.2014.00036.

8 Attention, Information-Seeking, and Active Sampling

Empirical Evidence and Applications for Learning

Avanti Dey and Jacqueline Gottlieb

Abstract: *In this chapter, we present an overview of the literature addressing the neuroscience of attention, information-seeking, and active sampling, and we discuss its potential significance for learning and learning progress. First, we review the emerging hypothesis that attention is an active mechanism for information sampling and exploration in the environment. We then turn to a discussion of how reward motivates attention and how attention can be employed to reduce uncertainty about knowledge of one's current state. We further consider the way rewards interact with other factors (including novelty, surprise, and task relevance). Throughout the review, we particularly focus on the distinction between extrinsic and intrinsic motivation, highlighting curiosity as a key example of the latter in motivating the search for intrinsically desirable information that benefits learning on both long and short timescales. Finally, we discuss the role of cognitive control in directing attention during learning, as well as the way neural systems underlying cognition and motivation have implications for informing techniques for teaching and learning in wider educational contexts.*

In the field of neuroscience, attention remains both one of the most intensively studied phenomena and the most complex. William James defined selective attention in his seminal work *The Principles of Psychology* (1890) as "the narrowing of the mind" and, over a century later, the study of selective attention continues to attract interest. However, despite being acknowledged as a pervasive cognitive function in both human and nonhuman species, significant questions remain about the nature of attention, including its purpose, and its neural mechanisms.

Gottlieb et al. (see Gottlieb & Balan, 2010; Gottlieb, 2012 for reviews) have argued that attention forms a significant component of decision-making, by which individuals select appropriate actions or sources of information. Specifically, they describe attention as involving a complex interaction between motor, perceptual, affective, and cognitive processes that allows an individual to target relevant information in the environment, and which may then be used to

This chapter was supported in part by grants from the National Eye Institute, National Institute for Mental Health, and the Human Frontier Science Program.

guide actions and decisions. They point to the role of attention in information-seeking as a critical aspect of the capacity for curiosity and exploration (Gottlieb et al., 2013, 2016), and contend that the act of seeking information can itself be rewarding, motivating the individual to continue to seek out rewarding information. These aspects of reward and motivation form recurring elements of models of learning (see Flagel et al., 2011; Ryan & Deci, 2000; and Wise, 2004 for reviews), suggesting that these components are essential in the enhancement of learning mechanisms.

However, much of the attentional neuroscience literature has focused on relatively simple forms of learning, and it remains unclear how existing theories and models can accommodate more complex forms of learning, both in naturalistic settings and over a longer period of time than is generally investigated in the laboratory. In this chapter, we present an overview of the literature that directly links attention to the active sampling of information, curiosity, and reward, and attempt to illustrate how the integration of these elements may be relevant to real-world learning.

Attention in Information-Selection and Active-Sampling

To successfully negotiate the world, we are constantly called upon to make attentional decisions, ranging from the simple (look right or left when crossing the street) to the very complex (choose a mate or a career path). Decision-making occupies most of our cognitive capacity, and its failure may result in devastating behavioral and psychiatric disorders. Gottlieb & Balan (2010) and Gottlieb (2012) have proposed that attention can be understood as a mechanism for seeking and selecting information in order to make decisions; we review the evidence from animal and machine learning fields to that effect in this section.

Significant progress in understanding the cognitive mechanisms of decision-making was made possible by the development of behavioral tasks suitable for use in experimental animals. In these tasks animals are trained to make simple decisions based on sensory evidence or rewards, and express these decisions through specific actions. This strategy has been particularly successful in investigations of the oculomotor system, wherein monkeys report decisions by making a saccade (a type of rapid eye movement). Most studies of oculomotor decisions have focused on the lateral intraparietal (LIP) area, a cortical area located at the interface between visual input and oculomotor output (e.g., Gold & Shadlen, 2007; Goldberg et al., 2006; Gottlieb & Goldberg, 1999; Sugrue et al., 2005). LIP has been an attractive target of investigation, because its neurons encode the direction of an upcoming saccade in a manner that depends on the evidence for that saccade, suggesting that they provide a window into the mechanisms of decision formation (Gold & Shadlen, 2007; Goldberg et al., 2006; Kable & Glimcher, 2009; Sugrue et al., 2005). Specifically, these neurons may be relevant for attentional decisions that select sources of information. Although some empirical and computational approaches have portrayed vision as starting with a passive input stage that simply registers the available information (Blake & Yuille, 1992; Tsotsos, 2011), the active control of eye movements makes it clear that people, like other animals, actively sample (or select) the information they are interested in. Information sampling is therefore a highly active process (Blake & Yuille, 1992; Tsotsos, 2011), in which the brain actively seeks out and focuses on interesting sources of information.

The central insight from studies of LIP is that the neurons reflect not merely the final outcome of a decision – the metrics of an upcoming saccade – but also the accumulation of evidence leading to that decision. In a typical paradigm, monkeys see a patch containing random dot motion directed toward one of several saccade targets and are rewarded for selecting the target whose location is congruent with motion direction (Britten et al., 1992). As expected, LIP neurons encode the direction of the upcoming saccade, responding more if the monkey plans a saccade toward the receptive field relative to the opposite direction. Importantly, these responses depend on the strength of the sensory evidence supporting the saccade. Thus, these findings led to a view of LIP as an integration point for multiple sources of evidence, which encodes the accumulation of that evidence into an evolving motor plan, culminating in the final selection of an action (Beck et al., 2008; Mazurek et al., 2003; Wang, 2008).

However, the question remains as to *how* neurons know which target to select. While several lines of research have linked target selection responses in LIP with simple decisions based on perceptual evidence or rewards (Kable & Glimcher, 2009; Platt & Glimcher, 1999; Sugrue et al., 2005; Yang & Shadlen, 2007), these studies have yet to consider the unique information sampling nature of gaze (Gottlieb et al., 2014) and leave unresolved questions about the selection process encoded by the cells (Gottlieb, 2012; Maunsell, 2004). An intuitive solution, therefore, is to consider that attention and gaze play essential roles in sampling information. That is, attention is the mechanism by which an active sensing policy coordinates with the decision maker's beliefs, goals, or actions.

Because questions of active sampling are relatively infrequent in the study of oculomotor control, it is useful to start by considering the computations that they may entail. Active sampling is a ubiquitous aspect of natural behavior and a core building block of the perception-action cycle (e.g., before deciding what to do at an intersection, we look at the traffic, traffic sign, or traffic light). We next describe three distinct features that guide attention that results in the determination of which stimulus to sample (Gottlieb, 2018).

Model-Based Selection

One of the most important features of active sampling policies is that they depend on prior knowledge of the task structure, whereby a hierarchical process of prior knowledge organizes sampling strategies. This knowledge is embodied in a task model that specifies the requisite states and actions, as well as the relation between stimuli and subsequent states. Based on this knowledge, the decision maker can then estimate the probability (or uncertainty) of competing actions and the meaning of sensory cues, as well as the information that the cues may bring about future states (e.g., the colors of the traffic light are associated with either crossing or waiting).

Dependence on Reward and Uncertainty

A second critical feature of active sampling policies is that two possible mechanisms are capable of distinguishing between informative and uninformative cues: the reward expectations associated with a cue and the uncertainty stemming from the prospect that a cue will alter the decision maker's beliefs about future states. These mechanisms may play differential roles according to the context (Johnson et al., 2014; Sullivan et al., 2012), and we will discuss these reward- and uncertainty-based aspects of attention more fully in a later section.

Prospective Nature

A final important aspect of information sampling is that it requires the agent to decide which stimulus to sample (i.e., what to look at) before performing a detailed analysis of the sampled information (Navalpakkam & Itti, 2005). For instance, a pedestrian must decide to look at a traffic light before knowing whether the light is red or green. To understand active sampling, therefore, we must think of shifts of gaze or attention as *proactive* acts that request specific types of information in order to obtain a better view of that information.

Active Sampling: Learning for Information Gains

There is evidence that decision makers direct their gaze and attention to aspects of the environment based on how much information they expect to *gain* and not necessarily on the mere existence of something. To examine this, Yang et al. trained participants to use visual scanning to infer which of two types of pattern (stripes or spots) was disguised underneath a masked visual display (Yang et al., 2016). Participants made a series of saccades before classifying the pattern and received information via the transient removals of the mask in a local region around their current fixation. To model optimal behavior, the authors used a so-called Bayesian active sampling model that worked by (1) updating its estimates of the posterior probability of each candidate pattern based on the information acquired in each successive fixation, and (2) estimating the expected information gains (EIG) of each potential fixation location based on its current beliefs and the known statistics of the candidate patterns. The key finding was that gaze allocation, while not completely at the level of optimal predictions, was strongly biased toward locations with high expected gains in information. The findings are consistent with previous investigations (Najemnik & Geisler, 2005; Renninger et al., 2007) and clearly illustrate how saccades may be guided by defined measures of EIG.

An encoding of the reliability (or validity) of a cue – defined as the probability that a cue will deliver correct information – has also been shown to affect gaze and attention in a separate series of studies using an extension of the Posner cueing paradigm in which a cue was systematically manipulated (Vossel et al., 2006, 2013, 2015). One key finding of these studies is that participants showed a robust sensitivity to reliability, such that the cueing effects on reaction times (i.e., the difference in response latency for target detection on valid versus invalid trials) increased in proportion of reliability. That is, participants adjusted the weight they afforded to a predictive cue based on its estimated reliability. Participants were also observed to flexibly update their estimates of cue reliability when tested in a dynamic regime in which this quantity unexpectedly changed throughout a session. This dynamic updating was successfully modeled using a hierarchical Bayesian framework that represented, at successive levels, beliefs about the immediate target location, beliefs about the current validity of the cue, and beliefs about the volatility of the environment (Vossel et al., 2015).

Recall the earlier discussion on the LIP area – could cue reliability and EIG be related to this area, which is responsible for information accumulation in decision-making and is sensitive to both rewards and informational factors? To examine this question, monkeys were trained on a novel paradigm in which they made two contingently related saccades on each trial (Foley et al., 2017) – a first saccade to gather information from a visual cue that signaled 0 percent, 50 percent, or 100 percent reward likelihoods, and a second saccade to report a decision based on that information. Monkeys received the cue information in a gaze-contingent fashion (i.e., only after making a saccade to a cue) and made their saccadic decision based on advance information regarding cue reliability. When given the choice to choose which cue to sample, the monkeys consistently elected to inspect the more accurate cue, verifying that they adopted a reliability-based sampling policy. Moreover, LIP neurons showed robust modulations by cue reliability in both forced choice trials (in which a single cue appeared inside their receptive field) and, importantly, in free-choice trials in which the monkeys had the opportunity to freely select a cue.

Information-seeking behavior has also been explored in so-called "noninstrumental paradigms," in which monkeys can simply learn in advance about a reward that they will receive but cannot take actions to modify those rewards. Bromberg-Martin and Hikosaka (2009) gave monkeys the opportunity to sample one of two cues that had different reliabilities in predicting the size of a reward that would be given at the end of the trial. If the monkeys chose the informative cue, this cue changed to one of two patterns that provided advance information about reward size. However, choosing the uninformative item meant that the two revealed patterns had only a random relation to reward size. Thus, while monkeys were free to observe cues of different reliabilities, they could take no action to alter the reward probability. The monkeys exhibited a consistent preference for the informative cues, which was found to be associated with a small increase of activity in midbrain dopamine (DA) cells. A subsequent study extended this finding by showing that monkeys are even willing to sacrifice juice reward to view predictive cues, and neurons in the orbitofrontal cortex (OFC) encoded the value that the monkeys placed on this information (Blanchard et al., 2015). Critically, the responses in DA and OFC cells arose *before* the monkeys discriminated the specific reward information, corresponding to when the sampling decisions are made.

Collectively, these findings suggest that the learning and updating of cue reliability involves large-scale interactions between several systems involved in attention and reward valuation. In humans, gaze is directed by the degree of information expected to be obtained and can be dynamically adjusted to reflect both local and global beliefs about the stimuli and the environment. In monkeys, explicit signals of cue reliability are encoded in parietal oculomotor cells and can contribute to the top-down orienting of attention and gaze. However, the research reviewed in this section highlights a significant gap in the literature: studies to date have largely investigated relatively simple tasks, either through cue-stimulus association or saccadic shifts in attention. Although this evidence has been crucial in linking together several aspects of decision-making that were long considered disparate (i.e., aspects of attention and active-sampling), it is important to point out that how these mechanisms may apply to more complex forms of learning across a range of environments is unclear.

Information Sampling in a Known Environment

In addition to selecting actions that harvest immediate rewards, agents can also select actions that have indirect benefits by virtue of facilitating *future* actions. For example, in order to get a cookie from a high shelf, a child may first pull up a chair and climb on it before reaching for and grasping the cookie. This type of information gathering action is a special type of intermediate step that obeys the imperative to reduce uncertainty and adjudicate among competing interpretations.

Many computational approaches are adept at modeling this type of information-seeking, and one in particular relies on partially observable Markov decision processes (POMDPs) (Dayan & Daw, 2008; Kaelbling et al., 1998; see Bialek et al., 2001; and Singh et al., 2004, for alternative representations). A POMDP is a mathematical formalism that describes a task as a series of states, each with its own set of possible actions and immediate or future outcomes (rewards or punishments). The states are "partially observable" in the sense that their identities are not deterministic but described by probability distributions, making POMDPs useful tools for measuring uncertainty and the value of new information.

For purposes of illustration, let us return to the example of crossing an intersection. In a POMDP, the agent performing the task would be described as starting in an initial state, from which they can choose two possible actions: "stop" or "go." However, the agent has uncertainty about the true nature of state. Rather than acting directly under this uncertainty, the agent can choose to obtain more information through an intermediate "observing action," such as looking at the traffic light. This action is modeled as a transition to a different state, where the probability distributions are more clearly separated and the agent can be certain whether the optimal action is to stop or to proceed. Regardless of which alternative turns out to be correct, the agent has a much higher likelihood of obtaining a reward after, rather than before, having taken the action.

Information Sampling in an Unknown Environment

It is not always the case that an agent can readily discern all the information available to them in a given task or situation. In the field of developmental robotics, an alternative mechanism for learning has been proposed, which tracks an agent's local learning progress (LP) in a task space that is either unfamiliar or unknown (Oudeyer et al., 2007, 2013; Schmidhuber, 2013). The central objective of developmental robotics is to design agents that can explore in open-ended environments and develop autonomously without a pre-programmed trajectory, based on their intrinsic interest. A system that has been particularly successful in this regard explicitly measures the agent's LP in an activity, defined as an improvement in its predictions of the consequences of its actions (Oudeyer et al., 2007) or in its ability to solve self-generated problems over time (Baranes & Oudeyer, 2013; Srivastava et al., 2013), and rewards activities in proportion to their ability to produce LP. This system produces a targeted search for information that drives the agent to learn and, in using a local measure of learning the system, avoids the difficulties associated with defining an absolute (and potentially unknowable) goal.

The advantage of this approach is that it has been used most successfully in real-world situations. It allows robots to efficiently learn repertoires of skills in high dimensions and under strong time constraints, and to avoid unfruitful activities that are either well-learned and trivial or random and unlearnable (Baranes & Oudeyer, 2013; Nguyen & Oudeyer, 2013; Ngo et al., 2012; Pape et al., 2012). Furthermore, the system self-organizes development and learning trajectories that share fundamental qualitative properties with infant development (Kaplan & Oudeyer 2011; Moulin-Frier & Oudeyer, 2012; Oudeyer & Kaplan, 2006; Oudeyer et al., 2007).

In sum, a system based on LP holds considerable promise for achieving efficient, intrinsically motivated exploration in large open-ended spaces. It must be noted, however, that while computationally powerful, this approach entails a complex meta-cognitive architecture for monitoring LP that still awaits definitive empirical evidence. The question remains, therefore, as to what extent informational actions such as task-related eye movements extend to tasks, and eventually real-life scenarios, in which not all aspects of a situation are known or anticipated.

Attention in Uncertainty, Reward, and Motivation

As reviewed in the previous section, studies show that attention-directed eye movements are directly linked to goal-directed behaviors in which an agent actively seeks out and acquires information to guide a forthcoming action. We turn now to a discussion of *how* attention is guided so as to sample information, focusing on two related factors: the intention to reduce *uncertainty* and the intention to obtain *rewards*. Such considerations are particularly relevant for situations in which the parameters of a task are not well-defined or exist outside of a laboratory setting. We discuss the interaction between cognition (attention) and motivation in learning, and the way in which attention is employed in order to reduce uncertainty and maximize reward in guiding exploratory action.

Extrinsic Reward and Attention: Reinforcement Learning

The primary goal of exploratory action is not to exert force on the world, but to alter the *beliefs* of the decision maker (sometimes called an *epistemic state* – that is, what the decision maker knows). For instance, we instinctively orient to a new sign in a storefront or to a strange bird perched on a tree, while in laboratory tasks, gaze is drawn to novel or uncertain stimuli in familiar scenes (Brockmole & Henderson, 2005a, 2005b; Yang et al., 2009). We can define this as "attention for learning," which allocates resources to uncertain rather than reliable cues (Gottlieb, 2012).

It has been previously noted that the brain must distinguish between at least two types of uncertainty to generate adaptive exploration (Oudeyer et al., 2007; Payzan-LeNestour & Bossaerts, 2011; Yu & Dayan, 2005). *Reducible* uncertainty is due to the observer's imperfect knowledge and can be eliminated by acquiring information (e.g., a person hears an ambulance siren and turns to find out where it is). Indeed, "attention for learning" seems to be specifically guided by this form of uncertainty, as it possible to obtain information that can inform future action. In contrast, *irreducible* uncertainty is a property of the task itself and cannot be reduced through the observer's effort (e.g., white noise on a television screen; Gottlieb, 2012).

While information-seeking is often geared toward uncertainty reduction, the motivations behind this process can be diverse and derive from either *extrinsic* or *intrinsic* factors. In extrinsically motivated contexts, information gathering is a means to an end (i.e., it is used to maximize the agent's progress toward a separate goal). Paradigmatic examples of this type of sampling are the eye movements that subjects make in natural behavior – such as glancing at the traffic light at a busy intersection (Tatler et al., 2011). In reinforcement learning (RL) terms, task-related information sampling can be considered a feature of exploitation (the ability to act based on known rules in order to obtain rewards rather than learn). The agent is engaged in a task that seeks to maximize an extrinsic reward (e.g., food or money), and information gathering is an intermediate step in obtaining this reward. It may also be the case that an agent wishes to reach a goal but must explore further to discover an appropriate strategy for reaching that goal (e.g., learning to drive).

Indeed, much of the early work in monkeys suggests that one mechanism of attentional selection is based on prior *instrumental* learning of stimulus-reward (Pavlovian) associations, in which an informative cue is, by definition, one that signals the more desirable action, and thus the reliability of a cue is closely correlated with the chance of success in the task. Saccade-related responses in LIP and the basal ganglia are enhanced for reward-associated visual cues. This learning is slow and enduring and, importantly, modifies salience automatically even when visual stimuli are irrelevant for actions, consistent with the phenomenon of value-driven attention capture reported in human observers (Anderson et al., 2011; Della Libera & Chelazzi, 2009; Hickey et al., 2010). It has been found that that target selection responses in LIP cells scale monotonically with the value of a planned saccade, such as when value is defined according to the magnitude or probability of a juice reward delivered for making that saccade (Kable & Glimcher, 2009; Sugrue et al., 2005). This result supports the idea that saccade decisions can be described in economic or reinforcement terms. This can also be phrased in the context of our traffic light example: If the pedestrian looks at the traffic light and takes the action signaled by that light (i.e., either stop or go), they have correctly estimated the state of the world and have a high chance of success in the task (i.e., high reward probability). However, should the pedestrian decide to look at a cloud, the actions will be chosen at random and are far less likely to have a high reward probability. Although the shift of attention in and of itself is not the reward-harvesting action and therefore not the agent's primary goal, these actions take on indirect reward value, because the eventual probability of success of the action sequence is larger if they start by sampling an informative rather than an uninformative cue.

However, it is important to note that, while informativeness is closely aligned with reward associations in some instrumental contexts, this relationship is not obligatory in all task conditions. These conditions, to which we alluded in the previous section, include *non-instrumental* paradigms in which agents may simply want to know, but cannot act on the outcome. Gottlieb et al. have also tested LIP responses in this non-instrumental context, where visual stimuli brought information about a reward but did not support a decision based on that reward (Peck et al., 2009). At the onset of a trial in this study, the monkeys had uncertainty about the trial's reward. They viewed a brief visual stimulus that resolved this uncertainty by signaling whether the trial would end in a reward or a lack of reward (i.e., brought "good" or "bad" news). After presenting a cue inside or opposite the receptive field of an LIP cell, the monkeys were trained to maintain fixation for a brief delay and then make a saccade to a separate target that could appear either at the same or at the opposite location. Thus, the cues did not allow for the monkeys to make an active choice but could potentially bias attention toward or away from their visual field location. The authors found that both positive and negative cues evoked a similar visual response shortly after their onset, suggesting that they both transiently attracted attention, but it was only cues bringing "good news" that produced sustained neural *excitation* at slightly longer delays, whereas cues bringing "bad news" produced sustained *suppression*. Moreover, saccades following a positive cue were facilitated if they were directed toward the cue-congruent location, suggesting that "good news" automatically attracted attention.

While these results are consistent with previously described reward modulations, they differ in that they were not based on instrumental rewards in which the reward was only delivered by making a saccade, but on mere stimulus-reward associations. In other words, learned reward associations are capable of modifying the salience, or the ability, of a stimulus to automatically bias attention.

The concepts of *surprise* and *novelty* have also been shown to determine the way in which we attend to and sample information in the environment, due to the key role played by expectations in orienting attention toward significant items (Friston et al., 2013). Studies by Itti and Baldi have shown that surprise, defined in the domain of visual features, attracts human saccades during free-viewing exploration (Baldi & Itti, 2010; Itti & Baldi, 2009). They demonstrated that human free-viewing patterns could be predicted with greater fidelity and flexibility relative to simpler intensity based on a Bayesian model that directly incorporated the extent to which a particular visual input changed the observers' beliefs. That is, it is not the mere presence of information that attracts our attention, but the extent to which the information confirms or violates our prior expectations.

Novelty, in contrast with surprise, is not context-specific but is defined by the total amount of exposure that observers had to a given observation, and can be considered as the dissimilarity between a stimulus and the representation of familiar stimuli encoded in the observer's memory (Barto et al., 2013). In the framework of RL, novelty is thought to act as an internal reward that is equivalent to extrinsic rewards – novel stimuli activate midbrain dopaminergic structures (Horvitz, 2000; Laurent, 2008; Wittmann et al., 2007, 2008), provide a bonus for organizing reward-dependent exploration (Kakade & Dayan, 2002; Laurent, 2008; Lopes & Oudeyer, 2012), and recruit attentional resources through reward-independent effects (Foley et al., 2014; Peck et al., 2009).

Indeed, in comparing novel and familiar cues, we have observed that reward-dependent attentional effects are much weaker or absent for newly learned items (Foley et al., 2014). Instead, LIP neurons show enhanced responses to novel visual cues, and this novelty enhancement persists for dozens of presentations for cues that signal either negative or positive outcomes. When first confronted with a novel cue, monkeys showed anticipatory licking, indicating that they expected to receive a reward following the cue, but this licking quickly extinguished if a cue turned out to signal a negative outcome. Strikingly, however, the novel cue continued to produce enhanced salience and LIP responses, suggesting that it continued to attract attention even after the monkeys had learned its negative reward associations.

This enhanced salience of rewarding stimuli has been linked to the concept of *savoring*, in which people obtain utility not only from the physical rewards that they receive, but also from potential "anticipatory feelings" toward future rewards. Daddaoua et al. (2016) suggested, that subjects may sometimes seek to obtain conditioned reinforcement from a positive Pavlovian cue. According to this view, the animals' preference in the observing task can be motivated by the prospect of receiving a positive signal associated with the informative option (i.e., a cue indicating 100 percent large reward likelihood). This interpretation is supported by learning models postulating that animals are motivated both by uncertainty reduction and by "liking" for specific items (Litman, 2007). In addition, it is consistent with a rich literature showing that animals automatically approach reward-predicting Pavlovian cues even when they are not rewarded for the approach actions (Castro & Berridge, 2014; Dayan et al., 2006; Flagel et al., 2011).

Intrinsic Reward and Attention: Curiosity

This leads us to a discussion of *intrinsically* motivated contexts, which entail the search for information as a goal in itself – a process we would intuitively call "curiosity" or "interest,"[1] in contrast to extrinsic motivation based on the

1 Note that although "curiosity" and "interest" are used somewhat interchangeably in the colloquial sense, the psychology literature has distinguished between them. For instance, Litman (2005, 2008) has suggested that interest constitutes a psychometrically distinct component of the construct of curiosity by tapping into an affective element, in contrast to a deprivation-driven component. Research has also suggested that the difference between the two terms may be a function of developmental trajectories, in which interest may have a developmental aspect independently of curiosity (Grossnickle 2015; Renninger & Hidi, 2016). Collectively,

promise of salient reward. The fact that animals, and particularly humans, seem to avidly seek out information without the promise of an external reward suggests that the brain itself generates intrinsic rewards that assign value to information, raising complex questions about the benefits and computations of such rewards. From a computational perspective, intrinsically motivated behaviors can be characterized as would any other goal-directed behaviors – as actions that seek to maximize an internal goal, formalized as a reward (value) function. However, characterizing these internal factors is much more difficult due to the fact that they may be determined by multiple factors related to different aspects of the individual's affective or cognitive state. For instance, when creating a painting, an individual may be motivated by the desire to please a partner (a social reward), a feeling of pleasure in looking at the colors on the canvas (an emotional reward), or a desire to learn more about how to blend colors (a cognitive reward). These factors can be viewed as "rewards" in the broad sense of the term, much in the same way as any factor that reinforces behavior and "makes you come back for more" (Thorndike, 1911). However, it remains a formidable challenge to identify which of these internal rewards come into play in any given context and how these processes can be understood in relation to real-life learning contexts.

Curiosity is a particular system of intrinsic motivation that motivates agents to learn. In the early 1950s, Berlyne's seminal work on curiosity resulted in the delineation of several dimensions of curiosity, including *specific epistemic curiosity* – the desire for a particular piece of information (Berlyne, 1960). Specifically, Berlyne described curiosity as a drive state, functioning much in the same way as a biological drive. Just as animals seek to fill gaps in their physical resources (e.g., energy, sex, or wealth) they seek to fill gaps in their knowledge by taking learning-oriented actions. This brings us back again to the imperative to minimize uncertainty about the state of the world, and suggests that this imperative is similar to a biological drive.

It is important to recognize, however, that, while biological drives are prompted by salient and easily recognizable signs (e.g., somatic signals for hunger or sex), recognizing and eliminating information gaps requires a radically different, knowledge-based mechanism. Loewenstein (1994) built on these ideas and proposed an "information gap" hypothesis to explain specific epistemic curiosity. According to the information gap theory, this type of curiosity arises because of a discrepancy between what the observer knows and what he would like to know, where knowledge can be measured with traditional measures of information. For example, consider a mystery novel where the author initially introduces ten suspects who are equally likely to have committed a

---

these findings suggest that curiosity and interest may correspond to different learning goals and require different mechanisms – although these distinctions have not been made in the neuroscience literature, for which reason we focus on the overarching construct of "curiosity" in this chapter.

murder, and the reader's goal is to identify the true culprit. The reader can be described as wanting to move from a state of high entropy (or uncertainty, with multiple possible alternative murderers) to one of low entropy (with a single culprit identified), and their curiosity arises through awareness of the difference between the current and the goal (reference) uncertainty states. Defined in this way, curiosity can be viewed as a deprivation phenomenon that seeks to fill a need similar to other biological drives.

Curiosity in Computational Modeling

A further hallmark of curiosity is that it generates not a random, but a structured pattern of investigation. In the studies discussed in the first section of this chapter, tasks were largely designed with fixed parameters for individuals from which to actively sample. However, efficient information-seeking in open-ended conditions poses significant computational challenges. These stem from the fact that the agent explores in conditions of limited knowledge and time, the fact that they are faced with vast numbers of possible tasks, and the fact that many of these tasks are random or unlearnable and would optimally be avoided (e.g., one would ideally not spend much effort in trying to predict the stock market from the traffic pattern). To explore efficiently under these conditions (i.e., in a way that increases knowledge), agents may rely in part on low-level heuristics such as novelty bias or random action selection, but also require systems of intrinsic motivation that assign value to learnable tasks (Baldassarre & Mirolli, 2013; Gottlieb et al., 2013; Kaplan & Oudeyer, 2007; Lopes & Oudeyer, 2012; Oudeyer et al., 2007; Schmidhuber, 2006).

Computational studies show that, in environments that change quickly or continuously, curious individuals can gain an advantage by acquiring new skills and discovering new environmental structures (Barto, 2013; Singh et al., 2010). However, because natural environments contain many possible tasks – including learnable, unlearnable, or impossible tasks of varying complexity – agents cannot possibly assign intrinsic value to *all* sources of information. Such a strategy would result in collecting disparate pieces of information with nearly no discovery of useful structures, especially given the constraints of time and energy over a biological life span. Therefore, a successful curiosity mechanism must assign value to possible endeavors systematically and selectively in a way that maximizes the long-term advantage that can accrue from intrinsically motivated exploration.

One mechanism that has successfully described this process is learning progress (LP), which integrates a framework for learning over varying timescales and the intrinsic reward it generates. Specifically, the LP hypothesis proposes that the brain, seen as a predictive machine constantly trying to anticipate what will happen next, is intrinsically motivated to pursue activities in which predictions are *improving* (i.e., where uncertainty is decreasing and learning is actually occurring; Oudeyer et al., 2016). This means that the organism loses interest in activities that are either too easy or too difficult to predict (i.e., where uncertainty is low, or where uncertainty is high but not reducible) and focuses specifically on learnable activities that are just beyond its current predictive capacities. Moreover, the LP hypothesis posits a causal link between learning and curiosity, proposing that experiencing learning in a given activity triggers an intrinsic reward, and thus that learning in itself causally influences state curiosity and intrinsic motivation via a closed, self-reinforcing feedback loop between learning and curiosity-driven intrinsic motivation. In this situation, the learner becomes fundamentally active and is motivated to search for niches of learning in which, in turn, memory retention is facilitated (Oudeyer et al., 2016).

Existing computational models of LP suggest that intrinsically motivated exploration and learning can efficiently guide autonomous skill acquisition in large, novel, or difficult task spaces. For instance, Baranes and Oudeyer (2013) have shown that intrinsically motivated goal exploration can allow robots to sample sensorimotor spaces by actively controlling the complexity of explored goals and avoiding those goals that are either too easy or unattainable. Such a method allows robots to learn vast repertoires of multi-dimensional, continuous action skills in complex environments. Such an approach also allows for more efficient learning of models in which the dynamics are non-stationary (Lopes & Oudeyer, 2012). Furthermore, systems of intrinsic motivation may also foster spontaneous exploration of novel skills and promote potential synergies among skills, thereby generating learning pathways toward certain skills that would have remained difficult to reach in isolation (Baranes & Oudeyer, 2013; Forestier & Oudeyer, 2016).

Information as Reward in Neuroscience

The studies reviewed thus far support an *information-as-reward* hypothesis, demonstrating that curiosity conforms to basic characteristics of reward-motivated behavior. Emerging neuroscientific evidence corroborates this hypothesis, suggesting that curiosity for information involves the concerted action of dopaminergic systems implicated in value and motivation, as well as cortical systems mediating cognitive processes of memory and attention. For instance, Kang et al. (2009) used functional magnetic resonance imaging (fMRI) – a technique that measures brain activity by detecting changes associated with blood flow – to observe neural activity in human observers who pondered trivia questions. After reading a question, subjects rated their curiosity and confidence regarding the question and, after a brief delay, were given the answer. The key analyses focused on activations during the anticipatory period – after the subjects had received the question but before they were given the answer.

Areas that showed activity related to curiosity during this epoch included the left caudate nucleus, bilateral inferior frontal gyrus (IFG), and loci in the putamen and globus pallidus. The authors also showed that subjects were willing to pay a higher price to obtain the answers to questions about which they were more curious. They concluded that the value of the information, experienced as a feeling of curiosity, is encoded in some of the same structures that evaluate material gains (Kang et al., 2009).

To further investigate the attentional component of curiosity, Baranes et al. (2015) adapted the procedure used by Kang et al. (2009) to incorporate eye-tracking. Subjects were presented with trivia questions and asked to rate their curiosity and confidence in the answer, while their eye movements were being tracked during the anticipation period. The authors reliably observed that questions eliciting higher curiosity were associated with faster anticipatory gaze shifts to the expected location of the answer. Furthermore, the magnitude of the eye movement effect was correlated with measures of curiosity-related personality traits (Risko et al., 2012). Finally, machine learning algorithms reliably read out curiosity states from the eye movement patterns, generalizing across individual observers and relying primarily on the anticipatory orienting of gaze.

Additional studies have shown that higher curiosity is associated with enhanced memory performance, possibly through the heightened activation of parahippocampal structures and its dopaminergic projections (Gruber et al., 2014; Kang et al., 2009). Moreover, people are more willing to wait and pay for information about which they are more curious (Kang et al., 2009), and that high-curiosity information is associated with activation in brain areas known to respond to rewards, including the nucleus accumbens and the caudate (Gruber et al., 2014; Kang et al., 2009). There is also a strong link between how valuable information is and the likelihood of remembering it. People are more likely to remember high-curiosity information; even incidental information presented during a high-curiosity state is better remembered later (Gruber et al., 2014; Kang et al., 2009; Mullaney et al., 2014). Such results corroborate well-known findings regarding the enhancing effect of reward on subsequent memory (e.g., Adcock et al., 2006). Thus, in addition to generating global signals of arousal and motivation, curiosity also recruits cognitive systems related to memory and attention.[2] This recruitment is clearly beneficial in allowing observers to discriminate, encode, and retain the valuable information. In addition, it may be critically important in motivating the observers to sample specific items.

---

2 It is important to note that the reward system also comprises a significant affective component (see Berridge & Kringelbach, 2008 for a review), which may be linked to the concept of "interest," as mentioned in a previous footnote (Germain & Hess, 2007; Hidi, 1990; Isaacowitz et al., 2006; Mather & Carstensen, 2003; Renninger & Hidi, 2011). However, how this component is directly linked to attention and information-seeking is not yet well understood, and is beyond the immediate scope of this chapter.

Attention, Cognitive Control, and Difficulty

In the final section of this chapter, we briefly discuss the neural interface of attention and cognitive control, and how the engagement of frontal regions of the brain can facilitate learning. Although a full discussion of the neural underpinnings of cognitive control is beyond the scope of this chapter, we specifically highlight how the studies discussed so far frame the interplay of cognitive and motivational systems that may facilitate learning.

It is well-established that the activation of attentional systems in the brain increases in response to demands placed on attentional performance, whether through distraction, sustained attention, or target shifting (see Sarter et al., 2006 for a review). Specifically, the more challenging the task, the greater the increase in coordinated activity between multiple neural regions underlying attention, control, and motivation. Attentional performance under challenging conditions, particularly the enhancement of attentional processes in response to *increasing* challenge, requires mechanisms that act to optimize input processing and the redistribution and focusing of processing resources. Such functions have been conceptualized as being orchestrated by "supervisory attentional systems" (Norman & Shallice, 1986; Stuss et al., 1995), a "central executive control" (Baddeley, 1986), or the anterior attention network (Posner, 1994; Posner & Dehaene, 1994). Prefrontal and anterior cingulate cortices, interacting with parietal areas, have been consistently identified as representing the core components of the brain's circuitry responsible for top-down control (Buschman & Miller, 2007; Dosenbach et al., 2008; Friedman-Hill et al., 2003; Gehring & Knight, 2002; Pessoa et al., 2003).

There is also evidence that the cortical cholinergic input system originating from the basal forebrain represents an essential component of neuronal systems mediating attentional functions and capacities (e.g., Chiba et al., 1995; Dalley et al., 2001; Everitt & Robbins, 1997). Moreover, this circuitry has been shown to be modulated in response to the effects of incentive and motivation on attentional performance and learning (Botvinick et al., 2001). That is, motivation appears to determine the degree of effort. To that effect, studies have reliably shown that manipulating the incentives associated with task performance elicits variation in neural activity associated with effortful cognitive control (Falkenstein et al., 1995; Gehring et al., 1993; Ullsperger & von Cramon, 2004).

Indeed, motivation appears to play a significant role in the degree of attention and effort devoted to a task (although it should be noted that the two types can be difficult to separate [Hidi, 2016]). However, it is not merely a linear relationship. Among the most influential theories of intrinsic motivation is the principle of optimal challenge – also referred to as the *autotelic principle* (Steels, 2004) – which states that people avoid activities that are too easy or too difficult (and produce, respectively, boredom and frustration) and instead focus on activities with an intermediate level of challenge (Berlyne, 1960; Csikszentmihalyi, 1997).

Similarly, the effects of reward responsiveness may also follow this inverted U-pattern, such that some level of external or internal reward may boost motivation toward better cognitive performance (Satterthwaite et al., 2012), whereas too much focus on reward may result in performance decrements (i.e., choking), thereby hindering performance (van Duijvenvoorde et al., 2016). Moreover, engagement in optimally challenging tasks can, at times, induce a highly pleasurable state of "flow," characterized by feelings of being relaxed, absorbed, and in control (Abuhamdeh & Csikszentmihalyi, 2012; Keller & Bless, 2008), suggesting that it triggers internal rewards.

In order to examine how difficulty affects learning in open-ended tasks, Gottlieb et al. developed a paradigm for systematically testing the choices of human observers in a free-play context (Baranes et al., 2015). Participants played a series of short computer games of variable difficulty and freely chose which game they wished to play without external guidance or rewards. Subjects were free to sample from a small or a large choice set of difficulty levels, and where they did or did not have the possibility to sample new games at a constant level of difficulty. The results showed that participants spontaneously adopted a structured exploration strategy that was largely guided by levels of difficulty, in which they (1) generally started with easier games and progressed to more difficult games, and (2) often repeated moderately and highly difficult games much more frequently than was predicted by chance, suggesting the tendency to practice.

Although, to our knowledge, there is little neuroscientific evidence that can speak to the neural underpinnings of such phenomena, we can reasonably hypothesize that the incorporation of difficulty and (intrinsic) reward into a free-exploration paradigm involves the complex coordination of multiple systems of attention, motivation, and reward. An individual begins a free exploration of the games and, having successfully completed a game, receives an "internal" reward. The individual is then motivated to continue to seek out more games, focusing attention on the slightly more difficult games, anticipating the promise of further internal reward for having successfully completed such a game. That is, accompanying the search through the space of games entails an increasingly heightened coordinated response between the multiple systems of cognition (attention) and motivation, and the individual continues to be rewarded through the successful learning (i.e., the completion of increasingly difficult games, or even the completion of the same game multiple times, thereby reinforcing their aptitude at that particular level).

Concluding Thoughts

Throughout this chapter, we have emphasized that attention is the primary mechanism by which agents seek out and sample an environment in order to acquire information (i.e., learn). Active sampling may be motivated by the desire to reduce uncertainty or by the desire to obtain reward. While extrinsic reward in the form of food or money has clear consequences for facilitating relatively simple forms of learning, intrinsic motivation, often in the form of (epistemic) curiosity, presents a new challenge for understanding what facilitates learning in less constrained and potentially unknown contexts.

Our understanding of the links between attention, information-seeking, reward, and motivation remains far from complete, and there are several open questions that remain to be addressed. These broadly include: (1) What determines how attention is related to learning and information-seeking? Is more attention allocated to more reliable cues, or is attention allocated to more uncertain stimuli in order to facilitate learning about them? How does the context of a known or an unknown environment determine this relationship? (2) What are the mechanisms that motivate attention? How critical are reward signals for motivating attention, and what is their source? How can we bridge the findings from psychology to neuroscience in understanding how curiosity and motivation interact with attention to promote learning and information-seeking? What determines an individual's degree of curiosity and motivation, and how can they be leveraged to inform learning? (3) How can existing biological and computational models incorporate the complex dynamism of attention, information-seeking, reward, and motivation? With many aspects of this interaction still unknown, how can a unifying framework be fruitfully applied to neuroscientific studies of attention and learning, and can it provide a bridge for cross-talk between the fields of neuroscience, psychology, and computation?

Findings reviewed in this chapter further suggest several important features that have implications for real-life learning. First, they highlight the importance of providing individuals with learning materials that are informationally engaging and have the right level of complexity and learnability. Second, they suggest the importance of personalized and active learning. Indeed, features like novelty or LP are fundamentally subjective, in the sense that they are a measure of the relation between a particular type of learning material and the state of knowledge of a particular learner at a given time of their learning trajectory. As a consequence, that which triggers curiosity and learning will be specialized across different individuals. Learners have also a fundamental capability that should be leveraged: as evidenced by the literature, the brain is intrinsically rewarded by features like novelty or LP, so motivated individuals will spontaneously and actively search for these features and select adequate learning materials if the environment and teacher provide an adequate range of options. Of course, these stipulations assume that the learning environment is a somewhat structured one (as in a classroom), and it is not clear how these many elements may interact in a less constrained environment.

In sum, we have described the role of attention in several relevant aspects of learning, setting the stage for future research to investigate how these various systems interact, what comprises their underlying mechanisms, and how they can be adapted into real-world, complex learning situations. In moving forward, it will be crucial to better understand the interaction between neural systems of cognition and motivation or reward. Specifically, converging research strands from psychology, neuroscience, and computational learning theory indicate that attention, curiosity, motivation, and reward are firmly interconnected across several dimensions, and that such connections have wide implications for learning and education.

References

Abuhamdeh, S. & Csikszentmihalyi, M. (2012). The importance of challenge for the enjoyment of intrinsically motivated, goal-directed activities. *Personality and Social Psychology Bulletin, 38*(3), 317–30. doi:10.1177/0146167211427147.

Adcock, R. A., Thangavel, A., Whitfield-Gabrieli, S., Knutson, B., & Gabrieli, J. D. (2006). Reward-motivated learning: Mesolimbic activation precedes memory formation. *Neuron, 50*(3), 507–17. doi:10.1016/j.neuron.2006.03.036.

Anderson, B. A., Laurent, P. A., & Yantis, S. (2011). Value-driven attentional capture. *Proceedings of the National Academy of Sciences of the United States of America, 108*(25), 10 367–71. doi:10.1073/pnas.1104047108.

Baddeley, A. D. (1986). *Working memory*. Oxford: Oxford University Press.

Baldassarre, G. & Mirolli, M. (2013). Intrinsically motivated learning systems: An overview. In *Intrinsically motivated learning in natural and artificial systems* (pp. 1–14). Berlin Heidelberg: Springer. doi:10.1007/978-3-642-32375-1_1.

Baldi, P. & Itti, L. (2010). Of bits and wows: A Bayesian theory of surprise with applications to attention. *Neural Networks, 23*(5), 649–66. doi:10.1016/j.neunet.2009.12.007.

Baranes, A. & Oudeyer, P. Y. (2013). Active learning of inverse models with intrinsically motivated goal exploration in robots. *Robotics and Autonomous Systems, 61*(1), 49–73. doi:10.1016/j.robot.2012.05.00.

Baranes, A., Oudeyer, P. Y., & Gottlieb, J. (2015). Eye movements reveal epistemic curiosity in human observers. *Vision Research, 117*, 81–90. doi:10.1016/j.visres.2015.10.009.

Barto, A. G. (2013). Intrinsic motivation and reinforcement learning. In *Intrinsically motivated learning in natural and artificial systems* (pp. 17–47). Berlin Heidelberg: Springer. doi:10.1007/978-3-642-32375-1_2.

Barto, A., Mirolli, M., & Baldassarre, G. (2013). Novelty or surprise? *Frontiers in Psychology, 4*. doi:10.3389/fpsyg.2013.00907.

Beck, J. M., Ma, W. J., Kiani, R., Hanks, T., Churchland, A. K., Roitman, J., ... Pouget, A. (2008). Probabilistic population codes for Bayesian decision making. *Neuron, 60*(6), 1142–52. doi:10.1016/j.neuron.2008.09.021.

Berlyne, D. E. (1960). *Conflict, arousal, and curiosity*. McGraw-Hill.

Berridge, K. C. & Kringelbach, M. L. (2008). Affective neuroscience of pleasure: Reward in humans and animals. *Psychopharmacology, 199*(3), 457–80. doi:10.1007/s00213-008-1099-6.

Bialek, W., Nemenman, I., & Tishby, N. (2001). Predictability, complexity, and learning. *Neural Computation, 13*(11), 2409–63. doi:10.1162/089976601753195969.

Blake, A. & Yuille, A. (1992). *Active vision*. Cambridge, MA: MIT Press.

Blanchard, T. C., Hayden, B. Y., & Bromberg-Martin, E. S. (2015). Orbitofrontal cortex uses distinct codes for different choice attributes in decisions motivated by curiosity. *Neuron, 85*(3), 602–14. doi:10.1016/j.neuron.2014.12.050.

Botvinick, M. M., Braver, T. S., Barch, D. M., Carter, C. S., & Cohen, J. D. (2001). Conflict monitoring and cognitive control. *Psychological Review, 108*(3), 624. doi:10.1037/0033-295X.108.3.624.

Britten, K. H., Shadlen, M. N., Newsome, W. T., & Movshon, J. A. (1992). The analysis of visual motion: A comparison of neuronal and psychophysical performance. *Journal of Neuroscience, 12*(12), 4745–65.

Brockmole, J. R. & Henderson, J. M. (2005a). Object appearance, disappearance, and attention prioritization in real-world scenes. *Psychonomic Bulletin & Review, 12*(6), 1061–7. doi:10.3758/BF03206444.

Brockmole, J. R. & Henderson, J. M.(2005b). Prioritization of new objects in real-world scenes: Evidence from eye movements. *Journal of Experimental Psychology–Human Perception and Performance, 31*(5), 857–68. doi:10.1037/0096-1523.31.5.857.

Bromberg-Martin, E. S. & Hikosaka, O. (2009). Midbrain dopamine neurons signal preference for advance information about upcoming rewards. *Neuron, 63*(1), 119–26. doi:10.1016/j.neuron.2009.06.009.

Buschman, T. J. & Miller, E. K. (2007). Top-down versus bottom-up control of attention in the prefrontal and posterior parietal cortices. *Science, 315*(5820), 1860–2.

Castro, D. C. & Berridge, K. C. (2014). Advances in the neurobiological bases for food "liking" versus "wanting." *Physiology & Behavior, 136*, 22–30. doi:10.1126/science.1138071.

Chiba, A. A., Bucci, D. J., Holland, P. C., & Gallagher, M. (1995). Basal forebrain cholinergic lesions disrupt increments but not decrements in conditioned stimulus processing. *Journal of Neuroscience, 15*(11), 7315–22.

Csikszentmihalyi, M. (1997). *Flow and the psychology of discovery and invention.* New York, NY: Harper Perennial.

Daddaoua, N., Lopes, M., & Gottlieb, J. (2016). Intrinsically motivated oculomotor exploration guided by uncertainty reduction and conditioned reinforcement in non-human primates. *Scientific Reports, 6.* doi:10.1038/srep20202.

Dalley, J. W., McGaughy, J., O'Connell, M. T., Cardinal, R. N., Levita, L., & Robbins, T. W. (2001). Distinct changes in cortical acetylcholine and noradrenaline efflux during contingent and noncontingent performance of a visual attentional task. *Journal of Neuroscience, 21*(13), 4908–14.

Dayan, P. & Daw, N. D. (2008). Decision theory, reinforcement learning, and the brain. *Cognitive, Affective, & Behavioral Neuroscience, 8*(4), 429–53. doi:10.3758/cabn.8.4.429.

Dayan, P., Niv, Y., Seymour, B., & Daw, N. D. (2006). The misbehavior of value and the discipline of the will. *Neural Networks, 19*(8), 1153–60. doi:10.1016/j.neunet.2006.03.002.

Della Libera, C. & Chelazzi, L. (2009). Learning to attend and to ignore is a matter of gains and losses. *Psychological Science, 20*(6), 778–84. doi:10.1111/j.1467-9280.2009.02360.x.

Dosenbach, N. U., Fair, D. A., Cohen, A. L., Schlaggar, B. L., & Petersen, S. E. (2008). A dual-networks architecture of top-down control. *Trends in Cognitive Sciences, 12*(3), 99–105. doi:10.1016/j.tics.2008.01.001.

Everitt, B. J. & Robbins, T. W. (1997). Central cholinergic systems and cognition. *Annual Review of Psychology*, *48*(1), 649–84. doi:10.1146/annurev.psych.48.1.649.

Falkenstein, M., Koshlykova, N. A., Kiroj, V. N., Hoormann, J., & Hohnsbein, J. (1995). Late ERP components in visual and auditory Go/Nogo tasks. *Electroencephalography and Clinical Neurophysiology/Evoked Potentials Section*, *96*(1), 36–43. doi:10.1016/0013-4694(94)00182-k.

Flagel, S. B., Clark, J. J., Robinson, T. E., Mayo, L., Czuj, A., Willuhn, I., ... Akil, H.,(2011). A selective role for dopamine in reward learning. *Nature*, *469*(7328), 53. doi:10.1038/nature09588.

Foley, N. C., Jangraw, D. C., Peck, C., & Gottlieb, J. (2014). Novelty enhances visual salience independently of reward in the parietal lobe. *Journal of Neuroscience*, *34*(23), 7947–57. doi:10.1523/jneurosci.4171-13.2014.

Foley, N. C., Kelly, S. P., Mhatre, H., Lopes, M., & Gottlieb, J. (2017). Parietal neurons encode expected gains in instrumental information. *Proceedings of the National Academy of Sciences of the United States of America*, *114*(16), E3315-E3323.

Forestier, S. & Oudeyer, P. Y. (2016). Curiosity-driven development of tool use precursors: A computational model. In *38th Annual Conference of the Cognitive Science Society (CogSci 2016)* (pp. 1859–64).

Friedman-Hill, S. R., Robertson, L. C., Desimone, R., & Ungerleider, L. G. (2003). Posterior parietal cortex and the filtering of distractors. *Proceedings of the National Academy of Sciences of the United States of America*, *100*(7), 4263–8. doi:10.1073/pnas.0730772100.

Friston, K., Schwartenbeck, P., FitzGerald, T., Moutoussis, M., Behrens, T., & Dolan, R. (2013). The anatomy of choice: active inference and agency. *Frontiers in Human Neuroscience*, *7*. doi:10.3389/fnhum.2013.00598.

Gehring, W. J., Goss, B., Coles, M. G., Meyer, D. E., & Donchin, E. (1993). A neural system for error detection and compensation. *Psychological Science*, *4*(6), 385–90. doi:10.1111/j.1467-9280.1993.tb00586.x.

Gehring, W. J. & Knight, R. T. (2002). Lateral prefrontal damage affects processing selection but not attention switching. *Cognitive Brain Research*, *13*(2), 267–79. doi:10.1016/s0926-6410(01)00132-x.

Germain, C. M. & Hess, T. M. (2007). Motivational influences on controlled processing: Moderating distractibility in older adults. *Aging, Neuropsychology, and Cognition*, *14*(5), 462–86. doi:10.1080/13825580600611302.

Gold, J. I. & Shadlen, M. N. (2007). The neural basis of decision making. *Annual Review of Neuroscience*, *30*, 535–74. doi:10.1146/annurev.neuro.29.051605.113038.

Goldberg, M. E., Bisley, J. W., Powell, K. D., & Gottlieb, J. (2006). Saccades, salience and attention: the role of the lateral intraparietal area in visual behavior. *Progress in Brain Research*, *155*, 157–75. doi:10.1016/S0079-6123(06)55010-1.

Gottlieb, J. (2012). Attention, learning, and the value of information. *Neuron*, *76*(2), 281–95. doi:10.1016/j.neuron.2012.09.034.

Gottlieb, J. (2018). Understanding active sampling strategies: empirical approaches and implications for attention and decision research. *Cortex*, *102*, 150–60. doi:10.1016/j.cortex.2017.08.019.

Gottlieb, J. & Balan, P. (2010). Attention as a decision in information space. *Trends in Cognitive Sciences*, *14*(6), 240–8. doi:10.1016/j.tics.2010.03.001.

Gottlieb, J. & Goldberg, M. E. (1999). Activity of neurons in the lateral intraparietal area of the monkey during an antisaccade task. *Nature Neuroscience*, *2*(10), 906–13. doi:10.1038/13209.

Gottlieb, J., Hayhoe, M., Hikosaka, O., & Rangel, A. (2014). Attention, reward, and information seeking. *Journal of Neuroscience, 34*(46), 15497–504. doi:10.1523/JNEUROSCI.3270-14.2014.

Gottlieb, J., Lopes, M., & Oudeyer, P. Y. (2016). Motivated cognition: Neural and computational mechanisms of curiosity, attention, and intrinsic motivation. In S. Kim, J. Reeve & M. Bong (Eds.), *Advances in motivation and achievement: Recent developments in neuroscience research on human motivation* (pp. 149–72). Bingley: Emerald Group Publishing.

Gottlieb, J., Oudeyer, P. Y., Lopes, M., & Baranes, A. (2013). Information-seeking, curiosity, and attention: computational and neural mechanisms. *Trends in Cognitive Sciences, 17*(11), 585–93. doi:10.1016/j.tics.2013.09.001.

Grossnickle, E. M. (2015). *The expression and enactment of interest and curiosity in a multiple source use task* (Doctoral dissertation). University of Maryland, College Park.

Gruber, M. J., Gelman, B. D., & Ranganath, C. (2014). States of curiosity modulate hippocampus-dependent learning via the dopaminergic circuit. *Neuron, 84*(2), 486–96. doi:10.1016/j.neuron.2014.08.060.

Hickey, C., Chelazzi, L., & Theeuwes, J. (2010). Reward changes salience in human vision via the anterior cingulate. *Journal of Neuroscience. 30*, 11096–103. doi:10.1523/JNEUROSCI.1026-10.2010.

Hidi, S. (1990). Interest and its contribution as a mental resource for learning. *Review of Educational Research, 60*(4), 549–71. doi:10.3102/00346543060004549.

Hidi, S. (2016). Revisiting the role of rewards in motivation and learning: Implications of neuroscientific research. *Educational Psychology Review, 28*(1), 61–93. doi:10.1007/s10648-015-9307-5.

Horvitz, J. C. (2000). Mesolimbocortical and nigrostriatal dopamine responses to salient non-reward events. *Neuroscience, 96*(4), 651–6. doi:10.1016/S0306-4522(00)00019-1.

Isaacowitz, D. M., Wadlinger, H. A., Goren, D., & Wilson, H. R. (2006). Selective preference in visual fixation away from negative images in old age? An eye-tracking study. *Psychology and Aging, 21*(1), 40. doi:10.1037/0882-7974.21.1.40.

Itti, L. & Baldi, P. (2009). Bayesian surprise attracts human attention. *Vision Research, 49*(10), 1295–306. doi:10.1016/j.visres.2008.09.007.

Johnson, L., Sullivan, B., Hayhoe, M., & Ballard, D. (2014). Predicting human visuomotor behavior in a driving task. *Philosophical Transactions of the Royal Society B: Biological Sciences, 369*(1636), 20130044. doi:10.1098/rstb.2013.0044.

Kable, J. W. & Glimcher, P. W. (2009). The neurobiology of decision: consensus and controversy. *Neuron, 63*(6), 733–45. doi:10.1016/j.neuron.2009.09.003.

Kaelbling, L. P., Littman, M. L., & Cassandra, A. R. (1998). Planning and acting in partially observable stochastic domains. *Artificial Intelligence, 101*(1), 99–134. doi:10.1016/s0004-3702(98)00023-x.

Kakade, S. & Dayan, P. (2002). Dopamine: Generalization and bonuses. *Neural Networks, 15*(4), 549–59. doi:10.1016/s0893-6080(02)00048-5.

Kang, M. J., Hsu, M., Krajbich, I. M., Loewenstein, G., McClure, S. M., Wang, J. T. Y., & Camerer, C. F. (2009). The wick in the candle of learning: Epistemic curiosity activates reward circuitry and enhances memory. *Psychological Science, 20*(8), 963–73. doi:10.2139/ssrn.1308286.

Kaplan, F. & Oudeyer, P.-Y. (2007). In search of the neural circuits of intrinsic motiva-
     tion. *Frontiers in Neuroscience*, *1*, 17

Kaplan, F. & Oudeyer, P.-Y. (2011). From hardware and software to kernels and enve-
     lopes: A concept shift for robotics, developmental psychology, and brain
     sciences. In J. L. Krichmar & H. Wagatsuma (Eds.), *Neuromorphic and
     brain-based robots* (pp. 217–50). Cambridge: Cambridge University Press.
     doi:10.1017/cbo9780511994838.011.

Keller, J. & Bless, H. (2008). Flow and regulatory compatibility: An experimental
     approach to the flow model of intrinsic motivation. *Personality and Social
     Psychology Bulletin*, *34*(2), 196–209. doi:10.1177/0146167207310026.

Laurent, P. A. (2008). The emergence of saliency and novelty responses from rein-
     forcement learning principles. *Neural Networks*, *21*(10), 1493–9. doi:10.1016/
     j.neunet.2008.09.004.

Litman, J. A. (2005). Curiosity and the pleasures of learning: Wanting and liking
     new information. *Cognition & Emotion*, *19*(6), 793–814. doi:10.1080/026999
     30541000101.

Litman, J. A. (2007). Curiosity as a feeling of interest and feeling of deprivation: The I/D
     model of curiosity. *Issues in the Psychology of Motivation*, 149–56. doi:10.1037/
     t27877-000.

Litman, J. A. (2008). Interest and deprivation factors of epistemic curiosity. *Personality
     and Individual Differences*, *44*(7), 1585–95. doi:10.1016/j.paid.2008.01.014.

Loewenstein, G. (1994). The psychology of curiosity: A review and reinterpretation.
     Psychological Bulletin, *116*(1), 75. doi:10.1037//0033-2909.116.1.75.

Lopes, M. & Oudeyer, P. Y. (2012). The strategic student approach for life-long explo-
     ration and learning. In *2012 IEEE International Conference on Development
     and Learning and Epigenetic Robotics (ICDL)* (pp. 1–8). IEEE. doi:10.1109/
     devlrn.2012.6400807.

Mather, M. & Carstensen, L. L. (2003). Aging and attentional biases for emotional
     faces. *Psychological Science*, *14*(5), 409–15. doi:10.1111/1467-9280.01455.

Maunsell, J. H. (2004). Neuronal representations of cognitive state: reward or atten-
     tion? *Trends in Cognitive Sciences*, *8*(6), 261–5. doi:10.1016/j.tics.2004.04.003.

Mazurek, M. E., Roitman, J. D., Ditterich, J., & Shadlen, M. N. (2003). A role for
     neural integrators in perceptual decision making. *Cerebral Cortex*, *13*(11),
     1257–69. doi:10.1093/cercor/bhg097.

Moulin-Frier, C. & Oudeyer, P. Y. (2012). Curiosity-driven phonetic learning. In *2012
     IEEE International Conference on Development and Learning and Epigenetic
     Robotics (ICDL)* (pp. 1–8). IEEE. doi:10.1109/devlrn.2012.6400583.

Mullaney, K. M., Carpenter, S. K., Grotenhuis, C., & Burianek, S. (2014). Waiting for
     feedback helps if you want to know the answer: The role of curiosity in the
     delay-of-feedback benefit. *Memory & Cognition*, *42*(8), 1273–84. doi:10.3758/
     s13421-014-0441-y.

Najemnik, J. & Geisler, W. S. (2005). Optimal eye movement strategies in visual search.
     Nature, *434*(7031), 387. doi:10.1016/j.ajo.2005.04.009.

Navalpakkam, V. & Itti, L. (2005). Modeling the influence of task on attention. *Vision
     Research*, *45*(2), 205–31. doi:10.1016/j.visres.2004.07.042.

Ngo, H., Luciw, M., Forster, A., & Schmidhuber, J. (2012). Learning skills from
     play: artificial curiosity on a katana robot arm. In *2012 International Joint*

Conference on Neural Networks (IJCNN) (pp. 1–8). IEEE. doi:10.1109/ ijcnn.2012.6252824.

Nguyen, S.M. & Oudeyer, P. Y. (2013). Socially guided intrinsic motivation for robot learning of motor skills. *Autonomous Robots, 36*(3), 273–94. doi:10.1007/ s10514-013-9339-y.

Norman, D. A. & Shallice, T. (1986). Attention to action. In *Consciousness and self-regulation* (pp. 1–18). NYC, NY: Springer US. doi:10.1007/ 978-1-4757-0629-1_1.

Oudeyer, P. Y., Baranes, A., & Kaplan, F. (2013). Intrinsically motivated learning of real-world sensorimotor skills with developmental constraints. In M. Mirolli & G. Baldassarre (Eds.), *Intrinsically motivated learning in natural and artificial systems* (pp. 303–65). Berlin Heidelberg: Springer. doi:10.1007/978-3-642-32375-1_13.

Oudeyer, P. Y., Gottlieb, J., & Lopes, M. (2016). Intrinsic motivation, curiosity, and learning: Theory and applications in educational technologies. *Progress in Brain Research, 229*, 257–84. doi:10.1016/bs.pbr.2016.05.005.

Oudeyer, P. Y. & Kaplan, F. (2006). Discovering communication. *Connection Science, 18*(2), 189–206. doi:10.1080/09540090600768567.

Oudeyer, P. Y., Kaplan, F., & Hafner, V. V. (2007). Intrinsic motivation systems for autonomous mental development. *IEEE Transactions on Evolutionary Computation, 11*(2), 265–86. doi:10.1109/TEVC.2006.890271.

Pape, L., Oddo, C. M., Controzzi, M., Cipriani, C., Förster, A., Carrozza, M. C. & Schmidhuber, J. (2012). Learning tactile skills through curious exploration. *Frontiers in Neurorobotics, 6*. doi:10.3389/fnbot.2012.00006.

Payzan-LeNestour, E. & Bossaerts, P. (2011). Risk, unexpected uncertainty, and estimation uncertainty: Bayesian learning in unstable settings. *PLoS Computational Biology, 7*(1), e1001048. doi:10.1371/journal.pcbi.1001048.

Peck, C. J., Jangraw, D. C., Suzuki, M., Efem, R., & Gottlieb, J. (2009). Reward modulates attention independently of action value in posterior parietal cortex. *Journal of Neuroscience, 29*(36), 11 182–91. doi:10.1523/jneurosci.1929-09.2009.

Pessoa, L., Kastner, S., & Ungerleider, L. G. (2003). Neuroimaging studies of attention: From modulation of sensory processing to top-down control. *Journal of Neuroscience, 23*(10), 3990–8. doi: 0270-6474/03/233990-09.00/0.

Platt, M. L. & Glimcher, P. W. (1999). Neural correlates of decision variables in parietal cortex. *Nature, 400*(6741), 233.

Posner, M. I. (1994). Attention: The mechanisms of consciousness. *Proceedings of the National Academy of Sciences of the United States of America, 91*(16), 7398–403. doi:10.1073/pnas.91. 16.7398.

Posner, M. I. & Dehaene, S. (1994). Attentional networks. *Trends in Neurosciences, 17*(2), 75–9. doi:10.1016/0166-2236(94)90078-7.

Renninger, K. A. & Hidi, S. (2011). Revisiting the conceptualization, measurement, and generation of interest. *Educational Psychologist, 46*(3), 168–84. doi:10.1080/00461520.2011.587723.

Renninger, K. A. & Hidi, S. (2016). *The power of interest for motivation and learning.* New York, NY; Routledge.

Renninger, L. W., Verghese, P., & Coughlan, J. (2007). Where to look next? Eye movements reduce local uncertainty. *Journal of Vision, 7*(3), 6. doi:10.1167/ 7.3.6.

Risko, E. F., Anderson, N. C., Lanthier, S., & Kingstone, A. (2012). Curious eyes: Individual differences in personality predict eye movement behavior in scene-viewing. *Cognition, 122*(1), 86–90. doi:10.1016/j.cognition.2011.08.014.

Ryan, R. M. & Deci, E. L. (2000). Intrinsic and extrinsic motivations: Classic definitions and new directions. *Contemporary Educational Psychology, 25*(1), 54–67. doi:10.1006/ceps.1999.1020.

Sarter, M., Gehring, W. J., & Kozak, R. (2006). More attention must be paid: The neurobiology of attentional effort. *Brain Research Reviews, 51*(2), 145–60. doi:10.1016/j.brainresrev.2005.11.002.

Satterthwaite, T. D., Ruparel, K., Loughead, J., Elliot, M. A., Gerraty, R. T., Calkins, M. E., ... Wolf, D. H. (2012). Being right is its own reward: load and performance related ventral striatum activation to correct responses during a working memory task in youth. *Neuroimage, 61*(3), 723–29.

Schmidhuber, J. (2006). Developmental robotics, optimal artificial curiosity, creativity, music, and the fine arts. *Connection Science, 18*(2), 173–87. doi:10.1080/09540090600768658.

Schmidhuber, J. (2013). Maximizing fun by creating data with easily reducible subjective complexity. In M. Mirolli & G. Baldassarre (Eds.), *Intrinsically motivated learning in natural and artificial systems* (pp. 95–128). Berlin Heidelberg: Springer. doi:10.1007/978-3-642-32375-1_5.

Singh, S., James, M. R., & Rudary, M. R. (2004). Predictive state representations: A new theory for modeling dynamical systems. In *Proceedings of the 20th Conference on Uncertainty in Artificial Intelligence* (pp. 512–19). AUAI Press.

Singh, S., Lewis, R. L., Barto, A. G., & Sorg, J. (2010). Intrinsically motivated reinforcement learning: An evolutionary perspective. *IEEE Transactions on Autonomous Mental Development, 2*(2), 70–82. doi:10.1109/TAMD.2010.2051031.

Srivastava, R. K., Steunebrink, B. R., & Schmidhuber, J. (2013). First experiments with PowerPlay. *Neural Networks, 41*, 130–36. doi:10.1016/j.neunet.2013.01.022.

Steels, L. (2004). The autotelic principle. *Lecture Notes in Computer Science, (3139)*, 231–42. doi:10.1007/978-3-540-27833-7_17.

Stuss, D. T., Shallice, T., Alexander, M. P., & Picton, T. W. (1995). A multidisciplinary approach to anterior attentional functions. *Annals of the New York Academy of Sciences, 769*(1), 191–212. doi:10.1111/j.1749-6632.1995.tb38140.x.

Sugrue, L. P., Corrado, G. S., & Newsome, W. T. (2005). Choosing the greater of two goods: neural currencies for valuation and decision making. *Nature Reviews. Neuroscience, 6*(5), 363. doi:10.1038/nrn1666.

Sullivan, B. T., Johnson, L., Rothkopf, C. A., Ballard, D., & Hayhoe, M. (2012). The role of uncertainty and reward on eye movements in a virtual driving task. *Journal of Vision, 12*(13), 19. doi:10.1167/12.13.19.

Tatler, B. W., Hayhoe, M. M., Land, M. F., & Ballard, D. H. (2011). Eye guidance in natural vision: Reinterpreting salience. *Journal of Vision, 11*(5), 5. doi:10.1167/11.5.5.

Thorndike, E. L. (1911). *Animal intelligence.* New York: Macmillan.

Tsotsos, J. K. (2011). *A computational perspective on visual attention.* Cambridge, MA: MIT Press. doi:10.7551/mitpress/9780262015417.001.0001.

Ullsperger, M. & von Cramon, D. Y. (2004). Neuroimaging of performance monitoring: Error detection and beyond. *Cortex, 40*(4), 593–604. doi:10.1016/s0010-9452(08)70155-2.

van Duijvenvoorde, A. C., Peters, S., Braams, B. R., & Crone, E. A. (2016). What motivates adolescents? Neural responses to rewards and their influence on adolescents' risk taking, learning, and cognitive control. *Neuroscience & Biobehavioral Reviews, 70*, 135–47. doi:10.1016/j.neubiorev.2016.06.037.

Vossel, S., Mathys, C., Daunizeau, J., Bauer, M., Driver, J., & Friston, K. J., & Stephan, K. E. (2013). Spatial attention, precision, and Bayesian inference: A study of saccadic response speed. *Cerebral Cortex, 24*(6), 1436–450. doi:10.1093/cercor/bhs418.

Vossel, S., Mathys, C., Stephan, K. E., & Friston, K. J. (2015). Cortical coupling reflects Bayesian belief updating in the deployment of spatial attention. *Journal of Neuroscience, 35*(33), 11 532–42. doi:10.1523/jneurosci.1382-15.2015.

Vossel, S., Thiel, C. M., & Fink, G. R. (2006). Cue validity modulates the neural correlates of covert endogenous orienting of attention in parietal and frontal cortex. *Neuroimage, 32*(3), 1257–64. doi:10.1016/j.neuroimage.2006.05.019.

Wang, X. J. (2008). Decision making in recurrent neuronal circuits. *Neuron, 60*(2), 215–34. doi:10.1016/j.neuron.2008.09.034.

Wise, R. A. (2004). Dopamine, learning and motivation. *Nature Reviews Neuroscience, 5*(6), 483.

Wittmann, B. C., Bunzeck, N., Dolan, R. J., & Düzel, E. (2007). Anticipation of novelty recruits reward system and hippocampus while promoting recollection. *Neuroimage, 38*(1), 194–202. doi:10.1016/j.neuroimage.2007.06.038.

Wittmann, B. C., Daw, N. D., Seymour, B., & Dolan, R. J. (2008). Striatal activity underlies novelty-based choice in humans. *Neuron, 58*(6), 967–73. doi:10.1016/j.neuron.2008.04.027.

Yang, H., Chen, X., & Zelinsky, G. J. (2009). A new look at novelty effects: Guiding search away from old distractors. *Attention, Perception, & Psychophysics, 71*(3), 554–64. doi:10.3758/app.71.3.554.

Yang, S. C. H., Lengyel, M., & Wolpert, D. M. (2016). Active sensing in the categorization of visual patterns. *eLife, 5*, e12215. doi:10.7554/elife.25660.

Yang, T. & Shadlen, M. N. (2007). Probabilistic reasoning by neurons. *Nature, 447*(7148), 1075. doi:10.1038/nature05852.

Yu, A.J. & Dayan, P. (2005). Uncertainty, neuromodulation, and attention. *Neuron, 46*(4), 681–92. doi:10.1016/j.neuron.2005.04.026.

9 Open Digital Badges and Reward Structures

Daniel T. Hickey and Katerina Schenke

Abstract: *In recent years, web-enabled credentials for learning have emerged, primarily in the form of Open Badges. These new credentials can contain specific claims about competency, evidence supporting those claims, links to student work, and traces of engagement. Moreover, these credentials can be annotated, curated, shared, discussed, and endorsed over digital networks, which can provide additional meaning. However, digital badges have also reignited the simmering debate over rewards for learning. This is because they have been used by some and characterized by many as inherently "extrinsic" motivators. Our chapter considers this debate in light of a study that traced the development and evolution of 30 new Open Badge systems. Seven arguments are articulated: (1) digital badges are inherently more meaningful than grades and other credentials; (2) circulation in digital networks makes Open Badges particularly meaningful; (3) Open Badges are particularly consequential credentials; (4) the negative consequences of extrinsic rewards are overstated; (5) consideration of motivation and badges should focus primarily on social activity and secondarily on individual behavior and cognition; (6) situative models of engagement are ideal for studying digital credentials; and (7) the motivational impact of digital credentials should be studied across increasingly formal "levels."*

Digital badges are a new kind of learning credential that can contain hyperlinks that provide easy access to relevant web-enabled information. In contrast to grades and degrees, digital badges can contain specific claims about competencies, details about how those competencies were acquired, and links to evidence such as completed work and traces of engagement. Recognizing

This research was primarily supported by grants from the John D. and Catherine T. MacArthur Foundation. Additional support was provided by a grant from the Indiana University Office of the Vice Provost for Research and by an assistantship from the Indiana University Department of Counseling and Educational Psychology. Individuals who contributed directly to the Design Principles Documentation Project included Christine Chow, Cindy Cogswell, Rebecca Itow, Nate Otto, Joshua Quick, Cathy Tran, James Willis III, and Suraj Uttamchandani. Rebecca Itow and Christopher Andrews assisted in the production of this manuscript.

the need for standardization in this new credentialing system, Open Badges are issued in compliance with an agreed-upon set of metadata standards that allow badges to work across multiple platforms and make it easy for earners to annotate, curate, and share their badges over social networks. Curation and sharing of Open Badges in social networks can increase recognition and meaning (including "likes" and comments). The metadata standards also make it possible for the information contained in Open Badges to be examined and verified by both humans and computers.

Open Badges were introduced in 2012, with significant backing from the Digital Media and Learning (DML) initiative at the John D. and Catherine T. MacArthur Foundation, in close collaboration with the Mozilla Foundation. That year, a team at Mozilla worked with innovators from Peer to Peer University to draft the initial set of metadata standards. Also that year, MacArthur funded 30 pioneering educational programs to create and issue Open Badges (with supplemental funding from the Bill and Melinda Gates Foundation [2011] for a subset of the winning proposals). These events led to broad media coverage, in both mainstream venues (e.g., Carey, 2012; Eisenberg, 2011) and education-related outlets (e.g., Kolowich, 2014; Young, 2012).

By 2017, the use of Open Badges had grown steadily around the world. The MacArthur initiative had evolved into an ambitious youth-oriented, city-specific badging platform known as *Project LRNG*.[1] A more sophisticated set of metadata standards (*Open Badges Specifications 2.0*) and the maintenance of these new standards was assumed by the IMS Global Learning Consortium, the world's leading organization for setting educational technology standards. While some began referring to Open Badges as "micro-credentials," many use the term "digital badges" or simply "badges."

Predictably, the introduction of Open Badges rekindled the long-running debate over incentives for learning and, more generally, reward structures in education. This is in part because badges can be used as evidence-free "extrinsic" incentives for learning. As we will elaborate, such incentives have been shown in hundreds of empirical studies to undermine intrinsically motivated learning and subsequent free-choice engagement. The concerns about badges have been raised in widely cited critiques by influential writers, (e.g., Kohn, 2014; Resnick, 2012), including one that had been central in MacArthur's larger ten-year, $250M initiative (Jenkins, 2012).

Our chapter will deeply explore these concerns over badges and motivation. The chapter opens with a summary of digital credentialing, an example badge system, and a summary of the concerns about badges and motivation. This is followed by an extended consideration of the motivational concerns in light of the conclusions drawn from a detailed study of all 30 Open Badge systems, funded in 2012 by the MacArthur Foundation. The chapter concludes with

---

1 Project LRNG's website can be accessed at www.lrng.org.

seven arguments about using Open Badges to recognize and motivate learning, including arguments about future research that might explore and resolve the motivational concerns in learning contexts.

Credentialing, Digital Credentials, and Endorsement

Traditionally, diplomas, degrees, and certificates (as well as their associated grades and transcripts) are formally endorsed by outside accrediting bodies established for that purpose. Over the last century, conventional accrediting practices emerged alongside routines for hiring employees and advancing students. As such, these practices are often taken for granted by stakeholders and have become been quite resistant to change (Olneck, 2015). Conventional credentialing practices rely primarily on analog documents (e.g., grades and transcripts) and communication (e.g., conversations, phone calls, and emails), making credentialing expensive and inflexible for institutions and invisible to most educators (Anderson & McGreal, 2012). Traditional credentials are also removed (i.e., "distal") from student learning experiences, and the admissions and hiring decisions associated with those credentials are practically invisible to students.

Because traditional credentialing practices are so distal, they push educators to introduce grades, points, mastery schemes, and other artificial means of recognizing and motivating learning that are closer (i.e., "proximal") to the learning experience. Arguably, this use of proximal motivators (which are not intrinsically meaningful) to give meaning to distal credentials is responsible for much of the practical debate over motivation and extrinsic rewards. Open Badges offer new opportunities to award credentials that achieve the goals of proximal assessment by attending to learners' interests and experiences, while also promising the kind of objective and aggregated evidence that admissions and hiring committees value. In this way, Open Badges have the potential to reduce the use of static credentials and promote a dynamic credentialing system that is more flexible, transparent, equitable, and motivational. Our chapter focuses on the motivational aspects of such a system.

An Example Open Badge System

An example of how Open Badges are being used to recognize and motivate learning was provided by the *Supporter to Reporter* (S2R) program. S2R is a youth sports journalism project in the United Kingdom that incorporated Open Badges as part of the initiative funded by MacArthur in 2012. Led by an educational non-profit organization known as *DigitalMe,* the S2R project had already been established in partnership with professional sporting associations,

Figure 9.1. *Content of a Supporter to Reporter Open Badge*

amateur sporting clubs, and schools across the United Kingdom.[2] DigitalMe created a sophisticated website where budding journalists and reporters could display various S2R badges that they earned by creating and posting increasingly sophisticated media accounts of sporting events and interviews. Entry-level badges could be earned for simply posting a brief account of an event, while the highest-level badges granted earners field-level access at professional matches. The S2R website also offered a comprehensive set of free curricular resources to teachers, mentors, and learners.

Figure 9.1 displays the contents of an actual S2R badge, including an image, title, description, date issued, and three hyperlinks. The first hyperlink is to the page at the S2R website shown in Figure 9.2. That page displays the criteria that the earner met, a description of the evidence contained within the badge, a description of who awarded the badge, and the number of likes, comments, and views. The second hyperlink goes to the actual evidence (a video interview of a star athlete featured at a school tournament), along with the number of views and comments posted. The third hyperlink (embedded in the image) is to the page posted by the badge issuer (in this case, the school tournament) that allows the badge to be verified.

Concerns over Digital Badges and Intrinsic Motivation

Although Open Badges have certainly made significant inroads into credentialing, they have yet to be embraced by many educators and schools, and therefore have yet to be recognized by many admissions officers, hiring managers, and recruiters (Fong et al., 2016). Whereas there are certainly

---

[2] The DigitalMe program's website can be accessed at www.digitalme.co.uk.

Figure 9.2. *Criteria for earning the Supporter to Reporter Open Badge*

other obstacles to the wider use of badges, the motivational concerns introduced earlier have generated resistance among some educators and schools. In
a widely cited critique, then-director of the MIT Media Lab, Mitch Resnick,
stated this concern over digital badges:

> The problem, for me, lies in the role of badges as motivators. In many
> cases, educators are proposing badge systems in order to motivate students.
> It's easy to understand why educators are doing this: most students get
> excited and engaged by badges. But toward what end? And for how long?
> I worry that students will focus on accumulating badges rather than making
> connections with the ideas and material associated with the badges – the
> same way that students too often focus on grades in a class rather than the
> material in the class, or the points in an educational game rather than the
> ideas in the game. Simply engaging students is not enough. They need to be
> engaged for the right reasons. (Resnick, 2012)

The influential education writer Alfie Kohn (2014) raised similar concerns in a keynote address at a London conference that was organized around Open Badges. Reflecting his several books on rewards for learning (e.g., Kohn, 1999), Kohn argued that prior research on extrinsic incentives had "already proven" that some of the most widely touted functions of badges (e.g., publically displaying competency, providing "pathways" for learning, and helping learners track their accomplishments) would have "devastating consequences for learning and learners, in both the near- and long-term."

A particularly stinging critique of digital badges came from media scholar Henry Jenkins (2012), who was an influential early participant in MacArthur's DML initiative. Jenkins worried that badges would be used in competitive "gamification" schemes that are antithetical to the informal "participatory cultures" (Jenkins et al., 2009) that the DML initiative had been promoting.

Empirical support for concerns about using digital badges as extrinsic motivators comes from studies of the "overjustification effect" (Lepper et al., 1973), whereby providing arbitrary (i.e., "extrinsic") incentives for activities that individuals already find intrinsically motivating leads to reduced intrinsic motivation and to post-incentive disengagement. The classic example in the Lepper et al. study involved rewarding young children for playing with felt-tipped colored pens. Lepper et al. promised some children a reward (a "good player" ribbon, the *expected reward* condition) for playing with the markers. Later, when the children were invited again to play with the markers in the absence of any reward, the children who played while expecting the reward (i.e., had been "overjustified") played significantly less than the *unexpected reward* (a ribbon that had not been promised during the previous play) children or the *no-reward* children. This phenomenon and many variants have been documented in hundreds of experimental studies and compiled in multiple meta-analyses (e.g., Deci et al., 1999). Evidence of the overjustification effect has led many to embrace these concerns and other core assumptions of self-determination theory (Deci & Ryan, 1985) and its broad implications for the way that learning is motivated and recognized (e.g., Cordova & Lepper, 1996).

Although concerns about using digital badges as extrinsic rewards have yet to be examined in empirical studies (cf., Abramovich et al., 2013), such uses have been widely discussed in the educational media (e.g., Ash, 2012) and among educational bloggers (e.g., Ferlazzo, 2012; Gerstein, 2013). Given the extensive prior research on the overjustification effect and the influence of commentators like Alfie Kohn (and his workplace counterpart Pink, 2011), these concerns appear to be significant obstacles to both the study of and broader use of Open Badges and digital credentials more generally. The seven arguments presented in this chapter, particularly the fourth argument, are intended to provide guidance for addressing these concerns in both practice and research.

The Design Principles Documentation Project

To explore the concerns about Open Badges and motivation to learn, we draw on our work in the Design Principles Documentation (DPD) Project. With funding from MacArthur, the DPD Project studied the 30 distinct badge system development efforts funded in 2012. The DPD Project documented the specific design practices and the more general design principles that emerged as each of the 30 efforts attempted to build badge systems in a diverse range of informal and formal educational contexts.

The DPD Project attempted to document the practical insights that emerged as each of the 30 efforts worked to bring their badge system to life, aiming to capture the *phronetic narrative* or "practical wisdom" (Halverson, 2004) that emerged as the individual projects designed and implemented their Open Badging systems. In doing so, the DPD Project aimed to capture the information that "evaporates" as technological features evolve and design teams dissolve (Kruchten, 2004). In other words, the study documented many of the most useful insights (e.g., seemingly good ideas that don't work out) that may have been lost in rapid iterating or as team members left. Useful complementary information about the MacArthur initiative and the 30 badge system designs can be found in Grant (2014).

Methods of the DPD Project

The DPD Project first carried out a content analysis to identify intended practices (described in each of the 30 proposals) for *recognizing*, *assessing*, *motivating*, and *studying* learning. The practices uncovered in each of the four areas were then organized (using a simple card sort) into more general badge design practices. In a series of structured interviews from 2012 to 2014, the project tracked whether each intended practice was implemented. In late 2014, after the badge design efforts had exhausted their funds and submitted a final report, the DPD Project attempted to determine whether each project had (1) created a functioning badge system where earners were actively earning badges, (2) created a partial badge system but not the larger learning ecosystem where badges were being earned by learners, or (3) suspended their efforts or otherwise had not created a fully functioning badge system. In late 2015, the DPD Project tried to determine which badge systems were "thriving" (i.e., new learners and badges being added, and badges being shared), "existing" (i.e., badges still earnable but no evidence of them being earned and shared), or "suspended" (i.e., no evidence of badges being offered). Partly to support the analyses presented in this chapter, the original proposals were then analyzed to derive four overarching types of badge systems that reflected the kinds of learning that the badges were intended to recognize (e.g., *competency-based*, *inquiry-based*, *participation-based*, or *hybrid*). The success with which the various practices were implemented and the relative success of the four different types of badge systems were used to derive more general principles for designing digital badge systems broadly and Open Badge systems specifically.

The DPD Project was ultimately a very complicated study, the findings of which are highly contextual. For example, eight of the 30 efforts were suspended without ever issuing any badges and nine of the 30 were deemed "partial" implementations. This introduced uncertainty as to whether particular practices were harder to implement (versus having been proposed within a badge system that was ultimately suspended because of other challenges). The motivational principles were particularly challenging to study, because most of the proposals did not specifically articulate their motivational practices or principles. This challenge required the DPD team to infer those principles based on the recognition and assessment practices that were more specifically articulated (Tran et al., 2014). As will be elaborated, inferring the motivational impact of the recognition and assessment practices necessarily required the DPD team to draw assumptions about the nature of learning and (therefore) motivation within each system.

The project's extended analyses of design practices for using Open Badges and the ultimate status of the 30 proposed Open Badging systems are detailed in a final project report (Hickey & Willis, 2017). These analyses resulted in 57 initial design principles regarding "where badges work better" and included 17 principles for motivating learning with digital badges.

The next section provides a consolidated summary of the principles for motivating learning in digital Open Badge systems. This is followed by a more theoretical consideration of those principles, in light of the relative success of the four types of proposed badge systems.

Badge Design Principles Derived from Motivational Practices

Naturally, most of the motivational design principles were derived from practices used to "add value" to badges. For example, of the 30 badge system designs, three proposed to *motivate learning with extrinsic rewards* (i.e., a video library, Amazon gift certificates, and NASA certificates). All three of these Open Badge systems were ultimately implemented, meaning that the system had progressed to the point of awarding badges to actual learners. However, only the video library was actually offered to badge earners (by the *Who Built America?* project, for earning an entire set of badges in a history teacher professional development project). Moreover, even though it was an extrinsic reward, it was not entirely unrelated to the learning. As of 2015, that reward had never been claimed by any participant. The Amazon gift certificates and the NASA certificates were not offered in the final iteration of their respective systems. Leaders of these two efforts reported, in interviews, that these incentives were not offered because of concerns about the possibility that they would impact intrinsic motivation. These observations and the general concerns about incentives led to the relatively straightforward motivational design principle that *badges work better when associated with intrinsically meaningful incentives rather than extrinsic rewards.*

Similar to extrinsic rewards, five of the 30 proposed badge systems intended to motivate learning by associating badges with course credit. Only one system, an alliance of after-school programs, succeeded in doing so. The alliance associated badges with course credit by drawing on an existing system of assessments and program quality reviews. But the after-school badge system was promptly suspended because the students and teachers felt that the badges were redundant with grades (elaborated in Davis & Singh, 2015). Detailed in the next section, this difficulty of associating badges with course grades was a central factor in the suspension of several systems, including all three of the proposed Open Badging environments associated with the Gates Foundation's *Project Mastery* initiative. These findings led to the potentially controversial principle that badges work better when learning is not motivated by formal course credit; these findings also supported the corresponding learning recognition principle *badges work better when they present unique information and evidence.*

One of the most challenging badge design practices to study was how to motivate learning with competition. Badges seem to naturally foster the public display of proficiency, which in turn may stimulate competition. The highest level S2R badge was both highly valued and hard to earn. Leaders of the S2R project reported that it certainly fostered competition among their most active participants, but there was no sort of "leader board" that prevented multiple participants from earning that badge. Several other systems succeeded in implementing such high-value badges. This included another youth journalism project (based in the United States) that motivated students with a comprehensive "All Star" badge (earners qualified for a field trip to Washington, DC). As we will elaborate, these badges were associated with "participation-based" learning; while earners recognized that they were competing to reach the highest level badge, there was no actual limit on the number of students who could earn it. In contrast, several competency-based systems proposed truly competitive point systems featuring actual leader boards. However, only one system, a gamified math drill and practice program, succeeded in doing so. This led to the tentative motivational principle that *badges probably work better when competition concerns basic skills or participation in social practices, rather than learning from inquiry.*

Of the 30 efforts, eight proposed to motivate learning with external opportunities. This included six efforts to formally associate their badges with internships, scholarships, and admissions. While three of those six implemented their badge system, none succeeded in securing any sort of agreement with institutions to award such opportunities, and none reported that their earners succeeded in using their badges to secure such opportunities on their own. In contrast, two of the six systems (including S2R) succeeded in issuing badges sufficiently rich with evidence that their earners were able to use the badges in successful applications for internships and admissions. These observations resulted in the design principle that *badges work better when they motivate learning by containing claims and evidence that will help earners secure opportunities and internships.*

A closely related badge design practice was to *motivate learning with external endorsements.* Of the 11 systems that proposed to do so, only five succeeded, including four that did so by drawing on existing institutional relationships. Just one of the efforts to secure endorsements from an external agency was successful in garnering support from an institution that could be explicitly stated on their badge.[3] For the other six efforts, it appeared that the inability to formalize external endorsements was a major factor in the suspension of those badge systems. These observations led to the motivational principle that *badges work better when they motivate as informal evidence-rich credentials that speak for themselves,* and to a corresponding recognition principle that *badges work better when external endorsements are based on existing institutional relationships.*

Two inter-related practices for adding value to badges were: motivate learning with internal opportunities and motivate learning with entry-level badges for initial accomplishments. Of the ten efforts that proposed doing so, eight of the nine whose badge systems were implemented succeeded in implementing basic "entry-level" badges that unlocked additional, more valued opportunities inside of the learning context. This resulted in two design principles that helped respond to motivational concerns: *Badges work better when they provide additional opportunities within the environment where the badges are issued,* and *badges work better when initial badges are easy to earn and provide access to more advanced badges.*

Of the 30 projects, nine proposed to motivate learning by displaying badges publicly. All six of these nine projects that implemented their badge systems were able to implement this practice. In most cases, this included giving earners control over if and how the badges were displayed and, in some cases, adding additional information about those badges (e.g., by adding comments to the S2R badge). These observations and the obvious value for self-determination led to the principle that *badges work better when learners control how their badges are displayed publicly.*

Two final motivational principles presented here concern two less obvious motivational practices for adding value to badges: *motivate learning by recognizing disciplinary identities,* and *motivate learning by engaging with disciplinary communities.* As elaborated in the final section of this chapter, contemporary theories of identity and motivation (Nolen et al., 2015; Oyserman, 2015) led the project to conclude that at least 13 of the 30 badge systems proposed one or both of these practices, and that all 10 of the 13 that implemented their badge system implemented these practices successfully. For example, the S2R "learning pathways" through the increasingly sophisticated

---

3 After extensive review, the National Oceanic and Atmospheric Administration allowed Planet Stewards to include the NOAA acronym (but not the NOAA logo) on their badges.

badges were named after directly relevant professional roles (journalist, producer, and coach), and the S2R effort invested significant energy in building relationships with local sporting clubs. These observations led to the design principle that *badges work better when used to help earners establish personal identities and engage with disciplinary and professional communities.*

The remainder of the motivational design principles were rather tentative and were mostly associated with the assumed motivational impact of various assessment and goal-setting practices. These practices proved rather difficult to implement, and the design principles that emerged generally suggested that such practices should start with modest ambition and be based on proven examples that have successfully been implemented by others.

Each of these principles seems worthy of further study and refinement in the context of designing new Open Badge systems. Before proposing a model for doing so, we introduce some crucial theoretical issues that need to be addressed in order to carry out such research in a manner that might advance this new field.

Badge Design Principles Derived from Comparing Types of Badge Systems

The DPD Project was able to identify four different types of proposed badge systems by considering (1) the types of learning to be recognized, (2) the types of assessments to be used, and (3) the likely motivational consequences of those recognition and assessment practices.

Competency-based badge systems. Analysis of the 30 proposed badge systems revealed that seven intended to issue badges for *competency-based* learning. These systems proposed to (1) award badges for self-paced individualized mastery of relatively specific competencies, (2) use largely summative assessments of those competencies as criteria for awarding badges, and (3) use badges as primarily external and extrinsic motivators for learning (by formally associating them with course credit or external opportunities). Of these seven efforts, only two succeeded in implementing a complete system, in 2014. By 2015, only one of the competency-based systems – Buzzmath, a gamification platform for drill and practice activities for middle school mathematics – was thriving. However, Buzzmath had decided not to use Open Badges (partly due to privacy concerns for minors); they offered internal badges on their website instead, as simple tokens of mastery.

There was a range of reasons why none of the seven competency-based badge systems created a thriving Open Badges system, and some of those reasons were explicitly motivational. For example, the Young Adult Library Services Administration successfully implemented Open Badges for mastery of the detailed competencies outlined by their organization. However, they reported that the badges were simply not valuable enough to motivate potential earners to (1) master those competencies, (2) generate evidence of that mastery, and (3) locate a qualified peer who was willing to review that evidence. More generally, it seemed that none of the competency-based Open Badge systems were sufficiently valued by the larger set of stakeholders so as to motivate the systemic changes needed (particularly to the assessment infrastructure) to support a thriving system. To this point, four of these efforts reported that the funding was insufficient to build the sophisticated technological tools needed to support self-paced mastery and the assessment of numerous competencies. This included three foundations that were provided additional support from the Gates Foundation.

These findings are timely because competency-based badges exemplify a broader trend toward *competency-based education* (CBE) within and outside of the United States. Most of the CBE variants (including "gamification") are organized around the self-paced mastery of specific measurable behaviors or mental associations (Everhart et al., 2014). CBE is often presented as an alternative to "traditional" schooling where credentials are said to be based on "seat time." Some influential observers have essentially equated the push to use Open Badges in educational settings with the movement toward CBE (e.g., Afterschool Alliance, 2015; American Council on Education, 2016; Blackburn et al., 2016; Duncan, 2011). Likewise, proponents of gamification have pointed out obvious connections with digital badges (e.g., Buckingham, 2014; Mallon, 2013; Metzger et al., 2016).

Notably, the three competency-based badge systems that received additional funding from the Gates Foundation were part of its *Project Mastery* initiative, which aimed to completely reorganize secondary learning around "proficiency-based pathways" (2011, p. 7). The DPD Project's findings regarding those three efforts were bolstered by a more extensive study from the Rand Corporation (Steele et al., 2014), which found that a central challenge for all three Gates-supported systems concerned *equity* in terms of who "benefits most under competency-based models" and that "educators at several sites reported that a competency-based approach may disproportionately favor highly motivated learners" (p. 49).[4] These concerns echo similar concerns in a report by the Carnegie Foundation, which concluded that CBE "may privilege some students over others, ... be fine for highly motivated students, ... [and] could speed the progress of more accomplished and affluent students ... while their peers are left to struggle and possibly fall further behind" (Silva et al., 2015, p. 26).

---

4 Other credentialing tensions reported by Steele et al. (2014) included equating evidence from anytime/anywhere learning with conventional criteria, determining who can authorize credit, maintaining a common definition of proficiency, and building a sustainable model. They also pointed to other tensions, including technical, financial, and logistical barriers to efficiency. These later tensions echo problems identified by Leuba (2015) whereby most learning management systems and student information systems are organized around courses, making it difficult to organize learning around competencies.

Inquiry-based badge systems. The DPD Project concluded that 12 of the 30 systems intended to issue badges for *inquiry-based* learning. These systems proposed to (1) award badges for completing larger projects or investigations that focused on higher-order conceptual understanding, (2) use more formative performance-based and portfolio-based assessment methods to evaluate that understanding, and (3) focus more on intrinsic sources of motivation like interest and curiosity. While these badge systems were intended to recognize both self-paced and group-based learning, their most salient feature was that the learning was organized around some sort of investigation or inquiry, typically around an extended project. For example, the teacher professional development activities for Who Built America? featured web-based historical investigations that included sophisticated portfolio assessment practices.

Of the 12 proposed inquiry-based badge systems, four had succeeded in implementing a complete Open Badge system by 2014, and four (including Who Built America?) appeared to be thriving in 2015. One notable commonality across the four thriving systems is that they found ways to minimize assessment demands. They did so by drawing on existing assessment practices, using computers, or significantly scaling back proposed practices for formally assessing learners' work. Conversely, a commonality across the eight efforts that did not implement badges or thrive was that they struggled to implement ambitious performance and portfolio assessment practices. Some of these assessment challenges were compounded by the realization that displaying evidence in Open Badges would direct additional scrutiny to the validity of that evidence, including the manner in which it was obtained.

These observations about the challenges of assessing inquiry-based learning and its many variants have important implications for motivation. Inquiry-oriented learning is presumed to be intrinsically motivating because it can be organized around Malone and Lepper's (1987) factors for "making learning fun" (*challenge, curiosity, control,* and *fantasy*). Because such intrinsically motivated learning is typically open-ended and idiosyncratic, it has always been challenging to assess efficiently and reliably (e.g., Shavelson et al., 1992). The difficulties of assessing inquiry-based learning appear to be heightened when the claims and web-enabled evidence are circulated widely in Open Badges. Thus, while the inquiry-based badge systems may assuage the concerns about using badges as extrinsic motivators, they introduced hurdles of their own in implementing the assessments needed to award those badges and in gathering the evidence to include in them.

Participation-based badge systems. Of the 30 badge systems, five proposed to award *participation-based* badges. These systems proposed to (1) award badges primarily for participation in social learning and group projects, (2) emphasize peer-assessment and "crowdsourced" assessment practices, and (3) rely more on social and cultural forms of motivation. The S2R system exemplified such Open Badge systems. Consider that the first two criteria for earning a badge in Figure 9.2 start with "Worked as part of." From the outset, the S2R badge system was designed to motivate earners to create media artifacts that would gain page views, likes, and comments from peers and the public. Like S2R, none of the participation-based badge systems proposed to assess and recognize *specific* competencies. Rather, most badges were awarded for completing a course or a project, typically for groups of learners; while specific competencies were often included, they tended to be more tacitly assessed.

All five of the participation-based efforts had successfully implemented an Open Badge system by 2014, and by 2015 four of the Open Badge systems appeared to be thriving. It seems that the proposed badges were sufficiently valued by stakeholders to introduce and sustain the assessments and other new practices that were needed, and were sufficiently valued by learners to motivate them to carry out the activities needed to earn them.

Generally speaking, the participation-based badge systems aimed to allow each badge to speak for itself. Rather than struggling to formalize external opportunities and endorsements, the participation-based systems invested in creating social networks where viewers could decide for themselves whether the information contained in a specific badge supported the claims made by that badge.

Hybrid badge systems. The five remaining badge systems were categorized as "hybrids" because they employed features for assessing, recognizing, and motivating learning that were consistent with all perspectives. Akin to the inquiry-based systems, these efforts also encountered mixed outcomes that reinforce the conclusions about keeping individual assessment practices manageable. While two of those systems were thriving in 2015, their results did not add new insights to the motivational issues explored in our chapter.

New badge design principles. Looking across types of badge systems, the limited success of competency-based badges, the mixed results for the inquiry-based and hybrid badges, and the success of the participation-based badges led to the design principle that *badges work better where learning, recognition, and assessment practices are primarily sociocultural*. By focusing more on social and cultural practices (versus individual practices), participation badges are relatively more consistent with the sociocultural perspectives that provided significant impetus for the MacArthur Foundation's larger DML initiative (e.g., Brown, 2012; Ito, 2012; Yowell, 2014). Similarly, the DPD Project was influenced by the new models of motivation that follow from sociocultural perspectives (Hickey, 2003; Nolen, et al., 2015; Yowell & Smylie, 1999).

While the participation-based badges did include claims for specific competencies, these competencies were generally *not* assessed in isolation from other competencies or social activity. Rather, the participation-based badge systems left it up to educators or experts to make the judgment that someone who completed the particular program, activity, or course had indeed demonstrated those competencies or understandings. This appears to support a sixth general conclusion: *Badges work better when awarded for completion of workshops, courses, or projects, rather than specific skills or competencies.*

The motivational appeal of participation-based badges was nicely articulated by S2R leader Lucy Neale Lewis. She stated that S2R "issues badges for taking on professional roles" and that "our supporters start off pretty low so we award badges for distance traveled rather than level achieved." Presaging the important new "Endorsements 2.0" feature (described later in this chapter), Neale also stated that

> Open Badge Academy is about getting endorsements after you have earned a badge. People can come and add endorsements to the evidence. For example, one of the ways you can earn a badge is for an internship. You earn the badge on completing the internship. You can add that you thought it went well. The employer can also add an endorsement, adding additional feedback; your peers can do that too. The idea is building trust via multipoint validation. We like to use the e-Bay comparison when we talk about badges.

These findings led us to conclude that participation-based learning is uniquely (and possibly ideally) suited to take full advantage of the unique affordance of Open Badges for recognizing and motivating that learning. While Open Badges certainly may be useful for recognizing and motivating competency-based and inquiry-based learning, these findings suggest that caution is in order and that particular care needs to be directed at managing the significant (though rather different) assessment challenges they present.

It is important to note that participation badges are sometimes conflated with "attendance badges," awarded for showing up at a conference or a class (e.g., Thigpen, 2014, p. 6). We strongly agree that evidence-free badges should not be awarded simply for showing up.[5] But this is very different than participation-based and "role-based" badges awarded for what Greeno (1998) and Hickey (2003) characterized as *engaged participation,* and which (ideally) contain evidence of that participation. In particular, we worry that conflating attendance and participation badges may obscure the significant motivational potential of the "entry-level" badges that most of the participation-based badge systems offer to new learners.

Seven Arguments about Motivating Learning with Digital Badges

Our general experience with the DPD Project and the findings we have shown lead us to advance the following five arguments about using Open Badges to

---

5 Bowen (2013) of Purdue University coined the term "carpetbadging" to refer to such practices, while Ravet (2015) characterized the practice as "spray and pray." This practice became widespread around 2013 and seems to have undermined the apparent value of digital badges for some stakeholders. The practice is encouraged by some commercial badge systems that make it cumbersome to upload unique evidence for each issued badge.

recognize and motivate learning. These are followed by two arguments about the systematic study of efforts to do so with Open Badges.

Argument #1: Digital Badges Are Inherently Meaningful

Arguably, the simmering tensions over extrinsic rewards and intrinsic motivation that were inflamed by digital badges are proxies for an enduring struggle between two antithetical paradigms of learning. The competency-based badge systems were generally consistent with traditional "associationist" perspectives that characterize knowledge in terms of specific behavioral or cognitive relationships (Anderson, 1982; Skinner, 1953). As such, associationist perspectives frame learning in terms of demonstrated mastery of those relationships, with relatively little concern about how learners form those relationships. As one influential proponent asserted, competency-based education is "agnostic as to the source of learning while maintaining clear and transparent learning standards" (Leuba, 2015).

In contrast, the inquiry-based badge systems were generally consistent with "constructivist" perspectives that characterize knowledge as higher-order cognitive schemata and conceptual understanding (Case, 1996). As such, constructivist perspectives frame learning as engaging in sense-making and exploration; such engagement is presumed to be necessary to reorganize prior knowledge in order to construct such schema. While this assumption underpins a vast array of approaches, these perspectives are united in their concern that extrinsic incentives will distort and undermine such intrinsically motivated engagement.

From our perspective, the enduring debate between associationist and constructivist perspective has been played out in the need to grade student work, and this need is largely driven by traditional credentialing practices. Early studies of the overjustification effect were a response to behaviorist educational practices, "token economies," and mastery learning schemes that had gained many adherents by the early 1970s (Greene et al., 1976). We assume that the overjustification effect can (and will) be replicated with digital badges that carry little meaning and are arbitrarily associated with certificates, degrees, or other distal motivators. But doing so ignores the fact that *digital* badges are intended to include detailed claims, evidence supporting those claims, and information about how that evidence was gathered. Such information can make digital badges more meaningful (i.e., "intrinsic") than the less meaningful (i.e., "extrinsic") rewards implicated in the overjustification effect.

Our point here is that the very design of digital badges encourages what Rieber (1996) called "endogenous" incentives that are directly relevant to the learning being incentivized while avoiding the "exogenous" incentives that are arbitrarily related.[6] We encourage constructivist skeptics to factor this

---

6 It is worth noting that some proponents of gamification make similar arguments about not offering arbitrary exogenous incentives, particularly for activity that is already appealing to learners (e.g., Nicholson, 2012).

into their concerns about Open Badges. Of course, our study suggested that intrinsically motivated constructivist learning presents its own challenges for obtaining evidence to include in digital badges. But we believe that it is inappropriate to equate digital and Open Badges with extrinsic rewards, CBE, or other related practices that are antithetical to constructivist approaches.

Argument #2: Open Digital Badges Are Particularly Meaningful

Our second argument is that the unique characteristics of Open Badges can make them particularly meaningful and (therefore) motivational. The Open Badges Specifications allow badge systems that let earners control if and where their badges are shared, and make them responsible for organizing and annotating their badge collections. It seems to us that Kohn (2014) overlooked the motivational value of such earner control when he equated earners sharing badges with teachers publicly posting grades.

As illustrated by participation-based badges and elaborated in Casilli and Hickey (2016), the transparency that Open Badges introduce means that their value and credibility can be "crowdsourced." This means that Open Badges make traditional approaches to validation (of the evidence) and accreditation (of value) less relevant. While this introduces new uncertainties for adding meaning and value to credentials, it also opens up vast new possibilities for doing so. Consider that most young people are now able to very quickly learn the norms of new social networks. In particular, most are quite adept at learning (and shaping) the norms in their smaller network of friends within those larger networks. We believe that similar networked learning will occur as Open Badges become more widely used. We also suspect learners who are disenfranchised by existing credentialing practices will be able to learn about and participate in these networked credentialing practices more successfully.

Argument #3: Open Badges Are Particularly Consequential Credentials

To reiterate, the DPD Project observed that most of the 30 badge design efforts struggled to (1) define learning outcomes and (2) design and implement assessments to generate evidence. This is not surprising, given that the introduction of assessments is typically quite consequential for the broader educational practices and ecosystems in which those assessments function (National Research Council, 2001; Shepard, 2000). This is because assessments push educators to think about the *processes* of learning instead of just the *practices* of teaching (Moss, 2003). As elaborated by Torrance (2012), these disruptions can be *transformative* (positively impacting the broader ecosystem), *conformative* (aligning the ecosystem to the assessments, which can be positive or negative, depending on the assessments), and *deformative* (negatively impacting the ecosystem).

Importantly, leaders of some of the 30 efforts reported that their assessment challenges were amplified by the recognition that they would be placing claims, evidence, and relevant information in Open Badges. Doing so makes this information public and readily accessible; leaders recognized that this transparency was likely to bring additional scrutiny to this information and the manner in which it was obtained. In this way, Open Badges are likely to enhance the positive and negative consequences of assessment practices for the broader ecosystem in which they function.

While their assessment challenges were different, both the competency-based systems and the inquiry-based systems struggled to overcome the challenges of designing and implementing their assessment systems. The competency-based systems struggled to design and implement the more summative assessments needed to provide evidence of numerous competencies, while the inquiry-based systems struggled to obtain convincing evidence of competency from completed work and learner-generated artifacts. In contrast, the participation-based systems focused more on exploiting the social recognition and motivation potential of Open Badges. In particular, these systems began exploring the way that social networks allow others to "like" and comment upon the badges and badge evidence. We believe that such "endorsement" practices have the potential to truly transform credentialing and its potential for motivating learning. We suspect that few stakeholders in the current credentialing enterprise have recognized the motivational potential of new "third party" endorsement made possible by *Open Badges Specifications 2.0* (described in Hickey & Otto, 2017). As argued in a foundational chapter on Open Badge endorsements:

> The intentionally open structure of badge endorsement provides opportunities for a variety of different types of endorsers, including community organizations, employers, standards bodies, and groups that are re-envisioning how the value of learning is defined. (Everhart, et al., 2016, p. 232)

These arguments about endorsement and open recognition were further advanced at an international conference in 2016. The *Bologna Open Recognition Declaration* (2016) asserted that Open Badges "had proved the power of a simple, affordable, resilient and trustworthy technology to create an open recognition ecosystem working across countries, educational sectors, work, social environments and technologies" and "demonstrated that we have the means and the opportunity to put an end to the disparities of the recognition landscape."

Argument #4: The Negative Consequences of Extrinsic Rewards Are Overstated

Despite our argument that Open Badges offer inherently meaningful incentives, it seems likely that Open Badges will still be used in ways that are relatively arbitrary and disconnected from engagement in learning. This seems particularly likely with the "closed" badge systems (e.g., *Buzzmath* and

ClassBadges.com).[7] Of course, behaviorally oriented theorists continue to dispute the empirical evidence against extrinsic incentives and question the very idea of intrinsically motivated engagement (Cameron et al., 2001). Furthermore, Hidi (2016) recently reviewed the evidence from neuroscience that documented the seemingly positive consequences of extrinsic rewards on brain activity. Hidi points out that while the social and educational psychological literature heavily emphasizes the negative effects of rewards on learning and motivation, the neuroscience literature suggests that our brains are "hardwired" to recognize and respond to rewards. As such, research that better understands the complicated nature of rewards is needed before any conclusive decisions about whether rewards are "good" or "bad" can be made.

Hidi's review bolsters the argument that even when badges function in a less meaningful and more arbitrary fashion, the potentially negative consequences for intrinsically motivated engagement in learning may be outweighed by other potentially positive consequences of extrinsic rewards. These include (1) the neurological response of individuals, (2) the behavioral engagement of individuals, and (3) the collective engagement of a learning community. In this way, badges can "jump-start" networked learning communities. If they do so, membership in and recognition by this community might motivate individual engagement that has all of the characteristics of intrinsic motivation. This "balancing" of incentives in actual learning contexts seems like a particularly fertile area for future research.

Argument #5: Focus Primarily on Social Activity and Secondarily on Individual Activity

For complex reasons, we believe that considering the motivational value of Open Badges by *starting* with their impact on the way that individuals behave or process information is problematic, because any coherent consideration of motivation in learning contexts must reconcile (1) knowing and learning at the level of the individual with (2) knowing and learning at the level of larger social and cultural activity. Starting one's consideration of Open Badges at the level of the individual, one inevitably encounters the antithetical tensions between the associationist and constructivist models of learning. This, in turn, leads to corresponding tensions over learning (i.e., having those associations versus using those structures) and *evidence of* learning (i.e., demonstrating specific associations versus applying conceptual structures). While methodological and theoretical coherence may still be possible (by choosing one perspective or the other), practical tensions that will likely undermine efforts to transform education or produce useful design principles for motivating engagement will almost certainly be introduced.

---

7 ClassBadges.com launched in 2013; as of January 2017 the site was available for free use but was no longer supported.

Another problem with starting one's consideration of badges and motivation with the behavior or cognition of individuals is that doing so necessarily characterizes social learning by "aggregating" assumptions about individual learning. This is why behavioral theorists use the notion of "meta-contingencies" (Lamal, 1990; Todorov, 2013), which characterizes social activity by aggregating assumptions about how contingencies (such as rewards) motivate individuals. Conversely, cognitive theorists like Bandura (2000) turn to aggregative characterizations of individual constructs like self-efficacy to characterize social activity in terms of "collective efficacy." In a cogent characterization of aggregative reconciliation of individual and social activity, Bandura (2000) asserted that "[t]here is no disembodied group mind that believes. Perceived collective efficacy resides in the minds of group members as the belief they have in common regarding their group's capability" (pp. 165–6).

In short, we contend that focusing on individual activity leads to aggregative reconciliation of social activity, and that this leads to an inaccurate and incomplete characterization of social activity. More specifically, we assume that social activity and human culture are indeed most accurately characterized with the notion of "disembodied group minds" (which was dismissed in Bandura, 2000, p. 165). Therefore, we believe that any effort to coherently and completely reconcile individual and social motivation for learning should start with social activity, and that this is particularly true with digitally networked learning.

Argument #6: Situative Models of Engagement Are Ideal for Studying Digital Credentials

Our sixth argument is rooted in the nature of learning in digital networks. While all of the 30 badge design efforts involved networked computers, they varied in the extent to which the actual learning was "socially networked." Back in 2008, Brown and Adler (2008) stated that "the Web 2.0 is creating a new kind of participatory medium that is ideal for supporting multiple modes of learning" and that "the most profound impact of the Internet, an impact that has yet to be fully realized, is its ability to support and expand the various aspects of social learning" (p. 18). Brown and Adler made a clear distinction between socially networked learning from prior "Cartesian" views of learning that treat knowledge as "a kind of substance and that pedagogy concerns the best way to transfer this substance from teachers to students" (p. 19). Consistent with Lucy Neale Lewis' characterization of "role-based" badges above, Brown and Adler advanced a "participatory" view of networked learning that "involves not only 'learning about' the subject matter but 'learning to be a full participant in the field'" (p. 19).

As articulated by Xenos and Foot (2008), Web 2.0 digital networks are defined by *transactive interactions* (where the website provides content and information that is tailored to the information visitors provide) and *shared control* (between the producers of content and the collective users, so that content and user experience are co-produced by the website creator and visitors). This means the disciplinary knowledge created and stored in these networks is highly bound to that context, and the networks themselves evolve rapidly in response to evolving user needs. This in turn means that the important disciplinary knowledge in these settings is highly *contextual* (takes much of its meaning from the context in which it is used) and highly *consequential* (has obvious consequences for disciplinary practice, because many of the practices take place in similarly networked contexts). In this way, digital social networks necessarily create multiple "disembodied group minds" that transcend individual participants.

In addition to affording a more coherent depiction of individual and social activity, situative perspectives offer a coherent way to study all forms of individual activity. The "situative synthesis" in Greeno (1998) treats all forms of individual knowing (i.e., the objective behavior of individuals *and* the way human minds appear to process information) as "special cases" of social activity. All learning is fundamentally situated in the social, technological, and material contexts where it is created, learned, and used. Put differently, this perspective suggests that individual knowledge is "secondary" to knowledge that is primarily social. This allows educational innovators to primarily focus on engaged participation in whatever disciplinary practices are the focus of the innovation. Contrary to many characterizations, this participation can occur in social isolation, as individuals use the socially constructed tools of the discipline with increasing success.

In learning contexts, credentials and incentives are likely to be accompanied by discourse among educators and learners when they are introduced, offered, and earned. This discourse can be more or less disciplinary (concerning the ideas, terms, content, resources, and practices that define the particular discipline). From a situative perspective, discourse that is more disciplinary is always better than discourse that is less disciplinary. While the theory behind this idea might be complex, its practical implication is quite simple: Is the discourse associated with the credential more or less disciplinary? If the discourse associated with the incentive concerns the discipline (e.g. "your connections between _____ and _____ were very strong") then the incentive is likely desirable. If the discourse does not concern the discipline (e.g., "you were late" or "you failed") then the incentive is likely undesirable.

Argument #7: Study Motivation and Digital Credentials at Three Levels

Our final argument is that the motivational consequences of digital badges should be understood and studied at three increasingly formal "levels." At the "close" level, one first examines the extent to which badges (introducing, offering, earning, or endorsing them) are associated with productive forms of disciplinary engagement. Engle and Conant's (2002) study of *productive disciplinary engagement* (PDE) suggests looking for discourse that makes connections between disciplinary knowledge (abstractions that experts "know" independent of context) and learners' nascent disciplinary practices (what experts "do" in particular disciplinary contexts where their expertise can be recognized). Likewise, Engle's (2006) study of *generative learning* points to discourse that (1) establishes common ground with content *and* differential trajectories of participation, (2) temporally frames engagement around prior experiences *and* future goals, and (3) journalistically frames participants as authors *and* contributors to a larger community.

At the second "proximal" level, one then examines whether PDE and generative learning is "echoed" in intrinsically motivated engagement and situational interest (Hidi & Anderson, 2014). Such engagement and situational interest can be readily captured using self-reports during or immediately after the activities associated with the badges. Because such self-reports can be automatically offered and analyzed in networked learning contexts, establishing baseline scores across multiple activities and learners on simple Likert-scale items is possible. The baselines can reveal scores that are relatively higher or lower than the baselines for particular activities carried out to earn badges.

At the third "distal" level, the credentialing system that emerges from iterative refinements across the close and proximal level systems can then be more formally evaluated by comparing such systems to a similar learning environment that does not include those credentials (or some other comparison environment that targets the same disciplinary standards) according to more stable, longer-term outcomes. These include changes in personal interest in the particular discipline (Hidi & Renninger, 2006), as well as changes in subsequent free-choice engagement in activities associated with the discipline.

A version of such a multi-level approach was employed in a quasi-experimental study of incentives and badges reported by Filsecker and Hickey (2014) that was carried out with the Quest Atlantis STEM educational video-game (Barab et al., 2007). This study compared badge-based incentives (classroom leader boards and avatar badges that offered special opportunities) with appeals to curiosity and challenge. Results across two matched pairs of classes revealed that the incentives were indeed associated with significantly higher levels of PDE (as indicated by increased and more appropriate use of targeted scientific concepts in player-submitted "field reports"), slightly higher levels of self-reported intrinsic motivation when completing those reports, and slightly more positive changes in self-reported individual interest in learning about the STEM discipline and problems.

As best illustrated in a similar study of multiple levels of assessment (Hickey & Zuiker, 2012), the "echoes" of impact across different kinds of evidence are useful for distinguishing systematic impact from innovation from the random variation that is usually present in authentic learning contexts. This provides useful evidence for guiding iterative refinements of recognition and assessment practices, which in turn can deliver useful design principles that can serve as the starting points for others.

This nascent "multiple-levels" model of motivation draws on some of the same ideas and concerns behind more well-known "multi-level" considerations (e.g., Chen & Kanfer, 2006; Järvelä et al., 2010). But the model proposed here diverges in its embrace of a situative synthesis, resolutely interventionist goals, and design-based research methods. The method is complex and presents tensions between interventionist goals for iterative refinement and naturalistic goals for generalizable results. But it accrues design principles that extend beyond particular projects. When these design principles are shared, along with examples and information about the most relevant features of the example context, these principles can be readily used and extended by others.

Fortunately, in networked learning settings, the discourse associated with credentials can be captured and searched by machines. We are particularly excited that digital badges promise to hold and organize evidence of learning (elaborated in Hickey & Willis, 2015). If the multi-level model summarized here is applied to digital badges, the evidence of learning contained in the issued badges is immediately useable to study motivation. When coupled with the forthcoming features of Open Badges 2.0, tremendous potential for transforming learning and education is promised.

Concluding Thoughts

Our primary conclusions from this research are represented by the seven design principles given. To reiterate, these conclusions emerged when considering the concerns that critics and skeptics have raised about the potentially negative consequences of digital badges for intrinsic motivation in light of the findings of the Design Principles Documentation Project. The DPD Project concluded that seven of the 30 badge system designs primarily intended to use badges as relatively extrinsic incentives (within competency-based ecosystems). But the fact that 23 other systems did not attempt to use badges in this manner suggests to us that the concerns about extrinsic rewards should be directed at the design of broader educational ecosystems rather than badges. Put differently, our evidence supports the conclusion that Open Badges have provided a new proxy for the enduring debate over reward structures in educational ecosystems; our argument is that equating badges and reward structures in this fashion is inappropriate and is impeding the important research and innovation required to identify needed principles for using digital credentials most effectively.

It is important to note that some leaders within the Open Badges community (particularly Ravet, 2014) have expressed concerns that introducing Open Badges into constructivist ecosystems might lead them to be transformed ("deformed" in Torrance, 2012) into competency-based ecosystems (and presumably the corresponding reward structures). Our data did not provide support for that concern, in that the inquiry-based systems did not report or appear to shift towards more specific measurable competencies because of badges. However, tension with conventional summative assessments has long been a central issue for proponents of inquiry-based education and other such constructivist approaches (e.g., Gardner, 1992). Thus, another general conclusion is that Open Badges provide both the impetus and the context for educators and innovators to make new progress on resolving these enduring tensions. To reiterate, we believe that situative theories and the new forms of evidence of learning contained in (and represented by) digital badges present a promising path forward in this regard.

Two rather nuanced conclusions may help guide future studies of badges and reward structures. Our first conclusion is that Open Badges are likely to draw additional scrutiny to claims and evidence, and to the manner in which such information is obtained. Our second conclusion is that the transparency afforded by this new scrutiny is likely to enhance the consequences of assessment practices for the larger educational ecosystems that those assessments serve. These consequences can be both positive and negative; some consequences might be positive from certain perspectives and negative from other perspectives. These nuances call for studies that are well-theorized and carefully designed, rather than simplistic comparison studies that introduce badges and then examine a few outcomes.

We close by reiterating that we did not reach any strong conclusions regarding competency-based versus inquiry-based badge systems. While the competency-based efforts had a particularly difficult time implementing their badge systems, most of those efforts also struggled more generally because they also had to overcome the fundamental orientation of their broader school systems towards courses and cohorts. Of course, our data did suggest that it was easier to issue badges for the completion of courses and projects with cohorts of learners, and provided some support for the concerns raised elsewhere about the limitations of self-paced competency-based education (and the reward structures that they call for). But we believe that self-paced competency-based learning is ideal for some learning goals and contexts, and is inevitable in many more contexts, regardless of concerns raised by others. We hope that this chapter provides helpful guidance for using digital badges across the entire range of educational approaches.

References

Abramovich, S., Schunn, C., & Higashi, R. M. (2013). Are badges useful in education? It depends upon the type of badge and expertise of learner. *Educational Technology Research and Development*, *61*(2), 217–32. doi: 10.1007/s11423-013-9289-2.

Afterschool Alliance (2015). *Digital badges in afterschool: Connecting learning in a connected world.* [Report]. Retrieved from www.afterschoolalliance.org/documents/DigitalBadgesInAfterschool.pdf.

American Council on Education (2016). *Quality dimensions for connected credentials.* Washington, DC. Retrieved from http://connectingcredentials.org/wp-content/uploads/2016/04/Quality-Dimensions-for-Connected-Credentials.pdf.

Anderson, J. R. (1982). Acquisition of cognitive skill. *Psychological Review, 89*(4), 369–406. doi: 10.1037/0033-295X.89.4.369.

Anderson, T. & McGreal, R. (2012). Disruptive pedagogies and technologies in universities. *Educational Technology & Society, 15*(4), 380–89.

Ash, K. (2012, June 13). "Digital badges" would represent student skill acquisition; Initiatives seek to give students permanent online records for developing specific skills. *Education Week Digital Directions 5*(3), pp. 24–25, 28, 30. Retrieved from https://www.edweek.org/dd/articles/2012/06/13/03badges.h05.html

Bandura, A. (2000). Exercise of human agency through collective efficacy. *Current Directions in Psychological Science, 9*(3), 75–8.

Barab, S., Zuiker, S., Warren, S., Hickey, D., Ingram-Goble, A., Kwon, E. J., ... Herring, S. C. (2007). Situationally embodied curriculum: Relating formalisms and contexts. *Science Education, 91*(5), 750–82. doi: 10.1002/sce.20217.

Blackburn, R. D., Porto, S. C., & Thompson, J. J. (2016). Competency-based education and the relationship to digital badges. In L. Y. Muilenburg & Z. L. Berge (Eds.), *Digital badges in education: Trends, issues, and cases* (pp. 30–8). New York, NY: Routledge.

Bologna Open Recognition Declaration (2016). Author. Retrieved from www.openrecognition.org.

Bowen, K. (2013). "Carpetbadging" – why metadata is so important when it comes to #openbadges [Twitter post]. Retrieved from https://twitter.com/kyledbowen/status/336577 520449245185.

Brown, J. S. (2012). *Cultivating the entrepreneurial learner in the 21st century.* [YouTube video]. Keynote address at the 2012 Digital Media and Learning Conference. Retrieved from https://www.youtube.com/watch?v=SoRV0BEwvEU.

Brown, J. S. & Adler, R. P (2008). Open education, the long tail, and learning 2.0. *EDUCAUSE Review, 43*(1), 16–20.

Buckingham, J. (2014). Open digital badges for the uninitiated. *The Electronic Journal for English as a Second Language, 18*(1), 1–11.

Cameron, J., Banko, K. M., & Pierce, W. D. (2001). Pervasive negative effects of rewards on intrinsic motivation: The myth continues. *The Behavior Analyst, 24*(1), 1–44.

Carey, K. (2012). Show me your badge. *The New York Times.* Retrieved from https://www.nytimes.com/2012/11/04/education/edlife/show-me-your-badge.html.

Case, R. (1996). Changing views of knowledge and their impact on educational research and practice. In D. R. Olson & N. Torrance (Eds.), *Handbook of education and human development* (pp. 75–99). Cambridge, MA: Blackwell.

Casilli, C. & Hickey, D. (2016). Transcending conventional credentialing and assessment paradigms with information-rich digital badges. *The Information Society, 32*(2), 117–29. doi: 10.1080/01972243.2016.1130500.

Chen, G. & Kanfer, R. (2006). Toward a systems theory of motivated behavior in work teams. *Research in Organizational Behavior, 27*, 223–67. doi: 10.1016/s0191-3085(06)27006-0.

Cordova, D. I. & Lepper, M. R. (1996). Intrinsic motivation and the process of learning: Beneficial effects of contextualization, personalization, and choice. *Journal of Educational Psychology, 88*(4), 715–30.

Davis, K. & Singh, S. (2015). Digital badges in afterschool learning: Documenting the perspectives and experiences of students and educators. *Computers & Education, 88,* 72–83. doi: 10.1016/j.compedu/2015.04.011.

Deci, E. L., Koestner, R., & Ryan, R. M. (1999). A meta-analytic review of experiments examining the effects of extrinsic rewards on intrinsic motivation. *Psychological Bulletin, 125*(6), 627–68. doi: 10.1037/0033-2909.125.6.627.

Deci, E. L. & Ryan, R. M. (1985). The general causality orientations scale: Self-determination in personality. *Journal of Research in Personality, 19*(2), 109–34. doi: 10.1016/0092-6566(85).

Duncan, A. (2011). Digital Badges for Learning. *Opening remarks and DML 2012 competition event transcript.* Retrieved from www.ed.gov/news/speeches/digital-badges-learning.

Eisenberg, A. (2011, November 19). For job hunters, digital merit badges. *The New York Times,* p. BU3. Retrieved from https://www.nytimes.com/2011/11/20/business/digital-badges-may-highlight-job-seekers-skills.html

Engle, R. A. (2006). Framing interactions to foster generative learning: A situative explanation of transfer in a community of learners classroom. *The Journal of the Learning Sciences, 15*(4), 451–498. http://doi.org/10.1207/s15327809jls1504

Engle, R. A. & Conant, F. R. (2002). Guiding principles for fostering productive disciplinary engagement: Explaining an emergent argument in a community of learners classroom. *Cognition and Instruction, 20*(4), 399–483. doi: 10.1207/S1532690XCI2004_1.

Everhart, D., Derryberry, A., Knight, E., & Lee, S. (2016). The role of endorsement in Open Badges ecosystems. In D. Ifenthaler, N. Belin-Mularski, & D. Mah, (Eds.), *Foundation of digital badges and micro-credentials* (pp. 221–35). New York, NY: Springer.

Everhart, D., Sandeen, C., Seymour, D., & Yoshino, K. (2014). *Clarifying competency-based education terms: A lexicon.* Blackboard.com. Retrieved from http://bbbb.blackboard.com/Competency-based-education-definitions.

Ferlazzo, L. (2012). The dangers of "gamification" in education. *Edublogs.* Retrieved from http://larryferlazzo.edublogs.org/2012/02/26/the-dangers-of-gamification-in-education/.

Filsecker, M. & Hickey, D. T. (2014). A multilevel analysis of the effects of external rewards on elementary students' motivation, engagement and learning in an educational game. *Computers & Education, 75,* 136–48. doi: 10.1016/j.compedu.2014.02.008.

Fong, J., Janzow, P., & Peck, K. (2016). *Demographic shifts in educational demand and the rise of alternative credentials.* University Professional and Continuing Education Association. Retrieved from http://upcea.edu/wp-content/uploads/2017/05/Demographic-Shifts-in-Educational-Demand-and-the-Rise-of-Alternative-Credentials.pdf.

Gardner, H. (1992). Assessment in context: The alternative to standardized testing. In B. R. Gifford & M. C. O'Connor (Eds.), *Changing assessments: Alternative views of aptitude, achievement, and instruction* (pp. 77–120). Boston, MA: Kluwer Academic Publishers.

Gates Foundation. (2011). *Supporting students: Investing in innovation and quality.* College Ready Monograph Series. Seattle, WA. Retrieved from https://docs.gatesfoundation.org/documents/supporting-students.pdf.

Gerstein, J. (2013). I Don't Get Digital Badges. *User generated education* [blog]. Retrieved from https://usergeneratededucation.wordpress.com/2013/03/16/i-dont-get-digital-badges.

Grant, S. (2014). *What counts As learning.* Digital Median and Learning Research Hub. Retrieved from https://dmlhub.net/publications/what-counts-learning.

Greene, D., Sternberg, B., & Lepper, M. R. (1976). Overjustification in a token economy. *Journal of Personality and Social Psychology, 34*(6), 1219–34. doi: 10.1037/0022-3514.34.6.1219.

Greeno, J. G. (1998). The situativity of knowing, learning, and research. *American Psychologist, 53*(1), 5–26. doi: 10.1037/0003-066X.53.1.5.

Halverson, R. (2004). Accessing, documenting, and communicating practical wisdom: The phronesis of school leadership practice. *American Journal of Education, 111*(1), 90–121. doi: 0195-6744/2004/11101-0004$05.00

Hickey, D. T. (2003). Engaged participation versus marginal nonparticipation: A stridently sociocultural approach to achievement motivation. *The Elementary School Journal, 103*(4), 401–29. doi: 0013-5984/2003/10304-0006$05

Hickey, D. T. & Otto, N. (2017). "Endorsement 2.0" is about to transform eCredentials. *EDUCAUSE Review [online].* Retrieved from https://er.educause.edu/articles/2017/2/endorsement-2-taking-open-badges-and-ecredentials-to-the-next-level.

Hickey, D. T. & Willis, J. E. (2015). Research designs for studying individual and collaborative learning with digital badges. In *Proceedings of the Second Annual Open Badges in Education Workshop*, Poughkeepsie, NY (pp. 36–40). Retrieved from http://ceur-ws.org/Vol-1358/paper5.pdf.

Hickey, D. T. & Willis, J. E. (2017). Where badges appear to work better. *Final Report of the Design Principles Documentation Project.* Indiana University. Center for Research on Learning and Technology. Retrieved from http://bit.ly/2DPDfinalreport.

Hickey, D. T. & Zuiker, S. J. (2012). Multilevel assessment for discourse, understanding, and achievement. *Journal of the Learning Sciences, 21*(4), 522–82. doi: 10.1080/10508406.2011.652320.

Hidi, S. (2016). Revisiting the role of rewards in motivation and learning: Implications of neuroscientific research. *Educational Psychology Review, 28*(1), 61–93. doi: 10.1007/s10648-015-9307-5.

Hidi, S. & Anderson, V. (2014). Situational interest and its impact on reading and expository writing. In A. Renninger, S. Hidi, & A. Krapp, (Eds.), *The Role of interest in learning and development* (pp. 215–38). New York, NY: Psychology Press. (Reprinted from 1992).

Hidi, S. & Renninger, K. A. (2006). The four-phase model of interest development. *Educational Psychologist, 41*(2), 111–27. doi: 10.1207/s15326985ep4102_4.

Ito, M. (2012). Reflections on DML 2012 and a vision of educational change. [blog post at *DML Central*]. Retrieved from http://dmlcentral.net/blog/mimi-ito/reflections-dml2012-and-visions-educational-change.

Järvelä, S., Volet, S., & Järvenoja, H. (2010). Research on motivation in collaborative learning: Moving beyond the cognitive–situative divide and combining individual and social processes. *Educational Psychologist, 45*(1), 15–27. doi: 10.1080/00461520903433539.

Jenkins, H. (2012). How to earn your skeptic "badge." *Confessions of an Aca-Fan. The official blog of Henry Jenkins.* Retrieved from http://henryjenkins.org/2012/03/how_to_earn_your_skeptic_badge.html.

Jenkins, H., Purushotma, R., Weigel, M., Clinton, K., & Robison, A. J. (2009). *Confronting the challenges of participatory culture: Media education for the 21st century.* Cambridge, MA: MIT Press.

Kohn, A. (1999). *Punished by rewards: The trouble with gold stars, incentive plans, A's, praise, and other bribes.* Boston, MA: Houghton Mifflin Harcourt.

Kohn, A. (2014). Keynote presentation at the 12th Annual e-Portfolio, Open Badges, and Identity Conference, London, England. Retrieved from www.youtube .com/watch?v=p_98XcxJqkw.

Kolowich, S. (2014). Can digital "badges" and "nanodegrees" protect job seekers from a first-round knockout? *Chronicle of Higher Education.* Retrieved from www .chronicle.com/article/Can-Digital-Badges-and/150257.

Kruchten, P. (2004). *The rational unified process: An introduction.* New York, NY: Addison-Wesley.

Lamal, P. A. (1990). *Behavioral analysis of societies and cultural practices.* New York, NY: Taylor & Francis.

Lepper, M. R., Greene, D., & Nisbett, R. E. (1973). Undermining children's intrinsic interest with extrinsic reward: A test of the "overjustification" hypothesis. *Journal of Personality and Social Psychology, 28*(1), 129–37.

Leuba, M. (2015). Competency-based education: Technology challenges and opportunities. *EDUCAUSE Review* [online]. Retrieved from http://er .educause.edu/articles/2015/10/competency-based-education-technology-challenges-and-opportunities.

Mallon, M. (2013). Gaming and gamification. *Public Services Quarterly, 9*(3), 210–21. doi: 10.1080/15228959.2013.815502.

Malone, T. W. & Lepper, M. R. (1987). Making learning fun: A taxonomy of intrinsic motivations for learning. In R. E. Snow & M. J. Farr (Eds.), *Aptitude, learning, and instruction, Vol. 3, conative and affective process analysis* (pp. 223–53). Hillsdale, NJ: Lawrence Erlbaum.

Metzger, E. C., Lubin, L., Patten, R. T., & Whyte, J. (2016). Applied gamification: Creating reward systems for organizational professional development. In D. Ifenthaler, N. Belin-Mularski, & D. Mah (Eds.) *Foundation of digital badges and micro-credentials* (pp. 457–66). NYC, NY: Springer International Publishing. doi: 10.1007/978-3-319-15425-1.

Moss, P. A. (2003). Reconceptualizing validity for classroom assessment. *Educational Measurement: Issues and Practice, 22*(4), 13–25. doi: 10.1111/j.1745-3992 .2003.tb00140.x

National Research Council. (2001). *Knowing what students know: The science and design of educational assessment.* Washington, DC: National Academies Press.

Nicholson, S. (2012). A user-centered theoretical framework for meaningful gamification. *Games, Learning & Society, 8*(1), 223–30.

Nolen, S. B., Horn, I. S., & Ward, C. J. (2015). Situating motivation. *Educational Psychologist, 50*(3), 234–47. doi: 10.1080/00461520.2015.1075399.

Olneck, M. (2015). Whom will digital badges empower? Sociological perspectives on digital badges. In D. T. Hickey, J. Jovanovic, S. Lonn, & J.E. Willis, III (Eds.), *Proceedings of the Second International Open Badges in Education Workshop* (pp. 5–11), Workshop, Poughkeepsie, NY. Retrieved from http://ceur-ws.org/ Vol-1358/paper1.pdf

Oyserman, D. (2015). *Pathways to success through identity-based motivation.* Oxford, UK: Oxford University Press.

Pink, D. H. (2011). *Drive: The surprising truth about what motivates us.* New York, NY: Penguin.

Ravet, S. (2014). #Openbadges for key competencies. *Learning futures: Reflections on learning, technologies, identities, and trust* [blog post]. Retrieved from http:// www.learningfutures.eu/2014/12/openbadges-for-key-competencies/

Ravet, S. (2015). #OpenBadges: Beyond "Spray and pray"! *Learning futures* [blog post]. Retrieved from www.learningfutures.eu/2015/02/openbadges-beyond-spray-and-pray.

Resnick, M. (2012). Still a badge skeptic [blog post]. Retrieved from http://hastac.org/blogs/mres/2012/02/27/still-badge-skeptic.

Rieber, L. P. (1996). Seriously considering play: Designing interactive learning environments based on the blending of microworlds, simulations, and games. *Educational Technology Research and Development*, *44*(2), 43–58. doi: 10.1007/BF02300540.

Shavelson, R. J., Baxter, G. P., & Pine, J. (1992). Research news and comment: Performance assessments: Political rhetoric and measurement reality. *Educational Researcher*, *21*(4), 22–7. doi: 10.3102/0013189X021004022.

Shepard, L. A. (2000). The role of assessment in a learning culture. *Educational Researcher*, *29*(7), 4–14.

Silva, E., White, T., & Toch, T. (2015). *The Carnegie Unit: A century-old standard in a changing educational landscape*. New York: Carnegie Foundation for the Advancement of Teaching. Retrieved from www.carnegiefoundation.org/resources/publications/carnegie-unit.

Skinner, B. F. (1953). *Science and human behavior*. Santa Monica, CA: Simon and Schuster.

Steele, J. L., Lewis, M., Santibanez, L., Faxon-Mills, S., Rudnick, B., Stecher, B., & Hamilton, L. (2014). *Competency-based education in three pilot programs: Examining implementation and outcomes*. Santa Monica, CA: RAND Corporation. Retrieved from www.rand.org/pubs/research_reports/RR732.html.

Thigpen, K. (2014). *Digital badge systems: The promise and potential*. Washington, DC: The Alliance for Excellent Education. Retrieved from http://all4ed.org/wp-content/uploads/2014/11/DigitalBadgeSystems.pdf.

Todorov, J. C. (2013). Conservation and transformation of cultural practices through contingencies and metacontingencies. *Behavior and Social Issues*, *22*, 64–73. doi: 10.521/bsi.v.22i0.4612.

Torrance, H. (2012). Formative assessment at the crossroads: Conformative, deformative and transformative assessment. *Oxford Review of Education*, *38*(3), 323–42. doi: 10.1080/03054985.2012.689693.

Tran, C., Schenke, K., & Hickey, D. T. (2014). Design principles for motivating learning with digital badges: Consideration of contextual factors of recognition and assessment. In J. L. Polman, E. A. Kyza, D. K. O'Neill, I. Tabak, W. R. Penuel, A. S. Jurow, ... L. D'Amico (Eds.), *Learning and becoming in practice: The International Conference of the Learning Sciences (ICLS) 2014, Volume 1* (pp. 1027–1032). Boulder, CO: The International Society of the Learning Sciences.

Xenos, M. & Foot, K. (2008). Not your father's Internet: The generation gap in online politics. In W. L. Bennett (Ed.), *Civic life online: Learning how digital media can engage youth*, (pp. 51–70). Cambridge, MA: The MIT Press.

Young, J. R. (2012). "Badges" earned online pose challenge to traditional college diplomas. *The Education Digest*, *78*(2), 48–52.

Yowell, C. M. (2014). Presentation at the Open Badges Summit to Reconnect Learning. Retrieved from http://vimeo.com/87127953.

Yowell, C. M. & Smylie, M. A. (1999). Self-regulation in democratic communities. *The Elementary School Journal*, *99*(5), 469–90. doi: 10.1086/461936.

10 The Promise and Peril of Choosing for Motivation and Learning

Erika A. Patall and Sophia Yang Hooper

Abstract: In this chapter, an overview of the concept of choice provision and a discussion of the benefits and detriments of providing choice for motivation and learning in educational contexts is discussed. A review of the theoretical perspectives explaining how and why choice may have benefits, and sometimes detriments, is provided. In reviewing the relevant theories and the corresponding empirical evidence, we highlight a diverse set of perspectives – motivational, cognitive, social, and neuroscientific – to provide a nuanced understanding of the role of choice in educational settings. We focus the second half of the chapter on areas of contention within choice theory and research, including a discussion of the conceptual confluence of choice and autonomy and the various characteristics of individuals, tasks, choices, classrooms, and cultures that predict divergent choice effects. In closing the chapter, we discuss the implications of this research for educational practice and make recommendations for future research.

A pressing concern for many teachers is how they can promote student motivation and create a classroom environment in which students are engaged and putting forth effort. Their concern with students' motivation is well justified. Motivated students – those who are interested in what they are learning, can see the value in academic tasks, and feel in control of their learning – inevitably learn more and are more persistent (Lepper et al., 2005; Murayama et al., 2013; Yeager et al., 2014). In contrast, students who struggle with motivation in class put forth less effort (e.g., Shen et al., 2010), have lower achievement (e.g., Leroy & Bressoux, 2016), and are more likely to be disruptive in the classroom (e.g., Brown-Wright et al., 2013) or to drop out of school altogether (Vallerand et al., 1997).

Providing students with opportunities to make choices and decisions regarding their academic work is one strategy that both psychologists and educators have identified as promising for supporting student motivation and promoting learning. According to psychological and educational theorists, choosing can lead to feelings of autonomy, control, interest, and value; enhanced memory; and more adaptive self-regulation, as well as to the subsequent learning that results from such experiences (e.g., Patall et al., 2008). Likewise, teachers report using choice provision as a motivational and instructional strategy because it increases interest, engagement, effort, self-regulation, and learning (Flowerday & Schraw, 2000).

Despite the potential of choice provision as a motivational and instructional strategy in the classroom, the role it plays in student motivation, engagement, and other important educational outcomes is surprisingly complex (e.g., Katz & Assor, 2007). The landscape of choice theory and research is teeming with explanations for when, why, and how providing choice will lead to benefits or detriments for students in the classroom. Accordingly, the significance of choice provision for students' motivation, engagement, and learning is examined in this chapter. We begin by providing an overview of the theoretical perspectives and research evidence attesting to the significant role choice plays in motivation and learning within educational settings. In our review, we attempt to highlight a diverse set of perspectives – including motivational, cognitive, and neuroscientific perspectives – to provide a nuanced understanding of the role of choice in educational settings. We highlight particularly thorny issues and areas of contention in the research and theory related to the role of choice in educational settings, including its confluence with autonomy and the conditions under which its effects diverge. Finally, we discuss the implications of this research for educational practice and make recommendations for future research.

Theory and Research Focused on Choice

Next, we will review theory and research relevant to the effects of choice from three distinct perspectives: motivation perspectives, cognitive perspectives, and neuroscience perspectives.

Motivation Perspectives

Choice has long been viewed as a powerful driver in many psychological theories of motivation (see Lewin, 1952 for an early example). Self-determination theory provides one of the more well-defined perspectives regarding the role of choice in motivation. According to self-determination theory, people tend to interact with the environment in ways that promote learning and mastery (Deci & Ryan, 1985; Ryan & Deci, 2000). However, this inclination toward growth and personal development is especially promoted under certain circumstances. Specifically, the theory posits that the satisfaction of three fundamental needs – for autonomy, competence, and relatedness – underlies people's optimal psychological functioning, including their psychological well-being, engagement in tasks, and internal forms of motivation such as intrinsic motivation (the propensity to engage in a behavior for its own sake or for enjoyment). The need for autonomy (deCharms, 1968) refers to the experience of volition and that behaviors are self-authored, self-endorsed, and consistent with personal interests and values. The need for competence (White, 1959) refers to the experience of effectance in one's pursuits. The need for relatedness (Baumeister & Leary, 1995) refers to the experience of connections and caring with others. Further, and important to understanding the role of choice, social contexts influence the extent to which these needs are satisfied and the subsequent adaptive outcomes that these psychological needs fuel (Ryan & Deci, 2000).

One such contextual factor is choice provision (e.g., Patall et al., 2008). In particular, the provision of choice is expected to primarily support one's experience of autonomy. Having the opportunity to make choices should theoretically lead to the experience that one has self-authored and thus endorse one's own behavior. However, choice has also been tied to the other needs: people feel competent when they have control over and have chosen the tasks they engage in (e.g., Henry, 1994; Henry & Sniezek, 1993; Langer, 1975), and people feel related to others to the extent that providing a choice and supporting autonomy communicates caring and respect (Deci & Ryan, 2014; Williams et al., 2016). In turn, self-determination theory holds that having choice should result in enhanced intrinsic motivation, engagement, and performance (Deci & Ryan, 1985; Ryan & Deci, 2000).

In line with self-determination theory, the importance of providing choices has also been emphasized in other motivation theories focused on academic pursuits. *Achievement goal orientation theorists* have suggested that support for autonomy in the form of choices regarding tasks, materials, learning methods, or pace of learning in the classroom may be one of a number of key instructional practices that lead students to adopt a mastery goal orientation (e.g., a focus on developing skills and learning; Ames, 1992). In contrast, restricting options and choices may lead students to adopt a performance goal orientation (e.g., a focus on demonstrating competence and performing better than others; Ames, 1992). *Academic expectancy-value theorists* also rely on the idea that supporting autonomy can have important motivating consequences. Specifically, they argue that opportunities for student decision-making in the classroom create a context in which value for a task may develop and lead to enhanced expectancies for success (Jacobs & Eccles, 2000), particularly during adolescence, when developmental changes lead students to want greater autonomy and more opportunities for decision-making (e.g., Eccles et al., 1993; Midgley & Feldlaufer, 1987). Finally, though they do not consistently emphasize the role of experiencing autonomy, *interest theorists* have also suggested that choice may be an important antecedent to students' motivation. In particular, theories focused on interest development posit that the provision of choices in the classroom should support situational interest, that is, the momentary experience of positive feelings and value for content that emerges out of the context (e.g., Hidi & Renninger, 2006) and the subsequent development of individual (personal) interest for a domain (Linnenbrink-Garcia et al. 2013; Schraw et al., 2001; Tsai et al., 2008).

A great deal of research has supported the notion that the provision of choice leads to adaptive student motivation and learning outcomes. Experimental and correlational research has routinely demonstrated that providing and perceiving task-related choices leads to students' enhanced feelings of autonomy, interest, enjoyment, and persistence on a task (e.g., Assor et al., 2002; Cordova & Lepper, 1996; Mouratidis et al., 2011; Patall et al., 2008, 2010, 2013) and to enhanced task value, effort, engagement, performance, subsequent learning, and perceived competence (e.g., Assor et al., 2002; Cordova & Lepper, 1996; Patall et al., 2008, 2010, 2013). A meta-analysis of 41 studies examining the effect of choice across a wide range of settings indicated that, on average, providing choice enhanced intrinsic motivation, perceived competence, effort, and task performance, among other outcomes (Patall et al., 2008).

Research specifically relevant to educational settings has also routinely demonstrated the motivational and learning benefits of choice provision. For example, in one study with elementary school children, those who were provided with various choices during a computerized math activity (such as the opportunity to choose their game name or various icons in the math game) demonstrated greater intrinsic motivation and learning (as measured by the number of problems answered correctly on a math test) than children who were not provided with choices (Cordova & Lepper, 1996). The benefits of choosing have been found to extend to forms of performance beyond content learning. Amabile and Gitomer (1984) found that children who were given the choice of which task materials to use when creating collages produced work that was assessed to be more creative than that produced by children given no choice. During the transition to junior high school, students were more likely to feel competent and to value schoolwork if they felt they had some autonomy about choosing the activity (Midgley & Feldlaufer, 1987). Linnenbrink-Garcia et al. (2013) found that, after controlling for students' initial individual interest or perceived competence for science, the perception of having choices supported talented adolescents' situational interest for a science course during a three-week summer program, as well as subsequent individual interest and perceived competence in science at the end of the program. Choice may also support the broader social-emotional climate. For example, in analyzing the transcripts of elementary and middle school student focus groups, Williams et al. (2016) found that student perceptions that teachers gave choices in their instruction communicated messages of trust, respect, and worth that influenced the students' engagement. Finally, in a classroom-based intervention providing causal evidence regarding the effects of providing students with choices in authentic classrooms, Patall et al. (2010) found that high school students reported higher intrinsic motivation to do homework, felt more competent regarding the homework, and performed better on a unit test after they received a choice between two options for each homework assignment in the unit, compared to a unit in which they did not have homework choices.

The motivational implications of having choices may also extend to educational outcomes beyond students' motivation and performance for a given task. In one demonstration of how the provision of choices within a classroom can broadly influence educational outcomes relevant to school success, Patall and Leach (2015) conducted a set of studies exploring the link between the provision of choice and academic dishonesty. They proposed that, given evidence suggesting that one of the primary functions of academic dishonesty is to preserve a sense of competence or control and solve motivational dilemmas such as a lack of interest (e.g., Ruedy et al., 2013), having choices in the classroom would likely mitigate the tendency to cheat. They found that the opportunity to make task choices (compared to not having task choices) mitigated undergraduate students' score misreporting for a task when the opportunity to misreport was available. Moreover, the results suggested that, although both having task choices and having the opportunity to misreport independently supported students' perceptions of control, competence, and interest, there were no additional psychological benefits of cheating beyond those that choosing provided when both opportunities were available. However, the benefits of choices may not be entirely desirable. A follow-up study (Patall & Leach, 2015) suggested that perceptions of having choice opportunities in the classroom may predict desirable beliefs about competence and control that lead to unfavorable attitudes toward cheating and less anticipated cheating behavior, but may also lead to perceptions of having greater opportunity to cheat that, in turn, predict more favorable attitudes toward cheating and greater anticipated cheating behavior.

In sum, a variety of motivation theories generally converge to suggest that, on average, the provision of choice in the classroom will support students' experience of autonomy, competence, relatedness, interest, and motivation, as well as a variety of learning and educational outcomes that follow from those motivational orientations.

Cognitive and Neuroscientific Perspectives

Beyond being a motivational tool to influence students' school outcomes, cognitive psychological theory and research suggest that making choices may also have a more direct relationship with memory and learning through various cognitive processes.

A pervasive finding within research on memory and learning is that self-chosen items are remembered better than experimenter-assigned items (e.g., Perlmuter et al., 1971; Takahashi, 1991; Watanabe & Soraci, 2004). A number of mechanisms have been proposed to explain this phenomenon. An early explanation for the self-choice effect on memory focused exclusively on motivational mechanisms similar to those previously described, suggesting that individuals perceive greater control over the situation, activate their motivation, and therefore improve performance in memory and learning tasks when given the opportunity to choose items to remember (Perlmuter & Monty, 1979; Perlmuter et al., 1971). Although extensive evidence has been provided linking the provision of choice to perceived control (e.g., Leotti et al., 2010), there is limited direct evidence for this mechanism specifically for learning outcomes.

A number of other explanations have been offered for the self-choice benefits to memory. The meta-memory hypothesis (Takahashi, 1992; Takahashi & Umemoto, 1987) suggests that choosing facilitates memory simply because individuals have an opportunity to choose easier items, options, or objects to remember. However, evidence suggesting that self-choice effects are found even when choices are constrained such that individuals cannot select easier items to remember (e.g., Watanabe, 2001) and that these effects emerge for both target items chosen and items that individuals are exposed to in the context of the task (e.g., Watanabe & Soraci, 2004) limits the applicability of this mechanism. Other hypotheses have emphasized the encoding advantages of choosing, suggesting, for example, that a greater level of distinctiveness of information is encoded when participants choose items to remember (e.g., Takahashi, 1997), that choice activates connective processing, which in turn improves memory (e.g., Hirano & Ukita, 2003), or that choice imparts memory benefits when there is a clear criterion for choosing and information is therefore better integrated into cognitive structures (e.g., Toyota, 2015).

Other plausible explanations for the effects of choice on memory include the multiple-cue hypothesis and the self-reference effect. According to the multiple-cue hypothesis (Watanabe, 2001), choice facilitates memory because it requires participants to pay attention to context items as well as target items while encoding information, which serve as additional retrieval cues and additional retrieval routes in subsequent remembering. A further argument of this hypothesis is that such benefits are unlikely when participants do not choose items to remember, because context items are not as closely attended to when there are no items to choose among. In line with this argument, Watanabe and Soraci (2004) revealed that when given choices of target items, undergraduate students recognized context items better than when they did not choose target items, though choice also produced greater false recognition of items they believed they had encountered. Moreover, when context items were presented as cues to individuals, such cues enhanced individuals' free recall of the target items.

The self-reference effect is another particularly plausible cognitive explanation with neuroscientific underpinnings (e.g., see Hidi et al., 2017, for review) of how choosing can support memory and learning. The self-reference effect refers to the phenomenon in which individuals memorize, encode, and retrieve information better when it is self-related or has been linked with the self (Rogers et al., 1977; Symons & Johnson, 1997). This self-reference effect occurs as a result of a number of biases that prioritize the processing of self-related information, including greater attention and effective encoding strategies such as enhanced elaboration and organization (e.g., Humphreys & Sui,

2015; Klein & Loftus, 1988). In terms of the link between the self-reference effect and choosing, to the extent that allowing individuals to make choices about learning stimuli encourages them to link stimuli with the self and take greater ownership of stimuli, choosing can trigger particularly strong self-reference effects for memory and learning (e.g., Cloutier and Macrae, 2008; Cunningham et al., 2011). In other words, the choosing process itself creates a "self-object association." In turn, this *self-involved* choosing process promotes memory encoding.

In research demonstrating the cognitive effects of choosing, Cloutier and Macrae (2008) asked pairs of participants to choose a series of numbered tickets, each of which listed a target word that was spoken aloud. The results of a subsequent memory test revealed that participants were better at remembering the words listed on the tickets they had personally chosen than those on tickets chosen by the other participant. Thus, even when the information was trivially connected to the self, choosing facilitated referencing information to the self and subsequent memory for that information. Similarly, Cunningham et al. (2011) demonstrated that undergraduate students were better at remembering self-chosen, self-owned shopping items (items identified as belonging to the self) than they were at remembering self-owned items assigned to them by someone else. Moreover, these authors concluded that this effect, in which choosing enhanced the self-reference effect beyond merely "owning" an item, was not simply due to participants choosing items they would be particularly good at remembering. Additional experiments revealed the same effect even when choices were an "illusion" and showed that participants were best at identifying owned items when they were chosen.

Beyond the benefits of allowing students to directly control specific items for later memory, research on metacognitive control has also demonstrated the benefits of allowing students to control what and how they study (e.g., Metcalfe, 2009). Research has consistently shown that honoring students' study choices (e.g., by the experimenter actually presenting what the student selected for restudy) produces superior learning than when study choices are not honored (e.g., Kornell & Metcalfe, 2006). Moreover, the benefits of honoring students' metacognitive choices emerge regardless of whether students choose to study items that they had more or less favorable assessments of in terms of prior learning (e.g., Kornell & Metcalfe, 2006). Son (2010) also found that the benefits of choosing extended to the way students study. Extensive evidence points to the limitations of massed study and to the benefits of spacing study over time (e.g., Cepeda et al., 2006). Son (2010) found that spacing study enhanced learning to a greater degree than massed study among both undergraduate students and elementary school students, particularly when it had been the students' own choice to space their learning. However, when spacing study had been forced on the student (i.e., they did not choose it), there was no performance benefit compared to massed study among undergraduate students and there were more limited benefits among elementary school children. Taken together, cognitive research on the effects of having choices has pointed to clear benefits for memory and learning through a diverse set of cognitive mechanisms.

Given the extensive research documenting the benefits of choosing for motivation and learning, it comes as little surprise that evidence has recently begun to emerge demonstrating the neuroscientific underpinnings of these effects (see Hidi, 2015; Leotti et al., 2010; Murayama et al., 2016 for reviews). This research has demonstrated that although choosing is inherently effortful and demanding (e.g., Nelson & Vohs, 2008), it is nonetheless also inherently rewarding and motivating at a neural level (e.g., Leotti & Delgado, 2011, 2014; Murayama et al., 2016).

Using functional magnetic resonance imaging (fMRI), Leotti and Delgado (2011) demonstrated that participants experienced increased activation of the bilateral ventral striatum and the midbrain (areas of the brain known to be associated with reward and the subjective experience of value) in response to being presented with a cue that indicated they would receive a choice rather than be forced to select a particular key in a computer task. Importantly, this increased activity in response to anticipated choice was observed even when the choice was irrelevant to the actual consequences of the key selected in the computer tasks and all keys had the same expected reward value. Neuroscientific evidence also suggests that the level of striatal activity, and therefore the subjective experience of reward, increases with the number of options available (e.g., Aoki et al., 2013; Fujiwara et al., 2013). Despite the basic rewarding properties of choice at the neural level, other neuroscientific evidence points to the limitations of choice under certain conditions. For example, Hsu et al. (2005) found that uncertainty in making choices correlated positively with activation in both the orbitofrontal cortex and amygdala, and negatively with the striatal system, suggesting that uncertainty in making decisions mitigates the anticipated reward value and benefits of making choices. Finally, there is some neuroscientific evidence to suggest that choosing serves as an adaptive motivational buffer against aversive experiences. Murayama et al. (2015) found that participants who were forced to accept certain options for a game experienced decreased activation in the ventromedial prefrontal cortex following failure feedback compared to the activation experienced following success feedback. This is indicative of an aversive experience because the ventromedial prefrontal cortex is also part of the reward network. However, this decrease in activation in response to failure feedback was not observed among participants who had made choices about the game. In other words, neural evidence suggests that choosing buffers against the aversive experience of receiving negative feedback.

Similarly, the benefits of choosing for performance are evident at the neural level. Using electroencephalography (EEG),[1] Legault and Inzlicht

---

1 EEG is a test used to detect, evaluate, and record electrical activity in the brain. Psychological researchers often use EEG to observe and compare brain activities under certain stimuli or situations.

(2013) demonstrated that, compared to participants who were pressured to engage in a particular task, participants who had the illusion that they had chosen to engage in a target task (in this case, the Stroop task) performed better and had a greater magnitude of error-related negativity (ERN), presumably an error-detection system that is critical to task improvement (e.g., Hajcak & Foti, 2008; Holroyd & Coles, 2002; Luu et al., 2000). Directly relevant to observations of a self-choice effect in studies of memory and learning, neuroscientific evidence points to the role of the striatum in the reward network and in facilitating declarative memory by regulating activity in the memory-related brain structure, the hippocampus (e.g., Lisman & Grace, 2005). Along these lines, recent evidence suggests that the provision of choice predicted greater striatal activity and better subsequent remembering after a 24-hour delay (Murty et al., 2015).

In sum, neuroscientific evidence complements the findings of behavioral research from motivational and cognitive perspectives, suggesting that having the opportunity to choose is inherently motivating and supportive of performance at a neural level under many circumstances. While the neuroscientific evidence regarding the specific mechanisms through which choice influences educational outcomes is still emerging, it seems likely that choosing may yield effects on educational outcomes through a variety of neural and cognitive mechanisms.

Difficult Issues in Understanding the Effects of Choice Provision

The theory and evidence we have presented thus far on the role of choice in students' motivation, engagement, and learning might suggest that the concept of choice is relatively straightforward and that choice has unequivocal benefits for students' academic functioning. In fact, though choice has routinely been equated with closely related concepts such as autonomy (e.g., Ryan & Deci, 2006) and control (e.g., Skinner, 1996), the effects of choice are not ubiquitously positive across all people and circumstances (see Katz & Assor, 2007 for another discussion). In this section, we discuss some of the most significant challenges that have complicated scholars' understanding of the function and effects of choice, and how choice can be used as a motivational and instructional tool.

The Distinction between Choice and the Related Concepts of Autonomy, Control, and Self-Determination

The opportunity and act of choosing is clearly related to the concepts of autonomy, control, and self-determination. However, its connection with these concepts has not always been clear.

Much of the confusion centers on the relationship between choice and autonomy. The act of making a personal choice is sometimes conflated with the concept of autonomy, and the two have sometimes even been considered interchangeable (e.g., Bandura, 1989; Iyengar & Lepper, 1999; Markus & Kitayama, 1991). Part of this confusion comes from the fact that "autonomy" is an umbrella term that has been used for a wide variety of constructs, though most frequently it is conceptualized in two ways: as independence and as volitional functioning (e.g., Soenens et al., 2007). According to many developmental and social-cultural theories of psychology, autonomy is the extent to which an individual engages in behaviors and makes decisions without relying on others (e.g., Bandura, 1989; Markus & Kitayama, 1991; Smetana et al., 2004; Van Petegem et al., 2012). In contrast to this conceptualization of autonomy as independence, self-determination theory defines autonomy as self-endorsed or volitional functioning, as opposed to pressured or controlled functioning (Ryan & Deci, 2000). From this perspective, autonomy reflects a phenomenological experience of one's behavior being consistent with personally valued interests, preferences, and needs. While research has routinely supported the proposition that self-endorsed functioning is related to greater motivation, greater well-being, and a variety of educational outcomes among students across various cultures (e.g., Chen et al., 2015; León et al., 2015; Patall et al., 2013; Reeve et al., 2003; Vansteenkiste et al., 2010), research has failed to definitively determine whether autonomy defined as independent functioning yields benefits (e.g., Beyers et al., 2003).

When autonomy is defined as merely acting and deciding independently, it is readily conflated with choice. To further complicate matters, when scholars or laypeople refer to perceptions of having choice, they are typically referring to *the experience* of having the "ability to exercise *control* over ourselves and our environment" (Iyengar, 2010, p. 7). In other words, they are usually referring to something that goes beyond the straightforward perception that an individual has options or has made a selection among them. Rather, they are referring to *the experience* of having freedom and control over decision-making and behavior (e.g., Deci & Ryan, 1985; Reeve et al., 2003). When conceptualized in this way, choosing can easily be conflated with the concept of autonomy as volitional functioning and with other motivational concepts such as perceived control (e.g., Skinner, 1996).

The problem is that, although the act of making a choice implies (at least some) independent functioning (aligning with one narrow conceptualization of autonomy), having and making choices does not always translate into feeling volitional. Likewise, feeling autonomous and in control does not necessarily require having chosen. Thus, rather than being synonymous with autonomy or control, the provision of choice may be most prudently conceptualized as a characteristic of the environment and the act of choosing as an imperfect cognitive-behavioral antecedent to feeling autonomous, competent, and in control (e.g., Henry, 1994; Langer, 1975; Leotti et al., 2010; Perlmuter & Monty, 1979; Skinner, 1996; Tafarodi et al., 1999). Maintaining this distinction is important because scholars are confronted with confusing empirical results when the concepts of choice, autonomy, self-determination, and control are viewed as interchangeable (e.g., Iyengar & Lepper, 1999; Katz & Assor, 2007; Moller et al., 2006; Schwartz, 2000). The imperfect nature of people's perceptions of the world (e.g., Dawes, 1976; Kahneman et al., 1982; Nisbett & Ross, 1980) means that having and making choices does not guarantee that an individual will perceive the opportunity to choose or experience a sense of autonomy and control. Moreover, many factors can influence the extent to which having choices translates into *feeling* volitional, a topic we discuss next.

Factors That Alter the Effects of Choosing

The cumulative evidence on choice suggests that, on average, having choices and making choices have benefits for students' motivation and performance (e.g., Patall et al., 2008). However, the effects of choice are not ubiquitously positive. Some studies find that choice may have no effect or even a negative effect on certain outcomes (Assor et al., 2002; Flowerday & Schraw, 2003; Flowerday et al., 2004; Overskeid & Svartdal, 1996; Parker & Lepper, 1992; Reeve et al., 2003). Although choice has been routinely found to be linked to the experience of autonomy (volitional functioning), perceived competence, control, interest-based motivation, and performance, moderators of those effects have often been found. Moreover, the links between choice and motivation focused on the utility value and the perceived importance of tasks, as well as behavioral and cognitive engagement, seem to be particularly tentative (e.g., Assor et al., 2002; Patall et al., 2010, 2013; Wang & Eccles, 2013). We discuss several key factors that may influence the effects of choice. These include the existing levels of interest, motivation, and competence of the chooser and environmental conditions that influence that motivation and those perceptions of competence, as well as the cultural context and the nature of the relationships among individuals involved in the decision-making process.

The role of existing interest and motivation in defining choice effects. The relationship between choosing, interest, and motivation is complex. We previously described how choice is a motivational tool that can be used by teachers and parents to build feelings of autonomy, motivation, and interest that perhaps did not previously exist. However, we also know that the motivational orientation of the student doing the choosing influences whether students want to bother with making a choice and how successful choosing will be for further motivation promotion (e.g., Patall, 2013). By the same token, the motivational quality of tasks and the extent to which choices tap into students' existing interests and motivation similarly influence the benefits of choosing (e.g., Katz & Assor, 2007; Patall, 2013; Patall et al., 2008). Why is this the case?

First, it comes as little surprise that students vary in their interests and motivation across time, people, tasks, and domains (e.g., Gottfried et al., 2001;

Hidi & Renninger, 2006; Schiefele, 2009). What is most relevant here, however, is that this variation in interest and motivation influences the extent to which students prefer to choose and benefit from choosing. While some limited evidence and theory suggest that providing choices may buffer against the negative outcomes that poorly motivated students display and that providing choices may therefore be particularly beneficial for those individuals who lack personal interest for the task at hand (Flowerday & Schraw, 2000; Schraw et al., 2001; Tsai et al., 2008), there is stronger evidence to suggest that optimally motivated students – those who have an existing interest in or value for the activity they are presented choices about – actually benefit most from having the opportunity to make choices (e.g., Mouratidis et al., 2011; Patall, 2013). For example, in one study (Patall, 2013), undergraduate students reported a greater preference for choosing aspects of a task in responses to scenarios that described a task that was more, compared to less, personally interesting. Moreover, Patall (2013) revealed, in a second study, that choosing aspects of a trivia game enhanced post-task interest for the game only for individuals high in initial individual interest for trivia games in general. Similarly, Mouratidis et al. (2011) found that elementary-age Greek physical education students with higher, compared to lower, relative autonomous motivation (i.e., motivation based to a great extent on interest, enjoyment, and value for course tasks) benefited significantly more from a need-supportive class in which teachers provided opportunities for making choices and working with other students. In other words, students must care about the domain or activity in the first place for choices to seem meaningful and worth the effort, and in order to maximize their desirable effects.

Second, the effects of choice have been found to vary based on the extent to which choices are designed to support a sense of freedom by allowing individuals to express the self and to act in accordance with their personal preferences and interests (e.g., Katz & Assor, 2007; Reeve et al., 2003). By the same token, when choices are administered in a controlling manner that leads an individual to make a particular choice, and there is therefore little opportunity to act in according with existing preferences and interests, choosing has little (if not a negative) effect on motivation and performance. In other words, choosing can be motivationally supportive because it provides an opportunity to express preferences and to act based on interests. However, when it does not successfully tap into students' existing interests or includes restrictions on self-expression, choosing is experienced as irrelevant, inconsequential, or controlling and is likely to backfire. This is because tasks being consistent with the students' interests and values so that behavior is self-endorsed is most critical to eliciting adaptive motivation and performance (e.g., Flowerday & Shell, 2015; Katz & Assor, 2007). Choice can be one means to accomplishing this end, especially when students' interests and preferences are explicitly considered in the design of choice opportunities and choices are not restricted in any way.

Finally, the role of interest and motivation comes into play when thinking about the nature of tasks themselves and the extent to which the tasks the individual is asked to make choices about are perceived to be interesting or boring (e.g., Patall, 2013; Tafarodi et al., 1999). Somewhat in contradiction to the interactions observed between choice and an individual's interest or motivation, research suggests that choosing is particularly powerful for tasks that are perceived as boring. There is more opportunity to improve the nature of the task by incorporating personal preferences and interests in the context of a motivationally deprived task. In line with this, many demonstrations of improved motivation and performance due to choice have involved neutral or lackluster activities, such as solving anagram puzzles and paired-associate word learning (e.g., Iyengar & Lepper, 1999; Monty et al., 1973; Perlmuter & Monty, 1973) or homework in a classroom context (Patall et al., 2010). In an explicit test of this, Patall (2013) found that choosing enhanced undergraduate students' interest, perceived competence, and value for a reading comprehension task when the reading passage was normatively boring but not when the passage was interesting. Further, Patall (2013) also provided some evidence to suggest that the context in which choice may yield the greatest benefits is one in which the individual has some initial motivation for the task *and* the task itself is boring and could be improved with personal choice. However, additional research is needed to better understand the interplay among these various factors.

Feelings of competence and conditions that support competence. Similarly, choosing exerts motivational and performance benefits through students' feelings of competence and control (e.g., Langer, 1975; Patall et al., 2008; Perlmuter & Monty, 1979; Ryan & Deci, 2000). However, feeling competent also appears to be a prerequisite if the benefits of choice are to be maximized. When choosing involves many options, options that are difficult to compare, or suboptimal strategies for making a decision, people eschew choice, and satisfaction with their choices is likely to be undermined (e.g., Katz & Assor, 2007; Iyengar & Lepper, 2000; Patall et al., 2014; Sethi-Iyengar et al., 2004). Decision-making research suggests that more efficacious individuals desire more options when making a choice, are more likely to look for pre-choice information that would help them make a decision, and benefit from having more options in terms of post-decision satisfaction and performance; the opposite is true of less efficacious individuals (e.g., Reed et al., 2012; Scheibehenne et al., 2010).

More directly relevant, competence seems to be a critical consideration when determining the effect of choosing on students' motivation and engagement. For example, Wang and Eccles (2013) found that student perceptions of being provided with choices at school during academic tasks positively predicted engagement for high achievers but negatively predicted engagement for low achievers. In a series of three studies of college students, Patall et al. (2014) found that the provision of choice enhanced perceived competence, intrinsic motivation, willingness to engage in the game again, and task per-formance when initial perceptions of competence were high; however, motivation diminished with choice when perceived competence was low. This pattern held whether initial perceived competence was simply measured, manipulated by altering the difficulty of the task, or manipulated with competence feedback. This pattern of findings seems to indicate that making choices can only be experienced as empowering – providing the individual with the sense that their behavior during the task was truly self-endorsed and that the task provided an opportunity to maximize skill development – when students feel equipped to make choices. When perceptions of competence are low, rather than being empowering, making task choices may be primarily experienced as overwhelming. Individuals who believe they have limited competence on a task likely feel ill-equipped to choose successfully and may therefore prefer to either have no opportunities for choice or to have another (ideally, more expert) person make decisions for them. Along these lines, research has begun to reveal the synergistic benefits of providing structure in the environment to support competence in combination with autonomy supports such as providing choice (e.g., Jang et al., 2010; Sierens et al., 2009; Vansteenkiste et al., 2012). For example, Vansteenkiste et al. (2012) found that high school students who experienced teaching marked by both high autonomy support (broadly defined and including choice provision) and clear expectations (support for competence) exhibited better academic motivation and self-regulated learning than students who experienced other teaching configurations of autonomy support and expectations.

Along similar lines, choice has the potential to backfire when students choose options that are not ideal for facilitating learning. For example, students may choose to study content that has already been learned well instead of focusing on more difficult material (e.g., Thiede et al., 2003) or may naively choose study strategies that are suboptimal compared to alternative strategies (e.g., Bjork et al., 2013). Therefore, either having the prerequisite expertise to choose well or having environmental scaffolds built into choices can be important for students. In a demonstration of this point, Thiede et al. (2003) showed that when more accurate judgments of text comprehension were induced, people studied more strategically (choosing to focus on texts for which they had performed poorly) and ultimately experienced better performance. In the absence of accurate judgments of comprehension, people's choices of what to study were random. This has particular implication for young students who may lack the relevant expertise or cognitive sophistication to make choices to facilitate learning (e.g., Son, 2005).

Overall, though choosing may support motivation, learning, and performance in situations in which an adolescent already feels competent about the task and is able to make a good decision, when those conditions are not met, choosing runs the risk of depleting motivation and hindering performance.

Cross-cultural and interpersonal context. As part of a broader controversy over the cultural significance of autonomy, cultural psychologists have argued that there are fewer benefits of choice provision and choosing among Eastern cultures, because autonomy and independence are Western-specific values that conflict with Easterners' interdependent sensibility (e.g., Iyengar & DeVoe, 2003; Markus & Kitayama, 1991). According to this theory, members of more interdependent Eastern cultures strive for in-group harmony and internalize the values of trusted others with whom they have close relationships (e.g., Markus & Kitayama, 1991). Consequently, being presented with choices made on their behalf by such persons would readily lead to a feeling that they can behave competently and in accordance with their personal values (i.e., their interdependent orientation). In contrast, exercising personal choice in a group context would be viewed as incongruent with group goals and less intrinsically motivating.

In the most widely cited example of this proposition (Iyengar & Lepper, 1999), one study showed that, although all children benefited from making personal choices relative to an experimenter assigning a task, motivation was most enhanced among Asian American children when their mothers made choices for them. This same condition undermined intrinsic motivation for European American children. In another example, Bao and Lam (2008) found, in a series of studies, that Chinese students' motivation and performance on academic tasks was enhanced when mothers or teachers made choices for them, but only if they felt close to their mother or teacher. When they did not feel close, making a personal choice enhanced their motivation and performance most strongly.

Building on the findings of Bao and Lam (2008), it is important to note that the broader interpersonal climate is an influential factor in determining the effect of choice regardless of culture. First, there are many conditions under which even Western students fully endorse the decisions of trusted others and may prefer to defer decisions to trusted parents or teachers (e.g., Van Petegem et al., 2012). Likewise, when the context (regardless of culture) prescribes a cooperative group orientation, personal choice may have less value. Hagger et al., (2014) found that after inducing an individualistic group norm, British undergraduate students in the personal choice condition exhibited greater intrinsic motivation than students who had aspects of the task selected for them. However, when the group norm prescribed collectivism, students assigned to the task by an in-group member were more intrinsically motivated than participants who made personal choices or had choices prescribed to them by an out-group member.

Moreover, choosing may assume different meanings depending on the interpersonal context. Consistent with this idea, developmental scholars have long noted that the benefits of adolescents' independent decision-making may depend on supportive relationships with parents (e.g., Grotevant & Cooper, 1986; Hill & Holmbeck, 1986). In line with this supposition, Roth et al. (2015)

found, in one study, that mothers' choice provision was more strongly related to adolescents' autonomous motivation when adolescents felt that their mothers provided high unconditional positive regard. Going further, supportive social relationships may attenuate the desire for choice by fostering internalization of others' values (e.g., Ryan & Deci, 2000). In one series of studies, Ybarra et al. (2012) found that American undergraduate students who were primed to think about supportive relationships (and the calm and security associated with such relationships) were less willing to pay to have a greater number of consumer product options to choose among than people who either were primed to think about unsupportive relationships or did not think about any relationship.

Taken together, the existing evidence suggests that the broader cultural and interpersonal context can change both the meaning and effects of choosing. When the cultural context emphasizes a group orientation or the students feel supported by trusted others, personal choice may play a less important role in supporting motivation and performance. By the same token, students may feel most empowered by the choice opportunities that others provide in the context of trusting, supportive relationships.

Implications for Educational Practice and Future Research

Choice holds a great deal of promise as an educational intervention. Choice has motivational implications for students' feelings of autonomy, competence, control, and intrinsic motivation. Choice has cognitive implications for students' memory and learning. Choice also has implications for the broader social environment of the classroom, predicting student perceptions of the social-emotional climate of the classroom or even academic dishonesty.

However, a review of the research on choice reveals that the effects of choosing are not always straightforward. Consequently, when implementing choice as a strategy to support educational outcomes, the following considerations become important.

- Is choice appropriate to the task?
  (Students may be more likely to benefit from choice when tasks are boring and the students need a motivational boost.)
- Are students prepared to choose?
  (Students are more likely to benefit from choosing if they care about the domain in the first place, and feel competent about the task and in making decisions about the task.)
- Do the classroom context and the choices provided support students' psychological needs?
  (Choices that allow students to express their interests, values, and preferences will be more successful. Likewise, contexts that scaffold students'

development of expertise and decision-making when existing competence is lacking will lead to the greatest benefits for students.)

- Does the social and cultural context emphasize a group orientation or facilitate trusting, supportive relationships?
  (Facilitating close, caring relationships is likely to benefit motivation, regardless of whether students make personal choices or would rather relinquish choice to others likely to be better decision-makers. However, educators should be cautious about providing choices in the context of an environment that emphasizes an interdependent orientation.)

Despite everything we know about choosing and its links with educational outcomes, there is still much research to be done to fully understand the benefits and detriments of choosing. A particularly important direction for future research involves the need to better understand developmental differences and the interplay among choices and other environmental supports for motivation (e.g., other autonomy supports, classroom structure, or positive student–teacher relationships) and learning (e.g., retrieval practice, desirable difficulty, or distributed practice). The effectiveness of interventions that involve providing choices to promote students' social and academic functioning depends on a clear understanding of how various strategies interact and influence the effects of each other. In line with this same goal of translating choice to the classroom, there is also a need to better understand the role of various individual differences that have rarely been the focus of study. These include understanding the role of level of risk for academic failure in explaining how students vary in their reactions to choice in educational contexts. Understanding how choice will affect the outcomes of various populations that exist within educational settings is critical for creating solid practical guidelines related to choice provision.

Finally, like all research, the research on choice provision is not perfect. In particular, choice research in field settings (e.g., the classroom or the home) has relied heavily on child and adolescent perceptions of the environment. There is a great need for observational data to extend our knowledge about choice provision in the field. A major task of future research will be to expand and synthesize across more diverse and rigorous research methods to explore questions of choice provision in field settings.

Concluding Thoughts

This chapter provided a brief review of the theoretical perspectives and research related to the effects of choice on students' educational outcomes. Overall, it highlighted that providing choices and choosing should have a prominent place in an arsenal of motivational and instructional tools. However, even though choice is to be valued for its inherently motivating and cognitively enriching qualities, there are limits to the benefits of choosing. The possibilities as well as the limits of choice both need to be understood, so that the provision of choice enables desirable educational outcomes.

References

Amabile, T. M. & Gitomer, J. (1984). Children's artistic creativity: Effects of choice in task materials. *Personality and Social Psychology Bulletin, 10*, 209–15. doi: 10.1177/0146167284102006.

Ames, C. (1992). Classrooms: Goals, structures, and student motivation. *Journal of Educational Psychology, 84*, 261–71. doi: 10.1037/0022-0663.84.3.261.

Aoki, R., Matsumoto, M., Yomogida, Y., Izuma, K., Murayama, K., Sugiura, A., ... Matsumoto, K. (2014). Social equality in the number of choice options is represented in the ventromedial prefrontal cortex. *Journal of Neuroscience, 34*, 6413–21.

Assor, A., Kaplan, H., & Roth, G. (2002). Choice is good, but relevance is excellent: Autonomy-enhancing and suppressing teacher behaviours predicting students' engagement in schoolwork. *British Journal of Educational Psychology, 72*, 261–78. doi: 10.1348/000709902158883.

Bandura, A. (1989). Human agency in social cognitive theory. *American Psychologist, 44*, 1175–1184. doi: 10.1037/0003-066X.44.9.1175.

Bao, X. & Lam, S. (2008). Who makes the choice? Rethinking the role of autonomy and relatedness in Chinese children's motivation. *Child Development, 79*, 269–83. doi: 10.1111/j.1467-8624.2007.01125.x.

Baumeister, R. F. & Leary, M. R. (1995). The need to belong: Desire for interpersonal attachments as a fundamental human motivation. *Psychological Bulletin, 117*, 497–529. doi: 10.1037/0033-2909.117.3.497.

Beyers, W., Goossens, L., Vansant, I., & Moors, E. (2003). A structural model of autonomy in middle and late adolescence: Connectedness, separation, detachment, and agency. *Journal of Youth and Adolescence, 32*, 351–65. doi: 10.1023/A:1024922031510.

Bjork, R. A., Dunlosky, J., & Kornell, N. (2013). Self-regulated learning: Beliefs, techniques, and illusions. *Annual Review of Psychology, 64*, 417–44.

Brown-Wright, L., Tyler, K. M., Graves, S. L., Thomas, D., Stevens-Watkins, D., & Mulder, S. (2013). Examining the associations among home–school dissonance, amotivation, and classroom disruptive behavior for urban high school students. *Education and Urban Society, 45*, 142–62. doi: 10.1177/0013124511408715.

Cepeda, N. J., Pashler, H., Vul, E., Wixted, J. T., & Rohrer, D. (2006). Distributed practice in verbal recall tasks: A review and quantitative synthesis. *Psychological Bulletin, 132*, 354–80. doi: 10.1037/0033-2909.132.3.354.

Chen, B., Vansteenkiste, M., Beyers, W., Boone, L., Deci, E. L., Van der Kaap-Deeder, J., ... Verstuyf, J. (2015). Basic psychological need satisfaction, need frustration, and need strength across four cultures. *Motivation and Emotion, 39*, 216–36. doi: 10.1007/s11031-014-9450-1.

Cloutier, J. & Macrae, N. (2008). The feeling of choosing: Self-involvement and the cognitive status of things past. *Consciousness and Cognition, 17*, 125–35. doi: 10.1016/j.concog.2007.05.010.

Cordova, D. I. & Lepper, M. R. (1996). Intrinsic motivation and the process of learning: Beneficial effects of contextualization, personalization, and choice. *Journal of Educational Psychology, 88*, 715–30. doi: 10.1037/0022-0663.88.4.715.

Cunningham, S. J., Brady-Van den Bos, M., & Turk, D. J. (2011). Exploring the effects of ownership and choice on self-memory biases. *Memory, 19*, 449–61. doi: 10.1080/09658211.2011.584388.

Dawes, R. M. (1976). Shallow psychology. In J. S. Carroll & J. W. Payne (Eds.), *Cognition and social behavior* (pp. xiii, 290). Oxford: Lawrence Erlbaum.

deCharms, R. (1968). *Personal causation.* New York, NY: Academic Press.

Deci, E. L. & Ryan, R. M. (1985). The general causality orientations scale: Self-determination in personality. *Journal of Research in Personality, 19*, 109–34. doi: 10.1016/0092-6566(85)90023-6.

Deci, E. L. & Ryan, R. M. (2014). Autonomy and need satisfaction in close relationships: Relationships motivation theory. In N. Weinstein (Ed.), *Human motivation and interpersonal relationships* (pp. 53–73). Dordrecht: Springer Netherlands. doi: 10.1007/ 978-94-017-8542-6_3.

Eccles, J. S., Midgley, C., Wigfield, A., Buchanan, C. M., Reuman, D., Flanagan, C., & MacIver, D. (1993). Development during adolescence: The impact of stage-environment fit on young adolescents' experiences in schools and in families. *American Psychologist, 48*, 90–101. doi: 10.1037/0003-066X.48.2.90.

Flowerday, T. & Schraw, G. (2000). Teacher beliefs about instructional choice: A phenomenological study. *Journal of Educational Psychology, 92*, 634–45. doi: 10.1037/0022-0663.92.4.634.

Flowerday, T. & Schraw, G. (2003). Effect of choice on cognitive and affective engagement. *The Journal of Educational Research, 96*, 207–15. doi: 10.1080/00220670309598810.

Flowerday, T., Schraw, G., & Stevens, J. (2004). The role of choice and interest in reader engagement. *The Journal of Experimental Education, 72*, 93–114. doi: 10.3200/JEXE.72.2.93-114.

Flowerday, T. & Shell, D. F. (2015). Disentangling the effects of interest and choice on learning, engagement, and attitude. *Learning and Individual Differences, 40*, 134–40. doi: 10.1016/j.lindif.2015.05.003.

Fujiwara, J., Usui, N., Park, S. Q., Williams, T., Iijima, K., Taira, M., ... Tobler, P. N. (2013). Value of freedom to choose encoded by the human brain. *Journal of Neurophysiology, 110*(8), 1915–29. doi: 10.1152/jn.01057.2012.

Gottfried, A. E., Fleming, J. S., & Gottfried, A. W. (2001). Continuity of academic intrinsic motivation from childhood through late adolescence: A longitudinal study. *Journal of Educational Psychology, 93*, 3–13. doi: 10.1037/0022-0663.93.1.3.

Grotevant, H. D. & Cooper, C. R. (1986). Individuation in family relationships. *Human Development, 29*, 82–100. doi: 10.1159/000273025.

Hagger, M. S., Rentzelas, P., & Chatzisarantis, N. L. D. (2014). Effects of individualist and collectivist group norms and choice on intrinsic motivation. *Motivation and Emotion, 38*, 215–23. doi: 10.1007/s11031-013-9373-2.

Hajcak, G. & Foti, D. (2008). Errors are aversive: Defensive motivation and the error-related negativity. *Psychological Science, 19*, 103–8. doi: 10.1111/ j.1467-9280.2008.02053.x.

Henry, R. A. (1994). The effects of choice and incentives on the overestimation of future performance. *Organizational Behavior and Human Decision Processes, 57*, 210–25. doi: 10.1006/obhd.1994.1012.

Henry, R. A. & Sniezek, J. A. (1993). Situational factors affecting judgments of future performance. *Organizational Behavior and Human Decision Processes, 54*, 104–32. doi: 10.1006/obhd.1993.1005.

Hidi, S. (2015). Revisiting the role of rewards in motivation and learning: Implications of neuroscientific research. *Educational Psychology Review, 28*(1), 61–93. doi: 10.1007/s10648-015-9307-5.

Hidi, S. & Renninger, K. A. (2006). The four-phase model of interest development. *Educational Psychologist, 41*, 111–27. doi: 10.1207/s15326985ep4102_4.

Hidi, S., Renninger, K. A., & Northoff, G. (2017). The development of interest and self-related processing. In F. Guay, H. W. Marsh, D. M. McInerney, & R. G. Craven (Eds.), *International advances in self research, Vol. 6: SELF – Driving positive psychology and well-being* (pp. 51–70). Charlotte, NC: Information Age Press.

Hill, J. P. & Holmbeck, G. N. (1986). Attachment and autonomy during adolescence. *Annals of Child Development, 3*, 145–89.

Hirano, T. & Ukita, J. (2003). Choosing words at the study phase: The self-choice effect on memory from the viewpoint of connective processing. *Japanese Psychological Research, 45*, 38–49.

Holroyd, C. B. & Coles, M. G. H. (2002). The neural basis of human error processing: Reinforcement learning, dopamine, and the error-related negativity. *Psychological Review, 109*, 679–709. doi: 10.1037/0033-295X.109.4.679.

Hsu, M., Bhatt, M., Adolphs, R., Tranel, D., & Camerer, C. F. (2005). Neural systems responding to degrees of uncertainty in human decision making. *Science, 310*, 1680–3.

Humphreys, G. W. & Sui, J. (2015). The salient self: Social saliency effects based on self-bias. *Journal of Cognitive Psychology, 27*, 129–40. doi: 10.1080/ 20445911.2014.996156.

Iyengar, S. (2010). *The art of choosing*. New York: Grand Central Publishing.

Iyengar, S. S. & DeVoe, S. E. (2003). Rethinking the value of choice: Considering cultural mediators of intrinsic motivation. In V. Murphy-Berman & J. J. Berman (Eds.), *Nebraska symposium on motivation. Cross-cultural differences in perspectives on the self* (Vol. 49, pp. 129–74). Lincoln: University of Nebraska Press.

Iyengar, S. S. & Lepper, M. R. (1999). Rethinking the value of choice: a cultural perspective on intrinsic motivation. *Journal of Personality and Social Psychology, 76*, 349.

Iyengar, S. S. & Lepper, M. R. (2000). When choice is demotivating: Can one desire too much of a good thing? *Journal of Personality and Social Psychology, 79*(6), 995–1006. doi: 10.1037/0022-3514.79.6.995.

Jacobs, J. E. & Eccles, J. S. (2000). Parents, task values, and real-life achievement-related choices. In C. Sansone & J. Harackiewicz (Eds.), *Intrinsic and Extrinsic Motivation: The Search for Optimal Motivation and Performance* (pp. 405–39). San Diego, CA: Academic Press.

Jang, H., Reeve, J., & Deci, E. L. (2010). Engaging students in learning activities: It is not autonomy support or structure but autonomy support and structure. *Journal of Educational Psychology, 102*, 588–600. doi: 10.1037/a0019682.

Kahneman, D., Slovic, P., & Tversky, A. (1982). *Judgment under uncertainty: Heuristics and Biases*. Cambridge, UK: Cambridge University Press.

Katz, I. & Assor, A. (2007). When choice motivates and when it does not. *Educational Psychology Review, 19*, 429. doi: 10.1007/s10648-006-9027-y.

Klein, S. B. & Loftus, J. (1988). The nature of self-referent encoding: The contributions of elaborative and organizational processes. *Journal of Personality and Social Psychology, 55*, 5–11. doi: 10.1037/0022-3514.55.1.5.

Kornell, N. & Metcalfe, J. (2006). Study efficacy and the region of proximal learning framework. *Journal of Experimental Psychology: Learning, Memory, and Cognition, 32*, 609–22. doi: 10.1037/0278-7393.32.3.609.

Langer, E. J. (1975). The illusion of control. *Journal of Personality and Social Psychology, 32*, 311.

Legault, L. & Inzlicht, M. (2013). Self-determination, self-regulation, and the brain: Autonomy improves performance by enhancing neuroaffective responsiveness to self-regulation failure. *Journal of Personality and Social Psychology, 105*(1), 123–38.

León, J., Núñez, J. L., & Liew, J. (2015). Self-determination and STEM education: Effects of autonomy, motivation, and self-regulated learning on high school math achievement. *Learning and Individual Differences, 43*, 156–63. doi: 10.1016/j.lindif.2015.08.017.

Leotti, L. A. & Delgado, M. R. (2011). The inherent reward of choice. *Psychological Science, 22*, 1310–18. doi: 10.1177/0956797611417005.

Leotti, L. A. & Delgado, M. R. (2014). The value of exercising control over monetary gains and losses. *Psychological Science, 25*, 596–604. doi: 10.1177/0956797613514589.

Leotti, L. A., Iyengar, S. S., & Ochsner, K. N. (2010). Born to choose: The origins and value of the need for control. *Trends in Cognitive Sciences, 14*, 457–63. doi: 10.1016/j.tics.2010.08.001.

Lepper, M. R., Corpus, J. H., & Iyengar, S. S. (2005). Intrinsic and extrinsic motivational orientations in the classroom: Age differences and academic correlates. *Journal of Educational Psychology, 97*, 184–96. doi: 10.1037/0022-0663.97.2.184.

Leroy, N. & Bressoux, P. (2016). Does amotivation matter more than motivation in predicting mathematics learning gains? A longitudinal study of sixth-grade students in France. *Contemporary Educational Psychology, 44–45*, 41–53. doi: 10.1016/j.cedpsych.2016.02.001.

Lewin, K. (1952). Selected theoretical papers. In *Field Theory in Social Science*. London: Social Science Paperbacks.

Linnenbrink-Garcia, L., Patall, E. A., & Messersmith, E. E. (2013). Antecedents and consequences of situational interest. *British Journal of Educational Psychology, 83*, 591–614. doi: 10.1111/j.2044-8279.2012.02080.x.

Lisman, J. E., & Grace, A. A. (2005). The hippocampal-VTA loop: Controlling the entry of information into long-term memory. *Neuron, 46*(5), 703–13. doi: 10.1016/j.neuron.2005.05.002.

Luu, P., Collins, P., & Tucker, D. M. (2000). Mood, personality, and self-monitoring: Negative affect and emotionality in relation to frontal lobe mechanisms of error monitoring. *Journal of Experimental Psychology: General, 129*, 43–60. doi: 10.1037/0096-3445.129.1.43.

Markus, H. R. & Kitayama, S. (1991). Culture and the self: Implications for cognition, emotion, and motivation. *Psychological Review, 98*, 224–53. doi: 10.1037/0033-295X.98.2.224.

Metcalfe, J. (2009). Metacognitive judgments and control of study. *Current Directions in Psychological Science, 18*, 159–63. doi: 10.1111/j.1467-8721.2009.01628.x.

Midgley, C. & Feldlaufer, H. (1987). Students' and teachers' decision-making fit before and after the transition to junior high school. *The Journal of Early Adolescence, 7*, 225–41. doi: 10.1177/0272431687072009.

Moller, A. C., Deci, E. L., & Ryan, R. M. (2006). Choice and ego-depletion: The moderating role of autonomy. *Personality and Social Psychology Bulletin, 32,* 1024–36. doi: 10.1177/0146167206288008.

Monty, R. A., Rosenberger, M. A., & Perlmuter, L. C. (1973). Amount of locus of choice as sources of motivation in paired-associate learning. *Journal of Experimental Psychology, 97,* 16.

Mouratidis, A. A., Vansteenkiste, M., Sideridis, G., & Lens, W. (2011). Vitality and interest–enjoyment as a function of class-to-class variation in need-supportive teaching and pupils' autonomous motivation. *Journal of Educational Psychology, 103,* 353–66. doi: 10.1037/a0022773.

Murayama, K., Izuma, K., Aoki, R., & Matsumoto, K. (2016). "Your choice" motivates you in the brain: The emergence of autonomy neuroscience. In S.-I. Kim, J. Reeve, & M. Bong (Eds.), *Recent developments in neuroscience research on human motivation* (Advances in Motivation and Achievement, Vol. 19, pp. 95–125). Bingley, UK: Emerald Group Publishing. doi: 10.1108/S0749-742320160000019004.

Murayama, K., Matsumoto, M., Izuma, K., Sugiura, A., Ryan, R. M., Deci, E. L., & Matsumoto, K. (2015). How self-determined choice facilitates performance: A key role of the ventromedial prefrontal cortex. *Cerebral Cortex, 25*(5), 1241–51. doi: 10.1093/cercor/bht317.

Murayama, K., Pekrun, R., Lichtenfeld, S., & vom Hofe, R. (2013). Predicting long-term growth in students' mathematics achievement: The unique contributions of motivation and cognitive strategies. *Child Development, 84,* 1475–90. doi: 10.1111/cdev.12036.

Murty, V. P., DuBrow, S., & Davachi, L. (2015). The simple act of choosing influences declarative memory. *Journal of Neuroscience, 35,* 6255–64. doi: 10.1523/JNEUROSCI.4181-14.2015.

Nelson, N. & Vohs, K. (2008). Making choices depletes the self's resources and impairs subsequent self-regulation. *NA-Advances in Consumer Research, 35,* 905–6.

Nisbett, R. E. & Ross, L. (1980). *Human inference: Strategies and shortcomings of social judgment.* New York: Prentice-Hall.

Overskeid, G. & Svartdal, F. (1996). Effect of reward on subjective autonomy and interest when initial interest is low. *The Psychological Record, 46,* 319–32.

Parker, L. E. & Lepper, M. R. (1992). Effects of fantasy contexts on children's learning and motivation: Making learning more fun. *Journal of Personality and Social Psychology, 62,* 625–33. doi: 10.1037/0022-3514.62.4.625.

Patall, E. A. (2013). Constructing motivation through choice, interest, and interestingness. *Journal of Educational Psychology, 105,* 522–34. doi: 10.1037/a0030307.

Patall, E. A., Cooper, H., & Robinson, J. C. (2008). The effects of choice on intrinsic motivation and related outcomes: A meta-analysis of research findings. *Psychological Bulletin, 134,* 270–300. doi: 10.1037/0033-2909.134.2.270.

Patall, E. A., Cooper, H., & Wynn, S. R. (2010). The effectiveness and relative importance of choice in the classroom. *Journal of Educational Psychology, 102,* 896–915. doi: 10.1037/a0019545.

Patall, E. A., Dent, A. L., Oyer, M., & Wynn, S. R. (2013). Student autonomy and course value: The unique and cumulative roles of various teacher practices. *Motivation and Emotion, 37,* 14–32. doi: 10.1007/s11031-012-9305-6.

Patall, E. A. & Leach, J. K. (2015). The role of choice provision in academic dishonesty. *Contemporary Educational Psychology, 42*, 97–110. doi: 10.1016/j.cedpsych.2015.06.004.

Patall, E. A., Sylvester, B. J., & Han, C. (2014). The role of competence in the effects of choice on motivation. *Journal of Experimental Social Psychology, 50*, 27–44. doi: 10.1016/j.jesp.2013.09.002.

Perlmuter, L. C. & Monty, R. A. (1973). Effect of choice of stimulus on paired-associate learning. *Journal of Experimental Psychology, 99*, 120–3. doi: 10.1037/h0034749.

Perlmuter, L. & Monty, R. A. (Eds.). (1979). *Choice and perceived control*. Hillsdale, NJ: Lawrence Erlbaum Associates.

Perlmuter, L., Monty, R. A., & Kimble, G. A. (1971). Effect of choice on paired-associate learning. *Journal of Experimental Psychology, 91*, 47–53. doi: 10.1037/h0031828.

Reed, A. E., Mikels, J. A., & Löckenhoff, C. E. (2012). Choosing with confidence: Self-efficacy and preferences for choice. *Judgment and Decision Making, 7*, 173–80.

Reeve, J., Nix, G., & Hamm, D. (2003). Testing models of the experience of self-determination in intrinsic motivation and the conundrum of choice. *Journal of Educational Psychology, 95*, 375–92. doi: 10.1037/0022-0663.95.2.375.

Rogers, T., Kuiper, N., & Kirker, W. (1977). Self-reference and the encoding of personal information. *Journal of Personality and Social Psychology, 35*, 677–88. doi: 10.1037/0022-3514.35.9.677.

Roth, G., Kanat-Maymon, Y., & Assor, A. (2015). The role of unconditional parental regard in autonomy-supportive parenting. *Journal of Personality, 84*, 716–25. doi: 10.1111/jopy.12194.

Ruedy, N. E., Moore, C., Gino, F., & Schweitzer, M. E. (2013). The cheater's high: The unexpected affective benefits of unethical behavior. *Journal of Personality and Social Psychology, 105*, 531–48. doi: 10.1037/a0034231.

Ryan, R. M. & Deci, E. L. (2000). Self-determination theory and the facilitation of intrinsic motivation, social development, and well-being. *American Psychologist, 55*, 68.

Ryan, R. M. & Deci, E. L. (2006). Self-regulation and the problem of human autonomy: Does psychology need choice, self-determination, and will? *Journal of Personality, 74*, 1557–86. doi: 10.1111/j.1467-6494.2006.00420.x.

Scheibehenne, B., Greifeneder, R., & Todd, P. M. (2010). Can there ever be too many options? A meta-analytic review of choice overload. *Journal of Consumer Research, 37*, 409–25. doi: 10.1086/651235.

Schiefele, U. (2009). Situational and individual interest. In K. R. Wentzel & A. Wigfield (Eds.), *Handbook of Motivation at School* (pp. 197–222). New York, NY: Routledge.

Schraw, G., Flowerday, T., & Lehman, S. (2001). Increasing situational interest in the classroom. *Educational Psychology Review, 13*, 211–24. doi: 10.1023/A:1016619705184.

Schwartz, B. (2000). Self-determination: The tyranny of freedom. *American Psychologist, 55*, 79–88. doi: 10.1037//0003-066X.55.1.79.

Sethi-Iyengar, S., Huberman, G., & Jiang, W. (2004). How much choice is too much? Contributions to 401(k) retirement plans. *Pension Design and Structure: New Lessons from Behavioral Finance, 83*, 84–7.

Shen, B., Wingert, R. K., Li, W., Sun, H., & Rukavina, P. B. (2010). An amotivation model in physical education. *Journal of Teaching in Physical Education, 29,* 72–84. doi: 10.1123/jtpe.29.1.72.

Sierens, E., Vansteenkiste, M., Goossens, L., Soenens, B., & Dochy, F. (2009). The synergistic relationship of perceived autonomy support and structure in the prediction of self-regulated learning. *British Journal of Educational Psychology, 79,* 57–68. doi: 10.1348/000709908X304398.

Skinner, E. A. (1996). A guide to constructs of control. *Journal of Personality and Social Psychology, 71,* 549–70. doi: 10.1037/0022-3514.71.3.549.

Smetana, J. G., Campione-Barr, N., & Daddis, C. (2004). Longitudinal development of family decision making: Defining healthy behavioral autonomy for middle-class African American adolescents. *Child Development, 75,* 1418–34. doi: 10.1111/j.1467-8624.2004.00749.x.

Soenens, B., Vansteenkiste, M., Lens, W., Luyckx, K., Goossens, L., Beyers, W., & Ryan, R. M. (2007). Conceptualizing parental autonomy support: Adolescent perceptions of promotion of independence versus promotion of volitional functioning. *Developmental Psychology, 43,* 633–46.

Son, L. K. (2005). Metacognitive control: Children's short-term versus long-term study strategies. *The Journal of General Psychology, 132,* 347–64. doi: 10.3200/GENP.132.4.347-364.

Son, L. K. (2010). Metacognitive control and the spacing effect. *Journal of Experimental Psychology: Learning, Memory, and Cognition, 36,* 255–62. doi: 10.1037/a0017892.

Symons, C. S. & Johnson, B. T. (1997). The self-reference effect in memory: A meta-analysis. *Psychological Bulletin, 121,* 371.

Tafarodi, R. W., Milne, A. B., & Smith, A. J. (1999). The confidence of choice: Evidence for an augmentation effect on self-perceived performance. *Personality and Social Psychology Bulletin, 25,* 1405–16. doi: 10.1177/0146167299259006.

Takahashi, M. (1991). The role of choice in memory as a function of age: Support for a metamemory interpretation of the self-choice effect. *Psychologia: An International Journal of Psychology in the Orient, 34,* 254–8.

Takahashi, M. (1992). Memorial consequences of choosing nonwords: Implication for interpretations of the self-choice effect. *Japanese Psychological Research, 34,* 35–8.

Takahashi, M. (1997). *The encoding process in human memory.* Kyoto: Kitaohji-Shobo.

Takahashi, M. & Umemoto, T. (1987). The study of selective memory in children: An interaction of academic successfulness and free choice. *Human Developmental Research, 3,* 167–76.

Thiede, K. W., Anderson, M. C., & Therriault, D. (2003). Accuracy of metacognitive monitoring affects learning of texts. *Journal of Educational Psychology, 95,* 66–73. doi: 10.1037/0022-0663.95.1.66.

Toyota, H. (2015). The role of word choice and criterion on intentional memory. *Perceptual and Motor Skills, 120*(1), 84–94. doi: 10.2466/22.PMS.120v12x2.

Tsai, Y.-M., Kunter, M., Lüdtke, O., Trautwein, U., & Ryan, R. M. (2008). What makes lessons interesting? The role of situational and individual factors in three school subjects. *Journal of Educational Psychology, 100,* 460–72. doi: 10.1037/0022-0663.100.2.460.

Vallerand, R. J., Fortier, M. S., & Guay, F. (1997). Self-determination and persistence in a real-life setting: Toward a motivational model of high school dropout. *Journal of Personality and Social Psychology*, *72*, 1161–76. doi: 10.1037/0022-3514.72.5.1161.

Van Petegem, S., Beyers, W., Vansteenkiste, M., & Soenens, B. (2012). On the association between adolescent autonomy and psychosocial functioning: Examining decisional independence from a self-determination theory perspective. *Developmental Psychology*, *48*, 76.

Vansteenkiste, M., Niemiec, C. P., & Soenens, B. (2010). The development of the five mini-theories of self-determination theory: An historical overview, emerging trends, and future directions. In *The decade ahead: Theoretical perspectives on motivation and achievement* (Vol. 16, Part A, pp. 105–65). Bingley, UK: Emerald Group Publishing Limited. doi: 10.1108/S0749-7423(2010)000016A007.

Vansteenkiste, M., Sierens, E., Goossens, L., Soenens, B., Dochy, F., Mouratidis, A., ... Beyers, W. (2012). Identifying configurations of perceived teacher autonomy support and structure: Associations with self-regulated learning, motivation and problem behavior. *Learning and Instruction*, *22*, 431–9. doi: 10.1016/j. learninstruc.2012.04.002.

Wang, M.-T. & Eccles, J. S. (2013). School context, achievement motivation, and academic engagement: A longitudinal study of school engagement using a multidimensional perspective. *Learning and Instruction*, *28*, 12–23. doi: 10.1016/ j.learninstruc.2013.04.002.

Watanabe, T. (2001). Effects of constrained choice on memory: The extension of the multiple-cue hypothesis to the self-choice effect. *Japanese Psychological Research*, *43*(2), 98–103.

Watanabe, T. & Soraci, S. A. (2004). The self-choice effect from a multiple-cue perspective. *Psychonomic Bulletin & Review*, *11*, 168–72.

White, R. W. (1959). Motivation reconsidered: The concept of competence. *Psychological Review*, *66*(5), 297–333. doi: 10.1037/h0040934.

Williams, J. D., Wallace, T. L., & Sung, H. C. (2016). Providing choice in middle grade classrooms: An exploratory study of enactment variability and student reflection. *The Journal of Early Adolescence*, *36*(4), 527–50. doi: 10.1177/0272431615570057.

Ybarra, O., Lee, D. S., & Gonzalez, R. (2012). Supportive social relationships attenuate the appeal of choice. *Psychological Science*, *23*, 1186–92. doi: 10.1177/0956797612440458.

Yeager, D. S., Henderson, M. D., Paunesku, D., Walton, G. M., D'Mello, S., Spitzer, B. J., & Duckworth, A. L. (2014). Boring but important: A self-transcendent purpose for learning fosters academic self-regulation. *Journal of Personality and Social Psychology*, *107*, 559–80. doi: 10.1037/a0037637.

PART III

Interest and Internal Motivation

11 Interest Development and Learning

K. Ann Renninger and Suzanne E. Hidi

Abstract: *Developing interest is a powerful support for deeper learning. The presence of even some interest beneficially affects individuals' attention and memory, as well as their motivation and meaningful engagement. In this chapter, we expand on previous descriptions of the relation between interest and its development as conceptualized in the Four-Phase Model of Interest Development (Hidi & Renninger, 2006; Renninger & Hidi, 2016). We explain that interest has a physiological basis, and therefore is universal – meaning that all persons, regardless of age or context, can be supported to develop at least some interest in topics to be learned. We describe how and when interest is likely to develop. We review findings which provide evidence that the structure of tasks and activities, as well as interactions with other people, may be helpful to interest development, and also that when these supports are mismatched with the learner's phase of interest, they may constrain or impede interest development. We point to interest as a determinant of learners' understanding, effort, and feedback preferences, and the coordination of their phase of interest development with their abilities to set and realize goals, feel self-efficacy, and self-regulate. We conclude by identifying some open questions concerning the process of interest development and learning.*

Conceptualized as a variable that develops, interest has two meanings. It refers to the psychological state of individuals as they are engaging with some content (e.g., physics, playing bridge, writing) and to their motivation to work with that content over time.[1] The components of interest include knowledge and value, which are usually accompanied by positive feelings. When people have

---

The editorial assistance provided by J. Melissa Running, Lauren Knudsen, and Eliana Yankelev is most appreciated. Research support from the Swarthmore College Faculty Research Fund is also gratefully acknowledged.

1 This chapter extends the detailed review of the beneficial effects of interest on motivation and meaningful engagement from Renninger and Hidi's (2016) book by explicitly considering how and when the development of interest is likely to occur. We point the interested reader to the book and do not reference it repeatedly in this chapter.

an interest, they are likely to search for relevant information, and continue to seek deeper understanding of the content and persevere, even when faced with difficulty (Hidi, 1990). They also are likely to be engaged in meaningful learning, as they are more attentive, more willing to expend greater effort, more able to pursue and realize goals, and more able to develop and effectively use strategies than when they have no interest.

Even if students enter a class without much (or any) interest, it is possible to support them to become interested and to learn. For example, Crouch et al. (2018) found that infusing life science content (e.g., optics, cell membrane potential) into an introductory physics course for life science students provided multiple and repeated opportunities for students to work with, reflect on, and make meaningful connections to physics.[2] The first-semester course used traditional physics examples, whereas the second-semester course used life science content as the examples for the lectures, problem sets, demonstrations, and assignments. Study results indicated that students who had little to no interest in physics at the beginning of their course-work and low performance in the traditional course, had their interest triggered and maintained by the introduction of the life science examples in the experimental second-semester course. Moreover, at the completion of the experimental course, the grades of those with less-developed interest were similar to those of students who had had more-developed interest in physics. These data illustrate how interest in a subject can be triggered to develop, and they indicate that triggering interest can positively affect learning, especially for students with less interest or low achievement.

Lo (2015) and Lo and Tierney (2017) reported similar effects in their study of role-play activity in a high school government course (see also Knogler et al., 2015; Rotgans & Schmidt, 2017a). Echoing the benefit of multiple encounters with life science examples in the physics course, Lo and Tierney pointed to the essential role of repeated opportunities to engage in meaningful activities about a given content (government) for learners whose interest has been "grabbed by an activity" but is not yet developed. In a large-scale study (39,192 ninth grade students), Jansen et al. (2016) showed that, once

---

2 Life science students are typically majors in biology who plan to pursue careers in medicine or biotechnology. In undergraduate physics education, reform practices have called for the development of introductory physics for the life sciences (IPLS) courses (e.g., Crouch & Heller, 2014; Meredith & Redish, 2013), specifying that IPLS courses need to enable life science students to (a) develop their physics-related quantitative skills and problem-solving abilities in life science contexts that are specific to their subsequent use, and (b) be in a position to use their physics understanding and skills when they enter a medical profession or medical research. They further suggest that these goals can be met if the IPLS course is responsive to the needs and experiences of life science students, as well as to the content of modern biology and modern chemistry. In other words, the goals for the IPLS course involve supporting students with an interest in life science content to develop enough of an interest in physics to meaningfully engage with the physics in life science content.

developed, interest predicted student achievement across five subject areas (biology, chemistry, German, math, and physics). Moreover, this effect held between persons (students with higher achievement also had higher interest) and within persons (students had higher achievement in the subject areas in which they had higher interest). These findings support Harackiewicz et al., (2016), who maintain that "cultivating interest should not be an afterthought" (p. 221).

Developments in affective neuroscience help explain these findings and provide additional insight. They suggest that all persons are hardwired to develop interest or engage in seeking behaviors (Panksepp, 1998), and that the process of searching for information, a characteristic of both interest and curiosity, is intrinsically rewarding (e.g., Gottlieb et al., 2013; Gruber et al., 2014; Marvin & Shohamy, 2016).[3] These findings also explain why interest leads to learning without extrinsic rewards. Furthermore, because interest has a physiological basis, these findings indicate that all persons may be supported to develop at least some interest in any content, regardless of their prior level of interest or background. In other words, interest is malleable, and the level or phase of a person's existing interest can be supported to develop further. The potential to develop and gain the benefit of interest is universal and is not exclusive to a gender, racial or ethnic group, or particular social status. As such, educators (e.g., teachers, parents, employers, curriculum and software developers) need to understand how to support interest development.

In reviewing the literature (Renninger & Hidi, 2011), we identified five approaches to the conceptualization of interest: development, emotion, value and feelings, task features, and vocational interests. We explained that there are characteristics of interest researchers tend to agree on: interest is always content specific, has affective and cognitive components, exists in the interaction of the person and the environment, may or may not be something about which a person is metacognitively aware, and has a biological basis. We also noted that differences among the conceptualizations reflect the focus of the research questions posed. A developmental conceptualization such as that of the four-phase model addresses questions associated with the triggering of attention and the search for information *over* time. Other conceptualizations

---

3 Investigators have established that the brain's reward circuitry is a hardwired, evolution-molded information processing mechanism fueled by the neurotransmitter dopamine (Ernst & Spear, 2009). The activation of the reward circuitry (by rewards or their expectations) influences behavior, enhances attention, reduces reaction time, and increases both memory and performance (e.g., Ernst et al., 2007; see Hidi, 2016). Moreover, intrinsic rewards that include information-seeking have been found to activate the reward circuitry just like external rewards (Kang et al., 2009). In their review of the literature, Gottlieb et al. (2013) suggested that "information search" is an intrinsic reward; that is, information has value in and of itself. They argued that there is a need to understand the nature of intrinsic rewards that motivate this type of activity as well as impact learning and, possibly, cognitive development. These findings are further supported by Gruber et al. (2014) and Marvin and Shohamy (2016).

assess attributes of interest development (e.g., emotion, value) at a *specific* time – information that provides additional detail about aspects of interest development, but may not address changes in development or the developmental process per se.

In the rest of this chapter, we explain that interest, conceptualized as a variable that develops, is a process of information search and learning. This includes consideration of how and when interest is likely to develop, and that the process of triggering interest occurs in each phase (a point that was not clearly stated in our previous work). Issues related to understanding and studying interest development are addressed, including measurement, individual factors (such as topic preferences of groups and age), and connections to content based on learners' phase of interest. Evidence is presented demonstrating that the structure of tasks and activities, in addition to interactions with other people, may contribute to interest development. We also note that a mismatch of such resources with the learners' phase of interest development may constrain or impede overall interest development as findings indicate that interest contributes to learner understanding, effort, and feedback preferences, as well as to the coordination of their phase of interest with their abilities to set and realize goals, be self-efficacious, and self-regulate. In concluding, open questions concerning the process of interest development and learning are identified.

To begin, we review the Four-Phase Model of Interest Development (Hidi & Renninger, 2006; Renninger & Hidi, 2011, 2016).

The Four-Phase Model of Interest Development

The Four-Phase Model of Interest Development describes phases in the developing and deepening of learner interest for particular content: triggered situational interest, maintained situational interest, emerging individual interest, and well-developed individual interest (see Table 11.1). Briefly, in the first phase of interest development (triggered situational interest), people's attention may be initially activated by environmental features that are incongruous or surprising, have some personal relevance, or capture their imagination (e.g., demonstrations with toys and magic), and that promote short-term information search (see Palmer et al., 2016). These features may be observed by individuals themselves, or others may encourage such attention. For example, educators may intervene by inserting novelty or surprise into lab assignments, demonstrations, or exhibits (Nieswandt & Horwitz, 2015). They also could promote students' or participants' attention to utility (Harackiewicz et al., 2016; Hulleman & Harackiewicz, 2009) or to specific elements of inquiry activity (Renninger et al., 2014). In this phase, individuals' feelings may be either positive or negative, and the level of their content-related knowledge

Table 11.1 *The four phases of interest development (Hidi & Renninger, 2006): Definitions and learner characteristics, revised and updated*

	Phases of interest development			
	Less-developed (earlier)		More-developed (later)	
	Phase 1: Triggered situational interest	Phase 2: Maintained situational interest	Phase 3: Emerging individual interest	Phase 4: Well-developed individual interest
Definition	• Psychological state resulting from short-term changes in cognitive and affective processing associated with a particular class of content	• Psychological state that involves focused attention to a particular class of content	• Psychological state *and* the beginning of a relatively enduring predisposition to seek re-engagement with a particular class of content over time	• Psychological state *and* a relatively enduring predisposition to re-engage with a particular class of content over time
Learner Characteristics	• Attends to content, if only fleetingly • May or may not be reflectively aware of the experience • May need support from others and/or instructional design to further engage • May experience either positive or negative feelings • Unlikely to persevere when confronted with difficulty • May simply want to be told what to do	• Re-engages content that previously triggered attention • Is developing knowledge of content • May be developing a sense of the content's value • Is likely to be able to be supported by others to find connections to content based on existing skills, knowledge, or prior experience • Is likely to have positive feelings • May not persevere when confronted with difficulty • May want to be told what to do	• Is likely to independently re-engage with content • Has stored knowledge and stored value • Is reflective about the content • Is focused on their own questions • Has positive feelings • May not persevere when confronted with difficulty • May not want feedback from others	• Independently re-engages with content • Has stored knowledge and stored value • Is reflective about the content • Is likely to recognize others' contributions to the content • Can self-regulate easily to reframe questions and seek answers • Has positive feelings • Can persevere through frustration and challenge in order to meet goals • Appreciates and may actively seek feedback

Note. From *The power of interest for motivation and engagement* by K. A. Renninger & S. E. Hidi, 2016, Table 1.2, p. 13. Copyright by Taylor and Francis, 2016. Reprinted with permission and updated for this chapter.

only has to be adequate for processing incoming information.[4] However, repeated opportunity to continue to engage with content increases the individuals' possibility of experiencing interest: the psychological state of interest.

Once an interest is triggered, it may or may not develop into a maintained situational interest. Encouragement to continue to work with content is critical for a person's interest to shift to a maintained situational interest. Maintained, or sustained, engagement can be supported by the structure of tasks or activities, or by other people. Hands-on activity, group work, computers, games, and the meaningfulness of tasks have all been identified as supporting individuals to re-engage in working with content (e.g., Mitchell, 1993; Swarat et al., 2012). As with triggered situational interest, the design of such tasks can be adjusted to focus participant attention on content (e.g., on science), and not only on the other people with whom they are working. For example, Master et al. (2016) reported that providing high school girls with a learning environment that did not fit stereotypes about girls and computer science, increased the girls' interest in computer science courses. In this phase, content knowledge and value starts to develop, and individuals are beginning to develop their ability to work with the content independently. Their feelings tend to be positive, and they benefit from support to continue engagement and from experiencing information search as rewarding.

As individuals begin to independently seek additional information about the content of their interest, they also begin to identify and create their own opportunities for doing so, and their phase of interest shifts to become an emerging individual interest. They may be supported in their search for information by having time and opportunity to explore, and working with others who already have a developed understanding of, and value for, the content (Azevedo, 2006; Nolen, 2007a, 2007b; Pressick-Kilborn & Walker, 2002; Pressick-Kilborn, 2015; Renninger & Hidi, 2002; Renninger & Riley, 2013; see also Xu et al., 2012). Although the information they seek may not be new to the discipline or content area, it is likely to be new to them (e.g., a budding fisherman may wonder: Why do the fish bite here in the lake rather than over there? See Renninger, 2000). In this phase, the development of content-related knowledge and value is increasingly coordinated. This phase of interest also marks a change from what could be considered primarily extrinsically driven to primarily intrinsically driven information search and involvement. Even if they encounter difficulties that result in negative emotions, individuals' feelings about the content are likely to be positive (see Fulmer & Frijters, 2011; O'Keefe & Linnenbrink-Garcia, 2014). In such cases, encouragement from others may be needed to identify strategies to persevere (Renninger et al., 2018).

---

4 Even though interest tends to be associated with positive feelings, negative feelings can also trigger interest and focus attention (Ainley, 2007; Hidi & Harackiewicz, 2000; Iran-Nejad, 1987). To enable an interest in some content to develop, negative feelings have to subside.

The continued development of interest into the fourth phase (well-developed individual interest) is primarily self-generated. Individuals in this phase are committed to deepening their understanding, and they are voluntarily involved in ongoing information search. Instructional conditions that challenge by encouraging the seeking of clarification, resolution, or deeper understanding can facilitate ongoing seeking behavior (e.g., Azevedo, 2006; Barron et al., 2014; Ito et al., 2010; Lipstein & Renninger, 2007). Persons with a well-developed interest are typically working to understand or expand on their thinking about particular information, and are likely to continue even if frustrated (e.g., successive failed experiments; see Neumann, 2006). They usually are able to anticipate strategies for working with content, know of others' approaches, and are resourceful in their search for related information. As such, they also can be expected to sustain long-term constructive and/or creative engagement, as long as they are given the time and latitude to do so (e.g., Azevedo, 2013a, 2013b; Izard & Ackerman, 2000; Renninger & Hidi, 2002). In this phase of interest, individuals' feelings are positive, even if frustrations arise (O'Keefe & Linnenbrink-Garcia, 2014); their interest, content knowledge, and value development continue to be coordinated; re-engagement becomes self-reinforcing; and educators and other authorities often acknowledge the depth and quality of their work (Hidi & Harackiewicz, 2000).

Rotgans and Schmidt (2017a) questioned whether there is a reliable distinction between emerging and well-developed individual interest. The answer is "yes" – investigations have confirmed the existence of four phases (e.g., Lipstein & Renninger, 2007; Michaelis & Nathan, 2016; Wang & Adescope, 2016). However, in some populations, there may be few persons who can be placed in this fourth phase of interest development. For example, Lipstein and Renninger (2007) found relatively few middle school students who had a developed interest in writing, and Rotgans and Schmidt (2017a) were not able to identify a shift to the fourth phase in their study of primary school science students. The result may have been due to the age of the participants, as well as to the time frame within which their study was conducted (four weeks). The number of persons who are likely to reach Phase 4 is also limited if the persons being studied are struggling learners (Cabot, 2014).

In summary, the development of interest is propelled by the triggering of attention and the information search that follows. In both earlier and later phases of interest development, the psychological state needs to be triggered. In earlier phases of interest development, this may take the form of making self-related connections to the content (see Hidi et al. Chapter 1) that can be facilitated by the structure of the environment or interacting with other people. In contrast, in later phases of interest, individuals have a foundation of content knowledge on which to build, and they are positioned to pursue information that other people or the task provide, as well as to initiate inquiries of their own.

Generally, interest can be expected to develop sequentially from earlier to later phases of interest as individuals recognize and engage with available opportunities and resources. Once triggered, an individual's skills, knowledge, and value may continue to increase. For example, in the card game of bridge, interest may continue to develop because of the interactions provided by the game itself, discussions with other players or people to whom the game is recounted, or information pursuit (e.g., reading about bridge, revisiting other options for the hands played). However, in any phase of interest development, interest can be expected to plateau or fall off if individuals have no opportunity to engage with content that allows them to further develop their understanding, have competing interests, or do not receive the support they need to make meaningful connections (see case material and discussion in Alexander et al., Chapter 13; Dohn & Dohn, 2017; Larson et al., Chapter 5; Renninger & Lipstein, 2006).

Further Issues Related to Interest Development

Issues central to understanding interest development include measurement, individual factors (such as topic preferences and age), and the connections to content that learners in different phases are in a position to make. Differences of genetic makeup, familial experience, or educator support appear to account for variations in what emerges as a developed interest for individuals, although specific research on these factors is still needed (see related discussions in Ainley & Ainley, 2015; Alexander et al., 2015; Crowley et al., 2015; Pressick-Kilborn, 2015; Sloboda, 1996; Xu et al., 2012). Two people who share an interest in some content such as the physics of optics, are often not interested in the same aspects. One might be interested in color e.g., how light takes on different colors, how separation of light into different colors works; whereas another might be interested in images, how eyes and instruments (e.g. eyeglasses, microscopes) form images, and how instruments help extend the capacity of human vision (see Krapp & Fink, 1992/2014; Renninger & Shumar, 2002). The two might also be in different phases of interest. Even if they are in the same phase of interest development, the time frame and characteristics of transitioning from one to another phase of interest are likely to vary (Renninger & Hidi, 2002; Renninger & Riley, 2013; Renninger et al., 2008). For example, we have observed that interest can be triggered and then maintained by a serendipitous event: once an apparently dead turtle triggered the interest of its middle-school-aged caretaker, he began to assume responsibility for its well-being and an interest in what this involved (Renninger & Hidi, 2002). In another study, with a participant of approximately the same age, the shift from triggered to maintained situational interest was observed to take four years – and then, within a few days, that participant's interest shifted again to become an emerging individual interest (Renninger & Riley, 2013).

Measuring the Development of Interest

There is no single method for assessing interest and its development. Depending on the research questions being addressed, many data sources can be used, including visual gaze (e.g., Gottlieb et al., 2013), facial expressions (e.g., Mortillaro et al., 2011), neuroscientific techniques (e.g., Gruber et al., 2014), observation (e.g., Renninger & Bachrach, 2015), artifact analysis (e.g., Nolen, 2007a), class enrollment and re-enrollment (e.g., Harackiewicz et al., 2002), descriptive information about context (e.g., Azevedo, 2013a, 2013b), participant engagement (e.g., Barron et al., 2014; Pressick-Kilborn, 2015), and self-reports (e.g., Tröbst et al., 2016). However, measuring the development of interest requires clarity about what needs to be measured (i.e., indicators of interest). In many situations, behavioral indicators (e.g., observed frequency of engagement), in addition to direct measures (e.g., asking, "How likely are you to talk about physics outside of school?"), allow triangulation of data and confirmation that participants are in a position to respond to questions about interest.

Given that different people engage with different interests in similar ways, four behavioral indicators can enable researchers and practitioners to distinguish between the phases of interest development or changes in interest over time. These indicators include whether an individual engages with the content (1) frequently, (2) with understanding and depth of knowledge, (3) voluntarily, and (4) independently. Together, these four indicators of engagement provide reliable information for educators: those with more-developed interest are easily identified by their frequent re-engagement with a subject, the depth of their engagement, and the likelihood that they will choose to engage with it both voluntarily and independently, given the opportunity. Those with less-developed interest do not re-engage with content in this way. Used in self-reporting, such as surveys and interviews, these behavioral indicators form a single factor (Alpha = 0.91, Renninger & Schofield, 2014). They also have been employed to identify interest in other data sources, such as observations (Renninger et al., 2014), videotapes of free play (Renninger & Wozniak, 1985), and log file analyses of online workshop participation (Renninger et al., 2011).

How much a person likes certain content has also been used frequently as an indicator of interest; however, "liking" distinguishes only between no interest and some interest. It does not effectively distinguish between earlier and later phases of interest development (see Ainley, 2017). Learners who are new to content may say that they like it "a lot," but so will those who have an already developed interest.

Because a person's interest is always in a particular content, practitioners and researchers who wish to assess the change in interest over time, or wish to establish the phase of interest a learner is in, may need to adapt their items or observational protocols to assess relevant behavior. For example, assessing interest in mathematics might include determining the frequency with which learners return to engagement, the likelihood that they will find and work on mathematical problems by themselves even if they are not assigned, and so forth. Setting up a comparison in the way that questions are posed can lead learners to think about mathematics in relation to other content (such as physics or German) and can be useful. Furthermore, some researchers aggregate their assessments to focus on earlier (less-developed interest) and later (more-developed interest) phases of interest, rather than on the four phases.

Individual Factors: Topic Preferences and Age

Reliable preferences for particular topics have been observed based on gender, group membership, and life experience. As demonstrated in the study of the physics class for life science students described earlier, topics that are known interests for particular groups can be used to both trigger their attention and then involve them in working with the challenges of disciplinary content. For example, the topic of health and caring for humans has been shown to enable (a) seventh grade girls to more effectively understand pumps, when presented in discussions of pumping blood to the heart rather than pumping oil to an oil-fired heating plant, whereas boys did not show this pattern (Hoffmann & Häussler, 1998); and (b) Latinx students to continue enrollment in undergraduate biology classes that focus on health and caring, because the content leads them to identify connections between the biology they are learning and their interest in using what they learn in their own communities (Thoman et al., 2015).

Another factor that can influence the development of interest is age (see Renninger, 2009). Before eight years of age, children can be expected to readily explore different types of content, at least in part because they are also less likely to compare what they are able to do with what other children can do. Sometime between eight and ten years of age, in addition to conforming to age-related norms, children begin engaging in self-other comparisons that may extend into adulthood (see Harter, 2003). Such comparisons often redirect their attention away from exploring and learning content and toward considerations of how they are achieving relative to other people. Their desire to achieve and to fit in with others has implications for the way children (as well as older individuals) may need to be supported to work with content that is new or that they have not already mastered (Renninger, 2009). Developing a new interest (or renewing a prior interest) at an older age requires the triggering and sustaining of interest. This can be accomplished using interventions that involve the learner in making links back to the self in ways that promote the self-related processing of information, such as those pointing to utility or relevance (see Hidi et al., Chapter 1; Hulleman et al., 2016). The use of life science as a context for learning physics provides an example. Another option to develop interest involves having learners work alongside other peers on projects or richly textured assignments that allow the ongoing triggering of interest (e.g., Knogler et al., 2015; Lo & Tierney, 2017; Rotgans & Schmidt, 2017a). If needed, these are contexts that can be readily adjusted so that the structure of the activity provides enough guidance, and other participants can model skills that will provide support for meaningful engagement (see Renninger et al., 2014). Older students have also been shown to be able to trigger their own interest – for example, by making an ostensibly boring task into a game (Sansone et al., 1992).

Connections to Content in Different Phases

In any of the four phases of interest development, individuals can be supported to experience the psychological state of interest. The frequency of a person's re-engagement affects the frequency with which they experience interest (Sansone & Thoman, 2005; Thoman et al., 2017). Moreover, repeated engagement is most likely to affect the experiencing of interest if it also contributes to the deepening of knowledge, value, and learning. Time on task without stretching understanding may not be sufficient. The presence of challenge and the opportunity to grow knowledge are critical.

Consider what the physics students of the Crouch et al. (2018) study related about the life science examples in their physics classes. Researchers asked the students to explain why the life science examples triggered their interest, and if they did not, why not. Students who had a less-developed interest in physics at the beginning of the course reported that the examples helped them make a meaningful connection to the physics content. For example, students with less-developed interest in physics reported:

- Physics is a hard subject to understand and master. However, physics tied in with subjects of personal interest such as biology really get you engaged in the material.
- The life science examples are naturally much more intriguing and feel more relevant to what I'm interested in, so I was naturally more keen to answer the questions.
- The life science examples played a major role in sparking my interest in understanding those concepts using physics. In high school, I learned those concepts, but it was not applied to life experiences. Using life science examples makes the concepts easier to understand because those physics concepts are now related to a real-life experience. As a pre-med student, using life science helped trigger my interest in physics.
- The use of life science examples greatly helped contextualize otherwise sometimes abstract ideas; they made the underlying concepts much more exciting, and I also expect to retain them better into the future since I can employ them to think about real-world issues.

Students with more-developed interest in physics reported that (a) the examples enabled them to see the connections between disciplines and (b) they knew the more obvious information about the life science examples, but were challenged and most interested when the examples enabled them to deepen their knowledge of some aspect of the examples' content and its functioning. For example, they explained:

- I got the most questions out of examples I was most familiar with in everyday life, particularly optics of vision, because here I was most able to find discrepancies between my own reasoning and how I used the concepts I was learning and sort them out.
- Knowing about the biological phenomena involved helped me better appreciate having a different approach than the one I had already learned. For example, I don't think screening in salt solution would have been as interesting to me if I hadn't already known a bit about DNA, proteins, and cells. I loved the [homework] problem asking us to calculate the electric forces between DNA molecules in pure water as screening was being introduced and we found that the electric forces should be too great for so much DNA to be packed together in the nucleus. This was a turning point for me, as I had never considered this before, but now that I had, it seemed to be a very significant problem. If I hadn't known anything about DNA, this would not have been as worthwhile of a problem.
- When we learned about immersion oil in microscopy, I had already had experience using this technique, and I knew that it was to increase the amount of light that went into the microscopy, but I didn't really understand how oil helped until we talked about the example in class. In general, I found that I was familiar with the examples used because of my previous courses in biology and chemistry, but I had a weak or incomplete understanding of the physics behind the examples until this class.

Students with less-developed interest, as well as those with more-developed interest, needed to be able to identify connections between their already existing knowledge base and the life science content; however, the connections that they were prepared to make varied. The life science examples represented different types of triggers for the two groups of students, and the examples were also differently effective (there were no apparent gender differences). In the experimental class, the use of life science examples benefited those with a less-developed interest in physics. On the other hand, they benefited those with a more-developed interest in physics only if their use enabled these students to think in new ways about what they already knew.

Perhaps it is not surprising that, over the course of the semester in the experimental class, there was a slight decline in the physics interest of the group of students with a more-developed interest in physics. It is possible that a more sophisticated treatment of the life science examples would have better engaged these students. Their open-ended responses suggest that the use of examples that pushed them to deepen their understanding of both the physics and the life science content might have been more effective. Similarly, if expert bridge players are forced into a game with novice players, they may lose interest in that game.

A critical consideration in understanding how and when interest is likely to develop in later phases has to do with the content that learners are encountering. They need to find the content in the tasks or discussions that they engage in to be both doable (given their level of ability) and challenging enough to be interesting. Moreover, for interest to continue to develop, the challenge needs to be one that learners are able to recognize and choose to engage with both voluntarily and independently. Triggers for continued involvement may come from the connections that can be made to disciplinary content, complex problem solving, or opportunities to engage in critical thinking with other people.

Even though interest develops through the structure of tasks and activities, or through interactions with other people, the effectiveness of task characteristics and interactions appears to be also dependent on educators' appreciation of the learners' present content knowledge (and related valuing; e.g., Turner et al., 2015; Xu et al., 2012). This is important information that can inform decision-making about how to design or what to say, so that learners can make or continue to deepen connections to content.

Interest and Its Coordination with Other Motivational Variables

The development of a new interest (even if it means overcoming aversion) begins with the triggering of attention to content. External support can contribute to the likelihood that individuals will continue to attend to new content. For example, structured and collaborative programming or activity can support initial engagement (Gutwill & Allen, 2012; Hidi et al., 1998); other well-developed interests (e.g., basketball) may be inserted as contexts for mathematical word problems or reading passages (Renninger et al., 2002; Walkington & Bernacki, 2014); or content that is familiar, such as optics, can be used to provide a foundation for developing a new interest in physics (Crouch et al., 2018; Hoffmann, 2002).

A person's attention could also possibly be triggered by curiosity instead of interest. If triggered by curiosity, a person might encounter, and recognize, a knowledge gap (Lowenstein, 1994). The exact relation between interest and curiosity is currently a point of debate (e.g., Grossnickle, 2016); although only interest has been shown to develop over time. Renninger and Hidi (2016) noted that curiosity and interest both involve information-seeking, but the basis and outcomes of the search differ. Whereas curiosity represents a desire to seek and learn new information by exploring novel and uncertain environments, individual interest is the motivation to seek and learn new information that is linked to some form of existing knowledge, which then continues to develop.

They also suggested that curiosity is similar to the earlier phases of interest development and, with external support, could be a trigger for interest.

The development of interest does not occur in a vacuum. Its development has been found to be coordinated with a number of motivational variables. Empirical support has established the existence of a reciprocal relation between interest and goal setting (Harackiewicz et al., 2008), self-efficacy (e.g., Hidi & Ainley, 2008), and self-regulation (e.g., Sansone & Thoman, 2005). That is, although these variables are distinct, it is only in earlier phases of interest that they may appear to be unrelated; in later phases of interest they are coordinated and mutually supportive of each other. Using within-person analyses, Lipstein and Renninger (2007) provided further elaboration on these relations in their study of middle school students' interest in writing. They found that the students' understanding, effort, feedback preferences, goals, self-efficacy, and self-regulation were distinct in each of the four phases of interest. These data were then used to develop portraits of the students in each phase of interest development.[5]

As depicted in Table 11.2, the student portraits indicate that, in general, participants with less-developed interest (triggered situational interest and maintained situational interest) are not likely to have much understanding of the task. In this case, students may think that writing requires a lot of effort. They want feedback on their writing, but need it to be directly related to their work – feedback they can work with. They do not identify as persons who pursue writing, and may not even think that developing an interest in writing is possible. Their self-efficacy, or belief in the possibility that they could be successful writers, is likely to be low, and so is their ability to self-regulate – to set goals for themselves in writing that they then strive to achieve. Such learners are likely to need support from the structure of the learning environment or from other people in order to make and sustain connections to writing, and find them rewarding.

Lipstein and Renninger (2007) further reported that, in contrast, those with more-developed interest in writing (emerging individual interest and well-developed individual interest) find working with writing rewarding. They voluntarily seek additional opportunities to continue to grow their knowledge, and have an understanding of writing that is quite developed (for a person in middle school). Although they recognize that they invest a lot of time on their writing, they do not feel that it is arduous. For them, feedback about the substance of what they are doing is preferred – as long as they continue to feel challenged and confident. Learners with more-developed interest in writing

---

5 Portraiture provides ethnographic narrative about the commonalities across multiple instances, rather than singling out a particular case for description (see Lawrence-Lightfoot & Davis, 1997). In the Lipstein and Renninger (2007) study, portraits were developed on the basis of responses from 72 (38 male, 34 female) middle school students, who completed both open-ended surveys and in-depth, semi-structured interviews.

Table 11.2 *Phases of interest in writing: Understanding, effort, feedback preferences, goals, self-efficacy, and self-regulation*

	Phases of Interest in Writing			
	Less-developed (earlier)		More-developed (later)	
	Phase 1: Triggered situational	Phase 2: Maintained situational	Phase 3: Emerging individual	Phase 4: Well-developed individual
Understanding	Most have little vision of writing as a purposeful activity (e.g., communication) or as a process; writing is associated with assignments	Most conceive of writing as a means toward some other end (e.g., emotional expression, success in school); many either articulate that writing has a purpose (e.g., communication) or that it is a process	Most articulate a purpose for writing (e.g., communication); some demonstrate an understanding of process instead	All describe a purpose for writing (e.g., communication) and demonstrate an understanding of writing as a process
Effort	Most feel that writing takes a lot of effort; perceive even small tasks as arduous	Most do not feel that writing takes an overwhelming amount of work; do not invest more effort in writing than other school assignments	Most expend a lot of effort and keep working until they are personally satisfied; do not feel that the work they put into writing is arduous	Most expend a lot of effort by choice and keep working until they and others are satisfied; do not feel that the work they put into writing is arduous
Feedback preferences	All want comments that require few changes and feel manageable; afraid of audience censure and being thought of as "stupid"	All want to hear positive feedback and specific directions to improve their work; look to teacher for standards for performance	All want their ideas to be heard and have their work appreciated; want audience reactions that are open-ended; do not want to hear specific directives or questioning of their decision-making	All want their ideas to be heard and want honest feedback in any form, whether reactive or constructive criticism; prefer initial feedback on content, followed by feedback about technique

Table 11.2 (*Cont.*)

Phases of Interest in Writing

	Less-developed (earlier)		More-developed (later)	
	Phase 1: Triggered situational	Phase 2: Maintained situational	Phase 3: Emerging individual	Phase 4: Well-developed individual
Goals	Most want to "get it done" or focus on grammar and other details	Most want to do things well (according to standard set by teacher)	Most want to do things well (according to a personal standard); may opt for work that exceeds level of readiness	All want to do things well (seem to embrace both personal and more universally accepted standards for writing); more aware than those in other phases of interest about the level of work that they are able to do
Self-efficacy	Most feel that they are poor writers (this perception is often reinforced by low grades)	Most are generally comfortable with their abilities as writers (this perception is often reinforced by high grades)	Most are confident in their abilities as writers (often, but not always, this perception is reinforced by grades)	Most are confident in their abilities as writers; have a realistic sense of their abilities relative to peers and published authors; do not need to have their abilities confirmed by others
Self-regulation	Most do not set goals for themselves as writers and do not identify strategies to be mastered	Most employ strategies that allow them to meet standards set by their teacher	Most tend to focus on phrasing and other stylistic concerns	All employ their own strategies as well as strategies suggested by others (e.g., outlining); they all seek feedback or help from others

Note. Adapted from tables 1 and 2 in "Putting things into words: The development of 12–15-year-old students' interest for writing," by R. Lipstein & K. A. Renninger, 2007, in P. Boscolo & S. Hidi (Eds.), *Motivation and writing: Research and school practice* (pp. 113–40). New York, NY: Elsevier.

typically identify as writers, have high self-efficacy about writing, and are able to self-regulate to set goals for themselves in their writing that they then work to achieve.

Renninger et al. (2018) clarify that a person with more-developed interest needs situations to be challenging but not overwhelming. Being overwhelmed by too much challenge can lead to a drop in self-efficacy and a change in the need for feedback. They describe the case of a ballerina named Emily, who had studied dance since she was four years old. Emily had a developed interest in ballet, but reported that she seriously considered quitting ballet after her teacher moved her into an advanced class of older students.

> [Emily] developed her ability to dance in the context of successively challenging classes, and is influenced by role models like her teacher and older classmates. Knowing that the advanced class was for the older and more developed dancers, Emily was very motivated to get into it ... But when she was asked to master steps she did not yet know, participation felt overwhelming, and the challenge affected her self-efficacy. Emily's motivation and her interest in ballet began to wane. Her mother's encouragement was critical to Emily's continued participation in the class, and the promise of pointe shoes signaled that her teacher thought the challenges of the class were within her reach. (Renninger et al., 2018, p. 118)

Even though Emily identified as a ballerina, her profile became similar to that of a person new to an interest when she had to face with the challenge of mastering steps that the older students were perfecting. She needed, and received, feedback and encouragement from other people (e.g., her mother, her teacher) to work with the challenge.

Similarly, analyzing the middle school students' interest in writing, Renninger and Lipstein (2006) found that students who described changes in their interest pointed to the challenges of their writing tasks, as well as to the presence or absence of support from other people. For example, those with only a triggered situational interest directly linked their interest to their perception that the writing assignments had become more difficult and to a feeling that they did not have the background needed to write effectively. For example,

> Ella[6] said that she had not always disliked writing: "Once I got to middle school and we started to have to analyze things, it just got harder." She commented that teachers did not really teach her how to write, but ... "they just kind of assume you know how to write." (p. 71)
>
> Tom reported that he had not always disliked writing: "In elementary school, I think I liked writing, but then when I got to high school, I did not like it as much." ... He also said that writing "got a lot harder because it started getting advanced." (p. 72)

---

6 All names are pseudonyms.

Those with a maintained situational interest showed more interest in writing and explained that they found themselves developing their interest because of the types of assignments (open-ended free writes) they were doing. They expressed a sense that they had the knowledge they needed and knew they could do the required tasks, in part because they were receiving confirmation of this from others. For example,

> Allison reported that, when she was younger, she did not like writing at all, but this year she began to really like to write. Asked about what she thought contributed to her changed feelings, she said that preparation for exams, essay writing, and other training during the last school year had made her feel more prepared: "When I went into the next year, it all came back to me and I knew how to write, and I knew what the different types of writing were." (p. 73)
>
> Matt described his transition to liking writing as gradual ... Matt mentioned the free writes that he had the opportunity to write this year. He reported that he "liked these a lot because we got to write something of our choice, and there was a minimal time limit, but you could spend more time if you wanted to." He focused in particular on one experience when he had been inspired because his dog had jumped on him and reopened an old scar, which reminded him of the hospital visit and what a farcical experience that had been ... He said, "I was kind of reluctant to read it [to the class], but then after I read it, people gave me a lot of responses and I felt a lot better." (p. 74)

Students with more-developed interest also pointed to the validation of their writing provided by other people. For example,

> Dave reported that he likes writing a lot, but that he has not always liked to write as much as he does now. When asked what changed his feelings about writing, he instantly responded that things changed for him in the third grade when "kids said that they liked my story about a spaceship and a little kid." The interviewer reflected back this sentiment, saying, "So, when somebody tells you that they like your writing then you like it more?" He enthusiastically responded, "Yeah." (p. 76)

The student interviews provide us with a better understanding of the relation of interest development to other motivational variables. They illustrate the coordination of learners' interest with their goals, feelings of self-efficacy, and self-regulation in each phase of interest development. They also further confirm that the structure of the environment and interactions with other people are critical supports for interest development. We note that these findings are also likely to apply to content other than writing.

Concluding Thoughts

In this chapter, we have explained that the presence of interest is always motivating and meaningfully engaging – and that interest is malleable. At any age, and in any context, interest can be encouraged to develop. The presence of even some interest can positively affect achievement, as we saw in the case of the life science students in physics. Interest provides support for the development of knowledge and coordinated valuing, and these reciprocally affect the outcomes.[7] Moreover, the phase of learners' interest development appears to be a determinant of their understanding, effort, and feedback preferences, in addition to being coordinated with their goals, feelings of self-efficacy, and likely self-regulation.

There are a number of issues that still need to be resolved, however (Ainley, 2017). In this chapter, based on our consideration of interest and learning, open questions include the following:

- What is the extent of the coordination of interest and other motivational variables in learning?
- What are generalizable practices for structuring tasks or interacting with other people that can provide support for the continued development of interest in different phases of interest development?
- What is the distinction between interest and curiosity, and does it affect learning?
- Does self-specificity provide an explanation of why some triggers for interest work and others do not?
- What are the conditions in which interest is arrested or falls off?

References

Ainley, M. (2007). Being and feeling interested: Transient state, mood, and disposition. In P. Schutz (Ed.), *Emotion in education* (pp. 141–57). New York, NY: Academic Press. https://doi.org/10.1016/B978-012372545-5/50010-1.

Ainley, M. (2017). Interest: Knowns, unknowns, and basic processes. In P. A. O'Keefe & J. M. Harackiewicz (Eds.), *The Science of interest* (pp. 3–24). New York, NY: Springer International Publishing.

Ainley, M. & Ainley, J. (2015). Early science learning experiences: Triggered and maintained interest. In K. A. Renninger, M. Nieswandt, & S. Hidi (Eds.), *Interest in mathematics and science learning* (pp. 17–33). Washington, DC: American Educational Research Association.

Alexander, J. M., Johnson, K. E., & Leibham, M. E. (2015). Emerging individual interests related to science in young children. In K. A. Renninger, M. Nieswandt, & S. Hidi (Eds.), *Interest in mathematics and science learning* (pp. 261–81). Washington, DC: American Educational Research Association.

Azevedo, F. S. (2006). Personal excursions: Investigating the dynamics of student engagement. *International Journal of Computers for Mathematical Learning, 11*(1), 57–98. doi: 10.1007/s10758-006-0007-6.

7 There has been some misunderstanding of how we conceptualize the role of knowledge in the four-phase model (e.g., Rotgans & Schmidt, 2017b). The model specifies that: interest supports the development of knowledge, interest can be an outcome of knowledge development, and interest and knowledge are reciprocally related.

Azevedo, F. S. (2013a). The tailored practice of hobbies and its implication for the design of interest-based learning environments. *The Journal of the Learning Sciences, 22*(3), 462–510. doi: 10.1080/10508406.2012.730082.

Azevedo, F. S. (2013b). Knowing the stability of model rockets: An investigation of learning in interest-based practices. *Cognition and Instruction, 31*(3), 345–74. doi: 10.1080/07370008.2013.799168.

Barron, B., Gomez, K., Pinkard, N., & Martin, C. (2014). *The digital youth network: cultivating digital media citizenship in urban communities.* Cambridge, MA: MIT Press.

Cabot, I. (2014). The Four-Phase Model of Interest Development: Elaboration of a measurement instrument. Poster presented in K. A. Renninger & S. E. Hidi (chairs), *Current approaches to interest measurement.* Philadelphia, PA: American Educational Research Association.

Crouch, C. H. & Heller, K. (2014). Introductory physics in biological context: An approach to improve introductory physics for life science students. *American Journal of Physics, 82*, 378–86. doi: 10.1119/1.4870079.

Crouch, C. H., Wisittanawat, P., Cai, M., & Renninger, K. A. (2018). Life science students' attitudes, interest, and performance in introductory physics for life sciences (IPLS): An exploratory study. *Physical Review Physics Education Research. 14*(1). https://doi.org/10.1103/PhysRevPhysEducRes.14 .010111.

Crowley, K., Barron, B., Knutson, K., & Martin, C. K. (2015). Interest and the development of pathways to science. In K. A. Renninger, M. Nieswandt, & S. Hidi (Eds.), *Interest in mathematics and science learning* (pp. 297–315). Washington, DC: American Educational Research Association.

Dohn, N. B. & Dohn, N. B. (2017). Integrating Facebook in upper secondary biology instruction: A case study of students' situational interest and participation in learning communication. *Research in Science Education, 47*(6), 1305–29. doi: 10.1007/s11165-016-9549-3.

Ernst, M. & Spear, L. P. (2009). Reward systems. In M. de Haan & M. R. Gunnar (Eds.), *Handbook of developmental social neuroscience* (pp. 324–41). New York, NY: Guilford Press.

Fulmer, S. M. & Frijters, J. C. (2011). Motivation during an excessively challenging reading task: The buffering role of relative topic interest. *Journal of Experimental Education, 79*(2), 185–208. doi: 10.1080/00220973.2010.481503.

Gottlieb, J., Oudeyer, P.-Y., Lopes, M., & Baranes, A. (2013). Information seeking, curiosity and attention: Computational and neural mechanisms. *Trends in Cognitive Science, 17*(11), 585–96. doi: 10.1016/j.tics.2013.09.001.

Grossnickle, E. M. (2016). Disentangling curiosity: Dimensionality, definitions, and distinctions from interest in educational contexts. *Educational Psychology Review, 28*(1), 23–60. doi: 10.1007/s10648-014-9294-y.

Gruber, M. J., Gelman, B. D., & Ranganath, C. (2014). States of curiosity modulate hippocampus-dependent learning via the dopaminergic circuit. *Neuron, 84*(2), 486–96. doi: 10.1016/j.neuron.2014.08.060.

Gutwill, J. P. & Allen, S. (2012). Deepening students' scientific inquiry skills during a science museum field trip. *Journal of the Learning Sciences, 12*(1), 130–81. doi: 10.1080/10508406.2011.555938.

Harackiewicz, J. M., Barron, K. E., Tauer, J. M., & Elliot, A. J. (2002). Predicting success in college: A longitudinal study of achievement goals and ability measures as predictors of interest and performance from freshman year through graduation. *Journal of Educational Psychology*, *94*(3), 562–75. doi: 10.1037//0022-0663.94.3.562.

Harackiewicz, J. M., Durik, A. M., Barron, K. E., Linnenbrink, L., & Tauer, J. M. (2008). The role of achievement goals in the development of interest: Reciprocal relations between achievement goals, interest, and performance. *Journal of Educational Psychology*, *100*(1), 105–22. doi: 10.1037/0022-0663.100.1.105.

Harackiewicz, J. M., Smith, J. L., & Priniski, S. J. (2016). Interest matters: The importance of promoting interest in education. *Policy Insights from the Behavioral and Brain Sciences*, *3*(2), 220–7. doi:10.1177/2372732216655542.

Harter, S. (2003). The development of self-representation during childhood and adolescence. In M. R. Leary & J. P. Tangney (Eds.), *Handbook of self and identity* (pp. 610–42). New York, NY: Guilford.

Hidi, S. (1990). Interest and its contribution as a mental resource for learning. *Review of Educational Research*, *60*(4), 549–71.

Hidi, S. (2016). Revisiting the role of rewards in motivation and learning: Implications of neuroscientific research. *Educational Psychology Review*, *28*(1), 61–93. doi: 10.1007/s10648-015-9307-5.

Hidi, S. & Ainley, M. (2008). Interest and self-regulation: Relationships between two variables that influence learning. In D. H. Schunk & B. J. Zimmerman (Eds.), *Motivation and self-regulated learning: Theory, research, and application* (pp. 77–109). Mahwah, NJ: Erlbaum.

Hidi, S. & Harackiewicz, J. M. (2000). Motivating the academically unmotivated: A critical issue for the 21st century. *Review of Educational Research*, *70*(2), 151–79. doi: 10.2307/1170660.

Hidi, S. & Renninger, K. A. (2006). The four-phase model of interest development. *Educational Psychologist, 41*(2), 111–27. doi: 10.1207/s15326985ep4102_4.

Hidi, S. E., Renninger, K. A., & Northoff, G. (2018). The development of interest and self-related processing. In F. Guay, H. W. Marsh, D. M. McInerney, & R. G. Craven (Eds.), *International advances in self research, Vol. 6: SELF – Driving positive psychology and well-being* (pp. 51–70). Charlotte, NC: Information Age Press.

Hidi, S., Weiss, J., Berndorff, J. D., & Nolan, J. (1998). The role of gender, instruction and a cooperative learning technique in science education across formal and informal settings. In L. Hoffman, A. Krapp, K. Renninger, & J. Baumert (Eds.), *Interest and Learning: Proceedings of the Seeon Conference on Interest and Gender* (pp. 215–27). Kiel: Institute for Science Education (IPN).

Hoffmann, L. (2002). Promoting girls' learning and achievement in physics classes for beginners. *Learning and Instruction*, *12*(4), 447–65. doi: 10.1016/S0959-4752(01)00010-X.

Hoffmann, L. & Häussler, P. (1998). An intervention project promoting girls' and boys' interest in physics. In L. Hoffmann, A. Krapp, K. A. Renninger, & J. Baumert (Eds.), *Interest and Learning: Proceedings of the Seeon Conference on Interest and Gender* (pp. 301–16). Kiel: Institute for Science Education (IPN).

Hulleman, C. & Harackiewicz, J. (2009). Promoting interest and performance in high school science classes. *Science, 326*(5698), 1410–12. doi: 10.1126/science.1177067.

Hulleman, C. S., Kosovich, J. J., Barron, K. E., & Daniel, D. B. (2016). Making connections: Replicating and extending the utility value intervention in the classroom. *Journal of Educational Psychology, 109*(3), 387–404. doi: 10.1037/edu0000146.

Iran-Nejad, A. (1987). Cognitive and affective causes of interest and liking. *Journal of Educational Psychology, 79*(2), 120–30. doi: 10.1037/0022-0663.79.2.120.

Ito, M., Baumer, S., Bittanti, M., Boyd, D., Cody, R., Herr-Stephenson, B., ... Tripp, L. (2010). *Hanging out, messing around, and geeking out: Kids living and learning with new media.* Cambridge, MA: MIT Press.

Izard, C. E. & Ackerman, B. P. (2000). Motivational, organizational, and regulatory functions of discrete emotions. In M. Lewis & J. M. Haviland-Jones (Eds.), *Handbook of emotions* (2nd ed., pp. 253–64). New York, NY: Guilford.

Jansen, M., Lüdtke, O., & Schroeders, U. (2016). Evidence for a positive relationship between interest and achievement: Examining between-person and within-person variation in five domains. *Contemporary Educational Psychology, 46,* 116–27. doi: 10.1016/j.cedpsych.2016.05.004.

Kang, M. J., Hsu, M., Krajbich, I. M., Loewenstein, G., McClure, S. M., Wang, J. T., & Camerer, C. F. (2009). The wick in the candle of learning: Epistemic curiosity activates reward circuitry and enhances memory. *Psychological Science, 20,* 963–73. doi: 10.1111/j.1467-9280.2009.02402.x.

Knogler, M., Harackiewicz, J. M., Gegenfurtner, A., & Lewalter, D. (2015). How situational is situational interest? Investigating the longitudinal structure of situational interest. *Contemporary Educational Psychology, 43,* 39–50. doi: 10.1016/j.cedpsych.2015.08.004.

Krapp, A. & Fink, B. (1992/2014). The development and function of interests during the critical transition from home to preschool. In K. A. Renninger, S. Hidi, & A. Krapp (Eds.), *The role of interest in learning and development* (pp. 397–431). Hillsdale, MJ: Erlbaum. doi: 10.4324/9781315807430.

Lawrence-Lightfoot, S. & Davis, J. H. (1997). *The art and science of portraiture.* San Francisco, CA: Jossey-Bass.

Lipstein, R. & Renninger, K. A. (2007). "Putting things into words": The development of 12–15-year-old students' interest for writing. In P. Boscolo & S. Hidi (Eds.), *Motivation and writing: Research and school practice* (pp. 113–40). New York, NY: Kluwer Academic/Plenum Press. doi: 10.1163/9781849508216_008.

Lo, J. C. (2015). Developing participation through simulations: A multi-level analysis of situational interest on students' commitment to vote. *The Journal of Social Studies Research, 39*(4), 243–54. doi: 10.1016/j.jssr.2015.06.008.

Lo, J. C. & Tierney, G. (2017). Maintaining interest in politics: 'Engagement First' in a U.S. high school government course. *Journal of Social Science Education, 16*(3), 62–73. doi: 10.2390/jsse-v16-i3-1572.

Lowenstein, G. (1994). The psychology of curiosity: A review and reinterpretation. *Psychology Bulletin, 116*(1), 75–98. doi: 10.1037/0033-2909.116.1.75.

Marvin, C. & Shohamy, D. (2016). Curiosity and reward: Valence predicts choice and information prediction errors enhance learning. *Journal of Experimental Psychology, 145*(3), 266–72. doi: 10.1037/xge0000140.

Master, A., Cheryan, S., & Meltzoff, A. N. (2015). Computing whether she belongs: Stereotypes undermine girls' interest and sense of belonging in computer science. *Journal of Educational Psychology*, *108*(3), 424–37. doi: 10.1037/edu0000061.

Meredith, D. C. & Redish, E. F. (2013). Reinventing physics for life-sciences majors. *Physics Today*, *66*(7), 38–43. doi: 10.1063/PT.3.2046.

Michaelis, J. E., & Nathan, M. J. (June, 2016). Observing and measuring interest development among high school students in an out-of-school robotics competition. American Society of Engineering Education (ASEE 2016) Pre-College Engineering Education Division paper, New Orleans, LA.

Mitchell, M. (1993). Situational interest: Its multifaceted structure in the secondary school mathematics classroom. *Journal of Educational Psychology*, *85*(3), 424–36. doi: 10.1037/0022-0663.85.3.424.

Mortillaro, M., Mehu, M., & Scherer, K. R. (2011). Subtly different positive emotions can be distinguished by their facial expressions. *Social Psychological and Personality Science*, *2*(3), 262–71. doi: 10.1177/1948550610389080.

Neumann, A. (2006). Professing passion: Emotion in the scholarship of professors at research universities. *American Educational Research Journal*, *43*(3), 381–424. doi: 10.3102/00028312043003381.

Nieswandt, M. & Horowitz, G. (2015). Undergraduate students' interest in chemistry: The roles of task and choice. In K. A. Renninger, M. Nieswandt, & S. Hidi (Eds.), *Interest in mathematics and science learning* (pp. 225–42). Washington, DC: American Educational Research Association.

Nolen, S. B. (2007a). Young children's motivation to read and write: Development in social contexts. *Cognition and Instruction*, *25*(2), 219–70. doi: 10.1080/07370000701301174.

Nolen, S. B. (2007b). The role of literate communities in development of children's interest in writing. In S. Hidi & P. Boscolo (Eds.), *Writing and motivation* (pp. 241–55). Oxford: Elsevier.

O'Keefe, P. A. & Linnenbrink-Garcia, L. (2014). The role of interest in optimizing performance and self-regulation. *Journal of Experimental Social Psychology*, *53*, 70–8. doi: 10.1016/j.jesp.2014.02.004.

Palmer, D. A., Dixon, J., & Archer, J. (2016). Identifying underlying causes of situational interest in a science course for preservice elementary teachers. *Science Education*, *100*(6), 1039–61. doi: 10.1002/sce.21244.

Panksepp, J. (1998). *Affective neuroscience: The foundations of human and animal emotion*. New York, NY: Oxford.

Pressick-Kilborn, K. (2015). Canalization and connectedness in development of science interest. In K. A. Renninger, M. Nieswandt, & S. Hidi (Eds.), *Interest in mathematics and science learning* (pp. 353–68). Washington, DC: American Educational Research Association.

Pressick-Kilborn, K. & Walker, R. (2002). The social construction of interest in a learning community. In D. M. McInerney & S. Van Etten (Eds.), *Research on sociocultural influences on learning and motivation* (pp. 153–82). Greenwich, CT: Information Age Publishing.

Renninger, K. A. (2000). Individual interest and its implications for understanding intrinsic motivation. In C. Sansone & J. M. Harackiewicz (Eds.), *Intrinsic motivation: Controversies and new directions* (pp. 373–404). San Diego, CA: Academic Press. doi: 10.1016/B978-012619070-0/50035-0.

Renninger, K. A. (2009). Interest and identity development in instruction: An inductive model. *Educational Psychologist, 44*(2), 1–14. doi: 10.1080/00461520902832392.

Renninger, K. A. (2010). Working with and cultivating interest, self-efficacy, and self-regulation. In D. Preiss & R. Sternberg (Eds.), *Innovations in educational psychology: Perspectives on learning, teaching and human development* (pp. 107–138). New York, NY: Springer.

Renninger, K. A., Austin, L., Bachrach, J. E., Chau, A., Emmerson, M., King, R., ... Stevens, S. J., (2014). Going beyond the "Whoa! That's Cool!" of inquiry: Achieving science interest and learning with the ICAN Intervention. In S. Karabenick & T. Urdan, (Eds.), *Motivation-based learning interventions, Vol. 18: Advances in motivation and achievement* (pp. 107–40). London: Emerald Group Publishing. doi: 10.1108150749-742320140000018017.

Renninger, K. A. & Bachrach, J. E. (2015). Studying triggers for interest and engagement using observational methods. *Educational Psychologist, 50*(1), 58–69. doi: 10.1080/00461520.2014.999920.

Renninger, K. A., Bachrach, J. E., & Posey. S. K. (2008). Learner interest and achievement motivation. *Social Psychological Perspectives: Advances in Motivation and Achievement, 15*, 461–91. doi: 10.1016/S0749-7423(08)15014-2.

Renninger, K. A., Cai, M., Lewis, M., Adams, M., & Ernst, K. (2011). Motivation and learning in an online, unmoderated, mathematics workshop for teachers. *Special Issue: Motivation and New Media. Educational Technology, Research and Development, 59*(2), 229–47. doi: 10.1007/sl1423-011-9195-4.

Renninger, K. A., Ewen, E., & Lasher, A. K. (2002). Individual interest as context in expository text and mathematical word problems. *Learning and Instruction 12*(4), 467–91. doi: 10.1016/s0959-4752(01)00012-3.

Renninger, K. A. & Hidi, S. (2002). Student interest and achievement: Developmental issues raised by a case study. In A. Wigfield & J. S. Eccles (Eds.), *Development of achievement motivation* (pp. 173–95). New York, NY: Academic Press. doi: 10.1016/b978-012750053-9/50009-7.

Renninger, K. A. & Hidi, S. (2011). Revisiting the conceptualization, measurement, and generation of interest. *Educational Psychologist, 46*(3), 168–84. doi: 10.1080/00461520.2011.587723.

Renninger, K. A. & Hidi, S. (2016). *The power of interest for motivation and engagement*. New York, NY: Routledge.

Renninger, K. A. & Lipstein, R. (2006). Come si sviluppa l'interesse per la scrittura; Cosa volgliono gli studenti e di cosa hannobisogno? [Developing interest for writing: What do students want and what do students need?] *Età Evolutiva, 84*, 65–83.

Renninger, K. A., Ren, Y., & Kern, H. M. (2018). Motivation, engagement, and interest: "In the end, it came down to you and how you think of the problem." In F. Fischer, C. E. Hmelo-Silver, S. R. Goldman, & P. Reimann (Eds.), *International handbook of the learning sciences* (pp. 116–26). New York, NY: Routledge.

Renninger, K. A. & Riley, K. R. (2013). Interest, cognition and the case of L- and science. In S. Kreitler (Ed.), *Cognition and motivation: Forging an interdisciplinary perspective* (pp. 352–82). Cambridge: Cambridge University Press.

Renninger, K. A. & Schofield, L. S. (2014). Assessing STEM interest as a developmental motivational variable. Poster presented in K. A. Renninger & S. E. Hidi (chairs), *Current Approaches to Interest Measurement*. Philadelphia, PA: American Educational Research Association.

Renninger, K. A. & Shumar, W. (2002). Community building with and for teachers: The Math Forum as a resource for teacher professional development. In K. A. Renninger & W. Shumar (Eds.), *Building virtual communities: Learning and change in cyberspace* (pp. 60–95). New York, NY: Cambridge University Press.

Renninger, K. A. & Wozniak, R. (1985). Effect of interest on attentional shift, recognition, and recall in young children. *Developmental Psychology, 21,* 624–32. doi:10.1037/0012-1649.21.4.624.

Rotgans, J. I. & Schmidt, H. G. (2017a). Interest development: Arousing situational interest affects the growth trajectory of individual interest. *Contemporary Educational Psychology, 49,* 175–84. doi: 10.1016./j.cedpsych/2017.02.003.

Rotgans, J. I. & Schmidt, H. G. (2017b). The relation between individual interest and knowledge acquisition. *British Educational Research Journal, 43*(2), 350–71. doi: 10.1002/berj.3268.

Sansone, C. & Thoman, D. B. (2005). Interest as the missing motivator in self-regulation. *European Psychologist, 10*(3), 175–86. doi: 10.1027/1016-9040.10.3.175.

Sansone, C., Weir, C., Harpster, L., & Morgan, C. (1992). Once a boring task always a boring task? Interest as a self-regulatory mechanism. *Journal of Personality and Social Psychology, 63*(3), 37990. doi:10.1037/0022-3514.63.3.379.

Schultz, W. (2007) Behavioural theories and the neurophysiology of reward. *Annual Review of Psychology, 57,* 87–115. doi: 10.1146/annurev.psych.56.091103.070229.

Sloboda, J. A. (1996). The acquisition of musical performance experience: Deconstructing the "talent" account of individual differences in musical expressivity. In K. A. Ericsson (Ed.), *The road to excellence: The acquisition of expert performance in the arts and sciences, sports, and games* (pp. 107–26). Mahwah, NJ: Lawrence Erlbaum Associates.

Swarat, S., Ortony, A., & Revelle, W. (2012). Activity matters: Understanding student interest in school science. *Journal of Research in Science and Teaching, 49*(4), 515–37. doi: 10.1002/tea.21010.

Thoman, D. B., Brown, E. R., Mason, A. Z., Harmsen, A. G., & Smith, J. L. (2015). The role of altruistic values in motivating underrepresented minority students for biomedicine. *BioScience, 65*(1), 183–88. doi: 10.1093/biosci/biu199.

Tröbst, S., Kleickmann, T., Lange-Schubert, K., Rothkopf, A., & Möller, K. (2016). Instruction and students' declining interest in science: An analysis of German fourth- and sixth-grade classrooms. *American Educational Research Journal, 53*(1), 162–93. doi: 10.3102/0002831215618662.

Turner, J. C., Kackar-Cam, H. Z., & Trucano, M. (2015). Teachers learning how to support student interest in mathematics and science. In K. A. Renninger, M. Nieswandt, & S. Hidi (Eds.), *Interest in mathematics and science learning* (pp. 243–60). Washington, DC: American Educational Research Association.

Walkington, C. A. & Bernacki, M. L. (2014). Motivating students by "personalizing" learning around individual interests: A consideration of theory, design, and implementation issues. In S. A. Karabenick & T. C. Urdan (Eds.),

Advances in motivation and achievement, Vol. 18: Motivational interventions (pp. 139–77). Bingley: Emerald Group Publishing Limited. doi: 10.1108/s0749-742320140000018004.

Wang, Z. & Adesope, O. (2016). Exploring the effects of seductive details with the 4-phase model of interest. *Learning and Motivation, 55*, 65–77. doi: 10.1016/j.lmot.2016.06.003.

Xu, J., Coats, L. T., & Davidson, M. L. (2012). Promoting student interest in science: The perspectives of exemplary African American teachers. *American Educational Research Journal, 49*(1), 124–54. doi: 10.3102/0002831211426200.

12 Online Affinity Networks as Contexts for Connected Learning

Mizuko Ito, Crystle Martin, Matthew Rafalow,
Katie Salen Tekinbaş, Amanda Wortman, and
Rachel Cody Pfister

Abstract: This chapter describes the ways in which online affinity networks motivate learning and support interest development. It builds on the model of "connected learning" that posits that learning is most resilient and meaningful when it is tied to social relationships and cultural identities, and spans in-school and out-of-school settings. The analysis draws from ethnographic case studies of youth-centered networks focused on fanfiction, knitting, professional wrestling, anime video remixers, Bollywood dance, YouTube vloggers, and communities surrounding two games, Little Big Planet 2 and StarCraft II. Factors that draw young people to online spaces to pursue their interests are diverse. For some, it is to find a safe space for a stigmatized interest. For others, it is because of an attraction to a narrow niche, leveling up, or technical specialization that is only accessible online. In all cases, however, high functioning online affinity networks are characterized by a strong set of shared values and culture that are the magnet for affiliation. In addition, a set of shared practices provide a focus of activity and engagement.

Amy was 17 years old when she was interviewed as part of Pfister's (2014, 2016) study of Ravelry.com (Ravelry), an online community for knitters and crocheters. Amy is an avid fiber crafter and pattern maker, and is also active on *Hogwarts at Ravelry*, a group within Ravelry focused on Harry Potter-related creations. Amy first learned to crochet from her grandmother and picked up knitting with her sister. Eventually she started to look online for designs and inspiration, and one of her friends introduced her to Ravelry. There she found a wealth of resources, new designs, and kindred spirits, including the sub-community of Harry Potter fans. One of Amy's hat designs, inspired by a hat in the sixth Harry Potter movie, has been "favorited" by 1,100 people and in the queue of more than 400 people as something that they would like to make.

We are grateful for the contributions to this research by Adam Ingram-Goble (Verve Mobile), Neta Kligler-Vilenchik (Hebrew University of Jerusalem), Ksenia Korobkova (University of California [UC], Irvine), Yong Ming Kow (City University of Hong Kong), Sangita Shresthova (University of Southern California [USC]), and Timothy Young (Twitch). This work was supported by two John D. and Catherine T. MacArthur Foundation grants.

She has begun selling her patterns on Ravelry and, with the support of her father, is planning to launch a blog and expand her business online. Her passion for the fiber arts has even sparked interest from her parents: her mother has started to crochet and her father has picked up knitting.

This chapter describes the ways in which online affinity networks motivate learning and support interest development in the context of shared culture and purpose. It builds on the model of "connected learning," which posits that learning is most resilient and meaningful when it is tied to social relationships and cultural identities, and spans in-school and out-of-school settings (Ito et al., 2013). Although Amy's story has much that is familiar to earlier generations, it is worth noting some important differences. In an earlier era, Amy would have pursued her interest in knitting and crocheting with her family, friends, and possibly, eventually, a local knitting circle or related group. She might have been able to find others in her local community who could introduce her to the intricacies of pattern design, but it is unlikely that she would have found a critical mass of knitters who were also Harry Potter fans. While she might have designed a Harry Potter-inspired hat based on her personal interest, she would not have been able to connect to an audience of thousands of other Harry Potter fans who also appreciated her design. It is also unlikely that she would have been able to sell and market her designs, given the niche nature of the audience and the lack of distribution channels in local communities. The online affinity network of Ravelry, and opportunities for online distribution and sales, vastly expanded Amy's ability to pursue a specialized interest, develop expertise, and connect this interest to future opportunities.

Factors that draw young people to online spaces to pursue their interests are diverse. For some, it is the need to find a safe space for a stigmatized interest. For others, it is an attraction to a narrow niche, leveling up, or technical specialization that is only accessible online. In all cases, however, high functioning online affinity networks are characterized by a strong set of shared culture and values that is the magnet for affiliation. In addition, a set of shared practices provides a focus of activity and engagement.

Young people like Amy are growing up in an environment of abundant connection to information, knowledge, and social interaction that offers new opportunities for learning and pursuing interests. Activities such as quickly googling for information, posting questions on specialized online forums, or publishing creative work online are now commonplace. It is easy to forget that these kinds of interactions have become widespread in the United States only in the last decade. These environments are a fertile ground for young people to engage in interest-driven learning, develop relationships centered on these interests, and contribute to shared causes and communities. They also provide unique case studies of interest development, learning, and motivation in which young people are connecting and contributing to communities where they feel a strong sense of affinity and belonging.

Building on a prior large-scale ethnographic study of online youth practices (Ito et al., 2010), the Leveling Up Study was designed to bring focus to online practices and networks that could bridge the divides between in-school and out-of-school learning. This chapter draws from ethnographic case studies of online affinity networks from the Leveling Up Study, as well as additional case studies from collaborating researchers in the Media, Activism, and Participatory Politics (MAPP) project. Our analysis pivots around how online affinity networks open up unique avenues for young people to find "their people" – peers and mentors who share an identity or interest. These case studies of affinity networks provide a lens through which to deepen our understanding of the relationships between social belonging, cultural affinity, learning, interests, and motivation.

After first describing the unique features of online affinity networks and how they relate to issues of learning and motivation, we describe the case study research that informs this chapter. In the second half of the chapter, we delve into the ethnographic material, illustrating how online affinity networks motivate participation and learning through shared culture and purpose.

Youth and Online Affinity Networks

Ever since its early days, the internet has been an avenue for people to connect with others around shared interests and identities, including fandoms, political discourse, gaming, and ethnic, religious, or LGBT identities. Rheingold (2000) described the unique bonding between participants in early online forums – like the Whole Earth 'Lectronic Link (The WELL) – in his book, *The virtual community*. Many other researchers followed in his footsteps by studying, for example, virtual worlds (Boellstorff, 2008; Kendall, 2002; Turkle, 2005), online groups of gamers (Nardi, 2010; Taylor, 2009), fans (Baym, 2000; Bury, 2005; Jenkins, 2008), and bloggers (Russell & Echchaibi, 2009). Eventually, internet platforms like MySpace and Facebook became mainstream, mirroring the everyday networks that we navigate in school, community, and workplace. At the same time, niche and interest-centered online communities also continued to proliferate, and they now encompass almost every imaginable affinity and pursuit. The internet has provided a new infrastructure for people to communicate and organize around interests and affinity with ease, and in a more pervasive way. For children and youth who have limited access to face-to-face affinity groups, the impact of online affinity networks is particularly profound.

In online affinity networks, young people are pursuing what, in our earlier Digital Youth research (Ito et al., 2010), we described as "interest-driven" learning and participation – they are going online to find information, communities, and learning resources that support specialized interests and affiliations that may not be available in their local communities. In our earlier study, LiveJournal was a gathering spot for these kinds of interactions, which later moved to platforms like Tumblr or Twitter. We contrasted this with "friendship-driven" forms of online communication that centered on MySpace and IM, and eventually text messages, Facebook, and Instagram. Teens might discuss romantic relationships and negotiate school-based popularity on Snapchat and Facebook, while they geek out on games, anime, or music on Tumblr and Twitter. While online affinity networks do utilize platforms like Facebook and Instagram, they also typically rely on sites and platforms that allow for more specialized forms of content creation, sharing, and reputation building. Young people describe how they segment their online identities between the friendship-driven and interest-driven platforms. For example, a young person's Facebook network might include both local school-based relationships and friends from online affinity networks, but they will also be connected to the affinity network through platforms and online communities focused on the interest area.

Online affinity networks share some characteristics with longstanding hobby and sports networks, but they are not characterized by the organizational contexts, infrastructures, and face-to-face relations that we associate with these place-based groups. We see continuity between place-based affinity networks and online affinity networks in that both support learning and participation centered on the pursuit of interests. What differentiates online affinity networks from the hobby and sports groups in a young person's local community is that they center on online space and infrastructure rather than brick-and-mortar organizations and settings. Although most hobby and interest groups now have some mix of online and place-based presence, online affinity networks are distinguished by their primary reliance on online infrastructure. We have identified three common features that characterize online affinity networks, which we elaborate in this section:

1. The network is *specialized*. It is centered on a specific affinity or interest, rather than being layered with other forms of affiliation. Organizations such as schools and workplaces can support affiliation based on specialized interests, but other affiliations and agendas come into play. In schools, teens negotiate romantic and peer relationships and academic competition, as well as pursue specialized interests. By contrast, in online affinity networks, teens' status centers on knowledge, expertise, and contribution to the interest area.
2. Involvement is *intentional*. It is a voluntary "chosen" affiliation, and not part of a formal professional, school, or governmental affiliation. While some online affinity networks may have formal markers of membership and leadership, contributions and involvement are driven by personal interest and choice. Participants move more fluidly in and out of engagement than in formal organizations that directly determine young people's academic and economic success.
3. Content sharing and communication takes place on *openly networked* online platforms. At least some dimension of every online affinity network

is discoverable on the "open" internet, without the gatekeeping of a financial transaction or formal institutional membership. Further, by definition, online affinity networks make use of digitally networked infrastructures that allow for broader visibility and access than place-based forms of communication.

As more and more young people go online, smartphones spread, and online affinity networks proliferate, we can expect that these networks will become more central to how young people socialize, learn, and pursue interests. In our earlier Digital Youth study, based on fieldwork in 2006–7, teens described a stigma associated with meeting new friends online – the pull of local relationships and the status and social capital derived from local place-based friendships exerted a much stronger influence on their online participation than did online affinity networks. This dynamic may be changing, however. Our current study was focused on active participants in online affinity networks, so it is not surprising that they were comfortable with making online friends through affinity groups. More recent survey research also indicates, however, that online friendships are becoming more and more commonplace. The majority of US teens now say they have met a new friend online (Lenhart et al., 2015). It is likely that the role of online affinity networks is growing in young people's lives.

How Affinity Networks Connect Interests to Learning

Researchers who study learning have increasingly recognized the role of culture, social relationships, and shared practice in the discovery of interests and the persistence in pursuing them. A growing body of research on the development of technical interests has documented how familial support (Crowley & Jacobs, 2002; Crowley et al., 2015), the availability of shared activities (Azevedo, 2011, 2013), and rapport with teachers and mentors (Maltese & Tai, 2010) play a more significant role than formal instruction in the development of scientific interests. Our research on young people and affinity networks reinforces these views of interest development. We draw from Azevedo's view that interests are an interaction between individual preferences and "lines of practice" – the ways in which interests are sustained over time through joint activities. We see an ongoing and dynamic interaction between individual inclinations and the network of relationships, affinities, and activities that are available in a young person's social world. Even when a young person has a strong personal passion for a particular interest area, involvement waxes and wanes depending on whether they feel a sense of belonging, have friends and mentors who share the interest, and have access to activities that sustain their involvement. We describe young people's personal predilection for an interest as an "affinity" in order to highlight its relational and culturally situated nature. A young person's demonstration of interest is grounded in personal preference as well as whether they can relate to the culture, people, and practices that embody the interest. Whether it is math, surfing, or knitting, interests cannot be separated from their culture, people, and places. These contextual features are fundamental drivers of young people's attraction to the area of interest.

We see our work on sociocultural contexts for interest development as complementary to psychological research that investigates how interest is triggered, sustained, and deepened (e.g., Renninger & Hidi, 2016), and we hope to build more bridges between these bodies of research. We see deepening interest as both "internally" developmental and as an "external" process of building connections that are relational, cultural, and practical in nature. In other words, robust interest is characterized by more rather than fewer situational ties; the focus of our investigation has been the development of these sociocultural ties and networks. In this we draw from a long tradition in sociocultural learning theory that recognizes how learning is part and parcel of belonging in situated practices (e.g., Brown, Collins, & Duguid, 1989; Cole, 1996; Lave & Wenger, 1991). Unlike the seminal case studies of situated learning in professional "communities of practice" (Lave & Wenger, 1991; Orr, 1990; Wenger, 1998), however, our cases center on networks of affinity and interests that are only loosely institutionalized. We draw broadly on sociocultural approaches in the learning sciences, but focus specifically on the unique forms of social learning that thrive in technology-enabled affinity networks.

How we support progression in learning and interest development is often viewed as a "pipeline" with a set of handoffs between educational institutions (see Figure 12.1). We argue that the network of informal supports is critically important to consider, in addition to the formal pipeline. Further, many informal supports, such as peer and family relationships or online affinity networks, transcend the boundaries of formal activities and organizational membership, and thus can be more resilient over time than relationships centered on a particular class, grade, or institution. If we return to the story of Amy, we can see that her process of developing interest and expertise relied on a growing network of relational supports, activities, and opportunities to share. Her online affinity network in *Hogwarts at Ravelry* helped fill gaps in her knowledge, as well as in her social and cultural supports, so that she could sustain her learning and interest in a unique specialization. Unlike an interest such as chess or basketball, which is often supported within schools and other community-based institutions, a specialization in knitting and pattern making would have been difficult to sustain without her online supports (see Figure 12.2).

The fundamental drivers of specialized, expert learning are the same as those we see in more traditional professional groups – learning in situ, sustained engagement with peers with related expertise, and productive social and cultural contributions. What differs is how Amy's interests are supported through an online, affinity-centered infrastructure that is only loosely institutionalized.

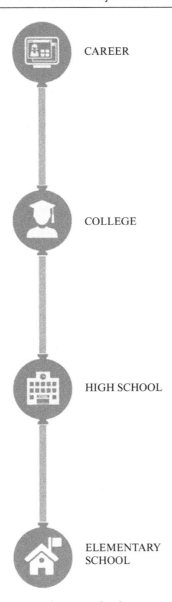

CAREER

COLLEGE

HIGH SCHOOL

ELEMENTARY
SCHOOL

Figure 12.1. *Learning and interest development as a pipeline, or progression.*
Image designed by Nat Soti.

An online affinity network is much more accessible than a formal professional
arts and crafts community or a community-based organization like a sports
team. Conversely, it has fewer ties to the local community and context of participants; this lack of support in the local community for a niche interest is
often what drives young people to online networks. In Amy's case, her family
provided local support for knitting, and the online setting enabled Amy to connect to a more specialized and expert community of Harry Potter-fan knitters.

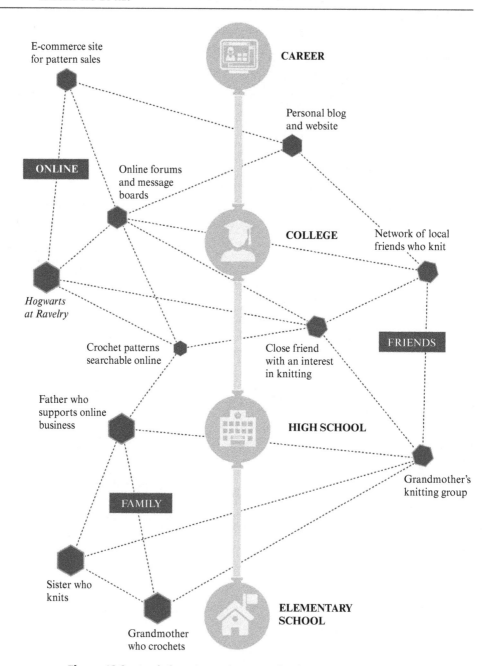

E-commerce site
for pattern sales

CAREER

Personal blog
and website

ONLINE

Online forums
and message
boards

COLLEGE

Network of local
friends who knit

*Hogwarts
at Ravelry*

Crochet patterns
searchable online

Close friend
with an interest
in knitting

FRIENDS

Father who
supports online
business

HIGH SCHOOL

Grandmother's
knitting group

FAMILY

Sister who
knits

**ELEMENTARY
SCHOOL**

Grandmother
who crochets

Figure 12.2. *Amy's learning and interest development as a process of network building. Image designed by Nat Soti.*

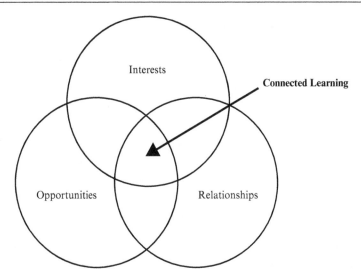

Figure 12.3. *Connecting the spheres of learning. Image designed by Katie Salen Tekinbaş.*

Our case studies of online affinity networks and connected learners like Amy enable us to understand these unique affordances of the online world, as well as reflect back on our assumptions about learning and interest development.

Although there are steps and pathways that young people traverse over time as they become more involved in an area of interest, connected learning is more appropriately conceived of as the growth of a network of connections than as a linear pathway or an internalization of skills and knowledge. Connected learners are situated within a set of personal and organizational relationships that knit together their interests and affinities, peer networks, and organizational sites of power and opportunity like schools, civic institutions, and workplaces (see Figure 12.3).

Online affinity networks can play a powerful role in connecting a young person's learning network, because they distill and make accessible a set of relationships and roles that are centered on personal interest and identities. For young people who do not have peers and mentors in their local community and organizations who share their interest, online affinity networks fill a vacuum in their connected learning network. Even with local supports for an interest, the online world can provide access to more depth and specialization. And when young people are able to connect the relationships and learning from their online affinity networks back to their local relationships and organizations, the outcomes can be transformational – opening up new educational pathways, civic engagements, and economic opportunity.

The Leveling Up Study

This chapter draws from case studies[1] of online affinity networks developed by researchers in the MacArthur Foundation-funded Connected Learning Research Network (CLRN) and Youth and Participatory Politics (YPP) Research Network.[2] The cases were not selected because they are typical of youth behaviors, but rather are positive examples that exhibit elements of connected learning. In this, the approach is akin to what those working in public health have described as a "positive deviance" model, which seeks out examples of practices in existing communities that can be spread and scaled to address systemic problems (Pascale et al., 2010). Our ethnographic case studies strategically sample from different populations and forms of social organization, combining in-depth, observational research with a comparative analysis that surfaces patterns and relationships between, as well as within, cases. We developed shared protocols and shared codes, using both a priori and emergent coding.[3] This cultural and practice-based analysis is still inter- pretive and qualitative in nature, and does not rest on the kinds of sampling approaches and claims for representativeness characteristic of quantitative research. But it does offer a way of analyzing patterns of social organiza- tion and cultural forms that exceed the bounds of conventional case-based

1 The case studies were conducted using different data-collection methodologies, and we have varying degrees of contextual information about our participants. In every case, if we know the information, then we have indicated age, gender, and participant-identified racial or ethnic identity. If this information is not indicated, then we did not know it for this participant due to the constraints of the particular case study. For example, in some of the studies that focus on online affinity networks, interviews were conducted over the phone or through online chat. In most cases, we derived this information from self-reports in background questionnaires admin- istered after most of our formal interviews. Although race is not the central analytic category in this chapter, there are times when we think it is relevant to our description, and we thought that if racial or ethnic identity were to be mentioned for some number of participants, then we needed to be symmetrical in our treatment and indicate racial identity for all respondents for whom we did have this information.

2 The Leveling Up project, part of the CLRN, and headed by Mizuko Ito at UC Irvine and Katie Salen Tekinbaş at UC Irvine, is the source of the majority of case studies. Members of the Leveling Up research team include: Adam Ingram-Goble of Verve Mobile; Ksenia Korobkova of UC Irvine; Yong Ming Kow of City University of Hong Kong; Crystle Martin of UC Irvine; Rachel Cody Pfister of UC San Diego; Matt Rafalow of UC Irvine; Amanda Wortman of UC Irvine; and Timothy Young of Twitch. Members of the MAPP project, led by Henry Jenkins at USC and part of the YPP network, have also contributed case material, including Neta Kligler-Vilenchik of Hebrew University of Jerusalem and Sangita Shresthova of USC.

3 The a priori coding scheme was derived from the framework and design principles developed by the CLRN in the report, *Connected learning: An agenda for research and design* (Ito et al., 2013). Each researcher coded the data they collected, and emerging themes were discussed often in coding meetings attended by all research team members. Analysis was facilitated by Dedoose, the first cloud-based qualitative analysis platform that is designed with an empha- sis on collaboration. Analysis of key constructs provided a pooled Cohen's Kappa of 0.91, indicating high inter-rater reliability. The case studies from the MAPP team, and Ito's prior research with anime fans, were not part of this more intensive research coordination process; that material was brought in more selectively, at a later phase of the analysis, to enrich the core findings established by the Leveling Up case analyses.

research. It is a form of qualitative "meta-analysis" that draws findings from across varied case research that addresses similar questions.

The Leveling Up project began in fall 2011, with the majority of the field-work taking place in 2012 and 2013. This work is unusual among qualitative field-based studies in that it includes cross-case analysis of a large number of complementary studies. The cases include a variety of affinity networks that make use of online spaces and employed research methods ranging from questionnaires, surveys, semi-structured interviews, and observation to content analyses of media, profiles, videos, and other online artifacts.[4] When we present ethnographic research in this chapter, we indicate from which of the case studies the example is drawn. To acknowledge young people as agents, we use the pseudonyms and ethnic and racial categories that our interviewees used to describe themselves. Here, we draw from five case studies conducted as part of the Leveling Up Study and from three other complementary cases of online affinity networks that were conducted as part of other research studies:

1. Ksenia Korobkova's *One Direction fanfiction* case study delved into an online fanfiction community, members of which are connected to each other in two ways: (1) with an online forum and other media outlets, and (2) through Directioner fan art.
2. The *Ravelry* case study, led by Rachel Cody Pfister, examined an online community and database for fiber crafting (knitting, crocheting, weaving, and spinning). The research focused on *Hogwarts at Ravelry*, an interest group that combines the interests of Harry Potter and fiber crafting to create a fictional universe.
3. Two gaming case studies examined the creative culture and practices among both players and industry game developers engaged with *LittleBigPlanet 2* and *StarCraft II*. Adam Ingram-Goble, Matthew Rafalow, Yong Ming Kow, Katie Salen Tekinbas, and Timothy Young collaborated on these two case studies.
4. The *professional wrestling fandom* case study, led by Crystle Martin, examined fan communities of professional wrestling, with a focus on fantasy wrestling through role-playing narratives.
5. The *anime music video (AMV) community* case study was conducted by Mizuko Ito as part of the earlier Digital Youth Study, and focused on a

4 Collectively, the Leveling Up research team conducted 166 semi-structured interviews and chronicled more than 1,500 hours of observation, which were cataloged in field notes. In addition, a demographic and media background survey was completed by 83 participants. Supplemental data from USC's Media, Activism, and Participatory Politics project include: 15 participant interviews, two expert interviews and 35 hours of observation for the Nerdfighter case study; and 120 interviews with dancers and choreographers globally (40 interviews in the United States), more than 200 hours of on-site observation, and extensive in-depth media analysis for the Bollywood case study. The Anime Music Video case study draws on 23 interviews, an online survey with 277 valid responses, and over 300 hours of observation at conventions and online.

sub-community of English-language fans of Japanese anime who create and share remixed videos.

6. The *Nerdfighter* case study, led by Neta Kligler-Vilenchik, was based on research from the MAPP project led by Henry Jenkins at USC, and part of the YPP network. It centered on an informal community formed around the YouTube vlog channel for brothers John and Hank Green. Many of the participants were high school and college age, united by a shared identity as "nerds" and a broad common goal of "decreasing world suck."

7. The *Bollywood dance* case study built on Sangita Shresthova's decade-long research on live Bollywood dance communities. This case study explored Bollywood dance as a participatory, interest-driven practice in the United States as it delves into the Hindi Film Dance competition scene on college campuses, and the online sharing of media related to these activities.

We sought out affinity networks and young people who exhibited "positive deviance" in that they were more likely than other affinity networks to exhibit elements of connected learning. We also sought out cases that represented a wide spectrum of online interests, taking care to include groups under-represented in research on online communities, specifically girls and black and Latino youth. The case studies of *StarCraft II* and *LittleBigPlanet 2* represent the more stereotypically "geeky" end of the spectrum, showcasing the state of the art in game development, networked community organization, and peer production. The *AMV* case also represents a highly tech savvy group, dominated by white and Asian young men. The case study of the *Nerdfighters*, from the MAPP project, describes a highly digitally activated geek community of predominantly young women that has pushed innovation in civic activation through digital networks. Our case study of professional wrestling fans represents an interest popular among black and Latino youth. The Bollywood case is centered on Asian young women. Two other cases were also selected because of their appeal to women and girls: the case study of the *One Direction (1D) fanfiction* affinity network taps into the energies of one of the most activated and mainstream fandoms for younger teenage girls, and *Ravelry* represents an older female age set, which has enabled us to look at intergenerational connections through an interest area that has stood the test of time.

Although encompassing a diverse range of interests and affinities, our case studies offer a window into the common characteristics of online affinity networks that support connected learning. These include strongly shared culture and practices, varied ways of contributing, high standards, and effective ways of providing feedback and help. Unlike much of the learning that young people encounter in school, affinity networks provide opportunities that are self-selected and intentional, and are also tied to contributions to social communities and authentic recognition in these communities. This can involve being a community organizer, publishing work online, competing in a public tournament, and providing feedback and expertise for others. Young people have historically had these kinds of opportunities for learning, contribution, and recognition in adult-sponsored athletics and the arts; the online world increases the possibilities, making these kinds of opportunities more varied, accessible, and youth driven.

Shared Culture and Purpose

Well-organized online affinity networks are successful in sustaining participation, deepening interests, and fueling learning because they are able to parlay participants' feelings of affinity into a sense of belonging and shared purpose. These contexts can be powerfully motivating, because they cultivate a niche or subcultural identity and engage participants in sometimes epic shared endeavors or friendly competition. We discuss these features of online affinity networks in terms of shared culture and shared purpose.

Shared Culture

At the heart of any affinity network is a set of shared interests, identities, culture, and values that binds participants together. Although online affinity networks exist for every imaginable interest area, they are particularly active and robust for groups that are specialized, lack a critical mass in local communities, and hold to high standards of knowledge and expertise. In other words, people tend to congregate in online affinity networks when they want to geek out with others who are passionate experts and they lack these relationships in their offline lives. They often feel a particularly profound sense of belonging to these groups because of this shared niche culture and identity.

For example, shared interests in fiber crafting and Harry Potter is a niche combination that lacks a critical mass in most local communities, but is a magnet for over 1,000 participants to connect on Ravelry. "We all belong here," said Amazon, a white, 28-year-old *Hogwarts at Ravelry* member based in Cleveland. Her description of why she loves *Hogwarts at Ravelry* captures how a shared passion for a niche interest binds members of an online affinity network:

> The camaraderie and instant friendship, especially in your own house, though interhouse love is also prevalent. I can talk to someone I've never met before and because of the history inherent at Hogwarts, we've passed each other in the halls a thousand times. We go to the same charms class. We know the same lingo, share the same inside jokes.

Amazon describes the unique pleasure of sharing cultural context and insider references with others with shared tastes, passions, and expertise. Rich content worlds like the Harry Potter series offer a treasure trove of specialized knowledge that provides ample fodder for geeking out and social organizing by engaged fan communities (Jenkins, 2012).

Anime fandom also supports a wide range of highly specialized affinity networks within the fandom. The AMV scene is one such niche, a network that centers around the specific practices of video remixing within the broader anime fandom. Gepetto, an 18-year-old from Brazil who had been an anime fan for some time, describes the moment when he first discovered AMVs. He was shocked to realize that the AMV was created by "a fan just like me." As he recounts this memory, he continues, "Actually, my heart is racing right now just remembering. Of course, I'm a weird person but it's still racing." After discovering AMVs, Gepetto went on to become an active participant in animemusicvideos.org, a center of gravity for the AMV community. "I love the forums, I love the chats, I love answering questions and having mine answered in turn. I could spend 24 hours straight discussing AMVs without so much as a coffee break." His ongoing interest and engagement is fueled by the shared referents and connoisseurship of anime, as well as by the deep technical expertise around video remixing that is discussed in the forums.

Competitive esports like *StarCraft II* represent a highly tuned arena for players and fans to compete in and strive for excellence. In these competitive affinity networks, young people will connect online or in tournaments outside their local community in order to pursue an ongoing challenge. Often their affinity network will include a mix of local peers as well as online networks that allow them to specialize and level up. Mona,[5] a 22-year-old Asian college student from New Jersey, vividly recalled how relationships forged through *StarCraft II* motivated her to do her best in game matches; she remembered "getting butterflies in my stomach because I have to play for my team and I don't want to let them down." Mark, a junior in high school from California, recalled how watching a *StarCraft II* tournament and feeling a part of a community that shared his passion provided the rush and drive to pursue his interest in *StarCraft II*. Remembering the tournament, he described, "I can't even emphasize how addicted that made me to *StarCraft* as a game. I saw that and I was like, this is it. This is the game that I'm going to play. This is the community that I want to be a part of and this is what I want to do for a really long time."

Another pull for young people to connect online comes if an interest is stigmatized. Online affinity networks provide an attractive safe haven, even when young people might have local friends who share the interests. This was true for both the One Direction fanfiction writers and the members of *The Wrestling Boards*, where some felt they needed to hide their interests from their local communities. Tween and teen obsession over boy bands is often culturally devalued, particularly among adults, and many fans of One Direction didn't share their interests with teachers and parents. Katie, a 15-year-old white girl in Australia, said that although she was a prolific writer, she did not feel comfortable telling her teachers about her fanfiction because they "wouldn't get it plus they would ask questions."

---

5 Real name used with permission.

Although many WWE fans came into the interest through their families, the interest is often stigmatized among peers. Jonathan, a white, 16-year-old participant on *The Wrestling Boards* from England, said that wrestling was viewed negatively in his area, and that "no one that I know likes WWE as they see it as being 'childish' or 'immature.'" WacoKid, a white and Native American male in his 30s from Texas, said that although conversations in his local community would sometimes reveal people's wrestling interests, it was generally something that people kept to themselves and did not openly discuss or participate in: "For the most part, WWE fans (or any pro wrestling fans) around here seem to be in the closet." For these fans, their wrestling interests were not just unsupported by their local communities but were something to be hidden.

Shared Purpose

Activity in online affinity networks is fueled by shared practices that give purpose to participation in the network. Unlike purely social online "hanging out," online affinity networks involve organized production, collaboration, and competition. These networks are examples of what Jenkins et al. (2009) have called "participatory culture" – "a culture with relatively low barriers to artistic expression and civic engagement, strong support for creating and sharing one's creations, and some type of informal mentorship whereby what is known by the most experienced is passed along to novices" (p. xi). In affinity networks, participants are not simply consuming media, but are actively involved in creation, circulation, curation, and commentary. We describe the shared practices of online affinity networks in two categories: collaborative production, and contests and challenges.

Collaborative production. Collaborative production offers members the opportunity to engage in meaningful and hands-on learning where they blend skills, envision new creations, and build affinity as they work toward the shared purpose of the community (Ito, 2012; Ito et al., 2013; Moran & John-Steiner, 2004; Searle, 2004).

In *The Wrestling Boards,* members role-play as wrestlers, write background stories for their characters, and carry out wrestling matches with other members through the coordinated exchange of creative writing and role-play. *Hogwarts at Ravelry* members similarly use role-playing and crafting to build a fantasy world that parallels the Hogwarts of the Harry Potter series. For example, in a discussion about moving a conversation to a different message board thread, Knitting Principal,[6] the leader of *Hogwarts at Ravelry* and a white woman from Idaho, switched to role-play and began *"waving wand frantically ... shouting WHOOSH!!!"* In other small moments, members "dropped their suitcases" in the discussion threads for their houses as new school years

---

6 Real screen name used with permission.

began and sometimes would "trip over broomsticks" lying around in classes. These small moments of role-play continually reinforce the fantasy world of the group. Images of crafted items are also abundant and help create a visual representation of the fantasy world; Hagrid's pumpkin patch was recreated through knit pumpkin toys and crocheted pot holders, and members filled the Great Hall's tables with images of crocheted food items at Thanksgiving.

The Bollywood Dance case study is of an online affinity network centered on production and competition in dance performance. Members of university dance teams combine specialized skills and work together to craft a Bollywood dance performance. Akash, a college student from California, used his engineering skills to build props, his musical interests to research and develop hip-hop inspired choreography, and his filmography interests to create introductory videos for his team's competitions. Neesha, a college student from Palo Alto, learned to use GarageBand to create sound mixes for her team. Other roles included costume designing, fundraising, and the creation of stories for performances.

The One Direction fan community of Wattpad centers on the production of fanfiction and media related to One Direction. While most fanfiction benefits from some type of collective feedback or suggestions, some authors also create "collab-accounts" through which multiple authors collaboratively author a work. It is also common for members to work collaboratively on a project through a "blending of skills" (Moran & John-Steiner, 2004, p. 11). For example, one person may write a fanfiction story and another person creates the book cover graphics to accompany it. Additionally, some members work together to collaboratively produce GIFs (short looping digital images) around their One Direction interests. Similarly, Nerdfighters use collab channels on YouTube to help overcome some of the challenges of online production. Creative production is a high-effort endeavor. Producing a video involves multiple stages of planning, scripting, filming, editing, posting, and tagging. By joining forces, young Nerdfighters lower the bar to entry for posting videos to YouTube, as well as the expectation of maintaining constantly updated content.

The *Sackboy Planet* affinity network also offers an example of how collaborative production involves combining and blending specialized knowledge and skills. The shared purpose of this affinity network is the construction of *LittleBigPlanet 2* game levels. *Sackboy Planet* members devote much of their creative energy to level design, *LittleBigPlanet 2*'s most innovative feature. Many complex skills go into level creation, including game design, programming, art, story development, and scripting. Players use the level design forum of *Sackboy Planet* to find others with whom to create levels; they post a thread asking others with specific skill sets to join forces and create a level. Co-creation presents opportunities for designers to combine their specific design skills and ideas in a way that can produce a collaborative and creative synergy. Ninjadude, a white 19-year-old from the United States, pointed out that collectively sharing insights and new ideas was an important part of level creation. When players asked him for help, he will "take a look at it and try to figure it out," and he has gone "in and helped them with specific things."

Sackboy Planet demonstrates how collaborative production can play a powerful role in supporting shared purpose through building connections and combining skills. Players acquire and advance their skills through meaningful activities, embodying their learning as they build, tinker, and troubleshoot levels. The complex and diverse skills required to build levels encourage players to form connections with others and combine their specialized knowledge, gain creative insights, and produce a more masterful level than any one player could build. This collaborative production advances individual learning, but it also advances the collective shared purpose through building affinity and producing more creative and more expert levels.

Contests and challenges. Contests and challenges are another category of collective practice that help motivate and structure engagement in most online affinity networks. They are particularly salient in affinity networks centered on competitive games like *StarCraft II*, whose online platform matches players based on past performance on "the ladder," providing continuous challenge, transparent ranking, and the potential for leveling up. In addition to this everyday play and practice, the *StarCraft II* community organizes a host of tournaments for different levels of players, including the pro leagues, the after-hours gaming league for working professionals, the *Collegiate Starleague*, and the *High School Starleague*. Another popular social format is "BarCraft," where players commandeer sports bars for after-work viewings of esports competitions. Social viewing of this kind is an important vehicle for players and fans to develop a more sophisticated understanding of sports. Games like *StarCraft* have earned the moniker "esports" because of similarities with traditional sports; esports has professional players, spectators and fans, and high-stakes competitions. Further, because players can compete at any time of day or night with comparatively little physical exhaustion, the performance and practice demands of esports are in some ways more relentless than traditional athletics.

Competition is a source of creative inspiration in *Over the Ropes,* the fantasy wrestling federation of *The Wrestling Boards*. Writers co-construct fantasy wrestling matches using role-play and narratives. At the beginning of a season, players describe their character's background, physical characteristics, wrestling style, moves, and appearance. If their wrestler is selected by the Booker, who manages the fantasy wrestling federation and can be selected from anyone in the community, the player spends the first part of the week role-playing dialogue with their opponent and co-constructing a storyline. Rubin, for example, role-played as his wrestler Trent Dixon and taunted his opponent, "Do whatever the hell you want, chuck in another seven guys for all I care, I'll just dismantle them in exactly the way I plan to do to Exterminator." The Booker awards points for quality, authenticity, and quantity. At the end of the week, the exchanges (or "feuds") between the two wrestlers are compiled into a narrative, with the winner determined by the number of points given by the Booker. Better collaboration results in a better storyline, meaning the accumulation of more points. The point system becomes a powerful way to reward collaborative competitions and group participation, and to motivate members to accumulate more wrestling knowledge and improve their writing abilities.

Similarly, a competitive narrative powers the fantasy world of *Hogwarts at Ravelry*. The penultimate competition is the House Cup, for which the different houses – or sub-communities of the group – compete. Members participate in classes and challenges that ask them to learn more about their Harry Potter interests, advance their crafting skills, and embody this learning through producing crafted items. Professor Briana,[7] an active community member from Utah, asked students to complete a star chart, wherein they would discover that major Harry Potter characters were named after stars and constellations. One herbology class assignment asked Mary, a 21-year-old white woman in Canada, to learn more about the magical herb gillyweed and craft an item with "bobbles" to represent it. Through this assignment, Mary drew on her knowledge of the fourth Harry Potter book, and she looked to a knitting book and then to her mother to learn the bobble stitch.

LittleBigPlanet players at times organize contests that would appeal to other players. For example, Jaron (27 years old, white, and from the United States) was "helping plan and execute the very first LBP Hunger Games competition." Ninjadude organized a contest that was a "caption contest," where the organizer would give a "blank scene that would be kind of funny and everyone would enter and put their caption on. What are the sack people in this thing thinking or saying?" This provided a very different type of participation in the *LittleBigPlanet 2* affinity network than the usual game playing and level creation, while still drawing on the shared interests of the players.

In the Bollywood dance scene, competitions are a growing force in structuring and motivating participation. They include both regional and national events, with Bollywood America as the penultimate competition. Thousands of dancers organize through Facebook and more specialized channels such as desidanceteams.com. Preparing for a competition is a major production, which includes not only choreographing and practicing dance, but fundraising, creating videos, and making props and costumes. This pride and excitement around creative competitions is also evident in Wattpad, where a range of official and community-sponsored challenges are an ongoing focus of attention for young writers. In particular, the annual Watty awards are a centerpiece of the competitive landscape of Wattpad. The AMV world also organizes around competitions. Most major anime conventions feature an AMV screening and competition, which is one of the most well-attended events. Xstylus, a

7 Real name used with permission.

28-year-old white male, describes the moment when his video was recognized as a winner at a major convention:

> The massive auditorium gave me a standing ovation. The only people who could ever come close to experiencing such a feeling are Hollywood directors having won an Academy Award for Best Picture. It was the finest, greatest, most moving moment of my entire existence. Nothing will ever top it. Ever.

Winning competitions is the penultimate form of recognition for video editors, and awards are proudly displayed on their online profiles. AMV also organizes an annual viewers' choice awards, in addition to a wide range of "top" lists and rankings, that is based on community scoring and reviews of videos.

Concluding Thoughts

Online affinity networks are a unique genre of social and cultural organization that has emerged with the growth of digital networks. These online networks share many similarities with affinity networks that are rooted in places, such as sports, creative groups, and other community-based organizations. What makes them unique, however, is that they are leveraging open online networks to create more specialized niches with relatively low barriers to participation. This means that young people today have the opportunity to connect with peers who share interests that may not have a critical mass in their local communities or in their families, and to go much deeper in these specialties. While our research indicates how online affinity networks can fuel the development of interest and expertise, few educational institutions are tapping into these networks. In addition, our research highlights the positive learning potential of online affinity networks, but we recognize that most young people are not reaping the learning benefits of these forms of engagement. Harnessing the learning potential of these networks for all youth would require more investigation and design research on how to effectively connect these communities of interest to our educational institutions, workplaces, and civic organizations.

References

Azevedo, F. S. (2011). Lines of practice: A practice-centered theory of interest relationships, cognition and instruction. *Cognition and Instruction, 29*(2), 147–84. doi: 10.1080/07370008.2011.556834.

Azevedo, F. S. (2013). The tailored practice of hobbies and its implication for the design of interest-driven learning environments. *Journal of the Learning Sciences, 22*(3), 462–510. doi: 10.1080/10508406.2012.730082.

Baym, N. (2000). *Tune in, log on: Soaps, fandom, and online community*. Thousand Oaks, CA: Sage Publications.

Boellstorff, T. (2008). *Coming of age in second life: An anthropologist explores the virtually human*. Princeton, NJ: Princeton University Press.

Brown, J. S., Collins, A., & Duguid, P. (1989). Situated cognition and the culture of learning. *Educational Researcher*, *18*(1), 32–42. doi: 10.3102/0013189X018001032.

Bury, R. (2005). *Cyberspaces of their own: Female fandoms online*. New York, NY: Peter Lang Publishing.

Cole, M. (1996). *Cultural psychology: A once and future discipline*. Cambridge, MA: The President and Fellows of Harvard College.

Crowley, K., Barron, B., Knutson, K., & Martin, C. K. (2015). Interest and the development of pathways to science. In K. A. Renninger, M. Nieswandt, & S. Hidi (Eds.), *Interest in mathematics and science learning*. Washington, DC: AERA.

Crowley, K. & Jacobs, M. (2002). Building islands of expertise in everyday family activity. In G. Leinhardt, K. Crowley, & K. Knutson (Eds.), *Learning conversations in museums* (pp. 333–56). Mahwah, NJ: Lawrence Erlbaum Associates.

Ito, M. (2012). Contributors versus leechers: Fansubbing ethics and a hybrid public culture. In M. Ito, D. Okabe, & I. Tsuji (Eds.), *Fandom unbound: Otaku culture in a connected world* (pp. 179–204). New Haven, CT: Yale University Press.

Ito, M., Baumer, S., Bittanti, M., Boyd, D., Cody, R., Herr-Stephenson, B., ... Tripp, L. (2010). *Hanging out, messing around, and geeking out: Kids living and learning with new media*. Cambridge, MA: MIT Press.

Ito, M., Guitiérrez, K., Livingstone, S., Penuel, B., Rhodes, J., Salen, K., ... Watkins, C. S. (2013). *Connected learning: An agenda for research and design*. Irvine, CA. Retrieved from http://dmlhub.net/publications/connected-learning-agenda-research-and-design.

Jenkins, H. (2008). *Convergence culture: Where old and new media collide*. New York, NY: New York University Press.

Jenkins, H. (2012). "Cultural acupuncture": Fan activism and the Harry Potter Alliance. *Transformative Works and Cultures*, *10*. doi: 10.1057/9781137350374_11.

Jenkins, H., Purushotma, R., Weigel, M., Clinton, K., & Robison, A. J. (2009). *Confronting the challenges of participatory culture: Media education for the 21st century*. Cambridge, MA: MIT Press.

Kendall, L. (2002). *Hanging out in the virtual pub: Masculinities and relationships online*. London: University of California Press.

Lave, J. & Wenger, E. (1991). *Situated learning: Legitimate peripheral participation*. New York, NY: Cambridge University Press.

Lenhart, A., Smith, A., Anderson, M., Duggan, M., & Perrin, A. (2015). *Teens, technology & friendships*. Washington, DC. Retrieved from www.pewinternet.org/files/2015/08/Teens-and-Friendships-FINAL2.pdf.

Maltese, A. V. & Tai, R. H. (2010). Eyeballs in the fridge: Sources of early interest in science. *International Journal of Science Education*, *32*(5), 669–85. doi: 10.1080/09500690902792385.

Moran, S. & John-Steiner, V. (2004). How collaboration in creative work impacts identity and motivation. In D. Miell & K. Littleton (Eds.), *Collaborative creativity: contemporary perspectives* (pp. 11–25). London: Free Association Books.

Nardi, B. (2010). *My life as a night elf priest: An anthropological account of world of warcraft*. Ann Arbor, MI: University of Michigan Press.

Orr, J. (1990). Sharing knowledge, celebrating identity: War stories and community memory in a service culture. In D. S. Middleton & D. Edwards (Eds.), *Collective remembering: Memory in society* (pp. 169–189). Beverly Hills, CA: Sage Publications.

Pascale, R., Sternin, J., & Sternin, M. (2010). *The power of positive deviance: How unlikely innovators solve the world's toughest problems.* Cambridge, MA: Harvard Business Review Press.

Pfister, R. C. (2014). *Hats for house elves: Connected learning and civic engagement in* Hogwarts at Ravelry. Irvine, CA: Digital Media and Learning Hub.

Pfister, R. C. (2016). *Unraveling Hogwarts: Understanding an affinity group through the lens of activity theory* (Unpublished doctoral dissertation). San Diego, CA.

Renninger, K. A. & Hidi, S. (2016). *The power of interest for motivation and engagement.* New York, NY: Routledge.

Rheingold, H. (2000). *The virtual community: Homesteading on the electronic frontier.* Cambridge, MA: MIT Press.

Russell, A. & Echchaibi, N. (Eds.). (2009). *International blogging: Identity, politics and networked publics.* New York, NY: Peter Lang Publishing.

Searle, R. H. (2004). Creativity and innovation in teams. In D. Miell & K. Littleton (Eds.), *Collaborative creativity: Contemporary perspectives* (pp. 175–88). London: Free Association Books.

Taylor, T. L. (2009). *Play between worlds: Exploring online game culture.* Cambridge, MA: MIT Press.

Turkle, S. (2005). *The second self: Computers and the human spirit.* Cambridge, MA: MIT Press.

Wenger, E. (1998). *Communities of practice: Learning, meaning, and identity.* New York, NY: Cambridge University Press.

13 Multiple Points of Access for Supporting Interest in Science

Joyce M. Alexander, Kathy E. Johnson,
and Carin Neitzel

Abstract: *The pipeline metaphor used to characterize dwindling interest in science and STEM-related careers has gradually been replaced by alternative models that convey complex pathways into, through and out of science by young men and women. In this chapter, we review literatures from educational psychology, cognitive development, and science education and present our own mixed methods approach to developing a model of the roles that children, parents and teachers play in launching, supporting, and sustaining pathways to science interest from early childhood to the transition to college. We use our longitudinal data to describe cases that illustrate these critical developmental inflection points. These rich cases illustrate the advantages of using qualitative methods, when possible, to augment developmental models derived from more quantitative approaches depicted through path diagrams, phase models, or Sankey diagrams. The cases discussed highlight critical roles that parents and teachers might play in nurturing science interests among males and females. Implications for future research and suggestions for practice are considered.*

> *Development, in fact, may be viewed best as a set of multiple developmental trajectories, and our task as developmentalists is to discover how the interplay between different trajectories of children and adults accounts for outcomes (Parke et al., 1994, p. 47).*

Very young children's interest in the natural world and their receptiveness to informal science learning opportunities would seem to bode well for nurturing later educational and career interests related to science. Yet in the United States, a stubborn gap persists in the numbers of jobs available related to science, technology, engineering, and mathematics (STEM) and the employees available to fill them (President's Council of Advisors on Science and Technology, 2012). In explaining the discrepancy between STEM interests early in childhood versus during the transition to postsecondary education,

This research was supported by grants from the National Science Foundation and by funding from the Noyce Foundation. We are tremendously grateful to the many graduate and undergraduate students, as well as the children (now young adults) and family members, who have participated enthusiastically in our research for many years.

the metaphor of a leaky pipeline frequently has been used (e.g., Institute for Higher Education Policy, 2015), though not without criticism (Metcalf, 2014). The notion of a pipeline implies that people flow passively through pipes, passing or not passing relevant benchmarks, and that women and individuals from underrepresented groups are particularly prone to leaking out along the way, yielding a flow into STEM fields that leaves much to be desired. The metaphor also suggests that effective policy might best be directed at patching the leaks – an approach that clearly has not met with much success despite millions of dollars invested in K–20 efforts, such as co-curricular programming, curricular reform, and expanding research opportunities (Committee on Equal Opportunity in Science and Engineering (CEOSE), 2015).

More recently the pipeline metaphor has begun to be replaced by the notion of pathways. Rather than an increasingly narrow trickle of graduates passing through a leaky pipe, the pathway metaphor recognizes that there are multiple routes into and through STEM education and careers, and that the notion of a pipeline fails to describe nearly half of the individuals who ultimately end up in traditional STEM occupations (Cannady et al., 2014). In this chapter, we describe our own developing model of the roles of children, parents, and teachers in launching, supporting, and sustaining pathways to science interest across developmental time.

We use the pathway framework to more deeply consider key transitions or points of inflection that may lead to a science interest in the first two decades of life. Some of these inflection points might be significant and aligned with critical milestones, such as experience with a robotics team at the transition to middle school or a summer research experience in high school. Others may be more innocuous and folded within the confines of early childhood family activities, discussions at science museums during middle childhood, or watching inspiring documentaries about scientific discoveries. Much of the research on STEM career pathways has taken advantage of national longitudinal samples that capture patterns of course-taking behaviors and selection of majors. Such analyses are far less apt to take into account students' interests, motivations, and goal orientation, or instructors' or parents' comfort with teaching or supporting children in learning about STEM fields and the resulting quality of instruction. Finally, such research typically fails to consider that early in adulthood, career decisions often unfold against a complex backdrop of other significant life events, such as finding a life partner and beginning to raise a family (Clausen, 1986; Kerckhoff, 1993; McAdams, 1988).

In the present chapter we use data from a longitudinal study of interest development, extending from early childhood through the transition to college, to consider such inflection points in detail. We dwell upon multiple points of access along the pathway to science interests and science learning that unfold throughout primary and secondary education, and use case study analyses to illuminate and evaluate the variations in on-ramps (opportunities to take up science interests) and off-ramps (factors that lead to the diminishment of science interests) that impact male and female students.[1]

In the next section we highlight some typical approaches or "prototypes" for describing and explaining pathways into science interests or STEM-related career plans, discussing unique strengths of each approach as well as potential drawbacks. Following this, we describe our own developing model of the roles of children, parents, and teachers in launching, supporting, and sustaining science interests across developmental time. The remaining sections are devoted to descriptions of key inflection moments that mark different access points for supporting science interests, augmented by more detailed cases that help illustrate these on-ramps and occasional off-ramps.

Depicting the Pathways To and Through STEM Interests

It is complicated to trace the on-ramps to science pathways based at home, in school, or through co-curricular experiences across developmental time partly because engagement with science means different things at different points in the first two decades of life. For example, consider three different socio-temporal contexts for a student's interaction with a natural history museum exhibit on dinosaurs. A five-year-old with an intense interest related to dinosaurs might attempt to soak up every detail of the exhibit, proudly announcing to her parents the facts that she's committed to memory from being read various library books, and insisting on dwelling for lengthy periods of time on interactive exhibit components with a willing parent. In contrast, that same child might engage with the exhibit far less enthusiastically and for considerably less time as a middle school student on a field trip surrounded by a crowd of friends who dismissively state that dinosaurs are for babies and therefore completely uncool. Finally, that same person, as a young woman visiting the museum the summer before she starts college to prepare for a future career as a paleontologist, might carefully critique the information provided, formulating questions to ask the museum educator and perhaps noticing gaps in the scientific knowledge base that beg to be filled by future scientists. Researchers concentrating on the interaction between the developmental level of the child and either science interests or science achievement can find it challenging to depict the complex changing patterns of relationships that evolve across socio-familial and educational settings.

---

1 Some organizations and affiliated researchers restrict the definition of STEM or science interests to a very narrow set (e.g., the National Science Foundation, 2011 focuses on mathematics, engineering, computer science, and physics). The Organisation for Economic Co-operation and Development (OECD, 2007), however, defines STEM professionals as including life science, health, and teaching professionals, adding those based on the biological sciences. We prefer this broader definition and use it in this chapter, as many early childhood activities involve engagement with the natural world and with animals, which may lay foundational knowledge related to biology.

There are three general approaches to addressing this challenge. Our intent is not to complete a thorough review of these alternative approaches, but rather to highlight a "prototype" for each and to consider the general strengths and weaknesses of each approach. Taken together, they highlight a series of inflection points that we propose the field consider as opportunities to initiate, sustain, or potentially diminish science interest and involvement in science-relevant activities over developmental time. The three general categories include Sankey diagrams, Phase theories, and structural equation modeling or path analyses.

Sankey Diagrams

Increasingly, researchers have turned to Sankey diagrams, originally developed to convey the flow of energy through a steam engine, to illustrate the relative proportions of individuals who traverse various pathways into (or away from) STEM careers. As an example, Cannady et al. (2014) present data from the 1988 National Educational Longitudinal Study to categorize science pathways for four groupings of individuals. The groups were created by crossing two well-known predictors of STEM career engagement: completion of calculus in high school and an expressed career interest related to STEM. The resultant data illustrates that all four pathways yielded some entrants into STEM careers, though at varying levels of frequency. As noted earlier, such alternative pathways are rarely considered in the traditional pipeline metaphor, leading Cannady et al. to champion the notion that some students "fall off the beaten path" to find their way into STEM careers despite the odds that seem to be against them at the conclusion of high school. Sadler et al. (2012) also have used Sankey diagrams to compare student career interests at the start and end of high school as a function of gender. Bergstrom et al. (2016) used Sankey diagrams to illustrate how individuals who leave one subdiscipline of STEM often end up with interests in other STEM-related disciplines (see Figure 13.1 for an illustration).

Sankey diagrams are a significant improvement over the pipeline metaphor, because they enable the reader to visualize the relative flow of individuals into and out of a science interest as a function of a category or "type" to which the individual belongs. Both the on-ramps and off-ramps are readily observable, and one can quickly glean information regarding the prevalence of each pathway from the relative widths of the lines used to depict them. The Sankey diagram is not useful for helping convey the underlying mechanism for *why* a particular individual traverses a path. The model also depends heavily on the validity of the categories used to group individuals and presumes that those categories are mutually exclusive. For example, Sadler et al. (2012) grouped individuals based on their career interests at particular time points in high school, which presumes that a student could not simultaneously harbor career interests for both medicine and engineering, for example, despite the

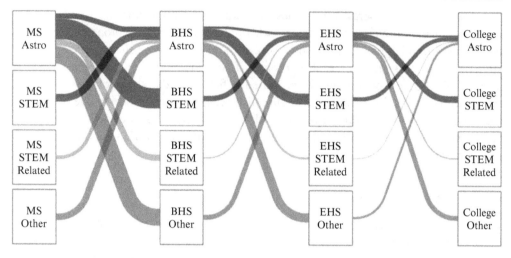

Figure 13.1. *Sankey diagram of inflow and outflow for students from middle school through college illustrating how students interested in one STEM subfield often move to another STEM subfield over developmental time. Reprinted with permission from "Evolution and persistence of students' astronomy career interests: A gender study," by Z. Bergstrom, P. Sadler, & G. Sonnert, 2016,* Journal of Astronomy & Earth Sciences Education, *3, p. 77–92. http://dx.doi.org/10.19030/jaese.v3i1.9690. Note:* MS refers to middle school, BHS refers to the beginning of high school, and EHS refers to the end of high school.

existence of career paths that span both, such as biomechanical and biomedical engineering.

Phase Models

A second way of depicting shifts over time in levels of interest in or depth of engagement with STEM is to focus on phases or stages that emerge over time. Development is reflected through temporal covariation with the phases or through an explicit recognition that some phase transitions cannot occur until a particular level of cognitive development has been achieved. Phase models can take into account both the developmental status of the individual and the individual's receptivity to different types of environmental influences at different points in time. For example, Hidi and Renninger's (2006) Four-Phase Model of interest development articulates a developmental continuum from *situational* to *individual* interests, with each phase marked by an initial emergence and a more stable period marked by varying levels of knowledge, value, and positive affect. Situational interests involve the focused attention and positive affective response that may suddenly be triggered (phase 1) and then maintained (phase 2) through supportive environmental conditions (Hidi & Baird, 1986; Hoffman, 2002; Mitchell, 1993). Eventually, individual interests emerge (phase 3) when the interest transitions to a more enduring psychological state accompanied by relevant stored knowledge, positive affect, and a sense of value that motivates re-engagement in activities aligned with the interest domain (Renninger, 1989, 2000; Renninger & Wozniak, 1985). Finally, a well-developed individual interest (phase 4) involves the enhancing and deepening of interest to the point where it serves as a foundation for self-regulated and independent learning and can be maintained in the face of frustration (Lipstein & Renninger, 2007). More recently, Renninger and Riley (2013) expanded this model to describe the four phases of interest development as a function of both learner characteristics and the needs that the learner has across open versus closed learning environments, as depicted in Table 13.1.

Phase models acknowledge that individuals (and, in this case, their levels of interest) change over time. They also allow researchers to consider different types of environmental support that might be fruitful in different phases of development. For example, Tytler et al. (2008) map out the factors associated with both home and school that influence students' engagement with STEM across the entire period of formal K–12 instruction. Phase models do not generally take into account individual differences, such as developmental level, levels of previously acquired knowledge, personality, or other sociocultural traits that may influence the rate of progress through the phases (see Alexander et al., 2015 for one exception). They also are inherently linear and may not adequately explain why some individuals might ultimately plateau at a particular phase, or even regress to an earlier phase.

Path Diagrams

Finally, many researchers have used path diagrams and traditional structural equation modeling to help explain pathways to STEM careers, STEM coursework in college, or variables related to STEM achievement. For example, Gottfried et al. (2016) analyzed the relation between parents' stimulation of children's curiosity at age eight years and children's subsequent science intrinsic motivation, science achievement, and intent to pursue science or "science acquisition." The model depicted in Figure 13.2 suggests that there is not a direct path between stimulation of curiosity during the elementary school years and science acquisition. Rather, the relation to science acquisition is indirect, emerging through the positive and significant direct relations between parents' stimulation of curiosity and both science intrinsic motivation and science achievement.

Structural equation models or path analyses permit researchers to consider multiple variables and constructs aligned with the individual and the environment. As these models are typically applied to longitudinal data sets, development is captured through changes in relations among variables over time. Individual constructs – such as gender, interest, motivation, and perceptions of teachers – can be examined in conjunction with behavioral variables (such

Table 13.1 *Depiction of learner characteristics and needs in interest development, generally, and across different types of learning environments*

	Phases of interest development		
Phase 1: Triggered situational	Phase 2: Maintained situational	Phase 3: Emerging individual	Phase 4:Well-developed individual
Learner characteristics			

• Attends to content, if only fleetingly
• Needs support to engage
  • from others
  • through instructional design
• May experience either positive or negative feelings
• May or may not be reflectively aware of triggered interest
	• Re-engages content that previously triggered attention
	• Is supported by others to find connections between skills, knowledge, and prior experience
	• Has positive feelings
	• Is developing knowledge of the content
	• Is developing a sense of the content's value
		• Is likely to independently re-engage with content
		• Has curiosity questions that lead to seeking answers
		• Has positive feelings
		• Has stored knowledge and stored value
		• Is very focused on his/her own questions
			• Independently re-engages with content
			• Has curiosity questions
			• Self-regulates easily to reframe questions and seek answers
			• Has positive feelings
			• Can persevere through frustration and challenge to meet goals
			• Recognizes others' contributions to the discipline
			• Actively seeks feedback

Needs/more closed learning environment			
• To have his/her ideas respected • To feel genuinely appreciated for his/her efforts • To have others understand how hard working with this content is • A limited number of concrete suggestions	• To have his/her ideas respected • To feel genuinely appreciated for efforts • Support to explore his/her own ideas	• To have his/her ideas respected • To feel genuinely appreciated for his/her efforts • To feel that his/her ideas and goals are understood • Feedback that enables him/her to see how goals can be more effectively met	• To have his/her ideas respected • Information and feedback • To balance his/her personal standards with more widely accepted standards in the discipline • To feel that his/her ideas have been heard and understood • Constructive feedback • Challenge

318

Needs/more open learning environment

- To have his/her ideas respected
- To feel genuinely appreciated for efforts made
- To know that he/she the content

- To have his/her ideas respected
- To feel genuinely appreciated for the efforts he/she have made
- To know what he/she have learned and what he/she still want to learn

- To have his/her ideas respected
- To express his/her ideas
- Not to be told to revise present efforts
- To feel that his/her ideas and goals are understood
- To feel genuinely appreciated for his/her efforts
- Feedback that enables him/her to see how his/her goals were met

- To have his/her ideas respected
- Information and feedback
- To balance his/her personal standards with more widely accepted standards in the discipline
- To feel that his/her ideas have been heard and understood
- Constructive feedback
- Challenge

Note. Reprinted with permission from Renninger, K. A., & Riley, K. (2013). Interest, cognition, and the case of L- and science. In S. Kreitler (Ed.), *Cognition and motivation: Forging an interdisciplinary perspective* (pp. 352–82). Cambridge: Cambridge University Press.

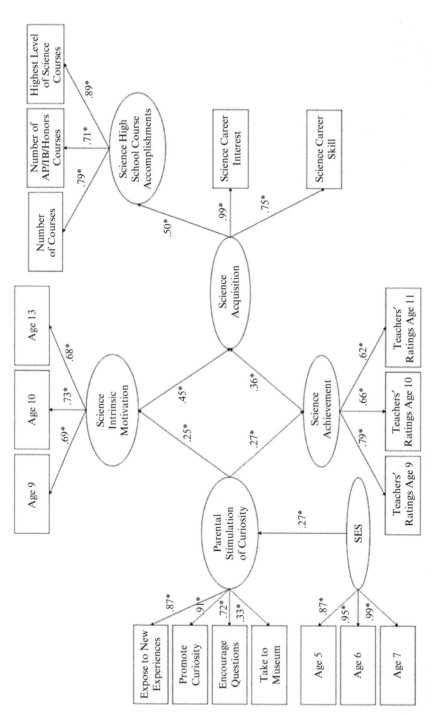

Figure 13.2. *SEM longitudinal progression model from parental stimulation of children's curiosity to high school science acquisition. Reprinted with permission from " Pathways from parental stimulation of children's curiosity to high school science course accomplishments and science career interest and skill," by A. E. Gottfried et al., 2016,* International Journal of Science Education, 38, *1972–95. http://ldx.doi.org/10.1080/09500693.2016.1220690.*

as course-taking patterns or selection of a college major) and environmental variables (such as parenting style or teacher attitudes). Path analyses depend on reliable and valid measurements of constructs when applied to longitudinal data sets. This is not a trivial issue when attempting to measure interest, engagement, or perceptions of STEM fields in individuals whose foundational knowledge of science and understanding of the nature of science is deepening over developmental time. Except for assessments of cognitive constructs such as processing speed, language, or nonverbal intelligence, available measures rarely offer specific forms that have been normed and validated for multiple age ranges. Such models also may be prone to gloss over variations in the sample based on socioeconomic status or multicultural identity, as the principal goal of the researcher is to control for such background variables in order to identify the most robust solution.

Mixed Methods Approaches: Gaining Insights through Case Analyses

We maintain that it is important for the field, if possible, to rely on mixed methods approaches when examining multiple points of access across developmental time for developing interests related to science. Such an approach depends on recruiting and maintaining a sample that is large enough to provide sufficient statistical power to yield outcomes that can be depicted as paths, phases, or patterns of flow. At the same time, individuals in the sample need to be assessed sufficiently frequently, and with enough attention to the surrounding family and school environments, to invite qualitative, case-based analyses. Such approaches are fairly rare across the three areas of literature that we believe are relevant to this topic: (1) educational research that uses large national longitudinal data sets to track patterns of course-taking behaviors and student attitudes that predict entry into STEM career fields (e.g., Maltese & Tai, 2011); (2) cognitive developmental studies of early knowledge construction or interest development (e.g., Mervis et al., 2003); and (3) social cognitive analyses of relations among key motivational and social variables that support identity development aligned with STEM fields (e.g., Harackiewicz et al., 2000). Our goal in this chapter is to bring together these three areas of literature and present a developmental model of the emergence of interests related to science. Our resulting model is depicted in Figure 13.3 as a point of reference.

Our longitudinal analysis of children's interests related to science had a unique focus on tracing children's interests and preferred activities over 14 years, considering the relative influences of parents, child characteristics, and teachers on interest trajectories over time. We recruited 215 children at age four, and tracked their interest and play behaviors bimonthly through interviews with parents until age eight. We traced early science learning opportunities, as

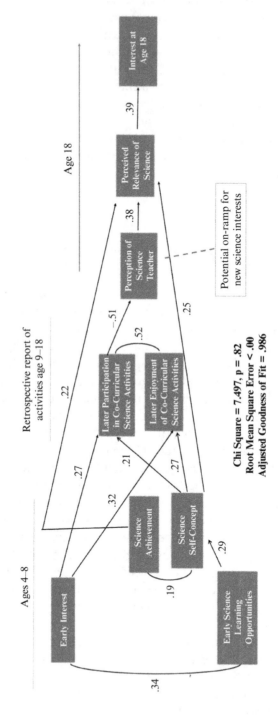

Figure 13.3. *Longitudinal mixed-methods model predicting science interests from age 4 to 18. From "Longitudinal predictors of science interests in young adult males and females," by J. M. Alexander et al., 2017, Presented at the Society for Research in Child Development conference, Austin, TX.*

well as parent support for children's interests related to science. At age eight, we measured science achievement and self-concept in a sub-sample of the group (the portion that had advanced to third grade by that time, given that our recruitment window spanned the kindergarten cut-off date for Indiana). At age 18, we reconnected with 82 of these young adults to learn more about their science-related out-of-school involvement, their perceptions of in-school science and teachers, and their current interests and career plans.

Our initial findings from early and middle childhood suggested a co-regulation model of interest development where both child and parent play significant, yet varied, roles across developmental time (Alexander et al., 2012, 2015; Johnson et al., 2004). Socializing agents in the child's environment (such as parents, older siblings, and teachers) interact with the child to foster and sustain interests, with parents playing larger roles in the early childhood years, and children (along with their teachers) taking on more responsibility for interest regulation and enhancement in elementary school. But children also play significant roles driving the direction and timing of these interactions. Thus, our co-regulation model is reminiscent of biopsychosocial, interactional, or conditional models in which adults influence children's behaviors, which subsequently exert a reciprocal influence on shaping adult behaviors (Chak, 2010; Gallagher, 2002; McDevitt & Ostrowski, 2009). Some aspects of our model align with behaviors that are suggested to parents for supporting general positive child trajectories: attention, encouragement, and helpful messages (see Holden, 2010; Holden also considers parent roles in initiating trajectories and moderating roadblocks and off-ramps). But, more specific to science, parents model behavior, encourage, select activities and toys, and allocate family time to attend events or activities important for interest support (e.g., Fredricks & Eccles, 2004; Jodl et al., 2001).

During elementary school, children assume more responsibility for the self-regulation of science interests as they gain proficiency as readers and constructors of knowledge. The peer networks established in school yield opportunities for social comparison, and children develop the ability to metacognitively reflect on their own interests. They may begin to see that their interests set them apart from their peers, supporting the role of early interests in self-concept development (see Leibham et al., 2013 for an extended consideration of the role of self-concept), and they ultimately may gravitate toward friends who share similar interests or suppress expression of interests that are dismissed or ignored by their peers. Parents may still play a role in regulating activities that occur in the evening, on weekends, or during breaks from school. They may also (if resources are available) seek out more competent mentors to support the child's interests. Thus, our co-regulation model focuses on the constant interaction between the child and the parent, which changes appropriately with development as children become more autonomous, but with a special emphasis on the early years and their critical role in interest development. Renninger (2009) has crafted a similar argument, suggesting that support for science interests prior to eight to ten years of age means that children develop a language for and experience within the domain before they start comparing themselves to others. This allows them to develop an identity as "a person who does science."

Although our model was intended to account for transitions between early childhood and middle childhood, other researchers have tackled the transitions from middle school to high school and beyond. Archer et al. (2012) followed a sample of children from age 10 to 14 and reported profound differences among families in terms of how they navigate the developmentally evolving task of supporting science aspirations. For example, some families were very science-friendly (approximately 15 percent of their sample) and embedded science in much of what they did together. Another 7.5 percent of families had children with a science interest even though their parents possessed little background or social capital related to science. Equally prevalent were parents who had significant social capital related to science but who were raising children with lower expressed interests, resulting in their perceived "pushing" of science-related activities. Approximately 27 percent of families had a child with a strong interest in science, but who pursued it on their own time with little family support and with no expressed desire to pursue a career in a scientific field. Finally, Archer et al. (2012) identified a group where science was quite peripheral to all members of the family (approximately 28 percent of families). Archer et al. conclude that children's aspirations and attitudes toward science are complex and socially embedded, with families ultimately determining the scope of what their children consider to be possible or desirable.

The developmental model proposed by Tytler et al. (2008; see Figure 13.4) examines the roles that parents can play in supporting science engagement during middle childhood and through the high school years. They suggest that a parent's most important role during middle childhood includes supporting their child's interest in math and science and nurturing the child's beliefs in their abilities in these areas. As children transition to high school, parents help associate positive value with math and science participation by providing opportunities for children to "reconnect" with STEM, including beginning to develop an understanding of the pathways to STEM careers. Teachers also play a critically important role during high school, as they are responsible for introducing new ways of thinking about science, fostering adolescents' beliefs in their ability to "do science," discussing the value of science to society, and providing a variety of challenging pedagogical environments. Such efforts help adolescents grow in their understanding of the relevance of science as well as their knowledge about the possible pathways to science careers.

In sum, the three developmental models just reviewed illustrate the evolving relationship between child and parent and the gradual reduction of influence between adults and children related to the development of science interest. They hint at phases of development, per our discussion in the previous section,

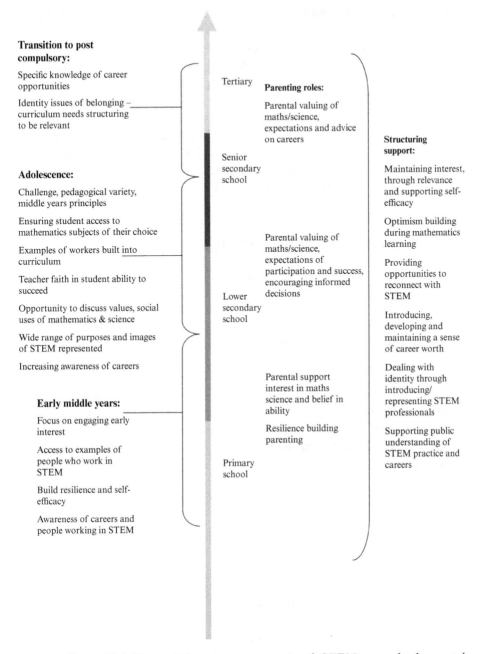

Transition to post compulsory:

Specific knowledge of career opportunities

Identity issues of belonging – curriculum needs structuring to be relevant

Adolescence:

Challenge, pedagogical variety, middle years principles

Ensuring student access to mathematics subjects of their choice

Examples of workers built into curriculum

Teacher faith in student ability to succeed

Opportunity to discuss values, social uses of mathematics & science

Wide range of purposes and images of STEM represented

Increasing awareness of careers

Early middle years:

Focus on engaging early interest

Access to examples of people who work in STEM

Build resilience and self-efficacy

Awareness of careers and people working in STEM

Tertiary

Senior secondary school

Lower secondary school

Primary school

Parenting roles:

Parental valuing of maths/science, expectations and advice on careers

Parental valuing of maths/science, expectations of participation and success, encouraging informed decisions

Parental support interest in maths science and belief in ability

Resilience building parenting

Structuring support:

Maintaining interest, through relevance and supporting self-efficacy

Optimism building during mathematics learning

Providing opportunities to reconnect with STEM

Introducing, developing and maintaining a sense of career worth

Dealing with identity through introducing/ representing STEM professionals

Supporting public understanding of STEM practice and careers

Figure 13.4. *Factors influencing engagement with STEM across developmental time. Reprinted with permission from* Opening up pathways: Engagement in STEM across the primary-secondary school transition, *by Tytler et al., 2008, Australian Department of Education, Employment, and Workplace Relations. Available at https://docs.education.gov.au/system/files/doc/other/ openpathinscitechmathenginprimsecschtrans.pdf.*

but also suggest longitudinal connections between early experiences and later science engagement.

In the remainder of this chapter, we examine three developmental time points – early childhood, middle childhood, and high school – that are prevalent in Figure 13.3 as potential inflection points. These inflection points are critical developmental times where the roles of parents, teachers, and the individuals themselves contribute to the formulation of potential on-ramps to science interests (see also Hidi et al., 2015 for a similar argument). Within each developmental time point, we use cases to highlight stories of opportunities to initiate, sustain, or diminish interests in science. The complexity of interacting forces on the development of science interests become clear.

Inflection Point 1: Early Childhood

Preschoolers, toddlers, and even infants display their emerging interests through play or through requests for persistent re-engagement with books, toys, or digital media associated with a particular domain. They may demonstrate a high degree of consistency in their preference for toys (Renninger & Wozniak, 1985) or persist in pursuing their interest during free play, even when that interest is not shared by older siblings (Leibham et al., 2005). DeLoache et al. (2007) reported that parents of very young children (ranging from 11 months to 6 years) reported that about one-third of children expressed extremely intense interests related to domains such as *airplanes* or *dinosaurs*. Of these early expressed interests, 37 percent were observed during the first year of life, and 90 percent were evidenced by age 24 months. Interestingly, they reported that extremely intense interests were much more common for boys than for girls. In examining the early emergence of interests in our own longitudinal sample, we similarly found that boys were six times as likely as girls to manifest early interests in what we termed conceptual domains such as *dinosaurs* or *horses*, those that often form the foundational knowledge for science (Johnson et al., 2004).

Indeed, our own longitudinal study had been inspired by reports of very young children who had acquired substantial conceptual information about dinosaurs (Chi & Koeske, 1983; Gobbo & Chi, 1986), as well as diary studies of early lexical development in toddlers with remarkable knowledge of object names aligned with science-relevant domains such as birds (Mervis et al., 2008). We originally were quite curious as to how such interests emerged, and thus attempted to carefully track any sustained interests that parents reported, regardless of the domain. Though it is highly unlikely that toddlers and preschoolers begin to associate domains such as dinosaurs, airplanes, or birds with the field of science until they begin school, it seems probable that the conceptual knowledge base developed – the names for things, the attributes of those things, and the manner by which those things might be related or considered as "of the same kind" doubtless provide some level of foundational support when biological or physical science concepts are eventually introduced.

In many cases, very early interests appear to originate within children – particularly boys. These blossoming interests may not necessarily be dependent on opportunities for support provided in the home (Alexander et al., 2012) but nor do they develop in a vacuum. We found that parent beliefs and interests could lay the foundation on which children's interests were expressed. Parents nurtured such interests once they had been observed by providing structure for engaging with the domain, reading relevant books (before children were capable of fluent reading), and providing exposure to additional sources of information. Neitzel et al. (2008) found that interest-related activities in the home also had a clear relation to the kinds of questions children asked and the ways children pursued information in kindergarten. Relatedly, Gottfried et al. (2016) argued for the critical role that parents can play in nurturing their children's curiosity, which subsequently is related to the child's development of science intrinsic motivation and facilitative of pathways into science. Indeed, exposing young children to experiences that foster awe regarding the natural world or that motivate children's curiosity (Engel, 2011; Klahr et al., 2013) appear to be critical roles that parents can play in nurturing initial pathways toward science interests.

In our first case study, the interplay between parent and child is obvious in determining and supporting Martin's interest in science.[2]

Case Study 1: Martin

From age four to eight, Martin's mother's phone interviews paint a picture of a typically developing little boy. Martin likes to draw, watch Scooby-Doo, pretend that he's a cowboy, and visit the Children's Museum. Martin's reading interests range from silly books to nonfiction works focused on salamanders or natural disasters. He loves Harry Potter around age eight and watches SpongeBob SquarePants. At each call, Martin's mother tells us he loves to be outside digging, feeding squirrels, on the trampoline, or in the clubhouse. His mother tells us that he likes to catch and identify caterpillars, butterflies, moths, cocoons, and bugs. He reads a variety of nonfiction animal and bug books. His interest in bugs starts to decrease, but toads and frogs soon take their place. She never identifies these outdoor interests as Martin's focus, instead mentioning that his interests tend to change often. It is not until much later that we learn the true nature of Martin's outdoor activities.

In middle school, Martin tells us that he started to develop an interest in science that "stood apart from other subjects," and notes that he began to see biology as

2 All names used in case studies have been changed to protect confidentiality.

applicable to everyday life and it just kind of "satisfied a need for curiosity." He volunteered at an animal shelter for four years (fifth to eighth grade; mom drove him downtown twice a week).

At age 18 Martin claims that he has always been good at science. "I was always outside a bunch as a kid so finding explanations for rainbows and rain, clouds ... just to have it explained to me in elementary school and later years was really neat and that I could apply it to everyday life." Martin admits that he did "plenty of experiments when I was little with my mom. She would always take us bug exploring and we would catch bugs without nets ... finding life under rocks." Martin's mother is now an early childhood educator who also teaches "bug classes" to elementary school children.

At age 18, Martin describes a rich set of outdoor activities as just part of what the family regularly did as he was growing up. We learn his grandfather was a farmer. His freshman year in college, he worked at a quarantine bug lab for the USDA. His career plan, now that he's in college, is to become an agricultural scientist studying agronomy, the science of how things grow and soil conditions.

Although, at age 18, Martin tells us he has been interested in outdoors activities "forever," his mother never identifies his plant and animal interests as primary interests during early childhood. The activities are there, but they are embedded throughout the transcripts as part of everyday life. Whether Martin's interest drives additional family activities is unclear, because Martin's activities align so well with his mother's interests. Martin's case illustrates well how early childhood science interests are often embedded in ordinary life events. Martin's case also illustrates how a well-informed parent can support these ordinary daily curiosity events.

Inflection Point 2: Middle Childhood and Activities In and Out of School

Many developmental models suggest that middle childhood is a critical time for the development of science interests. Our quantitative model (Figure 13.3) illustrates that the child's science self-concept at age eight relates directly to their perceptions of the relevance of science at age 18 as well as continued participation in science activities. In addition, age eight science achievement relates directly to age 18 perceived relevance of science. In a retrospective study of scientists and graduate students illustrating the importance of middle childhood, Dabney et al. (2013) found that 25 percent of doctoral students and 42 percent of scientists reported that the first remembered interest in science was at some point between kindergarten and fifth grade. Scientists and doctoral students in the physical sciences reported that their interest was initiated by something other than a family member 80 to 82 percent of the time. This begs the question of whether school-related or out-of-school activities play the more important role in the development of science-related interests in middle childhood.

Initiating New Pathways to Science Interests in Middle Childhood

Because of changes in the *Elementary and Secondary Education Act* in 2001, most US states do not emphasize school-related science exposure in early elementary school. Exposure begins in late elementary because this is the first time science is included in required standardized testing, per the 2001 No Child Left Behind Act. It makes sense that increased exposure to science in late elementary school could trigger new interests. As an example, Falk et al. (2016) followed a group of children across the fifth and sixth grades. They found that interest in earth/space science, life science, and technology/engineering increased significantly between the ages of 10 and 12 years. Students had transitioned from one day of science exposure a week in fifth grade to science exposure every day in sixth grade. This lends credence to the role that classes and exposure can play in the development of science interests. Unfortunately, their data also revealed a decrease in STEM participation outside of school over the same time frame for these individuals. This suggests that creating opportunities for on-ramps into new science interests does not necessarily mean children will pursue them outside of school during middle childhood.

Continuing to be involved in out-of-school activities during the middle childhood years is touted as a potential "inoculation" against losing an existing STEM interest (Lee, 1998; Potvin & Hasni, 2014). New out-of-school activities in middle childhood can also open opportunities for interests to develop and flourish, and have been argued to be a critical foundation for positive attitudes toward STEM or later science careers (Afterschool Alliance, 2017; Aschbacher et al., 2010; Bell et al., 2009; McCreedy & Dierking, 2013). For example, Falk and Needham (2013) reported that individuals who participated in free-choice STEM experiences as youth were significantly more likely to grow up to be adults who participated in both free-choice and career-oriented STEM activities. Basu and Barton (2007) similarly found that youth engagement in science-related activities led to positive attitudes toward science, positive views of agency related to science learning, and supportive social relationships around science. Not surprisingly, students who participated in lower-quality informal learning programs tended to have lower scientific reasoning skills than students who participated in enriched informal learning programs (Gerber et al., 2001). Relatedly, Bergstrom et al. (2016) found that students who spend their free time engaged in activities like tinkering, reading, or watching non-fiction TV (or sci-fi series) are more likely to focus on an astronomy career interest at the end of high school than those who do not, regardless of gender. In fact, Bergstrom et al. (2016) argued that out-of-school activities are better predictors of astronomy career interests than the typical traditional academic indicators of readiness (such as SAT scores) and the completion of high school physics and calculus.

As an important caveat to this discussion, Falk et al. (2016) maintain that it is important to consider available resources when examining interest development. Some communities possess fewer resources and thus offer fewer opportunities for children to have positive STEM experiences outside of school (Alexander et al., 2007; Archer et al., 2012; Downey et al., 2004) or home (George & Kaplan, 1998; Tenenbaum & Callanan, 2008; Tenenbaum & Leaper, 2003). Archer et al. (2012) suggest that by age ten, children from working-class families have been disadvantaged because of fewer community opportunities and are less likely to engage with STEM interests, even if they enjoy science. According to Archer et al. (2012) family social capital and habitus is defined as the ways and settings in which families operate, impinge upon, and define each family's relationship with science. This results in girls, in particular, seeing potential careers as engineers or physicists as simply incongruent with their current self-views (Archer et al., 2013).

Interestingly, when we examined our case study data carefully, we could identify no obvious cases where a science interest in middle childhood was initiated by an out-of-school activity and sustained when there were no indications of science-related interests in the home in early childhood. There were a few minor exceptions, but most pathways to STEM interests were related to in-school activities. For example, Keisha took a computer class at the suggestion of one of her friends in seventh grade. As Keisha notes:

KEISHA: I thought it was the coolest thing! We got to learn how to do PowerPoint and Access, and I was good at it, so I liked it, and just kind of kept going with it.

INTERVIEWER: Why do you think you kept going?

KEISHA: Pretty soon I could help other people, so I felt like I was needed.

It was not until her junior year of high school that Keisha considered this interest as a potential career opportunity. During her junior year, her mom introduced her to a friend who "teaches teachers about technology" so they can use technology effectively in their classroom. Keisha told us, "I thought that was something I could see myself doing."

In a second case, Ava developed an interest in X-rays and magnetic resonance imaging and admits, at age 18, that she is set for her career to work in a "healthcare setting because it'll never go away. There's always going to be people that are going to need help." When asked how and when her interest began, she tells us it began when she was in eighth grade because she had been having back issues for several years. After multiple diagnosis attempts, it was determined that she had hairline fractures in her spine from her long involvement in gymnastics. Technically, this was an out-of-school activity that triggered an enduring science interest, but the personal meaningfulness and intense family involvement were more likely the triggers and sustaining forces. As these case details illustrate, given the age and restricted mobility opportunities in middle childhood, middle-class children rely heavily on parents to play significant roles in the support of their interests. Interestingly, in our data, the task of introducing new science topics for students to explore seems to consistently fall to teachers (or a more knowledgeable doctor, in one case).

When students did mention examples of out-of-school activities related to science, they usually were tied to early childhood experiences. Thus, for our middle-class sample, middle childhood seems to be more critical for sustaining emerging (or previously demonstrated) interests in science, which is consistent with the inoculation theme introduced earlier (Lee, 1998; Potvin & Hasni, 2014). Importantly, this task does not seem to be about sustaining interest in a particular subfield of science. Rather, it seems to be more about sustaining the awe, curiosity, and wonder related to the overarching domain of science (see also Engel, 2015). Parents are particularly well positioned to help facilitate this, given their constant and varied opportunities to interact with their children across multiple contexts. It is not surprising that Gottfried et al. (2016) found that parent stimulation of curiosity was significantly related to science motivation and achievement and goals for the future. Similarly, Leibham et al. (2005) found that differences in parental beliefs about the importance of supporting curiosity in learning (measured at age five) were critical for predicting which children would continue their science-related interest two years later.

Opportunities to Sustain an Existing Interest Related to Science

The case study of John helps illustrate the evolving role of family support, the role of early self-concept in continued science engagement, and the important role that others (particularly teachers) play in high school.

Case Study 2: John

At age four, John is fascinated with construction. He pretends to farm and plays with his Tonka construction trucks. As he grows, John expresses the typical interests you might expect from a young boy – basketball, painting, music, playing cards, and hockey. But building and construction activities persist as a common theme. At the age of five, he begins to dabble in woodworking and receives his own set of tools. He uses his own tools to mimic the big construction projects his dad is always doing. He builds his own squirrel trap and uses scrap wood to build a picture frame and a puzzle. His TV watching revolves around nonfiction documentaries about garbage trucks and other kinds of large construction equipment. He pretends that he has a recycling business and watches home improvement shows on his own.

> *By the time John is six, his parents estimate that 75 percent of his free play revolves around the construction theme. He constructs speedways for his Hot Wheels cars and plays with trains, but his favorite activity is to go to construction sites and watch the big equipment in action. He borrows videos from the library about construction and visits the John Deere store with his family. With the transition to school, his goal is to drive a backhoe, and his mother estimates that he has read just about everything out there about construction that is appropriate for his age. By the age of eight he has built a bridge in his garage that he uses for his remote control cars.*
>
> *At age 18, John accurately recalls this early fascination with construction and admits that it hasn't gone away. He watches YouTube videos to learn how to fix things such as engines, and he continually takes things apart to reverse-engineer their construction. He has known "since he was old enough to consider" that he wanted to be an engineer. He credits a great Algebra II high school teacher (followed by a series of good math teachers) for really sparking his interest in math. He chose to take chemistry (three years), biology, and college-level physics while in high school. He likes the "logical process-based part of science" and learning about how things work. He doesn't like memorizing or "arbitrary" parts of science. He did not like biology. He has a mind for the scientific process and likes to apply these principles to everyday life to help him solve problems. If engineering doesn't work out, he's considering becoming a mechanic or a conservationist. He sees himself as having a carpentry hobby throughout life.*

The Role of Family and Science Self-Concept

John's case illustrates well the developmental changes suggested in Figure 13.3. His major interests in how things work and engineering have been there "always," according to John. John's case reflects a child that displayed high science interest and a heavy dose of early science-related experiences, and continues down that path. As John's cognitive abilities developed, he noticed that taking things apart became more interesting. In fourth grade he got "interested enough to start to work to understand them (engines) rather than just look at them as something cool." He supports this interest with self-sought content from YouTube, though this behavior really resurfaced as a sophomore in high school now that he is "old enough and capable enough to do it on my own." John also reports that middle childhood allowed him to begin to consider engineering as a career, noting that, "I really started to understand what an engineer does (in middle school)." John also credits a nonfiction book his family owned on how things work for strengthening his interest, "It had exploded views of things like a ship and a truck – pretty detailed models. That just sort of evolved into research on my own and taking things apart."

Research by Eccles et al. has convincingly demonstrated that out-of-school choices made by elementary school children (and their families) regarding activities can influence their beliefs about personal ability and utility beliefs about the activities (e.g., Dickhauser & Steinsmeier-Pelster, 2003; Eccles et al., 2015; Renninger, 2009) and cognitive abilities (e.g., Eccles et al., 1998). Simpkins et al. (2006) illustrated that these beliefs then influenced later choices and behaviors. In fact, they found that youth who believed they were skilled in a domain or had an interest in a domain were more likely to continue to pursue this endeavor during adolescence than their peers. Together, these studies and John's case study illustrate a potent role for an early positive self-concept in determining possible pathways toward later science involvement.

The Role of Teachers and Peers

John credits his Algebra II teacher for reawakening his interest in mathematics in high school (a key predictor of continued involvement in science, particularly in pipeline models of science involvement). He also participates in several co-curricular math-related activities in high school that lead to a growing sense of competence and high self-concept in the mathematics area. School classes also play a critical role in John's future science plans. John does not like the "fact-based classes like biology and anatomy that require a lot of memorizing. That's why I liked chemistry so much because it's more about the process than even memorizing facts." He considers himself the top or one of the top students in his class in chemistry. This positive feedback seems to sustain his interest in pursuing science in general, though he did not report that he has any specific plans for pursuing chemistry as a field of study.[3]

Circumstances that Diminish Existing Science Interest

Despite the suggestion that off-ramps are more likely as children age, there is surprisingly little research documenting the exact causes of loss of science interest in the middle childhood years. Some have hypothesized that low-quality science-related experiences might be contributing. Others have hypothesized that low-quality out-of-school experiences are the problem. Suter (2017) examined the relationships between out-of-school activity participation and science scores from the Programme for International Student Assessment (PISA, 2006), a large data set spanning 72 countries. Students showed more positive attitudes toward science but lower PISA science scores when they spent more time in after-school science-related programs compared to students with little after-school participation. Similarly, Lin and Schunn

---

3 As further indication of the significant role of others, John does admit his parents pushed him a bit to take lessons he did not really like. For example, when he was four, his mother put him in piano class but he did not enjoy it. He admits that he was "just doing it because my mom would get me toys if I practiced a bunch." Now he considers that time well invested because "after years of practice becoming good enough to play interesting music ... that's probably the point where I really started to enjoy it rather than sort of do it."

(2016), in a large study of middle school students from the United States, found that students had higher interest in science but lower science reasoning ability when they spent more time in after-school science programs. Finally, Knapp (2007) argued that many out-of-school programs are staffed by guides who report feeling unqualified to teach science and hold no STEM-related degrees. He argued that these individuals may not be prepared to correct misconceptions and, in fact, may unintentionally endorse them.

In the case below, Elijah remembers how his involvement in out-of-school science activities ended.

Case Study 3: Elijah

Elijah's mother tells us, when we first meet him, that Elijah loves to make things out of Play-Doh. He loves to play pretend role model games and fishing. He also loves to have a story read to him. He does not have a favorite topic; he will read anything. Around the age of five, Elijah discovers Pokémon cards. He continues to enjoy Pokémon cards for the next year, but Power Rangers are also a favorite. At age six-and-a-half, he moves onto Yu-Gi-Oh! cards, and loves watching the television show and dueling with the card decks. Elijah's profile reveals no interest in science-related television or reading. There is very little reference to science-related topics at all.

But there was a moment in third or fourth grade when Elijah might have gone down a different path. He remembers being in 4-H, "but it didn't really appeal to me. I was never much of an outdoorsy guy." He did get into the LEGO robotics competition, however, but stopped after two years. Did he know why? "I remember one awful time when I was taking the thing to a competition and dropped it … that was heartbreaking as a kid." Whether this was a reconstruction or the real reason he stopped going is unknown, but Elijah never re-engages with science in a tangible way.

At the age of 18, Elijah is very much into games. He loves role-play games like Dungeons & Dragons and card-based games like Magic: The Gathering. He is an avid reader and completer of logic puzzles. Elijah tell us he has been an avid reader all his life. In high school, Elijah reports that he doesn't find science "terribly interesting … because I don't like any subject where there's only one right answer." He reports sleeping through biology class. His environmental science class was at least "applicable to the real world. But I had an awful teacher … these were my worst classes."

Negotiating off-ramps for parents and teachers can be very challenging (Holden, 2010). Holden (2010) argues that parents play a central role in mediating a negative event. This could happen through pre-arming the child to help them envision what they would do if something negative happened. Second, parents might help interpret the negative situation and manage the child's reactions while the negative event is happening to avoid the off-ramp altogether. Finally, after an event, parents can counteract any negative aftereffects and work to repair any damage to self-concept. In Elijah's case, his parents were not around during this event, so the teacher or out-of-school activity leader was thrust into this role. Such instructors manage many students at once and it takes a perceptive adult and the time to manage an off-ramp incident while it is happening. Unless teachers know their students very well, they likely lack the skill for mediation based on the child's developmental level and personality. Issues with lack of effective training related to STEM and instruction makes this off-ramp probable during the middle childhood years.

Inflection Point 3: The High School Years

As suggested by the model presented in Figure 13.3, high school presents a third inflection point for supporting pathways aligned with interests in science. Developmentally, children have significantly more autonomous time away from parents, and their social networks are far more likely to include significant interactions with teachers and peers. Students can choose some of their courses in high school and are far less likely to be involved in out-of-school science-related activities, as research has suggested that adolescents spend most of their time hanging out with friends, working, or engaging in school-affiliated extracurricular activities (though some of these may be science related; Simpkins et al., 2006). Overall, as argued by Osborne et al. (2010), enrollment data indicate that there is a steep decline in the number of science-related courses taken during the high school years. Some students report science as uninteresting and unimportant, difficult, or full of rote-learning opportunities not connected to real life. High school is also a key time in which adolescents ponder whether they are a "science person" or not as they consider career options (Rosser & Lane, 2002; Subotnik et al., 2009). Science in high school is fundamentally different than the science of early childhood. As one of our participants so eloquently said, "I really liked science before they added the math."

Initiating New Pathways to Science Interests in High School

Given this backdrop of overall declining interest in science during high school, what are options for initiating new pathways to science? Ellen's case, detailed below, illustrates how high school can be a potential on-ramp for interests in science, particularly for girls.

Ellen shares with us that in high school much of her science and math exposure as a child was related to her older brother. Her parents, brother, and aunt all have science-related careers. This suggests that Ellen's family provided a

Case Study 4: Ellen

Ellen is a bright eight-year-old scoring the highest in our sample on reading (about two standard deviations [SD] above the mean) and mathematics (about three SD above the mean). However, science was about the furthest thing from Ellen's mind when she was young. She loved doing puzzles and mazes and pretending to be a princess. She loved the Disney characters and played with Barbie dolls most of the time. She now reads books about princesses and ballerinas and loves playing with her friends. She also loves being on the playground and enjoys board games, chasing butterflies, and observing real bugs. Barbie dolls continue as her favorite plaything, but she receives a roller coaster- building game for the home computer at age six that evolves to become a major interest. At age seven, Ellen has added playing keyboard music to her repertoire, though fantasy and dress-up are still preferred activities. She begins gymnastics by age eight and enjoys crafts such as making jewelry and pottery. Ellen's early science interest score was approximately one SD below the mean compared to other girls from age four to eight.

She remembers liking math in first grade when she got separated into an accelerated group that was working on multiplication tables and long division. Upon reflection, she thinks her interest grew because her older brother was "the same (as she is), very into math, very into science, tinkering." She thinks her parents thought "just a continuation of, oh here's another smart kid, let's teach her math." Ellen's brother is six years older, and by the time she was in elementary school, he was competing in the Science Olympiad. She was not trying to emulate him "but he was a role model ... and I discovered I had an interest in the (areas) and I enjoyed them."

Ellen reports that her interest in the human body began in high school, though she is not sure what sparked it. She just "woke up one day and was like it would be cool to build robotic arms." She self-initiated reading and then "saw this as a viable career option." She has a real curiosity for the area. She does not want to do "cut and dry research fields or mathematics or be a professor." Instead she wants to "go out and create" with her science.

She attended an engineering camp in high school for two weeks at a local college, where a small group of students worked together on a project. Ellen's group made a remote-controlled glove that could control the workings of a type of crane found in arcade games. She was also a counselor at a summer science day camp for two years.

As a sophomore in high school, Ellen settled on a career in biomedical engineering. "I want to work with prosthetics." Ellen indicates that she might also consider a career as a computer programmer, because she "feels like every video game enthusiast always entertains being a game designer." She taught herself basic programming in Python. Both of Ellen's parents are doctors – her mother is an optometrist and her father is a flight surgeon, "so obviously medical interests run in the family."

rich environment in which a science interest might develop, but Ellen did not show an inkling of interest in science during early childhood. As a result, and illustrative of our model, her mother reports very average (typical of girls) ratings of science-related activities both inside and outside the home from age four to seven. Ellen did start to do some science-related activities during middle childhood, but the reported number is well below the mean (about one SD), even for females.

In high school, however, the data are very different and it is clear from our quantitative data that Ellen's teachers had something to do with this sudden interest in science. She reports highly positive attitudes toward her high school science teachers (approximately one-and-a-half SD above the mean for females) and very low anxiety about science (two SD below the mean for females). She scores high on the subscale measuring attitudes about science's value to society (two SD above the mean for females) and reports a high level of desire to do science (including extra assignments, reading, and challenging work; about two SD above the mean for females). In fact, as we catch up with her at age 18, she is now a freshman at a small college known for its emphasis on engineering and STEM.

The strong positive influence of high school teachers on potential career options is clearly evident in the literature. Olson (2009) suggests that high school is a critical time for future scientists and engineers to develop their career discipline focus. Maltese and Tai (2010) found that 40 percent of practicing scientists indicated that high school-based factors played an important role in sparking their initial interest in science. These factors included teacher encouragement and teacher personal attitudes (not being dismissive, and being excited about content and the abilities of students to learn).

In fact, there are a variety of studies suggesting that teacher behaviors are critical to supporting pathways toward science careers (i.e., Azevedo, 2015; Bulunuz & Jarrett, 2015; Crowley et al., 2015; Maltese & Harsh, 2015). Enjoyment of science and class activities seems particularly important (Correll, 2001). Teachers who are inspiring, enthusiastic, or who have positive attitudes are more likely to promote sustained development of science interests or science involvement (e.g., Pressick-Kilborn, 2015; Riegle-Crumb et al., 2010; Turner et al., 2015). Interestingly, Aschbacher et al. (2010) identified a group of middle school students who found their science teachers inspiring. Even if these students did have one poor teacher over the four years of the study, they persisted in their science interests and career plans because they saw the challenging class as the outlier, not the rule.

Lyon and colleagues (2012), reporting on Project Exploration in Chicago, found that students often pursued STEM activities beyond high school and continued to be involved as adults, if given the right opportunities to stay connected. The Project Exploration program was built around student curiosity questions and has a goal of making science more accessible. It was relationship-rich and provided access to experts in science. What is most interesting about this project is that, even for those who did not continue into STEM careers, participants continued to demonstrate ongoing engagement with STEM as adults, whether through public policy advocacy or volunteering, or as a significant aspect in their parenting.

Our quantitative model and our qualitative case studies suggest a potential on-ramp for science interests in high school. In our model, there is a positive relation between the perception of the science teacher, through perceived relevance of science, through to science interest at age 18. This new on-ramp is particularly used by the girls in our sample. Although there were gender-based differences in science interests between ages four and eight between boys and girls, there are no gender-related differences in science interests in our sample at age 18. High school presents an excellent opportunity to engage or re-engage students to consider lifetime involvement in STEM. According to our participants, critical to this opportunity are high-quality, content-savvy teachers and exciting curriculum that engages learners in considering the possibilities science presents in meaningful ways.

Sustaining an Active Interest Despite Less-than-Ideal Circumstances

Our next case study illustrates an important caveat to our discussion. We found it interesting that some of our participants maintained an interest in science despite a negative view of school science. In Alicia's case, there is significant support in the home for early science interests. Those early interests are clearly related to later enjoyment of science in high school and course choices. However, this connection is not driven by teachers.

Case Study 5: Alicia

At age four, Alicia loves collecting and sorting plant seeds. She asks her mom to tell her the names of the seeds, which Mom is happy to do. Mom reports that "bug" was one of her first words, clearly noticing her daughter's interest in bugs. The interest wanes a bit as school starts. She still collects tiny flowers and seeds, but bugs and seeds are no longer identified as her primary interest. Around age six, Alicia watches Bill Nye on television, reads books about dinosaurs, bugs, and other science topics, and borrows science videos occasionally from the library. Seed collecting continues to be a minor interest through age seven, when her mother reports that Alicia likes to garden in the summer. Her mother reports, when Alicia is eight, that the family took a visit to a special garden in a state far away with many amazing species of flowers and animals. Videos and reading preferences for flowers and bugs continue through age eight-and-a-half, though it does not rise to the level of her "primary interest." Alicia's early science interest score was two SD above the mean for females.

At age 18, Alicia reports a high interest in star navigation and plants. She recalls that this interest began when she was very young and her father would take her outside and show her the stars. She is in the process of creating an accurate star map in her room with glow-in-the-dark stars (over 1,800 so far and not yet one-quarter done). She explains that her interest in planets was recently reinforced when she took a high school earth-space science course. In addition, she has taken biology, human-body systems, medical interventions, marine biology, zoology, and astronomy in high school. She reports having watched video documentaries since she was little. She also expresses an interest in the human body (how it is built and functions). She believes that interest started when she began at a magnet high school as a freshman. Alicia also has an enduring interest in art and uses art as a tool to better understand her science interests. She shares a story from her earth-space science course where she drew Jupiter and everyone was amazed. Similarly, she believes her biomed class has made her drawing much better because "if you don't figure out how the skeletal structure works, if you're drawing people, your figures aren't going to be that great."

When asked what has kept her interested in the human body, Alicia notes that she thinks it will help her get a job and "everyone" tells her she should become a doctor. She also notes that her mother is interested in radiology and has been taking some late-career classes in it.

She recalls that when she was little she wanted to know how everything worked. She thinks she stayed interested in science because her elementary school had an outdoor lab in which they often did activities. But nothing quite like that was available in high school. She is currently an active aquarium keeper with over 75 fish, which relates to her personal interest in marine biology. When she got into high school her interest in biology and earth science was reinforced further by thinking about a future career and realizing that she likes animals. She never actually mentions the teachers when she references any of these science classes, just the content.

Alicia notes that she has not yet settled on a career choice but is considering a career in agriculture or natural resources because she thinks a career as a park ranger would be interesting, through kind of dangerous. She is also interested in being a doctor (it will be good to help people) or an art teacher. She also admits that she is considering a career in science or engineering. Upon reflection, however, she adds that being in science or engineering might be a problem, because "girls don't go into (science) because they receive so much sexual harassment and I'm not capable of dealing with that."

Illustrative of her enduring science interest and supportive family environment, Alicia ends up at a science-related magnet school and takes far more science courses in high school than 99 percent of our sample. At age 18, Alicia has a positive view of science's value to society (about one SD above the mean for females) and reports enjoying her science-related, out-of-school activities (about two SD above the mean for females). Her rating of her teachers is about average for the sample and not what you might expect from someone who has grown up in this science-rich environment. Her science self-concept is high, almost the highest in the sample, and her value and perceived relevance of biology is the highest we see in the sample, while chemistry is relegated to "not so interesting or relevant."

Alicia seems to be one of the individuals in our sample whose rich out-of-school science activities creates a problem for her in-school science experience. In all her comments about taking so many science courses, she never once mentions a teacher as a positive influence, except when they have noticed her exceptional artwork. She refers multiple times to the opportunity to learn new content. For example, "In my class we look at X-rays a lot. I like to think about it a lot." This negative relation between participation in co-curricular science activities and perception of the science teacher illustrates the tension between formal and informal science opportunities, suggesting that some students with early science interests may not need teacher support to maintain or expand their science interests.

Circumstances that Might Diminish Science Interests in High School

The next case study, Sam, nicely illustrates a key developmental inflection point that is implicit in Figure 13.3. Sam's case illustrates the potential off-ramps for science-related interests in high school.

Case Study 6: Sam

At age four, Sam is most interested in computers and Hot Wheels. His parents are actively involved in music, so there is always music in the house. Sam loves to read about airplanes, trains, and cars, and he especially loves the car books that are interactive. He picks out car books at the library, focusing on those with detailed construction equipment drawings. He talks with his parents about NASCAR races he watches on TV. He builds cars out of LEGO. He often pretends that he has a store or a garage sale, or is on a construction site. He races his cars. Within the next two months, Sam's interests expand as he begins to play T-ball and hockey. But over the next year, we see that cars are a recurring theme for Sam. His family attends their first NASCAR race. He looks up Jeff Gordon on the Internet and sends him a picture of Sam and his family at the race. Sam's early science interest score was 0.8 SD above the mean for boys.

At the age of six, Sam discovers baseball cards after a vacation where they spent some time watching baseball. Baseball cards continue to be an interest as school starts; cars remain in his repertoire, but at a much lower level. Sam is often found dividing his cards into teams and then pretending that the teams are playing each other. Sam's baseball interest grows as his mother borrows baseball books from the *library and buys more baseball cards, and Sam often talks about baseball players and teams while the family is traveling. He plays baseball multiple days a week and his pretend play revolves around the theme of baseball card store ownership.*

At age 18, Sam reports significant activities related to sports (basketball, baseball, bowling, and tennis) that were consistent across the years. The science activities he reports tended to be localized to individual, unique experiences, except for visiting the zoo, which happened a couple times per month, since he lived nearby. Sam admits he has always been good at math and that he still likes collecting things. In fact, he now buys and sells baseball and other cards as his hobby. He has taken physics, biology, and chemistry in high school. He reports that physics (his freshman year) was particularly grueling and he was often frustrated by it. He rates science overall as a three out of five in terms of fun and reports some poor experiences in class.

As his career goal, now that he is a sophomore in college, he states that he really wants to be a math teacher. He did a "shadowing experience" with a teacher and loved it. He reports a strong desire to help students and he is passionate about this career choice. He tells us he could imagine a future where he uses science in his job, but it would not be his first choice. He has taken up the bass and played in a high school band. But, he ... wants to stay involved in baseball, which he "really got into" in fifth or sixth grade. So, he figures as a teacher he can be a baseball coach on the side.

Sam's case illustrates the anatomy of a science interest off-ramp. Sam relates a story about taking physics as a freshman. He doesn't remember much about the class other than trying to keep himself from failing. He assumes there is something he probably learned in class that he might eventually use, but "I wouldn't be able to come up with a specific example." He notes that the negative physics experience came on the heels of a "horrific science teacher" in middle school. He does not elaborate what he means. He does not believe he is good in science (either in general or in specific courses) and would have a hard time imagining himself in a career that used science. "It's certainly not my first option, not even close." He also has a limited vision of science careers, seeing them "more as doing things in a laboratory rather than being in open spaces."

Interestingly, when Sam is later asked if he has ever visited a science museum, his answer betrays his unhappy relationship with science.

INTERVIEWER: "What would you expect to see there?"

SAM: "I think that, due to my past experiences with science, I would probably expect it to look similar to a classroom, a science classroom. Of course, I can't expect that, but it's my own fault because of my ignorance. I think reaching beyond the past experiences maybe I would see some things related to weather ... I know that's kind of a stupid answer."

Our data is hardly the first to find that, by high school, some students who previously had positive views about science are no longer interested in science-related careers. There has been a significant amount of research over the years illustrating that students' attitudes toward and interest in science decrease across the school years, with some level of stability in science interest reached by approximately age 14 (e.g. Gottfried et al., 2001; Osborne et al., 2003; Said et al., 2016; Tytler, 2014). Interestingly, Vedder-Wiess and Fortus (2011) have suggested that declining interest in STEM during adolescence may not be inevitable and may occur only in a subset of youth, driven more by school than home environments. Sam's case certainly illustrates this point.

Our data suggest an important off-ramp – a negative correlation between ongoing science involvement and perceptions of school science teachers. Aschbacher et al. (2010) reported that students who were originally interested in science but lost that interest often blamed school experiences and teachers who failed to support their science interests. Similarly, Krapp and Prenzel (2011) found that students who were well prepared academically for a science career did not pursue that option because they reported losing their interest during school. Our data (see Figure 13.3) suggest that adolescents who report high out-of-school science involvement are likely to rate their teachers as low in ability to make science interesting, low in clarity of presentation, and low in willingness to give individual help (these students may need a different type of help than other students).

Vedder-Wiess and Fortus (2011) have blamed lack of motivation to learn science on more traditional lecture-based classrooms instead of student-focused or democratic classrooms with more choice and autonomy. Lyons (2006) claims that students are simply turned off by the autocratic way science is presented in their classes. In many cases, students who are interested in STEM report that their classes in school are boring (Cleaves, 2005) and they simply do not enjoy their science classes (Osborne et al., 2003).

Aschbacher et al. (2010) have also proposed other viable reasons why high school students might lose interest in science. These include a lack of interesting extracurricular school clubs or competing interests associated with other family priorities. Females also report feeling less welcome in science-related clubs (Bergstrom et al., 2016). According to Aschbacher et al. (2010) students may also experience a growing and more realistic perception of what science careers entail as they age, perhaps sensing for the first time that the career path will be too difficult (illustrating again the critical role of self-concept). At the very least, students sense that such activities no longer entail just the awe of "staring at the stars" and instead require deep math and science understandings (Bergstrom et al., 2016).

Although not strictly STEM related, Sam's story of his interest in music illustrates many of the themes in the model we have presented. As Sam says, "So I've always kind of dabbled in music just because I've always had the resources available." His family's home has a significant recording studio in it, which is related to his father's profession. He says it was always around, but he didn't really get into it until "high school because I started to realize I've got to find things on my own and develop my own interests ... so, I picked up a bass one day and kind of just taught myself how to play." He sustained his interest through real skill development and growing competence, and is now doing actual concerts, which he considers "quite a thrill."

Concluding Thoughts

Our review and description of cases associated with our developmental model of science interest pathways reaffirm the complex array of factors that can impact interests in science at the developmental transition to career choices. Whether documented as Sankey diagrams or path analyses, or through developmental phase models, the potential exists, at nearly every developmental time period, for a positive experience with science to trigger a more sustained interest, or a negative experience to begin to weaken the interest. Our own work combines the advantages of both the quantitative path analyses with a more case-based approach that reveals aspects of development akin to the phase models. Additionally, our cases represent individuals who move in and out of science interests, much like Sankey diagrams, but without the requirement of individuals being restricted by existing, mutually exclusive categories. The resulting model diminishes the relevance of traditional pipeline arguments for the development and support of science interests.

We also reaffirm the importance of researchers reading broadly and attempting to integrate findings across literature in educational psychology, cognitive development, and science education. This literature (and the professional meetings associated with it) has typically been associated with different groups of researchers whose paths rarely cross, despite grappling with similar constructs to address questions pertaining to science interests at varying levels of analysis.

Science interests and the supports they need change throughout developmental time. Very early in childhood, interests seem most prone to arise spontaneously and become manifest through behaviors such as curiosity questioning, scientific word learning, and preferences for repeated engagement with toys and types of books. Parents are critical for nurturing these early interests through the provision of opportunities to engage with relevant content in the home, answering or inspiring additional curiosity questions, or through informal science learning opportunities in the community. Evidence also suggests that parents can help instill a sense of wonder, awe, and curiosity in their children, which seems to provide a powerful inoculation that protects students from interest loss as school begins, even if adverse formal science education experiences ensue.

With the transition to school and developing fluency in reading, children are increasingly able to self-regulate their interest-related activities and knowledge. However, unstructured time for pursuing interests becomes an increasingly scarce commodity as out-of-school activities expand in middle and high school. Early elementary school seems a critical time by which children should accrue positive experiences with science, as it lays the foundation for science self-concept and supports children to see themselves as "someone who likes science." A positive self-concept and continued involvement in out-of-school science activities also helps buffer negative experiences with science and maintain science interests.

High school clearly is a time when students begin to evaluate relations among their perceived academic strengths, interests, and career goals. More flexibility in course selection provides opportunities to build a strong foundation in mathematics and science, or begin to shift to other pursuits. High school science teachers appear to play a particularly pivotal role for girls, given that we found no differences in science interests for males and females at the transition to college, despite significant differences in middle childhood. High school teachers must help students move beyond the general sense of awe and curiosity related to science to begin to see the role that mathematics and formal scientific inquiry play in actually doing science and undergirding science careers. Teachers can also support high school students by introducing a variety of STEM careers and ways in which scientific inquiry is used outside of laboratories. Some of our participants who were least interested in science viewed science as based entirely in a laboratory – the domain of individuals wearing white lab coats. Teachers can expand the way students think about science by illustrating the many ways science plays a role in society.

What might these patterns mean for practitioners intending to capitalize on what we know about the role of learner motivation in designing science curricula? Osborne and Dillon (2008) maintain that all nations should do whatever they can to ensure that only the highest quality science educators are engaged in instruction for students in elementary and lower secondary school. Furthermore, they argue that science teachers should emphasize engagement for students younger than 14 years. Evidence would suggest that this is best achieved through opportunities for extended investigative work and hands-on experimentation, and not through a stress on the acquisition of vocabulary (Tytler et al., 2008).

Our findings also suggest that the period between preschool and second grade is important to the early formation of self-concept and opens the door for further engagement in science. It seems critical that we invest in science education that can cultivate a sense of awe or wonder in children during the preschool and elementary school years. Gottfried et al. (2016) found that parental simulation of curiosity was extremely important for facilitating children's trajectories into science. For children from homes in which parents are not able to provide this support, it is critical that teachers are well positioned to assume this role. Inculcating a healthy sense of awe and wonder about the natural and physical world, coupled with an understanding of the roles that science and mathematics play in helping us understand that which we are curious about, seems a particularly promising combination for supporting individuals' progress along pathways to deepening science interests.

References

Afterschool Alliance. (2017). *STEM-ready America: Inspiring and preparing students for success with afterschool and summer learning.* Washington, DC. Stemreadyamerica.org. Available at http://stemreadyamerica.org/read-the-compendium/.

Alexander, J. M., Johnson, K. E., & Kelley, K. (2012). Longitudinal analysis of the relations between opportunities to learn about science and the development of interests related to science. *Science Education, 96,* 763–86. doi: 10.1002/sce.21018.

Alexander, J. M., Johnson, K. E., & Leibham, M. E. (2015). Emerging individual interests related to science in young children. In K. A. Renninger, M. Nieswandt, & S. Hidi (Eds.), *Interest in mathematics and science learning* (pp. 261–80). Washington, DC: American Educational Research Association. doi: 10.3102/978-0-935302-42-4.

Alexander, K. L., Entwiscle, D. R., & Olson, L. S. (2007). Lasting consequences of the summer learning gap. *American Sociological Review, 72,* 167–80. doi: 10.1177/000312240707200201.

Archer, L., DeWitt, J., Osborne, J., Dillon, J., Willis, B., & Wong, B. (2012). Science aspirations, capital, and family habitus: How families shape children's engagement and identification with science. *American Educational Research Journal, 49,* 881–908. doi: 10.3102/0002831211433290.

Archer, L., DeWitt, J., Osborne, J., Dillon, J., Willis, B., & Wong, B. (2013). "Not girly, not sexy, not glamorous": Primary school girls' and parents' constructions of science aspirations. *Pedagogy, Culture, and Society, 21,* 171–94. doi: 10.1080/14681366.2012.748676.

Aschbacher, P. R., Li, E., & Roth, E. J. (2010). Is science me? High school students' identities, participation, and aspirations in science, engineering, and medicine. *Journal of Research in Science Teaching, 47,* 564–82. doi: 10.1002/tea.20353.

Azevedo, F. S. (2015). Sustaining interest-based participation in science. In K. A. Renninger, M. Nieswandt, & S. Hidi (Eds.), *Interest in mathematics and science learning* (pp. 281–96). Washington, DC: American Educational Research Association. doi: 10.3102/978-0-935302-42-4.

Basu, S. J. & Barton, A. C. (2007). Developing a sustained interest in science among urban minority youth. *Journal of Research in Science Teaching, 44,* 466–89. doi: 10.1002/tea.20143.

Bell, P., Lewenstein, B., Shouse, A. W., & Feder, M. A. (Eds.). (2009). *Learning science in informal environments: People, places, and pursuits.* Washington, DC: National Academy Press. doi: 10.17226/12190.

Bergstrom, Z., Sadler, P., & Sonnert, G. (2016). Evolution and persistence of students' astronomy career interests: A gender study. *Journal of Astronomy & Earth Sciences Education, 3*, 77–92. http://dx.doi.org/10.19030/jaese.v3i1.9690.

Bulunuz, M. & Jarrett, O. S. (2015). Play as an aspect of interest development in science. In K. A. Renninger, M. Nieswandt, & S. Hidi (Eds.), *Interest in mathematics and science learning* (pp. 153–72). Washington, DC: American Educational Research Association. doi: 10.3102/978-0-935302-42-4.

Cannady, M. A., Greenwald, E., & Harris, K. N. (2014). Problematizing the STEM pipeline metaphor: Is the STEM pipeline metaphor serving our students and the STEM workforce? *Science Education, 98*, 443–60. doi: 10.1002/sce.21108.

Chak, A. (2010). Adult response to children's exploratory behaviours: An exploratory study. *Early Child Development and Care, 180*, 633–46. http://dx.doi.org/10.1080/03004430802181965.

Chi, M. T. H. & Koeske, R. D. (1983). Network representation of a child's dinosaur knowledge. *Developmental Psychology, 19*, 29–39. http://dx.doi.org/10.1037/0012-1649.19.1.29.

Clausen, J. A. (1986). *The life course: A sociological perspective.* Englewood Cliffs, NJ: Prentice-Hall.

Cleaves, A. (2005). The formation of science choices in secondary school. *International Journal of Science Education. 27*, 471–86. http://dx.doi.org/10.1080/0950069042000323746.

Committee on Equal Opportunity in Science and Engineering (CEOSE) (2015). *2013–2014 Biennial report to congress: Broadening participation in today's STEM workforce.* Arlington, VA: National Science Foundation. Available at www.nsf.gov/od/oia/activities/ceose/documents/2013-2014 CEOSE Biennial Report to Congress_Final Version_09-08-2015.pdf.

Correll, S. (2001). Gender and the career choice process: The role of biased self-assessments. *American Journal of Sociology, 106*, 1691–730. https://doi.org/10.1086/321299.

Crowley, K., Barron, B., Knutson, K., & Martin, C. K. (2015). Interest and the development of pathways to science. In K. A. Renninger, M. Nieswandt, & S. Hidi (Eds.), *Interest in mathematics and science learning* (pp. 297–314). Washington, DC: American Educational Research Association. doi: 10.3102/978-0-935302-42-4.

Dabney, K. P., Chakraverty, D., & Tai, R. H. (2013). The association of family influence and initial interest in science. *Science Education, 97*, 395–409. doi: 10.1002/sce.21060.

DeLoache, J. S., Simcock, G., & Macari, S. (2007). Planes, trains, automobiles – and tea sets: Extremely intense interests in very young children. *Developmental Psychology, 43*, 1579–86. doi: 10.1037/0012-1649.43.6.1579.

Dickhauser, O. & Steinsmeier-Pelster, J. (2003). Gender differences in the choice of computer science courses: Applying an expectancy-value model. *Social Psychology of Education, 6*, 173–89. doi: 10.1023%2FA%3A1024735227657.pdf.

Downey, D. B., Von Hippel, P. T., & Broh, B. A. (2004). Are schools the great equalizer? Cognitive inequality during the summer months and the school year. *American Sociological Review, 69*, 613–35. https://doi.org/10.1177/000312240406900501.

Eccles, J. S., Fredricks, J. A., & Epstein, A. (2015). Understanding well-developed interests and activity commitment. In K. A. Renninger, M. Nieswandt, & S. Hidi (Eds.), *Interest in mathematics and science learning* (pp. 315–30). Washington, DC: American Educational Research Association. doi: 10.3102/978-0-935302-42-4.

Eccles, J. S., Wigfield, A., & Schiefele, U. (1998). Motivation. In N. Eisenberg (Ed.), *Handbook of child psychology* (Vol. 3, 5th ed., pp. 1017–95). New York, NY; Wiley. doi: 10.1002/9780470147658.

Elementary and Secondary Education Act (2001). The no child left behind act of 2001. Accessed from www2.ed.gov/policy/elsec/leg/esea02/107-110.pdf.

Engel, S. (2011). Children's need to know: Curiosity in schools. *Harvard Educational Review, 81*, 625–645. https://doi.org/10.17763/haer.81.4.h054131316473115.

Engel, S. (2015). *The hungry mind: The origins of curiosity in childhood*. Cambridge, MA: Harvard University Press.

Falk, J. H. & Needham, M. D. (2013). Factors contributing to adult knowledge of science and technology. *Journal of Research in Science Teaching, 50*, 431–52. doi: 10.1002/tea.21080.

Falk, J. H., Staus, N., Dierking, L. D., Penuel, W., Wyld, J., & Bailey, D. (2016). Understanding youth STEM interest pathways within a single community: The *Synergies* project. *International Journal of Science Education, 6*, 369–84. http://dx.doi.org/10.1080.21548455.2015.1093670.

Fredricks, J. A. & Eccles, J. S. (2004). Parental influences on youth involvement in sports. In M. Weiss (Ed.), *Developmental sport and exercise psychology: A lifespan perspective* (pp. 145–64). Morgantown, WV: Fitness Information Technology.

Gallagher, K. C. (2002). Does child temperament moderate the influence of parenting on adjustment? *Developmental Review, 22*, 623–43. https://doi.org/10.1016/S0273-2297(02)00503-8.

George, R. & Kaplan, D. (1998). A structural model of parent and teacher influences on science attitudes of eighth graders: Evidence from NELS:88. *Science Education, 82*, 93–109. doi: 10.1002/(SICI)1098-237X(199801)82:1<93::AID-SCE5>3.0.CO;2-W.

Gerber, B. L., Cavallo, A. M., & Marek, E. A. (2001). Relationships among informal learning environments, teaching procedures, and scientific reasoning ability. *International Journal of Science Education, 23*, 535–49. http://dx.doi.org/10.1080/09500690116971.

Gobbo, C., & Chi, M. T. H. (1986). How knowledge is structured and used by expert and novice children. *Cognitive Development, 1*, 221–37. https://doi.org/10.1016/S0885-2014(86)80002-8.

Gottfried, A. E., Fleming, J. S., & Gottfried, A. W. (2001). Continuity of academic intrinsic motivation from childhood through late adolescence: A longitudinal study. *Journal of Educational Psychology, 93*, 3–13. http://dx.doi.org/10.1037/0022-0663.93.1.3.

Gottfried, A. E., Preston, K. S., Gottfried, A. W., Oliver, P. H., Delany, D. E., & Ibrhahim, S. M. (2016). Pathways from parental stimulation of children's curiosity to high school science course accomplishments and science career interest and skill. *International Journal of Science Education, 38*, 1972–95. http://dx.doi.org/10.1080/09500693.2016.1220690.

Harackiewicz, J. M., Barron, K. E., Tauer, J. M., Carter, S. M., & Elliott, A. J. (2000). Short-term and long-term consequences of achievement goals in college: Predicting continued interest and performance over time. *Journal of Educational Psychology*, *92*, 316–30. http://dx.doi.org/10.1037/0022-0663 .92.2.316.

Hidi, S. & Baird, W. (1986). Interestingness – A neglected variable in discourse processing. *Cognitive Science*, *10*, 179–94. doi: 10.1207/s15516709cog1002_3.

Hidi, S. & Renninger, K. A. (2006). The four phase model of interest development. *Educational Psychologist*, *41*, 111–27. http://dx.doi.org/10.1207/ s15326985ep4102_4.

Hidi, S., Renninger, K. A., & Nieswandt, M. (2015). Conclusions: Emerging issues and themes in addressing interest in learning mathematics and science. In K. A. Renninger, M. Nieswandt, & S. Hidi (Eds.), *Interest in mathematics and science learning* (pp. 385–96). Washington, DC: American Educational Research Association. doi: 10.3102/978-0-935302-42-4.

Hoffman, L. L. (2002). Promoting girls' interest and achievement in physics classes for beginners. *Learning and Instruction*, *12*, 447–65. https://doi.org/10.1016/ S0959-4752(01)00010-X.

Holden, G. W. (2010). Childrearing and developmental trajectories: Positive pathways, off-ramps, and dynamic processes. *Child Development Perspectives*, *4*, 197–204. doi: 10.1111/j.1750-8606.2010.00148.x.

Institute for Higher Education Policy. (2015). *Diversifying the STEM Pipeline: The Model Replication Institutions Program*. Washington, DC. Available at www .ihep.org/sites/default/files/uploads/docs/pubs/report_diversifying_the_ stem_pipeline_report.pdf.

Jodl, K. M., Michael, A., Malanchuk, O., Eccles, J. S., & Sameroff, A. (2001). Parents' roles in shaping early adolescents' occupational aspirations. *Child Development*, *72*, 1247–65. doi: 10.1111/1467-8624.00345.

Johnson, K. E., Alexander, J. M., Spencer, S., Leibham, M. E., & Neitzel, C. (2004). Factors associated with the early emergence of intense interests within conceptual domains. *Cognitive Development*, *19*, 325–43. https://doi.org/10.1016/j .cogdev.2004.03.001.

Kerckhoff, A. C. (1993). *Diverging pathways: Social structure and career deflections*. New York, NY: Cambridge University Press.

Klahr, D., Matlen, B., & Jirout, J. (2013). Children as scientific thinkers. In G. J. Feist & M. E. Gorman (Eds.), *Handbook of the psychology of science* (pp. 243–7). New York, NY: Springer.

Knapp, D. (2007). A longitudinal analysis of an out of school science experience. *School Science and Mathematics*, *107*(2), 44–51. doi: 10.1111/j.1949- 8594.2007.tb17767.x.

Krapp, A. & Prenzel, M. (2011). Research on interest in science: Theories, methods, and findings. *International Journal of Science Education*, *33*, 27–90. http:// dx.doi.org/10.1080/09500693.2010.518645.

Lee, J. D. (1998). Which kids can "become" scientists? Effects of gender, self-concepts, and perceptions of scientists. *Social Psychology Quarterly*, *61*, 199–219. www .jstor.org/stable/2787108.

Leibham, M. E., Alexander, J. M., & Johnson, K. E. (2013). Science interests in pre-school boys and girls: Relations to later self-concept and science achievement. *Science Education, 97*, 574–93. doi: 10.1002/sce.21066.

Leibham, M. E., Alexander, J. M., Johnson, K. E., Neitzel, C. L., & Reis-Henrie, F. P. (2005). Parenting behaviors associated with the maintenance of pre-schoolers' interests: A prospective longitudinal study. *Applied Developmental Psychology, 26*, 397–414. https://doi.org/10.1016/j.appdev.2005.05.001.

Lin, P.-Y. & Schunn, C. D. (2016). The dimension and impact of informal science learning experiences on middle schoolers' attitudes and abilities in science. *International Journal of Science Education, 38*, 2551–72. http://dx.doi.org/10.1080/09500693.2016.1251631.

Lipstein, R. L. & Renninger, K. (2007). Interest for writing: How teachers can make a difference. *English Journal, 96*(4), 79–85. www.jstor.org/stable/30047170.

Lyon, G. H., Jafri, J., & St. Louis, K. (2012, Fall). Beyond the pipeline: STEM pathways for youth development. *Afterschool Matters*, 48–57. Available at https://eric.ed.gov/?id=EJ992152.

Lyons, T. (2006). Different countries, same science classes: Students' experiences of school science in their own words. *International Journal of Science Education, 28*, 591–613. http://dx.doi.org/10.1080/09500690500339621.

Maltese, A. V. & Harsh, J. A. (2015). Students' pathways of entry into STEM. In K. A. Renninger, M. Nieswandt, & S. Hidi (Eds.), *Interest in mathematics and science learning* (pp. 203–24). Washington, DC: American Educational Research Association. doi: 10.3102/978-0-935302-42-4.

Maltese, A. V. & Tai, R. H. (2010). Eyeballs in the fridge: Sources of early interest in science. *International Journal of Science Education, 32*, 669–85. http://dx.doi.org/10.1080/09500690902792385.

Maltese, A. & Tai, R. S. (2011). Pipeline persistence: Examining the association of educational experiences with earned degrees in STEM among U.S. students. *Science Education, 95*, 877–907. doi: 10.1002/sce.20441.

McAdams, D. P. (1988). *Power, intimacy, and the life story: Personological inquiries into identity*. New York, NY: Guilford Press.

McCreedy, D. & Dierking, L. D. (2013). *Cascading influences: Long-term impacts of informal STEM experiences for girls*. Philadelphia, PA. The Franklin Institute Science Museum. Available at www.fi.edu/sites/default/files/cascading-influences.pdf.

McDevitt, M. & Ostrowski, A. (2009). The adolescent unbound: Unintentional influence of curricula in ideological conflict seeking. *Political Communication, 26*, 11–29. http://dx.doi.org/10.1080/10584600802622811.

Mervis, C. B., Pani, J. R., & Pani, A. M. (2003). Transaction of child cognitive-linguistic abilities and adult input in the acquisition of lexical categories at the basic and subordinate levels. In D. H. Rakison & L. M. Oakes (Eds.), *Early category and concept development: Making sense of the blooming, buzzing confusion* (pp. 242–74). New York, NY: Oxford University Press.

Metcalf, H. (2014). Disrupting the pipeline: Critical analyses of student pathways through postsecondary STEM education. *New Directions for Institutional Research, 158*, 77–93. doi: 10.1002/ir.20047.

Mitchell, M. (1993). Situational interest: Its multifaceted structure in the secondary school mathematics classroom. *Journal of Educational Psychology*, *85*, 424–36. http://dx.doi.org/10.1037/0022-0663.85.3.424.

National Science Foundation. (2011). *Science and engineering degrees: 1966–2008 NSF 11–316*. Arlington, VA: NSF. Available at www.nsf.gov/statistics/nsf11316/pdf/nsf11316.pdf.

Neitzel, C., Alexander, J. M., & Johnson, K. E. (2008). Children's early interest-based activities in the home and subsequent information contributions and pursuits in kindergarten. *Journal of Educational Psychology*, *100*, 782–97. http://dx.doi.org/10.1037/0022-0663.100.4.782.

OECD (2007). *Education at a glance 2007: OECD indicators*. Paris: Organisation for Economic Cooperation and Development. Available at www.oecd.org/education/skills-beyond-school/40701218.pdf.

Osborne, J. F. & Dillon, J. (2008). *Science education in Europe: Critical reflections*. London: Nuffield Foundation. Available at www.nuffieldfoundation.org/sites/default/files/Sci_Ed_in_Europe_Report_Final.pdf.

Osborne, J., Simon, S., & Collins, S. (2003). Attitudes toward science: A review of the literature and its implications. *International Journal of Science Education*, *25*, 1049–79. http://dx.doi.org/10.1080/0950069032000032199.

Parke, R. D., Ornstein, P. A., Rieser, J. J., & Zahn-Waxler, C. (1994). The past as prologue: An overview of a century of developmental psychology. In R. D. Parke, P. A. Ornstein, J. J. Reiser, & C. Z. Waxler (Eds.), *A century of developmental psychology* (pp. 1–70). Washington, DC: American Psychological Association.

PISA (Programme for International Student Assessment). (2006). Paris: OECD (Organisation for Economic Co-operation and Development).

Potvin, P. & Hasni, A. (2014). Interest, motivation and attitude towards science and technology at K–12 levels: A systematic review of 12 years of educational research. *Studies in Science Education*, *50*, 85–129. http://dx.doi.org/10.1080/03057267.2014.881626.

President's Council of Advisors on Science and Technology. (2012). *Engage to excel: Producing one million additional college graduates with degrees in Science, Technology, Engineering, and Mathematics*. Available at https://obamawhitehouse.archives.gov/sites/default/files/microsites/ostp/pcast-engage-to-excel-final_2-25-12.pdf.

Pressick-Kilborn, K. (2015). Canalization and connectedness in the development of science interest. In K. A. Renninger, M. Nieswandt, & S. Hidi (Eds.), *Interest in mathematics and science learning* (pp. 353–68). Washington, DC: American Educational Research Association. doi: 10.3102/978-0-935302-42-4.

Renninger, K. A. (1989). Individual differences in children's play interest. In L. T. Winegar (Ed.), *Social interaction and the development of children's understanding* (pp. 147–72). Norwood, NJ: Ablex.

Renninger, K. A. (2000). Individual interest and its implications for understanding intrinsic motivation. In C. Sansone & J. M. Harackiewicz (Eds.), *Intrinsic and extrinsic motivation: The search for optimal motivation and performance* (pp. 373–404). San Diego, CA: Academic Press.

Renninger, K. A. (2009). Interest and identity development in instruction: An inductive model. *Educational Psychologist, 44*(2), 1–14. http://dx.doi.org/10.1080/0046152090 2832392.

Renninger, K. A. & Riley, K. (2013). Interest, cognition, and the case of L- and science. In S. Kreitler (Ed.), *Cognition and motivation: Forging an interdisciplinary perspective* (pp. 352–82). Cambridge: Cambridge University Press.

Renninger, K. A. & Wozniak, R. H. (1985). Effect of interest on attentional shift, recognition, and recall in young children. *Developmental Psychology, 21*(4), 624–32. http://dx.doi.org/10.1037/0012-1649.21.4.624.

Riegle-Crumb, C., Moore, C., & Ramos-Wada, A. (2010). Who wants to have a career in science or math? Exploring adolescents' future aspirations by gender and race/ethnicity. *Science Education, 95*, 458–76. doi: 10.1002/sce.20431.

Rosser, S. V. & Lane, E. O. (2002). Key barriers for academic institutions seeking to retain female scientists and engineers: Family-unfriendly policies, low numbers, stereotypes, and harassment. *Journal of Women and Minorities in Science and Engineering, 8*, 163–91. doi: 10.1615/JWomenMinorScienEng.v8.i2.40.

Sadler, P. M., Sonnert, G., Hazari, Z., & Tai, R. (2012). Stability and volatility of STEM career interest in high school: A gender study. *Science Education, 96*, 411–27. doi: 10.1002/sce.21007.

Said, Z., Summers, L. R., Abd-El-Khalick, F., & Wang, S. (2016). Attitudes toward science among grades 3 through 12 Arab students in Qatar: Findings from a cross-sectional national study. *International Journal of Science Education, 38*, 621–43. http://dx.doi.org/10.1080/09500693.2016.1156184.

Simpkins, S. D., Davis-Kean, P. E., & Eccles, J. S. (2006). Math and science motivation: A longitudinal examination of the links between choices and beliefs. *Developmental Psychology, 42*, 70–83. http://dx.doi.org/10.1037/0012-1649.42.1.70.

Subotnik, R. F., Tai, R. H., Rickoff, R. & Almarode, J. (2009). Specialized public high schools of science, mathematics, and technology and the STEM pipeline: What do we know now and what will we know in 5 years? *Roeper Review, 32*:1, 7–16. http://dx.doi.org/10.1080/02783190903386553.

Suter, L. E. (2017). Using international comparative data in achievement in educational research. In D. Wyse, N. Selwyn, E. Smith, & L. E. Suter (Eds.), *The BERA/Sage handbook of educational research* (pp. 313–335). Thousand Oaks, CA: Sage Publications.

Tenenbaum, H. R. & Callanan, M. A. (2008). Parent's science talk to their children in Mexican-descent families residing in the USA. *International Journal of Behavioral Development, 32*, 1–12. https://doi.org/10.1177/0165025407084046.

Tenenbaum, H. R. & Leaper, C. (2003). Parent-child conversations about science: The socialization of gender inequities? *Developmental Psychology, 39*, 34–47. http://dx.doi.org/10.1037/0012-1649.39.1.34.

Turner, J. C., Kackar-Cam, H. Z., & Trucano, M. (2015). Teachers learning how to support student interest in mathematics and science. In K. A. Renninger, M. Nieswandt, & S. Hidi (Eds.), *Interest in mathematics and science learning* (pp. 243–60). Washington, DC: American Educational Research Association. doi: 10.3102/978-0-935302-42-4.

Tytler, R. (2014). Attitudes, identity and aspirations toward science. In N. G. Lederman & S. K. Abell (Eds.). *Handbook of research on science education* (pp. 82–103). New York, NY: Routledge.

Tytler, R., Osborne, J., Williams, G., Tytler, K., & Clark, J. C. (2008). *Opening up pathways: Engagement in STEM across the primary-secondary school transition.* Australian Department of Education, Employment, and Workplace Relations. Available at https://docs.education.gov.au/system/files/doc/other/openpathinscitechmathenginprimsecschtrans.pdf.

Vedder-Wiess, D. & Fortus, D. (2011). Adolescents' declining motivation to learn science: Inevitable or not? *Journal of Research in Science Teaching, 48,* 199–216. doi: 10.1002/tea.20398.

14 Predicting Academic Effort

The Conscientiousness × Interest Compensation (CONIC) Model

Ulrich Trautwein, Benjamin Nagengast,
Brent Roberts, and Oliver Lüdtke

Abstract: Academic effort is a key construct in research on motivational variables such as interest and in research on conscientiousness, one of the Big Five domains of human personality. Surprisingly, the two lines of research have rarely been brought together. In this chapter, we describe the differences and similarities in the theoretical foundation of the two constructs and review research on their predictive power for academic effort. We then introduce the Conscientiousness × Interest Compensation (CONIC) model which postulates that conscientiousness and interest (partly) compensate for each other in predicting academic effort. Subsequently, we present empirical evidence for the model. In the final section of the chapter, we formulate some next steps in a research program on conscientiousness and interest.

What is the most important factor influencing academic effort? Why do some students persevere on a given task whereas others give up quickly? Ask a few psychologists, and you will get a number of different answers, depending on the specialization of each respondent. Two of the most likely answers include "conscientiousness" and "interest." At the same time, however, chances are high that no single respondent will mention both of these constructs. The reason for this is both easy and troubling: the constructs of interest and conscientiousness stem from very different lines of thinking about academic effort, which have rarely been brought together in an explicit way. The fact that different fields independently developed unique ways of thinking about motivation makes this an interesting mystery – one that should be resolved as soon as possible, given its implications for theory and practice.

More specifically, psychologists who focus on the study of motivation emphasize the role of interest but do not include conscientiousness in their thinking. A good example is the well-known review by Pintrich (2003) on key constructs in what he called "motivational science." Whereas interest

This chapter is informed by the authors' prior research (especially Trautwein et al., 2015) and partly adapts this material. Preparation of the chapter was supported by a grant from the Ministry of Science, Research, and the Arts Baden-Württemberg.

figured prominently as one of five key families of social-cognitive constructs used in research on student motivation, conscientiousness was not mentioned at all. Conversely, for a long time, scholars specializing in personality psychology have focused on the so-called Big Five personality constructs (neuroticism, extraversion, openness, conscientiousness, and agreeableness; see Costa & McCrae, 1992; Goldberg, 1993; McCrae & Costa, 2003), of which conscientiousness is most closely associated with academic effort and achievement (e.g., De Raad & Schouwenburg, 1996); social-cognitive constructs such as personal interests have been ignored altogether or treated as consequences of underlying personality dimensions (e.g., McCrae & Costa, 2008).

In our view, these silo practices constitute a significant limitation to research on academic effort that needs to be overcome. Integrating the divergent lines of thinking about both conscientiousness and interest will lead to a better understanding of students' academic effort, and will contribute to a broader perspective on how to develop sustained effort in students.

In our own prior research and ongoing work, we have started to integrate classic personality constructs as conceptualized in the Big Five and social-cognitive variables such as self-concept and interest (e.g., Rieger et al., 2017; Roberts & Nickel, 2017; Trautwein et al., 2009, 2015). The present chapter focuses on two constructs only, namely conscientiousness and interest, and their unique and combined power to predict academic effort. More specifically, we propose a compensatory effects model, the CONIC model, as a theoretical foundation for studying conscientiousness and interest as predictors of academic effort. To this end, we will first describe the two constructs of interest and conscientiousness. We will then discuss the compensatory effects model and present results from empirical studies. Finally, we will illuminate some theoretical and practical implications.

Psychology of Motivation: Interest

Interest has been a key concept in educational and psychological research for a long time, and this research has yielded a large body of knowledge on the characteristics of interest, its origins and development, and its power to trigger and sustain academic behavior (e.g., Eccles & Wigfield, 2002; Hidi & Ainley, 2008; Krapp, 2002; Renninger et al., 2015). In an influential review by Pintrich (2003), interest was included in the list of the five most important social-cognitive constructs in the domain of motivation science.

Interest research is a highly productive, yet somewhat complex and fragmented, research field with several different, albeit overlapping, lines of theorizing (e.g., Wigfield & Eccles, 2000). In addition to what can be characterized as "stand-alone" approaches (e.g., Krapp, 2002; Hidi & Renninger, 2006), interest has been integrated into broader theories, such as self-determination theory (Deci & Ryan, 2002) and expectancy-value theory (Eccles & Wigfield, 2002). Despite some differences between approaches, there is some consensus with regard to a number of central characteristics of interest (also see Renninger & Hidi, 2016), which are described next.

First, individual interest relates to specific content. More specifically, interest can be defined as a relatively stable evaluative orientation toward certain domains (Eccles & Wigfield, 2002; Schiefele, 1991) and "a relatively enduring predisposition to re-engage with particular content over time" (Hidi & Ainley, 2008, p. 88). Hence, individual interest is strongly domain-specific (Bong, 2001; Eccles et al., 1993) and has to be differentiated from other constructs such as curiosity (Renninger & Hidi, Chapter 11). Students often have favorite subjects at school and will happily volunteer reasons for preferring mathematics or sports, even if their objective performance in both subjects is the same. In fact, correlations among interest in different subjects are typically much lower than correlations among grades or test scores in those same subjects (e.g., Jansen et al., 2016; Nagy et al., 2006). In particular, a strong distinction is made between *verbal* subjects and *mathematical* subjects, with students tending to report more interest in one or the other (Nagy et al., 2006; see also Marsh, 1986). Empirical evidence indicates that the domain specificity of interest increases with students' age (Denissen et al., 2007).

Second, interest seems to consist of both affective and cognitive components. According to Renninger and Hidi (2011), affect, value, and knowledge are core components of interest, although their importance varies across different phases of interest development. According to the Munich Interest School (e.g., Krapp, 2002; Schiefele, 1991), two aspects or components of individual interest can be distinguished: feeling-related and value-related valences. Similarly, expectancy-value theory (Eccles & Wigfield, 2002) distinguishes between intrinsic value and attainment value. Intrinsic value (sometimes called "interest value") is defined as the enjoyment one gains from doing a task. Attainment value has similarities with value-related valences as described by Schiefele (1991). When instruments distinguish between affective elements of interest (e.g., "I really like mathematics") and more value-related aspects (e.g., "mathematics is important to me"), the resulting correlations are typically quite high (Gaspard et al., 2015; Trautwein et al., 2012).

Third, there is a need to distinguish between individual interest as a relatively stable orientation towards certain domains and the more momentary experience of interest in a specific situation (see Hidi & Renninger, 2006; Krapp, 2002; Tsai et al., 2008), for which terms such as "situational interest" or "interest experience" have been used. This momentary state of interest is always a function of characteristics of both the individual and the situation. Interest experience is a momentary manifestation of a latent disposition (Krapp, 2002) in that the psychological state of interest is more likely to be triggered when content is perceived as relevant to one's already existing individual interests. However, interest experience can also be predominantly prompted by situational characteristics (such as in the first phase of the "four phases of interest development"; Hidi & Renninger, 2006), which can "trigger" interest even if the domain is new to the individual or the individual is unaware of the association with already existing interests.

Fourth, interest-driven engagement is typically associated with positive feelings, although negative affect can be associated with the early phases of interest development (see Ainley & Hidi, 2014; Renninger & Hidi, 2016). In fact, researchers have consistently emphasized the feeling-related aspects of interest (e.g., Krapp, 2002; Renninger & Hidi, 2011) or have even equated individual interest with emotion (see Reeve et al., 2015). Equally important, it is postulated that interest-driven engagement may protect students from experiencing the exhaustion that typically occurs when engaging in cognitive endeavors (Reeve et al., 2015; Thoman et al., 2011).

Fifth, there is a stable and substantial association between interest and positive academic outcomes, such as academic effort and academic attainment. This association was documented in an early meta-analysis by Schiefele et al. (1992) and thereafter in a large number of articles, book chapters, and books, including some of our own work (e.g., Jansen et al., 2016; Trautwein & Lüdtke, 2007; Trautwein et al., 2006). In fact, given robust evidence for a positive association between interest and academic outcomes, research has shifted toward identifying processes that underlie this positive association.

Sixth, to date, there is no single standardized and widely accepted instrument for assessing individual interest. Instead, many different questionnaires with good face validity and generally good psychometric quality have been used. The most common measures being used are self-reports, and – given that students are aware of their own interests, but these are less easily observed by external observers – this approach seems to be most appropriate for this field of research, at least for well-established individual interest (Renninger & Hidi, 2016).

Personality Psychology: Conscientiousness

The other key personal characteristic considered in this chapter is the personality trait of conscientiousness. Personality traits are defined as relatively enduring, automatic individual patterns of thoughts, feelings, and behaviors that arise in specific situations (Roberts, 2009). Individuals reporting high levels of conscientiousness tend to exhibit self-control, goal-directed behavior, make plans, delay gratification, and follow norms and rules (John et al., 2008;

John & Srivastava, 1999). Conscientiousness has also been characterized as a family of constructs that describe individual differences in the propensity to be self-controlled, responsible, hardworking, orderly, and rule-abiding (Roberts et al., 2014).

Together with neuroticism, extraversion, agreeableness, and openness to experience (the latter sometimes labeled imagination, intellect, or culture), conscientiousness is one of the traits included in the Big Five model of personality (Digman, 1990; Funder, 1991; Goldberg, 1993), the most frequently used trait model in personality psychology.

In the present context, the following characteristics of the psychological construct of conscientiousness are of particular importance. First, conscientiousness is a trait, which means that it is not domain-specific (e.g., McCrae & Costa, 2008). In fact, the cross-time and cross-situational consistency of feelings, thoughts, and behaviors are a cornerstone of the definition of a "trait," although there is some discussion of the extent to which traits are "decontextualized." It is true that all traits, whether conscientiousness or the remaining Big Five traits, arise in response to situations (Roberts, 2009). The relevant question is how to best define and operationalize trait-evoking situations at more or less aggregate levels (Fleeson & Gallagher, 2009). Different scholastic disciplines provide excellent opportunities to test the cross-domain consistency of the predictive effects of traits such as conscientiousness, which is a family of traits that is highly relevant to achievement settings, such as those found in school and at work. Therefore, the different domains and contexts of students' educational experiences provide an ideal laboratory to test the cross-domain consistency of personality traits. For example, with regard to students' academic effort, there is evidence to show that students high in conscientiousness tend to work hard across a wide range of subjects (e.g., Trautwein & Lüdtke, 2007). Hence, in stark contrast to the construct of interest, the motivational force that comes with conscientiousness is not linked to a specific domain or subject.

Second, efforts to map out the dimensions that belong within the domain of conscientiousness are still ongoing (Roberts et al., 2014). Work on the lower-order structure of conscientiousness has revealed anywhere from two (DeYoung et al., 2007) to ten dimensions (Roberts et al., 2014). The consensus is that conscientiousness is made up of at least four facets: orderliness, self-control, industriousness, and responsibility. Other facets, such as conventionality, persistence, and punctuality, while identified in some research, are not as unequivocally supported as facets of conscientiousness. Broadly speaking, these sub-dimensions can be organized into reactive and proactive domains (Jackson et al., 2010). The reactive dimensions are best expressed in the facet of self-control, which reflects the propensity to inhibit impulses. The proactive dimensions are best represented by the facet of industriousness, or the propensity to pursue goals even in the face of temporary setbacks. Of these dimensions, industriousness (i.e., the tendency to work hard, aspire to excellence, and persist in the face of challenges) is perhaps most closely related to academic effort.

Third, the use of the term "trait" implies that the construct of conscientiousness tends to be highly stable. Indeed, empirical research points to substantial correlational stability for conscientiousness (or its constitutive dimensions) even after longer periods of time (Roberts & DelVecchio, 2000). At the same time, the traditional notion of traits as in-born characteristics that do not systematically change in response to interaction with the environment (see McCrae & Costa, 2008) has been challenged. For instance, the neo-socioanalytic model of personality (see Roberts & Nickel, 2017) proposes that personality traits have a tendency to show relatively large life course patterns of change, such that most people become more agreeable, conscientious, and emotionally stable with age. Moreover, these patterns of change are not solely due to genetic factors, but appear to arise in response to environmental factors.

Fourth, conscientiousness-prompted actions do affect emotional experiences, despite the fact that the construct itself has no clear link to positive or negative emotional states. In particular, conscientiousness is related to implementation behaviors that bring about positive affect and satisfaction (Hill et al., 2014). Conscientiousness also helps immunize people from experiencing certain forms of negative affect, specifically guilt (Hill et al., 2014). The positive experiences brought about through implementation behaviors (e.g., industriousness) are thought to lead to accomplishments, such as winning academic awards (e.g., Lüdtke et al., 2011), that bring pride and satisfaction. Conversely, by avoiding negative experiences like marital discord and a diminished financial standing (Xu et al., 2015), highly conscientious individuals avoid negative experiences and the guilt that sometimes comes with failure (Fayard et al., 2012). In contrast to interest and the emotional experience of activities one is passionate about, there is little evidence that conscientiousness is directly linked to positive emotional experiences such as joy or happiness (Fayard et al., 2012).

Fifth, conscientiousness is particularly relevant for education, as it is the most robust personality trait predictor of academic success and academic effort that is independent of cognitive ability (Poropat, 2009). A relatively large body of literature has shown that conscientiousness is associated with a wide variety of academic outcomes (De Raad & Schouwenburg, 1996; Poropat, 2009), although there are many fewer studies with high school students than college students (for an exception, see Spengler et al., 2013). Noftle and Robins (2007) summarized the results of 20 studies examining the association between conscientiousness and GPA or college grades. Conscientiousness was significantly positively related to the academic outcome variable in 15 of these 20 studies; the mean effect size was 0.26. Similarly, the relatively few studies that have examined the association between conscientiousness and academic outcomes in high school students have generally found positive links. Some more recent studies have provided empirical support for the notion that these positive associations are mediated by academic effort (Bidjerano & Dai, 2007; De Raad & Schouwenburg, 1996; Noftle & Robins, 2007).

Sixth, in contrast to individual interest, where the instruments are oftentimes tailored to the research question or project, there is a greater tendency among personality researchers to use only a few standardized questionnaires to assess conscientiousness, such as the NEO-PI and the NEO-FFI (Costa & McCrae, 1992), as well as the BFI (John et al., 2008). Despite some debates about measurement issues (e.g., Marsh et al., 2010), these instruments have proved to be reliable and valid. When testing the associations among conscientiousness and academic variables (such as academic effort), it is of critical importance that measures of conscientiousness do not just report these behaviors. In fact, most personality inventories take into account that conscientiousness consists of a set of feelings, thoughts, and behaviors and, thus, cannot be reduced to just the behavioral aspect (see Jackson et al., 2012). Another advantage of personality traits is that they can be validly assessed with either self-report or observer report. For educational research, this means that sources other than the students themselves, such as parents or teachers, can be tapped to provide valid information about students' levels of conscientiousness (Göllner et al., 2017). In fact, some research has shown that teacher ratings of personality, and particularly of behaviors linked to conscientiousness, are quite useful for predicting life outcomes. For example, in a series of studies based on a longitudinal cohort from Luxembourg, teacher ratings of students' school-based conscientiousness predicted outcomes such as educational attainment, occupational status, physical health, and even longevity above and beyond family socioeconomic status and the students' cognitive ability (Spengler et al., 2015a, 2015b, 2016).

In sum, conscientiousness is a family of traits that shows continuity across time and is relevant across situations, including educational domains. The constituent elements of the domain of conscientiousness include facets that are particularly relevant for educational effort, such as industriousness. Moreover, research has shown that these facets predict many important emotional and behavioral outcomes that are related to success in school and life.

Interest and Conscientiousness as Predictors of Academic Effort: The CONIC Model

In this section, we introduce the *CONscientiousness Interest Compensation* (CONIC) model. The CONIC model describes the association between conscientiousness and individual interest, and explains how they work together to predict academic effort. It is based on the theoretical distinctions described earlier in the chapter. In this section, we synthesize these distinctions and discuss their consequences for predicting academic effort. Finally, we describe empirical support for the CONIC model.

Interest and conscientiousness are considered to be powerful predictors of academic effort. At the same time, interest and conscientiousness differ in how they are conceptualized. In fact, the existing literature suggests that the two constructs may belong to different layers of personality and are located at different levels of analysis (e.g., Asendorpf & van Aken, 2003; Jackson et al., 2012; McCrae & Costa, 2008; Roberts & Nickel, 2017; but see Kandler et al., 2014). For instance, McAdams and Pals (2006) differentiated between dispositional traits and characteristic adaptations (including values and other motivational concerns), highlighting conceptual and developmental differences between traits (high stability, low plasticity in response to contextual variables, and high domain generality; see McCrae & Costa, 2008) and characteristic adaptations (more amenable to external influences, more likely to change over time, and more situation-anchored). Similarly, Asendorpf and van Aken (2003) differentiated between "core" and "surface" characteristics, with traits (including conscientiousness) constituting the core of personality (and having relatively high "immunity to environmental influences"; p. 636) and constructs (such as self-worth, self-perceived peer acceptance, and loneliness) constituting the surface characteristics, which exhibit "high (but not total) susceptibility to environmental influences" (p. 636). According to Winter et al. (1998) who differentiated between "traits" and "motives," "motives refer to people's wishes and desires" (p. 231), whereas traits refer to people's "stylistic and habitual patterns of cognition, affect, and behavior" (Emmons, 1989, p. 32). Hence, in contrast to traits, which describe "how" individuals behave across situations, interests describe "what" individuals want to do.

Interestingly, individual interests in school subjects have not been explicitly addressed in the discussion of how constructs at different levels (traits/core characteristics versus characteristic adaptations/surface characteristics) relate to each other. In addition, the extent to which core and surface characteristics differ, in terms of stability and susceptibility, has become subject to a number of recent empirical studies (e.g., Rieger et al., 2017). Nevertheless, given the theoretical differences between the constructs, speaking of different layers of personality is justified.

What are the implications of the relative conceptual independence of conscientiousness and individual interest for their combined predictive effect on academic effort? We propose the CONIC model to account for these relations. According to the CONIC model, both conscientiousness and interest uniquely contribute to explaining academic effort when both constructs are simultaneously considered. In regression analyses, this "additive" effect would be reflected in statistically significant and positive regression weights for both interest and conscientiousness when simultaneously entered into the regression equation. More importantly, however, the CONIC model also

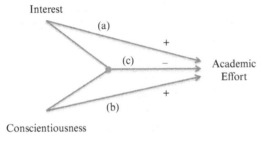

Figure 14.1. *Graphical depiction of the CONIC model*

postulates a *compensatory mechanism*. The compensatory interaction means that conscientiousness and individual interest can (partly) compensate for one another. In other words, individual interest will be less important for academic effort among students who are high in conscientiousness, and conscientiousness will be of less importance for students who have high interest. Statistically speaking, support for a compensatory effect (also called an *"interference or antagonistic effect"*; Cohen et al., 2003, p. 285) is found when the sign of the interaction is opposite to that of the two main effects. In such an interaction, the two predictors compensate for each other to a certain extent.

A graphical depiction of the CONIC model is provided in Figure 14.1, in which both interest (path a) and conscientiousness (path b) predict academic effort. Moreover, they interact with each other (path c) in predicting academic effort, indicating a compensatory effect. Domain interest plays an important motivational role for students who are low in conscientiousness.

Empirical Support for the CONIC Model

Both interest and conscientiousness are believed to be associated with academic effort and achievement, and there is substantial empirical support for this claim. However, the bulk of existing studies are what can be called "single predictor" studies: they include either interest or conscientiousness as a predictor, but not both. Alternatively, even if both interest and conscientiousness are used as predictors, possible interaction effects are not considered.

A growing body of research can be considered to directly or indirectly test the CONIC model. We first report findings from studies originating in our own lab, followed by related research from other colleagues.

Scrutinizing the CONIC model: our research program. We first tested the unique and interactive effects of interest and conscientiousness in a series of four studies published by Trautwein et al. (2015). The starting point of the analyses was rather exploratory in nature: We probed for potential interaction effects, but did not directly specify whether compensatory or synergistic interactions were expected. Moreover, we did not originally use the term "CONIC model." However, because the results of all four studies were in line with what we now call the CONIC model, we treat them as support for this model.

The first of the four studies (Study 1) was a re-analysis of a large data set – 2,557 eighth grade students from 133 classes in 99 non-academic track (non-Gymnasium) schools in two German states (Baden-Wuerttemberg and Saxony) – in which we were able to test the predictive effect of interest and conscientiousness in three subjects (mathematics, English, and German). We used latent moderated structural (LMS) equation modeling to predict academic effort (Klein & Moosbrugger, 2000). The interaction term had a significant regression weight in all three subjects (math: $B = -0.20$, German: $B = -0.17$, English: $B = -0.22$), indicating that conscientiousness and interest mutually moderated each other's predictive effects on academic effort. The interaction term explained 2–3 percent of the variance in academic effort, over and above the main effects. The significant interaction effects are plotted in Figure 14.2, in which we can see that students high in both conscientiousness and interest

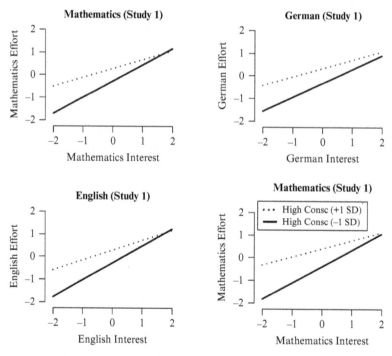

Figure 14.2. *Plots of the moderating effect of conscientiousness on the relationship between interest and effort. Depicted are simple slopes at +1 SD from the mean of conscientiousness. All effects are between-student effects. The independent variable (interest; x-axis) and dependent variable (effort; y-axis) range from −2 to +2 SD of the mean (see Aiken & West, 1991). From "Using individual interest and conscientiousness to predict academic effort: Additive, synergistic, or compensatory effects?" by U. Trautwein, O. Lüdtke, N. Nagy, A. Lenski, A. Niggli, & I. Schnyder, 2015,* Journal of Personality and Social Psychology, *109, pp. 142–62. Copyright by the American Psychological Association, reprinted with permission.*

reported the highest academic effort, whereas students low on both conscientiousness and interest reported the lowest effort. More importantly, however, the figure illustrates a compensation effect: at very high levels of individual interest, conscientiousness did not "add" much to academic effort, and students high in interest reported above-average academic effort, even if their conscientiousness was low.

In Study 2, we applied the same analytical approach as in Study 1 to re-analyze a data set encompassing a sample of 415 high school students from 20 classes in academic track schools in which students filled out a conscientiousness measure, as well as interest and academic effort scales for math and English. In this study, the interaction term had a significant regression weight in math ($B = -0.20$) but not in English ($B = -0.04$), indicating that conscientiousness and interest mutually moderated each other's predictive effects on academic effort in mathematics but not in English. As can be seen in Figure 14.2, the significant interaction effect was again of a compensatory nature.

In Study 3, a sample of 1,025 high school students from 51 grade seven and grade ten classrooms were asked to report their interest in a set of five subjects, as well as the academic effort they typically invested in those subjects. For each of the five subjects, we investigated whether there was a significant interaction between conscientiousness and academic interest in predicting academic effort. In all five subjects, conscientiousness and interest statistically significantly predicted academic effort. Furthermore, we found support for the compensatory effects model in the three "main subjects" (math, German, and English). For the other two subjects (biology and a second foreign language), no compensatory effect was found.

More importantly, however, using a multi-level design, we complemented the analyses at the between-student level with analyses at the within-student level. Over time, most students develop specific interest profiles, exhibiting a marked interest in some subjects and a dislike of others. These interest profiles are likely to correspond with academic effort profiles, with students putting more effort into their favorite subjects and less effort into their least-liked subjects. At the same time, students high in conscientiousness can be expected to report more academic effort overall than students low in conscientiousness.

We tested for possible interaction effects using multi-level modeling. The CONIC model predicts a weaker relationship between interest and academic effort among students high in conscientiousness than students low in conscientiousness (as conscientiousness can compensate for lack of interest) and vice versa. Indeed, conscientiousness partly explained the variation in the interest slope across students; more specifically, the cross-level interaction effect Conscientiousness × Domain-Specific Interest proved to be significant ($B = -0.04$, $p = 0.006$). Figure 14.3 illustrates the significant interaction between conscientiousness and domain-specific interest.

Finally, in Study 4, we examined whether the compensatory effects model also holds when interest experience – rather than individual interest – is

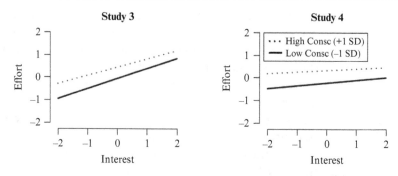

Figure 14.3. *Plots of the moderating effect of conscientiousness on the relationship between interest and effort. Depicted are simple slopes at +1 SD from the mean of conscientiousness. Both effects are within-student effects. The independent variable (interest; x-axis) and dependent variable (effort; y-axis) range from −2 to +2 SD of the mean. From "Using individual interest and conscientiousness to predict academic effort: Additive, synergistic, or compensatory effects?" by U. Trautwein, O. Lüdtke, N. Nagy, A. Lenski, A. Niggli, & I. Schnyder, 2015,* Journal of Personality and Social Psychology, *109, pp. 142–62. Copyright by the American Psychological Association, reprinted with permission.*

examined. Our major research question concerned the degree to which conscientiousness moderates the association between interest experience and academic effort. To that end, we tested whether students high in conscientiousness were more likely to invest academic effort on days in which their interest experience was comparatively low. More specifically, we investigated how interest experience and conscientiousness predicted academic effort in French as a foreign language on a day-to-day basis. The sample consisted of 1,530 students in 89 classrooms in three Swiss cantons. Results from multi-level modeling showed that the cross-level interaction Conscientiousness × Interest Experience significantly predicted academic effort ($B = -0.03$, $p = 0.002$), again supporting the predictions of the CONIC model. The interaction effect is illustrated in Figure 14.3 ("Study 4"). Both high conscientiousness and high interest experience were associated with high academic effort. However, they also compensated for each other, as indicated by the (relatively) high academic effort scores when only conscientiousness or interest experience was high.

More recently, we found additional empirical support for the CONIC model in a study by Rieger et al. (2018). In this study, we were interested in whether the CONIC model would also find empirical support in a longitudinal study. More specifically, we were interested in whether changes in academic effort, from one time point to the next, can be predicted by interest, conscientiousness, and the interaction between the two variables. To test the CONIC model in a longitudinal study, we re-analyzed data from a large school achievement study in Germany (pooled N across time points was 3,876 students from 99 schools) encompassing four time points (from grades five to eight: T1, T2, T3, and T4). We again applied LMS equation modeling. In these analyses, the effect of the interaction between interest and conscientiousness on the change in academic effort was significantly negative for five out of a total of nine prediction models, and negative (but not significant) in the other four models. In line with the predictions of the CONIC model, the significant interactions indicated that conscientiousness and interest moderated each other's predictive effects on the change in academic effort across all three school subjects. Thus, the positive effect of conscientiousness on the development of academic effort was stronger when interest was low – or vice versa, the positive effect of interest on the development of academic effort was stronger when conscientiousness was low. Thus, the results of the study lend further support to the CONIC model.

In an additional study (Song et al., 2017), we tested whether the CONIC model would still hold when, on the basis of expectancy-value theory (Eccles & Wigfield, 2000; also see Gaspard et al., 2015), we replaced interest with utility value (one of the other three value components in expectancy-value theory) in the prediction models. Furthermore, in this study, we tested whether the CONIC model would also hold when predicting academic achievement instead of academic effort as the outcome variable. We re-analyzed data from a study (Gaspard et al., 2017) that was originally planned to examine dimensions and facets of expectancy and value beliefs. The study provided data from 830 students in grades five through 12 from 51 classes in two German academic track schools. In addition to conscientiousness and domain interest in four school subjects (German, English, mathematics, and biology; we also measured interest in physics in some grade levels, but do not report on those data here), we also measured students' perceived utility value (e.g., "Knowing the contents in [school subject] will be helpful for my future career") for these subjects. Furthermore, we used teacher-assigned school grades in these subjects, in addition to a domain-specific academic effort scale. Again, LMS regression analysis was applied, and the results provided further support for the CONIC model. The Conscientiousness × Interest interaction term was significant in all four school subjects. Extending previous results, the interaction term was also predictive of achievement in two of the four domains. Furthermore, when interest was replaced by utility value, we found the same pattern of results: the Conscientiousness × Utility Value interaction term was a significant predictor of academic effort in all four school subjects. Furthermore, it statistically significantly predicted school grades in two of the four school subjects. Hence, the pattern of results was in support of the CONIC model, and it indicates that the model might be generalizable to related predictors (utility value instead of interest) and outcomes (school grades instead of academic effort).

Related research from other labs. The association among interest, conscientiousness, and academic effort has also been investigated by other research groups. Importantly, in work by Sansone et al. (e.g., Sansone et al., 1999, 2010), conscientiousness and interest were conceptualized within a larger framework of self-regulation. Sansone et al. differentiate between goals-defined motivation (the what and why of activity engagement) and experience-defined motivation (the interest experienced during the activity). As argued by Sansone et al. (2010, p. 201), "individuals may differ in the extent to which motivation to reach goals and motivation based on the experience are attended to and considered important. When individuals characteristically weigh goals-defined motivation as more important, such as in the case of individuals high in conscientiousness, the lack of motivation derived from the boring experience is not as critical for their persistence." Sansone et al. found support for this assumption in a series of lab experiments in which both conscientiousness and interest experience were assessed.

Also of interest in this context is a recent article by Di Domenico and Fournier (2015). These researchers examined conscientiousness, autonomous motivation, and intelligence as predictors of academic performance (cumulative GPA) in a sample of 271 undergraduate students. Although not identical, a high score in autonomous motivation is typically closely associated with high interest. In regression analyses, the authors found intelligence and conscientiousness to be statistically significant unique predictors of academic performance. Autonomous motivation did not have a statistically significant unique effect on the outcome, but the Conscientiousness × Autonomous Motivation interaction term was negative and statistically significant, indicating that conscientiousness compensated for low levels of autonomous motivation.

Concluding Thoughts

Over a set of studies, we developed and found empirical support for the CONIC model, which postulates that conscientiousness and interest can compensate for each other in predicting academic effort. Despite being a "young model," the empirical support for the CONIC model is substantial. We were able to replicate the effect in several independent data sets. Moreover, the CONIC model was robust against variations in the predictor variables (individual interest, interest experiences, and utility value), outcomes (academic effort and achievement), and designs (within-person and between-person). Furthermore, a pattern of results in line with the CONIC model has been reported by other researchers (see Di Domenico & Fournier, 2015; Sansone et al., 2010). Finally, the CONIC model complements earlier work by our lab (see Trautwein & Lüdtke, 2007; Trautwein et al., 2006), in which we showed that conscientiousness is particularly important in situations characterized by low external supervision or control (i.e., homework versus in-school learning, as well as varying levels of perceived teacher monitoring of homework completion). Still, there is a need for additional research that replicates our findings and tests their generalizability across predictor variables (e.g., does the CONIC model hold for all sub-facets of conscientiousness?), outcome variables (e.g., different modes of self-regulation), and research designs (e.g., various lab settings).

Why do conscientiousness and interest (partly) compensate for each other? In the chapter introduction, we highlighted several differences between conscientiousness and interest that lend plausibility to the argument that they are part of different modes of regulation. Most importantly, whereas interest is a powerful energizing factor that attracts individuals to take action, behavior prompted by conscientiousness can instead feel like it results from a "pushing" force. While the activity itself is the goal in interest-driven activities, high conscientiousness pushes individuals to work hard on tasks even when there is no immediate incentive, but rather long-term goals. Assuming that activities triggered by conscientiousness versus interest represent two different modes of regulation that can both lead to high effort, it seems likely that they can compensate for each other. However, future studies are needed to get a better understanding of how the two presumed modes of regulation complement each other and how they impact the quality of academic learning.

The empirical support for the CONIC model has theoretical implications for both personality psychology and motivational psychology. With regard to personality psychology, the clear empirical support for the substantial domain-specificity of academic behavior is of high interest. Conscientiousness, as one of the Big Five "super factors," did predict academic behavior across several domains; however, interest proved to be a similarly important predictor. In our view, whereas the Big Five personality factors help describe typical patterns of feeling, thoughts, and behaviors, they are only partly able to predict the "direction" in individuals' lives. This is also evidenced when comparing long-term effects of the Big Five and, for instance, vocational interests (see Stoll et al., 2017). Vocational interests add to the predictive power of the Big Five for important life course outcomes – and oftentimes are the more powerful predictors. In our view, academic domains such as those studied in our research are an ideal opportunity to study the cross-domain stability of personality in the future, within and beyond the framework of the CONIC model.

Finally, the CONIC model might also contribute to educational practice by overcoming a problematic divide between practitioners who emphasize the need to strengthen "personality factors" and those who seek to make school "interesting." Our research indicates that both factors play a crucial role in determining academic effort, and individual interest might be particularly important when conscientiousness is low.

References

Ainley, M. & Hidi, S. (2014). Interest and enjoyment. In R. Pekrun & L. Linnenbrink-Garcia (Eds.), *International handbook of emotions in education* (pp. 205–27). New York, NY: Routledge.

Asendorpf, J. & van Aken, M. A. G. (2003). Personality-relationship transaction in adolescence: Core versus surface personality characteristics. *Journal of Personality, 71*, 629–66. doi: 10.1111/1467-6494.7104005.

Bidjerano, T. & Dai, D. Y. (2007). The relationship between the big-five model of personality and self-regulated learning strategies. *Learning and Individual Differences, 17*, 69–81. doi: 10.1016/j.lindif.2007.02.001.

Bong, M. (2001). Between- and within-domain relations of academic motivation among middle and high school students: Self-efficacy, task value, and achievement goals. *Journal of Educational Psychology, 93*, 23–34. doi: 10.1037//0022-0663.93.1.23.

Cohen, J., Cohen, P., West, S. G., & Aiken, L. S. (2003). *Applied multiple regression/correlation analysis for the behavioral sciences*. Mahwah, NJ: Lawrence Erlbaum Associates.

Costa, P. T. & McCrae, R. R. (1992). *Revised NEO Personality Inventory (NEO PI-R) and NEO Five Factor Inventory (NEO-FFI). Professional Manual*. Odessa, FL: Psychological Assessment Resources.

De Raad, B. & Schouwenburg, H. C. (1996). Personality in learning and education: A review. *European Journal of Personality, 10*, 303–36. doi: 10.1002/(SICI)1099-0984(199612)10:5<303::AID-PER262>3.3.CO;2-U.

Deci, E. L. & Ryan, R. M. (Eds.). (2002). *Handbook of self-determination research*. New York, NY: University of Rochester Press.

Denissen, J. J. A., Zarrett, N. R., & Eccles, J. S. (2007). I like to do it, I'm able, and I know I am: Longitudinal couplings between domain-specific achievement, self-concept, and interest. *Child Development, 78*, 430–47. doi: 10.1111/j.1467-8624.2007.01007.x.

DeYoung, C. G., Quilty, L. C., & Peterson, J. B. (2007). Between facets and domains: 10 aspects of the Big Five. *Journal of Personality and Social Psychology, 93*(5), 880.

Di Domenico, S. I. & Fournier, M. A. (2015). Able, ready, and willing: Examining the additive and interactive effects of intelligence, conscientiousness, and autonomous motivation on undergraduate academic performance. *Learning and Individual Differences, 40*, 156–62. doi: 10.1016/j.lindif.2015.03.016.

Digman, J. M. (1990). Personality structure: Emergence of the five-factor model. In M. R. Rosenzweig & L. W. Porter (Eds.), *Annual review of psychology* (Vol. 41, pp. 417–46). Palo Alto, CA: Annual Reviews.

Eccles, J. S. & Wigfield, A. (2002). Motivational beliefs, values, and goals. *Annual Review of Psychology, 53*, 109–32. doi: 10.1146/annurev.psych.53.100901.135153.

Eccles, J., Wigfield, A., Harold, R., & Blumenfeld, P. (1993). Age and gender differences in children's self and task perceptions during elementary school. *Child Development, 64*, 830–47. doi: 10.2307/1131221.

Emmons, R. A. (1989). Exploring the relations between motives and traits: The case of narcissism. In D. Buss & N. Cantor (Eds.), *Personality psychology: Recent trends and emerging directions* (pp. 32–44). New York, NY: Springer.

Fayard, J. V., Roberts, B. W., Robins, R. W., & Watson, D. (2012). Uncovering the affective core of conscientiousness: The role of self-conscious emotions. *Journal of Personality, 80*, 1–32.

Fleeson, W. & Gallagher, P. (2009). The implications of Big Five standing for the distribution of trait manifestation in behavior: Fifteen experience-sampling studies and a meta-analysis. *Journal of Personality and Social Psychology, 97*, 1097–114. doi: 10.1037/a0016786.

Funder, D. (1991). Global traits: A neo-Allportian approach to personality. *Psychological Science, 2*, 31–9. doi: 10.1111/j.1467-9280.1991.tb00093.x.

Gaspard, H., Häfner, I., Parrisius, C., Trautwein, U., & Nagengast, B. (2016). Assessing task values in five subjects during secondary school: Measurement structure and mean level differences across grade level, gender, and academic subject. *Contemporary Educational Psychology.* Advance online publication. doi: 10.1016/j.cedpsych.2016.09.003.

Gaspard, H., Häfner, I., Parrisius, C., Trautwein, U., & Nagengast, B. (2017). Assessing task values in five subjects during secondary school: Measurement structure and mean level differences across grade level, gender, and academic subject. *Contemporary Educational Psychology, 48*, 67–84. doi: 10.1016/j.cedpsych.2016.09.003.

Goldberg, L.R. (1993). The structure of phenotypic personality traits. *American Psychologist, 48*, 26–34. doi: 10.1037//0003-066X.48.1.26.

Göllner, R., Roberts, B.W., Damian, R.I., Lüdtke, O., Jonkmann, K., & Trautwein, U. (2017). Whose "storm and stress" is it? Parent and child reports of personality development in the transition to early adolescence. *Journal of Personality, 83*(3), 376–87. doi: 10.1111/jopy.12246.

Hidi, S. & Ainley, M. (2008). Interest and self-regulation: Relationships between two variables that influence learning. In D. H. Schunk & B. J. Zimmerman (Eds.), *Motivation and self-regulated learning: Theory, research, and applications* (pp. 77–109). New York, NY: Routledge.

Hidi, S. & Renninger, K. A. (2006). The four-phase model of interest development. *Educational Psychologist, 41*, 111–27. doi: 10.1207/s15326985ep4102_4.

Hill, P. L., Nickel, L.B., & Roberts, B.W. (2014). Are you in a healthy relationship? Linking conscientiousness to health via implementing and immunizing behaviors. *Journal of Personality, 82*, 485–92.

Jackson, J. J., Hill, P. L., & Roberts, B. W. (2012). Misconceptions of traits continue to persist: A response to Bandura. *Journal of Management, 38*, 745–52. doi: 10.1177/0149206312438775.

Jackson, J. J., Wood, D., Bogg, T., Walton, K. E., Harms, P. D., & Roberts, B. W. (2010). What do conscientious people do? Development and validation of the Behavioral Indicators of Conscientiousness (BIC). *Journal of Research in Personality, 44*(4), 501–11.

Jansen, M., Lüdtke, O., & Schroeders, U. (2016). Evidence for a positive relation between interest and achievement: Examining between-person and within-person variation in five domains. *Contemporary Educational Psychology, 46*, 116–27.

John, O. P., Naumann, L. P., & Soto, C. J. (2008). Paradigm shift to the integrative Big-Five trait taxonomy: History, measurement, and conceptual issues. In O. P. John, R. W. Robins, & L. A. Pervin (Eds.), *Handbook of personality: Theory and research* (pp. 114–58). New York, NY: Guilford Press.

John, O. P. & Srivastava, S. (1999). The big five trait taxonomy: History, measurement, and theoretical perspectives. In L. A. Pervin & O. P. John (Eds.), *Handbook of personality: Theory and research* (2nd ed., pp. 102–38). New York, NY: Guilford Press.

Kandler, C., Zimmermann, J., & McAdams, D. P. (2014). Core and surface characteristics for the description and theory of personality differences and development. *European Journal of Personality, 28*, 231–43. doi: 10.1002/per.1952.

Klein, A. & Moosbrugger, H. (2000). Maximum likelihood estimation of latent interaction effects with the LMS method. *Psychometrika, 65*, 457–74. doi: 10.1007/BF02296338.

Krapp, A. (2002). Structural and dynamic aspects of interest development: Theoretical considerations from an ontogenetic perspective. *Learning and Instruction, 12*, 383–409. doi: 10.1016/S0959-4752(01)00011-1.

Lüdtke, O., Roberts, B., Trautwein, U., & Nagy, G. (2011). A random walk down university avenue: Life paths, life events, and personality trait change at the transition to university life. *Journal of Personality and Social Psychology, 101*(3), 620–37. doi: 10.1037/a0023743.

Marsh, H. W. (1986). Verbal and math self-concepts: An internal/external frame of reference model. *American Educational Research Journal, 23*, 129–49.

Marsh, H. W., Lüdtke, O., Muthén, B., Asparouhov, T., Morin, A. J. S., Trautwein, U., & Nagengast, B. (2010). A new look at the big five factor structure through exploratory structural equation modeling. *Psychological Assessment, 22*, 471–91. doi: 10.1037/a0019227.

McAdams, D. P. & Pals, J. L. (2006). A new Big Five: Fundamental principles for an integrative science of personality. *American Psychologist, 61*, 204–17. doi: 10.1037/0003-066X.61.3.204.

McCrae, R. R. & Costa, P. T., Jr. (2003). *Personality in adulthood: A five-factor theory perspective* (2nd ed.). New York, NY, US: Guilford Press. http://dx.doi.org/10.4324/9780203428412.

McCrae, R. R. & Costa, P. T., Jr. (2008). Empirical and theoretical status of the Five-Factor Model of personality traits. In G. J. Boyle, G. Matthews, & D. H. Saklofske (Eds.), *The Sage handbook of personality theory and assessment* (pp. 273–94). London: Sage.

Nagy, G., Trautwein, U., Baumert, J., Köller, O., & Garrett, J. (2006). Gender and course selection in upper secondary education: Effects of academic self-concept and intrinsic value. *Educational Research and Evaluation, 12*, 323–45. doi: 10.1080/13803610600765687.

Noftle, E. E. & Robins, R. W. (2007). Personality predictors of academic outcomes: Big Five correlates of GPA and SAT scores. *Journal of Personality and Social Psychology, 93*, 116–30. doi: 10.1037/0022-3514.93.1.116.

Pintrich, P. R. (2003). A motivational science perspective on the role of student motivation in learning and teaching contexts. *Journal of Educational Psychology, 95*, 667–86.

Poropat, A. E. (2009). A meta-analysis of the five-factor model of personality and academic performance. *Psychological Bulletin, 135*, 322–38. doi: 10.1037/a0014996.

Reeve, J., Lee, W., & Won, S. (2015). Interest as emotion, as affect, and as schema. In K. A. Renninger, M. Nieswandt, & S. Hidi (Eds.), *Interest in mathematics and science learning* (pp. 79–92). Washington, DC: American Educational Research Association.

Renninger, K. A. & Hidi, S. (2011). Revisiting the conceptualization, measurement, and generation of interest. *Educational Psychologist*, *46*, 168–84.

Renninger, K. A. & Hidi, S. (2016). *The power of interest for motivation and engagement*. New York, NY: Routledge.

Renninger, K. A., Nieswandt, M., & Hidi, S. (Eds.). (2015). *Interest in mathematics and science learning*. Washington, DC: AERA.

Rieger, S., Göllner, R., Spengler, M., Trautwein, U., Nagengast, B., & Roberts, B. W. (2017). Social cognitive constructs are just as stable as the Big Five between grades 5 and 8. *AERA Open*, *3*(3), 1–9.

Rieger, S., Göllner, R., Spengler, M., et al. (2018). *The development of students academic effort: Unique and joint effects of conscientiousness and individual interest*, under review.

Roberts, B. W. (2009). Back to the future: Personality and assessment and personality development. *Journal of Research in Personality*, *43*, 137–45.

Roberts, B. W. & DelVecchio, W. F. (2000). The rank-order consistency of personality traits from childhood to old age: A quantitative review of longitudinal studies. *Psychological Bulletin*, *126*, 3–25.

Roberts, B. W., Lejuez, C., Krueger, R. F., Richards, J. M., & Hill, P. L. (2014). What is conscientiousness and how can it be assessed? *Developmental Psychology*, *50*(5), 1315–30.

Roberts, B. W. & Nickel, L. B. (2017). A critical evaluation of the Neo-Socioanalytic Model of personality. In J. Specht (Ed.), *Personality development across the lifespan* (pp. 157–77). San Diego, CA: Elsevier.

Sansone, C., Thoman, D. B., & Smith, J. L. (2010). Interest and self-regulation: Understanding individual variability in choices, effort, and persistence over time. In R. H. Hoyle (Ed.), *Handbook of personality and self-regulation* (pp. 192–217). West Sussex: Wiley-Blackwell.

Sansone, C., Wiebe, D. J., & Morgan, C. L. (1999). Self-regulating motivation: The moderating role of hardiness and conscientiousness. *Journal of Personality*, *67*, 701–33.

Schiefele, U. (1991). Interest, learning, and motivation. *Educational Psychologist*, *26*, 299–323. doi: 10.1207/s15326985ep2603&4_5.

Schiefele, U., Krapp, A., & Winteler, A. (1992). Interest as a predictor of academic achievement: A meta-analysis of research. In K. A. Renninger, S. Hidi, & A. Krapp (Eds.), *The role of interest in learning and development* (pp. 183–212). Hillsdale, NJ: Lawrence Erlbaum.

Song, J., Gaspard, H., Nagengast, B., & Trautwein, U. (2018). Predicting academic effort and achievement: Generalizability of the Conscientiousness × Interest Compensation (CONIC) model across domains, outcomes, and predictors, submitted for publication.

Spengler, M., Brunner, M., Damian, R. I., Lüdtke, O., Martin, R., & Roberts, B. W. (2015a). Does it help to be a responsible student? Student characteristics and behaviors at age 12 predict occupational success 40 years later over and above childhood IQ and parental SES. *Developmental Psychology*, *51* (9), 1329–40.

Spengler, M., Lüdtke, O., Martin, R., & Brunner, M. (2013). Personality is related to educational outcomes in late adolescence: Evidence from two large-scale achievement studies. *Journal of Research in Personality*, *47*, 613–25.

Spengler, M., Roberts, B. W., Lüdtke, O., Martin, R. & Brunner, M. (2015b). The kind of student you were in elementary school predicts mortality. *Journal of Personality*. doi: 10.1111/jopy.12180.

Spengler, M., Roberts, B. W., Lüdtke, O., Martin, R., & Brunner, M. (2016). Student characteristics and behaviors in childhood predict self-reported health in middle adulthood. *European Journal of Personality*, *30*(5), 456–66.

Stoll, G., Rieger, S., Lüdtke, O., Nagengast, B., Trautwein, U., & Roberts, B. W. (2017). Vocational interests assessed at the end of high school predict life outcomes assessed 10 years later over and above IQ and Big Five personality traits. *Journal of Personality and Social Psychology*, *113*(1), 167–84. doi: 10.1037/pspp0000117.

Thoman, D. B., Smith, J. L., & Silva, P. J. (2011). The resource replenishment function of interest. *Social Psychological and Personality Science*, *2*, 592–99.

Trautwein, U. & Lüdtke, O. (2007). Students' self-reported effort and time on homework in six school subjects: Between-student differences and within-student variation. *Journal of Educational Psychology*, *99*, 432–44. doi: 10.1037/0022-0663.99.2.432.

Trautwein, U. & Lüdtke, O. (2009). Predicting homework motivation and homework effort in six school subjects: The role of person and family characteristics, classroom factors, and school track. *Learning and Instruction*, *19*, 243–58. doi: 10.1016/j.learninstruc.2008.05.001.

Trautwein, U., Lüdtke, O., Kastens, C. & Köller, O. (2006). Effort on homework in grades 5 through 9: Development, motivational antecedents, and the association with effort on classwork. *Child Development*, *77*(4), 1094–111. doi: 10.1111/j.1467-8624.2006.00921.x.

Trautwein, U., Lüdtke, O., Nagy, N., Lenski, A., Niggli, A., & Schnyder, I. (2015). Using individual interest and conscientiousness to predict academic effort: Additive, synergistic, or compensatory effects? *Journal of Personality and Social Psychology*, *109*, 142–62. doi: 10.1037/pspp0000034.

Trautwein, U., Lüdtke, O., Roberts, B. W., Schnyder, I., & Niggli, A. (2009). Different forces, same consequence: Conscientiousness and competence beliefs are independent predictors of academic effort and achievement. *Journal of Personality and Social Psychology*, *97*, 1115–28. doi: 10.1037/a0017048.

Trautwein, U., Lüdtke, O., Schnyder, I. & Niggli, A. (2006). Predicting homework effort: Support for a domain-specific, multilevel homework model. *Journal of Educational Psychology*, *98*(2), 438–56. doi: 10.1037/0022-0663.98.2.438.

Trautwein, U., Marsh, H.W., Nagengast, B., Lüdtke, O., Nagy, G., & Jonkmann, K. (2012). Probing for the multiplicative term in modern expectancy-value theory: A latent interaction modeling study. *Journal of Educational Psychology*, *104*, 763–77. doi: 10.1037/a0027470.

Tsai, Y.-M., Kunter, M., Lüdtke, O., Trautwein, U., & Ryan, R. (2008). What makes lessons interesting? The role of situation and person factors in three school subjects. *Journal of Educational Psychology*, *100*, 460–72. doi: 10.1037/0022-0663.100.2.460.

Wigfield, A. & Eccles, J. S. (2000). Expectancy-value theory of achievement motivation. *Contemporary Educational Psychology*, *25*, 68–81. doi: 10.1006/ceps.1999.1015.

Winter, D. G., John, O. P., Stewart, A. J., Klohnen, E. C., & Duncan, L. E. (1998). Traits and motives: Toward an integration of two traditions in personality research. *Psychological Review*, *105*, 230–50. doi: 10.1037//0033-295X.105.2.230.

Xu, Y., Beller, A. H., Roberts, B. W., & Brown, J. R. (2015). Personality and young adult financial distress. *Journal of Economic Psychology*, *51*, 90–100.

15 Reconceptualizing Intrinsic Motivation

Excellence as Goal

Barry Schwartz and Amy Wrzesniewski

Abstract: *There is a long history of thought and research in the social sciences that views human beings as engaged in entirely instrumental activities in pursuit of goals that typically give them pleasure. This view makes a sharp distinction between "means" and "ends," and treats the relation between means and ends as essentially arbitrary. Forty years of research on "intrinsic motivation" presents a different view, suggesting that some activities are themselves ends. In this chapter, we argue that distinguishing between intrinsic and extrinsic motivation has been important, but that the current understanding of the distinction is not adequate to capture the most important dimensions of difference between these two types of motives. We suggest a modification of the distinction, between activities that are pursued for consequences that bear an intimate relation to the activities themselves, and those that are purely instrumental. We call the former class of activities "internally motivated," and argue that while they are not necessarily pleasurable, they yield lasting effects on well-being that instrumental consequences typically do not. Further, we argue that internally motivated activities differ from intrinsically motivated ones, in which the sheer pleasure of the activity motivates its pursuit. We discuss evidence from both laboratory research and field studies, including a longitudinal study of West Point cadets, in support of our arguments.*

The pursuit of excellence leads not only to better performance but also to greater well-being. In the golden era of learning theory in psychology, in the middle of the twentieth century, research methods were developed for studying the behavior of rats and pigeons that were meant to produce general principles that applied to the instrumental, goal-directed behavior of all organisms (Schwartz, 1978; Skinner, 1953). Rats would press levers, negotiate mazes, and run down alleys, or pigeons would peck at illuminated disks for food or water. The central idea behind these methods was that since the relation between the response and the reward – the means and the end – was completely arbitrary, it would be representative of all instrumental, goal-directed activity.

This chapter extends Schwartz & Wrzesniewski (2016). The two chapters have much in common, but the earlier one focuses on the relation between internal motivation and what Aristotle called "*eudaimonia,*" whereas this one considers methodological and conceptual challenges to distinguishing internal motivation, intrinsic motivation, and instrumental motivation.

The relation was "arbitrary" because the response required to produce the food or water could be anything of which the organism was capable, and no relation between that response and the outcome had existed for the organism prior to the experiment. Rats pressing levers for food could be a stand-in for people working in factories or offices for their paychecks.

An assumption that helped justify these methods was that the purely instrumental relation between means and ends (lever press and food) for the rat is what characterized most human activity. Yes, some means might be more pleasant than others (rats seemed to "enjoy" running in exercise wheels, for example), but this was an incidental fact, a mere detail, that got in the way of understanding the far more general relation between means and ends. Without a paycheck, people wouldn't work. With a paycheck, it hardly mattered what work people did. In making this assumption, learning theorists were following in the hallowed tradition of Smith (1776, 1937), the father of modern economics, and Taylor (1911, 1967), the father of what came to be called "scientific management" (see Schwartz et al., 1978 for elaboration).

We think this view of the relation between means and ends continues to dominate the layperson's thinking about human motivation. To get CEOs to serve the interests of the company, give them company shares as a significant part of compensation. To get students to work hard in school, give them frequent tests and grades – and even better, rewards like pizza parties – if they do well. To get car salespeople to put maximum effort into closing deals, pay them commissions. And to get doctors to do all that is necessary, but only what is necessary, for high-quality patient care, pay them bonuses for good, but efficient, medical outcomes.

There is little doubt that much human activity is instrumental in just the way that rat lever-pressing or pigeon key-pecking is. But pure, arbitrary instrumentality is not the only possible relation between means and ends. Aristotle (1988), for example, had quite a different view. As evidenced by his masterwork of moral philosophy, *Nicomachean ethics*, Aristotle thought that most human activities had ends, or goals (*teloi*), that were specific to them. It was the human *telos* to pursue excellence, and what "excellence" meant was very much specific to the activity in question. The *telos* of the builder was to produce excellent buildings. The *telos* of the doctor was to cure disease. The *telos* of the athlete was to produce outstanding athletic performances. Of course, in each of these cases the performer might earn a livelihood, but it was earning a livelihood that was incidental to human activity and achieving the activity-specific *telos* that was central to it, at least among people who rightly understood the point of their activities. Certainly, many of the things that people do are instrumental; they are means to an end. But for Aristotle, the ultimate end to which all activities lead is flourishing (*eudaimonia*), and that requires excellences that are intimately related to the activities of those who pursue them.

Aristotle's teleological framework for understanding human nature is probably foreign to most modern students of human behavior. But with a little bit of translation, his ideas can be related to modern conceptions. In this chapter, we will try to do the translating, specifically in relation to motivation. Partly in response to the instrumentalist assumptions of learning theory, it has become commonplace to distinguish between "intrinsic" and "extrinsic" motivation. Extrinsically motivated activity is directed to some other end – it is a means to that end. It is instrumental, like the rat's lever press. Intrinsically motivated activity is an end in itself. Extrinsically motivated activity is work; intrinsically motivated activity is play. Extrinsically motivated activity is all about achieving some instrumental goal; intrinsically motivated activity *is* the goal (see Deci, 1975; Deci & Ryan, 1985; Lepper et al., 1973; Pink, 2011; see Hidi, 2016, for a recent review of the literature).

We believe that while the above distinction between intrinsic and extrinsic motivation offers a much richer view of human motivation than the purely instrumental view that it replaces, it fails to capture important distinctions that should be made between various types of relations among motives, actions, and consequences. In this chapter, we will try to make some of these distinctions and clarify what the terms "intrinsic" and "extrinsic" ought to mean. In particular, we present a view intended to enrich the concept of intrinsic motivation by suggesting that "intrinsically motivated" behavior frequently has goals aside from the pleasure of engaging in the behavior. The consequences of intrinsically motivated behavior often matter; it is just that the consequences that matter have a special relation to the behavior that produces them. And because the use of the terms "intrinsic" and "extrinsic" is already rather fraught, we will introduce a slightly different terminological distinction in order to describe a fuller conceptualization of the nature of human motivation.

"Intrinsic" and "Extrinsic" Motivation

Psychologists have long realized that to understand human behavior, we need to know not only what someone does, but why they do it. Motives matter. Different types of motives have different effects on behavior even when the motives seem to point in the same direction. For example, Lepper et al. (1973) showed that giving nursery school children awards for drawing made them less interested in drawing, which they liked to do, and led them to draw less interesting pictures than if they weren't given awards. And Deci (1971, 1975) showed that giving college students money for solving puzzles made them less interested in working on such puzzles, which they enjoyed, when money was not available. Similarly, Gneezy and Rustichini (2000) showed that adding a fine to the social sanctions already associated with parents coming late to pick up their children from daycare weakened those social sanctions and increased lateness, rather than strengthening those social sanctions and reducing lateness. In the first two cases, it might be said that the rewards that were added to the already enjoyable activities of drawing and puzzle-solving instrumentalized the activities, turning "play into work," and thus made the activities less enjoyable. Analogously, the fine for lateness instrumentalized that activity and thus gave parents permission to come late, since they were "paying" for it.

What *should* happen to the performance of demanding, effortful activities when intrinsic and extrinsic motives are combined? Logic would suggest that if you have one reason for doing something, adding a second reason to do the same thing would be even better, rendering motivation more tenacious, follow-through stronger, and outcomes better (see Cerasoli et al., 2014 for a meta-analysis of this very question, and Hidi, 2016, for a recent review). Schools and workplaces are full of systems that attempt to tap people's intrinsic motives to act (e.g., because engaging in the activity is the moral, interesting, or meaningful thing to do), while also providing rewards intended to spark extrinsic motives to pursue the same acts (e.g., grades, bonuses, or promotions). Yet – as shown by the studies of nursery school children's drawing and daycare parents coming to fetch their kids, and in a direct challenge to this assumption – a substantial body of research suggests that far from boosting motivation, holding extrinsic motives can undermine whatever intrinsic motives may have been operating, leading to drops in overall motivation, persistence, and performance (Deci et al., 1999; Deci & Ryan, 2014; Frey & Oberholzer-Gee, 1997; Frey, 1994; Kiviniemi et al., 2002; and see Murayama et al., 2010 for evidence on the neural basis of this undermining effect and Hidi, 2016 for a review of the neuroscientific evidence). In short, this work suggests that salient instrumental incentives may trigger extrinsic motives, which act to undermine motivation that would otherwise be based in the value and reward of doing the activity or engaging in the act for the sake of objectives that are intimately connected to the act itself. This effect, labeled the "motivational crowding out effect" by economists (Frey, 1994) and the "overjustification effect" by psychologists (Lepper, et al., 1973), has been demonstrated across a range of experimental contexts (Deci et al., 1999), though there are arguments that question both the reliability and the interpretation of such studies (Cerasoli et al., 2014; Eisenberger & Cameron, 1996; Lacetera et al., 2012).

Much of the existing literature in the psychology of motivation treats intrinsic and extrinsic motivation as if there is a stark categorical distinction between them (but see Gerhart & Fang, 2015). It is assumed that behavior is either intrinsically motivated or extrinsically motivated. In addition, intrinsic motivation is usually associated with the pleasure that derives from simply engaging in the activity, rather than with the consequences of the activity. That is, the nursery school kids love to draw whether or not the end result is a nice picture. It is worth noting that this definition of intrinsic motivation rules out the possibility of being intrinsically motivated to do anything that is *not* pleasurable, an untenable definitional state of affairs to which we will return. What is more, researchers also often use the consequences of behavior as an indication of what motivates the behavior (e.g., if a student gets an "A" on an exam, she is assumed to be motivated by the grades). So, for example, an instrumental consequence may be added to a situation in an effort to improve performance (e.g., a gift certificate for high scores on a standardized test). If that consequence influences behavior (e.g., students do better on the test), researchers conclude that instrumental incentives work, and infer (since the incentives worked) that the behavior was instrumentally motivated in the first place. This presumption renders it impossible to discern the presence of intrinsic motives in cases where actions have produced any sort of instrumental outcome. Finally, it is generally assumed that intrinsic motivation leads to better performance than extrinsic, though interestingly, nearly every intervention designed to increase motivation focuses on the extrinsic. Though a recent meta-analysis suggests that extrinsic rewards can boost performance even when intrinsic motivation is present (Cerasoli et al., 2014), it is still unclear whether rewards *increase* intrinsic motivation or act as a supplementary boost.

We think that the assumptions that intrinsic motivation is entirely about the activity and not its consequence, and that the presence of an instrumental consequence rules out the possibility that an activity is intrinsically motivated, are mistaken in ways that lead to oversimplification of what is an extremely complex set of relations between motives, actions, and consequences. Here, we attempt to clarify some of these relations and delineate some important distinctions, leading to a series of questions for both theoretical and empirical analysis.

The Idea of a "Practice"

Imagine a second grade teacher who enjoys her work and is good at it. Her work produces a family of consequences for her. She gets pleasure from the minute-to-minute, day-to-day character of her job and from interacting with young kids. She gets satisfaction from knowing that she is an excellent teacher – that she does the job well. She gets satisfaction from evidence that kids are learning and are enthusiastic. She enjoys respect and admiration from her peers. She enjoys respect and admiration from parents. She enjoys respect and admiration from society at large. She appreciates her nice salary and benefits as well as her job security. She is pleased that she can leave her workplace at three in the afternoon. She likes that she has lots of vacation days and the entire summer off.

Thus, this teacher's work has multiple consequences. Which of them serve also as motives? We can identify several possibilities: pleasure in the activity, pursuit of excellence, status and acclaim, salary, job security, and benefits, and the desire to have a positive impact on others. Which of these motives count as "intrinsic"? And what are the criteria for establishing a motive as intrinsic?

We think these questions can be profitably addressed from a framework developed by neo-Aristotelian philosopher Alasdair MacIntyre. In *After virtue* (1981), MacIntyre introduces the idea of a "practice," which he defines as

> any coherent and complex form of socially established cooperative human activity through which goods internal to that form of activity are realized in the course of trying to achieve those standards of excellence which are appropriate to, and partially definitive of, that form of activity, with the result that human powers to achieve excellence, and human conceptions of the ends and goods involved, are systematically extended (p. 175).

This definition is complex, and requires elucidation. We will do so by examining several of its important features. First, practices are complex. The card game of bridge is a practice, whereas Rochambeau ("rock, paper, scissors") is not. The game of tennis is a practice, whereas hitting a tennis ball over the net is not. Gardening is a practice, whereas planting flowers is not.

Second, practices are characterized by the pursuit of excellence or, at least, competence. People who engage in practices strive to be good at them. Third, what constitutes excellence is itself defined by standards internal to the practice, largely established by practitioners themselves. Thus, one is perfectly free to say something like, "I don't know much about art, but I know what I like." But one is not entitled to expect that anyone (especially artists) will care what one likes or interpret one's likes and dislikes as an indication of the quality of the art. In another domain, the quality of a search engine in presenting users with exactly the information they seek (the *telos* of search engine design, after all) need have nothing to do with the profits it generates for shareholders. Software designers engaged in the practice seek search engine excellence. Shareholders, and software designers who are not "practitioners," seek profitability.

The concept of excellence is necessarily imprecise. First, if MacIntyre is right, excellence is a moving target since, as practices develop, the standards of excellence among practitioners change. And second, each practice has standards of excellence that are peculiar to it. There is no abstract standard of excellence that unites instances of excellence across different practices. Moreover, there is room for disagreement – both among practitioners, and between practitioners and non-practitioners – about what excellence means (see Kuhn, 1977 for a parallel argument about judgments of the excellence of scientific theories among practicing scientists). Nonetheless, however imprecise "excellence" may be, in MacIntyre's (and Aristotle's) telling, only activities that have standards of excellence can be practices.

A fourth feature of practices, most important for purposes of this chapter, is that practitioners pursue goods or ends that are internal to the practice itself. In other words, there is an intimate relation between the ends of the practice and the means to achieve those ends. For our hypothetical second grade teacher, educating students and engendering in them enthusiasm for learning are internal to the practice. Salary and benefits, job security, and summers off are not. These ends could be achieved in other ways, through any number of other occupations; the relations between the teacher's teaching and these ends are purely instrumental. Not even praise and admiration from parents and peers is unambiguously internal to the practice. Perhaps praise for excellence *as a teacher* is; praise for excellence more generally is not.

Finally, in MacIntyre's conception, practices and the goals toward which they are aimed develop. As people – gardeners, bridge players, biologists, teachers, software engineers, or psychologists – continue to practice, standards of excellence change. That is, what it means to be an excellent psychologist in 2017 is likely quite different from what it meant to be an excellent psychologist in 1967. The line between what is and is not a practice is sometimes fuzzy, and some activities may be practices at one point in their development but not at another. But we think the differences between prototypical practices and mere instrumental activities are clear. And we also think MacIntyre's framework enables us to discern whether a given participant in a practice is a true practitioner or not.

It is worth noting that there is no mention of pleasure in MacIntyre's account of practices. Of course, our second grade teacher may derive pleasure from her day-to-day activities, but that is just icing on the cake. As Aristotle (1988, No. Book X, section 3) writes, "there are many things that we would be keen about even if they brought no pleasure … [And] we should choose these even if no pleasure resulted." Nussbaum (1990) observes in commenting on this passage that, "even if in fact pleasure is firmly linked to excellent action as a necessary consequence, it is not the end *for which* we act" (p. 57). In other words, not every consequence of an act is a motive for the act. What makes the second grade teacher's activities "internally motivated" is that she is pursuing aims that are internally and intimately related to teaching – aims that cannot be achieved in any other activity. The crucial point here is that participation in a practice is not aimless. It is not "play." Results matter. Indeed, results matter critically. But the route to achieving those results also matters. As we pointed out recently (Wrzesniewski et al., 2014), a "practicing" gardener pursues a beautiful and bountiful garden, but will not hire someone else to produce and maintain that garden. The "practicing" painter pursues a striking work of art, but will not hire someone else to paint it. The "practicing" doctor wants to be the one who cures disease and eases suffering, the "practicing" teacher wants to be the one who opens up and inspires young minds, and so on.

Competitive games have winners and losers, and people who love the games want to win. Indeed, if they are practitioners pursuing excellence, they *should* want to win. But they should not want to win by cheating. If they cheat, they are treating the ends as external to the activities that produce them. As practitioners pursuing excellence, the cheaters are cheating themselves. One of us (B. S.) discovered the difference between playing a game for amusement and distraction and playing a game to pursue excellence when he taught his seven-year-old granddaughter to play rummy. Rummy is a rather simple game, but playing it well requires that you notice which cards have been discarded and which have been picked up by your opponent, in an effort to construct your opponent's unseen hand, so you can avoid discarding cards that will improve that hand. When granddad pointed this out to granddaughter, by showing her cards he had withheld that she needed, she asked how he knew she needed those cards. He explained, thinking that her development as a rummy player was about to accelerate. She threw down her cards, exclaiming, "I thought we were playing a game, not thinking." Thus ended her career as a rummy player.

It is perhaps an unfortunate accident that early research on intrinsic motivation focused on the drawings of four-year-olds and the puzzle-solving of college students. Neither of these activities is a practice, and both are rather effortless. Thus, the focus was on pleasure in the activity – engaging in the activity "for its own sake" – rather than on pursuit of excellence in the activity. But even in these cases, we doubt that the pre-schooler would be pleased if others did the drawing and handed it to her, or the college student would be pleased to get handed already-solved puzzles. Pre-schoolers want pleasing pictures *that they drew*, and college students want solved puzzles *that they solved*. In other words, we think that the framework of means and ends is as characteristic of "intrinsically" motivated behavior as it is of "extrinsically" motivated behavior. The critical distinction between these two categories of means-ends relation is in the connection between means and ends. With so-called "intrinsically motivated" behavior, the relation between means and ends is anything but arbitrary.

From "Intrinsic"/"Extrinsic" to "Internal"/"Instrumental"

To focus on the relation between means and ends, rather than on how pleasurable an activity may be, we prefer the term "internal" to "intrinsic" and the term "instrumental" to "extrinsic" (Wrzesniewski et al., 2014). Both of our terms acknowledge that consequences matter, and focus on the relation between the consequences that matter and the activities that produce them. An instrumental relation means that a particular act producing a particular consequence is a mere matter of contingency. The instrumentally motivated actor is after the consequence and will presumably choose whatever route to that consequence is most efficient and convenient. The internally motivated actor cares about both the activity and the consequence, as well as the relation between them.

We believe that our suggestion that consequences also matter to internally motivated activities calls attention to the most salient characteristics of those activities, while at the same time honoring the distinction that previous researchers have made between intrinsic and extrinsic motivation. In reality, the pursuit of excellence in many, if not most, activities involves long periods of intense training that are often anything but pleasurable. Learning anatomy is not fun for most medical students. Weight training is not fun for most competitive athletes. If one takes "pleasure in the activity" as the hallmark of intrinsic motivation, then it is implausible to imagine – given the perseverance necessary in the face of obstacles and challenges, and the sheer boredom that often accompanies some of what it takes to achieve excellence – that any pursuit of excellence could be regarded as intrinsically motivated. Young people searching for their "calling" (see Wrzesniewski et al., 1997) may use the pleasure they get from pursuing various activities as diagnostic of whether they are "called" to them, and may thus wrongly reject many activities that demand high effort at not especially pleasurable tasks as not right for them. Duckworth's concept of "grit" captures well the point we are after (Duckworth & Gross, 2014; Duckworth & Seligman, 2005; Duckworth et al., 2007, 2010). Grit, Duckworth tells us, has two components. One is perseverance – commitment for the long haul. The second is engagement, which will not always be pleasurable, but will keep people working at things that are hard. Grit turns out to predict success in a wide variety of domains better than various kinds of aptitude tests typically used for this purpose. The reason, we suspect, is that grit enables people to withstand the countless hours of deliberate practice, much of it focused on aspects of an activity that people do poorly, that are a key ingredient in the development of expertise (Ericcson et al., 1993).

Our point in invoking grit is that it highlights the importance of perseverance even in activities that are internally motivated. Our view is that pleasure should not be seen as the hallmark of whether motivation is internal or instrumental. Rather, we see pleasure as an affective state that often accompanies engaging in activities that are internally motivated, but that need not accompany such activities. Nor do we think that experiencing pleasure disqualifies an activity as internally motivated (e.g., "she gardens because it gives her pleasure. Therefore, gardening is instrumental in the pursuit of pleasure."). We think a focus on pleasure distracts us from the main point, which is a distinction between behavior whose motivating consequences are intimately related to the acts and behavior whose motivating consequences are arbitrarily related to the acts.

What Motivates the Second Grade Teacher?

With the distinction between internal and instrumental and MacIntyre's conception of practices in mind, let us revisit our second grade teacher. As we said above, she appreciates interacting with and inspiring her students, seeing evidence that they are learning, gaining the approval of parents and peers, and having a nice salary and benefits, job security, and ample time off. Her work provides her with many attractive consequences. But which of them are motives? And which of the motives are internal to the activities?

It is obvious that the development of her students is internal to the practice of teaching. What else could excellence in pursuit of the *telos* of education mean if not this? And it is equally obvious that her salary and benefits, and the other trappings of the job, are instrumental. She certainly appreciates all these features of her job, but would she continue to do her job if they disappeared? And would she willingly switch jobs if she found another occupation that provided similar salary and benefits?

The matter of status and approval from colleagues and parents is less clear. Does she want status, or status as an educator? If the former, then she might switch jobs if something became available that offered higher status. If the latter, then arguably what she wants is excellence as a teacher, and the acclaim she gets is just a by-product of her pursuit of the *telos* of education. It is possible, though, that what she wants is the status with or without the excellence that normally produces it, in which case she might put more effort into self-promotion than self-improvement. The distinction here may be subtle, but we think it is a key to understanding the distinction we made some years ago between attitudes toward work as a "career" and attitudes toward work as a "calling" (Wrzesniewski et al., 1997). People with careers are interested in rising in the hierarchy and attaining the status and other benefits that come with advancement. But they are interested in advancement per se, rather than advancement that is simply a by-product of excellent practice in their particular chosen occupation. People with callings, in contrast, certainly appreciate recognition, but they would want any recognition they get to be for excellence in the particular work they have chosen to do.

To illustrate this subtle distinction, imagine that the school in which our teacher works, influenced by the No Child Left Behind (NCLB) Act, adopts a set of standardized tests that assess student progress. Imagine further that status and acclaim will come to teachers whose students do best on these tests. Finally, imagine that our teacher believes that these tests, as metrics, are misguided, both as ways to measure educational attainment and as goals for teachers to strive to achieve. What will this teacher do? If she is motivated by status and the prospects for advancement (i.e., she has a "career"), she will play by the new rules and do whatever she can to help her students excel on the tests. If she is motivated by the *telos* of education (i.e., she has a "calling"), she will continue teaching as before, even if it means foregoing the opportunity to achieve the respect and approval of peers and parents.[1] Indeed, she might even

---

1 But not all parents. One of us (A. W.) was thrilled when her daughter's veteran kindergarten teacher – with more than 25 years of experience honing her craft – explained at back-to-school night that she had little interest in the regimented, test-directed instructional system at use in the school, and instead planned to teach as she always had, with a single goal to guide her. That goal? "To make your children love learning." She assured us that all the rest would follow, which it did, in abundance, that year. Here was, quite clearly, a teacher dedicated to the *telos* of her practice.

agitate to get the school to abandon these tests, suggesting that in relying on them, the school is losing sight of the true *telos* of the practice of education.

Our analysis of the second grade teacher suggests some of the complexity in assessing the nature of the motivation underlying job performance, and the difficulty of identifying motives as internal or instrumental. We think it is more realistic to imagine the distinction between internal and instrumental as a continuum rather than as categorical. Praise from parents and peers is less "instrumental" than salary and benefits. Moreover, some aspects of the teacher's work that may seem quite instrumental may not be. She may value the time off she has for the opportunities it gives her to develop lesson plans and become an even better teacher. Does this make the frequent school holidays and vacations less instrumental? We think probably it does.

More generally, it seems clear to us that some goods are only attainable through the particular activity, some are attainable through the activity but also through some other activities (they are internal to success at a practice, but not unique to it), and some are completely arbitrary in their relation to a practice – a rule imposed from without rather than a connection that is built in.

Why and When Internal Motives Are Better Than Instrumental Motives

There is a widely held belief – almost a presumption – that internal motives will produce better performance than instrumental motives. How could this not be true? Internal motives drive people to achieve excellence in the activity. Instrumental motives will only yield this result if the instrumental outcomes depend on excellence. If a teacher is working principally for salary, benefits, and time off, she will only be an excellent teacher if these aspects of her job depend on it.

We think this view is true in general, but not universally. We think that for certain kinds of work, instrumental motives may be just as powerful as internal ones. If the work involves relatively simple, routinized tasks, in which performance is easily assessed, instrumental motives will probably do the job (see Cerasoli et al., 2014). Smith's (1776, 1937) famous pin factory, the example with which he celebrates the productive efficiency that accompanies the division of labor, features work structured in exactly this way. The tasks are simple, repeated over and over, easily monitored, with little training required. One might say that the division of labor was invented with an eye toward economizing on the need for employees who had a *telos*. For complex jobs that require flexibility and discretion, internal motives might be needed, or at least be very helpful. Deskilling the task also decreases the need for workers with such motives. And it has the added benefit of putting control of the work in the hands of the manager, who organizes the instrumental incentives, instead of in the hands of the worker, who may or may not have the needed internal motives (Marglin, 1976).

We think Aristotle (and MacIntyre) would be less impressed with the pin factory than Smith was. For Aristotle, excellence required doing the right thing, at the right time, in the right way, for the right reasons. Nussbaum (1990) calls this "the priority of the particular." Can all this "rightness" be measured and quantified in a way that enables one to reward good performance with instrumental incentives? Given the complexity of most work, and the improvisation and unrewarded effort it requires, we doubt it. Even in the simplest work, unexpected obstacles, challenges, and opportunities to act with excellence abound. One of us (A. W.) has shown that even in situations requiring relatively simple and well-defined work (as in the case of hospital janitors), those employees who seem guided by the *telos* of hospital work grasp opportunities to step outside their well-defined occupational roles to do what is needed, or would be helpful, in unforeseen circumstances (Wrzesniewski & Dutton, 2001). Employees who work with this *telos* in mind end up sounding a lot like someone striving to become excellent in a practice, and they develop complex systems for discerning what kind of response is needed, and when (see Schwartz, 2015; Schwartz & Sharpe, 2011).

We think that even rather simple and easily measured work benefits from what are sometimes called "incomplete contracts." Few work contracts specify precisely what is to be done and how it is to be done. The contracts leave room for people to use their discretion when a situation calls for it. Incomplete contracts may be inevitable, and trying to make them complete almost always results in reduced employee effectiveness (Hirsch, 1976). But it is worth pointing out that there is much less danger in relying on incomplete contracts if employees are guided by internal motives than if they are guided by instrumental ones. Indeed, some of the research we have described on how extrinsic motives can undermine intrinsic motives (Deci, 1975; Lepper et al., 1973) – or as economists prefer to describe it, how extrinsic motives can crowd out moral motives (Frey & Oberhlozer-Gee, 1997) – may suggest that the more complete one makes an employee contract, the more one threatens the aim of employees to pursue the *telos* of their occupation. We see this when dedicated teachers start teaching to the test as their employment status comes to depend more and more on student test performance. The problem with standardized tests is probably not the tests themselves, but the uses to which the test results are put, i.e., the instrumental outcomes for teachers that depend on student test performance.

In a recent review and argument along these lines, Stroebe (2016) discusses the explosive growth of reliance on student course evaluations to assess the quality of university instruction. Stroebe provides evidence that course evaluations have become commonplace in universities across the United States and that they are increasingly being used in faculty assessments for promotion and tenure. He then notes the paradox that, whereas students are reporting spending less and less time on their coursework (a drop of almost 75 percent over the last 50 years), their grades are getting higher and higher (grades have inflated by about 25 percent over the last 25 years). Thus, students are apparently working less but "learning" more. Stroebe then presents a persuasive argument that decreased work, improved grades, and increased emphasis on course evaluations are related. He suggests that an implicit "contract" between students and their teachers has developed whereby students provide positive course evaluations of their teachers in exchange for low workloads and high grades. Though, of course, other interpretations of these findings are possible, the one most hopeful interpretation – that students are giving high ratings to courses and getting good grades because they are learning more – is contradicted by evidence that positive student evaluations of introductory courses are uncorrelated (or in some studies, even negatively correlated) with student grades in more advanced courses.

Stroebe's review should give those who embrace "accountability" via course evaluations pause. But from the point of view of the arguments in this chapter, the problem is less with the evaluations per se than with the uses to which they are put. Feedback to teachers about how they are doing (in addition to student performance on exams) is crucial if teachers are to improve. Feedback is not the problem; the problem is the instrumentalization of that feedback – its consequences for promotion and tenure. One might imagine that if critical feedback has no consequences, the teachers will just ignore it. But this will not be the case for teachers with the *telos* of educating and inspiring students. For real "practitioners," the feedback is the point; the consequences for career development are secondary.

It is a truism in management theory that, as a manager, you should "be careful what you measure, for what you measure is what you will get" (e.g., Kerr, 1975). We are suggesting a qualification to that truism by suggesting that what you measure is what you will get primarily if you instrumentalize what is being measured. The potential of this instrumentalization to undermine the core aims of nearly any pursuit is, we feel, consequential and potentially quite damaging.

To conclude this section of the chapter, the possibility that the relative merits of internal and instrumental motives may depend on the nature of the activity that is required helps explain why much of the criticism leveled at the use of extrinsic incentives has focused on tasks that require judgment, flexibility, and creativity (e.g., Collins & Amabile, 1999; Schwartz & Sharpe, 2011). Though the empirical status of this criticism is somewhat controversial, the idea behind it is that when desired activities can be precisely specified and measured, relying on instrumental consequences may not impair performance, and may even enhance it. It is when flexibility and intelligent variation are required that internal motives come more into their own (see Schwartz, 1982, for some evidence consistent with this view).

The West Point study. Testing the assumption that the pursuit of *telos* in an activity can be undermined by the presence of more instrumental motives was our aim when we embarked on a study that assessed the long-term impact of different types of motives on outcomes in a real-world setting. We wanted to find a setting in which both internal and instrumental motives were possible, and where the outcomes at stake were of great significance to the lives of participants and to the wider world as well. And so we studied West Point cadets, chosen because they voluntarily undertake a grueling nine-year commitment when they matriculate at the United States Military Academy at West Point (Wrzesniewski et al., 2014). West Point has traditionally been the preeminent training ground for military leadership in the United States. After four years of undergraduate and military leadership education, involving a difficult physical component, graduates of West Point become commissioned military officers – second lieutenants – with a five-year commitment of military service. It is a significant undertaking, and one that requires a great deal of motivation and effort. It was the structure of the motivation of cadets, and their impact on the outcomes the cadets experienced, to which we turned our attention.

While one might expect that all West Point cadets matriculate out of a motivation to serve their country as military leaders – an internal motive, impossible to separate from the activity itself – it is also true that a West Point education and military officership can yield better career opportunities later – an instrumental motive. We followed 10,238 West Point cadets from ten consecutive entering classes for periods of up to 14 years to learn what happens to them as a function of their original motives to attend. The strength of their various motives was measured twice upon entry to West Point, and fell into categories reflecting internal and instrumental motives, among other types. We found that for key educational and career outcomes, those with stronger internal motives, who were there because they deeply desired training as military leaders who would serve the country, were more likely to graduate from West Point and become commissioned officers, to be identified as eligible for early promotion in their first five years as a military officer, and to remain in the military up to six years (the end of the window we measured) after their commitment to the country was fulfilled. In contrast, those with stronger instrumental motives were less likely to be identified as eligible for early promotion or to remain after their mandatory military service period was up.

Most striking, however, were our findings regarding the combined effects of internal and instrumental motives. For every outcome – graduation, early promotion eligibility, and remaining in the military – instrumental motives weakened the positive effects of internal motives.[2] The undermining of internal motives by instrumental motives significantly hurt cadets' chances of ever graduating from West Point and becoming military officers. Even when cadets

---

2 Instrumental and internal motives were measured using two separate surveys administered at different times close to the start of cadets' time at West Point. Cadets rated the strength of their agreement with a number of motives that could have led them to matriculate. The motives that represented – conceptually and psychometrically – instrumental and internal aims were used to assess these motivations.

who had successfully become military officers were internally motivated, the mere presence of instrumental motives made consideration for early promotion and the likelihood of staying in the military less probable. While our results could be interpreted to mean that internal motives can help dampen the negative effects of instrumental motives, the story here is clear – salient instrumental motives, either on their own or in combination with internal motives, harm individual and institutional outcomes. And we hasten to point out that, unlike most laboratory studies in which the effects of adding instrumental motives are assessed in the short term, in the West Point study, motivational differences at age 18 were manifested up to 15 years later.

While the example of West Point cadets is rather specific, other evidence from individuals drawn from a range of occupations suggests that seeing work as a calling, in which the internal aims of the work are ends in and of themselves, corresponds with higher job and life satisfaction, as well as with more time spent at work and fewer days of work missed (Wrzesniewski et al., 1997). Others find that those who see work as a calling – whether they be classical musicians, zookeepers, or administrative assistants – are more engaged with, involved in, and motivated to stay in their jobs, even if they are no longer paid (see Bunderson & Thompson, 2009; Dobrow, 2013; Schabram & Maitlis, 2016; Wrzesniewski et al., 1997). Indeed, people for whom the internal aims of their job are their motives for working are also more identified with and attached to the organizations in which they work (Cardador et al., 2011). Finally, while evidence on whether those with callings are better performers on the job is still thin, data showing a positive (and predictive) effect of callings on performance is growing (see Hall & Chandler, 2005; Wrzesniewski et al., 2017).

Diagnosing Motivation: Methodological Issues

The story about motivation we have told here is a complex one. Everything people do has multiple consequences, but not every consequence is a motive. Some motives are clearly internal, some are clearly instrumental, and some are ambiguous. Some activities are poorly served by recruiting instrumental motives; others are well served. What can be done to make sense of a messy domain like this one? Can we rely on the standard analytic and experimental toolkit that characterizes the work of empirical scientists to clarify the relevant issues?

Consider, again, the second grade teacher. What might we do to determine which of the consequences of her work are motives? An obvious move would be to introduce a performance bonus based on her students' standardized test scores. If scores go up, we infer instrumental motivation. If not, then we infer internal motivation (or that the teacher is incapable of raising test scores). The strategy seems straightforward enough, and countless efforts to find instrumental incentives that will improve the school performance of students have just this character: introduce material incentives into the classroom and observe whether performance improves.

This kind of research on outcomes is essential if one is interested in determining whether one's interventions make a difference. But what the literature on motivational competition teaches us is that just because an instrumental incentive *can* affect behavior does not mean that it previously *was* affecting behavior. In other words, one can't infer from the fact that instrumental incentives had effects that the behavior in question was motivated by instrumental incentives prior to the intervention. Motivational competition shows us that incentives change not only behavior, but also the motivational structure that supports the behavior. The nursery-school children in the Lepper et al. (1973) study did not draw to get awards until their drawing got them awards. So the introduction of instrumental incentives can *create* a phenomenon rather than reveal it.

Smith (1776, 1937) realized this 250 years ago, when he wrote of people consigned to work on assembly lines that:

> The man whose life is spent in performing a few simple operations ...
> has no occasion to exert his understanding, or to exercise his invention
> in finding out expedients for difficulties which never occur. He naturally
> *loses*, therefore, the habit of such exertion and generally *becomes* as stupid
> and ignorant as it is possible for a human creature to be. (p. 615, emphasis
> added)

Smith's point was that factory work changes people (see also Kohn & Schooler, 1982 for evidence on this point). What was the man like before he entered the factory and "lost" the habit of invention and creativity? How intelligent was he before the factory made him "become as stupid and ignorant as it is possible for a human creature to be"? And so it is with instrumental incentives. Manipulating them to see if they work is one thing. Manipulating them to draw inferences about the motivational structure influencing the people who are subjected to the manipulation is quite another. And so, the tools we normally rely on to analyze complex phenomena may fail us when it comes to diagnosing motivation (see Schwartz, 2015 for an extended discussion of this point). The tools we use to "diagnose" may actually be creating motivational structure rather than diagnosing it. Changing the structure of work may change the structure of motivation of those who do the work. Thus, in attempting to assess motivation, we are attempting to assess a moving target, with measurement tools that may alter what they are measuring.

The same possibility arises when we use motivational tools to encourage performance. MacIntyre (1981) discusses the challenge of inspiring a young person to develop skill at chess. The problem with chess, as with many other complex activities (like, for example, learning to play the piano or learning to read) is that the *telos* of the activity may not become apparent until the child has reached a certain level of proficiency. So how does one instill that level of proficiency? MacIntyre imagines bribing the child with treats for good moves or winning games until a point is reached at which the *telos* of the game takes over. But the lesson of research on the overjustification effect and motivational crowding out is that the very bribes used to help create a sense of the *telos* of chess may prevent it from appearing. Given this possibility, it may be more promising to make the early steps toward proficiency in a complex practice as engaging as they can be, so that instrumental incentives are not required to keep the child engaged.

Our proposal about the dynamic nature of motivation is not meant to suggest that efforts to do analytic research will tell us nothing fundamental. Indeed, some such efforts may help us understand behavior energized by multiple motives. Return, again, to our second grade teacher. Suppose that instead of adding material incentives for high test scores, we removed personal contact with the children. The teacher would videotape her lessons and the videos would be played for the kids. If it were to turn out that, under these conditions, the teacher's behavior was less energetic and her lessons were less inspired, we might infer that a substantial part of what motivated the teacher was the prospect of daily interactions with her students. Treating this result as an *essential* fact about teacher motivation might be unwarranted, but treating it as at least a *contingent* fact would be perfectly justified (though we hasten to add that diagnosing what is essential and what is merely contingent is not a simple matter).

Concluding Thoughts

In this chapter, we have argued that engaging in and pursuing excellence in activities for reasons that underscore the purpose of the activities themselves marks a meaningful departure from the instrumental reasons so often assumed to be driving activities. What is more, to be internally motivated to pursue an activity need not be based in the pleasure that activity brings. Indeed, the opportunity to develop and grow in that activity can be an even more powerful and long-lasting motive than pleasure (Ryan & Deci, 2001; Wrzesniewski et al., 2014).

Often, if not always, the pursuit of excellence leads to better performance. But perhaps even more importantly, it leads to greater well-being. Rather than well-being resulting from the pursuit of pleasure or pleasurable ends (the focus of hedonic approaches to well-being), we align with a view of well-being that is based in Aristotle's conception of *eudaimonia* – the pursuit of excellence in the practices one undertakes. The depth, range, and nature of the well-being that results from deep engagement in activities, for ends that are inextricably connected to the activities themselves, is apparent in studies of work as a calling. In callings, as in any practice undertaken for the sake of the *telos* of the practice itself, well-being results from its pursuit, as well as from its ends (see Bunderson & Thompson, 2009; Cardador et al., 2011; Dobrow, 2013; Hall & Chandler, 2005; Wrzesniewski et al., 1997, 2017). Indeed, in a study of animal shelter workers, all of whom thought of their work as a calling, those who described their calling in terms of constituting a practice in which they were developing and investing to excel in the work thrived relative to those who understood their callings through the contribution they stood to make or the identity they enacted in the work (Schabram & Maitlis, 2016). In other words, the self-help truism that "it's the journey, not the destination" is neither completely true nor completely false. The "journey" matters, but, as we have been arguing throughout this chapter, the "destination" matters too.

The stability of well-being that depends not on the fleeting pleasure gotten from instrumental outcomes, but rather resides in the activity itself, makes all the difference in understanding what it is that makes work, play, or any other activity worth doing. It is possible that current efforts to measure well-being that are deployed by psychologists and other social scientists have the hedonic (rather than the *eudaimonic*) framework built into them, with their focus on the experience of positive and negative affect, so that pleasure seems even more important to well-being than it would if measures of well-being were differently constructed. Thus, a different set of tools for measuring well-being might provide even more impressive evidence for a *eudaimonic* conception of a life well-lived than is presently suggested by the evidence, though the importance to well-being of the sorts of experiences we have focused on in this chapter is impressive, even with the deck stacked against it.

References

Aristotle (1988). *The Nicomachean ethics* (David Ross, trans.). Oxford: Oxford University Press.

Bunderson, J. S. & Thompson, J. A. (2009). The call of the wild: Zookeepers, callings, and the double-edged sword of deeply meaningful work. *Administrative Science Quarterly, 54*, 32–57. doi: 10.2189/asqu.2009.54.1.32.

Cardador, M. T., Dane, E., & Pratt, M. G. (2011). Linking calling orientations to organizational attachment via organizational instrumentality. *Journal of Vocational Behavior, 79*, 367–78. doi: 10.1016/j.jvb.2011.03.009.

Cerasoli, C. P., Nicklin, J. M., & Ford, M. T. (2014). Intrinsic motivation and extrinsic incentives jointly predict performance: A 40-year meta-analysis. *Psychological Bulletin, 140*, 980–1008. doi: 10.1037/a0035661.

Collins, M. A. & Amabile, T. M. (1999). Motivation and creativity. In R.M. Sternberg (Ed.), *Handbook of creativity* (pp. 297–312). New York, NY: Cambridge University Press.

Deci, E. L. (1971). Effects of externally mediated rewards on intrinsic motivation. *Journal of Personality and Social Psychology, 18*, 105–15. doi: 10.1037/h0030644.

Deci, E. L. (1975). *Intrinsic motivation*. New York, NY: Plenum Press. doi: 10.1007/978-1-4613-4446-9.

Deci, E. L., Koestner, R., & Ryan, R. M. (1999). A meta-analytic review of experiments examining the effects of extrinsic rewards on intrinsic motivation. *Psychological Bulletin, 125*, 627–68. doi: 10.1037/0033-2909.125.6.627.

Deci, E. L. & Ryan R. M. (1985). *Intrinsic motivation and self-determination in human behavior*. New York, NY: Plenum. doi: 10.1007/978-1-4899-2271-7.

Deci, E. L. & Ryan, R. M. (2014). The importance of universal psychological needs for understanding motivation in the workplace. In M. Gagné (Ed.), *The Oxford Handbook of Work Engagement, Motivation, and Self-Determination Theory*, (pp. 13–32). New York, NY: Oxford University Press.

Dobrow, S. R. (2013). Dynamics of calling: A longitudinal study of musicians. *Journal of Organizational Behavior, 34*, 431–52. doi: 10.1002/job.1808.

Duckworth, A. L. & Gross, J. J. (2014). Self-control and grit: Related but separable determinants of success. *Current Directions in Psychological Science, 23*, 319–25. doi: 10.1177/0963721414541462.

Duckworth, A. L., Kirby, T., Tsukayama, E., Berstein, H., & Ericsson, K. (2010). Deliberate practice spells success: Why grittier competitors triumph at the National Spelling Bee. *Social Psychological and Personality Science, 2*, 174–81. doi: 10.1177/1948550610385872.

Duckworth, A. L., Peterson, C., Matthews, M. D., & Kelly, D. R. (2007). Grit: Perseverance and passion for long-term goals. *Journal of Personality and Social Psychology, 92*, 1087–101. doi: 10.1037/0022-3514.92.6.1087.

Duckworth, A. L. & Seligman, M. E. P. (2005). Self-discipline outdoes IQ predicting academic performance in adolescents. *Psychological Science, 16*, 939–44. doi: 10.1111/j.1467-9280.2005.01641.x.

Eisenberger, R. & Cameron, J. (1996). Detrimental effects of reward: Reality or myth? *American Psychologist, 51*, 153–1166. doi: 10.1037/0003-066X.51.11.1153.

Ericcson, K. A., Krampe, R. T., & Tesch-Romer, C. (1993). The role of deliberate practice in the acquisition of expert performance. *Psychological Review 100*, 363–406. doi.org/10.1037/0033-295X.100.3.363.

Frey, B. S. (1994). How intrinsic motivation is crowded out and in. *Rationality and Society, 6*, 334–52. doi: 10.1177/1043463194006003004.

Frey, B. S. & Oberholzer-Gee, F. (1997). The cost of price incentives: An empirical analysis of motivation crowding out. *American Economic Review, 87*, 746–55.

Gerhart, B. & Fang, M. (2015). Pay, intrinsic motivation, extrinsic motivation, performance, and creativity in the workplace: Revisiting long-held beliefs. *Annual Review of Organizational Psychology and Organizational Behavior, 2*, 489–521. doi: 10.1146/annurev-orgpsych-032414-111418.

Gneezy, U. & Rustichini, A. (2000). A fine is a price. *Journal of Legal Studies, 29*, 1–17. doi: 10.1086/468061.

Hall, D. T. & Chandler, D. E. (2005). Psychological success: When the career is a calling. *Journal of Organizational Behavior, 26*, 155–76. doi: 10.1002/job.301.

Hidi, S. (2016). Revisiting the role of rewards in motivation and learning: Implications of neuroscientific research. *Educational Psychology Review, 28*, 61–93. doi: 10.1007/s10648-015-9307-5.

Hirsch, F. (1976). *Social limits to growth*. Cambridge, MA: Harvard University Press. doi: 10.4159/harvard.9780674497900.

Kerr, S. (1975). On the folly of rewarding A while hoping for B. *Academy of Management Journal, 18*, 769–83. doi: 10.2307/255378.

Kiviniemi, M. T., Snyder, M., & Omoto, A. M. (2002). Too many of a good thing? The effects of multiple motivations on task fulfillment, satisfaction, and cost. *Personality and Social Psychology Bulletin, 28*, 732–43. doi: 10.1177/0146167202289003.

Kohn, M. L. & Schooler, C. (1982). Job conditions and personality: A longitudinal assessment of their reciprocal effects. *American Journal of Sociology, 87*, 1257–86. doi: 10.1086/227593.

Kuhn, T. S. (1977). Objectivity, value judgment, and theory choice. In Kuhn, T. S. (Ed.), *The essential tension* (pp. 320–39). Chicago, IL: University of Chicago Press.

Lacetera, N., Macis, M., & Slonim, R. (2012). Will there be blood? Incentives and displacement effects in pro-social behavior. *American Journal of Economic Policy, 4*,186–223. doi: 10.1257/pol.4.1.186.

Lepper, M. R., Greene, D., & Nisbett, R. E. (1973). Undermining children's intrinsic interest with extrinsic rewards: A test of the "overjustification hypothesis". *Journal of Personality and Social Psychology, 28*, 119–37. doi: 10.1037/h0035519.

MacIntyre, A. (1981). *After virtue*. Notre Dame, IN: University of Notre Dame Press.

Marglin, S. (1976). What do bosses do? In A. Gorz (Ed.), *The division of labour* (pp. 13–54). London: Harvester Press.

Murayama, K., Matsumoto, M., Izuma, K., & Matsumoto, K. (2010). Neural basis of the undermining effect of extrinsic reward on intrinsic motivation. *Proceedings of the National Academy of Sciences of the United States of America, 107*, 20911–16. doi: 10.1073/pnas.1013305107.

Nussbaum, M. (1990). *Love's knowledge*. Oxford: Oxford University Press.

Pink, D. H. (2011). *Drive: The surprising truth about what motivates us*. New York, NY: Penguin.

Ryan, R. M. & Deci, E. L. (2001). On happiness and human potentials: A review of research hedonic and eudaimonic well-being. *Annual Review of Psychology, 52*, 141–66. doi: 10.1146/annurev.psych.52.1.141.

Schabram, K. & Maitlis, S. (2016). Negotiating the challenges of a calling: Emotion and enacted sensemaking in animal shelter work. *Academy of Management Journal, 60*, 584–609. doi: 10.5465/amj.2013.0665.

Schabram, K. & Maitlis, S. (2017). Negotiating the challenges of a calling: Emotion and enacted sensemaking in animal shelter work. *Academy of Management Journal, 60*, 584–609. doi: 10.5465/amj.2013.0665.

Schwartz, B. (1978). *The psychology of learning and behavior*. New York, NY: Norton.

Schwartz, B. (1982). Reinforcement induced behavioral stereotypy: How not to teach people to discover rules. *Journal of Experimental Psychology: General, 111*, 23–59. doi: 10.1037/0096-3445.111.1.23.

Schwartz, B. (2015). *Why we work*. New York, NY: Simon & Schuster.

Schwartz, B., Schuldenfrei, R., & Lacey, H. (1978). Operant psychology as factory psychology. *Behaviorism, 6*, 229–54.

Schwartz, B. & Sharpe, K. (2011). *Practical wisdom: The right way to do the right thing*. New York, NY: Riverhead.

Schwartz, B. & Wrzesniewski, A. (2016). Internal motivation, instrumental motivation, and eudaimonia. In J. Vitterso (Ed.), *Handbook of eudaimonic well-being* (pp. 123–34). New York, NY: Springer.

Skinner, B. F. (1953). *Science and human behavior*. New York, NY: MacMillan.

Smith, A. (1776/1937). *The wealth of nations*. New York, NY: Modern Library.

Stroebe, W. (2016). Why good teaching evaluations may reward bad teaching: On grade inflation and other unintended consequences of student evaluation. *Perspectives on Psychological Science, 11*, 800–16. doi: 10.1177/174569161 6650284.

Taylor, F. W. (1911/1967). *Principles of scientific management*. New York, NY: Norton.

Wrzesniewski, A., Berg, J. M., Grant, A. M., Kurkoski, J., & Welle, B. (2017). Dual mindsets at work: Achieving long-term gains in happiness. Working paper.

Wrzesniewski, A. & Dutton, J. E. (2001). Crafting a job: Revisioning employees as active crafters of their work. *Academy of Management Review, 26*, 179–201.

Wrzesniewski, A., McCauley, C. R., Rozin, P., & Schwartz, B. (1997). Jobs, careers, and callings: People's relations to their work. *Journal of Research in Personality, 31*, 21–33. doi: 10.1006/jrpe.1997.2162.

Wrzesniewski, A., Schwartz, B., Cong, X., Kane, M., Omar, A., & Kolditz, T. (2014). Multiple types of motives don't multiply the motivation of West Point cadets. *Proceedings of the National Academy of Sciences of the United States of America, 111*, 10 990–5. doi: 10.1073/pnas.1405298111.

PART IV

Curiosity and Boredom

16 Curiosity and Learning

A Neuroscientific Perspective

Matthias J. Gruber, Ashvanti Valji, and
Charan Ranganath

Abstract: *Curiosity – the intrinsic desire to acquire new information – is a key factor for learning and memory in everyday life. To date, there has been very little research on curiosity and, therefore, our understanding of how curiosity impacts learning is relatively poor. In this chapter, we give an overview of psychological theories of curiosity and how initial research has focused on curiosity as a specific personality characteristic (i.e. trait curiosity). We then review recent findings on curiosity emerging in experimental psychology and cognitive neuroscience. Rather than examining trait curiosity, this recent line of research explores how temporary states of curiosity affect cognitive processes. Recent findings suggest that curiosity states elicit activity in the brain's dopaminergic circuit and thereby enhance hippocampus-dependent learning for information associated with high curiosity but also for incidental information encountered during high-curiosity states. We speculate how this new line of curiosity research could help to better understand the mechanisms underlying curiosity-related learning and potentially lead to a fruitful avenue of translating laboratory-based findings on curiosity into educational settings.*

> I have no special talents. I am only passionately curious.
>
> Albert Einstein

Epistemic curiosity – the intrinsic desire to acquire new knowledge – enhances learning (for a review, see Renninger & Hidi, 2016), and it is a strong predictor of academic achievement and job performance (Mussel, 2013; von Stumm et al., 2011). Despite the importance of curiosity to everyday learning, until recently, the topic had been largely ignored in experimental psychology and cognitive neuroscience, and we lack an understanding of the cognitive and neural processes underlying the nebulous concept of curiosity. Fortunately,

Work on this manuscript was supported by a COFUND Fellowship from the European Commission and the Welsh Government for M.J.G., a PhD studentship from the School of Psychology at Cardiff University for A.V., and a Vannevar Bush Faculty Fellowship to C.R. (Office of Naval Research Grant N00014-15-1-0033). Any opinions, findings, and conclusions or recommendations expressed in this material are those of the author(s) and do not necessarily reflect the views of the Office of Naval Research or the US Department of Defense.

new experimental research has begun to shed some light on how curiosity modulates brain activity and memory processes. In this chapter, we will give an overview of what is known about curiosity. We will start by reviewing theories of curiosity and early research on curiosity as a personality trait. Subsequently, we will review research from experimental psychology and cognitive neuroscience showing how momentary states of curiosity affect learning and memory processes. Finally, we will propose how a neuroscience-based framework of curiosity can stimulate hypothesis-driven research on curiosity, and we will speculate about how future findings could be used for educational settings.

Psychological Theories on Curiosity and Curiosity as a Personality Trait

In 1891, William James (1891) was the first to describe curiosity as an instinct that evolved to facilitate survival and adaptation through active exploration of the environment. However, it was not until the 1950s that the behaviorist D.E. Berlyne started the first series of experimental research on curiosity (Berlyne, 1950). Berlyne categorized curiosity along several dimensions: "epistemic and perceptual curiosity," where the former refers to the drive and desire for knowledge and the latter to exploratory behavior that enhances perception of the environment (Berlyne, 1954). Another dimension introduced by Berlyne (1960) was "specific and diversive curiosity." Specific curiosity relates to the desire to reduce uncertainty by searching for a particular piece of information that is lacking. In contrast, diversive curiosity refers to the seeking of information or stimulation that is novel, complex, or surprising in order to reduce feelings of boredom and increase arousal (Berlyne, 1960, 1966). Berlyne (1960) suggested that complexity, surprise, uncertainty, and novelty activate the "curiosity drive" and subsequently increase aversive arousal levels. The desire to resolve uncertainty is thought to be fulfilled through information-seeking, a behavior that is proposed to reduce arousal and satisfy curiosity. A limitation of this theory by Berlyne is that it poses a paradox between the assertion that curiosity is aversive, and the fact that people frequently and intentionally look for opportunities that spark their curiosity. If curiosity merely raises levels of aversiveness, it would be sensible to avoid exposure to situations that spark such curiosity.

Alternate accounts, such as incongruity theory, define curiosity as the propensity to make sense of the environment instigated by violated expectations (Loewenstein, 1994). Along the same lines, optimal arousal theory (Berlyne, 1967; Hebb, 1949, 1955) proposed the existence of an "optimal level of incongruity," such that slight expectancy violations stimulate curiosity, whilst higher states of incongruity create a fear-like response. In contrast to drive theories, the optimal arousal account argues that "moderate levels of curiosity" are sought out as they are "more pleasurable" than high and low levels which are more aversive. However, this idea fails to explain why, if pleasurable levels of curiosity are preferred, people try to resolve their curiosity (Loewenstein, 1994). Therefore, Loewenstein (1994) proposed the information gap theory to better explain voluntary exposure to curiosity and its situational determinants. He characterized specific epistemic curiosity as a "cognitively induced deprivation that results from the perception of a gap in one's knowledge" (p. 76). Like drive theories, information gap theory frames curiosity as a motivation to seek information in order to eliminate an aversive state. However, Loewenstein (1994) additionally proposed that, "satisfying curiosity is in itself pleasurable," and that pleasure, "compensates for the aversiveness of the curiosity itself" (Loewenstein, 1994, p. 90) (for other related theoretical accounts, see Litman, 2005; Spielberger & Starr, 1994).

Adopting these early ideas on dissociating between various underlying factors of epistemic curiosity (Berlyne, 1954; Loewenstein, 1994), subsequent research focused on developing various personality questionnaires to measure different facets of trait curiosity. Most questionnaires include general self-report statements about an individual's curiosity. One of the most prominent questionnaires, the Epistemic Curiosity Scale (ECS) developed by Litman and Spielberger (2003), measured the two constructs of diversive and specific epistemic curiosity that were originally introduced by Berlyne (1960). Furthermore, extending beyond contemporary models of curiosity (Loewenstein, 1994; Spielberger & Starr, 1994), Litman and Jimerson (2004) suggested that curiosity and our intent to seek out information could be elicited both by aversive feelings of deprivation and by positive emotional feelings of interest, which led to the two factor interest and deprivation Epistemic Curiosity scale (Litman, 2008).

Contrary to the research investigating different factors that induce curiosity, Kashdan and colleagues have focused on the nature and processes underlying trait curiosity. Kashdan et al. (2009) developed the Curiosity and Exploration Inventory-II (CEI-II), which measures two processes underlying curiosity: (a) stretching, which is the initial desire to obtain information and seek out new opportunities, and (b) embracing, which is the actual willingness and readiness to embrace unpredictable and novel situations (Kashdan et al., 2009; for an earlier version of the inventory, see Kashdan et al., 2004). Interestingly, this line of research has shown how trait curiosity is positively related to well-being and personal growth (e.g., Kashdan & Steger, 2007).

In addition to refining the measurement of specific aspects of trait curiosity, it has also been recently suggested that trait curiosity can be understood as a critical component of the "openness to experience" trait – one of the Big Five personality traits (i.e., neuroticism, agreeableness, extraversion, conscientiousness, and openness to experience) (DeYoung, 2014; Woo et al., 2014). In particular, Woo et al. (2014) developed a hierarchical measure of the openness to experience scale that attempts to dissociate the multiple factors that contribute to this global trait. The scale highlights curiosity as an important factor within "openness to intellectual experiences," which contains the facets "intellectual efficiency," "ingenuity," and "curiosity" (for further measures of curiosity, e.g., see the Ontario Test of Intrinsic Motivation [OTIM; Day, 1971] and Melbourne Curiosity Inventory [MCI; Naylor, 1981]).

In understanding the various concepts underlying trait curiosity, a crucial question is whether there is any relationship between trait curiosity and learning abilities. As expected, some studies that investigate the association between personality traits and learning mostly support positive relationships. For example, Hassan et al. (2015) found a mediating role of epistemic curiosity on learning. Additionally, Mussel (2013) showed that trait curiosity positively correlated with performance in work settings, potentially suggesting a facilitating role of curiosity on learning. Similarly, curiosity measures that are applicable to educational settings have also been shown to influence learning (Grossnickle, 2016; Renninger & Hidi, 2016; von Stumm et al., 2011). For example, Kashdan and Yuen (2007) studied the relationship between perceived school qualities, school grades, and trait curiosity using the CEI (an earlier version of the CEI-II). The authors found that Chinese students scoring high in trait curiosity outperformed students who were low in trait curiosity, but only when they believed their school provided a challenging environment in which to learn. Highly curious individuals showed greater academic success in more challenging environments but, critically, they performed more poorly in less challenging environments (Kashdan & Yuen, 2007).

In conclusion, several theories have highlighted different types of curiosity and speculated how curiosity is accompanied by aversive and positive feelings. Questionnaires measuring trait curiosity have attempted to dissociate different types and factors underlying curiosity. Critically, initial studies showing that trait curiosity positively correlates with learning success stress the importance of better harnessing curiosity in the classroom (Ainley et al., 2002; Grossnickle, 2016; Hidi, 2016; Mussel, 2013).

The Neural Mechanisms Underlying Curiosity States

Instead of focusing on curiosity traits, a recent series of studies has started to investigate how momentary states of curiosity can affect learning and memory. In this part, we will describe the current research on such curiosity states and explain how the findings are consistent with the literature on the way extrinsic rewards affect learning and memory.

Epistemic Curiosity States

Kang and colleagues (2009) conducted the first study that investigated the neural mechanisms underlying curiosity states. In order to manipulate

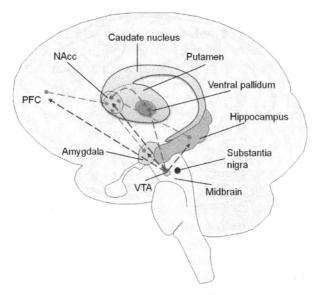

Figure 16.1. *Mesolimbic pathway. The arrows projecting from the VTA to the hippocampus, amygdala, PFC and NAcc represent Dopaminergic input. The arrows projecting from the hippocampus, amygdala and PFC to the NAcc represent glutamatergic input. Arrows projecting from the NAcc to the ventral pallidum and from the ventral pallidum to the VTA represent GABAergic inputs that subsequently stimulate the dopaminergic neurons in the midbrain (VTA). From "The hippocampal-VTA loop: Controlling the entry of information into long-term memory," by J.E. Lisman and A.A. Grace, 2005,* Neuron, *46 (5), 703–713; and "Dopamine and adaptive memory," by D. Shohamy and R.A. Adcock, 2010,* Trends in Cognitive Sciences, *14 (10), 464–472.*

curiosity in a lab setting, participants were presented with a set of trivia questions that elicited either high or low epistemic curiosity. Participants' brain activation underlying curiosity was measured via functional magnetic resonance imaging (fMRI).[1] During the fMRI phase of the experiment, participants were required to read the trivia questions, silently guess the answers, and rate their curiosity, and then rate their confidence in knowing the answer. Each trivia question was subsequently shown again, this time followed by the correct answer. After participants had completed the fMRI task, they reported their initial answers to the trivia questions. Based on previous findings showing that activation in the striatum signals reward anticipation (Adcock et al., 2006; Knutson et al., 2001; see Figure 16.1), the authors speculated that activation in the striatum could correlate with

---

1 A non-invasive technique, fMRI allows the indirect measure of neural activity throughout the whole brain while a participant performs a task or rests inside the scanner. Compared to other methods in cognitive neuroscience, fMRI has a very high spatial resolution, allowing inferences to be made about the contribution of specific brain areas in certain tasks.

curiosity. Consistent with this idea, Kang et al. (2009) found that when trivia questions were presented for the first time, increased activity for high-compared to low-curiosity questions were observed in the prefrontal cortex (PFC), the parahippocampal gyri (PHG), and importantly the caudate nucleus – a region within the striatum. Kang et al. (2009) suggested that the relationship between activity in the caudate nucleus and participants' reported curiosity is consistent with Loewenstein's (1994) information gap theory, which proposes that curiosity is associated with the anticipation of rewarding information (i.e., satisfies a knowledge gap). The assumption that curiosity satisfaction is rewarding led Kang et al. (2009) to conduct another behavioral study in which they demonstrated that participants were willing to sacrifice "scarce resources," such as "waiting time" or "limited tokens," to learn answers to questions that piqued their curiosity (see also Marvin & Shohamy, 2016).

The fMRI findings by Kang et al. (2009) suggest that high curiosity is related to the rewarding value of information, which in turn facilitates learning of the new information. To test this prediction, Kang and colleagues conducted a follow-up experiment in which a memory test for answers to previously seen trivia questions was administered one to two weeks after learning. Results showed that increased curiosity was associated with increased recollection of answers to trivia questions that were initially unknown. The authors speculated the findings imply that curiosity might stimulate brain regions associated with memory in response to unknown answers, and thereby enhance memory for correct, previously unknown, trivia answers (Kang et al., 2009).

In addition, growing literature on extrinsic motivation and memory has shown that motivational state by itself can facilitate learning and memory (Shohamy & Adcock, 2010). More specifically, the hippocampus (a critical area in the brain's memory circuit) together with two critical reward-related regions – the nucleus accumbens (NAcc) and the substantia nigra/ventral tegmental area (SN/VTA) complex – have been found to be highly connected and are thought to form a functional loop that regulates learning (Kahn & Shohamy, 2013; Lisman & Grace, 2005). Thereby, VTA dopaminergic neurons enhance long-term potentiation (LTP) in the hippocampus, which then leads to enhanced memory consolidation (for reviews, see Lisman & Grace, 2005; Lisman et al., 2011; Otmakhova et al., 2013; Shohamy & Adcock, 2010). A seminal fMRI study by Adcock et al. (2006) tested, for the first time, how such reward- and memory-related regions affect memory retention. In their study, cues signalled either a high or low monetary reward for successfully memorizing upcoming neutral visual stimuli. Participants showed increased memory performance for visual scenes that followed high- compared to low-reward cues. During the encoding phase, high-reward cues predictive of later remembered scenes showed increased activity in the hippocampus and brain regions receptive to reward anticipation, such as the NAcc and the SN/VTA (for converging findings, see Murty & Adcock, 2014; Wittmann et al., 2005; Wolosin et al., 2012). Crucially, these findings illustrate that activity (elicited by reward cues) *prior* to the encoding of upcoming information leads to reward-related memory enhancements, specifically, via activity and interactions between the SN/VTA and hippocampus (Adcock et al., 2006).

The findings on the relationship between reward states and memory by Adcock et al. (2006), together with the findings by Kang et al. (2009) on the involvement of the reward-related areas during states of epistemic curiosity, raise the question of whether curiosity states enhance long-term memory similar to the way reward states do (Gruber et al., 2014). Therefore, we followed up the initial findings by Kang et al. (2009) and addressed the question of whether this specific functional loop supporting reward-related memory benefits involving the hippocampus, NAcc, and SN/VTA predicted memory enhancements for upcoming information during states of curiosity (Gruber et al., 2014). The experimental procedure was adopted from Kang et al. (2009) and involved an initial screening phase, a study phase, and a surprise memory test. In the screening phase, participants rated both the likelihood of knowing the correct answer to each trivia question and their curiosity about the answer to each question. Trivia questions for which the answers were unknown were included in the remaining phases of the experiment. In the study phase, in which we used fMRI to measure brain activity, trials began with the presentation of a selected trivia question. Participants had to wait 14 seconds until the correct answer was revealed. During this anticipation period, a neutral image was also presented (further details follow). During the final phase, memory for the trivia answers and neutral images was tested – after a short delay in this fMRI experiment and after a one-day delay in a behavioral follow-up experiment.

In both same-day and one-day-delayed memory tests, we found that participants exhibited better memory for answers to questions that they were more curious about (in line with Kang et al., 2009). The fMRI results indicated that, when trivia questions were presented, activity in the critical reward-related regions (i.e., SN/VTA and NAcc) linearly increased with participants' curiosity ratings. This suggests that key regions of the dopaminergic circuit involved during extrinsic reward anticipation also correlate with the level of curiosity (cf., Adcock et al., 2006; Knutson et al., 2001). In contrast, however, once curiosity had been satisfied (i.e., when the answer was shown), these two regions no longer showed an increase of activation for high-compared to low-curiosity states. The findings underscore the role of anticipatory activity during curiosity states ahead of upcoming information. To further extend the findings by Kang et al. (2009), we then asked whether activity during curiosity states (i.e., activity elicited by the trivia questions) predicts later memory for upcoming high- or low-curiosity information. We found that activation in the right hippocampus and bilateral NAcc during the presentation of high-compared to low-curiosity questions predicted later memory improvements for answers to high-compared to low-curiosity questions (Gruber et al., 2014).

In contrast, activity *during* the presentation of high- and low-curiosity answers did not predict the curiosity-related memory improvements. These findings, which are consistent with studies on extrinsic reward anticipation, demonstrate that anticipatory activity elicited in the NAcc and the hippocampus during states of high curiosity facilitate the learning of the upcoming information associated with high curiosity.

Investigating how the characteristics of the anticipation period enhance memory for upcoming high-curiosity information, Mullaney et al. (2014) hypothesized that the duration and unpredictability of waiting periods ahead of upcoming high-curiosity information could increase participants' anticipation about information and subsequently facilitate learning. In line with their predictions, answers presented after a fixed four-second delay and after a random delay, compared to a no-delay condition, increased memory performance for answers to high-curiosity questions (Mullaney et al., 2014). In addition, Baranes et al. (2015) recorded eye movements during curiosity states and found that states of high curiosity, elicited by the presentation of a trivia question, were associated with participants' anticipatory gaze toward the location of the answer. In another recent study, Marvin and Shohamy (2016) found that the positive relationship between curiosity and willingness to wait for the associated answer to a high-curiosity trivia question is independent of the valence of the trivia question (i.e., information associated with negative, neutral, or positive emotions). Together, these findings suggest that harnessing states of high curiosity via anticipating information leads to memory enhancements for high-curiosity information.

Perceptual Curiosity States and Uncertainty

In addition to studies on epistemic curiosity states, Jepma and colleagues explored the neural mechanisms underlying perceptual curiosity (Jepma et al., 2012). The authors used blurred visual stimuli, as compared to clear visual stimuli, to induce perceptual curiosity. They found that blurred compared to clear visual stimuli increased activation in conflict and arousal regions, including the anterior insular cortex and the anterior cingulate cortex. The authors therefore speculated that this finding is in line with early drive theories (Berlyne, 1954, 1960, 1966) assuming curiosity is an aversive state that subsequently increases arousal. During relief of perceptual curiosity, Jepma et al. (2012) found increased activation in the striatum (i.e., caudate nucleus, putamen, and NAcc) for conditions in which visual stimuli disambiguated blurred images compared to visual stimuli that failed to resolve the identity of blurred images. This latter finding suggests that reducing perceptual uncertainty, through access to information that resolves uncertainty, might be in itself rewarding. The results by Jepma et al. (2012) might seem contradictory to our study on epistemic curiosity (Gruber et al., 2014) that show increased activity in the striatum and hippocampus during anticipation rather than during processing of the actual (uncertainty reducing) information. However, these differences in findings might potentially not be driven by the type of curiosity, but might be due to different levels of uncertainty about the anticipated information in the two studies. In the study by Jepma et al. (2012), the correct information (i.e., a clear image) was not often revealed, leading to high uncertainty about whether curiosity might be satisfied. On the contrary, in our study (Gruber et al., 2014) trivia questions were followed by the correct answer in most cases, leading to high certainty that curiosity would be satisfied. In line with theoretical accounts and non-human animal findings on dopamine functions (Lisman et al., 2011; Shohamy & Adcock, 2010), high certainty to receive upcoming information is likely to drive dopaminergic activity during anticipatory states, whereas high uncertainty about presentation of upcoming information might drive dopaminergic activity during processing of the actual awaited information via resolving uncertainty and leading to surprise (cf., Chiew et al., 2016; Marvin & Shohamy, 2016). Future studies need to systematically address the role of uncertainty in curiosity and the way uncertainty affects learning and memory for high-curiosity information. Interestingly, a nascent line of curiosity research in non-human animals suggests that resolving uncertainty activates dopaminergic neurons in the midbrain associated with reward. For example, Bromberg-Martin and Hikosaka (2009) found that advance information elicits dopaminergic activity in a way similar to primary rewards (e.g., food, water). In addition, Daddaoua et al. (2016) showed that intrinsically motivated behaviors are, in part, elicited by events associated with uncertainty that needs to be resolved.

Importantly, while recent findings suggest that curiosity-inducing information might stimulate dopaminergic regions in a similar fashion as primary rewards, it is conceivable that other brain regions and networks might code the differential attributes of secondary rewards (e.g., information) and primary rewards (cf., Blanchard et al., 2015; Bouret & Richmond, 2010). Although curiosity research in humans has started to demonstrate broad commonalities between curiosity and reward processes, the dissociations between them and their unique contributions to learning and memory still remain to be explored.

Curiosity States Benefit Learning of Incidental Information

In our fMRI experiment, we showed that hippocampal activity during high-curiosity states predicts the memory advantage for upcoming high-curiosity information (Gruber et al., 2014). Furthermore, we explored whether a high-curiosity state could even facilitate learning for incidentally encoded information that is presented during a high-curiosity state. To address this question, we presented a neutral, incidental image of a face during the 14-second-long anticipation period. Participants had to make an incidental encoding judgment on the face image in order to ensure similar levels of encoding throughout the experiment. Finally, as a surprise to participants, we tested their memory not only for the trivia answers but also for the incidental face images. Interestingly, we found that neutral face stimuli were better recognized when these faces were presented during states of high compared to low curiosity. Because participants did not expect the later surprise memory test, it is unlikely that they used deeper encoding strategies for faces presented during high- compared to low-curiosity states. In line with this speculation, activity following faces did not differ between high- and low-curiosity states, suggesting that a memory enhancement for incidental faces might not be purely driven by stimulus-related factors (Gruber et al., 2014).

We therefore further investigated whether the activation when curiosity is elicited (via a trivia question) might predict the later memory advantage for incidental faces encountered during states of high curiosity. Although brain activation across all participants did not predict the memory improvement for incidental faces, we found that *individual variations* in question-related activity showed a positive correlation with the later memory advantage for incidental faces. Specifically, the level of activation in the SN/VTA and hippocampus predicted the magnitude of the curiosity-driven memory enhancements for incidental faces. In addition, between-participants variations in the level of communication (i.e., functional connectivity) between the SN/VTA and the hippocampus also predicted the magnitude of the memory enhancement for incidental faces. Importantly, this suggests that curiosity activates critical regions within the dopaminergic circuit and hippocampus in preparation for upcoming information, *regardless* of whether information that a participant was initially curious about or other information is presented when anticipating high-curiosity information.

Importantly, one day later we replicated the curiosity-driven memory advantage for incidental faces when faces were tested in a recognition test (Gruber et al., 2014), suggesting that curiosity-driven memory enhancements for incidental information might be persistent across time and might potentially undergo enhanced memory consolidation (cf., Kang et al., 2009; Marvin & Shohamy, 2016; further elaboration of this finding is presented later). In addition, unpublished data from our laboratory indicates that curiosity-driven memory enhancements for incidental faces are not evident for all types of recognition memory, but these memory enhancements seem to be specific for recollection that is accompanied by retrieving contextual-spatial details (Gruber et al., 2015). In addition, unpublished data from our laboratory also suggests that curiosity-driven memory enhancements are especially pronounced when the incidental information is presented early during the anticipation period. That is, we found curiosity-driven memory enhancements for incidental faces when face images were presented directly after the presentation of the trivia question (i.e., early in the anticipation period) but not when face images were presented directly prior to the presentation of the trivia answer (i.e., late in the anticipation period) (Gruber et al., 2015). These findings, again, are in line with the idea that incidental information might show memory enhancements that are driven by processes related to eliciting a curiosity state (i.e., temporally contiguous to the trivia question) but not necessarily driven by processes related to satisfying a curiosity state (i.e., temporally contiguous to the trivia answer). Although these initial findings of how curiosity states benefit learning of incidental information are intriguing, future research is needed to better understand the generalizability of these findings and how they can potentially translate to educational settings.

Similarities Between How Curiosity and Reward States Benefit Learning of Neutral Information

Consistent with the curiosity-related memory advantage for incidental information, studies that investigate how other types of salient states influence memory have shown converging findings. For example, several studies that elicit reward states via monetary incentives also demonstrated memory enhancements of temporally contiguous neutral or non-rewarded information. In a study by Mather and Schoeke (2011), the authors showed that reward-related memory enhancements in young and old adults spread from rewarded to neighboring non-rewarded trials. Furthermore, in an elegant design by Murayama and Kitagami (2014), the authors showed that neutral images of objects showed memory enhancements when these images preceded an unrelated, rewarded reaction-time task. In addition, Loh et al. (2016) demonstrated that memory enhancements for rewarded information presented during representationally rich contexts also led to memory enhancements of neutral, non-rewarded information presented in the same high-reward context. Together, the findings on how curiosity and reward states enhance memory for temporally contiguous information are in line with rodent studies showing that mere novelty exposure – a different type of salience that activates the dopaminergic circuit – can enhance memory retention for originally weakly encoded information (Moncada & Viola, 2007; Redondo & Morris, 2011; Wang et al., 2010). In addition, two recent studies in humans have shown that memory enhancements for rewarded information can also spread to semantically related, non-rewarded information even if the semantically associated information is not temporally contiguous (Oyarzún et al., 2016; Patil et al., 2016). It would be highly relevant to investigate whether this spreading of memory enhancements via semantically associated information would also be evident when curiosity (instead of rewards) facilitates learning (e.g., whether memory enhancements are evident for neutral, low-curiosity information that is semantically linked to information associated with high curiosity).

Curiosity States and Memory Consolidation

One important point about how curiosity might benefit memory is that curiosity states seem to lead to better memory retention. Recent studies have suggested that information associated with high curiosity is still better remembered one day and up to at least two weeks after it has been studied (Gruber et al., 2014; Kang et al., 2009; Marvin & Shohamy, 2016; McGillivray et al., 2015). While only one study, by McGillivray et al., (2015), investigated memory performance after both immediate and delayed memory tests, their results seem to indicate that the magnitude of curiosity-driven memory enhancements does not change over time. These findings are in line with our own findings showing memory benefits for high-curiosity trivia answers and incidental faces presented during high-curiosity states in an immediate, but also one-day delayed, memory test (Gruber et al., 2014). Critically, these findings suggest that curiosity does not lead to a mere immediate short-lived memory benefit but seems to enhance memory retention across time.

Although future research on curiosity and memory would need to investigate the underlying neural processes associated with enhanced memory retention, theories and work in rodents suggest that rewards lead to increased memory consolidation processes via dopaminergic modulation of hippocampal functions (for further reading, see Düzel et al., 2009; Lisman & Grace, 2005; Shohamy & Adcock, 2010). Furthermore, recent human fMRI studies on reward and memory that investigated neural activity during *post*-learning rest periods or during sleep have shown that increases in *post*-learning neural dynamics predict later memory advantages for high-reward information (Gruber et al., 2016; Igloi et al., 2015; Murty et al., 2017). The findings on reward and memory suggest that neural processes happening *after* learning facilitate memory consolidation to build strong and more permanent memory traces for highly salient information (for further reviews, see Miendlarzewska et al., 2016; Murty & Dickerson, 2016). Future research would need to address whether curiosity enhances neural consolidation mechanisms in a similar way, as well as how enhanced consolidation for high-curiosity information can be optimally harnessed in educational settings.

Curiosity-Based Learning Might Not Require Any Additional Extrinsic Rewards

Another important factor in our understanding of how curiosity increases memory retention concerns its relationship to extrinsic rewards (Hidi, 2016). Research suggests that it is still widely believed that rewards might help foster intrinsic motivation (Murayama et al., 2017). However, research suggests that the opposite is likely to be the case (Murayama et al., 2010). Most relevant, Murayama and Kuhbandner (2011) conducted a study in which they investigated how the interplay between reward and curiosity influences memory retention. Participants received high and low monetary incentives in order to successfully encode answers to trivia questions. Importantly, when the trivia material was associated with low curiosity, participants indeed better remembered low-curiosity trivia answers for which they received high compared to low reward. In contrast, however, high-curiosity trivia material did not benefit from the additional high-reward incentive. The findings suggest that when learning is driven by curiosity, additional extrinsic motivation might not be effective and necessary. It might also be the case that, in some circumstances, reward undermines the beneficial effects of curiosity (Murayama et al., 2010). Further research is needed to better understand how curiosity and reward interact to facilitate learning and memory retention.

Future Directions and Implications for Education

A Neuromodulatory Framework of Curiosity

Despite the importance of curiosity and learning in real life, curiosity has never been a widely studied topic. As we reviewed here, psychological theories on curiosity primarily sparked initial research on trait curiosity. However, studies in experimental psychology and cognitive neuroscience on curiosity states provide promising findings that might help develop an increased interest in hypothesis-driven curiosity research. In this chapter, we focused on recent findings that have started to uncover how curiosity states shape learning and memory (for alternative reviews and current models on the influence of curiosity on information-seeking, see Gottlieb et al., 2013; Kidd & Hayden, 2015; Oudeyer & Kaplan, 2009).

The recent findings on curiosity and memory seem to support the idea that the neurocognitive mechanisms of curiosity states resemble mechanisms associated with reward anticipation that depend on the dopaminergic circuit and, thereby, benefit hippocampal functions to facilitate learning and memory. Such a neural framework of curiosity allows us to generate specific predictions about curiosity and learning. In particular, theories and findings in humans and non-human animals on the neural mechanisms of reward anticipation can guide the generation of hypotheses about how curiosity might influence learning and memory (cf., Marvin & Shohamy, 2016). In addition to reward anticipation, it has recently been shown that there is a variety of other extrinsically and intrinsically salient processes affecting hippocampal functions via dopaminergic modulation: for example, novelty, exploration, and choice (Düzel et al., 2010; Lisman & Grace, 2005; Murty et al., 2015). Importantly, these processes are strongly linked to curiosity, and a systematic investigation of how these processes share commonalities might hold the promise to elucidate the underlying factors of how curiosity affects memory. In addition, it is highly conceivable that other neuromodulators (such as noradrenaline or acetylcholine) thought to affect hippocampal functions via arousal and novelty (Mather et al., 2016; Ranganath & Rainer, 2003) might potentially underlie the neural mechanisms of how curiosity facilitates learning. Importantly, future research on curiosity states could borrow from theories and findings on how neuromodulation affects hippocampus-dependent learning.

Future Directions

The neuromodulatory framework of how curiosity might affect hippocampus-dependent learning has the potential to guide further research on curiosity and memory. Here, we propose several potential directions that would help us better understand the neural mechanisms of curiosity, and their impact on learning and memory specifically in educational settings.

What are the neurocognitive processes that overlap or dissociate between the various types of curiosity? Over the last decades, theories on curiosity have proposed different types (e.g., epistemic versus perceptual curiosity; Berlyne, 1960) and different facets of curiosity (e.g., interest-based versus deprivation-based curiosity; Litman, 2008). It is not known, however, to what degree these different types and facets of curiosity potentially share the same cognitive and neural mechanisms, or whether these different types of curiosity facilitate learning and memory processes in a similar way. To refine our understanding of the commonalities and differences between curiosity types and their underlying facets, future research in cognitive neuroscience can elucidate the extent to which these various hypothesized types of curiosity differ or share similar neural mechanisms, and how they ultimately benefit memory in potentially different ways.

How does curiosity interact with other processes in support of learning? Initial evidence has suggested that when curiosity is satisfied, other processes that are either independent of curiosity or interact with curiosity might benefit memory (e.g., valence and the actual interestingness of or surprise about the information, or interest and expert knowledge about a topic; cf., Marvin & Shohamy, 2016; McGillivray et al., 2015). Again, in line with a neuromodulatory framework of curiosity, predictions about the interactions between curiosity and other related processes (e.g., interestingness, surprise) could be derived from the human and non-human animal literature investigating the interactions between reward anticipation and other reward-related processes (e.g., reward consumption or reward-prediction errors) (cf., Marvin & Shohamy, 2016; McGillivray et al., 2015). In addition, educational research has suggested that the concepts of curiosity and interest can be differentiated and are not interchangeable terms (Grossnickle, 2016; Hidi, 2016). The four-phase model of interest development by Hidi and Renninger (2006) proposes that initial situational interest stimulated by curiosity can lead to a "well-developed individual interest" in a topic. Therefore, it would be highly relevant for people in educational settings to understand how the neural mechanisms between curiosity and interest differ, and how these two factors may differentially influence learning and memory.

Are the beneficial effects of curiosity states influenced by trait curiosity? It has been shown that individual variations in curiosity traits might show relationships with learning and academic success (e.g., Kashdan & Yuen, 2007; von Stumm et al., 2011). In our initial fMRI experiment (Gruber et al., 2014), we found large individual variations in the extent to which curiosity states facilitated learning of incidental information. These individual variations were driven by activation in the SN/VTA and hippocampus. It is unclear whether these variations might have been driven by variations in individuals' general trait curiosity. To date, there is very little evidence on the relationship between curiosity states and trait curiosity (Spielberger & Starr, 1994). In other words, it is not clear whether somebody who scores high on a curiosity trait questionnaire might also benefit the most from a high-curiosity state during learning. Initial studies using EEG and eye-tracking (Baranes et al., 2015; Begus et al., 2016; Mussel et al., 2016) suggest that curiosity traits and their states could show a relationship. However, future research would need to elucidate the extent to which curiosity traits and states share similar structural and functional neural mechanisms, and how the interplay between curiosity traits and states facilitate learning. This research would be important for educational settings, to understand how students who show generally low or high trait curiosity might best benefit from being in high-curiosity states when they learn new material.

How do curiosity-related memory enhancements spread across incidental, non-curiosity-related information? States associated with curiosity and reward enhance memory for incidental information presented during such salient states. Furthermore, it has been shown that reward enhances memory for non-rewarded information that is semantically associated with rewarded information (Oyarzún et al., 2016; Patil et al., 2016). It would be crucial to better understand the temporal characteristics of how curiosity states can benefit memory for neutral or semantically associated information. For example: What is the maximum duration for a curiosity state in order to benefit memory for incidental information encountered during the curiosity state? Do curiosity-related memory benefits spread to information that is semantically associated with high-curiosity information? How does initial curiosity for a topic develop into interest for a given topic (cf., Hidi & Renninger, 2006)? Translating these findings into educational settings could potentially be very fruitful. For example, in the classroom, is curiosity sparked at the start of a lesson sufficient to accelerate learning for specific types of incidental information encountered throughout the lesson? It would be interesting to explore how often curiosity needs to be sparked within a lesson to maximize the influence of curiosity on learning.

Concluding Thoughts

Recent promising developments in our understanding of the neurocognitive mechanisms of curiosity suggest that curiosity seems to recruit the dopaminergic circuit similarly to reward anticipation processes and, thereby, facilitates hippocampus-dependent learning. Our proposed neuromodulatory framework of curiosity provides a fruitful approach to stimulate and guide further research on the neural and cognitive components of curiosity. The recent resurgence of research on curiosity has started to shed light on how curiosity benefits learning and memory. For education, a better understanding of the mechanisms underlying curiosity-based learning might help (a) inform teachers and policymakers of *why* curiosity is important for learning, (b) find *how* curiosity can be harnessed in the most effective way in the classroom, and (c) improve educational training on the role of curiosity and learning in the classroom. Ultimately, a potentially very promising translational research avenue will be to further study laboratory-based findings in the classroom in order to test the generalizability of the beneficial effects of curiosity in applied settings. Such applied research findings can then, in turn, inform theories and guide future laboratory-based research on curiosity. Developing such a "closed-loop" approach between curiosity research in the laboratory and applied settings could be a very promising way to increasingly harness the benefits of curiosity in today's classrooms, and thereby improve teaching strategies and guide educational policymaking.

References

Adcock, R. A., Thangavel, A., Whitfield-Gabrieli, S., Knutson, B., & Gabrieli, J. D. E. (2006). Reward-motivated learning: Mesolimbic activation precedes memory formation. *Neuron, 50*(3), 507–17. doi: 10.1016/j.neuron.2006.03.036.

Ainley, M., Hidi, S., & Berndorff, D. (2002). Interest, learning, and the psychological processes that mediate their relationship. *Journal of Educational Psychology, 94*(3), 545–61. doi: 10.1037/0022-0663.94.3.545.

Baranes, A., Oudeyer, P. Y., & Gottlieb, J. (2015). Eye movements reveal epistemic curiosity in human observers. *Vision Research, 117*, 81–90. doi: 10.1016/j.visres.2015.10.009.

Begus, K., Gliga, T., & Southgate, V. (2016). Infants' preferences for native speakers are associated with an expectation of information. *Proceedings of the National Academy of Sciences of the United States of America, 113*(44), 12397–402. doi: 10.1073/pnas.1603261113.

Berlyne, D. E. (1950). Novelty and curiosity as determinants of exploratory behavior. *British Journal of Psychology, 41*, 68–50.

Berlyne, D. E. (1954). A theory of human curiosity. *British Journal of Psychology*, *3*, 180–91.

Berlyne, D. E. (1960). *Conflict, arousal, and curiosity*. New York, NY: McGraw-Hill Book Company.

Berlyne, D. E. (1966). Curiosity and exploration. *Science*, *153*(3731), 25–33. doi: 10.1126/science.153.3731.25.

Berlyne, D. E. (1967). Arousal and reinforcement. In D. Levine (Ed.), *Nebraska Symposium on Motivation* (Vol. 15, pp. 1–110). Lincoln, NE: University of Nebraska Press.

Blanchard, T. C., Hayden, B. Y., & Bromberg-Martin, E. S. (2015). Orbitofrontal cortex uses distinct codes for different choice attributes in decisions motivated by curiosity. *Neuron*, *85*(3), 602–14. doi: 10.1016/j.neuron.2014.12.050.

Bouret, S. & Richmond, B. J. (2010). Ventromedial and orbital prefrontal neurons differentially encode internally and externally driven motivational values in monkeys. *The Journal of Neuroscience*, *30*(25), 8591–601. Retrieved from www.jneurosci.org/content/30/25/8591.abstract.

Bromberg-Martin, E. S. & Hikosaka, O. (2009). Midbrain dopamine neurons signal preference for advance information about upcoming rewards. *Neuron*, *63*(1), 119–26. doi: 10.1016/j.neuron.2009.06.009.

Chiew, K. S., Stanek, J. K., & Adcock, R. A. (2016). Reward anticipation dynamics during cognitive control and episodic encoding: Implications for dopamine. *Frontiers in Human Neuroscience*, *10*, 555. doi: 10.3389/fnhum.2016.00555.

Daddaoua, N., Lopes, M., & Gottlieb, J. (2016). Intrinsically motivated oculomotor exploration guided by uncertainty reduction and conditioned reinforcement in non-human primates. *Scientific Reports*, *6*. doi: 10.1038/srep20202.

Day, H. I. (1971). The measurement of specific curiosity. In H. I. Day, D. E. Berlyne, & D. E. Hunt (Eds.), *Intrinsic motivation: A new direction in education*. New York, NY: Hold, Rinehart, & Winston.

DeYoung, C. G. (2014). Openness/intellect: A dimension of personality reflecting cognitive exploration. In R. J. Larsen & M. L. Cooper (Eds.), *The APA handbook of personality and social psychology: Personality processes and individual differences* (Vol. 3, pp. 369–99). Washington, DC: American Psychological Association.

Düzel, E., Bunzeck, N., Guitart-Masip, M., & Düzel, S. (2010). Novelty-related motivation of anticipation and exploration by dopamine (NOMAD): Implications for healthy aging. *Neuroscience & Biobehavioral Reviews*, *34*(5), 66–9. doi: 10.1016/j.neubiorev.2009.08.006.

Düzel, E., Bunzeck, N., Guitart-Masip, Wittmann, B., Schott, B. H., & Tobler, P. N. (2009). Functional imaging of the human dopaminergic midbrain. *Trends in Neurosciences*, *32*(6), 321–8. doi: 10.1016/j.tins.2009.02.005.

Gottlieb, J., Oudeyer, P. Y., Lopes, M., & Baranes, A. (2013). Information-seeking, curiosity, and attention: Computational and neural mechanisms. *Trends in Cognitive Sciences*, *17*(11), 585–93. doi: 10.1016/j.tics.2013.09.001.

Grossnickle, E. M. (2016). Disentangling curiosity: Dimensionality, definitions, and distinctions from interest in educational contexts. *Educational Psychology Review*, *28*(1), 23–60. doi: 10.1007/s10648-014-9294-y.

Gruber, M. J., Gelman, B. D., & Ranganath, C. (2014). States of curiosity modulate hippocampus-dependent learning via the dopaminergic circuit. *Neuron*, *84*(2), 486–96. doi: 10.1016/j.neuron.2014.08.060.

Gruber, M. J., Ritchey, M., Wang, S.-F., Doss, M. K., & Ranganath, C. (2016). Post-learning hippocampal dynamics promote preferential retention of rewarding events. *Neuron*, *89*(5), 1110–20. doi: 10.1016/j.neuron.2016.01.017.

Gruber, M., Yonelinas, A., & Ranganath, C. (2015). *States of curiosity benefit later recollection of incidental information.* Poster presented at the Annual Cognitive Neuroscience Society Meeting. San Francisco, CA.

Hassan, M. M., Bashir, S., & Mussel, P. (2015). Personality, learning, and the mediating role of epistemic curiosity: A case of continuing education in medical physicians. *Learning and Individual Differences*, *42*, 83–9. doi: 10.1016/j.lindif.2015.07.018.

Hebb, D. O. (1949). *The organization of behavior: A neuropsychological theory.* New York, NY: Wiley.

Hebb, D. O. (1955). Drives and the C. N. S. (conceptual nervous system). *Psychological Review*, *62*(4), 243–54. doi: 10.1037/h0041823.

Hidi, S. (2016). Revisiting the role of rewards in motivation and learning: Implications of neuroscientific research. *Educational Psychology Review*, *28*(1), 61–93. doi: 10.1007/s10648-015-9307-5.

Hidi, S. & Renninger, K. A. (2006). The four-phase model of interest development. *Educational Psychologist*, *41*(2), 111–127. doi: 10.1207/s15326985ep4102_4.

Igloi, K., Gaggioni, G., Sterpenich, V., & Schwartz, S. (2015). A nap to recap or how reward regulates hippocampal-prefrontal memory networks during daytime sleep in humans. *eLife*, *4*, e07903. doi: 10.7554/eLife.07903.

James, W. (1891). *The principles of psychology*, Vol II. London: Macmillan.

Jepma, M., Verdonschot, R. G., van Steenbergen, H., Rombouts, S. A. R. B., & Nieuwenhuis, S. (2012). Neural mechanisms underlying the induction and relief of perceptual curiosity. *Frontiers in Behavioral Neuroscience*, *6*(February), 1–9. doi: 10.3389/fnbeh.2012.00005.

Kahn, I. & Shohamy, D. (2013). Intrinsic connectivity between the hippocampus, nucleus accumbens, and ventral tegmental area in humans. *Hippocampus*, *23*(3), 187–92. doi: 10.1002/hipo.22077.

Kang, M. J., Hsu, M., Krajbich, I. M., Loewenstein, G., McClure, S. M., Wang, J. T., & Camerer, C. F. (2009). The wick in the candle of learning. *Psychological Science*, *20*(8), 963–74. doi: 10.1111/j.1467-9280.2009.02402.x.

Kashdan, T. B., Gallagher, M. W., Silvia, P. J., Winterstein, B. P., Breen, W. E., Terhar, D., & Steger, M. F. (2009). The Curiosity and Exploration Inventory-II: Development, factor structure, and psychometrics. *Journal of Research in Personality*, *43*(6), 987–98.

Kashdan, T. B., Rose, P., & Fincham, F. D. (2004). Curiosity and exploration: Facilitating positive subjective experiences and personal growth opportunities. *Journal of Personality Assessment*, *82*(3), 291–305. doi: 10.1207/s15327752jpa8203_05.

Kashdan, T. B. & Steger, M. F. (2007). Curiosity and pathways to well-being and meaning in life: Traits, states, and everyday behaviors. *Motivation and Emotion*, *31*(3), 159–73.

Kashdan, T. B. & Yuen, M. (2007). Whether highly curious students thrive academically depends on perceptions about the school learning environment: A study of Hong Kong adolescents. *Motivation and Emotion*, *31*(4), 260–70. doi: 10.1007/s11031-007-9074-9.

Kidd, C. & Hayden, B. Y. (2015). The psychology and neuroscience of curiosity. *Neuron*, *88*(3), 449–60. doi: 10.1016/j.neuron.2015.09.010.

Knutson, B., Adams, C. M., Fong, G. W., & Hommer, D. (2001). Anticipation of increasing monetary reward selectively recruits nucleus accumbens. *Journal of Neuroscience, 21*, 1–5.

Lisman, J. E. & Grace, A. A. (2005). The hippocampal-VTA loop: Controlling the entry of information into long-term memory. *Neuron, 46*(5), 703–13. doi: 10.1016/j.neuron.2005.05.002.

Lisman, J., Grace, A. A., & Duzel, E. (2011). A neoHebbian framework for episodic memory; role of dopamine-dependent late LTP. *Trends in Neurosciences, 34*(10), 536–47. doi: 10.1016/j.tins.2011.07.006.

Litman, J. A. (2005). Curiosity and the pleasures of learning: Wanting and liking new information. *Cognition & Emotion, 19*(6), 793–814. doi: 10.1080/02699930541000101.

Litman, J. A. (2008). Interest and deprivation factors of epistemic curiosity. *Personality and Individual Differences, 44*(7), 1585–95. doi: 10.1016/j.paid.2008.01.014.

Litman, J. A. & Jimerson, T. L. (2004). The measurement of curiosity as a feeling of deprivation. *Journal of Personality Assessment, 82*(2), 147–57.

Litman, J. & Spielberger, C. (2003). Measuring epistemic curiosity and its diversive and specific components. *Journal of Personality Assessment, 80*(1), 75–86. doi: 10.1207/S15327752JPA8001_16.

Loewenstein, G. (1994). The psychology of curiosity: A review and reinterpretation. *Psychological Bulletin, 116*(1), 75–98. doi: 10.1037//0033-2909.116.1.75.

Loh, E., Kumaran, D., Koster, R., Berron, D., Dolan, R., & Duzel, E. (2016). Context-specific activation of hippocampus and SN/VTA by reward is related to enhanced long-term memory for embedded objects. *Neurobiology of Learning and Memory, 134, Part,* 65–77. doi: 10.1016/j.nlm.2015.11.018.

Marvin, C. B. & Shohamy, D. (2016). Curiosity and reward: Valence predicts choice and information prediction errors enhance learning. *Journal of Experimental Psychology: General, 145*(3), 266–72. doi: 10.1037/xge0000140.

Mather, M., Clewett, D., Sakaki, M., & Harley, C.W. (2016). Norepinephrine ignites local hot spots of neuronal excitation: How arousal amplifies selectivity in perception and memory. *Behavioral and Brain Sciences, 39.* doi: 10.1017/S0140525X15000667.

Mather, M. & Schoeke, A. (2011). Positive outcomes enhance incidental learning for both younger and older adults. *Frontiers in Neuroscience, 5*(129). doi: 10.3389/fnins.2011.00129.

McGillivray, S., Murayama, K., & Castel, A. D. (2015). Thirst for knowledge: The effects of curiosity and interest on memory in younger and older adults. *Psychology and Aging, 30*(4), 835–41. doi: 10.1037/a0039801.

Miendlarzewska, E. A., Bavelier, D., & Schwartz, S. (2016). Influence of reward motivation on human declarative memory. *Neuroscience & Biobehavioral Reviews, 61*, 156–76. doi: 10.1016/j.neubiorev.2015.11.015.

Moncada, D. & Viola, H. (2007). Induction of long-term memory by exposure to novelty requires protein synthesis: Evidence for a behavioral tagging. *The Journal of Neuroscience, 27*(28), 7476–81. doi: 10.1523/JNEUROSCI.1083-07.2007.

Mullaney, K. M., Carpenter, S. K., Grotenhuis, C., & Burianek, S. (2014). Waiting for feedback helps if you want to know the answer: The role of curiosity in the delay-of-feedback benefit. *Memory & Cognition, 42*(8), 1273–84. doi: 10.3758/s13421-014-0441-y.

Murayama, K. & Kitagami, S. (2014). Consolidation power of extrinsic rewards: Reward cues enhance long-term memory for irrelevant past events. *Journal of Experimental Psychology: General, 143*(1), 15–20. doi: 10.1037/a0031992.

Murayama, K., Kitagami, S., Tanaka, A., & Raw, J. (2017). People's naiveté about how extrinsic rewards influence intrinsic motivation. *Motivation Science, 2*(3), 138–142. doi: 10.1037/mot0000040.

Murayama, K. & Kuhbandner, C. (2011). Money enhances memory consolidation – but only for boring material. *Cognition, 119*(1), 120–4. doi: 10.1016/j.cognition .2011.01.001.

Murayama, K., Matsumoto, M., Izuma, K., & Matsumoto, K. (2010). Neural basis of the undermining effect of monetary reward on intrinsic motivation. *Proceedings of the National Academy of Sciences of the United States of America, 107*(49), 20911–16. doi: 10.1073/pnas.1013305107.

Murty, V. P. & Adcock, R. A. (2014). Enriched encoding: Reward motivation organizes cortical networks for hippocampal detection of unexpected events. *Cerebral Cortex, 24*(8), 2160–8. doi: 10.1093/cercor/bht063.

Murty, V. P. & Dickerson, K. C. (2016). Motivational influences on memory. In S. Kim, J. Reeve, & M. Bong (Eds.), *Recent developments in neuroscience research on human motivation* (Vol. 19, pp. 203–27). Bingley, UK: Emerald Group Publishing Limited. doi: 10.1108/S0749-742320160000019019.

Murty, V. P., DuBrow, S., & Davachi, L. (2015). The simple act of choosing influences declarative memory. *The Journal of Neuroscience, 35*(16), 6255–64. Retrieved from www.jneurosci.org/content/35/16/6255.abstract.

Murty, V. P., Tompary, A., Adcock, R. A., & Davachi, L. (2017). Selectivity in post-encoding connectivity with high-level visual cortex is associated with reward-motivated memory. *The Journal of Neuroscience, 37*(3), 537–45. Retrieved from www.jneurosci.org/content/37/3/537.abstract.

Mussel, P. (2013). Introducing the construct curiosity for predicting job performance. *Journal of Organizational Behavior, 34*, 453–72.

Mussel, P., Ulrich, N., Allen, J. J., Osinsky, R., & Hewig, J. (2016). Patterns of theta oscillation reflect the neural basis of individual differences in epistemic moti-vation. *Scientific Reports, 6*. doi: 10.1038/srep29245.

Naylor, F. D. (1981). A state-trait curiosity inventory. *Australian Psychologist, 16*(2), 172–83. doi: 10.1080/00050068108255893.

Otmakhova, N., Duzel, E., Deutch, A. Y., & Lisman, J. (2013). The hippocampal-VTA loop: The role of novelty and motivation in controlling the entry of information into long-term memory. In G. Baldassarre & M. Mirolli (Eds.), *Intrinsically motivated learning in natural and artificial systems* (pp. 235–54). Berlin, Heidelberg: Springer.

Oudeyer, P. Y. & Kaplan, F. (2009). What is intrinsic motivation? A typology of com-putational approaches. *Frontiers in Neurorobotics, 3*, 1–14. doi: 10.3389/ neuro.12.006.2007.

Oyarzún, J. P., Packard, P. A., de Diego-Balaguer, R., & Fuentemilla, L. (2016). Motivated encoding selectively promotes memory for future inconsequential semantically-related events. *Neurobiology of Learning and Memory, 133*, 1–6. doi: 10.1016/j.nlm.2016.05.005.

Patil, A., Murty, V. P., Dunsmoor, J. E., Phelps, E. A., & Davachi, L. (2016). Reward retroactively enhances memory consolidation for related items. *Learning and Memory*, *24*(1), 65–70. doi: 10.1101/lm.042978.

Ranganath, C. & Rainer, G. (2003). Neural mechanisms for detecting and remembering novel events. *Nature Reviews Neuroscience*, *4*(3), 193–202.

Redondo, R. L. & Morris, R. G. M. (2011). Making memories last: The synaptic tagging and capture hypothesis. *Nature Reviews Neuroscience*, *12*(1), 17–30. Retrieved from doi: 10.1038/nrn2963.

Renninger, K. A., & Hidi, S. E. (2016). *The power of interest for motivation and engagement*, New York: Routledge.

Shohamy, D. & Adcock, R. A. (2010). Dopamine and adaptive memory. *Trends in Cognitive Sciences*, *14*(10), 464–72. doi: 10.1016/j.tics.2010.08.002.

Spielberger, C. D. & Starr, L. M. (1994). Curiosity and exploratory behavior. In H. F. O'Neil Jr. & M. Drillings (Eds.), *Motivation: Theory and research* (pp. 221–43). Hillsdale, NJ: Lawrence Erlbaum Associates, Inc.

von Stumm, S., Hell, B., & Chamorro-Premuzic, T. (2011). The hungry mind. *Perspectives on Psychological Science*, *6*(6), 574–88. doi: 10.1177/1745691611421204.

Wang, S.-H., Redondo, R. L., & Morris, R. G. M. (2010). Relevance of synaptic tagging and capture to the persistence of long-term potentiation and everyday spatial memory. *Proceedings of the National Academy of Sciences of the United States of America*, *107*(45), 19 537–42. doi: 10.1073/pnas.1008638107.

Wittmann, B. C., Schott, B. H., Guderian, S., Frey, J. U., Heinze, H. J., & Düzel, E. (2005). Reward-related fMRI activation of dopaminergic midbrain is associated with enhanced hippocampus-dependent long-term memory formation. *Neuron*, *45*(3), 459–67. doi: 10.1016/j.neuron.2005.01.010.

Wolosin, S. M., Zeithamova, D., & Preston, A. R. (2012). Reward modulation of hippocampal subfield activation during successful associative encoding and retrieval. *Journal of Cognitive Neuroscience*, *24*, 1532–47.

Woo, S. E., Chernyshenko, O. S., Longley, A., Zhang, Z.-X., Chiu, C.-Y., & Stark, S. E. (2014). Openness to experience: Its lower level structure, measurement, and cross-cultural equivalence. *Journal of Personality Assessment*, *96*(1), 29–45. doi: 10.1080/00223891.2013.806328.

17 Curiosity

Nature, Dimensionality, and Determinants

Jordan Litman

Abstract: *Curiosity has been a popular subject of inquiry by psychological scientists for over a century. Nevertheless, its nature, dimensionality, and determinants all remain surprisingly poorly understood. While there is general agreement on a "broad strokes" understanding of curiosity as a desire for new knowledge, the precise character of that desire and the specific behaviors it may motivate continue to spark considerable disagreement and debate. In this chapter, I discuss both previous and contemporary theory and research on curiosity as a psychological construct. I describe curiosity in terms of two types: D-type and I-type. D-type curiosity is theorized to reflect an uncomfortable "need to know" that becomes increasingly bothersome until satisfied by obtaining the desired specific pieces of missing information. I-type curiosity is theorized to be a more relaxed "take it or leave it" attitude towards the discovery of new information, in which the aim is simply to have fun while learning. Qualitative differences between I-type and D-type curiosity experiences – being motivated either to induce situational interest or reduce situational uncertainty, respectively – are hypothesized to translate into significant quantifiable differences in the extent to which each type of curiosity energizes behavior. Specifically, D-type curiosity is hypothesized to be associated with both more intense levels of state-curiosity and greater persistence in subsequent information-seeking behavior as compared to I-type curiosity. Finally, future directions for research are discussed.*

Historically, the experience and expression of curiosity has been conceptualized in terms of one of two ostensibly opposite and mutually exclusive motives for seeking out new information. The first account, commonly known as *curiosity drive theory*, viewed curiosity as an uncomfortable state of uncertainty brought about from exposure to novel, complex, or ambiguous stimuli. By gathering new knowledge about such stimuli, uncertainty could be reduced or eliminated, which was theorized to sate curiosity and be rewarding (e.g., Berlyne, 1950, 1960; Litman & Jimerson, 2004). The second account, typically referred to as the *optimal level of arousal theory of curiosity*, was based on evidence that in the absence of novel, complex, or ambiguous stimuli, individuals frequently chose to seek them out. This alternate account of curiosity claimed that people were motivated to maintain an "optimal" degree of arousal, which was pleasurable, achieved by interactions with stimuli capable of inducing situational interest (e.g., Day, 1971; Kashdan et al., 2004). In keeping with this approach, being over-aroused by extremely unusual stimuli or under-aroused (i.e., bored) by overly familiar stimuli was theorized to be unpleasant (Berlyne, 1967; Leuba, 1955).

However, the drive and optimal arousal models of curiosity both fell short in that neither could comprehensively account for information-seeking behavior. If uncertainty was always intolerably distressing, it would be easier to try to avoid it entirely (Frenkel Brunswick, 1949; Furnham & Marks, 2013). On the other hand, if uncertainty was initially pleasurable, but investigation would unavoidably lead to over-familiarity and boredom, then why bother to learn anything new? This debate remained essentially unresolved for decades, with arguments for both a drive account (e.g., Loewenstein, 1994) and an optimal arousal account (e.g., Spielberger & Starr, 1994) touted well into the latter part of the twentieth century, coupled with the insistence that one view necessarily excluded the other. By the end of the twentieth century, the most common definition of curiosity was little more than a sheepish admission that no agreement on a meaningful definition exists (Keller et al., 1994). Unfortunately, disagreements on the nature of curiosity have persisted into the twenty-first century (Grossnickle, 2014).

Interest and Deprivation Curiosity

In response to the long-standing lack of agreement among curiosity theorists, Litman and Jimerson (2004) posited that the seemingly contrary ideas espoused by the drive and optimal arousal perspectives were, in fact, *not* incompatible at all. Indeed, there is considerable evidence that suggests most motivational systems involve *both* reduction- and induction-oriented behaviors. Hunger and subsequent eating behavior, for example, can be stimulated by the uncomfortable pangs associated with a specific nutritional deficit, but can also be activated by the pleasing sight or smell of food (e.g., Cornel et al., 1989; Herman & Polivy, 2004; Lowe & Butryn, 2007). Likewise, strictly psychological or social motives, such as desires for academic or job-related achievement, can involve striving to reduce a deficiency due to a perceived discrepancy between a current situation and a preferred one (i.e., feed-back self-regulation), as well as working toward the attainment of a brand new goal without identifying any particular deficiency in one's condition (i.e., feed-forward self-regulation; Carver & Scheier, 1998; Locke & Latham, 2002; Mullaney et al., 2014).

Based on these ideas, Litman and Jimerson (2004) reasoned that different types of curiosity could be aroused when individuals discover opportunities to learn something new, based solely on the expectation that this new information would generate pleasurable experiences of situational *interest*

(Litman & Spielberger, 2003; Renninger & Hidi, 2011). Alternatively, curiosity can also be activated when individuals decide they are missing key pieces of information needed to better understand something, in which case curiosity reflects a feeling of *deprivation* attributed to the present lack of desired knowledge (Litman, 2008, 2010; Litman et al., 2010; Loewenstein, 1994).[1] According to Litman and Jimerson (2004), experiences of interest-type (I-type) curiosity are expressed in situations where individuals do not feel they are missing any important pieces of information, per se, but rather find an opportunity to learn something new that is anticipated to be aesthetically pleasing or entertaining (e.g., getting to hear a new anecdote expected to be amusing). Deprivation-type (D-type) curiosity, on the other hand, is activated when individuals become aware that they have an incomplete understanding of something they want to make sense of (c.f., Chater & Loewenstein, 2016). If the missing information is found, it can be incorporated into a relevant repertoire of knowledge, eliminate a specific knowledge gap, and result in improved comprehension (e.g., being able to figure or find out the solution to a stymying logical problem).

Accordingly, D-type curiosity is theorized to reflect an uncomfortable "need to know" that becomes increasingly bothersome until satisfied by obtaining the desired specific pieces of missing information (Litman, 2005, 2008). By contrast, I-type curiosity is theorized to be a more relaxed "take it or leave it" attitude toward the discovery of new information, more broadly speaking, in which the aim is simply to have fun while learning.[2] These qualitative

---

1 Intuitively, experiences of interest and curiosity overlap but imply meaningfully different phenomena, even though both lay and scientific definitions commonly conflate the two. Hidi and Anderson (1992) posited that curiosity and interest differed in at least two important ways. First, curiosity is always associated with seeking *new* information, whereas this is not prerequisite for interest. Second, both reduction and induction accounts are based on evidence that increased contact with a curiosity-arousing stimulus always reduces curiosity; however, there is no evidence to suggest that interest declines similarly, and in fact, may intensify with greater contact. Put more precisely, interest tends to involve direct interaction with information perceived as *available*, whereas curiosity always involves a desire for information perceived as (presently) *unavailable*. In this context, I-type curiosity could be construed as a special case of situational interest, where the emphasis is on gathering new information anticipated to generate situational interest as evidenced by increased positive affect and sustained engagement, akin to aesthetic appreciation (c.f., Renniger & Hidi, 2016). On the other hand, Silvia (2005) has compellingly argued that situational interest can involve being engaged or immersed in a particular subject without positive affect. Using the Silvia definition, one could also make the case that D-type curiosity is a special case of interest as sustained attention aimed at completing knowledge sets. In this case, subsequent states of positive affect would be attributed to the reward associated with successfully reducing knowledge discrepancies rather than aesthetic appreciation.

2 One reasonable question to ask is whether I-type curiosity and D-type curiosity might as well be labeled as "Diversive Curiosity" and "Specific Curiosity," (Day, 1971) or as "Breadth" and "Depth" (Ainley, 1987; Langevin, 1971); the former suggests seeking out a relatively wide range of new information (i.e., simply seeking novelty might satisfy one's curiosity), while the latter suggests seeking out a very narrow range of information. However, there are several reasons why this explanation is less satisfactory than one rooted in the I/D distinction. First, there is no definitive or consistent way to scale the degree to which any unknown is relatively

differences between I-type and D-type curiosity experiences – i.e., being motivated either to induce situational interest or reduce situational uncertainty, respectively – are hypothesized to translate into significant quantifiable differences in the extent to which each type of curiosity energizes behavior. Specifically, D-type curiosity is hypothesized to be associated with both more intense levels of state curiosity and with greater persistence in subsequent information-seeking behavior as compared to I-type curiosity (Litman et al., 2005).[3]

Psychometric Assessment, Correlates, and Dimensionality of I-type and D-type Curiosity

Psychometric research has been particularly helpful in the study of curiosity for two major reasons. First, although many outward information-seeking behaviors can be directly observed, the specific thoughts, feelings, and experiential states that underlie and give rise to their expression are far more difficult to measure directly. Second, psychometric research on curiosity has been useful for empirically evaluating the construct validity of theoretical ideas about its nature and dimensionality (e.g., Ainley, 1987), as well as for facilitating identification of the most valid and reliable indicators of curiosity (c.f., Gerbing & Anderson, 1988). As theoretical views on the nature of curiosity have evolved to reflect consideration of distinct "feelings of interest" and "feelings of deprivation," researchers have developed several new psychometric instruments, specially designed to assess individual differences in the experience and expression of Interest (I) type curiosity and Deprivation (D) type curiosity (see Litman & Silvia, 2006 for a detailed review and discussion).

---

broad or narrow in scope, nor has there ever been one developed. These labels have always been a greater source of confusion than clarity – indeed, Berlyne (1966) did not even consider "diversive exploration" to be motivated by curiosity, but rather an expression of *sensation seeking*. Second, the Diversive/Breadth and Specific/Depth labels do not impart any information about the relevant emotional-motivational experiences that might be involved in their arousal or satiation, making them functionally equivalent. In short, the concepts of I-type curiosity and D-type curiosity, and their distinction in experience and expression, *encompass and extend* beyond the less clear differentiation between Diversive/Breadth and Specific/Depth.

3 My use of the term "type" is occasionally a source of some feather-ruffling. My curiosity "types" are not meant to refer to people who are theorized to display *only* I-type *or* D-type curiosity. Rather, the term is meant to describe two relatively distinct subsets of emotional-motivational experiences and behavioral expressions that are found to diverge into meaningfully different, but not orthogonal, categories. The underlying determinants of this categorical distinction among indicators of curiosity are shorthand labels for two correlated dimensions of personality, in keeping with contemporary trait theory (c.f., Cloninger, 2009). More precisely, the terms "I-type" and "D-type" are overly simple descriptors for two broad dimensions of our sociocultural understanding of curiosity, and the complex interaction between those ideas and the activity of two specific brain systems that are implicated in appetite and pleasure (i.e., "wanting" and "liking," respectively; addressed in a later section of the chapter), including the relative magnitude of their activity and the distinct subjective experiences that follow.

Additionally, in keeping with the state-trait theory of curiosity (Spielberger & Starr, 1994), this line of research has also helped clarify the strength of the relationships between estimates of individual differences in I-type and D-type curiosity as dispositional traits and the degree to which such tendencies are predictive of the arousal of corresponding emotional-motivational curiosity states in real time (Litman et al., 2005).

Research on the interrelations among psychometric instruments designed to assess I-type and D-type curiosity have yielded three major sets of findings critical to evaluating their psychological meaningfulness. First, research has demonstrated that measures of I-type and D-type curiosity are moderately to strongly positively correlated with one another, as would be expected, given their shared association with desiring and seeking out new information (Litman & Silvia, 2006). Indeed, if they were only very weakly related, it would suggest that they mapped onto completely different constructs rather than psychologically distinct experiences and expressions of a common domain. Second, and consistent with the above finding, both I-type curiosity and D-type curiosity have been found to be either very weakly related or essentially uncorrelated with measures of conceptually unrelated constructs, such as extrinsic motives for material compensation and facets of Big Five Agreeableness, such as Compliance and Modesty (Litman et al., 2010; Litman & Mussel, 2013). The third major finding in psychometric research is that both types of curiosity are found to be associated with differences in individuals' orientations toward new knowledge, their use of relevant self-regulatory strategies, and their choices in setting self-directed learning goals. I-type curiosity and D-type curiosity are also found to differ in relation to the experience and expression of positive and negative affectivity, in regard to desired information the magnitude of association with measures of conceptually relevant personality constructs (e.g., Big Five Openness), the intensity of experienced curiosity states, and the degree to which subsequent information-seeking behaviors are expressed.

Highly consistent with the theorized differences between I-type curiosity and D-type curiosity reviewed in the previous section, I-type curiosity is positively associated with orientations toward knowledge that manifest in novelty seeking and being more tolerant of ambiguity; self-regulatory strategies that involve optimistic appraisals about seeking the unknown and greater willingness to take risks in so doing; and setting learning-goals aimed primarily at learning new knowledge just for the fun of it. I-type curiosity is associated with positive affectivity and Big Five Openness. However, relative to its D-type counterpart, I-type curiosity is also associated with the arousal of generally lower intensity curiosity states and the expenditure of less effort when given opportunities to actually seek out new information capable of satisfying it. In sum, I-type curiosity appears to correspond to exploring new things for the carefree pursuit of pleasure, but also corresponds to a relatively weak motive and less knowledge-seeking behavior, as compared to D-type curiosity. Quite different from I-type curiosity, D-type curiosity is found positively associated with using caution, deliberation, and judiciousness in the self-regulation of thinking and reasoning, and with setting learning-goals that define successful achievement on the basis of gaining knowledge that is objectively accurate and useful. D-type curiosity shows small positive associations to negative affectivity (consistent with an unsatisfied need-like condition) and is uncorrelated with positive affect. Although, like I-type curiosity, D-type curiosity is also positively related to Big Five Openness, it shows equally strong or stronger overlap with Conscientiousness (i.e., persistence). Also quite different from I-type curiosity, on the average, D-type curiosity is associated with the arousal of very intense curiosity states and the exertion of greater effort when given opportunities to seek out new information expected to satiate its arousal (Koo & Choi, 2010; Lauriola et al., 2015; Litman, 2008, 2010; Litman et al., 2005, 2010; Richards et al., 2013). Overall, these findings are highly consistent with the theorized distinction between I-type curiosity and D-type curiosity.

Psychometric studies of curiosity have also been especially helpful in elucidating its higher-order and lower-order dimensionality. Factor analytic research of curiosity measures has found that I-type and D-type curiosity may be conceptualized as higher-order factors that can be further differentiated into several lower-order dimensions (Litman & Silvia, 2006), each of which appear to map onto seeking out different "formats" of new information, including epistemic ideas, facts, or solutions to problems (Litman, 2012; Mussel et al., 2012); sensory-perceptual stimulation (Collins et al., 2004); information about other people's experiences and feelings (Litman & Pezzo, 2007, 2012); and knowledge about the nature of one's inner self (Litman et al., 2017). These lines of factor analytic research have also shed some light on the degree to which I-type curiosity and D-type curiosity may differentiate in regard to the forms of knowledge each motivates seeking out.

While I-type curiosity has been shown to manifest in seeking out virtually all forms of information (Litman & Silvia, 2006), D-type curiosity has been found to play a uniquely important role as a major theme in *intellectual* curiosity (Gruber et al., 2014; Powell et al., 2016) and inquisitiveness about *individuals in the social world* – both the self (i.e., intrapersonal) and others (i.e., interpersonal) – as evidenced by their degree of overlapping variance, common correlates, and shared reactions to uncertainty (e.g., Han et al., 2013). Additionally, the lower-order dimensions of curiosity identified in past research have also been found to further subdivide into factors on the basis of selectively targeted "sources" of new knowledge. In the case of intrapersonal curiosity (i.e., inquisitiveness about the inner self), for example, there is evidence of three distinct sub-factors, which include exploring the meaning of events from one's past, pondering one's identity and purpose in life, and endeavoring to make sense of one's feelings and motives (Litman et al., 2017).

Although psychometric studies of I-type curiosity and D-type curiosity have been extraordinarily helpful in clarifying curiosity's nature and dimensionality, as noted in the beginning of this section, a major caveat of such research is that it provides mainly *indirect* glimpses of the relevant emotional-motivational states. To conduct a more direct investigation of state curiosity, we must consider not only the nature of the I-type and D-type constructs and their cross-contextual indicators, but also how these constructs *interact with situational phenomena in real time*. In the next section, theory and research findings on the situational determinants of curiosity as an emotional-motivational state, including the association between state curiosity and measures of the thoughts and feelings that are theorized to define the underlying traits, will be addressed.

Situational Determinants of State Curiosity: The Role of Metamemory and Trait Curiosity in the Activation of State Curiosity

Beginning in the late twentieth and early twenty-first century, along with a reassessment of the nature of curiosity and how to more precisely measure it, new theoretical and empirical work in this area also examined the situational determinants of curiosity as a transient emotional-motivational state, including the chain of underlying processes activated by those determinants. Historically, the arousal of state curiosity has been attributed to encounters with stimulus-events characterized as *novel, complex,* or *ambiguous* (e.g., Berlyne, 1950, 1960, 1966). These three terms describe situations in which individuals are most likely to recognize that some information pertaining to a relevant stimulus is missing, pointing to a discrepancy between information that is available and information that is currently unavailable but desired to be known. This conceptualization of the situational determinants of state curiosity suggests that the primary function of curiosity is to energize seeking out and obtaining new information capable of resolving recognized discrepancies in our available knowledge (Litman, 2005; Loewenstein, 1994).[4] However, the stimulus conditions (e.g., novelty) that coincide with discrepancies in knowledge are not *physical* properties like shape or texture, because the extent to which something is regarded as relatively novel, complex, or ambiguous will depend entirely on the past experiences and available knowledge of the individual perceiver (Dember, 1960; Dember & Earl, 1957; Markey & Loewenstein, 2014). Knowledge discrepancies are therefore difficult to precisely control,

---

4 This view is actually somewhat in opposition to the "positive psychological" definition, which has tended to describe curiosity as a very general positive emotional-motivational approach system oriented primarily toward the overarching end goal of personal growth. Such theoretical approaches also tend to conflate curiosity with other constructs such as *play* and *creativity* (e.g., Kashdan, 2004). See Görlitz (1987) for a great deal of discussion on the pros and cons of taking this theoretical approach.

suggesting that consideration of the processes underlying their identification will be central to understanding the degree to which curiosity states are likely to be aroused.

Based on the idea that finding knowledge discrepancies requires an individual to evaluate differences between that which is known and unknown, Loewenstein (1994) reasoned that we identify discrepancies by explicit memory control and monitoring processes. In short, determining the magnitude of a knowledge discrepancy – or "information gap" which is a *metacognitive judgment*. As to the impact of that judgment, Loewenstein (1994) hypothesized that the degree to which curiosity is aroused will be inversely related to the magnitude of the perceived knowledge discrepancy. His prediction was rooted in the concept of the *approach gradient* (Miller, 1959), which holds that the intensity of motive-states peaks as one approaches goal achievement. Accordingly, Loewenstein reasoned that the greater the discrepancy, the further away individuals will perceive themselves from accomplishing their goal of discrepancy resolution, hence the anticipated inverse relationship between size of information gap and intensity of state curiosity.

Prior research has shown that metacognitive judgments about the otherwise unretrievable contents of memory via explicit search correspond (albeit imperfectly) to the actual contents of our memory, suggesting that we are able to make generally accurate judgments about what we know and don't know (Koriat, 1998; Koriat & Levy-Sadot, 1999). Crucially, arriving at these judgments is not merely a cold cognitive process. The subjective states that accompany these processes, which individuals mindfully monitor and assess in order to arrive at a judgment, have a clear and distinctive affective component that may be thought of as a "metacognitive feeling state." Moreover, along with awareness and affect, metacognitive judgments about the contents of one's memory are found to energize engaging in either more or less *subsequent* cognitive effort expenditure, in terms of relevant memory search, retrieval, and evaluation of what (if anything) was retrieved. As such, we can consider the end result of these metacognitive processes to generate a specific, subjective *metacognitive experience* (ME) that reflects a categorically distinct form of metacognitive, affect-laden "knowing"[5] (Efklides, 2006, 2009, 2011).

---

5 Relatively recent work on the concept of knowledge-emotions (e.g., D'Mello & Graesser, 2014; Silvia, 2017) offers a viable framework for addressing the nature of curiosity as a cognitive-affective process that has potential to build on previous work on the role of MEs and state curiosity by endeavoring to account for cognitive processes that carry with them inherent affective meaning. However, at present this approach is not well suited to the study of curiosity; studies of "interest" as a knowledge-emotion overlap with – but do not differentiate between – I-type and D-type curiosity as described in this chapter. Related work on "confusion" and "impasse-driven learning" (e.g., VanLehn, 1988), which is aimed at resolving confusion through problem solving, may point to important analogs associated with expressions of D-type curiosity. I anticipate that work on knowledge-emotion and impasse-driven learning will prove to become important ideas in future work on curiosity.

One possible ME an individual might arrive at is to determine that no information is missing (i.e., aware of no appreciable discrepancy). Such determinations result in an "I *know* this" ME, characterized by varying degrees of confidence and surety in having access to the relevant knowledge. Other times, after a memory search an individual may conclude "I *don't know* this," which also involves subjective feelings that one is certain the information is *not* stored in memory. Both "know" and "don't know" MEs tend to be made rapidly and both typically result in discontinuation of further memory search. Finally, each tends to be predictive of relative recall or recognition accuracy in the expected direction (e.g., Koriat & Lieblich, 1974; Maril et al., 2001, 2005).

Other MEs involve determining that the targeted information is indeed stored *somewhere* in memory, but can only be *partially* retrieved, generating a *"feeling of knowing."* Like "don't know" MEs, "feeling of knowing" also involves unsuccessful attempts to retrieve specific targets. However, unlike "don't know" states, "feeling of knowing" MEs are found to result in the retrieval of *some* knowledge from long-term storage, such as a close associate (Brown & McNeill, 1966; Hart, 1965; Mangan, 2000), to be further processed in working memory. Closely related to "feeling of knowing" is the tip-of-the-tongue (TOT) ME, which gives rise to very intense feelings that retrieval of the presently unavailable target is imminent (Brown, 1991; Burke & James, 2000; Widner et al., 2005). Similar to "feeling of knowing" MEs, TOTs also involve either the incomplete activation of a target or the retrieval of strong associates rather than the desired target. Typically, greater overall activation and more robust affective experiences are associated with TOTs as compared to "feeling of knowing." Both "feeling of knowing" and TOT are positively correlated with recognition accuracy in subsequent memory tests. Particular to these "partial retrieval" MEs, both require individuals to carefully evaluate whatever they had retrieved into working memory – a situation that results in troublesome uncertainty and cognitive conflict that individuals are motivated to eliminate. Consequently, as compared to "don't know" or "know" MEs, TOT and "feeling of knowing" MEs are found to motivate individuals to expend additional time and effort searching for the desired target (Maril, et al., 2001, 2005).

In keeping with Loewenstein's (1994) theoretical views about the impact of perceived relative magnitude of knowledge gaps on state curiosity, we would expect individuals to feel relatively close to their goal of discrepancy elimination during "feeling of knowing" and (especially) TOT MEs and experience very high levels of curiosity. However, during "don't know" MEs, individuals should feel relatively far from eliminating their knowledge discrepancy and, therefore, feel less curious. Finally, given that a "know" ME suggests that no appreciable amount of information is perceived as missing (i.e., essentially zero knowledge discrepancy), very little or no state curiosity should be activated. Only a few studies have tested these hypotheses to date, but they have all found essentially the same results: individuals experience more intense levels of state curiosity for learning new information when they report partial retrieval MEs (e.g., TOTs), an intermediate degree of curiosity for "don't know" MEs, and the lowest levels of state curiosity when they have "know" MEs (Gruber et al., 2014; Kang et al., 2009; Litman et al., 2005; Loewenstein, 1992, 1994; Metcalfe et al., 2017).

Building on Loewenstein's (1994) theoretical and empirical work, Litman et al. (2005) asked participants whether they knew the answers to a series of general knowledge questions and examined the relationships between "know," "don't know," and TOT states for correct answers, self-reports of how much they wanted to find out the answers (i.e., state curiosity), and actual information-seeking behavior, based on tracking which answers each participant chose to look up by actively seeking them at the end of the study. Additionally, they examined whether individual differences in dispositional levels of I-type and D-type curiosity (in this case, intellectual or epistemic curiosity, as measured by two self-report scales) were positively associated with the intensity of state curiosity experiences and, as would be predicted by the state-trait theory of personality and emotional-motivational states (Spielberger & Starr, 1994).

First, consistent with Loewenstein's (1994) predictions, Litman and colleagues found that the highest levels of state curiosity were associated with TOT MEs, an intermediate level of state curiosity was aroused during "don't know" MEs, and the lowest levels were found for "know" MEs. Moreover, as would be expected, the extent to which participants engaged in information-seeking behavior at the conclusion of the study followed this pattern as well. In determining whether trait levels of I-type or D-type curiosity predicted the intensity levels of curiosity states, separate path analyses conducted for each ME (i.e., TOT, "don't know," and "know") revealed that the relationships between state and trait curiosity depended on the specific ME that was reported.

When participants reported TOT MEs, the intensity of associated curiosity states was significantly predicted by the D-type scale but *not* the I-type scale; when participants reported "don't know" MEs, state curiosity was predicted by the I-type scale but *not* the D-type. For "know" MEs, state curiosity levels were found to be unrelated to *either* I-type or D-type curiosity. The relationships between the trait and state measures of curiosity that were empirically found are highly instructive in that they offer some additional insight into the relative affective tone of the curiosity states that were activated during the TOT and "don't know" MEs. These findings suggested that during TOT MEs, state curiosity tended to involve bothersome feelings associated with perceived information deprivation, as evidenced by the significant relationship with D-type trait curiosity. This is also consistent with prior work on TOTs that have described these MEs as characterized by feelings such as "tingling, torment, or turmoil" (Schwartz et al., 2000, p. 19). In contrast, during "don't know" MEs, curiosity states were more likely to involve pleasurable feelings of situational interest, given the significant relationship to I-type trait curiosity. Thus, Litman et al.'s (2005) study not only further demonstrated that MEs influence the extent to which state curiosity is aroused, it also provided evidence that MEs can influence the *affective tone and subjective experience of state curiosity* as well, consistent with the I/D distinction.

Additionally, Litman et al.'s (2005) findings raised important questions about why partial retrieval MEs (e.g., TOTs) and "don't know" MEs would be differentially related to D- or I-type curiosity, respectively; the findings also raised questions about why *neither* I- or D-type trait curiosity was predictive of levels of inquisitiveness for "know" MEs. First, D-type curiosity experiences are theorized to involve tension and reflect a motive to seek specific pieces of information in order to solve problems and reduce uncertainty; as previously noted, partial retrieval MEs (especially TOTs) are found to generate considerable cognitive conflict associated with approaching closure of a knowledge gap in order to arrive at an accurate conclusion, which is highly consistent with the concept of D-type curiosity. Second, D-type curiosity is theorized to correspond to an especially intense desire for missing information and greater determination and perseverance in resolving unknowns; partial retrieval MEs are found associated with especially strong levels of state curiosity and also to predict continued searching for targeted information in memory, which is also highly consistent with the D-type concept. Thus, both theoretical and empirical assessments of curiosity and metacognition suggest that partial retrieval MEs may underlie activation of D-type curiosity states.

Turning to the degree of state curiosity associated with "don't know" MEs, why would there be a unique association with I-type curiosity but not D-type? Unlike partial retrieval MEs, "don't know" states do not involve being explicitly aware of having retrieved *any* potentially relevant knowledge, and therefore should not be associated with experiences of cognitive conflict or being motivated to continue searching in hopes of resolving uncertainty. It is therefore quite reasonable to expect that individuals would only be likely to choose to search for the missing information based on its expected ability to stimulate pleasurable states of situational interest, once discovered. As such, these findings are consistent with both the theorized affective nature of I-type curiosity and the hypothesized strength of I-type curiosity as a relatively weaker motive to seek out new information. Thus, the findings suggest that "don't know" MEs may underlie activation of I-type curiosity states.

Lastly, the lack of *any* significant relationship between state and trait curiosity for "know" states raised questions about what, if anything, could be inferred about the nature of the curiosity states associated with this ME? One possibility is that being curious about the correct answers during "know" MEs might reflect a desire for *performance feedback* (Park et al., 2007). Put another way, if these answers were believed to have been already known *and* successfully retrieved, the only new information to be gained in seeking them out would be verification of questioned accuracy. Measures of relative certainty for a "know" ME that were taken in the study were negatively associated with levels of state curiosity, so this interpretation is logical. Although desiring performance feedback information could be construed as a kind of curiosity (i.e., wondering "how many did I get right?"), it might reflect acting primarily on ulterior motives associated with, say, self-esteem protection rather than a desire to learn new knowledge for its own sake.

Although the above commentary is primarily concerned with epistemic (i.e., intellectual) curiosity, as previously noted, D-type curiosity has been found to overlap with curiosity about other people (Han et al., 2013; Litman & Pezzo, 2007), and also about the inner self (Litman et al., 2017), pointing to a common motive of closing knowledge gaps across these different expressions of inquisitiveness (Litman et al., 2017). Accordingly, although most research on metacognitive processes has focused on linguistic representations of knowledge (i.e., words), the findings of several studies indicate that individuals engage in similar MEs for other kinds of information as well, including odors (Jönsson & Olsson, 2003) and visual images. There is also evidence that such monitoring processes are activated when attempting to solve mathematical or logical problems (Metcalfe & Wiebe, 1987), thus these phenomena are of potential value in studying many (if not all) dimensions of curiosity. In studies of sensory-perceptual curiosity, in which respondents attempt to arrive at a meaningful interpretation of an image, information gap magnitude has been operationalized in terms of the ratio of visual information that is available to that which is unavailable or blurred. These studies have also found that when individuals are working with a relatively small knowledge gap, they tend to experience greater levels of state curiosity (Jepma et al., 2012; Markey & Loewenstein, 2014).

Recent research also finds that even visual attention directed toward desired knowledge is reinforced via the anticipated satiation of curiosity states (Baranes et al., 2015). Moreover, studies that have examined experiences of subjective activation have found evidence of improved memory for the relevant linguistic or visual information that was learned in the process of satiating those curiosity states (e.g., Gruber et al., 2014; Jepma et al., 2012; Kang et al., 2009; McGillivray et al., 2015). Thus, there is a growing body of evidence that suggests satiating curiosity is a highly rewarding experience that plays an important role in directing our attention to new sources of knowledge and in successfully encoding that knowledge into memory, pointing to an *incentive-salience model* of curiosity and learning (e.g., Berridge, 2007, 2012; Berridge & Robinson, 1998; Fowler, 1967; Marvin & Shohamy, 2016).

Research findings on the situational determinants of curiosity that utilize the information gap/ME approach are highly consistent with findings on the nature and dimensionality of curiosity. However, while a consideration of the role of MEs, such as those reviewed in this section, provides a potentially fruitful set of methodological approaches to studying the situational determinants of emotional-motivational states of I-type and D-type curiosity, a clearer understanding of the neuroanatomical systems that ultimately underlie these cognitive-affective processes remains unclear but has attracted a great deal of attention recently by neuroscientists (Gottlieb et al., 2013; Kidd & Hayden, 2015). As such, the latest theory and research on likely candidates for the major brain substrates of curiosity beg some consideration, and will be addressed in the next section.

Underlying Neural Mechanisms: Advances in Neuroscience and Our Understanding of Reward Systems Involved in Curiosity

As with many phenomena of relevance to psychologists, identifying the major neurobiological systems that underlie the activation of emotional-motivational curiosity states, and the subsequent reward experienced by satiating such states, has been of great interest, particularly over the last decade. As noted in the first section, drive-based and optimal-arousal-based approaches to conceptualizing curiosity remain quite popular to this day. However, due to their many limitations, and to new findings in the field of affective neuroscience, these approaches have been largely abandoned as explanatory theories for emotional-motivational states and consequent experiences of reward when satiated (see Litman, 2005 for more commentary); curiosity should not be treated as an exception.

Recent research has suggested that an incentive-salience approach to evaluating curiosity may help clarify the nature of its experience and expression. In keeping with this approach, work by Berridge and colleagues on *wanting* and *liking*, a complex neural system that underlies the arousal of different appetites and their satiation, has been especially enlightening. "Wanting" refers to mesolimbic dopamine receptor activity and is theorized to underlie experiences of desire that motivate expressions of behavioral approach; "liking" corresponds to the activity of opioid receptors in the nucleus accumbens, for which greater activity corresponds to higher levels of hedonic impact (Berridge, 2012; Berridge & Robinson, 1998). Additionally, the amygdala, strongly implicated in subjective experiences of tension and distress (Shin & Liberzon, 2010), and the prefrontal cortex, which plays an important role in impulse-modulation and associative learning (Berridge & Robinson, 2003a, 2003b), are major components of the complete wanting-liking system.

The wanting and liking system has been implicated in desire and pleasure for food, water, drugs, and even sensory stimulation (e.g., Berridge & Winkielman, 2003). Berridge and colleagues find that greater wanting activation (i.e., appetite) corresponds to greater liking activity (i.e., pleasure) in response to receipt of the rewarding stimulus. Moreover, very high levels of wanting activation can create incentives for potential rewards akin to an organism being drawn to the desired stimulus as if it was a "motivational magnet." When wanting is high in a given situation, it may elicit compulsive approach; in the face of delayed reward, as when faced with momentary goal frustration (i.e., partial reinforcement effects), high levels of wanting activation correspond to response perseveration, which may be construed as "determination" to continue pursuing a wanted stimulus even if satiation is uncertain (c.f., Anselme, 2015).

However, research on wanting and liking finds that while the associated processes work cooperatively, their activity and impact on behavior can also be dissociated, meaning there can be a relative disparity between wanting and liking activity, which does not necessarily change in a one-to-one ratio (i.e., it is possible to be relatively high in one while being lower in the other). This finding points to a mechanism by which individuals can experience a wide range of different subjective states attributed to mismatches between the intensity of appetites and the subsequent pleasure derived from their satiation (Berridge, 2004; Berridge & Robinson, 2003a, 2003b). Although liking will tend to be greater when preceded by higher levels of wanting (i.e., the old adage "hunger is the best spice" turns out to have a basis in neuroscience), rewarding stimuli can generate pleasure in the absence of any appreciable appetite. Using hunger and food consumption to illustrate these ideas, experiencing a high degree of wanting activation followed by equally high levels of liking might map onto conditions of sodium or glucose deprivation, for which the associated intense craving is expected to result in extreme pleasure once satiated by the desired nutrient, while low levels of wanting followed by relatively higher levels of liking would be analogous to snacking on chips or sweets in the absence of nutrient deprivation, because the salty or sweet taste is still inherently pleasurable. In short, research shows that while greater wanting makes a pleasurable stimulus more motivationally salient, more attractive, and more rewarding when attained, the experience of desire is dissociable from the hedonic (i.e., pleasure) value of a desired stimulus.

Regarding the subjectively felt affective experiences associated with wanting and liking, Berridge (2004, 2009) posits that liking is the primary neural substrate of pleasure from reward, and explicitly differentiates it from wanting (i.e., desire). However, Berridge tends to hedge his bets on attributing any specific subjective affective experience to wanting – at least in regard to dopamine receptor activity – and he describes it purely in relation to motivational intensity as evidenced by behavioral choice and the expenditure of effort in the pursuit of a reward (e.g., Berridge & Robinson, 2003a, 2003b). This begs the question of what affective experience might be tentatively hypothesized as an analog of wanting.

As previously noted, another critical brain region in wanting and liking is the amygdala, the activation of which is strongly implicated in subjective experiences of tension, distress, and anxiety (e.g., Shin & Liberzon, 2010). In past research, lesions of the amygdala have been found to reduce or eliminate wanting specific stimuli, though such lesions have no impact on liking (Berridge & Robinson, 1998). Related research also finds that amygdala stimulation can increase incentive salience – including guiding organisms to targeting and selecting a specific desired stimulus, even at the cost of eschewing other possible rewards. (Kumar et al., 2014; Mahler & Berridge, 2012; Robinson et al., 2014). By contrast, amygdala stimulation can reduce the hedonic experiences that reflect liking, indicating that amygdala activity is central to wanting but not to liking (Kumar et al., 2014). Thus, consideration of the role the amygdala plays in wanting and liking potentially elucidates how the neural substrates of desire and reward map onto the conventional idea that appetites become gradually more uncomfortable as they increase in intensity, and that satiating such appetites with the relevant "to be liked" stimulus brings about pleasure and, for more intense appetites, hedonic experience in the form of *both* pleasure and relief.

According to Litman (2005, 2010), the qualitative and quantitative differences found between I-type and D-type curiosity reflect subjective experiences that emerge due to the degree of an individual's initial wanting of new information and the relative degree of subsequent liking that results from learning it. In this context, the high levels of wanting activation are theorized to underlie the affective tone of emotional-motivational D-type curiosity states (i.e., increasingly bothersome until sated), the intensity of the associated emotional-motivational states (i.e., strong), the expected degree or likelihood of engaging in information-seeking behaviors energized by those states (more persistence and greater likelihood, respectively), while approximately matched levels of liking account for the magnitude of reward value experienced when the desired knowledge is obtained (high degree of pleasure).

Accordingly, relatively low levels of initial wanting are theorized to underlie the affective tone of emotional-motivational I-type curiosity states (generally pleasant), the intensity of the associated emotional-motivational states (modest), and the expected degree or likelihood of engaging in information-seeking behaviors energized by those states (less determined and lower likelihood, respectively), while comparatively high levels of liking account for the magnitude of reward value when desired knowledge is obtained (moderate degree of pleasure). Litman (2005) reasoned that these same wanting and liking processes might also correspond to the phenomenon of *processing fluency* (e.g., Reber et al., 2004); I-type in regard to aesthetic appreciation and D-type in terms of sense-making (Chater & Loewenstein, 2016; Chatterjee & Vartanian, 2014).

Although the degree to which the neuroscience of wanting and liking maps onto the experience and expression of curiosity is still very much in its infancy, recent research has been promising. Gruber et al. (2014), for example, found strong evidence that dopamine activity was positively associated with information search that reflected a desire to find out answers to questions, while earlier work by Biederman and Vessel (2006) has shown that opioid activity occurs when we learn new information and incorporate it with knowledge stored in memory.

Concluding Thoughts

The preceding sections of this chapter addressed in some detail the long road in transitioning from early work on the nature and dimensionality of curiosity and different methodological approaches to studying its major situational determinants and subsequent outcomes to the current state of the science in the twenty-first century. In brief, the archaic and incompatible drive and arousal theories have begun to diminish in importance as explanatory models, while new work that builds on the relatively recently proposed I/D model, which incorporates and extends beyond classic approaches, has gained ground and proven to be quite fruitful. Moreover, the I/D model has shown promise in guiding the development of new valid and reliable psychometric instruments. Reconceptualizing novelty, complexity, and ambiguity in terms of metamemory rather than stimulus features has broken new ground in the study of curiosity's determinants (e.g., Metcalfe et al., 2017), and helped guide new work on the underlying reward mechanisms involved in curiosity based on the methods of contemporary affective neuroscience (e.g., Gruber et al., 2014). Given that recent advances in a range of fields (such as psychometrics, assessment, metamemory, and neuroscience) over the last decade have opened many new paths to be explored in furthering our scientific understanding of curiosity, in the remainder of this chapter I will elaborate on a few specific recommendations for scientists looking to conduct new research on curiosity.

Developmental Course of the Experience and Expression of I-type and D-type Curiosity

Along with a re-evaluation of the nature, dimensionality, situational determinants, and underlying mechanisms associated with the experience and expression of curiosity, there has been a renewed interest in exploring the developmental course of curiosity (e.g., Jirout & Klahr, 2012; Oudeyer & Smith, 2016). In consideration of the I/D distinction and earlier work in this area (e.g., Henderson & Moore, 1979; Penny & McCann, 1964), Piotrowski et al. (2014) recently developed and validated new psychometric tools for assessing I-type and D-type dimensions of curiosity in children as young as three years of age. Building on the psychometric work by Piotrowski, Litman et al. (2014), Sullivan and Litman (2017, Manuscript in preparation) very recently began re-evaluating archival data on the facial expressions of *infants*, previously identified as conveying cognitive-perceptual engagement, and which have been variously labeled as expressing either "curiosity" or "interest."

Sullivan and Litman (2017, Manuscript in preparation) discovered two expressions in particular "leapt out" as potential indicators that may discriminate between I-type and D-type curiosity, respectively: one labeled as "Open Wonder" (OW) and a second that has been labeled as "Knit Brow" (KB) (Sullivan & Lewis, 2003). The OW face is notable for raised brows, and wide open eyes, which are the common expressions of positively valenced interest in adults (e.g., Kenza et al., 2015; Reeve, 1993), and for an absence of tension, as measured by stable vagal tone. The OW face is typically accompanied by positive affective vocalizations and little fussing. Quite different from the OW face, the KB expression was marked by lowering of the brows, and is typically found in situations hallmarked by challenge and uncertainty, accompanied by evidence of some tension on the basis of an unstable vagal tone. Moreover, when KB faces are displayed, infants will appear to engage in intense concentration (i.e., negatively valenced "interest"). Consistent with this interpretation of KB faces, in adults such expressions are commonly associated with the exertion of mental effort (e.g., Schwartz, 2005). If indeed these faces can be more clearly validated as expressions of infant I-type and D-type curiosity, it would provide a very useful tool for assessing the developmental course of experiences and expressions of I-type and D-type forms of inquisitiveness.

What is especially exciting is that there is clear evidence of the importance of these same facial expressions in inquisitive adults that has also been largely overlooked in regard to curiosity. Specifically, there are two highly relevant forms of non-manual grammatical facial expressions used cross-culturally in sign language when asking questions of others: the "Yes/No" (Y/N) expression and the "Who/What/Why/When/Where?" (Wh?) (Nguyena & Ranganath, 2010; Zeshan, 2004). The Y/N face is characterized by raised brows and wide eyes, quite similar to the infant OW expression, and is explicitly used to make queries when the inquisitive person has a complete lack of any appreciable knowledge relative to the topic in question. The Wh? face is characterized by lowered brows and narrowed eyes, and is explicitly aimed at inquiring about highly specific details to "flesh out" a partially known or understood topic for which there are specific information gaps to be filled; it is very similar to the infant KB expression. Moreover, all of these facial expressions show considerable overlap with expressions empirically found to be associated with thinking and problem solving in previous research (e.g., King, 1996).

While it has been generally recognized that facial expressions are important for conveying both ideas and emotion to others in sign language (e.g., Benitez-Quiroz et al., 2014; Elliott & Jacobs, 2013), the degree of potential overlap between the Y/N and Wh? faces and interest/curiosity – and their apparent relatedness to distinct expressions of I-type and D-type curiosity as described in this chapter – has not been explored. Research is currently underway that will investigate the role of these "questioning" expressions in infants and adults, which point as potential windows into "the face of curiosity" (Litman et al., 2017, Manuscript in preparation).

Thoughts on Curiosity in the Digital Age of Information

An especially important idea to keep in mind moving forward on studying curiosity into the twenty-first century is that due to the extraordinary access to information ushered in by the digital era of modern information technology, Millennials (and their younger siblings, "Generation Z," as they are sometimes labeled) are able to chase new ideas or immerse themselves in research in a way that has simply not been possible for previous generations. Modern information storage and exchange has effectively created an "age of information," radically altering the potential to explore the new, as well as delve much more deeply into any given topic, and to do so with far greater anonymity and freedom from social constraints (e.g., Schneider et al., 2013; Spielberger & Starr, 1994) that might inhibit inquisitiveness from being expressed.

In the "information age," individuals can easily search for almost anything they are curious about. This has impacted how we seek out and utilize information relevant to the arts, the sciences, human interaction, entertainment, investigation, design – virtually everything! This greater access to information has been transformative, opening the floodgates on our ability to act on I- and D-types of curiosity in ways only just beginning to be understood and utilized. Bearing these notions in mind, if the twenty-first century can be defensibly construed of as the "Information Age," it has surely ushered in a "Curiosity Age" as well.

References

Ainley, M. D. (1987). The factor structure of curiosity measures: Breadth and depth of interest curiosity styles. *Australian Journal of Psychology*, *39*, 53–9. doi: 10.1080/00049538708259035.

Anselme, P. (2015). Incentive salience attribution under reward uncertainty: A Pavlovian model. *Behavioural Processes*, *111*, 6–18. doi: 10.1016/j.beproc.2014.10.016.

Baranes, A, Oudeyer, P., & Gottlieb, J. (2015). Eye movements reveal epistemic curiosity in human observers. *Vision Research*, *117*, 81–90. doi: 10.1016/j.visres.2015.10.009.

Benitez-Quiroz, C. F., Gökgöz, K., Wilbur, R. B., & Martinez, A. M. (2014). Discriminant features and temporal structure of nonmanuals in American Sign Language. *PLoS ONE*, *9*, e86268. doi: 10.1371/journal.pone.0086268.

Berlyne, D. E. (1950). Novelty and curiosity as determinants of exploratory behavior. *British Journal of Psychology*, *41*, 68–80.

Berlyne, D. E. (1960). *Conflict, arousal, and curiosity*. New York, NY: McGraw-Hill. doi: 10.1037/11164-000.

Berlyne, D. E. (1966). Curiosity and exploration. *Science*, *153*, 25–33. doi: 10.1126/science.153.3731.25.

Berlyne, D. E. (1967). Arousal and reinforcement. In D. Levine (Ed.), *Nebraska symposium on motivation* (pp. 1–110). Lincoln, NE: University of Nebraska Press.

Berridge, K. C. (2004). Pleasure, unfelt affect, and irrational desire. In A. S. R. Manstead, A. H. Fischer, & N. Frijda (Eds.), *Feelings and emotions: The Amsterdam symposium* (pp. 43–62). Cambridge, UK: Cambridge University Press. doi: 10.1017/CBO9780511806582.015.

Berridge, K. C. (2007). The debate over dopamine's role in reward: The case for incentive salience. *Psychopharmacology, 191*, 391–431. doi: 10.1007/s00213-006-0578-x.

Berridge, K. C. (2009). Wanting and liking: Observations from the neuroscience and psychology laboratory. *Inquiry: An Interdisciplinary Journal of Philosophy, 52*, 78–398. doi: 10.1080/00201740903087359.

Berridge, K. C. (2012). From prediction error to incentive salience: Mesolimbic computation of reward motivation. *European Journal of Neuroscience, 35*, 1124–43. doi: 10.1111/j.1460-9568.2012.07990.x.

Berridge, K. C. & Robinson, T. E. (1998). The role of dopamine in reward: Hedonics, learning, or incentive salience? *Brain Research Reviews, 28*, 308–67. doi: 10.1016/S0165-0173(98)00019-8.

Berridge, K. C. & Robinson, T. E. (2003). Parsing reward. *Trends in Neurosciences, 26*, 507–13. doi: 10.1016/S0166-2236(03)00233-9.

Berridge, K. C. & Winkielman, P. (2003). What is an unconscious emotion? *Cognition & Emotion, 17*, 181–211. doi: 10.1080/02699930302289.

Biederman, I. & Vessel, E. A. (2006). Perceptual pleasure and the brain. *American Scientist, 94*, 249–255. doi: 10.1511/2006.59.995.

Brown, A. S. (1991). A review of the tip-of-the-tongue experience. *Psychological Bulletin, 109*, 204–23. doi: 10.1037/0033-2909.109.2.204.

Brown, R. & McNeill, D. (1966). The "tip-of-the-tongue" phenomenon. *Journal of Verbal Learning and Verbal Behavior, 5*, 325–37. doi: 10.1016/S0022-5371(66)80040-3.

Burke, D. M. & James, L. E. (2000). Phonological priming effects on word retrieval and tip-of-the-tongue experiences in young and older adults. *Journal of Experimental Psychology: Learning, Memory and Cognition, 26*, 1378–91. doi: 10.1037/0278-7393.26.6.1378.

Carver, C. S. & Scheier, M. F. (1998). *On the self-regulation of behavior.* New York, NY: Cambridge University Press. doi: 10.1017/CBO9781139174794.

Chater, N. & Loewenstein, G. (2016). The under-appreciated drive for sensemaking. *Journal of Economic Behavior & Organization, 126*, 137–54. doi: 10.1016/j.jebo.2015.10.016.

Chatterjee, A. & Vartanian, O. (2014). Neuroaesthetics. *Trends in Cognitive Sciences, 18*, 370–5. doi: 10.1016/j.tics.2014.03.003.

Cloninger, S. (2009). Conceptual issues in personality theory. In P. J. Corr & G. Matthews (Eds.), *The cambridge handbook of personality psychology* (pp. 3–26). New York, NY: Cambridge University Press. doi: 10.1017/CBO9780511596544.004.

Collins, R. P., Litman, J. A., & Spielberger, C. D. (2004). The measurement of perceptual curiosity. *Personality and Individual Differences, 36*, 1127–41. doi: 10.1016/S0191-8869(03)00205-8.

D'Mello, S. K. & Graesser, A. C. (2014). Confusion. In R. Pekrun & L. Linnenbrink-Garcia (Eds.), *International handbook of emotions in education* (pp. 289–310). New York, NY: Routledge.

Day, H. I. (1971). The measurement of specific curiosity. In H. I. Day, D. E. Berlyne, & D. E. Hunt (Eds.), *Intrinsic motivation: A new direction in education* (pp. 99–112). New York, NY: Holt, Rinehart & Winston.

Dember, W. N. (1960). *The psychology of perception*. New York, NY: Henry Holt & Co.

Dember, W. N. & Earl, R. W. (1957). Analysis of exploratory, manipulative, and curiosity behaviors. *Psychological Review, 64*, 91–6. doi: 10.1037/h0046861.

Efklides, A. (2006). Metacognition and affect: What can metacognitive experiences tell us about the learning process? *Educational Research Review, 1*, 3–14. doi: 10.1016/j.edurev.2005.11.001.

Efklides, A. (2009). The role of metacognitive experiences in the learning process. *Psicothema, 21*, 76–82.

Efklides, A. (2011). Interactions of metacognition with motivation and affect in self-regulated learning: The MASRL model. *Educational Psychologist, 46*, 6–25 doi: 10.1080/00461520.2011.538645.

Elliott, E. A. & Jacobs, A. M. (2013). Facial expressions, emotions, and sign languages, *Frontiers in Psychology*, 1–4. doi: 10.3389/fpsyg.2013.00115.

Fowler, H. (1967). Satiation and curiosity: Constructs for a drive and incentive-motivational theory of exploration. In K. W. Spence (Ed.), *The psychology of learning and motivation: Advances in research and theory* (Vol. 1, pp. 157–227). New York, NY: Academic Press. doi: 10.1016/S0079-7421(08)60514-9.

Frenkel-Brunswick, E. (1949). Tolerance toward ambiguity as a personality variable. *American Psychologist, 3*, 268.

Furnham, A. & Marks, J. (2013). Tolerance of ambiguity: A review of the recent literature. *Psychology, 4*, 717–28. doi: 10.4236/psych.2013.49102.

Gerbing, D. W. & Anderson, J. C. (1988). An updated paradigm for scale development incorporating unidimensionality and its assessment. *Journal of Marketing Research, 25*, 186–192. doi: 10.2307/3172650.

Görlitz, D. (1987). *Curiosity, imagination, and play: On the development of spontaneous cognitive and motivational processes*. Hillsdale, NJ: Lawrence Erlbaum.

Gottlieb, J., Oudeyer, P. Y., Lopes, M., and Baranes, A. (2013). Information seeking, curiosity, and attention: Computational and neural mechanisms. *Trends in Cognitive Science, 17*, 585–593. doi: 10.1016/j.tics.2013.09.001.

Grossnickle, E. M. (2014). Disentangling curiosity: Dimensionality, definitions, and distinctions from interest in educational contexts. *Educational Psychology Review, 26*, 1–38.

Gruber, M. J., Gelman, B. D. & Ranganath, C. (2014). States of curiosity modulate hippocampus-dependent learning via the dopaminergic circuit. *Neuron, 84*, 486–496. doi: 10.1016/j.neuron.2014.08.060.

Han, C., Li, P., Warren, C., Feng, T., Litman, J., & Li, H. (2013). Electrophysiological evidence for the importance of interpersonal curiosity. *Brain Research, 15*, 45–54. doi: 10.1016/j.brainres.2012.12.046.

Hart, J. T. (1965). Memory and the feeling-of-knowing experience. *Journal of Educational Psychology, 56*, 208–216. doi: 10.1037/h0022263.

Henderson, B. & Moore, S. G. (1979). Measuring exploratory behavior in young children: A factor-analytic study. *Developmental Psychology, 15*, 113–19. doi: 10.1037/0012-1649.15.2.113.

Herman, C. P. & Polivy, J. (2004). The self-regulation of eating: Theoretical and practical problems. In R. F. Baumeister & K. D. Vohs (Eds.), *Handbook of self-regulation: Research, theory, and applications* (pp. 492–508). New York, NY: The Guilford Press.

Hidi, S., & Anderson, V. (1992). Situational interest and its impact on reading and expository writing. In K. A. Renninger, S. Hidi, & A. Krapp (Eds.), *The role of interest in learning and development* (pp. 215–238). Hillsdale, NJ: Lawrence Erlbaum Associates, Inc.

Jepma, M., Verdonschot, R. G., van Steenbergen, H., Rombouts, S. A., & Nieuwenhuis, S. (2012). Neural mechanisms underlying the induction and relief of perceptual curiosity. *Frontiers in Behavioral Neuroscience, 6,* 1–9. doi: 10.3389/fnbeh.2012.00005.

Jirout, J. & Klahr, D. (2012). Children's scientific curiosity: In search of an operational definition of an elusive concept. *Developmental Review, 32,* 125–160. doi: 10.1016/j.dr.2012.04.002.

Jönsson, F. U. & Olsson, M. J. (2003). Olfactory metacognition. *Chemical Senses, 28,* 651–8. doi: 10.1093/chemse/bjg058.

Kang, M. J., Hsu, M., Krajbich, I. M., Loewenstein, G., McClure, S. M., Wang, J. T., & Camerer, C. F. (2009). The wick in the candle of learning: Epistemic curiosity activates reward circuitry and enhances memory. *Psychological Science, 20,* 963–973. doi: 10.1111/j.1467-9280.2009.02402.x.

Kashdan, T. B. (2004). Curiosity. In C. Peterson and M. E. P. Seligman (Eds.), *Character strengths and virtues: A handbook and classification* (pp. 125–41). Washington, DC: American Psychological Association and Oxford University Press.

Kashdan, T. B., Rose, P., & Fincham, F. D. (2004). Curiosity and exploration: Facilitating positive subjective experiences and personal growth opportunities. *Journal of Personality Assessment, 82,* 291–305. doi: 10.1207/s15327752jpa8203_05.

Keller, H., Schneider, K., & Henderson, B. (1994). *Curiosity and exploration.* Berlin: Springer-Verlag. doi: 10.1007/978-3-642-77132-3.

Kenza, B., Mohamed, B., & Hacene, B. (2015). *Facial expressions of interest's emotion.* Paper presented at the 2015 International Conference on Applied Research in Computer Science and Engineering (ICAR). Beirut. doi: 10.1109/ARCSE.2015.7338133.

Kidd, C. & Hayden, B. Y. (2015). The psychology and neuroscience of curiosity. *Neuron, 88,* 449–60. doi: 10.1016/j.neuron.2015.09.010.

King, J. K. (1996). *Reflections of thought: Cognitive facial expressions in the human interface.* IEEE International Workshop on Robot and Human Communication, 195–200.

Koo, D.-M. & Choi, Y.-Y. (2010). Knowledge search and people with high epistemic curiosity. *Computers in Human Behavior, 26,* 12–22. doi: 10.1016/j.chb.2009.08.013.

Koriat, A. (1998). Metamemory: The feeling of knowing and its vagaries. In M. Sabourin & F. Craik (Eds.), *Advances in psychological science, Vol. 2: biological and cognitive aspects* (pp. 461–79). Hove: Psychology Press/Erlbaum.

Koriat, A. & Levy-Sadot, R. (1999). Processes underlying metacognitive judgment: Information-based and experience-based monitoring of one's own knowledge. In S. Chaiken & Y. Trope (Eds.), *Dual-Process theories in social psychology* (pp. 483–502). New York, NY: Guilford Press.

Koriat, A. & Lieblich, I. (1974). What does a person in a "TOT" state know that a person in a "don't know" state doesn't know? *Memory & Cognition, 2,* 647–55. doi: 10.3758/BF03198134.

Kumar, P., Berghorst, L. H., Nickerson, L. D., Dutra, S. J., Goer, F. K., Greve, D. N., & Pizzagalli, D. A. (2014). Differential effects of acute stress on anticipatory and consummatory phases of reward processing. *Neuroscience 266*, 1–12. doi: 10.1016/j.neuroscience.2014.01.058.

Langevin, R. L. (1971). Is curiosity a unitary construct? *Canadian Journal of Psychology, 25*, 360–74. doi: 10.1037/h0082397.

Lauriola, M., Litman, J. A., Mussel, P., De Santis, R., Crowson, H. M., & Hoffman, R. R. (2015). Epistemic curiosity and self-regulation. *Personality and Individual Differences, 83*, 202–7. doi: 10.1016/j.paid.2015.04.017.

Leuba, C. (1955). Toward some integration of learning theories: The concept of optimal stimulation. *Psychological Reports, 1*, 27–33. doi: 10.2466/pr0.1955.1.g.27.

Litman, J. A. (2005). Curiosity and the pleasures of learning: Wanting and liking new information. *Cognition and Emotion, 19*, 793–814. doi: 10.1080/02699930541000101.

Litman, J. A. (2008). Interest and deprivation dimensions of epistemic curiosity. *Personality and Individual Differences, 44*, 1585–95. doi: 10.1016/j.paid.2008.01.014.

Litman, J. A. (2010). Relationships between measures of I- and D-type curiosity, ambiguity tolerance, and need for closure: An initial test of the wanting-liking model of information-seeking. *Personality and Individual Differences, 48*, 397–402. doi: 10.1016/j.paid.2009.11.005.

Litman, J. A. (2012). Epistemic curiosity. In S. Norbert (Ed.), *Encyclopedia of the sciences of learning* (pp. 1162–5). New York, NY: Springer-Verlag.

Litman, J. A., Crowson, H. M., & Kolinski, K. (2010). Validity of the interest- and deprivation-type epistemic curiosity distinction in non-students. *Personality and Individual Differences, 49*, 531–6. doi: 10.1016/j.paid.2010.05.021.

Litman, J. A., Hutchins, T. L., & Russon, R.K. (2005). Epistemic curiosity, feeling-of-knowing, and exploratory behaviour. *Cognition and Emotion, 19*, 559–82. doi: 10.1080/02699930441000427.

Litman, J. A. & Jimerson, T. L. (2004). The measurement of curiosity as a feeling-of-deprivation. *Journal of Personality Assessment, 82*, 147. doi: 10.1207/s15327752jpa8202_3.

Litman, J. A. & Mussel, P. (2013). Development and validation of German translations of interest- and deprivation-type epistemic curiosity scales. *Journal of Individual Differences, 34*, 59–68. doi: 10.1027/1614-0001/a000100.

Litman, J. A. & Pezzo, M. V. (2007). Dimensionality of interpersonal curiosity. *Personality and Individual Differences, 43*, 1448–59. doi: 10.1016/j.paid.2007.04.021.

Litman, J. A. & Pezzo, M. V. (2012). Interpersonal curiosity. In: S. Norbert (Ed.), *Encyclopedia of the sciences of learning* (pp. 1634–5). New York, NY: Springer-Verlag.

Litman, J. A., Robinson, O. C., & Demetre, J. (2017). Intrapersonal curiosity: Inquisitiveness about the inner self. *Self and Identity, 16*, 231–250. doi: 10.1080/15298868.2016.1255250.

Litman, J. A., Russon, R. K., & Litman, N. M. (2017). *The face of curiosity: An appraisal process approach.* Institute of Human and Machine Cognition, Ocala, FL.

Litman, J. A. & Silvia, P. J. (2006). The latent structure of trait curiosity: Evidence for interest and deprivation curiosity dimensions. *Journal of Personality Assessment, 86*, 318–28. doi: 10.1207/s15327752jpa8603_07.

Litman, J. A. & Spielberger, C. D. (2003). Measuring epistemic curiosity and its diversive and specific components. *Journal of Personality Assessment, 80*, 75–86. doi: 10.1207/S15327752JPA8001_16.

Locke, E. A. & Latham, G. P. (2002). Building a practically useful theory of goal setting and task motivation. *American Psychologist, 57*, 705–17. doi: 10.1037/0003-066X.57.9.705.

Loewenstein, G. (1994). The psychology of curiosity: A review and reinterpretation. *Psychological Bulletin, 116*, 75–98. doi: 10.1037/0033-2909.116.1.75.

Lowe, M. R. & Butryn, M. L. (2007). Hedonic hunger: A new dimension of appetite? *Physiology & Behavior, 91*, 432–9. doi: 10.1016/j.physbeh.2007.04.006.

Mahler, S. V. & Berridge, K. C. (2012). What and when to "want"? Amygdala-based focusing of incentive salience upon sugar and sex. *Psychopharmacology, 221*, 407–26. doi: 10.1007/s00213-011-2588-6.

Mangan, B. (2000). What feeling is the "feeling of knowing?" *Consciousness and Cognition, 9*, 538–44. doi: 10.1006/ccog.2000.0488.

Maril, A., Simons, J. S., Weaver, J. J., & Schacter, D. L. (2005). Graded recall success: An event-related fMRI comparison of tip-of-the-tongue and feeling-of-knowing. *Neuroimage, 24*, 1130–8. doi: 10.1016/j.neuroimage.2004.10.024.

Maril A., Wagner, A., & Schacter, D. (2001). On the tip of the tongue: An event-related fMRI study of semantic retrieval failure and cognitive conflict. *Neuron, 31*, 653–60. doi: 10.1016/S0896-6273(01)00396-8.

Markey, A. & Loewenstein, G. (2014) Curiosity. In R. Pekrun & L. Linnenbrink-Garcia (Eds.), *International handbook of emotions and education* (pp. 228–42). New York, NY: Routledge.

Marvin, M. B. & Shohamy, D. (2016). Curiosity and reward: Valence predicts choice and information prediction errors enhance learning. *Journal of Experimental Psychology: General, 145*, 266–72. doi: 10.1037/xge0000140.

McGillivray, S., Murayama, K., & Caste, A. D. (2015). Thirst for knowledge: The effects of curiosity and interest on memory in younger and older adults. *Psychology and Aging, 30*, 835–41. doi: 10.1037/a0039801.

Metcalfe, J., Schwartz B. L., & Bloom, P. A. (2017). The tip-of-the-tongue (TOT) state and curiosity. *Cognitive Research: Principles and Implications, 2*, 31–8.

Metcalfe, J. & Wiebe, D. (1987). Intuition in insight and noninsight problem solving. *Memory & Cognition, 15*, 238–46. doi: 10.3758/BF03197722.

Miller, N. A. (1959). Liberalization of basic S-R concepts: Extensions to conflict behavior, motivation, and social learning. In S. Koch (Ed.), *Psychology: The study of a science* (pp. 196–292). New York, NY: McGraw-Hill.

Mullaney, K. M., Carpenter, S. K., Grotenhuis, C., & Burianek, S. (2014). Waiting for feedback helps if you want to know the answer: The role of curiosity in the delay-of-feedback benefit. *Memory & Cognition, 42*, 1273–84. doi: 10.3758/s13421-014-0441-y.

Mussel, P., Spengler, M., Litman, J. A., & Schuler, H. (2012). Development and validation of the German work-related curiosity scale. *European Journal of Psychological Assessment, 28*, 109–17. doi: 10.1027/1015-5759/a000098.

Nguyen, T. D. & Ranganath, S. (2010). Facial expressions in American Sign Language: Tracking and recognition. *Pattern Recognition, 4*, 665–76.

Oudeyer, P. & Smith L. B. (2016). How evolution may work through curiosity-driven developmental process. *Topics in Cognitive Science, 8*, 492–502. doi: 10.1111/tops.12196.

Park, G., Schmidt, A. M., Scheu, C., & DeShon, R. P. (2007). A process model of goal orientation and feedback seeking. *Human Performance, 20*, 119–45. doi: 10.1080/08959280701332042.

Penny, R. K. & McCann, B. (1964). The children's reactivity curiosity scale. *Psychological Reports, 15*, 323–334. doi: 10.2466/pr0.1964.15.1.323.

Piotrowski, J. T., Litman, J. A., & Valkenburg, P. (2014). Measuring epistemic curiosity in young children. *Infant and Child Development, 23*, 542–33. doi: 10.1002/icd.1847.

Powell, C., Nettelbeck, T., & Burns, N. R. (2016). Deconstructing intellectual curiosity. *Personality and Individual Differences, 95*, 147–51. doi: 10.1016/j.paid.2016.02.037.

Reber, R., Schwarz, N., & Winkielman, P. (2004). "Processing fluency and aesthetic pleasure: Is beauty in the perceiver's processing experience?" *Personality and Social Psychology Review. 8*, 364–82. doi: 10.1207/s15327957pspr0804_3.

Reeve, J. (1993). The face of interest. *Motivation and Emotion, 77*, 353–75. doi: 10.1007/BF00992325.

Renninger, K. A. & Hidi, S. (2011). Revisiting the conceptualization, measurement, and generation of interest. *Educational Psychologist, 46*, 168–84. doi: 10.1080/00461520.2011.587723.

Renninger, K. A. & Hidi, S. (2016). *The power of interest for motivation and learning.* New York: Routledge.

Richards, J. B., Litman, J. A., & Roberts D. H. (2013). Performance characteristics of measurement instruments of epistemic curiosity in third-year medical students. *Medical Science Educator, 23*, 355–63. doi: 10.1007/BF03341647.

Robinson, M. J. F., Warlow, S. M., & Berridge, K. C. (2014). Optogenetic excitation of central amygdala amplifies and narrows incentive motivation to pursue one reward above another. *The Journal of Neuroscience, 34*, 16 567–80. doi: 10.1523/JNEUROSCI.2013-14.2014.

Schneider, A., von Krogh, G., & Jäger, P. (2013). 'What's coming next?' Epistemic curiosity and lurking behavior in online communities. *Computers in Human Behavior, 29*, 293–303. doi: 10.1016/j.chb.2012.09.008.

Schwartz, B. L., Travis, D. M., Castro, A. M., & Smith, S. M. (2000). The phenomenology of real and illusory tip-of-the-tongue states. *Memory & Cognition, 28*, 18–27. doi: 10.3758/BF03211571.

Schwartz, N. (2005). When thinking feels difficult: Meta-cognitive experiences in judgment and decision making. *Medical Decision Making, 25*, 105–12. doi: 10.1177/0272989X04273144.

Shin, L. M., & Liberzon, I. (2010). The neurocircuitry of fear, stress, and anxiety disorders. *Neuropsychopharmacology, 35*(1), 169–91. doi: 10.1038/npp.2009.83.

Silvia, P. J. (2005). What is interesting? Exploring the appraisal structure of interest. *Emotion, 5*, 89–102. doi: 10.1037/1528-3542.5.1.89.

Silvia, P. (2017). Knowledge emotions: Feelings that foster learning, exploring, and reflecting. In R. Biswas-Diener & E. Diener (Eds.), *Noba Textbook Series: Psychology*. Champaign, IL: DEF publishers. doi: nobaproject.com.

Spielberger, C. D. & Starr, L. M. (1994). Curiosity and exploratory behavior. In H. F. O'Neil, Jr., & M. Drillings (Eds.), *Motivation: Theory and research* (pp. 221–43). Hillsdale, NJ: Lawrence Erlbaum Associates.

Sullivan, M. W. & Lewis, M. (2003). Emotional expressions of young infants and children: A practitioner's primer. *Infants and Young Children, 16*, 120–42. doi: 10.1097/00001163-200304000-00005.

Sullivan, M. & Litman, J. A. (2017). *Infant expressions of I- and D-type epistemic curiosity within the first two months of life.* Newark, NJ: Rutgers University.

VanLehn, K. (1988) Toward a theory of impasse-driven learning. In H. Mandl. & A. Lesgold (Eds.), *Cognitive science: Learning issues for intelligent tutoring systems* (pp. 19–41). New York, NY: Springer. doi: 10.1007/978-1-4684-6350-7_2.

Widner, R. L., Otani, H., & Winkelman, S. E. (2005). Tip-of-the-tongue experiences are not merely strong feeling-of-knowing experiences. *The Journal of General Psychology, 132,* 392–407. doi: 10.3200/GENP.132.4.392-407.

Zeshan, U. (2004). Interrogative constructions in signed languages: Cross-linguistic perspectives. *Language, 80,* 7–39.

18 The Role of Curiosity and Interest in Learning and Motivation

Da-Jung Diane Shin, Hyun Ji Lee, Glona Lee, and Sung-il Kim

Abstract: *Curiosity and situational interest are powerful driving forces in learning and motivation that lead students to learn more effectively. In this chapter, we elucidate curiosity and situational interest by focusing on (1) conceptual definitions and characteristics, (2) antecedents, (3) cognitive and behavioral outcomes, and (4) strategies to foster them in school. Curiosity is a short-lasting, aversive state that desires an acquisition of specific information. Its properties contrast with those of situational interest, which is an overall positive affect and a general preference for a topic. Whereas curiosity and situational interest are stimulated by similar contextual features (such as collative variables), triggering curiosity requires one to perceive an information gap between what one knows and what one wants to know. Despite these differences, ample evidence displays that both curiosity and situational interest positively impact students' learning, motivation, creativity, and well-being once triggered. Thus, in closing, integrative and specific pedagogical guidelines to enhance students' curiosity and situational interest in education practice are suggested.*

When we encounter something novel, uncertain, or outside our expectations, we often feel an urge to find out more about it. This psychological state, termed curiosity, is driven by an information gap and has been recognized as an important motivator for learning. For a long time, curiosity has been considered to be synonymous with interest (Rotgans & Schmidt, 2014; Silvia, 2006). Only recently have some researchers acknowledged the need to conceptually distinguish the two constructs. Interest has been posited as intrinsic motivation, and components of interest have been found to share common characteristics with those of curiosity (Grossnickle, 2016; Markey & Loewenstein, 2014; Renninger & Hidi, 2016). In classrooms, curiosity and interest are both

This work was supported by the Ministry of Education of the Republic of Korea and by the National Research Foundation (NRF-2015S1A5B6036594) of Korea.

positively and negatively affected by similar factors and, when triggered, both curiosity and interest can have an energizing effect on student learning. For these reasons, it seems, the two concepts have not often been differentiated in educational research or in practice. Nonetheless, separating them may be possible, and this could be vital for refining theories surrounding curiosity and interest and their application in education. Furthermore, understanding the shared and unique properties of the two constructs may shed light on how, both independently and together, they influence student learning and motivation, and what should be done to promote them in the classroom.

The purpose of this chapter is to further the understanding of curiosity and interest in educational settings by reviewing relevant research. First, the conceptual definitions of curiosity and interest are reviewed. Second, the underlying mechanisms of curiosity and interest are examined through a systematic review that addresses the common situational determinants of curiosity and situational interest, and identifies unique antecedents of curiosity that are not related to interest. In addition, the contribution of individual differences to the elicitation of curiosity and interest is noted. Third, the role of curiosity and interest in motivation and learning are discussed. In this section, the current understanding of the behavioral and cognitive outcomes of curiosity and interest in the context of education are reviewed. Finally, we discuss classroom variables that can facilitate or suppress student curiosity and interest, and suggest specific ways to promote these two psychological states. As such, we seek to establish educational implications and future directions for both research and practice.

Definitions of Curiosity and Interest

Curiosity and interest have frequently been conceptualized as synonymous. The two concepts are often used interchangeably in scholarly research and in everyday conversation (Grossnickle, 2016; Renninger & Hidi, 2016; Rotgans & Schmidt, 2014). This lack of distinction may be due in part to the similarities in their characteristics. For example, curiosity and interest can be triggered by similar factors and can lead to comparable cognitive and behavioral outcomes, such as increased attention, engagement, and exploration (Kidd & Hayden, 2015; Loewenstein, 1994; Renninger & Hidi, 2011). Nonetheless, with increasing attention being paid to the potency of curiosity in learning and the theoretical need to differentiate curiosity from interest, the discussion of the conceptual divide between curiosity and interest has recently turned heated among education researchers. From our point of view, curiosity and interest are related but not interchangeable constructs. Thus, in this section, we first describe the traditional concept of interest, and then the distinctive characteristics of curiosity that set the two apart.

Interest

Interest has been conceptualized in various ways in the past, but it can be thought of as a preference for a certain activity, topic, or domain (Bergin, 2016). This preference can be either generated by specific stimuli in the environment or developed as a part of enduring characteristics. The former is termed situational interest and arises from attention-grabbing stimuli (Hidi & Harackiewicz, 2000; Mitchell, 1993), while the latter is individual interest – a relatively stable predisposition that causes individuals to gravitate toward certain classes of stimuli (Durik & Harackiewicz, 2007; Hidi & Harackiewicz, 2000). In an effort to explain how interest develops, Hidi and Renninger (2006; see Renninger & Hidi, 2016 for a more detailed discussion) proposed that an individual's situational interest can develop into longer-term individual interest with an increase in value and relevant knowledge. The Four-Phase Model of Interest Development describes situational and individual interests as evolving through consecutive phases of triggered situational interest, maintained situational interest, emerging individual interest, and well-developed individual interest (Hidi & Renninger, 2006). In other words, interest develops in conjunction with the development of knowledge and value, but it also may fall off or regress if continued engagement with the content of interest is not supported.

Curiosity

Although educational research has addressed curiosity, there is no single widely accepted definition of the concept (Grossnickle, 2016; Kidd & Hayden, 2015). While early philosophical discourse on curiosity regarded it as a passion or as being appetitive, the contemporary definition chiefly sees it as a desire for information in the absence of extrinsic reward (Jirout & Klahr, 2012; Markey & Loewenstein, 2014). However, these definitions are too broad and lead to conceptual confusion between curiosity and interest. Therefore, more specific definitions of curiosity need to be investigated in order to illustrate its uniqueness.

Curiosity can be categorized as either "state" or "trait." State curiosity is associated with temporal arousal and the feeling of wanting to know something in a given context as a result of curiosity-evoking stimuli. This type of curiosity is often mistaken for situational interest, because the two appear to be very similar in terms of engagement. However, while situational interest embraces any information regarding topics or activities of interest and has no specific limitation in its duration, state curiosity usually revolves around the acquisition of specific information and does not last for a significant length of time, usually only until the situation in question has been resolved or the participant withdraws (Grossnickle, 2016; Markey & Loewenstein, 2014). Also, while situational interest is typically associated with the experience of positive affect, state curiosity is usually accompanied by the discomfort of knowledge deprivation or cognitive disequilibrium (Berlyne, 1954; Loewenstein, 1994).

Trait curiosity, on the other hand, refers to an individual's tendency to seek new knowledge and experiences (Grossnickle, 2016; Kashdan et al., 2004; Litman & Silvia, 2006; Loewenstein, 1994). Trait curiosity is thought to impact an individual's experience of state curiosity, as those with high trait curiosity will feel curious with increased frequency and intensity (Litman & Silvia, 2006).

Both trait curiosity and state curiosity have been further subdivided by some researchers. Trait curiosity has been partitioned into cognitive curiosity, physical thrill seeking, and social thrill seeking (Reio et al., 2006); and interest-type and deprivation-type curiosity (Litman, 2010). State curiosity has been separated into perceptual and epistemic curiosity (Berlyne, 1954). For the purpose of the present chapter, we will mainly focus on state (epistemic) curiosity because of its close connection to situational interest.

Underlying Mechanisms of Curiosity and Interest

Despite the different definitions and characteristics of curiosity and interest, there exists a large overlap in the underlying mechanisms, both environmental and personal. However, it is possible to further separate curiosity from interest by identifying its unique antecedents.

Situational Determinants of Curiosity and Interest

Sources of situational interest. Situational interest is known to be elicited by a wide range of contextual features (Anderson et al., 1987; Hidi & Baird, 1988). For example, Bergin (1999) introduced a list of determinants that influence interest in classroom settings and divided them into individual (i.e., belongingness, emotions, competence, utility-goal relevance, and background knowledge) and situational factors (i.e., hands-on activities, discrepancy, novelty, food, social interaction, modeling, games and puzzles, content, biophilia, fantasy, humor, and narrative). Typically, situational interest can be divided into triggered situational interest and maintained situational interest, depending on the duration and relevance (Hidi & Renninger, 2006; Renninger & Hidi, 2016). Relatively superficial task characteristics – such as surprising information, character identification, personal relevance, or task intensity – have been discussed as sources of triggered situational interest (Schraw et al., 2001; Schraw & Lehman, 2001), whereas more meaningful and relevant features – such as project-based learning, group work, or tutoring – are considered to be sources of maintained situational interest (Mitchell, 1993). It can then be concluded that situational factors grabbing an individual's attention trigger situational interest, and that situational and individual factors containing some form of personal value maintain it.

By dividing situational interest into its triggered and maintained forms, the similarity between situational interest – particularly triggered situational interest – and state curiosity becomes more apparent. Triggered situational interest and state curiosity are generated by contextual features that grab the attention (as opposed to meaningful features) and have the possibility to develop into maintained situational interest and individual interest. Common situational determinants of interest and curiosity include novelty, discrepancy, puzzles, uncertainty, and incongruous and surprising information. Curiosity and interest research has been influenced by the pioneering work of Daniel Berlyne, a psychologist who extensively studied the causes of both constructs (e.g., Berlyne, 1954, 1960). He suggested that collative variables – such as novelty, ambiguity, complexity, and surprisingness – are factors that trigger curiosity and interest. Numerous studies have utilized these variables in different ways to generate both interest and curiosity (e.g., Iran-Nejad, 1987; Kim, 1999; Silvia, 2006). Rather than having a direct influence on emotional aspects (through humor, fantasy, food, or task intensity) or self-relevant aspects (through character identification, personal relevance, or involvement), these variables prompt individuals to pay attention to the content by creating a disequilibrium in their schema (Ginsburg & Opper, 1969; Markey & Loewenstein, 2014). The curiosity and triggered situational interest evoked by these sources can thus be considered similar.

Unique cause of curiosity. Although curiosity and situational interest share some triggering factors, identifying specific antecedents of curiosity allows it to be distinguished from interest. The information gap theory suggested by Loewenstein (1994) has gained support for its explanation of the causes of curiosity (Kang et al., 2009; Loewenstein, 1994). His theory stands out from other theories that deal with both curiosity and interest by investigating the roots of curiosity. In doing so, he pinpointed the information gap – the discrepancy between an individual's current knowledge level and the level of knowledge they seek to attain – as a unique direct cause of curiosity. Researchers have supported this proposition and demonstrated that the most important factors leading to curiosity are the reference point of knowledge and deprived knowledge caused by curiosity-evoking stimuli (Kang et al., 2009; Markey & Loewenstein, 2014). Therefore, while interest may be provoked by the novelty or game-like features of a task that is informationally complete, curiosity is experienced only when the individual in question perceives that information is missing. Quizzes or trivia questions are typically used to evoke curiosity because they highlight the missing information (Kang et al., 2009; Stahl & Feigenson, 2015). This exposure to the unknown then creates a sense of discomfort or deprivation, which naturally instills the desire to learn more.

Individual Differences

Although both state curiosity and situational interest are primarily affected by environmental factors, they can be influenced by enduring individual factors, such as trait curiosity and individual interest.

Trait curiosity. Individuals with high trait curiosity are more prone to seek, notice, and become absorbed in curiosity-evoking experiences (Kashdan et al., 2004). Although curiosity can be experienced by most individuals depending on the situation, trait curiosity is expected to influence the frequency, and perhaps the intensity, of these experiences by increasing the awareness of and interactions with curiosity-evoking stimuli (Grossnickle, 2016). Several studies have provided empirical evidence that state curiosity is associated with trait curiosity and situational interest (Kashdan & Steger, 2007; Litman et al., 2005; Silvia, 2008). In a study by Kashdan and Steger (2007), where both trait curiosity and daily state curiosity were measured, correlations were found to be significant at 0.42. Litman and his colleagues (2005) compared their two measures of trait curiosity, the Epistemic Curiosity (EC) scale and the Curiosity as a Feeling-of-Deprivation (CFD) scale, to the state curiosity experienced in three feeling-of-knowing states: "don't know," "tip-of-the-tongue (TOT)," and "I know." They found that their measures of trait curiosity correlated significantly with state curiosity in curiosity-evoking situations. In addition, when trait curiosity and situational interest are examined, trait curiosity has been found to positively predict situational interest when participants are engaged in complex tasks (Silvia, 2008). This process was mediated by appraisals related to coherence and comprehensibility.

Individual interest. Individual interest involves an individual's positive attitude and stored content knowledge for, as well as the understanding and high value of, certain activities or topics (Hidi, 2006). When individual interest arises – not necessarily a conscious decision – individuals desire to engage in the task and generate their own questions and answers, and this engagement tends to be effortless (Hidi & Renninger, 2006). Because individual interest is related to spontaneous engagement, developed value, and stored knowledge, it is assumed to influence state curiosity and situational interest by providing more opportunities to interact with curiosity- and interest-evoking situations (Hidi & Renninger, 2006). For example, individual interest has been found to display a strong correlation with information-seeking, a behavior also demonstrated by individuals with high curiosity (Schiefele, 1991). In addition, more knowledge increases search efficiency and facilitates the acquisition of information (Brucks, 1985). Therefore, individual interest can help maintain curiosity until a successful resolution of curiosity is made by attaining desired information.

Consequences of Curiosity and Interest

Despite the conceptual distinction between curiosity and interest, they both have been found to be associated with similar positive outcomes in learning contexts. Researchers have consistently displayed the association between interest and adaptive outcomes, such as enhanced attention, persistence, and performance (Ainley et al., 2002; Hidi, 1990; Schiefele, 1991). Recent studies have demonstrated the beneficial effects of curiosity on attention, memory, and personal well-being (Gruber et al., 2014; Kang et al., 2009; Kashdan & Steger, 2007). In this section, the overlapping educational benefits of curiosity and interest are discussed in more detail.

Attention and Memory

Curiosity and interest have been found to capture a learner's attention (Shirey & Reynolds, 1988). Several studies have utilized objective indicators of attention – including pupil dilation, eye movement, and reaction time – to demonstrate the effect of curiosity and interest on attention (Beatty, 1982; Gottlieb et al., 2013; Kang et al., 2009). In a study by Kang et al. (2009), questions that more strongly evoked curiosity lead to increased pupil dilation. In addition, eye movement has been shown to be guided by the bias toward curiosity-evoking stimuli, indicating that curiosity drives people to pay attention to them (Gottlieb et al., 2013). Young children more frequently fixate on items they are interested in (Renninger & Wozniak, 1985), and students have been found to pay more attention to interesting rather than uninteresting text (Anderson et al., 1987). In a study that investigated the relationship between text-based interest and attention using reading time, participants spent less time reading interesting text compared to the uninteresting text (McDaniel et al., 2000). Researchers interpreted that the faster reading time means less cognitive demand when reading due to the automatic attention allocation (Hidi, 1995; McDaniel et al., 2000). The benefit of this is that the remaining cognitive resources can be used to improve memory and learning.

A number of studies on curiosity and interest have illustrated the links to memory. Neuroscience studies have revealed that the brain regions related to memory, such as the hippocampus, are activated when students are highly curious (e.g., about blurry pictures or the answers to trivia questions) or when their guesses about answers are incorrect (Gruber et al., 2014; Jepma et al., 2012; Kang et al., 2009). These studies have also shown that students were better at recalling answers or even irrelevant information associated with questions that provoked high curiosity, highlighting the powerful effect of curiosity on memory. A recent behavioral study illustrated the effect of curiosity on memory by demonstrating that the recall of interesting questions was high regardless of the provision of monetary rewards, whereas the recall of uninteresting questions was moderated by monetary reward (Murayama & Kuhbandner, 2011). Interest has also been found to influence memory and learning (Hidi, 1990; Schraw & Lehman, 2001). Researchers have shown that objects of interest or interesting text are better recalled compared to uninteresting objects or text (Renninger & Wozniak, 1985; Wade et al., 1993). In a study conducted by McDaniel et al. (2000), efficient processing of interesting information due to the automatic attention allocation resulted in better memory and learning of the content. Both individual and situational interest in text-based learning have been found to predict the text recall rate (Ainley et al., 2002).

Motivation and Achievement

Curiosity and interest can function as motivators in academic settings either directly or indirectly. It has been claimed that curious individuals experience flow-like engagement in rewarding situations (Kashdan et al., 2004). In a flow state, children lose track of time and become deeply engaged in their task with a sense of control (Nakamura & Csikszentmihalyi, 2014). Thus, they are thought to self-regulate their cognitive resources to focus on the present task. In addition, curiosity has been linked to a greater use of resources and effort (Kang et al., 2009). In Kang and colleagues' behavioral study, undergraduates rated their level of curiosity in trivia questions. If they desired to know the answers, they were asked to spend scarce resources (i.e., limited tokens or waiting time). It was found that students were more likely to spend resources to fill in information for questions that provoked a higher state of curiosity. Indeed, when individuals become curious, they are more motivated to seek unknown information (Loewenstein, 1994). This motivation to gain information is so powerful that even young infants are known to engage in exploration when faced with unexpected situations (Stahl & Feigenson, 2015). Several studies agree that exploratory behavior deriving from curiosity is associated with better learning and achievement (Kashdan & Yuen, 2007; Marvin & Shohamy, 2016; Von Stumm et al., 2011). For example, Von Stumm et al. (2011) proposed curiosity as the third determinant of academic performance. They found that even though intelligence is the strongest predictor of academic performance, the combination of curiosity and effort can be just as influential.

Like curiosity, interest has been found to motivate learners and to eventually result in better performance (Ainley et al., 2002). The positive association between interest and motivational constructs – such as engagement, perceived competence, and cognitive processing – have been reported by existing studies (Durik & Harackiewicz, 2007; Hidi, 1990; Schiefele, 1991). In an investigation that tested the effects of situational and individual interest in math, both were found to be positively associated with task engagement, perceived competence, and performance (Durik & Harackiewicz, 2007). Interest has also been found to be associated with the use of effective learning strategies – such as elaboration, information-seeking, and critical thinking – and a positive attitude toward learning content (Schiefele, 1991). Similar to curiosity, motivation triggered by interest leads to better learning (Ainley et al., 2002; Hoffmann, 2002). Ainley et al. (2002) demonstrated that individual and situational interest could predict test scores for corresponding topics either directly or indirectly via positive affect and persistence. Situational interest, in particular, has been known to prompt even unmotivated students to learn (Hidi & Harackiewicz, 2000). An intervention study that generated situational interest using modified instruction showed that girls who received interesting instructions performed significantly better than those in the control group, despite a general lack of interest in science (Hoffmann, 2002). Therefore, both curiosity and interest serve as motivation for learning and influence academic success.

Creativity

Curiosity and interest researchers have demonstrated a similar relationship between the two constructs and creativity (Day & Langevin, 1969; Karwowski, 2012; Maw & Maw, 1970). Curious people tend to prefer novelty (Kashdan et al., 2004; Loewenstein, 1994), and this tendency is thought to lead to novelty-finding and novelty-producing, which can be considered important processes for creativity (Schweizer, 2006). In addition to this, tolerance for ambiguity and risk taking, which are aspects of curiosity, have been recognized as necessary for creativity (Kaufman & Beghetto, 2009). This relationship between curiosity and creativity has long been recognized. For example, Day and Langevin (1969) proposed that curiosity and intelligence had a positive influence on creativity, and Maw and Maw (1970) also noted the association between curiosity and creativity in younger students. These researchers demonstrated that highly curious students were more adaptive and creative thinkers compared to less curious students. More recently, an empirical study expanded on the role of curiosity in creativity by examining curiosity in relation to two creativity-related self-concepts: creative self-efficacy and creative personal identity (Karwowski, 2012). The results showed a strong correlation between curiosity and both self-beliefs, implying that individuals with high curiosity are more likely to believe that they are creative.

Previous research has also identified the positive effect of interest on creativity. For example, in a study conducted by Amabile (1985), participants were asked to write a poem after being given intrinsic or extrinsic reasons for engaging in the task. Those who were exposed to intrinsic reasons (e.g., because I enjoy the opportunity; because I like writing) showed more creativity in their writing. In addition, the positive affect generated by enjoyment and satisfaction with work has been found to have a linear relationship with creativity (Amabile et al., 2005). Interested individuals attempt to satisfy their intrinsic needs with positive affect, and this, in turn, increases their knowledge and creativity (Fredrickson, 1998). Although the underlying mechanisms that lead to creativity may differ, both curiosity and interest motivate individuals to seek and explore new things, causing them to think and act in creative ways (Kashdan & Silvia, 2009).

Psychological Well-Being

Interest and curiosity have been recognized as being positively associated with various forms of well-being, such as life satisfaction, in various domains (Park et al., 2004; Ryan & Deci, 2000). In work environments, individuals were more productive and reported feeling less exhausted when they were working for the pleasure of learning new things and the enjoyment of challenge at work (Fernet et al., 2004). Moreover, individuals who engage in activities for the sake of interest in, curiosity with, and satisfaction from the task itself were found to have healthier lifestyles (Pelletier et al., 2004). In other research, individuals who participated in religious activities out of their own interest and for intrinsic reasons were found to experience positive changes, whereas those who participated for extrinsic reasons did not (Ryan et al., 1993). Participation for intrinsic reasons was negatively associated with negative psychological states such as anxiety or depression, and positively associated with outcomes like self-esteem and self-actualization. Participation for extrinsic reasons demonstrated the opposite trend. Consequently, general intrinsic motivation, which comes from interest and curiosity, can be seen to be associated with psychological well-being (Ryan & Deci, 2000).

Researchers have also tested the relationship between curiosity and life satisfaction and found similar results. A study that looked at the relationship between different character strengths and life satisfaction reported that individuals who are curious and interested in experiences and seek novelty are associated with greater life satisfaction (Park et al., 2004). Information-seeking and feedback-seeking behaviors, which can arise from curiosity, have also been found to be correlated with job satisfaction (Wanberg & Kammeyer-Mueller, 2000). In another study, the effect of curiosity on well-being was tested in an educational setting, with participants asked to write a diary entry daily for 21 days (Kashdan & Steger, 2007). It was found that individuals with high trait curiosity were more likely to search for and detect meaning in life and to experience life satisfaction. Furthermore, curious people seek challenges, and this tendency is accompanied by the self-perception of their competence, that is, the belief that they are capable of acquiring valuable knowledge (Kashdan & Silvia, 2009). As a result, they explore and adopt growth-oriented behaviors, which eventually increases their well-being (Kashdan & Steger, 2007).

Fostering Curiosity and Interest

Although there is widespread acceptance that curiosity and interest are valuable forms of motivation that should be promoted in educational settings to benefit students, many researchers have documented a dramatic drop in student curiosity and interest when they move on to higher grades (e.g., Kim et al., 2015). A primary goal of school should be, therefore, to become the primary motivational environment where the development of epistemic curiosity and academic interest is encouraged. Previous literature on curiosity and interest has provided suggestions for how to encourage student inquiries and ways in which their curiosity and interest can be fostered in the classroom. Here we will identify some of the factors that affect curiosity and interest in the classroom, and recommend strategies to increase their influence in this setting.

Learning Content

Perhaps the most obvious yet important way of fostering student curiosity and interest is to provide them with topics, activities, and materials that can spark their curiosity and interest. Unfortunately, learning materials presented at schools are typically under-stimulating, fail to stoke the imagination, and discourage curious inquiry. This is because, even though research has identified the psychological underpinnings of curiosity and interest, the actual incorporation of these into educational materials has been much slower. We will thus revisit the antecedents of curiosity and interest, and suggest how they can be utilized in educational content to improve learning.

Providing ill-defined problems. The structure of a problem can affect learning experiences of students. That is, some problems may instill learners to only engage superficially without feeling curious or interested, while other problems may not only trigger learners' curiosity and interest, but also encourage them to make deeper inferences to solve their curiosity and interest. Types of problems can be distinguished by well-defined problems (i.e., those with one correct, agreed-upon solution) and ill-defined problems (i.e., those with conflicting assumptions and where several different solutions are possible; Schraw et al., 1995). As opposed to well-defined problems where students' thoughts are meant to converge and be guided in a uniform direction, ill-defined problems open the possibility to inquire into diverse ways (Chin & Chia, 2006; Smith, 1988), and thereby support interest and curiosity-guided exploration. In line with this, a case study by Chin and Chia (2006) found that ill-defined problems stimulated students to pose questions that led them to explore their own independent inquiries.

Therefore, teachers should provide students with problems or tasks that possess multiple solutions and solution paths, and fewer parameters (Chin & Chia, 2006). The examples of these may constitute creative writing, inference making, debating, and solving problems in real-life contexts. Given an ill-defined problem, students can freely guess and explore without worrying about providing wrong answers, and can resolve curiosity in their own ways. This autonomous problem-solving process, by resolving one's curiosity, is an important source for the generation of interest (Iran-Nejad, 1987; Kim, 1999).

Incorporating collative variables. The decisions a teacher makes regarding the focus and characteristics of content and the activities used to deliver that content have important ramifications on curiosity and interest development (Pressick-Kilborn, 2015). Effective materials that can ignite student curiosity and interest are generally characterized as vivid, well organized, optimally novel, and challenging. That is, learning materials should incorporate sources of curiosity and interest – such as collative variables that encompass novelty, uncertainty, and surprise – to achieve an optimal level of both in students (Bergin, 1999; Berlyne, 1954, 1960; Durik et al., 2015). For example, vivid texts containing rich imagery, suspense, engaging themes, and intriguing information that surprises the reader have a positive influence on student interest and learning (Bergin, 1999; Garner, 1992). Personal relevance and meaningfulness are also important sources of interest that can be incorporated into learning materials (Pressick-Kilborn, 2015). Teachers can use authentic materials from real life to facilitate personal relevance and emphasize the value of learning about them to increase students' interest (Durik et al., 2015; Pressick-Kilborn, 2015). At the same time, however, the materials should be designed and formulated in a coherent manner to guide the learners' thoughts and imagination (Hidi & Baird, 1988; Schraw et al., 2001). It is important to note that texts including irrelevant but highly interesting content can interfere with learning by diverting student attention (Harp & Mayer, 1998; Hidi, 1990). Thus, collative features in learning materials must be chosen with caution to maintain coherence with the target content knowledge.

Materials that induce an information gap are another important source of curiosity. When children perceive a gap between what they know and what they want to know, a sense of deprivation encourages them to seek the information (Loewenstein, 1994). Thus, learning materials that are designed to create an information gap in children can serve to generate curiosity. Riddles, puzzles, and trivia questions have been found to be especially effective, because the missing information is presented in a salient manner (Kang et al., 2009; Loewenstein, 1994). This is because, even when appropriate material is presented, curiosity will not arise if children fail to recognize the information gap (Loewenstein, 1994). For instance, Loewenstein (1994) stated that curiosity could not be generated if children are overly confident about their knowledge and believe that they know the answer when they actually do not. In this case, teachers can guide the students to guess the answer and provide feedback.

Providing tasks of optimal difficulty. Certain levels of prior knowledge are necessary for both curiosity and interest. Previous studies suggest that an optimal level of knowledge (not too high nor too low) is needed to instigate curiosity (Kang et al., 2009; Loewenstein, 1994). An appropriate level of prior knowledge for the given material helps students make more inferences regarding the content, which is the genesis of curiosity and interest (Grossnickle, 2016; Kim, 1999). This aligns with Piaget's moderate novelty principle, which posits that an object should be neither too familiar nor too novel to grab a student's attention (Ginsburg & Opper, 1969; Grossnickle, 2016).

A level of difficulty that is too high will act as a barrier to curiosity and interest. For instance, in a study by Acee and his colleagues (2010), the presentation of completely familiar and easy content resulted in task-focused boredom stemming from meaninglessness and tediousness, while too novel and difficult content brought about self-focused boredom associated with frustration and dissatisfaction. In line with this study, Kang et al. (2009) reported that the relationship between curiosity and students' confidence in their knowledge followed an inverted U-shape function, indicating that curiosity was the highest when confidence regarding current knowledge was optimal. Thus, learning materials that do not match the students' level can result in boredom, anxiety, or frustration and may even lead to withdrawal (Chak, 2002).

One way to craft materials of optimal difficulty is to introduce the unfamiliar through the familiar (Hoffmann, 2002; Schraw et al., 2001; Xu et al., 2012). That is, teachers can use students' prior knowledge, past experience, and interests in familiar contexts to connect to new ones. Alternatively, when introducing novel concepts, teachers can provide students with the appropriate background knowledge to facilitate their understanding and the perception of the information gap in learning. Forming a meaningful connection with the learning materials would boost student curiosity and interest. If teachers can make an effort to supply information that can provoke interest and engagement, these materials will serve as direct primary sources for curiosity and interest in students.

Learning Context

Individuals with a curiosity mindset have a better tolerance for ambiguity (Kashdan et al., 2011). They are more likely to consider difficulties as challenges than as threats (Hodgins & Knee, 2002). It is a concept similar to "embracing" – a willingness to embrace the novelty and uncertainty, and to gain new experiences and knowledge (Kashdan et al., 2009). The curiosity mindset is important in learning, because it enables individuals to value curiosity and information-seeking under uncertain situations instead of avoiding them (Kashdan, 2007; Silvia, 2006). The curiosity mindset can be fostered by encouraging questions, permitting errors, guiding exploration, and experiencing successful resolution. We thus present some specific strategies for establishing a learning context that welcomes questions and exploration.

Establishing a nonthreatening environment. An environment or practice that intimidates students discourages them from becoming curious and expanding on their interests. Threatening elements in the classroom – such as overt competition, a focus on normative evaluation, or a controlling instructional style – may induce anxiety, which is a psychological state known to hinder interest and exploration (Ames & Archer, 1988; Stefanou et al., 2004). Even if learning materials are devised to increase student curiosity and interest, Lee (2016) suggested that anxiety due to an upcoming competitive test might deter students from deeply engaging in learning, thus lowering the effect of curiosity-evoking material on curiosity. In particular, a threatening environment that generates anxiety can be harmful to student curiosity and interest in two ways: first, by weakening informational processing and attentional control due to overloading the students' cognitive capacity with worry (Eysenck et al., 2007; Lee, 2016), and second, by limiting exploratory behavior due to repeated experiences of failure to satisfy the need for knowledge (Peters, 1978).

Therefore, teachers need to establish a safe and nonthreatening environment where students can focus more on the content to be learned and where they feel comfortable asking questions and exploring knowledge further. For example, in a real-life classroom, students with high trait curiosity ask more questions when they perceive their instructor to be patient, accepting, gentle, and warm; whereas their rate of questioning falls to a level reflecting low trait curiosity when they perceive their instructor to be impatient, critical, harsh, and cold (Peters, 1978).

Permitting errors. Curiosity involves errors in its own process (Loewenstein, 1994). That is, curiosity is evoked when students detect an error or a discrepancy in their thoughts, beliefs, and behaviors, and the process of resolving curiosity through exploration accompany risks of failure. Mistakes and errors lead to a violation of expectation (surprise) and create an information gap that facilitates active information-seeking. Thus, without acknowledging one's error as an essential part of the learning process, the growth of curiosity is unlikely. A learning environment that turns students' errors and failures into valuable learning opportunities empowers students to be resilient to failures, explore persistently, and try to reduce errors. Since normative assessment makes students feel anxious regardless of its valence (Kim et al., 2010), negative feedback in response to errors is likely to elicit shame and make students avoid novel and challenging tasks. On the other hand, informative feedback regarding errors would encourage reflexive awareness of the information gap and promote deeper exploration.

Providing autonomy. In most learning environments, students merely follow the curriculum and instructions set by their teachers. In these circumstances, students may not develop a sense of ownership over their learning (Stefanou et al., 2004). Students are often found to express their curiosity or interest when they are not participating in teacher-directed activities. This observation can be utilized to nurture curiosity in the classroom by allowing students to freely make choices (about such things as topics, homework, assessments, and learning activities) and to make their own inquiries. Choice is a major driver of increases in the sense of self-determination (Deci et al., 1991), and it has been shown to increase student interest (especially in otherwise low-interest students) and performance outcomes (Ryan & Deci, 2000; Schraw et al., 2001). It has been reported that when students are given a chance to choose what they want to learn, they exhibit a greater ownership, interest, confidence, and sense of value in a task (Patall, 2013). The sense of having a choice is so powerful that it can even weaken the negative feelings associated with undesired activities (Patall et al., 2010). In addition, providing students with opportunities to generate and answer their own questions enhances their perceived ability to close information gaps and further elevates their levels of curiosity and interest (Markey & Loewenstein, 2014).

As can be seen, students often develop a good idea of what they want to know when they are given a sense of freedom. Nevertheless, precautions should be taken when providing choices in the classroom. For example, offering too many choices can burden students with cognitive overload (Patall et al., 2008). Because the act of choosing is effortful and draws on cognitive resources, the provision of too many choices can lead to fatigue and can adversely affect student learning (Muraven & Baumeister, 2000). This cognitive depletion can also negatively affect curiosity and interest, both of which require sufficient cognitive resources to engage in learning activities.

Facilitating social interaction. An important way in which students can develop their curiosity and interest is through social interaction (Bergin, 2016). In the classroom, students not only acquire knowledge and values, but also learn how to expand and refine their inquiries or preferences for specific topics, by interacting with teachers and their peers. In particular, a growing consensus holds that friends and peer groups are an important context where students' beliefs and preferences are socialized (Bergin, 2016; Ryan, 2001). Students tend to feel interested in a task or activity that allows them to socialize, especially with their friends (Bergin, 1999, 2016). When working together in a group, students can stimulate each other's curiosity and interest by sharing their thoughts, preferences, and questions on the topic or problem. At the same time, students' prior interest and curiosity can be cultivated with the support of peers. A recent study reported that peer responsiveness contributes positively to the maintenance of interest among adolescents (Thoman et al., 2012). Therefore, teachers should create the social realm of learning, where students can work together and interact with each other to solve problems and engage in academic tasks.

Role of the teacher. A study has shown that, given a list of qualities to be encouraged in students, teachers are quick to agree that curiosity is an essential element of the classroom. When teachers are asked to come up with the qualities on their own, however, only a few mention curiosity (Engel, 2011). As indicated by this result, teachers often fail to actively encourage curiosity in the classroom. Instead, they subtly push aside student inquiries during instructional practice in an effort to meet the standards of mandated curricula.

Instilling curiosity and interest in children is best achieved when teachers themselves are curious and interested, such as when they are excited, involved, self-directed, and trying new things (Engel, 2011; Pressick-Kilborn, 2015). Xu et al. (2012) determined that exemplary science teachers who promote student interest must have a genuine interest in science, in promoting student interest in science, and in forming strong relationships with their students. When teachers themselves are curious and interested, students are more likely to model their behavior. For instance, Engel (2011) introduced a study in which she found that children who observed teachers showing an interest in exploring a topic further and deviating from the task at hand exhibited increasingly more curious exploration compared to children who watched teachers adhering to conventional instruction. Furthermore, a recent study has demonstrated that spending time with an enthusiastic teacher in the classroom significantly boosts a student's interest in the course (Kim & Schallert, 2014; Long, 2003). This research emphasizes that a teacher has a powerful effect on the development of curiosity and interest in students. These two important constructs may well emerge in the interaction between students and teachers, with a supportive relationship between the two providing students with a foundation for their curiosity and interest to bloom.

Concluding Thoughts

In this chapter, we have discussed the possible distinction between curiosity and interest by outlining their conceptual definitions and identifying their shared and unique underlying mechanisms. We have also summarized the current understanding of the educational merits of the two constructs and introduced ways to promote curiosity and interest in an educational context.

To date, curiosity and interest have not been firmly distinguished from each other, and research on curiosity in an educational context is still in its early stages. In addition, as opposed to interest, for which the development and influence on students have been extensively studied and widely validated (Ainley et al., 2002; Durik & Harackiewicz, 2007; Hidi & Renninger, 2006), there remain significant gaps in theories and empirical evidence regarding curiosity in educational settings. As conceptual clarity is a necessary step toward the empirical advancement of the theories, more work is needed to investigate the similarities and differences between curiosity and interest in terms of their respective definitions, antecedents, and consequences for achieving their effective utilization in the classroom.

References

Acee, T. W., Kim, H., Kim, H. J., Kim, J. I., Chu, H. N. R., Kim, M., ... The Boredom Research Group. (2010). Academic boredom in under- and over-challenging situations. *Contemporary Educational Psychology, 35*, 17–27. doi: 10.1016/j.cedpsych.2009.08.002.

Ainley, M., Hidi, S., & Berndorff, D. (2002). Interest, learning, and the psychological processes that mediate their relationship. *Journal of Educational Psychology*, *94*, 545–61. doi: 10.1037//0022-0663.94.3.545.

Amabile, T. M. (1985). Motivation and creativity: Effects of motivational orientation on creative writers. *Journal of Personality and Social Psychology*, *48*, 393–9. doi: 10.1037/0022-3514.48.2.393.

Amabile, T. M., Barsade, S. G., Mueller, J. S., & Staw, B. M. (2005). Affect and creativity at work. *Administrative Science Quarterly*, *50*, 367–403. doi: 10.2189/asqu.2005.50.3.367.

Ames, C. & Archer, J. (1988). Achievement goals in the classroom: Students' learning strategies and motivation processes. *Journal of Educational Psychology*, *80*, 260–7. doi: 10.1037/0022-0663.80.3.260.

Anderson, R. C., Shirey, L. L., Wilson, P. T., & Fielding, L. G. (1987). Interestingness of children's reading material. In R. E. Snow & M. J. Farr (Eds.), *Aptitude, learning, and instruction: Cognitive and affective process analyses* (pp. 287–99). Hillsdale, NJ: Lawrence Erlbaum Associates.

Beatty, J. (1982). Task-evoked pupillary responses, processing load, and the structure of processing resources. *Psychological Bulletin*, *91*, 276–92. doi: 10.1037/0033-2909.91.2.276.

Bergin, D. A. (1999). Influences on classroom interest. *Educational Psychologist*, *34*, 87–98. doi: 10.1207/s15326985ep3402_2.

Bergin, D. A. (2016). Social influences on interest. *Educational Psychologist*, *51*, 7–22. doi: 10.1080/00461520.2015.1133306.

Berlyne, D. E. (1954). A theory of human curiosity. *British Journal of Psychology: General Section*, *45*, 180–91. doi: 10.1111/j.2044-8295.1954.tb01243.x.

Berlyne, D. E. (1960). *Conflict, arousal, and curiosity*. New York, NY: McGraw-Hill. doi: 10.1037/11164-000.

Brucks, M. (1985). The effects of product class knowledge on information search behavior. *Journal of Consumer Research*, *12*, 1–16. doi: 10.1086/209031.

Chak, A. (2002). Understanding children's curiosity and exploration through the lenses of Lewin's field theory: On developing an appraisal framework. *Early Child Development and Care*, *172*, 77–87. doi: 10.1080/03004430210874.

Chin, C. & Chia, L. G. (2006). Problem-based learning: Using ill-structured problems in biology project work. *Science Education*, *90*(1), 44–67. doi: 10.1002/sce.20097.

Day, H. I. & Langevin, R. (1969). Curiosity and intelligence: Two necessary conditions for a high level of creativity. *Journal of Special Education*, *3*, 263–74. doi: 10.1177/002246696900300305.

Deci, E. L., Vallerand, R. J., Pelletier, L. G., & Ryan, R. M. (1991). Motivation and education: The self-determination perspective. *Educational Psychologist*, *26*, 325–46. doi: 10.1207/s15326985ep2603&4_6.

Durik, A. M. & Harackiewicz, J. M. (2007). Different strokes for different folks: How individual interest moderates the effects of situational factors on task interest. *Journal of Educational Psychology*, *99*, 597–610. doi: 10.1037/0022-0663.99.3.597.

Durik, A. M., Hulleman, C. S., & Harackiewicz, J. M. (2015). One size fits some: Instructional enhancements to promote interest. In K. A. Renninger,

M. Nieswandt, & S. Hidi (Eds.). *Interest in mathematics and science learning* (pp. 49–62). Washington, DC: American Educational Research Association.

Engel, S. (2011). Children's need to know: Curiosity in schools. *Harvard Educational Review, 81,* 625–45.

Eysenck, M. W., Derakshan, N., Santos, R., & Calvo, M. G. (2007). Anxiety and cognitive performance: Attentional control theory. *Emotion, 7,* 336–53. doi: 10.1037/1528-3542.7.2.336.

Fernet, C., Guay, F., & Senecal, C. (2004). Adjusting to job demands: The role of work self-determination and job control in predicting burnout. *Journal of Vocational Behavior, 65,* 39–56. doi: 10.1016/S0001-8791(03)00098-8.

Fredrickson, B. L. (1998). What good are positive emotions? *Review of General Psychology, 2,* 300–19. doi: 10.1037/1089-2680.2.3.300.

Garner, R. (1992). Learning from school texts. *Educational Psychologist, 27,* 53–63.

Ginsburg, H. P. & Opper, S. (1969). *Piaget's theory of intellectual development: An introduction.* Englewood Cliffs, NJ: Prentice-Hall.

Gottlieb, J., Oudeyer, P. Y., Lopes, M., & Baranes, A. (2013). Information-seeking, curiosity, and attention: Computational and neural mechanisms. *Trends in Cognitive Sciences, 17,* 585–93. doi: 10.1016/j.tics.2013.09.001.

Grossnickle, E. M. (2016). Disentangling curiosity: Dimensionality, definitions, and distinctions from interest in educational contexts. *Educational Psychology Review, 28,* 23–60. doi: 10.1007/s10648-014-9294-y.

Gruber, M. J., Gelman, B. D., & Ranganath, C. (2014). States of curiosity modulate hippocampus-dependent learning via the dopaminergic circuit. *Neuron, 84,* 486–96. doi: 10.1016/j.neuron.2014.08.060.

Harp, S. F. & Mayer, R. E. (1998). How seductive details do their damage: A theory of cognitive interest in science learning. *Journal of Educational Psychology, 90,* 414–34. doi: 10.1037/0022-0663.90.3.414.

Hidi, S. (1990). Interest and its contribution as a mental resource for learning. *Review of Educational Research, 60,* 549–71. doi: 10.3102/00346543060004549.

Hidi, S. (1995). A reexamination of the role of attention in learning from text. *Educational Psychology Review, 7,* 323–50. doi: 10.1007/BF02212306.

Hidi, S. (2006). Interest: A unique motivational variable. *Educational Research Review, 1,* 69–82. doi: 10.1016/j.edurev.2006.09.001.

Hidi, S. & Baird, W. (1988). Strategies for increasing text-based interest and students' recall of expository texts. *Reading Research Quarterly, 23,* 465–83. doi: 10.2307/747644.

Hidi, S. & Harackiewicz, J. M. (2000). Motivating the academically unmotivated: A critical issue for the 21st century. *Review of Educational Research, 70,* 151–79. doi: 10.3102/00346543070002151.

Hidi, S. & Renninger, K. A. (2006). The four-phase model of interest development. *Educational Psychologist, 41,* 111–27. doi: 10.1207/s15326985ep4102_4.

Hodgins, H. S. & Knee, C. R. (2002). The integrating self and conscious experience. In E. L. Deci & R. M. Ryan (Eds.), *Handbook of self-determination research* (pp. 87–100). Rochester, NY: University of Rochester Press.

Hoffmann, L. (2002). Promoting girls' interest and achievement in physics classes for beginners. *Learning and Instruction, 12,* 447–65. doi: 10.1016/S0959-4752(01)00010-X.

Iran-Nejad, A. (1987). Cognitive and affective causes of interest and liking. *Journal of Educational Psychology, 79*, 120–30. doi: 10.1037/0022-0663.79.2.120.

Jepma, M., Verdonschot, R. G., Van Steenbergen, H., Rombouts, S., & Nieuwenhuis, S. (2012). Neural mechanisms underlying the induction and relief of perceptual curiosity. *Frontiers in Behavioral Neuroscience, 6*(5), 1–9. doi: 10.3389/fnbeh.2012.00005.

Jirout, J. & Klahr, D. (2012). Children's scientific curiosity: In search of an operational definition of an elusive concept. *Developmental Review, 32*, 125–60. doi: 10.1016/j.dr.2012.04.002.

Kang, M. J., Hsu, M., Krajbich, I. M., Loewenstein, G., McClure, S. M., Wang, J. T. Y., & Camerer, C. F. (2009). The wick in the candle of learning: Epistemic curiosity activates reward circuitry and enhances memory. *Psychological Science, 20*, 963–73. doi: 10.1111/j.1467-9280.2009.02402.x.

Karwowski, M. (2012). Did curiosity kill the cat? Relationship between trait curiosity, creative self-efficacy and creative personal identity. *Europe's Journal of Psychology, 8*, 547–58. doi: 10.5964/ejop.v8i4.513.

Kashdan, T. B. (2007). Social anxiety spectrum and diminished positive experiences: Theoretical synthesis and meta-analysis. *Clinical Psychology Review, 27*, 348–65. doi: 10.1016/j.cpr.2006.12.003.

Kashdan, T. B., Afram, A., Brown, K. W., Birnbeck, M., & Drvoshanov, M. (2011). Curiosity enhances the role of mindfulness in reducing defensive responses to existential threat. *Personality and Individual Differences, 50*, 1227–32. doi: 10.1016/j.paid.2011.02.015.

Kashdan, T. B., Gallagher, M. W., Silvia, P. J., Winterstein, B. P., Breen, W. E., Terhar, D., & Steger, M. F. (2009). The curiosity and exploration inventory-II: Development, factor structure, and initial psychometrics. *Journal of Research in Personality, 43*, 987–98. doi: 10.1016/j.jrp.2009.04.011.

Kashdan, T. B., Rose, P., & Fincham, F. D. (2004). Curiosity and exploration: Facilitating positive subjective experiences and personal growth opportunities. *Journal of Personality Assessment, 82*, 291–305. doi: 10.1207/s15327752jpa8203_05.

Kashdan, T. B. & Silvia, P. J. (2009). Curiosity and interest: The benefits of thriving on novelty and challenge. In C. R. Snyder & S. J. Lopez (Eds.), *Handbook of positive psychology* (2nd ed., pp. 367–74). New York, NY: Oxford University Press.

Kashdan, T. B. & Steger, M. F. (2007). Curiosity and pathways to well-being and meaning in life: Traits, states, and everyday behaviors. *Motivation and Emotion, 31*, 159–73. doi: 10.1007/s11031-007-9068-7.

Kashdan, T. B., & Yuen, M. (2007). Whether highly curious students thrive academically depends on perceptions about the school learning environment: A study of Hong Kong adolescents. *Motivation and Emotion, 31*, 260–70. doi: 10.1007/s11031-007-9074-9.

Kaufman, J. C. & Beghetto, R. A. (2009). Beyond big and little: The four C model of creativity. *Review of General Psychology, 13*, 1–12. doi: 10.1037/a0013688.

Kidd, C. & Hayden, B. Y. (2015). The psychology and neuroscience of curiosity. *Neuron, 88*, 449–60. doi: 10.1016/j.neuron.2015.09.010.

Kim, S. (1999). Causal bridging inference: A cause of story interestingness. *British Journal of Psychology, 90*, 57–71. doi: 10.1348/000712699161260.

Kim, S., Jiang, Y., & Song, J. (2015). The effects of interest and utility on mathematics engagement and achievement. In K. A. Renninger, M. Nieswandt, & S. Hidi (Eds.), *Interest in mathematics and science learning* (pp. 63–78). Washington, DC: American Educational Research Association.

Kim, S., Lee, M., Chung, Y., & Bong, M. (2010). Comparison of brain activation during norm-referenced versus criterion-referenced feedback: The role of perceived competence and performance-approach goals. *Contemporary Educational Psychology*, *35*, 141–52. doi: 10.1016/j.cedpsych.2010.04.002.

Kim, T. & Schallert, D. L. (2014). Mediating effects of teacher enthusiasm and peer enthusiasm on students' interest in the college classroom. *Contemporary Educational Psychology*, *39*, 134–44. doi: 10.1016/j.cedpsych.2014.03.002.

Lee, H. J. (2016). *Effects of violation-of-expectation and anxiety on curiosity*. Unpublished master's thesis. Korea University. Retrieved from http://dcollection.korea.ac.kr/jsp/common/DcLoOrgPer.jsp?sItemId=000000068794.

Litman, J. A. (2010). Relationships between measures of I- and D-type curiosity, ambiguity tolerance, and need for closure: An initial test of the wanting-liking model of information-seeking. *Personality and Individual Differences*, *48*, 397–402. doi: 10.1016/j.paid.2009.11.005.

Litman, J. A., Hutchins, T. L., & Russon, R. K. (2005). Epistemic curiosity, feeling-of-knowing, and exploratory behaviour. *Cognition & Emotion*, *19*, 559–82. doi: 10.1080/02699930441000427.

Litman, J. A. & Silvia, P. J. (2006). The latent structure of trait curiosity: Evidence for interest and deprivation curiosity dimensions. *Journal of Personality Assessment*, *86*, 318–28. doi: 10.1207/s15327752jpa8603_07.

Loewenstein, G. (1994). The psychology of curiosity: A review and reinterpretation. *Psychological Bulletin*, *116*, 75–98. doi: 10.1037/0033-2909.116.1.75.

Long, J. F. (2003). *Connecting with the content: How teacher interest affects student interest in a core course* (Doctoral dissertation, Ohio State University). Retrieved from https://etd.ohiolink.edu/rws_etd/document/get/osu1056140146/inline.

Markey, A. & Loewenstein, G. (2014). Curiosity. In R. Pekrun & L. Linnenbrink-Garcia (Eds.), *International handbook of emotions in education* (pp. 246–64). London and New York, NY: Routledge.

Marvin, C. B. & Shohamy, D. (2016). Curiosity and reward: valence predicts choice and information prediction errors enhance learning. *Journal of Experimental Psychology–General*, *145*, 266–72. doi: 10.1037/xge0000140.

Maw, W. H. & Maw, E. W. (1970). Self-concepts of high-curiosity and low-curiosity boys. *Child Development*, *41*, 123–9. doi: 10.2307/1127394.

McDaniel, M. A., Waddill, P. J., Finstad, K., & Bourg, T. (2000). The effects of text-based interest on attention and recall. *Journal of Educational Psychology*, *92*, 492–502. doi: 10.1037/0022-0663.92.3.492.

Mitchell, M. (1993). Situational interest: Its multifaceted structure in the secondary school mathematics classroom. *Journal of Educational Psychology*, *85*, 424–36. doi: 10.1037/0022-0663.85.3.424.

Muraven, M. & Baumeister, R. F. (2000). Self-regulation and depletion of limited resources: Does self-control resemble a muscle? *Psychological Bulletin*, *126*, 247. doi: 10.1037//0033-2909.126.2.247.

Murayama, K. & Kuhbandner, C. (2011). Money enhances memory consolidation – But only for boring material. *Cognition*, *119*, 120–4. doi: 10.1016/j.cognition.2011.01.001.

Nakamura, J. & Csikszentmihalyi, M. (2014). The concept of flow. In M. Csikszentmihalyi (Ed.), *Flow and the foundations of positive psychology* (pp. 239–63). Dordrecht: Springer.

Park, N., Peterson, C., & Seligman, M. E. P. (2004). Strengths of character and well-being. *Journal of Social and Clinical Psychology*, *23*, 603–19. doi: 10.1521/jscp.23.5.603.50748.

Patall, E. A. (2013). Constructing motivation through choice, interest, and interestingness. *Journal of Educational Psychology*, *105*, 522–34. doi: 10.1037/a0030307.

Patall, E. A., Cooper, H., & Robinson, J. C. (2008). The effects of choice on intrinsic motivation and related outcomes: A meta-analysis of research findings. *Psychological Bulletin*, *134*, 270–300. doi: 10.1037/0033-2909.134.2.270.

Patall, E. A., Cooper, H., & Wynn, S. R. (2010). The effectiveness and relative importance of choice in the classroom. *Journal of Educational Psychology*, *102*, 896–915. doi: 10.1037/a0019545.

Pelletier, L. G., Dion, S. C., Slovinec-D'Angelo, M., & Reid, R. (2004). Why do you regulate what you eat? Relationships between forms of regulation, eating behaviors, sustained dietary behavior change, and psychological adjustment. *Motivation and Emotion*, *28*, 245–77. doi: 10.1023/b:moem.0000040154.40922.14.

Peters, R. A. (1978). Effects of anxiety, curiosity, and perceived instructor threat on student verbal-behavior in college classroom. *Journal of Educational Psychology*, *70*, 388–95. doi: 10.1037/0022-0663.70.3.388.

Pressick-Kilborn, K. (2015). Canalization and connectedness in the development of science interest. In K. A. Renninger, M. Nieswandt, & S. Hidi (Eds.), *Interest in mathematics and science learning* (pp. 353–67). Washington, DC: American Educational Research Association.

Reio, T. G., Petrosko, J. M., Wiswell, A. K., & Thongsukmag, J. (2006). The measurement and conceptualization of curiosity. *Journal of Genetic Psychology*, *167*, 117–35. doi: 10.3200/GNTP.167.2.117-135.

Renninger, K. A. & Hidi, S. (2011). Revisiting the conceptualization, measurement, and generation of interest. *Educational Psychologist*, *46*, 168–84. doi: 10.1080/00461520.2011.587723.

Renninger, K. A. & Hidi, S. (2016). Interest, attention, and curiosity. In K. A. Renninger & S. Hidi (eds.), *The Power of Interest for Motivation and Engagement* (pp. 32–51). New York, NY: Routledge.

Renninger, K. A. & Wozniak, R. H. (1985). Effect of interest on attentional shift, recognition, and recall in young children. *Developmental Psychology*, *21*, 624–32. doi: 10.1037/0012-1649.21.4.624.

Rotgans, J. I. & Schmidt, H. G. (2014). Situational interest and learning: Thirst for knowledge. *Learning and Instruction*, *32*, 37–50. doi: 10.1016/j.learninstruc.2014.01.002.

Ryan, A. M. (2001). The peer group as a context for the development of young adolescent motivation and achievement. *Child Development*, *72*(4), 1135–50. doi: 10.1111/1467-8624.00338.

Ryan, R. M. & Deci, E. L. (2000). Intrinsic and extrinsic motivations: Classic definitions and new directions. *Contemporary Educational Psychology*, *25*, 54–67. doi: 10.1006/ceps.1999.1020.

Ryan, R. M., Rigby, S., & King, K. (1993). Two types of religious internalization and their relations to religious orientations and mental health. *Journal of Personality and Social Psychology*, *65*, 586–96. doi: 10.1037/0022-3514.65.3.586.

Schiefele, U. (1991). Interest, learning, and motivation. *Educational Psychologist, 26*, 299–323. doi: 10.1080/00461520.1991.9653136.

Schraw, G., Dunkle, M. E., & Bendixen, L. D. (1995). Cognitive processes in well-defined and ill-defined problem solving. *Applied Cognitive Psychology, 9*(6), 523–38. doi: 10.1002/acp.2350090605.

Schraw, G., Flowerday, T., & Lehman, S. (2001). Increasing situational interest in the classroom. *Educational Psychology Review, 13*(3), 211–24. doi: 10.1023/A:1016619705184.

Schraw, G. & Lehman, S. (2001). Situational interest: A review of the literature and directions for future research. *Educational psychology review, 13*, 23–52. doi: 10.1023/A:1009004801455.

Schweizer, T. S. (2006). The psychology of novelty-seeking, creativity and innovation: Neurocognitive aspects within a work-psychological perspective. *Creativity and Innovation Management, 15*, 164–72. doi: 10.1111/j.1467-8691.2006.00383.x.

Shirey, L. L. & Reynolds, R. E. (1988). Effect of interest on attention and learning. *Journal of Educational Psychology, 80*, 159–66. doi: 10.1037/0022-0663.80.2.159.

Silvia, P. J. (2006). *Exploring the psychology of interest*. New York, NY: Oxford University Press.

Silvia, P. J. (2008). Appraisal components and emotion traits: Examining the appraisal basis of trait curiosity. *Cognition & Emotion, 22*, 94–113. doi: 10.1080/02699930701298481.

Smith, G. F. (1988). Towards a heuristic theory of problem structuring. *Management Science, 34*(12), 1489–506. doi: 10.1287/mnsc.34.12.1489.

Stahl, A. E. & Feigenson, L. (2015). Observing the unexpected enhances infants' learning and exploration. *Science, 348*, 91–4. doi: 10.1126/science.aaa3799.

Stefanou, C. R., Perencevich, K. C., DiCintio, M., & Turner, J. C. (2004). Supporting autonomy in the classroom: Ways teachers encourage student decision making and ownership. *Educational Psychologist, 39*(2), 97–110. doi: 10.1207/s15326985ep3902_2.

Thoman, D. B., Sansone, C., Fraughton, T., & Pasupathi, M. (2012). How students socially evaluate interest: Peer responsiveness influences evaluation and maintenance of interest. *Contemporary Educational Psychology, 37*(4), 254–65. doi: 10.1016/j.cedpsych.2012.04.001.

Von Stumm, S., Hell, B., & Chamorro-Premuzic, T. (2011). The hungry mind. *Perspectives on Psychological Science, 6*, 574–88. doi: 10.1177/1745691611421204.

Wade, S. E., Schraw, G., Buxton, W. M., & Hayes, M. T. (1993). Seduction of the strategic reader: Effects of interest on strategies and recall. *Reading Research Quarterly, 28*, 92–114. doi: 10.2307/747885.

Wanberg, C. R. & Kammeyer-Mueller, J. D. (2000). Predictors and outcomes of proactivity in the socialization process. *Journal of Applied Psychology, 1*, 373–85. doi: 10.1037//0021-9010.85.3.373.

Xu, J., Coats, L. T., & Davidson, M. L. (2012). Promoting student interest in science: The perspectives of exemplary African American teachers. *American Educational Research Journal, 49*, 124–54. doi: 10.3102/0002831211426200.

19 Boredom

Thomas Goetz, Nathan C. Hall, and Maike Krannich

Abstract: This chapter examines boredom – an emotion often described as one of the plagues of modern societies. In educational settings, boredom is also often experienced. The chapter first outlines how boredom is defined and operationalized including current approaches to differentiating specific types of boredom. We further review the extent to which boredom has been investigated in the research literature and how it has been assessed. Empirical evidence on the prevalence of boredom in students is outlined, and preliminary findings on the frequency of boredom experiences in teachers is highlighted. Theoretical considerations and empirical findings are subsequently addressed concerning the effects and causes of academic boredom, as are relevant conceptual frameworks and findings on how to most effectively cope with boredom in educational settings. Implications for the prevention and reduction of boredom in the classroom following from empirical literature are then discussed. Finally, we outline potential next steps in research on academic boredom.

Is boredom an emotion, cognition, motivational orientation, or a form of fatigue? Is it a unique experience or simply an absence of interest? These and other questions related to the experience of boredom are currently being explored across research domains, and the answers depend largely on disciplinary perspective. What is clear, however, is that research on the topic of boredom has increased substantially over the past decade, particularly with respect to its definition and the extent to which it can be defined as an emotion, even though it is not a prototypical emotional experience like anxiety or happiness (e.g., Ekman, 1984; Rosch, 1978; Shaver et al., 1987). The component process model of emotions accounts for varied approaches to defining and describing boredom (Kleinginna & Kleinginna, 1981; Scherer, 2000). It suggests that individuals' emotions are perhaps best understood in terms of their underlying processes. From this perspective, boredom is regarded as, indeed, a unique emotional experience consisting of five underlying components: *affective* (unpleasant, aversive sensation), *cognitive* (altered perceptions of time), *motivational* (desire to withdraw), *physiological* (low arousal), and *expressive* (vocal, facial, postural expressions; Pekrun et al., 2010).

According to this component perspective, boredom is a stand-alone emotional experience and not simply the absence of positive emotions or interest (see Pekrun et al., 2010). This assertion is supported by three main arguments, the first being the existence of numerous affective states not experienced as positive that also would not be described as boredom (e.g., anger, anxiety, hopelessness). Second, although lack of interest may represent an important antecedent of boredom experiences, the two constructs are not identical: whereas lack of interest is affectively neutral, boredom is typically described as having a negative valence (e.g., the "torments of boredom"; Berlyne, 1960, p. 192). Third, although the construct of boredom does overlap with lack of interest or enjoyment, it is important to consider discrepant motivational consequences (e.g., due to affective load; Goetz & Frenzel, 2006). Whereas enjoyment or lack of interest does not indicate a clear intention to engage in or withdraw from an activity, boredom is consistently found to correspond with a self-reported desire to leave the situation.[1]

Research has also examined the conceptual dimensions underlying boredom experiences. The most well-known of these considerations is the circumplex model of affect (Russell, 1980; see also Watson & Tellegen, 1985), in which emotional states are defined according to the two orthogonal dimensions: valence and arousal.

Boredom is consistently classified as an unpleasant emotional state of relatively low negative *valence* (e.g., Fisher, 1993; Perkins & Hill, 1985). Despite there is support for this assumption in the literature (e.g., Goetz et al., 2007), research concerning the *arousal* dimension of boredom is mixed. For example, whereas several studies classify boredom as a low-arousal emotion (e.g., Mikulas & Vodanovich, 1993), others suggest the opposite (e.g., Berlyne, 1960; London et al., 1972). As such, there is ongoing debate as to how this emotion is best understood in terms of arousal (Pekrun et al., 2010).

One explanation for these inconsistent findings is that arousal is not well-defined as a construct and may itself be multidimensional in nature, with the varied assessments employed capturing only specific elements of this underlying component (see Schimmack & Reisenzein, 2002; Watson et al., 1999). Another possibility is that boredom is not ideally represented as a single

---

1 Thus, similar to the way that lack of approach tendencies can be distinguished from avoidance orientations in achievement goal research (Pekrun et al., 2010), it is also possible to differentiate between emotion-oriented constructs, in a manner.

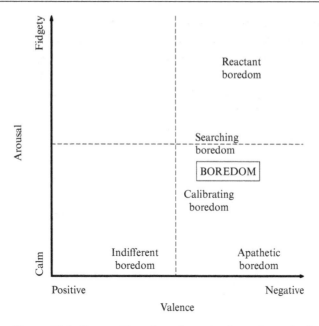

Figure 19.1. *Types of boredom along the dimensions of valence and arousal (Goetz et al., 2014a)*

construct but is better understood as an umbrella term encompassing different "types" of boredom.[2]

In line with this assumption, a recent empirical study by Goetz and colleagues (2014a) examined boredom using in vivo assessments in real-life settings. Support for different types of boredom was found in both achievement and non-achievement contexts (see Figure 19.1). Following from qualitative research on the phenomenology of boredom (i.e., students describing how boredom feels as they experience it; Goetz & Frenzel, 2006), these findings suggest that not only do different types of boredom exist in academic achievement settings, but they can be reliably differentiated based on the underlying dimensions of valence and arousal.

In Figure 19.1, the *average* level of valence and arousal when experiencing boredom in real-life settings (i.e., "BOREDOM") is plotted in relation to the five postulated and observed boredom types. This average boredom experience is located in the lower right quadrant – a classification based on valence and arousal consistent with previous definitions of boredom (e.g., Russell, 1980). Although this classification may be useful in identifying a prototypic boredom experience, Goetz et al. (2014a) argue that this boredom descriptor

---

2 This idea was implied in psychoanalytic literature as early as the 1930s ("*... it is probable that the conditions and forms of behavior called 'boredom' are psychologically quite heterogeneous*"; Fenichel, 1951, p. 349) and echoed over six decades later by Phillips (1993), who proposed that boredom was not a single entity but consisted instead of multiple "boredoms" (p. 78).

is more accurately understood as a composite variable averaging across disparate types of boredom that differ in valence and arousal. More specifically, they suggest that individuals may experience up to five discrete types of boredom in academic settings: (1) *indifferent boredom* (relaxed, withdrawn, indifferent), having a slightly positive valence and very low arousal; (2) *calibrating boredom* (uncertain, receptive to change or distraction), having a slightly negative valence and still relatively low arousal, but higher arousal than indifferent boredom; (3) *searching boredom* (somewhat restless, active pursuit of change or distraction), with a slightly negative valence and higher arousal than indifferent boredom; (4) *reactant boredom* (highly restless, motivated to leave the situation for specific alternatives), having a high negative valence and relatively high arousal; and (5) *apathetic boredom* (highly aversive), characterized by high negative valence and very low arousal.

Goetz et al. (2014a) report that these five boredom types were found to differ in how they were experienced (phenomenology), and were also differentially related to other emotions (e.g., positive relation between indifferent boredom and enjoyment, negative relation between reactant boredom and enjoyment). All five types were also specifically described by participants as experiences of boredom.

Above and beyond existing operational definitions of boredom based on component approaches, ongoing research based on dimensional approaches suggests that different "types" of boredom may be experienced by students. Whereas these types may differ based on valence and arousal, they nonetheless share essential elements of the common operational definition of this emotion. In other words, whereas there exists significant variance within students' experience of boredom with respect to multiple types of "boredoms," these differences do not qualitatively contradict, but rather serve to clarify, the psychological processes underlying this emotion.

Boredom in academic domains is often referred to as an *academic emotion*; a classification used to describe emotions experienced in educational settings that directly correspond with learning, classroom behavior, and achievement (Pekrun et al., 2002). For example, *academic boredom* is experienced during learning activities, such as homework completion or classroom exercises.

Summary

The component process model of emotions proposes that boredom can be operationalized as a specific emotion consisting of a unique combination of *affective, cognitive, motivational, physiological,* and *expressive* components. Boredom is thus best regarded as not simply reflecting the absence of positive emotions or interest. In dimensional approaches, boredom is commonly defined as low in arousal and of slightly negative valence. However, recent research suggests that individuals' experiences of boredom can differ on these dimensions. In other words, individuals seem to experience different types of boredom. The term "academic boredom" refers to boredom (including subtypes of boredom) as experienced in the context of learning and achievement.

How Extensively Has Academic Boredom Been Investigated?

To illustrate the growing research interest related to boredom in academic settings, we next outline the article frequencies resulting from two literature searches on the topic (see Figures 19.2 and 19.3). We first searched for publications in which the word "boredom" appeared in the title or abstract, then expanded our search to the subcategory "academic boredom" (with "boredom" AND "academic" in the title or abstract). The search was conducted via the international databases PsycINFO and ERIC, with papers appearing in both searches counted once (non-English publications with English titles or abstracts were included). The number of publications is displayed in the figures in ten-year periods, with publication rates presented as the number of relevant papers per 10,000 publications. The change in publication rates concerning "boredom" and "academic boredom" is indicated relative to the overall increase in scientific publications, as is the number of publications in these domains relative to the total number of publications.

Figure 19.2 shows the results of the literature search for "boredom," revealing it to be of relatively consistent scientific interest over a 50-year period (1966–2015). Figure 19.3 outlines the results of the literature search on

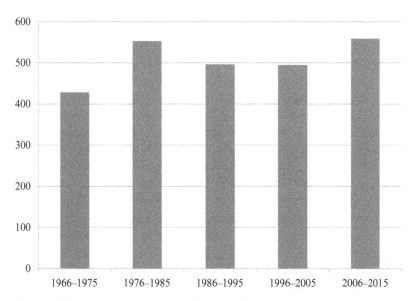

Figure 19.2. *Number of papers on "boredom" per 10,000 publications in PsycINFO and ERIC databases*

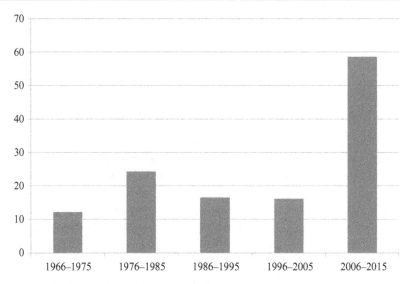

Figure 19.3. *Number of papers on "academic boredom" per 10,000 publications in PsycINFO and ERIC databases*

"academic boredom," showing scientific interest in the topic to have strongly increased after 2005.

Academic boredom has primarily been assessed through interviews (e.g., Farrell et al., 1988; Goetz et al., 2007; Kanevsky & Keighley, 2003) and standardized questionnaires (e.g., Daschmann et al., 2011). In addition to single-item measures (e.g., Geiwitz, 1966; Gjesme, 1977; Perkins & Hill, 1985; Shaw et al., 1996), questionnaire research has increasingly utilized multi-item scales to assess various facets of academic boredom (see Table 19.1; for detailed descriptions of existing measures, see reviews by Vodanovich, 2003b and Vodanovich & Watt, 2016). Arguably the most commonly employed measure of academic boredom is from the Achievement Emotions Questionnaire (AEQ; Pekrun et al., 2011; sample item: *"I get so bored I have problems staying alert"*). Domain-specific versions of the AEQ have also been developed to examine boredom in different subject areas (sample item: *"I can't concentrate in [DOMAIN] class because I am so bored"*; for a math-specific version, see Pekrun et al., 2005). Descriptive statistics for the AEQ boredom scale and empirically observed relations with other academic variables (e.g., emotions, self-concept, achievement) are outlined in Pekrun et al. (2011; university students) and Goetz et al. (2010; high school students). For example, findings in a sample of 973 eighth grade students in the mathematics domain (AEQ-M) found boredom to have significant positive and negative correlations ($p < 0.001$) of -0.68 with enjoyment, -0.43 with pride, 0.52 with anxiety, 0.74 with anger, -0.42 with academic self-concept, and -0.28 with academic achievement (Goetz et al., 2010).

Table 19.1 *Self-report measures of boredom*

Scale	Reference
Academic Boredom Scale (ABS)[*]	Acee et al. (2010)
Boredom Coping Scale (non-academic context)	Hamilton et al. (1984)
Boredom Experience Scale	van Tilburg and Igou (2012)
Boredom Proneness Scale	Farmer and Sundberg (1986)
Boredom subscale; Achievement Emotions Questionnaire (AEQ; mathematics-related version: AEQ-M)[*]	Pekrun et al. (2011)
Boredom Susceptibility Scale (subscale of the Sensation Seeking Scale)	Zuckerman (1979)
Class-Related Boredom (short version from the AEQ-M)[*]	Goetz et al. (2010)
Coping with Boredom Scale (academic context)[*]	Nett et al. (2010); Nett et al. (2011)
Dutch Boredom Scale	Reijseger et al. (2013)
Free Time Boredom Scale	Ragheb and Merydith (2001)
Homework Boredom Scale (based on the AEQ-M)[*]	Goetz et al. (2012)
Leisure Boredom Scale	Iso-Ahola and Weissinger (1990)
Multidimensional State Boredom Scale	Fahlman et al. (2013)
Occupational Boredom Scales	Grubb (1975); Lee (1986)
Precursors to Boredom Scales (academic context)	Daschmann et al. (2011); Tze et al. (2016)
Relational Boredom Scale (interpersonal relationships)	Harasymchuk and Fehr (2012)
Sexual Boredom Scale	Watt and Ewing (2010)
State Boredom Measure	Todman (2013)

[*]Scales explicitly developed for the context of learning and achievement

Summary

Research interest on boredom, as reflected by publication rates in psychology and empirical educational research, has remained consistent since the 1960s. However, the proportion of publications exploring academic boredom strongly increased after 2005. These results underscore the consistent importance of research on boredom and, moreover, indicate a growing research emphasis specifically on boredom in academic settings. Existing empirical findings concerning academic boredom are based primarily on data from standardized interviews and questionnaires, with the boredom scale of the Achievement Emotions Questionnaire (Pekrun et al., 2011) being arguably the most commonly utilized measure.

How Intensively Is Boredom Experienced by Students and Teachers?

International research has consistently found boredom to be one of the most frequently experienced emotions in academic settings (e.g., United States: Csikszentmihalyi & Larson, 1984; Asia: Won, 1989; Europe: Goetz et al., 2014a; Africa: Vandewiele, 1980). Recent findings indicate that boredom is more often experienced in academic settings than in non-academic contexts (Chin et al., 2017). For example, Larson and Richards' (1991) study of fifth and ninth grade students indicated that boredom was experienced 32 percent of the time in class. Similarly, Goetz et al. (2007) reported that ninth grade students were bored almost half of the time. Research with older students is comparable. Nett et al.'s (2011) study of 11th grade students indicated that they were bored 58 percent of the time during math class, using real-time data collection methods (experience sampling).

In a study by Goetz and Nett (2012), in which post-secondary students were asked how strongly they experienced specific emotions in learning and achievement settings (retrospective questionnaire, Likert scale: "1" *not at all* to "5" *very strongly*), the mean levels of 3.02 for boredom, 2.90 for anxiety, and 3.30 for enjoyment showed boredom to be experienced just as intensively as anxiety. With respect to boredom across disciplines, a study with German eighth and 11th grade students examined the emotions of boredom, anxiety, and enjoyment in the domains of German (native language), mathematics, physics, history, and music (for data set information, see Haag & Goetz, 2012). Mean boredom levels were once again above the scale midpoint, and were higher than for enjoyment and anxiety, in each subject area.

There is, at present, a lack of research on teachers' boredom, likely following from early findings suggesting experiences of boredom to be infrequent among teachers (Frenzel et al., 2016). However, recent studies suggest that boredom is much more pronounced in teachers than initially assumed. Findings from Goetz et al. (2015) do indicate that, similar to their students, teachers also tend to consistently report higher levels of boredom as compared to anxiety.

Summary

Findings from studies employing both retrospective and real-life assessment methods provide consistent empirical evidence of students' academic boredom as a frequently and intensively experienced emotion in academic settings. These findings have been found to hold across grade levels, cultures, and academic disciplines. Further, academic boredom is more pronounced in teachers than initially assumed.

Does Boredom Matter? The Consequences of Academic Boredom

Theoretical Considerations

In an attempt to explain the mechanisms by which academic boredom impacts learning and achievement, Pekrun's (2006) control-value theory of achievement emotions was employed to consider the effects of boredom on performance. Findings indicate that boredom is mediated in large part by (1) students' achievement motivation, (2) accessibility of cognitive resources, and (3) learning strategies, including their higher-order self-regulation of learning strategies. Concerning *motivation*, Pekrun's theory suggests that boredom corresponds with a desire to leave or avoid boredom-inducing situations. Since avoidance and intrinsic motivation tend to be inversely related, boredom is considered to impair engagement and persistence, mostly functioning as avoidance motivation. With respect to *cognitive resources*, boredom is assumed to redirect attention toward more rewarding and highly valued pursuits. Boredom is thus hypothesized to reduce the cognitive resources available for the "boring" task, resulting in attention deficits. Finally, boredom impacts *learning strategies* and *self-regulation* by contributing to less frequent use of cognitive and metacognitive learning strategies and, thus, shallow information processing. Specifically, boredom is hypothesized to reduce students' use of deep learning strategies (e.g., cognitive elaboration). Boredom is additionally expected to inhibit students' abilities to regulate their learning with respect to goal setting, selecting cognitive and metacognitive strategies, and monitoring their progress.

Given the negative impact of boredom on cognitive resources, learning strategies, motivation, and self-regulation, it is not surprising that boredom is consequently hypothesized to have negative effects on academic performance with respect to both simple and complex tasks (Pekrun et al., 2010). Although there is little empirical evidence, Vodanovich (2003a) has also hypothesized that boredom may benefit learning and achievement outcomes in some circumstances by encouraging creativity (e.g., holistic thinking), self-reflection (e.g., refocusing attention on alternate learning activities in which greater success is possible), innovation (e.g., seeking variety and change), as well as relaxation (e.g., renewing cognitive resources, well-being). The assertion that boredom could have specific benefits for learning and achievement is also consistent with evolutionary research pointing to the need to be able to disengage during prolonged exposure to non-rewarding situations (Bornstein et al., 1990).

Empirical Findings

Findings from qualitative and quantitative research to date consistently indicate that higher levels of boredom correspond with lower levels of attention (e.g., Farmer & Sundberg, 1986), achievement-striving (e.g., Jarvis & Seifert, 2002), and learning strategy use (e.g., Pekrun et al., 2011). Experimental studies also show boredom to predict poorer task performance and greater variability in achievement levels over time (e.g., Ahmed et al., 2013; Hamilton et al., 1984; Kass et al., 2001). Research by Wallace et al. (2003) further showed boredom proneness to correspond with more frequent reports of common cognitive failures, such as distractibility memory lapses.

Although there aren't a lot of studies directly examining the relation between boredom and academic achievement, existing studies suggest that higher levels of boredom correspond with poorer achievement (e.g., Daniels et al., 2009; Goetz et al., 2010; Pekrun et al., 2010, 2011). The observed correlations between boredom and academic performance are typically around –0.30 across subject domains (cf., Goetz & Hall, 2013). Moreover, longitudinal work indicates that boredom and achievement have reciprocal effects over time, with boredom having consistently negative effects on later performance that, in turn, contributes to subsequent boredom (e.g., Pekrun et al., 2014).

In their recent meta-analysis, Tze and colleagues (2016) found that boredom had a modest yet consistent negative relationship with academic outcomes ($\bar{r} =$ –0.24) such as learning strategy use and achievement. The strongest relations were observed between boredom and achievement motivation indicators (e.g., self-efficacy). It is important to note, however, that the observed overall relationship between boredom and achievement may be attenuated, considering that boredom is hypothesized to result from tasks that either over- or under-challenge a person (Krannich et al., 2016).

Summary

From a theoretical perspective, boredom is assumed to be detrimental for learning behavior and academic achievement due to its negative effects on cognitive resources, motivation, and learning strategies. Despite the hypothesized potential benefits of boredom (e.g., creativity, innovation), empirical findings consistently show modest negative relations between boredom and academic outcomes.

What Are the Causes of Academic Boredom?

Theoretical Considerations

When considering the potential antecedents of academic boredom, three theoretical models are of particular relevance (see Figure 19.4): Pekrun's

(2006) control-value theory and Robinson's (1975) model specifically concern boredom in learning and achievement settings, with a third model by Hill and Perkins (1985) addressing individuals' experiences of boredom more generally. Additionally, antecedent variables (e.g., isolation) identified as predictive of boredom in scattered empirical studies are informative (e.g., Fisher, 1993).

Pekrun's (2006) **control-value theory**. This theory posits that individuals' perceptions of personal control and value concerning achievement activities and outcomes represent the most important psychosocial antecedents of boredom in achievement settings. *Subjective control* refers to an agent's perceived causal influence over actions and outcomes (Skinner, 1996), whereas *subjective value* concerns the perceived valences and personal relevance thereof. Pekrun's theory posits that boredom is most reliably elicited when achievement activities are perceived as lacking importance or value. This model thus hypothesizes a negative relationship between the frequency and intensity of boredom in academic activities and the subjective value of these activities. In this respect, boredom differs from other positive (e.g., joyful experience connected to importance) and negative (e.g., anxiety about importance) emotions that are assumed to be *more* intensively experienced with increasing value.

In terms of subjective control, Pekrun's (2006) theory further assumes that the relationship between feelings of boredom and subjective control is curvilinear, with higher levels of boredom expected when perceived control is very low or very high, and less likely when perceived control is at a moderate level. In other words, it is proposed that boredom is most likely to occur when a learning or achievement task is not sufficiently challenging (high control) or, conversely, when task demands exceed capabilities (low control; Acee et al., 2010; Krannich et al., 2016).[3] Concerning more distal boredom antecedents, Pekrun's model asserts that elements of the social environment (such as classroom goal structures or parental support) may also impact students' perceptions of control and value (proximal antecedents) that, in turn, more directly predict student boredom. For example, parental support in a given subject area would be expected to increase the students' perceived value of that domain, resulting in lower boredom levels.

Robinson's (1975) **model of academic boredom**. This model proposes that three critical types of variables serve as antecedents to academic boredom. The first is the *monotony* of class activities; the second is students' perceived *uselessness* of these activities (cf., value in Pekrun's model); and the third is the *social environment*. This model thus asserts that, in addition to the learning environment at home and school (e.g., available learning resources and

---

3 This perspective contrasts with "flow" theory as proposed by Csikszentmihalyi (1975), which instead asserts that boredom should occur only when capabilities significantly exceed demands (i.e., high perceived control).

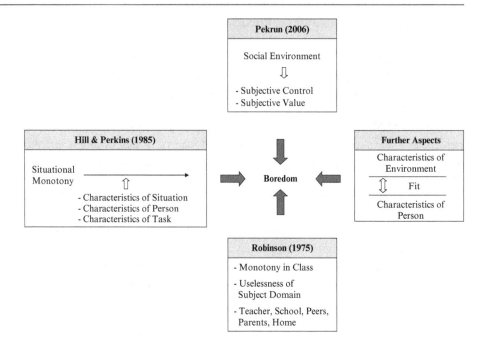

Figure 19.4. *Theoretical assumptions on the antecedents of achievement boredom*

amenities), the interest and value for learning – as well as specific subject matter demonstrated by teachers, peers, and parents – can have a significant impact on students' boredom experiences.

Hill and Perkin's (1985) **general boredom model**. The main underlying assumption in this model is that boredom is primarily the result of *monotonous situations*. However, this model further asserts that this effect is moderated by (a) *situational* characteristics (i.e., allows for additional or alternative stimulation), (b) *personal* characteristics (e.g., extroverts are more inclined to seek out more stimulating activities), and (c) *task* characteristics (i.e., some tasks afford greater flexibility than others concerning alternate activities).

Additional antecedents of boredom experiences. In addition to the antecedent variables outlined above (e.g., subjective control and value), other possible predictors of academic boredom – partially overlapping with those outlined in the preceding theoretical models – have been proposed as well (see Smith, 1981). These include *environmental characteristics* (e.g., monotony, isolation, lack of alternatives; Fisher, 1993) and *dispositional characteristics* (e.g., boredom susceptibility, age, extraversion; e.g., Farmer & Sundberg, 1986). The *fit* between the two (e.g., suboptimal stimulation, difficulty, content) has increasingly been a focus since the 1980s (e.g., O'Hanlon, 1981). To better reflect the combined contributions of existing research on boredom antecedents, a conceptual heuristic is presented in Figure 19.4.

Empirical Findings

Research on the antecedents of academic boredom indicates that high levels of *subjective control* (e.g., academic self-concept, self-efficacy) correspond with less boredom. In educational settings, challenging tasks can reduce perceptions of control. The relationship observed between subjective control and boredom tends to be negatively linear (not curvilinear as is often assumed), because tasks at school tend to pose significant challenges (are not extremely easy to solve) thereby preventing very high perceptions of control (e.g., Dicintio & Gee, 1999; Goetz et al., 2006, 2012). Similarly, negative correlations between boredom and subjective *value* (intrinsic and extrinsic) have been reported (e.g., Goetz et al., 2006; Pekrun et al., 2010, 2011).

Additionally, achievement *motives* and mastery achievement *goals* have been found to correspond with lower boredom (e.g., Duda et al., 1992; Goetz et al., 2016; Jagacinski & Duda, 2001; Pekrun et al., 2006, 2009), with greater *teaching quality* (e.g., enthusiasm, elaborative instruction, clarity) typically also corresponding to lower student boredom (e.g., Frenzel et al., 2007; Goetz et al., 2013). Finally, *task characteristics*, including monotony and repetition, as well as lack of complexity, variety, and intellectual stimulation, have also been empirically linked to greater boredom (e.g., Scerbo, 1998).

Summary

Following from three primary theoretical models and scattered empirical findings, antecedents of academic boredom are typically classified as involving the environment or situation (e.g., teaching), the individual (e.g., appraisals), and/or the fit between individual differences and the learning environment (e.g., content versus interests). Available evidence suggests that students who experience lower boredom levels report higher levels of subjective control and value (Pekrun, 2006), are motivated to both perform well and pursue content mastery, and tend to have effective instructors who facilitate engaging classroom environments as opposed to monotonous learning experiences.

How Can We Cope with Academic Boredom?

Theoretical Considerations

In contrast to voluminous literature on coping with stress and negative affect (e.g., Lazarus & Folkman, 1984, 1987; Skinner et al., 2003), surprisingly little research has examined the strategies individuals use to cope with boredom

Table 19.2 *Classification of students' strategies for coping with boredom*

Type of coping	Approach coping	Avoidance coping
Cognitive	Changing one's perception of the situation	Focusing on thoughts not related to the situation
Behavioral	Taking actions to change the situation	Taking actions not related to the situation

(Daniels et al., 2015; Nett et al., 2010; Sansone et al., 1992; Strain & Graesser, 2012; Vodanovich, 2003b). Although the most straightforward strategy often mentioned in the research literature on boredom is simply to quit the boring activity (Berlyne, 1960; see also Miller & Wrosch, 2007), this response is not always possible (e.g., at school) and can lead to negative results (e.g., achievement deficits). Thus, to address the present research gap on various other ways in which students can effectively and efficiently cope with boredom in educational settings, recent studies have explored whether existing models of coping behavior can be effectively applied to academic boredom.

For example, in preliminary research by Nett et al. (2010, 2011), a 2 × 2 classification system from stress research by Holahan et al. (1996) was adapted to examine whether boredom could also be differentiated based on two dimensions: (1) strategies that aim to either approach or avoid the situation, and (2) strategies that are cognitive versus behavioral in nature (see Table 19.2; empirical results based on this classification system are given later). Examples for each coping strategy type include responses to the statement "When I am bored in mathematics class ..." such as "... I make myself aware of the importance of the issue" (*cognitive approach*), "... I ask my teacher for more interesting tasks" (*behavioral approach*), "... I study for another subject" (*cognitive avoidance*), and "... I talk to my classmates" (*behavioral avoidance*).

Empirical Findings

Despite limited research on the types and effects of students' strategies for coping with boredom, scattered existing findings are nonetheless revealing. For example, a study by Vandewiele (1980) suggested various specific strategies used by students (13 to 14 years old) to prevent boredom, including reading (20%), doing homework (9%), visiting friends (9%), listening to music (8%), participating in sports (6%), and playing games (4%). Similarly, Harris (2000) found university students (mean age of 28 years) to cope with non-academic boredom mainly by reading (39%), daydreaming (26%), socializing (21%), watching television (20%), doing physical activity (18%), doing something new (16%), sleeping (15%), organizing (14%), cleaning (10%), listening to music (9%), or studying (7%).

With respect to coping strategies for academic boredom, Goetz et al. (2007) found German ninth graders to report coping with boredom in class primarily through distraction (86%), acceptance (23%), increasing attention (15%), and relaxation (8%). The two most common strategies reported for coping with academic boredom can thus be classified as cognitive avoidance and cognitive approach strategies, according to the conceptual framework outlined in Table 19.2. To more intensively explore the applicability of this coping model to academic boredom, Nett et al. (2010) developed the *Coping with Boredom Scale* with a sample of German secondary students (fifth to tenth grade) and identified three groups of students based on their reported boredom-related coping strategies.

The first group identified by Nett et al. (2010) prefers cognitive approach strategies (*reappraisers*; e.g., bolstering perceived value of class content), the second focuses mainly on behavioral approach strategies (*criticizers*; e.g., suggesting more engaging activities to the instructor), and the third relies primarily on behavioral avoidance (*evaders*; e.g., engaging in unrelated activities). An analysis of group differences on academic outcomes showed that reappraisers experience less boredom and demonstrate a more adaptive academic profile (cognitions, emotions, motivation) as compared to the other groups. Follow-up studies have recently replicated these findings in both Chinese and Canadian university student samples (Daniels et al., 2015; Tze et al., 2013). In sum, existing findings suggest that, although cognitive avoidance may be a common response to academic boredom, students who attempt to cognitively reframe boring content as more interesting or important are less likely to be bored and experience less academic difficulties. This is also in line with findings by Sansone et al. (1992), from the perspective of self-regulation of motivation, that illustrate how adopting strategies that enhance interest in an assigned activity (e.g., focusing on the challenge afforded) can make the activity more positive in nature (see also Sansone, 2009; Sansone et al., 2015).

Summary

Despite numerous conceptual models for classifying strategies of coping with stress, theoretical frameworks that attempt to categorize the types of strategies students used to cope with academic boredom are limited. In their 2 × 2 classification system, Nett et al. (2010, 2011) differentiate boredom-related coping strategies along the dimensions of approach versus avoidance and cognitive strategies versus behavioral strategies – a model validated internationally with both secondary and post-secondary students. Preliminary findings based on this framework show cognitive avoidance to be the most frequently used coping strategy, with cognitive approach strategies proving consistently effective for reducing boredom.

How Can Academic Boredom Be Reduced?

Following from the aforementioned theoretical approaches and findings are numerous potential avenues for reducing or preventing academic boredom. Perhaps the most empirically validated approach for minimizing boredom is to *enhance students' perceived value of, and personal interest in, academic tasks and content* by, for example, highlighting the relevance of classroom activities to students' daily lives (cf., Durik & Harackiewicz, 2007; Hidi & Renninger, 2006; Hulleman & Harackiewicz, 2009; Renninger & Hidi, 2016). Likewise, existing research underscores the importance of *adequately matching task demands to student competencies* to maintain optimal perceptions of academic control in students (e.g., Krannich et al., 2016; Preckel et al., 2010). *Demonstrating enthusiasm while teaching* has also been consistently found to contribute to student enjoyment – an emotion incompatible with academic boredom that should also contribute to greater achievement-striving (Keller et al., 2016; Pressick-Kilborn, 2015; Xu et al., 2014).

It is also important to support the diagnostic competencies of teachers *to better identify when students are bored*, as well as consider the underlying causes so as to better modify class content and activities to reduce boredom experiences. Although there exist no published studies to date on how accurate teachers are in evaluating their students' boredom, recent research indicates that parents can quite accurately judge the intensity and frequency of their children's boredom, as well as specific antecedent variables (Nett et al., 2016). Given the specific familiarity of teachers with students' learning behavior and expressed emotions in class, teachers could also be expected to be highly accurate when evaluating their students' boredom levels. Similarly, intervention efforts could focus on helping students better identify and anticipate their own feelings of boredom, as well as *informing students of effective strategies for coping with boredom*. Despite potential awkwardness for teachers in acknowledging suboptimal instruction or learning tasks, it is expected that – by addressing individual differences in student interests and achievement levels, the inevitable mismatch with class activities, and specific strategies for reducing boredom levels – students can assume more responsibility for their feelings of boredom in class and assume more control over their academic development.

Concluding Thoughts

Given cumulative empirical evidence showing academic emotions (including academic boredom) to be organized primarily in a domain-specific manner (e.g., Goetz et al. 2007), the domain-specific assessment of academic boredom is highly recommended to most effectively evaluate boredom in students during academic activities (e.g., in mathematics versus language classes). Future studies employing real-time (state) assessments of academic boredom (i.e., experience sampling method; Goetz et al., 2014a; Larson & Richards, 1991; Nett et al., 2011) are also strongly recommended to reduce bias due to subjective beliefs (see Goetz et al., 2014b; Robinson & Clore, 2002). The use of more objective measures of academic boredom, such as physiological markers or facial expression recognition, are also encouraged to validate findings obtained from self-report research.

Empirical findings suggest that the experience of boredom may take different forms, and that specific subtypes of boredom can be differentiated along the dimensions of valence and arousal (Goetz et al., 2014a). Further study of the prevalence, antecedents, effects, and generalizability of *specific types of boredom* within and across subject areas is encouraged in order to shed light on how educators can address boredom. Cultural as well as developmental differences (e.g., elementary school children versus older adults) in the meaning of academic boredom also warrant additional research (e.g., cognitive interviewing of self-report boredom measures; see Frenzel et al., 2012; Karabenick et al., 2007).

Future experimental or longitudinal studies on the *antecedents and effects of boredom* would help clarify the causal nature of the relationships. Further research into the possibility that different types of boredom (e.g., indifferent versus reactant boredom; Goetz et al., 2014a) may have different antecedents and effects is also needed.

Additionally, given limited research on how learners *cope with academic boredom*, more studies are necessary to evaluate effective boredom coping strategies. Such studies should refer to existing models in the fields of coping, emotion regulation, and self-regulated learning (see Nett et al., 2010).

Concerning the *assessment of academic boredom*, future studies are encouraged to distinguish between trait and state measures (e.g., retrospective self-perceptions versus real-time experiences; cf., Kahneman, 2011) and, if possible, triangulate data from varied assessments (such as facial expressions, neuroimaging, physiological indicators, and physical activity) that are less subject to response bias (Harley et al., 2012).

Considering that nearly all published research on academic boredom to date has focused on students, research on *boredom in teachers* is also warranted, particularly given recent findings showing this emotion to be frequently experienced by teachers in classroom settings (Becker et al., 2015). Given the considerable amount of existing research illustrating the various negative consequences of academic boredom, it is anticipated that efforts to examine boredom in teachers could contribute to both teacher well-being and student learning.

Finally, following from the aforementioned suggested research directions is the development of targeted *interventions for reducing and preventing academic boredom* for both students and teachers. For example, control-enhancing programs might be developed (e.g., Hall et al., 2007) or programs that aim to foster students' self-regulation competencies (e.g., Goetz & Bieg, 2016).

References

Acee, T. W., Kim, H., Kim, H. J., Kim, J.-I., Chu, H. R., Kim, M., ... Wicker, F. W. (2010). Academic boredom in under- and over-challenging situations. *Contemporary Educational Psychology*, *35*(1), 17–27.

Ahmed, W., van der Werf, G., Kuyper, H., & Minnaert, A. (2013). Emotions, self-regulated learning, achievement in mathematics: A growth curve analysis. *Journal of Educational Psychology*, *105*, 150–61.

Becker, E. S., Keller, M. M., Goetz, T., Frenzel, A. C., & Taxer, J. L. (2015). Antecedents of teachers' emotions in the classroom: An intraindividual approach. *Frontiers in Psychology*, *6*, 635.

Berlyne, D. E. (1960). *Conflict, arousal, and curiosity*. New York, NY: McGraw-Hill Book Company.

Bornstein, R. F., Kale, A. R., & Cornell, K. R. (1990). Boredom as a limiting condition on the mere exposure effect. *Journal of Personality and Social Psychology*, *58*, 791–800.

Chin, A., Markey, A., Bhargava, S., Kassam, K. S., & Loewenstein, G. (2017). Bored in the USA: Experience sampling and boredom in everyday life. *Emotion*, *17*(2), 359–68.

Csikszentmihalyi, M. (1975). *Beyond boredom and anxiety*. San Francisco, CA: Jossey-Bass.

Csikszentmihalyi, M. & Larson, R. (1984). *Being adolescent*. New York, NY: Basic Books.

Daniels, L. M., Stupnisky, R. H., Pekrun, R., Haynes, T. L., Perry, R. P., & Newall, N. E. (2009). A longitudinal analysis of achievement goals: From affective antecedents to emotional effects and achievement outcomes. *Journal of Educational Psychology*, *101*, 948–63.

Daniels, L. M., Tze, V. M. C., & Goetz, T. (2015). Examining boredom: Different causes for different coping profiles. *Learning and Individual Differences*, *37*, 255–61.

Daschmann, E. C., Goetz, T., & Stupnisky, R. H. (2011). Testing the predictors of boredom at school: Development and validation of the Precursors to Boredom Scales. *British Journal of Educational Psychology*, *81*, 421–40.

Dicintio, M. J. & Gee, S. (1999). Control is the key: Unlocking the motivation of at-risks students. *Psychology in the Schools*, *36*, 231–7.

Duda, J. L., Fox, K. R., Biddle, S. J., & Armstrong, N. (1992). Children's achievement goals and beliefs about success in sport. *British Journal of Educational Psychology*, *62*, 313–23.

Durik, A. M. & Harackiewicz, J. M. (2007). Different strokes for different folks: How individual interest moderates the effects of situational factors on task interest. *Journal of Educational Psychology*, *99*, 597–610.

Ekman, P. (1984). Expression and the nature of emotion. In K. S. Scherer & P. Ekman (Eds.), *Approaches to emotion* (pp. 319–43). Hillsdale, NJ: Erlbaum.

Fahlman, S. A., Mercer-Lynn, K. B., Flora, D. B., & Eastwood, J. D. (2013). Development and validation of the multidimensional state boredom scale. *Assessment*, *20*(1), 68–85.

Farmer, R. & Sundberg, N. D. (1986). Boredom proneness: The development and correlates of a new scale. *Journal of Personality Assessment, 50,* 4–17.

Farrell, E., Peguero, G., Lindsey, R., & White, R. (1988). Giving voice to high school students: Pressure and boredom, ya know what I'm sayin'? *American Educational Research Journal, 25*(4), 489–502.

Fenichel, O. (1951). On the psychology of boredom. In D. Rapaport (Ed.), *Organization and pathology of thought: Selected sources* (pp. 349–61). New York, NY: Columbia University Press.

Fisher, C. D. (1993). Boredom at work: A neglected concept. *Human Relations, 46*(3), 395–417.

Frenzel, A. C., Pekrun, R., Dicke, A.-L., & Goetz, T. (2012). Beyond quantitative decline: Conceptual shifts in adolescents' development of interest in mathematics. *Developmental Psychology, 48*(4), 1069–82.

Frenzel, A. C., Pekrun, R., & Goetz, T. (2007). Perceived learning environment and students' emotional experiences: A multilevel analysis of mathematics classrooms. *Learning and Instruction, 17,* 478–93.

Frenzel, A. C., Pekrun, R., Goetz, T., Daniels, L. M., Durksen, T. L., Becker-Kurz, B., & Klassen, R. (2016). Measuring teachers' enjoyment, anger, and anxiety: The Teacher Emotions Scales (TES). *Contemporary Educational Psychology, 46,* 148–63.

Geiwitz, P. J. (1966). Structure of boredom. *Journal of Personality and Social Psychology, 3,* 592–600.

Gjesme, T. (1977). General satisfaction and boredom at school as a function of the pupils' personality characteristics. *Scandinavian Journal of Educational Research, 21*(3), 113–46.

Goetz, T., Becker, E. S., Bieg, M., Keller, M. M., Frenzel, A. C., & Hall, N. C. (2015). The glass half empty: How emotional exhaustion affects the state-trait discrepancy in self-reports of teaching emotions. *PLoS ONE, 10*(9): e0137441.

Goetz, T. & Bieg, M. (2016). Academic emotions and their regulation via emotional intelligence. In A. A. Lipnevich, F. Preckel, & R. D. Roberts (Eds.), *Psychosocial skills and school systems in the 21st century: Theory, research, and practice* (pp. 279–98). New York, NY: Springer.

Goetz, T., Cronjaeger, H., Frenzel, A. C., Lüdtke, O., & Hall, N. C. (2010). Academic self-concept and emotion relations: Domain specificity and age effects. *Contemporary Educational Psychology, 35,* 44–58.

Goetz, T. & Frenzel, A. C. (2006). Phänomenologie schulischer Langeweile [Phenomenology of boredom at school]. *Zeitschrift für Entwicklungspsychologie und Pädagogische Psychologie, 38*(4), 149–53.

Goetz, T., Frenzel, A. C., Hall, N. C., Nett, U., Pekrun, R., & Lipnevich, A. (2014a). Types of boredom: An experience sampling approach. *Motivation and Emotion, 38,* 401–19.

Goetz, T., Frenzel, A. C., & Pekrun, R. (2007). Regulation von Langeweile im Unterricht. Was Schuelerinnen und Schueler bei der "Windstille der Seele" (nicht) tun [Regulation of boredom in class. What students (do not) do when experiencing the "Windless Calm of the Soul"]. *Unterrichtswissenschaft*, *35*(4), 312–33.

Goetz, T., Frenzel, A. C., Pekrun, R., Hall, N. C., & Lüdtke, O. (2007). Between- and within-domain relations of students' academic emotions. *Journal of Educational Psychology*, *99*(4), 715–33.

Goetz, T., Haag, L., Lipnevich, A. A., Keller, M. M., Frenzel, A. C., & Collier, A. P. M. (2014b). Between-domain relations of students' academic emotions and their judgments of school domain similarity. *Frontiers in Psychology*, *5*, 1153.

Goetz, T. & Hall, N. C. (2013). Emotion and achievement in the classroom. In J. Hattie and E. M. Anderman (Eds.), *International guide to student achievement* (pp. 192–5). New York, NY: Routledge.

Goetz, T., Luedtke, O., Nett, U. E., Keller, M., & Lipnevich, A. A. (2013). Characteristics of teaching and students' emotions in the classroom: Investigating differences across domains. *Contemporary Educational Psychology*, *38*, 383–94.

Goetz, T. & Nett, U. E. (2012). *Boredom in university students*. Codebook, University of Konstanz, Konstanz.

Goetz, T., Nett, U. E., Martiny, S. E., Hall, N. C., Pekrun, R., Dettmers, S., & Trautwein, U. (2012). Students' emotions during homework: Structures, self-concept antecedents, and achievement outcomes. *Learning and Individual Differences*, *22*(2), 225–34.

Goetz, T., Pekrun, R., Hall, N. C., & Haag, L. (2006). Academic emotions from a social-cognitive perspective: Antecedents and domain specificity of students' affect in the context of Latin instruction. *British Journal of Educational Psychology*, *76*(2), 289–308.

Goetz, T., Sticca, F., Pekrun, R., Murayama, K., & Elliot, A. J. (2016). Intraindividual relations between achievement goals and discrete achievement emotions: An experience sampling approach. *Learning and Instruction*, *41*, 115–25.

Grubb, E. A. (1975). Assembly line boredom and individual differences in recreation participation. *Journal of Leisure Research*, *7*, 256–69.

Haag, L. & Goetz, T. (2012). Mathe ist schwierig und Deutsch aktuell. Vergleichende Studie zur Charakterisierung von Schulfächern aus Schülersicht [Math is difficult and German up to date: A study on the characterization of subject domains from students' perspective]. *Psychologie in Erziehung und Unterricht*, *59*, 32–46.

Hall, N. C., Perry, R. P., Goetz, T., Ruthig, J. C., Stupnisky, R. H., & Newall, N. E. (2007). Attributional retraining and elaborative learning: Improving academic development through writing-based interventions. *Learning and Individual Differences*, *17*, 280–90.

Hamilton, J. A., Haier, R. J., & Buchsbaum, M. S. (1984). Intrinsic enjoyment and boredom coping scales: Validation with personality, evoked potential, and attention measures. *Personality and Individual Differences*, *5*, 183–93.

Harasymchuk, C. & Fehr, B. (2012). Development of a prototype-based measure of relational boredom. *Personal Relationships*, *19*, 162–81.

Harley, J. M., Bouchet, F., & Azevedo, R. (2012). *Measuring learners' unfolding, discrete emotional responses to different pedagogical agent scaffolding strategies.* Paper presented at the annual meeting of the American Educational Research Association, Vancouver.

Harris, M. B. (2000). Correlates and characteristics of boredom proneness and boredom. *Journal of Applied Social Psychology*, *30*(3), 576–98.

Hidi, S. & Renninger, A. (2006). The four-phase model of interest development. *Educational Psychologist*, *41*, 111–27.

Hill, A. B. & Perkins, R. E. (1985). Towards a model of boredom. *British Journal of Psychology*, *76*, 235–40.

Holahan, C. J., Moos, R. H., & Schaefer, J. A. (1996). Coping, stress resistance, and growth: Conceptualizing adaptive functioning. In M. Zeidner & N. S. Endler (Eds.), *Handbook of coping: Theory, research, applications* (pp. 24–43). New York, NY: John Wiley & Sons.

Hulleman, C. S. & Harackiewicz, J. M. (2009). Promoting interest and performance in high school science classes. *Science*, *326*(5958), 1410–12.

Iso-Ahola, S. E. & Weissinger, E. (1990). Perceptions of boredom in leisure: Conceptualization reliability, and validity of the Leisure Boredom Scale. *Journal of Leisure Research*, *22*, 1–17.

Jagacinski, C. M. & Duda, J. L. (2001). A comparative analysis of contemporary achievement goal orientation measures. *Educational and Psychological Measurement*, *61*, 1013–39.

Jarvis, S. & Seifert, T. (2002). Work avoidance as a manifestation of hostility, helplessness, and boredom. *Alberta Journal of Educational Research*, *48*, 174–87.

Kahneman, D. (2011). *Thinking, fast and slow*. London: Allen Lane.

Kanevsky, L. & Keighley, T. (2003). On gifted students in school: To produce or not to produce? Understanding boredom and the honor in underachievement. *Roeper Review*, *26*, 20–8.

Karabenick, S. A., Woolley, M. E., Friedel, J. M., Ammon, B. V., Blazevski, J., Bonney, C. R., ... Kelly, K. L. (2007). Cognitive processing of self-report items in educational research: Do they think what we mean? *Educational Psychologist*, *42*(3), 139–51.

Kass, S. J., Vodanovich, S. J., Stanny, C. J., & Taylor, T. M. (2001). Watching the clock: Boredom and vigilance performance. *Perceptual and Motor Skills*, *92*, 969–76.

Keller, M. M., Woolfolk Hoy, A. E., Goetz, T., & Frenzel, A. C. (2016). Teacher enthusiasm: Reviewing and redefining a complex construct. *Educational Psychology Review*, *28*, 743–69.

Kleinginna, P. R. & Kleinginna, A. M. (1981). A categorized list of emotion definitions, with suggestions for a consensual definition. *Motivation and Emotion*, *5*, 345–79.

Krannich, M., Goetz, T., & Lipnevich, A.A. (2016). *The effects of boredom due to being over- or underchallenged on students' occupational choice intentions*. Paper presented at the Annual Meeting of the American Educational Research Association, Washington, DC.

Larson, R.W. & Richards, M. H. (1991). Boredom in the middle school years: Blaming schools versus blaming students. *American Journal of Education*, *99*(4), 418–43.

Lazarus, R. S. & Folkman, S. (1984). *Stress, appraisal, and coping*. New York, NY: Springer.

Lazarus, R. S. & Folkman, S. (1987). Transactional theory and research on emotions and coping. *European Journal of Personality*, *1*(3), 141–69.

Lee, T. W. (1986). Toward the development and validation of a measure of job boredom. *Manhattan College Journal of Business*, *15*, 22–8.

London, H., Schubert, D. S., & Washburn, D. (1972). Increase of autonomic arousal by boredom. *Journal of Abnormal Psychology*, *80*(1), 29–36.

Mikulas, W. L. & Vodanovich, S. J. (1993). The essence of boredom. *The Psychological Record*, *43*(1), 3–12.

Miller, G. E. & Wrosch, C. (2007). You've gotta know when to fold 'em: Goal disengagement and systemic inflammation in adolescence. *Psychological Science*, *18*(9), 773–7.

Nett, U. E., Daschmann, E. C., Goetz, T., & Stupnisky, R. (2016). How accurately can parents judge their children's boredom in school? *Frontiers in Psychology*, *7*, 770.

Nett, U. E., Goetz, T., & Daniels, L. (2010). What to do when feeling bored? Students' strategies for coping with boredom. *Learning and Individual Differences*, *20*, 626–38.

Nett, U. E., Goetz, T., & Hall, N. C. (2011). Coping with boredom in school: An experience sampling perspective. *Contemporary Educational Psychology*, *36*(1), 49–59.

O'Hanlon, J. F. (1981). Boredom: Practical consequences and a theory. *Acta Psychologica*, *49*, 53–82.

Pekrun, R. (2006). The control-value theory of achievement emotions: Assumptions, corollaries, and implications for educational research and practice. *Educational Psychology Review*, *18*, 315–41.

Pekrun, R., Elliot, A. J., & Maier, M. A. (2006). Achievement goals and discrete achievement emotions: A theoretical model and prospective test. *Journal of Educational Psychology*, *98*, 583–97.

Pekrun, R., Elliot, A. J., & Maier, M. A. (2009). Achievement goals and achievement emotions: Testing a model of their joint relations with academic performance. *Journal of Educational Psychology*, *101*, 115–35.

Pekrun, R., Goetz, T., Daniels, L. M., Stupnisky, R. H., & Perry, R. P. (2010). Boredom in achievement settings: Exploring control-value antecedents and performance outcomes of a neglected emotion. *Journal of Educational Psychology*, *102*(3), 531–49.

Pekrun, R., Goetz, T., & Frenzel, A. C. (2005). *Achievement Emotions Questionnaire – Mathematics (AEQ-M) – User's Manual*. University of Munich: Department of Psychology.

Pekrun, R., Goetz, T., Frenzel, A. C., Barchfeld, P., & Perry, R. P. (2011). Measuring emotions in students' learning and performance: The achievement emotions questionnaire (AEQ). *Contemporary Educational Psychology*, *36*(1), 36–48.

Pekrun, R., Goetz, T., Titz, W., & Perry, R. P. (2002). Academic emotions in students' self-regulated learning and achievement: A program of qualitative and quantitative research. *Educational Psychologist*, *37*(2), 91–105.

Pekrun, R., Hall, N. C., Goetz, T., & Perry, R. P. (2014). Boredom and academic achievement: Testing a model of reciprocal causation. *Journal of Educational Psychology*, *106*(3), 696–710.

Perkins, R. E. & Hill, A. B. (1985). Cognitive and affective aspects of boredom. *British Journal of Psychology*, *76*(2), 221–34.

Phillips, A. (1993). *On kissing, tickling, and being bored: Psychoanalytic essays on the unexamined life*. Cambridge, MA: Harvard University Press.

Preckel, F., Goetz, T., & Frenzel, A. (2010). Ability grouping of gifted students: Effects on academic self-concept and boredom. *British Journal of Educational Psychology, 80*, 451–72.

Pressick-Kilborn, K. J. (2015). Canalization and connectedness in the development of science interest. In K. A. Renninger, S. Hidi, & M. Nieswandt (Eds.), *Interest in mathematics and science learning* (pp. 353–67). American Educational Research Association, Washington, DC.

Ragheb, M. G. & Merydith, S. P. (2001). Development and validation of a unidimensional scale measuring free time boredom. *Leisure Studies, 20*, 41–59.

Reijseger, G., Schaufeli, W. B., Peeters, M. C. W., Taris, T. W., van Beek, I., & Ouweneel, E. (2013). Watching the paint dry at work: Psychometric examination of the Dutch Boredom Scale. *Anxiety, Stress & Coping: An International Journal, 26*, 508–25.

Renninger, K. A. & Hidi, S. (2016). *The power of interest for motivation and learning*. New York, NY: Routledge.

Robinson, M. D. & Clore, G. L. (2002). Belief and feeling: Evidence for an accessibility model of emotional self-report. *Psychological Bulletin, 128*(6), 934–60.

Robinson, W. P. (1975). Boredom at school. *British Journal of Educational Psychology, 45*, 141–52.

Rosch, E. (1978). Principles of categorization. In E. Rosch & B. B. Lloyd (Eds.), *Cognition and categorization* (pp. 27–48). Hillsdale, NJ: Erlbaum.

Russell, J. A. (1980). A circumplex model of affect. *Journal of Personality and Social Psychology, 39*(6), 1161–78.

Sansone, C. (2009). What's interest got to do with it?: Potential trade-offs in the self-regulation of motivation. In J. Forgas, R. Baumeister, and D. Tice (Eds.), *Psychology of self-regulation: Cognitive, affective, and motivational processes* (pp. 35–51). New York, NY: Psychology Press.

Sansone, C., Thoman, D., & Fraughton, T. (2015). The relation between interest and self-regulation in mathematics and science. In K. A. Renninger, M. Nieswandt, & S. Hidi (Eds.), *Interest in mathematics and science learning* (pp. 111–31). Washington, DC: American Educational Research Association.

Sansone, C., Weir, C., Harpster, L., & Morgan, C. (1992). Once a boring task always a boring task? Interest as a self-regulatory mechanism. *Journal of Personality and Social Psychology, 63*, 379–90.

Scerbo, M. W. (1998). What's so boring about vigilance? In R. R. Hoffman, M. F. Sherrick, & J. S. Warm (Eds.), *Viewing psychology as a whole: The integrative science of William N. Dember* (pp. 145–66). Washington, DC: American Psychological Association.

Scherer, K. R. (2000). Emotions as episodes of subsystems synchronization driven by nonlinear appraisal processes. In M. D. Lewis & I. Granic (Eds.), *Emotion, development, and self-organization* (pp. 70–99). Cambridge: Cambridge University Press.

Schimmack, U. & Reisenzein, R. (2002). Experiencing activation: Energetic arousal and tense arousal are not mixtures of valence and activation. *Emotion, 2*, 412–17.

Shaver, P., Schwartz, J., Kirson, D., & O'Connor, C. (1987). Emotion knowledge: Further exploration of a prototype approach. *Journal of Personality and Social Psychology, 52*(6), 1061–86.

Shaw, S. M., Caldwell, L. L., & Kleiber, D. A. (1996). Boredom, stress and social control in the daily activities of adolescents. *Journal of Leisure Research, 28*(4), 274–92.

Skinner, E. A. (1996). A guide to constructs of control. *Journal of Personality and Social Psychology, 71*, 549–70.

Skinner, E. A., Edge, K., Altman, J., & Sherwood, H. (2003). Searching for the structure of coping: A review and critique of category systems for classifying ways of coping. *Psychological Bulletin, 129*(2), 216–69.

Smith, R. P. (1981). Boredom: A review. *Human Factors, 23*, 329–40.

Strain, A. C. & Graesser, A. C. (2012). *Cognitive reappraisal to alleviate boredom during learning.* Paper presented at the annual meeting of the American Educational Research Association, Vancouver.

Todman, M. (2013). The dimensions of state boredom: Frequency, duration, unpleasantness, consequences and causal attributions. *Educational Research International, 1*(1), 32–40.

Tze, V. M. C., Daniels, L. M., & Klassen, R. M. (2016). Evaluating the relationship between boredom and academic outcomes: A meta-analysis. *Educational Psychological Review, 28*, 119–44.

Tze, V. M. C., Daniels, L. M., Klassen, R. M., & Li, J. C. (2013). Canadian and Chinese university students' approaches to coping with academic boredom. *Learning and Individual Differences, 23*, 32–43.

Van Tilburg, W. A. P. & Igou, E. R. (2012). On boredom: Lack of challenge and meaning as distinct boredom experiences. *Motivation and Emotion, 36*, 181–94.

Vandewiele, M. (1980). On boredom of secondary school students in Senegal. *Journal of Genetic Psychology, 137*, 267–74.

Vodanovich, S. J. (2003a). On the possible benefits of boredom: A neglected area in personality research. *Psychology and Education – An Interdisciplinary Journal, 40*, 28–33.

Vodanovich, S. J. (2003b). Psychometric measures of boredom: A review of the literature. *Journal of Psychology, 137*(6), 569–95.

Vodanovich, S. J. & Watt, J. D. (2016). Self-report measures of boredom: An updated review of the literature. *Journal of Psychology: Interdisciplinary and Applied, 150*(2), 196–228.

Wallace, J. C., Vodanovich, S. J., & Restino, B. M. (2003). Predicting cognitive failures from boredom proneness and daytime sleepiness scores: An investigation within military and undergraduate samples. *Personality and Individual Differences, 34*, 635–44.

Watson, D. & Tellegen, A. (1985). Toward a consensual structure of mood. *Psychological Bulletin, 98*(2), 219–35.

Watson, D., Wiese, D., Vaidya, J., & Tellegen, A. (1999). The two general activation systems of affect: Structural findings, evolutionary considerations, and psychobiological evidence. *Journal of Personality and Social Psychology, 76*, 820–38.

Watt, J. D. & Ewing, J. E. (2010). Toward the development and validation of a measure of sexual boredom. *Journal of Sex Research, 33*, 57–66.

Won, H. J. (1989). *The daily leisure of Korean school adolescents and its relationship to subjective well-being and leisure functioning.* Doctoral dissertation, University of Oregon, Department of Leisure Studies and Services.

Xu, J., Du, J., & Fan, X. (2014). Emotion management in online group work reported by Chinese students. *Educational Technology Research and Development 62*(6), 795–819.

Zuckerman, M. (1979). *Sensation seeking: Beyond the optimal level of arousal.* Hillsdale, NJ: Erlbaum.

20 The Costs and Benefits of Boredom in the Classroom

Jhotisha Mugon, James Danckert, and
John D. Eastwood

Abstract: *Boredom has traditionally been viewed as detrimental to learning. We present an alternative perspective. The vast majority of past research on academic boredom has examined judgments about the boringness of a situation and the propensity to feel bored, rather than actual state boredom. While retrospective judgments about the boringness of a task may be a cause of later disengagement, we argue that in-the-moment state boredom is a consequence of disengagement. This claim flows from our definition of boredom as the uncomfortable feeling associated with the unfulfilled desire to be mentally engaged. We propose that in-the-moment feelings of boredom can be an aid to learning. First, boredom is an immediate process indicator of a failure in learning, which can signal the need to correct disengaged, ineffectual learning. Second, boredom is an uncomfortable feeling, so it motivates an engagement of mental resources as a means of eliminating boredom. We believe our theoretical analysis points towards fruitful future empirical inquiry, clarifies the interpretation of existing findings, and highlights areas where theory development and conceptual precision are needed.*

The primary goal of this chapter is to explore boredom's role in the classroom. To begin, we need to be clear on what we mean by "boredom," as this term has been variously used in the scholarly literature. We define boredom as *the negatively valenced feeling associated with being cognitively disengaged.*[1] We contend that the state of being unable to deploy cognitive resources so as to become engrossed with either internal thought or external tasks is an intrinsically negative feeling. Just as the negative feeling of pain in response to tissue

---

1 The first part of this definition is phenomenological, i.e., what it feels like to be bored. Below we will offer a more nuanced articulation of what boredom feels like, so that it can be distinguished from other negatively valenced feelings. The second part of this definition is sub-personal and describes the cognitive mechanisms that underpin the feeling of boredom.

John D. Eastwood's research was supported in part by the Natural Sciences and Engineering Research Council of Canada.

damage is innate, so too is the negative feeling of boredom in response to being cognitively disengaged. Because boredom is a negatively valenced feeling, it is inherently aversive. That is, whenever possible, we try to avoid feeling bored. We categorize boredom as a feeling because it not only involves both cognitive and affective components, it is also an in-the-moment subjective experience. In our view, the feeling of boredom is commonly, and unhelpfully, conflated with the judgment that something is itself boring. Imagine attending a lecture on insects, a topic of which you have considerable knowledge and interest. As the lecture begins, you quickly realize that the talk is pitched at a very basic level that is well below your own expertise. Therefore, you use the lecture as an opportunity to work out the organizational structure of a paper you have been struggling with all week. To the extent that you were able to engage your cognitive resources in the task of outlining your paper, we would say that, by definition, you were not bored. That is, your cognitive resources were engaged, albeit not with the lecture. However, when a friend asks about the lecture over dinner conversation later, you might report that the lecture was boring and that you were bored during the lecture. In this case – we suggest – it is, in fact, more accurate to say that the lecture was (potentially) boring, but that you did not actually feel bored because you found an outlet in which to successfully immerse yourself. Alternatively, imagine that during the lecture you were not able to engage your cognitive resources in the task of outlining your paper. In this instance, all options in front of you – the lecture itself or your own internal thoughts – are insufficient to satisfy your desire to be engaged. We would say that, in that moment, you were bored. If your friend happened to be with you during the lecture, you could have reported your in-the-moment feeling of boredom. After the fact (once again, over dinner) you might retrospectively report that you felt bored during the lecture and that the lecture was boring, but you would not, at the time of reporting, be feeling bored.[2] When a lecture, or anything else, is judged to be boring, such judgment is essentially expressing disdain or disgust for that object and a motivation to try to avoid it in the future.

This distinction between the retrospective, summary evaluation about how boring a given situation was and in-the-moment feelings of boredom is a critical jumping-off point for the present chapter. This distinction highlights the need for both conceptual and measurement precision when considering the topic of boredom in the classroom. In our view, the vast majority of research on academic boredom has, to date, examined students' retrospective, summary evaluations about how boring a learning situation was. Yet, models of academic boredom posit a key role for in-the-moment feelings of boredom

---

2 Note that, in this case, boredom was not the result of lack of interest in the content, but rather was related to how the content was presented. We might say that situational interest or the psychological state of interest did not occur, but the predisposition to engage with insect-related content was nevertheless present.

(Pekrun et al., 2009). Therefore, a complete understanding of academic boredom requires that we broaden our empirical investigations to include an examination of in-the-moment feelings of boredom, not just retrospective judgments about the boringness of a situation. In the present chapter, we sketch out some preliminary ideas about the way that in-the-moment feelings of boredom might operate in a learning context. In doing so, *we propose the counterintuitive claim that in-the-moment feelings of boredom can be an aid to learning*.

The secondary goal of this chapter is to clarify the concept of "interest" as it relates to in-the-moment feelings of boredom, judgments about an activity's boringness, and the engagement of cognitive resources in a learning context. Just like the term "boredom," so too the term "interest" has been used in a variety of different ways in the scholarly literature. Renninger and Hidi (2016) helpfully distinguish between interest as the "psychological state of a person while engaging with some type of content" and interest as the "cognitive and affective motivational predisposition to re-engage with that content over time" (p. 8). This could be boiled down to a "state" that occurs in response to engaging with some content and a "predisposition" that motivates future engagement with that content. Renninger and Hidi (2016) suggest that these two aspects of interest are interdependent and co-occurring; however, from a functional and experiential point of view they are distinct aspects of the "whole" of interest. The precise way in which the psychological state (response to content) and the predisposition (motivation to engage) are manifested and interrelated at a given point in time is less well developed in their model. For example, while washing dishes with your friend after dinner you might report that you are very interested in insects (you have motivation to engage with content about insects in the future), but the degree to which it could be said that you are currently experiencing the psychological state of interest (in response to insect-related content) is not obvious. A clear strength of Renninger and Hidi's model is their articulation of how interest develops over time. Namely, they map the progression from a triggered situational interest to a maintained situational interest to an emerging individual interest and, finally, to a well-developed individual interest. This model focuses more on explaining how interest changes and develops over time, and less on the issue of first causes.

The response to engagement with some content cannot *cause* engagement with that content – it is, by definition, a consequence of engagement. Moreover, motivation to re-engage with content cannot occur until *after* some initial engagement has already occurred – it is, by definition, the propensity to do something again in the future. In short, interest cannot cause that very first initial engagement with whatever content one might consider (insects or otherwise). To get interest started, one needs some pre-interest mechanism. For example, it has been argued that we are born with a propensity to pay attention to certain kinds of things and to find them interesting – for instance, things that are complex, ambiguous, or surprising (e.g., Berlyne, 1974; see also

Hidi, 1990 for a review in the domain of education). Moreover, the affective neuroscience literature has established that mammals are hardwired to engage in seeking behavior (e.g., Alcaro & Panksepp, 2011). However, insofar as interest is an experience that results from engagement with a particular content (a response and a desire for re-engagement), it would seem problematic to call the attentional bias to attend to surprising objects an interest, nor can we call the neurological imperative to engage in seeking behavior an interest.[3] In this chapter, we propose a potentially surprising pre-interest mechanism that serves to get interest started: boredom. To be clear, we do not propose that boredom is the only pre-interest mechanism that causes triggered situational interest. However, we believe it is one important route to interest and engagement. Our contention is that boredom can motivate the engagement of a learner's cognitive resources and that, once those cognitive resources become engaged with some particular content, it is then possible for new interest to develop and deepen engagement.[4] Comparing boredom to curiosity, which may be thought of as another pre-interest mechanism, can further elucidate the manner in which we think boredom can cause interest. Whereas boredom motivates the *engagement of a learner's cognitive resources* (i.e., *a content-free push*), curiosity motivates the *engagement with some particular content* (i.e., *a content-specific pull*).[5] Both serve to elicit initial engagement but from different "sides" of engagement. Boredom emphasizes the undesirable state of the learner; whereas, in the case of curiosity, the emphasis is on the desired content that the learner is moving toward. Once boredom or curiosity gets some particular content "in front of a learner" so to speak, interest may develop, motivating sustained engagement with that content over time.

To be clear, our counterintuitive claim that boredom can be an aid to learning is not directly supported by existing empirical research – the research

---

3 We will leave it to interested researchers to take a stance on this particular definitional issue – perhaps there is a case to be made for considering these inborn attentional orienting mechanisms and seeking behaviors to be interests. Our argument about the role of boredom in *causing* interest does not depend on this definitional issue being resolved in any particular manner.

4 As we hope will become clear over the course of the chapter, this claim about boredom causing engagement, and thus interest, is actually a re-statement or unpacking of the earlier counterintuitive claim that boredom can be an aid to learning. Our claim is predicated on our definition of boredom as an unfulfilled desire for cognitive engagement (see the next section). Nevertheless, because boredom is aversive, people may become preoccupied with making the negative feeling go away rather than taking the time to respond to the need expressed in boredom. For example, the bored individual may simply seek relief through shutting down and sleeping, so that the aversive feeling is eliminated without actually resolving the underlying problem signaled by boredom.

5 We acknowledge the considerable debate and research regarding curiosity and its relation with interest (Renninger & Hidi, 2016). Here we make use of a particular understanding of curiosity to deepen the reader's understanding of our claim about boredom. Moreover, we find it notable that some have argued that curiosity, like boredom, can involve an aversive feeling. However, our claim about boredom causing interest does not hinge on accepting any particular way of thinking about curiosity.

needed to test the proposal that in-the-moment feelings of boredom can be an aid to learning simply does not yet exist. In the chapter, we present empirical findings that highlight key gaps in the literature and offer some indirect support for our counterintuitive proposal. However, our principal strategy is to conduct a careful analysis and synthesis of existing findings and concepts. In this regard, we view our contribution to be primarily theoretical. We believe our theoretical analysis points toward fruitful future empirical inquiry, clarifies the interpretation of existing findings, and highlights areas needing theory development.

In the following sections, we focus on articulating the basic cognitive mechanisms underlying boredom, interest, and engagement (including attentional processes). Further, we seek to elucidate how boredom, interest, and engagement are related in the moment. That is, we are concerned with the micro development of boredom, interest, and engagement over a period of minutes. We review the minimal existing neurological findings on boredom and provide a tentative interpretation of these early results.

What Is Boredom?

Earlier we defined boredom as *the negatively valenced feeling associated with being cognitively disengaged*. In the present section we unpack this definition. It is common to hear researchers bemoan the fact that "boredom" lacks a clear definition. Notwithstanding legitimate and useful debate on how best to define boredom, we believe this complaint is overstated and reflects the fact that researchers have typically not grounded their definition or measuring tools in boredom theory. Indeed, we found considerable overlap in the definition of boredom across distinct theoretical models (Fahlman et al., 2013). After carefully examining the psychodynamic, arousal, cognitive, and existential theories of boredom, we discovered that all models converge on the following phenomenological definition: *Boredom is a negatively valenced feeling that involves the unfulfilled desire for satisfying activity and is associated with aversive high and low arousal, negative affect, difficulty concentrating, and the feeling that time is passing slowly.* We then conducted a modified grounded theory analysis (Strauss & Corbin, 1998) on participants' descriptions of boredom. Four key themes emerged: (1) a disconnection or struggle to engage in one's surrounding environment, (2) a negative or undesirable experience, (3) emotional and cognitive experiences, and (4) changes in time perception. Thus, results of the empirical grounded theory analysis were entirely consistent with the theoretical review, suggesting that laypersons use the term "boredom" in a manner that is very similar to that used by boredom researchers.

We have also (Eastwood et al., 2012) argued that the state of cognitive disengagement underpins boredom and can explain the subjective experience of boredom. In this manner, we expanded our definition of boredom to include both subjective experience and the underlying cognitive processes that give rise to that subjective experience. The most contentious aspect of this definition is the assertion that boredom, by definition, encompasses both high arousal and low arousal. Some have suggested that boredom is exclusively a state of low arousal (e.g., Russell, 1980; Vogel-Walcutt et al., 2012). In fact, the majority of research on academic boredom has been predicated on the idea that boredom is a state of low arousal (e.g., Pekrun, 2006). We disagree with this definition of boredom. Elsewhere we have argued that including high arousal as part of the experience of boredom has more utility and is more consistent with existing theory and data (e.g., Eastwood et al., 2012; Fahlman et al., 2013; Merrifield & Danckert, 2014).

Part of the disagreement regarding arousal may reflect different ideas as to where the definitional boundaries should be placed around a dynamic phenomenon. Moreover, there is the related question of where to put the definitional boundaries between boredom itself and the antecedents and consequences of boredom. Consider, for example, the definition of boredom offered by Vogel-Walcutt and colleagues (2012):

> State boredom occurs when an individual experiences *both* the (objective) neurological state of low arousal *and* the (subjective) psychological state of dissatisfaction, frustration, or disinterest in response to the low arousal. (p. 102; emphasis added)

Dissatisfaction and frustration are negatively valenced feelings that are associated with *high* arousal (Russell, 1980); moreover, in the definition offered, it appears that the high arousal is a later stage in a dynamic unfolding of affect and arousal over time. Thus, it would appear that, despite the authors' statements to the contrary, this definition embraces both the idea that boredom is dynamic and that it may involve high arousal.

Whether or not boredom is associated with high or low arousal may depend on the stage of boredom during a given episode or the environmental situation at hand. For example, increased arousal may reflect an attempt to engage attention with an under-stimulating task. If repeated attempts to engage attention fail, then low arousal may ensue. On the other hand, variations between high and low arousal may depend on contextual factors. More specifically, certain situations are too challenging while others do not offer any challenge – leading to different levels of arousal but similar disengagement with the situation (Klapp, 1986). Indeed, consistent with others (e.g., Berlyne, 1960; Bernstein, 1975; Eastwood et al., 2012; Fenichel, 1953; Greenson, 1951; Hamilton, 1981; O'Hanlon, 1981; Smith, 1981; Thackray, 1981), we argue that it is precisely the contrasting or oscillating experiences of agitation and restlessness on one hand, and lethargy and fatigue on the other, that are key to distinguishing boredom from other neighboring emotional states.

A central reason that including both high and low arousal in the conceptualization of boredom is important is that, without doing so, it becomes conceptually difficult to distinguish boredom from apathy – a state of indifference.[6] In our view, the bored individual is anything but indifferent; they exhibit a strong, restless desire for engagement (Eastwood et al., 2012; Merrifield & Danckert, 2014) and, from a purely psychometric point of view, we have previously shown that boredom is indeed distinct from apathy (Goldberg et al., 2011).

What Is Happening in the Bored Brain?

Recent attempts have been made to explore the neural networks associated with being bored. This has been done either directly (Danckert & Merrifield, 2016) or indirectly, while exploring the state of flow (Ulrich et al., 2014) or examining the influence of boredom on future purchasing behavior (Dal Mas & Wittmann, 2017) using functional magnetic resonance imaging (fMRI).[7] Such neuroimaging work further helps refine our understanding of how best to define boredom. Although *highly speculative* at this point, existing data suggest that *the bored individual may be stuck in their internal thoughts and bodily sensations, unable to shift attention successfully to the environment around them.*

Three important brain systems are key to understanding boredom: the *default mode network* (DMN), the *central executive network* (CEN), and the *salience network* (SN; Menon & Uddin, 2010). The DMN is associated with off-task thinking, attentional disengagement from external tasks, and engagement with internal thought processes. It is chiefly comprised of the medial parietal cortex, posterior cingulate cortex, and ventromedial prefrontal regions (Andrews-Hanna, 2012; Greicius et al., 2003; Mason et al., 2007; Weissman et al., 2006). Research has shown that the DMN is implicated in internally focused thoughts, mind wandering, and lapses in attention (Andrews-Hanna 2012; Christoff et al., 2009; Fox et al., 2015; Mason et al., 2007; Weissman

6 Barbalet (1999) makes a similar point in the context of distinguishing boredom from ennui. For example: "Boredom, but not ennui, is a feeling that expresses a dissatisfaction with the lack of interest in an activity or condition. Boredom, in its irritability and restlessness (conditions not present in ennui), is not a feeling of acceptance of or resignation toward a state of indifference, as ennui is. Boredom, therefore, is not a passive surrender to those conditions that provoke it. The elements of active discomfort are what characterize boredom … [Boredom] is a restless and irritable feeling about an absence of interest" (pp. 634–5). The agitated feeling seen in boredom "expresses the subject's distress at their finding no interest in their activities or circumstances."

7 fMRI is a metabolic imaging technique that measures changes in the blood-oxygen-level-dependent (BOLD) signal when participants are engaged in a particular task. The general idea is that when a particular area of the brain is involved in a task it will have higher metabolic needs. Differences then in oxy- and deoxyhemoglobin can be measured with fMRI highlighting brain regions more involved in a given task. By looking at these differences, researchers can infer which areas and brain networks are involved in specific tasks or the experience of specific emotions.

et al., 2006). The CEN, comprising frontal cortical areas and lateral poste-rior parietal areas, is active when a person is attentionally engaged with exter-nal stimuli (Christoff et al., 2009; Collette & Van der Linden, 2002; Ulrich et al., 2014). When attention is not engaged with any external stimuli or task, increased activation is seen in the DMN with concomitant decreases in acti-vation of the CEN (Andrews-Hanna et al., 2012; Buckner, et al., 2008). The SN, which prominently includes the insular cortex (or insula), has been shown to be important for switching between the DMN and the CEN in response to salient and goal-relevant information (Menon & Uddin, 2010; Sidlauskaite et al., 2014; Uddin, 2015). One prominent theory regarding the anterior insula suggests that this brain region is important for representing our conscious, embodied experience of the here and now (Craig, 2009). We next review find-ings related to boredom with respect to these three key neurological systems.

Neuroimaging research suggests that when we are engaged with a task, there is a concomitant increase in frontal executive system activity (i.e., the CEN) and a decrease in DMN activity, whereas the opposite is associated with being bored (Danckert & Merrifield, 2016; Ulrich et al., 2014, 2015). Ulrich and colleagues (2014) contrasted the experience of boredom with that of flow – a state of optimal engagement in which one is fully focused on the task at hand. Participants in this study completed a series of mathematical questions that were either too easy, presumably leading to boredom; too hard, leading to cognitive overload; or just right (problems titrated to an individual's ability), leading to a state of flow. When participants were in a flow state, the CEN was active and there was decreased activation in the DMN, and there was also increased activity in the insular cortex, further highlighting participants' engagement in the here and now. In contrast, when participants were bored during the easy mathematical questions, the researchers observed increased activity in the DMN and decreased activity in the CEN. It is not that par-ticipants were not engaged in any task – they were solving math questions. However, because the questions were too easy, solving them did not occupy participants' cognitive resources and, thus, participants were able to divert surplus cognitive resources to off-task, internal thoughts, leading to increased activity in the DMN.

We (Danckert & Merrifield, 2016) showed more directly that when an indi-vidual is bored, their brain activity is distinct from what we observe when they are simply "doing nothing." When watching a boring movie of two men hanging laundry, activity in the insular cortex was anticorrelated with the DMN.[8] That is, activity in the insula was negatively correlated with activity

---

8 Unlike traditional imaging studies in which brain activation is subtracted across two condi-tions to highlight which regions are more active in one task vs another, this study used an approach known as independent components analysis. Here we discover which brain areas or networks show correlated activity (i.e., they fluctuate across time in synchrony with one another, thus forming a network) and which areas do not show coordinated activity with other networks. Two possibilities arise here – activity could be random (not associated with any

in the DMN. This relationship – when the DMN is active, the insula is deactivated – was not evident during a rest condition when no movie was present (Danckert & Merrifield, 2016). Inducing boredom led to the downregulation of the insula, in contrast to the upregulation of this region during a flow state, as observed in Ulrich and colleagues' (2015) study (note that both studies showed upregulation of the DMN when bored). During the resting condition, participants simply fixated on a cross on the screen while trying not to fall asleep. There were no other relevant stimuli in the environment for participants to engage with. In contrast, during the boredom condition, participants were required to watch the movie. Because the anterior insular cortex is responsible for representing saliency and interacts with the CEN, it may be that the anticorrelated activation observed when participants were bored represents failed attempts to engage with the movie. That is, participants tried to engage, but there is only so much one can do to engage with a movie in which two men hang laundry! Successful engagement, were it possible, would involve the SN signalling the CEN that there is something worthwhile to engage with; the DMN would be downregulated at the same time. This is not what we see. When bored, insula activity fails to successfully engage the CEN and downregulate the DMN – we're stuck in the boredom of the moment.

In a more recent study, people were asked to do a very simple task (decide if the frame around a picture was blurry or not) that was presumably also very boring, prior to making decisions about how much they would be willing to pay to download music (Dal Mas & Wittmann, 2017). These purchasing decisions were also made after having done a more challenging visual search task or a task that simply asked them which images they liked more. When bored, people were willing to pay more for music – as though they were desperate for any stimulation to rescue them from the boring task. Activity in the caudate nucleus – a subcortical structure known to be important for representing reward value (Aupperle et al., 2015; Knutson et al., 2001) – was associated with decisions to download music and avoid the boring task. Activity in the insular cortex was associated with how willing people were to pay to avoid boredom – the higher the willingness to pay to avoid boredom, the more activity was seen in the insula (Dal Mas & Wittmann, 2017). So on one hand, failures to engage are reflected in the downregulation of the insula (Danckert & Merrifield, 2016), while on the other, an increased desire to engage (by paying more to *avoid* boredom) is associated with the upregulation of the insula (Dal Mas & Wittmann, 2017).

If the insular cortex is important for switching between the large-scale neural networks involved in off-task thinking on the one hand (i.e., the DMN), and in goal-directed behavior on the other (i.e., the CEN), then boredom may

---

network across time) or anticorrelated with another network. Regions that are anticorrelated show fluctuations in activity in the opposing direction to an identified network. For our example, when the DMN shows an increase in activity, the insula shows a decrease, and vice versa.

represent a kind of interminable present. Certainly, when bored, we often complain about being *stuck* in the moment.

Is Boredom a Cause or a Consequence of Disengagement?

There is a wealth of cross-sectional, correlational research showing that boredom with the material at hand is negatively correlated with successful learning. In a recent meta-analysis of 29 empirical studies, Tze and collaegues (2016) found that academic boredom had significant negative correlations with motivation (r = –0.40), study strategies or behaviors (r = –0.35), and achievement (r = –0.16). These findings are relatively well established and non-controversial. Their interpretation, however, is not. We maintain that whether boredom is a cause or a consequence of disengagement in the learning context depends on what is meant by the term "boredom." In the previous sections on the definition and neuroimaging correlates of boredom, we specifically developed a definition and a conceptualization of the *in-the-moment state of boredom*. As foreshadowed in the introduction, a central claim of this chapter is that the vast majority of research into the link between boredom and academic performance has not examined in-the-moment state boredom, but rather *retrospective judgments about the boringness of a situation*.[9] In our view, the distinction between these two ways of conceptualizing and measuring boredom is critical when asking: "Is boredom a cause or a consequence of disengagement in a learning context?" In short, we argue that boredom as a retrospective judgment about the boringness of a task may be a *cause* of disengagement, and boredom as an in-the-moment state may be a *consequence* of disengagement.

Retrospective Judgments of Task Boringness as a Cause of Disengagement

Next we review longitudinal research that has examined the relation between boredom and learning outcomes over time. We review these studies in some methodological detail in order to illustrate that they have measured retrospective judgments of task boringness rather than in-the-moment state boredom.

Pekrun et al. (2010; Study 5) asked undergraduate students to report their level of course-related boredom (e.g., "The material bores me to death" with response options ranging from "strongly agree" to "strongly disagree") approximately 20 weeks into a 26-week course of study. Thus, although this measure may reflect judgments about the boringness of a task at a specific time point, it does not assess in-the-moment state boredom. Subsequent achievement levels

---

9 A notable exception to our generalization is the work of Goetz and colleagues (2007), in which they *did* examine in-the-moment state academic boredom. However, they did not look at the relation between state boredom and performance.

(i.e., final course grades) were obtained upon completion of the course of study. Analyses indicated that boredom was a significant negative predictor of achievement, even after controlling for achievement levels prior to starting the course (see also Daniels et al., 2009 who reported comparable findings using self-report items such as "When studying for this course, I feel bored"). These studies have the advantage of establishing prediction over time; however, they are not able to examine whether changes in academic boredom are related to changes in academic outcomes.

Ahmed et al. (2013) asked seventh grade students to report their level of boredom (e.g., "I get bored of studying math" with response options ranging from "not at all" to "very much") while "attending math class," "studying math," and "completing math tests" at three time points: in the fall, winter, and spring. The question posed to participants (Do you get bored of studying math?) may have elicited retrospective judgments about the boringness of math tasks, or it may have elicited retrospective reports of previous state experiences of boredom. However, in either case, the question does not assess in-the-moment state affect, but rather something more akin to a dispositional statement about how the situation makes them feel. At each time point, students also reported their use of "shallow" cognitive learning strategies such as rehearsal, "deep" cognitive learning strategies such as elaboration, and "meta-cognitive" learning strategies such as monitoring. The authors found that boredom levels increased over the academic year and that students who started with higher boredom levels had steeper increases in boredom over time. With respect to learning strategies, the shallow, deep, and meta-cognitive strategies all decreased over the academic year. Moreover, math achievement was shown to decrease over time. Importantly, results showed that increases in boredom were associated with decreases in shallow learning strategies and achievement. Similarly, Tze et al. (2014) asked undergraduate students to report their level of boredom (e.g., "The material bored me to death") during the previous week while "studying" and "in class" at five time points during a course. Although this measure may reflect judgments about the boringness of a task during a particular week, it does not assess in-the-moment state boredom. Thus, contrary to what the authors claim, this cannot be considered a measure of state boredom. At each time point, students also reported their "vigor," "absorption," "dedication," and "effort regulation." The authors found that in-class boredom increased over time. In contrast, boredom experienced during studying did not change. Students' effort regulation showed a linear decrease over time. Finally, an increase in in-class boredom was associated with a decrease in effort regulation. These studies have the advantage of examining the correlations between *changes* in key variables over time; however, they are not able to isolate the temporal precedence of changes. Once again, however, the most important point is that they did not measure the in-the-moment experience of boredom, but rather retrospective judgments about the boringness of a situation or dispositional judgments about how the situation makes students feel.

Pekrun et al. (2014), asked undergraduate students to report their level of boredom (e.g., "When studying for this course I feel bored") over the course of two academic terms at five different time points. This question would appear to assess generalized, dispositional judgments about how a situation makes the participant feel rather than assessing state boredom. The experimental design employed by the authors allowed them to examine reciprocal influences of boredom on achievement and vice versa. Compared to several alternative models, the reciprocal effects model, in which boredom negatively predicts subsequent achievement *and* achievement negatively predicts subsequent boredom, was the best fitting model. These findings are arguably the most illuminating to date on the temporal links between boredom and academic achievement. However, as with the other studies reviewed, we argue that in-the-moment state boredom was not assessed.

In summary, we suggest the claim that in-the-moment state boredom *causes* disengagement and poor academic achievement is not supported by existing findings. Instead, existing research supports the notion that beliefs, judgments, or dispositional reports about the boringness of a situation may cause disengagement and poor academic achievement. The claim that the majority of research on boredom in a learning context has been about retrospective judgments about the boringness of a situation, rather than about the in-the-moment state of boredom, is further bolstered by examining the definition of boredom found in this literature.

Pekrun and colleagues (2010) differentiate between boredom and lack of interest by looking at the motivation associated with the two states. They define boredom as involving a desire to avoid the activity that elicited the experience. They state "Boredom implies that the activity acquires negative intrinsic value, thus inducing motivation to avoid engagement [with that activity]" (p. 533), whereas "lack of interest per se should leave the motivation to perform an activity unaffected (other things being equal)" (p. 533). We contend that what is being offered here is a definition of a judgment of the boringness of a situation, rather than state boredom per se.

Consider the following illustrative example. Imagine someone engaging in the sport of rock climbing. As they reach up to take hold of a crevice in the rock above them, excruciating pain radiates down their fingers into their elbow. Because pain is aversive, the person is motivated to alleviate their suffering, so they alter their hand position in the crevice. In so doing, they have learned a new strategy (based on the pain feedback) and actually progressed in the skill of rock climbing. The aversiveness of the feeling is not the same thing as saying the activity is aversive. However, beliefs, judgments, or dispositional reports about the painfulness of rock climbing may indeed cause subsequent disengagement (a disinclination to attempt a certain route up the rock face) and thus stagnation in the development of rock climbing skill. The emotional state associated with beliefs, judgments, or dispositional reports of the boring-ness of a situation might be conceptualized as "disgust" or "contempt" rather than boredom (see Miller, 1997 for an elaboration of the distinction between disgust and boredom). Feeling boredom while doing an activity is aversive and thus students will be strongly motivated to avoid the state of boredom. Several different strategies to avoid feeling bored might be pursued, including avoiding the activity that elicited boredom, pursuing some other more exciting activity, or redoubling efforts to engage. As we will discuss later, Nett and colleagues (2010, 2011) have shown that cognitive approach strategies, where participants attempt to change the meaning of the task at hand and thereby maintain engagement, are the most effective ways of coping with boredom. In fact, if boredom is defined as motivation to avoid engagement with a boring task, then it is incoherent to propose cognitive approach boredom coping strategies, as such strategies would amount to recommending that the way to cope with boredom is to not be bored. While we believe that students will – perhaps more often than not – cope with boredom by avoiding the task at hand, in our view it is problematic to define boredom as the motivation to avoid the task at hand.

Thus, from both a measurement and a definitional point of view, it would appear that the majority of research into academic boredom has not evaluated the role of in-the-moment state boredom. On the one hand, the fact that previous work has largely focused on retrospective judgments of task boringness in no way undercuts the value of this work; existing work has been immensely informative. On the other hand, lack of investigation into state boredom represents a key limitation, especially in light of the fact that some models of academic boredom are based on conceptualizing boredom as a state. For example, Pekrun's (2009) model postulates that boredom might divert cognitive resources (e.g., Ellis & Ashbrook, 1988) from the academic task at hand or hinder the self-regulation of cognition, perhaps by increasing the adoption of shallow information processing strategies (Pekrun et al., 2010). In order to establish that boredom as a state *emotion* has a negative academic impact, it is necessary to examine the moment-to-moment unfolding of the learning process. That is, in-the-moment changes in state boredom must be shown to precede and predict in-the-moment changes in academic performance as a result of interrupted cognitive processes or resources. The key point we wish to highlight is the timescale at which this question needs to be examined. Assuming state emotions fluctuate over the course of minutes or hours, state boredom cannot, by definition, have an impact on achievement days or weeks later via a diversion of cognitive resources.

State Boredom as a Consequence of Disengagement

To our knowledge, definitive longitudinal or experimental research on the in-the-moment impact of state boredom on academic performance has not been conducted. However, there is a small amount of research examining how state boredom and attention are related over a period of minutes. Presumably attention is centrally important to the learning process and may be a key mechanism linking boredom and performance.

Hunter and Eastwood (2016) asked participants to report their current boredom at various points during a sustained attention task. Correlational findings were most consistent with the notion that state boredom was a *consequence* rather than a *cause* of attention failures. Numerically speaking, attention failures were more robustly correlated with subsequent state boredom ratings compared to boredom ratings made prior to a failure on the task. Similarly, Damrad-Frye and Laird (1989) demonstrated that manipulations of attentional engagement caused feelings of boredom. The authors had participants listen to an audio recording of an article and judge how bored they felt under three different conditions: conscious distraction (i.e., loud, clearly notable noise in the adjacent room), unconscious distraction (i.e., just-noticeable noise in the adjacent room), and no distraction. Participants who listened to the article under conditions of unconscious distraction reported the highest levels of boredom. Damrad-Frye and Laird argued that in both distraction conditions participants were aware of their difficulty focusing attention on the audio recording; however, in the just-noticeable noise condition, participants attributed their inattention to the article rather than to the distraction. To our knowledge, these are the only two studies that speak directly to the possibility of in-the-moment attentional disengagement causing state boredom (although see Carriere et al., 2008 for a similar causal account with trait boredom and trait attention). We are not aware of any research establishing the opposite causal arrow – that state boredom causes attentional disengagement. In addition, we believe there are compelling theoretical reasons to think disengagement comes before, or is part of, the boredom experience (Eastwood et al., 2012). Clearly, however, more empirical research is needed to resolve these issues.

How Might In-the-Moment State Boredom Be an Aid to Learning?

Conceptualizing in-the-moment state boredom as *the negatively valenced feeling associated with being cognitively disengaged* (rather than as a cause of disengagement) suggests three ways in which boredom can be an aid to learning. First, boredom can be thought of as an immediate process indicator of a failure in the learning context, which can inform both teacher and student that a change is needed to facilitate learning. In other words, boredom provides immediate feedback about the learning process that can guide alternative learning strategies. If the boredom signal was not present, both student and teacher might persist in a disengaged, ineffectual learning process without even knowing that learning was being hindered until the time had come to test skill and knowledge acquisition.

Second, based on the idea that it is biologically advantageous for people to maximally engage their cognitive resources, it is reasonable to conceptualize the state of being cognitively disengaged (i.e., bored) as inherently aversive. Therefore, whenever possible, people will try to avoid feeling bored. This desire is adaptive and can motivate learning, because when one is bored, one is incapable of learning; having one's cognitive resources engaged would both eliminate boredom and facilitate learning. In this way of thinking, the goal of the educator is not to eliminate boredom, but rather to use boredom as an aid to help maximize the engagement of the learner's cognitive resources with the content. However, because boredom is so aversive, students tend to seek the quickest and easiest way of becoming cognitively engaged and, unfortunately, this often results in students focusing attention on something other than the task at hand (e.g., acting out in class). So, in this sense, boredom is an early, in-the-moment indicator that learning is failing, but is *not* itself a direct cause of learning failure. State boredom can push us back into a state of effective learning if we have the capacity to heed its message. Responding adaptively to the boredom signal is not an easy task for either educators or students. Importantly, however, it is a different task from trying to *eliminate* state boredom from the classroom.

Third, as we mentioned in the introduction, we propose that in-the-moment state boredom can be thought of as a pre-interest mechanism that causes triggered situational interest. Our claim is that boredom motivates the engagement of a learner's cognitive resources, and once those resources become engaged with some particular content, interest can then develop and deepen engagement with that content over time. Essentially, we are arguing what might initially seem a surprising claim; namely, that boredom can cause engagement with content, and subsequent engagement with content causes interest. The need for a pre-interest mechanism to facilitate initial engagement with content is supported by our earlier logic, which suggested, by definition, that the psychological state of interest can't come before initial engagement and determine our focus of attention. Moreover, the power of initial engagement to give rise to interest is supported by research findings demonstrating that the mere act of attending to or engaging with certain content can change the way that content is affectively coded. That is, existing empirical research suggests that we like things we deliberately pay attention to; we dislike things we deliberately avoid paying attention to; and we find boring things that are difficult for us to pay attention to.[10]

On the one hand, researchers have demonstrated what has been called the "mere exposure effect"; namely, we judge neutral objects more positively after we pay attention to them (Yagi et al., 2009), and the more frequently

---

10 However, the mere act of paying attention to some particular content is typically not able to override our dislike for that content. That is, we often pay attention to things we do not like without any shift in our affective evaluation of that content.

we encounter a particular object, the more we may like it (Bornstein, 1989; Zajonc, 1968). Furthermore, the very act of gazing at an object contributes to our increased preference for that object (Shimojo et al., 2003). Perhaps most relevant for the argument we are developing here, Nunoi and Yoshikawa (2016) demonstrated that deeply processed stimuli were more preferred compared to stimuli that were processed shallowly. Strikingly, this preference effect was evident up to six weeks after processing the material, suggesting that the level of processing may contribute to the development of stable interests over time. On the other hand, objects that we actively ignore are subsequently responded to more slowly – an effect that has been termed "negative priming" (Fox, 1995; Tipper, 1985). Moreover, objects that we actively ignore because they are a distraction to our task at hand are subsequently judged more negatively. This effect, called "distractor devaluation," appears to be mediated by inhibitory attentional processes (Fenske & Raymond, 2006; Gollwitzer et al., 2014). For example, in the initial demonstration of distractor devaluation, Raymond et al., (2003) presented a target and a distractor stimulus on screen and asked participants to determine whether the target appeared on the left or the right. Next they presented the target, the distractor stimulus, or a novel stimulus, by itself, and asked participants to provide an affective rating of the stimulus. Results indicated that the previously ignored distractor was judged more negatively than the target that had been focused on and never-seen-before stimulus. Finally, as we discussed earlier, the work of Damrad-Frye and Laird (1989) demonstrates that stimuli we struggle to focus our attention on become less interesting, and this difficulty in processing appears to give rise to more generalized feelings of boredom. Namely, participants who listened to a recording under conditions of mild distraction reported the highest levels of boredom and the lowest levels of interest in the recording. Damrad-Frye and Laird (1989) argued that participants attributed their inattention to the recording itself rather than to the distraction. Taken together these empirical findings lend support to the idea that attention can precede boredom and interest.

Responding Adaptively to Boredom

A central component to our argument is the idea that in-the-moment state boredom can be adaptive in the learning context if students and educators are able to respond effectively to the signal of boredom that flags when disengagement has already occurred. In this section we review existing empirical research on the topic of coping with boredom in an academic setting.

Nett et al. (2010) developed a self-report boredom coping scale (BCS) based on the idea that students could use approach or avoidance strategies to cope with boredom in the classroom. They proposed that these approach or avoidance responses could be further broken down into cognitive or behavioral strategies. Thus, four strategies were proposed: (1) cognitive approach – in which students attempted to change their perception and value of the situation; (2) cognitive avoidance – in which students tried to distract or entertain themselves with thoughts not associated with their current situation; (3) behavioral approach – in which students took action to modify the learning situation; and (4) behavioral avoidance – in which students took action to avoid the boring situation. Factor analysis of results from grade five to grade ten German students confirmed a four-factor model for this scale. Next, based on participants' responses, Nett and colleagues identified three dominant boredom coping profiles among the research participants: *reappraisers, criticizers,* and *evaders*. Reappraisers preferred a cognitive approach strategy to boredom coping. Criticizers were characterized by a preference for behavioral approach strategies, but also employed cognitive and behavioral avoidance strategies. Finally, the evaders preferred cognitive and behavioral avoidance strategies. These distinct kinds of coping differed in efficacy. In particular, reappraisers reported that they were less frequently bored and experienced more positive emotional, motivational, and cognitive outcomes compared to the criticizers and evaders. The evaders, on the other hand, were the most frequently bored and experienced the least positive emotional, motivational, and cognitive outcomes compared to the other two groups. This highlights the effectiveness of using cognitive approach strategies in coping with boredom.

In a subsequent study, Nett and colleagues (2011) examined whether students' self-reported proneness to using specific boredom coping strategies (traits) predicted the actual use of these strategies when bored in the classroom (state) and whether this, in turn, had an effect on reported levels of state boredom. Individuals who reported a preference for adopting either behavioral avoidance or cognitive approach strategies tended to actually use these strategies when bored in the classroom. Interestingly, those who typically adopt a cognitive approach to tasks tended to do so even when not bored. This suggests that a cognitive approach strategy may be optimal for successful engagement with a task at hand, and may ultimately allow students to *prevent* state boredom.

However, are these results replicable in different cultural contexts? Tze et al. (2013) assessed whether the BCS possessed the same factor structure and psychometric properties when used with samples of Canadian and Chinese university students. Furthermore, they sought to determine whether different academic boredom coping profiles are evident in different cultures. In terms of the utility of the BCS in a Chinese sample, they found mixed support. That is, although a similar four-factor model was an adequate fit to the data (cognitive approach, behavioral approach, cognitive avoidance, behavioral avoidance), the factor loadings were not the same for the Chinese and Canadian samples, suggesting that the coping strategies do not behave in the same manner across different cultural groups. Given this variance, Tze and colleagues were not able to directly compare coping profiles of Chinese and Canadian students. Moreover, the coping profiles observed within the Canadian sample were different than the profiles observed within Nett and colleagues' original sample of German students. Although Tze and colleagues did not replicate previous coping profiles, when considered at the level of coping strategies, they did find that approach strategies were the most effective way to respond to boredom for both Canadian and Chinese students. Taken together, the clear message that emerges is that approach strategies appear to be the most effective way to respond to boredom within the classroom (less clear, but probable, is the conclusion that high levels of avoidance strategies are disadvantageous). Second, although the exact conclusions concerning cultural differences in academic boredom coping are far from clear, there is sufficient evidence to suggest that cross-cultural differences do exist, prompting the need for further research to establish the nature of those differences.

Daniels et al. (2015) approached the question of how students cope with boredom from a different angle. They sought to determine whether there is a relation between boredom coping profiles and students' *beliefs* about what causes boredom in the classroom, as measured by the Precursors to Boredom Scale (PBS; Dashmann et al. 2011). The impetus for this analysis was the notion that different kinds of boredom coping might be employed for different kinds of perceived causes of boredom. Dashmann and colleagues proposed eight different perceived causes of boredom among students: *monotony, lack of meaning, opportunity costs, being over- or under-challenged, lack of involvement, teacher dislike,* and *generalized (trait) boredom.* Daniels and colleagues found that cognitive approach strategies were negatively correlated with perceived causes of boredom, whereas cognitive and behavioral avoidance strategies were positively correlated with perceived causes of boredom. Furthermore, reappraisers reported lower levels of perceived causes of boredom compared to criticizers and evaders; whereas there was no significant difference in levels of the various perceived causes of boredom between the criticizers and evaders. It is not entirely clear how to interpret these findings. Presumably individuals who report fewer or lower levels of various perceived causes of boredom are essentially saying that they do not experience boredom as much as those who report higher levels of perceived causes of boredom. Thus, as in other research reviewed, high levels of cognitive approach strategies and low levels of avoidance strategies are more adaptive; in this case, because they are associated with lower levels of perceived boredom precursors (and thus presumably lower levels of boredom). However, given that the BCS purports to measure how a student copes when experiencing boredom, finding that reappraisers report lower levels of perceived causes of boredom points out the possibility that individuals high in adaptive boredom coping actually experience less boredom. This possibility is bolstered by Nett and colleagues' (2011) finding that levels of trait cognitive approach strategies predicted their use in the classroom even when students were not currently experiencing boredom, and that actual cognitive approach strategies in the classroom were negatively correlated with state boredom. The term "boredom coping," then, might be a misnomer, in that effective coping strategies are in fact addressing the underlying cause of disengagement rather than managing the symptoms or outcomes of disengagement (i.e., boredom).[11] Indeed, the view we take in this chapter is that boredom is a signal that a problem has occurred rather than a cause of problems. This signal can usefully cue students and teachers to engender the state of cognitive approach and minimize the state of avoidance, thereby promoting engaged learning and preventing continued boredom.

Concluding Thoughts

The central, counterintuitive claim of this chapter is that state boredom can be an aid to learning. In this regard, we view boredom as akin to physical pain. It is highly adaptive that we experience pain. In fact, there is a medical condition known as congenital analgesia in which the individual is incapable of feeling pain. People with this condition are at significant risk of injury and death, as they do not have the early warning signal that tells them they need to stop what they are doing and protect their body. Similarly, without boredom, we would lack the early warning signal that tells us we are attentionally disengaged. Boredom is an "in-the-moment" process indicator that learning is not happening. Boredom not only alerts us to the failure of learning, it also informs us that the present learning strategy or context is ineffective and therefore – by the process of elimination – can guide us toward more effective learning. Moreover, because the state of being attentionally disengaged (i.e., bored) is highly aversive, it strongly motivates the learner to *become* engaged. However, just like the individual in pain may seek pain reduction strategies that are counterproductive in the long run, so too the bored student may seek to avoid boredom in ways that further jeopardize learning. Clearly, it is not an easy task to respond adaptively to the boredom signal, and this represents a critically important challenge for students and teachers. The research reviewed here suggests that cognitive approach strategies may be the most effective responses to academic boredom. Further, just because it is adaptive that we experience pain, it does not follow that we ought to seek out or cultivate pain. Again, similarly, we are not claiming that it is a good idea to *facilitate* boredom in the classroom. Rather, we are saying that the concern should not be

11 Notably, an earlier, more general Boredom Coping Scale developed by Hamilton et al. (1984) has been similarly critiqued as actually assessing the propensity to experience boredom rather than skill at dealing with boredom once it occurs (e.g., Eastwood et al., 2007; Vodanovich & Watt, 2016).

the boredom itself, but rather we should seek to remediate the underlying conditions that have elicited boredom. The notion that state boredom can be an aid to learning can be brought into sharper relief if we compare it to two other emotional states that are not conducive to learning; namely, apathy and disgust. A student who is in a state of apathy will not be motivated to change the present circumstances and, thus, is likely to persist in learning situations that are suboptimal. A student who is in a state of disgust will be motivated to escape the present circumstances and, thus, is likely to avoid learning situations that could be beneficial. In contrast, a student who is in a state of boredom is receiving direct feedback about a failure of the learning process and is motivated to eliminate boredom. By employing cognitive approach strategies, students may be able to both halt boredom and improve learning outcomes.

References

Ahmed, W., van der Werf, G., Kuyper, H., & Minnaert, A. (2013). Emotions, self-regulated learning, and achievement in mathematics: A growth curve analysis. *Journal of Educational Psychology*, *105*(1), 150.

Alcaro, A. & Panksepp, J. (2011). The SEEKING mind: Primal neuro-affective substrates for appetitive incentive states and their pathological dynamics in addictions and depression. *Neuroscience & Biobehavioral Reviews*, *35*(9), 1805–20.

Andrews-Hanna, J. R. (2012) The brain's default network and its adaptive role in internal mentation. *Neuroscientist*, *18*, 251–70.

Aupperle, R. L., Melrose, A. J., Francisco, A., Paulus, M. P., & Stein, M. B. (2015). Neural substrates of approach-avoidance conflict decision-making. *Human Brain Mapping*, *36*(2), 449–62.

Barbalet, J. M. (1999). Boredom and social meaning. *The British Journal of Sociology*, *50*(4), 631–46.

Berlyne, D. E. (1960). *Conflict, arousal, and curiosity*. New York, NY: McGraw-Hill Book Company. doi: 10.1037/11164-000.

Berlyne, D. E. (Ed.). (1974). *Studies in the new experimental aesthetics: Steps toward an objective psychology of aesthetic appreciation*. Oxford: Hemisphere.

Bernstein, H. E. (1975). Boredom and the ready-made life. *Social Research*, *42*, 512–37.

Bornstein, R. F. (1989). Exposure and affect: Overview and meta-analysis of research, 1968–1987. *Psychological Bulletin*, *106*(2), 265–89.

Buckner, R. L., Andrews-Hanna, J. R., & Schacter, D. L. (2008) The brain's default network: Anatomy, function, and relevance to disease. *Annals of the New York Academy of Sciences* (*1124*), 1–38.

Carriere, J. S., Cheyne, J. A., & Smilek, D. (2008). Everyday attention lapses and memory failures: The affective consequences of mindlessness. *Consciousness and Cognition*, *17*(3), 835–47.

Christoff, K., Gordon. A. M., Smallwood, J., Smith, R., & Schooler, J. W. (2009). Experience sampling during fMRI reveals default network and executive system contributions to mind-wandering. *Proceedings of the National Academy of Sciences*, *106*(21), 8719–24.

Collette, F. & Van der Linden, M. (2002). Brain imaging of the central executive component of working memory. *Neuroscience & Biobehavioral Reviews*, *26*(2), 105–25.

Craig, A. D. (2009). How do you feel – now? The anterior insula and human awareness. *Nature Reviews Neuroscience*, *10*(1), 59–70.

Dal Mas, D. E. & Wittmann, B. C. (2017). Avoiding boredom: Caudate and insula activity reflects boredom-elicited purchase bias. *Cortex*, *92*, 57–69.

Damrad-Frye, R. & Laird, J. D. (1989). The experience of boredom: The role of the self-perception of attention. *Journal of Personality and Social Psychology*, *57*(2), 315.

Danckert, J. & Merrifield, C. (2016). Boredom, sustained attention and the default mode network. *Experimental Brain Research*, *236*(9), 1–12.

Daniels, L. M., Stupnisky, R. H., Pekrun, R., Haynes, T. L., Perry, R. P., & Newall, N. E. (2009). A longitudinal analysis of achievement goals: From affective antecedents to emotional effects and achievement outcomes. *Journal of Educational Psychology*, *101*(4), 948.

Daniels, L. M., Tze, V. M., & Goetz, T. (2015). Examining boredom: Different causes for different coping profiles. *Learning and Individual Differences*, *37*, 255–61.

Dashmann, E. C., Goetz, T., & Stupnisky, R. H. (2011). Testing the predictors of boredom at school: Development and validation of the precursors to boredom scales. *British Journal of Educational Psychology*, *81*(3), 421–40.

Eastwood, J. D., Cavaliere, C., Fahlman, S. A., & Eastwood, A. E. (2007). A desire for desires: Boredom and its relation to alexithymia. *Personality and Individual Differences*, *42*(6), 1035–45.

Eastwood, J. D., Frischen, A., Fenske, M. J., & Smilek, D. (2012). The unengaged mind defining boredom in terms of attention. *Perspectives on Psychological Science*, *7*(5), 482–95.

Ellis, H. C. & Ashbrook, P. W. (1988). Resource allocation model of the effect of depressed mood states on memory. In K. Fiedler & J. Forgas (Eds.), *Affect, cognition, and social behavior* (pp. 25–43). Toronto: Hogrefe International.

Fahlman, S. A., Mercer-Lynn, K. B., Flora, D. B., & Eastwood, J. D. (2013). Development and validation of the multidimensional state boredom scale. *Assessment*, *20*(1), 68–85.

Fenichel, O. (1953). On the psychology of boredom. In O. Fenichel (Ed.), *The collected papers of Otto Fenichel* (Vol. 1, pp. 292–302). New York, NY: W. W. Norton.

Fenske, M. J. & Raymond, J. E. (2006). Affective influences of selective attention. *Current Directions in Psychological Science*, *15*(6), 312–16.

Fox, E. (1995). Pre-cuing target location reduces interference but not negative priming from visual distractors. *Quarterly Journal of Experimental Psychology*, *48*(1), 26–40.

Fox, K. C., Spreng, R. N., Ellamil, M., Andrews-Hanna, J. R., & Christoff, K. (2015). The wandering brain: Meta-analysis of functional neuroimaging studies of mind-wandering and related spontaneous thought processes. *Neuroimage*, *111*, 611–21.

Goldberg, Y. K., Eastwood, J. D., LaGuardia, J., & Danckert, J. (2011). Boredom: An emotional experience distinct from apathy, anhedonia, or depression. *Journal of Social and Clinical Psychology*, *30*(6), 647–666.

Gollwitzer, P. M., Martiny-Huenger, T., & Oettingen, G. (2014). Affective consequences of intentional action control. *Advances in Motivation Science*, *1*, 49–83.

Greenson, R. R. (1951). Apathetic and agitated boredom. *Psychoanalytic Quarterly*, *20*, 346–7.

Greicius, M. D., Krasnow, B., Reiss, A. L., & Menon, V. (2003). Functional connectivity in the resting brain: a network analysis of the default mode hypothesis. *Proceedings of the National Academy of Sciences*, *100*(1), 253–8.

Hamilton, J. A. (1981). Attention, personality, and the self-regulation of mood: Absorbing interest and boredom. *Progress in Experimental Personality Research*, *10*, 281–315.

Hamilton, J. A., Haier, R. J., & Buchsbaum, M. S. (1984). Intrinsic enjoyment and boredom coping scales: Validation with personality, evoked potential, and attention measures. *Personality and Individual Differences*, *5*(2), 183–93.

Hidi, S. (1990). Interest and its contribution as a mental resource for learning. *Review of Educational Research*, *60*(4), 549–71.

Hunter, A. & Eastwood, J. D. (2016). Does state boredom cause failures of attention? Examining the relations between trait boredom, state boredom, and sustained attention. *Experimental Brain Research*, *236*(9), 1–10.

Klapp, O. E. (1986). *Overload and boredom: Essays on the quality of life in the information society*. Westport, CT: Greenwood Publishing Group.

Knutson, B., Adams, C. M., Fong, G. W., & Hommer, D. (2001). Anticipation of increasing monetary reward selectively recruits nucleus accumbens. *Journal of Neuroscience*, *21*(16), RC159–RC159.

Mason, M. F., Norton, M. I., Van Horn, J. D., Wegner, D. M., Grafton, S. T., & Macrae, C. N. (2007). Wandering minds: the default network and stimulus-independent thought. *Science*, *315*(5810), 393–5.

Menon, V. & Uddin, L. Q. (2010). Saliency, switching, attention, and control: A network model of insula function. *Brain Structure and Function*, *214*(5–6), 655–67.

Merrifield, C. & Danckert, J. (2014). Characterizing the psychophysiological signature of boredom. *Experimental Brain Research*, *232*(2), 481–91.

Miller, W. I. 1997. *The anatomy of disgust*. Cambridge: Harvard University Press.

Nett, U. E., Goetz, T., & Daniels, L. M. (2010). What to do when feeling bored? Students' strategies for coping with boredom. *Learning and Individual Differences*, *20*(6), 626–38.

Nett, U. E., Goetz, T., & Hall, N. C. (2011). Coping with boredom in school: An experience sampling perspective. *Contemporary Educational Psychology*, *36*(1), 49–59.

Nunoi, M. & Yoshikawa, S. (2016). Deep processing makes stimuli more preferable over long durations. *Journal of Cognitive Psychology*, *28*:6, 756–63.

O'Hanlon, J. F. (1981). Boredom: Practical consequences and a theory. *Acta Psychologica*, *49*, 53–82.

Pekrun, R. (2006). The control-value theory of achievement emotions: Assumptions, corollaries, and implications for educational research and practice. *Educational Psychology Review*, *18*(4), 315–41.

Pekrun, R., Elliot, A. J., & Maier, M. A. (2009). Achievement goals and achievement emotions: Testing a model of their joint relations with academic performance. *Journal of Educational Psychology*, *101*(1), 115.

Pekrun, R., Goetz, T., Daniels, L. M., Stupnisky, R. H., & Perry, R. P. (2010). Boredom in achievement settings: Exploring control-value antecedents and performance outcomes of a neglected emotion. *Journal of Educational Psychology*, *102*(3), 531.

Pekrun, R., Hall, N. C., Goetz, T., & Perry, R. P. (2014). Boredom and academic achievement: Testing a model of reciprocal causation. *Journal of Educational Psychology*, *106*(3), 696.

Raymond, J. E., Fenske, M. J., & Tavassoli, N. T. (2003). Selective attention determines emotional responses to novel visual stimuli. *Psychological Science*, *14*(6), 537–42.

Russel, J. A. (1980). A circumplex model of affect. *Journal of Personality and Social Psychology*, *39*, 1161–78.

Renninger, K. A. & Hidi, E. S. (2016). *The Power of interest for motivation and engagement*. New York, NY: Routledge.

Shimojo, S., Simion, C., Shimojo, E., & Scheier, C. (2003). Gaze bias both reflects and influences preference. *Nature Neuroscience*, *6*(12), 1317–22.

Sidlauskaite, J., Wiersema, J. R., Roeyers, H., Krebs, R. M., Vassena, E., Fias, W., ... Sonuga-Barke, E. (2014). Anticipatory processes in brain state switching: Evidence from a novel cued-switching task implicating default mode and salience networks. *NeuroImage*, *98*, 359–65.

Smith, R. P. (1981). Boredom: A review. *Human Factors: The Journal of the Human Factors and Ergonomics Society*, *23*, 329–40.

Strauss, A. & Corbin, J. (1998). *Basics of qualitative research: Techniques and procedures for developing grounded theory* (2nd ed.). Thousand Oaks, CA: Sage.

Thackray, R. I. (1981). The stress of boredom and monotony: A consideration of the evidence. *Psychosomatic Medicine*, *43*(2), 165–76.

Tipper, S. P. (1985). The negative priming effect: Inhibitory priming by ignored objects. *Quarterly Journal of Experimental Psychology*, *37*(4), 571–90.

Tze, V. M., Daniels, L. M., & Klassen, R. M. (2016). Evaluating the relationship between boredom and academic outcomes: A meta-analysis. *Educational Psychology Review*, *28*(1), 119–44.

Tze, V. M., Daniels, L. M., Klassen, R. M., & Li, J. C. H. (2013). Canadian and Chinese university students' approaches to coping with academic boredom. *Learning and Individual Differences*, *23*, 32–43.

Tze, V. M., Klassen, R. M., & Daniels, L. M. (2014). Patterns of boredom and its relationship with perceived autonomy support and engagement. *Contemporary Educational Psychology*, *39*(3), 175–87.

Uddin, L. Q. (2015). Salience processing and insular cortical function and dysfunction. *Nature Reviews Neuroscience*, *16*, 55–61.

Ulrich, M., Keller, J., & Grön, G. (2015). Neural signatures of experimentally induced flow experiences identified in a typical fMRI block design with BOLD imaging. *Social Cognitive and Affective Neuroscience*, *11*(3), 496–507. doi: 10.1093/scan/nsv133.

Ulrich, M., Keller, J., Hoenig, K., Waller, C., & Grön, G. (2014) Neural correlates of experimentally induced flow experiences. *NeuroImage*, *86*, 194–202.

Vodanovich, S. J. & Watt, J. D. (2016). Self-report measures of boredom: An updated review of the literature. *The Journal of Psychology, 150*(2), 196–228.

Vogel-Walcutt, J. J., Fiorella, L., Carper, T., & Schatz, S. (2012). The definition, assessment, and mitigation of state boredom within educational settings: A comprehensive review. *Educational Psychology Review, 24*(1), 89–111.

Weissman, D. H., Roberts, K. C., Visscher, K. M., & Woldorff, M. G. (2006). The neural bases of momentary lapses in attention. *Nature Neuroscience, 9*(7), 971–8.

Yagi, Y., Ikoma, S., & Kikuchi, T. (2009). Attentional modulation of the mere exposure effect. *Journal of Experimental Psychology: Learning, Memory, and Cognition, 35*(6), 1403.

Zajonc, R. B. (1968). Attitudinal effects of mere exposure. *Journal of Personality and Social Psychology, 9*(2, pt. 2), 1.

PART V

Goals and Values

21 Motivated Memory

Integrating Cognitive and Affective Neuroscience

Kimberly S. Chiew and R. Alison Adcock

Abstract: A growing body of literature indicates that motivation can critically shape long-term memory formation in the service of adaptive behavior. In the present chapter, we review recent cognitive neuroscience evidence of motivational influences on memory, with a focus on anatomical pathways by which neuromodulatory networks support encoding-related activity in distinct subregions of the medial temporal lobe. We argue that engagement of distinct neural circuits as a function of motivational context at encoding leads to formation of different memory representations, supporting different patterns of adaptive behavior. We present a novel neurocognitive model, the Interrogative/Imperative *model of information-seeking, to account for pursuit of learning goals. Interrogative or imperative modes of information-seeking are often, but not necessarily, associated with approach or avoidance motivation, respectively. We also discuss additional influences on motivated memory encoding, including intrinsic motivation, curiosity, choice, and cognitive control processes. Taken together, this body of research suggests that the nature of memory representations depends on an individual's neurophysiological response to, rather than extrinsic qualities of, a given motivational manipulation or context at the time of encoding. Finally, we discuss potential applications of these research findings to real-life educational settings and directions for future research.*

Motivation is critical to learning and memory, and there is widespread use of strategies to motivate learning in the classroom, many of which rely on intuition. However, empirical neuroscience research has only recently begun to examine the large repertoire of motivated behaviors and memory processes

This research was supported in part by a postdoctoral fellowship to Kimberly S. Chiew awarded by the Canadian Institutes of Health Research. The content is solely the responsibility of the authors and does not necessarily represent the official views of the Canadian Institutes of Health Research.

central to education, positioning itself to provide evidence-based solutions. Early work in neuroscience focused on relatively simple forms of associative learning. These included Pavlovian stimulus-stimulus learning (where a motivationally significant stimulus is associated with a previously neutral stimulus; for example, the sound of a bell with a food reward) and instrumental stimulus-response learning (where the strength of a behavior is modified by rewarding or punishing consequences; for example, learning to press a button to receive a food reward). Using such models has yielded rich psychology and neuroscience literature on motivation in associative learning. More recently, these investigations have been augmented by new lines of cognitive neuroscience research that address a common intuition among educators: motivation plays a critical role in the way information is learned and encoded into long-term memory.

The recognition that motivational influences can act on long-term memory processing by the medial temporal lobe (MTL) represents an important advance in memory research. Learning and memory over extended timescales (i.e., multiple days or years) is essential to adaptive behavior and cannot be accounted for by the Pavlovian or instrumental associative learning mechanisms historically studied in the context of motivation. In the present chapter, we review emerging cognitive neuroscience evidence regarding motivational effects on learning and memory formation. We discuss several factors important to motivational contexts and their impact on neural activity and cognition, including incentive salience, expectation, extrinsic versus intrinsic motivation, curiosity, and choice. Although this new research area opens many questions, based on present evidence we argue that distinct motivational states serve as adaptive contexts for learning, engaging distinct neural circuitry to support memory encoding and, thus, leading to distinct forms of memory representation. Importantly, present evidence suggests that an individual's neurophysiological response to a motivational manipulation is critical in determining the nature of the encoded memory representation, rather than extrinsic qualities of the incentive. Finally, we discuss the implications of these basic scientific findings regarding motivation and learning in applied settings, such as educational or managerial environments.

Motivation and Memory Encoding: Core Neural and Psychological Substrates

The MTL areas of the brain have long been recognized as critical to the encoding and retrieval of declarative long-term memory (Squire et al., 1991; Tulving & Markowitsch, 1998). The MTL comprises sub-structures that play complementary, yet distinct, roles in these processes; these structures include the hippocampus (and surrounding cortical regions: the perirhinal, parahippocampal, and entorhinal cortices; reviewed in Davachi, 2006). Decades of research in both animal and human models suggest that the hippocampus plays an essential role in binding elements of an episode into an interrelated, multimodal long-term memory (Eichenbaum, 2000; Tulving & Murray, 1985; Tulving, 2002). More recent evidence has refined this account, suggesting that overlying cortical regions represent distinct aspects or features of an episode to be bound together: the perirhinal cortex selectively supports memory for items previously encountered, and the parahippocampal cortex supports memory for the environmental context in which the items were encountered. The hippocampus thus binds item and context memory together to produce a coherent memory episode (Davachi, 2006; Konkel & Cohen, 2009; Ranganath, 2010).

Largely distinct from the research literature investigating the MTL and long-term memory, a separate body of affective neuroscientific research has sought to characterize the modulatory neurotransmitter dopamine and its effects on motivated behavior. Widespread evidence suggests that the mesolimbic and mesocortical dopamine pathways, which primarily originate in the ventral tegmental area (VTA) and associated nuclei in the midbrain and project widely to regions in the limbic system and cerebral cortex, critically support motivated pursuit of a broad range of rewards, such as food and sex (Olds & Milner, 1954; Willner & Scheel-Krüger, 1991). Given the opportunity to directly self-stimulate the VTA (i.e., through a button press), rodents forego other biologically relevant rewards to continue self-stimulation, providing direct evidence for a critical role of the VTA in motivation and reinforcement (Olds & Milner, 1954). Neuroimaging studies in humans, using functional magnetic resonance imaging (fMRI), have likewise observed increased mesolimbic activity during anticipation and pursuit of reward relative to non-reward outcomes, typically using secondary rewards such as money (Carter et al., 2009; Knutson et al., 2005).

Functional relationships between the mesolimbic dopamine system and the MTL are well positioned to support motivated learning. Animal studies have long demonstrated anatomical connectivity between the VTA and hippocampus (Amaral & Cowan, 1980; Samson et al., 1990). Novel stimuli can elicit midbrain dopamine neuron activity, and dopamine released in the hippocampus stabilizes long-term potentiation,[1] supporting learning of new information (reviewed in Lisman & Grace, 2005), including single-trial learning (Neugebauer et al., 2009; O'Carroll et al., 2006; reviewed further in Shohamy & Adcock, 2010).

Despite these findings in learning and memory and the robust link between dopamine and motivation, the potential effects of motivational manipulations on encoding into long-term memory and their supporting neural circuitry have only recently begun to be investigated. Wittmann et al. (2005) examined

---

1 Long-term potentiation refers to a persistent increase in synaptic strength based on recent patterns of neuronal firing at that synapse.

incidental memory (with a three-week delay between encoding and retrieval) for reward predictive and non-reward predictive picture stimuli, and observed a subsequent memory benefit for stimuli that predicted reward over those that did not. The researchers found that this memory benefit was associated with enhanced activity, both in the dopaminergic midbrain and in the hippocampus, at the time of encoding. Likewise, a seminal experiment from our laboratory (Adcock et al., 2006) examined neural activity during memory encoding as a function of a reward incentive manipulation. In contrast to incidental memory encoding in the study by Wittmann and colleagues (2005), participants intentionally encoded picture stimuli in anticipation of receiving monetary incentive (signaled prior to each picture stimulus with a high versus low value reward cue) for successfully remembering each in a recognition test 24 hours later. Recognition memory was superior for stimuli associated with high versus low value cues. Additionally, encoding of high (versus low) value stimuli was associated with enhanced anticipatory activity in the VTA as well as the hippocampus. Importantly, on a trial-by-trial basis, functional connectivity between the VTA and hippocampus at the time of encoding predicted subsequent memory success.

In addition to mesolimbic and MTL regions, research has indicated a role for higher cortical regions in motivated memory encoding. The lateral prefrontal cortex (PFC) is robustly innervated by dopamine (Goldman-Rakic & Friedman, 1991; Sawaguchi & Goldman-Rakic, 1991), may provide informational input to the dopaminergic midbrain to support adaptive behavior (Ballard et al., 2011), and plays a fundamental role in supporting cognitive control processes (Miller & Cohen, 2001); accordingly, recognition of the contributions of such PFC-based control processes to memory encoding is steadily growing (Blumenfeld & Ranganath, 2007; Wang & Morris, 2010). In a recent study from our laboratory, lateral PFC activity and hippocampal connectivity were associated with the encoding of surprising information under reward anticipation (Murty et al., 2016); similarly, PFC and VTA co-activation has been observed during reward-motivated memory encoding (Cohen et al., 2014). Together, these findings indicate a role for PFC-based control processes, potentially as mediators of interactions between neuromodulatory and MTL memory systems, in supporting motivated memory encoding. Neuroanatomical circuitry associated with motivated memory encoding is shown in Figure 21.1.

Taken together, these studies suggest that manipulating motivation through reward anticipation can lead to enhanced encoding and long-term memory via dopaminergic input from the VTA to the hippocampus, with potential modulation via the PFC. Wittmann and colleagues (2005) characterized enhanced memory for reward-signaling stimuli as a function of VTA and hippocampal activity. Adcock and colleagues (2006) observed that anticipatory activity in mesolimbic dopamine system regions – that is, activity elicited prior to the presentation of stimuli to be remembered – predicted enhanced memory. This

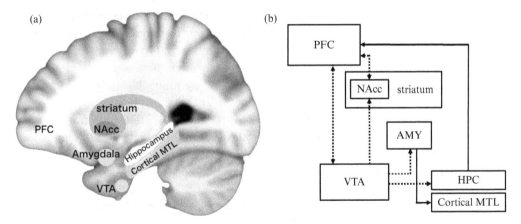

Figure 21.1. *Key neuroanatomical circuitry associated with reward-motivated memory encoding shown in terms of (a) an anatomical schematic and (b) proposed connections between regions. Note that these diagrams are not intended to be comprehensive, but instead highlight key regions and connections for clarity. Mesolimbic dopamine neurons primarily originating in the VTA project widely to limbic and cortical targets (indicated by dashed arrow pathways). Under reward incentive, the hippocampus (HPC) receives dopaminergic input from the VTA and critically supports long-term memory formation. In contrast, under punishment motivation, the amygdala (AMY) is engaged and connects to cortical MTL regions. The VTA also projects to the nucleus accumbens (NAcc), a region within the ventral striatum associated with encoding reward value, and to the PFC, involved in the maintenance of information and control processes critical to memory encoding*

time course of activity parallels psychological conceptualizations of motivation as a sustained state that might enhance learning (Dweck, 1986; Schunk et al., 2014; Utman, 1997), in contrast to prior observations of memory enhancement in response to transient signals of reward, novelty, surprise, or distinctiveness (Parkin, 1997; Tulving & Kroll, 1995). This observation further suggests that a motivational state can serve as an encoding context for memory independent of stimulus features, optimizing memory for different aspects of information depending on the goals that are active at the time of encoding.

Effects of Incentive Valence on Motivated Memory Encoding

Although early studies examining motivational effects on declarative long-term memory primarily manipulated motivation using rewards, the associative learning literature also has a rich history of characterizing the effects of punishments or threats on behavior using both classical (Pavlovian) and instrumental conditioning (Colwill & Rescorla, 1986; Mackintosh, 1983; Rescorla & Wagner, 1972). By emphasizing avoidance of undesired outcomes instead of approach to desired outcomes, threat- or punishment-oriented motivational contexts might differ from reward-oriented motivational contexts in terms of relevant information and adaptive behavior, leading to different learning and memory outcomes. A recent study from our laboratory sought to clarify this issue, investigating episodic memory encoding following the encoding paradigm used in Adcock et al. (2006), but under threat of punishment via electric shock instead of reward incentives (Murty et al., 2012). Recognition memory was enhanced under high versus low threat of punishment, but encoding under these conditions was associated with activity in neural regions distinct from those observed under reward-motivated encoding (e.g., in Adcock et al., 2006). Specifically, Murty and colleagues observed that successful memory encoding under threat of punishment was associated with enhanced anticipatory activity in the amygdala and enhanced connectivity between the amygdala and the parahippocampal and orbitofrontal cortices. This finding contrasts with successful reward-motivated memory encoding, which was instead associated with enhanced VTA activation and VTA-hippocampal connectivity (Adcock et al., 2006; Wittmann et al., 2005). Observed patterns of differential neural engagement associated with reward- versus punishment-motivated encoding are summarized in Figure 21.2.

Given that, as noted above, different substructures within the MTL may support distinct aspects of declarative memory (Davachi, 2006; Eichenbaum

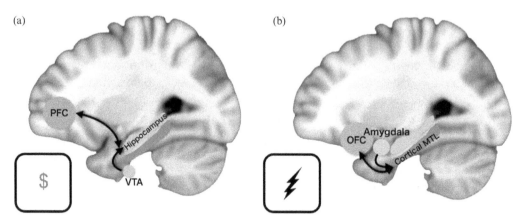

Figure 21.2. *Reward- versus punishment-motivated memory encoding was characterized by differential connections between neuromodulatory centers, MTL regions, and the neocortex. (a) Reward-motivated memory encoding (using money) was associated with enhanced VTA activity and connectivity to the hippocampus (Adcock et al., 2006), as well as enhanced hippocampus–PFC connectivity (Murty et al., 2016). (b) In contrast, under threat of punishment (electric shock), memory encoding was associated with enhanced amygdala activity and connectivity to cortical MTL regions (specifically, parahippocampal cortex; Murty et al., 2012) and cortical MTL–OFC connectivity (Murty et al., 2016).*

et al., 2007), the dissociable patterns of MTL activity observed in association with encoding success under reward- versus punishment-motivated encoding have important downstream implications for the potential nature of the memory representations encoded. The perirhinal and parahippocampal MTL cortices are linked to the encoding of item and context memory, respectively, but are thought to support relatively isolated, unitized representations of this information; in contrast, the hippocampus is thought to critically bind item and context information together into a coherent declarative memory episode. Thus, under punishment-motivated encoding, the absence of enhanced hippocampal engagement (as observed by Murty et al., 2012) means that, although simple recognition may still be enhanced, benefits to relational memory (i.e., dependent on item-context binding) would not be predicted.

Behavioral evidence consistent with this prediction was observed in another recent study from our laboratory (Murty et al., 2011), in which we investigated spatial memory performance under approach versus avoidance motivation using a virtual reality version of the Morris water task, requiring participants to navigate to correct platforms while avoiding incorrect platforms. Participant performance was assessed under reward (monetary incentives) or punishment (threat of electric shock) motivation, relative to a no-incentive baseline condition. We observed that, relative to the baseline, in the reward incentive condition performance improved, but under punishment incentives performance was impaired. Given that Morris task performance depends on relational memory for the platforms and their spatial locations relative to one another – processes that have been robustly linked to hippocampal function (Burgess et al., 2002) – this pattern of performance is consistent with the hypothesis that reward (or approach) motivation might specifically promote hippocampally dependent memory, while punishment (or avoidance) motivation might not.

Beyond Reward and Punishment: Interrogative and Imperative Goal States

Limitations of the Valence Account of Motivated Encoding

Although differences have been observed in neural circuitry and behavioral outcome as a function of motivational valence, it is important to note that objective descriptors of external incentives (i.e., rewards or punishments) alone cannot determine motivational states (Higgins, 1998; Strauman & Wilson, 2010). Beyond goal valence (i.e., approach versus avoidance), factors such as situational context, other characteristics of the extrinsic incentives (i.e., salience) or individual differences may influence the nature of the motivational state evoked, the neural circuitry engaged, and the behavioral outcome elicited. Despite growing recognition of the complex relationships between the valence of external incentives, the motivational states they may elicit, and the corresponding influence on behavior, these complexities have only recently begun to be systematically explored.

One well-characterized example of a putative disconnect between extrinsic incentive, anticipated motivational state, and behavioral outcomes is the phenomenon of "choking under pressure" (Baumeister, 1984; Beilock & Carr, 2001). In contrast to enhanced task performance under incentives, choking is characterized by performing more poorly than expected, given an anxious desire to perform well in a high-reward situation (Beilock & Carr, 2001). Arguably, this pattern of performance might reflect a situation where failing to obtain a high-stakes reward is interpreted as a threat or punishment, leading to a motivational state and behavioral outcome more typically associated with a punishment orientation. This situation and the choking outcome might in turn depend on aspects of the reward (i.e., salience or stakes) and individual variability (i.e., in tendencies toward stress or anxiety).

An important finding from different literature – Murty et al.'s (2011) investigation of reward versus punishment motivation on spatial memory encoding – supports the idea that individual variability may play a critical role in determining motivational outcome. In addition to the main effects of incentive valence previously described, individual variability in physiological arousal during the task, characterized using measures of skin conductance level (SCL), appeared to modulate the effect of motivational incentives on spatial memory performance. Specifically, increased SCL arousal in response to reward incentives was associated with decreased performance, both within and across subjects. In contrast, under punishment incentives, SCL arousal was globally elevated and did not correlate with memory performance. These observations were interpreted as evidence that high arousal could negate or reverse the benefits of reward incentives on spatial memory, and further suggest that any opportunity to gain reward that elicits a high state of physiological arousal might result in paradoxical encoding of memory representations similar to those encoded under threat of punishment.

The Interrogative/Imperative Model of Information-Seeking

Our laboratory proposed the *interrogative/imperative model of information-seeking* to account for the complexities observed in the research reviewed in this chapter's previous section. This model is summarized in Figure 21.3. It goes beyond valenced incentives to consider motivational contexts as adaptive modes of information-seeking; this model thus permits more specific predictions regarding the effects of different motivational contexts on learning and memory (Murty & Adcock, 2017). In part, this model was proposed to address observations that extrinsic incentive structures do not sufficiently characterize motivational states (Higgins, 1998). It asserts that goals can be primarily

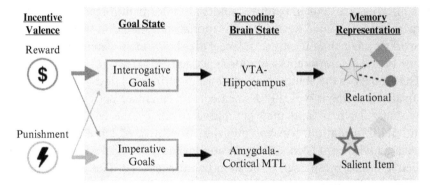

Figure 21.3. *The interrogative/imperative model of information-seeking and its predictions regarding the effects of motivation on MTL-dependent memory. This model predicts that reward- and punishment-valenced incentives generally (but not exclusively) drive interrogative versus imperative information-seeking goal states, respectively. These goal states in turn are associated with the engagement of discrete neural circuits during encoding, including different subregions of the MTL, ultimately leading to the formation of different memory representations. Memories encoded in an interrogative state are predicted to be richly detailed and highly relational, while memories encoded in an imperative state are predicted to be relatively sparse and centered on salient items. From "Distinct medial temporal lobe network states as neural contexts for motivated memory formation," by V. P. Murty and R. A. Adcock, 2017, in D. E. Hannula and M. C. Duff (eds.), The hippocampus from cells to systems, pp. 467–501.*

associated with interrogative or imperative modes of information-seeking. Within this framework, an imperative mode is thought to be elicited when goal states are highly salient, urgent, and unambiguous; information-seeking in this model is thought to be relatively restricted and in the service of immediate goal outcomes, with additional information being of limited utility. In contrast, the interrogative mode is thought to be elicited when goal states are diffuse, low-urgency, or conflicting; this context elicits expansive information-seeking, supporting both immediate and more remote adaptive behavior. As such, the interrogative/imperative model of information-seeking predicts that learning in a high-threat or, more generally, a high-urgency situation tends to be limited, while learning in a low-threat or low-urgency situation might lead to greater exploration and thus improved retention of contextual information. By this account, valence is incompletely predictive, so that the anticipation of reward more often leads to an interrogative state, whereas the threat of punishment typically leads to an imperative state. However, other factors, including incentive salience (discussed in more detail later in the chapter) and individual differences (such as trait anxiety and stress reactivity) may also contribute to the goal state evoked. Ultimately, Murty and Adcock (2017) argue that interrogative and imperative modes of information-seeking reflect the brain systems recruited during a motivational state, and that these modes and networks, rather than incentive valence, are the primary determinants of the nature of the memory representations encoded.

The model has the ability to account for experimental findings that reward-motivated learning is typically associated with enhanced activity in the VTA–hippocampal circuit and may be characterized by the encoding of more relational information, whereas punishment-motivated learning is typically associated with enhanced activity in an amygdala–cortical MTL circuit and is characterized by sparser, more item-based encoding. The model's predictions are also consistent with broader experimental evidence relating differential neural substrates to distinct patterns of motivated, adaptive behavior. In addition to being linked with enhanced declarative memory, activity in the mesolimbic dopamine system has been associated with both motor and cognitive exploratory behaviors (Düzel et al., 2010). This is consistent with the conception of this system as supporting information-seeking in an interrogative mode. In contrast, the central amygdala is thought to play a critical role in mediating physiological arousal and responses to threat, including freezing and inhibitory behaviors (Choi et al., 2010; Davis, 1992) and fear conditioning behaviors (LaBar et al., 1998; LeDoux, 2003). This profile of behavior under threat is associated with restricted information-seeking, consistent with the decreased utility of additional information-seeking in an imperative state.

Open Questions Facing the Interrogative/Imperative Model

Although the interrogative/imperative model of information-seeking can potentially account for a range of empirical observations regarding adaptive memory under different motivational contexts, open questions remain. One currently unresolved aspect of this model concerns *incentive salience*, the extent to which a person perceives a stimulus to be rewarding. Attribution of incentive salience is related to both the sensory representation and the learned significance of a stimulus: making it, for example, an object of desire or "wanting," and associating it with specific behaviors as motivated responses (Berridge, 2007; Berridge & Robinson, 1998). A stimulus must, by definition, have incentive salience to elicit any motivated behavior. High levels of incentive salience would be expected to engender an imperative goal state irrespective of the valence of the incentive. Such high-saliency, imperative goal states have typically been associated with compulsive, inflexible behaviors: for example, those that characterize drug addiction (Everitt et al., 2001; Flagel et al., 2009) and often result in impaired performance, such as "choking under pressure" (Beilock & Carr, 2001; Mobbs et al., 2009). These patterns of behavior in response to highly salient stimuli are consistent with our model's conceptualization of imperative information-seeking.

Neuroanatomical evidence suggests that brain regions assumed to be associated with *both* interrogative and imperative modes are implicated in supporting incentive salience. In rodent models, processing of incentive salience has been associated both with activity in the central amygdala (Mahler & Berridge, 2009, 2012), a critical node of the proposed imperative network, and the mesolimbic dopamine system (Berridge, 2007), which is thought to underlie interrogative information-seeking. Further, these brain regions have been argued to operate synergistically, with the amygdala increasing gain in mesolimbic dopaminergic regions and amplifying incentive salience (Mahler & Berridge, 2012; Phillips et al., 2008). It should be noted that amygdala nuclei are selectively implicated in learning or acquisition of salience. For example, a human neuroimaging study of a high-stakes reward task with over-learned cues showed that "choking" behavior during active avoidance was associated with activation in ventral, dopamine-rich midbrain regions, but not activation in the amygdala (Mobbs et al., 2009). Similarly, during a punishment-motivated memory encoding task (Murty et al., 2012), significant amygdala activity was observed during subsequently remembered versus forgotten trials, but was not observed in analyses collapsing across memory success and failure. This finding suggests that amygdala activation might specifically be associated with successful (but not unsuccessful) motivated memory formation.

An additional open question is the extent to which different modes of information-seeking might be characterized by the interplay of activity in different neuromodulator systems. The midbrain–hippocampal circuit associated with the interrogative mode of information-seeking is primarily innervated by dopamine, but dopaminergic modulation is also associated with punishment processing and avoidance behavior more consistent with an imperative information-seeking mode (Carter et al., 2009; Maia & Frank, 2011; Oleson et al., 2012). It has been proposed that distinct populations of dopamine neurons play different modulatory roles in the adaptive control of behavior (Bromberg-Martin et al., 2010), and such cell-level differences may account for the observed behavioral outcomes. Meanwhile, norepinephrine is a candidate neuromodulator supporting imperative processing, due to its role in arousal and stress response (Aston-Jones & Bloom, 1981; Morilak et al., 2005) and its innervation of the amygdala (Berridge & Waterhouse, 2003). The complex role of the norepinephrine system in higher cognitive processes beyond threat and arousal is increasingly recognized, and norepinephrine may mediate the balance between exploratory and exploitative behaviors (Aston-Jones & Cohen, 2005). Moreover, this system may work in concert with other neuromodulatory systems, including the dopaminergic system, to support adaptive behavior (Briand et al., 2007; Cools, 2008; Verguts & Notebaert, 2009). Thus, it may be proposed that dopamine and norepinephrine interact to regulate interrogative and imperative modes of information-seeking via distinct pathways engaging different MTL subcomponents, leading to differential memory representations. In this conception, the neuromodulatory systems are synergistic;

however, to the degree that memory representations emphasize some aspects of experience, the effects of interrogative versus imperative motivational states on memory may be competitive. Research specifically testing this hypothesis is ongoing, but preliminary data suggest that neural substrates and behavioral elements play overlapping roles in both information-seeking modes.

Having a new framework that relates motives specific to information-seeking to memory formation introduces many questions for future research, and may help account for a broad range of existing empirical observations of motivated behavior and learning in both animal and human models. Importantly, the interrogative/imperative framework clarifies the adaptive value of information under different motivational contexts and makes specific predictions about the nature of the memory representations encoded. For example, it predicts that variation in the urgency or salience of a reward anticipation state (induced via experimental manipulation or considered through examination of trait differences) will lead to increased engagement of the amygdala–cortical MTL circuitry and memory outcomes previously associated with punishment motivation. Further, it is currently unknown whether reward-enhanced versus punishment-impaired relational (spatial) memory performance (as behaviorally observed in Murty, 2011) is associated with activity in VTA–hippocampal and amygdala–cortical MTL circuits, respectively, as has been observed in our other studies of declarative memory encoding under reward and punishment motivation (Adcock et al., 2006; Murty et al., 2012). These issues and others remain to be addressed by ongoing research.

Beyond Extrinsic Incentives: Intrinsic Influences on Motivated Learning

Thus far, our review of motivational influences on declarative learning and memory has primarily focused on experimental work manipulating motivation via the use of extrinsic incentives such as money. In addition to such extrinsic motivators, intrinsic motivation – that is, motivation to volitionally engage in a task for its own sake or satisfaction (Ryan & Deci, 2000) – also serves as an important influence on learning and behavior. While intrinsic motivation is an important construct in the social psychology literature, it has been relatively underexplored in the cognitive neuroscience literature, given the challenges of experimentally manipulating and characterizing intrinsic motivation. Recent studies have begun to address this gap, delineating the cognitive and neural mechanisms supporting intrinsic motivation and its effects on performance, as well as potential interactions between intrinsic and extrinsic motivation.

Neural Characterizations of Intrinsic Motivation

While there are methodological challenges in investigating the neural basis of intrinsic motivation, a number of recent studies have elegantly addressed this question with psychological paradigms amenable to functional neuro-imaging. Murayama and colleagues (Murayama et al., 2010) investigated neural activity associated with the *undermining effect*, a well-characterized interaction between intrinsic and extrinsic motivation, and provided hints regarding the neural basis of intrinsic motivation. The undermining effect is a phenomenon whereby intrinsic motivation tends to decrease after extrinsic rewards have been given and then withdrawn (Deci, 1971; Deci et al., 1999). Murayama and colleagues developed an fMRI-compatible, intrinsically inter-esting "stopwatch" task (requiring participants to stop within 50 milliseconds of a five-second time limit) and examined the effects of a reward incentive manipulation on task engagement and neural activity, both during the first session (with the incentive manipulation) and in a subsequent, no-incentive session. Individuals who had received reward incentives showed decreased task engagement in the subsequent session, consistent with an undermining effect; this change in behavior was accompanied by reduced neural activity in regions associated with value representation and task maintenance (i.e., anterior stria-tum, PFC). Together, this pattern of findings suggests that both extrinsic and intrinsic motivators can engage reward- and task performance-related brain circuitry, but when extrinsic rewards are introduced and then taken away, the intrinsic value associated with task performance (and related neural activation) decreases, undermining behavioral engagement.

A recent study from our laboratory demonstrated a more direct charac-terization and enhancement of the neural activity associated with internally derived motivation of a different sort (MacInnes et al., 2016). Using an inno-vative technique – *cognitive neurostimulation*,[2] or volitional activation of neuromodulatory source nuclei using self-generated thoughts and imagery – together with real-time fMRI feedback from the VTA, we demonstrated that participants were able to learn to volitionally sustain VTA activation via self-generated motivational strategies over the course of an experimen-tal session (shown in Figure 21.4). Importantly, learned VTA activation was not observed in a visual control condition, in a false feedback condition, or in response to feedback from a different dopamine-rich region, the nucleus accumbens. Further, the learned enhancement in VTA activation was accom-panied by increased functional connectivity with the hippocampus, identified previously as a downstream target of mesolimbic dopamine and implicated in motivated memory using studies of extrinsic reward incentive (Adcock et al., 2006; Murty & Adcock, 2014; Wolosin et al., 2012). Taken together, these find-ings suggest that participants who learn to volitionally sustain VTA activity via self-generated motivational strategies could intentionally promote mem-ory encoding via the hippocampus. This neuroanatomical characterization of internally generated motivation is highly analogous to the circuitry identified

---

2 "Cognitive neurostimulation," a term developed by our laboratory and first introduced in MacInnes et al. (2016), refers to the activation of neuromodulatory source nuclei using only thoughts and imagery, without external aids.

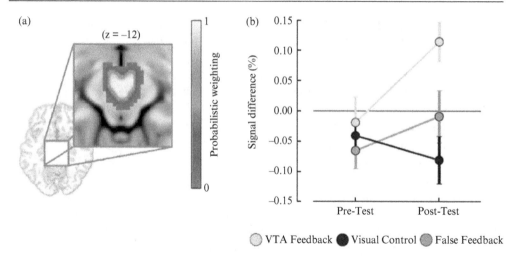

Figure 21.4. *Sustaining VTA activation and VTA feedback. MacInnes and colleagues (2016) demonstrated that participants can learn to volitionally enhance and sustain VTA activation using intrinsic, self-generated motivational strategies and fMRI feedback. (a) Participants up-regulated and received feedback from the VTA, anatomically defined using a probabilistic region of interest (ROI). (b) Following training (pre- to post-test), participants who received VTA feedback were more successful in enhancing VTA activity (in activation versus control trials) than participants who received a visual control, false feedback manipulation or feedback from the nucleus accumbens (for full results, refer to MacInnes et al., 2016). From "Cognitive neurostimulation: Learning to volitionally sustain ventral tegmental area activation," by J. J. MacInnes, K. C. Dickerson, N. Chen, and R. A. Adcock, 2016, Neuron 89(6), pp. 1331–42.*

during reward anticipation under external motivators (Adcock et al., 2006; Wittmann et al., 2005) and holds much promise as a safe, efficient method of enhancing dopaminergic function without the side effects associated with external interventions. Whether the effects of cognitive neurostimulation can enhance learning and memory outcomes similarly to reward-enhanced declarative learning remains to be tested.

Curiosity and Information Search: Intrinsic Motivation to Learn?

Intrinsic motivation to learn can act as a powerful driver of human behavior. Arguably, the most important behaviors supported by intrinsic motivation are learning behaviors dedicated to seeking new information. Although information-seeking behaviors can be deployed in the service of a larger goal, information-seeking can also be experienced as an end in itself – this process has been conceptualized as characteristic of both *curiosity* (Gottlieb et al., 2013) and *interest* (Hidi & Renninger, 2006), constructs that are often referred to interchangeably, but are beginning to be understood as separable[3] (Grossnickle, 2016). Recent work has begun to characterize the concept of information search – the desire to learn what is unknown – in terms of fundamental cognitive and neural mechanisms. These investigations have suggested overlap in the neurocognitive mechanisms supporting extrinsic and intrinsic motivation to learn.

Neuronal recordings in primates indicate that advance informative cueing about upcoming rewards has been associated with phasic activity in the dopaminergic midbrain, including the VTA (Bromberg-Martin & Hikosaka, 2009); this has been interpreted as evidence for the intrinsic motivational value of information. Complementary findings have been observed in the human cognitive neuroscience literature, where neuroimaging studies have identified enhanced mesolimbic dopamine system activity in association with increasing levels of curiosity. In one of the first investigations of curiosity within a neurocognitive perspective (Kang et al., 2009), participants were scanned using fMRI as they read trivia questions and silently guessed the answers. Neural activity associated with questions eliciting high versus low levels of curiosity was contrasted, which revealed that higher levels of curiosity were associated with increased activity within the caudate, a brain region associated with reward anticipation (Delgado et al., 2000, 2003). Additionally, high versus low curiosity during incorrect guesses was associated with enhanced activity in frontal and MTL regions associated with memory encoding. Along with these neural findings, in a separate behavioral study, Kang and colleagues observed enhanced memory for incorrect answers soliciting high versus low curiosity (Kang et al., 2009). Taken together, these findings were interpreted as evidence that curiosity enhances memory for surprising new information via a midbrain–MTL–frontal circuit similar to the dopaminergic circuit previously associated with memory enhancement via external reward incentives.

Additional evidence that curiosity enhances memory via neural circuitry previously associated with the processing of extrinsic rewards was illustrated in a study by Gruber et al. (2014). This study expanded on findings by Kang et al. (2009) in that it investigated neural activity associated with curiosity-related anticipatory states and subsequent memory benefits, both for target stimuli (answers to trivia questions that participants were curious about) and incidental stimuli (faces presented during an anticipatory period between

---

3 The distinction between curiosity and interest has yet to be clearly delineated in the cognitive neuroscience literature, but has been of growing interest in other literature, such as that of educational psychology (as discussed at length in Grossnickle, 2016). Comprehensive discussion of the distinction between curiosity and interest is beyond the scope of the present chapter. Instead, it should be noted that information-seeking as discussed here can be considered characteristic of both curiosity and interest, and that the neuroscience studies described here as investigating curiosity or information-seeking do not explicitly attempt to disentangle these constructs from interest; in neuroscience literature, this empirical distinction has yet to be made.

trivia question and answer). Gruber et al. observed that high versus low curiosity during the anticipation period between question and answer was associated with enhanced activity in the midbrain and nucleus accumbens, regions previously characterized as part of the mesolimbic dopamine system. Notably, memory for incidentally encoded face stimuli was enhanced under high versus low curiosity states; individual variability in curiosity-enhanced memory was associated with anticipatory activity in the midbrain and hippocampus, as well as functional connectivity between these regions (Gruber et al., 2014). This finding parallels a key finding from our laboratory: enhanced memory for stimuli encoded under extrinsic reward incentive is associated with enhanced anticipatory activity in the midbrain and hippocampus, as well as enhanced connectivity between these regions (Adcock et al., 2006). Similar memory benefits and engagement of common neural circuitry in association with encoding under reward anticipation and curiosity anticipation further suggest that extrinsic and intrinsic motivation support learning via common neural mechanisms.

New research from our laboratory (Stanek et al., in preparation) has built upon these observations to develop a more nuanced characterization of brain activity and potential memory enhancement during a state of curiosity. Given findings suggesting that curiosity may benefit memory via similar neural circuitry to reward anticipation, we sought to examine whether curiosity-related benefits to memory could likewise be characterized by sustained, anticipatory neural signal. We developed a curiosity-eliciting trivia-question paradigm similar to that used by Gruber et al. (2014), but different in that it permitted the separation of neural activity during distinct temporal phases of the curiosity signal: cue (i.e., curiosity-eliciting trivia question), anticipation, and outcome (receipt of the answer to the trivia question). Our paradigm also included an action response manipulation to systematically characterize how action might impact motivated learning, given prior research findings that action contingency might enhance striatal activation specifically associated with reward reinforcement processes (Tricomi et al., 2004). This paradigm contrasts with Gruber et al. (2014), whose paradigm required an incidental button-press on each trial to receive the trivia question response.

Using this paradigm, robustly enhanced memory was observed for high versus low curiosity-eliciting information. Memory benefit was also observed for information requiring a response action (versus no response action). Interestingly, the action-related memory benefit was more pronounced for low- versus high-curiosity information, paralleling findings that motivational manipulations such as monetary incentive might benefit memory more for uninteresting versus interesting information (Murayama & Kuhbandner, 2011). In terms of neural findings, high versus low curiosity-eliciting cues led to enhanced activity in mesolimbic reward-processing regions and memory-related MTL regions, as well as in the PFC; activity in many of these regions was also associated with enhanced subsequent memory. These findings are

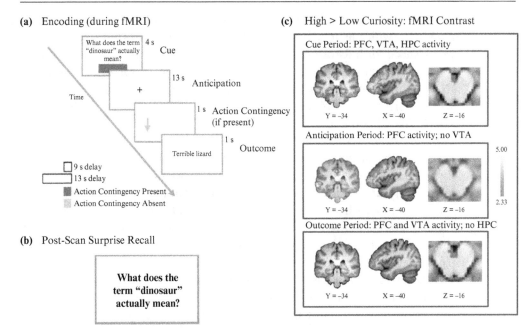

Figure 21.5. *Curiosity-enhanced memory encoding. Stanek et al. (in preparation) characterized brain regions supporting curiosity-enhanced memory encoding using fMRI. (a) A trivia-question paradigm with cue, variable anticipation, and outcome phases and an action-contingency manipulation was used to elicit curiosity for subsequent answers at encoding. (b) Following the encoding phase, participants recalled as many answers as possible to the trivia questions seen during the encoding phase. (c) A robust memory benefit was observed for low- and high-curiosity answers. This was accompanied by enhanced PFC, VTA, and HPC engagement at cue: PFC activity was maintained through anticipation and outcome, VTA activity decreased during the anticipation period and returned during the outcome phase, and HPC engagement decreased at the outcome stage*

summarized in Figure 21.5. Stanek and colleagues' design also dissociated activity at the cue, anticipation, and outcome phases of curiosity: at the time of a curiosity-eliciting cue, the midbrain and hippocampus showed activation related to memory enhancement, but a sustained curiosity signal during the anticipation period prior to outcome was seen primarily in the PFC instead of in the mesolimbic regions. Interestingly, curiosity effects in the PFC were greater for no-action than action trials, paralleling our behavioral results where the enhancement of memory by curiosity was greater in no-action trials.

These studies are just beginning to characterize the neural mechanisms by which intrinsic motivation to learn can lead to enhanced memory, but already suggest an important takeaway point: the neural circuitry engaged during curious anticipation is highly consistent with the neural circuitry elicited during reward anticipation or the interrogative mode of information-seeking.

Additionally, Stanek and colleagues demonstrated that action contingency is associated with memory benefit, and that this benefit might be particularly pronounced for information that is not intrinsically motivating to learn (i.e., low-curiosity information). This result complements prior work suggesting that extrinsic motivational manipulations might benefit memory specifically when information itself is not of intrinsic value (Murayama & Kuhbandner, 2011). These findings converge on action-related recruitment of the dopaminergic and striatal circuits associated with reinforcement (Tricomi et al., 2004) and suggest that the additional utility of action-based approaches to learning, in real-life settings such as the classroom or workplace, is greatest for intrinsically uninteresting information. These findings also raise interesting questions about whether action requirements could have undercutting effects on curiosity, similar to extrinsic rewards. Finally, as noted at the beginning of this section, information-seeking may be driven by both curiosity and interest. These constructs have not been clearly distinguished in the neuroscience literature, despite separation in the educational psychology literature (Grossnickle, 2016); examining whether curiosity and interest are separable in terms of neurobiological substrates also remains to be addressed by future research.

Choice and Control Processes Influence Motivated Memory Encoding

The research described earlier considers motivated action mainly in terms of its interactions with other forms of motivation in shaping learning and memory. However, compared to the passive intake of information, self-driven or active processes are theorized to provide an increasingly wide range of benefits to learning and memory. Much research investigating active learning has been conducted from an educational psychology perspective in classroom settings, as opposed to a fundamental neurocognitive perspective (e.g., Freeman et al., 2014; Hake, 1998). However, the emergence of new research on the cognitive and neural mechanisms of decision processes, including volitional choice and cognitive control, supports the growing recognition that action and memory processes must interact to support the learning and implementation of adaptive, goal-directed behavior.

Effects of Volition and Choice on Memory Encoding

One line of research has investigated the online control of behavior and related brain activity during exploratory learning (Voss et al., 2011a, 2011b) and has shown that the ability to implement volitional control has important effects on subsequent memory. Voss and colleagues developed a novel paradigm that manipulated the extent to which participants could volitionally control object viewing within a stimulus array (i.e., via a "moving window," controlled with a computer mouse, through which stimuli were viewed) presented for a predetermined time period. Volitional control was associated with subsequent memory benefit, as well as with enhanced functional connectivity between the hippocampus (associated with memory encoding) and the PFC and parietal regions (associated with executive control; Voss et al., 2011a). Additionally, Voss and colleagues observed spontaneous adjustments in behavior during exploratory learning, which were associated with hippocampal activity and connectivity with frontocerebellar circuits. Specifically, when exploring a visual array, "spontaneous revisitation" of previously visited objects (i.e., using the moving window, which was participant-controlled with a computer mouse) was associated with enhanced hippocampal activity and subsequent memory for those objects (Voss et al., 2011b). Importantly, amnesic patients with hippocampal damage failed to display volition-related memory benefits (Voss et al., 2011a) and displayed fewer revisitation behaviors than the controls (Voss et al., 2011b). Taken together, these observations in healthy and lesioned participants indicate not only that the hippocampus is essential for learning, but also that the hippocampus communicates with regions associated with executive control to support specific, adaptive behaviors leading to optimal learning under volitional control.

Voss and colleagues' studies elegantly illustrate that agency over learning may offer memory benefits supported by MTL memory systems. However, these studies employed a volitional exploration paradigm that combined multiple potential benefits to memory, including control of study content, order, and timing. In a follow-up study, Markant et al. (2014) systematically manipulated each of these factors using a series of behavioral experiments to pinpoint the specific cognitive mechanisms by which self-directed study leads to enhanced memory. Markant and colleagues observed that the advantage of self-directed over passive learning was present even when volitional control determined only the timing, but not the order or content, of study material. The authors argue that the memory advantage for self-directed study might be related to the ability to match stimulus presentation to the current attentional or preparatory state to optimize learning.

Research investigating the neurobiological basis of this memory advantage suggests that a sense of agency or choice might enhance memory through the same mesolimbic dopamine pathways implicated in reward processing and motivated behavior. Perception of agency or choice has been behaviorally characterized as subjectively rewarding and associated with activity in mesolimbic dopamine regions associated with reward processing, including the caudate and ventral striatum (Leotti & Delgado, 2011; Tricomi et al., 2004). A recent study directly investigated whether the perception of choice was associated with enhanced declarative memory and characterized the neurobiological mechanisms associated with this effect using fMRI (Murty et al., 2015). Participants were presented with two occluded stimuli on each trial and either freely chose to reveal, or were directed to reveal, one of the two stimuli. Importantly, participant choice had no influence on the stimulus content revealed, leading Murty and colleagues to contrast memory behavior and neural activity as a function of perceived choice, in addition to controlling for actual stimulus content. Free choice was associated with robust benefits in memory performance, enhanced anticipatory activity in the striatum, and subsequent connectivity between the striatum and hippocampus during stimulus encoding. These findings were interpreted as a novel observation of the neural mechanisms supporting active learning, but are also consistent with prior observations indicating that engagement of the mesolimbic dopamine system (whether elicited via action contingency or motivational context) and mesolimbic input to the hippocampus can support memory encoding.

Control Processes Influence Task Performance and Memory Encoding

In addition to choice, the implementation of cognitive control itself might impact how information is encoded and represented in memory. As previously noted, PFC-based control processes are recognized to play a contributing role in memory encoding (Blumenfeld & Ranganath, 2007), particularly during self-directed exploration (Voss et al., 2011a). However, direct interactions between controlled task performance and memory encoding are just beginning to be characterized in the research literature. A hallmark of increased cognitive control is increased attention to task-relevant information, which might lead to a benefit for such information in long-term memory (Chun & Turk-Browne, 2007). Consistent with this prediction, a recent study demonstrated enhanced incidental memory for stimuli in a task-switching paradigm that were presented under conditions – including advance preparation time, volitional task switching, and reward incentives – eliciting enhanced top-down control (Richter & Yeung, 2015). Similarly, incidental memory for task-relevant stimuli in a Stroop paradigm was superior for stimuli presented during incongruent versus congruent trials (eliciting higher versus lower control, respectively; Krebs et al., 2015). Functional neuroimaging in the latter study identified a conflict-triggered lateral PFC region predictive of subsequent retrieval success. Further, this PFC region displayed connectivity with hippocampal and parahippocampal MTL regions associated with memory encoding; PFC–MTL functional coupling was stronger during high versus low control (incongruent versus congruent) trials, providing evidence that top-down control might influence subsequent memory via PFC input to MTL regions supporting memory encoding.

As we have argued elsewhere, characterizing the role of motivation in adaptive behavior will require the integration of observations across multiple cognitive domains (Chiew et al., 2016). Recent work has extended the investigation of motivational influences on memory to examine cognitive control-memory interactions as a potential mechanism for these effects. Both control and memory processes are necessary for motivated, adaptive behavior and, although an extensive body of work has characterized the effects of motivational influences on cognitive control and task performance (Botvinick & Braver, 2015; Chiew & Braver, 2013; Cools, 2008), for the most part, this literature has developed separately from research examining the effects of motivation on declarative memory. In an early investigation integrating these questions, Richter and Yeung (2015) used reward incentives to elicit increased top-down control in a task-switching paradigm and examined the effects on subsequent memory for task stimuli. The authors observed that reward-enhanced task performance was associated with enhanced memory for task-relevant stimuli. Although these findings offer exciting preliminary evidence that motivation exerts effects on both controlled task performance and subsequent memory, further work is needed to clarify whether motivational contexts produce these shifts coherently and synergistically in multiple domains. It also remains to be determined whether changes in control-memory interactions differ under rewarding versus punishing motivational contexts, as has been observed separately in both the memory domain (i.e., Murty et al., 2012, 2016; and reviewed here) and the control domain (Braver et al., 2009; Stürmer et al., 2011). In particular, to our knowledge, no existing investigations of the effects of cognitive control on subsequent memory have separately characterized item and relational memory measures. Finally, the effects of punishment or high salience reward incentives on controlled task performance and subsequent memory will inform an integrated account of how motivational context influences these diverse cognitive processes to shape memory.

Developing a coherent account of the role of motivation and cognition across both control and memory domains has important implications for our understanding of goal-directed, adaptive behavior. Cognitive control and learning processes are intimately intertwined: goal pursuit is not only dependent on online performance in the present moment, but also requires that we learn from past situations to inform and refine our adaptive behavior in future. At present, the mechanistic basis of these processes is not well-characterized; thus, considering the role of cognitive control in motivated memory is an exciting new research direction that holds much promise in advancing our understanding of the multiple timescales of adaptive behavior.

Motivated Memory Research: Potential Applications to Real-Life Educational Settings

Taken together, the research findings reviewed in this chapter provide evidence that motivational influences can profoundly affect the nature of memory representations, and that these effects are supported by neuromodulatory input, particularly from the mesolimbic dopaminergic system, to MTL structures involved in memory encoding. Additionally, empirical evidence indicates that motivated learning and memory outcomes depend on a number of factors, including valence, salience, extrinsic incentives, intrinsic curiosity, motor demands, choice, and cognitive control processes. Each of these factors represents a source of variance that can be potentially manipulated to optimize learning and memory in real-life settings such as educational and workplace environments.

The first conclusion we wish to highlight from this research is that different motivational contexts (i.e., rewarding versus punishing) are associated with the encoding of distinct memory representations. Specifically, motivational states that are characterized by high urgency or salience, perception of threat, or anxiety (even if not actually associated with extrinsic punishment incentives) are predicted to promote an imperative mode of information-seeking. This mode of information-seeking may not be optimal for learning in the educational setting: while an imperative mode may lead to enhanced item memory, experimental evidence suggests that this kind of processing may result in suboptimal or even impaired relational memory encoding. Interrogative processing, on the other hand, may enhance relational memory (Murty et al., 2011). Hallmarks of relational memory include its richness of detail and high levels of contextualization; these characteristics support the role of relational memory in conceptual knowledge (Kumaran et al., 2009; Shohamy & Turk-Browne, 2013) and might be critical to both the advancement of knowledge and development of the critical thinking skills that education seeks to foster. Accordingly, educators might consider teaching strategies that encourage an interrogative learning mode while discouraging an imperative learning mode (i.e., minimizing the use of threats or punishments to motivate students, especially with those already tending toward anxiety or those facing high-urgency problems in other domains of their lives).

A second finding emerging from the reviewed research literature with potentially important implications for applied settings is that motivational processes enhancing memory can be anticipatory – in other words, they can be induced ahead of the information to be learned. Benefits of anticipatory motivation have been observed both with extrinsic and intrinsic motivators, such as curiosity, as well as with both intentionally and incidentally encoded stimuli (Adcock et al., 2006; Gruber et al., 2014). Although states of curiosity offer robust benefits to learning (Gruber et al., 2014; Kang et al., 2009; Stanek et al., in preparation), extrinsic motivators can also improve memory when used judiciously, as they may benefit memory for uninteresting material (Murayama & Kuhbandner, 2011). However, extrinsic motivators also have the potential to undermine intrinsic motivation (Murayama et al., 2010); thus, it appears that their use should be aimed at reinforcing beneficial processes like control and attention rather than outcomes. Assessing the application of these findings in naturally occurring educational settings – for example, exploring the potential impact of putting students in a motivated, anticipatory state (using gentle incentives or prizes, sparking curiosity, or using information-incidental manipulations like upbeat music) before presenting new information – should be explored.

A third finding emerging from the reviewed literature is that action and volition might play important roles in enhancing learning and subsequent memory.

Volitional control over a learning context leads to enhanced memory compared to passive intake of information (Markant et al., 2014; Murty et al., 2015), even if the learner does not control information content or order. When considered together with Murayama et al.'s observation that external incentives might boost memory for uninteresting material (Murayama & Kuhbandner, 2011), this observation suggests the potential availability of multiple strategies to help encourage learning when the material itself does not intrinsically appeal. Additionally, evidence from Stanek and colleagues (in preparation) suggests that action might be particularly beneficial to learning for information that is not interesting. Such a strategy would avoid the potential problem, presented by extrinsic rewards, of undermining future learning in the same context, an outcome that remains to be tested experimentally.

Concluding Thoughts

Advances in cognitive neuroscience have allowed us to move beyond intuition and toward a more mechanistic account of how motivation might be beneficial to declarative, long-term learning and memory. A growing body of evidence has characterized the memory representations and neural circuitry associated with encoding under different motivational contexts, with a particular focus on interactions between mesolimbic pathways associated with reward motivational processing and MTL regions supporting memory function. This work has supported the development of theoretical frameworks positing different adaptive learning modes and has generated specific predictions for future research. Additionally, neuroimaging studies have indicated that information search, choice, and volitional action might promote activity in mesolimbic pathways historically associated with reward anticipation and processing, leading to benefits in declarative memory similar to those observed under the influences of extrinsic reward incentives. Finally, given recent evidence suggesting that controlled task performance can influence downstream memory, we point to a need for future research to investigate the effect of motivation on such control-memory interactions. Such work would advance an understanding of goal pursuit, in terms of both present performance and adaptive learning to support future behavior. Although many open questions remain, extant research is rapidly laying a foundation for understanding the biological mechanisms underlying adaptive cognition and behavior, and stands available to inform evidence-based strategies for enhancing learning in educational settings.

References

Adcock, R. A., Thangavel, A., Whitfield-Gabrieli, S., Knutson, B., & Gabrieli, J. D. E. (2006). Reward-motivated learning: Mesolimbic activation precedes memory formation. *Neuron*, *50*(3), 507–17. doi: 10.1016/j.neuron.2006.03.036.

Amaral, D. G. & Cowan, W. M. (1980). Subcortical afferents to the hippocampal formation in the monkey. *The Journal of Comparative Neurology, 189*(4), 573–91. doi: 10.1002/cne.901890402.

Aston-Jones, G. & Bloom, F. E. (1981). Activity of norepinephrine-containing locus coeruleus neurons in behaving rats anticipates fluctuations in the sleep-waking cycle. *Journal of Neuroscience, 1*(8), 876–86.

Aston-Jones, G. & Cohen, J. D. (2005). An integrative theory of locus coeruleus-norepinephrine function: Adaptive gain and optimal performance. *Annual Review of Neuroscience, 28*, 403–50. Retrieved from www.ncbi.nlm.nih.gov/entrez/query.fcgi?cmd=Retrieve&db=PubMed&dopt= Citation&list_uids=16022602.

Ballard, I. C., Murty, V. P., Carter, R. M., MacInnes, J. J., Huettel, S. A., & Adcock, R. A. (2011). Dorsolateral prefrontal cortex drives mesolimbic dopaminergic regions to initiate motivated behavior. *Journal of Neuroscience, 31*(28), 10340–6. doi: 10.1523/JNEUROSCI.0895-11.2011.

Baumeister, R. F. (1984). Choking under pressure: Self-consciousness and paradoxical effects of incentives on skillful performance. *Journal of Personality and Social Psychology, 46*(3), 610–20. Retrieved from www.ncbi.nlm.nih.gov/pubmed/6707866.

Beilock, S. L. & Carr, T. H. (2001). On the fragility of skilled performance: What governs choking under pressure? *Journal of Experimental Psychology: General, 130*(4), 701–25. doi: 10.1037/0096-3445.130.4.701.

Berridge, C. W. & Waterhouse, B. D. (2003). The locus coeruleus-noradrenergic system: Modulation of behavioral state and state-dependent cognitive processes. *Brain Research Reviews, 42*(1), 33–84.

Berridge, K. C. (2007). The debate over dopamine's role in reward: The case for incentive salience. *Psychopharmacology, 191*(3), 391–431. doi: 10.1007/s00213-006-0578-x.

Berridge, K. C. & Robinson, T. E. (1998). What is the role of dopamine in reward: Hedonic impact, reward learning, or incentive salience? *Brain Research Reviews, 28*(3), 309–69. doi: 10.1016/S0165-0173(98)00019-8.

Blumenfeld, R. S. & Ranganath, C. (2007). Prefrontal cortex and long-term memory encoding: An integrative review of findings from neuropsychology and neuroimaging. *The Neuroscientist, 13*(3), 280–91. doi: 10.1177/1073858407299290.

Botvinick, M. & Braver, T. (2015). Motivation and cognitive control: From behavior to neural mechanism. *Annual Review of Psychology, 66*, 83–113. doi: 10.1146/annurev-psych-010814-015044.

Braver, T. S., Paxton, J. L., Locke, H. S., & Barch, D. M. (2009). Flexible neural mechanisms of cognitive control within human prefrontal cortex. *Proceedings of the National Academy of Sciences of the United States of America, 106*(18), 7351–6. Retrieved from www.ncbi.nlm.nih.gov/entrez/query.fcgi?cmd=Retrieve&db=PubMed&dopt=Citation&list_uids=19380750.

Briand, L. A., Gritton, H., Howe, W. M., Young, D. A., & Sarter, M. (2007). Modulators in concert for cognition: Modulator interactions in the prefrontal cortex. *Progress in Neurobiology, 83*(2), 69–91. doi: 10.1016/j.pneurobio.2007.06.007.

Bromberg-Martin, E. S. & Hikosaka, O. (2009). Midbrain dopamine neurons signal preference for advance information about upcoming rewards. *Neuron, 63*(1), 119–26. doi: 10.1016/j.neuron.2009.06.009.

Bromberg-Martin, E. S., Matsumoto, M., & Hikosaka, O. (2010). Dopamine in motivational control: Rewarding, aversive, and alerting. *Neuron, 68*(5), 815–834. doi: 10.1016/j.neuron.2010.11.022.

Burgess, N., Maguire, E. A., & O'Keefe, J. (2002). The human hippocampus and spatial and episodic memory. *Neuron, 35*(4), 625–41.

Carter, R. M., MacInnes, J. J., Huettel, S. A., & Adcock, R. A. (2009). Activation in the VTA and nucleus accumbens increases in anticipation of both gains and losses. *Frontiers in Behavioral Neuroscience, 3*, 21. doi: 10.3389/neuro.08.021.2009.

Chiew, K. S. & Braver, T. S. (2013). Temporal dynamics of motivation-cognitive control interactions revealed by high-resolution pupillometry. *Frontiers in Psychology, 4*, 15. Retrieved from www.ncbi.nlm.nih.gov/entrez/query.fcgi?cmd=Retrieve&db= PubMed&dopt=Citation&list_uids=23372557.

Chiew, K. S., Stanek, J. K., & Adcock, R. A. (2016). Reward anticipation dynamics during cognitive control and episodic encoding: Implications for dopamine. *Frontiers in Human Neuroscience, 10*, 555. doi: 10.3389/fnhum.2016.00555.

Choi, J.-S., Cain, C. K., & LeDoux, J. E. (2010). The role of amygdala nuclei in the expression of auditory signaled two-way active avoidance in rats. *Learning & Memory (Cold Spring Harbor, NY), 17*(3), 139–47. doi: 10.1101/lm.1676610.

Chun, M. M. & Turk-Browne, N. B. (2007). Interactions between attention and memory. *Current Opinion in Neurobiology, 17*(2), 177–84. doi: 10.1016/j.conb.2007.03.005.

Cohen, M. S., Rissman, J., Suthana, N. A., Castel, A. D., & Knowlton, B. J. (2014). Value-based modulation of memory encoding involves strategic engagement of fronto-temporal semantic processing regions. *Cognitive, Affective & Behavioral Neuroscience, 14*(2), 578–92. doi: 10.3758/s13415-014-0275-x.

Colwill, R. M. & Rescorla, R. A. (1986). Associative structures in instrumental learning. *Psychology of Learning and Motivation, 20*, 55–104.

Cools, R. (2008). Role of dopamine in the motivational and cognitive control of behavior. *Neuroscientist, 14*(4), 381–95. doi: 10.1177/1073858408317009.

Davachi, L. (2006). Item, context, and relational episodic encoding in humans. *Current Opinion in Neurobiology, 16*(6), 693–700. doi: 10.1016/j.conb.2006.10.012.

Davis, M. (1992). The role of the amygdala in fear and anxiety. *Annual Review of Neuroscience, 15*(1), 353–75. doi: 10.1146/annurev.ne.15.030192.002033.

Deci, E. L. (1971). Effects of externally mediated rewards on intrinsic motivation. *Journal of Personality and Social Psychology, 18*(1), 105–15. doi: 10.1037/h0030644.

Deci, E. L., Koestner, R., & Ryan, R. M. (1999). A meta-analytic review of experiments examining the effects of extrinsic rewards on intrinsic motivation. *Psychological Bulletin, 125*(6), 627–68. doi: 10.1037/0033-2909.125.6.627.

Delgado, M. R., Locke, H. M., Stenger, V. A., & Fiez, J. A. (2003). Dorsal striatum responses to reward and punishment: Effects of valence and magnitude manipulations. *Cognitive, Affective, & Behavioral Neuroscience, 3*(1), 27–38. doi: 10.3758/CABN.3.1.27.

Delgado, M. R., Nystrom, L. E., Fissell, C., Noll, D. C., & Fiez, J. A. (2000). Tracking the hemodynamic responses to reward and punishment in the striatum. *Journal of Neurophysiology, 84*(6). Retrieved from http://jn.physiology.org/content/84/6/3072.short.

Düzel, E., Bunzeck, N., Guitart-Masip, M., & Düzel, S. (2010). Novelty-related motivation of anticipation and exploration by dopamine (NOMAD): Implications for healthy aging. *Neuroscience & Biobehavioral Reviews*, *34*(5), 660–9. doi: 10.1016/j.neubiorev.2009.08.006.

Dweck, C. S. (1986). Motivational processes affecting learning. *American Psychologist*, *41*(10), 1040–8. doi: 10.1037/0003-066X.41.10.1040.

Eichenbaum, H. (2000). A cortical-hippocampal system for declarative memory. *Nature Reviews Neuroscience*, *1*(1), 41–50.

Eichenbaum, H., Yonelinas, A. P., & Ranganath, C. (2007). The medial temporal lobe and recognition memory. *Annual Review of Neuroscience*, *30*(1), 123–52. doi: 10.1146/annurev.neuro.30.051606.094328.

Everitt, B. J., Dickinson, A., & Robbins, T. W. (2001). The neuropsychological basis of addictive behaviour. *Brain Research Reviews*, *36*(2), 129–38. doi: 10.1016/S0165-0173(01)00088-1.

Flagel, S. B., Akil, H., & Robinson, T. E. (2009). Individual differences in the attribution of incentive salience to reward-related cues: Implications for addiction. *Neuropharmacology*, *56*, 139–48. doi: 10.1016/j.neuropharm.2008.06.027.

Freeman, S., Eddy, S. L., McDonough, M., Smith, M. K., Okoroafor, N., Jordt, H., & Wenderoth, M. P. (2014). Active learning increases student performance in science, engineering, and mathematics. *Proceedings of the National Academy of Sciences*, *111*(23), 8410–15. doi: 10.1073/pnas.1319030111.

Goldman-Rakic, P. S., & Friedman, H. R. (1991). The circuitry of working memory revealed by anatomy and metabolic imaging. In H. S. Levin, H. M. Eisenberg & A. L. Benton (Eds.) *Frontal lobe function and dysfunction* (pp. 72–90). Oxford: Oxford University Press.

Gottlieb, J., Oudeyer, P.-Y., Lopes, M., & Baranes, A. (2013). Information-seeking, curiosity, and attention: Computational and neural mechanisms. *Trends in Cognitive Sciences*, *17*(11), 585–93.

Grossnickle, E. M. (2016). Disentangling curiosity: Dimensionality, definitions, and distinctions from interest in educational contexts. *Educational Psychology Review*, *28*(1), 23–60.

Gruber, M. J., Gelman, B. D., & Ranganath, C. (2014). States of curiosity modulate hippocampus-dependent learning via the dopaminergic circuit. *Neuron*, *84*(2), 486–96. doi: 10.1016/j.neuron.2014.08.060.

Hake, R. R. (1998). Interactive-engagement versus traditional methods: A six-thousand-student survey of mechanics test data for introductory physics courses. *American Journal of Physics*, *66*(1), 64–74.

Hidi, S. & Renninger, K. A. (2006). The four-phase model of interest development. *Educational Psychologist*, *41*(2), 111–27. doi: 10.1207/s15326985ep4102_4.

Higgins, E. T. (1998). *Promotion and prevention: Regulatory focus as A motivational principle* (pp. 1–46). Washington, DC: The National Academy of Sciences. doi: 10.1016/S0065-2601(08)60381-0.

Kang, M. J., Hsu, M., Krajbich, I. M., Loewenstein, G., McClure, S. M., Wang, J. T., & Camerer, C. F. (2009). The wick in the candle of learning: Epistemic curiosity activates reward circuitry and enhances memory. *Psychological Science*, *20*(8), 963–73. doi: 10.1111/j.1467-9280.2009.02402.x.

Knutson, B., Taylor, J., Kaufman, M., Peterson, R., & Glover, G. (2005). Distributed neural representation of expected value. *Journal of Neuroscience*, *25*(19). Retrieved from www.jneurosci.org/content/25/19/4806.short.

Konkel, A. & Cohen, N. J. (2009). Relational memory and the hippocampus: Representations and methods. *Frontiers in Neuroscience, 3*, 23.

Krebs, R. M., Boehler, C. N., De Belder, M., & Egner, T. (2015). Neural conflict–control mechanisms improve memory for target stimuli. *Cerebral Cortex, 25*(3), 833–43. doi: 10.1093/cercor/bht283.

Kumaran, D., Summerfield, J. J., Hassabis, D., & Maguire, E. A. (2009). Tracking the emergence of conceptual knowledge during human decision-making. *Neuron, 63*(6), 889–901. doi: 10.1016/j.neuron.2009.07.030.

LaBar, K. S., Gatenby, J. C., Gore, J. C., LeDoux, J. E., & Phelps, E. A. (1998). Human amygdala activation during conditioned fear acquisition and extinction: A mixed-trial fMRI study. *Neuron, 20*(5), 937–45. doi: 10.1016/S0896-6273(00)80475-4.

LeDoux, J. (2003). The emotional brain, fear, and the amygdala. *Cellular and Molecular Neurobiology, 23*(4/5), 727–38. doi: 10.1023/A:1025048802629.

Leotti, L. A. & Delgado, M. R. (2011). The inherent reward of choice. *Psychological Science, 22*(10), 1310–18. doi: 10.1177/0956797611417005.

Lisman, J. E. & Grace, A. A. (2005). The hippocampal-VTA loop: Controlling the entry of information into long-term memory. *Neuron, 46*(5), 703–13. doi: 10.1016/j.neuron.2005.05.002.

MacInnes, J. J., Dickerson, K. C., Chen, N., & Adcock, R. A. (2016). Cognitive neurostimulation: Learning to volitionally sustain ventral tegmental area activation. *Neuron, 89*(6), 1331–42. doi: 10.1016/j.neuron.2016.02.002.

Mackintosh, N. J. (1983). *Conditioning and associative learning*. Oxford: Clarendon Press.

Mahler, S. V. & Berridge, K. C. (2009). Which cue to "want"? Central amygdala opioid activation enhances and focuses incentive salience on a prepotent reward cue. *The Journal of Neuroscience: The Official Journal of the Society for Neuroscience, 29*(20), 6500–13. doi: 10.1523/JNEUROSCI.3875-08.2009.

Mahler, S. V. & Berridge, K. C. (2012). What and when to "want"? Amygdala-based focusing of incentive salience upon sugar and sex. *Psychopharmacology, 221*(3), 407–26. doi: 10.1007/s00213-011-2588-6.

Maia, T. V. & Frank, M. J. (2011). From reinforcement learning models to psychiatric and neurological disorders. *Nature Neuroscience, 14*(2), 154–62. doi: 10.1038/nn.2723.

Markant, D., DuBrow, S., Davachi, L., & Gureckis, T. M. (2014). Deconstructing the effect of self-directed study on episodic memory. *Memory & Cognition, 42*(8), 1211–24. doi: 10.3758/s13421-014-0435-9.

Miller, E. K. & Cohen, J. D. (2001). An integrative theory of prefrontal cortex function. *Annual Review of Neuroscience, 24*(1), 167–202. doi: 10.1146/annurev.neuro.24.1.167.

Mobbs, D., Hassabis, D., Seymour, B., Marchant, J. L., Weiskopf, N., Dolan, R. J., & Frith, C. D. (2009). Choking on the money: Reward-based performance decrements are associated with midbrain activity. *Psychological Science, 20*(8), 955–62. doi: 10.1111/j.1467-9280.2009.02399.x.

Morilak, D. A., Barrera, G., Echevarria, D. J., Garcia, A. S., Hernandez, A., Ma, S., & Petre, C. O. (2005). Role of brain norepinephrine in the behavioral response to stress. *Progress in Neuro-Psychopharmacology and Biological Psychiatry, 29*(8), 1214–24.

Murayama, K. & Kuhbandner, C. (2011). Money enhances memory consolidation – But only for boring material. *Cognition, 119*(1), 120–4. doi: 10.1016/j.cognition.2011.01.001.

Murayama, K., Matsumoto, M., Izuma, K., & Matsumoto, K. (2010). Neural basis of the undermining effect of monetary reward on intrinsic motivation. *Proceedings of the National Academy of Sciences of the United States of America, 107*(49), 20 911–6. doi: 10.1073/pnas.1013305107.

Murty, V. P. & Adcock, R. A. (2014). Enriched encoding: reward motivation organizes cortical networks for hippocampal detection of unexpected events. *Cerebral Cortex, 24*(8), 2160–8. doi: 10.1093/cercor/bht063.

Murty, V. P. & Adcock, R. A. (2017). Distinct medial temporal lobe network states as neural contexts for motivated memory formation. In D. E. Hannula & M. C. Duff, (Eds.), *The hippocampus from cells to systems* (pp. 467–501). Cold Spring, NY: Springer International Publishing.

Murty, V. P., DuBrow, S., & Davachi, L. (2015). The simple act of choosing influences declarative memory. *Journal of Neuroscience, 35*(16), 6255–64. Retrieved from www.jneurosci.org/content/35/16/6255.short.

Murty, V. P., LaBar, K. S., & Adcock, R. A. (2012). Threat of punishment motivates memory encoding via amygdala, not midbrain, interactions with the medial temporal lobe. *Journal of Neuroscience, 32*(26), 8969–76. Retrieved from www.jneurosci.org/content/32/26/8969.short.

Murty, V. P., LaBar, K. S., & Adcock, R. A. (2016). Distinct medial temporal networks encode surprise during motivation by reward versus punishment. *Neurobiology of Learning and Memory, 134*, 55–64. doi: 10.1016/j.nlm.2016.01.018.

Murty, V. P., LaBar, K. S., Hamilton, D. A., & Adcock, R. A. (2011). Is all motivation good for learning? Dissociable influences of approach and avoidance motivation in declarative memory. *Learning & Memory (Cold Spring Harbor, NY), 18*(11), 712–7. doi: 10.1101/lm.023549.111.

Neugebauer, F., Korz, V., & Frey, J. U. (2009). Modulation of extracellular monoamine transmitter concentrations in the hippocampus after weak and strong tetanization of the perforant path in freely moving rats. *Brain Research, 1273*, 29–38. doi: 10.1016/j.brainres.2009.03.055.

O'Carroll, C. M., Martin, S. J., Sandin, J., Frenguelli, B., & Morris, R. G. M. (2006). Dopaminergic modulation of the persistence of one-trial hippocampus-dependent memory. *Learning & Memory, 13*(6), 760–9. doi: 10.1101/lm.321006.

Olds, J. & Milner, P. (1954). Positive reinforcement produced by electrical stimulation of septal area and other regions of rat brain. *Journal of Comparative and Physiological Psychology, 47*(6), 419–27. doi: 10.1037/h0058775.

Oleson, E. B., Gentry, R. N., Chioma, V. C., & Cheer, J. F. (2012). Subsecond dopamine release in the nucleus accumbens predicts conditioned punishment and its successful avoidance. *Journal of Neuroscience, 32*(42). Retrieved from www.jneurosci.org/content/32/42/14804.short.

Parkin, A. J. (1997). Human memory: Novelty, association and the brain. *Current Biology.* doi: 10.1016/S0960-9822(06)00400-3.

Phillips, A. G., Vacca, G., & Ahn, S. (2008). A top-down perspective on dopamine, motivation and memory. *Pharmacology Biochemistry and Behavior, 90*(2), 236–49.

Ranganath, C. (2010). Binding items and contexts: The cognitive neuroscience of episodic memory. *Current Directions in Psychological Science*, *19*(3), 131–7.

Rescorla, R. A. & Wagner, A. R. (1972). A theory of Pavlovian conditioning: Variations in the effectiveness of reinforcement and nonreinforcement. *Classical Conditioning II: Current Research and Theory*, *2*, 64–99.

Richter, F. R. & Yeung, N. (2015). Corresponding influences of top-down control on task switching and long-term memory. *Quarterly Journal of Experimental Psychology (Hove)*, *68*(6), 1124–47. doi: 10.1080/17470218.2014.976579.

Ryan, R. M. & Deci, E. L. (2000). Intrinsic and extrinsic motivations: Classic definitions and new directions. *Contemporary Educational Psychology*, *25*(1), 54–67. doi: 10.1006/ceps.1999.1020.

Samson, Y., Wu, J. J., Friedman, A. H., & Davis, J. N. (1990). Catecholaminergic innervation of the hippocampus in the cynomolgus monkey. *The Journal of Comparative Neurology*, *298*(2), 250–63. doi: 10.1002/cne.902980209.

Sawaguchi, T. & Goldman-Rakic, P. S. (1991). D1 dopamine receptors in prefrontal cortex: Involvement in working memory. *Science*, *251*(4996), 947–50. Retrieved from www.ncbi.nlm.nih.gov/entrez/query.fcgi?cmd=Retrieve&db=PubMed&dopt=Citation&list_uids=1825731.

Schunk, D. H., Meece, J. L., & Pintrich, P. R. (2014). *Motivation in education: Theory, research, and applications*. London: Pearson Education Limited.

Shohamy, D., & Adcock, R. A. (2010). Dopamine and adaptive memory. *Trends in Cognitive Sciences*, *14*(10), 464–72.

Shohamy, D. & Turk-Browne, N. B. (2013). Mechanisms for widespread hippocampal involvement in cognition. *Journal of Experimental Psychology: General*, *142*(4), 1159–70. doi: 10.1037/a0034461.

Squire, L. R., Zola-Morgan, & Stuart. (1991). The medial temporal lobe memory system. *Science*, *253*(5026). Retrieved from http://search.proquest.com/docview/213549918?pq-origsite=gscholar.

Strauman, T. J. & Wilson, W. A. (2010). Behavioral activation/inhibition and regulatory focus as distinct levels of analysis. In R. H. Hoyle (Ed.), *Handbook of personality and self-regulation* (pp. 447–73). New York, NY: Guilford Press.

Stürmer, B., Nigbur, R., Schacht, A., & Sommer, W. (2011). Reward and punishment effects on error processing and conflict control. *Frontiers in Psychology*, *2*, 335.

Tricomi, E. M., Delgado, M. R., & Fiez, J. A. (2004). Modulation of caudate activity by action contingency. *Neuron*, *41*(2), 281–92. doi: 10.1016/S0896-6273(03)00848-1.

Tulving, E. (2002). Episodic memory: From mind to brain. *Annual Review of Psychology*, *53*(1), 1–25.

Tulving, E. & Kroll, N. (1995). Novelty assessment in the brain and long-term memory encoding. *Psychonomic Bulletin & Review*, *2*(3), 387–90. doi: 10.3758/BF03210977.

Tulving, E. & Markowitsch, H. J. (1998). Episodic and declarative memory: Role of the hippocampus. *Hippocampus*, *8*(3), 198–204. doi: 10.1002/(SICI)1098-1063(1998)8:3<198::AID-HIPO2>3.0.CO;2-G.

Tulving, E. & Murray, D. (1985). Elements of episodic memory. *Canadian Psychology*, *26*(3), 235–8.

Utman, C. H. (1997). Performance effects of motivational state: A meta-analysis. *Personality and Social Psychology Review*, *1*(2), 170–82. doi: 10.1207/s15327957pspr0102_4.

Verguts, T. & Notebaert, W. (2009). Adaptation by binding: A learning account of cognitive control. *Trends in Cognitive Sciences*, *13*(6), 252–257. doi: 10.1016/j. tics.2009.02.007.

Voss, J. L., Gonsalves, B. D., Federmeier, K. D., Tranel, D., & Cohen, N. J. (2011a). Hippocampal brain-network coordination during volitional exploratory behavior enhances learning. *Nature Neuroscience*, *14*(1), 115–20. doi: 10.1038/ nn.2693.

Voss, J. L., Warren, D. E., Gonsalves, B. D., Federmeier, K. D., Tranel, D., & Cohen, N. J. (2011b). Spontaneous revisitation during visual exploration as a link among strategic behavior, learning, and the hippocampus. *Proceedings of the National Academy of Sciences of the United States of America*, *108*(31), E402-9. doi: 10.1073/pnas.1100225108.

Wang, S.-H. & Morris, R. G. M. (2010). Hippocampal-neocortical interactions in memory formation, consolidation, and reconsolidation. *Annual Review of Psychology*, *61*, 49–79.

Willner, P. & Scheel-Krüger, J. (1991). *The mesolimbic dopamine system: From motivation to action*. Wiley Chichester. Washington, DC: The National Academy of Sciences.

Wittmann, B. C., Schott, B. H., Guderian, S., Frey, J. U., Heinze, H.-J., & Düzel, E. (2005). Reward-related fMRI activation of dopaminergic midbrain is associated with enhanced hippocampus-dependent long-term memory formation. *Neuron*, *45*(3), 459–67. doi: 10.1016/j.neuron.2005.01.010.

Wolosin, S. M., Zeithamova, D., & Preston, A. R. (2012). Reward modulation of hippocampal subfield activation during successful associative encoding and retrieval. *Journal of Cognitive Neuroscience*, *24*(7), 1532–47. doi: 10.1162/ jocn_a_00237.

22 Conceptualizing Goals in Motivation and Engagement

Susan Bobbitt Nolen

Abstract: *This chapter describes different approaches to the concept of goals in different theoretical explanations of motivation and engagement, considers their limitations, and points out tensions among explanations. Approaches to understanding goals and motivation have varied considerably. Psychological theories, focusing on individual differences or on the effects of context on individuals, aim to predict the relationship of goals to actions and beliefs across settings. More situated approaches have taken the position that individuals are always in context and that the focus of research should be the activity system or the individual-in-context. Research from this perspective investigates how goals arise within activity systems as individuals interact with people and objects over time. Different approaches have led to differences in research questions and methods. The chapter is organized around metatheoretical questions common to the study of goals across theoretical perspectives, including which goals should be studied and promoted in educational settings, the nature of the relationship between individual and context, and the relation of goals to the meaning of activity.*

Motivation theories are constructed by humans to explain why people do things and to predict their future behavior. Not surprisingly, goals are a major focus of attention in these theories. It is easier to explain someone's behavior (e.g., repetitively hitting small balls with a metal club from the same spot) if you know what the person is trying to accomplish (a longer or more accurate golf shot). Clearly the golfer is focused on improving, but why? One set of explanations involves whether the goal is self-referenced (personal improvement) or other-referenced (becoming a superior golfer relative to others). Even that goal is of limited use in explaining the behavior, however, unless one knows

Thanks to colleagues and students who have contributed to my thinking about goals over the years, especially Ilana S. Horn and Chris Ward. Thanks to Dennis McInerney for helpful comments on an earlier draft.

that long, accurate shots lead to better scores in golf games. The explanation for the behavior comes from knowing something about competitive games, about golf in particular, and about the nature and use of golf ranges – all cultural knowledge of social practices. One could also say that the goal (more accurate or longer shots) arises from the person's participation in the social practice of golf. Other explanations might focus on personality characteristics of the individual (perhaps she is very competitive across most contexts), interests (in the game or in the access it provides to business deals), or beliefs (perhaps she believes that effortful practice will lead to greater competence). There could also be situational factors at play (annual company tournament next weekend). Knowing a person's goal, then, is one piece of the puzzle that is motivation. But only one.

Goals are particularly salient in the study of achievement motivation. The very label "achievement motivation" implies striving for a goal. Murray (1938) defined the need for achievement as striving to accomplish something difficult; rapidly manipulating and organizing people, things, and ideas; overcoming obstacles; and outperforming others or oneself – goals primarily reflecting Western culture's focus on individual merit. In early work on achievement motivation, this undifferentiated cluster of goals was largely unexamined in the psychological literature until goal theorists began to posit that different goals or definitions of success (achievement) led to different strategies, responses to failure, and satisfaction with learning. Work in this area, which became known collectively as achievement goal theory, maintained a focus on individual cognition as the driver of behavior, with social context theorized as sets of variables that might influence those cognitions (Ames, 1992; Anderman & Maehr, 1994; Maehr & Midgley, 1991). For example, the TARGET framework has emphasized the role of tasks, authority, recognition, grouping, evaluation, and time (Lüftenegger et al., 2014).

Sociocultural approaches, such as situative theory or cultural-historical activity theory, consider the phenomenon of motivated action from a different angle. Individuals are not theoretically separated from contexts, but are considered as part of activity systems, along with other people and the material, conceptual, and behavioral aspects of social practice. Goals arise through participation in social practice. In the golf example, the goal of longer or more accurate shots makes sense only in the context of the social practice of the game. Our understanding of the individual's motive for hitting golf balls at the range would also be informed by knowing who she participates with, their relationships, and the extent to which a certain level of expertise is important to individuals' identity within and beyond the group. For a member of a competitive golf team who is striving to become a professional golfer, the meaning and object of the activity, along with the level of engagement, would be different than for the weekend recreational player. Identity, power relations among individuals, individual and collective agency, emotional relations, and the relationship of the local activity system to other activity systems to which it is related (or in which it is embedded) all contribute to a situated understanding of motive.

In school settings, as in sport, goals may be conceptualized as individual phenomena or as situated in social practice. A child learning to read and write, for example, could be characterized as mastery-oriented, if focused on personal improvement in skill, or performance-oriented, if concerned about relative performance in reading or writing tasks relative to peers. Understanding how and why the child takes this approach can be enhanced by knowing how skilled reading and writing are defined and enacted in the child's class or school or by how literacy skill is related to social status and identity within the class or at home (Nolen, 2007). In this chapter, I will describe different approaches to the concept of goals in different theoretical explanations of motivation and engagement, consider their limitations, and point out tensions between explanations.

Which Goals?

An enduring question among motivation researchers has been to identify the particular goals most involved in having a motivation to learn. Most of this work has been conducted by those taking an achievement goal theory approach. This approach, as applied to educational settings, emerged from conversations among several theorists – including John Nicholls, Carol Dweck, Marty Maehr, Carole Ames, and Glynn Roberts – in the late 1970s at the University of Illinois. They divided then-current aspects of achievement motivation, based on the work of Murray and Atkinson (Atkinson & Litwin, 1960; Atkinson & Raphelson, 1956; Atkinson & Reitman, 1956; Murray, 1938, 1943), into two goals, intentions, or reasons for learning: (1) the goal of learning new things, mastery, performing one's best, or improving skill (variously labeled task, mastery, or learning goals) and (2) the goal of demonstrating or establishing high ability (variously labeled ego, performance, or ability goals and defined with or without reference to normative ability). Over time, the definitions of each goal were refined and narrowed to improve theoretical clarity and to enable more reliable and valid measures of the individual constructs. The measures used by Elliott and his colleagues (Elliot et al., 2011) are an example of this narrowing, where a task orientation is defined as striving for correct answers or an improved score on an exam.[1]

---

1 The use of the word "goal" in psychological theories is a bit slippery. One might have a particular goal or outcome in mind in a particular situation (e.g., I want to improve my understanding of the concept of attachment), but motivation psychologists also focus on general approaches or ways of thinking about learning situations, often called "goal orientations" or "orientations," but just as often shortened to "goals" (e.g., in my classes, I aim to understand as much material as possible). This can be confusing to individual readers as well as leading to theoretical fuzziness (D. McInerney, personal communication, March 28, 2017). This ambiguity is, in part, a result of attempts by psychologists to describe ways of thinking about learning situations (orientations) as individual differences or traits. Another possibility would be to consider

The original theorists ultimately went their separate ways, and their theories developed along somewhat different pathways. Differences included whether the two kinds of goals were generally uncorrelated dimensions of achievement or a typology of persons or contexts, whether or not definitions of success varied, and whether demonstration of ability was important to both kinds of goals or only to performance goals (Senko et al., 2011). Other researchers (e.g., Joan Duda [Duda, 1995], Andrew Elliot [Elliot & Harackiewicz, 1996], and Paul Pintrich [Pintrich et al., 1998]) took up the ideas and developed them further, exploring approach-avoidance contrasts and creating trichotomous, or even "quadchotomous" versions of the theory (Elliot et al., 2011). Throughout, however, the goals studied were variations on the original theme.

Other theorists have questioned this narrow focus as failing to capture important information about the variety of goals related to learning and their interaction (e.g., Boekaerts et al., 2006; King & McInerney, 2014; Mansfield, 2012; Wentzel, 1996). Theories are cultural products, and the focus on mastery and performance goals has been associated with Western, educated, industrial, rich, and democratic (WEIRD) societies (King & McInerney, 2014). Cross-cultural research has aimed to test the universality of these and other possible achievement goals (King et al., 2014; King & McInerney, 2014; McInerney et al., 1997; Zusho & Clayton, 2011) and, along with interview and open-ended survey studies (Lee & Bong, 2016; Urdan & Mestas, 2006), has explored their definitions, salience, and relationships in different populations.

Wentzel (2000) argued that goals can be conceptualized along several dimensions, including their content, achievement orientation, proximity, or difficulty. Wentzel and others have argued that goal contents are important to understand, because not all goals for learning are related to school achievement as it is usually defined. Learners may engage in learning activities in order to adhere to rules or conform, to help others, to have fun, or to gain access to further education or employment (Mansfield, 2012). Students often pursue multiple goals in school, but understanding how these goals synergize or conflict in particular contexts has received little attention in the psychological literature (Boekaerts et al., 2006).

To understand this multiplicity of goals, some authors have hypothesized a hierarchical structure, with the upper levels populated by more general, long-term, or ideal goals and the lower levels by context-specific action plans or short-term goals (Carver & Scheier, 2000; Lee & Bong, 2016; Michou et al., 2014). Lee and Bong (2016) used open-ended survey responses to obtain more emic views of goals among Korean middle schoolers. They reported

---

the goals set in particular situations as belonging to different categories (e.g., in Algebra class, I try to understand as much as possible, but in psychology, I just want to get a good grade).

both situational and societal influences. Distal goals reflected norms of Korean society, where education is seen as a means to life success; social status goals were by far the most prevalent. But "When describing their more immediate achievement goals, the students responded that they studied to gain knowledge; to improve ability; and because it was useful, interesting, and satisfying" (p. 290). As in previous studies using methods other than forced-choice surveys, performance and social status goals were rare. The proximal-distal dimension is an important distinction often ignored in studies of achievement goals, although (in earlier work) immediate, situated goals have been found to predict achievement behavior better than more general goals (Nolen, 1988).

Others have proposed a more phenomenological approach, where the hierarchies are individual causal beliefs (e.g., if I am good at reading, I will have more friends) rather than goals (Wentzel, 2000). In this view, contextual factors might emphasize one version of causality or another, and students might adopt these beliefs, influencing the goals they set.

Which Goals Should Educators Encourage?

Once a set of goals for achievement or learning are identified, the question naturally arises regarding which goals are the most beneficial for learning. Although most correlational studies have found positive effects on interest, satisfaction with learning, and continuing motivation for task or mastery orientations, achievement goal theorists have spent considerable time debating the value of performance-approach goals (seeking to perform better than others or establish high relative ability). Some evidence from a series of longitudinal studies of college undergraduates found that mastery goals positively predicted interest and persistence in the major, but performance goals predicted positive effects on achievement (Harackiewicz et al., 1997, 1998). Other studies have suggested that having both mastery and performance goals seemed optimum, at least in college undergraduates: the so-called "multiple goal" hypothesis (Senko et al., 2011).

But it is one thing to *have* both kinds of goal, and another to try to induce them. Other theorists have warned against promoting performance goals in educational settings, citing their roots in normative achievement and suggesting that they create motivational winners and losers (Kaplan & Middleton, 2002; Midgley et al., 2001). Not everyone can be above average. Indeed, a consistent finding has been that classrooms emphasizing relative performance are associated with lower motivation to learn and, sometimes, with lower achievement (Butler, 1987, 2006; Covington & Omelich, 1984; Linnenbrink, 2005). These studies and recommendations assume particular relationships between individuals and contexts, which I take up in the next section.

The Roles of the Individual and Context, or "Where Do Goals Reside?"

Goals as Individual Differences

Socio-cognitive theories like those described above assume that goals are properties of individuals. Some theories postulate that individuals have stable, general orientations to learning that they employ across settings. Countless studies have employed correlational designs using self-report (mostly survey) data to examine the relationships among various goals, and between goals and other outcomes, with the individual as the unit of analysis. When groups have been studied, students' perceptions of their learning contexts have been averaged across units, usually classrooms. Although some studies have focused on specific classes or subject areas, many have used broadly worded instruments, asking students for generalizations about their goals "in school." Some researchers have attempted to identify goal profiles based on the levels of various goals. In this body of work, the assumption is that goals are in students' heads and that they resemble stable personality traits.

Little is known about how goals arise in people's heads. Some studies have investigated the role of parents and schools as "socializing agents." Usually these studies analyze surveys of students' perceptions of parent goals (e.g., Gonida & Cortina, 2014; Kim et al., 2010; Luo et al., 2013; Vedder-Weiss & Fortus, 2013) or teacher goals or behavior (Lüftenegger et al., 2014; Nolen, 2003). Most of these studies have used the individual as the unit of analysis, ignoring possible impacts of clustering on results in classroom settings (for exceptions, see Nolen, 2003; Thorkildsen & Nicholls, 1998). Results have been similar to other survey studies of goals, with relatively small amounts of variance in motivation accounted for by perceptions of teacher behavior or goals.

Cultural differences and similarities. A number of researchers have investigated the universality of goals across cultures, within and between countries. These studies have ranged from administering (sometimes) translated forms of standard measures of goal orientation to people in different cultural groups and then comparing various forms of invariance across groups. Zusho and Clayton (2011) and King and McInerney (2014) have provided extensive theoretical and methodological reviews of this work, which I will not replicate here. It is worth noting, however, that both sets of researchers argue for a universalist metatheory in which it is assumed that there are core motivational processes in all humans that are, nonetheless, acted upon by culture to produce somewhat different results. The most careful and extensive work to date using a goal theory is that of Dennis McInerney and his colleagues (e.g., Ali et al., 2014; Magson et al., 2014; McInerney, 2008; McInerney & Ali, 2013; McInerney et al., 1997, 1998; Nelson et al., 2006). They have systematically used etic methods (from the perspective of an outsider to a group) and emic methods (seeking the perspective of an insider) together to develop and test a hierarchical theory of goals, across a variety of Western (or colonial) and Indigenous groups, in both urban and remote settings. They have found, in large part, structural invariance across these groups in measures of a variety of goals that support the proposed hierarchical structure. Furthermore, the motivational profiles of Indigenous and non-Indigenous groups are strikingly similar. From a scientific, universalist perspective this is heartening. However, as McInerney (2003) argues, it remains to be explained why, if motivation is so similar across groups, some groups perform better academically than others, and why some individuals in historically under-performing groups nonetheless perform well. He goes on to suggest that historic and present racism, structural inequality in educational opportunity, and other factors may moderate the impact of individual goals on achievement.

Context Influences Goals

The role of context in studies of goals for learning has usually been assumed to be stable and unidirectional. That is, context (as a set of variables) is presumed to influence students' goals in stable and predictable ways. In educational settings, teachers' actions or practices (often assessed via self-report) are a usual target of investigation. Researchers have described learning-oriented classrooms as sharing certain characteristics hypothesized to promote mastery goals (e.g., meaningful tasks, tolerance of mistakes, cooperative learning, pressing for understanding). Classrooms in which teachers emphasize relative performance, competition, correct answers are predicted to either lead to performance avoidance or academic alienation. In these studies, perceptions of these contextual variables are measured via self-report along with individual goals, and correlations among them are tested based on the assumption that context influences motivation. Lüftenegger and colleagues (2014), for example, used structural equation modeling to investigate how students' perceptions of the learning climate impact mastery motivation. Using a scale based on Ames' (1992) TARGET framework, the researchers found small but significant positive relationships between perceptions of the classroom goal structure and students' mastery motivation nine months later. In a study using growth curve modeling to investigate the impact of a learning-focused summer program on mastery and performance orientation in and after the program, O'Keefe et al. (2013) found similar small but significant impacts.

These common research designs and measurement choices may explain why, despite careful and exacting research on the nature and behavior of the specific variables in goal theories, the proportion of variance explained in important outcomes remains fairly small. Further, the implications for educational practice of socio-cognitive research on goals remain what they were at the beginning: foster a mastery, learning, and task orientation in classrooms and do not highlight performance differences (Ames & Ames, 1984; Nicholls & Burton, 1982; Park et al., 2016; Senko & Tropiano, 2016).

However, little work has explored the processes involved in fostering a mastery orientation. Park et al. (2016) found that teachers who reported using practices assumed to foster a performance-oriented climate in primary grades classrooms had negative effects on student learning, but that teachers who reported fostering a mastery-oriented climate did not have the opposite effect. A number of descriptive dimensions of learning-focused classrooms have been put forth – from supporting autonomy to treating mistakes as a natural part of learning to making classroom work more meaningful for students. But how those characteristics might operate on motivation, and what factors can interfere with positive outcomes, have yet to be explored. In a descriptive study using hierarchical linear modeling to account for cluster effects, Nolen (2003) found that the shared perception of a learning-oriented classroom including many recommended characteristics predicted a substantial portion of between-class differences in science achievement but only a small proportion of variance in task orientation. Intervention research has been similarly unable to make a convincing link between context and task or mastery motivation. In a critique of a recent special section on using socio-cognitive interventions to increase motivation, Schwartz et al. (2016) called for the collection of process data between intervention and measures of its impact to uncover the mechanisms that explain both why an intervention worked for some students and why it did not work for others. Careful classroom observation studies of the link between teacher practices and student goals, as in the work of Julianne Turner and her colleagues (Meyer et al., 1997; Turner, 1995; Turner et al., 2011), remain rare.

Situative and Sociocultural Approaches: Learner-in-Context

Another way to conceptualize relations between the individual and the context is that they are part of the same unit. That is, individuals are always embedded in a context, and individuals and contexts co-develop through interaction. In this view, learners, teachers, material and conceptual resources, relationships, and identities are all part of systems of activity. This co-constitutive relationship makes it difficult to conceptualize goals as a property of individual cognition. Rather, goals and other motives arise through interaction in and between activity systems. The goals of the golfer practicing her swing at the range are understood not as residing in the head of the golfer, but in the relation of the golfer to the social activity of golfing and the golfer's identity within the local practice of that activity. Consider three golfers practicing side-by-side. Suppose all are trying to improve their distance and accuracy over their previous levels. An achievement goal theorist might describe them all as having a mastery-approach goal that is self-referenced. However, one golfer is an occasional, recreational golfer getting ready for a game with friends, one plays weekly in a league with the same group of acquaintances, and the third is a member of a competitive golf team hoping to improve enough to become a professional golfer. The reason for their practice is thus embedded in the contexts of play, in relation to their identities as golfers, given how central or peripheral being a golfer is to their sense of self and the relationship of their skill level to membership in the group.

In a situative approach, the relationship of the motivated activity to the person's identity in a particular context is an important contributor to both the nature and strength of their goals. Drawing on social theories (e.g., Holland, 2010; Holland et al., 1998; Holland & Lave, 2001; Wenger, 1998), identities are seen as co-constructed through interaction in social contexts. Both narrative identity (a person's own concept of self) and positional identity (an individual's position within a social context) are important in an understanding of goals. In a longitudinal study of novice teachers (Horn et al., 2008; Nolen et al., 2009, 2011), we found that individual learning goals were particular to their contexts, and to their positional identities or desired identities in those contexts. When a particular teaching strategy was seen as central to the practice in a particular department, for example, and a novice wished to be seen as a full member of that department, she might set a goal to master the strategy as a means to membership. She might also be willing to set a provisional mastery goal if someone with whom she identified (a trusted mentor, for example) promoted that practice, suspending her initial disbelief in its utility. Goals might also arise from the individual's narrative identity. Novice teachers in our study cast most decisions about their goals for learning teaching practices in terms of becoming "the kind of teacher" they wanted to be. This, in turn, was informed by their developing sense of the teacher's role, their conception of good teaching, and their sense of their own knowledge gaps. Those conceptions were co-developed with others through interaction in classes, field experiences, and ultimately in the schools where they found employment after graduation (Horn et al., 2008; Nolen et al., 2009).

Identity, then, is continually negotiated in social context. But the contexts themselves are also continually changing through those interactions (Hand & Gresalfi, 2015; Hickey & Granade, 2004; Horn, 2005). In an intervention study of experienced teachers, Turner and her colleagues (2011) describe both individual change in practice and a change in what was considered normal practice in teaching middle school math within that department. Teachers renegotiated both their teacher identities and their community practices through interactions with students and in sense-making discussions with colleagues and the researchers. Goals evolved throughout the year-long intervention as some teachers' visions of possible teaching selves evolved.

Goals and the Meaning of Activity

Goals imply valued end states that require certain actions for their accomplishment. Thus, goals not only provide impetus but also meaning to activity. In the example of three golfers practicing at the golf range, the nature of the learning goal (enable participation in the social activity of the weekly golf league, become a professional golfer) imbues the activity of range practice with more or less importance, leading perhaps to differences in time invested, the intensity or extensiveness of the practice, whether the golfer seeks the assistance of a coach, and so on. This is an individual analysis of the relationship between goals and motivation from an individual or psychological perspective, involving both issues of timescale and the contents and individual value of the goal.

Timescale and the Meaning of Activity

Goals entail imagining the future. Timescale thus becomes an additional facet of goals with implications for motivation. Early experimental work on goal-setting compared proximal goals with distal goals, finding the former increased motivation and self-efficacy in initially amotivated students (Bandura & Schunk, 1981). These findings have been replicated and extended to other populations and settings. Proximal goals are theorized to provide more clearly attainable targets leading to clearer progress feedback, both of which should support increased self-efficacy and motivation. Other researchers have taken an individual-difference approach to timescale, characterizing the ability to focus on more distal goals as a personality trait (future time perspective) linked to increased motivation to learn (Lens et al., 2012; Schuitema et al., 2014). The ability to clearly imagine distal goals (e.g., becoming a professional golfer), along with the links between more proximal goals and the distal goal, provides a context for the meaning of present activity. Although this means that proximal goals are seen as instrumental to the end goal, motivational effects are greatest when the end goals themselves are intrinsic and highly valued (Lee et al., 2010; Vansteenkiste et al., 2008). The ability to imagine connections between valued future goals or identities and current activity provides a person-centered set of meanings for that activity.

Meaning of Activity as Socially Constructed

A sociocultural or situative analysis looks beyond individual goals and values for the meaning of motivated activity. From this perspective, an understanding of why people set certain short- and long-term goals is built on knowledge of societal and local value systems, as well as on the person's identities within those systems. As important are the local meanings of certain kinds of participation, given the individual's narrative and positional identity within a local activity system or community of practice. I once was asked to help discover what was motivating a low-status student to become increasingly disruptive, with behaviors leading to banishment from certain areas and, ultimately, suspension from school. Observation revealed that his "disruptive" behaviors were almost identical to the joking behavior of a very popular student. In fact, he appeared to be imitating that student as a strategy aimed at the goal of gaining popularity. For the teacher and other students, those same joking behaviors had different meanings: disruptive (and punishable) when performed by the low-status student and entertaining (and rewarded through laughter and smiles) when performed by the high-status student. Understanding the low-status student's goals (and intervening appropriately in the situation) depended on understanding the local meaning of his behaviors and his position in the social system of the classroom.

Understanding teachers' motives to learn or reject new practices provides another example of the utility of a situative analysis of goals. Take the goal of learning to conduct the discussion practice known as Socratic seminar in a high school history class. For a practicing teacher, this goal may be motivated by curriculum mandates (extrinsic), a desire to support students' critical reading of texts (instrumental, valued goal), or the teacher's personal enjoyment of discussion (intrinsic). For a *student* teacher, the proximal goal may be to master a particular teaching practice; this may, in turn, be seen as a step along a path to the long-term goal of becoming a good history teacher (a mastery goal leading to a future identity). Thus far, the explanations rest on individual interests and values. The meaning of the activity (conducting Socratic seminars), however, is also a function of the social context (a high school history department) and the individual's position in it. The practicing teacher likely has some authority to conduct classroom activities as he sees fit, but is held accountable to parents and administrators for fulfilling their goals for student learning. The student teacher is a guest in someone else's classroom, in a department with its own history and norms. If discussion-based practice runs counter to prevailing instructional norms, students might be reluctant to participate, leading the student teacher to doubt her skill or the worth of the practice. Using Socratic seminar itself could be interpreted (by the supervising teacher) as disruptive, the attempt as rebellious, and the student teacher as unprofessional. At the same time, the student teacher's university instructors might promote Socratic seminar as a valuable strategy and urge her to try again. In this case, how are we to understand the student teacher's motives and goals? Clearly her motivation to persist in mastering the practice will depend on a number of factors, including her positionality in both university and field placement, her understanding of the practice, her ongoing relationship with the supervising teacher and the students, and the perceived risks and benefits of persistence. Focusing only on the nature of the goal (mastery) without understanding the (multiple) contexts of activity misses much that could explain her behavior.

Complicating the analysis further, local meanings are not static but evolve over time through the interactions of the individuals in the setting and in relation to larger societal contexts. Supervising teachers' views of particular practices might change as they watch student teachers successfully engaging students in new ways, for example, leading to changes in the mentor–novice relationships and a more collaborative approach to learning new practices. In the same context, different activities with different social contracts can change the meaning of activity and highlight particular goals. Children as young as five, for example, can differentiate between competitions (e.g., a spelling bee) and learning activities in a classroom (Thorkildsen, 1989), and the appropriateness of competition versus cooperation in each. In individual competition, a goal of winning or performing better than others is appropriate to the social context. In a learning activity, a goal of understanding or improving is more desirable. At the same time, if the learning activity has little meaning or interest for participants, as in the traditional math instruction settings described by Boaler and Greeno (2000), students may instead seek to limit effort and investment.

Differences in Meaning Afford or Constrain (Access to) Goals

Local meanings. Even relatively straightforward-seeming goals (such as to learn mathematics or to learn to read and write) are socially constructed, enmeshed in both cultural norms and values and in individuals' positions within social contexts. To begin with, the nature of the goal – what it means to "learn mathematics" – varies across settings. It may mean "learn to compute quickly with few errors," or it may mean "learn to think quantitatively" or to "describe the universe symbolically." Learning to write may be learning to produce error-free text to the teacher's specifications or learning to communicate complex ideas and feelings to others. The local meaning of activity is likely to influence learners' goals and strategies, their success, and their interactions with others. In a classroom setting, a child's position, access to certain kinds of instruction, and social relationships may all be influenced by their ability as defined locally. "Good readers" may get more choice in reading material, status for being better than others, or introduced to more complex or interesting forms of text. Different students will have access to "good reader" identities if "good reading" is defined as fluent oral reading or as thinking and responding to ideas presented in text, for example (Nolen, 2007). When learning mathematics is defined as "making sense of numbers," children approach math tasks differently and develop different mathematical identities than if errorless computation using standard algorithms is the definition of success (Cobb et al., 1989, 2009). Put a different way, social definitions of academic success carry with them resources and opportunities for participation in particular ways because those definitions are created through social practice.

Meanings in larger systems. Beyond the local setting, the meaning of activity is negotiated in larger cultural systems. Powerful cultural narratives provide ready-made goals that are often promoted uncritically by powerful others, including the media, educators, parents, and philanthropists. "Doing well in school" is promoted as a key to "climbing the ladder of success." Finishing high school is merely a step toward a college degree. "Doing better" than one's parents means attaining a certain level of education, a certain kind of job, and a certain level of financial security. Jones and Vagle (2013) argue that promoting these and similar goals "construct[s] classist hierarchies in schools and classroom practice" that may inadvertently "alienate the very students they hope to inspire" (p. 129). Interestingly, goal theories have either largely ignored culture or investigated whether the goals identified as most important in the educational systems of WEIRD countries translate across cultural boundaries. Almost no attention has been paid to the ways in which the achievement goals reflected in goal theories *are* cultural constructs, nor have most theorists turned a critical lens on their origins or implications.[2]

Individuals' goals can either reflect or stand in opposition to the values promoted by cultural systems. Although there may be some universal, evolutionarily important underlying motives (e.g., interest, competence, relatedness), goals as subjectively experienced position individuals and groups in relation to the norms, resources, and social structures in which they live, learn, and work. Na'Ilah Nasir and her colleagues (Nasir, 2011; Nasir & Cooks, 2009; Nasir et al., 2009) argue that engagement and identity development are shaped by material and social resources in particular contexts. Nasir (2011) describes how resources in school and community provide adolescents with models of African American identity, goals, and strategies that range from academic success to success on the street. Individual students, she claims, draw from these models, interacting with adults and peers in ways that then support or constrain their development toward particular identities. Her analysis provides an account of motivation and engagement that includes both individuals and social contexts, processes, and structures. Her data provide recognizable examples of human interactions that can inform attempts to engage students academically while acknowledging influences in and out of school.

Learners face inevitable clashes between competing narratives that require them to try to sort through goals promoted in school (e.g., apply to a prestigious but distant university) and obligations to family, the need to earn income now versus the hope of a "better" job later, and the needs of friends and maintaining peer relationships versus pleasing teachers and parents. In a multicultural society, learners must negotiate competing cultural expectations, changing definitions of success, and the structural impediments of racism, sexism, ableism, and religious discrimination. Theories that focus on a small

---

2 An exception to this is the cultural historical approach of Roth (2011).

number of goals expected to relate in similar specific ways across all contexts may not be sufficient to either explain how goals function "in the wild" or inform interventions to promote motivation to learn.

Concluding Thoughts

In this chapter, I have described various approaches to the study of goals in research on motivation and engagement. In considering the role of goals in psychological and situative theories, I have noted metatheoretical questions that have been addressed by researchers from various perspectives, including which goals should be studied and promoted in educational settings and the nature of the relationship between individual and context. I have argued that goals are not context-free, but instead are aspects of activity systems drawn from cultural models, and that, when adopted, goals position individuals in relation to those ongoing social structures. Goals can be understood in relation to the meaning(s) of activity; the same action can be pursued for multiple reasons in the same setting by different individuals, depending in part on their individual sense of those meanings. But the responses of others to those actions will depend on *their* interpretations of the underlying motives and, thus, will contribute to the ongoing development of the collective meaning system.

Research that examines the relationships of individual goals to the meaning systems in which they reside could shed light on the question of which goals to promote in particular educational contexts. But such research would do well to consider the multiple goals individuals might bring to those settings, how their identities in and out of those settings might contribute to their decisions to take up or reject promoted goals, and how the goals available in specific settings to specific people change through ongoing interaction and negotiation. In the end, a better understanding of the processes involved in the development and pursuit of goals might be the most useful goal for motivation researchers.

References

Ali, J., McInerney, D. M., Craven, R. G., Yeung, A. S., & King, R. B. (2014). Socially oriented motivational goals and academic achievement: Similarities between native and Anglo Americans. *The Journal of Educational Research, 107*(2), 123–37. doi: 10.1080/00220671.2013.788988.

Ames, C. (1992). Classrooms: Goals, structures, and student motivation. *Journal of Educational Psychology, 84*(3), 261.

Ames, C. & Ames, R. (1984). Goal structures and motivation. *The Elementary School Journal, 85*(1), 39–52. doi: 10.1086/461390.

Anderman, E. M. & Maehr, M. L. (1994). Motivation and schooling in the middle grades. *Review of Educational Research, 64*(2), 287–309.

Atkinson, J. W. & Litwin, G. H. (1960). Achievement motive and test anxiety conceived as motive to approach success and motive to avoid failure. *The Journal of Abnormal and Social Psychology*, *60*(1), 52–63. doi: 10.1037/h0041119.

Atkinson, J. W. & Raphelson, A. C. (1956). Individual differences in motivation and behavior in particular situations. *Journal of Personality*, *24*, 349–63. doi: 10.1111/j.1467-6494.1956.tb01274.x.

Atkinson, J. W. & Reitman, W. R. (1956). Performance as a function of motive strength and expectancy of goal-attainment. *The Journal of Abnormal and Social Psychology*, *53*(3), 361–6. doi: 10.1037/h0043477.

Bandura, A. & Schunk, D. H. (1981). Cultivating competence, self-efficacy, and instrinsic interest through proximal self-motivation. *Journal of Personality and Social Psychology*, *41*, 586–98.

Boaler, J. & Greeno, J. G. (2000). Identity, agency, and knowing in mathematical worlds. In J. Boaler (Ed.), *Multiple perspectives on mathematics teaching and learning* (pp. 45–82). Stamford, CT: Ablex.

Boekaerts, M., de Koning, E., & Vedder, P. (2006). Goal-directed behavior and contextual factors in the classroom: An innovative approach to the study of multiple goals. *Educational Psychologist*, *41*(1), 33–51.

Butler, R. (1987). Task-involving and ego-involving properties of evaluation: Effects of different feedback conditions on motivational perceptions, interest, and performance. *Journal of Educational Psychology*, *79*(4), 474–82.

Butler, R. (2006). Are mastery and ability goals both adaptive? Evaluation, initial goal construction, and the quality of task engagement. *British Journal of Educational Psychology*, *76*(3), 595–611.

Carver, C. S. & Scheier, M. F. (2000). On the structure of behavioral self-regulation. In M. Boekaerts, P. R. Pintrich, & M. Zeidner (Eds.), *Handbook of self-regulation*. (pp. 41–84). San Diego, CA: Academic Press.

Cobb, P., Gresalfi, M., & Hodge, L. L. (2009). An interpretive scheme for analyzing the identities that students develop in mathematics classrooms. *Journal for Research in Mathematics Education*, *40*(1), 40–68.

Cobb, P., Yackel, E., & Wood, T. (1989). Young children's emotional acts while doing mathematical problem-solving. In D. B. McLeod & V. M. Adams (Eds.), *Affect and mathematical problem solving: A new perspective*. New York, NY: Springer-Verlag.

Covington, M. V. & Omelich, C. L. (1984). Task-oriented versus competitive learning structures: Motivational and performance consequences. *Journal of Educational Psychology*, *76*(6), 1038–50.

Duda, J. L. (1995). Motivation in sport settings: A goal perspective approach. In G. C. Roberts (Ed.), *Motivation in sport and exercise*. (pp. 57–91). Champaign, IL: Human Kinetics Books.

Elliot, A. J. & Harackiewicz, J. M. (1996). Approach and avoidance achievement goals and intrinsic motivation: A mediational analysis. *Journal of Personality and Social Psychology*, *70*(3), 461–75.

Elliot, A. J., Murayama, K., & Pekrun, R. (2011). A 3 × 2 achievement goal model. *Journal of Educational Psychology*, *103*(3), 632–48. doi: 10.1037/a0023952.

Gonida, E. N. & Cortina, K. S. (2014). Parental involvement in homework: Relations with parent and student achievement-related motivational beliefs and achievement. *British Journal of Educational Psychology, 84*(3), 376–96. doi: 10.1111/bjep.12039.

Hand, V. M. & Gresalfi, M. (2015). The joint accomplishment of identity. *Educational Psychologist, 50*(3), 190–203. doi: 10.1080/00461520.2015.1075401.

Harackiewicz, J. M., Barron, K. E., Carter, S. M., Lehto, A. T., & Elliot, A. J. (1997). Predictors and consequences of achievement goals in the college classroom: Maintaining interest and making the grade. *Journal of Personality and Social Psychology, 73*(6), 1284–95.

Harackiewicz, J. M., Barron, K. E., Carter, S. M., Lehto, A. T., & Elliot, A. J. (1998). Rethinking achievement goals: When are they adaptive for college students and why? *Educational Psychologist, 33*(1), 1–21.

Hickey, D. T. & Granade, J. B. (2004). The influence of sociocultural theory on our theories of engagement and motivation. In D. McInerney & S. Van Etten (Eds.), *Big theories revisited* (Vol. 4, pp. 200–23). Greenwich, CT: Information Age Publishing.

Holland, D. (2010). Symbolic worlds in time/spaces of practice: Identities and transformations. In B. Wagoner (Ed.), *Symbolic transformation: The mind in movement through culture and society*. (pp. 269–83). New York, NY: Routledge/Taylor & Francis Group.

Holland, D., Lachicotte, W., Skinner, D., & Cain, C. (1998). *Identity and agency in cultural worlds*. Cambridge, MA: Harvard University Press.

Holland, D. & Lave, J. (Eds.). (2001). *History in person: Enduring struggles, contentious practice, intimate identities*. Albuquerque, NM: School of American Research Press.

Horn, I. S. (2005). Learning on the job: A situated account of teacher learning in high school mathematics departments. *Cognition and Instruction, 23*(2), 207–36. doi: 10.1207/s1532690xci2302_2.

Horn, I. S., Nolen, S. B., Ward, C. J., & Campbell, S. S. (2008). Developing practices in multiple worlds: The role of identity in learning to teach. *Teacher Education Quarterly, 35*(3), 61–72.

Jones, S. & Vagle, M. D. (2013). Living contradictions and working for change: Toward a theory of social class-sensitive pedagogy. *Educational Researcher, 42*(3), 129–41. doi: 10.3102/0013189X13481381.

Kaplan, A. & Middleton, M. J. (2002). Should childhood be a journey or a race? Response to Harackiewizc, et al. (2002). *Journal of Educational Psychology, 94*(3), 646–8.

Kim, J.-I., Schallert, D. L., & Kim, M. (2010). An integrative cultural view of achievement motivation: Parental and classroom predictors of children's goal orientations when learning mathematics in Korea. *Journal of Educational Psychology, 102*(2), 418–37. doi: 10.1037/a0018676.

King, R. B., Ganotice, F. A., Jr., & Watkins, D. A. (2014). A cross-cultural analysis of achievement and social goals among Chinese and Filipino students. *Social Psychology of Education, 17*(3), 439–55.

King, R. B. & McInerney, D. M. (2014). Culture's consequences on student motivation: Capturing cross-cultural universality and variability through personal investment theory. *Educational Psychologist, 49*(3), 175–98.

Lee, M. & Bong, M. (2016). In their own words: Reasons underlying the achievement striving of students in schools. *Journal of Educational Psychology, 108*(2), *274–94*. doi: 10.1037/edu0000048.

Lee, J. Q., McInerney, D. M., Liem, G. A. D., & Ortiga, Y. P. (2010). The relationship between future goals and achievement goal orientations: An intrinsic–extrinsic motivation perspective. *Contemporary Educational Psychology*, *35*(4), 264–79. doi: 10.1016/j.cedpsych.2010.04.004.

Lens, W., Paixao, M. P., Herrera, D., & Grobler, A. (2012). Future time perspective as a motivational variable: Content and extension of future goals affect the quantity and quality of motivation. *Japanese Psychological Research*, *54*(3), 321–33. doi: 10.1111/j.1468-5884.2012.00520.x.

Linnenbrink, E. A. (2005). The dilemma of performance-approach goals: The use of multiple goal contexts to promote students' motivation and learning. *Journal of Educational Psychology*, *97*(2), 197–213. doi: 10.1037/0022-0663.97.2.197.

Lüftenegger, M., van de Schoot, R., Schober, B., Finsterwald, M., & Spiel, C. (2014). Promotion of students' mastery goal orientations: Does target work? *Educational Psychology*, *34*(4), 451–69.

Luo, W., Aye, K., Hogan, D., Kaur, B., & Chan, M. (2013). Parenting behaviors and learning of Singapore students: The mediational role of achievement goals. *Motivation & Emotion*, *37*(2), 274–85. doi: 10.1007/s11031-012-9303-8.

Maehr, M. L. & Midgley, C. (1991). Enhancing student motivation: A school-wide approach. *Educational Psychologist*, *26*(3–4), 399–427.

Magson, N. R., Craven, R. G., Nelson, G. F., Yeung, A. S., Bodkin-Andrews, G. H., & McInerney, D. M. (2014). Motivation matters: Profiling indigenous and non-indigenous students' motivational goals. *Australian Journal of Indigenous Education*, *43*(2), 96–112.

Mansfield, C. (2012). Rethinking motivation goals for adolescents: Beyond achievement goals. *Applied Psychology: An International Review*, *61*(4), 564–84. doi: 10.1111/j.1464-0597.2012.00506.x.

McInerney, D. M. (2003). Motivational goals, self-concept and sense of self: What predicts academic achievement? In H. W. Marsh, R. G. Craven, & D. M. McInerney (Eds.), *International advances in self research*. Greenwich, CT: Information Age Publishing.

McInerney, D. M. (2008). Personal investment, culture and learning: Insights into school achievement across Anglo, aboriginal, Asian and Lebanese students in Australia. *International Journal of Psychology*, *43*(5), 870–9. doi: 10.1080/00207590701836364.

McInerney, D. M. & Ali, J. (2013). Indigenous motivational profiles: Do they reflect collectivism? A cross-cultural analysis of similarities and differences between groups classified as individualist and collectivist cultures. In R. Craven, G. Bodkin-Andrews, & J. Mooney (Eds.), *Indigenous peoples* (pp. 211–32). Charlotte, NC: Information Age Publishing.

McInerney, D. M., Hinkley, J., Dowson, M., & Van Etten, S. (1998). Aboriginal, Anglo, and immigrant Australian students' motivational beliefs about personal academic success: Are there cultural differences? *Journal of Educational Psychology, 90*(4), 621–9.

McInerney, D. M., Roche, L. A., McInerney, V., & Marsh, H. W. (1997). Cultural perspectives on school motivation: The relevance and application of goal theory. *American Educational Research Journal*, *34*(1), 207–36. doi: 10.2307/1163347.

Meyer, D. K., Turner, J. C., & Spencer, C. A. (1997). Challenge in a mathematics classroom: Students' motivation and strategies in project-based learning. *The Elementary School Journal*, *97*(5), 501–21. doi: 10.1086/461878.

Michou, A., Vansteenkiste, M., Mouratidis, A., & Lens, W. (2014). Enriching the hierarchical model of achievement motivation: Autonomous and controlling reasons underlying achievement goals. *British Journal of Educational Psychology*, *84*(4), 650–66.

Midgley, C., Kaplan, A., & Middleton, M. J. (2001). Performance-approach goals: Good for what, for whom, under what circumstances, and at what cost? *Journal of Educational Psychology*, *93*(1), 77–86.

Murray, H. A. (1938). *Explorations in personality: A clinical and experimental study of fifty men of college age*. Oxford: Oxford University Press.

Murray, H. A. (1943). *Thematic apperception test*. Cambridge, MA: Harvard University Press.

Nasir, N. S. (2011). *Racialized identities: Race and achievement among African American youth*. Palo Alto, CA: Stanford University Press.

Nasir, N. S. & Cooks, J. (2009). Becoming a hurdler: How learning settings afford identities. *Anthropology & Education Quarterly*, *40*(1), 41–61. doi: 10.1111/j.1548-1492.2009.01027.x.

Nasir, N. S., McLaughlin, M. W., & Jones, A. (2009). What does it mean to be African American? Constructions of race and academic identity in an urban public high school. *American Educational Research Journal*, *46*(1), 73–114.

Nelson, G. F., O'Mara, A. J., McInerney, D. M., & Dowson, M. (2006). Motivation in cross-cultural settings: A Papua New Guinea psychometric study. *International Education Journal*, *7*(4), 400–9.

Nicholls, J. G. & Burton, J. T. (1982). Motivation and equality. *Elementary School Journal*, *82*(4), 367–78.

Nolen, S. B. (1988). Reasons for studying: Motivational orientations and study strategies. *Cognition and Instruction, 5*(4), 260–287.

Nolen, S. B. (2003). Learning environment, achievement, and motivation in high school science. *Journal of Research in Science Teaching*, *40*(4), 347–68.

Nolen, S. B. (2007). The role of literate communities in the development of children's interest in writing. In P. Boscolo & S. Hidi (Eds.), *Writing and motivation* (pp. 241–55). Oxford: Elsevier.

Nolen, S. B., Horn, I. S., Ward, C. J., & Childers, S. (2011). Assessment tools as boundary objects in novice teachers' learning. *Cognition and Instruction*, *29*(1), 88–122.

Nolen, S. B., Ward, C. J., Horn, I. S., Childers, S., Campbell, S. S., & Mahna, K. (2009). Motivation development in novice teachers: The development of utility filters. In M. Wosnitza, S. A. Karabenick, A. Efklides, & P. Nenniger (Eds.), *Contemporary motivation research: From global to local perspectives* (pp. 265–78). Ashland, OH: Hogrefe & Huber.

O'Keefe, P. A., Ben-Eliyahu, A., & Linnenbrink-Garcia, L. (2013). Shaping achievement goal orientations in a mastery-structured environment and concomitant changes in related contingencies of self-worth. *Motivation and Emotion*, *37*(1), 50–64.

Park, D., Gunderson, E. A., Tsukayama, E., Levine, S. C., & Beilock, S. L. (2016). Young children's motivational frameworks and math achievement: Relation to teacher-reported instructional practices, but not teacher theory of intelligence. *Journal of Educational Psychology*, *108*(3), 300–13. doi: 10.1037/edu0000064.

Pintrich, P. R., Ryan, A. M., & Patrick, H. (1998). The differential impact of task value and mastery orientation on males' and females' self-regulated learning. In A. K. L. Hoffmann, K. A. Renninger, & J. Baumert (Eds.), *Interest and learning* (pp. 337–52). Kiel: Institute for Science Education (IPN).

Roth, W.-M. (2011). Object/motives and emotion: A cultural-historical activity theoretic approach to motivation in learning and work. In D. M. McInerny, R. A. Walker, & G. A. Liem (Eds.), *Sociocultural theories of learning and motivation: Looking back, looking forward.* (Vol. 10, pp. 43–63). Charlotte, NC: Information Age Publishing.

Schuitema, J., Peetsma, T., & van der Veen, I. (2014). Enhancing student motivation: A longitudinal intervention study based on future time perspective theory. *The Journal of Educational Research, 107*(6), 467–81. doi: 10.1080/00220671.2013.836467.

Schwartz, D. L., Cheng, K. M., Salehi, S., & Wieman, C. (2016). The half empty question for socio-cognitive interventions. *Journal of Educational Psychology, 108*(3), 397–404. doi: 10.1037/edu0000122.

Senko, C., Hulleman, C. S., & Harackiewicz, J. M. (2011). Achievement goal theory at the crossroads: Old controversies, current challenges, and new directions. *Educational Psychologist, 46*(1), 26–47. doi: 10.1080/00461520.2011.538646.

Senko, C. & Tropiano, K. L. (2016). Comparing three models of achievement goals: Goal orientations, goal standards, and goal complexes. *Journal of Educational Psychology, 108*(8), 1178–92. doi: 10.1037/edu0000114.

Thorkildsen, T. A. & Nicholls, J. G. (1998). Fifth graders' achievement orientations and beliefs: Individual and classroom differences. *Journal of Educational Psychology, 90*(2), 179–201. doi: 10.1037/0022-0663.90.2.179.

Turner, J. C. (1995). The influence of classroom contexts on young children's motivation for literacy. *RRQ, 30*(3), 409–41.

Turner, J. C., Warzon, K. B., & Christensen, A. (2011). Motivating mathematics learning: Changes in teachers' practices and beliefs during a nine-month collaboration. *American Educational Research Journal, 48*(3), 718–62. doi: 10.3102/0002831210385103.

Urdan, T. & Mestas, M. (2006). The goals behind performance goals. *Journal of Educational Psychology, 98*(2), 354–65. doi: 10.1037/0022-0663.98.2.354.

Vansteenkiste, M., Timmermans, T., Lens, W., Soenens, B., & Van den Broeck, A. (2008). Does extrinsic goal framing enhance extrinsic goal-oriented individuals' learning and performance? An experimental test of the match perspective versus self-determination theory. *Journal of Educational Psychology, 100*(2), 387–97. doi: 10.1037/0022-0663.100.2.387.

Vedder-Weiss, D. & Fortus, D. (2013). School, teacher, peers, and parents' goals emphases and adolescents' motivation to learn science in and out of school. *Journal of Research in Science Teaching, 50*(8), 952–88. doi: 10.1002/tea.21103.

Wenger, E. (1998). *Communities of practice: Learning, meaning, and identity.* Cambridge: Cambridge University Press.

Wentzel, K. R. (1996). Social goals and social relationships as motivators of school adjustment. In J. Juvonen & K. R. Wentzel (Eds.), *Social motivation: Understanding children's school adjustment* (pp. 226–47). New York, NY: Cambridge University Press.

Wentzel, K. R. (2000). What is it that I'm trying to achieve? Classroom goals from a content perspective. *Contemporary Educational Psychology, 25*(1), 105–15. doi: 10.1006/ceps.1999.1021.

Zusho, A. & Clayton, K. (2011). Culturalizing achievement goal theory and research. *Educational Psychologist, 46*(4), 239–60.

23 Achievement Goal Orientations

A Person-Oriented Approach

Markku Niemivirta, Antti-Tuomas Pulkka,
Anna Tapola, and Heta Tuominen

Abstract: In this chapter, we describe the principles of a person-oriented approach to studying individual differences (and similarities), and how it can be applied to the study of students' achievement goal orientations. First, we briefly illustrate the approach, which provides a way of looking at the relative emphasis of different achievement goal orientations, thereby explicitly addressing the issue of multiple goals and their associations with important outcomes. Second, we give a comprehensive review of studies that have applied such an approach to investigating students' achievement goals. The diversity in conceptualizations, methods, and study samples in the studies complicates the interpretation of the findings, but some generalizations can nevertheless be made. Based on the review, we conclude that students with qualitatively different achievement goal orientation profiles can clearly be identified, and that the extracted profiles are rather similar across studies. Further, it seems that such profiles are relatively stable over time and meaningfully associated with learning and various educational outcomes (e.g., academic achievement, self-perceptions, well-being, task-related motivation, and performance). The review also contributes to the debate concerning the advantages of endorsing different goals. Finally, we raise some methodological concerns, discuss implications for learning, and provide suggestions for future research.

In this chapter, we will explore a way of studying motivation that focuses on the profiles of students' preferred goals and related outcomes in achievement contexts. We argue that taking into account the relative emphasis of different goals or goal orientations provides us with valuable information about individual differences in motivation and how those differences are associated with various academic and personal outcomes. This so-called person-oriented approach is well suited for the study of group and individual differences within and over time, as it is predicated on the assumption that the population

This research was supported by the University of Helsinki, the Academy of Finland, and the Jenny and Antti Wihuri Foundation.

is heterogeneous with respect to the patterns of variables. Variables are considered less as agents and outcomes and more as properties of individuals and their environment (Laursen & Hoff, 2006). In the following, we will first briefly describe and illustrate the person-oriented approach, after which we will review a body of research that has resulted from such an approach to investigating students' achievement goals and goal orientations.

What Is a Person-Oriented Approach?

When we refer to motivation in everyday discussions, we tend to describe individuals or groups of individuals: "he was not motivated to do the task," "she has always displayed immense interest in mathematics," "the team clearly lacked confidence," and so on. Yet, in research, we are inclined to discuss the constructs: interest seems to predict course choices, anxiety interferes with task performance, and confidence contributes to achievement above and beyond intelligence. This is rather natural since, in research, we are mostly interested in the constructs that describe and refer to the psychological phenomena we believe to represent the various aspects of motivation. Most studies are designed correspondingly: we measure different types of variables and then link those variables to each other through correlations and regressions. Such an approach can be labeled as variable-oriented. Within this approach, models and hypotheses are formulated in terms of variables and variable relations, use statistical methods that focus on variable relations, and treat variables as the main units of analysis (Bergman & Magnusson, 1997). For example, we could hypothesize that two independent facets of perfectionism (Stoeber & Otto, 2006), goal level and discrepancy (i.e., perceived dissatisfaction with goal attainment), differently predict task performance. Accordingly, we would conduct a study where we first measure participants along the two measures of perfectionism, have them then perform a task, and, finally, regress the performance scores on the measures of perfectionism. The obtained regression coefficients would thus inform us about the extent to which change in one facet independently predicts the change in task performance.

Alternatively, we could also focus more on the individuals instead of variables, and hypothesize that there are groups of individuals that are similar to each other, but different from the others in terms of the level of the facets of perfectionism. For example, some may set high goals and be satisfied with their attainments, some may set high goals and be unsatisfied with their attainments, and yet some may set low goals and still be satisfied with their attainments. These three different groups might then also differ in their task performance. Thus, instead of examining relations among variables within a sample, we would be more interested in examining the heterogeneity of the sample across variables. In practice, we would first group the participants according to their perfectionism profiles, and then examine group differences on task performance. Through this, we would gain information about how people with different perfectionism profiles succeeded in the task. This approach can be labeled as person-oriented. Within this approach, the focus is on score profiles across the variables, instead of variables as such. Models and hypotheses are formulated in terms of individuals and variable configurations, and statistical methods that focus on individuals and groups of individuals are used.

We can thus differently approach the same targets of interest with different implications for the potential outcomes. Although there is no clear consensus on the terms "variable-oriented" and "person-oriented" (Bergman & Trost, 2006), the difference between these approaches is not just the methods used. The person-oriented approach is often linked to the holistic-interactionistic paradigm introduced by Magnusson (1988) and further developed by Bergman and Magnusson (1997), which views the individual as an active agent in the person-environment system. Its core tenets suggest that there is lawfulness and structure both in intra-individual constancy and change, and in inter-individual differences in constancy and change; that this lawfulness and structure can be described as patterns of the involved factors; and that some patterns occur more frequently, some less frequently, than expected based on theory (see von Eye & Bogat, 2006).

Consider, for instance, our example of perfectionism above. Perfectionistic strivings refer to individual tendencies to set high standards and, simultaneously, to critically evaluate personal achievements in relation to those standards. This implies that a person with extreme levels in both facets – who strives for high goals but is seldom satisfied with the outcomes – can be considered as a perfectionist. However, as those facets of perfectionism tend to be empirically uncorrelated, people are likely to display different combinations of the two: they may be high or low in both, in neither, or in just one of them. Indeed, empirical studies demonstrate this to be the case (Rice & Slaney, 2002).

In addition to describing similarities and differences across individuals and groups of individuals, the person-oriented approach is also well suited for analyzing development and change over time. Here, the interest is more in the stability and change of the patterning of variables, rather than in the stability of variables as such. For example, instead of examining stability coefficients and changes in mean levels of the facets of perfectionism, one would investigate whether the same number of groups was identified in different measurement points, whether the identified profiles were similar over time, and the extent to which members in each group remained in the same group. The patterning of the groupings and membership frequencies could then be analyzed using cross-tabulation or configural frequency analysis (CFA; von Eye, 1990). Stability is present if similar profiles and groups are identified at the different measurement points, and if members are likely to stay in similar groups over time. In contrast, qualitative shifts (i.e., changes in individuals' profiles) are present if people move from one group to another.

To summarize, in some cases, score or variable profiles may be a theoretically more appropriate and empirically more accurate way of describing certain phenomena than simple scores or variables, and the examination of score con-figurations may be more informative than the analyses of variable relation-ships. A person-oriented approach may thus provide us with a view that goes beyond mere variable relationships, and inform us more thoroughly about the similarities and differences between and within individuals and groups of indi-viduals. However, it is important that the given theoretical stance both justify the approach and provide substantive grounds for interpreting the results. As it is always possible to identify profiles or form groups in the data, any solutions derived from such person-oriented analyses need to be meaningful in relation to the underlying theoretical framework. Naturally, variable- and person-oriented approaches should not be taken as methodological rivals, but rather as complementary approaches with different foci (see Niemivirta, 2002a).

In the remaining parts of the chapter, we will first describe the way such a person-oriented approach can be applied to the study of differences (and similarities) in how students orient themselves to learning and performance in achievement settings, and then review a set of findings obtained from such studies.

Achievement Goals Versus Achievement Goal Orientations

As noted already in the title of this chapter, our focus is on students' achieve-ment goal *orientations*. Thus, we explicitly differentiate between goals and goal orientations. This view follows the early work on achievement goals by Nicholls (1989) and Dweck (1992), who jointly and independently set the stage for this line of research. Such a view is also integrated into the so-called adaptive model of learning, which seeks to describe the dynamics of students' self-regulation in the context of learning and achievement (Boekaerts & Niemivirta, 2000), and thus provides the broader theoretical framework for our approach. Let us illustrate this briefly.

Classroom events comprise frequent unfolding episodes that focus on learning and performance – students are expected to both attain and demonstrate their competence. From the student's point of view, such repeated episodic events represent coping situations, each packed with challenges, expectations, and demands that measure the availability and sufficiency of the student's personal resources. When a student encounters such a situation, they first seek to identify and interpret the features of the situation. The resulting situational construal – a function of the student's prior experiences, goals, and beliefs (i.e., "theory"), and of the features of the situation (i.e., "data") – then influences how the stu-dent appraises the event's subjective relevance and their personal resources to cope with it. These appraisals, in turn, result in outcomes such as emotions, motivational states, and action tendencies that set the stage for further activity.

As noted, the goals we hold partly guide our interpretations and responses to specific situations, and they may become manifested on various levels of action (Vallacher & Wegner, 1987). For example, the goal might be the action itself (e.g., the enjoyment of jogging), the outcome of the action (e.g., the euphoric feeling afterward), or subsequent consequences (e.g., better health). The early work on achievement goals made a similar distinction between different levels of goals as well. For Nicholls (1984), the key issue was how the students define success in achievement situations. He argued that individuals commonly define success either in a self-referenced fashion (e.g., in terms of learning something new or performing better than before) or based on normative comparison (e.g., doing better than others). Thus, when striving to increase competence in the former sense, students are said to be task-involved, and when seeking to demonstrate competence in the latter sense, they are said to be ego-involved. These particular goal states were assumed to be elicited in part as a function of the situational setting (e.g., competitive versus individualized task instruction) and to influence differentially further task choice and attainment. Importantly, Nicholls (1989) further argued that while situationally induced conceptions of success become manifested in task- and ego-involvement, individuals also differ in their commitment to those criteria of success, and thus also in their proneness to the two types of involvement. Task-oriented individuals would be inclined to approach tasks in the self-referenced fashion, whereas ego-oriented individuals would do so in a normative fashion. The former would seek to increase their competence, whereas the latter would seek to validate their competence.

Also, Dweck (1992) made a distinction between specific goals as the outcomes individuals strive for and the more superordinate goals behind the particular outcomes individuals strive for. She further argued that the adoption of goals in achievement situations emerges as a function of individual differences and situational factors. That is, people bring to a situation certain goal tendencies, but goal tendencies can also be fostered by the situation (e.g., when they provide cues that increase the salience or value of particular goals).

Following the above, our view thus focuses on individual differences in the proneness to favor certain goals and outcomes. While more specific goals represent objects, events, states, or experiences one seeks to attain, goal orientations reflect individual differences in the preferences for certain types of desired end-states. In a sense, then, they could be seen as knowledge structures we do not need to be constantly conscious about, but which may become activated as a function of the situation or our perception of it: the higher the accessibility, the stronger the preference and the easier it becomes activated based on the current situational setting and environmental cues (see also Pintrich, 2000).

Unfortunately, much of the empirical research has not made such a differentiation explicit, or has considered it as irrelevant (see Elliot, 1999). Yet, many studies that refer to achievement goals seem to have treated them as orientations (e.g., more generalized tendencies), either in how they have been operationalized or measured, or in how the results have been interpreted. It is thus virtually impossible to unambiguously categorize studies into ones that have focused on goals per se and ones that have focused on goal orientations. This also applies to studies conducted following the person-oriented approach, which makes it difficult to differentiate between studies where "person-orientation" refers to a theoretically and methodologically argued stance and studies that merely use person-oriented methods for analyses (e.g., clustering of participants). Due to this, we will in the following sections first look into this research as a whole, without a detailed separation of specific types of studies, and then in our concluding summaries, we will make certain differentiating aspects explicit.

Different Classes of Goals and Goal Orientations

In order to understand how achievement goals (i.e., specific goals associated with the desire to attain or demonstrate competence) and achievement goal orientations (i.e., dispositional tendencies to prefer certain types of goals and outcomes over some others in achievement-related settings) contribute to students' achievement-related responses and actions, we need to identify the kinds of goals that students are likely to endorse in achievement settings.

The early research identified two types of goals that formed the grounds for later advancements: goals or goal states with a focus on increasing competence, and goals or goal states with a focus on demonstrating competence (i.e., task- and ego-involvement by Nicholls [1984], learning and performance goals by Dweck & Leggett [1988], respectively). Task-involved children endorsing learning goals seemed to consider errors and setbacks as part of the learning process and tools for improvement, whereas ego-involved children endorsing performance goals seemed to perceive errors as indications of failure and, subsequently, lack of competence. Thus, the adoption of either type of goal resulted in qualitatively different cognitive and affective processes in an achievement setting.

As an educational psychologist (see Thorkildsen & Nicholls, 1998, for a discussion on the different approaches to studying achievement-related motivation and behavior), Nicholls sought to understand more comprehensively the various ways students may adjust to or cope with the demands of achievement situations, and thus also acknowledged goals that are not directly targeted at increasing or demonstrating competence, but which may still cover a substantive part of students' achievement-related behavior in the classroom. These included work avoidance (e.g., trying to avoid effort and preferring easy assignments) and academic alienation (e.g., trying to disregard rules and expectations by "goofing off" and "beating the system"), which empirically often merged into one, (work) avoidance orientation. Note that such goals have often been disregarded in contemporary research based on the argument that they, rather, represent the absence of an achievement goal than the presence of one (Elliot & Thrash, 2001), yet the research clearly suggests that they indeed belong to the goals students themselves identify and subscribe to in achievement contexts (Dowson & McInerney, 2001; Lemos, 1996; Pulkka & Niemivirta, 2015).

The classification of goals put forth by Dweck and Nicholls was later followed by new elaborations. Inconsistent findings associated with performance goals led to an explicit bifurcation of performance goals into approach (i.e., a desire to demonstrate competence) and avoidance (i.e., a desire to avoid demonstrating incompetence) forms (Elliot & Harackiewicz, 1996; Middleton & Midgley, 1997; Skaalvik, 1997). Later, the approach-avoidance distinction was also applied to mastery goals, suggesting the differentiation of mastery-approach goals (i.e., desire to learn) and mastery-avoidance goals (i.e., desire to avoid failure to learn or deterioration in skill) dimensions (Elliot & McGregor, 2001; Pintrich, 2000). However, given the somewhat limited and inconsistent findings, the separation of mastery goals has not received unreserved agreement in the research field (see Bong, 2009).

Other developments concerning students' mastery strivings included a class of goals that, on the one hand, describe a desire of improving one's skills and succeeding at school (like the original mastery goal), but that, on the other hand, grounds on extrinsic criteria (e.g., grades) for evaluating mastery (unlike the original mastery goal). Such goals have been referred to as outcome goals (Grant & Dweck, 2003) or mastery-extrinsic goals (Niemivirta, 2002b, 2004). Despite some differences in conceptual nuances, empirical findings commonly suggest that while such goals are related to some positive and adaptive patterns of coping and behavior (e.g., commitment, effort, academic achievement) they may also induce performance-concerns (e.g., fear of failure), likely due to the more explicit instrumental criteria for mastery (Grant & Dweck, 2003; Niemivirta, 2002b; Tuominen-Soini et al., 2011).

In our own work, we have focused on five orientations – the Helsinki 5[1] – that, in our view, represent a comprehensive array of goals and outcomes relevant in the classroom: mastery-intrinsic, mastery-extrinsic, performance-approach, performance-avoidance, and (work) avoidance goal orientations, respectively. They refer to the expectations embedded in achievement-related contexts (i.e., to learn and to demonstrate what has been learned), the different psychological functions associated with such expectations (i.e., self-improvement, self-enhancement, and self-protection), and the overall responses to those demands (i.e., accept the expectations or detach from them). They also tap both the individual and instrumental values (or lack thereof) attached to such expectations. Importantly, however, we believe that since we all identify and acknowledge the different ways of orienting ourselves to the academic ethos – the "educational tasks set for us" – a better understanding of them and their role in relation to other educational outcomes requires the examination of

1 This anecdotal label for our set of orientations was proposed by Professor Mary Ainley when she served as the honorable opponent for the doctoral defense of one of the authors.

their relative weight. Dweck (1996) acknowledged this differentiation and expressed it aptly when she stated that "virtually all people share the basic classes of goals ... People differ, however, in the relative emphasis they place on them and on the means they use to pursue them" (p. 353).

We may thus have a common understanding of the different goals and their meaning, but there are differences in which goals we follow or find relevant for ourselves. It is natural for any human being to experience joy in learning, to feel good about succeeding in front of others, or to feel bad about failing in public, but the personal significance of these experiences may vary significantly. The preferences for such experiences are also likely to vary as a function of the situation, but it is still probable that we exhibit tendencies to prefer some experiences over others. That is, we are oriented toward the environment in specific contexts in idiosyncratic ways, which makes certain interpretations of and responses to the situation more likely than others. The patterning of these orientations thus serves as a motivational lens through which we view the situations, and becomes manifested in our goal and outcome preferences. In the following, we will explore the patterning of such tendencies.

Achievement Goal Orientation Profiles

Methodologically, different approaches have been used to study the effects of multiple goals on educational outcomes that do not fully qualify as examples of a person-oriented approach. These would include studies looking at the interaction effects of goals through multiple regressions (e.g., Harackiewicz et al., 1997; Kaplan & Midgley, 1997) and studies classifying participants using median splits (e.g., Pintrich, 2000). The latter approach does indeed produce groups, but the number of groups is arbitrary in the sense that any continuous variable can be split into two based on the median, and, thus, the resulting classification does not represent the "true" empirical clustering of cases within a sample. Conventional cluster analysis is already a more sophisticated technique, although this common procedure is prone to bias because of the problems in determining the number of clusters (Pastor et al., 2007). More recent studies have used model-based approaches, such as latent class clustering and latent profile analysis, which have several advantages over the traditional methods, including statistical criteria for determining the appropriate number of classes (Nylund et al., 2007).

Types of Profiles

Studies examining students' achievement goals from a person-oriented approach (see Appendix for a comprehensive summary of these studies) started to appear in the 1990s, and their number has been constantly increasing (see

Table 23.1 *Summary of the classification methods used in the reviewed studies*

| | Year of publishing | | | | | | |
Method	1991–1995	1996–2000	2001–2005	2006–2010	2011–2015	2016–	Total
Median split	2	2	3	3	1		11
Cluster analysis	2	3	5	13	10	3	36
Model-based			1	3	11	8	23
Total	4	5	9	19	22	11	70

Note. "Total" is total *N* of studies. The study of Lau and Roeser (2008) using inverse factor analysis is excluded from this table.

Table 23.2 *Summary of the level of schooling and the number of profiles extracted in the reviewed studies*

| | Number of profiles | | | | | | |
School level	2	3	4	5	6	≥7	Total
Elementary/primary school		9	5	1			15
Middle/lower secondary/junior high school		4	8	1	4	2	19
High/upper secondary/ vocational school	1		6	2	3	1	13
College/university/adult studies	1	6	11	1	1	1	21
Total	2	19	30	5	8	4	68

Note. Studies using median split procedures are excluded from this table. Some studies included several samples or educational contexts, and they are classified into several cells accordingly.

Table 23.1). The review of the literature reveals that different conceptualizations, different analytical methods, as well as participants of different ages and from various educational contexts make the interpretation and generalization of the results challenging (see also Wormington & Linnenbrink-Garcia, 2017). Regarding methodology, 16 percent of the reviewed studies employed median split procedures, slightly over half used cluster analysis, and about one-third utilized model-based techniques (see Table 23.1). With respect to the participants, approximately one-third of the reviewed studies included university students, nearly as many studies examined middle or lower secondary school students, and slightly fewer studies included elementary and high school students (see Table 23.2).

In the early work on goal profiles, researchers differentiated mainly between mastery and performance goals, and used these two for clustering the students (this was the case in 11 percent of the reviewed studies) but, later, the trichotomous (i.e., mastery, performance-approach, and performance-avoidance) model (Elliot & Harackiewicz, 1996) gained popularity (30 percent of the reviewed studies). The 2×2 goal model (Elliot & McGregor, 2001), a common framework within the variable-oriented studies, has been utilized in 8 percent of the reviewed person-oriented studies, while the 3×2 goal model (Elliot, et al., 2011) has been used in only one person-oriented study.

Work-avoidance goals were included, with different kinds of combinations of other goals, in one-third of the studies: along with mastery and performance goals in 11 percent, along with mastery, performance-approach, and performance-avoidance goals in 6 percent, and as part of the Helsinki 5 (Niemivirta, 2002b) in 14 percent of the reviewed studies, respectively. Some studies have included other goals as well, such as social goals, and they have been used as clustering variables along with academic goals in 16 percent of the reviewed studies (Gonçalves et al., 2017; Korpershoek et al., 2015; Litalien et al., 2017; Valle et al., 2003).

Naturally, both conceptual revisions and more eclectic approaches have led to an increased complexity in the possible goal combinations, which adds to the difficulty of comparing classification solutions and the resulting profiles across the studies. Some generalizations can nevertheless be made. When exploring multiple goals, determining the number of distinct profiles becomes an essential issue. In most cases (see Appendix), the number of identified profiles has varied between three and six, with the vast majority of studies including three or four profiles (see Table 23.2).

Certain profiles seem to be rather common across studies, almost irrespective of the age of the participants or their level of schooling. These would include a predominantly mastery goal profile (e.g., learning-oriented, mastery-oriented, task-oriented) with relatively low values on any type of performance goal (Niemivirta, 2002b; Peixoto et al., 2016; Schwinger et al., 2016; Tapola et al., 2014), a predominantly performance goal profile (e.g., low-mastery/high-performance, performance-oriented; Gonçalves et al., 2017; Pintrich, 2000; Tapola & Niemivirta, 2008; Valle et al., 2003), and a combined mastery and performance-approach goal profile (e.g., multiple goals cluster, success-oriented, approach group; Daniels et al., 2008; Luo et al., 2011; Pulkka & Niemivirta, 2013a; Tuominen-Soini et al., 2008; Turner et al., 1998). In addition, profiles with moderate (e.g., moderate multiple goals, indifferent; Jansen in de Wal et al., 2016; Pulkka & Niemivirta, 2013b; Schwinger et al., 2016; Tuominen-Soini et al., 2011) and low levels of achievement goals (e.g., low-mastery/low-performance, low-motivation, disengaged, disaffected; Conley, 2012; Daniels et al., 2008; Gonçalves et al., 2017; Liu et al., 2009; Pintrich, 2000; Tuominen-Soini et al., 2008) have often been found. Finally, studies including a work-avoidance orientation have usually found a work-avoidant profile (e.g., avoidance-oriented, work-avoidance group) with relatively low values on mastery and performance goal orientations (Kolić-Vehovec et al., 2008; Ng, 2009; Niemivirta, 2002b; Tapola & Niemivirta, 2008; Veermans & Tapola, 2004).

The number and types of goal profiles extracted naturally depend on the types of achievement goals taken into consideration and the method used for extracting the different profiles, but nevertheless it seems rather clear that certain combinations of achievement goals are common and they represent differences in how students orient toward achievement settings. The next questions are: How stable are these profiles, and how do they contribute to learning and other educational outcomes?

Stability of Profiles

Although the person-oriented approach to studying achievement goal orientations has become more popular, as yet only a few studies have investigated the stability and change in goal orientation profiles. The existing findings are rather mixed implicating to the variations by study sample and choice of methods. Some studies show that among young elementary school students, only about one-third or even less hold the same profile over the school years (Schwinger & Wild, 2012; Schwinger et al., 2016; Veermans & Tapola, 2004), while some others suggest that as many as 80 percent of students display stable profiles from fifth to sixth grade (Jansen in de Wal et al., 2016) or 75 percent across the transition from elementary to lower secondary school (Tuominen et al., 2018, manuscript submitted for publication). In secondary and higher education, the proportion of students displaying identical profiles within and between academic years has varied from 60 to 75 percent (Lee et al., 2017; Pulkka & Niemivirta, 2013a; Tuominen-Soini et al., 2011), and half of the students have shown profile stability even across an educational transition from lower to upper secondary school (Tuominen-Soini et al., 2012).

Note, also, that although some students do show a change in their motivational profile over time, the majority of them seem to move to a neighboring group with a fairly similar profile (e.g., from mastery- to success-oriented), and substantial qualitative shifts (e.g., from mastery- to avoidance-oriented) are rare (Gonçalves et al., 2017; Pulkka & Niemivirta, 2013a; Tuominen-Soini et al., 2011, 2012). We can thus conclude that stability in goal orientation profiles is more frequent than significant changes, even across educational transitions (Gonçalves et al., 2017; Tuominen et al., 2018, manuscript submitted for publication; Tuominen-Soini et al., 2012).

Although part of the changes detected in different studies are "genuine" in the sense that they reflect true changes either in the individual or in their relations with the surrounding world – for instance, maturation, changes in calibrating one's competence perceptions, transitions to new educational contexts, changing social environment, and identity development – the instability observed in some studies is more likely due to the methodology. For example, all the studies displaying low stability have classified students according to their goal profiles separately at different time points, thus ignoring the dependence of the measures across time points, while the studies exhibiting higher stability have taken this non-independence explicitly into account. One must thus exercise caution when interpreting the findings and drawing inferences from them. Nevertheless, it does not seem premature to conclude that students' achievement goal orientation profiles do not randomly fluctuate, but rather seem relatively stable over time. This supports our view of such profiles as tendencies to view and approach achievement settings in particular ways. If this is the case, different achievement goal profiles should also influence students' achievement-related activities and experiences, and thus contribute to various educational outcomes. We will review such findings next.

Achievement Goal Orientation Profiles and Educational Outcomes

We have examined, in a series of our studies, the kinds of achievement goal orientation profiles that can be identified among students of different ages and how those profiles are associated with various educationally relevant outcomes. Using the Helsinki 5 model and robust model-based classification methods, we have found considerable consistency in the profiles across studies and various academic contexts (i.e., elementary, secondary, and higher education). Usually we have found groups with a dominant tendency toward mastery (mastery-oriented students), performance (success-oriented students, performance-oriented students), and avoidance (avoidance-oriented students), as well as a group of students without a dominant tendency toward any specific achievement goal orientation (indifferent students). Mastery-oriented and success-oriented students both emphasize learning and achievement, but success-oriented students are also likely to endorse performance-related goals. Indifferent students represent a "typical" student who seeks to do what is expected (to learn and perform well), but also tries to minimize the required effort. Compared to the others, avoidance-oriented students display lower mastery aspirations and aim more at minimizing the effort and time spent on studying.

In the following sections, we will first describe findings from our own studies following the above scheme, after which we will reflect on other studies on similar themes and draw some general conclusions.

Profile Differences in Relation to Motivation

Using a nationally representative sample of folk high school students, we investigated how groups of students with different achievement goal orientation profiles differ with respect to task-specific motivation (i.e., situational interest, self-efficacy, and claimed self-handicapping) during a problem-solving task (Niemivirta et al., 2013).[2] The groups differed in terms of how they interpreted, experienced, and approached learning and performance situations. Compared to the others, mastery- and success-oriented students anticipated the task to be more interesting and reported higher self-efficacy, whereas students emphasizing performance-related orientations claimed more self-handicaps. Students' task-specific motivation partly mediated the effects of achievement goal orientations on performance: mastery- and success-oriented students' confidence in their own abilities seemed to support their task engagement.

Similarly, other studies have demonstrated support for the merits of high mastery goals (i.e., a dominant mastery goal) and high approach goals (i.e., a combination of mastery and performance-approach goals) profiles in terms of motivational outcomes (see Table 23.3 for an overview of the commonly found goal profiles and how they are linked to various outcomes). Mastery-oriented students seem to express a high overall level of motivation, such as high self-efficacy, intrinsic motivation, value of studying, and perceived ability (Kolić-Vehovec et al., 2008; Schwinger et al., 2016; Tuominen-Soini et al., 2012). Similarly, success-oriented students, or students striving for both mastery and performance, also show high intrinsic motivation, commitment, self-efficacy, and task value (Korpershoek et al., 2015; Luo et al., 2011; Schwinger et al., 2016), but they are more likely to attribute learning and success to fixed abilities (Gonçalves et al., 2017; Tapola & Niemivirta, 2008) and they express higher concern for failure (Tuominen-Soini et al., 2011). Both of these groups of students nevertheless demonstrate higher persistence and effort, and report using more effective learning strategies than the others (Niemivirta, 1998; Tuominen-Soini et al., 2008; Valle et al., 2003). Compared to the above groups, students with a relative emphasis on performance goals, particularly when performance-approach goals are coupled with performance-avoidance goals, seem to exhibit less-positive patterns of motivation, such as academic withdrawal, low self-esteem, and inferior effort regulation (Luo et al., 2011; Tapola & Niemivirta, 2008). Also students with moderate or low goal profiles display rather unfavorable patterns of motivational beliefs, such as low agency beliefs, high academic withdrawal, high fear of

---

2 In the Finnish educational system, the folk high schools provide adult education that generally does not grant academic degrees. The courses typically focus on social sciences, art subjects, and languages.

Table 23.3 *Summary of the most commonly identified achievement goal profiles, their characteristics, and associations with academic and emotional outcomes*

	Predominantly mastery	Predominantly performance	Combined mastery and performance	Average	Low	Work-avoidant
Characteristics of the profile	High mastery, low other goals (e.g., mastery-oriented)	High performance, low mastery (e.g., performance-oriented)	High mastery and high performance-approach (e.g., success-oriented)	Moderate all goals (e.g., indifferent)	Low mastery and low performance (e.g., low motivation, disengaged)	High work avoidance, low other goals (e.g., avoidance-oriented)
Motivation	High self-efficacy High intrinsic motivation Commitment and effort in relation to educational goals	Relatively low self-efficacy High fear of failure	High self-efficacy High intrinsic motivation Commitment and effort in relation to educational goals High fear of failure	High academic withdrawal and fear of failure	Low self-efficacy Relatively low commitment and effort	Low commitment and effort Relatively high academic withdrawal
Academic achievement	High (mostly)	Moderate	High	Relatively low	Low	Low
Self-perceptions	Positive	Moderate	Positive	Moderate	Moderate	Relatively negative
Emotions/affect	High positive affect (enjoyment) Low negative affect (anxiety) High interest	High negative affect (anxiety, frustration)	High positive affect (enjoyment) High negative affect (anxiety, worry) High interest	Moderate negative affect	Low positive affect (enjoyment, enthusiasm) Relatively high negative affect (boredom, distress)	High negative affect (anxiety, boredom) Low interest
Academic and general well-being	High engagement High school value Low burnout Low depressive symptoms	Moderate well-being	High engagement High school value High school burnout (exhaustion, inadequacy)	Relatively low engagement and school value Moderate well-being	Moderate well-being Slightly pronounced cynicism	Low engagement Low school value High school burnout (cynicism, inadequacy) Depressive symptoms

Table 23.3 (*Cont.*)

	Predominantly mastery	Predominantly performance	Combined mastery and performance	Average	Low	Work-avoidant
Perceptions of and responses to the learning environment	Positive evaluations of course materials and teaching. High participation. Moderate satisfaction. Low preferred emphasis on ability and evaluation	Relatively high preferred emphasis on ability and evaluation	Moderate evaluations of course materials. Positive evaluations of teaching. High participation. Moderate satisfaction. High perceived and preferred emphasis on learning, individualistic work, and task variety; relatively high preferred emphasis on ability and evaluation	Moderate evaluations of course materials and teaching. Moderate participation. Moderate satisfaction		Low evaluations of course materials and teaching. Low participation. Low satisfaction. Relatively low perceived emphasis on learning, individualistic work, and task variety; low preferred emphasis on individualistic work
Task-related motivation and performance under different conditions	Increase in situational interest during task. Maintaining high self-efficacy and affect even in demanding or ego-involving task conditions	High self-handicapping and low self-efficacy in ego-involving condition	Decrease in situational interest during task			Low and stable situational interest. Self-handicapping and low self-efficacy in ego-involving condition

failure, and a dysfunctional attributional profile (Gonçalves et al., 2017; Tuominen-Soini et al., 2011), although it is the avoidance-oriented students that systematically show the most maladaptive patterns of motivation – relatively low valuing of school, low effort, and high academic withdrawal (Kolić-Vehovec et al., 2008; Niemivirta, 1998; Tapola & Niemivirta, 2008; Tuominen-Soini et al., 2011).

Profile Differences in Relation to Achievement

Regarding learning and achievement, there has been some debate over the relative benefits of holding mastery versus performance-approach goals (Harackiewicz et al., 2002; Kaplan & Middleton, 2002; Senko et al., 2011). It would seem that, surprisingly often, the adoption of performance goals contributes to better academic achievement than a focus on mastery, although this appears to depend on both the sample in question (e.g., age and educational context) and the criteria used for achievement. From the person-oriented approach, it is of particular interest to see whether taking into account the different combinations of goals could shed some light into this debate.

In one of our studies, we investigated how lower secondary school students with distinct achievement goal orientation profiles differed in terms of academic achievement, and found that both mastery- and success-oriented students performed equally well in school (Tuominen-Soini et al., 2011). The indifferent students' academic achievement was relatively inferior, but they still fared better than the avoidance-oriented students. Interestingly, similar differences were detected among the upper secondary school students, but with one distinction: success-oriented students' achievement was even higher than that of the mastery-oriented students. Considering the fact that the academic track of our upper secondary school is considerably selective and rather performance-focused by nature, this difference might implicate to a contextual effect.

On the whole, regarding the contribution of achievement goal orientation profiles to achievement in general, and the relative benefits of mastery versus performance strivings in particular, the findings seem threefold. Studies have demonstrated that (1) mastery-oriented students display the highest academic achievement (Gonçalves et al., 2017; Meece & Holt, 1993; Schwinger & Wild, 2012); (2) students emphasizing both mastery and performance-approach goals attain the best grades (Pastor et al., 2007; Tuominen-Soini et al., 2008) and; (3) these two groups perform equally well in school (Daniels et al., 2008; Pintrich, 2000; Tanaka, 2007). It seems that striving primarily for mastery is especially beneficial in terms of achievement among young students in the elementary school context (Meece & Holt, 1993; Schwinger et al., 2016; Zhang et al., 2016), while emphasizing both mastery and performance (e.g., high multiple goals or a success-oriented profile) might be most profitable in educational contexts that are relatively selective or performance-focused and competitive, such as the academic track of upper secondary school or higher education (Tuominen-Soini et al., 2011). In turn, students with predominantly performance-oriented, moderate, or low goal profiles generally receive lower grades than the two above-mentioned groups (Conley, 2012; Gonçalves et al., 2017; Pastor et al., 2007; Tuominen-Soini et al., 2008; Valle et al., 2003), followed by the avoidance-oriented students, who rather systematically display the lowest levels of academic achievement and performance (Niemivirta, 1998; Niemivirta et al., 2013; Tuominen-Soini et al., 2008). Note, however, that some studies have not found notable differences in academic achievement (Korpershoek et al., 2015; Schwinger et al., 2016; Tapola et al., 2014), particularly when the focus was on a specific task performance (Niemivirta, 2002b; Niemivirta et al., 2013; Tapola et al., 2014).

Thus, is seems that the emphasis on mastery is consistently beneficial when it comes to school achievement, although its coupling with performance goals might be particularly favorable in certain contexts. Then again, this effect does not necessarily extend to specific task performances. In fact, if students' mastery tendencies and task characteristics do not match (e.g., the task seems irrelevant for learning or focuses on trivialities), such tendencies may even turn out to be counterproductive (Pulkka & Niemivirta, 2015; see also Senko et al., 2013).

To some extent, then, this goes against some of the conclusions drawn from the findings of variable-oriented studies (as described earlier). That is, a dominant emphasis on performance does not seem to have any advantage over mastery tendencies. Considering the fact that, in some contexts, striving for performance along with mastery might result in added value, it is of importance to deliberate these observations with our findings concerning students' well-being. If the focus on performance implicates ability concerns and entails the urge to validate one's competence, such strivings might not come without consequences.

Profile Differences in Relation to Well-Being

In our studies, both mastery- and success-oriented students have been shown to be highly engaged in studying and finding their schoolwork meaningful, although success-oriented students' stronger concerns with performance seem to make them more vulnerable to emotional distress and school burnout (Tuominen-Soini et al., 2008, 2012). For some students, achievement may come with a price. That is, striving for performance and success may, even in the presence of striving for mastery, entail some unfavorable concomitants: being rather stressed and emotionally exhausted, and feeling inadequate as a student. Compared to mastery- and success-oriented students, the indifferent students report relatively low school value and engagement. However, despite not thriving in school, they do not seem to have any particular problems either. In stark contrast to mastery-oriented students, avoidance-oriented students are characterized by relatively low levels of school value and engagement, and a high level of cynicism toward school.

Findings of other studies are in line with this example, lending support once again for the adaptiveness of high mastery and combined mastery and performance-approach goal profiles (see Table 23.3). Mastery-oriented students tend to exhibit an adaptive pattern of adjustment and well-being, such as positive self-perceptions, high engagement and enjoyment, and low negative affect (Daniels et al., 2008; Tapola & Niemivirta, 2008; Tuominen-Soini et al., 2012; Turner et al., 1998). Students simultaneously emphasizing mastery and performance have been shown to value studying and to be engaged in school and committed to their educational goals but, also, to experience anxiety, stress, and even depressive symptoms somewhat more than their mastery-oriented peers (Daniels et al., 2008; Luo et al., 2011; Pintrich, 2000; Tuominen-Soini et al., 2008).

The profile in which mainly performance goals are emphasized, especially if performance-avoidance goals are high, seems to contribute to less positive emotional outcomes, such as anxiety and negative affect (Luo et al., 2011; Pintrich, 2000; Tapola & Niemivirta, 2008; Valle et al., 2015). However, holding a dominant performance-approach goal orientation is associated with more adaptive outcomes than not emphasizing any achievement goal orientation; students with low goal profiles display less adaptive patterns of motivation and learning (Bouffard et al., 1995; Daniels et al., 2008; Liu et al., 2009). Students displaying moderate achievement goal profiles express passivity and lack of engagement to some degree but, based on their manifest levels of well-being, they do not seem to experience serious psychological distress (Tuominen-Soini et al., 2011). Finally, students emphasizing mainly avoidance tendencies manifest the most negative outcomes in terms of emotion and well-being, such as adjustment problems, cynicism, depressive symptoms, low school value, and low school engagement (Kolić-Vehovec et al., 2008; Niemivirta, 2002b; Tuominen-Soini et al., 2008, 2012).

Profile Differences in Relation to the Perceptions of the Learning Environment

Student motivation should not only be seen as an educational outcome, but also as a mediator that filters the influence of the learning environment on the student. That is, if achievement goal orientation profiles represent a motivational lens through which the students interpret the events embedded in the academic context, it is also likely that students' perceptions of the learning environment and instructional practices vary as a function of their goal orientation profiles. Based on our studies, this also seems to be the case. In a series of studies on university students (Pulkka & Niemivirta, 2013a, 2013b, 2015), we found that students with predominantly mastery or combined mastery–performance profiles found the courses more interesting; were more satisfied with the courses in general; reported investing more effort into their studying and active participation; and gave the most positive evaluations of the quality of pedagogical materials, teaching methods, and assessment methods when compared to low goal or avoidance-oriented groups.

When examining how differently oriented elementary school students perceived their learning environment and what sort of instructional practices they preferred (Tapola & Niemivirta, 2008), we found that students emphasizing predominantly mastery goals, and students emphasizing both mastery and performance goals, perceived their classroom as relatively more learning focused than those high in either performance- or work-avoidance goals, who, in turn, viewed their classroom as providing less variety in task structure (e.g., possibilities for alternative task formats and activities). Similar patterns of differences were also found with respect to preferences. While performance-oriented students preferred public evaluation practices more than the other groups did, avoidance-oriented students showed the least interest in challenging and task-focused classroom work.

Other studies investigating similar issues seem to echo our findings. Compared to the others, mastery-oriented and mastery–performance-oriented students seem to perceive their classroom as cooperative and meaningful (Koul et al., 2012), and tend to evaluate teaching, evaluation, clarity of goals, and appropriateness of the workload more positively (Cano & Berben, 2009). This suggests that mastery-focused students not only have had more positive experiences during the courses, but also that they generally take a more positive stance on achievement situations. In a sense, then, these findings agree with the model of adaptive learning (Boekaerts & Niemivirta, 2000) in that, in principle, similar conditions and pedagogical settings may be viewed and experienced differently depending on the students' motivational lenses, and the perceived match contributes to students' evaluations.

Profile Differences in Task-Related Motivation and Performance as a Function of Situation

In previous examples, we have looked at how students with different achievement goal orientation profiles experience their learning environment, and how they differ in terms of achievement or task performance. However, only a few studies have examined the interaction of those, that is, how students' task-related motivation and performance vary as a function of their achievement goal orientation under different task situations or pedagogical conditions. After all, one important assumption of this approach is that specific situations may differently contribute to the responses of students with dissimilar achievement goal orientation profiles.

In one study, we found that students' situational appraisals in different task conditions varied as a function of their goal orientation profiles (Niemivirta, 2002b). For example, in an "ego-involving condition" with an emphasis on normative performance, both performance- and avoidance-oriented students reported using self-handicapping strategies more often than mastery-oriented students did, while no differences were found in the "task-involving condition" emphasizing exploration and learning. Moreover, while the context moderated performance- and avoidance-oriented students' self-efficacy (i.e., their self-efficacy was lower in the ego-involving condition), it did not influence mastery-oriented students' self-efficacy, which may be taken as an indication of the adaptiveness of the focus on mastery. Interestingly, though, no such interaction effects were found in relation to actual task performance.

In another study examining changes in students' task-related interest under two instructional conditions (i.e., science simulation with either abstract or concrete task elements), we found that, irrespective of the condition, both the overall level and change in situational interest were somewhat different for students with different goal orientation profiles (Tapola et al., 2014). On average, mastery-oriented students reported slight but steady increases in their situational interest toward the end of the task, while for success-oriented students, the change was steadily decreasing. In contrast, avoidance-oriented students' situational interest was lowest and relatively stable in both conditions. However, the patterns of changes characterizing each goal orientation group were somewhat more evident in the abstract condition, thus supporting the assumption of the interaction between achievement goal orientation group and task condition.

It thus seems that while students striving for mastery and students striving for performance goals may both show equal task performance and affect in ordinary task situations (Tanaka, 2007), students emphasizing mastery might be more likely to maintain positive self-perceptions (e.g., self-efficacy) and affect (e.g., high situational interest, low anxiety) in demanding task conditions involving complex tasks or performance pressure, for example. In a sense, these results could be taken to support the view that students' situational appraisals and reactions parallel their achievement goal orientation profiles, and that they may partly follow from the efforts to adapt to the psychological demands of the situation as experienced by the student.

Concluding Thoughts

In this chapter, we have described the principles of a person-oriented approach to studying individual differences (and similarities) and how it can be applied to the study of students' achievement goal orientations. Such an approach in the present context is theoretically justified by the argument that students, through experiences and in interaction with their environment, develop a motivational mind-set that reflects their approach and orientation toward achievement settings. This mind-set, then, becomes manifested in the students' achievement goal orientation profiles, that is, the patterning of goals and related outcomes they prefer and strive for.

Studies following this line of logic and rationale have been increasing in number in recent years and, although they may differ to some extent in whether their study design is theory-driven or whether they just apply person-oriented methods (e.g., classify participants using cluster analysis), the overall findings in terms of the different profiles identified seem rather robust. Students with qualitatively different profiles are clearly identified. Some students emphasize mastery, some performance, some avoidance, and some different combinations of these. Such profiles also seem relatively stable, thus lending support for conceptualizing them as dispositional characteristics. This does not, however, imply that they should be taken as fixed entities, but rather as generalizations that set the stage for new experiences and contribute to students' responses somewhat differently depending on the context.

The person-oriented approach provides a way of looking at the relative emphasis of different achievement goal orientations, thereby explicitly addressing the issue of multiple goals and their associations with important outcomes (see Table 23.3). The present review thus provides insight into "which orientation is good for what" and contributes to the debate concerning the advantages of endorsing different goals. For example, the findings suggest that students' tendency to validate and demonstrate their personal qualities may be associated with some desired educational outcomes (such as engagement, valuing of school, and academic achievement), but it may also be linked to some adjustment problems and socio-emotional vulnerability, even when such performance-focused goals and outcomes are pursued along with mastery-focused goals.

The findings also have implications for learning. For example, it would seem that goal configurations or goal orientation profiles partly contribute to where the learner's mental energy and focus are directed in achievement-related situations: whether the focus is mainly on the task itself (mastery) or on its outcomes (performance). In the mastery mode, the "state of being involved" is important and rewarding in its own right, while the performance mode is instrumental in the aim of excelling or demonstrating superiority over others. Depending on the emphasis given to different goals and outcomes, then, students would seem to be inclined to engage under very different psychological mind-sets: while emphasis on mastery seems to facilitate concentration and commitment to learning, emphasis on performance is more likely accompanied with greater emotional vulnerability due to concerns with students proving their adequacy. Then again, if students considered those consequences immaterial, they might completely detach from the task (avoidance). This, in turn, would likely depend on whether the disengagement was due to a complete lack of interest and personal relevance (alienation) or due to repeated exposure to emotionally negative and discouraging learning experiences (self-protective withdrawal). The validity of this assumption, however, remains an open question, as current research informs us rather little about the different reasons for disengagement and avoidance.

The diversity in conceptualizations and operationalizations, analyses used, and characteristics of the participants naturally complicates the interpretation and generalization of the results, but also the approach itself (i.e., classification and use of resulting groups in drawing inferences about motivational differences) brings about the risks of oversimplifying the underlying phenomena and misunderstanding the nature of the findings and their implications. From the theoretical point of view, we have already cautioned the reader to not consider achievement goal orientation profiles as fixed entities or trait-like characteristics, and similar awareness should also be extended to what commonly follows from the employed methodology. For example, the types of profiles extracted depend on the classification method applied, type of measures used, and sets of orientations included in the analysis. Already the criteria for deciding the most appropriate or valid number of groups may make a crucial difference, and even if model-based techniques accompanied by specific statistical criteria were used, the choice of the final solution always involves some degree of subjective decision-making. Similarly, the interpretation of profiles and labeling them accordingly are subject to judgment. The labels are often formulated to reflect substantively meaningful variation in both the absolute level and relative emphasis of different orientations. This is not, however, meant to be categorical in the sense that all the individuals in the given group were "of this kind," but should rather be understood as a descriptive and pragmatic way of illustrating some core features of each group in comparison to others. For example, for a group to be labeled as avoidance-oriented, the absolute level of work avoidance would not need to be extremely high, if the relative level was high compared to both the other orientations within the group and the level of work avoidance in other groups. It might thus be the one distinguishing feature of the group, which would then become salient through corresponding labeling. Both researchers and readers should bear this in mind and exercise caution when looking into the findings.

This also has important practical implications. Considering the extensive and rather systematic findings on the different motivational profiles and how they are linked to learning, achievement, and well-being, it would clearly be of relevance if teachers and educators were able to identify such tendencies in students. However, this should not lead to stigmatizing the students with corresponding labels and treating them as groups of individuals having invariable motivational mind-sets with different normative values attached to them. As research shows, despite the observed stability of different profiles, the context does matter. Certain tendencies do not result in similar responses in all situations, and the emphasis of different orientations may change as a function of the context. The key question from the educators' perspective would then be how to structure the environment so that it provided the most optimal fit with all different tendencies. A failure safe and supportive environment would likely benefit all students, but certain procedures and activities might also be of particular relevance for some students. Mastery-oriented students might appreciate facilitation and cultivation of personal interests, performance-oriented students might value challenging tasks with minimal emphasis on social comparison, and avoidance-oriented students might become more engaged through meaningful and personalized tasks. Although this conclusion is yet without unambiguous evidence, it would seem that pedagogical practices focusing on mastery are advantageous for all students, with given individual differences additionally addressed through personification. Naturally, this is a very challenging task, particularly since we know that pedagogical delivery itself is subject to students' interpretations, due to which future research should address more thoroughly what sort of practices are the most beneficial, for whom, and under what conditions.

In this chapter, we have provided a rather comprehensive review of the studies investigating students' achievement goals and goal orientations from a person-oriented perspective. Despite the growing interest in this line of research, many open questions remain, thereby providing suggestions for future research. Longitudinal designs would be valuable in order to provide more insight into both the stability and fluctuation of motivational profiles over time, and their long-term adaptiveness in relation to different academic (e.g., learning and achievement) and personal (e.g., well-being and aspirations) outcomes. More research is also needed on how individual goal configurations are manifested in specific learning situations and under different conditions (e.g., high versus low stakes tasks, tasks varying in personal relevance or utility). Similarly important would be to more precisely take into account the role of other personal factors (e.g., temperament) and the situation (e.g., fluctuations in motivational states), as well as their interaction in producing different responses and learning outcomes, both during tasks and over time. Finally, developmental studies should also be implemented that look at the early antecedents and sources of different tendencies (e.g., parenting), as well as their influence on the development of other motivational factors (e.g., interests and competence perceptions). Although these suggestions imply rather complex and demanding study designs, we are confident that complementing them with a person-oriented approach would provide some added value in addressing the likely heterogeneity in situational dynamics and developmental trajectories.

Appendix: Summary of studies examining achievement goal orientation profiles

Studies using median split procedures

Study	Measures	Domain	Sample, N, Country	Method	Number of profiles: their labels
Pintrich & Garcia, 1991	Intrinsic and extrinsic (i.e., mastery and performance) goal orientations (MSLQ; Pintrich et al., 1993)	General	College students,[b] N = 263, USA	Quartile split	9: Intrinsic and extrinsic goal orientations were split into the lowest quartile, middle 50 percent, and highest quartile, and these two three-level categorical variables were crossed, resulting in nine cells
Bouffard et al., 1995	Learning and performance goal orientations (LPOQ; Ames & Archer, 1988; Pintrich & De Groot, 1990; Bouffard et al., 1995)	General, course-specific	College students, N = 702, Canada	Median split	4: High learning/high performance (HLHP); high learning/low performance (HLLP); low learning/high performance (LLHP); low learning/low performance (LLLP)
Bouffard et al., 1998	Learning and performance goal orientations (LPOQ; Bouffard et al., 1995)	General, course-specific	Junior (N = 408), middle (N = 323), and senior (N = 341) high school students, Canada	Median split	4: High learning/high performance (HLHP); high learning/low performance (HLLP); low learning/high performance (LLHP); low learning/low performance (LLLP)
Pintrich, 2000	Mastery and performance goal orientations (Midgley et al., 1998)	Mathematics	Eighth and ninth graders from junior high school, N = 150, USA	Median split	4: High-mastery/low-performance; high-mastery/high-performance; low-mastery/high-performance; low-mastery/low-performance

(*Cont.*)

Study	Measures	Domain	Sample, *N*, Country	Method	Number of profiles: their labels
Haydel & Roeser, 2002	Task mastery, ego-approach, and ego-avoidance orientations (PALS; Midgley et al., 2000; and implicit theories of intelligence, self-confidence in science ability)[a]	Science	Tenth and 11th graders from high school, *N* = 403, USA	Median split	4: Mastery-oriented (incremental intelligence beliefs and a mastery orientation); ego-oriented (entity intelligence beliefs, an ego orientation, and high confidence); helpless (entity intelligence beliefs, an ego orientation, and low confidence); unclassified
Roeser et al., 2002	Task, ego-approach, and ego-avoidance goal orientations (PALS; Midgley et al., 1995; and intelligence is fixed, academic mastery efficacy)[a]	Course-specific (social studies and science)	Sixth, seventh, and eighth graders from middle school, *N* = 62, USA	Median split	3: Mastery-oriented; ego-oriented; helpless
Shih, 2005	Mastery, performance-approach, and performance-avoidance goals (Elliot & Church, 1997)	General	Sixth graders from elementary school, *N* = 242, Taiwan	Median split	4: High mastery/low performance-approach; low mastery/high performance-approach; high/high; low/low 4: High performance-approach/ low performance-avoidance; low performance-approach/high performance-avoidance; high/high; low/ low

590

Study	Goal measure	Context	Sample	Method	Groups
Ng, 2006	Mastery, performance-approach, and work avoidance goals	Course assignment-specific	Adult distance learners, $N = 168$, Hong Kong	Median split	4: Mastery-focused learners; performance-focused learners; balanced-goal learners; performance-anxious learners
Lau & Lee, 2008	Mastery and performance-approach goals (Greene et al., 2004; and perceived instrumentality)[a]	General	Eighth-graders from secondary schools, $N = 925$, Hong Kong	Median split	4: High mastery/high performance-approach; high mastery/low performance-approach; low mastery/high performance-approach; low mastery/low performance-approach goal groups
Koul et al., 2009	Mastery and performance goal orientations (Niemivirta, 1998)	General	University students, $N = 867$, Thailand	Median split	4: High mastery/high performance; high mastery/low performance; low mastery/high performance; low mastery/low performance
Sideridis & Kaplan, 2011	Mastery, performance-approach, and performance-avoidance goals (Elliot & Church, 1997)	Solving puzzles	University students, $N = 97$, Greece	Median split	4: Mastery-oriented; performance approach–oriented; performance avoidance–oriented; amotivated

Studies using cluster analysis or model-based techniques

Study	Measures	Domain	Sample, N, country	Method	Number of profiles: their labels
Meece & Holt, 1993	Task-mastery, ego-social, and work-avoidant goals (Meece et al., 1988)	Science	Fifth and sixth graders, $N = 257$, USA	Cluster analysis	3: High mastery (high on mastery but low on other goals); combined mastery-ego (high on both mastery and ego, low on work-avoidant goals); low mastery-ego (low on mastery-ego, but high on work-avoidant goals)
Seifert, 1995	Mastery and performance goal orientations (Seifert, 1995)	General	Fifth graders, $N = 79$, Canada	Cluster analysis	3: Both mastery- and performance-oriented; mastery-oriented; moderately performance-oriented but not mastery-oriented
Niemivirta, 1998	Learning, performance, and avoidance orientations (Niemivirta, 1998)	General	Seventh graders from junior high school, $N = 485$, Finland	Cluster analysis	3: Learning-oriented; performance-oriented; avoidance-oriented
Turner et al., 1998	Learning and ability goals (PALS; Midgley & Maehr, 1991; and negative affect, deep strategy, self-efficacy, action after failure, preference for difficulty)[a]	Mathematics	Fifth and sixth graders from elementary school, $N = 160$, USA	Cluster analysis	4: Learning-oriented; success-oriented; uncommitted; avoidant

Study	Constructs (measure)	Domain	Sample	Method	Number and description of clusters
Bembenutty, 1999	Task, performance-approach, and performance-avoidance goal orientations (PALS; Midgley et al., 1997)	Mathematics	College students, N = 102, USA	Cluster analysis	3: High mastery; combined high mastery and high performance-approach; low mastery, low performance-approach, and low performance-avoidance
Suárez Riveiro et al., 2001	Task, self-enhancing ego, self-defeating ego, and work-avoidance orientations (Skaalvik, 1997)	General	University students, N = 595, Spain	Cluster analysis	3: High self-enhancing/self-defeating/work-avoidance and medium task goals; high task/self-defeating and medium self-enhancing/work-avoidance goals; high task, medium work-avoidance and low self-enhancing/self-defeating goals
Niemivirta, 2002b	Mastery-intrinsic, mastery-extrinsic, performance-approach, performance-avoidance, and work-avoidance orientations (Niemivirta, 2002b)	General	Ninth graders from junior high school, N = 143, Finland	Latent class cluster analysis	3: Learning-oriented; avoidance-oriented; performance-oriented
Sideridis & Tsorbatzoudis, 2003	Mastery, performance-approach, task avoidance, and positive social experiences (Elliot & Church, 1997; Lethwaite & Piparo, 1993; Ablard & Lipschultz, 1998; Thorkildsen & Nicholls, 1998; Eccles et al., 1983; Wigfield & Guthrie, 1997; and other cognitive and motivational variables)[a]	Mathematics	Fifth and sixth graders from elementary school, N = 58, Greece	Cluster analysis	3: Amotivated/disengaged-low achievers; motivated-high achievers; avoidant/uncommitted-low achievers

Study	Measures	Domain	Sample, *N*, country	Method	Number of profiles: their labels
Valle et al., 2003	Learning, performance, and social reinforcement goals (Hayamizu & Weiner, 1991)	General	University students, *N* = 609, Spain	Cluster analysis	3: Predominance of performance goals (PG); predominance of multiple goals (MG); predominance of learning goals (LG)
Veermans & Tapola, 2004	Learning, performance, and avoidance orientations (Niemivirta, 1998)	General	Primary school students followed from third to sixth grade,[b] *N* = 21, Finland	Cluster analysis	3: Avoidance; learning; performance-avoidance
Smith & Sinclair, 2005	Task, performance approach, and performance-avoidance goals (PALS; Midgley et al., 1998)	General	Final year high school students, *N* = 588, Australia	Cluster analysis	7: Average multi-goal; approach; task; disengaged; strong multi-goal; task/approach; avoid/approach
Brdar et al., 2006	Learning, performance, and work-avoidance goal orientations (Niemivirta, 1996, 1998)	General	High school students, *N* = 1057, Croatia	Cluster analysis	4: Learning-oriented; work-avoidance-oriented; performance-/learning-oriented; performance-/work-avoidance-oriented

Fortunato & Goldblatt, 2006	Learning, performance-approach, and performance-avoidance goal orientations (VandeWalle, 1997)	General	Undergraduate students, N = 311, USA	Cluster analysis	4: Fear-based achievers; low achievers; moderate achievers; high achievers
Woodrow, 2006	Task, performance-approach, and performance-avoidance goal orientations (PALS; Midgley et al., 1997; and language test, integrative, intensity, anxiety in class, anxiety out of class, self-efficacy in class, self-efficacy out of class, cognitive strategies, social strategies, metacognitive strategies)[a]	English	Asian students taking English courses at intensive language centers prior to university entry, N = 275, Australia	Cluster analysis, profile analysis using multidimensional scaling (PAMS)	2: Adaptive learning; less adaptive learning
Levy-Tossman et al., 2007	Mastery, performance-approach, and performance-avoidance goals (PALS; Midgley et al., 2000)	General	Seventh graders from junior high school, N = 203, Israel	Cluster analysis	6: Medium-low mastery and performance-approach, low performance-avoidance; medium mastery, low performance; medium-low mastery, medium performance; medium-high mastery, high performance; high mastery, medium performance-approach, medium-low performance-avoidance; high mastery and performance-approach, medium performance-avoidance

Study	Measures	Domain	Sample, N, country	Method	Number of profiles: their labels
Pastor et al., 2007	Mastery-approach, performance-approach, performance-avoidance, and mastery-avoidance goals (Elliot & McGregor, 2001)	General, semester-specific	College students, N = 1868, USA	Latent profile analysis	Two-, three-, and four-factor conceptualizations were used: five profiles were needed to classify students in the two- and three-factor conceptualizations and six profiles in the four-factor conceptualization. The majority of students were represented in clusters with moderate to high levels on goal orientations. No profile emerged that was low in mastery-approach, and with one exception in the four-factor conceptualization, no profile emerged that was high on avoidance measures.
Tanaka, 2007	Learning, achievement, performance-approach, and performance-avoidance orientations (Niemivirta, 1999)	General	Ninth graders from junior high school, N = 109, Japan	Cluster analysis	3: HL–HP (high learning/high performance goal group); HL–LP (high learning/low performance goal group); LL–LP (low learning/low performance goal group)
Daniels et al., 2008	Mastery and performance-approach goals (MSLQ; Pintrich et al., 1993)	Course-specific (introductory psychology)	College students, N = 1002, Canada	Cluster analysis	4: High mastery/performance (multiple goals); dominant mastery; dominant performance; low mastery/performance (low motivation)
Kolić-Vehovec et al., 2008	Mastery, performance, and work-avoidance orientations (Rijavec & Brdar, 2002; Niemivirta, 1998)	General	University students, N = 352, Croatia	Cluster analysis	4: Mastery; mastery–performance; performance–work-avoidance; work-avoidance

596

Study	Constructs	Domain	Sample	Method	Profiles
Lau & Roeser, 2008	Task mastery, ego approach, ego avoidance, and work avoidance goals (PALS; Midgley et al., 2000; task values, classroom emotions, test anxiety, competence-beliefs, context beliefs, regulatory processes, cognitive abilities)[a]	Science	High school students, N = 318, USA	Inverse factor analysis	4: Boys: able and confident; anxious and ego-involved; intrinsically motivated and task-involved; able but work avoidant. 4: Girls: able; positive perception of classroom; confident and task-involved; anxious and ego-involved
Ng, 2008	Mastery-development, performance-approach (Ames & Archer, 1988; Bouffard et al., 1995; Meece et al., 1988; Young, 1997), work-related, social enhancement, and social affiliation goals[a]	Course-specific	Adult distance learners, N = 797, Hong Kong	Cluster analysis	4: Mastery-focused learners; multiple-goal learners with a work focus; multiple-goal learners with a performance focus; multiple-goal learners with multiple focuses
Tapola & Niemivirta, 2008	Learning, performance, and avoidance orientations (Niemivirta et al., 2001)	General	Sixth graders from elementary school, N = 208, Finland	Latent class cluster analysis	4: Learning-oriented; achievement-oriented; performance-oriented; avoidance-oriented
Tuominen-Soini et al., 2008	Mastery-intrinsic, mastery-extrinsic, performance-approach, performance-avoidance, and work-avoidance orientations (Niemivirta, 2002b)	General	Ninth graders from lower secondary school and second-year students from general upper secondary school, N = 1321, Finland	Latent profile analysis	6: Indifferent; mastery-oriented; performance-oriented; success-oriented; disengaged; avoidance-oriented
Cano & Berbén, 2009	Mastery-approach, mastery-avoidance, performance-approach, and performance-avoidance goals (Elliot & McGregor, 2001)	Mathematics	University students, N = 680, Spain	Cluster analysis	4: Low achievement goals (AG), specifically on mastery goals; low AG but moderately high mastery approach; high AG but low performance approach; high AG, specifically performance approach

Study	Measures	Domain	Sample, *N*, country	Method	Number of profiles: their labels
Dina & Efklides, 2009	Mastery, performance-approach, and performance-avoidance goal orientations (Midgley et al., 1998; and math ability, mathematics self-concept, attitude toward mathematics, test anxiety)[a]	Mathematics	Seventh and ninth graders from junior high school, *N* = 870, Greece	Cluster analysis	8: High attitude/high self-concept/high mastery/high performance-approach; high ability/high anxiety; high performance/low ability; low attitude/low self-concept/low mastery; high ability/high attitude/low anxiety/low performance-avoidance; high performance/low ability/high anxiety/low attitude/low self-concept; low goals/low attitude/low self-concept/low anxiety; low anxiety
Liu et al., 2009	Mastery-approach, mastery-avoidance, performance-approach, and performance-avoidance goals (Elliot & McGregor, 2001)	Project work	Secondary Two students, *N* = 491, Singapore	Cluster analysis	4: Moderately; highly; moderately high; low
Ng, 2009	Mastery, performance-approach, and work-avoidance goals (Ames, 1992; Meece et al., 1988; Young, 1997)	Course assignment–specific (essay)	Adult distance learners, *N* = 441, Hong Kong	Cluster analysis	3: Performance-focused; work-avoidant; multiple-goal learners
van der Veen & Peetsma, 2009	Mastery and performance-approach orientation (Seegers et al., 2002)	Mathematics	First graders from lowest level of secondary school, *N* = 735, Netherlands	Cluster analysis	4: Low mastery–low performance-approach; low mastery–high performance-approach; high mastery–low performance-approach; high mastery–high performance-approach

Study	Goal constructs	Domain	Sample	Analysis	Profiles
Luo et al., 2011	Mastery, performance-approach, and performance-avoidance goals (PALS; Midgley et al., 1998, 2000)	Mathematics	Secondary Three students, $N = 1697$, Singapore	Latent class cluster analysis	4: Diffuse (moderate multiple); moderate mastery (moderate mastery/low performance approach and avoidance); success-oriented (moderate mastery/high performance approach and avoidance); approach (high mastery and performance approach/low performance avoidance)
Tuominen-Soini et al., 2011	Mastery-intrinsic, mastery-extrinsic, performance-approach, performance-avoidance, and work-avoidance orientations (Niemivirta, 2002b)	General	Ninth graders from lower secondary school,[b] $N = 530$ and second-year students from general upper secondary school,[b] $N = 519$, Finland	Latent profile analysis	4: Indifferent; success-oriented; mastery-oriented; avoidance-oriented
Núñez et al., 2011	Learning, performance, and social reinforcement goals[a] (Hayamizu & Weiner, 1991)	General	Primary and secondary school students with learning disabilities, $N = 259$, Spain	Cluster analysis	4: Profile with predominance of performance and social-reinforcement-seeking goals (PSG); profile with generalized low motivation (LowM); multiple goal profile (MG); profile with predominance of learning goals (LG)
Bembenutty, 2012	Task, performance-approach, and performance-avoidance goal orientations (PALS; Midgley et al., 1997)	General	Preservice teachers enrolled in an educational psychology course at a college, $N = 169$, USA	Latent class analysis	4: Moderate mastery, low performance, moderate avoidance; high mastery, low performance, low avoidance; high mastery, low performance, moderate avoidance; high mastery, moderate performance, moderate avoidance

(Cont.)

Study	Measures	Domain	Sample, N, country	Method	Number of profiles: their labels
Berger, 2012	Mastery-approach, challenge-mastery, performance-approach, performance-avoidance, and work-avoidance goals (Elliot & McGregor, 2001; Grant & Dweck, 2003)	Professional mathematics	Vocational school students, N = 263, Switzerland	Latent profile analysis	4: Low mastery and challenge-mastery but high work-avoidance; a standard profile with no peak on any goals; high mastery but low performance and work-avoidance goals; high mastery, performance-approach, and performance-avoidance goals
Conley, 2012	Mastery, performance-approach, and performance-avoidance goals (PALS; Midgley et al. 2000; and task values, competence beliefs)[a]	Mathematics	Seventh graders from middle school, N = 1870, USA	Cluster analysis	7: Low cluster; average-traditional; average-high cost; average-multiple goals; high-low cost; high-high cost; high-all
Jang & Liu, 2012	Mastery-approach, performance-approach, mastery-avoidance, and performance-avoidance goals (AGQ; Elliot & McGregor, 2001)	Mathematics	Secondary Two students, N = 480, Singapore	Cluster analysis	5: High multiple goals; high mastery approach; low multiple goals; high mastery avoidance; low performance goals
Koul et al., 2012	Mastery, performance-approach, and performance-avoidance goal orientations (Niemivirta, 1998; and GPA scores, perceptions of classroom learning environment, and levels of classroom anxiety)[a]	Biology and physics	High school students, N = 1538, Thailand	Cluster analysis	2: Students with higher GPA scores and high levels of mastery goals; students with lower GPA scores, high levels of performance-approach and performance-avoidance goals, and high levels of classroom anxieties
Schwinger & Wild, 2012	Mastery, performance-approach, and performance-avoidance goals (Nicholls et al., 1985; Köller & Baumert, 1998)	Mathematics	Students followed from third to seventh grade,[b] N = 302, Germany	Latent profile analysis	3: High multiple goals; moderate multiple goals; primarily mastery-oriented
Tuominen-Soini et al., 2012	Mastery-intrinsic, mastery-extrinsic, performance-approach, performance-avoidance, and work-avoidance orientations (Niemivirta, 2002b)	General	Ninth graders followed from lower to upper secondary school,[b] N = 579, Finland	Latent profile analysis	4: Indifferent; success-oriented; mastery-oriented; avoidance-oriented

Study	Construct (measure)	Domain	Sample	Analysis	Results
Dela Rosa & Bernardo, 2013	Mastery-approach and performance-approach orientations (Harackiewicz et al., 1997)	Algebra	University students, N = 900, Philippines	Cluster analysis	4: Predominantly performance-approach; predominantly mastery-approach; multiple goals; low achievement goal
Pulkka & Niemivirta, 2013a	Mastery-intrinsic, mastery-extrinsic, performance-approach, performance-avoidance, and work-avoidance orientations (Niemivirta, 2002)	General	First and second year students from the National Defense University,[b] N = 169, Finland	Latent class cluster analysis	4: Mastery-oriented; success-oriented; avoidance-oriented; indifferent
Pulkka & Niemivirta, 2013b	Mastery-intrinsic, mastery-extrinsic, performance-approach, performance-avoidance, and work-avoidance orientations (Niemivirta, 2002b)	General	First and second year students from the National Defense University, N = 167, Finland	Latent class cluster analysis	4: Mastery-oriented; success-oriented; indifferent; avoidance-oriented
Shim & Finch, 2014	Mastery, performance-approach, and performance-avoidance goals (PALS; Midgley et al., 2000; and social development, social demonstration-approach, and social demonstration-avoidance goals)[a] (Ryan & Shim, 2008)	General	Middle school students, N = 440, USA	Confirmatory factor latent class analysis	6: Class 1 was totally mastery- and development-goals-oriented; class 2 was mastery-oriented in the academic sphere but showed high pursuit of all social goals; classes 3 and 4 both had moderately high academic achievement goals, but class 3 had lower social goals compared to class 4; class 5 had the lowest achievement goals; class 6 had low academic achievement goals but relatively high values for social development, approach, and avoidance goals compared to class 5

(Cont.)

Study	Measures	Domain	Sample, N, country	Method	Number of profiles: their labels
Tapola et al., 2014	Mastery-intrinsic, mastery-extrinsic, performance-approach, performance-avoidance, and work-avoidance orientations (Niemivirta, 2002b)	General	Fourth, fifth, and sixth graders from elementary school, $N = 140$, Finland	Latent class cluster analysis	3: Success-oriented; mastery-oriented; avoidance-oriented
Dull et al., 2015	Mastery and performance goals (Duncan & McKeachie, 2005; Pintrich et al., 1993)	Accounting	University students, $N = 521$, USA	Cluster analysis	4: Multiple-goal; mastery; performance; low motivation
Flanagan et al., 2015	Self-approach, self-avoidance, task-approach, task-avoidance, other-approach, and other-avoidance goals (AGQ; Elliot et al., 2011)	Course-specific	University students, $N = 286$, England, Australia, and Singapore	Cluster analysis	4: Very high mastery; high–very high all goals; moderately high mastery; very–extremely high all goals
Inglés et al., 2015	Learning, achievement, and social reinforcement goals[a] (Hayamizu & Weiner, 1991)	General	Compulsory secondary education students, $N = 2022$, Spain	Cluster analysis	4: High generalized motivation; low generalized motivation; predominance of learning and achievement goals; predominance of social reinforcement goals
Korpershoek et al., 2015	Mastery, performance, extrinsic, and social motivation[a] (McInerney & Ali, 2006)	General	Ninth graders from secondary school, $N = 7257$, Netherlands	Multi-level latent class analysis	6: Above average on all scales; below average on all scales; average scores on mastery and social and above average scores on performance and extrinsic; above average scores on mastery and social; two clusters with extremely low scores on performance and to a lesser extent on extrinsic

Study	Goals/constructs	Domain	Sample	Analysis	Profiles
Valle et al., 2015a	Learning, performance-approach, and performance-avoidance goals (Skaalvik, 1997)	General	University students, $N = 2556$, Spain	Cluster analysis	7: LG (learning goals); LG/P-AvG (learning goals/performance-avoidance goals); P-AvG (performance-avoidance goals); HM-MG (high motivation by multiple goals); P-ApG/P-AvG (performance-approach goals/performance-avoidance goals); LM (Low Motivation); LG/PApG (learning goals/performance-approach goals)
Valle et al., 2015b	Learning, performance-approach, and performance-avoidance goals (Núñez et al., 1997)	General	Fourth, fifth, and sixth graders from elementary school, $N = 535$, Spain	Cluster analysis	3: Low multiple goals; high multiple goals; predominantly learning goals
Jansen in de Wal et al., 2016	Mastery approach, performance approach, and performance avoidance orientation (Seegers et al., 2002)	Language and mathematics	Fifth and sixth graders from elementary school,[b] $N = 722$, Netherlands	Latent profile analysis, latent transition analysis	3: Multiple goals; approach-oriented; moderate/indifferent; similar goal profiles could be discerned at all measurement waves for both language and mathematics
Peixoto et al., 2016	Task, self-enhancing ego, self-defeating ego, and avoidance orientation (Skaalvik, 1997; Pipa et al., 2016)	General	Fifth and seventh graders, $N = 695$, Portugal	Cluster analysis	4: Self-defeating-oriented; self-enhancing-oriented; disengaged; task-oriented
Regueiro et al., 2016	Acquisition, competence and control goals, goals of interest in subjects, performance-avoidance, performance-approach, work-avoidance, social recognition goals, obtaining future work goals, and punishment-avoidance goals (Núñez et al., 1997)[a]	General	High school students, $N = 714$, Spain	Latent profile analysis	5: Moderate learning goals; unmotivated; failure avoidance; positive goals; multiple goals

(*Cont.*)

Study	Measures	Domain	Sample, *N*, country	Method	Number of profiles: their labels
Schwinger et al., 2016	Mastery, performance-approach, and performance-avoidance goals (Spinath et al., 2002)	Mathematics	Third and fourth graders from elementary school,[b] *N* = 542, Germany	Latent profile analysis	5: High multiple goals; moderate multiple goals; primarily mastery-oriented; moderately performance-oriented; amotivated (all profiles were not prevalent at each measurement wave)
Wilson et al., 2016	Mastery, performance-approach, and performance-avoidance goals (PALS; Midgley et al., 2000)	General	Third graders from elementary school, *N* = 195, USA	Cluster analysis	4: Mastery; multi-goal; avoidant; low motivation
Zhang et al., 2016	Mastery, performance-approach, and performance-avoidance goals (Midgley et al., 2000; Köller & Baumert, 1998; Schwinger & Wild, 2006)	General	Fourth graders from elementary school, *N* = 4387, Germany	Latent class analysis	3: Mastery-oriented; high multiple; low mastery
Zhou, 2016	Mastery-approach, performance-approach, performance-avoidance, and mastery-avoidance goals (Elliot & Murayama, 2008)	Task-specific	University students, *N* = 105, China	Cluster analysis	3: Mastery-approach-focused; approach-oriented; avoidance-oriented
Gonçalves et al., 2017	Mastery, performance-approach self-presentation, performance-approach competitive, and performance-avoidance goals (PALS; Midgley et al., 2000) and social responsibility, prosocial friendship-oriented, and prosocial learning-oriented goals (Wentzel, 1993)[a]	General	Ninth graders from basic education and tenth graders from secondary school,[b] *N* = 386, Portugal	Latent class cluster analysis	6: Overall moderate; disaffected; performance-oriented; mastery-social-oriented; overall high non-competitive; performance-mastery-oriented
Lee et al., 2017	Mastery-approach, performance-approach, and performance-avoidance goals (PALS; Midgley et al., 2000)	Anatomy	University students,[b] *N* = 121, USA	Latent profile analysis	3: Very-low performance; low performance; moderate performance (all profiles had similarly high levels of mastery)

| Litalien et al., 2017 | Task, effort, competition, social power, affiliation, social concerns, praise, and token reward goals (ISM; McInerney & Ali, 2006)[a] | General | High school students, $N = 7848$, Hong Kong | Latent profile analysis | 5: Mastery-competition-oriented; moderately motivated; mastery-social-oriented; social power and rewards-oriented; mastery-oriented (males)/moderately unmotivated (females) |
| Tuominen et al., 2018 | Mastery-intrinsic, mastery-extrinsic, performance-approach, performance-avoidance, and work-avoidance orientations (Niemivirta, 2002b) | General | Sixth graders from elementary school and seventh graders from lower secondary school,[b] $N = 419$, Finland | Latent profile analysis, latent transition analysis | 4: Indifferent; success-oriented; mastery-oriented; avoidance-oriented |

Note. This summary comprises altogether 71 studies in peer-reviewed, English-language journals that meet the criteria of clustering students on the basis of achievement goals or goal orientations, and follow a person-oriented approach with corresponding methods. Studies within the field of sports psychology are excluded from this summary. A search was conducted using various databases (e.g., PsycINFO, ERIC, Scopus) for the years 1990–2017. References that were published in a scholarly journal and that described an empirical study were selected. The reference lists for all relevant articles were examined to locate additional studies. Also, a manual search for articles from key authors in the field was conducted.
[a]Other variables were used for classification in addition to achievement goals or goal orientations.
[b]The study includes longitudinal analysis of achievement goal orientation profiles.

References

Ablard, K. E. & Lipschultz, R. E. (1998). Self-regulated learning in high-achieving students: Relations to advanced reasoning, achievement goals, and gender. *Journal of Educational Psychology, 90*, 94–101. doi: 10.1037/0022-0663.90.1.94

Ames, C. (1992). Classrooms: Goals, structures, and student motivation. *Journal of Educational Psychology, 84*, 261–71. doi: 10.1037/0022-0663.84.3.261

Ames, C. & Archer, J. (1988). Achievement goals in the classroom: Students' learning strategies and motivation processes. *Journal of Educational Psychology, 80*, 260–7. doi: 10.1037//0022-0663.80.3.260

Bembenutty, H. (1999). Sustaining motivation and academic goals: The role of academic delay of gratification. *Learning and Individual Differences, 11*(3), 233–57. doi: 10.1016/S1041-6080(99)80002-8

Bembenutty, H. (2012). Latent class analysis of teacher candidates' goal orientation, perception of classroom structure, motivation, and self-regulation. *Psychology Journal, 9*(3), 97–106.

Berger, J. (2012). Uncovering vocational students' multiple goal profiles in the learning of professional mathematics: Differences in learning strategies, motivational beliefs, and cognitive abilities. *Educational Psychology, 32*(4), 405–25. doi: 10.1080/01443410.2012.674663

Bergman, L. R. & Magnusson, D. (1997). A person-oriented approach in research on developmental psychopathology. *Development and Psychopathology, 9*(2), 291–319.

Bergman, L. R. & Trost, K. (2006). The person-oriented versus the variable-oriented approach: Are they complementary, opposites, or exploring different worlds? *Merrill-Palmer Quarterly, 52*, 601–32.

Boekaerts, M. & Niemivirta, M. (2000). Self-regulated learning: Finding a balance between learning goals and ego-protective goals. In M. Boekaerts, P. R. Pintrich, & M. Zeidner (Eds.), *Handbook of self-regulation* (pp. 417–50). San Diego, CA: Academic Press.

Bong, M. (2009). Age-related differences in achievement goal differentiation. *Journal of Educational Psychology, 101*, 879–96. doi: 10.1037/a0015945

Bouffard, T., Boisvert, J., Vezeau, C., & Larouche, C. (1995). The impact of goal orientation on self-regulation and performance among college students. *British Journal of Educational Psychology, 65*(3), 317–29.

Bouffard, T., Vezeau, C., & Bordeleau, L. (1998). A developmental study of the relation between combined learning and performance goals and students' self-regulated learning. *British Journal of Educational Psychology, 68*(3), 309–19.

Brdar, I., Rijavec, M., & Loncaric, D. (2006). Goal orientations, coping with school failure and school achievement. *European Journal of Psychology of Education, 21*(1), 53–70. doi: 10.1007/BF03173569

Cano, F. & Berben, A. B. G. (2009). University students' achievement goals and approaches to learning in mathematics. *British Journal of Educational Psychology, 79*(1), 131–53. doi: 10.1348/000709908X314928

Conley, A. M. (2012). Patterns of motivation beliefs: Combining achievement goal and expectancy-value perspectives. *Journal of Educational Psychology*, *104*(1), 32–47. doi: 10.1037/a0026042

Daniels, L. M., Haynes, T. L., Stupnisky, R. H., Perry, R. P., Newall, N. E., & Pekrun, R. (2008). Individual differences in achievement goals: A longitudinal study of cognitive, emotional, and achievement outcomes. *Contemporary Educational Psychology*, *33*(4), 584–608. doi: 10.1016/j.cedpsych.2007.08.002

Dela Rosa, E. D. & Bernardo, A. B. I. (2013). Testing multiple goals theory in an Asian context: Filipino university students' motivation and academic achievement. *International Journal of School & Educational Psychology*, *1*(1), 47–57. doi: 10.1080/21683603.2013.782594

Dina, F. & Efklides, A. (2009). Student profiles of achievement goals, goal instructions and external feedback: Their effect on mathematical task performance and affect. *European Journal of Education and Psychology*, *2*, 235–62.

Dowson, M. & McInerney, D. M. (2001). Psychological parameters of students' social and work avoidance goals: A qualitative investigation. *Journal of Educational Psychology*, *93*, 35–42. doi: 10.1037/0022-0663.93.1.35

Dull, R. B., Schleifer, L. L. F., & McMillan, J. J. (2015). Achievement goal theory: The relationship of accounting students' goal orientations with self-efficacy, anxiety, and achievement. *Accounting Education*, *24*(2), 152–74. doi: 10.1080/09639284.2015.1036892

Duncan, T. G. & McKeachie, W. J. (2005). The making of the motivated strategies for learning questionnaire. *Educational Psychologist*, *40*, 117–28.

Dweck, C. S. (1992). The study of goals in psychology. *Psychological Science*, *3*, 165–7.

Dweck, C. S. (1996). Capturing the dynamic nature of personality. *Journal of Research in Personality*, *30*, 348–62. doi: 10.1006/jrpe.1996.0024

Dweck, C. S. & Leggett, E. L. (1988). A social-cognitive approach to motivation and personality. *Psychological Review*, *95*, 256–73. doi: 10.1037/0033-295X.95.2.256

Eccles, J., Adler, T. F., Futterman, R., Goff, S. B., Kaczala, C. M., Meece, J., & Midgley, C. (1983). Expectancies, values and academic behaviors. In J. T. Spence (Ed.), *Achievement and achievement motives* (pp. 75–146). San Francisco, CA: W. H. Freeman.

Elliot, A. J. (1999). Approach and avoidance motivation and achievement goals. *Educational Psychologist*, *34*, 169–89. doi: 10.1207/s15326985ep3403_3

Elliot, A. J. & Church, M. A. (1997). A hierarchical model of approach and avoidance achievement motivation. *Journal of Personality and Social Psychology*, *72*, 218–32. doi: 10.1037/0022-3514.72.1.218

Elliot, A. J. & Harackiewicz, J. M. (1996). Approach and avoidance achievement goals and intrinsic motivation: A mediational analysis. *Journal of Personality and Social Psychology*, *70*, 461–75. doi: 10.1037/0022-3514.70.3.461

Elliot, A. J. & McGregor, H. A. (2001). A 2 × 2 achievement goal framework. *Journal of Personality and Social Psychology*, *80*, 501–19. doi: 10.1037/0022-3514.80.3.501

Elliot, A. J. & Murayama, K. (2008). On the measurement of achievement goals: Critique, illustration, and application. *Journal of Educational Psychology*, *100*, 613–28. doi: 10.1037/0022-0663.100.3.613

Elliot, A. J., Murayama, K., & Pekrun, R. (2011). A 3 × 2 achievement goal model. *Journal of Educational Psychology, 103*, 632–48. doi: 10.1037/a0023952

Elliot, A. J. & Thrash, T. M. (2001). Achievement goals and the hierarchical model of achievement motivation. *Educational Psychology Review, 13*, 139–56. doi: 1009057102306

Flanagan, M. J., Putwain, D. W., & Caltabiano, M. L. (2015). The relationship between goal setting and students' experience of academic test anxiety. *International Journal of School & Educational Psychology, 3*(3), 189–201. doi: 10.1080/21683603.2015.1060910

Fortunato, V. J. & Goldblatt, A. M. (2006). An examination of goal orientation profiles using cluster analysis and their relationships with dispositional characteristics and motivational response patterns. *Journal of Applied Social Psychology, 36*(9), 2150–83. doi: 10.1111/j.0021-9029.2006.00099.x

Gonçalves, T., Niemivirta, M., & Lemos, M. S. (2017). Identification of students' multiple achievement and social goal profiles and analysis of their stability and adaptability. *Learning and Individual Differences, 54*, 149–59. doi: 10.1016/j.lindif.2017.01.019

Grant, H. & Dweck, C. S. (2003). Clarifying achievement goals and their impact. *Journal of Personality and Social Psychology, 85*, 541–53. doi: 10.1037/0022-3514.85.3.541

Greene, B. A., Miller, R. B., Crowson, H. M., Duke, B. L., & Akey, K. L. (2004). Predicting high school students' cognitive engagement and achievement: Contributions of classroom perceptions and motivation. *Contemporary Educational Psychology, 29*, 462–82. doi: 10.1016/j.cedpsych.2004.01.006

Harackiewicz, J. M., Barron, K. E., Carter, S. M., Lehto, A. T., & Elliot, A. J. (1997). Predictors and consequences of achievement goals in the college classroom: Maintaining interest and making the grade. *Journal of Personality and Social Psychology, 73*(6), 1284–95. doi: 10.1037/0022-3514.73.6.1284

Harackiewicz, J. M., Barron, K. E., Pintrich, P. R., Elliot, A. J., & Thrash, T. M. (2002). Revision of achievement goal theory: Necessary and illuminating. *Journal of Educational Psychology, 94*, 638–45. doi: 10.1037/0022-0663.94.3.638

Hayamizu, T. & Weiner, B. (1991). A test of Dweck's model of achievement goals as related to perceptions of ability. *Journal of Experimental Education, 59*, 226–34.

Haydel, A. M. & Roeser, R. W. (2002). On motivation, ability, and the perceived situation in science test performance: A person-centered approach with high school students. *Educational Assessment, 8*(2), 163–89. doi: 10.1207/S15326977EA0802_05

Inglés, C. J., Martínez-Monteagudo, M. C., García-Fernández, J. M., Valle, A., Núñez, J. C., Delgado, B., & Torregrosa, M. S. (2015). Motivational profiles Spanish students of compulsory secondary education: Differential analysis of academic self-attributions. *Anales De Psicología, 31*(2), 579–88. doi: 10.6018/analesps.31.2.173281

Jang, L. Y. & Liu, W. C. (2012). 2 × 2 achievement goals and achievement emotions: A cluster analysis of students' motivation. *European Journal of Psychology of Education, 27*(1), 59–76. doi: 10.1007/s10212-011-0066-5

Jansen in de Wal, J., Hornstra, L., Prins, F. J., Peetsma, T., & Van der Veen, I. (2016). The prevalence, development and domain specificity of elementary school students' achievement goal profiles. *Educational Psychology*, *36*(7), 1303–22. doi: 10.1080/01443410.2015.1035698

Kaplan, A. & Middleton, M. (2002). Should childhood be a journey or a race? Response to Harackiewicz et al. (2002). *Journal of Educational Psychology*, *94*, 646–8. doi: 10.1037/0022-0663.94.3.646

Kaplan, A. & Midgley, C. (1997). The effect of achievement goals: Does level of perceived academic-competence make a difference? *Contemporary Educational Psychology*, *22*, 415–35. doi: 10.1006/ceps.1997.0943

Kolić-Vehovec, S., Rončević, B., & Bajšanski, I. (2008). Motivational components of self-regulated learning and reading strategy use in university students: The role of goal orientation patterns. *Learning and Individual Differences*, *18*(1), 108–13. doi: 10.1016/j.lindif.2007.07.005

Köller, O. & Baumert, J. (1998). Ein Deutsches Instrument zur Erfassung von Zielorientierungen bei Schülerinnen und Schülern [A German instrument for assessing students' goal orientations]. *Diagnostica*, *44*, 173–81.

Korpershoek, H., Kuyper, H., & van der Werf, G. (2015). Differences in students' school motivation: A latent class modelling approach. *Social Psychology of Education*, *18*(1), 137–63. doi: 10.1007/s11218-014-9274-6

Koul, R., Clariana, R. B., Jitgarun, K., & Songsriwittaya, A. (2009). The influence of achievement goal orientation on plagiarism. *Learning and Individual Differences*, *19*(4), 506–12. doi: 10.1016/j.lindif.2009.05.005

Koul, R., Roy, L., & Lerdpornkulrat, T. (2012). Motivational goal orientation, perceptions of biology and physics classroom learning environments, and gender. *Learning Environments Research*, *15*(2), 217–29. doi: 10.1007/s10984-012-9111-9

Lau, K. & Lee, J. (2008). Examining Hong Kong students' achievement goals and their relations with students' perceived classroom environment and strategy use. *Educational Psychology*, *28*(4), 357–72. doi: 10.1080/01443410701612008

Lau, S. & Roeser, R. W. (2008). Cognitive abilities and motivational processes in science achievement and engagement: A person-centered analysis. *Learning and Individual Differences*, *18*(4), 497–504. doi: 10.1016/j.lindif.2007.11.002

Laursen, B. & Hoff, E. (2006). Person-centered and variable-centered approaches to longitudinal data. *Merrill-Palmer Quarterly*, *52*(3), 377–89.

Lee, Y.-K., Wormington, S. V., Linnenbrink-Garcia, L., & Roseth, C. J. (2017). A short-term longitudinal study of stability and change in achievement goal profiles. *Learning and Individual Differences*, *55*, 49–60. doi: 10.1016/j.lindif.2017.02.002

Lemos, M. S. (1996). Students' and teachers' goals in the classroom. *Learning and Instruction*, *6*(2), 151–71.

Lethwaite, R. & Piparo, A. J. (1993). Goal orientations in young competitive athletes: Physical achievement, social-relational, and experiential concerns. *Journal of Research in Personality*, *27*, 103–17.

Levy-Tossman, I., Kaplan, A., & Assor, A. (2007). Academic goal orientations, multiple goal profiles, and friendship intimacy among early adolescents. *Contemporary Educational Psychology*, *32*(2), 231–52. doi: 10.1016/j.cedpsych.2006.06.001

Litalien, D., Morin, A. J., & McInerney, D. M. (2017). Achievement goal profiles among adolescent males and females. *Developmental Psychology*, *53*(4), 731–751. doi: 10.1037/dev0000288

Liu, W. C., Wang, C. K. J., Tan, O. S., Ee, J., & Koh, C. (2009). Understanding students' motivation in project work: A 2 × 2 achievement goal approach. *British Journal of Educational Psychology*, *79*(1), 87–106. doi: 10.1348/000709908X313767

Luo, W., Paris, S. G., Hogan, D., & Luo, Z. (2011). Do performance goals promote learning? A pattern analysis of Singapore students' achievement goals. *Contemporary Educational Psychology*, *36*(2), 165–76. doi: 10.1016/j.cedpsych.2011.02.003

Magnusson, D. (1988). *Individual development from interactional perspective*. Hillsdale, NJ: Erlbaum.

McInerney, D. M. & Ali, J. (2006). Multidimensional and hierarchical assessment of school motivation: Cross-cultural validation. *Educational Psychology*, *26*, 717–34. doi:10.1080/01443410500342559

Meece, J. L., Blumenfeld, P. C., & Hoyle, R. H. (1988). Students' goal orientations and cognitive engagement in classroom activities. *Journal of Educational Psychology*, *80*, 514–23. doi: 10.1037/0022-0663.80.4.514

Meece, J. L. & Holt, K. (1993). A pattern analysis of students' achievement goals. *Journal of Educational Psychology*, *85*(4), 582–90. doi: 10.1037/0022-0663.85.4.582

Middleton, M. J. & Midgley, C. (1997). Avoiding the demonstration of lack of ability: An underexplored aspect of goal theory. *Journal of Educational Psychology*, *89*, 710–18. doi: 10.1037/0022-0663.89.4.710

Midgley, C., Kaplan, A., Middleton, M. J., Maehr, M. L., Urdan, T., Anderman, L. H., ... Roeser, R. (1998). The development and validation of scales assessing students' achievement goal orientations. *Contemporary Educational Psychology*, *23*, 113–31. doi: 10.1006/ceps.1998.0965

Midgley, C. & Maehr, M. L. (1991). *Patterns of adaptive learning survey*. Ann Arbor, MI: University of Michigan.

Midgley, C., Maehr, M. L., Hicks, L., Roeser, R. W., Urdan, T. U., Anderman, E., & Kaplan, A. (1995). *Patterns of adaptive learning survey (PALS) Manual*. Ann Arbor, MI: University of Michigan.

Midgley, C., Maehr, M. L., Hicks, L., Roeser, R. W., Urdan, T. U., Anderman, E. Kaplan, A., Arunkumar, R., & Middleton, M. (1997). *Patterns of adaptive learning survey (PALS)*. Ann Arbor, MI: University of Michigan.

Midgley, C., Maehr, M. L., Hruda, L., Anderman, E. M., Anderman, L., Freeman, K. E., Gheen, M., Kaplan, A., Kumar, R., Middleton, M. J., Nelson, J., Roeser, R., & Urdan, T. (2000). *Manual for the Patterns of Adaptive Learning Scales (PALS)*. Ann Arbor: University of Michigan.

Ng, C. C. (2006). The role of achievement goals in completing a course assignment: Examining the effects of performance-approach and multiple goals. *Open Learning*, *21*(1), 33–48. doi: 10.1080/02680510500472189

Ng, C. C. (2008). Multiple-goal learners and their differential patterns of learning. *Educational Psychology*, *28*(4), 439–56. doi: 10.1080/01443410701739470

Ng, C. C. (2009). Profiling learners' achievement goals when completing academic essays. *Educational Psychology*, *29*(3), 279–95. doi: 10.1080/01443410902797988

Nicholls, J. G. (1984). Achievement motivation: Conceptions of ability, subjective experience, task choice, and performance. *Psychological Review*, *91*, 328–46.

Nicholls, J. G. (1989). *The competitive ethos and democratic education*. Cambridge, MA: Harvard University Press.

Nicholls, J. G., Patashnick, M., & Nolen, S. (1985). Adolescents' theories of education. *Journal of Educational Psychology*, *77*, 683–92. doi: 10.1037/0022-0663.77.6.683

Niemivirta, M. (1996). *Intentional and adaptive learning modes – The self at stake*. Paper presented at the 2nd European Conference on Educational Research, Sevilla, Spain.

Niemivirta, M. (1998). Individual differences in motivational and cognitive factors affecting self-regulated learning: A pattern-oriented approach. In P. Nenniger, R. S. Jäger, A. Frey, & M. Wosnitza (Eds.), *Advances in motivation* (pp. 23–42). Landau: Verlag Empirische Pädagogik.

Niemivirta, M. (1999). *The self at work: Generalized and task-specific self-appraisals in motivation and performance*. Paper presented at the 8th European Conference for Research on Learning and Instruction, Gothenburg, Sweden.

Niemivirta, M. (2002a). Individual differences and developmental trends in motivation: Integrating person-centered and variable-centered methods. In P. R. Pintrich & M. L. Maehr (Eds.), *Advances in motivation and achievement* (Vol. 12, pp. 241–75). Amsterdam: JAI Press.

Niemivirta, M. (2002b). Motivation and performance in context: The influence of goal orientations and instructional setting on situational appraisals and task performance. *Psychologia*, *45*(4), 250–70. doi: 10.2117/psysoc.2002.250

Niemivirta, M. (2004). *Habits of mind and academic endeavors: The correlates and consequences of achievement goal orientations*. Helsinki, Finland: Helsinki University Press.

Niemivirta, M., Pulkka, A.-T., Tapola, A., & Tuominen-Soini, H. (2013). Tavoiteorientaatioprofiilit ja niiden yhteys tilannekohtaiseen motivaatioon ja päättelytehtävässä suoriutumiseen [Achievement goal orientation profiles and their relations to task-specific motivation and performance]. *Kasvatus [The Finnish Journal of Education]*, *44*(5), 533–47.

Niemivirta, M., Rijavec, M., & Yamauchi, H. (2001). Goal orientations and action-control beliefs: A cross-cultural comparison among Croatian, Finnish, and Japanese students. In A. Efklides, J. Kuhl, & R. M. Sorrentino (Eds.), *[Trends and prospects in motivation research]* (pp. 163–83). Dordrecht: Kluwer.

Núñez, J. C., González-Pienda, J. A., González-Pumariega, S., García, M., & Roces, C. (1997). *Cuestionario para la Evaluación de Metas Académicas [Evaluation of Academic Goals Questionnaire]*. Oviedo: Departamento de Psicología. Universidad de Oviedo.

Núñez, J. C., González-Pienda, J. A., Rodríguez, C., Valle, A., Gonzalez-Cabanach, R., & Rosário, P. (2011). Multiple goals perspective in adolescent students with learning difficulties. *Learning Disability Quarterly*, *34*(4), 273–86. doi: 10.1177/0731948711421763

Nylund, K. L., Asparouhov, T., & Muthén, B. O. (2007). Deciding on the number of classes in latent class analysis and growth mixture modeling: A Monte

Carlo simulation study. *Structural Equation Modeling*, *14*, 535–69. doi: 10.1080/10705510701575396

Pastor, D. A., Barron, K. E., Miller, B. J., & Davis, S. L. (2007). A latent profile analysis of college students' achievement goal orientation. *Contemporary Educational Psychology*, *32*(1), 8–47. doi: 10.1016/j.cedpsych.2006.10.003

Peixoto, F., Monteiro, V., Mata, L., Sanches, C., Pipa, J., & Almeida, L. S. (2016). "To be or not to be retained … that's the question!" Retention, self-esteem, self-concept, achievement goals, and grades. *Frontiers in Psychology*, *7*: 1550. doi: 10.3389/fpsyg.2016.01550

Pintrich, P. R. & de Groot, E. V. (1990). Motivational and self-regulated learning components of classroom academic performance. *Journal of Educational Psychology*, *82*, 33–40. doi: 10.1037//0022-0663.82.1.33

Pintrich, P. R. & Garcia, T. (1991). Student goal orientation and self-regulation in the college classroom. In M. L. Maehr, & P. R. Pintrich (Eds.), *Advances in motivation and achievement*, (Vol. 7, pp. 371–402). Greenwich: JAI Press.

Pintrich, P. R. (2000). Multiple goals, multiple pathways: The role of goal orientation in learning and achievement. *Journal of Educational Psychology*, *92*(3), 544–55. doi: 10.1037/0022-0663.92.3.544

Pintrich, P. R., Smith, D. A. F., Garcia, T., & McKeachie, W. J. (1993). Reliability and predictive validity of the Motivated Strategies for Learning Questionnaire (MSLQ). *Educational and Psychological Measurement*, *53*(3), 801–13.

Pipa, J., Peixoto, F., Mata, L., Monteiro, V., & Sanches, C. (2016). The goal orientations scale (GOS): Validation for Portuguese students. *European Journal of Developmental Psychology*, *14*, 477–88. doi: 10.1080/17405629. 2016.1216835

Pulkka, A.-T. & Niemivirta, M. (2013a). Adult students' achievement goal orientations and evaluations of the learning environment: A person-centred longitudinal analysis. *Educational Research and Evaluation*, *19*(4), 297–322. doi: 10.1080/13803611.2013.767741

Pulkka, A.-T. & Niemivirta, M. (2013b). In the eye of the beholder: Do adult students' achievement goal orientation profiles predict their perceptions of instruction and studying? *Studies in Educational Evaluation*, *39*(3), 133–43. doi: 10.1016/j.stueduc.2013.06.002

Pulkka, A.-T. & Niemivirta, M. (2015). The relationships between adult students' achievement goal orientations, self-defined course goals, course evaluations, and performance. *Journal for Educational Research Online*, *7*(3), 28–53.

Regueiro, B., Núñez, J. C., Valle, A., Piñeiro, I., Rodríguez, S., & Rosário, P. (2016). Motivational profiles in high school students: Differences in behavioural and emotional homework engagement and academic achievement. *International Journal of Psychology*. doi: 10.1002/ijop.12399

Rice, K. G. & Slaney, R. B. (2002). Clusters of perfectionists: Two studies of emotional adjustment and academic achievement. *Measurement and Evaluation in Counseling and Development*, *35*, 35–48.

Rijavec, M. & Brdar, I. (2002). Coping with school failure and self-regulated learning. *European Journal of Psychology of Education*, *17*, 177–94.

Roeser, R. W., Strobel, K. R., & Quihuis, G. (2002). Studying early adolescents' academic motivation, social-emotional functioning, and engagement in learning: Variable- and person-centered approaches. *Anxiety, Stress & Coping, 15*(4), 345–68. doi: 10.1080/1061580021000056519

Ryan, A. & Shim, S. S. (2008). An exploration of young adolescents' social achievement goals and social adjustment in middle school. *Journal of Educational Psychology, 100*, 672–87. doi: 10.1037/0022-0663.100.3.672

Schwinger, M., Steinmayr, R., & Spinath, B. (2016). Achievement goal profiles in elementary school: Antecedents, consequences, and longitudinal trajectories. *Contemporary Educational Psychology, 46*, 164–79. doi: 10.1016/j.cedpsych.2016.05.006

Schwinger, M. & Wild, E. (2006). Die Entwicklung von Zielorientierungen im Fach Mathematik von der 3. bis 5. Jahrgangsstufe [The development of goal orientations in mathematics from 3rd to 5th grade]. *Zeitschrift für Pädagogische Psychologie, 20*, 269–78.

Schwinger, M. & Wild, E. (2012). Prevalence, stability, and functionality of achievement goal profiles in mathematics from third to seventh grade. *Contemporary Educational Psychology, 37*(1), 1–13. doi: 10.1016/j.cedpsych.2011.08.001

Seegers, G., van Putten, C. M., & de Brabander, C. J. (2002). Goal orientation, perceived task outcome and task demands in mathematics tasks: Effects on students' attitude in actual task settings. *British Journal of Educational Psychology, 72*, 365–84. doi: 10.1348/000709902320634366

Seifert, T. L. (1995). Characteristics of ego- and task-oriented students: A comparison of two methodologies. *British Journal of Educational Psychology, 65*, 125–38. doi: 10.1111/j.2044-8279.1995.tb01136.x

Senko, C., Hama, H., & Belmonte, K. (2013). Achievement goals, study strategies, and achievement: A test of the "learning agenda" framework. *Learning and Individual Differences, 24*, 1–10. doi: 10.1016/j.lindif.2012.11.003

Senko, C., Hulleman, C. S., & Harackiewicz, J. M. (2011). Achievement goal theory at the crossroads: Old controversies, current challenges, and new directions. *Educational Psychologist, 46*(1), 26–47. doi: 10.1080/00461520.2011.538646

Shih, S. (2005). Taiwanese sixth graders' achievement goals and their motivation, strategy use, and grades: An examination of the multiple goal perspective. *Elementary School Journal, 106*(1), 39–58.

Shim, S. S. & Finch, W. H. (2014). Academic and social achievement goals and early adolescents' adjustment: A latent class approach. *Learning and Individual Differences, 30*(1), 98–105. doi: 10.1016/j.lindif.2013.10.015

Sideridis, G. D. & Kaplan, A. (2011). Achievement goals and persistence across tasks: The roles of failure and success. *Journal of Experimental Education, 79*(4), 429–51. doi: 10.1080/00220973.2010.539634

Sideridis, G. D. & Tsorbatzoudis, C. (2003). Intra-group motivational analysis of students with learning disabilities: A goal orientation approach. *Learning Disabilities: A Contemporary Journal, 1*(1), 8–19.

Skaalvik, E. M. (1997). Self-enhancing and self-defeating ego orientation: Relations with task and avoidance orientation, achievement, self-perceptions, and anxiety. *Journal of Educational Psychology*, *89*, 71–81. doi: 10.1037/0022-0663.89.1.71

Smith, L. & Sinclair, K. E. (2005). Empirical evidence for multiple goals: A gender-based, senior high school student perspective. *Australian Journal of Educational and Developmental Psychology*, *5*, 55–70.

Spinath, B., Stiensmeier-Pelster, J., Schöne, C., & Dickhäuser, O. (2002). *Die skalen zur erfassung von lern- und leistungsmotivation (SELLMO) [Scales for the measurement of learning and achievement motivation]*. Göttingen: Hogrefe.

Stoeber, J. & Otto, K. (2006). Positive conceptions of perfectionism: Approaches, evidence, challenges. *Personality and Social Psychology Review*, *10*(4), 295–319. doi: 10.1207/s15327957pspr1004_2

Suárez Riveiro, J. M., Cabanach, R. G., & Valle Arias, A. (2001). Multiple-goal pursuit and its relation to cognitive, self-regulatory, and motivational strategies. *British Journal of Educational Psychology*, *71*(4), 561–72. doi: 10.1348/000709901158677

Tanaka, K. (2007). Relations between general goal orientations and task-specific self-appraisals. *Japanese Psychological Research*, *49*(4), 235–47. doi: 10.1111/j.1468-5884.2007.00350.x

Tapola, A., Jaakkola, T., & Niemivirta, M. (2014). The influence of achievement goal orientations and task concreteness on situational interest. *Journal of Experimental Education*, *82*(4), 455–79. doi: 10.1080/00220973.2013.813370

Tapola, A. & Niemivirta, M. (2008). The role of achievement goal orientations in students' perceptions of and preferences for classroom environment. *British Journal of Educational Psychology*, *78*(2), 291–312. doi: 10.1348/000709907X205272

Thorkildsen, T. A., & Nicholls, J. G. (1998). Fifth graders' achievement orientations and beliefs: Individual and classroom differences. *Journal of Educational Psychology*, *90*, 179–201. doi: 10.1037/0022-0663.90.2.179

Tuominen, H., Niemivirta, M., Lonka, K., & Salmela-Aro, K. (2018). Stability and change in goal orientation profiles across the transition from elementary to secondary school: A latent transition analysis. Manuscript submitted for publication.

Tuominen-Soini, H., Salmela-Aro, K., & Niemivirta, M. (2008). Achievement goal orientations and subjective well-being: A person-centred analysis. *Learning and Instruction*, *18*(3), 251–66. doi: 10.1016/j.learninstruc.2007.05.003

Tuominen-Soini, H., Salmela-Aro, K., & Niemivirta, M. (2011). Stability and change in achievement goal orientations: A person-centered approach. *Contemporary Educational Psychology*, *36*(2), 82–100. doi: 10.1016/j.cedpsych.2010.08.002

Tuominen-Soini, H., Salmela-Aro, K., & Niemivirta, M. (2012). Achievement goal orientations and academic well-being across the transition to upper secondary education. *Learning and Individual Differences*, *22*(3), 290–305. doi: 10.1016/j.lindif.2012.01.002

Turner, J. C., Thorpe, P. K., & Meyer, D. K. (1998). Students' reports of motivation and negative affect: A theoretical and empirical analysis. *Journal of Educational Psychology*, *90*(4), 758–71. doi: 10.1037/0022-0663.90.4.758

Vallacher, R. R. & Wegner, D. M. (1987). What do people think they're doing? Action identification and human behavior. *Psychological Review, 94*(1), 3–15.

Valle, A., Cabanach, R. G., Nunez, J. C., Gonzalez-Pienda, J., Rodríguez, S., & Pineiro, I. (2003). Multiple goals, motivation and academic learning. *British Journal of Educational Psychology, 73*(1), 71–87. doi: 10.1348 /000709903762869923

Valle, A., Núñez, J. C., Cabanach, R. G., Rodríguez, S., Rosário, P., & Inglés, C. J. (2015a). Motivational profiles as a combination of academic goals in higher education. *Educational Psychology, 35*(5), 634–50. doi: 10.1080/01443410.2013.819072

Valle, A., Pan, I., Núñez, J. C., Rodríguez, S., Rosário, P., & Regueiro, B. (2015b). Multiple goals and homework involvement in elementary school students. *The Spanish Journal of Psychology, 18*, 1–11. doi: 10.1017/sjp.2015.88

van der Veen, I. & Peetsma, T. (2009). The development in self-regulated learning behaviour of first-year students in the lowest level of secondary school in the Netherlands. *Learning and Individual Differences, 19*(1), 34–46. doi: 10.1016/j. lindif.2008.03.001

VandeWalle, D. (1997). Development and validation of a work domain goal orientation instrument. *Educational and Psychological Measurement, 57*, 995–1015.

Veermans, M. & Tapola, A. (2004). Primary school students' motivational profiles in longitudinal settings. *Scandinavian Journal of Educational Research, 48*(4), 373–95. doi: 10.1080/0031383042000245780

von Eye, A. (1990). Configural frequency analysis of longitudinal multivariate responses. In A. von Eye (Ed.), *Statistical methods in longitudinal research* (pp. 545–70). New York, NY: Academic Press.

von Eye, A. & Bogat, G. A. (2006). Person-oriented and variable-oriented research: Concepts, results, and development. *Merrill-Palmer Quarterly, 52*, 390–420.

Wentzel, K. R. (1993). Motivation and achievement in early adolescence: The role of multiple classroom goals. *Journal of Early Adolescence, 13*, 4–20. doi: 10.1177/0272431693013001001

Wigfield, A. & Guthrie, J. T. (1997). Relations of children's motivation for reading to the amount and breadth of their reading. *Journal of Educational Psychology, 89*, 420–32. doi: 10.1037/0022-0663.89.3.420

Wilson, T. M., Zheng, C., Lemoine, K. A., Martin, C. P., & Tang, Y. (2016). Achievement goals during middle childhood: Individual differences in motivation and social adjustment. *The Journal of Experimental Education, 84*(4), 723–43. doi: 10.1080/00220973.2015.1094648

Woodrow, L. J. (2006). A model of adaptive language learning. *Modern Language Journal, 90*(3), 297–319. doi: 10.1111/j.1540-4781.2006.00424.x

Wormington, S. V. & Linnenbrink-Garcia, L. (2017). A new look at multiple goal pursuit: The promise of a person-centered approach. *Educational Psychology Review, 29*, 407–45. doi: 10.1007/s10648-016-9358-2

Young, A. J. (1997). I think, therefore I'm motivated: The relations among cognitive strategy use, motivational orientation and classroom perceptions over time. *Learning and Individual Differences, 9*, 249–83. doi: 10.1016/S1041-6080(97)90009-1

Zhang, Y., Watermann, R., & Daniel, A. (2016). Are multiple goals in elementary students beneficial for their school achievement? A latent class analysis. *Learning and Individual Differences, 51*, 100–10. doi: 10.1016/j.lindif.2016.08.023

Zhou, M. (2016). University students' emotion during online search task: A multiple achievement goal perspective. *The Journal of Psychology: Interdisciplinary and Applied, 150*(5), 576–90. doi: 10.1080/00223980.2016.1143797

24 Expectancy-Value Theory and Its Relevance for Student Motivation and Learning

Emily Q. Rosenzweig, Allan Wigfield, and Jacquelynne S. Eccles

Abstract: In this chapter we review Eccles and colleagues' expectancy-value theory (EVT) of motivation and discuss its relevance for understanding and improving student learning. According to EVT, students' expectancies for success and task values are two critical factors impacting their motivation, academic performance, and choice of activities. Recent research has suggested that students' perceptions of the negative consequences of completing a task, called cost, also impact their academic outcomes. Thus we review the construct of perceived cost alongside our review of expectancies and values throughout this chapter. We define expectancies, task values, and cost, explain how these constructs develop over time and relate to one another, and discuss how they predict students' academic behavior, performance, and choice. We then review research regarding intervention studies that have improved students' academic outcomes by targeting their expectancies, values, and/or perceptions of cost. We conclude by listing questions that future research needs to address.

Eccles and colleagues' (1983) expectancy-value theory (EVT) of achievement motivation identifies students' expectancies for success and task values as important determinants of their motivation and subsequent academic outcomes. EVT provides a framework for understanding how students' perceptions of themselves, how others see them, and aspects of their educational environment subsequently impact their educational choices, aspirations, and achievement. Using this framework, researchers and educational practitioners

Research on the development of children's expectancies and values was conducted by Jacquelynne S. Eccles, Allan Wigfield, and colleagues with support from a National Institute of Child Health and Human Development (NICHD) grant. Other research discussed in this chapter was supported by a National Institute of Mental Health grant, NICHD grants, a National Science Foundation (NSF) Interagency Educational Research Initiative grant, an NSF Graduate Research Fellowship, and grants from the Spencer Foundation. The writing of this chapter was supported in part by a NSF Social, Behavioral, and Economic Sciences Postdoctoral Fellowship to the first author.

have developed interventions to change students' expectancies and values for learning in order to improve their academic outcomes. In this chapter, we review EVT and discuss its implications for understanding and improving students' learning. We review research showing how students' expectancies and task values develop over time and impact various learning outcomes. Following this, we provide a brief review of intervention studies guided by EVT, discussing two of our own intervention studies in more depth for the purposes of illustration. We conclude with a discussion of issues and questions that we believe the next generation of research based in EVT still needs to address.

EVT: Tenets, Development, and Relation to Learning Outcomes

Over the past century, many psychologists have posited that individuals' expectancies and task values are critical for understanding why they choose to pursue the activities that they do (Higgins, 2007; Lewin, 1938; Pekrun, 1993, 2000, 2009;[1] Rokeach, 1973; Tolman, 1932). Atkinson (1957) was the first researcher to develop a formal mathematical model of how individuals' expectancies and values determine their motivation. He suggested that individual's achievement on academic tasks is determined by their overall motive to achieve or avoid failure, probability of success on the task (i.e., expectancy), and incentive to complete the task (i.e., task value). Atkinson viewed probabilities of success and incentive values as inversely related, so individuals value tasks more if they have lower probabilities of succeeding at them.

Eccles-Parsons and her colleagues (1983) built on Atkinson's (1957) theory of motivation and proposed a much-expanded EVT model. Like Atkinson, they hypothesized that students' motivation to pursue achievement tasks (e.g., putting forth effort to do assignments or to practice a skill, choosing to pursue certain activities that help build skills, using strategies to improve skills) is determined most proximally by their expectancies for success on a task and the extent to which they value it (see Figure 24.1 for depiction of the EVT model;[2] see Eccles-Parsons et al., 1983; Eccles & Wigfield, 2002; Wigfield & Eccles, 1992; Wigfield et al., 2016 for reviews). In contrast to Atkinson's work, Eccles and her colleagues defined expectancies and values in terms of students' subjective appraisals of tasks, rather than only in terms of objective quantities such as probabilities of success or incentives.

---

1 Pekrun calls his model a control-value model, because he focuses on students' perceptions of control over outcomes rather than their expectancies for success. Control beliefs and expectancies relate positively, and other aspects of Pekrun's model are similar to Eccles and colleagues' model, on which we focus in this chapter.

2 Note that Figure 24.1 differs from prior depictions (e.g., Wigfield et al., 2017) in that we changed the term "child" to the term "student" to be consistent with our focus throughout this chapter.

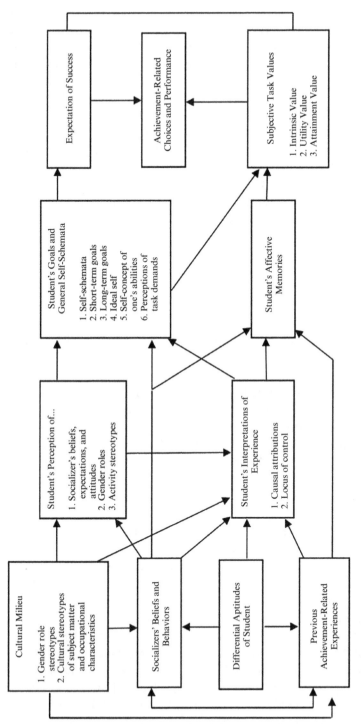

Figure 24.1. *Eccles-Parsons et al.'s expectancy-value theory. Adapted from Wigfield, Rosenzweig, & Eccles (2017), Achievement values. In A. Elliot and C. S. Dweck (Eds.),* Handbook of Competence and Motivation *(2nd ed.) pp. 116–34. New York, NY: Guilford.*

Eccles-Parsons et al. (1983) defined expectancies for success as individuals' beliefs about how well they will perform on future achievement tasks. A major factor influencing expectancies for success is students' beliefs about their ability. Although ability beliefs are conceptually distinct from expectancies, the two constructs often overlap empirically (Eccles & Wigfield, 1995). Thus, many EVT researchers combine measures of ability beliefs with measures of expectancies, or instead of measuring expectancies. It should be noted that ability beliefs and expectancies for success are part of a larger constellation of individuals' beliefs about competence, including the motivational construct of self-efficacy. Bandura (1997) and Pajares (1996) posited that expectancies for success are distinct from self-efficacy, which they defined as students' beliefs about their capabilities to do the actions necessary to complete a given task. However, self-efficacy overlaps with expectancies in much empirical research, and researchers sometimes measure self-efficacy in place of expectancies or ability beliefs (Bong & Skaalvik, 2003; Wigfield & Eccles, 2000).

Task value refers to how much an individual wants to pursue a task. Eccles-Parsons and her colleagues defined task value as comprising three components: intrinsic value, attainment value, and utility value (Eccles-Parsons et al., 1983; see Eccles, 2005; Wigfield et al., 2017 for reviews). Intrinsic value refers to the extent to which a student enjoys completing a task or the consequences of completing a task. Attainment value concerns the extent to which a student finds a task to be personally meaningful or important. Utility value describes the extent to which a student believes a task will be useful for current or future goals. A critical difference between Atkinson's (1957) model and that of Eccles and colleagues is that, in the latter, expectancies and values are posited to relate positively to one another. That is, students who believe that they will perform well on a task often also value the task more. Additionally, students who perceive that they may not perform well on a task might devalue the task to protect their own self-worth. Much empirical work done in real-world achievement settings (as compared to the laboratory tasks Atkinson tended to use) shows that individuals' expectancies and values are positively related (Eccles & Wigfield, 1995, 2002; Jacobs et al., 2002; Meece et al., 1990; Wigfield et al., 1997).

Consider the example of Rebecca, a high school junior who wants to pursue a job in the medical field. She needs to choose between three after-school activities: playing the saxophone in the band, participating in the robotics club, or receiving extra tutoring in her history class. In order to decide which extracurricular activity to do, Rebecca would consider whether she believes she will be successful in each of the activities (i.e., her expectancies for success). For example, she believes that she would do very well in the band, because she feels competent to play the saxophone and she expects that she will contribute to the sound of the group. She believes she would be somewhat successful at raising her history grade if she received the extra tutoring. In contrast, she has never built a robot before so she does not necessarily expect that she will succeed in robotics club. Rebecca also considers the extent to which the activities are useful, interesting, or important to her (task value). For example, she does not like history, but the tutoring would be useful for raising her grade. She would enjoy participating in the band or robotics club, and both would be useful to her for her college applications. The robotics club also would be useful because it is aligns with her future career goals. However, Rebecca cares more about whether she is a good friend than with whether she prepares for her career or raises her history grade. Thus she might have very high attainment value for playing in the band, because she could spend the most time with her friends.

Another way in which Eccles and colleagues extended Atkinson's (1957) work was to include in their model information about the antecedents of expectancies and task values. In EVT, expectancies and values are impacted by many different factors. As Figure 24.1 shows, the most proximal influences are students' ability beliefs, goals, memories, and perceptions of the demands of different achievement tasks. Impacting those factors are students' stereotypes and beliefs about different academic domains, and their interpretations of their previous experiences. One step further back in the model is a set of broader influences, including cultural norms, socializer's beliefs and values, students' levels of intelligence or ability on different tasks, and students' other personal experiences (see Eccles, 2005; Eccles-Parsons et al., 1983; Meece et al., 1990; Wigfield & Eccles, 1992, 2000, for reviews). Beyond those noted in the figure, researchers have posited that additional factors also impact expectancies and values. For example, students make decisions in complex social environments where making one choice entails giving up another; they are not always aware of all choices available to them (Eccles, 2005; Wigfield et al., 2017). Conceptualizing the different antecedents of expectancies and task values is useful, because it demonstrates that students' perceptions of these constructs are malleable. That is, students' expectancies and task values can change as a function of interactions with others and experiences in educational environments.

Cost and Its Role Within EVT

Let us assume that Rebecca has the highest combination of expectancy and value for playing in the band compared to the other two activities. Will she definitely join the band? Recent work within EVT suggests that in some circumstances, it may be incorrect to draw such a conclusion. That is because expectancies and task values address only whether or not a student is motivated *positively* to pursue a given task. It is also critical to understand students' perceptions of why they might *not* want to pursue that task. To this end, EVT researchers have suggested that students' valuing of a task is influenced by their perceptions regarding the negative consequences of engaging with a task, called cost (Eccles, 2005; Flake et al., 2015; Wigfield & Eccles, 1992). Eccles-Parsons et al. (1983) described cost in their original conceptualization of EVT, but it received little attention in the early studies of the theory. Researchers have studied cost further since that time, but most of that work has been done within the past five years (see Barron & Hulleman, 2015; Wigfield et al., 2017, for review). There remains much work to do in order to understand the construct of cost and its implications for student learning.

Cost refers to any negative consequences of engaging with a task, and Eccles (2005) defined it more specifically as "what the individual must give up to do a task ... as well as the anticipated effort one will need to put into task completion" (p. 113). Any individual is likely to perceive many different types of negative consequences for a particular task. Thus researchers studying cost agree that it has multiple dimensions. The three dimensions of cost researchers most frequently discuss in the literature are: (a) effort cost, students' perceptions of the amount of effort required to complete a task; (b) emotional cost, students' perceptions of the negative emotional or psychological consequences of pursuing a task; and (c) loss of valued alternatives cost, students' perceptions of valued activities they must give up in order to pursue a task (Barron & Hulleman, 2015; Battle & Wigfield, 2003; Eccles, 2005; Flake et al., 2015; Gaspard et al., 2015a; Perez et al., 2014; Wigfield et al., 2017). Researchers have developed more detailed measures of cost that assess these dimensions (Battle & Wigfield, 2003; Flake et al., 2015; Gaspard et al., 2015a; Perez et al., 2014). However, different researchers have posited that there are other dimensions of cost that are important, including students' perceptions of cost as a result of needing to fulfill others' expectations (Johnson & Safavian, 2016), cost associated with other activities taking away time and effort from the target activity (Flake et al., 2015), perceptions of ego threat as a result of task failure (Lu et al., 2011), and financial cost (Battle & Wigfield, 2003; Wigfield et al., 2017). More research is needed to determine if these other dimensions of cost are particularly salient to students and if they are distinct from the three types of cost noted above.

To illustrate cost, we return to the example of Rebecca. There is cost associated with participation in each after-school activity. For example, Rebecca believes that the band requires too much practice at home (effort cost), and it would take time that could be spent on her schoolwork, or developing her other interests such as robotics (loss of valued alternatives cost). However, because Rebecca likes the band very much and can only choose one extracurricular activity, the loss of valued alternatives cost would be much higher for her if she did robotics club or the history tutoring versus playing in the band. Additionally, Rebecca is concerned about fitting in at the robotics club because few women are in it, and she believes she might be perceived as unintelligent if she goes to the tutoring (emotional cost). She does not have those same concerns with joining the band.

How would Rebecca integrate her perceptions of cost, expectancy, and task value to decide which activity to complete? Although researchers agree that Rebecca would consider all three of these factors, to date they have not reached a clear consensus on precisely how she would do so. Researchers have debated exactly how cost relates to expectancies and values in the EVT model.

Eccles-Parsons and colleagues (1983) introduced cost in their original presentation of the EVT model, but they did not clearly situate cost with respect to other constructs in the theory. They described cost as a mechanism by which task value influenced students' motivation and achievement, but they also wrote that the cost of engaging in an activity might be weighed against its benefits to impact whether or not students decided to value the activity. This suggests that Eccles et al. (1983) may have perceived cost as impacting task values rather than being a pathway by which task values impacted achievement (Barron & Hulleman, 2015; Wigfield et al., 2017).

Later, both Eccles (2005) and Wigfield and Eccles (1992, 2000) located cost alongside attainment, utility, and intrinsic value as a component of task values, rather than a distinct construct that negatively influences task values. Many other researchers have treated cost as a component of task values since then (e.g., Conley, 2012; Gaspard et al., 2015a; Perez et al., 2014; Safavian & Conley, 2016; Trautwein et al., 2012). This conception implies that cost's primary impact is to reduce the extent to which a student values a task. Recently some EVT researchers have suggested that cost might be a separate facet of the expectancy-value model alongside expectancies and task values. For instance, Barron and Hulleman (2015) proposed that the EVT model should be renamed as the expectancy-value-cost model. This conception would imply that students weigh cost, expectancies, and task values as independent factors, instead of considering cost as a part of task values.

Wigfield et al. (2017) reviewed research on this debate and concluded that cost might be distinct from value rather than being a component of it. However, they cautioned that more research was needed before drawing conclusions about whether cost is a separate facet that should be included in the name of the model. The exact role of cost in EVT cannot be determined until researchers conduct careful theoretical and empirical analyses that take into account the way that cost is defined and measured. We omit cost from Figure 24.1 for now, because its location within EVT is still under investigation, see Wigfield et al. (2017) for a figure showing how they believe cost influences students' overall task value for a given activity. Nonetheless, cost impacts in important ways students' course outcomes and learning behaviors. Thus we discuss cost alongside expectancies and task values throughout the remainder of this chapter, while acknowledging that its exact role within EVT is not yet clear.

Development of Students' Expectancies, Values, and Perceptions of Cost

Students' expectancies, task values, and perceptions of cost change and evolve as they progress through development and through different levels of schooling. Researchers first explored this topic by examining different-aged students' responses to items measuring their expectancies and task values. An initial goal of this work was to determine at what point in development students could perceive expectancies and/or task values as distinct (Eccles & Wigfield, 1995; Eccles et al., 1993). Their factor analyses of children's expectancies and values showed that expectancies and values were empirically distinct in children as young as six years old. Additionally, six-year-old students' expectancies and task values in one academic subject area were distinct from those in other subject areas (e.g., expectancies for success in math versus reading). Eccles et al. (1993) found that children in fourth grade and younger did not distinguish among interest, attainment, and utility value; items measuring these all loaded on one factor. Eccles and Wigfield (1995) showed that for students in fifth grade and older the three components of value formed separate factors.

There are also mean-level changes in motivation that occur across all students over time. Many researchers in different countries have reported that students' expectancies and task values decline starting in elementary school through the end of high school (e.g., Fredricks & Eccles, 2002; Frenzel et al., 2010; Gaspard et al., 2017; Jacobs et al., 2002; Watt, 2004), although recent work also shows different patterns of change in different students (Archambault et al., 2010; see further discussion below). Gaspard et al. (2017) showed that German students' perceptions of cost increase during this time period (Gaspard et al., 2017).

Various reasons for these declines have been offered (Eccles et al., 1998; Wigfield et al., 2015). First, many (but not all; see Heyman et al., 1992) very young children tend to be optimistic with respect to their ability to accomplish different tasks, and report valuing them highly. As students receive more evaluative feedback they become more accurate and realistic in their assessments of their abilities, leading to declines in perceptions of ability and expectancies for success of many students (Jacobs et al., 2002). Second, students' interests become more differentiated over time, so they may show less motivation for some domains, whereas they develop their interests and abilities in others (Hidi & Renninger, 2006; Krapp, 2002). Third, Eccles and Midgley (1989) and Wigfield et al. (1996), among others, discussed how the educational environments students encounter as they go through school focus too much on normative comparisons of students' performance, do not provide enough autonomy support to meet early adolescents' growing needs for it, and disrupt students' social networks, among other things. These school environment changes can negatively impact many students' expectancies and values for various academic tasks and subject areas.

For many years, EVT researchers focused on this overall decline in students' motivation. However, more recent research has suggested that the conclusion of inevitable, overall decline among all students is oversimplified (see Wigfield et al., 2016, for a review). Rather than all students' motivation declining in all academic domains over time, many factors differentially affect how expectancies, values, and cost change over time. This includes academic domain, students' gender and/or ethnicity, and the type of motivational construct being assessed (Fredricks & Eccles, 2002; Gaspard et al., 2017; Gottfried et al., 2001; Wang & Pomerantz, 2009). Even within one academic subject and one motivational construct, there are individual differences in students' trajectories of change over time: Researchers conducting person-centered analyses have found that there are many different trajectories of motivational development that students follow, some of which include increased motivation rather than declines (Archambault et al., 2010; Musu-Gillette et al., 2015). Thus a decline in motivation is not inevitable, or even likely, for all students in all subjects.

How Expectancies, Values, and Cost Relate to Learning Outcomes

Many researchers have demonstrated that expectancies and task values are critical predictors of educational outcomes in many academic domains in elementary school through college (e.g., Denissen et al., 2007; Durik et al., 2006; Meece et al., 1990; Musu-Gillette et al., 2015; Pintrich & DeGroot, 1990; Rosenzweig & Wigfield, 2017; Simpkins et al., 2006; Xiang et al., 2004). Outcomes impacted by expectancies and task values include grades, test scores, course-taking intentions and patterns, choices of extracurricular activities, college majors, and academic engagement. These relations have been found in large-scale longitudinal studies as well as cross-sectional ones. For example, Durik et al. (2006) demonstrated that elementary school students' reports of the importance of reading predicted how many English courses they took in high school. Additionally, their reports of intrinsic value for reading predicted how much they read books for leisure in high school, as well as what courses they took. Simpkins et al. (2006) demonstrated that elementary school students' engagement in math activities predicted their later motivation for math and science, which predicted the number of courses they took in those fields over time. Additionally, Musu-Gillette et al. (2015) found that students' high school math expectancies and utility value predicted their choices to pursue math-related majors in college.

Expectancies and values do not influence all outcomes similarly. Typically, students' expectancies predict more strongly achievement and academic performance compared to task values (e.g., Bong et al., 2012; Durik et al., 2006; Meece et al., 1990; Musu-Gillette et al., 2015; Rosenzweig & Wigfield, 2017). Task values, on the other hand, tend to be relatively stronger predictors of students' course-taking intentions and choices (e.g., Durik et al., 2006; Eccles, 1987; Meece et al., 1990; Rosenzweig & Wigfield, 2017). Beyond direct impacts, students' expectancies and task values predict course outcomes indirectly because they relate positively to each other. Thus they can impact course outcomes and choices via indirect effects through one another. For example, students who value a task highly also likely have higher expectancies for success on the task. As just noted students' expectancies directly predict outcomes like grades, and so their values can indirectly predict grades through their positive relations with both contiguous and later expectancies for success (e.g., Meece et al., 1990).

Students' perceptions of cost also predict their educational outcomes. Cost has been found to predict negatively students' achievement (Conley, 2012; Jiang et al., 2018; Trautwein et al., 2012) and course-taking intentions or choices (Battle & Wigfield, 2003; Perez et al., 2014). Some work suggests that cost might be a particularly important factor that distinguishes students who are at risk for underachievement. Conley (2012) conducted cluster analyses of middle school students' perceptions of self-efficacy, task values, and cost in math. She found seven groups of students. The groups of students whose patterns of motivation included high cost performed worse in math than did their peers; further, Conley stated that cost was particularly important for distinguishing groups of students with adaptive vs. maladaptive patterns of motivational beliefs, values, and goals. Additionally, Jiang et al. (2018) reported that Korean high school students' perceptions of cost predicted a variety of outcomes associated with maladaptive academic functioning, including avoidance intentions, performance avoidance goal adoption, procrastination, disorganization, and negative classroom affect. In many cases cost predicted these outcomes more strongly than expectancies or task values.

Expectancies, task values, and cost also relate to motivational constructs outside of EVT, and those constructs predict students' academic behavior and performance. For example, having high utility or intrinsic value can help students develop interest in a field over time, and interest is a strong predictor of students' engagement with coursework and academic performance (Harackiewicz et al., 2002; Hulleman & Harackiewicz, 2009). Having higher task values and expectancies also relates positively to students using self-regulated learning strategies and negatively to students' academic anxiety (Pintrich & DeGroot, 1990; Wolters et al., 1996). Additionally, expectations, values, and cost relate reciprocally to students' goal orientations for learning. Students' expectancies or related beliefs such as self-efficacy predict positively their adoption of both mastery and performance approach goals for learning[3]

---

3 Typically, mastery goals are defined as goals in which students desire to develop competence, either by learning and improving one's skills as much as possible (mastery approach goals) or by avoiding failures to learn or to develop one's skills (mastery avoidance goals). Conversely, performance goals are defined as those in which students desire to demonstrate competence, either by trying to outperform others as much as possible (performance approach goals) or by trying to avoid being outperformed by others (performance avoidance goals; Elliot, 1999; Elliot & Church, 1997; see Senko, 2016, for review).

(see Nolen, Chapter 22), and vice versa; these beliefs also predict negatively students' adoption of performance avoidance goals for learning (e.g., Bong et al., 2014; Elliot & Church, 1997). Task values predict positively students' adoption of mastery approach goals (see Wigfield & Cambria, 2010, for review). There is less work on cost, but Jiang et al. (2018) showed that perceptions of cost predicted positively students' adoption of performance avoidance goals. Researchers debate the precise relations of achievement goals with performance, but in general students who adopt performance avoidance goals tend to perform more poorly in school (see Senko, 2016; Senko et al., 2011, for review).

Finally, there are interactive effects of expectancies, values, and cost in predicting outcomes, but the nature of these interactions has not been consistent across all research. Many researchers, including several who used data from large representative international samples, reported that students' task values impacted their course outcomes more strongly when their expectancies were higher (Guo et al., 2015a; Nagengast et al., 2011, 2013; Trautwein et al., 2012). However, others have reported that task values impacted students' learning outcomes more strongly when their expectancies were *lower* (Guo et al., 2015b; Hensley, 2014; Lee et al., 2013, 2014). The populations studied, type of outcome being measured, or other aspects of instruction might explain why different interactions were observed between these sets of studies. Few researchers have evaluated interactions with cost, but Trautwein et al. (2012) found that expectancies and cost showed an interaction in predicting German middle school students' achievement on a math standardized test. Specifically, students' perceptions of expectancies predicted achievement more strongly as cost decreased.

Summary

Students' expectancies for success, task values, and perceptions of cost impact strongly their educational achievement outcomes and course-taking patterns. There remains more work to be done on precisely how these constructs interrelate to predict students' outcomes, particularly with respect to cost. However, the work that has been done provides a useful framework for understanding how students' beliefs and values directly impact their subsequent academic behavior and choice, and the variety of school environment, socialization, and cultural factors that influence students' expectancies, values, and cost perceptions. Further, the research on the development of students' expectancies, values, and cost perceptions shows that these variables are malleable: They change over time within students, differ as a function of various individual characteristics, and can change as a result of students experiencing different educational and family environments. Thus it may be possible to change these variables in order to improve students' educational outcomes. That is the topic of the next section.

Using EVT in Interventions to Improve Student Learning

Researchers have developed a variety of instructional intervention programs that have attempted to improve students' expectancies, task values, and/or perceptions of cost in order to improve their academic outcomes. In this section we present several representative examples of this work, including two examples of our own studies. Our aim is to demonstrate the breadth of the work that has been done on this topic and to illustrate directions for future research to build on this work; see Lazowski and Hulleman (2016), Rosenzweig and Wigfield (2016), and Tibbetts et al. (2016) for more complete reviews of interventions targeting students' motivation.

There are many variations in how intervention researchers have targeted constructs from EVT. We organize this section in accordance with the *level* at which interventions were done. We begin with interventions that targeted whole classrooms or schools, and then we discuss interventions targeting individuals. Another distinction to make is the extent to which interventions are theoretically specific or theoretically eclectic; we provide examples of both. Theoretically eclectic interventions target students' expectancies and/or task values in addition to other motivational constructs outside of EVT, such as interest. These differ from theoretically specific interventions, which target either a single motivational construct from EVT (e.g., perceived cost) or two or more constructs from EVT (e.g., expectancies and task values).

Classroom- or School-Level Interventions

Classroom- or school-level interventions have targeted motivational constructs, either from EVT only (e.g., Yang & Wu, 2012) or from EVT in addition to constructs from other motivational theories (e.g., Falco et al., 2010; Marinak, 2013; Morgen et al., 2008). Concept-Oriented Reading Instruction (CORI) (see Guthrie et al., 2004 for review), which we will discuss, is a good example of a theoretically eclectic intervention targeting students' motivation at the school or classroom level. An example of a theoretically specific intervention at this level is the CareerStart intervention (Orthner et al., 2013; Wooley et al., 2013). CareerStart aimed to improve middle school students' perceptions of value by emphasizing the relevance of their coursework for their future careers. Although the authors did not state directly that they were targeting utility value, their items assessed utility value, and their definition of value referred only to the utility type of value grounded in expectancy-value theory. In this school-level intervention, teachers of all core academic subjects in a school provided students with examples of how course content from their subject would be useful in careers from the local labor market where their school was located. Compared to control students, this intervention improved students' utility value and perceptions of the importance of school, as well as their math achievement.

Although many school- or classroom-level interventions involve teachers changing their instructional practices, in some interventions researchers provide materials to the classrooms or schools. An example is the Motivation in Mathematics (MoMA) Intervention implemented by Gaspard and colleagues (2015a). This theoretically specific intervention targeted German high school students' task values; the students attended Gymnasium, the highest academic level in German schools. The initial MoMa study included 82 ninth grade math classes, which were assigned randomly to the intervention group or to a waiting control group. In intervention classes, students watched a one-hour presentation by research staff focused on the importance of effort for student success. Then they read and evaluated quotations from other students regarding how they thought math related to their lives. Students in classes that received the intervention reported higher utility, intrinsic, and attainment value for mathematics after five months compared to students in the control group, with female students showing the strongest benefits (Gaspard et al., 2015b). Students in intervention classes also earned higher math test scores compared to a control condition (Brisson et al., 2017). However, one unexpected finding was that the intervention negatively impacted students' motivation for non-mathematics subjects. That is, intervention group students reported lower scores than did control group students on a composite measure of task values for German (the participants' native language) and English (a foreign language) six weeks after the intervention (Gaspard et al., 2016). Gaspard et al. explained this by stating that one way students develop a frame of reference to understand their expectancies and values in one domain is by contrasting them with their beliefs and values in other domains (Marsh, 1986; Möller & Marsh, 2013). Improving students' value of math may cause students to report having lower value for unrelated subjects, in order to see themselves more clearly as people who value math. Researchers should explore further the possibility that interventions might reduce students' motivation for non-targeted subjects.

Individual-Level Interventions

Instead of targeting whole schools or classroom, much intervention research grounded in EVT has targeted individual students. Most individual-level interventions do not ask teachers to change their instructional practices, because it would be difficult for a teacher to administer an intervention only to some students in a class without other students noticing. Thus individual-level interventions are typically administered as homework assignments, out-of-school activities, or in-class writing activities.

Weisgram and Bigler (2006, 2007) conducted theoretically eclectic intervention studies in which they aimed to improve female students' expectancies (measured in terms of self-efficacy) and value for science and engineering, in addition to their interest in these subjects and their perceptions of gender discrimination. The interventions were delivered to students in the form of workshops or camps outside of school time. Students completed hands-on activities designed to improve their science self-efficacy, and they received information about scientific careers designed to increase their task values. The authors found, in their 2006 study, that the programs improved students' self-efficacy or utility value compared to a group of students who did not attend. However, in their 2007 study, they found that the positive effects of similar workshops on utility value and self-efficacy were limited to students who attended and also received additional information about gender discrimination, which was unrelated to EVT.

Acee and Weinstein (2010) conducted an intervention that targeted three components of task values. The authors designed a 100-minute session delivered on the computer in which college statistics students completed tasks designed to help them re-appraise their perceptions of intrinsic value, attainment value, and utility value. For example, students brainstormed a list of skills they could develop by studying statistics in order to increase their attainment value. Students were randomly assigned to the intervention condition or a control condition; students in the intervention group reported higher perceived task values for statistics and were more likely to access a supplemental website about statistics compared to students in the control condition. Students in one class of the two that provided the sample for the intervention also earned higher statistics test scores.

An increasing number of researchers have conducted theoretically specific interventions that target students' perceptions of utility value, by asking students to think about the way that the lessons they are learning in a course relate to their lives (see Harackiewicz & Canning, Chapter 25, for further discussion). Utility value intervention researchers have demonstrated that if students engage in one to eight brief reflective writing intervention activities about this topic over the course of several months, their perceptions of utility value, interest, and achievement in a variety of academic courses can improve (Harackiewicz et al., 2016; Hulleman & Harackiewicz, 2009; Hulleman et al., 2010, 2016). These activities have taken different forms across different studies (e.g., homework essay assignments, in-class essay assignments, evaluating quotations from other students). An important issue in this research is that the effects of these interventions are often moderated by student-level variables (see Rosenzweig & Wigfield, 2016 for review). In general, students who benefit most from utility value interventions are those who begin the intervention at a greater risk for underachievement, such as African American or first-generation college students, students with low expectancies for success or prior performance, or students with low initial interest in a subject (Harackiewicz et al., 2016; Hulleman & Harackiewicz, 2009; Hulleman et al., 2010, 2016). It will be important for future work to address why such interventions are more effective for some students than others, and if they can be modified to be successful for all students.

Two Intervention Examples from Our Own Work

We discuss two examples of our intervention work. Our goal is to illustrate different ways that EVT can be used to guide interventions that attempt to improve student outcomes, and to discuss issues in these interventions that researchers should address in future research.

First, we describe the CORI intervention (Guthrie et al., 2004, 2012, 2013), a theoretically eclectic school- or classroom-level intervention implemented by teachers in students' reading classes. CORI integrates reading strategy instruction and teaching practices to enhance students' motivation. The elementary school version of CORI aimed to improve students' overall reading motivation, reading strategy use, and reading comprehension, and the books and other reading materials in CORI dealt with plant and animal ecology. In middle school, CORI targeted students' motivation and comprehension for reading information texts in the areas of science and social studies, focusing on topics like the Civil War and animal and plant adaptations to their environment (Guthrie & Klauda, 2014; Guthrie et al., 2004, 2012, 2013). At both levels, CORI included teaching practices designed to enhance students' self-efficacy (or competence beliefs more broadly) and valuing of reading (more later). The intervention also included teaching practices designed to enhance motivational variables from other theories of motivation, such as students' intrinsic motivation and prosocial motivation (Guthrie et al., 2004, 2012, 2013).

Most CORI studies have used quasi-experimental designs, in which schools were randomly assigned to CORI or to different kinds of control groups. Guthrie and Klauda (2014) used the particularly powerful switching replication design, in which all students experienced both CORI and the districts' traditional instruction, in different orders. In this design, students acted as their own controls. In all versions of CORI, teachers received professional development in which they learned the various teaching practices that were part of the CORI program, and they implemented CORI for four to 12 weeks.

As noted above, CORI included daily teaching practices to increase students' reading comprehension and strategy use, such as asking students to summarize texts. Teachers also embedded, in their instruction, daily practices to support different constructs associated with students' motivation to read. To target students' expectancies (measured in terms of self-efficacy or competence beliefs in different versions of CORI), teachers provided students with reading materials that they could comprehend, gave them assignments at which they could succeed, and provided feedback designed to give them information about how to improve. To target task values, in elementary school, teachers began by engaging students in hands-on activities related to the topic to generate their situational interests. Then, they built on these activities by having students generate their own questions about the activities, and they provided students with interesting texts to read that related directly to the hands-on activities and the questions they posed. In middle school, teachers targeted the valuing of reading by emphasizing the relevance of course material for students' lives and by describing to students why skills in information text reading were important to master. In addition, at both elementary and middle school, CORI teachers provided students with many choices about what materials to read and what assignments to do (to foster intrinsic motivation for reading), and allowed for much social interaction around reading, given the importance of peers in children and early adolescents' lives.

Much research has shown that students receiving CORI had higher reading motivation, reading engagement, reading comprehension, reading strategy use, word recognition, and later reading grades compared to students in control classrooms (e.g., Guthrie & Klauda, 2014; Guthrie et al., 2004, 2007, 2013). Interestingly, in one version of CORI conducted at the elementary school level, students in CORI classrooms showed higher post-test reading comprehension and reading strategy use than did students in a condition that focused directly on enhancing students' comprehension and strategy use but did not include motivation supports (Guthrie et al., 2004). Furthermore, CORI has been shown to benefit both struggling readers (Guthrie et al., 2009) and African American students (Guthrie et al., 2012) to the same extent as other students. These are two groups that traditionally struggle to achieve high reading comprehension in school.

The CORI intervention is one of very few interventions that used a strong, eclectic theoretical rationale in its design and enhanced a variety of motivational variables, including expectancy-related constructs, task values, and intrinsic motivation. Guthrie, Wigfield, and colleagues had the goal of improving students' motivation generally, but they did not train teachers to be "motivation-supportive" in a general sense. Rather, as just discussed, they taught teachers to implement particular instructional practices that aligned with motivational constructs from EVT and other theories, choosing these practices with respect to prior research grounded in those theories.

The design and results of the CORI studies also illustrate several important and ongoing issues that should be addressed in future intervention research. First, as just noted, CORI benefited both high- and low-achieving students to the same extent, whereas many other EVT interventions only benefited students who were at risk for underachievement (e.g., Hulleman & Harackiewicz,

2009). The reason these different patterns of effects occurred is unclear, because not enough research has addressed how and why different students respond differently to various types of interventions. This is important because the fact that CORI benefited both high and low achievers means it is not lessening the achievement gap between these groups. Second, the motivation supports in CORI were implemented in somewhat large doses, because the intervention practices occurred every day for at least one month. It is unclear whether CORI would be effective if its implementation were briefer, in line with the brief utility value interventions discussed above. Third, CORI allows for a fair amount of teacher control over how it is implemented; this contrasts with interventions like Success for All (Borman et al., 2007) that are highly scripted. Instructional fidelity is assessed in CORI, but teachers can implement the instructional practices in different ways, and so arrive at fidelity in different ways. Guthrie and colleagues have argued that giving teachers some control over how they implement CORI should enhance their own motivation to utilize CORI practices effectively. Like students, teachers also need autonomy. However, it is unclear how "flexible" intervention programs such as CORI compare to scripted interventions with respect to fidelity and outcomes; this is an important future direction for intervention researchers to explore.

The second intervention we describe is a theoretically specific intervention to reduce students' perceptions of cost in an introductory college physics course (Rosenzweig, 2017). In this study, Rosenzweig (2017) targeted only students' perceptions of cost, rather than a variety of motivational constructs as CORI had. The cost-reduction intervention was implemented by researchers and delivered to college physics students online as part of their course homework assignments. This study is one of the very first to target the cost aspect of EVT.

In the study, college physics students were randomly assigned to the intervention condition, a control condition in which they did not complete an activity, or one of two other conditions.[4] Students received the intervention or control activities during two seven-minute to 15-minute sessions that occurred one month apart. In the intervention condition, in order to reduce cost, Rosenzweig (2017) encouraged students to re-attribute their cost experiences (see Walton & Cohen, 2007, 2011). As such, students were asked to read quotations from their peers pointing to the fact that their peers' cost experiences were common to others and were short term in nature. Participating students evaluated the quotations and then wrote a quotation describing how they overcame cost experiences of their own.

Interestingly, rather than showing overall effects on all students, the cost intervention differentially impacted different groups of students. Female students and students with low prior achievement reported significantly lower

---

4 The other two conditions were an additional control condition in which students summarized what they were learning, and a utility value intervention condition in which students wrote about the relevance of course material to their lives.

cost after receiving the cost intervention, compared to a control condition in which students completed only surveys. Female intervention group students earned higher exam scores, and took more STEM courses in the semester following the intervention, and students with low prior achievement who received the intervention earned higher exam scores. There were no significant differences on these outcomes between conditions for high-achieving students or male students. Each of these variables was assessed in separate analyses, so it is important to note that low-achieving students might include both male and female students, and so on.

This is one of the first studies to show that EVT-based interventions can reduce any students' perceptions of cost, although effects were limited to only certain students. This work also demonstrates that EVT-based interventions do not need to be long or require many resources to impact students. Finally, as is the case with a variety of the brief social psychological-based interventions discussed earlier (e.g., Harackiewicz et al., 2016; Hulleman & Harackiewicz, 2009; Hulleman et al., 2010, 2016) this work illustrates the importance of considering moderating variables that might cause interventions to impact students differently. A critical issue for future brief interventions of these types is to determine which moderator variables appear to modify the effects of which interventions.

Summary

In summary, the research shows that different kinds of interventions based in EVT – from relatively brief ones focused on single constructs to more intensive ones focused on several motivational constructs and implemented over several weeks – are effective in improving students' motivation and achievement in different subject areas. There are also remaining questions, concerning for whom these programs might work best and how they might be effectively implemented, that have not been explored in intervention research to date; we discuss some of these questions and issues in the final section.

Concluding Thoughts

EVT provides a theoretical framework that can be used to develop intervention protocols to improve (at least some) students' motivation and learning. We are very encouraged with these results; however, there are at least four questions that subsequent studies need to answer in order to understand how EVT, and interventions based in it, can be used most effectively to improve student motivation and various educational outcomes.

The first question that needs to be explored is: *What are the most critical dimensions of cost and how do they impact students' choices of activities and their performance outcomes?* Research has demonstrated that cost relates to students' achievement and choices but, presently, the dimensions of cost that are most salient to students, and whether those same dimensions are equally salient to all, is unclear. For example, it is possible that emotional cost is more salient to female or African American students, who are often exposed to stereotypes suggesting that they typically have worse performance in certain academic domains (Eccles, 2007; Steele, 1997). Additionally, even though new, expanded measures of cost have been developed by Gaspard and colleagues (2015b), Flake and colleagues (2015), and Perez and colleagues (2014), critical dimensions of cost have possibly not been included in these new measures. Further study of the relations of cost, task values, and expectancies is needed. This will require careful theoretical arguments about how these constructs should be defined, how they may relate, and how distinct they are, in addition to systematic factor analytic work using measures of the cost, the components of task values, and various competence-related beliefs, including (but not limited to) expectancies. This research should be done with large and diverse samples at different points in development. Third, researchers are just beginning to explore the impacts of cost on students' adaptive and maladaptive educational outcomes.

The second question is: *For whom do different instructional practices designed to enhance motivation work or (sometimes) work against, and why?* As the intervention examples illustrated, many efforts to improve students' motivation in the classroom do not benefit all students to the same extent (see also Canning & Harackiewicz, Chapter 25, p. 635). Although many researchers have reported that there are moderators impacting the effectiveness of expectancy-value-theory-grounded interventions, this work has not yet generated a systematic understanding of these moderators or the reason different moderators emerge in different EVT-based interventions. It is critical to understand the role of moderating variables in order to understand why certain motivation-supportive instructional practices are effective for some students but not others, how the effects of the interventions may vary across different educational contexts (see Kaplan et al., 2012), and which practices may be effective for all students. Attention to this issue will help ensure that interventions do not show undermining effects for some students, and will help researchers decide which interventions to implement for given groups of students.

The third question is: *What is the best length and dosage for implementing EVT-based interventions?* There is an assumption underlying intervention research that interventions will be more effective if they last longer or are implemented in a higher dosage during the time period over which they are administered. Many researchers have argued that their mixed or null results were due to not implementing the intervention long enough or intensively enough (e.g., Kim & Hodges, 2012; Moote et al., 2013; Star et al., 2014). However, few researchers have actually evaluated the effects of intervention length or dosage empirically, and the relationship between intervention length and dosage may be more complex than simply "more is better" (see Rosenzweig & Wigfield,

2016 for more detailed discussion). This is because there are many aspects of intervention length and dosage: for length, there is the time period over which an intervention lasts and the length of each session; for dosage, factors include the number of intervention sessions administered, the number of ways a given motivational construct is supported in a given intervention session, the number of topics covered in each session, and the amount of material presented in each session. Having more of one or another element will possibly produce better outcomes but, for others, there is no clear relationship to students' outcomes.

Another possibility is that the type of intervention conducted interacts with length or dosage. For example, an intervention may be effective after only one session if it targets a thought that students repeatedly have in school, such as "I don't think this is useful." However, an intervention predicated on students learning through experience, such as one designed to raise students' expectancies of success by encouraging them to have mastery experiences, might need to include many sessions before the intervention's lesson is realized. Similarly, a briefer intervention tailored to students' needs may be more effective than a longer one that is not personalized (Song & Keller, 2001).

Finally, the fourth question is: *How can teachers best align their instruction with EVT?* It would be optimal for teachers to understand and utilize EVT-based teaching practices (and those from other motivational theories) consistently in their classroom practice. Educational policies and practices in many school districts, such as the strong foci on testing and accountability, may make it difficult to do so (see Wigfield et al., 2018, for discussion of how practices based in EVT and other theories sometimes conflict with and sometimes correspond to national educational policies). We recommend that researchers explore further how teachers can implement motivation-supportive instructional techniques in their classroom with minimal time and resources. We also recommend that researchers explore whether it may be beneficial for teachers to target motivation interventions to specific struggling students, rather than implementing interventions with whole classrooms.

References

Acee, T. W. & Weinstein, C. E. (2010). Effects of a value-reappraisal intervention on statistics students' motivation and performance. *The Journal of Experimental Education, 78*(4), 487–512. doi: 10.1080/00220970903352753.

Archambault, I., Eccles, J. S., & Vida, M. N. (2010). Ability self-concepts and subjective value in literacy: Joint trajectories from grades 1–12. *Journal of Educational Psychology, 102*(4), 804–16. doi: 10.1037/a0021075.

Atkinson, J. W. (1957). Motivational determinants of risk-taking behavior. *Psychological Review, 64*, 359–72. doi: 10.1080/00220970903352753.

Bandura, A. (1997). *Self-efficacy: The exercise of control.* New York, NY: W. H. Freeman.

Barron, K. E. & Hulleman, C. S. (2015). Expectancy-value-cost model of motivation. In J. S. Eccles & K. Salmelo-Aro (Eds.), *International encyclopedia of social and behavioral sciences: Motivational psychology* (2nd ed., pp. 503–9). New York, NY: Elsevier. doi: 10.1016/B978-0-08-097086-8.26099-6.

Battle, A. & Wigfield, A. (2003). College women's value orientations toward family, career, and graduate school. *Journal of Vocational Behavior, 62*, 56–75. doi: 10.1016/S0001-8791(02)00037-4.

Bong, M., Cho, C., Ahn, H. S., & Kim, H. J. (2012). Comparison of self-beliefs for predicting student motivation and achievement. *Journal of Educational Research, 105*, 336–52.

Bong, M., Hwang, A., Noh, A., & Kim, S. I. (2014). Perfectionism and motivation of adolescents in academic contexts. *Journal of Educational Psychology, 106*(3), 711–29. doi: 10.1080/00220671.2011.627401.

Bong, M. & Skaalvik, E. M. (2003). Academic self-concept and self-efficacy: How different are they really? *Educational Psychology Review, 15*(1), 1–40. doi: 10.1023/A:1021302408382.

Borman, G. D., Slavin, R. E., Cheung, A. C. K., Chamberlain, A. M., Madden, N. A., & Chambers, B. (2007). Final reading outcomes of the national randomized field trial of Success for All. *American Educational Research Journal, 44*, 701–31.

Brisson, B. M., Dicke, A.-L., Gaspard, H., Häfner, I., Flunger, B., Nagengast, B., & Trautwein, U. (2017). Short intervention, sustained effects: Promoting students' math competence beliefs, effort, and achievement. *American Educational Research Journal.* doi: 10.3102/0002831217716084.

Conley, A. M. (2012). Patterns of motivation beliefs: Combining achievement goal and expectancy-value perspectives. *Journal of Educational Psychology, 104*(1), 32–47. doi: 10.1037/a0026042.

Denissen, J. J., Zarrett, N. R., & Eccles, J. S. (2007). I like to do it, I'm able, and I know I am: Longitudinal couplings between domain-specific achievement, self-concept, and interest. *Child Development, 78*(2), 430–47. doi: 10.1111/j.1467-8624.2007.01007.x.

Durik, A. M., Vida, M., & Eccles, J. S. (2006). Task values and ability beliefs as predictors of high school literacy choices: A developmental analysis. *Journal of Educational Psychology, 98*, 382–93. doi: 10.1037/0022-0663.98.2.382.

Eccles, J. S. (1987). Gender roles and women's achievement-related decisions. *Psychology of Women Quarterly, 11*, 135–72. doi: 10.1111/j.1471-6402.1987.tb00781.x

Eccles, J. S. (2005). Subjective task values and the Eccles et al. model of achievement related choices. In A. J. Elliott & C. S. Dweck (Eds.), *Handbook of competence and motivation* (pp. 105–21). New York, NY: Guilford.

Eccles, J. S. (2007). Where are all the women? Gender differences in participation in physical science and engineering. In S. J. Ceci & W. M. Williams (Eds.), *Why aren't more women in science? Top researchers debate the evidence* (pp. 199–210). Washington, DC: American Psychological Association. doi: 10.1037/11546-016.

Eccles, J. S. & Midgley, C. (1989). Stage/environment fit: Developmentally appropriate classrooms for early adolescents. In R. Ames & C. Ames (Eds.), *Research on motivation in education* (Vol. 3, pp. 139–81). New York, NY: Academic Press.

Eccles, J. S. & Wigfield, A. (1995). In the mind of the achiever: The structure of adolescents' academic achievement related-beliefs and self-perceptions. *Personality and Social Psychology Bulletin, 21*, 215–25.

Eccles, J. S. & Wigfield, A. (2002). Motivational beliefs, values, and goals. *Annual Review of Psychology, 53*(1), 109–32. doi: 10.1146/annurev.psych.53.100901.135153.

Eccles, J. S., Wigfield, A., Harold, R., & Blumenfeld, P. B. (1993). Age and gender differences in children's self- and task perceptions during elementary school. *Child Development, 64*, 830–47. doi: 10.1111/j.1467-8624.1993.tb02946.x.

Eccles, J. S., Wigfield, A. & Schiefele, U. (1998). Motivation to succeed. In W. Damon & N. Eisenberg (Eds.), *Handbook of child psychology: Social, emotional, and personality development* (pp. 1017–95). Hoboken, NJ: John Wiley & Sons Inc.

Eccles-Parsons, J. S., Adler, T. F., Futterman, R., Goff, S. B., Kaczala, C. M., Meece, J. L., & Midgley, C. (1983). Expectancies, values, and academic behaviors. In J. T. Spence (Ed.), *Achievement and achievement motivation* (pp. 75–146). San Francisco, CA: W. H. Freeman.

Elliot, A. J. (1999). Approach and avoidance motivation and achievement goals. *Educational Psychologist, 34*(3), 169–89. doi: 10.1207/s15326985ep3403_3.

Elliot, A. J. & Church, M. A. (1997). A hierarchical model of approach and avoidance achievement motivation. *Journal of Personality and Social Psychology, 72*(1), 218–32. doi: 10.1037/0022-3514.72.1.218.

Falco, L. D., Summers, J. J., & Bauman, S. (2010). Encouraging mathematics participation through improved self-efficacy: A school counseling outcomes study. *Educational Research and Evaluation, 16*(6), 529–49. doi: 10.1080/13803611.2011.555101.

Flake, J. K., Barron, K. E., Hulleman, C., McCoach, D. B., & Welsh, M. E. (2015). Measuring cost: The forgotten component of expectancy-value theory. *Contemporary Educational Psychology, 41*, 232–44. doi: 10.1016/j.cedpsych.2015.03.002.

Fredricks, J. & Eccles, J. S. (2002). Children's competence and value beliefs from childhood through adolescence: Growth trajectories in two male sex-typed domains. *Developmental Psychology, 38*, 519–33. doi: 10.1037/0012-1649.38.4.519.

Frenzel, A. C., Goetz, T., Pekrun, R., & Watt, H. M. (2010). Development of mathematics interest in adolescence: Influences of gender, family, and school context. *Journal of Research on Adolescence, 20*(2), 507–37. doi: 10.1111/j.1532-7795.2010.00645.x.

Guo, J., Marsh, H. W., Parker, P. D., Morin, A. J. S., & Yeung, A. S. (2015b). Expectancy–value in mathematics, gender and socioeconomic background as predictors of achievement and aspirations: A multi-cohort study. *Learning and Individual Differences, 37*, 161–8. doi: 10.1016/j.lindif.2015.01.008.

Guo, J., Parker, P. D., Marsh, H. W., & Morin, A. J. (2015a). Achievement, motivation, and educational choices: A longitudinal study of expectancy and value using a multiplicative perspective. *Developmental Psychology, 51*(8), 1163–76. doi: 10.1037/a0039440.

Gaspard, H., Dicke, A., Flunger, B., Brisson, B., Häfner, I., Nagengast, B., & Trautwein, U. (2015a). Fostering adolescents' value beliefs for mathematics with a relevance intervention in the classroom. *Developmental Psychology, 51*(9), 1226–40. doi: 10.1037/dev0000028.

Gaspard, H., Dicke, A. L., Flunger, B., Häfner, I., Brisson, B. M., Trautwein, U., & Nagengast, B. (2016). Side effects of motivational interventions? Effects of an intervention in math classrooms on motivation in verbal domains. *AERA Open*, *2*(2), 1–14. doi: 10.1177/2332858416649168.

Gaspard, H., Dicke, A., Flunger, B., Schreier, B., Häfner, I., Trautwein, U., & Nagengast, B. (2015b). More value through greater differentiation: Gender differences in value beliefs about math. *Journal of Educational Psychology*, *107*(3), 663–77. doi: 10.1037/edu0000003.

Gaspard, H., Häfner, I., Parrisius, C., Trautwein, U., & Nagegast, B. (2017). Assessing task values in five subjects during secondary school: Measurement structure and mean level differences across grade level, gender, and academic subject. *Contemporary Educational Psychology*, *48*, 67–84. doi: 10.1016/j.cedpsych.2016.09.003.

Gottfried, A. E., Fleming, J. S., & Gottfried, A. W. (2001). Continuity of academic intrinsic motivation from childhood through late adolescence: A longitudinal study. *Journal of Educational Psychology*, *93*(1), 3–13. doi: 10.1037/0022-0663.93.1.3.

Guthrie, J. T. & Klauda, S. L. (2014). Effects of classroom practices on reading comprehension, engagement, and motivations for adolescents. *Reading Research Quarterly*, *49*, 387–416. doi: 10.1002/rrq.81.

Guthrie, J. T., Klauda, S. L., & Ho, A. (2013). Modeling the relationships among reading instruction, motivation, engagement, and achievement for adolescents. *Reading Research Quarterly*, *48*, 9–26. doi: 10.1002/rrq.035.

Guthrie, J. T., Klauda, S., & Morrison, D. (2012). Motivation, achievement, and classroom contexts for information book reading. In J. T. Guthrie, A. Wigfield, & S. L. Klauda (Eds.), *Adolescents' engagement in academic literacy* (pp. 1–51). College Park: University of Maryland.

Guthrie, J. T., McRae, A., Coddington, C. S., Klauda, S. L., Wigfield, A., & Barbosa, P. (2009). Impacts of comprehensive reading instruction on diverse outcomes of low- and high-achieving readers. *Journal of Learning Disabilities*, *42*(3), 195–214. doi: 10.1177/0022219408331039.

Guthrie, J. T., McRae, A. C., & Klauda, S. L. (2007). Contributions of Concept-Oriented Reading Instruction to knowledge about interventions for motivations in reading. *Educational Psychologist*, *42*, 237–50. doi: 10.1080/00461520701621087.

Guthrie, J. T., Wigfield, A., Barbosa, P., Perencevich, K. C., Taboada, A., Davis, M. H., ... Tonks, S. (2004). Increasing reading comprehension and engagement through concept-oriented reading instruction. *Journal of Educational Psychology*, *96*(3), 403–23. doi: 10.1037/0022-0663.96.3.403.

Guthrie, J. T., Wigfield, A., & Klauda, S. L. (2012). *Adolescents' engagement in academic literacy*. Retrieved March 29, 2017, from www.corilearning.com/research-publications.

Guthrie, J. T., Wigfield, A., & Perencevich, K. (Eds.). (2004). *Motivating reading comprehension: Concept oriented reading instruction*. Malwah, NJ: Lawrence Erlbaum.

Harackiewicz, J. M., Barron, K. E., Tauer, J. M., & Elliot, A. J. (2002). Predicting success in college: A longitudinal study of achievement goals and ability measures as predictors of interest and performance from freshman year through graduation. *Journal of Educational Psychology, 94*(3), 562–75. doi: 10.1037/0022-0663.94.3.562.

Harackiewicz, J. M., Canning, E. A., Tibbetts, Y., Priniski, S. J., & Hyde, J. S. (2016). Closing achievement gaps with a utility-value intervention: Disentangling race and social class. *Journal of Personality and Social Psychology, 111*(5), 745–65. doi: 10.1037/pspp0000075.

Hensley, L. C. (2014). Reconsidering active procrastination: Relations to motivation and achievement in college anatomy. *Learning and Individual Differences, 36*, 157–64. doi: 10.1016/j.lindif.2014.10.012.

Heyman, G. D., Dweck, C. S., & Cain, K. M. (1992). Young children's vulnerability to self-blame and helplessness: Relationships to beliefs about goodness. *Child Development, 63*, 401–15.

Hidi, S. & Renninger, K. A. (2006). The four-phase model of interest development. *Educational Psychologist, 41*(2), 111–27.

Higgins, E. T. (2007). Value. In A. W. Kruglanski & E. T. Higgins (Eds.), *Handbook of social psychology* (2nd ed., pp. 454–72). New York, NY: Guilford Press.

Hulleman, C. S., Godes, O., Hendricks, B. L., & Harackiewicz, J. M. (2010). Enhancing interest and performance with a utility value intervention. *Journal of Educational Psychology, 102*, 880–95. doi: 10.1037/a0019506.

Hulleman, C. S. & Harackiewicz, J. M. (2009). Promoting interest and performance in high school science classes. *Science, 326*(5958), 1410–12. doi: 10.1126/science.1177067.

Hulleman, C. S., Kosovich, J. J., Barron, K. E., & Daniel, D. B. (2016). Making connections: Replicating and extending the utility value intervention in the classroom. *Journal of Educational Psychology*. Advance online publication. doi: 10.1037/edu0000146.

Jacobs, J., Lanza, S., Osgood, D. W., Eccles, J. S., & Wigfield, A. (2002). Changes in children's self-competence and values: Gender and domain differences across grades one through 12. *Child Development, 73*, 509–27. doi: 10.1111/1467-8624.00421.

Jiang, Y., Rosenzweig, E. Q., & Gaspard, H. (2018). An expectancy-value-cost approach in predicting students' academic motivation and achievement. *Contemporary Educational Psychology, 54*, 139–52. doi: 10.1016/j.cedpsych.2018.06.005.

Johnson, M. L. & Safavian, N. (2016). What is cost and is it always a bad thing? Furthering the discussion concerning college-aged students' perceived costs for their academic studies. *Journal of Cognitive Education and Psychology, 15*(3), 368–90. doi: 10.1891/1945-8959.15.3.368.

Kaplan, A., Katz, I., & Flum, H. (2012). Motivation theory in educational practice: Knowledge claims, challenges, and future directions. In K. R. Harris, S. Graham, & T. Urdan (Eds.), *Educational psychology handbook: Vol. 2: Individual differences in cultural and contextual factors* (pp. 165–94). Washington, DC: American Psychological Association.

Kim, C. & Hodges, C. B. (2012). Effects of an emotion control treatment on academic emotions, motivation and achievement in an online mathematics course. *Instructional Science, 40*, 173–92. doi: 10.1007/s11251-011-9165-6.

Krapp, A. (2002). Structural and dynamic aspects of interest development: Theoretical considerations from an ontogenetic perspective. *Learning and Instruction*, *12*(4), 383–409. doi: 10.1016/S0959-4752(01)00011-1.

Lazowski, R. A. & Hulleman, C. S. (2016). Motivation interventions in education: A meta-analytic review. *Review of Educational Research*, *86*(2), 602–40. doi: 10.3102/0034654315617832.

Lee, J., Bong, M., & Kim, S. (2014). Interaction between task values and self-efficacy on maladaptive achievement strategy use. *Educational Psychology*, *34*, 538–60. doi: 10.1080/01443410.2014.895296.

Lee, J., Lee, M., & Bong, M. (2013). High value with low perceived competence as an amplifier of self-worth threat. In D. M. McInerney, H. W. Marsh, R. G. Craven, & F. Guay (Eds.), *Theory driving research* (pp. 205–31). Charlotte, NC: Information Age. doi: 10.13140/2.1.3704.1282.

Lewin, K. (1938). *The conceptual representation and the measurement of psychological forces*. Durham, NC: Duke University Press.

Lu, K. M., Pan, S, Y., & Cheng, J. W. (2011). Examination of a perceived cost model of employees' negative feedback-seeking behavior. *The Journal of Psychology: Interdisciplinary and Applied*, *145*, 573–94. doi: 10.1080/0022 3980.2011.613873.

Marinak, B. A. (2013). Courageous reading instruction: The effects of an elementary motivation intervention. *Journal of Educational Research*, *106*(1), 39–48. doi: 10.1080/00220671.2012.658455.

Marsh, H. W. (1986). Verbal and math self-concepts: An internal/external frame of reference model. *American Educational Research Journal*, *23*, 129–49. doi: 10.3102/00028312023001129.

Meece, J. L., Wigfield, A., & Eccles, J. S. (1990). Predictors of math anxiety and its consequences for young adolescents' course enrollment intentions and performances in mathematics. *Journal of Educational Psychology*, *82*, 60–70.

Möller, J. & Marsh, H. W. (2013). Dimensional comparison theory. *Psychological Review*, *120*, 544–60. doi: 10.1037/a0032459.

Moote, J. K., Williams, J. M., & Sproule, J. (2013). When students take control: Investigating the impact of the crest inquiry-based learning program on self-regulated processes and related motivations in young science students. *Journal of Cognitive Education and Psychology*, *12*, 178–96. doi: 10.1891/1945-8959.12.2.178.

Morgan, P. L., Fuchs, D., Compton, D. L., Cordray, D. S., & Fuchs, L. S. (2008). Does early reading failure decrease children's reading motivation? *Journal of Learning Disabilities*, *41*(5), 387–404.

Musu-Gillette, L. E., Wigfield, A., Harring, J. & Eccles, J. S. (2015). Trajectories of change in student's self-concepts of ability and values in math and college major choice. *Educational Research and Evaluation*, *21*(4), 343. doi: 10.1080/13803611.2015.1057161.

Nagengast, B., Marsh, H. W., Scalas, L. F., Xu, M. K., Hau, K. T., & Trautwein, U. (2011). Who took the "x" out of expectancy–value theory? A psychological mystery, a substantive-methodological synergy, and a cross-national generalization. *Psychological Science*, *22*, 1058–66. doi: 10.1177/0956797611415540.

Nagengast, B., Trautwein, U., Kelava, A., & Lüdtke, O. (2013). Synergistic effects of expectancy and value on homework engagement: The case for a within-person perspective. *Multivariate Behavioral Research, 48*, 428–60. doi: 10.1080/00273171.2013.775060.

Orthner, D. K., Jones-Sanpei, H., Akos, P., & Rose, R. A. (2013). Improving middle school student engagement through career-relevant instruction in the core curriculum. *Journal of Educational Research, 106*(1), 27–38. doi: 10.1080/00220671.2012.658454.

Pajares, F. (1996). Self-efficacy beliefs in academic settings. *Review of Educational Research, 66*, 543–78. doi: 10.3102/00346543066004543.

Pekrun, R. (1993). Facets of adolescents' academic motivation: A longitudinal expectancy– value approach. In P. Pintrich & M. L. Maehr (Eds.), *Advances in motivation and achievement* (Vol. 8, pp. 139–89). Greenwich, CT: JAI Press.

Pekrun, R. (2000). A social-cognitive, control value theory of achievement emotions. In J. Heckhausen (Ed.), *Motivational psychology of human development* (pp. 143–63). Oxford: Elsevier.

Pekrun, R. (2009). Emotions at school. In K. R. Wentzel & A. Wigfield (Eds.), *Handbook of motivation at school* (pp. 575–604). New York, NY: Routledge.

Perez, T., Cromley, J. G., & Kaplan, A. (2014). The role of identity development, values, and costs in college STEM retention. *Journal of Educational Psychology, 106*, 315–29. doi: 10.1037/a0034027.

Pintrich, P. R. & De Groot, E. V. (1990). Motivational and self-regulated learning components of classroom academic performance. *Journal of Educational Psychology, 82*(1), 33–40. doi: 10.1037/0022-0663.82.1.33.

Rokeach, M. (1973). *The nature of human values.* New York, NY: The Free Press.

Rosenzweig, E. (2017). *More useful, or not so bad? Evaluating The effects of interventions to reduce perceived cost and increase utility value with college physics students* (Doctoral dissertation). doi: 10.13016/M2G293.

Rosenzweig, E. Q. & Wigfield, A. (2016a). STEM motivation interventions for adolescents: A promising start, but farther to go. *Educational Psychologist, 51*(2), 146–63. doi: 10.1080/00461520.2016.1154792.

Rosenzweig, E. Q. & Wigfield, A. (2017). What if reading is easy but unimportant? How students' patterns of affirming and undermining motivation for reading information texts predict different reading outcomes. *Contemporary Educational Psychology, 48*, 133–48. doi: 10.1016/j.cedpsych.2016.09.002.

Safavian, N. & Conley, A. (2016). Expectancy-value beliefs of early-adolescent Hispanic and non-Hispanic youth: Predictors of mathematics achievement and enrollment. *AERA Open, 2*(4), 1–17. doi: 10.1177/2332858416673357.

Senko, C. (2016). Achievement goal theory: a story of early promises, eventual discords, and future possibilities. In K. R. Wentzel & D. B. Miele (Eds.), *Handbook of motivation of school* (2nd ed., pp. 75–95). New York, NY: Routledge.

Senko, C., Hulleman, C. S., & Harackiewicz, J. M. (2011). Achievement goal theory at the crossroads: Old controversies, current challenges, and new directions. *Educational Psychologist, 46*(1), 26–47. doi: 10.1080/00461520.2011.538646.

Simpkins, S. D., Davis-Kean, P. E., & Eccles, J. S. (2006). Math and science motivation: A longitudinal examination of the links between choice and beliefs. *Developmental Psychology, 42*, 70–83. doi: 10.1037/0012-1649.42.1.70.

Song, S. H. & Keller, J. M. (2001). Effectiveness of motivationally adaptive computer-assisted instruction on the dynamic aspects of motivation. *Educational Technology Research and Development, 49*(2), 5–22. doi: 10.1007/BF02504925.

Star, J., Chen, J. A., Taylor, M. W., Durkin, K., Dede, C., & Chao, T. (2014). Evaluating technology-based strategies for enhancing motivation in mathematics. *International Journal of STEM Education, 1*(7), 1–19. doi: 10.1186/2196-7822-1-7.

Steele, C. M. (1997). A threat in the air: How stereotypes shape intellectual identity and performance. *American Psychologist, 52*(6), 613. doi: 10.1037/0003-066X.52.6.613.

Tibbetts, Y., Harackiewicz, J. M., Priniski, S. J., & Canning, E. A. (2016). Broadening participation in the life sciences with social–psychological interventions. *CBE-Life Sciences Education, 15*(3), es4. doi: 10.1187/cbe.16-01-0001.

Tolman, E. C. (1932). *Purposive behavior in animals and men.* New York, NY: Appleton-Century-Crofts.

Trautwein, U., Nagengast, B., Nagy, G., Jonkmann, K., Marsh, H. W., & Ludtke, O. (2012). Probing for the multiplicative term in modem expectancy-value theory: A latent interaction modeling study. *Journal of Educational Psychology, 104*, 763–77. doi: 10.1037/a0027470.

Walton, G. M. & Cohen, G. L. (2007). A question of belonging: Race, social fit, and achievement. *Journal of Personality and Social Psychology, 92*(1), 82–96. doi: 10.1037/0022-3514.92.1.82.

Walton, G. M. & Cohen, G. L. (2011). A brief social-belonging intervention improves academic and health outcomes of minority students. *Science, 331*(6023), 1447–51. doi: 10.1126/science.1198364.

Wang, Q. & Pomerantz, E. M. (2009). The motivational landscape of early adolescence in the United States and China: A longitudinal investigation. *Child Development, 80*(4), 1272–87. doi: 10.1111/j.1467-8624.2009.01331.x.

Watt, H. (2004). Development of adolescents' self-perceptions, values, and task perceptions. *Child Development, 75*, 1556–74. doi: 10.1111/j.1467-8624.2004.00757.x.

Weisgram, E. S. & Bigler, R. S. (2006a). Girls and science careers: The role of altruistic values and attitudes about scientific tasks. *Journal of Applied Developmental Psychology, 27*(4), 326–48. doi: 10.1016/j.appdev.2006.04.004.

Weisgram, E. S. & Bigler, R. S. (2006b). The role of attitudes and intervention in high school girls' interest in computer science. *Journal of Women and Minorities in Science and Engineering, 12*, 325–36. doi: 10.1615/JWomenMinorScienEng.v12.i4.40.

Weisgram, E. S. & Bigler, R. S. (2007). Effects of learning about gender discrimination on adolescent girls' attitudes toward and interest in science. *Psychology of Women Quarterly, 31*(3), 262–9. doi: 10.1111/j.1471-6402.2007.00369.x.

Wigfield, A. & Cambria, J. (2010). Expectancy-value theory: retrospective and prospective. In T. Urdan, & S. A. Karabenick (Eds.), *Advances in motivation and achievement. The next decade of research in motivation and achievement,* Vol. 16A (pp. 35–70). London: Emerald. doi: 10.1108/S0749-7423(2010)000016A005.

Wigfield, A. & Eccles, J. S. (1992). The development of achievement task values: A theoretical analysis. *Developmental Review, 12*(3), 265–310. doi: 10.1016/0273-2297(92)90011-P.

Wigfield, A. & Eccles, J. S. (2000). Expectancy-value theory of achievement motivation. *Contemporary Educational Psychology, 25*, 68–81. doi: 10.1006/ceps.1999.1015.

Wigfield, A, Eccles, J. S., Fredricks, J., Simpkins, S., Roeser, R., & Schiefele, U. (2015). Development of achievement motivation and engagement. In R. Lerner (series Ed.) and M. Lamb (vol. Ed.), *Handbook of child psychology and developmental science* (7th ed., Vol. 3, pp. 657–700). New York, NY: Wiley.

Wigfield, A., Eccles, J. S., & Pintrich, P. R. (1996). Development between the ages of 11 and 25. In D. Berliner & R. Calfee (Eds.), *Handbook of educational psychology* (pp. 148–85). New York, NY: Macmillan.

Wigfield, A., Eccles, J. S., Yoon, K. S., Harold, R. D., Arbreton, A., Freedman-Doan, C., & Blumenfeld, P. C. (1997). Changes in children's competence beliefs and subjective task values across the elementary school years: A three-year study. *Journal of Educational Psychology, 89*, 451–69. doi: 10.1037/0022-0663.89.3.451.

Wigfield, A., Rosenzweig, E. Q., & Eccles, J. (2017). Competence values. In A. Elliot, C. Dweck, & D. Yeager (Eds.) *Handbook of competence and motivation: Theory and application* (2nd ed.). New York, NY: Guilford Press.

Wigfield, A., Tonks, S. M., & Klauda, S. L. (2016). Expectancy-value theory. In K. R. Wentzel & D. B. Miele (Eds.), *Handbook of motivation of school* (2nd ed., pp. 55–74). New York, NY: Routledge.

Wigfield, A., Turci, L., Cambria, J. & Eccles, J. S. (2018). Motivation in education. In R. Ryan (Ed.), *Oxford handbook of motivation* (2nd ed.). New York: Oxford University Press.

Wolters, C. A., Yu, S. L., & Pintrich, P. R. (1996). The relation between goal orientation and students' motivational beliefs and self-regulated learning. *Learning and Individual Differences, 8*(3), 211–38. doi: 10.1016/S1041-6080(96)90015-1.

Woolley, M. E., Rose, R. A., Orthner, D. K., Akos, P. T., & Jones-Sanpei, H. (2013). Advancing academic achievement through career relevance in the middle grades: A longitudinal evaluation of CareerStart. *American Educational Research Journal, 50*(6), 1309–35.

Xiang, P., McBride, R. E., & Bruene, A. (2004). Fourth graders' motivation in an elementary physical education running program. *The Elementary School Journal, 104*(3), 253–66. doi: 10.1086/499752.

Yang, Y. C. & Wu, W. I. (2012). Digital storytelling for enhancing student academic achievement, critical thinking, and learning motivation: A year-long experimental study. *Computers and Education, 59*(2), 339–52. doi: 10.1016/j.compedu.2011.12.012.

25 Utility Value and Intervention Framing

Elizabeth A. Canning and Judith M. Harackiewicz

Abstract: Students often lose interest in critical introductory courses that act as gateways to successive courses and careers. Utility value writing interventions have been designed to help students find the personal relevance and value of course material in order to promote interest and performance. However, little is known about how best to implement the intervention in terms of how to frame it, particularly in multi-level classrooms where students enter the course with different goals, challenges, and educational backgrounds. In this chapter, we review the research on utility value writing interventions and discuss differential findings across educational contexts. Using a case study in two-year colleges, we consider psychological (e.g., confidence, engagement) and cognitive (linguistic indicators of cognitive processing) mechanisms for the success of the intervention, as well as how the intervention can be beneficial for students with varying levels of interest and performance. We conclude with implications for intervention framing and directions for future research.

When students encounter subjects that do not seem important or useful, they may become disengaged, lacking the motivation to do well. Cultivating interest is paramount for motivating students in introductory courses, because interest is linked to more time studying, greater investment in learning, and academic performance (Harackiewicz et al., 2016; Hidi & Harackiewicz, 2000; Renninger & Hidi, 2011). Introductory-level college courses are the gatekeepers for many fields and careers, and serve to provide all students with enough general background in the subject to study more advanced topics. However, students in introductory courses have varied academic backgrounds and interest levels. In a college-level introductory biology course, some students may have taken advanced biology courses in high school, whereas other students enter the

This research was supported by a National Institutes of Health grant. Elizabeth Canning was supported by a National Science Foundation Graduate Research Fellowship Program grant, and by the Institute of Education Sciences, US Department of Education, through an award to the University of Wisconsin-Madison. We also thank Sara Goldrick-Rab and the Wisconsin HOPE Lab for funding this research.

course with more limited backgrounds. Likewise, some students are fascinated by biology from day one, while others need to be supported to recognize that the material is interesting or relevant. Cultivating interest in such multi-level class-rooms can be difficult for instructors. For instance, students who are struggling to keep up with the material may lose interest if the material is too difficult. In contrast, students who are doing well in a class may become bored or frustrated if the material is not novel or challenging enough. How can instructors promote interest and achievement without discouraging some and boring others?

One way to develop interest in introductory courses is to highlight the value of course material (Hulleman & Harackiewicz, 2009). One type of value that predicts interest, effort, and performance is utility value (UV) – the percep-tion that a task is useful and relevant, beyond the immediate situation, for other tasks or aspects of a person's life (Eccles & Wigfield, 2002; Wigfield & Cambria, 2010). For instance, a student may find a lesson on genetics to be important for their personal goal of becoming a doctor or because it helps them understand a parent's disease. If educators can help students find utility value in a subject, regardless of students' performance levels, educators may be able to promote interest and achievement.

Our approach is based in expectancy-value theory (Eccles & Wigfield, 2002), which forms the basis for one type of intervention that aims to use perceptions of utility value to promote interest and achievement. In this chapter, we review the research that led to the development of these interventions, as well as recent intervention research conducted in a number of educational contexts. Finally, we explore possible mechanisms for the success of these interventions, as well as how they can be beneficial for students with varying levels of interest and performance.

Expectancy-Value Theory

Eccles' expectancy-value model (Eccles & Wigfield, 2002) argues that academic performance, task engagement, course choices, and career plans are influenced by two factors: students' expectations for success and the value they attach to the task. Many studies have documented the importance of both expectancy (e.g., confidence) and value-related beliefs (e.g., valuing a task as useful or meaningful). When students expect to do well in a course and perceive value in course topics, they develop greater interest in the course, work harder, perform better, persist longer, and are more likely to take additional courses (Eccles & Wigfield, 2002; Wigfield & Cambria, 2010). Eccles (Eccles, 2009; Eccles et al., 1983) identified four types of task values: intrinsic (the inherent enjoyment of a task), utility (the importance or usefulness of a task for other tasks and goals), attainment (the importance to one's self concept or identity of doing well in a task) and cost (the negative aspects of engaging in a task).[1]

---

1 More recent conceptualizations of the expectancy-value framework consider cost to be a dis-tinct construct, independent of task values (Barron & Hulleman, 2015).

Of the four subjective task values, perceived utility value has been shown to be particularly effective in fostering a variety of outcomes, including interest (Hulleman et al., 2010; Husman et al., 2004; Wigfield & Cambria, 2010), task engagement (Husman & Lens, 1999; Raved & Assaraf, 2011), and academic achievement (Bong, 2001; Durik et al., 2006; Hulleman & Harackiewicz, 2009). For example, Hulleman and colleagues (2008) found that perceptions of utility value, measured early in a class, predicted subsequent interest in the course and positively predicted students' final grade in the course. More recently, Hulleman and colleagues (2017) found that the self-reported frequency with which students made connections between course material and their lives was positively related to perceptions of utility value and continued interest in the course. Although much of the research on utility value has been correlational (Hulleman et al., 2008; Wigfield & Cambria, 2010), recent field studies have shown that interventions designed to enhance perceptions of utility value can also increase interest, course performance, and subsequent course-taking in a domain (see Harackiewicz & Priniski, 2018).

Utility Value Interventions

Experimental research suggests that promoting perceptions of utility value is possible with simple interventions that have students write short essays about the relevance of course topics to their own lives. The critical component of this intervention is the writing assignment, which typically instructs students to discuss course material and explain how that material applies to them personally. This type of assignment encourages students to think about course material in new ways, which can facilitate learning as well as foster interest in the course topic.

UV interventions typically work best for students who doubt their competence or have a history of poor performance (Hulleman & Harackiewicz, 2009; Hulleman et al., 2010). For example, Hulleman and Harackiewicz (2009) implemented a UV intervention for high school students by having them write about the personal relevance of their science schoolwork. They found that students with less confidence in their science class, measured early in the semester, reported higher interest at the end of the semester and had higher grades in the UV condition, relative to a control condition, whereas confident students made no significant gains with the intervention. In addition, Hulleman et al. (2010) implemented the same intervention in an introductory psychology class. They found that students who had performed poorly on an early exam and who wrote about utility value reported more interest in the course at the end of the semester when compared to those in the control group. Similarly, a UV intervention improved grades for low-performing male students in an introductory psychology course (Hulleman et al., 2017). Another study of UV interventions in a college biology course varied the number of UV assignments that students received (Canning et al., 2018). Students who completed at least one UV writing assignment earned higher grades in the course, were more likely to enroll in the second semester of the course sequence, and were less likely to abandon their STEM major, on average, compared to students in the control condition. Furthermore, giving students more choice in the UV assignment has been shown to enhance the effectiveness of the intervention (Rosenzweig et al., 2018).

Implementing a Utility Value Intervention to Address Achievement Gaps

More recently, UV interventions have been used to promote performance for underrepresented students who struggle in introductory science courses. Harackiewicz and colleagues (2016) implemented a UV intervention in an introductory biology course that was a gateway to all biomedical science majors. Most students in this course intend to major in a STEM field and many are pre-medical or pre-health students. The intervention consisted of three 500-word essay assignments emailed to students throughout the semester. Students completed the essays as homework assignments and turned them in online for course credit. Students were randomly assigned to receive either the UV writing assignments (in which they wrote about how the course material was relevant and useful to them) or control essays (in which they summarized course material). The UV intervention was successful in reducing the achievement gap for underrepresented minority (URM) students by 40 percent and for URM students who were also first-generation (FG-URM) college students by 61 percent (Harackiewicz et al., 2016).

Why was the UV intervention particularly effective for FG-URM students? To answer this question, the researchers examined several individual difference variables collected at the beginning of the semester (before the intervention was implemented) and analyzed the content of the essays for clues about mechanism. The FG-URM students entered the course with a unique motivational profile compared to other students taking the course. They began the course with the least preparation in biology and the lowest incoming GPAs; however, they were the most motivated to do well in the course and to use what they learned to give back to their families and communities. The UV assignments were engaging for all students, but FG-URM students became particularly engaged with the assignments, writing longer essays than any other group of students. This increased engagement mediated the intervention effects on course grade. The intervention was particularly successful for FG-URM students in this context, because it provided the opportunity for them to connect course material to their personal goals of giving back to their families and communities. Indeed, the analysis of UV essay content revealed that FG-URM students wrote more about social and familial themes.

Initially, the UV assignments may have triggered interest by engaging emotions and thoughts about family, friends, and communities. As students became wrapped up in the assignments (as evidenced by their increased essay length), their interest in biology may have been sustained, likely contributing to increased course performance by the end of the course. By the time students enroll in this biology course, they have already made it through a difficult chemistry sequence, and so their interest in the field is likely quite high. Even with high levels of interest in biology, the UV intervention may have prompted a motivational process that gave FG-URM an extra boost of support. Perhaps the UV intervention provides an opportunity for disadvantaged students to overcome other barriers (such as lower preparation and prior grades) by tapping into personal values that contribute to interest. In sum, the UV intervention has been successful at promoting interest and learning in several experimental field studies implemented in high school science classrooms and four-year institutions; however, it has yet to be tested in more diverse contexts.

Multi-Level Classrooms: A Case Study of Two-Year Colleges

Two-year colleges represent a different educational context, in which students have varying levels of preparation and face different challenges. Students at two-year colleges face many personal, financial, and structural challenges that contribute to higher drop-out rates and delayed degree completion (Bailey et al., 2006; Crosta, 2013; Goldrick-Rab, 2010; Karp & Bork, 2014). For example, two-year college students are more likely to come from disadvantaged backgrounds, have families to care for, and work full-time compared to students at four-year colleges (Horn & Nevill, 2006; Horn & Skomsvold, 2011). It may be particularly difficult for students at two-year colleges to remain motivated and stay engaged in their courses given these external pressures, especially in (high-pressure) difficult introductory-level courses.

Courses in two-year colleges are smaller and much more variable in class composition (e.g., in terms of age, high school preparation, full-time versus part-time) than courses in four-year institutions. On average, students in this educational context come to college with less academic preparation and lower high school grades than students who attend four-year colleges and universities. For example, most two-year colleges enroll students with a variety of educational backgrounds. These students are less likely to have earned a high school diploma, many lack adequate writing skills, and almost half enroll in remedial or developmental education courses (Bailey et al., 2010; Horn & Nevill, 2006; Perin, 2013; Perin et al., 2003). Utility value interventions may be particularly powerful in these contexts, if they help students become more involved and engaged in their studies. However, intervention effects may be more variable in the two-year context, given the diversity of students' academic backgrounds. It may therefore be necessary to adapt the typical UV writing assignment for it to be effective in this context.

The UV intervention may be more difficult for less prepared students, because it requires them to construct essays that synthesize course material. Students must have a basic understanding of the material in order to perceive its utility and be able to write about it. Moreover, as implemented in previous studies at four-year institutions, the UV writing assignments require a high level of conceptual work and writing skills, which might prove more challenging for students with less academic preparation. Therefore, in the two-year college context, students may need additional support in learning to think about connections and generating their own examples of UV. Providing students with examples of UV connections may be particularly important in this context. The standard UV intervention implemented in previous research contains minimal external support (Harackiewicz et al., 2016), with only general or hypothetical examples of UV connections that students might write about. However, framing the intervention with more personalized examples may be necessary in the two-year college context, to help students discover and write about personally relevant connections.

Directly Communicated Utility Value Information

Framing the UV intervention is difficult, because studies have found that providing examples of UV connections (i.e., directly communicated UV information) can sometimes be threatening for students who lack confidence in their ability to do well (Canning & Harackiewicz, 2015; Durik & Harackiewicz, 2007; Durik et al., 2015a, 2015b). In one experiment, Durik and Harackiewicz (2007) tested the effects of directly communicated UV information by teaching participants a mental math technique and presenting information about how the technique could be useful in everyday life (e.g., "You might use mental math to figure out tips at restaurants or to manage your bank transactions"). They found that participants with high initial interest reported more interest in the technique after receiving a message with such examples. However, they also found some evidence that the UV manipulation undermined interest for individuals with low initial interest. Other studies have replicated these effects and found that participants with less confidence in their math ability actually showed less interest in the math technique after being told about its utility value, whereas participants with high confidence showed more interest in UV conditions (Canning & Harackiewicz, 2015; Durik et al., 2015b). Therefore, providing examples of UV connections can be threatening for students with low confidence, but can be beneficial for students with high confidence.

Canning and Harackiewicz (2015) tested different strategies to reduce the threat of directly communicated UV information, so that less confident students could benefit from this type of support. One experimental condition tested whether the combination of both directly communicated utility value and self-generated utility value (i.e., writing a short essay about the utility value of the material), might have a synergistic effect for interest and performance. Using the same mental math paradigm as Durik and Harackiewicz (2007), participants in this study were given information about how a novel multiplication technique could be useful in everyday life and then were instructed to write about how the technique could be useful to them personally. Canning and Harackiewicz (2015) found that the combination of directly communicated UV information and self-generated utility value was particularly effective for less confident participants. This combination increased interest in the task and performance on a subsequent multiplication test for individuals low in confidence, relative to either type of utility value alone. In other words, self-generated utility value was most effective for less confident students when combined with examples of UV information.

Directly communicated UV information might be too threatening by itself for individuals who lack confidence (Durik et al., 2015a, 2015b), but once these individuals were given the chance to process the information in their own words, as facilitated by the self-generated UV writing intervention, directly communicated utility value proved to be helpful, boosting the efficacy of the self-generated UV intervention. These results indicate that providing examples of UV information in combination with the opportunity to generate personal examples is necessary for less confident individuals to internalize the value of the task, increasing perceived utility value, performance, and interest.

Another strategy hypothesized to reduce the threat of directly communicated UV information is to change the source of the information. Varying the source could change the way the same information is perceived. For instance, information communicated by an older or more experienced student might be less threatening than the same information from a teacher. Peer tutoring, in which students teach other students, has been shown to be particularly effective in increasing engagement and learning (Greenwood et al., 1989; King et al., 1998). Framing the UV intervention with UV examples from peers rather than from the instructor may be most effective for students with low confidence or with a history of low performance, because these students are less likely to find value on their own. Utility value examples from peers may trigger interest compared to the same information presented from the instructor, which students may tune out or ignore. Then, when students write their own essay, they can begin working with the course material, facilitating learning, and come to value the topic for themselves.

Ultimately, UV interventions aim to have students generate personal examples of utility value, and it may be easier for students to come up with their own connections when they first see that other students can make them. Eccles suggests that perceptions of utility value can promote motivation and achievement because students find the material personally valuable, suggesting that UV connections need to be personal to be effective (Eccles et al., 1983). It could be that when a peer indicates their own perception of the utility of the material, the student who receives this information integrates it into their own evaluation of the material more readily than if an instructor presents the same information. Thus, UV examples from a peer could help students generate more value for themselves in the writing exercises, facilitating interest in the topic and ultimately improving performance in the course.

Implementing a Utility Value Intervention in Two-Year Colleges

Canning and colleagues (Canning, 2016; Canning et al., under review) compared two different ways of framing the UV intervention, with the goal of helping two-year college students find value in their coursework. The UV intervention was implemented in introductory courses across six different two-year college campuses. They tested two ways of framing the UV intervention against a control assignment, based on the procedures employed by Harackiewicz and colleagues (2016). In the control condition, the assignment instructions had students summarize the main points covered in the course. In the two UV writing conditions, students were asked to explain how course topics were relevant to their own lives or were useful to them. Both UV writing assignments contained examples of UV connections that students might write about, with only the framing of the examples differing between the UV conditions. In an instructor-framed UV condition, these examples were presented as being generated by the instructor, whereas a student-framed UV condition presented conceptually similar UV connections in the form of quotations from former students in the course.

Contrary to previous findings, students struggling in the course became less interested and perceived less utility value overall in UV conditions, compared to the control. Even though all students, on average, were articulating more utility value in their essays, as intended, struggling students did not benefit from this type of writing. In fact, the UV interventions caused these students to care less about doing well, lose confidence in their performance, and doubt their preparedness for the class (i.e., students reported that their high school education did not provide the right background for the course). Clearly, the UV intervention did not have its desired effect in this context. The UV interventions may have been somewhat threatening for students who were already struggling to keep up with the material. In contrast, the UV interventions benefited high-performing students by increasing their sense of belonging in the course and confirming their perceptions of preparedness for the course.

Moreover, the framing of the UV examples had a polarizing effect for students. High-performing students reported more interest in the course when UV examples were framed from former students in the course, rather than from the instructor. This type of UV assignment was hypothesized to be most effective, particularly for struggling students, but instead, it was only effective for students who were doing well in the course. UV information from other students made the course material more interesting and relevant for high-performing students. In addition, high-performing students reported that they cared more about doing well after receiving UV information from other students. In contrast, the same UV examples had a negative effect on grades for students struggling in the course. These students seemed to become disengaged from the assignment (i.e., wrote shorter essays) and reported that they cared less about doing well in the course. In other words, this intervention had the opposite effect than was intended for this group.

The results of this study are surprising, because the UV intervention did not help struggling students, as previous research has shown. Utility value interventions are not a one-size-fits-all approach for motivating students. Making personal connections with the course material can be motivating for students doing well in the course, but can sometimes be threatening for students who have not yet mastered the material. The intervention was effective in promoting perceptions of value, as hypothesized, but these perceptions did not promote interest or performance for students who were struggling in the course. It may be that the UV intervention depends on a higher level of content mastery than previously recognized. This study raises important questions about the mechanism of the UV intervention. Why did the UV intervention have negative effects for struggling students in two-year colleges, yet positive effects for struggling students in four-year institutions?

Mechanism: Building Confidence

Expectancy-value theory suggests that task values have the most influence on attitudes and behavior when perceived competence is high (Eccles & Wigfield, 2002). Students struggling to keep up in a course lack the confidence or competence piece that is essential in the expectancy-value model. When students doubt their ability to do well, the perception of value can be threatening, resulting in lower interest and perceived utility value in the course material.

However, less competent performers can benefit from UV interventions in a way that is consistent with expectancy-value theory if they first develop confidence (Canning & Harackiewicz, 2015; Durik et al., 2015b). One way to develop confidence is by demonstrating competence. As implemented in previous research, the UV assignment instructions had students first answer a scientific question and then discuss the relevance of the topic. In other words, when properly implemented, the UV intervention asks students to provide scientific details and analysis in their essays, in addition to explaining why the material is relevant to their lives. Thus, students must first master the material and then personalize the information, which may build confidence.

In previous research, UV interventions seem to have worked both by promoting value and by indirectly boosting the confidence of low performers. For example, in the laboratory, a UV intervention increased perceptions of mastering the material, which led to an increase in perceived utility value, interest, and performance for students with low confidence (Canning & Harackiewicz, 2015). In a psychology classroom, a UV intervention boosted confidence about learning the material, which led to increased course performance for the lowest-performing students (Hulleman et al., 2017). Increased confidence may be the mechanism that explains why UV interventions have been helpful for struggling students in previous research.

However, this confidence-building process may not have occurred when the UV intervention was implemented in two-year colleges. In fact, implementing the UV intervention in this context actually decreased confidence (i.e., performance expectations) for low performers and made them question their preparedness for the course (i.e., perceptions of an adequate high school education). Without the confidence gained from mastering the course material, these students were not able to benefit from finding value. Indeed, some analyses suggest that students in UV conditions may not have synthesized the material as much as students in the control. A linguistic analysis of essay content revealed that low-performing students in UV conditions were not using language indicative of cognitive processing, whereas high-performing students were. In other words, the less confident students may have focused more on the personal aspect of the assignment and neglected the scientific aspect of the assignment. Additionally, students were not writing about the content of the course as much as students in previous studies (Harackiewicz et al., 2016). Many of the essays contained personal narratives without any substantive scientific information, and this could be even more costly for students at risk of performing poorly in the course. This lack of content synthesis could explain why these students were not benefiting from the UV intervention in this study as previous research had found (Harackiewicz et al., 2016; Hulleman & Harackiewicz, 2009). It will be important to test this idea more directly in future research.

These findings pose an important limitation of UV interventions: students may need to have some degree of background knowledge in the course topic and demonstrate their competence in their essays in order for the intervention to be effective. For instance, in a recent laboratory study that varied whether or not students were asked to write a content summary before writing about value, students with low confidence reported more perceived utility value and were more engaged with the assignment when they first wrote a summary of the material before writing about the utility of the material (Priniski et al., 2016). In other words, students with low confidence benefited from synthesizing the content by summarizing the material before they completed the UV writing. This finding supports the hypothesis that struggling students in two-year colleges may not have synthesized the course material enough to benefit from the intervention.

One strategy to strengthen the UV intervention for students who struggle with course material is to provide students with more concrete instructions about how to choose a topic for their essay. For example, the typical UV assignment instructs students to pose a scientific question and then answer the question using material from the course. Many of the two-year college students posed questions that asked for a definition, instead of questions that required content synthesis (e.g., "What is evolution?" versus "How is evolution different from natural selection?"). These types of definition questions usually lead to shorter essays and do not lend themselves to an in-depth discussion of the material. In contrast, questions that stem from curiosity and interest are likely to go beyond reiterating definitions from a textbook and facilitate continued engagement with the course material (Renninger, 2000, 2009). Once students feel comfortable demonstrating their competence, they may be able to spend more time and attention thinking about UV connections and pose questions related to personal curiosity, rather than trying to master fundamentals like definitions. In UV conditions, some students posed a question about the relevance of the material that did not require very much course content to answer (e.g., "Why is evolution relevant to humans?"). This type of question focuses solely on the value piece of the assignment and does not require students to deepen their understanding of the material. If students can first demonstrate their understanding of the material by synthesizing the content, perhaps students could benefit from the UV aspect of the assignment. Content synthesis may be a necessary precursor for the UV intervention to facilitate learning and interest development.

Another limitation of the UV intervention is that students may need to have adequate writing skills in order for the intervention to be effective. For example, in previous implementations of the UV intervention in biology courses at a four-year institution (Harackiewicz et al., 2016), students typically had already met the composition requirements for their major by the time they enrolled in the course. In contrast, many two-year college students do not have very much experience with college-level writing. A lack of experience might explain the negative effects of the intervention for students who were struggling in these courses. The UV intervention might have more positive effects in this context if it were implemented after students had a chance to more fully develop their writing skills. Students may need some experience with college-level writing in order for the UV intervention to be effective. This is another issue that should be examined in future research.

Implications for Framing Utility Value Interventions

Framing UV interventions can be challenging, because there is increasing evidence that directly communicated UV information can be threatening for students who lack confidence in their ability to do well (Canning & Harackiewicz,

2015; Durik & Harackiewicz, 2007; Durik et al., 2015b). Telling students about the usefulness of the course material may hinder interest development and inhibit performance for students who doubt their abilities. However, providing students with UV examples can actually boost the effectiveness of the UV intervention when implemented without threat (Canning & Harackiewicz, 2015; Gaspard et al., 2015). Therefore, more research is needed to understand how to reduce the threat of such UV information.

Framing UV information in the form of student quotes did not offset the negative effects of directly communicated UV information; instead, this seemed to make it worse for students who were performing poorly in the course. The student-framed UV examples were hypothesized to promote engagement with the assignment for struggling students; however, these students became more disengaged with these examples, writing shorter essays and indicating less interest overall in the course. It might be that students were comparing themselves to the students who ostensibly wrote the UV examples, and this social-comparison process may have inhibited interest development. The student-framed UV examples had no grammatical errors and contained language similar to the instructor-framed UV examples; therefore, it is likely that students believed the authors of the examples to be high-achieving students. A well-developed UV example from another student can be threatening for students who believe they don't perform well compared to others. Indeed, comparisons with high-achieving peers can lead to lower academic self-competence (Altermatt & Pomerantz, 2005; Marsh, 1987). For struggling students, the student-framed UV examples may be yet another signal that they lack adequate skills to do well in the course. In contrast, high-achieving students might believe they perform better than or equal to other students, and so the student-framed UV examples may not be as threatening. In fact, the student-framed UV examples were beneficial for students performing well in the course and increased their interest in the course.

One possible way to reduce the threat of UV examples is to acknowledge that UV information may be hard to generate. For instance, the student-framed UV examples might be less threatening if they contained language about struggling with the assignment (e.g., "At first I couldn't think of any reasons why natural selection is relevant to me, but once I thought about it, I realized that learning about natural selection is useful for a lot of things"). If students who are struggling with the course see that other students have a hard time generating UV examples, they might gain the confidence to fully engage with the assignment, potentially facilitating interest and performance. It will be important to test this idea in future research.

Future Directions

Our review of UV intervention research suggests that the effects of UV interventions are more variable than originally thought and that the effectiveness of the interventions may depend on the students' level of preparation. In some contexts, such as four-year college biology classes (Harackiewicz et al., 2016), students were able to overcome weak backgrounds in the content area, because the intervention tapped other motivational processes that led to increased engagement. In other contexts, such as two-year colleges, students' lack of preparation, particularly with college-level writing, may have limited the efficacy of the intervention. In future studies, researchers should be aware of and measure differences in preparation as a potentially important moderator of intervention effectiveness.

One interesting feature of UV interventions that still needs to be explored is the role of the instructor. Feedback on the writing (i.e., correcting grammar and style), the scientific content (i.e., making sure the content is factual), and the UV connection (i.e., ensuring that the connection was specific to the writer and not to humans in general) may not be feasible for all instructors. In some implementations of the UV intervention, essays were graded for accuracy of scientific content and students received feedback in the form of individualized written commentary (Canning et al., 2018; Harackiewicz et al., 2016), whereas less feedback has been provided in other studies (Hulleman et al., 2010, 2017). This factor has not been varied systematically, however. It is important to know whether feedback on the assignment is an integral part of the intervention or whether simply completing the assignment thoughtfully is sufficient for its impact. Moreover, feedback on the assignment may be more important in contexts in which students need more guidance with the essay. This question should be addressed in future research.

It could also be the case that the instructor may be able to enhance the writing intervention if the relevance of course topics is integrated into course lectures and discussions. We know from previous research on directly communicated utility value that the types of connections communicated and highlighted during a learning tutorial greatly impact student motivation (Canning & Harackiewicz, 2015; Durik et al., 2015b). Perhaps the writing intervention is most effective when instructors emphasize a variety of connections in their lectures or only focus on applications that students can use in their daily life. To date, UV intervention studies have not been conducted on a large enough scale to examine instructor differences as moderators to the intervention, but this is an important future direction.

Another avenue for future research is the exploration of different intervention types. What is the best method for encouraging students to think about UV connections? Perhaps there are other ways to promote utility value without relying solely on a writing assignment, which has been the typical method of implementation in classrooms (Harackiewicz et al., 2012). For instance, Gaspard et al. (2015) implemented a UV intervention in ninth grade math courses consisting of a 90-minute presentation that emphasized the utility of mathematics and the importance of effort and ability beliefs. Following the presentation, students either wrote a short essay or evaluated interview quotations. Students who evaluated quotations reported higher utility value than those who wrote an essay, indicating that essay writing may not be the best method for implementation. Another possibility is to implement the UV intervention as an informal in-class assignment, rather than have students submit a formal essay in which they may be concerned about structure and grammar instead of focusing on generating UV connections. Perhaps even small group discussions would be effective. Different intervention types may be more effective in some contexts than others, and this will be important as researchers begin to test UV interventions in a variety of contexts (Priniski et al., 2018).

Concluding Thoughts

Given the early success with the UV intervention in college biology and psychology courses, it is important to begin testing the UV intervention in other contexts. Implementing a UV intervention in multi-level classrooms, such as those typical in two-year colleges, can be challenging. Testing the UV intervention in more diverse settings can reveal important limitations of the intervention, which provide more insight into the mechanism of the intervention. First, and most critical from both a theoretical and a practical perspective, students struggling in introductory courses may need to build confidence by having a chance to demonstrate their competence before they can benefit from utility value. Future studies should attend to how much course content students are synthesizing in their essays. In order for the UV intervention to have an impact on learning, students need to deepen their understanding of the course content before they connect it to their lives. Both aspects of the assignment are necessary for the intervention to promote interest and learning.

Second, until the most effective way to present UV information in a non-threatening manner is clear, UV examples may be too threatening to implement with students who struggle with the course material. Other forms of supporting the intervention (such as extra help with organizing essays and with writing skills) may be more beneficial for these students, rather than providing examples of UV connections. Until we learn more about the most effective way to frame UV assignments, it may be better to provide minimal UV examples and let students generate their own examples of utility value.

Finally, UV interventions are not a one-size-fits-all approach for motivating students. Utility value interventions should be tailored for the context and designed to complement current instructional practices (Harackiewicz & Priniski, 2018). What works at four-year institutions may not be effective in contexts such as two-year colleges, which tend to be very different places than traditional four-year institutions in terms of demographics, structure, resources, and campus culture (Bailey et al., 2015). By adapting interventions to fit within a given context, we may be able to promote interest and achievement for students struggling in introductory courses in many different educational contexts.

References

Altermatt, E. R. & Pomerantz, E. M. (2005). The implications of having high-achieving versus low-achieving friends: A longitudinal analysis. *Social Development*, *14*(1), 61–81. doi: 10.1111/j.1467-9507.2005.00291.x.

Bailey, T., Jeong, D. W., & Cho, S.-W. (2010). Referral, enrollment, and completion in developmental education sequences in community colleges. *Economics of Education Review*, *29*(2), 255–70. DOI: 10.1016/j.econedurev.2009.09.002.

Bailey, T. R., Jaggars, S. S., & Jenkins, D. (2015). *Redesigning America's community colleges: A clearer path to student success* (1st ed.). Cambridge, MA: Harvard University Press.

Bailey, T. R., Leinbach, T., & Jenkins, D. (2006). *Is student success labeled institutional failure? Student goals and graduation rates in the accountability debate at community colleges.* New York, NY: Columbia University, Teachers College, Community College Research Center.

Barron, K. E. & Hulleman, C. S. (2015). Expectancy-value-cost model of motivation. In J. D. Wright (Ed.), *International encyclopedia of the social & behavioral sciences* (2nd ed., Vol. 8, pp. 503–9). Oxford: Elsevier Ltd. DOI: 10.1016/B978-0-08-097086-8.26099-6.

Bong, M. (2001). Role of self-efficacy and task value in predicting college students' course performance and future enrollment intentions. *Contemporary Educational Psychology*, *26*(4), 553–70. DOI: 10.1006/ceps.2000.1048.

Canning, E. A. (2016). *Testing a utility-value intervention in two-year colleges* (Unpublished doctoral dissertation). University of Wisconsin-Madison, Madison, WI.

Canning, E. A. & Harackiewicz, J. M. (2015). Teach it, don't preach it: The differential effects of directly communicated and self-generated utility value information. *Motivation Science*, *1*(1), 47–71. DOI: 10.1037/mot0000015.

Canning, E. A., Harackiewicz, J. M., Priniski, S. J., Hecht, C. A., Tibbetts, Y., & Hyde, J. S. (2018). Improving performance and retention in introductory biology with a utility-value intervention. *Journal of Educational Psychology*, *110*(6), 834–49. DOI: 10.1037/edu0000244.

Canning, E. A., Priniski, S. J., & Harackiewicz, J. M. (under review). Unintended consequences of framing a utility-value intervention in two-year colleges.

Crosta, P. (2013). *Characteristics of early community college dropouts.* New York, NY: Columbia University, Teachers College, Community College Research Center.

Durik, A. M. & Harackiewicz, J. M. (2007). Different strokes for different folks: How individual interest moderates the effects of situational factors on task interest. *Journal of Educational Psychology*, *99*(3), 597–610. DOI: 10.1037/0022-0663.99.3.597.

Durik, A. M., Hulleman, C. S., & Harackiewicz, J. M. (2015a). One size fits some: Instructional enhancements to promote interest. K. A. Renninger, M. Nieswandt, & S. E. Hidi (Eds.), *Interest in mathematics and science learning* (pp.49–62). Washington, DC: American Educational Research Association.

Durik, A. M., Shechter, O., Noh, M., Rozek, C., & Harackiewicz, J. (2015b). What if I can't? Success expectancies moderate the effects of utility value information on situational interest and performance. *Motivation & Emotion*, *39*(1), 104–18. DOI: 10.1007/s11031-014-9419-0.

Durik, A. M., Vida, M., & Eccles, J. S. (2006). Task values and ability beliefs as predictors of high school literacy choices: A developmental analysis. *Journal of Educational Psychology*, *98*(2), 382–93. DOI: 10.1037/0022-0663.98.2.382.

Eccles, J. (2009). Who am I and what am I going to do with my life? Personal and collective identities as motivators of action. *Educational Psychologist*, *44*(2), 78–89. DOI: 10.1080/00461520902832368.

Eccles, J., Adler, T. F., Futterman, R., Goff, S. B., Kaczala, C. M., Meece, J. L., & Midgley, C. (1983). Expectations, values, and academic behaviors. In J. T. Spence (Ed.), *Perspective on achievement and achievement motivation* (pp. 75–146). San Francisco, CA: Freeman.

Eccles, J. & Wigfield, A. (2002). Motivational beliefs, values, and goals. *Annual Review of Psychology*, *53*(1), 109–32. DOI: 10.1146/annurev.psych.53.100901.135153.

Gaspard, H., Dicke, A.-L., Flunger, B., Brisson, B. M., Hafner, I., Nagengast, B., & Trautwein, U. (2015). Fostering adolescents' value beliefs for mathematics with a relevance intervention in the classroom. *Developmental Psychology*, *51*(9), 1226–40. DOI: 10.1037/dev0000028.

Goldrick-Rab, S. (2010). Challenges and opportunities for improving community college student success. *Review of Educational Research*, *80*(3), 437–69.

Greenwood, C. R., Delquadri, J. C., & Hall, R. V. (1989). Longitudinal effects of classwide peer tutoring. *Journal of Educational Psychology*, *81*(3), 371–83. DOI: 10.1037/0022-0663.81.3.371.

Harackiewicz, J. M., Canning, E. A., Tibbetts, Y., Priniski, S. J., & Hyde, J. S. (2016). Closing achievement gaps with a utility value intervention: Disentangling race and social class. *Journal of Personality and Social Psychology*, *111*(5), 745–65. DOI: 10.1037/pspp0000075.

Harackiewicz, J. M. & Priniski, S. J. (2018). Improving student outcomes in higher education: The science of targeted intervention. *Annual Review of Psychology*. *69*(1), 409–35.

Harackiewicz, J. M., Rozek, C. S., Hulleman, C. S., & Hyde, J. S. (2012). Helping parents to motivate adolescents in mathematics and science: An experimental test of a utility value intervention. *Psychological Science*, *23*(8), 899–906. DOI: 10.1177/0956797611435530.

Harackiewicz, J. M., Smith, J. L., & Priniski, S. J. (2016). Interest matters: The importance of promoting interest in education. *Policy Insights from the Behavioral and Brain Sciences*, *3*(2), 220–7.

Hidi, S. & Harackiewicz, J. M. (2000). Motivating the academically unmotivated: A critical issue for the 21st century. *Review of Educational Research*, *70*(2), 151–79. DOI: 10.2307/1170660.

Horn, L. & Nevill, S. (2006). *Profile of undergraduates in U.S. postsecondary education institutions: 2003–04 with a special analysis of community college students (NCES 2006-184)*. Washington, DC: Department of Education, National Center for Education Statistics.

Horn, L. & Skomsvold, P. (2011). *Community college student outcomes: 1994–2009 (NCES 2012-253)*. Washington, DC: U.S. Department of Education, National Center for Education Statistics.

Hulleman, C. S., Durik, A. M., Schweigert, S. B., & Harackiewicz, J. M. (2008). Task values, achievement goals, and interest: An integrative analysis. *Journal of Educational Psychology*, *100*(2), 398–416. DOI: 10.1037/0022-0663.100.2.398.

Hulleman, C. S., Godes, O., Hendricks, B. L., & Harackiewicz, J. M. (2010). Enhancing interest and performance with a utility value intervention. *Journal of Educational Psychology*, *102*(4), 880–95. DOI: 10.1037/a0019506.

Hulleman, C. S. & Harackiewicz, J. M. (2009). Promoting interest and performance in high school science classes. *Science*, *326*(5958), 1410–12.

Hulleman, C. S., Kosovich, J. J., Barron, K. E., & Daniel, D. (2017). Making connections: Replicating and extending the utility value intervention in the classroom. *Journal of Educational Psychology*. *109*(3), 387–404. DOI: 10.1037/edu0000146.

Husman, J., Derryberry, W. P., Crowson, H. M., & Lomax, R. (2004). Instrumentality, task value, and intrinsic motivation: Making sense of their independent interdependence. *Contemporary Educational Psychology*, *29*(1), 63–76. DOI: 10.1016/S0361-476X(03)00019-5.

Husman, J. & Lens, W. (1999). The role of the future in student motivation. *Educational Psychologist*, *34*(2), 113–25. DOI: 10.1207/s15326985ep3402_4.

Karp, M. & Bork, R. (2014). *"They never told me what to expect, so I didn't know what to do": Defining and clarifying the role of a community college student*. New York, NY: Columbia University, Teachers College, Community College Research Center.

King, A., Staffieri, A., & Adelgais, A. (1998). Mutual peer tutoring: Effects of structuring tutorial interaction to scaffold peer learning. *Journal of Educational Psychology*, *90*(1), 134–52. DOI: 10.1037/0022-0663.90.1.134.

Marsh, H. W. (1987). The big-fish-little-pond effect on academic self-concept. *Journal of Educational Psychology*, *79*(3), 280–95. DOI: 10.1037/0022-0663.79.3.280.

Perin, D. (2013). Literacy skills among academically underprepared students. *Community College Review*, *41*(2), 118–36. DOI: 10.1177/0091552113484057.

Perin, D., Keselman, A., & Monopoli, M. (2003). The academic writing of community college remedial students: Text and learner variables. *Higher Education*, *45*(1), 19–42.

Priniski, S. J., Harackiewicz, J. M., Canning, E. A., & Tibbetts, Y. (2016). *Understanding utility value interventions: The devil is in the methodological "details."* Poster presented at the American Educational Research Association, Washington, DC.

Priniski, S. J., Hecht, C. A., & Harackiewicz, J. M. (2018). Making learning personally meaningful: A new framework for relevance research. *Journal of Experimental Education*, *86*(1), 11–29. DOI: 10.1080/00220973.2017.1380589.

Raved, L. & Assaraf, O. B. Z. (2011). Attitudes towards science learning among 10th-grade students: A qualitative look. *International Journal of Science Education*, *33*(9), 1219–43. DOI: 10.1080/09500693.2010.508503.

Renninger, K. A. (2000). Individual interest and its implications for understanding intrinsic motivation. In C. Sansone & J. M. Harackiewicz (Eds.), *Intrinsic and extrinsic motivation: The search for optimal motivation and performance* (pp. 461–91). New York, NY: Academic Press.

Renninger, K. A. (2009). Interest and identity development in instruction: An inductive model. *Educational Psychologist*, *44*(2), 105–18. DOI: 10.1080/00461520902832392.

Renninger, K. A. & Hidi, S. (2011). Revisiting the conceptualization, measurement, and generation of interest. *Educational Psychologist, 46*(3), 168–84. DOI: 10.1080/00461520.2011.587723.

Rosenzweig, E. Q., Harackiewicz, J. M., Priniski, S. J., Hecht, C. A., Canning, E. A., Tibbetts, Y., & Hyde, J. S. (2018). Choose your own intervention: Using choice to enhance the effectiveness of a utility-value intervention. *Motivation Science*. Advance online publication. DOI: 10.1037/mot0000113.

Wigfield, A. & Cambria, J. (2010). Students' achievement values, goal orientations, and interest: Definitions, development, and relations to achievement outcomes. *Developmental Review, 30*(1), 1–35. DOI: 10.1016/j.dr.2009.12.001.

PART VI

Methods, Measures, and Perspective

26 Motivation and Learning

Measures and Methods

Mary Ainley and John Ainley

Abstract: *In this chapter we examine measures and methods that have come to prominence over the last two decades exploring how they build on, and are shaped by, relevant theory. In addition, we identify how contemporary measures and methods have expanded as researchers investigate interactive influences of person and context. First, the importance of distinguishing levels of generality and specificity in definitions of motivation constructs is explored. Second, we examine attempts to define the type of relation between motivation constructs and learning, for example, mediation relations and reciprocal relations. As specific research is considered we direct attention to the types of analytic procedures that have been used to test hypotheses and assess models of the relations between motivation and learning. In particular we highlight the development of research methods that go beyond the range of insights into motivation and learning that can be achieved using only self-report questionnaires.*

In the preface to the 12th volume (*New directions in measures and methods*) in the series *Advances in Motivation and Achievement*, Pintrich and Maehr (2002) wrote: "As in all scientific endeavors, a field makes progress not just because of new theoretical perspectives or ideas, but also because of the development of new methodologies" (p. xii). Pintrich and Maehr highlighted the attention researchers were giving to the theoretical underpinnings of new measures and new methods, and to the need for simultaneous consideration of both person and context, "allowing for both personal construals as well as contextual shaping and scaffolding behavior" (p. x).

In this chapter we examine some of the measures and methods that have come to prominence over the last two decades, exploring how they build on, and are shaped by, relevant theory. In addition, we identify how contemporary measures and methods have expanded as researchers increasingly have focused on investigating interactive influences of person and context in relations between motivation and learning, and motivation and achievement. We consider, first, the importance of distinguishing levels of generality and specificity in definitions of motivation constructs and, second, attempts to define the type of relation between motivation constructs and learning (for example, mediation relations and reciprocal relations). As specific research is considered, we will also give due attention to the types of analytic procedures that have been used to test hypotheses and assess models of the relations between motivation and learning. In particular, we highlight the development of research methods that go beyond the range of insights into motivation and learning that can be achieved using only self-report questionnaires.

Distinguishing Learning and Achievement

Across the literature reviewed for this chapter, various terms are used to denote behavior that is considered to be affected or influenced by motivation: "learning," "performance," "achievement," and "academic achievement." While there is some association between the types of studies and usage, it is not uncommon to find these terms being used interchangeably or in ways that are not consistent with generally accepted definitions. A report published by the US National Board for Professional Teaching Standards (2011) pointed to the "profoundly different ideas" represented by the terms "student learning" and "student achievement." This report defined achievement as "the status of subject-matter knowledge, understandings, and skills at one point in time," while student learning was defined as "the growth in subject-matter knowledge, understanding, and skills over time" (p. 9). At the heart of this distinction is the assumption that learning represents change or growth in knowledge, understanding, and skills, while a focus on achievement directs attention to the level of knowledge, understanding, or skill at a specific point in time.

When learning is investigated as achievement (defined as the current level of knowledge, understanding, and skills), the research models generally concern students' motivation as a general orientation, predisposition, or trait. Students' typical or generalized level of motivation is assessed as a predictive factor for their level of achievement at a given point in time. For example, when motivation variables are included in large international studies of student achievement (e.g., Trends in International Mathematics and Science Study [TIMSS], Programme for International Student Assessment [PISA]), it is students' typical or generalized level of motivation that is being evaluated. Variables such as students' general interest in science, personal valuing of science, and future motivation in science are modeled as predictors of science achievement, as measured through well-developed tests of scientific knowledge and understanding (e.g., OECD, 2006).

When learning as a change in knowledge, understanding, or skills is approached either as the process or as the outcome variable, a number of motivation perspectives may inform the research model. First, the motivational variable may be represented at the typical or generalized level, or it may be specified as a particular state or set of states operating in the particular learning context. In more complex models, it may involve the assessment of both the generalized orientation or predisposition and a specific state or set of states that play out across the course of a learning activity.

Second, investigating learning as change involves a temporal dimension, so that a prior level of knowledge, understanding, or skills can be compared with a later level of knowledge, understanding, or skills (Martin, 2015). The extent of the time lapse can vary from a short-term learning activity (such as a classroom event) to more extended longitudinal research for which students may be revisited over a number of years.

Third, generating measures of change over time requires that the two or more measures of achievement are vertically equated (Betebenner & Linn, 2010). If the measures are based on the same assessment instrument, then one can't be sure of the effect of practice or experience on the result and, if the time difference is large, the test on the second occasion may no longer be appropriately targeted. If the measures are based on different assessment instruments, there is a need to establish that the two assessments measure the same construct and, preferably, are vertically linked. There is also a consequential need to use appropriate methods for generating measures of achievement change. Traditionally, gain scores have been used, but recently, more sophisticated longitudinal data analytic methods (such as growth modeling) have been used (Shanley, 2016). Anderman et al. (2015) reviewed five types of growth models: student gain score models, covariate adjustment models, student percentile gain models (i.e., single-wave, value-added models), univariate value-added response models, and multivariate value-added response models.

Hence, when considering the relation between motivation and learning, it is critical to acknowledge whether the focus is learning as outcome or process, or as achievement.

Generality and Specificity of Motivation Constructs

One of the distinguishing features of the literature on motivation and learning in the last two decades has been the attention given to the generality of motivation constructs. This is a critical development, as it highlights a number of important shifts in emphasis. First, there is an increased focus on the character of motivational constructs in terms of whether they represent trait-like phenomena or whether they represent psychological states. Second, there is an associated increase in consideration of both person and situation or context. Along with these shifts in focus, it is currently common to see the bifurcation between traits and states loosened and replaced with more dynamic interaction models in which the explanatory constructs for both motivation and context are represented at multiple levels of generality and specificity. These levels can vary from referencing schooling, learning in general, a particular learning domain, a particular course, a particular class within a course, or a particular activity within a class. Specific point-in-time measures may refer to the whole activity just completed or to the very localized "right now."

The achievement motivation literature over the last two decades illustrates these changing perspectives in research on motivation and learning. In their influential review of motivation terminology, Murphy and Alexander (2000) used the example of achievement goals to argue that there was an inherent contradiction in motivation constructs. If achievement goals are orientations this is inconsistent with evidence that the educational context influences achievement goals.

> On the one hand, if students' goal orientations are truly orientations (i.e., motivational traits), then it is unclear what effect any manipulation of the instructional context should have on them. On the other hand, if sociocontextual factors have the power to transform students' perspectives on academic tasks, then it seems unlikely that the researchers are dealing with a motivational trait (p. 42).

Part of the issue here concerns the model of traits – in particular, the interpretation of traits as fixed dispositions. Using the same example of achievement goals, Pintrich (2000) suggested that the issue is one of identifying the interplay between intra-individual stability and contextual sensitivity. He argued for a distinction between general, global, and task-specific achievement goals, which amounts to identifying different forms of person and situation interaction. "Strong contexts can overwhelm chronically accessible traits, but in the absence of strong cues in the environment, then traits may influence behavior more" (Pintrich, 2000, p. 102). Ainley and Hidi (2002) built on this idea to draw attention to the dynamic character of motivation when they suggested that "the challenge is then to be able to identify within particular achievement domains the critical form(s) of interdependence between person and situation" (p. 47). The last two decades have witnessed a range of research focusing on motivation as a dynamic construct implicating both person and situation. Hence, there are several perspectives on the character of motivation when relations between motivation and learning are considered.

Generalized, Habitual Trait-like Phenomena

One major perspective conceptualizes motivation constructs as generalized or habitual ways of responding to a particular class of events. These perspectives view motivation as traits or dispositions; for example, in self-determination theory, intrinsic motivation is viewed as "an inherent organismic propensity" (Ryan & Deci, 2000, p. 58). Sometimes, to give emphasis to the construct as being more malleable than the relatively stable traits defined in mainstream personality literature, the motivation construct is referred to as a predisposition; for example, individual interest in Hidi and Renninger's four-phase model of interest development (Hidi & Renninger, 2006; Renninger & Hidi, 2011). In other literature, such as the achievement goals literature, the motivation construct is referred to as both disposition and orientation (Urdan & Mestas, 2006). Hence, from this perspective, motivation is a source of energy and direction for action in relation to a general class of situations or across a range of like contexts.

Psychological States

At the other end of the generality continuum are constructs that are based around levels of motivation operating in specific situations or at a specific point in time. In some settings, the individual is asked to reflect on the motivation experienced while undergoing a task they have just completed, or at the most specific level students are asked to report on their motivation at a particular point in time while they are engaged in a learning task.

A major question in understanding the dynamics of motivation concerns the relative balance of constructs at these different levels of generality. Awareness of such distinctions is critical when translating research findings into practice. Understanding what is happening in a specific learning context implicates, first, what the learner brings to the task in the form of achievement goal orientations, intrinsic motivation, individual interest, self-concept, and a range of other general motivation constructs. Second, there is the motivation arising from the learner encountering the learning context. This motivation may arise directly from the level of general motivation for the domain, or it may be a response to features of the learning context, to the presence of peers, or to features of the specific learning activity. Recently this was demonstrated in a three-week study (Knogler et al., 2015) separating the effects of individual and situational interest. Using latent state-trait analysis, Knogler et al. assessed variance due to individual interest, variance due to cross-situational consistency in situational interest, and variance due to situation-specific situational interest. While all of these factors contributed to levels of situational interest, the researchers were able to highlight the critical role played by situation-specific factors.

Similar attention to both the person and the personal response to the context can be seen in the design and inclusion of a set of "embedded interest items" in PISA 2006 measures. Most of the measures used in large international assessments such as PISA 2006 (OECD, 2006) use relatively small numbers of items that refer to motivation at a general level. In addition to items measuring general interest in science, PISA 2006 included a set of items to probe students' interest in learning more about the specific content of the science problems they had just been working on as part of the assessment of their science achievement. These PISA 2006 science assessments covered a number of different science topics, and situation-specific interest was measured by asking students whether they would like to find out more about the topic they had just answered questions on. For example, following questions dealing with tooth decay students were asked whether they were interested in finding out more about "what tooth decay bacteria look like under a microscope." In total, there were 52 of these embedded or situation-specific interest items spread over 18 topic units. In secondary analyses of the PISA 2006 data set,

Drechsel and colleagues (2011) applied multidimensional item response models to establish a general measure of science interest and two situation-specific, interest-in-science dimensions (living systems, and physical and technological systems). The PISA 2006 Technical Report indicated that the embedded (or situation-specific) interest measures were associated quite strongly (correlation coefficients around 0.5) with the general measures of interest in science and enjoyment of science (OECD, 2009). Separate secondary analyses of these data (Ainley & Ainley, 2011) modeled relations between interest in specific science topics and more general constructs (such as personal value of science, enjoyment of science, and interest in learning science), demonstrating strong predictive relations between the more general measures and the more specific measures of interest in particular science topics. These reports clearly show that inclusion of situation-specific interest items in PISA 2006 provides further indication of the need to consider specific motivation arising from the topic, as well as student's general motivation, when understanding the role of motivation in learning and achievement.

In sum, both general motivation for the domain and motivation arising from features of the situation will impact the character and intensity of motivation experienced at any point in time across a learning activity – at the beginning, at different points during the activity, and at the end, after the activity has been completed. All of these levels are part of the "dynamic" of motivation.

Measures of motivation (be they state or trait) are typically based on combinations of indicators that may be self-reported responses to items, on-task indicators of responses to individual tasks, or observations by others. However, the most commonly used form of motivation measure continues to be some form of self-report.

Self-Report Measures

One of the early and most widely known contributions to the measurement of achievement motivation was McClelland's Thematic Apperception Test (TAT; see McClelland et al., 1953). Content, in the form of stories generated by participants, was scored for achievement imagery. As a projective test, this method assessed participants' underlying or general motivation to achieve. The restrictions the TAT method placed on the conduct of research produced a climate, in the middle of the twentieth century, in which researchers were receptive to technological developments in printing and computing. Advances in printing machines and photocopiers allowed cheap production of questionnaires that could be administered to large groups. Advances in computing and statistical analysis allowed these larger volumes of data to be processed quickly and efficiently. In motivation research, these developments had a major impact on the form of measurement. Numerous self-report questionnaires – such as the Motivated Strategies for Learning Questionnaire (MSLQ; Pintrich et al.,

1991), Patterns of Adaptive Learning Scale (PALS; Midgley et al., 2000), Intrinsic Motivation Inventory (IMI; Ryan & Deci, 2000), and Achievement Goal Questionnaire (AGQ; Elliot & McGregor, 2001) – are now available to measure a wide range of motivation constructs.

Self-report using scales or questionnaires based on Likert or other rating scales is the most common form of measurement in research on motivation and learning. In their review of motivation terminology, Murphy and Alexander (2000) concluded that "most researchers relied on self-report or self-perception measures to ascertain participants' motivations" (p. 36). A decade later, Wigfield and Cambria (2010) took another look at the research relating motivation and "achievement outcomes," specifically focusing on achievement values, goal orientations, and interest as the motivation variables. They reported that the field was still dominated by self-report measures. A survey of measures of self-efficacy in publications from 2000 to 2010 (Klassen & Usher, 2010) reported that "more than 90 percent of studies investigating self-efficacy relied on surveys and questionnaires" (p. 11).

Scale Construction

In the construction of motivation scales, several indicators of one underlying dimension are often used to provide greater assurance that the underlying dimension is being measured, rather than something that reflects the particular context. Three issues are important in combining indicators in measures of motivation. First is the need to establish the dimensionality of the set of indicators, so as to know whether they form one or more unidimensional constructs. Second is a requirement for item response categories to be correctly ordered in terms of their association with the composite score. Third is the ability to demonstrate that the particular combination of indicators produces a valid measure of the underlying motivational state or trait. Traditionally, measures have combined scores based on responses from individual items as sums or averages, in which each item contributes equally to the overall score.

Modern methods of analysis weight the contribution of items to the composite score. One approach uses confirmatory factor analysis (CFA; Brown, 2014), while another uses item response theory (IRT) approaches such as partial credit or rating scale analysis (Bond & Fox, 2015; Schulz, 2009). These methods provide measures that reflect the underlying trait more accurately and reliably than sums of item scores.

At the same time, the widespread use of self-report measures has attracted criticism and there are several contemporary reviews examining issues of reliability and validity, item development, scoring assumptions, statistical analysis, and interpretation (e.g., Fulmer & Frijters, 2009; Greene, 2015; Karabenick et al., 2007). We will refer to a couple of the issues concerning the validity of self-report measures.

Validity and Self-Report Measures

Researchers reporting strong reliability, generally internal consistency, for their scales is common. However, important validity issues – such as the correspondence between item content as intended by the researcher, and the meaning and interpretation of items by participants – are not always addressed. Motivation constructs are often treated as if they have wide application and common understandings across the educational spectrum, from the primary level to the college and undergraduate level. Research papers referencing findings that come from a range of educational levels to support their predictions, without necessarily considering whether item content might be interpreted differently by students from different educational levels, are not uncommon. Karabenick et al. (2007) drew attention to this important validity issue when advocating the use of cognitive techniques, including interviews, to improve the validity of self-report measures. From their interview data, Karabenick et al. cite the example of responses to the item "Learning new ideas and concepts is very important." They report that "many students struggled with the word 'concepts.' Among the elementary students, 30 percent misread, struggled to read, or asked what the word meant during the interview process. When asked to read the item aloud, students often misread 'concepts' as 'compares,' 'conpact' [*sic*], or 'components.' One student also then asked, 'What are concepts?'" (p. 146).

The application of what Karabenick et al. refer to as "cognitive pretesting" involves qualitative procedures (such as interviewing) to examine the way respondents process item content and "whether respondents' cognitive processes during test performance mirror those intended by test designers" (p. 140). These techniques concern the validity of individual scale items rather than focusing just on the total scale score. They are not limited to pretesting for scale development, but can also be used to confirm how an existing scale is working. Among the questions posed in interviews, respondents are asked to describe in their own words what an item is "trying to find out from you" and, after reporting an answer to an item, asks them to "explain why you chose that answer."

The approach proposed by Karabenick et al. (2007) was adopted by Frenzel et al. (2012) to explore whether there are significant changes in meaning of the concept "interest in mathematics" across grade five to grade nine students. This study is important for our discussion because, while investigating interest in mathematics, it explores whether the often-cited decline in motivation observed from primary to secondary school is associated with changes in the meaning of interest in mathematics contingent on students' developmental level. Frenzel et al. considered the possibility that there may be qualitative or structural changes in the interest in mathematics concepts from grade five to grade nine. More specifically, the study considers the domain-specific concept of individual interest in mathematics and presents a longitudinal comparison of levels of interest in mathematics – that is, whether there are "age-related shifts in students' concepts of what it means to be interested" (p. 1070).

Structural equation modeling (SEM) techniques were used to assess measurement invariance and to model the latent variable structure across these data. To test their assumption of age-related changes in the meaning of interest in mathematics, Frenzel et al. (2012) predicted that the latent structure of interest in mathematics would not be invariant across grades. In their analyses of these grade-level data, the item intercepts, structural weights, and error variances were set to be equal, thereby assessing whether there was any loss in fit when the structure of the concept "interest in mathematics" was assumed to be invariant. A small but significant loss of fit was observed when these equality constraints were implemented, supporting the overall prediction of change in the structure of the concept.

The quality of this change in construct meaning was followed up using interviews of a smaller number of students, some in grade five and some in grade nine. Content analysis of the interview responses indicated a shift in the relative proportions of cognitive and affective comments. "It is important to note that the observed shifts were not simply uniform trends. Rather, the importance of emotional experiences for participants' concepts of interest was less pronounced in older adolescents, compared with younger adolescents, while the importance of cognitive components of the construct (thirst for knowledge and autonomous task choice) was more pronounced for older adolescents" (p. 1077).

Application of techniques such as "cognitive pretesting" represents a divergence from the more common assumption that scores on a test of interest in mathematics (or some other motivation construct) can be directly compared across age levels or cultures. Statistical procedures have been used in international studies of achievement to investigate whether the structure of the measures is equivalent across countries – that is, whether students from different countries understand and respond to questionnaire items (such as interest in science or interest in mathematics) in the same way. Information from multiple-group CFA can provide information about the extent of similarity of measurement models (i.e., the way specific items relate to a construct) with different constraints across countries. When scaling data across countries, the assumption is that a set of items measure a given construct in the same, or at least a very similar, way across countries. Multiple-group modeling can be used to test this assumption (e.g., Schulz, 2009). There may also be differences in the extent to which participants respond in socially desirable ways and the extent to which they agree with items (Bertling et al., 2016).

Several approaches have been employed to improve cross-cultural comparability of motivation and attitudinal measures, including forced-choice item formats and anchoring vignettes (Brown & Maydeu-Olivares, 2013; Van de Vijver & He, 2016). Forced-choice items require respondents to choose their most preferred option from two equally desirable options. Sets of forced-choice items can be used to develop a scale reflecting an underlying construct. When used in PISA 2012, it was claimed that this approach "essentially eliminated the huge difference between within- and between-country correlations found for self-reported ratings of motivation" (Van de Vijver & He, 2016, p. 245). Anchoring vignettes involve the presentation of hypothetical situations, and participants' responses are used to infer underlying perceptions that may bias their responses to other attitude questions (Kyllonen & Bertling, 2014). This has also been used in some of the PISA 2012 field trials (Van de Vijver & He, 2016).

Another aspect of validity concerns the course of motivation across the elapsed time for any specific learning activity. How well does self-report at the end of a learning activity capture the motivation that was in play as the learning activity was being performed? What is the relation between general motivation and the specific motivation aroused during a learning activity? Which is the most appropriate measure (or combination of measures) to iden-tify the relation between motivation and learning? Consideration of this type of question has resulted in approaches that focus on real-time designs (includ-ing various forms of self-report and extended interview protocols) to assess motivation, thereby identifying how motivation relates to learning processes and outcomes. These real-time designs are making significant changes to the landscape of measures and methods in research on motivation and learning.

Real-Time Measures

Earlier we referred to motivation, in the context of learning and achievement, as a dynamic system implicating what the student brings to a learning activity in the form of general motivation, and the dynamic states that arise as students engage with a learning activity in a particular context. General motivation for the domain and features of the specific situation will impact the character and intensity of motivation experienced at any point in time across a task – at the beginning, at different points during the task, and at the end after the task has been completed. All of these levels are part of the "dynamic" of motivation. Consideration of this dynamic character of motivation in relation to learning has prompted the development of a number of research approaches that go beyond assessments using the more common self-report questionnaires.

One of the earliest examples of real-time measurement of motivation is the experience sampling method (ESM; Larson & Csikszentmihalyi, 1983). ESM was devised to document students' goals, thoughts, feelings, and behavior in real time. Students carried "beepers" with them everywhere during waking hours and were contacted at random intervals. When contacted, they were required to provide information about what they were doing and about aspects of their thoughts and feelings regarding their current activity. This technique has been used in a number of studies by Csikszentmihalyi et al. (e.g., Hunter & Csikszentmihalyi, 2003) and has also been adopted and developed further by later researchers to obtain real-time assessment of students' motivation (e.g., Lewalter & Krapp, 2008).

Influenced by reports using ESM, a number of papers included in Pintrich and Maehr's (2002) *New directions in measures and methods* volume were suggesting measures of motivation that involved real-time assessment – for example, Boekaerts' On-line Motivation Questionnaire (Boekaerts, 2002); Ainley and Hidi's (2002) real-time interactive computer assessment; and Järvelä's (Järvelä et al., 2002) dynamic assessment. Each of these approaches will be described, with examples of contemporary research, to demonstrate the importance of considering motivation as a situated or interactive person and task phenomenon when investigating relations between motivation and learning.

The On-Line Motivation Questionnaire

Boekaerts (2002) designed the On-line Motivation Questionnaire (OMQ) to access students' situation-specific motivational appraisals "while the learning process is unfolding" (p. 81). Immediately after the task has been introduced, student appraisals of the situation are recorded using rating scales. A second part of the questionnaire is completed when the student finishes or withdraws from the task. Location of the assessment within the context of a specific learning task means that the motivation inherent in students' immediate appraisals in response to particular learning situations is recorded and interpreted in a more dynamic way than is possible simply with general motivation measures. The OMQ has been used by Boekaerts et al. in a variety of situations, including comparing examination and exercise settings, and different types of classroom problems (e.g., Boekaerts, 1999, 2007; Crombach et al., 2003).

Real-Time Interactive Computer Assessment

At the same time that the OMQ was being developed and, again, influenced by the success of the ESM, Ainley and Hidi (e.g., Ainley et al., 2002) developed an interactive computer format to allow the recording of indicators of students' motivation across the course of a learning task. This development was based on the assumption that there are many sources of students' motivation in any learning situation. Students bring general motivation to a learning activity in the form of orientations and predispositions, which interact with their perception of the learning activity as presented to them. Because the task extends across time, whether a small or larger interval, there is potential for motivation to change across the course of engaging with the learning activity. This may mean that the general motivation persists across the learning activity or – in response to features of the activity and the context in which it occurs – that motivation may increase, decrease, or fluctuate across the time interval.

The potential of interactive computer technology allowed probes to be introduced at critical points in the learning activity to assess what participants were thinking and feeling, in order to identify changing patterns of motivation.

Initial studies involved identifying relations between interest – both individual interest in the domain and situational interest for the topic – and performance on reading tasks (e.g., Ainley et al., 2005). Later versions were developed to identify relations between interest and problem solving, making use of the computer potentials that allow students to explore a range of information to present a solution to the open-ended problem (e.g., Ainley et al., 2008).

Other researchers have adapted these techniques to explore motivation in elementary mathematics classes (Tulis & Ainley, 2011), in challenging mathematics and reading tasks (Tulis & Fulmer, 2013), and in secondary biology dissection classes (Holstermann et al., 2012). While the research referenced so far has generally involved specific classroom tasks, the same type of design has been used to assess motivation (situational interest) as it plays out across a full-day workshop for college-age students (Rotgans & Schmidt, 2011). Simultaneously, other research programs are using real-time approaches to identify how sets of variables, including motivation, contribute to learning. For example, research into self-regulated learning by Azevedo et al. (Moos & Azevedo, 2008) experimented with forms of scaffolding (no scaffolding, conceptual scaffolding) as undergraduate students engaged with a 30-minute hypermedia task on the circulatory system. In addition to pretesting for prior knowledge and motivation, motivation measures were introduced at regular intervals during the hypermedia session. At the end of the task knowledge of the circulatory system and motivation were assessed. Under both experimental conditions, motivation showed a significant increase across the task. Having a sequence of motivation assessments across the course of the task enabled the researchers to describe how motivation changed across the task. Azevedo's research program (Azevedo, 2015) has extended this approach and is incorporating multiple forms of real-time measures, such as video and audio recordings, think-alouds, eye-tracking devices, facial expression monitoring, and physiological sensors.

Similar types of real-time measures involving data captured as part of computer-based assessments are also being considered as the basis for measures of attitudes and behaviors in the context of international large-scale assessments (Bertling et al., 2016). Process data in the form of, for example, response time data are being collected to complement self-report questionnaires. As international assessments move to digital recording through the use of laptop computers and a range of tablet devices, scenario-based tasks allow the recording of behavioral indicators, which (in combination with the self-report responses) provide wider sources of information concerning motivational states.

Dynamic Assessment and Socially Shared Regulation

A complementary but quite different perspective has developed out of Järvelä's support for dynamic assessment in the study of motivation and achievement.

Järvelä et al. (2002) suggested that the dynamic character of motivation required forms of assessment "embedded in the continuous learning and performance episodes in a natural learning setting" (p. 208). This approach focuses on person–environment interactions following Vygotsky's proposals concerning the zone of proximal development and its role in learning (Vygotsky, 1978). Järvelä et al. have developed this approach into what is now referred to as "a situative perspective on regulation of learning" (Järvenoja et al., 2015), which examines processes from both individual and group levels. In this way they explore questions concerning the contribution of motivation processes occurring at the level of the individual, as a function of both the context and the dynamics of the collaborative learning exercise. "Extending the interdependence of individual and social regulation to include contextual features, the regulation of learning can be understood as an interactive process not only between individual learners and groups but also between people and learning contexts" (p. 206). Video records of group participation in particular learning activities are used to establish key patterns of regulation by describing layers of interaction. At the first layer, "motivationally or emotionally meaningful episodes" are identified. At the second layer, these episodes are categorized in terms of the strategies and purposes they represent in that learning situation. The third layer involves identifying the sequence of "causes, actions, and effects" of the strategies and purposes. The final layer involves applying a full second-by-second analysis of the video record to provide a multilayered description of the socially shared regulation of learning processes. Effective employment of this method has become possible through recent developments in recording techniques and microanalytic protocols. As Järvenoja et al. (2015) suggest, research into the regulation of learning incorporating motivation and emotion processes is "just beginning."

In short, what we have described in this focus on issues of generality and specificity is how closely intertwined they are, with the increasing emphasis on motivation and learning as interactive relations between person and context. There is minimal emphasis on context when motivation is only measured as a generalized or habitual individual difference factor to assess its contribution to achievement. However, once specificity is introduced into the definition and measurement of the motivation construct, the character of the situation is already part of the relation being modeled.

New Designs and Analyses

Attention to these issues of generality and specificity of motivation constructs has been associated with different designs that make use of new multivariate analytic procedures. A number of specific developments in designs will be explored here – in particular, structural equation modeling, latent profile analysis, and multi-level modeling.

Structural Equation Modeling

Studies of motivation have employed a number of multivariate statistical methods to analyze data. The sophistication of these methods has grown from multiple regression through path analysis to various forms of structural equation modeling (SEM) (Kaplan, 2009; Marsh & Hau, 2007). Multiple regression is used to investigate the relationship between two or more predictor variables and an outcome variable by means of a linear equation that provides the best fit. The magnitudes of the regression coefficients represent the relationships between the predictors and outcome if the effects of the other predictor variables are held constant (hence the term "other things equal"). Path analysis is an extension of multiple regression that estimates the magnitude and significance of hypothesized causal connections between sets of measured (or manifest) variables. It considers the relationships among predictors, as well as the relationships between predictors and one or more outcomes. These are typically represented in the form of a path diagram and can be used to test hypotheses such as mediation. SEM can be seen as a development of path analysis that includes latent variables (such as motivation) inferred from measured variables. SEM, therefore, includes analyses of the relationships between latent variables (the "structural" part of the model), and between observed indicators and the latent variables to which they relate (the "measurement" part of the model).

Applications of SEM in research have grown since the mid-1990s. Hershberger (2003) noted the rapid growth in the use of SEM between 1994 and 2001 – a growth that has increased further since then. Noting the growth in popularity of tools related to SEM, Marsh and Hau (2007) stressed the importance of relating new methods of analysis to well-grounded theory concerning the issues under investigation. This applies particularly to issues concerning causality, given that SEM is often applied to correlational data. As Marsh and Hau note, longitudinal studies usually provide a stronger basis for testing causality than cross-sectional studies, but even longitudinal studies have limitations when inferences about causality are being sought. Examining some examples of SEM in motivation research is worthwhile.

Frenzel et al. (2012) used SEM to model the latent variable structure in a study of age-related changes in the meaning of interest in mathematics across grades. The results confirmed the prediction of a change in the structure of the concept "interest in mathematics" across grades. Directionality of effects in the relation between motivation and learning has always been problematic. Marsh and Martin (2011) used SEM to investigate the relations between, and the causal ordering of, academic self-concept and academic achievement. Basing their analyses on a reciprocal effects model, they concluded that increases in academic self-concept are related to improved academic achievement through both direct and indirect paths. Scherer et al. (2016) analyzed data from PISA 2012 for Australia, Canada, and the United States to investigate student perceptions of instructional quality and the relationship of those perceptions to achievement. They identified three factors across all three countries in students' perceptions of instructional quality: teacher support, cognitive activation, and classroom management. Moreover, they reported that, whereas self-concept and motivation were related to all three factors of perceived instructional quality, achievement was related to perceived classroom management. Tempelaar et al. (2007) used SEM to investigate the achievement motivations of university students, and were able to identify generic and subject-specific achievement motivations. They were able to show differences between subjects regarded as difficult and subjects regarded as less difficult in aspects such as cognitive competence. Gogol et al. (2017) examined a model of affective-motivational constructs: academic self-concept, interest, and anxiety within and between school subjects for grade nine students. They concluded that a major part of individual differences in subject-specific measures of affective-motivational constructs in relation to achievement indicators was explained by students' global appraisals of subjects. The contribution of subject-specific components was considerably smaller.

Latent Profile Analysis

Latent profile analysis (LPA) and latent class analysis (LCA) aim to identify groups of respondents who have similar characteristics. These approaches focus on person-centered analyses (rather than variable-centered analyses) and use latent variables as the basis for classifying individuals. The techniques have a similar purpose to cluster analysis, but have the advantage of basing categories on explicit models and latent variables. In LPA, the latent variables are based on continuous measures; in LCA, the latent variables are based on categorical measures. Tuominen-Soini et al. (2011) used LPA to examine the stability of achievement goal orientations, both across a four-month period for grade nine students and across the transition for students from grade 11 to grade 12. Four goal orientation profiles were identified: indifferent, success-oriented, mastery-oriented, and avoidance-oriented. The researchers suggest that these findings indicate substantial stability in achievement goal orientations across the targeted time intervals. Schwinger et al. (2016) investigated the achievement goal profiles of German elementary school students across seven measurement waves from grade two to grade four. Analyses were based on three goal measures: mastery, performance approach, and performance avoidance. LPA indicated five classes based on goal profiles (high multiple goals, moderate multiple goals, primarily mastery oriented, moderately performance oriented, and amotivated). It was also possible to identify how goal profiles changed over time; the antecedents of goal profiles, in terms of gender and implicit theories of intelligence; and associations between the goal profiles, intrinsic motivation, and achievement outcomes.

Multi-level Models

Many settings involve studies of students nested in classes and classes within schools. In these circumstances, the use of multi-level analysis provides important perspectives on influences operating at student, classroom, or school levels. These perspectives might not be evident in student-level analyses alone. In addition, the application of multi-level methods of analysis can provide more appropriate estimates of standard errors and, therefore, of statistical significance. Lüdtke et al. (2009) argue that multi-level analyses are especially important in studies of learning environments where student ratings of the environment should be aggregated to the classroom level and analyzed at that level. However, studying the effects of the learning environment presents a series of methodological challenges. Ludtke et al. discuss crucial elements in research that use student reports to gauge the impact of the learning environment on student outcomes. From a conceptual point of view, it is argued that ratings aggregated at the relevant level (e.g., class or school), and not individual student ratings, are of primary interest.

These analytic procedures are increasingly being used in research on the relation between motivation and learning when researchers are interested in causality interpretations.

Longitudinal Designs

Longitudinal designs include temporal separation between administrations of measures, which facilitates closer identification of specific relations between motivation and learning or achievement. Two types of relation between motivation and learning – mediation effects and reciprocal effects – are increasingly featured in the research literature.

Mediation Effects

Following the popularization of mediation analyses in experimental social psychology (e.g., Baron & Kenny, 1986; Judd & Kenny, 2010), many instances of research into relations between motivation and learning have been published, hypothesizing that the influence of one motivation variable on learning is mediated by another specified variable. This is underpinned by shifts in theoretical perspectives on the nature of motivation, as described by Eccles et al. (1998):

> The view of motivation has changed dramatically over the last half of the twentieth century, going from a biologically based drive perspective to a behavioral mechanistic perspective, and then to a cognitive-mediational/ constructivist perspective. The conception of the individual as a purposeful, goal-directed actor who must coordinate multiple goals and desires across multiple contexts within both short- and long-range time frames currently is prominent (p. 1074).

Hence, over the last two decades, mediation models have become very common in research on motivation and learning.

One of the important assumptions required for a valid test of mediation is temporal separation between variables. The mediation relation involves the effect of the independent variable operating through its effect on the mediator, which in turn affects the outcome. In their classic treatment of mediation, Baron and Kenny (1986) made it clear that mediation involves a causal model. The independent variable is causally related to the mediator and, simultaneously, the mediator is causally related to the outcome or dependent variable. Partial mediation can be identified, as well as full mediation. Demonstration of a mediation effect provides insight into the mechanism through which the initial variable exerts its effect on the outcome variable. As they caution: "Mediation is not defined statistically; rather statistics can be used to evaluate a presumed mediational model" (Kenny, 2016). Effective implementation of this type of research design depends on a strong theory of the relations between motivation and learning, as well as a design that separates the assessment of variables in time. The importance of this feature of mediation designs can be seen in some cases of apparent contradiction between findings. Consider the following example.

Mega et al. (2014) used Pekrun's control-value theory of achievement and achievement emotions (e.g., Pekrun et al., 2007) to hypothesize that self-regulated learning strategies and motivation function as mediators between achievement emotions and achievement. A large number of undergraduate participants (5,805) completed a computerized self-report questionnaire that included items relating to all three main predictor variables in a single administration. Predictor variables were measured at the general level as habitual tendencies related to study. The questionnaire included five facets of self-regulated learning (SRL); emotions questions consisting of positive and negative emotions referring to the self, academic achievement, and study time; and motivation questions incorporating five motivational beliefs. Using SEM, each of the subscales for the three main predictors was tested to establish latent predictor variables, which were then assessed for fit to the hypothesized model of emotions predicting SRL and motivation, which in turn predicted academic achievement. The model showed acceptable fit, and the authors concluded that the influence of achievement emotions on achievement was mediated by the influence of achievement emotions (especially positive emotions) on SRL and motivation.

However, to justify interpretation of the causal relation implicit in mediation requires some temporal separation of the predictor and mediation variables, which was not the case in this research. While the SEM results show an acceptable fit of these data to the model, alternative hypotheses have not been excluded. For example, what level of fit would result if the model posited emotion as mediator? The latter was reported in earlier research (Pekrun et al., 2009), which included temporal separation between the assessment of predictor and mediator variables: emotions mediated the effect of achievement goals (a subcomponent of the motivation measure in Mega et al.'s study) on academic achievement. Pekrun et al. (2009) measured undergraduate students' achievement goals for an exam that they knew they were going to sit a week later. One day before the exam, students reported how they felt about their preparation for the exam. The model in this case proposed that achievement goals as representations of desired outcomes trigger a range of processes, including the emotions experienced while preparing for the exam. "Achievement emotions are viewed as mediators that explain *how* achievement goals influence performance attainment" (Pekrun et al., 2009, p. 119).

Research that is able to identify mediation processes as the nature of relations between motivation and learning has the advantage of pointing to ways that research findings can guide the development of interventions.

In the same paper that identified emotions as mediators of the effects of achievement goals on achievement, Pekrun et al. (2009) pointed to potential reciprocal effects of emotions, achievement goals, and achievement: "Performance can influence students' emotions and goals, thus implying reciprocal effects of goals, emotions, and performance" (p. 118). In the next section, we take up the issue of identifying reciprocal relations.

Reciprocal Effects

Another positive outcome for understanding the relation between motivation and learning has come from the use of longitudinal designs that allow the untangling of the set of effects constituting reciprocal relations. Within a learning context, simple unidirectional causal relations are likely to be rare. More often, the pattern is one of reciprocal effects whereby the level of a motivation factor influences a future outcome, which in turn influences the level of motivation. Knowledge of the way such relations work provides some guidance for practitioners concerning the design of effective interventions. For example, Marsh et al. (2005) have linked the potential for detecting reciprocal effects to judicious use of longitudinal designs and advances in SEM. In their research on self-concept, interest, and mathematics achievement, they argued that "the reciprocal effects model implies that academic self-concept, interest, and academic achievement are reciprocally related and mutually reinforcing. Improved academic self-concepts and interest will lead to better achievement, and improved achievement will lead to better academic self-concepts and interest ... The reciprocal effects model suggests that the most effective strategy is to improve academic self-concept, interest, and achievement simultaneously" (p. 413).

To examine how reciprocal effects are implicated in the relation between motivation and learning, we will consider an example of research into the potential reciprocal relations between achievement goals, interest, and academic performance in undergraduate students by Harackiewicz et al. (2008).

Reciprocal effects can only be detected from a sequence of multiple measures of the same variables. In the Harackiewicz et al. study, there were five measurement points across a full semester. Data collection commenced in the first semester of the introductory psychology program. The sequence of measures was: T1 (first week of the semester), achievement goals and individual interest in the domain of psychology; T2 (three weeks into the semester), achievement goals and situational interest (catch-1); T3 (two weeks before the end of the semester), situational interest (catch-2 and hold); T4 (end of the semester), final exam; T5 (seven semesters later), records of performance and participation in psychology courses. In addition, each of the instructors had conducted a first exam between T2 and T3. Of particular interest are the findings concerning the form of the relations between achievement goals, interest, and performance. In addition to evidence that the effects of initial individual interest in the domain (T1) on situational interest early in the course (T2 catch-1) were mediated by mastery achievement goals, there was evidence of reciprocal effects of interest and performance:

> The analyses with first exam performance reveal the reciprocal effects of interest and performance, notably that early interest predicted exam performance and grades, and that early exam performance predicted subsequent situational interest (both catch and hold), controlling for initial interest. These results are consistent with the idea that students perform well on tasks they find interesting and that they become more interested in activities when they have performed well on them (p. 119).

In sum, advances in longitudinal designs and the application of a range of new statistical modeling procedures have expanded investigations and are yielding significant insights into the character of the relations that link motivation and learning.

Concluding Thoughts

In this chapter, we have examined measures and methods that have come to prominence over the last two decades in research investigating relations between motivation and learning. While still heavily dependent on self-report questionnaires, the field has expanded to include a range of real-time behavioral indicators, and we have highlighted a range of these new measures and methods. As well as noting that these measures and methods are closely linked to contemporary theories, we have explored how increasingly they include interactive influences of person and context in their focus. Together, the developments in measures and methods demonstrate, first, an increasing awareness that measures and methods need to mirror the levels of generality and specificity inherent in the motivation constructs being investigated and, second, that with appropriate designs researchers are able to examine more closely the specific types of relations that link motivation and learning. As such, research that draws on the strengths of the new measures and methods should add to the understanding of the power of motivation to provide energy and direction for learning, and this, in turn, can be used to inform educational practices.

References

Ainley, M. & Ainley, J. (2011). Student engagement with science in early adolescence: The contribution of enjoyment to students' continuing interest in learning about science. *Contemporary Educational Psychology, 36*(1), 4–12. doi: 10.1016/j.cedpsych.2010.08.001.

Ainley, M., Corrigan, M., & Richardson, N. (2005). Students, tasks and emotions: Identifying the contribution of emotions to students' reading of popular culture and popular science texts. *Learning and Instruction, 15*(5), 433–47.

Ainley, M., Enger, L., & Kennedy, G. (2008). The elusive experience of 'flow': Qualitative and quantitative indicators. *International Journal of Educational Research, 47,* 109–21. doi: 10.1016/j.ijer.2007.11.011.

Ainley, M. & Hidi, S. (2002). Dynamic measures for studying interest and learning. In P. R. Pintrich & M. L. Maehr (Eds.), *New directions in measures and methods* (Vol. 12, pp. 43–76). Amsterdam: JAI, Elsevier Science.

Ainley, M., Hidi, S., & Berndorff, D. (2002). Interest, learning, and the psychological processes that mediate their relationship. *Journal of Educational Psychology, 94*(3), 545–61. doi: 10.1037//0022-0663.94.3545.

Anderman, E. M., Gimbert, B., O'Connell, A. A., & Riegel, L. (2015). Approaches to academic growth assessment. *British Journal of Educational Psychology, 85,* 138–53.

Azevedo, R. (2015). Defining and measuring engagement and learning in science: Conceptual, theoretical, methodological, and analytical issues. *Educational Psychologist, 50*(1), 84–94. doi: 10.1080/00461520.2015.1004069.

Baron, R. M. & Kenny, D. A. (1986). The moderator-mediator variable distinction in social psychological research: Conceptual, strategic, and statistical considerations. *Journal of Personality and Social Psychology, 51,* 1173–82.

Bertling, J., Marksteiner, M., & Kyllonen, P. C. (2016). General noncognitive outcomes. In S. Kuger, E. Klieme, N. Jude, & D. Kaplan (Eds.), *Assessing contexts of learning: An international perspective.* (pp. 255–81). Cham: Springer.

Betebenner, D. W. & Linn, R. L. (2010). *Growth in student achievement: Issues of measurement, longitudinal data analysis, and accountability.* Princeton, NJ: Educational Testing Service.

Boekaerts, M. (1999). Motivated learning: Studying student * situation transactional units. *European Journal of Psychology of Education, 14*(1), 41–55.

Boekaerts, M. (2002). The on-line motivation questionnaire: A self-report instrument to assess students' context sensitivity. In P. R. Pintrich & M. L. Maehr (Eds.), *New directions in measures and methods* (Vol. 12, pp. 77–120). Oxford: Elsevier Science.

Boekaerts, M. (2007). Understanding students' affective processes in the classroom. In P. Schutz & R. Pekrun (Eds.), *Emotion in education* (pp. 37–56). Amsterdam: Elsevier.

Bond, T. G. & Fox, C. M. (2015). *Applying the Rasch model: Fundamental measurement in the human sciences.* (3rd ed.). New York, NY: Routledge.

Brown, A. L. & Maydeu-Olivares, A. (2013). How IRT can solve problems of ipsative data in forced-choice questionnaires. *Psychological Methods, 18*(1), 36–52. doi: 10.1037/a0030641.

Brown, T. A. (2014). *Confirmatory factor analysis for applied research* (2nd ed.). New York: Guilford Publications.

Crombach, M. J., Boekaerts, M., & Voeten, M. J. M. (2003). Online measurement of appraisals of students faced with curricular tasks. *Educational and Psychological Measurement, 63*(1), 96–111. doi: 10.1177/0013164402239319.

Drechsel, B., Carstensen, C., & Prenzel, M. (2011). The role of content and context in PISA interest scales: A study of the embedded interest items in the PISA 2006 science assessment. *International Journal of Science Education, 33*(1), 73–95. doi: 10.1080/09500693.2010.518646.

Eccles, J. S., Wigfield, A., & Schiefele, U. (1998). Motivation to succeed. In N. Eisenberg (Ed.), *Handbook of child psychology: Social, emotional, and personality development.* (Vol. 3, pp. 1017–96). New York, NY: Wiley.

Elliot, A. J. & McGregor, H. A. (2001). A 2 X 2 achievement goal framework. *Journal of Personality and Social Psychology, 80*(3), 501–19. doi: 10.1037//0022-3514.80.3.501.

Frenzel, A. C., Pekrun, R., Dicke, A.-L., & Goetz, T. (2012). Beyond quantitative decline: Conceptual shifts in adolescents' development of interest in mathematics. *Developmental Psychology, 48*(4), 1069–82. doi: 10.1037/a0026895.

Fulmer, S. M. & Frijters, J. C. (2009). A review of self-report and alternative approaches in the measurement of student motivation. *Educational Psychology Review, 21*, 219–46. doi: 10.1007/s10648-009-9107-x.

Gogol, K., Brunnera, M., Martin, R., Preckel, F., & Goetz, T. (2017). Affect and motivation within and between school subjects: Development and validation of an integrative structural model of academic self-concept, interest, and anxiety. *Contemporary Educational Psychology, 49*, 46–65. doi: 10.1016/j.cedpsych.2016.11.003.

Greene, B. A. (2015). Measuring cognitive engagement with self-report scales: Reflections from over 20 years of research. *Educational Psychologist, 50*(1), 14–30. doi: 10.1080/00461520.2014.989230.

Harackiewicz, J. M., Durik, A. M., Barron, K. E., Linnenbrink-Garcia, L., & Tauer, J. M. (2008). The role of achievement goals in the development of interest: Reciprocal relations between achievement goals, interest, and performance. *Journal of Educational Psychology, 100*(1), 105–22. doi: 10.1037/ 0022-0663.100.1.105.

Hershberger, S. L. (2003). The growth of structural equation modeling 1994–2001. *Structural Equation Modeling: A Multidisciplinary Journal, 10*, 35–46.

Hidi, S. & Renninger, K. A. (2006). The four-phase model of interest development. *Educational Psychologist, 41*(2), 111–27.

Holstermann, N., Ainley, M., Grube, D., Roick, T., & Bögeholz, S. (2012). The specific relationship between disgust and interest: Relevance during biology class dissections and gender differences. *Learning and Instruction, 22*, 185–92. doi: 10.1016/j.learninstruc.2011.10.005.

Hunter, J. P. & Csikszentmihalyi, M. (2003). The positive psychology of interested adolescents. *Journal of Youth and Adolescence, 32*, 27–35.

Järvelä, S., Salonen, P., & Lepola, J. (2002). Dynamic assessment as a key to understanding student motivation in a classroom context. In P. R. Pintrich & M. L. Maehr (Eds.), *New directions in measures and methods* (Vol. 12, pp. 207–40). Oxford: Elsevier Science.

Järvenoja, H., Järvelä, S., & Malmberg, J. (2015). Understanding regulated learning in situative and contextual frameworks. *Educational Psychologist, 50*(3), 204–19. doi: 10.1080/00461520.2015.1075400.

Judd, C. M. & Kenny, D. A. (2010). Data analysis in social psychology: Recent and recurring issues. In S. Fiske, D. T. Gilbert, & G. Lindzey (Eds.), *Handbook of social psychology* (pp. 115–39). Hoboken, NJ: John Wiley & Sons.

Kaplan, D. (2009). *Structural equation modeling: Foundations and extensions.* Los Angeles, CA: Sage.

Karabenick, S. A., Woolley, M. E., Friedel, J. M., Ammon, B. V., Blazevski, J., Bonney, C. R., & Kelly, K. L. (2007). Cognitive processing of self-report items in educational research: Do they think what we mean? *Educational Psychologist, 42*(3), 139–51. doi: 10.1080/00461520701416231.

Kenny, D. A. (2016). Mediation. Retrieved from http://davidakenny.net/cm/mediate .htm.

Klassen, R. M. & Usher, E. L. (2010). Self-efficacy in educational settings: Recent research and emerging directions. In T. C. Urdan & S. A. Karabenick (Eds.), *Advances in motivation and achievement. The decade ahead: Theoretical perspectives on motivation and achievement* (Vol. 16A, pp. 1–33). Bingley: Emerald.

Knogler, M., Harackiewicz, J. M., Gegenfurtner, A., & Lewalter, D. (2015). How situational is situational interest? Investigating the longitudinal structure of situational interest. *Contemporary Educational Psychology, 43*, 39–50. doi: 10.1016/j.cedpsych.2015.08.004.

Kyllonen, P. C. & Bertling, J. (2014). Innovative questionnaire assessment methods to increase cross-country comparability. In L. Rutkowski, M. von Davier, & D. Rutkowski (Eds.), *Handbook of international large-scale assessment: background, technical issues, and methods of data analysis.* Boca Raton, FL: CRC Press.

Larson, R. W. & Csikszentmihalyi, M. (1983). The experience sampling method. *New Directions for Methodology of Science & Behavioral Science, 15*, 41–56.

Lewalter, D. & Krapp, A. (2008). The role of contextual conditions of vocational education for motivational orientations and emotional experiences. *European Psychologist, 9*(4), 210–21. doi: 10.1027/1016-9040.9.4.210.

Lüdtke, O., Robitzsch, A., Trautwein, U., & Kunter, M. (2009). Assessing the impact of learning environments: How to use student ratings of classroom or school characteristics in multilevel modelling. *Contemporary Educational Psychology, 34*(2), 120–31. doi: 10.1016/j.cedpsych.2008.12.001.

Marsh, H. W. & Hau, K. (2007). Applications of latent-variable models in educational psychology: The need for methodological-substantive synergies. *Contemporary Educational Psychology, 32*(1), 151–70. doi: 10.1016/j.cedpsych.2006.10.008.

Marsh, H. W., Koller, O., Trautwein, U., Ludtke, O., & Baumert, J. (2005). Academic self-concept, interest, grades, and standardized test scores: Reciprocal effects models of causal ordering. *Child Development, 76*(2), 397–416.

Marsh, H. W. & Martin, A. J. (2011). Academic self-concept and academic achievement: Relations and causal ordering. *British Journal of Educational Psychology, 81*, 59–77. doi: 10.1348/000709910X503501.

Martin, A. J. (2015). Growth approaches to academic development: Research into academic trajectories and growth assessment, goals, and mindsets. *British Journal of Educational Psychology, 85*, 133–7. doi: 10.1111/bjep.12071.

McClelland, D. C., Atkinson, J. W., Clark, R. A., & Lowell, E. L. (1953). *The achievement motive.* New York, NY: Appleton-Century.

Mega, C., Ronconi, L., & De Beni, R. (2014). What makes a good student? How emotions, self-regulated learning, and motivation contribute to academic achievement. *Journal of Educational Psychology, 106*(1), 121–31. doi: 10.1037/a0033546.

Midgley, C., Maehr, M. L., Hruda, L. Z., Anderman, E., Anderman, L., Freeman, K. E., ... Urdan, T. (2000). *Manual for the patterns of adaptive learning scale.* Ann Arbor, MI: University of Michigan.

Moos, D. C. & Azevedo, R. (2008). Exploring the fluctuation of motivation and use of self-regulatory processes during learning with hypermedia. *Instructional Science, 36*, 203–31. doi: 10.1007/s11251-007-9028-3.

Murphy, P. K. & Alexander, P. A. (2000). A motivated exploration of motivation terminology. *Contemporary Educational Psychology, 25*, 3–53. doi: 10.1006/ceps.1999.1019.

OECD (Organisation for Economic Co-operation and Development). (2006). *Assessing scientific, reading, and mathematical literacy: A framework for PISA 2006.* Paris: OECD.

OECD (Organisation for Economic Co-operation and Development). (2009). *PISA 2006 Technical report.* Paris: OECD.

Pekrun, R., Elliot, A. J., & Maier, M. A. (2009). Achievement goals and achievement emotions: Testing a model of their joint relations with academic performance. *Journal of Educational Psychology, 101*, 115–35. doi: 10.1037/a0013383.

Pekrun, R., Frenzel, A. C., Goetz, T., & Perry, R. P. (2007). The control-value theory of achievement emotions: An integrative approach to emotions in education. In P. A. Schutz & R. Pekrun (Eds.), *Emotion in education* (pp. 13–36). San Diego, CA: Academic.

Pintrich, P. R. (2000). An achievement goal theory perspective on issues in motivation terminology, theory, and research. *Contemporary Educational Psychology, 25*, 92–104. doi: 10.1006/ceps.1999.1017.

Pintrich, P. R. & Maehr, M. L. (Eds.). (2002). *New directions in measures and methods: Advances in motivation and achievement* (Vol. 12). Oxford: Elsevier Science.

Pintrich, P. R., Smith, D., Garcia, T., & McKeachie, W. (1991). *A manual for the use of the Motivated Strategies for Learning Questionnaire (MSLQ).* Ann Arbor, MI: The University of Michigan.

Renninger, K. A. & Hidi, S. (2011). Revisiting the conceptualization, measurement, and generation of interest. *Educational Psychologist, 46*(3), 168–84. doi: 10.1080/00461520.2011.587723.

Rotgans, J. I. & Schmidt, H. G. (2011). Situational interest and academic achievement in the active-learning classroom. *Learning and Instruction, 21*, 58–67. doi: 10.1016/j.learninstruc.2009.11.001.

Ryan, R. M. & Deci, E. L. (2000). Intrinsic and extrinsic motivations: Classic definitions and new directions. *Contemporary Educational Psychology, 25*, 54–67. doi: 10.1006/ceps.1999.1020.

Scherer, R., Nilsen, T., & Jansen, M. (2016). Evaluating individual students' perceptions of instructional quality: An investigation of their factor structure, measurement invariance, and relations to educational outcomes. *Frontiers in Psychology, 7*, 110. doi: 10.3389/fpsyg.2016.00110.

Schulz, W. (2009). Questionnaire construct validation in the international civic and citizenship education study. *IERI Monograph Series, 2*, 85–107.

Schwinger, M., Steinmayr, R., & Spinath, B. (2016). Achievement goal profiles in elementary school: Antecedents, consequences, and longitudinal trajectories. *Contemporary Educational Psychology*, *46*(1), 164–79. doi: 10.1016/j.cedpsych.2016.05.006.

Shanley, L. (2016). Evaluating longitudinal mathematics achievement growth: Modeling and measurement considerations for assessing academic progress. *Educational Researcher, 45*(6), 347–57. doi: 10.3102/0013189X16662461.

Student Learning, Student Achievement Task Force. (2011). *Student learning, student achievement: How do teachers measure up?* Retrieved from https://eric.ed.gov/?id=ED517573.

Tempelaar, D. T., Gijselaers, W. H., van der Loeff, S. S., & Nijhuis, J. F. (2007). A structural equation model analyzing the relationship of student achievement motivations and personality factors in a range of academic subject-matter areas. *Contemporary Educational Psychology*, *32*(1), 105–31. doi: 10.1016/j.cedpsych.2006.10.004.

Tulis, M. & Ainley, M. (2011). Interest, enjoyment and pride after failure experiences? Predictors of students' state-emotions after success and failure during learning in mathematics. *Educational Psychology: An International Journal of Experimental Educational Psychology, 31*(7), 779–807. doi: org/10.1080/01443410.2011.608524.

Tulis, M. & Fulmer, S. M. (2013). Students' motivational and emotional experiences and their relationship to persistence during academic challenge in mathematics and reading. *Learning and Individual Differences, 27*, 35–46. doi: 10.1016/j.lindif.2013.06.003.

Tuominen-Soini, H., Salmela-Aro, K., & Niemivirta, M. (2011). Stability and change in achievement goal orientations: A person-centered approach. *Contemporary Educational Psychology, 36*, 82–100. doi: 10.1016/j.cedpsych.2010.08.002.

Urdan, T. C. & Mestas, M. (2006). The goals behind performance goals. *Journal of Educational Psychology, 97*(2), 354–65. doi: 10.1037/0022-0663.98.2.354.

Van de Vijver, F. J. R. & He, J. (2016). Bias assessment and prevention in noncognitive outcome measures in context assessments. In S. Kuger, E. Klieme, N. Jude, & D. Kaplan (Eds.), *Assessing contexts of learning: An international perspective.* (pp. 229–53). Cham: Springer.

Vygotsky, L. S. (1978). *Mind in society: The development of higher mental processes.* Cambridge, MA: Harvard University Press.

Wigfield, A. & Cambria, J. (2010). Students' achievement values, goal orientations, and interest: Definitions, development, and relations to achievement outcomes. *Developmental Review, 30*, 1–35. doi: 10.1016/j.dr.2009.12.001.

27 Addressing the Challenge of Measuring Student Engagement

Jennifer A. Fredricks, Tara L. Hofkens, and Ming-Te Wang

Abstract: *Student engagement is a relatively new construct that describes concepts as varied as classroom behaviors, emotional reactions, motivational beliefs, self-regulatory processes, metacognitive strategies, school belonging and interactions with instructional materials. This chapter reviews a variety of methods to measure student engagement including self-report surveys, teacher ratings, interviews, administrative data, observations, experience sampling methods, and real-time measures. The authors outline the strengths and limitations of each method. Next, we present two examples from our own research on approaches to measuring engagement. The goal of these cases is to illustrate how we have addressed some of the challenges with measurement, as well as showing the importance of choosing a measurement technique that aligns with the research questions. First, we describe the results of a qualitative study to develop a new subject-specific measure of engagement. Next, information on the predictive validity of an observational measure to assess engagement at the class-level is presented. The chapter concludes with a discussion of measurement limitations, future directions, and implications for policy and practice.*

The term "student engagement" is used to describe such varied concepts as classroom behaviors, emotional reactions, motivational beliefs, self-regulatory processes, metacognitive strategies, school belonging, and interactions with instructional materials. Over the past two decades, there has been an explosion of interest in the construct of student engagement. This increase is based on evidence linking engagement to indicators of positive academic adjustment (e.g., class attendance) and lower risk behavior (e.g., delinquency; Christenson et al., 2012; Fredricks et al., 2004; Wang & Fredricks, 2014). Moreover, engagement appears to hold tremendous potential as a locus for interventions, as it is assumed to be malleable, responsive to changes in social and academic factors, and influenced by personal characteristics (Appleton et al., 2008; Skinner & Pitzer, 2012).

As enthusiasm for the construct has grown, so too have concerns about inconsistencies in the definition and measurement of engagement (Appleton et al., 2008;

This chapter was supported in part by a grant from the National Science Foundation (1315943).

Azevedo, 2015; Fredricks & McColskey, 2012). The literature on engagement is also hampered by its limited attention to the theory that underpins the choice of measures (Azevedo, 2015; Sinatra et al., 2015). Too often the method for assessing engagement has driven the conceptualization of the construct, rather than the construct definition and theoretical framework determining the way to assess engagement (Sinatra et al., 2015). This lack of definitional and theoretical clarity has made it difficult to examine specific hypotheses about the relation between context and engagement, and to compare findings across studies.

Engagement has been studied in different hierarchal contexts (i.e., prosocial institutions, schools, classrooms, and discrete learning activities) and at different grain sizes, ranging from engagement at the macro-level (i.e., engagement in school or specific courses) to engagement at the micro-level (i.e., engagement in a discrete task or learning activity; Sinatra et al., 2015; Skinner & Pitzer, 2012). Whether there is a best measure of engagement is often unclear, given these different contexts and grain sizes. In this chapter, we review various methods to measure engagement, and we discuss the strengths and limitations of each approach. We then present two examples from our own research to illustrate different approaches to measuring engagement and the way we have addressed some of the challenges with measurement. We conclude with a discussion of limitations, future directions, and implications for policy and practice.

What Is Engagement?

There is broad agreement that engagement is a multidimensional construct describing the quality of involvement in an activity or learning context. The most prevalent conceptualization is that engagement consists of three distinct, yet interrelated, dimensions (Fredricks et al., 2004). *Behavioral engagement* has been defined in terms of involvement in classroom and school contexts, positive conduct, and absence of disruptive behaviors (Fredricks et al., 2004). *Emotional engagement* focuses on positive and negative reactions to teachers, classmates, academics, or school; a sense of belonging; and identification with school or subject domains (Finn, 1989; Voelkl, 1997). Finally, *cognitive engagement* is defined as the level of students' cognitive investment in learning, which includes being self-regulated and using deep learning strategies (Fredricks et al., 2004; Meece et al., 1988).

Recently, additional dimensions to the tripartite model of engagement have been proposed, though more research is necessary to determine if they are unique components. For example, some scholars have added social engagement as a fourth dimension, which has been defined by the quality of social interactions with peers and teachers in classroom tasks and in the broader school context (Rimm-Kaufman et al., 2015; Wang et al., 2016). Additionally, Reeve and Tseng (2011) proposed agentic engagement – which includes proactive, intentional, and constructive contributions to learning – as an additional dimension of engagement. Finally, we note that interest can be a component of meaningful engagement, and that many of the measurement issues are the same for both of these constructs (see Renninger & Hidi, 2016).

Most studies include surveys in which engagement and disengagement are operationalized and measured on a single continuum, with lower levels of engagement indicating disengagement. However, some researchers have begun to view engagement and disengagement as separate and distinct constructs that are associated with distinct learning outcomes (Skinner et al., 2009; Wang et al., 2015, 2016). Researchers also differ on whether they only include characteristics (i.e., indicators such as effort or enjoyment), or whether they also include antecedents (i.e., facilitators such as teacher or peer support) and outcomes (such as grades or discipline) in the operationalization and measurement of student engagement (Lam et al., 2012; Skinner & Pitzer, 2012).

An unanswered question in studies of engagement concerns its relation to motivation. Motivational scholars examine the question of why people act, think, and do what they do. In general, motivational theories have explained these motives in terms of individuals' underlying beliefs, goals, and values (Eccles & Wigfield, 2002). In contrast, engagement scholars have placed a greater emphasis on an individual's interaction with context (Fredricks et al., 2004). In other words, an individual is engaged in something (i.e., a task, activity, or relationship), and their engagement is conceptualized as indistinguishable from the thing with which they are engaging. Engagement is considered to be malleable and responsive to the variations in context that schools can target in interventions (Fredricks et al., 2004; Wang & Degol, 2014). Engagement also tends to be thought of in terms of action, or the behavioral, emotional, and cognitive manifestations of motivation (Skinner et al., 2009).

Methods for Studying Engagement

In the next section, we review different methods for studying engagement, at both the macro- and micro-levels, and highlight the strengths and limitations of each approach. We also provide some examples of ways the methods can be employed together.

Self-Reports

The most common way to assess engagement in school and in specific subject areas is self-reporting. In this methodology, students typically respond to a series of Likert-type questions about their behaviors, attitudes, and experiences. Surveys, in particular, are practical, and can be given to large and diverse samples of children in classroom settings at a relatively low cost. This makes it possible to gather data on both engagement and contextual factors at multiple times, to compare results across schools, and to test different models of the relation between contextual factors and engagement over time. Collecting data on students' perceptions may be a more valid way of understanding how students make meaning of their experiences than other methods (e.g., teacher report) that can be highly inferential (Appleton et al., 2008).

Despite these strengths, there are concerns about researchers' reliance on self-report methodologies, which are based on the assumption that engagement is stable and can be measured outside of students' actual involvement in learning tasks (Greene & Azevedo, 2010). In responding to survey items, students need to aggregate their perceptions and reflect on their experiences over numerous learning tasks. As a result, self-report methods often do not align with actual or real-time behaviors or strategy use (Greene, 2015; Winne & Perry, 2000). The validity of students' self-report responses also depends on students' level of reading comprehension, making it difficult to use this method to assess engagement for students who read below grade level.

Additional limitations of self-report surveys were outlined in Fredricks and McColskey's (2012) review of measures to assess elementary through high school students' engagement. They reported that of the 14 self-report surveys identified in the review, nine measured engagement at the school level and only five measured engagement in specific subject areas. Second, only five of the measures included items to reflect a multidimensional conceptualization of engagement, with most including only one or two of the dimensions. Third, there was often a mismatch between the choice of items and theoretical conceptions of engagement, with similar items often being used to assess different dimensions of engagement. Finally, they noted that there was limited evidence to support the construct and predictive validity of these survey measures.

Teacher Ratings

There are a few examples of teacher rating scales that have been developed by researchers to assess student engagement at the school and classroom level (Fredricks & McColskey, 2012). Some of these rating scales include items about behavioral and emotional engagement (Skinner et al., 2009), while others include items that reflect a multidimensional model of engagement (i.e., behavioral, emotional, and cognitive; Wang et al., 2016; Wigfield et al., 2008). Teacher rating scales may be more appropriate than self-report methods for younger children due to reading demands and their limited literacy skills (Fredricks & McColskey, 2012). They also are easy to collect and allow for comparison across students. Ratings of student behavior have also been used by researchers and practitioners to identify and screen for behaviors that either support or impede academic and social functioning (e.g., Lane et al., 2012). For example, the Systematic Screening for Behavioral Disorders is an evidence-based teacher rating scale that has been used to identify students who are at risk for internalizing (e.g., not talking to other students) and externalizing (e.g., displays aggression towards objects and persons) behaviors (Walker & Severson, 1992).

Another benefit of using teacher ratings is that they allow scholars to examine the correspondence between students' and teachers' perceptions of engagement in the classroom. Teachers tend to be more accurate reporters of behavioral engagement because these indicators are directly observable. In contrast, emotional and cognitive engagement tend to be more difficult for teachers to assess since students can mask their emotions and teachers have to infer how students engage cognitively with a task based on behavioral indicators (Skinner et al., 2009). Additionally, there are concerns that teachers may both overestimate and underestimate actual behaviors about potential rater bias as a result of both student characteristics (e.g., disability, gender, and socioeconomic status) and teacher characteristics (e.g., knowledge of disability and prior experience; Mason et al., 2014).

Interviews and Focus Groups

A few studies have used qualitative techniques including individual interviews and focus groups with teachers and students to assess engagement and disengagement in school (e.g., Blumenfeld et al., 2005; Conchas, 2001; Fredricks et al., 2016). These methods can describe both the "how" (the ways that teachers and students conceptualize and make meaning of engagement) and the "why" (the process by which psychological and contextual factors influence engagement over time). Qualitative methods have several strengths including enabling researchers to (1) collect data based on participants' own categories and meanings in their own words, (2) study a limited number of cases in depth, (3) describe in rich detail engagement as embedded in local contexts, and (4) identify and describe the contextual factors related to engagement (Johnson & Onwuegbuzie, 2004).

Despite these benefits, qualitative methods have some limitations. Because of the larger resources that are necessary for collecting and analyzing interview data, studies using these methods often include only a small number of participants, which can raise concerns about the generalizability of their findings to other settings. The knowledge, skills, and biases of the interviewer also can impact the quality, depth, and type of responses. As a result, interviewers need to be well-trained and have strong interpersonal skills (Tolan & Deutsch, 2015). Finally, there are questions about the reliability (stability and consistency) and validity of interview findings, especially with more open-ended interview protocols (Fredricks & McColskey, 2012).

Administrative (or Institutional) Data

Another method for collecting data on engagement is to use administrative, or institutional, data that have already been collected and is available in school records. Examples include attendance, truancy, credits earned, homework completion, graduation rates, problem behaviors, and assignment submissions (Appleton et al., 2008; Mandernach, 2015). One benefit of using administrative data to assess engagement is that it is collected on all students and is easily accessible. In addition, these indicators tend to be meaningful and easily understood by practitioners, and are often aligned with district and school priorities. However, one concern is that there is often not a clear demarcation between indicators and outcomes of engagement, such as grades, discipline, and number of credits. This lack of clear demarcation between indicators and outcomes makes it more difficult to explore the consequences of engagement (Lam et al., 2012). Additionally, there are concerns about potential biases in reporting of some indicators of disengagement by student characteristics (e.g., race, socioeconomic status, special education status). For example, low-socioeconomic-status students; minorities, especially African American students; and boys have been overrepresented in school disciplinary sanctions (e.g., office referrals, suspensions, and expulsions; Skiba et al., 2002). Finally, administrative data are typically indicators of behavioral engagement and disengagement and provide limited insight into the other dimensions of engagement.

Observational Methods

Another technique to assess engagement is to observe the level of engagement for individual children or for whole classes of students. The majority of these observational measures assess whether indicators of behavioral engagement such as on-task behavior, compliance, attention, participation, and disruptive behavior are present or absent during a defined time interval (Ponitz et al., 2009; Rimm-Kaufman et al., 2009; Volpe et al., 2005). Some studies score the average engagement of students in a class (e.g., Pianta et al., 2007), while others aggregate individual measures of behavioral engagement to form a single global indicator of behavioral engagement at the classroom level (e.g., Briesch et al., 2015).

Aggregating individual ratings to the classroom level assumes that student engagement is relatively homogeneous. However, recent studies using person-centered approaches show that student engagement can be quite different for each individual in the classroom or school based on personal characteristics and individual interactions with context (Wang & Decol, 2014; Wang & Peck, 2013). Given that individual differences in student engagement are associated with different learning outcomes, it might be inappropriate to aggregate individual measures of student engagement to create a global indicator at the classroom level.

Rather than assessing engagement with prespecified observational categories, other studies have used narrative and discourse analysis to measure engagement (Engle & Conant, 2002; Gresalfi, 2009; Nystrand & Gamarond, 1991; Ryu & Lombardi, 2015). This literature has been informed by sociocultural views of learning, and has focused on the processes by which students come to engage in groups, activities, and communities through the sharing and negotiating of norms, values, and resources (Ryu & Lombardi, 2015). These studies have observed the quality of instructional discourse between the individual and the group in a specific course, and have assessed teacher questioning and the development of student argumentation as evidence of disciplinary and substantive engagement.

Observational methods can provide a rich description of both engagement and learning environments. This information can be used to suggest emerging patterns of engagement that warrant further exploration, as well as to identify potential triggers of engagement and disengagement. Because observations are grounded in practice, these measures of student engagement are also useful to practitioners and can provide deep insight into a particular case (Renninger & Bachrach, 2015). Furthermore, these techniques can enhance our understanding of the unfolding of engagement in real time within both individual and group contexts (Fredricks & McColskey, 2012).

Despite these benefits, there also are several challenges with observational methods. Scholars need to make decisions about the appropriate time frame (e.g., continuous duration, momentary time sampling, or partial or whole interval recording), the setting in which observations are conducted (e.g., whole class, small group work, or seat work), the unit of analysis (i.e., individual or classroom level), the level of specificity (i.e., predetermined categories or more descriptive techniques), and the level of obtrusiveness (i.e., low intrusiveness or high obstructiveness) (Waxman et al., 2004; Wood et al., 2016). Observations can be time-consuming to conduct and analyze. Since these techniques tend to involve only a small number of students or contexts, there are questions about the generalizability of such findings to different social and cultural contexts (Waxman et al., 2004).

There are also concerns about the reliability of observational methods and potential observer biases, as the quality of the observation depends on the observer's ability to capture and make sense of what was observed (Turner & Meyer, 2000). Furthermore, individual observational measures focus on behavioral indicators and provide limited information on the quality of effort, participation, or thinking (Fredricks et al., 2004). Finally, there is limited information on the predictive validity of these observational techniques and the relation between these indicators and achievement-related outcomes (Fredricks & McColskey, 2012).

Experience Sampling

Another way to collect data on student engagement in specific courses and learning contexts is to use the experience sampling method (ESM; Shernoff et al., 2003; Uekawa et al., 2007; Yair, 2000). In this methodology, individuals carry smart phones or electronic pagers or alarm watches for a set time period. In response to ESM signals on their devices, students fill out a self-report questionnaire that asks about their location, activities, and cognitive and affective responses. ESM grew out of research on "flow," a high level of engagement in which individuals are so deeply absorbed in a task that they lose awareness of time and space (Shernoff & Csikzentmihalyi, 2009). One benefit of ESM is that it allows researchers to examine engagement as it occurs in real time and in specific contexts, which reduces problems with recall failure and answering in socially desirable ways (Hektner et al., 2007). Additionally, this technique can be used to compare engagement levels both within and across contexts. For example, using ESM techniques, researchers have found that high school students report the lowest levels of engagement in classroom settings and the highest levels of engagement in organized out-of-school contexts (Larson, 2000; Larson & Kleiber, 1993).

Despite these benefits, there are some challenges with this methodology. ESM requires a large time investment from respondents, and the success of the method depends largely on participants' ability and willingness to comply. Moreover, because this methodology requires frequent responses to survey items, there are concerns about hasty completion, exaggeration, and deliberation falsification (Shernoff et al., 2003). Since the data collected through this technique is relatively limited, it also provides limited insight into individual characteristics and aspects of classroom context that may help explain variations in engagement. Furthermore, there are concerns that the multidimensional nature of engagement may not be adequately captured by the small number of items included in ESM studies (Fredricks & McColskey, 2012). Finally, there are questions about the feasibility of using ESM techniques in classroom settings so that data collection is not disruptive and distracting.

Real-Time Measures

Engagement is assumed to be dynamic, fluctuating, and context dependent, although several of the measures (i.e., self-report, teacher report, and administrative data) assess engagement in one context at one point in time. Recently, a few scholars have attempted to account for the unfolding of engagement over time by using real-time measures in the context of discrete learning activities (Gobert et al., 2015; Miller, 2015; Shen et al., 2009). For example, some scholars have used log files, or the electronic interactions that occur as students work in online learning environments, to measure behavioral and cognitive engagement

(Azevedo et al., 2010; Gobert et al., 2015). Some examples of indicators of engagement collected through log files include (1) the number of posts to a discussion board, (2) the number of pages viewed in an online resource, (3) the number of edits made during a writing task, and (4) the number of times reading a text. Additionally, log files can provide information on disengagement in terms of the extent to which a student takes advantage of the properties in an online system to complete the task rather than deeply thinking through the material, and the amount of time a student is off task, such as when a student is surfing the Internet for material unrelated to the learning task (Azevedo et al., 2010; Gobert et al., 2015; Henrie et al., 2015). Another real-time method used to collect data on engagement involves eye tracking techniques, which record patterns of eye movement, such as whether a student fixates on a work or object, whether a student looks back and forth over a text, or whether a student skips a word (Boucheix et al., 2013; Duchowski, 2007; Miller, 2015). The assumption with eye tracking data is that people look longer at some words or images because they are thinking more deeply about these objects or are more cognitively engaged (Miller, 2015).

The electroencephalogram (EEG) technique is another method that has been used to collect data on engagement in real time. In this neurological test, electrodes are placed on the scalp to measure electrical activity produced by the brain during authentic learning activities (Antonenko et al., 2010). Brain activity detected from EEG data has been positively associated with speed and accuracy while solving chemistry problems (Stevens et al., 2008) and with the level of difficulty of a reading passage (Mostow et al., 2011). These studies suggest that EEG methods can provide an accurate measure of cognitive effort, which is a key indicator of cognitive engagement.

Other researchers have used devices to measure physiological phenomena associated with an emotional response or experience. One example is a bracelet that has been used to measure galvanic skin response (e.g., Arroyo et al., 2009; McNeal et al., 2014; Poh et al., 2010). Others have used galvanic skin response techniques in combination with blood pressure readings and electroencephalography to measure emotional engagement (Shen et al., 2009).

There are several benefits to using these newer real-time measures to assess engagement. First, these measures are more precise and give information on engagement levels as it occurs in real time in the context of a discrete learning activity. This allows researchers to collect large amounts of data over very short time periods, and to assess and model changes in engagement over time. Additionally, these techniques do not require participants to stop an activity to respond to survey questions (Miller, 2015). There also are potential practical applications to using these techniques. For example, scientists are using facial recognition and physiological data on emotional engagement to build adaptive learning systems that can apply behavioral strategies and emotional support to bolster learning (Kapoor et al., 2007; Shen et al., 2009). Although these initial efforts are intriguing, there still remain significant questions about how to reliably collect real-time data on emotions and use this information to build adaptive systems that can intervene with students to positively impact learning.

Despite these benefits, there are some limitations and many methodological questions concerning the use of real-time measures. Physiological devices can be complex and expensive, although technological advances continue to improve affordability (D'Mello & Graesser, 2012).

Some physiological devices are difficult to use in real educational settings, either because the devices themselves are cumbersome or because the physiological phenomena they are measuring are affected by other physiological processes, like sweating or movement (Henrie et al., 2015). Furthermore, data on nervous system arousal can be difficult to interpret without supplemental self-report or observational information that indicates whether the physiological arousal detected is indicative of positive or negative emotions (Henrie et al., 2015).

Because these methods are relatively new, there are also questions about the appropriate sampling frequency, time between observations, and level of granularity. These methods result in large volumes of data, and there are few guidelines on how to select the appropriate unit of analysis, how to ensure the validity of these data, and how to discover patterns and relationships in these data. Moreover, these methods are best suited to well-structured tasks that are often presented on a computer (Miller, 2015) or in highly controlled experimental settings (Antonenko et al., 2010). As a result, it is not clear whether, and if so how, this technique can be used in more complex and less structured learning environments and classroom tasks. Finally, the way these techniques can account for individual and contextual factors that may explain variations in student engagement is unclear.

Case Examples

In the next sections of this chapter, we describe two examples from our own research to show how we have combined different methods in order to address some of the methodological challenges involved in measuring engagement.

First, we describe how we used interviews and focus groups to develop and validate the Math and Science Engagement Scales (Wang et al., 2016). As we noted earlier, there are only a few multidimensional measures of engagement that have been developed for use in specific subject areas. This has made it difficult to examine which aspects of engagement are general and which aspects of engagement are subject specific. Our goal in this work was to use qualitative methods to help us better understand the way potential respondents of survey measures (i.e., teachers and students) conceptualize engagement and the language they use to describe its indicators. Talking to the potential respondents may increase the validity of the scales by helping determine points of convergence and divergence between researchers and the target population, as well as by identifying potential unexplored or untapped aspects of the construct (Gelhbach & Brinkworth, 2011).

In the second example, we present preliminary observational data on students' behavioral engagement drawn from a study of secondary school students' engagement in mathematics classes. Specifically, we describe how we used observational approaches to measure behavioral engagement at the classroom level, and how we tested the predictive validity of these methods by examining the relation between behavioral engagement and academic achievement. The aim of this observational study was to examine how students' behavioral engagement in mathematics classes contributes to mathematics achievement at the student level. Observational methods are useful for informing our understanding of how classroom-level processes shape the outcomes of individual students using data that has a higher degree of face validity than aggregated student self-reports.

Case 1: Using Qualitative Methods to Develop and Validate the Math and Science Engagement Scales

In this section, we present an example of how we used both interviews and focus groups to develop and validate the Math and Science Engagement Scales (Wang et al., 2016). We used the steps outlined by Gelhbach and Brinkworth (2011) to develop our student self-report measure of engagement and enhance the ecological validity of our scales. First, we reviewed the academic literature for different conceptualizations of student engagement, existing survey instruments of engagement, and related constructs. Next, we conducted in-depth interviews with 34 middle and high school teachers, and conducted interviews and focus groups with 106 middle and high school students, to learn how they conceptualized engagement and disengagement in math and science, as well as the factors that influenced their levels of engagement and disengagement (see Fredricks et al., 2016 for more discussion of this method).

We wanted to consider how both teachers and students described engagement and disengagement with little prompting from interviewers. So we next asked more directed probing questions to see if their responses aligned with the conceptualizations of engagement as a multidimensional construct that have been outlined in the research literature and include behavioral, emotional, and cognitive components. We then compared indicators that were derived from a qualitative analysis of the interviews and focus groups against findings from our literature review and previous measures. The purpose of this comparison was to determine whether teachers and students included or excluded the same dimensions of engagement as researchers, as well as the language they used to describe this construct.

In our initial list of survey items, we included indicators that were mentioned by either students or teachers but were not identified in the research, as well as items from prior measures of engagement that were not mentioned in the interviews. To ensure that our list of items corresponded to the construct of engagement, we had eight experts rate the items on both clarity and relevance. As a result of this feedback, we changed the wording of some items, added items about basic levels of behavioral engagement and the use of surface-level cognitive strategies, and dropped items that might be misinterpreted by students (see Fredricks et al., 2016 for more examples). Finally, we cognitively pretested the revised items with several focus groups of low- and high-achieving middle and high school students to assess the validity of these items. These interviews revealed that students did not understand the wording of some of our items, and they thought some items did not apply to both math and science (e.g., memorizing steps of a problem only applies to math). As a result of this feedback, we deleted some items and changed the wording to better reflect students' understanding and language.

We found that many of the indicators developed through the qualitative analysis overlapped with and validated current conceptualizations of engagement, including indicators of behavioral engagement (e.g., paying attention), affective or emotional engagement (e.g., enjoyment), and cognitive engagement (e.g., applying or connecting ideas). However, our qualitative analysis also revealed additional indicators – such as negative emotions like frustration and anger, and doing extra to learn more – that have tended not to be included in other measures of engagement. Furthermore, our qualitative analysis supported the inclusion of a social dimension of engagement, which has not typically been included in engagement measures. Indicators included items that reflect social affective (e.g., caring about others' ideas) and social cognitive (e.g., building on others' ideas) dimensions of group interactions. Our qualitative interviews also revealed some differences in the way students and teachers conceptualize engagement. For example, students were more likely to discuss competence (showing their mastery of math and science) as indicative of engagement, and were less likely than teachers to talk about engagement in terms of cognitive indicators.

Findings from our qualitative analysis also raise questions about the extent to which engagement is domain general and the extent to which it varies across subject areas. For example, many of the indicators (like attention and effort) were not necessarily unique to math and science and have been included in other measures of engagement. However, we also noted some aspects of engagement that have been less likely to be included in prior measures and may be more specific to math and science (such as being frustrated, solving problems in different ways, and building on ideas). Finally, our interviews revealed some domain-specific differences in the indicators of engagement. For example, students were more likely to discuss negative emotions (such as boredom, frustration, and anxiety in math) and to include social indicators (such as sharing and contributing to others' ideas in science).

In sum, the use of qualitative methods helped us validate the conceptualization of engagement outlined in the literature. Talking to the potential respondents of a survey increased the ecological validity of the construct by determining points of convergence and divergence between researchers and the target population, as well as by identifying potential unexplored or untapped aspects of this construct. Information from these interviews suggested ways to revise current measures to include aspects of engagement that are not typically included in current self-report surveys (e.g., social engagement) and to adapt wording of items to more closely reflect the language teachers and students use to describe this construct. Finally, the use of qualitative methods raised some questions to explore in future work on the potential differences between raters (i.e., teachers and students) in conceptualizations of engagement, and differences in the indicators of engagement across domains. For example, it is not clear whether the more socially focused indicators of engagement would exist in all other subject areas, or whether they are more common in math and science because of the instructional emphasis on collaboration, complex problem solving, abstract reasoning, and argumentation and explanation (Sinatra et al., 2015).

Case 2: Measuring Engagement with Observational Techniques

In this case, we describe how we developed and used an observational measure of adolescents' behavioral engagement at the classroom level in our longitudinal STEM engagement study. Studying engagement at the classroom level can enhance our understanding of students' engagement in groups, which may, in turn, help us understand how students' engagement as a group contributes to variance in student outcomes. Since student engagement is usually conceptualized and measured at the student level, researchers interested in measuring or studying classroom-level engagement often aggregate student self-reports. However, whether the data produced by aggregating individual self-reports accurately captures student engagement at the classroom level is unclear. Students' reports of their academic behaviors are susceptible to social desirability bias, and students may be limited in their ability to accurately reflect upon and assess their past experiences. In addition, aggregating student-level data to predict student-level outcomes does not allow for heterogeneity within classrooms, or for the fact that student perceptions and aggregated composites of classroom engagement may differentially predict student outcomes. Observational assessment has the potential to address these limitations by providing real-time, *in situ* assessments of engagement based on behavioral evidence assessed by an outside observer at the classroom level.

In order to investigate the reliability and validity of using observer reports to study student outcomes, we included an observational assessment of students' behavioral engagement in mathematics. Specifically, we used the engagement dimension of the Classroom Assessment Scoring System for secondary school students (CLASS-S), an observational tool that provides an assessment of classroom quality in terms of emotional climate, classroom management, and instructional supports for learning processes (Pianta et al., 2007). The CLASS-S framework has been adapted for secondary classrooms and includes a global measure of students' behavioral engagement in class. Specifically, the measure captures "the extent to which all students in class are focused and participating in the learning activity presented or facilitated by the teacher" (p. 109), and is assessed with behavioral indicators of engagement like responding, asking questions, volunteering, actively listening, and lacking off-task behavior (Pianta et al., 2012). In large-scale validation studies, the engagement dimension of CLASS-S has been shown to have fair inter-rater agreement (exact or adjacent agreement of 76.6 percent) and has been indicated by raters as easy to score (Kane et al., 2014). Classroom engagement scores on CLASS-S have also been linked to middle school teachers' value-added scores on state standardized tests in New York (Grossman et al., 2013). Thus, there is preliminary evidence that observational measures of student engagement predict important achievement outcomes.

During the 2015–16 academic school year, we videotaped 33 math classrooms consisting of 33 teachers and 492 fifth, seventh, and ninth grade students. The student sample was 41 percent Caucasian, 52 percent African American, and 49 percent female. 54 percent of students qualified for free or reduced-price school lunches. The average class size was 15 students. One morning class period taught by each math teacher in the study was observed. The videotapes were scored for students' behavioral engagement in class by having raters certified in CLASS-S divide the lesson into two consecutive 20-minute segments, code the segments separately, and then average the scores from the two coded segments. All video segments were coded by two raters, and the final score for each class period was calculated by averaging across the scores assigned by each rater. The coding team attended weekly reliability meetings and attained high reliability on the engagement dimension (Interclass correlation = 0.856). Additionally, we collected student demographics and achievement information from school records at the end of the academic year (see Table 27.1 for descriptive statistics).

To examine the relationship between observational scores of classroom behavioral engagement and student achievement in mathematics, we ran multi-level regression models in Mplus (Version 7.3; Muthén & Muthén, 1998–2014), which allowed us to account for the clustering of students within classrooms. First, we ran a fully unconditional model (Model 1) to estimate the proportion of variance of students' mathematics course grades that were within- and between-class components. Next, in Model 2, we added characteristics at the student level, including student gender, race (binary indicator of Caucasian or non-Caucasian), socioeconomic status (binary indicator of ineligibility for free or reduced-price lunch), and prior achievement (students' grade point average from the previous academic year [2014–15]). Finally, in Model 3, we added observer ratings of students' behavioral engagement at the classroom level.

Table 27.1 *Descriptive statistics of student- and classroom-level predictors and achievement outcomes (N = 492 secondary school students)*

Variable	N	Percent	Mean	SD	Range from	to
Student-level predictors						
Female	240	48.78				
Race						
Caucasian	185	40.57				
African American	237	51.97				
Asian	8	1.75				
Hispanic or Latinx/a	3	0.66				
Multi-racial	21	4.61				
Other	2	0.44				
Free or reduced-price lunch	264	53.66				
Previous achievement	362		3.22	0.80	0	4.0
Classroom-level predictor						
Observer report of student (behavioral) engagement	33		4.29	1.15	2.0	6.5
Student Outcomes						
Math course grade 2015–16	409		84.57	11.62	19.0	100.0

Our results demonstrate the relation between students' behavioral engagement and mathematics achievement (see Table 27.2). First, the intra-class correlation of 0.40 in the fully unconditional model (Model 1) confirms that a significant amount of variance in individual student's math achievement is explained at the classroom level. Second, Model 3 reveals that observational reports of students' behavioral engagement in mathematics class positively predict students' math course grades, even after controlling for student gender, minority status, and indicators of socioeconomic status and previous achievement. Specifically, every one-point increase in students' overall behavioral engagement in mathematics class was associated with a 3.83 increase in mathematics grades.

In sum, we found that observational methods were a useful tool for assessing classroom engagement and demonstrated good predictive validity. Observational scores were determined by a trained rater over 40 minutes of a class period and demonstrated high face validity. In addition to overcoming the potential for bias or inaccurate assessment inherent in student self-reports, observational methods had the additional advantage of being amenable to administrators and teachers because video recording did not result in loss

Table 27.2 *Hierarchical linear models predicting math achievement with student covariates and observer reports of students' behavioral engagement*

	Model 1: Fully unconditional model		Model 2: Covariates only		Model 3: Observational report of student behavioral engagement	
	β	(SE)	β	(SE)	β	(SE)
Fixed effects	77.23**	(2.04)	75.57**	(2.07)	75.88**	(1.88)
Level 1: Student						
Female			3.39*	(1.12)	3.38*	(1.11)
White			5.68**	(1.44)	5.44**	(1.45)
Free or reduced-price lunch			−3.55**	(0.96)	−3.58**	(0.97)
Previous GPA			−0.06	(0.04)	−0.04**	(0.04)
Level 2: Classroom						
Observational report of student behavioral engagement					3.83**	(1.00)
Random effects						
Between level variance, u_0	108.43*	(37.17)	77.81**	(29.01)	55.20*	(22.80)
Within level variance, r	160.31**	(28.73)	149.87**	(26.97)	150.61**	(27.08)
Intra-class correlation	0.403		0.320		0.313	
Pseudo R-squared						
Level 1			0.065		0.065	
Level 2			0.282		0.491	

*$p < 0.05$
**$p < 0.001$

of instructional time. Despite these strengths, it is worth noting that we do not know how much the presence of the video camera changed instruction, teacher–student interactions, or students' engagement in class. It is also not clear how typical the class period was for that class or group of students. In order to address these issues, future studies should conduct observations over multiple days of instruction.

Concluding Thoughts

In this chapter, we have pointed to the challenges of assessing engagement. When possible, we recommend using multiple methods to assess engagement, and we recognize that the integration of different methodologies adds additional complexity, such as the appropriate time frame and the temporal sequence for collecting different types of data. There are also questions about how variations in the learning environment influence the measures that are appropriate for assessing engagement. Much of the research using real-time measures has been conducted in very structured learning contexts, and there are questions about whether and how these findings generalize to other learning tasks or settings. Furthermore, there are practical challenges with assessing engagement in classroom contexts in a way that is unobtrusive and does not disrupt the flow of learning.

There are also questions about how to best integrate results from different methodologies. To date, there are few examples of ways to triangulate data collected from different methods, or how to reconcile discrepant and sometimes contradictory information about engagement levels provided by different methods. For example, prior research has shown only moderate correlations between teachers' and students' reports of students' engagement, with higher correlations for behavioral than emotional engagement (Skinner et al., 2009). Teachers may be better able to report on behavioral engagement because these indicators are more likely to be directly observable, whereas students may be better reporters of their emotional and cognitive engagement. However, even though students may have "better access" to these internal states than observers and teachers, they may not always be aware of them – especially younger children – in which case combining student self-report and interview data with teacher, observer, or physiological data can help get a more holistic and accurate assessment of engagement levels.

A continuing challenge in measuring engagement is the lack of definitional clarity about engagement (Azevedo, 2015; Fredricks & McColskey, 2012). This makes it difficult to compare and meaningfully interpret findings across different methodologies. Engagement research has come out of a variety of theoretical and disciplinary traditions, which has led to large variations in both the operationalization and the measurement of this construct. In future research, scholars need to more clearly articulate how they define engagement, describe how their conceptualization is similar or different from other related educational constructs, and articulate the theoretical framework underpinning the measurement of this construct. Furthermore, it is critical that both theory and research questions drive the choice of method, as opposed to the assessment technique determining the theoretical perspective and questions.

One of the reasons that engagement has had such appeal is that it represents a shift from a focus on individual characteristics to consideration of contextual factors that can be targeted in an intervention (Fredricks & McColskey, 2012; Wang & Degol, 2014). Unfortunately, methods used to assess engagement do so in one context and at one point in time, which has made it difficult to answer questions regarding the malleability of this construct and identify the source of engagement (Sinatra et al., 2015). On one hand, macro-level measures are much easier to administer, but often measure engagement outside of a learning context and fail to capture the dynamic and fluctuating nature of engagement. On the other hand, micro-level measures are more precise and assess engagement in real time in the context of real learning activities, but are also more difficult to administer and often lack the contextual information that could help explain engagement processes (Azevedo, 2015).

Implications for Policy and Practice

This chapter highlights different ways of conceptualizing and measuring student engagement, and the strengths and weakness of each. Given the potential importance of engagement for policy and practice and the variety of options for measuring engagement, it is important that scholars choose methods that match the theoretical conception and goals of the study.

More research is needed on which methods and survey instruments can be most easily adopted for use in policy and practice. One of the challenges with using measures of engagement to inform policy and practice is that these methods are not often easily accessible to educators and policymakers in a way that allows for comparison. To help address this concern, Fredricks et al. (2011) reviewed 21 survey and observational measures of engagement, and they provided information on the usage, administration, populations studied, measurement, and psychometric properties of these measures in a way that is more accessible to practitioners and policymakers.

Presently, many school districts use administrative data collected on student disengagement as part of an early warning system. Their goal is to identify students who are struggling earlier in their school career and use this data to direct students to appropriate interventions (Balfanz et al., 2007). However, there are questions about which indicators of disengagement can best identify those students who are most at risk, how school districts can collect and integrate this data into a school-based data system, and how educators should interpret this information and develop appropriate intervention plans (Appleton, 2012).

The measurement approaches outlined in this chapter can also be used to monitor engagement at the classroom, school, and district levels (Fredricks & McColskey, 2012). For example, the Institute for Research and Reform in Education collects survey data on student engagement as part of a structured process for planning, capacity building, and continuous school improvement (Connell et al., 2009). The Gwinnett County Public Schools have also been collecting survey data on student engagement as part of efforts to evaluate the effectiveness of district initiatives to increase student engagement (Appleton, 2012).

Furthermore, teachers can use these measures to track students' engagement in different instructional environments (i.e., whole class, small group, seat work, or large discussions) and different subject areas. Teachers can use data on engagement to more effectively design and implement learning experiences for their students, as well as to identify students who may need more individualized support. For example, the Instructional Practices Inventory is an observational tool that was developed for teacher leaders to collect data on engagement at the school level and to facilitate discussion of this data to influence instructional design and student learning (Valentine, 2005). The field would benefit immensely from additional examples of the ways educators and administrators have used engagement data to reflect on and make changes to their instructional strategies and school policies. Finally, in order for data on engagement to inform practice, educators will need to be provided with dedicated time, opportunities to collaborate with their peers, and professional development related to collecting, analyzing, and using engagement data.

References

Antonenko, P. Paas, F., Grabner, R. & van Gog, T. (2010). Using electroencephalography to measure cognitive load. *Educational Psychology Review, 22*, 425–38. doi: 10.1007/s10648-010-9130-y.

Appleton, J. J. (2012). Systems consultation: Developing the assessment-to-intervention link with the student engagement instrument. In S. Christenson, A. Reschly, & C. Wylie (Eds.), *Handbook of research on student engagement* (pp. 725–42). New York, NY: Springer.

Appleton, J. J., Christenson, S. L., & Furlong, M. J. (2008). Student engagement with school: Critical conceptual and methodological issues of the construct. *Psychology in the Schools, 45*, 369–86. doi: 10.1002/pits.20303.

Arroyo, I., Cooper, D. G., Burleson, W., Woolf, B. P., Muldner, K., & Christopherson, R. (2009). Emotion sensors go to school. *Conference on Artificial Intelligence in Education, 200*, 17–24.

Azevedo, R. (2015). Defining and measuring engagement and learning in science: Conceptual, theoretical, methodological, and analytical issues. *Educational Psychologist, 50*, 84–94. doi: 10.1080/00461520.2015.1004069.

Azevedo, R., Moos, D., Johnson, A., & Chauncey, A. (2010). Measuring cognitive and metacognitive regulatory processes used during hypermedia learning: Issues and challenges. *Educational Psychologist, 45*, 210–23. doi: 10.1080/00461520.2010.515934.

Balfanz, R., Herzog, L., & MacIver, P. J. (2007). Preventing student disengagement and keeping students on graduation path in urban middle grade schools: Early identification and effective interventions. *Educational Psychologist, 42*, 223–35. doi: 10.1080/00461520701621079.

Blumenfeld, P., Modell, J. Bartko, W. T., Secada, W., Fredricks, J., Friedel, J., & Paris, A. (2005). School engagement of inner city students during middle childhood. In C. R. Cooper, C. Garcia Coll, W. T. Bartko, H. M. Davis & C. Chatman (Eds.), *Developmental pathways through middle childhood: Rethinking diversity and contexts as resources* (pp. 145–70). Mahwah, NJ: Lawrence Erlbaum.

Boucheix, J. M., Lowe, R. K., Putri, D. K., & Groff, J. (2013). Cueing animations: Dynamic signaling aids information extraction and comprehension. *Learning and Instruction, 25*, 71–84. doi: 10.1016/j.learninstruc.2012.11.005.

Briesch, A. M., Hemphill, E. M., Volpe, R. J., & Daniels, B. (2015). An evaluation of observational methods for measuring response to class-wide intervention. *School Psychology Quarterly, 30*, 37–49. doi: 10.1037/spq0000065.

Christenson, S., Reschly, A., & Wylie C. (Eds.). (2012). *Handbook of research on student engagement*. New York, NY: Springer.

Conchas, G. Q. (2001). Structuring failure and success: Understanding the variability in Latino school engagement. *Harvard Educational Review, 71*, 475–504. doi: 10.17763/haer.71.3.280w814v1603473k.

Connell, J. P., Klem, A., Lacher, T., Leiderman, S., & Moore, W. (2009). *First things first: Theory, research, and practice*. Howell, NJ: Institute for Research and Reform in Education.

D'Mello, S. & Graesser, A. (2012). Dynamics of affective states during complex learning. *Learning and Instruction, 22*, 145–57. doi: 10.1016/j.learninstruc .2011.10.001.

Duchowski, A. (2007). *Eye tracking methodology: Theory and practice* (2nd ed.). New York, NY: Springer.

Eccles, J. S. & Wigfield, A. (2002). Motivational beliefs, values, and goals. *Annual Review of Psychology, 53*, 109–32. doi: 10.1146/annurev.psych.53.100901.135153.

Engle, R. A. & Conant, F. R. (2002). Guiding principles for fostering productive disciplinary engagement: Explaining an emergent argument in a community of learners' classroom. *Cognition and Instruction, 20*, 399–483. doi: 10.1207/ S1532690XCI2004_1.

Ferguson, R. F. & Danielson, C. (2014). How framework for teaching and tripod 7Cs evidence distinguish key components of effective teaching. *Designing Teacher Evaluation Systems*, 98–143.

Finn, J. D. (1989). Withdrawing from school. *Review of Educational Research, 59*, 117–42. doi: 10.3102/00346543059002117.

Fredricks, J. A., Blumenfeld, P. C. & Paris, A. (2004). School engagement: Potential of the concept: State of the evidence. *Review of Educational Research, 74*, 59–119. doi: 10.3102/00346543074001059.

Fredricks, J. A. & McColskey, W. (2012). The measurement of student engagement: A comparative analysis of various methods and student self-report instruments. In S. Christenson, A. L. Reschy, & C. Wylie (Eds.), *Handbook of research on student engagement* (pp. 763–83). New York, NY: Springer.

Fredricks, J., McColskey, W., Meli, J., Mordica, J., Montrosse, B., & Mooney, K. (2011). *Measuring student engagement in upper elementary through high school: A description of 21 instruments.* (Issues & Answers Report, REL 2010–No. 098). Washington, DC: US Department of Education, Institute of Education Sciences, National Center for Education. Available at http://ies.ed.gov/ncee/ edlabs/projects/project.asp?projectID=268.

Fredricks, J. A., Wang, M. T., Schall, J., Hofkens, T., Snug, H., Parr, A., & Allerton, J. (2016). Using qualitative methods to develop a survey of math and science engagement. *Learning and Instruction, 43*, 5–15. doi: 10.1016/ j.learninstruc.2016.01.009.

Gelhbach, H. & Brinkworth, M. E. (2011). Measure twice: cut down error: A process for enhancing the validity of survey scales. *Review of General Psychology, 15*, 380–7. doi: 10.1037/a0025704.

Gobert, J. D., Baker, R. S., & Wixon, M. B. (2015). Operationalizing and detecting disengagement within online science microworlds. *Educational Psychologist, 50*, 43–57. doi: 10.1080/00461520.2014.999919.

Greene, B. (2015). Measuring cognitive engagement with self-report scales: Reflections from over 20 years of research. *Educational Psychologist, 50*, 13–40. doi: 10.1080/00461520.2014.989230.

Greene, J. A. & Azevedo, R. (2010). The measurement of learners' self-regulated cognitive and metacognitive processes while using computer-based learning environments. *Educational Psychologist, 45*, 203–9. doi: 10.1080/00461520.2014.989230.

Gresalfi, M. S. (2009). Taking up opportunities to learn: Constructing dispositions in mathematics classrooms. *Journal of the Learning Sciences, 18,* 327–69. doi: 10.1080/10508400903013470.

Grossman, P., Loeb, S., Cohen, J. & Wyckoff, J. (2013). Measure for measure: The relationship between measures of instructional practice in middle school English language arts and teachers' value-added scores. *American Journal of Education, 50*, 4–36. doi: 10.1086/669901.

Hektner, J. M., Schmidt, J. A., & Csikzentmihalyi, M. (2007). *Experience sampling method: Measuring the quality of everyday life.* Thousand Oaks, CA: Sage Publications.

Henrie, C. R., Halverson, L. R., & Graham, C. R. (2015). Measuring student engagement in technology-mediated learning: A review. *Computers and Education, 90*, 36–53. doi: 10.1016/j.compedu.2015.09.005.

Johnson, R. W. & Onwuegbuzie, A. J. (2004). Mixed methods research: A research paradigm whose time has come. *Educational Researcher, 33*, 14–26. doi: 10.3102/0013189X033007014.

Kane, T., Kerr, K., & Pianta, R. (2014). *Designing teacher evaluation systems: New guidance from the measures of effective teaching project.* New York, NY: John Wiley & Sons.

Kapoor, A., Burleson, W., & Picard, R. W. (2007). Automatic prediction of failure. *International Journal of Human Computer Studies, 65*, 724–6. doi: 10.1016/j.ijhcs.2007.02.003.

Lam, S., Wong, B. P. H., Yang, H. & Liu, Y. (2012). Understanding student engagement with a contextual model. In S. Christenson, A. L. Reschy, & C. Wylie (Eds.), *Handbook of research on student engagement* (pp. 403–19). New York, NY: Springer.

Lane, K. L., Menzies, H. M, Oakes, W. P., & Kalberg, J. R. (2012). *Systematic screenings of behavior to support instruction: From preschool to high school.* New York, NY: Guilford Press.

Larson, R. W. (2000). Toward a psychology of positive youth development. *American Psychologist, 55*, 170–83. doi: 10.1037/0003-066X.55.1.170.

Larson, R. W. & Kleiber, D. (1993). Daily experiences of adolescents. In P. H. Tolan & B. J. Cohler (Eds.), *Handbook of clinical research and practice with adolescents* (pp. 125–45). Oxford: John Wiley.

Mandernach, J. (2015). Assessment of student engagement in higher education: A synthesis of literature and assessment tools. *International Journal of Learning, Teaching, and Educational Research, 12*, 1–14.

Mason, B., Gunersel, A. B., & Ney, E. (2014). Cultural and ethnic bias in teacher ratings of behavior: A criterion-focused review. *Psychology in the Schools, 51*, 1017–30. doi: 10.1002/pits.21800.

McNeal, K. S., Spry, J. M., Mitra, R., & Tipton, J. L. (2014). Measuring student engagement, knowledge, and perceptions of climate change in an introductory environment geology course. *Journal of Geoscience Education, 62*, 655–67. doi: 10.5408/13-111.1.

Meece, J., Blumenfeld, P. C., & Hoyle, R. H. (1988). Students' goal orientation and cognitive engagement in classroom activities. *Journal of Educational Psychology, 80*, 514–23. doi: 10.1037/0022-0663.80.4.514.

Miller, B. W. (2015). Using reading times and eye-movements to measure cognitive engagement. *Educational Psychologist, 50*, 31–42. doi: 10.1080/00461 520.2015.1004068.

Mostow, J., Chang, K. M., & Nelson, J. (2011, June). Toward exploiting EEG input in a reading tutor. In *International conference on artificial intelligence in education* (pp. 230–7). Berlin and Heidelberg: Springer.

Muthén, L. K. & Muthén, B. O. (1998–2014). *Mplus user's guide. Seventh edition.* Los Angeles, CA: Muthén & Muthén.

Nystrand, M. & Gamoran, A. (1991). Instructional discourse, student engagement, and literature achievement. *Research in the Teaching of English, 25*, 261–90.

Pianta, R. C., Hamre, B. K., Haynes, N. J., Mintz, S. L., & La Paro, K. M. (2007). *Classroom Assessment Scoring System Manual, Middle/Secondary Version.* Charlottesville, NC: University of Virginia Press.

Pianta, R. C., Hamre, B. K., & Mintz, S. L. (2012). *Classroom Assessment Scoring System (CLASS): Secondary class manual.* Charlottesville, VA: Teachstone.

Poh, M., Swenson, N. C., & Picard, R. W. (2010). A wearable sensor for unobtrusive, long-term assessment of electrodermal activity. *IEE Transactions on Biomedical Engineering, 57*, 1243–57.

Ponitz, C. C., Rimm-Kaufman, S. E., Grimm, K. J., & Curby, T. W. (2009). Kindergarten classroom quality, behavioral engagement, and reading achievement. *School Psychology Review, 38*, 102–20.

Reeve, J. M. & Tseng, C. (2011). Agency as a fourth aspect of students' engagement with learning activities. *Contemporary Educational Psychology, 36*, 357–67. doi: 10.1016/j.cedpsych.2011.05.002.

Renninger, K. A. & Bachrach, J. E. (2015). Studying triggers for interest and engagement using observational methods. *Educational Psychologist, 50*, 58–69. doi: 10.1080/00461520.2014.999920.

Renninger, K. A. & Hidi, S. (2016). *The power of interest for motivation and learning.* New York, NY: Routledge.

Rimm-Kaufman, S. E., Baroody, A. E., Larsen, R. A., Curby, T. W., & Abruy, T. (2015). To what extent do teacher-student interaction quality and student gender contribution to fifth graders' engagement in mathematics learning? *Journal of Educational Psychology, 107*, 17–185. doi: 10.1037/a0037252.

Rimm-Kaufman, S. E., Curby, T. W., Grimm, K. J., Nathanson, L., & Brock, L. (2009). The contribution of children's self-regulation and classroom quality to children's adaptive behaviors in the kindergarten classroom. *Developmental Psychology, 45*, 958–72. doi: 10.1037/a0015861.

Ryu, S. & Lombardi, D. (2015). Coding classroom interactions for collective and individual engagement. *Educational Psychologist, 50,* 70–83. doi: 10.1080/00461520.2014.1001891.

Shen, L., Wang, M., & Shen, R. (2009). Affective e-Learning: Using "emotional" data to improve learning in pervasive learning environment. *Educational Technology & Society, 12*(2), 176–89.

Shernoff, D. J. & Csikszentmihalyi, M. (2009). Flow in schools: Cultivating engaged learners and optimal learning environments. In R. Gilman, E. S. Huebner, & M. Furlong (Eds.), *Handbook of positive psychology in schools* (pp. 131–45). New York, NY: Routledge.

Shernoff, D. J., Csikzentmihalyi, M., Schneider, B., & Shernoff, E. S. (2003). Student engagement in high schools from the perspective of flow theory. *School Psychology Quarterly, 18,* 158–76. doi: 10.1521/scpq.18.2.158.21860.

Sinatra, G., Heddy, B. C., & Lombard, D. (2015). The challenge of defining and measuring student engagement in science. *Educational Psychologist, 1,* 1–13. doi: 10.1080/00461520.2014.1002924.

Skiba, R. J., Michael, R. S., Nardo, A. C., & Peterson, R. L. (2002). The color of discipline: Sources of racial and gender disproportionality in school punishment. *The Urban Review, 34,* 317–42. doi: 10.1023/A:1021320817372.

Skinner, E. A., Kindermann, T. A., & Furrer, C. J. (2009). A motivational perspective on engagement and disaffection. Conceptualization and assessment of children's behavioral and emotional participation in academic activities in the classroom. *Educational and Psychological Measurement, 69,* 493–525. doi: 10.1177/0013164408323233.

Skinner, E. A. & Pitzer, J. R. (2012). Developmental dynamics of student engagement, coping, and everyday resilience. In S. Christenson, A. L. Reschy, & C. Wylie (Eds.), *Handbook of research on student engagement* (pp. 21–45). New York, NY: Springer.

Stevens, R. H., Galloway, T. L., Berka, C., Johnson, R., & Sprang, M. (2008). Assessing student's mental representations of complex problem spaces with EEG technologies. In *Proceedings of the Human Factors and Ergonomics Society Annual Meeting* (Vol. 52, no. 3, pp. 167–71). Thousand Oaks, CA: SAGE Publications.

Tolan, P. H. & Deutsch, N. L. (2015). Mixed methods in developmental science. In R. Lerner (Ed.), *Handbook of child psychology and developmental science* (Vol. 1, 7th ed., 1–45), Hoboken, NJ: Wiley.

Turner, J. C. & Meyer, D. K. (2000). Studying and understanding the instructional context of classroom: Using our past to forge our future. *Educational Psychologist, 35,* 69–85. doi: 10.1207/S15326985EP3502_2.

Uekawa, K., Borman, K., & Lee, R. (2007). Student engagement in the U.S. urban high school mathematics and science classrooms: Findings on social organization, race, and ethnicity. *Urban Review, 39,* 1–43. doi: 10.1007/s11256-006-0039-1.

Valentine, J. (2005). *The instructional practices inventory: A process for profiling student engaged learning for school improvement.* Columbia, MO: University of Missouri, Middle Level Leadership Center. Retrieved at http://mllc.missouri.edu/Upload%20Area-Docs/IPI%20Manuscript%2012-07.pdf.

Voelkl, K. E. (1997). Identification with school. *American Journal of Education, 105,* 204–319. doi: 10.1086/444158.

Volpe, R. J., DiPerna, J. C., Hintze, J. M., & Shapiro, E. S. (2005). Observing students in classroom settings: A review of seven coding schemes. *School Psychology Review, 34*(4), 454–74.

Walker, H. & Severson, H. (1992). *Systematic Screening for Behavioral Disorders (SSBD)*. (2nd ed.). Technical Manual. Longmont, CA: Sopris West.

Wang, M. T., Chow, A., Hofkens, T., & Salmela-Aro, K. (2015). The trajectories of student emotional engagement and school burnout with academic and psychological development: Findings from Finnish adolescents. *Learning and Instruction, 36*, 57–65. doi: 10.1016/j.learninstruc.2014.11.004.

Wang, M. T. & Degol, J. (2014). Staying engaged: Knowledge and research needs in student engagement. *Child Development Perspectives, 8*, 137–43. doi: 10.1111/cdep.12073.

Wang, M. T. & Fredricks, J. A. (2014). The reciprocal links between school engagement and youth problem behavior during adolescence. *Child Development, 85*, 722–37. doi: 10.1111/cdev.12138.

Wang, M. T., Fredricks, J. A., Ye, F., Hofkens, T., & Schall, J. (2016). The math science engagement scale: Development, validation, and psychometric properties. *Learning and Instruction, 43*, 16–26. doi: 10.1016/j.learninstruc.2016.01.008.

Wang, M. T. & Peck, S. C. (2013). Adolescent educational success and mental health vary across school engagement profiles. *Developmental Psychology, 49*, 1266–76. doi: 10.1037/a0030028.

Waxman, H. C., Tharp, R. G., & Hilberg, R. S. (2004). Future directions for classroom observation research. In H. C. Waxman, R. S. Hilberg, & R. G. Tharp (Eds.), *Observational research in U.S. classrooms: New approaches for understanding cultural and linguistic diversity* (pp. 266–77). Cambridge: Cambridge University Press.

Wigfield, A., Guthrie, J. T., Perencevich, K. C., Taboada, A., Klauda, S. L., McRae, A., & Barbosa, P. (2008). Role of reading engagement in mediating the effects of reading comprehension instruction on reading outcomes. *Psychology in the Schools, 45*, 432–45. doi: 10.1002/pits.20307.

Winne, P. H. & Perry, N. E. (2000). Measuring self-regulated learning. In M. Boekaerts, P. Pintrich, & M. Zeidner (Eds.), *Handbook of self-regulation* (pp. 531–66). San Diego, CA: Academic Press.

Wood, B. K., Hojnoski, R. L., Laracy, S. D., & Olson, C. L. (2016). Comparison of observational methods and their relation to ratings of engagement in young children. *Topics in Early Childhood Special Education, 35*(4), 211. doi: 10.1177/0271121414565911.

Yair, G. (2000). Educational battlefields in America: The tug of war over students' engagement with instruction. *Sociology of Education, 73*, 247–69. doi: 10.2307/2673233.

28 Measuring Motivation in Educational Settings

A Case for Pragmatic Measurement

Jeff J. Kosovich, Chris S. Hulleman,
and Kenneth E. Barron

Abstract: A reality of conducting motivation research in educational settings is that there are tensions between technical standards of research and practical constraints of a given situation. Although adherence to standards for high-quality measurement is critical for good-quality data to be collected, measurement also requires substantial resources to ensure quality. In the current chapter, we discuss several examples of real data collected in different educational settings using a pragmatic measurement framework. Based on contemporary measurement perspectives, the pragmatic measurement framework emphasizes building evidence-based arguments to support the use and interpretation of a measure. Example 1 explores college students' attitudes toward general education classes. Example 2 tracks students' classroom motivation over several time points. Example 3 assesses experimental differences from an online motivation intervention. Together the three examples cover a range of possible research questions that researchers may encounter. As a whole, this chapter demonstrates that important and meaningful insights can be gained using pragmatic approaches to measurement. Importantly, we discuss the trade-offs that researchers or other measure users must consider when adopting a pragmatic approach to measurement.

Critical to any empirical investigation is the quality of its measurement. Regardless of whether a researcher adopts a descriptive, correlational, experimental, quantitative, or qualitative approach to answering a given research question, valid measurement is essential for drawing meaningful conclusions from research. However, commonly accepted practices for ensuring measurement quality can be at odds with other situational constraints of a research study. Consider the three scenarios below, which each highlight a tension between the technical standards of measurement and the practical constraints of the situation.

Scenario One: Undergraduate students often enroll in five classes per semester to fulfill major, minor, general education, and degree requirements. *Question:* How do students differ motivationally across a variety of coursework and why might those differences exist? *Measurement Tension:* Can we

This research was supported by the US Department of Education through a grant to the University of Virginia and by two National Science Foundation grants. The opinions expressed are those of the authors and do not represent views of the Institute of Education Sciences, the US Department of Education, or the National Science Foundation.

collect data on students' motivation in a way that provides high-quality data but does not frustrate students (i.e., does not require them to fill out the same lengthy survey for each class in which they are enrolled)?

Scenario Two: Research has demonstrated that student motivation declines from year to year, starting in first grade and continuing through high school (Jacobs et al., 2002). *Question:* Are the patterns of motivational decline consistent throughout the school year or are there high points and low points? *Measurement Tension:* How can multiple types of motivation be measured frequently throughout the school year without disrupting class time or frustrating students?

Scenario Three: Motivation interventions can help improve student motivation and academic success (Lazowski & Hulleman, 2016). *Question:* If researchers were asked to develop a brief motivation intervention that could be delivered in a class in 15 minutes or less, could they effectively change students' motivation? *Measurement Tension:* How can measures of motivation be included to evaluate the effectiveness of an intervention in 15 minutes or less?

Each of these scenarios describes different real-world questions that "measure users" (i.e., researchers, practitioners, policymakers, measure developers) may have regarding student motivation. Each scenario also identifies tensions between the technical demands of high-quality measurement and situational constraints that may make it difficult to answer the proposed questions. Although motivation plays a critical role in students' education, it is rarely assessed as often or as comprehensively as learning or achievement. Situational constraints in educational settings and applied research often limit how much, if any, information can be collected about students' motivation.

The purpose of our chapter is to describe the use of a flexible method of assessing measure quality in applied settings. We refer to this set of methods as *pragmatic measurement* (c.f., Kosovich, 2017, Paper 3). This approach seeks to minimize the resources required for data collection (e.g., class time, participant fatigue) while maximizing the quality of the data being collected (i.e., validity; aka "practical measurement"; Yeager et al., 2013). We divided our chapter into three major parts. In Part One, we focus on general approaches to measurement and provide an introduction on how pragmatic measurement can complement more common measurement practices. In Part Two, we introduce three case studies in which pragmatic measurement was used. In Part Three, we discuss the scholarly and practical implications of pragmatic measurement in the pursuit of educational motivation.

Part One: Approaches to Measuring Motivation

What Is Measurement and How Is It Done?

The essence of measurement is to systematically and accurately capture a particular phenomenon (AERA et al., 2014). To do this, measure users need to ensure that responses to the measure correspond to the phenomenon under study – e.g., a measure designed to assess math self-efficacy should be distinct from items to assess content knowledge in math (i.e., construct validity). Users also need to ensure that the measure elicits consistent responses – e.g., several different math self-efficacy questions should yield relatively similar responses from an individual (i.e., reliability). Ensuring that a measure is fulfilling its intended purpose is also known as *validation,* and validation for measures – whether they are self-report, behavioral, interview, or otherwise – is the foundation of most research. However, the situational constraints of conducting measurement in applied settings (e.g., time constraints in classrooms) are often underappreciated in validation work, and can have far-reaching consequences for data collection, analyses, and conclusions drawn from the data. For example, in Scenario One (i.e., measuring motivation for five different classes), asking a student to fill out the same questionnaire five consecutive times would likely lead to frustration or disengagement. The frustration could be further exacerbated by lengthy questionnaires. Thus, when developing or adopting a particular measure, users must consider the quality of the measure as it fulfills technical standards (e.g., construct validity and reliability) and consider more pragmatic concerns (e.g., if completing the measures will frustrate participants).

When used for research purposes, measure development frequently occurs in several iterative steps (Schmeiser & Welch, 2006). First, items are identified that can be used to collect data (e.g., self-report questions, components of a checklist). The content of the items is reviewed by various experts for theoretical soundness, coherence, or other characteristics important for the scale (e.g., accurate translation from another language). Items are then piloted with potential participants by directly completing the measure or discussing the measure with developers. For quantitative measures, various statistical procedures are conducted to assess whether the measure produces reliable scores (i.e., the items are consistent with each other or themselves over time), whether the items form distinct factors (i.e., items relate to each other more highly than they relate to items from other constructs), whether the items correlate or predict other theoretically important constructs in similar ways (i.e., correspond with similar constructs and diverge from less similar constructs), or whether the items predict outcomes (i.e., show that they meet a particular criterion). Qualitative measures require rigorous training of users in order to minimize bias and ensure proper measure deployment. Measures frequently undergo these and more complex processes multiple times during the course of development until a final useable measure is developed.

This common approach to measurement, which focuses on meeting the technical demands of providing high-quality validity evidence, does not generally account for the practical constraints of a typical classroom. The resulting measures may be able to produce high-quality information under ideal or controlled circumstances, but may break down once introduced to applied settings. The goal of this chapter is to demonstrate that useful information can be gleaned from measures that have balanced these technical and pragmatic considerations of conducting measurement in applied settings.

Pragmatic Measurement

Although the groundwork for pragmatic measurement exists in contemporary measurement theory, common measurement practices frequently adhere to outdated perspectives. One common example of this outdated knowledge is an exaggerated reliance on Cronbach's alpha coefficients (Sijtsma, 2009). Cronbach's alpha (α) is one of the most widely cited and reported reliability coefficients, yet there are volumes of research dedicated to debunking its usefulness. Even if a more appropriate coefficient is used, at least two items are required for their calculation (Traub & Rowley, 1991). However, the underlying goal of calculating reliability coefficients is not to achieve a specific number (as many users are inclined to think), but to demonstrate evidence of consistency (AERA et al., 2014). The overreliance on alpha and other outdated perspectives can severely limit the validation methods that are available to users interested in conducting measurement.

Pragmatic measurement is an approach to ensure that sound data on specific phenomena can be collected under variable and constrained circumstances, especially when widely accepted validation methods may be unreasonably burdensome (Kosovich, 2017). We formally define pragmatic measurement as balancing psychometric concerns and situational constraints to produce maximally informative and minimally intrusive measures. For example, in one study, faculty indicated that the researchers could spend no more than three minutes of class time per week conducting measurement (Yeager et al., 2013). Such constraints could be prohibitively restrictive if researchers are unwilling to compromise on the number of constructs measured, the number of items dedicated to any given construct, or the mode of measurement. Although the measurement standards (AERA et al., 2014) acknowledge situational constraints, the role of those factors is frequently underappreciated in common practice.

Pragmatic measurement is an argument-based approach to validation (Kane, 1992, 2013) that draws from contemporary perspectives to pursue the underlying goal of measurement. The elegance of Kane's argument-based approach is that it requires measure users to identify the intended purposes of the measure (e.g., to compare group differences) and to identify the assumptions they are making about the measure (e.g., the measure is sensitive to group differences; for examples, see Bell et al., 2012; Goldstein & Flake, 2016). The pragmatic measurement perspective adds the additional step of explicitly identifying potential constraints that could undermine the use of the measure and incorporating those constraints in selecting (or designing) and deploying the measure. We chose to build the pragmatic measurement perspective from Kane's framework, because it is derived from a highly influential line of validation philosophy (Cronbach & Meehl, 1955; Messick, 1989) that guides contemporary measurement recommendations (AERA et al., 2014). Having a pragmatic perspective, we also adopted Kane's framework because of its flexibility as a general validation tool (i.e., argument-based validation is not limited to a single type of measure, construct, or domain).

For example, the authors' previous work (Kosovich, 2017; Kosovich et al., 2017) identified prediction as an important use of a set of motivation measures. As evidence to using shorter measures rather than longer measures, the authors compared different versions of the scale (i.e., longer and shorter composites) to evaluate the amount of information lost. As would be expected, the shorter measures tended to explain less variance in outcomes. However, the decrease in variance explained was small in general, and proportionally smaller than the number of items eliminated from the longer scale. Based on those results, the authors concluded that, while the brief measures did not technically perform as well as the longer measures, the overall benefits of shortening the scales outweighed the cost (by a factor of eight to one).

Rather than finding the scale with the highest reliability or the lowest standard error, the goal of our research on pragmatic measurement is to find the scale that performs well enough technically and meets the constraints of the situation. In Part Two, we present three scenarios in which users might experience a tension between the situational constraints and technical demands of validation. The scenarios were selected to be representative of common uses of measurement in education research. Briefly introduced in the beginning of the chapter (i.e., student motivation across multiple classes, changes in motivation over time, and a time-restricted online motivation intervention), each scenario contains a measurement tension due to particular situational constraints that could be resolved by adopting the pragmatic measurement approach.

Part Two: Case Studies of Using Pragmatic Measures in Motivation Research

In the following sections, we consider three examples of pragmatic measurement in action. In Scenario One, the challenge from a pragmatic perspective was collecting data on multiple motivation constructs in five different domains in consecutive questionnaires. Not only would overly lengthy questionnaires likely lead to student disengagement, but questionnaire length was limited by the survey administrators. As a result, the researchers needed to produce brief measures that could capture a breadth of motivation constructs and a breadth of academic domains. In Scenario Two, the challenge was collecting data several times in a single semester. Students tend to object to repeatedly responding to the same questionnaire, thus necessitating the usage of relatively brief measures. In Scenario Three, the challenge was implementing an intervention and collecting data to assess the intervention in no more than

15 minutes. Again, brief measures were required and it was necessary to compile alternative validity evidence for the quality of the measures. These scenarios describe three common methodological approaches in motivational research (group differences, change over time, and interventions) and how the use of pragmatic measures of motivation can inform work on each.

Given the growing interest in motivation constructs, what kind of motivation should practitioners and policymakers assess? There are numerous motivational perspectives (Pintrich, 2003), which can certainly confuse those not familiar with the field. In an effort to integrate different facets of motivation (Atkinson, 1964; Lewin et al., 1944; Raynor, 1982; Vroom, 1964), an expectancy-value-cost framework (Barron & Hulleman, 2015) offers a perspective on motivation that can be used to organize the array of motivation constructs (Eccles, 1983; Hulleman et al., 2016a). According to the expectancy-value-cost framework, achievement behavior is most proximally determined by three major factors that can conceptually answer three questions (Barron & Hulleman, 2015). The first factor, *expectancy,* is an individual's perception that they can succeed at a task; it answers the question "Can I do this?" The second factor, *value*, is an individual's perception that engaging with a task is worthwhile; it answers the question "Do I want to do this?" The third major factor, *cost*, is focused on an individual's perception that there are psychological, physical, or other barriers preventing success; it answers the question "Is something preventing me from succeeding?"

Expectancies, values, and costs can be used in the first step of deciding which aspects of motivation are most salient in a particular context. For example, educators might predict that students would be most motivated in general education courses that are most similar to their college major (e.g., to a biology major, a science course would be more motivating than a classical literature course). Individuals would likely feel more confident about (i.e., expectancy), find more meaning in (i.e., value), and be less anxious about (i.e., cost) courses that align with their interests or major. Without measuring motivation, it is difficult to tell if such a prediction is accurate. However, measuring motivation in detail is also probably unnecessary. The expectancy-value-cost framework historically employs brief measures to understand the role of motivation in education (Kosovich, 2017), and in each of the three scenarios, some version of a pragmatic measure of expectancy, value, or cost is included. These examples are meant to showcase the utility of pragmatic measures, not the methods for designing pragmatic measures (for examples, see Kosovich, 2017; Yeager et al., 2013).

Scenario 1: Motivation for General Education

Post-secondary students are often required to take a variety of general education courses, many of which are not necessarily related to their major or their future plans in an obvious way. Because motivation is theorized to be (e.g., Eccles et al., 1983) and empirically shown to be (e.g., Jacobs et al., 2002) domain specific, students are more likely to be more motivated for some courses than for others. Presumably, students are more motivated for classes and activities related to their major. However, most research looking at student motivation across multiple domains does so for younger students and for more general topics (e.g., math, reading, sports). We were interested in answering two questions about college students' motivation: (1) How does students' motivation vary across their general education coursework? and (2) How does students' motivation for general education coursework compare to their major coursework? We explore the answer to these two questions using pragmatic measures of motivation in education (Barron et al., 2014).

A representative sample of students from a large university ($n = 808$) were asked to respond to an 18-item pragmatic measure of motivation (see Appendix 28.A). The measure asked about students' motivation in their major as well as in the five general education *areas* (i.e., academic domains). At the university under study, the five general education areas were (1) critical thinking and communication skills, (2) arts and humanities, (3) math and natural science, (4) history and social science, and (5) intrapersonal and interpersonal development. For each area and for their major, students were asked to rate their interest (e.g., "Area One courses interest me"), importance (e.g., "The topics and skills taught in Area One courses are important to me"), and expectancy (e.g., "I can do well in my Area One courses") for that area using a "1" (strongly disagree) to "6" (strongly agree) Likert scale.

Figure 28.1 presents the means and confidence intervals for students' interest, importance, and expectancy across areas and for their major. Despite using only one item per construct and measuring only three constructs, a number of interesting patterns emerged from the data. First – as might be expected – students tend to report higher motivation for their majors than for the general education areas. Second, students report the lowest interest for Area One (critical thinking and communication) and Area Three (math and natural science). Third, students report higher importance for Area Five (intrapersonal and intrapersonal development) than for the other areas. Finally, students report substantially lower expectancy for Area Three than for the other areas.

Students also were grouped into one of six curricular areas based on their declared major: (1) arts and letters, (2) business, (3) education, (4) integrated science and technology (ISAT), (5) science and math, and (6) visual and performing arts. A seventh group comprised "undeclared" majors. The next step was to assess the extent to which students' motivation was higher for areas more similar to their major. For example, we expected that students with science and math majors to give Area Three (math and natural science) the highest ratings on interest and importance, because that area matches the coursework of their college and major (see Figures 28.2, 28.3, and 28.4 for average ratings of interest, importance, and expectancy, respectively).

Students' ratings of different general education areas did differ by their major. For example, students with visual and performing arts majors reported

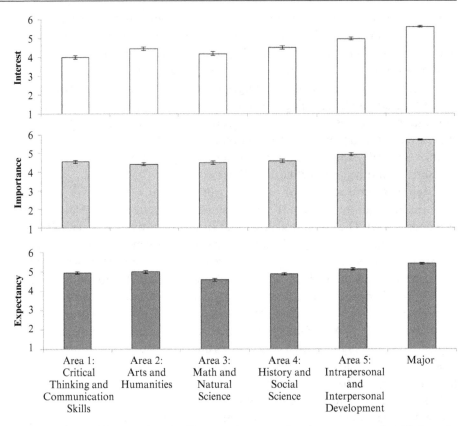

Figure 28.1. *Students' self-reported interest (top), importance (middle), and expectancy (bottom) by general education area plus major. All measures used a six-point Likert scale ranging from "1" (strongly disagree) to "6" (strongly agree).*

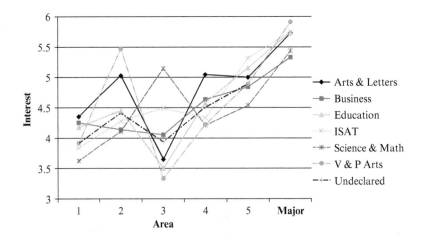

Figure 28.2. *Average ratings of interest, based on declared major. Each line shows the average interest of students grouped into one of six curricular areas based on their declared major (as well as undeclared students) for each general education area and their respective major. Students tended to report the highest interest for areas most similar to their major.*

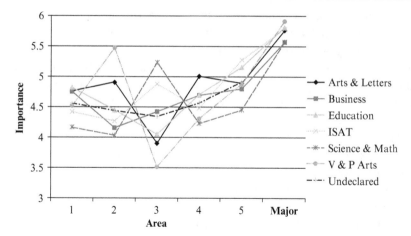

Figure 28.3. *Each line shows the average importance ratings of students grouped into one of six curricular areas based on their declared major (as well as undeclared students) for each general education area and their respective major. Students tended to report the highest value for areas most similar to their major.*

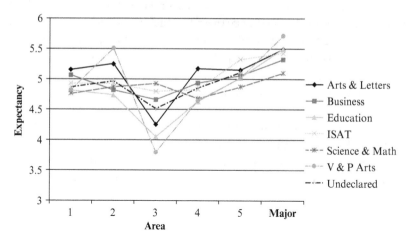

Figure 28.4. *Each line shows the average expectancy of students grouped into one of six curricular areas based on their declared major (as well as undeclared students) for each general education area and their respective major. Students tended to report the highest expectancy for areas most similar to their major.*

higher motivation for Area Two (arts and humanities) than for any other major, and they also reported the lowest motivation for Area Three (math and natural science). Science and math majors, along with ISAT majors, reported the exact opposite pattern, with the lowest motivation for Area Two and the highest motivation for Area Three. Another interesting but also alarming result was that education majors tended to have the lowest expectancy across areas, especially in Area Three.

Scholarly significance. The findings in this scenario offer a number of interesting and potentially important findings about motivation in higher education using single-item motivation measures. First, students' motivation for general education coursework varies by curricular area. Students from all majors indicated high motivation for Area Five (interpersonal and intrapersonal development) coursework, perhaps because students are able to see the relevance of studying intrapersonal and interpersonal phenomena beyond their major. Students tended to indicate the lowest interest in the foundational coursework comprising Area One (critical thinking and communication), the lowest importance for coursework in Area Two (arts and humanities), and the lowest expectancy for Area Three (math and natural science) coursework. Second, students' motivation for general education was indeed lower than their motivation for their major coursework. Third, there was significant variability in attitudes toward Area Two and Area Three, where higher interest, importance, and expectancy were found among students whose majors were most closely aligned with the area coursework. Therefore, not only is differentiating among components of the general education curriculum important, but recognizing that attitudes toward each component are related to a student's academic major is also important. These results highlight possible interventions to enhance students' motivation for their general education coursework. Area Two showed the lowest importance overall, which means that many students – particularly those with a natural science bent – might benefit from an intervention that aims to increase value for the arts and humanities. Area Three showed the lowest expectancy overall, indicating that many students might benefit from an expectancy-increasing intervention.

These relatively simple but striking results highlight an instance in which pragmatic measurement can contribute to discussions about education and much-needed course reform efforts. These measures functioned as a brief assessment that could uncover patterns in this particular educational context. Although they do not provide explicit, diagnostic information, the data identify places that may be worthy of more lengthy assessments or other forms of inquiry (e.g., focus groups, observations).

Scenario 2: Short-Term Repeated Measures

Our next scenario demonstrates that pragmatic measures can provide benefits when considering motivation over several points of time. Motivational theory suggests that motivation is dynamic, and that it is a culmination of prior experiences and attitudes combined with present contexts (Eccles et al., 1983). Students who demonstrate low achievement are also likely to diverge motivationally from students who demonstrate high achievement. As a result, monitoring motivation over time is important – how students feel about a class is likely to be different at the end of a semester than at the beginning. For example, a common finding in the motivational literature is that motivation declines over time. The pattern has been documented repeatedly, particularly in research from the expectancy-value framework that spans first grade through the end of high school (Jacobs et al., 2002).The implications of decreasing motivation for a particular domain mean the individuals are less likely to pursue the domain in the future, are likely to perform worse in the domain, and are likely to have a continued decline in their motivation. However, the majority of research examining motivational change occurs at a yearly timescale and ignores shorter time intervals. A concern with more frequent measurement is that participants will become fatigued or will disengage with the general research process.

Our second example addresses this gap in the literature by examining how students' expectancy and value change over the course of a semester, and whether that change is consistent across individuals (for the full study results, see Kosovich et al. 2017). Students' ($n = 389$) motivation was measured three times over the course of a semester, during week three (time one), week nine (time two), and week 14 (time three). We used eight items adapted from Eccles et al. (1983) to capture students' expectancy (five items; e.g., "I expect to do well in this class") and value (three items; e.g., "What I am learning in this class is relevant to my life"). Analyses were conducted using a parallel process model (Byrne, 2012), which examines the patterns of two or more constructs over time. The model provides *growth parameters* that include the level of each construct at the first time point (i.e., an intercept) and the rate of change in the construct for one time interval (i.e., a slope).

First, we found that the general declining trajectory in prior research was replicated in the current study. On average, expectancy and value both declined over the course of the semester. Importantly, the slopes were highly correlated ($r = 0.83$, $p < 0.01$) suggesting that expectancy and value change in tandem. However, the variability in expectancy slopes was statistically significant, while the variability in value slopes was not. In other words, not all individuals declined in their expectancies; some increased, some decreased, and some remained stable. Individuals were more homogeneous in their value trajectory, but the change that was present was highly related to expectancy. Second, growth parameters were uncorrelated with final exam scores. However, value intercepts and expectancy slopes both predicted end-of-semester, self-reported continuing interest. Thus, at the end of the semester, individuals with higher initial value showed greater interest, and individuals who increased in expectancy over time also reported higher interest at the end of the semester. Finally, concurrent exam scores were able to explain about 52 percent of the variation in expectancy slopes. Specifically, students who performed better on exams also reported more steeply increasing expectancies (rather than just higher).

Scholarly significance. Although we know that motivation changes over the long term, there is little research illuminating the short-term dynamics of motivation change (see Holstermann et al., 2012 for an example). Even when researchers repeatedly measure motivation over extremely short periods of time, they typically do not analyze change or variation among the individual time points (e.g., Hektner & Csikszentmihalyi, 1996; Rotgans & Schmidt, 2011). The results of this scenario show that although expectancy and value decline over the semester, the nature of that decline is complex. Variability in expectancy slopes was related to concurrent exam performance, supporting the link between perceptions of ability and performance (e.g., Bandura & Schunk, 1981). Indeed, many students' expectancy increased despite an average decline. The lack of variability in value slopes was also interesting, suggesting either that value is less susceptible to feedback about value or that feedback about value is simply not communicated to students. We know from our previous research that effective value feedback can lead to improvements in expectancy, value, interest, and performance later in the semester (Hulleman et al., 2010a, 2016b; Hulleman & Harackiewicz, 2009). It is worth noting that expectancy and value measures can be considered pragmatic measures, as they tend to be relatively brief. In the current example, eight items were used to measure expectancy and value, but fewer items have been used for the same types of analyses in other studies (e.g., Jacobs et al., 2002; Kosovich, 2017; Kosovich et al., 2015, 2017).

Perhaps most important are the effects of growth parameters on continuing interest. At a generic level, the results support hypothesized mechanisms for interest development and maintenance (Hidi & Renninger, 2006; Renninger & Hidi, 2016). First, Hidi and Renninger hypothesize that interest is more likely to develop and be sustained when individuals perceive meaningfulness in the content. Congruent with that hypothesis, we found that individuals who see greater usefulness in the topic at the beginning of the semester are more likely to maintain or increase interest. Similarly, interest maintenance and development require support from external sources, such as competence feedback. Congruent with that hypothesis, we found that consistent change in expectancy predicted later interest, controlling for prior interest.

Scenario 3: Online Motivation Interventions

The first two scenarios demonstrated instances where pragmatic measurement could be used to monitor natural patterns in a situation and provide useful information to relevant stakeholders (e.g., researchers, administrators). The third scenario takes another step, leveraging pragmatic measurement as a way to include assessments despite significant situational constraints. Researchers, practitioners, and policymakers are continually introducing new programs, initiatives, and curriculum (e.g., educational interventions) in hopes that they will improve student learning outcomes. In recent years, researchers have demonstrated that utility value interventions can increase students' interest in STEM, academic performance, and subsequent course taking (see Lazowski & Hulleman, 2016; Rosenzweig & Wigfield, 2016; Tibbetts et al., 2016 for reviews of this work). An important but difficult aspect of introducing and maintaining such interventions is assessing whether or not they bring about the expected changes in new contexts. Adopting interventions can be disruptive for classroom routines and can be time consuming. Including comprehensive assessments in addition to interventions may only add to the disruption and frustration. Once again, pragmatic measurement can provide a method for including useful measures without undermining the goal of the research or data collection. Utility value interventions tend to be relatively brief activities (e.g., 30 minutes) that ask students to write a short essay reflecting on ways that class material might be relevant or useful to their lives (Harackiewicz et al., 2014; Hulleman, 2007; Hulleman & Harackiewicz, 2009; Hulleman et al., 2010b, 2016b). Recent versions have been adapted to be delivered online (Hulleman et al., 2016b). In this third scenario, the researchers were given 15 minutes to complete the intervention and all relevant assessments.

This example includes a sample of algebra and geometry students ($n = 797$) from an accredited, online high school in the southeastern United States. The classes were self-paced and consisted of approximately ten topic modules for students to complete. Students received an e-mail from their course instructors asking them to volunteer their time by completing an online activity about how math was related to their lives. The study procedure was (1) a consent form; (2) a five-item baseline motivation questionnaire (self-efficacy and interest); (3) a ten- to 15-minute intervention; and (4) an eight-item follow-up questionnaire (self-efficacy, interest, utility value, and cost). We assessed participants' perceptions of utility value using one item, interest was measured with three items (e.g., "I am interested in taking more math classes in the future"; $\alpha = 0.89$), self-efficacy was measured with two items (e.g., "I am confident that I can figure out even the hardest concepts in algebra/geometry class"; $\alpha = 0.90$), and perceived cost was measured with two items (e.g., "I'm unable to put in the time needed to do well in algebra/geometry"; $\alpha = 0.87$). Participants responded using a five-point Likert scale from "1" (Not at All) to "5" (Extremely). Students who opted in to the study were randomly assigned to a utility value intervention or a control activity (for full details, see Rosenzweig et al., in press). The primary dependent measure was students' perceived utility value for the course. We also analyzed students' scores on the other motivational constructs to determine whether the interventions improved motivation broadly, instead of specifically improving utility value.

To model the effects of the intervention conditions on the different outcomes, we ran a series of multiple hierarchical linear regressions. We regressed each outcome on a set of dummy codes, which represented each condition relative to the control groups. We included students' course type, pretest competence beliefs, and pretest interest as covariates in the model. The results of the study showed that all three groups of students who received a utility value intervention reported higher utility value than the control groups (see Figure 28.5). Consistent with work by Gaspard et al. (2015), the condition

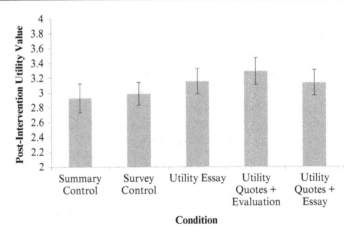

Figure 28.5. *Results of a utility value intervention study. Students were assigned to one of five experimental conditions (two control groups and three intervention groups). The summary group summarized material from class, whereas the survey group simply completed an extended self-report survey. The "utility essay" condition required students to write a brief essay about the usefulness of their course material, the "utility quotes and evaluation" condition required students to read a series of quotes and reflect on them, and the "utility quotes and essay" condition required the students to read a series of quotes and reflect on them and to write a brief essay about the usefulness of their course materials.*

in which individuals were asked to evaluate quotes rather than write an essay reported higher motivation after the intervention. There were no significant main effects of condition on post-test interest, cost, or self-efficacy, compared to either of the control conditions.

Scholarly significance. In this research we explored whether we could raise students' perceived utility value for math in online math courses through utility value interventions. To our knowledge, this is one of the first studies to demonstrate that utility value interventions can increase high school students' perceived utility value for learning math in online courses. Relative to the control conditions, the utility intervention that provided examples and non-essay tasks (i.e., the "utility quotes and evaluation" condition) increased students' utility value the most. Our findings support prior research suggesting that raising students' perceptions of utility value by asking them to make specific and personal connections to their course material is possible (e.g., Hulleman & Harackiewicz, 2009; Hulleman et al., 2010a, 2016b). We extend prior work to show that these interventions raise utility value for students in online courses, a growing segment of K–12 education that has been understudied in intervention research.

Furthermore, this research explored the boundary for how brief a utility value intervention can be and still produce positive effects for students. In this case, completing the intervention materials themselves took five to ten minutes, which is one-third of the length of time of most other interventions and less than one-tenth of the time of the Gaspard et al. (2015) intervention. This reinforces the notion that when interventions target specific psychological processes, they can have powerful effects despite minimal dosage (Yeager & Walton, 2011).

Part Three: Scholarly and Practical Implications

The three scenarios discussed in Part Two highlight cases in which pragmatic measurement can help answer motivation questions. The perspective allows users to identify the information that would support the use of the measure, rather than simply recommending a general checklist of requirements that may or may not be important. It also allows for more rapid measure development and use of measures, because it prioritizes the most important evidence rather than a generalized checklist of requirements. Additionally, the pragmatic measurement perspective also gives individuals the opportunity to collect some data (rather than none) if they do not have the resources to implement or develop a full-length scale. Importantly, with this perspective we emphasize the usability of data that are *good enough*, recognizing that measures and data are rarely ever ideal for the applied researcher, practitioner, or policymaker. Finally, the perspective can reduce the burden of frequent responding on participants by minimizing the demands of completing a measure.

Benefits and Applications of Pragmatic Measurement

The first scenario illuminated patterns of motivation across five general academic areas, students' major, and the correspondence between the two. Although the analyses were relatively simple, they were able to provide a substantial amount of information. This is one core use of pragmatic measures – to collect a breadth of information from a large group of individuals to inform practitioners. The results of the study in the first scenario could form a foundation for researchers or practitioners to launch more targeted inquiries. For example, why are education majors consistently reporting lower expectancies than other majors across academic areas?

The second scenario represented a more nuanced look at motivation over time. The results of the study not only further theoretical knowledge, but bring to light important points for practitioners. For example, the uniformity of the decline in utility value suggests that students may share similar experiences in a psychology class that does not foster value for the class material. Tracking fluctuations would be one obvious use of pragmatic measures. The research design in the second scenario still represented motivation only at the beginning, middle, and end of the semester. A major question is how motivation fluctuates at a more micro level, such as from week to week. Experience sampling methods can be used to examine motivation change in more narrow time intervals (e.g., Hektner & Csikszentmihalyi, 1996), but that method is intense and can be demanding for participants. A balance of the two might be a weekly three-item survey at the beginning or end of class. Such an exercise would be feasible with much larger sample sizes and could potentially be implemented at a much larger scale (e.g., a college or school district).

In the third scenario, we were able to assess motivation before and after an intervention within a 15-minute time frame. The brief measures allowed us to quickly assess several potential motivation factors that may be important to online high school math students. The results of the study demonstrated that even a 15-minute exercise may be sufficient for altering student motivation. From a pragmatic standpoint, these results could lead to negotiating for a longer intervention time slot, to gaining more buy-in from skeptical instructors or administrators, or to shortening other lengthier versions.

Beyond these three applications, pragmatic measures should have additional utility for other purposes (see Table 28.1). One would be routinely using pragmatic motivation assessment in teaching practice. Our research suggests that at least some measures of motivation do not require advanced statistical modeling to lead to accurate conclusions about results (Kosovich, et al., 2015). This could allow teachers or administrators to monitor motivation throughout the school year and develop curricular changes that might support motivation during common declines. Similarly, it could provide another source of information to identify students who are struggling with material or experiencing other issues. For example, students who report particularly high cost (e.g., feeling overwhelmed by their coursework) may benefit from time-management instruction or tutoring. If students have an anonymous outlet to inform instructors that they are not confident with the material, the instructor has the opportunity to spend extra time on a particular subject. By extension, the measures could be used to identify ideal times to implement interventions by instructors or researchers. As described by Yeager et al. (2013), changes to the classroom (e.g., interventions) could also be monitored and assessed by those same measures. Our suggestions here begin to highlight potential applications of pragmatic measurement, but moving forward carefully and considering the trade-offs that may accompany users' adoption of the pragmatic perspective is important.

Trade-Offs and Drawbacks of Pragmatic Measurement

Unfortunately, the benefits mentioned in this chapter come without some of the methodological rigor present in more ideal measurement studies. First and foremost, electing to use brief measures precludes some of the most powerful statistical methods for conducting validation. For example, *confirmatory factor analyses* require at least three items per scale to test the statistical quality of items (Kline, 2011), and *item response theory* models may require even more

Table 28.1 *Current and potential uses supported by pragmatic measurement*

Current uses	Measure type
General Motivation Tracking (Example 1: This Chapter: Barron, et al., 2014)	Self-report
Short-Term Repeated Measures (Example 2: This Chapter; Kosovich et al., 2017)	Self-report
Intervention Development & Refinement (Example 3: This Chapter; Rosenzweig et al., in prep)	Self-report, open-ended
Monitoring Potential Improvements to Classroom Activities (Yeager et al., 2013)	Self-report
Intervention Fidelity Assessment (Wormington et al., under review)	Rubric coding & profile analysis
Experience Sampling	Self-report, open-ended
Digital Learning Systems (Krumm et al., 2016)	Digital analytics (e.g., page views)
Potential uses	**Measure type**
Large-sample interviews	Interview, open-ended
Observational checklists	Observation
Variance-capturing covariate inventory (broad list of items covering non-central but relevant sources of variance)	Any

items for useful estimates (Embretson & Reise, 2000). Such techniques allow researchers to identify item bias, whereby items tend to favor one particular group or context over another for reasons unrelated to the underlying construct. The inability to identify bias means that group differences could be true differences or simply differences in item interpretation. There are many instances in which users may wish to compare groups on a particular measure. However, items containing substantial bias (i.e., characteristics that lead the measure to overestimate some groups' construct levels) may lead to inaccurate conclusions about the data. For example, does the measure miss critical aspects of an experience that would differentiate one group from another? Alternatively, is the measure focused on some critical aspects of an experience that would differentiate one group from another? Again, this is a notable concern, and developers need to do whatever is possible to minimize such problems. In the case of pragmatic measurement, a different measurement mode (e.g., qualitative interviews to support a Likert measure) may be able to identify some potential problems with a scale.

At a more basic level, using a single-item measure prevents the calculation of reliability coefficients (e.g., Cronbach's alpha). This is doubly problematic because, all else equal, scales can display lower reliability simply by including fewer items. Items that are unreliable and items that are biased can lead to false conclusions from the data. Furthermore, shortened scales are less likely to capture the full breadth of the construct under study (i.e., content validity), making it possible for overly brief measures to miss critical aspects of the construct. Such concerns are important and can lead to the attenuation, masking, or exaggeration of relationships or differences. Thus, considering both the evidence supporting (or not) the use of pragmatic measures, as well as the consequences of inaccurate conclusions, is important.

There is a nontrivial trade-off between different factors related to conducting measurement. Pragmatic measures can be used to reduce intrusion into day-to-day routines, but doing so may result in lost information or inconsistent data. Adopting a pragmatic measurement approach can also reduce the likelihood that students become frustrated by the length of the assessment, but doing so may exclude a variety of statistical tools for assessing the measure's quality. The result is a need to find balance between the various considerations.

Concluding Thoughts

Although we have found many instances of research that we would classify as using pragmatic measurement, there is no cohesive framework or body of literature on the practice. Moving forward, we are working to consolidate the existing research and to identify important considerations that need to be addressed more directly. For now, we simply advocate for identifying situational constraints in addition to the typical uses of the measure. The most critical endeavor to undertake is to develop a specific method for considering the pros and cons of different decisions users may make. The method or framework then needs to be applied to different types of measurement (e.g., interviews, observations). The mode of measurement selected by researchers and practitioners has implications for the questions that can be answered, the implementation methods that are used to collect the data, and the conclusions that can be drawn from that data.

Self-Report

Self-report measures have the benefit of collecting data about individuals' personal experiences. Quantitative self-report measures (e.g., Likert scales, survey ratings) are able to compile data on a broad array of constructs from large groups of individuals with relative efficiency. Such measures do not allow users to probe answers for greater understanding, may fail to capture actual thought processes, may suffer from wording effects, and may frustrate participants with tedium (Bowman, 2010; Duckworth & Yeager, 2015; Paulhus, 1984; Schwarz & Oyserman, 2001). In contrast, more qualitative self-report measures (e.g., open-ended survey questions, interviews, focus groups) are able to delve into participant responses and response processes, and allow researchers to establish a rapport with the participants. Developing pragmatic self-report measures may be able to strike a balance between the benefits and drawbacks of these different approaches.

Observation

Another set of methods that can compensate for or complement the shortcomings of self-report measures are observational measures (Renninger & Bachrach, 2015), which vary in their degree of flexibility or structure. Observations (e.g., note-taking, video, artifact analysis) are desirable, because they avoid the subjectivity or desirable responding in self-report and they can avoid participant fatigue. However, observational measures can be less desirable in that they are at risk for observer biases, require rigorous observer training (Bill and Melinda Gates Foundation, 2013), require more time for individuals to conduct the observations, and (in the case of less-structured observations) require more intense effort to analyze (Fredricks & McColsky, 2012). More structured observational measures (e.g., rubrics, checklists) can reduce the data collection and analysis burden, but also may not be as readily able to capture unique occurrences or unexpected phenomena.

Non-Human Observation

A somewhat different type of observation involves non-human observational tools, which can provide detailed data that depart substantially from the previous types of measures (e.g., Krumm et al., 2016). Non-human observational tools, like eye tracking and response times, can be collected with little to no burden on the part of the participants. More complex measures like fMRI are more intrusive but may provide much more comprehensive information. Ultimately, these types of measures may prove useful but are also more removed from the direct psychological experiences of individuals.

Different modes of measurement have their own benefits and drawbacks, but all measurement requires validation. An unreliable measure can hide relationships between constructs or produce spurious ones. An interviewer who has not been trained on a protocol may inadvertently influence the participant to respond in a desirable way. Thus, ensuring the technical integrity of measures is indispensable in conducting measurement. However, factors surrounding the measurement (e.g., limited data collection time or participant fatigue) could undermine validity in spite of excellent technical specifications (e.g., Wise & DeMars, 2005). Thus, potential implementation obstacles, such as the time available to complete a measure, need to be considered as the measures are being developed.

This chapter focused on self-reported quantitative data because the bulk of our research uses this type of measure. However, assessing pragmatic measurement's applicability to other quantitative approaches is important. Even more so is the need to examine pragmatic approaches to qualitative data. Miniature interviews or highly specific lines of questioning could provide a wealth of information for quantitative and qualitative researchers alike. Developing methods that maintain high-quality qualitative design for applied situations may be a significant hurdle.

In addition to the many suggestions we put forth in this chapter, we expect that many other viable ideas are simply not yet conceived. There are many instances in which pragmatic measurement could be used to supplement or refine existing projects. For example, collecting measures to serve as covariates is an important but secondary concern in many studies. Thus, if we can develop pragmatic covariate measures that effectively serve as proxies for longer measures, we can either measure additional covariates of interest or simply reduce the effort required from participants. Alternatively, we can increase the frequency of mixed-methods research by providing pragmatic supplemental measures for quantitative or qualitative researchers.

We end our discussion with a cautionary note. Pragmatic measurement is meant to foster innovation in research through flexible measurement practices. By pushing users to think more deeply about their purpose for measuring a construct and about evidence that supports the use of a measure for those purposes, we can push the bounds of knowledge in new and interesting ways. However, users must be wary of carelessly adopting the first convenient set of items available. Our push for pragmatic measurement is in no way an endorsement for poor-quality measurement work, nor is it a free pass for the widespread usage of brief or single-item measures. Every decision made about a scale introduces a trade-off between the technical and the pragmatic aspects of measurement and research. On the one hand, shortening a scale has the potential to drastically reduce its statistical integrity or the scope of conclusions that can be drawn. On the other hand, failing to take situational factors into consideration may invalidate the data collected in spite of previous technical quality. The pragmatic perspective does not eliminate these trade-offs – it brings them to the forefront of validation instead.

References

AERA, APA, & NCME. (2014). *Standards for educational and psychological testing.* Washington, DC: American Educational Research Association.

Atkinson, J. W. (1964). *An introduction to motivation.* Princeton, NJ: D. Van Nostrand Company.

Bandura, A. & Schunk, D. H. (1981). Cultivating competence, self-efficacy, and intrinsic interest through proximal self-motivation. *Journal of Personality and Social Psychology, 41*(3), 586–98. doi: 10.1037/0022-3514.41.3.586.

Barron, K. E., Grays, M., & Hulleman, C. S. (2014). *Assessing motivation in general education.* Poster presented at the Annual Meeting of the American Educational Research Association, Philadelphia, PA.

Barron, K. E. & Hulleman, C. S. (2015). Expectancy-value-cost model of motivation. In J. D. Wright (Ed.) *International encyclopedia of the social & behavioral sciences* (Vol. 8, pp. 503–9). Elsevier. doi: 10.1016/B978-0-08-097086-8.26099-6.

Bell, C. A., Gitomer, D. H., McCaffrey, D. F., Hamre, B. K., Pianta, R. C., & Qi, Y. (2012). An argument approach to observation protocol validity. *Educational Assessment, 17*(2–3), 62–87. doi:10.1080/10627197.2012.715014.

Bill and Melinda Gates Foundation. (2013). *Ensuring fair and reliable measures of effective teaching*. Retrieved from www.edweek.org/media/17teach-met1.pdf.

Bowman, N. A. (2010). Can 1st-year college students accurately report their learning and development? *American Educational Research Journal, 47*(2), 466–96. doi:10.3102/0002831209353595.

Byrne, B. M. (2012). *Structural equation modeling with Mplus: Basic concepts, applications, and programming*. Multivariate applications series. New York, NY: Routledge.

Cronbach, L. J. & Meehl, P. (1955). Construct validity in psychological tests. *Psychological Bulletin, 52*, 281–302.

Duckworth, A. L. & Yeager, D. S. (2015). Measurement matters: Assessing personal qualities other than cognitive ability for educational purposes. *Educational Researcher, 44*(4), 237–51. doi: 10.3102/0013189X15584327.

Eccles, J. S. (1983). Expectancies, values, and academic behaviors. In J. T. Spence (Ed.), *Achievement-related motives and behaviors* (pp. 119–46). San Francisco, CA: W. H. Freeman.

Eccles, J. S., Adler, T., Futterman, R., Goff, S. B., Kaczala, C. M., Meece, J. L., & Midgley, C. (1983). Expectancies, values, and academic behaviors. In J. T. Spence (Ed.), *Achievement and achievement motivation* (pp. 75–146). San Francisco, CA: W. H. Freeman.

Embretson, S. E. & Reise, S. P. (2000). *Item response theory for psychologists*. Mahwah, NJ: Lawrence Erlbaum Associates.

Fredricks, J. A. & McColsky, W. (2012). The measurement of student engagement: A comparative analysis of various methods and student self-report instruments. In S. L. Christenson, A. L. Reschly, & C. Wylie (Eds.), *Handbook of research on student engagement* (pp. 763–82). New York, NY: Springer. doi: 10.1007/978-1-4614-2018-7_37.

Gaspard, H., Dicke, A., Flunger, B., Brisson, B. M., Häfner, I., Nagengast, B., & Trautwein, U. (2015). Fostering adolescents' value beliefs for mathematics with a relevance intervention in the classroom. *Developmental Psychology, 51*(9), 1226–40. doi: 10.1037/dev0000028.

Goldstein, J. & Flake, J. K. (2016). Towards a framework for the validation of early childhood assessment systems. *Educational Assessment, Evaluation and Accountability, 28*(3), 273–93. doi: 10.1007/s11092-015-9231-8.

Harackiewicz, J. M., Canning, E. A., Tibbetts, Y., Giffen, C. J., Blair, S. S., Rouse, D. I., & Hyde, J. S. (2014). Closing the social class achievement gap for first-generation students in undergraduate biology. *Journal of Educational Psychology, 106*(2), 375–89. doi: 10.1037/a0034679.

Hektner, J. M. & Csikszentmihalyi, M. (1996). A longitudinal exploration of flow and intrinsic motivation in adolescents. In *Annual Meeting of the American Educational Research Association*, NYC, New York.

Hidi, S. & Renninger, K. A. (2006). The four-phase model of interest development. *Educational Psychologist, 41*(2), 111–27. doi: 10.1207/s15326985ep4102_4.

Holstermann, N., Ainley, M., Grube, D., Roick, T., & Bögeholz, S. (2012). The specific relationship between disgust and interest: Relevance during biology class dissections and gender differences. *Learning and Instruction, 22*(3), 185–92. doi: 10.1016/j.learninstruc.2011.10.005.

Hulleman, C. S. (2007). *The role of utility value in the development of interest and achievement*. University of Wisconsin-Madison. Retrieved from http://files .eric.ed.gov/fulltext/ED498264.pdf.

Hulleman, C. S., Barron, K. E., Kosovich, J. J., & Lazowski, R. A. (2016). Expectancy-value models of achievement motivation in education. In A. A. Lipnevich, F. Preckel, & R. D. Robers (Eds.), *Psychosocial skills and school systems in the twenty-first century: Theory, research, and applications.* (pp. 241–78). Basel, Switzerland: Springer. doi: 10.1007/978-3-319-28606-8.

Hulleman, C. S., Godes, O., Hendricks, B. L., & Harackiewicz, J. M. (2010). Enhancing interest and performance with a utility value intervention. *Journal of Educational Psychology 102*, 880–95. doi:10.1037/a0019506.

Hulleman, C. S. & Harackiewicz, J. M. (2009). Promoting interest and performance in high school science classes. *Science, 326*(5958), 1410–12. doi: 10.1126/science.1177067.

Hulleman, C. S., Kosovich, J. J., Barron, K. E., & Daniel, D. B. (2016). Making connections: Replicating and extending the utility value intervention in the classroom. *Journal of Educational Psychology. 109*(3), 387–404. doi: 10.1037/edu0000146.

Hulleman, C. S., Schrager, S. M., Bodmann, S. M., & Harackiewicz, J. M. (2010). A meta-analytic review of achievement goal measures: Different labels for the same constructs or different constructs with similar labels? *Psychological Bulletin, 136*(3), 422–49. doi: 10.1037/a0018947.

Jacobs, J. E., Lanza, S., Osgood, D. W., Eccles, J. S., & Wigfield, A. (2002). Changes in children's self-competence and values: Gender and domain differences across grades one through twelve. *Child Development, 73*(2), 509–27. doi: 10.1111/1467-8624.00421.

Kane, M. T. (1992). An argument-based approach to validity. *Psychological Bulletin, 112*(3), 527–35.

Kane, M. T. (2013). Validating the interpretations and uses of test scores. *Journal of Educational Measurement, 50*(1), 1–73. doi: 10.1111/jedm.12000.

Kline, R. B. (2011). *Principles and practice of structural equation modeling* (3rd ed.). New York: The Guilford Press.

Kosovich, J. J. (2017). *Pragmatic measurement for education science: A method-substance synergy of validation and motivation.* Charolottesville, VA: University of Virginia.

Kosovich, J. J., Flake, J. K., & Hulleman, C. S. (2017). Short-term motivation trajectories: A parallel process model of expectancy-value. *Contemporary Educational Psychology. 49*(3), 130–139. doi: 10.1016/j.cedpsych.2017.01.004.

Kosovich, J. J., Hulleman, C. S., Barron, K. E., & Getty, S. (2015). A practical measure of student motivation: Establishing validity evidence for the expectancy-value-cost scale in middle school. *The Journal of Early Adolescence, 35*(5–6), 790–816. doi: 10.1177/0272431614556890.

Kosovich, J. J., Hulleman, C. S., & Flake, J. K. (2017). *Practical measurement: An argument-based approach to exploring alternative psychometric validity evidence.* Poster presented at the annual Society for Research on Educational Effectiveness, Washington, DC.

Krumm, A. E., Beattie, R., Takahashi, S., D'Angelo, C., Feng, M., & Cheng, B. (2016). Practical measurement and productive persistence: Strategies for using digital learning system data to drive improvement. *Journal of Learning Analytics*, *3*(2), 116–38. doi: 10.18608/jla.2016.32.6.

Lazowski, R. A. & Hulleman, C. S. (2016). Motivation interventions in education: A meta-analytic review. *Review of Educational Research*, *86*(2), 602–40. doi: 10.3102/0034654315617832.

Lewin, K., Dembo, T., Festinger, L., & Sears, P. S. (1944). Level of aspiration. In J. M. Hunt (Ed.), *Personality and the behavior disorders* (pp. 333–78). New York, NY: Ronal Press. doi: 10.1037/10319-006.

Messick, S. (1989). Meaning and values in test validation: The science and ethics of assessment. *Educational Researcher*, *18*(2), 5–11.

Paulhus, D. L. (1984). Two-component models of socially desirable responding. *Journal of Personality and Social Psychology*, *46*(3), 598–609. doi: 10.1037//0022-3514.46.3.598.

Pintrich, P. R. (2003). A motivational science perspective on the role of student motivation in learning and teaching contexts. *Journal of Educational Psychology*, *95*(4), 667–86. doi: 10.1037/0022-0663.95.4.667.

Raynor, J. O. (1982). Future orientation, self-evaluation, and achievement motivation: Use of an expectancy × value theory of personality functioning and change. In N. T. Feather (Ed.), *Expectations and actions: Expectancy-value models in psychology* (pp. 97–124). Hillsdale, NJ: Erlbaum.

Renninger, K. A. & Bachrach, J. E. (2015). Studying triggers for interest and engagement using observational methods. *Educational Psychologist, 50*(March), 58–69. doi: 10.1080/00461520.2014.999920.

Renninger, K. A. & Hidi, S. (2016). *The power of interest for motivation and engagement.* Abingdon: Routledge. Retrieved from http://works.swarthmore.edu/fac-education/91.

Rosenzweig, E. Q., Hulleman, C. H., Barron, K. E., et al. (in press). Promises and pitfalls of adapting utility value interventions for online mathematics courses. *Journal of Experimental Education*. doi: 10.1080/00220973.2018.1496059.

Rosenzweig, E. Q. & Wigfield, A. (2016). STEM motivation interventions for adolescents: A promising start, but further to go. *Educational Psychologist*, *51*(2), 146–63. doi: 10.1080/00461520.2016.1154792.

Rotgans, J. I. & Schmidt, H. G. (2011). The role of teachers in facilitating situational interest in an active-learning classroom. *Teaching and Teacher Education*, *27*(1), 37–42. doi: 10.1016/j.tate.2010.06.025.

Schmeiser, C. B. & Welch, C. J. (2006). Test development. In R. L. Brennan (Ed.), *Educational measurement* (4th ed., pp. 307–53). Westport, CT: Praeger Publishers.

Schwarz, N. & Oyserman, D. (2001). Asking questions about behavior: Cognition, communication, and questionnaire construction. *American Journal of Evaluation*, *22*(2), 127–60. doi: 10.1177/109821400102200202.

Sijtsma, K. (2009). On the use, the misuse, and the very limited usefulness of Cronbach's alpha. *Psychometrika*, *74*(1), 107–20. doi: 10.1007/s11336-008-9101-0.

Tibbetts, Y., Harackiewicz, J. M., Canning, E. A., Boston, J. S., Priniski, S. J., & Hyde, J. S. (2016). Affirming independence: Exploring mechanisms underlying a values affirmation intervention for first-generation students. *Journal of Personality and Social Psychology*, *110*, 635–59. doi: 10.1037/pspa0000049.

Traub, R. E. & Rowley, G. L. (1991). Understanding reliability. *Educational Measurement: Issues and Practice*, *10*(1), 37–45. doi: 10.1111/j.1745-3992.1991.tb00183.x.

Vroom, V. H. (1964). *Work and motivation: Classic readings in organizational behavior*. New York, NY: John Wiley & Sons.

Wise, S. L. & DeMars, C. (2005). Low examinee effort in low-stakes assessment: Problems and potential solutions. *Educational Assessment*, *10*(1), 1–17.

Yeager, D. S., Bryk, A., Muhich, J., Hausman, H., & Morales, L. (2013). *Practical measurement*. Palo Alto, CA: Carnegie Foundation for the Advancement of Teaching. www.carnegiefoundation.org/resources/publications/practical-measurement/.

Yeager, D. S. & Walton, G. M. (2011). Social-psychological interventions in education: They're not magic. *Review of Educational Research*, *81*(2), 267–301. doi: org/10.3102/0034654311405999.

Appendix 28.A: General Education Survey

We are interested in how students view [the university]'s general education program, *The Human Community*. This survey assesses your attitudes toward general education coursework at [the university]. For each section below, think about the courses you will take or have already taken to fulfill your general education requirements. Respond to each item using the following scale:

1	2	3	4	5	6
Strongly disagree	Disagree	Slightly disagree	Slightly agree	Agree	Strongly agree

Area One: Skills for the Twenty-First Century

Area One is the cornerstone of The Human Community at [the university] in that students develop skills that facilitate inquiring, learning, thinking, and communicating in their personal, academic, and civic lives.

Students at [the university] typically fulfill their Area One requirement by taking coursework in the areas of **critical thinking**, **oral communication**, and **writing**.

1. Area One courses interest me.
2. The topics and skills taught in Area One courses are important to me.
3. I can do well in my Area One courses.

Area Two: Arts and Humanities

Area Two shows students what it means to live lives enriched by reflection, imagination, and creativity. It does so by offering each individual a multidisciplinary experience within the arts and humanities, those areas of endeavor humans have long valued for their intrinsic worth that invite a deeper appreciation of the human experience.

Students at [the university] typically fulfill their Area Two requirement by taking coursework in areas such as **history**, **art**, **music**, **theater**, and **literature**.

4. Area Two courses interest me.
5. The topics and skills taught in Area Two courses are important to me.
6. I can do well in my Area Two courses.

Area Three: The Natural World

Area Three provides students with the opportunity to develop problem-solving skills in science and mathematics at the college level. Students will be introduced to a substantial body of scientific facts, concepts, models, and theories and will also gain experience in using basic mathematics to obtain knowledge about the natural world.

Students at [the university] typically fulfill their Area Three requirement by taking coursework in areas such as **mathematics**, **chemistry**, **physics**, **astronomy**, **biology**, and **geology**.

7. Area Three courses interest me.
8. The topics and skills taught in Area Three courses are important to me.
9. I can do well in my Area Three courses.

Area Four: Social and Cultural Processes

Area Four helps students become critical thinkers about their own societies and the larger global community. These courses examine the key social and cultural processes and structures that shape the human experience.

Students at [the university] typically fulfill their Area Four requirement by taking coursework in areas such as **economics**, **history**, **political science**, **anthropology**, and **sociology**.

10. Area Four courses interest me.
11. The topics and skills taught in Area Four courses are important to me.
12. I can do well in my Area Four courses.

Area Five: Individuals in the Human Community

Area Five helps students learn about themselves as individuals and as members of different communities. Students explore how individuals develop and function in the social, psychological, emotional, physical, and spiritual dimensions.

Students at [the university] typically fulfill their Area Five requirement by taking coursework in areas such as **health**, **kinesiology**, **psychology**, and **sociology**.

13. Area Five courses interest me.
14. The topics and skills taught in Area Five courses are important to me.
15. I can do well in my Area Five courses.

Now that you have indicated your attitudes toward general education, we would like to know about your attitudes toward your major courses. Respond to the next three items using the scale below. *If you have not yet declared a major, select "7" as your response.*

1	2	3	4	5	6	7
Strongly disagree	Disagree	Slightly disagree	Slightly agree	Agree	Strongly agree	I haven't declared a major yet

16. My major courses interest me.
17. The topics and skills taught in my major courses are important to me.
18. I can do well in my major courses.

29 An Integrative Perspective for Studying Motivation in Relation to Engagement and Learning

Lisa Linnenbrink-Garcia and
Stephanie V. Wormington

Abstract: Several decades of research highlight the benefits of various motivational beliefs (e.g., perceived competence, achievement goals, task value) in supporting students' learning and engagement. Much of this research utilizes a variable-focused approach, examining how different forms of motivation uniquely and independently predict educational outcomes. In contrast, a person-oriented approach allows one to examine how motivational processes combine to shape academic engagement and achievement. Person-oriented approaches are especially promising in that they allow one to simultaneously consider variations in several motivational indicators to better understand the multiple ways that students utilize motivational resources to support engagement and achievement. This chapter presents an integrative, person-oriented approach to studying student motivation. Specifically, the approach (1) draws from multiple theoretical perspectives to operationalize motivation, and (2) utilizes person-oriented analyses to model how motivational components combine to shape learning and engagement. Based on prior research and our own work, preliminary conclusions regarding what motivates students and which combinations of motivation are most and least adaptive are discussed. Implications for translating integrative research into effective classroom practices to support student motivation are considered.

For both teachers and researchers, supporting student motivation and learning remains a central aim in education. Indeed, many educators in K-12 and higher education settings struggle to teach in a way that helps all students stay engaged and learn. Motivation researchers have spent decades refining frameworks for understanding motivation, and documenting the link between motivation and learning-related outcomes (for a recent review, see Linnenbrink-Garcia & Patall, 2016). Many of the lessons gleaned from motivation research have the potential to directly inform classroom practice; however, as in much of educational research, there is a disconnect between motivation theory and classroom practice (Linnenbrink-Garcia et al., 2016). One potential reason for this disconnect is that there are multiple theories of motivation, each providing distinct but complementary insights into what drives students in the classroom. This approach means that motivational research is frequently conducted using a single motivational framework. Focusing on a single theory often fails to explicitly consider how many different motivational factors synergistically affect students' learning and engagement – and can lead to a mismatch between both how researchers study motivation and what educators observe in their classrooms. In other words, students enter classrooms with myriad reasons to learn or to disengage, and these reasons are not necessarily captured by one particular motivational theory.

Accordingly, a basic premise of our chapter is that there is a need to integrate across motivational theories, both to better understand student motivation as it plays out in the classroom *and* to provide educators with clearer guidelines about ways to effectively support student motivation. The central argument for this integrative perspective is simple: motivation as it exists in the classroom is often much more complex and nuanced than motivation as it is presented in research papers. As a result, there is a disconnect between the information that motivation research provides and the information that educators can apply to support their students. Consider, for instance, two fifth grade students in a language arts class. Both students are concerned with showing their teacher that they are the best writer in class. One student also enjoys writing, sees herself as good at writing, and has a goal to develop her writing skills. The other student, conversely, neither sees himself as a good writer nor finds writing interesting. Would we expect both students to receive equally high grades in class, pursue writing in the future, or persevere through challenging class assignments? More importantly, how should a language arts teacher support both students' learning and engagement during class?

Integrating across motivational theories partially addresses the gap between theory and practice, as it can provide a more complete picture of the sundry reasons students are or are not motivated in the classroom. However, simply measuring diverse forms of motivation does not provide insight into what motivates particular students or which combination(s) of motivational factors lead to the greatest learning and engagement. We argue that researchers must not only consider multiple forms of motivation simultaneously, but also use an analytic approach that models the way that different combinations (or profiles) of motivation predict student engagement and learning. By considering how multiple forms of motivation function in concert with each other, researchers can begin to understand ways to design educational contexts that support the potentially multiple beneficial patterns of motivation. Moreover, understanding how various combinations of motivation relate to academic engagement and achievement has the potential to provide much clearer guidelines for educators working to support student motivation, engagement, and learning in their classrooms.

In light of these concerns, we propose an integrative approach to studying student motivation that consists of two components: (1) drawing from multiple theoretical perspectives to operationalize motivation, and (2) utilizing person-oriented analyses to model how motivational components combine to shape learning and engagement. After providing a brief overview of motivation and the major motivational theories on which our work is based, we describe a person-oriented perspective and highlight its utility for understanding how multiple types of motivation combine to shape students' learning and engagement. We then describe our integrative motivational research, drawing from a series of studies conducted in elementary school through college, as an illustrative example of the potential of an integrative approach for studying motivation. Based on prior research and our own work, we share preliminary evidence regarding what motivates students and which combinations of motivation are most and least adaptive. We conclude by considering the potential implications and difficulties of translating integrative research into effective classroom practices to support student motivation.

What is Motivation? An Integrative Perspective

From striving to make the honor role to pursuing a long-held interest in math, students can be driven to learn for a multitude of reasons. Researchers have developed numerous theories to operationalize motivation, with thousands of studies documenting how different types of motivation relate to students' thoughts, feelings, and outcomes in school. While each theory focuses on related but distinct motivating factors, most current theoretical perspectives consider forms of motivation that can be described as both initiating and sustaining behavior (Schunk et al., 2014). One useful framework for considering types of motivation divides constructs between two fundamental motivational questions: "Can I do this?" (i.e., competence-related beliefs) and "Do I want to do this, and why?" (i.e., value-related beliefs; Wigfield et al., 2006).

We contend that these two motivational questions serve as a useful anchor point for selecting motivational constructs across motivational theories. That is, researchers should include types of motivation that capture both competence-related beliefs and value-related beliefs when adopting an integrative perspective. With the plethora of constructs available, capitalizing on the predictive power across theories by identifying types of motivation that relate to different types of student outcomes is important. Whether a student feels confident that they can succeed in physics class, for instance, should relate to their final course grade (Schunk & Pajares, 2005). Whether a student finds value in learning about physics, on the other hand, may relate to their likelihood of enrolling in future science-related courses (Wigfield & Cambria, 2010). Considering both types of indicators provides a more complete picture of the way motivation relates to learning and behavior. At the same time, researchers should avoid unnecessary overlap among constructs. For instance, the added predictive value of including multiple indicators of competence-related beliefs is likely to be relatively small. An integrative perspective, in our view, involves fully capturing students' motivation as parsimoniously as possible.

There is no single optimal approach for integrating across motivational theories, and a thorough overview of all current motivational theories and constructs is beyond the scope of the current chapter (for recent reviews, see Linnenbrink-Garcia & Patall, 2016; Usher, 2016; Wigfield et al., 2015). To illustrate one potential approach, we present our integrative research and briefly describe the motivational theories that inform our work: social cognitive theory, achievement goal theory, expectancy-value theory, and interest theory. These four theories encompass many, but not all, of the major modern motivational theories. For instance, we do not draw from Deci and Ryan's (1985) prominent self-determination theory, even though it includes related but distinct motivational constructs, such as an intrinsic motivation. In this way, our approach is not meant to be all-encompassing; rather, our goal is to include constructs that provide a rich but parsimonious snapshot of student motivation.

Social Cognitive Theory

Whether students believe they can successfully complete a task is a key determinant of their subsequent behavior. Bandura's (1986) social cognitive theory highlights students' self-efficacy as a key component of motivation. *Self-efficacy* refers to individuals' beliefs about their capacities to successfully execute behaviors at particular levels or on a given task. In academic settings, self-efficacy refers to students' beliefs about their ability to learn, develop skills, or master material. For example, a student may feel confident that they can solve a particular math problem, read and understand a passage, or learn to conduct a science experiment. Self-efficacy is associated with a variety of educational indicators, including students' choices; effort and willingness to persist on a task; strategy use; emotions; and achievement (Bandura, 1986; Bandura et al., 1996; Pajares, 1996; Usher, 2016).

Achievement Goal Theory

Students may also enter the classroom with goals to increase their knowledge or to display their knowledge to others. Achievement goal theory, another prominent motivational theory, focuses on the purposes that underlie achievement-related decisions and behavior (Anderman & Wolters, 2006; Maehr & Zusho, 2009). While there is some variation in how these purposes are conceptualized (see Linnenbrink-Garcia et al., 2012a; Maehr & Zusho, 2009), goal theorists generally agree on two main types of goals: *mastery goals* (a focus on developing competence) and *performance goals* (a focus on demonstrating competence). Mastery goals and performance goals can be further differentiated based on approach or avoidance tendencies. Since there is less work and clarity around mastery-avoidance goals (a focus on avoiding not learning as much as possible; Elliot & McGregor, 1999; Madjar et al., 2011), we focus on the other three types of goals in our work: mastery-approach goals (a focus on developing competence), performance-approach goals (a focus on demonstrating competence to others), and performance-avoidance goals (a focus on avoiding appearing incompetent; Elliot, 1999; Middleton & Midgley, 1997). Achievement goals are related to key academic outcomes, including engagement and persistence, self-regulation, other forms of motivation (e.g., self-efficacy, interest), emotions, and achievement (for reviews, see Anderman & Wolters, 2006; Hulleman et al., 2010; Linnenbrink-Garcia & Barger, 2014). Mastery goals are generally positively related to adaptive indicators, such as other forms of motivation, positive emotions, self-regulation, and (at least to some extent) achievement. Performance-approach goals are linked to both positive and negative emotions, and show mixed relations with self-regulation and achievement. Performance-avoidance goals are generally negatively related to achievement and self-regulation, and are positively associated with negative emotions.

Expectancy-Value Theory

Students often find certain subject areas or topics to be particularly interesting, useful, or important to their identity. Expectancy-value theory, a third prominent perspective on motivation, highlights students' expectancies for success and perceived value as critical motivational components (Atkinson, 1957; Eccles, 1983). *Expectancies* refer to students' beliefs about whether they will be capable of succeeding at a task. Expectancies are part of a larger family of competence-related beliefs, including self-efficacy as described in social cognitive theory (Bandura, 1986). Values can be differentiated into four primary components: (1) *intrinsic value*, or finding a particular task or domain enjoyable and interesting; (2) *utility value*, or the usefulness of a task or subject area; (3) *attainment value*, or the personal importance of doing well on a particular task or in a particular domain for one's identity; and (4) *cost,* or the perceived drawbacks of engaging in a particular task or domain due to high effort needed for success, lost opportunities to engage in other tasks or domains, and psychological or emotional tolls. Both expectancies and values predict behaviors (such as academic and career choices, engagement, and achievement), with expectancies most strongly related to achievement and values most strongly related to choice (Wigfield & Cambria, 2010).

Interest Theory

Finally, students often find some topics, courses, or domains more interesting than others. Interest can be conceptualized both as a psychological state (e.g., the state of a person while engaged in a task) and as a relatively more enduring motivational disposition (Renninger & Hidi, 2016). Paralleling the other motivational theories described in this chapter, we focus on interest as a motivational disposition, with a specific focus on individual interest – a form of interest that is relatively stable and sustained in a given area.[1] Individual interest is characterized by positive emotions, such as enjoyment, personal meaningfulness, knowledge, and continued engagement over time. However, similar to the other motivational theories described earlier, individual interest can change over time, depending on the degree to which it is supported by the environment. Individual interest is related to behavioral and choice-related outcomes, such as increased attention, cognitive processing, persistence, and course choice (Harackiewicz et al., 2008; Renninger & Hidi, 2016; Schiefele, 2001, 2009; Wigfield & Cambria, 2010).

Our Integrative Approach to Studying Student Motivation

Drawing from these four major theoretical perspectives, we identified three broad families of motivational constructs as critical to foster in the class-room (see Table 29.1): perceived competence (representing self-efficacy and expectancies), task value (also representing individual interest), and achievement goals (mastery-approach, performance-approach, and performance-avoidance; see also Linnenbrink-Garcia & Wormington, 2017). Recall that our primary aims in adopting an integrative perspective were to (1) include constructs that address the motivational questions of "Can I do this?" and "Do I want to do this, and why?" and (2) capture a representative, parsimonious picture of student motivation. Perceived competence taps into the question of "Can I do this?" (i.e., competence-related beliefs), while task value and achievement goals address the question of "Do I want to do this, and why?" (i.e., value-related beliefs). We next describe each individual component (perceived competence, task value, and achievement goals) and our decision-making process for collapsing across constructs.

Perceived competence. Perceived competence refers to whether students believe they can be successful on a given task, in a given situation, or in a given domain. Perceived competence encompasses both self-efficacy (from social cognitive theory) and expectancies (from expectancy-value theory). While there are important theoretical distinctions among competence-related constructs (see Bong & Skaalvik, 2003; Schunk & Pajares, 2005), we view this family of beliefs as largely similar and showing similar relations to learning outcomes.

Task value. Task value considers whether a student values a given task or domain because it is interesting, enjoyable, useful, or important to them. As such, task value includes interest value, attainment value, and utility value

---

1 Interest researchers also study situational interest, which refers to interest that emerges from and is supported by the context (Hidi & Renninger, 2006; Renninger & Hidi, 2016). However, individual interest is more aligned with the other motivational constructs discussed in this chapter; thus, we limit our focus to individual interest.

Table 29.1 *Motivational constructs from social cognitive theory, expectancy-value theory, interest theory, and achievement goal theory*

	Can I do this?	Do I want to do this, and why?
Social cognitive theory	Self-efficacy	
Achievement goal theory		Mastery-approach goals Performance-approach goals Performance-avoidance goals
Expectancy-value theory	Expectancies	Task value
Interest theory		Individual interest

(from expectancy-value theory). Task value can also reasonably be considered to represent individual interest (from interest theory), given that both task value and individual interest include an interest/enjoyment component and a meaning/value component (Linnenbrink-Garcia & Wormington, 2017; Wigfield & Eccles, 2000). Though there are theoretical distinctions between individual interest and task value, there is also a great deal of overlap and consistency in how they relate to learning outcomes.[2]

Achievement goals. Achievement goals assess students' desires to develop their competence, demonstrate their competence to others, or avoid demonstrating incompetence. In this category, we include three distinct types of goals: mastery goals, performance-approach goals, and performance-avoidance goals. We view achievement goals as largely distinct from task value indicators, though the two groups of motivational indicators are reciprocally related (see Harackiewicz et al., 2008; Linnenbrink & Pintrich, 2000). Specifically, achievement goals assess the aim or focus of engagement, while task value captures students' emotional response and perceptions of the relative importance of a domain. Performance-approach goals and performance-avoidance goals are also related to different outcomes and display different patterns of relations than task value indicators. Thus, at least at this point, we include all four constructs (task value, mastery goal orientations, performance-approach goal orientations, and performance-avoidance goal orientations) to capture the complexity of the value-related elements of motivation.

---

2 As noted by Renninger and Hidi (2016), this conceptualization of individual interest as similar to task value does not fully capture interest as described in Hidi and Renninger's (2006) four-phase model of interest development. Specifically, unlike task value, interest need not be something of which one is consciously aware. Task value also excludes the knowledge element that is an important part of individual interest. Finally, task value does not capture the developing nature of interest, as conceptualized within the four-phase model. However, similar to our contention that self-efficacy and expectancies can reasonably be captured by perceived competence, we also contend that task value and individual interest are similar enough that they can reasonably be captured by the construct of task value.

What is a Person-Oriented Approach and How Can it Add to an Integrative Perspective?

Thus far, we have argued for the need to integrate across theories to include a range of motivational constructs. However, studying multiple forms of motivation simultaneously raises analytical challenges. A *person-oriented approach* can serve as a useful analytic technique to capture students' multifaceted motivation and understand the way many motivational factors simultaneously relate to learning and engagement. In this section, we first describe person-oriented approaches in contrast to more common variable-oriented approaches. Then, we briefly review person-oriented motivation research and describe how we have applied person-oriented analyses to our integrative motivational work.

Person-Oriented versus Variable-Oriented Approaches

The majority of motivation studies utilize a statistical framework generally referred to as a variable-oriented perspective. Within a variable-oriented perspective, researchers examine how specific motivational constructs (such as self-efficacy or mastery goals) relate to academic outcomes (such as engagement or achievement). Variable-oriented findings have yielded useful information on the relative benefits and detriments of individual types of motivation. For example, Wolters (2004) examined how middle school students' achievement goals (mastery, performance-approach, and performance-avoidance goals) and self-efficacy related to choice, effort, persistence, procrastination, learning strategies, and course grade. His findings identified which types of motivation most strongly predicted which types of academic outcomes. Mastery goals were related to all outcomes except course grade, and self-efficacy was associated with choice, persistence, and course grade. Performance-approach goals, on the other hand, were only related to course grade. Based on these results, one might conclude that multiple forms of motivation – including mastery goals, self-efficacy, and performance-approach goals – are important for supporting multiple indicators of academic success.

Variable-oriented analyses are well-suited to isolate unique effects and generalize across an entire sample of students. Applied to practice, variable-oriented analyses provide findings that would apply, on average, across a teacher's entire classroom or set of classrooms. However, if we recall that motivational constructs are not isolated in classrooms (e.g., teachers cannot control for other variables when trying to support a particular form of motivation in the classroom) and students do not all hold the same motivational beliefs (e.g., there might be a variety of combinations of different levels of motivation among students in a classroom), there are several challenges to consider when translating variable-oriented research findings to the classroom. Several of these difficulties are due to two assumptions on which variable-oriented analyses are based.

First, variable-oriented analyses examine the way each type of motivation *uniquely* predicts outcomes by controlling for other levels of motivation. For instance, variable-oriented analyses could inform us about how strongly students' interest in social studies relates to their final grade in a social studies course regardless of how competent they feel in class. This approach can present difficulties for multiple reasons. When numerous motivational variables are included as predictors, they each compete to predict unique variance in the outcome variable. However, decades of research suggest that many types of motivation are highly correlated with one another. Including highly related predictors together in a model may lead to what researchers refer to as multicollinearity; when multicollinearity occurs, important but highly related predictors may cancel each other out, emerge as non-significant, or switch signs. From a researcher perspective, multicollinearity presents a statistical problem in which results may be obscured due to statistical suppression; indeed, multicollinearity is an ongoing concern within the field for some motivational constructs, such as performance-approach and performance-avoidance goals (Law et al., 2012; Linnenbrink-Garcia et al., 2012a). From an educator perspective, multicollinearity might obscure information about the variety of forms of motivation that effectively support students' learning and prompt educators to overlook ways to support critical forms of motivation in their classroom. In other words, a variable-oriented approach may not provide the full picture of which forms of motivation are most strongly associated with student engagement and, consequently, which motivational factors teachers should focus on supporting in the classroom.

Second, variable-oriented analyses provide information on the way motivational variables predict learning and engagement across an entire sample. In other words, they assess general patterns of relations between variables that apply, on average, to all individuals studied. However, theory and practical experience suggest that students may have multiple reasons for engaging in class, and that understanding students' overall pattern of motivation is crucial for predicting their academic success (e.g., Pintrich, 2000). Within achievement goal theory, there is substantial debate about whether it is most adaptive when students simultaneously endorse both mastery and performance-approach goals or mastery goals alone (see Barron & Harackiewicz, 2001; Harackiewicz et al., 2002). Within expectancy-value theory, researchers have returned to Atkinson's original notion of an interaction between expectancy and values, and have begun to consider whether students need both high expectancies for success and value to be successful (e.g., Nagengast et al., 2011; Trautwein et al., 2012). Despite the theoretical importance, variable-oriented research often either ignores how various forms of motivation combine to shape academic outcomes or only considers interactions between two forms of motivation within a single framework. Even if researchers were interested in modeling interactions among more forms of motivation, they would likely face challenges; higher-order interactions require a substantial sample size, are difficult to interpret, and may lead researchers to discuss patterns of motivation endorsed by very few students. From a practical perspective, a variable-oriented approach is more limited in terms of describing patterns of motivation as they occur within students in the classroom. As such, teachers may view variable-oriented findings as less useful because they may not align with students' complex, multifaceted patterns of motivation.

A person-oriented perspective bypasses many of these challenges, making it a particularly fruitful approach to studying student motivation and to making recommendations for educational practice. Person-oriented analyses examine the way predictors combine at the level of the individual, identify common combinations of predictors (i.e., profiles), and compare profiles on outcomes of interest (Bergman et al., 2003; Laursen & Hoff, 2006; Marsh & Hao, 2007). Applied to motivation, a person-oriented approach involves creating groups or profiles of students based on several different motivational factors. To illustrate, let us return to our example of the two fifth grade language arts students. Both students reported high performance-approach goals, but differed with respect to their competency beliefs, mastery goals, and value. Even though they appear the same on some forms of motivation (i.e., performance-approach goals), person-oriented analyses would place these two students into different motivational profiles, because they display different overall patterns of motivation. By comparing students from these two profiles to one another, researchers would be able to answer the original question of which student will be most successful in class. Ultimately, person-oriented research may also provide recommendations on how a teacher could best support both students' learning, because it acknowledges that these students may have different needs, strengths, and challenges in the classroom.

Besides capturing students' multiple reasons for being motivated in a situation, a person-oriented approach can be particularly useful with an integrative theoretical perspective because it allows researchers to model the relations among motivation constructs across theoretical frameworks that may be conceptually related to one another. Accordingly, researchers who employ an integrated person-oriented approach to studying motivation should be better equipped to make more comprehensive suggestions for practice. Specifically, a person-oriented approach can help researchers better understand the way different combinations of motivations function together to predict key academic outcomes. Doing so is likely to reveal multiple beneficial pathways to success and, thus, would help teachers better understand which forms of motivation to support in the classroom and which patterns of motivation displayed by students may indicate that they are at greater risk academically. Moreover, by integrating across theories, this approach could help streamline the diverse motivational literature to provide a more comprehensive and integrated set of suggestions for information practice. Thus, we contend that person-oriented analyses are a useful tool, not only for researchers interested in adopting an integrative motivational perspective and translating research findings into practice, but also for educators who are interested in applying motivational research in their classrooms.

Related research. Person-oriented motivation research has blossomed in the past decade, most notably within self-determination theory (e.g., Hayenga & Corpus, 2010; Vansteenkiste et al., 2009; Wormington et al., 2012) and achievement goal theory (e.g., Bembenutty, 1999; Cano & Berben, 2009; Luo et al., 2011; Ng, 2006; Pulkka & Niemivirta, 2013). However, even with accumulating evidence, there has been little synthesis across person-oriented findings, or integration of person-oriented studies into the more mainstream variable-oriented literature (but, see Wormington & Linnenbrink-Garcia, 2016). Even fewer person-oriented studies have integrated across motivational frameworks, and there is little consistency among integrative studies as to which motivational and non-motivational constructs they used to create profiles (Bräten & Olaussen, 2005; Conley, 2012; Dina & Efklides, 2009; Lau & Roeser, 2008; Nelson et al., 2015; Seifert & O'Keefe, 2001; Shell & Husman, 2008; Shell & Su, 2013; Turner et al., 1998). While some researchers focus solely on motivational constructs to create profiles (e.g., Bräten & Olaussen, 2005; Conley, 2012), others draw more broadly to consider motivation alongside factors such as cognitive strategy use and emotional well-being (e.g., Turner et al., 1998) or social goals (Seifert & O'Keefe, 2001). Despite a lack of consistency, the growing number of studies provides evidence that person-oriented analyses are a useful tool for researchers interested in integrating across motivational theories to predict student engagement and learning.

In our own work, we integrated across social cognitive theory, expectancy-value theory, interest theory, and achievement goal theory to create profiles of perceived competence, task value, and achievement goals. We examined these integrative motivational profiles in a series of studies among samples varying by age, demographic characteristics, educational setting, and academic domain (Linnenbrink-Garcia et al., 2018; Wormington, 2016; Wormington et al., 2014; for additional details, see Linnenbrink-Garcia & Wormington, 2017). In this series of studies, we examined fifth grade students' general school motivation, middle school students' mathematics and social studies motivation, high school students' mathematics motivation in online courses, and college students' science motivation. In each sample, we also compared students in different profiles with respect to academic engagement and achievement. Strikingly similar profiles emerged across studies, with very similar patterns of profiles in relation to academic outcomes. There were also several sample-specific profiles and differences in the prevalence of certain profiles. Together, this work suggests that some profiles we identified may represent common motivational patterns. However, it is also critical to acknowledge findings that are limited to a specific set of students, domains, or educational contexts. Next, we summarize our findings to date across studies.

Across diverse samples, we found three consistent profiles, with a fourth profile emerging in all but one study. One profile of highly motivated students reported moderate-high to high levels of all forms of motivation we assessed – students in this profile felt competent in their ability to be successful, valued the subject area or schoolwork, and endorsed both mastery and performance (approach and avoidance) goals. A second profile of students also reported high perceived competence, task value, and mastery goals – they differed from the first profile because they did not also pursue performance-approach and performance-avoidance goals. Students who were high in all forms of motivation, or who had high levels of more intrinsic forms of motivation (task value, mastery goals) and perceived competence, reported equally high engagement and achievement, suggesting that both motivational profiles can support students' engagement in their schoolwork and high achievement.

A less adaptive, but equally common, profile consisted of students who reported mean levels of all forms of motivation around the midpoint of the scale; these students reported average perceived competence, task value, and achievement goals. Finally, across some samples, we found a profile with low performance goals and moderate to low perceived competence, task value, and mastery goals. Students in both the average profile and the profile characterized by low performance goals were generally less engaged and lower achieving than those in the first two profiles (characterized by high levels of all forms of motivation or high levels of intrinsic motivation and high perceived competence). As noted earlier, we also found several profiles that were specific to a particular sample; these profiles often reflected slight variations from the primary ones identified, but were not consistently identified across studies.

Taken together, our findings highlight the utility of adopting an integrative perspective and utilizing person-oriented analyses for capturing students' motivation and its relation to engagement and achievement. Based on consistent evidence from several samples and academic contexts, we can begin to draw preliminary conclusions that may be of use to the research and educational communities alike. One potentially illuminating finding, based on our evidence, is that endorsing performance goals (both approach and avoidance) may be adaptive as long as students also endorse high levels of competence beliefs, value, and mastery goals. However, the endorsement of performance goals alongside high competence beliefs, value, and mastery goals is not more beneficial than having high competence, value, and mastery *without* also endorsing performance goals. For researchers, this finding speaks squarely to the debate surrounding the benefits or drawbacks of performance-approach goal endorsement (Midgley et al., 2001; Senko et al., 2011). For educators, our results suggest that teachers need not be concerned with either dampening or amplifying each student's natural proclivity toward performance goals; rather, it seems critical to create a classroom that fosters feelings of competence, interest in and valuing of the subject, and a desire to develop competence over time.

Implications and Cautions for Using an Integrative Perspective on Motivation

As a field and within our own work, person-oriented motivational research is still in its nascence. Even in its early stages, however, we see substantial promise in the insights that integrative motivational research could hold for both research and practice. For researchers, person-oriented approaches provide a way to feasibly study motivation much more broadly, address theoretical questions regarding the optimal combinations of motivation, and bypass statistical obstacles (such as multicollinearity or interpreting higher-order interactions). Person-oriented findings can also be integrated with the much more extensive variable-oriented literature to provide additional nuance. For instance, our own work suggests that whether performance-approach goals are adaptive depends on accompanying competence beliefs, value, and mastery goals.

For practitioners, integrative motivational research provides examples of types of students (i.e., motivational profiles) that teachers might encounter in their classrooms. This focus on the student, rather than on motivational variables, can facilitate a better translation between what educators read about from motivation research and what they implement to support students in their classrooms. Specifically, a person-oriented approach allows researchers to provide a more descriptive account of different combinations of motivation than teachers might typically observe in students. With empirical research providing evidence that some of these combinations lead to greater engagement and learning, educators could use these descriptive profiles to identify students who may be more at risk given their current displays of motivation. As noted earlier, person-oriented research also makes it easier for researchers to integrate across theories and may also facilitate clearer, more concise recommendations for classroom practice that integrate across theoretical silos. This is key, as the current state of motivational research presents many challenges in providing a clear, concise, and accurate account of the motivational literature. The complexity of messages across theoretical approaches frequently leads to the decision to oversimplify motivational research, such as teaching teachers about intrinsic versus extrinsic motivation but not about other motivational constructs. An integrated, person-oriented account has the potential to retain more of the nuance regarding different forms of motivation, while also narrowing down the implications for the way these different forms of motivation can be applied in educational practice (see, for example, our work on creating five motivational design principles based on multiple motivational theories, Linnenbrink-Garcia et al., 2016).

Moving forward, we see potential for person-oriented research to guide both researchers and educators in tailoring the supports they provide for students displaying different patterns of motivation. This tailoring may take the form of implementing different social-psychological interventions based on a student's current motivational profile, allocating support and resources toward the most at-risk groups of students, or customizing classroom activities to best fit with students' multifaceted motivational beliefs. Of course, additional research should be conducted before making any of the above recommendations for practice, particularly with respect to interventions. Critically, our work and that of other researchers has focused solely on description – identifying motivational profiles that demonstrate more and less adaptive patterns of achievement, engagement, and learning. To take the next step toward determining which resources or interventional supports students with different motivational profiles may benefit from the most, our field requires much more in-depth study of mechanisms (i.e., why some combinations of motivational beliefs are associated with more or less beneficial academic outcomes) and experimental evidence examining whether intervention effects vary as a function of motivational profiles.

As an additional caveat, any attempt to label students comes with very real dangers, particularly for students in less adaptive profiles. Let us be explicit: we strongly believe that person-oriented analysis should not be treated as a diagnostic tool. Not only would doing so run the risk of a phenomenon akin to the Pygmalion effect[3] (Rosenthal & Jacobson, 1968), but our work suggests that treating motivational profiles as fixed or stable is inaccurate. In the integrative studies described earlier, we also examined how students shifted between motivational profiles between consecutive semesters or school years. Approximately half of students shifted between profiles regardless of the sample, context, and amount of time between measurement points (Linnenbrink-Garcia et al., 2012b, 2014; Wormington, 2016; Wormington et al., 2014). This level of stability aligns with the few person-oriented motivation studies that have also measured profile membership longitudinally (e.g., Corpus & Wormington, 2014; Hayenga & Corpus, 2010; Lee et al., 2017; Tuominen-Soini et al., 2011, 2012). As such, even a student holding a less adaptive combination of motivations at one time point does not indicate that they will retain those same levels of motivation indefinitely. We have begun to examine factors that predict these profile shifts, which will provide important information for targeting interventions and supports toward students in less adaptive profiles. Until that work is conducted and the body of person-oriented research is more robust, we urge researchers and educators to consider integrative person-oriented motivation research as a promising tool, but treat findings as preliminary.

As an integrative motivational perspective becomes more prominent, there are several additional considerations to keep in mind. For one, there may be

---

3 The Pygmalion effect refers to a classic study in which teachers were provided with information about whether students were "intellectual bloomers." Although membership in the bloomer group was randomly assigned (e.g., it did not reflect students' actual ability), these experimenter-generated indicators of intelligence predicted students' subsequent achievement, presumably through differential teacher expectations.

a more predictive or parsimonious combination of motivational variables to consider other than our suite of perceived competence, task value, and achievement goals. Researchers should think carefully in making their own decisions about the motivational predictors they do or do not include, which may vary based on their particular sample or research questions. Also of note, our work has primarily considered achievement and engagement as indicators of student learning. Of course, student learning is not limited to how engaged or disengaged students are during the class period or to their final grade in a course. In addition, we have not systematically examined how our findings might vary based on individual and contextual characteristics. As such, two of our goals moving forward are to broaden our operationalization of student learning, and to consider differences in profile membership and how the profiles relate to academic outcomes among diverse learners in diverse educational contexts. Both efforts should provide a more complete picture of students' motivation and facilitate a conversation with teachers who interface with a broader group of students in a more varied set of educational contexts.

Concluding Thoughts

In conclusion, an integrated motivational perspective has the potential to help address the gap between motivational theory and classroom practice. By combining across theories and using person-oriented analyses, an integrative approach can help researchers better model the way multiple forms of motivation function together to shape key academic outcomes. It also has the potential to guide researchers in tailoring interventions, and better inform researchers and educators about more or less adaptive combinations of motivation. Finally, an integrative motivational perspective may help educators see the connection between motivation theory and the forms and variations in motivation they observe in their students daily. There is more work to be done on this approach, but we are excited about the possibilities for shaping both theory and practice.

References

Anderman, E. M. & Wolters, C. A. (2006). Goals, values, and affect: Influences on student motivation. In P. A. Alexander & P. H. Winne (Eds.), *Handbook of educational psychology* (pp. 369–89). Mahwah, NJ: Lawrence Erlbaum Associates Publishers. doi: 10.4324/9780203874790.ch17.

Atkinson, J. W. (1957). Motivational determinants of risk-taking behavior. *Psychological Review*, *64*, 359–72. doi: 10.1037/h0043445.

Bandura, A. (1986). *Social foundations of thought and action: A social cognitive theory*. Englewood Cliffs, NJ: Prentice Hall.

Bandura, A., Barbaranelli, C., Caprara, G. V., & Pastorelli, C. (1996). Multifaceted impact of self-efficacy beliefs on academic functioning. *Child Development, 67*, 1206–22. doi: 10.1111/j.1467-8624.1996.tb01791.x.

Barron, K. E. & Harackiewicz, J. M. (2001). Achievement goals and optimal motivation: Testing multiple goal models. *Journal of Personality and Social Psychology, 80*, 706–22. doi: 10.1037/0022-3514.80.5.706.

Bembenutty, H. (1999). Sustaining motivation and academic goals: The role of academic delay of gratification. *Learning and Individual Differences, 11*, 233–57. doi: 10.1016/S1041-6080(99)80002-8.

Bergman, L. R., Magnusson, D., & El Khouri, B. (2003). *Studying individual development in an interindividual context: A person-oriented approach.* Mahwah, NJ: Lawrence Erlbaum Associates.

Bong, M. & E. M. Skaalvik (2003). Academic self-concept and self-efficacy: How different are they really? *Educational Psychology Review, 15*(1), 1–40. doi: 10.1023/A:1021302408382.

Bräten, I. & Olaussen, B. S. (2005). Profiling individual differences in student motivation: A longitudinal cluster-analytic study in different academic contexts. *Contemporary Educational Psychology, 30*, 359–96. doi: 10.1016/j.cedpsych.2005.01.003.

Cano, F. & Berbén, A. B. G. (2009). University students' achievement goals and approaches to learning in mathematics. *British Journal of Educational Psychology, 79*, 131–53. doi: 10.1348/000709908X314928.

Conley, A. M. (2012). Patterns of motivation beliefs: Combining achievement goal and expectancy-value perspectives. *Journal of Educational Psychology, 104*, 32–47. doi: 10.1037/a0026042.

Corpus, J. H. & Wormington, S. V. (2014). Profiles of intrinsic and extrinsic motivations in elementary school: A longitudinal analysis. *Journal of Experimental Education, 82*, 480–501. doi: 10.1080/00220973.2013.876225.

Deci, E. L. & Ryan, R. M. (1985). *Intrinsic motivation and self-determination in human behavior.* New York: Plenum.

Dina, F. & Efklides, A. (2009). Student profiles of achievement goals, goal instructions and external feedback: Their effect on mathematical task performance and affect. *European Journal of Education and Psychology, 2*, 235–62.

Eccles, J. S. (1983). Expectancies, values, and academic behaviors. In J. T. Spence (Ed.), *Achievement and achievement motives* (pp. 75–146). San Francisco, CA: Freeman.

Elliot, A. J. (1999). Approach and avoidance motivation and achievement goals. *Educational Psychologist, 34*, 169–89. doi: 10.1207/s15326985ep3403_3.

Elliot, A. J. & McGregor, H. A. (1999). Test anxiety and the hierarchical model of approach and avoidance achievement motivation. *Journal of Personality and Social Psychology, 80*, 501–19. doi: 10.1037/0022-3514.76.4.628.

Harackiewicz, J. M., Barron, K. E., Pintrich, P. R., Elliot, A. J., & Thrash, T. M. (2002). Revision of achievement goal theory: Necessary and illuminating. *Journal of Educational Psychology, 94*, 638–45. doi: 10.1037/0022-0663.94.3.638.

Harackiewicz, J. M., Durik, A. M., Barron, K. E., Linnenbrink-Garcia, L., & Tauer, J. M. (2008). The role of achievement goals in the development of interest: Reciprocal relations between achievement goals, interest, and performance. *Journal of Educational Psychology*, *100*, 105–22. doi: 10.1037/0022-0663.100.1.105.

Hayenga, A. O. & Corpus, J. H. (2010). Profiles of intrinsic and extrinsic motivation: A person-centered approach to motivation and achievement in middle school. *Motivation and Emotion*, *34*, 371–83. doi: 10.1007/s11031-010-9181-x.

Hidi, S. & Renninger, K. A. (2006). The four-phase model of interest development. *Educational Psychologist*, *41*, 111–27. doi: 10.1207/s15326985ep4102_4.

Hulleman, C. S., Schrager, S. M., Bodmann, S. M., & Harackiewicz, J. M. (2010). A meta-analytic review of achievement goal measures: Different labels for the same constructs or different constructs with similar labels? *Psychological Bulletin*, *136*, 422–49. doi: 10.1037/a0018947.

Lau, S. & Roeser, R. W. (2008). Cognitive abilities and motivational processes in science achievement and engagement: A person-centered analysis. *Learning and Individual Differences*, *18*, 497–504. doi: 10.1016/j.lindif.2007.11.002.

Laursen, B. & Hoff, E. (2006). Person-centered and variable-centered approaches to longitudinal data. *Merrill-Palmer Quarterly*, *52*, 377–89. doi: 10.1353/mpq.2006.0029.

Law, W., Elliot, A. J., & Murayama, K. (2012). Perceived competence moderates the relation between performance-approach and performance-avoidance goals. *Journal of Educational Psychology*, *104*, 806–19. doi: 10.1037/a0027179.

Lee, Y.-K., Wormington, S. V., Linnenbrink-Garcia, L., & Roseth, C. (2017). A short-term longitudinal study of stability and change in achievement goal profiles. *Learning and Individual Differences*, *55*, 49–60. doi: 10.1016/j.lindif.2017.02.002.

Linnenbrink, E. A. & Pintrich, P. R. (2000). Multiple pathways to learning and achievement: The role of goal orientation in fostering adaptive motivation, affect, and cognition. In C. Sansone & J. M. Harackiewicz (Eds.), *Intrinsic and extrinsic motivation: The search for optimal motivation and performance* (pp. 195–227). New York, NY: Academic Press.

Linnenbrink-Garcia, L. & Barger, M. M. (2014). Achievement goals and emotions. In R. Pekrun & L. Linnenbrink-Garcia (Eds.), *International handbook of emotions in education* (pp. 142–61). New York, NY: Routledge.

Linnenbrink-Garcia, L., Middleton, M. J., Ciani, K. D., Easter, M. A., O'Keefe, P. A., & Zusho, A. (2012a). The strength of the relation between performance-approach and performance-avoidance goal orientations: Theoretical, methodological, and instructional implications. *Educational Psychologist*, *47*, 281–301. doi: 10.1080/00461520.2012.722515.

Linnenbrink-Garcia, L. & Patall, E. A. (2016). Motivation. In E. Anderman & L. Corno (Eds.), *Handbook of educational psychology* (3rd ed., pp. 91–103). New York, NY: Taylor & Francis.

Linnenbrink-Garcia, L., Patall, E. A., & Pekrun, R. (2016). Adaptive motivation and emotion in education: Research and principles for instructional design. *Policy Insights from Behavioral and Brain Sciences*, *3*, 228–36.

Linnenbrink-Garcia, L., Perez, T., & Wormington, S. V. (2014). *Development of undergraduates' motivation in science: A person-centered approach*. Poster presented at the International Conference on Motivation, Helsinki.

Linnenbrink-Garcia, L., Riggsbee, J., Hill, N. E., Snyder, K. E., & Ben-Eliyahu, A. (2012b). *Motivational profiles of upper elementary school students: Stability and change in relation to academic engagement*. Paper presented at the annual meeting of the American Educational Research Association, Vancouver.

Linnenbrink-Garcia, L. & Wormington, S. V. (2017). Key challenges and potential solutions for studying the complexity of motivation in schooling: An integrative, dynamic person-oriented perspective. *British Journal of Educational Psychology Monograph Series, 12*, 89–108.

Linnenbrink-Garcia, L., Wormington, S. V., Snyder, K. E., Riggsbee, J., Perez, T., Ben-Eliyahu, A., & Hill, N. E. (2018). Multiple pathways to success: An examination of integrative motivational profiles among upper elementary and college students. *Journal of Educational Psychology, 110*, 1026–48. doi: 10.1037/edu0000245.

Luo, W., Paris, S. G., Hogan, D., & Luo, Z. (2011). Do performance goals promote learning? A pattern analysis of Singapore students' achievement goals. *Contemporary Educational Psychology, 36*, 165–76. doi: 10.1016/j.cedpsych.2011.02.003.

Madjar, N., Kaplan, A., & Weinstock, M. (2011). Clarifying mastery-avoidance goals in high school: Distinguishing between intrapersonal and task-based standards of competence. *Contemporary Educational Psychology, 36*, 268–79. doi: 10.1016/j.cedpsych.2011.03.003.

Marsh, H. W. & Hao, K. T. (2007). Applications of latent-variable models in educational psychology: The need for methodological-substantive synergies. *Contemporary Educational Psychology, 32*, 151–71. doi: 10.1016/j.cedpsych.2006.10.008.

Maehr, M. L. & Zusho, A. (2009). Achievement goal theory: The past, present, and future. In K. Wentzel (Ed.), *Handbook of motivation at school* (pp. 77–104). New York, NY: Routledge.

Middleton, M. J. & Midgley, C. (1997). Avoiding the demonstration of lack of ability: An underexplored aspect of goal theory. *Journal of Educational Psychology, 89*, 710–18. doi: 10.1037/0022-0663.89.4.710.

Midgley, C., Kaplan, A., & Middleton, M. (2001). Performance-approach goals: Good for what, for whom, under what circumstances, and at what cost? *Journal of Educational Psychology, 93*, 77–86. doi: 10.1037/0022-0663.93.1.77.

Nagengast, B., Marsh, H. W., Scalas, L. F., Xu, M. K., Hau, K. T., & Trautwein, U. (2011). Who took the "×" out of expectancy-value theory? A psychological mystery, a substantive-methodological synergy, and a cross-national generalization. *Psychological Science, 22*, 1058–66. doi: 10.1177/0956797611415540.

Nelson, K. G., Shell, D. F., Husman, J., Fishman, E. J., & Soh, L. K. (2015). Motivational and self-regulated learning profiles of students taking a foundational engineering course. *Journal of Engineering Education, 104*, 74–100. doi: 10.1002/jee.20066.

Ng, C. (2006). The role of achievement goals in completing a course assignment: Examining the effects of performance-approach and multiple goals. *Open Learning, 21*, 33–48. doi: 10.1080/02680510500472189.

Pajares, F. (1996). Self-efficacy beliefs in academic settings. *Review of Educational Research, 66*, 543–78. doi: 10.2307/1170653.

Pintrich, P. R. (2000). Multiple goals, multiple pathways: The role of goal orientation in learning and achievement. *Journal of Educational Psychology, 92*, 544–55. doi: 10.1037/0022-0663.92.3.544.

Pulkka, A. T. & Niemivirta, M. (2013). Adult students' achievement goal orientations and evaluations of the learning environment: A person-centered longitudinal analysis. *Educational Research and Evaluation, 19,* 297–322. doi: 10.1080/13803611.2013.767741.

Renninger, K. A. & Hidi, S. E. (2016). *The power of interest for motivation and engagement.* New York, NY: Routledge/Taylor & Francis.

Rosenthal, R. & Jacobson, L. (1968). *Pygmalion in the classroom.* New York, NY: Holt, Rinehart & Winston.

Schiefele, U. (2001). The role of interest in motivation and learning. In J. Collis & S. Messick (Eds.), *Intelligence and personality: Bridging the gap in theory and measurement* (pp. 163–94). Mahwah, NJ: Erlbaum.

Schiefele, U. (2009). Situational and individual interest. In K. R. Wentzel & A. Wigfield (Eds.), *Handbook of motivation at school* (pp. 197–222). New York, NY: Routledge.

Schunk, D. H., Meece, J. L., & Pintrich, P. R. (2014). *Motivation in education: Theory, research, and applications* (4th ed.). Upper Saddle River, NJ: Merrill Prentice Hall.

Schunk, D. H. & Pajares, F. (2005). Competence perceptions and academic functioning. In A. J. Elliot & C. S. Dweck (Eds.), *Handbook of competence and motivation* (pp. 85–104). New York, NY: Guilford Press.

Seifert, T. L. & O'Keefe, B. A. (2001). The relationship of work avoidance and learning goals to perceived competence, externality, and meaning. *British Journal of Educational Psychology, 71,* 81–92. doi: 10.1348/000709901158406.

Senko, C., Hulleman, C. S., & Harackiewicz, J. M. (2011). Achievement goal theory at the crossroads: Old controversies, current challenges, and new directions. *Educational Psychologist, 46,* 26–47. doi: 10.1080/00461520.2011.538646.

Shell, D. F. & Husman, J. (2008). Control, motivation, affect, and strategic self-regulation in the college classroom: A multidimensional phenomenon. *Journal of Educational Psychology, 100,* 443–59. doi: 10.1037/0022-0663.100.2.443.

Shell, D. F. & Soh, L. (2013). Profiles of motivated self-regulation in college computer science courses: Differences in major versus required non-major courses. *Journal of Science Education and Technology, 22,* 899–913. doi: 10.1007/s10956-013-9437-9.

Trautwein, U., Marsh, H. W., Nagengast, B., Lüdtke, O., Nagy, G., & Jonkmann, K. (2012). Probing for the multiplicative term in modern expectancy–value theory: A latent interaction modeling study. *Journal of Educational Psychology, 104,* 763–77. doi: 10.1037/a0027470.

Tuominen-Soini, H., Salmela-Aro, K., & Niemivirta, M. (2011). Stability and change in achievement goal orientations: A person-centered approach. *Contemporary Educational Psychology, 36,* 82–100. doi: 10.1016/j.cedpsych.2010.08.002.

Tuominen-Soini, H., Salmela-Aro, K., & Niemivirta, M. (2012). Achievement goal orientations and academic well-being across the transition to upper secondary education. *Learning and Individual Differences, 22,* 290–305. doi: 10.1016/j.lindif.2012.01.002.

Turner, J. C., Thorpe, P. K., & Meyer, D. K. (1998). Students' reports of motivation and negative affect: A theoretical and empirical analysis. *Journal of Educational Psychology, 90,* 758–71. doi: 10.1037/0022-0663.90.4.758.

Usher, E. L. (2016). Personal capability beliefs. In E. Anderman & L. Corno (Eds.), *Handbook of educational psychology* (3rd ed., pp. 146–59). New York, NY: Taylor & Francis.

Vansteenkiste, M., Soenens, B., Sierens, E., Luyckx, K., & Lens, W. (2009). Motivational profiles from a self-determination perspective: The quality of motivation matters. *Journal of Educational Psychology, 101*, 671–88. doi: 10.1037/a0015083.

Wigfield, A. & Cambria, J. (2010). Students' achievement values, goal orientations, and interest: Definitions, development, and relations to achievement outcomes. *Developmental Review, 30*, 1–35. doi: 10.1016/j.dr.2009.12.001.

Wigfield, A. & Eccles, J. S. (2000). Expectancy-value theory of achievement motivation. *Contemporary Educational Psychology, 25*, 68–81. doi: 10.1006/ceps.1999.1015.

Wigfield, A., Eccles, J. S., Fredricks, J. A., Simpkins, S., Roeser, R. W., & Schiefele, U. (2015). Development of achievement motivation and engagement. In R. Lerner (series Ed.) and M. Lamb & C. Garcia Coll (vol. Eds.), *Handbook of child psychology and developmental science* (7th ed., Vol. 3, pp. 657–700). New York, NY: Wiley.

Wigfield, A., Eccles, J. S., Schiefele, U., Roeser, R. W., & Davis-Kean, P. (2006). Development of achievement motivation. In N. Eisenberg, W. Damon, & R. M. Lerner (Eds.), *Handbook of child psychology, Vol. 3: Social, emotional, and personality development* (6th ed., pp. 933–1002). Hoboken, NJ: John Wiley & Sons.

Wolters, C. A. (2004). Advancing achievement goal theory: Using goal structures and goal orientations to predict students' motivation, cognition, and achievement. *Journal of Educational Psychology, 96*, 236–50. doi: 10.1037/0022-0663.96.2.236.

Wormington, S. V. (2016). *Smooth sailing or choppy waters? Patterns and predictors of motivation in on-line mathematics courses* (Doctoral dissertation). Retrieved from *Proquest*. https://mvlri.org/blog/is-there-more-than-one-path-to-success-in-math-patterns-and-predictors-of-students-motivation-and-achievement-in-online-math-courses/

Wormington, S. V., Barger, M. M., & Linnenbrink-Garcia, L. (2014). *One size fits all? longitudinal, profile-centered examinations of adolescents' motivation in mathematics and social studies*. Poster presented at the annual meeting of the American Educational Research Association, Philadelphia, PA.

Wormington, S. V., Corpus, J. H., & Anderson, K. G. (2012). A person-centered investigation of academic motivation and its correlates in high school. *Learning and Individual Differences, 22*, 429–38. doi: 10.1016/j.lindif.2012.03.004.

Wormington, S. V. & Linnenbrink-Garcia, L. (2016). A new look at multiple goal pursuit: The promise of a person-centered approach. *Educational Psychology Review*, 1–39. doi: 10.1007/s10648-016-9358-2.

30 Affordances and Attention

Learning and Culture

Duane F. Shell and Terri Flowerday

Abstract: In this chapter, we draw on Gibson's (1979) description of affordances to consider cultural differences in motivation and learning. We develop the argument that affordances are at the heart of cultural differences. We address the way culture influences both what and how people learn from the affordances that are available to them in their physical and social environments. Brain processes of neural plasticity and psychological learning mechanisms of repetition and connection drawn from the Unified Learning Model (Shell et al., 2010) are used to explain how our brain and memory store knowledge of affordances, as well as the actions needed to take advantage of these affordances. We then discuss the way attention sits at the intersection of motivation and learning, as well as how motivated attention leads to individual and cultural differences in knowledge and use of affordances, both implicitly and volitionally. Finally, the emergence of cultural differences in attention, learning, knowing, and motivation are discussed, with an emphasis on the impact of culture on learning in school.

Simon (1969) once noted that if you wanted to know what path an ant would take across the beach, you would know more from studying the beach than from studying the ant. This reflects Gibson's (1979) notion of affordances: "The affordances of the environment are what it offers the animal, what it provides or furnishes, either for good or ill" (p. 127). Back to Simon's ant, the terrain of the beach has specific hills and valleys. These characteristics of the beach terrain "afford" the ant the opportunity for some movements, but also, exclude doing other movements. Within the affordances of a specific environment, there also is the possibility of variation in the way different ants will move. If we were to observe a group of ants walking across the beach, it would immediately become apparent that although all are traversing the same beach, all are not traversing it in exactly the same way. There is a finite set of affordances available on the beach, yet individual ants are not necessarily experiencing all of them in exactly the same manner. There may be considerable variation in what each ant "knows" about the beach and in the exact movements used to traverse it. Thus, as noted in more recent ecological psychology theories (e.g., Chemero, 2003; Stoffregen, 2003), affordances involve an interaction between the organism and the environment. The environment may constrain what is possible to do or to learn, but the organism's characteristics also constrain the specific affordances it can take advantage of. The beach may be the same beach, but the affordances on the beach are not only different for different ants, they are also different for you and me.

In this chapter, we draw on Gibson's (1979) description of affordances to anchor our examination of cultural differences in motivation and learning. We argue that Gibson's conception of affordances is at the heart of cultural differences. The environment affords possibilities that may be perceived and acted on, and people living in different physical environments perceive and experience different affordances. Just consider the environmental differences between the Amazon rain forest and the Sahara desert. The people in these environments have different affordances available. Just as physical environments provide varying affordances, so too social environments provide differing affordances. Consider the different experiences of majority and minority group residents of the same city. The affordances available in these social environments can be quite distinct, even if these individuals are sharing a similar physical environment. Such sociocultural differences are reflected in religions, stories, and transmitted knowledge with a culture. Moreover, each individual in the group has unique personal experience and knowledge derived in part from the affordances each has perceived and taken advantage of in the past. This unique personal knowledge subsequently can affect the affordances they are able to use in the future.

The notion that individuals may take advantage of only some of the affordances available in an environment because of the individual's unique personal characteristics is at the heart of learning, especially the way motivation influences learning. Our goal in this chapter is to address how cultural differences affect motivation and learning, especially how they affect the way persons learn from the affordances available to them. To begin, we will discuss the neurological processes involved in learning and the psychological learning theory, the unified learning model (ULM; Shell et al., 2010), derived from these neurological processes, which explains how our brain and memory store knowledge of affordances and the actions needed to take advantage of these affordances. We then will discuss how attention sits at the intersection of motivation and learning, and is the determining mechanism for individual differences in knowledge and use of affordances. Finally, we examine the emergence of cultural differences in learning, knowing, and motivation, with an emphasis on learning in school.

Learning

The Neurobiology of Learning

Neural plasticity is the basic underlying process of brain and neurological learning and development (Kandel et al., 2012). Neural plasticity refers to the changes that occur in the neural connections of the brain at both the physical and functional levels. These changes occur both in the interconnections of neurons, through the creating and pruning of synapse connections between neurons, and in the efficiencies of existing connections, via changes in myelination and neurotransmitter properties at synapse junctions. Although the specifics of the biological mechanisms involved in neural plasticity are not fully known, new research is beginning to detail them (e.g., Stuchlik, 2014). However, the basics of neural plasticity mechanisms have been known for some time. Hebb (1949) was the first to articulate the basic principle of neural plasticity: associations between neurons that fire together are strengthened and associations between neurons that don't fire together are weakened. Subsequent neurological research has confirmed that Hebb's simple "use it or lose it" principle accurately describes how neural plasticity occurs in the brain (see Caporale & Dan, 2009; Kandel et al., 2012; Shors, 2014). Neurons that are active at the same time have their connections created or strengthened. Neurons that are not active at the same time are not connected or, if connected, have their connections weakened.

Neural plasticity accounts for the specific interconnections of neurons in the brain that change over time and are typically described as brain development. However, it is more accurate to describe neural plasticity as learning. Neural plasticity is not maturational or age graded. Neural plasticity is driven by stimulation. Neurons activate or fire in response to stimulation. Stimulation comes from sensory input and from internal activation via proprioceptive feedback, the sympathetic and parasympathetic regulatory systems, and emotions. Finally, stimulation also comes from retrieval of memories or motor neuron activation when these are activated by pattern matching to incoming stimuli or by the aforementioned internal activators.

We can think of the connections between neurons as recording the history of their repeated co-stimulation (see Corbetta, 2012). The strength of the connection reflects the number of times the neurons have been stimulated together (thereby having their connection strength increased) versus the number of times the neurons have been stimulated separately (thereby having their connection strength decreased). This historical record is biologically encoded in the brain via processes of long-term potentiation (LTP), synapse formation, synapse pruning, myelination, and changes in neurotransmitters at the synapse junction (Blumenfeld-Katzir et al., 2011; Driemeyer et al., 2008; Kandel et al., 2012; Miendlarzewska et al., 2016; Stuchlik, 2014).

The Unified Learning Model

Neural plasticity provides a mechanism for the brain and nervous system to perform two critical survival functions: (1) to allow accurate perception and understanding of the world around us and (2) to allow functional behavior in that world, presumably so that the organism can stay alive and reproduce

(Shell et al., 2010). These two functions are reflected in Gibson's (1979) definition of affordances. To survive, an animal must be able to perceive the affordances available and know what action to take to utilize them. Hence the need for an organism to have a way to store and remember affordances, and remember how to act to take advantage of known affordances. By biologically encoding a historical record of neuron co-stimulation, neural plasticity allows neuron connections to record what the organism knows about the world around it from past sensory input and what behaviors have been successful for the organism in meeting survival goals.

The unified learning model (Shell et al., 2010) translates these processes of Hebbian neural plasticity into two cognitive learning mechanisms: (1) *repetition*, the repeated exposure to sensory input, bodily sensations, retrieval of knowledge from long-term memory, or personal experience for declarative knowledge and repeated practice for procedural knowledge and (2) *connection*, the formation of larger units of meaning such as concepts or schema for declarative knowledge and development of stimulus-motor response patterns leading to automaticity for procedural knowledge. Shell et al. argue that repetition and connection are able to fulfill the aforementioned survival processes because of statistical learning. The strengthening and weakening of a neural connection each time the connection is repeated or not repeated can be represented as frequency counts. The statistical law of large numbers then says that as the number of repetitions increases, the frequency distribution will come to reflect the accurate probability distribution of whatever was being counted. In the case of neuron connections, these repetitions reflect the affordances that the organism has experienced. So as the organism experiences repeated affordances, their understanding of their world will become more accurate and their behavior will become more functional and successful. At the psychological level, repetition will ultimately produce declarative knowledge, which accurately reflects the probability distribution of whatever knowledge is being represented in a concept/schema and procedural knowledge, which accurately reflects the probability of successfully producing the desired behavior in a given context.

Numerous studies have shown that statistical learning occurs at the neurological level (e. g., Kirkham et al., 2002; Mitchel & Weiss, 2011; Schapiro et al., 2016; Turk-Browne et al., 2008). Studies have also shown that the learning of declarative knowledge and procedural knowledge follows statistical regularities (Kóbor et al., 2017). Language learning especially has been shown to follow statistical learning (Erickson & Thiessen, 2015). As noted by Shell in his contribution to Wang et al. (2013), statistical learning by neuronal connections allows each member of a cultural group, with their individually unique experience, to tend toward similar shared knowledge representations and similar recognizable behavior patterns. This is because, within the same physical or social environment, every person's unique experiences are bound by the physical and social affordances available in the shared environment. Hence, they are all moving toward the same statistical regularities present in the affordances of that environment. This provides a basic explanation for cultural differences in knowledge and understanding. The shared environment differs across cultures, regions, and peoples. So, within each specific culture, the members will tend toward a shared understanding of their experienced environment but, because these experienced environments differ across cultures and peoples, members of different cultures will have different declarative and procedural knowledge.

Cognitive Processing Limitations on Learning

Statistical learning through the law of large numbers can explain how persons within a shared physical and cultural environment come to have similar knowledge. If neural plasticity was a passive process driven from the environment, something like direct perception of affordances (see Chemero, 2003; Stoffregen, 2003), then ultimately members of a shared environment would have little individual variation. Mathematically, the law of large numbers says that all should be moving toward the same statistical representations given similar amounts of repetition (e.g., Kolmogorov, 1950). Individual differences would be almost solely a function of variation in the number of repetitions. This clearly is not true. Although, with repetition, knowledge may be tending toward an accurate probability distribution of affordances, there can be considerable individual difference in knowledge among the members of the same cultural group despite shared affordances in their common social and physical environments (e.g., Na et al., 2010).

Individual differences occur because humans cannot directly perceive the totality of the affordances in their environment. Miller's (1956) well-known "Magical Number 7 ± 2" was an early exploration of capacity limitations on information processing, immediate memory (short-term memory), and attention span. Subsequent studies of working memory (Baddeley, 1986; Cowan, 2010) and cognitive load (Sweller et al., 2011) have substantiated that limitations and constraints on what can be attended and processed exist at all levels of cognitive processing. Basically, the affordances available at any one time contain far more information than could possibly be attended, perceived, and processed.

These processing limitations have a profound effect on statistical learning. Shell et al. (2010) note the particularly critical role of the third learning mechanism proposed in the ULM: attention. Because of capacity limitations, attention can focus on only a sample of the possible information available. This means that on any given encounter with the environment, attention selects only a sample of the information available in affordances. So, even though all members of an environment may share the common available affordances, they are each sampling uniquely from the information available in those affordances. These individual differences in what they attend mean that each person's knowledge of affordances, and their neural representations of these affordances, are not updating based on the totality of information in the affordances. The person's knowledge and neural representations are updating based only on the information that was in their individually attended samples. Sampling theory and the law of large numbers dictate that, mathematically, all combinations of unique samples would still tend toward the same probabilities in the affordances. If attended samples of affordances were random, which might occur if neural plasticity was a passive process of recording sensory input, then there would be little difference between updating based on all information available versus samples. All combinations of unique samples would ultimately produce identical encoding of the information available in the affordances. But, attended samples are not random – they are biased by the individual's unique knowledge, resulting from their past history of learning from experienced affordances.

Attention, Learning, and Motivation

Attention and Learning

To understand the way attention affects learning, we need to revisit neural plasticity. The actual biochemical processes of neural plasticity in the brain and nervous system are not under any sort of volitional control. One cannot tell a dendrite to grow or a nerve to myelinate. As we have discussed, these processes occur due to neuron stimulation resulting from repetition and connection. And one cannot directly tell a neuron to repeatedly stimulate or connect to another neuron. One can, however, volitionally direct cognitions and behaviors that will indirectly trigger neuron stimulation.

Within the psychological and educational literature, there is a long history of research into and identification of cognitive processes and behaviors that have been shown to influence learning and subsequent achievement in educational settings. These include, among others, self-regulated learning (e.g., Boekaerts & Cascallar, 2006; Schunk & Zimmerman, 2013), study/learning strategies (e.g., Weinstein et al., 2000), knowledge building (e.g., Bereiter & Scardamalia, 2014), metacognition (e.g., Brown et al., 1983), and engagement (e.g., Sinatra et al., 2015). These behaviors and cognitions all serve to trigger ULM learning mechanisms. General learning strategies (such as note-taking, re-reading, summarizing, and paraphrasing) all involve repetition. Sometimes these are literally repetition as in rehearsal strategies. The more sophisticated strategies, however, also primarily serve to either revisit or retrieve information multiple times or in multiple formats. Knowledge-building and other deep learning strategies (such as elaboration and organization, as well as summarizing) serve the ULM mechanism of connection. These strategies interconnect multiple pieces of learned information with strategies (like matrix notes) attempting to make connections overt (e.g., Jairam et al., 2012). From the perspective of the ULM, these strategic learning methods are ways, at the cognitive and behavioral level, to indirectly trigger the neural processes involved in Hebbian neural plasticity by making students repeat and connect information.

More detailed examination of these strategic learning methods, however, indicates that they all involve attention. At both the neurological and cognitive level, repetition and connection are processes within the cognitive architecture and neural system. As discussed in the ULM (Shell et al., 2010), if information is attended, it is maintained in active cognition or working memory. In the brain, attention triggers processes such as LTP that maintain neuron activity (Kandel et al., 2012). Maintaining the information allows the information to be repeatedly attended. This retention is automatic once we attend to the information. We don't decide to retain the information or not; we only decide to attend. Similarly, attended information triggers automatic pattern-matching retrieval from long-term memory. So we will retrieve information from memory if it matches anything in current attention. This constitutes another form of repetition. Again, we do not decide to do pattern-match retrieval; we only attend.

Similarly, if two pieces of information are attended together, they will be automatically associated and stored as connected information. This is a function of the well-known learning mechanism of contiguity (e.g., Matzel et al., 1988; or more recently, Mayer & Fiorella, 2014), which reflects the Hebbian neural learning principle of "fire together; wire together." Subsequently, if either of the connected pieces of information is later attended, both will be retrieved from memory (or stimulated in the neurological system); thus their connection is repeated, even if only one was attended. Again, this is an automatic process. We do not decide to connect information, we only attend to information that is simultaneously in active cognition and working memory.

It is clear from the workings of these neuro-cognitive processes that although the ULM specifies three mechanisms of learning (attention, repetition, and connection), attention is the only one that is under volitional control. What we attend dictates whether repetition and connection occur at the neuro-cognitive level. Thus, we can reconceptualize the behaviors and cognitions subsumed under strategic learning, knowledge building, self-regulation, engagement, and studying as attention directing activities. Basically, they are ways, at the macro level of cognition and behavior, that we make ourselves focus our volitional attention. When I tell myself to "repeat" something, I am making myself attend. When I make a matrix outline, I am making myself attend to connections. When I relate something I am learning to prior knowledge, I am bringing the new information into contiguity with what I already know to make myself attend to both together.

Motivation and Attention

Because of the role attention plays in determining the information from available affordances that is sampled and learned, the cognitive and neurological factors that influence attention play a significant role in learning. In the ULM, Shell et al. (2010) expanded on the premise first proposed by Brooks and Shell (2006): the role of motivation in learning is to direct attention in working memory (see also Anselme, 2007 for a similar view). There are multiple ways that attention and motivation intersect.

Motivation and attention in System 1. Motivation and attention first intersect in what Kahneman (2011) called "System 1." Cognitive processes in System 1 include those that are part of the neurological and cognitive architecture. System 1 processes are not under volitional control. We have noted some of these before, such as the neurochemical processes of neural plasticity and basic biological functioning. Attention is directed automatically by System 1 processes, such as internal homeostatic drive mechanisms like thirst or hunger, and other proprioceptive and internal neural stimulation, such as pain (Horvitz, 2000). These automatic attention directors play critical roles in survival and underlie much classical and operant conditioning (Schultz, 2015). Anselme (2007) notes these as causal factors of the motivation that drives anticipatory attention. They direct attention toward those behaviors that can alleviate the drive by, say, providing food or water. These internal attention mechanisms are motivated through the primary System 1 motivator: the dopaminergic "reward system" (Hidi, 2016; Horvitz, 2000; Schultz, 2015). The reward system "computes" the value of possible environmental rewards, the prediction error of whether attained reward matches expected reward, contingency information for reward signals, and salience of stimuli (Bromberg-Martin et al., 2010; Hidi, 2016; Yin et al., 2008). Basically, the reward system provides a motivational boost for attending to those affordances that can most successfully reduce the biological drive.

Also, at System 1, attention can be directed automatically by aspects of the sensory environment, especially novelty and salience (see Knudsen, 2007). This is where the environmental aspects of affordances come into play. Physical environments have different salient attributes that need to be attended to for survival. These are the properties of the "beach" in Simon's (1969) example. Different beaches will make certain physical properties of terrain, temperature, and so forth salient, and the regularities of the environment dictate what is novel or out of the ordinary. Because of the critical importance of attending to the environment for survival, the brain has evolved automatic mechanisms for directing attention to salient and novel sensory inputs (Knudsen, 2007). Motivationally, this "bottom-up" automatic attention also interacts with the dopaminergic "reward system" (see Bromberg-Martin et al., 2010; Horvitz, 2000; Miendlarzewska et al., 2016; Schultz, 2015; Yin et al., 2008), which can provide a motivational boost to attend to particular inputs, especially novel and salient inputs that meet the needs of biological drive.

These System 1 attention mechanisms are impacted by emotion, which is distinct from the dopaminergic reward system but interacts with it. Emotion's role appears to be providing subtlety to rewards, especially degrees of pleasure or pain (Vuilleumier, 2005, 2015) that are distinct from the information provided by the reward system. Although not as well understood as the reward system, emotion appears to affect attention through the amygdala and its projections to the prefrontal cortical areas (Vuilleumier, 2005, 2015).

Also in System 1, there is evidence that neurons compute confidence estimations in decision-making (Kiani & Shadlen, 2009) and that confidence is encoded in neuron firing rates as part of the attractor networks in decision-making, with multiple confidence networks allowing decision monitoring and change (Deco et al., 2013). These confidence networks interconnect with the reward system to compute confidence in receiving rewards (Deco et al., 2013). In a revision to the original ULM (Shell et al., 2010), Shell et al. (2015) proposed, and computationally modeled, self-efficacy as being integrated with knowledge itself in memory. They proposed that self-efficacy modulates connection strength as a function of certainty in the accuracy of knowledge or the likelihood of success at attaining outcomes. This self-efficacy modulation mirrors how neuron firing rate modulates the strength of neural connections. This self-efficacy modulation biases attention toward those actions with the best chance at being successful in attaining desired rewards.

Motivation and attention in System 2. These aforementioned System 1 attentional processes serve the two primary functions of the brain. Novelty and salience serve to direct attention to potentially important aspects of the environment that are likely to have significance for understanding the world and for survival. Homeostatic drive mechanisms serve to direct attention to biological survival needs and motivate action to alleviate these needs. The motivation from the dopaminergic reward system, emotion, and confidence estimation serve to motivate these immediate attention directors. However, we are not motivated only by the immediate situation.

We can only store what we attend to, primarily that which is salient and novel. The information that was attended was linked to its value and utility for alleviating drive mechanisms via the reward system (Berridge & Kringelbach, 2008; Bromberg-Martin et al., 2010) and, perhaps, emotion (Vuilleumier, 2005, 2015). The initial tagging of these environmental features by the reward system makes them more likely to be noticed and attended in the future. Behaviors that were successful at attaining reward (reinforcement) are strengthened and associated with the environmental stimuli signaling that they should be done. Thorndike (1913) called this the "law of effect." The connections between stimuli and behaviors leading to reward are strengthened each time the behavior is successful in attaining the reward. Because of statistical learning, these connections will ultimately come to reflect the relative probability of success of the behavior in attaining the reward versus its failure.

These interactions of the reward system with learning anchor the first group of cognitive or knowledge-based motivators. Reward or reinforcement requires that we remember two things: first, the contingency of the reward on behavior; second, the magnitude or amount of the reward or its value. These two aspects of the dopaminergic reward system are reflected in social learning/cognitive theories (Bandura, 1986; Rotter, 1966; Weisz & Stipek, 1982) and in control theories of behavior (Skinner, 1996) as outcome expectancies (contingency) and value. In social learning/cognitive theories, outcome expectancies and value are seen as the memory record of past experienced rewards/reinforcement. Looked at in another way, they are the memory record of past activation of the reward system. Expectancies and value are motivating because they contain information about the likelihood that a behavior will lead to a desired outcome. Rotter's (1966) locus of control construct was theoretically conceptualized as the generalization of specific expectancies to produce an overall belief that rewards/reinforcement were contingently related to one's behavior (internal locus of control) or not (external locus of control). Similar notions of contingency are present in future time perspective (FTP) theories in the constructs of instrumentality (which reflects the relationship of present behaviors to achieving future goals) and connectedness (which, like locus of control, reflects a general belief that the future is contingently connected to the present [Husman et al., 2015; Husman & Lens, 1999; Husman & Shell, 2008]). FTP theories also recognize a future valence aspect, similar to value, that reflects the valuing of future goals/outcomes relative to present goals/outcome (Husman & Lens, 1999; Husman & Shell, 2008). It is the memory record of contingency, and the magnitude of experienced reward reflected in outcome expectancies and their associated value, that allows for computation of prediction error by the reward system for discrepancies from the reward expected. Note that this tight coupling of cognitive motivators to the reward system informational components of contingency and reward value in social learning/cognitive and FTP theories are not present in what has been termed modern expectancy-value theory (Eccles & Wigfield, 2002). Modern expectancy-value theory has different definitions of expectancy and value that do not correspond directly to these reward system informational components.

The reward system and its cognitive analogs, outcome expectancy and value, provide information on contingency of behavior to rewarding outcomes and the value (magnitude) of the contingent reward. As Bandura (1997) notes, however, this does not mean that one is capable of doing the contingent behavior. Bandura (1986, 1997) argued that having a strong outcome expectancy for a high value reward is not motivating if one does not believe one could successfully do the contingent behavior. He called this belief self-efficacy, which is the confidence one has in being able to successfully produce a cognitive or overt behavior. Research examining self-efficacy and outcome expectancies together (Shell et al., 1989, 1995) has supported Bandura's contention that self-efficacy is more strongly predictive of achievement than outcome expectancy. As noted previously, there is some evidence that self-efficacy has an actual neurological underpinning (Deco et al., 2013).

Emotions also have a memorial component. Just like the information about contingency and value connected to knowledge by the reward system, emotions connect nuances surrounding pleasure and pain to knowledge (Vuilleumier, 2005, 2015). Emotions are associated with stored information and impact the way memories are retrieved (Pekrun, 2006). Pekrun (2006) has theorized and found evidence to support the idea that emotion, expectancy, and value are interconnected at the cognitive level, mirroring interconnections between emotion and the reward system at the neurological level. He and his colleagues have also found that emotion influences attention in early sensory processing (Kuhbandner et al., 2011).

Interest has been described, similarly to affordances, as an interaction between the person and environment (Hidi & Renninger, 2006). Interest has also been shown to affect attention (Hidi & Renninger, 2006; Renninger & Hidi, 2016). In relation to affordances, situational interest derives from environmental novelty or salience (Renninger & Hidi, 2016); thus, it may serve to provide a motivational boost to sustaining attending to these aspects of the environment, perhaps by tapping the dopaminergic reward system or emotions (Renninger & Hidi, 2016). Interest itself, however, would seem to be distinct from the specific informational components in the neural reward system of value, contingency, and prediction error. At the cognitive level, individual interest is clearly distinct from the cognitive representations of reward as outcome expectancies and value. Individual interest may reflect the history of that which has been experienced as interesting (Hidi & Renninger, 2006). Like other top-down motivators, personal interest may then boost attention by recruiting activation of the reward system or emotions.

Finally, humans and other animals are goal directed or, as Tolman (1932) called it, purposive. Some goals are directed "bottom up" by System 1 level homeostatic drive mechanisms (e.g., goals to get food when hungry) or by sensory inputs (e.g., goals to explore novel stimuli). As Bandura (1986, 1997) noted, however, people have personal agency. We are active, volitional directors of our behavior and pursue our own personal goals. We are not just passive responders to System 1 motivators. Volitional goals exist in what Kahneman (2011) called System 2, or volitional, cognition. Most of these volitional goals are divorced from basic biological needs. In the ULM (Shell et al., 2010), goals motivate attention because we are motivated to do what is necessary to achieve the goal. Hence, we direct attention to that which will move us toward the goal. The other previously discussed cognitive motivators can be viewed as supporting goal directed attention. Value tells us how much reward is associated with the goal, expectancy tells us what behaviors are contingently related to the goal, and self-efficacy tells us the probability that we can successfully do the contingent behaviors. Emotion tells us how pleasant achieving the goal will be. Although the retrieval of expectancies, values, and self-efficacy from memory may be automatic by pattern matching to current active or working memory contents, these motivators do not necessarily produce automatic behavior. They are used for decision-making, to decide between alternative goals and alternative ways of achieving chosen goals. This allows volitional control of directing and sustaining attention in the face of competing motivators.

Social Learning and Attention

We have discussed the learning of affordances and motivation primarily from the perspective of direct experience. Humans, however, learn not only from their own personal experience, but also from other people. Social learning includes vicarious experience from observing others (Bandura, 1986, 2016) and from verbal interaction (Bandura, 1986; Vygotsky, 1980). Bandura (1986) has demonstrated that vicarious learning leads to the same progression of skill as actual practice, indicating that vicarious experience triggers the same neural statistical learning as direct behavior. When learning vicariously, people do not just learn procedural knowledge or behavior, they also learn expectancies, value, and self-efficacy from observation. Again, the effects appear to be identical to having actually received the reward or been successful themselves.

Berridge and Kringelbach (2008) have noted that much of what we find "intrinsically motivating" has no real connection to basic System 1 survival motivators in the reward system. Although a learned motivator such as money could arguably be seen as a means to procuring something like food that would alleviate a homeostatic drive, many things that we find enjoyable and motivating have no connection to any sort of survival function. For example, we have learned to find things such as art rewarding for its own sake. Similarly, the associated emotional feelings of pleasure have no basis in any physical property of the stimulus or activity; we have learned to feel the emotional reactions. So where did we learn these motivators? We learned them from other people.

That humans are social animals has long been noted. Various genetic bases for social affiliation have been proposed in evolutionary psychology (e.g., Seyfartha & Cheney, 2013). Any genetic underpinnings might be expected to have produced neurological motivating mechanisms for social functions and social learning, but the research into these is in its infancy (e.g., Feldman et al., 2016; Harmon-Jones & Inzlicht, 2016; Numan, 2014; Striepens et al., 2014). So, the neurological basis for motivation and attention in social functioning has yet be fully identified. Social interactions do appear to trigger reactions in the dopaminergic reward and emotion systems (Striepens et al., 2014), suggesting that social interactions may receive motivational boosts from those that trigger attention to socially relevant people and behaviors. But, social interactions also appear to direct attention independently of the reward system through other neural mechanisms such as the oxytocin pathway (Feldman et al., 2016; Striepens et al., 2014). It is clear that social cognitions direct attention.

In relation to affordances, for humans, the social/cultural environment often provides more affordances than the physical environment. It is true that many people's primary concerns are meeting basic survival mechanisms. For these people, social affordances tend to be heavily focused on environmental affordances that fulfill basic needs. But, in technologically advanced societies, social affordances can be quite different from the affordances in the environment and can be focused on socially constructed objects, behaviors, rewards, and motivations. For these people, the balance of the interaction between the person and the environment in affordances tilts toward the person.

Regardless of the focus of these social affordances, the majority of knowledge that humans learn is what Vygotsky (1980) called *socially constructed*. This knowledge is not a property of the physical environment; rather, it is a property of the social environment. Parents and other adults direct children's attention, and emphasize and repeat what is important. They model behaviors, tell stories, and introduce the child to cultural and social traditions and institutions (like religion). They explain the meaning of stimuli and actions in the world. They explain the meaning of feelings. These types of social knowledge transmissions are carried on by teachers in formal schooling. Our understanding of affordances in the physical environment is filtered through these socially constructed meanings. Others in our social group have guided our attention in ways that dictate the content of the affordance samples that we are attending.

The effects of socially learned, socially directed, and what might be called socially filtered affordances on attention are profound. Although we have been discussing motivation and attention primarily from the "bottom-up" System 1 perspective, the effects of "top-down" processes are even greater (Knudsen, 2007; Sarter et al., 2001). As discussed by Shell et al. (2010) in the ULM, incoming sensory information (and internal stimuli from homeostatic drive, proprioceptive, or pain) triggers retrieval of stored knowledge from long-term memory. These incoming stimuli trigger attention, but the activated long-term memory knowledge can reinforce or override the incoming stimuli and, thus, either sustain or redirect attention. This long-term memory knowledge was initially tagged with reward values or emotions, and is connected in memory with cognitive motivators. As the knowledge is activated, these associated motivators are also activated. Neurologically, retrieved information can stimulate the dopaminergic reward system and emotions via top-down neural projections into brain areas associated with the reward system and emotion (Bourgeois et al., 2016; Sarter et al., 2001). As discussed by Anderson (2016), retrieved knowledge that was previously rewarded can compete for attention even when irrelevant to the current task. These top-down influences have been called the prior knowledge effect (Shell et al., 2010). Existing knowledge biases attention to stimuli that correspond and reinforce current knowledge. This creates a self-fulfilling loop in which people attend more to information consistent with current knowledge, thus increasing the strength of that knowledge. Piaget (1971) noted this process as assimilation; we assimilate new information by incorporating it into existing knowledge. Thus, differences in culture-based, socially constructed knowledge cause perceptions of particular affordances to differ.

Culture, Affordances, and Learning

Park and Huang (2010) note that there is growing evidence in support of cultural influences on neural functioning. These influences are especially evident with regard to activation of the ventral visual cortex, an area associated with perceptual processing, including attention. Consistent with the ULM (Shell et al., 2010), Park and Huang note that the method of culture-based knowledge transfer – in the form of repeated experiences, thoughts, and perspectives – influences the way in which neural pathways get wired and are activated. The prior knowledge constructed from these experiences exerts top-down influences on attention. Sometimes referred to as "ways of knowing" (Warner, 2006), these well-established patterns influence the way members of a culture interpret and assimilate new information and, ultimately, the long-term memory knowledge that is created. These ways of knowing constitute social/cultural affordances and provide socially constructed meanings for interacting with physical affordances in the environment.

For example, many indigenous cultures understand the physical world as living parts of a larger whole. In Western thought, animals and plants are alive in different ways, and rocks are not alive. Many indigenous cultures understand the rocks to be alive, the waters to be alive, and the clouds to be alive: those are fundamentals taught from childhood. Furthermore, all things are related. Nothing exists in isolation; things done to one aspect of creation are done to every aspect. The connection is distinct. Much like the Western tradition of discrete categorization, it is the goal of science to organize, categorize, and isolate variables as a means of better understanding all the parts. People from Western cultures direct attention to focal points – key aspects of phenomena. However, people from indigenous cultures may attend to contextual factors. These basic perceptual functions influence the way learning takes place. It seems clear that the affordances available in the environment can be very different for indigenous and non-indigenous people.

Deloria and Wildcat (2001) speak to this issue. The identity and perspectives of Native American students are inextricably linked to places of ancestral culture and experience. They explain that "there is no such thing as isolation from the rest of creation, and the fact of this relatedness provides a basic context within which education in the growth of personality and the acquisition of technical skills can occur" (p. 45). They emphasize that "indigenous people represent a culture emergent from a place, and they actively draw on the power of that place" and "behavior, beliefs, values, symbols, and material products" are emergent from these diverse places (p. 31). These are powerful social/cultural affordances.

Clearly, differences in cultural experience, and the corresponding allocation of attention and practiced behavior, shape learning and knowledge development. Mooney et al. (2016) confirm that "our cultural experiences, beliefs, and values play a large part in whom we are, how we see ourselves, and what we think is important" (p. 13). And, for Aboriginal students, "identity is influenced by their environment and reinforced by significant others, including the broader Aboriginal community" (p. 13). Emotion, as displayed in facial expressions, is not universal. Culture influences the way emotion is expressed on the face and how it is interpreted by others (Jack et al., 2009). The communication of emotion, therefore, may be misinterpreted among persons from different cultural backgrounds. Indigenous communities maintain a shared identification with a specific land or place. Indigenous students may "hold beliefs, have perceptions and experiences, and design goals that are different from mainstream, majority educators" (McInerney & Flowerday, 2016, p. 1). Relationships, community, and place will likely be themes. Cajete (2015), a leading Native American scholar, reminds us that "relationship, respect, and responsibility are primary indigenous values, because they lay the foundations for positive communal processes" (p. 64).

Recall that affordances involve interaction between the person and the environment. These cultural differences lead to dramatically different affordance interaction. When traveling across the northern plains of South Dakota, a tourist might be noticing the flat, grassy landscape, the seemingly endless blue sky, and the occasional rocky butte. They may be looking at road signs, noticing locations of nearby gas stations, or simply wondering when the next town might appear. An indigenous person traveling across the same grassy plain could be searching the sky for eagles, listening to the meadowlarks, giving thanks for the clouds moving in from the west, greeting buttes as relatives, and offering a prayer to a sacred location as it is approached. The connection to place is central for indigenous people, and a seemingly empty landscape can be alive with memories, stories, and spiritual relationships. The physical affordances of the environment are the same, but attention may be directed in different ways and, therefore, the experienced affordance is very different.

We can now use the lens of the ULM (Shell et al., 2010) to specify the mechanism for cultural influences on learning. To recap: the knowledge that we have stored in memory is the result of the learning of information available in physical and social affordances in our environment. We have learned this knowledge through repetition and connection of information that we have attended. Because of statistical learning, our knowledge tends toward accurate representation of the statistical regularities present in the affordances. But the statistical regularities in our knowledge reflect only the information in the samples of the information from the affordances that we have attended. What we have attended is a function of motivation. This motivation derives from internal biological and neurological processes and from social learning.

How different cultures define rewards affects which things people learn to pay attention to for rewards. That which is defined as beautiful or valuable is subjective and differing across cultures. But the effect on things people might think of as intrinsic properties of physical stimuli is perhaps even more profound. Take something like taste. At a basic chemical level, taste sensory organs can detect certain properties (e.g., sweet, bitter, salty). But the combinations of these that we find pleasing is a function of culture and the food we have learned to eat. People in different cultures find different foods pleasant and desirable, because each culture identifies different affordances in the food to be rewarding.

The cultural norms transmitted by social interaction produce a cultural sampling bias in any encounter with affordances in the physical or social environment. These sampling biases affect the knowledge from available affordances that is repeated and connected, which leads to different cumulative probabilities in the person's knowledge of the world and expected successful behavior for attaining reward. Once learned, this culturally biased knowledge affects all future attention and biases all new attended samples, directing attention to those aspects of affordances that reinforce the existing knowledge.

Motivation, Culture, and Learning in School

When we consider motivation and learning in educational settings, it is clear that we cannot directly employ findings specific to what is known about the mechanisms of neural plasticity to practice. Recall that the goal of neural learning is to allow accurate understanding, and this is accomplished through statistical learning and storage of the history of repeated stimulations. However, for the brain to accomplish this, people need to interact with the world and extract information from available affordances. We cannot directly stimulate a neuron; we must obtain our information from the world.

As previously discussed, our perceptions of available affordances are filtered through social learning. Although much of the social knowledge and social interaction affecting perceptions of affordances occurs informally in homes and social groups, the main avenue for instruction about perceiving and responding to affordances is school. Formal schooling is especially important for societies in which the balance of knowledge has shifted heavily toward mathematics, science, and engineering (the so-called STEM fields), philosophy, and literature. As noted by Vygotsky (1980), the knowledge of these fields is not a property of the affordances of the physical environment; the knowledge is the property of the affordances of the social environment.

The affordances of the physical environment are not passively perceived directly, and neither are the socially determined affordances. Students in schools do not simply store the knowledge presented by teachers or react to the instructional materials provided. Students are active directors of their own attention, even if they are not always aware that this is the case. We draw on one of our recent studies to provide an illustration. We found that situational interest influenced reading time, which subsequently influenced learning (Flowerday & Shell, 2015). This could be interpreted, as situational interest often is, as an indication that some affordance in the reading material captured interest and, thus, directed attention and subsequent effort (indicating repetition and connection) to relevant information in the reading. But we know that attention to affordances is not solely a function of properties of the environment. Flowerday and Shell also found that topic interest (an indicator of knowledge-based or personal interest) influenced situational interest. This would reflect the System 2, top-down biasing of attention; the person's knowledge influenced whether they saw information in the text as interesting. In this example, we can see the interaction between the person and the environment in affordances (Chemero, 2003; Stoffregen, 2003). The ability of the environment to capture interest is partly a function of what the person is predisposed to seeing as interesting, based on prior responses to the affordances of their environment. Given this, it is clear that cultural differences in personal knowledge might exert a considerable impact on affordances in the school environment that trigger situational interest and attention.

In the same way that the affordances in school are specialized, socially constructed knowledge, the motivators that direct student attention in school are generally not directly connected to any sort of basic System 1 survival motivators in the dopaminergic reward system, such as rewards leading to alleviating hunger. Affordances in school typically are not going to have any intrinsic motivation in relation to survival or biological pleasure. They are going to be rewarding or motivating because, as Berridge and Kringelbach (2008) discuss, they have been given value through social interaction and social learning. This means that the rewarding properties of school affordances must be transmitted by teachers and other adults, and learned by students. Prior cultural knowledge that students have acquired from their communities and parents, about important rewards and motivation, may be at odds with what the teachers and the school view as rewarding.

The classroom is its own environment and, as such, provides certain affordances. Within this classroom environment, however, students bring their own prior knowledge based on their own experiences. Through System 1 biasing, these prior knowledge effects may have more influence on attention than System 2 motivators that may be present in school. Mooney et al. (2016) found significant differences between Aboriginal and non-Aboriginal students on factors of cultural diversity, cultural identity, and Aboriginal perspective. Aboriginal students were less likely to demonstrate behaviors associated with engagement. Deloria and Wildcat (2001) note that in traditional tribal education, accomplishments are not seen as individual that are seen as the accomplishments of the family. Flowerday (2016) notes that when teaching motivation theories to students, it is critical to ask them to "relate motivation to their lived experiences so they can make connections to the theoretical constructs" (p. 119). For indigenous students, this often means relating ideas to experiences in their family or community. Mooney et al. (2016) found that Aboriginal students were less likely to demonstrate behaviors associated with engagement. Rubie-Davis and Peterson (2016) found that Maori students had higher levels of performance goal orientation than their European peers, perhaps because achieving at high levels brings honor to their families. Also, Maori students felt the need to outperform peers as a means of demonstrating their competence in an environment which underestimates their abilities.

Flowerday et al. (2018) found that, in typical elementary and middle-school classrooms, ethnic minority students need to have higher levels of System 2 motivated self-directed learning to achieve the same level of math performance as white students. This higher System 2 motivated self-direction may be needed to overcome mismatches between their own prior cultural knowledge and the knowledge assumed by the classroom environment. Since the classroom environment is more compatible with white majority student prior knowledge, those students can be successful with less System 2 motivated self-directed learning than ethnic minority students, because they have more compatible System 1 automatic attention match between the classroom and their personal prior knowledge.

Concluding Thoughts

Although statistical learning is well established in many neurological (e.g., Kirkham et al., 2002; Mitchel & Weiss, 2011; Schapiro et al., 2016; Turk-Browne et al., 2008) and behavioral/cognitive (Erickson & Thiessen, 2015; Kóbor et al., 2017) studies, the argument by Shell et al. (2010) in the ULM that statistical learning is sufficient to explain all learning is untestable at present. The Hebb (1949) neural plasticity mechanisms of repetition and connection are well established as the neural processes of learning. But we cannot yet watch the specific biological processes at the neural level in real-time to see change after each repetition or to see these changes unfold across the life span. Also, neuroscience has only begun to examine how cultural experience affects the way information is processed by the brain.

Really getting at the heart of motivation and learning in school, as well as their neurological foundations, will require the examination of these processes in real classrooms with real content, which is beyond present technology. While we wait for new research technologies, we see a need to dig deeper into the processes of motivation and strategic self-regulation at the cognitive and behavioral levels. Our work has been looking at understanding how the combined and joint influences of motivation drive different patterns of strategic self-regulation (Nelson et al., 2015; Peteranetz et al., 2017; Shell & Husman, 2008; Shell & Soh, 2013). These studies employ profiling or person-centered methods. We have especially been using these to examine cultural and ethnic differences in profiles (Flowerday et al., 2018). We have also been trying to examine the dynamics of change in aspects of motivation across classes or school years to better understand how specific motivational constructs evolve, and how individual constructs might be associated with other aspects of motivated self-regulation profiles and differences in classroom environments (Flanigan et al., 2017; Peteranetz et al., 2018). In respect to cultural differences, we have been examining motivational beliefs among Native American students in the Southwest, and how these beliefs change from fifth to sixth grade.

Perhaps the biggest challenge is to somehow connect these macro-level efforts (that use primarily survey questionnaires) to more micro-level, fine-grained, real-time assessments that could potentially link our self-report and behavioral assessments more closely to underlying cognitive and neurological mechanisms. Our initial forays into this (Eck et al., 2016) have found that student motivated self-regulation profiles (Nelson et al., 2015; Shell & Soh, 2013) could be linked to real-time student trace data during a Wiki assignment. The ULM learning processes of repetition (indicated by multiple viewing, editing, or commenting on the same page) and connection (indicated by viewing, editing, or commenting on multiple unique pages) differed for students adopting different motivated self-regulation profiles during the course. Furthermore, such efforts will be needed to move our understanding of the role of culture in motivation, learning, and attention forward.

References

Anderson, B. A. (2016). The attention habit: How reward learning shapes attentional selection. *Annals of the New York Academy of Science, 1369*, 24–39. doi: 10.1111/nyas.12957.

Anselme, P. (2007). Some conceptual problems with the classical theory of behavior. *Behavioural Processes, 75*, 259–75.

Baddeley, A. (1986). *Working memory.* Oxford: Clarendon Press.

Bandura, A. (1986). *Social foundations of thought and action: A social cognitive theory.* Englewood Cliffs, NJ: Prentice-Hall.

Bandura, A. (1997). *Self-efficacy: The exercise of control.* New York, NY: W. H. Freeman/Times Books/ Henry Holt & Co.

Bandura, A. (2016). The power of observational learning through social modeling. In R. J. Sternberg, S. T. Fisk, & D. J. Foss (Eds.), *Scientists making a difference: One hundred eminent behavioral and brain scientists talk about their most important contributions* (pp. 235–9). New York, NY: Cambridge University Press.

Bereiter, C. & Scardamalia, M. (2014). Knowledge building and knowledge creation: One concept, two hills to climb. In S. C. Tan, H. Y. So, & J. Yeo (Eds.), *Knowledge creation in education* (Education Innovation Series). Singapore: Springer. doi: 10.1007/978-981-287-047-6_3.

Berridge, K. C. & Kringelbach, M. L. (2008). Affective neuroscience of pleasure: Reward in humans and animals. *Psychopharmacology (Berl), 199*(3): 457–80. doi: 10.1007/s00213-008-1099-6.

Blumenfeld-Katzir, T., Pasternak, O., Dagan, M., & Assaf, Y. (2011). Diffusion MRI of structural brain plasticity induced by a learning and memory task. *PLoS ONE 6*(6): e20678. doi: 10.1371/journal.pone.0020678.

Boekaerts, M. & Cascallar, E. (2006). How far have we moved toward the integration of theory and practice in self-regulation? *Educational Psychology Review, 18*(3), 199–210.

Bourgeois, A., Chelazzi, L., & Vuilleumier, P. (2016). How motivation and reward learning modulate selective attention. *Progress in Brain Research, 229*, 325–42. doi: 10.1016/bs.pbr.2016.06.004.

Bromberg-Martin, E. S., Matsumoto, M., & Hikosaka, O. (2010). Dopamine in motivational control: Rewarding, aversive, and alerting. *Neuron, 68*(5), 815–34. doi: 10.1016/j.neuron.2010.11.022.

Brooks, D. W. & Shell, D. F. (2006). Working memory, motivation, and teacher-initiated learning. *Journal of Science Education and Technology*, *15*(1), 17–30.

Brown, A. L., Bransford, J. D., Ferrara, R. A., & Campione, J. C. (1983). Learning, remembering, and understanding. In J. H. Flavell & E. M. Markman (Eds.), *Handbook of child psychology* (4th ed., Vol. 3). New York, NY: Wiley.

Cajete, G. A. (2015). *Indigenous community: Rekindling the teaching of the seventh fire.* St. Paul, MN: Living Justice Press.

Caporale. N. & Dan, Y. (2009). Spike timing-dependent plasticity: A Hebbian learning rule. *Annual Review of Neuroscience*, *31*, 25–46.

Chemero, A. (2003). An outline of a theory of affordances. *Ecological Psychology*, *15*(2), 181–95.

Corbetta, M. (2012). Functional connectivity and neurological recovery. *Developmental Psychobiology*, *54*, 239–53.

Cowan, N. (2010). The magical mystery four: How is working memory capacity limited, and Why? *Current Directions in Psychological Science*, *19*(1): 51–7. doi: 10.1177/0963721409359277.

Deco, G., Rolls, E. T., Albantakis, L., & Romo, R. (2013). Brain mechanisms for perceptual and reward-related decision making. *Progress in Neurobiology*, *103*, 194–213.

Deloria, Jr., V. & Wildcat, D. (2001). *Power and place: Indian education in America.* Golden, CO: Fulcrum Resources.

Driemeyer, J., Boyke, J., Gaser, C., Buchel, C., & May, A. (2008) Changes in gray matter induced by learning – Revisited. *PLoS ONE 3*(7): e2669. doi: 10.1371/journal.pone.0002669.

Eccles, J. S. & Wigfield, A. (2002). Motivational beliefs, values, and goals. *Annual Review of Psychology*, *53*(1), 109–32.

Eck, A., Soh, L.-K., & Shell, D. F. (2016). Investigating differences in wiki-based collaborative activities between student engagement profiles in CS1. *Proceedings of the 47th ACM Technical Symposium on Computer Science Education (SIGCSE'2016)* (pp. 36–41). New York, NY: ACM. doi: 10.1145/2839509.2844615.

Erickson, L. C. & Thiessen, E. D. (2015). Statistical learning of language: Theory, validity, and predictions of a statistical learning account of language acquisition. *Developmental Review*, *37*, 66–108.

Feldman, R., Monakhov, M., Pratt, M., & Ebstein, R. P. (2016). Oxytocin pathway genes: Evolutionary ancient system impacting on human affiliation, sociality, and psychopathology. *Biological Psychiatry*, *79*(3), 174–84. doi: 10.1016/j.biopsych.2015.08.008.

Flanigan, A. E., Peteranetz, M. S., Shell, D. F., & Soh, L.-K. (2017). Implicit intelligence beliefs of computer science students: exploring change across the semester. *Contemporary Educational Psychology*, *48*, 179–96. doi: 10.1016/j.cedpsych.2016.10.003.

Flowerday, T. (2016). Using motivation to teach motivation. In M. C. Smith & N. DeFrates-Densch (Eds.), *Challenges and innovations in educational psychology teaching and learning* (pp. 109–22). Charlotte, NC: Information Age Publishing.

Flowerday, T. & Shell, D. F. (2015). Disentangling the effects of interest and choice on learning, engagement, and attitude. *Learning and Individual Differences*, *40*, 134–40. doi: 10.1016/j.lindif.2015.05.003.

Flowerday, T., Shell, D. F., & Moreno, R., (2018). Using profiles of motivated strategic self-regulation to understand mathematics achievement of ethnically diverse elementary school students. Manuscript submitted for publication.

Gibson, J. J. (1979). *The ecological approach to visual perception.* Boston, MA: Houghton Mifflin.

Harmon-Jones, E. & Inzlicht, M. (Eds.) (2016). *Social neuroscience: Biological approaches to social psychology.* New York, NY: Routledge, Psychology Press.

Hebb, D. O. (1949). *The organization of behavior: A neuropsychological theory.* New York, NY: Wiley & Sons.

Hidi, S. (2016). Revisiting the role of rewards in motivation and learning: Implications of neuroscientific research. *Educational Psychology Review, 28,* 61–93. doi: 10.1007/s10648-015-9307-5.

Hidi, S. & Renninger, K. A. (2006). The four-phase model of interest development. *Educational Psychologist, 41,* 111–27.

Horvitz, J. C. (2000). Mesolimbocortical and nigrostriatal dopamine responses to salient non-reward events. *Neuroscience, 96*(4), 651–6.

Husman, J., Brem, S. K., Banegas, S., Duchrow, D. W., & Haque, S. (2015). Learning and future time perspective: The promise of the future–rewarding in the present. In M. Stolarski, N. Fieulaine, & W. van Beek (Eds.), *Time perspective theory; Review, research and application: Essays in Honor of Philip G. Zimbardo* (pp. 131–41). Springer International Publishing. doi: 10.1007/978-3-319-07368-2_8.

Husman, J. & Lens, W. (1999). The role of the future in student motivation. *Educational Psychologist, 34*(2), 113–25.

Husman, J. & Shell, D. F. (2008). Beliefs and perceptions about the future: A measurement of future time perspective. *Learning and Individual Differences, 18,* 166–75.

Jack, R. E., Blais, C., Scheepers, C., Schyns, P. G., & Caldara, R. (2009). Cultural confusions show that facial expressions are not universal. *Current Biology, 19*(18), 1543–8. doi: 10.1016/j.cub.2009.07.051.

Jairam, D., Kiewra, K. A., Kauffman, D. F., & Zhao, R. (2012). How to study a matrix. *Contemporary Educational Psychology, 37,* 128–35.

Kahneman, D. (2011). *Thinking fast and slow.* New York, NY: Farrar, Straus, & Giroux.

Kandel, E. R., Schwartz, J. H., Jessell, T. M., Siegelbaum, S. A., & Hudspeth, A. J. (2012). *Principles of neural science* (5th ed.). New York, NY: McGraw-Hill.

Kiani, R. & Shadlen, M. N. (2009). Representation of confidence associated with a decision by neurons in the parietal cortex. *Science, 324,* 759–64.

Kirkham, N. Z., Slemmer, J. A., & Johnson, S. P. (2002). Visual statistical learning in infancy: Evidence for domain-general learning mechanism. *Cognition, 83,* B35–B42. doi: 10.1016/S0010-0277(02)00004-5.

Kóbor, A., Janacsek, K., Takács, A., & Nemeth, D. (2017). Statistical learning leads to persistent memory: Evidence for one-year consolidation. *Scientific Reports, 7,* Article number: 760. doi: 10.1038/s41598-017-00807-3.

Kolmogorov, A. N. (1950). *Foundations of the theory of probability.* New York, NY: Chelsea Publishing.

Kuhbandner, C., Lichtenfeld, S., & Pekrun, R. (2011). Always look on the broad side of life: Happiness increases the breadth of sensory memory. *Emotion, 11*(4), 958–64. doi: 10.1037/a0024075.

Knudsen, E. I. (2007). Fundamental components of attention. *Annual Review of Neuroscience, 30,* 57–78. doi: 10.1146/annurev.neuro.30.051606.094256.

Matzel, L. D., Hel, F. P., & Miller, R. R. (1988). Information and expression of simultaneous and backward associations: Implications for contiguity theory. *Learning and Motivation, 19,* 317–44.

Mayer, R. E. & Fiorella, L. (2014). Principles for reducing extraneous processing in multimedia learning: Coherence, signaling, redundancy, special contiguity, and temporal contiguity principles. In R. E. Mayer (Ed.), *The Cambridge handbook of multimedia learning* (2nd ed., pp. 279–315). New York, NY: Cambridge University Press.

McInerney, D. M. & Flowerday, T. (2016). Indigenous issues in education and research: Looking forward. *Contemporary Educational Psychology, 47,* 1–3.

Miendlarzewska, E. A., Bavelier, D., & Schwartz, S. (2016). Influence of reward motivation on human declarative memory. *Neuroscience and Biobehavioral Reviews, 61,* 156–76.

Miller, G. A. (1956). The magical number seven, plus or minus two: Some limits on our capacity for processing information, *Psychological Review, 63,* 81–97.

Mitchel, A. D. & Weiss, D. J. (2011). Learning across senses: Cross-modal effects in multisensory statistical learning. *Journal of Experimental Psychology: Learning, Memory, & Cognition, 37,* 1081–91.

Mooney, J., Seaton, M., Kaur, G., Marsh, H. W., & Yeung, A. S. (2016). Cultural perspectives on Indigenous and non-indigenous Australian students' school motivation and engagement. *Contemporary Educational Psychology, 47,* 11–23.

Na, J., Grossmann, I., Varnum, M. E. W., Kitayama, S., Gonzalez, R., & Nisbett, R. E. (2010). Cultural differences are not always reducible to individual differences. *Proceedings of the National Academy of Sciences of the United States of America, 107*(14), 6192–7. doi: 10.1073/pnas.1001911107.

Nelson, K. G., Shell, D. F., Husman, J., Fishman, E. J., & Soh, L. K. (2015). Motivational and self-regulated learning profiles of students taking a foundational engineering course. *Journal of Engineering Education, 104*(1), 74–100. doi: 10.1002/jee.20066.

Numan, M. (2014). *Neurobiology of social behavior: Toward an understanding of the prosocial and antisocial brain.* Oxford: Academic Press.

Park, D. C. & Huang, C. M. (2010). Culture wires the brain: A cognitive neuroscience perspective. *Perspectives on Psychological Science, 5*(4), 391–400.

Pekrun, R. (2006). The control-value theory of achievement emotions: Assumptions, corollaries, and implications for educational research and practice. *Educational Psychology Review 18*(4), 315–41.

Peteranetz, M. S., Flanigan, A. E., Shell, D. F., & Soh, L.-K. (2017). Computational creativity exercises: An avenue for promoting learning in computer science. *IEEE Transactions on Education, 60*(4), 305–13. doi: 10.1109/TE.2017.2705152.

Peteranetz, M. S., Flanigan, A. E., Shell, D. F., & Soh, L.-K. (2018). Career aspirations, perceived instrumentality, and achievement in undergraduate computer science courses. *Contemporary Educational Psychology, 53,* 27–44. doi: 10.1016/j.cedpsych.2018.01.006.

Piaget, J. (1971). *Genetic epistemology.* New York, NY: W.W. Norton.

Renninger, K. A. & Hidi, S. (2016). *The power of interest for motivation and engagement.* New York, NY: Routledge.

Rotter J. B. (1966), Generalized expectancies for internal versus external control of reinforcement. *Psychology Monographs, 80,* 1–28.

Rubie-Davis, C. M. & Peterson, E. R. (2016). Relations between teachers' achievement over- and underestimation and students' beliefs for Maori and Pakeha students. *Contemporary Educational Psychology, 47,* 72–83.

Sarter, M., Givens, B., & Bruno, J. P. (2001). The cognitive neuroscience of sustained attention: Where top-down meets bottom-up. *Brain Research Reviews, 35,* 146–60.

Schapiro, A. C., Turk-Browne, N. B., Norman, K. A., & Botvinick, M. M. (2016). Statistical learning of temporal community structure in the hippocampus. *Hippocampus, 26*(1), 3–8. doi: 10.1002/hipo.22523.

Schultz, W. (2015). Neuronal reward and decision signals: From theories to data. *Physiological Review, 95,* 853–951. doi: 10.1152/physrev.00023.

Schunk, D. H. & Zimmerman, B. J. (2013). Self-regulation and learning. In W. M. Reynolds, G. E. Miller, & I. B. Weiner (Eds.), *Handbook of psychology* (Vol. 7, pp. 45–68). Hoboken, NJ: John Wiley & Sons.

Seyfartha, R. M. & Cheney, D. L. (2013). Affiliation, empathy, and the origins of theory of mind. *Proceedings of the National Academy of Sciences of the United States of America, 110* (Supplement 2), 10349–56. doi: 10.1073/pnas.1301223110.

Shell, D. F., Brooks, D. W., Trainin, G., Wilson, K., Kauffman, D. F., & Herr, L. (2010). *The unified learning model: How motivational, cognitive, and neurobiological sciences inform best teaching practices.* Dordrecht, Netherlands: Springer.

Shell, D. F., Colvin, C., & Bruning, R. H. (1995). Self-efficacy, attribution, and outcome expectancy mechanisms in reading and writing achievement: Grade level and achievement level differences. *Journal of Educational Psychology, 87,* 386–98. doi: 10.1037/0022-0663.87.3.386.

Shell, D. F. & Husman, J. (2008). Control, motivation, affect, and strategic self-regulation in the college classroom: A multidimensional phenomenon. *Journal of Educational Psychology, 100*(2) 443–59.

Shell, D. F., Murphy C. C., & Bruning, R. H. (1989). Self efficacy and outcome expectancy mechanisms in reading and writing achievement. *Journal of Educational Psychology, 81,* 91, 100. doi: 10.1037/0022-0663.81.1.91.

Shell, D. F. & Soh, L.-K. (2013). Profiles of motivated self-regulation in college computer science courses: Differences in major versus required non-major courses. *Journal of Science Education and Technology, 22*(6), 899–913.

Shell, D. F., Soh, L.-K., & Chiriacescu, V. (2015). Modeling self-efficacy as a dynamic cognitive process with the Computational-Unified Learning Model (C-ULM): Implications for cognitive informatics and cognitive computing. *International Journal of Cognitive Informatics and Natural Intelligence, 9*(3), 1–24. doi: 10.4018/IJCINI.2015070101.

Shors, T. J. (2014). The adult brain makes new neurons, and effortful learning keeps them alive. *Current Directions in Psychological Science, 23*(5) 311–18.

Simon, H. A. (1969). *The sciences of the artificial.* Cambridge, MA: MIT Press.

Sinatra, G. M., Heddy, B. C., & Lombardi, D. (2015). The challenges of defining and measuring student engagement in science. *Educational Psychologist, 50,* 1–13, doi: 10.1080/00461520.2014.1002924.

Skinner, E. A. (1996). A guide to constructs of control. *Journal of Personality and Social Psychology, 71,* 549–70.

Stoffregen, T. A. (2003). Affordances as properties of the animal–environment system. *Ecological Psychology*, *15*(2), 115–34.

Striepens, N., Matusch, A., Kendrick, K. M., Mihov, Y., Elmenhorst, D., Becker, B., ... Bauer, A. (2014). Oxytocin enhances attractiveness of unfamiliar female faces independent of the dopamine reward system. *Psychoneuroendocrinology*, *39*, 74–87.

Stuchlik, A. (2014). Dynamic learning and memory, synaptic plasticity and neurogenesis: An update. *Frontiers in Behavioral Neuroscience*, *8*(Article 106), 1–6. doi: 10.3389/fnbeh.2014.00106.

Sweller, J., Ayres, P. L., & Kalyuga, S. (2011), *Cognitive load theory*. New York, NY: Springer. doi: 10.1007/978-1-4419-8126-4.

Thorndike, E. L. (1913). *The psychology of learning*. New York, NY: Mason-Henry Press.

Tolman, E. C. (1932). *Purposive behavior in animal and men*. New York, NY: The Century Company.

Turk-Browne, N. B., Scholl, B. J., Chun, M. M., & Johnson, M. K. (2008). Neural evidence of statistical learning: Efficient detection of visual regularities without awareness. *Journal of Cognitive Neuroscience*, *21*, 1934–45.

Vuilleumier, P. (2005). How brains beware: Neural mechanisms of emotional attention. *Trends in Cognitive Science*, *9*, 585–94.

Vuilleumier, P. (2015). Affective and motivational control of vision. *Current Opinion in Neurology*, *28*, 29–35.

Vygotsky, L. S. (1980). *Mind in society: The development of higher psychological processes*. Cambridge, MA: Harvard University Press.

Wang, Y., Fariello, G., Gavrilova, M. L., Kinsner, W., Mizoguchi, F., Patel, S., ... Tsumoto, S. (2013). Perspectives on cognitive computers and knowledge processors. *International Journal of Cognitive Informatics and Natural Intelligence*, *7*(3), 1–24. doi: 10.4018/ijcini.2013070101.

Warner, L. S. (2006). Native ways of knowing: Let me count the ways. *Canadian Journal of Native Education*, *29*(2), 149.

Weinstein, C. E., Husman, J., & Dierking, D. R. (2000). Interventions with a focus on learning strategies. In M. Boekaerts, P. R. Pintrich, & M. Zeidner (Eds.), *Handbook of self-regulation* (pp. 727–47). San Diego, CA: Academic Press.

Weisz, J. R. & Stipek, D. J. (1982). Competence, contingency, and the development of perceived control. *Human Development*, *25*, 250–81.

Yin, H. H., Ostlund, S. B., & Balleine, B. W. (2008). Reward-guided learning beyond dopamine in the nucleus accumbens: The integrative functions of cortico-basal ganglia networks. *European Journal of Neuroscience*, *28*(8), 1437–48. doi: 10.1111/j.1460-9568.2008.06422.x.

Index

CPSIA information can be obtained
at www.ICGtesting.com
Printed in the USA
LVHW010950141122
733071LV00005B/86

9 781316 630792